Annotated Bibliographies of
Old and Middle English Literature

VOLUME VII

THE MIDDLE ENGLISH LYRIC AND SHORT POEM

Annotated Bibliographies of Old and Middle English Literature

ISSN 1353-8675

General Editor: T. L. Burton

Editorial Assistants:
Sabina Flanagan and Rosemary Greentree

Already Published

VOLUME I
The Language of Middle English Literature
David Burnley and Matsuji Tajima

VOLUME II
Ancrene Wisse, the Katherine Group, and the Wooing Group
Bella Millet

VOLUME III
Visions of the Other World in Middle English
Robert Easting

VOLUME IV
Old English Prose of Secular Learning
Stephanie Hollis and Michael Wright

VOLUME V
Old English Wisdom Poetry
Russell Poole

VOLUME VI
Old English Prose Translations of
King Alfred's Reign
Greg Waite

Annotated Bibliographies of
Old and Middle English Literature

VOLUME VII

THE MIDDLE ENGLISH LYRIC AND SHORT POEM

ROSEMARY GREENTREE

D. S. BREWER

© Rosemary Greentree 2001

All Rights Reserved. Except as permitted under current legislation
no part of this work may be photocopied, stored in a retrieval system,
published, performed in public, adapted, broadcast,
transmitted, recorded or reproduced in any form or by any means,
without the prior permission of the copyright owner

First published 2001
D. S. Brewer, Cambridge

ISBN 0 85991 621 9

D. S. Brewer is an imprint of Boydell & Brewer Ltd
PO Box 9, Woodbridge, Suffolk IP12 3DF, UK
and of Boydell & Brewer Inc.
PO Box 41026, Rochester, NY 14604-4126, USA
website: http://www.boydell.co.uk

A catalogue record for this book is available
from the British Library

Library of Congress Cataloging-in-Publication Data

Greentree, Rosemary.
  The Middle English lyric and short poem / Rosemary Greentree.
    p. cm. – (Annotated bibliographies of Old and Middle English literature, ISSN 1353–8675; v. 7)
  Includes bibliographical references and indexes.
  ISBN 0–85991–621–9 (alk. paper)
    1. English poetry – Middle English, 1100–1500 – Bibliography. 2. English poetry – Middle English, 1100–1500 – History and criticism – Bibliography.
  I. Title. II. Series
Z2012.G835 2001
[PR311]
016.821'040901–dc21   00–068885

This publication is printed on acid-free paper

Typeset by Joshua Associates Ltd, Oxford
Printed in Great Britain by
St Edmundsbury Press Ltd, Bury St Edmunds, Suffolk

Contents

General Editor's Preface	vii
Acknowledgements	viii
Abbreviations	ix
Manuscripts	x
Bibliographical Introduction	1
General Introduction	5
Defining the ME Lyric	5
Collections of Lyrics	13
Trends in Criticism	18
Individual Scholars	21
Individual Lyrics	23
The Isolable Lyrics	26
The Mundane Lyrics	32
Conclusions	35
Annotations of Editions	39
Other Works that Supply Editions of Lyrics	84
Annotations of Critical Works	86
Works Cited but not Annotated	402
Index of Scholars and Critics	404
Subject Index	410
Index of First Lines	436
Temporary Index of First Lines not noted in *IMEV* or *SIMEV*	535

For Russell,
James and Andrew

General Editor's Preface

The last two decades have seen an explosion in the production of annotated bibliographies in the humanities, motivated in part by the sheer impossibility of keeping up with the mass of critical literature produced since the fifties. They fill a need, felt by students and teachers at all levels, for reliable, concise, yet detailed guides to what has been written. Medieval English literature has been no exception to this general trend, with annotated bibliographies of many of the major authors and areas appearing in the last twenty years, or being now in preparation.

The primary aim of the current series of some two dozen volumes is to produce an annotated bibliography for every area of medieval English literary studies for which such a tool is not already in existence or in preparation. One of the major benefits of the series is thus to focus attention not only on those of the more popular areas not covered in other bibliographies, but also on those hitherto marginalized. The individual volumes contribute to our knowledge of our cultural heritage by showing, through a summary and evaluation of all known writings on the area in question, why that area is worthy of closer study, what sorts of interest it has already provoked, and what are the most fruitful directions for future research in it.

One of the distinguishing features of this series is the chronological arrangement of items, as opposed to the alphabetical arrangement more commonly adopted. Chronological arrangement facilitates the reading of annotations in the same order as the publication of the items annotated, and thus gives readers at one sitting a sense of the development of scholarship in the field. At the same time, the convenience of alphabetical arrangement is retained through the index of scholars and critics, which allows readers to locate with ease all items by a particular writer.

Each bibliography in the series is concentrated on a relatively small, reasonably self-contained area, defined on generic lines. This concentration leads to a second distinguishing feature of the series: the fullness and detail both of the annotations themselves and of the introductory sections. With the aim of letting the original authors speak for themselves the authors of the bibliographies keep their annotations as neutral as can reasonably be hoped; in the introductory sections, however, they offer critical analyses of the works annotated, drawing attention to the major trends in scholarship, showing which approaches have been most influential, which are exhausted, and which are most in need of further development.

The editorial work for the series has been assisted since 1991 by grants from the Australian Research Council and the University of Adelaide, to both of which bodies grateful acknowledgement is made here.

T.L. BURTON

Acknowledgements

The years spent with the bibliography have led me to incur many debts of gratitude, and it is a pleasure to acknowledge these now.

Much of that time has been spent in libraries, using their varied resources. The librarians of the Barr Smith Library at the University of Adelaide, in particular Alan Keig, Maria Albanese, Mary Georgopoulos and all in the Interlibrary Loan department, have searched tirelessly, sometimes with few clues to guide them; the librarians of Northwestern University found some of the more elusive references. I am grateful for their enterprise, stamina, and successes. I was also fortunate to be able to call on an informal library network, of widely scattered friends, who traced or eliminated some very resistant articles, and sustained my efforts – my thanks go to Janet Williams, Dallas Simpson, Frank Schaer, and Steve McKenna for their generous assistance. For help in translating some German works, I am indebted to Trudy Brown, Anna Ivey, and Hans Renner.

The bibliography has gained much from the advice of Tom Burton, the general editor of the series and the guidance of Philip Waldron; they have been creative and encouraging. Eva Sallis's perspectives, on the course of the work and later on the annotations and introduction, were inspiring. Another group of friends also read the introduction and offered some welcome insights – for these I thank Dorothy Hudson, Judith Smith, and Elizabeth and Brian Steveson.

A particular pleasure and valued part of the preparation was attendance at a Summer Institute on the medieval lyric, offered by the National Endowment for the Humanities, at Northwestern University, Evanston, IL, in 1995. The seminars and discussions, arranged by William D. Paden, offered some exciting opportunities to learn more of the lyrics of other European languages, and their effects on the ME lyrics. For assistance in attending the Institute, I am most grateful to the National Endowment for the Humanities, the Department of English, and the Faculty of Arts, to the University of Adelaide who awarded a travel grant for my journey and the George Murray Travelling Scholarship, and to the Australian Federation of University Women who awarded the Cathy Candler Scholarship. The experience was an enriching and stimulating one, which enabled me to meet scholars I might not have known, and to explore paths I might not otherwise have taken.

Without the care of Sam Humble, Lehonde Hoare, and Christopher Dibden I could not have completed the bibliography. My friends, especially Dorothy Hudson and Pauline Payne, and my family have supported and encouraged me through all its stages. My sons, James and Andrew, have offered thoughts from legal and scientific points of view, and Andrew devised an essential numbering system. My husband Russell is always a source of patience, strength, and love. To all, my sincere thanks.

Abbreviations

Add.	Additional
AN	Anglo-Norman
AS	Anglo-Saxon
Archiv	*Archiv für das Studium der neueren Sprachen und Literaturen*
BL	British Library
BrownXIII	*English Lyrics of the XIIIth Century*
BrownXIV	*Religious Lyrics of the XIVth Century*
BrownXV	*Religious Lyrics of the XVth Century*
CMERS	Center for Medieval and Early Renaissance Studies
IMEV	*Index of Middle English Verse*
ME	Middle English
MHG	Middle High German
MnE	Modern English
MRTS	Medieval and Renaissance Texts and Studies
MS	Manuscript
NT	New Testament
OE	Old English
OF	Old French
OIr	Old Irish
ON	Old Norse
OT	Old Testament
RMERV	*Register of Middle English Religious Verse*
RobbinsH	*Historical Poems of the XIVth and XVth Centuries*
RobbinsS	*Secular Lyrics of the XIVth and XVth Centuries*
SIMEV	*Supplement to the Index of Middle English Verse*

Manuscripts

In their references to the following manuscripts, the authors of works annotated use any of the forms listed here.

Auchinleck MS	Edinburgh, National Library of Scotland, Advocates 19.2.1
Bannatyne MS	Edinburgh, National Library of Scotland, Advocates 1.1.6
Devonshire MS	London, BL Add. 17492
Fairfax /Fayrfax MS	London, BL Add. 5465
Findern MS	Cambridge University Library Ff.1.6
John Grimestone's Preaching Book	Edinburgh, National Library of Scotland, Advocates 18.7.21
Henry VIII's MS	London, BL Add. 31922
Richard Hill's Commonplace Book	Oxford, Balliol College, 354
Loscombe MS	London, Wellcome Historical Library, 406
Ritson MS	London, BL Add. 5665
Simeon MS	London, BL Add. 22283
Shanne MS	London, BL Add. 38599
Thornton MS	London, BL Add. 31042
Vernon MS	Oxford, Bodleian Library, English Poetry a.1
Humphrey Wellys's/ Welles's Anthology	Oxford, Bodleian Library, Rawlinson C. 813

Bibliographical Introduction

This bibliography aims to offer a neutral, chronological survey of editions and criticism of the ME lyrics and short poems. Most editions and criticism are of the twentieth century, but it includes some nineteenth-century editions in current use. The coverage of works published until 1995 is complete, as far as possible, and I have also annotated a few works of 1996 and 1997 that were easily accessible. Some publications with promising titles were unfortunately not available. I have noted these, with any information obtainable from reviews or other bibliographies, but have had to mark them 'not seen.' The purpose of the annotations is to summarize the content of each work and to convey its style and the author's voice by means of quotations. Although the length of an annotation is usually a guide to the work's importance in the critical discourse, this is not always the case, since an outline of the contents of longer works is more useful than an attempt to note all the details. There is more attention to editions that are scholarly rather than popular or modernized versions, and to literary criticism, rather than manuscript or musical studies, but each category is represented, with some flexibility.

The bibliography relies on *IMEV* and *SIMEV* as reference sources, to provide the numbers used to identify most poems and standard forms of their first lines. The numbers used for identification are set in italics, to avoid confusion with numbers of annotations (in bold), or page numbers (in regular type). The index of first lines lists poems noted in *IMEV* and *SIMEV*, as they are cited in those indexes. A temporary index lists poems not noted in either index of ME verse, in the form cited by those who describe them.

IMEV and *SIMEV* have also been used as guides to the historical and geographical boundaries of the bibliography, and as ever, the interpretation of these boundaries is flexible, since those of the two indexes are not identical. Although *IMEV* lists poems generally of the period 1100 to 1500, *SIMEV* admits poems of later date and includes a wider range of material, in particular Middle Scots works. These variations are demonstrated in collections which include many works omitted from *IMEV* but included in *SIMEV*, such as Chambers and Sidgwick, **18**, and in the series of songs (classified as sixteenth-century pieces) collected by Flügel, **7**, **8**, **15**, and by Padelford and Benham, **20**, many of which are noted in *SIMEV* but not *IMEV*. In all cases, the poems are in the style of other ME lyrics. *SIMEV* lists more Scots works than *IMEV*; one may note for instance a greatly increased corpus of works of William Dunbar.

Numerous comparisons in the criticism of the ME lyrics and short poems bring references to poems of known authors, such as Chaucer and Middle Scots poets, and to poems written in other languages, such as Latin and Celtic works, and lyrics of troubadours and trouvères. Many annotations include such references, but none is concerned exclusively with them, although the works of the known poets are often regarded as part of the ME lyric corpus, or to be closely related. Considerations of time and space must supervene over any attempt to include all such critical material, and the ready availability of bibliographies of criticism of Chaucer, Henryson, Dunbar, and other identified authors ensures that references to criticism devoted entirely to their poems would be redundant. The bibliographies include Russell Peck's on Chaucer's lyrics, the general bibliographies of Chaucer criticism, that of Walter Scheps and J. Anna Looney, on the Middle Scots poets, and Florence Ridley's 'Middle Scots Writers' in *A Manual of the Writings in Middle English*. The need to set boundaries that are practical, although inevitably flexible, means for instance that there are no annotations of works such as Wimsatt's *Chaucer and His French Contemporaries*, which does not mention the ME lyric directly, although it offers much illumination to the study of the genre. I have, however, annotated Dronke's essay, **649**, in which extensive references to lyrics in other languages provide a context for 'Westron wynde when wylle thou blow' [*3899.3*], which Dronke mentions rather briefly. Similarly, there are numerous observations about musical settings and performances, but since the focus of the bibliography is literary criticism, I have not annotated works concerned solely with the musical aspects of ME lyrics.

Some of the works annotated refer to many poems, with varying degrees of emphasis, and it is necessary to show the range of the authors' allusions, but avoid misrepresenting their significance. The lists of numbers that follow the annotations demonstrate the range, by noting all the poems mentioned in a work, using numbers from *IMEV*, *SIMEV*, and the temporary index. Thus the list includes poems an author has cited in comparisons or to explain the context of poems, sometimes in quite brief references. The text of the annotation suggests the author's emphasis. The index of first lines directs the reader only to references in the text of annotations.

Since the poems are scattered widely, in manuscripts and in criticism, it was not possible to examine every source in every edition. It has been necessary to concentrate on editions in current use, and on those which supply scholarly apparatus. Thus I have not sought out 'popular' editions, nor all the editions prepared for teaching purposes, some of which have a circulation limited to the institution of their preparation. Among 'popular' editions I include those prepared without notes, often with partial or complete translations to MnE, which are generally intended for recreational reading rather than study, such as collections of love lyrics and Christmas carols. I have annotated some editions in which the lyrics occupy a section of a general anthology, and a very few that offer MnE translations, generally because there are references to them elsewhere in the literature.

I have used titles of poems only when this can be useful, as in the case of Brook's titles of the Harley lyrics, since these frequently occur in the critical discourse, and prevent the confusion of poems with similar first lines. It is not surprising that many authors have used a range of forms, and I have been guided by their choices. When more than one form of a name is in use, I have tried to avoid incongruity between text and quotation within an annotation by following the author's preference, for example, for the 'Song of Songs' or 'Canticle of Canticles'; the 'Welles' or 'Wellys' anthology; the 'Fairfax' or 'Fayrfax' MS, and so on. The list of manuscripts includes the titles that frequently appear in criticism.

The annotations are divided into those of editions and those of critical works, and are arranged chronologically. Other divisions, of subjects or particular periods of time, tend to be artificial and unhelpful, and it is difficult to apply them to the lyrics and their varied criticism. The introductory section 'Trends in Criticism' offers a guide to the annotations. It outlines the general tendencies in critical approaches through a comparison of works of the early and late periods of the bibliography, and also presents summaries of the work of particular scholars and studies of particular poems. The indexes of scholars, subjects, and first lines will assist the reader to trace other matters of interest.

scope of this discussion. Parts of Langer's description fit the ME lyric in particular as well as the lyric in general. Exceptions – poems called lyrics that have traces of plot, characters or argument, or lacking exploitation of language – point up the slippery nature of the ME lyric.

The works encompassed in the term 'ME lyric' are so numerous and varied that a study of the whole genre must be general and remain at its surface, often relying on metaphors and analogies, whereas more detailed study is confined to particular sections of the genre. Such studies are superficial or deep, in structural, not evaluative senses. We must accept the diverse nature of the poems and the use of analogies as a tool to examine them, and question the worth of any idea of coherence in the genre. John Burrow's observations acknowledge the range of the ME lyric:

> Lack of order is nowhere more apparent than in the large and varied body of work commonly known as the Middle English Lyric. The term 'lyric' in this context usually means no more than a short poem, preferably in stanzas . . . but it is hardly possible to speak in general about 'lyrics' so loosely defined. (**777**: 61)

All examinations confirm these perceptions; indeed they offer more reasons to support them.

Although a term such as 'lyric' is difficult to define (demonstrated in Burke's extended explorations of his thought processes) discussion and understanding are possible. When a general explanation is accepted, it is paradoxical that definition of a part of an area already defined should prove more difficult. The teasing complexities of the boundaries of ME and of the Middle Ages present problems in themselves, and the poems gathered in the term 'ME lyric' cover a much more disparate range than any enclosed by Burke's definition or Langer's descriptive remarks. The further extension of this range, in the poems related and linked to them, presents the greatest obstacle to a compact universal definition. Exploration is as much constrained as expanded by the notions that accompany the term, something to be recognized before those notions are either developed or discarded.

'Lyric' and 'lyrical' are general constructs, more recent than the ME poems they describe, and not applied during the period of composition, although there were specific terms such as *virelai*, carol, and roundel. In their current use, 'lyric' and 'lyrical' carry associations of their use both before and after the Middle Ages. 'Lyric' was first applied to Greek strophic works, accompanied by the music of the lyre, which suggests a certain consistency in form. Its application to more recent works carries the burden of the definition 'first advanced by Ruskin in the nineteenth century as "the expression by the poet of his own feelings" (*OED*) [which] does not apply to the short poems of the medieval period' (McNamer, **958**: 299), and implies consistency in content. The whole genre now known as the ME lyric shows little uniformity in form or content, although there is consistency in groups within it. There are similarities in thought and structure within the lyrics of religious and secular love, in the prayers and meditations, in the lyrics of instruction, and in the songs of merrymaking. (At an extreme, some of James Ryman's carols conform to the use of similar or even identical first lines, as in the series of dialogues between the Child Jesus and the Virgin, each beginning 'Shall I' [*3092–7*], and the two hymns to the Virgin with the opening lines, 'O closed gate of Ezechiel / O plentevous mounte of Daniel' [*2404–5*].) However, poems in any one group may hardly resemble those in the others, and it is hard to relate all the works to one category of 'lyric.'

Judgemental idiosyncrasy and subjectivity encumber the adjective 'lyrical.' It is possible to accept a poem as a lyric, but not to find it lyrical, since 'lyrical' now has connotations of effusion of the poet's emotion, and conscious striving to convey effects of beauty. The ME lyrics must frequently disappoint expectations of personal, emotional, delightful works. Some poems placed in the category 'ME lyric,' such as the instructions for finding the date of Easter ['In March after þe fyrst C,' *1502*], will not be found lyrical in any of those senses. Similarly, there are lyrical qualities in works of all periods, including some not classified as lyrics. Most characteristic in general understanding of the term 'lyric' is the linking of poetry and music. Related to this must be a concept of music, heard or unheard. The comments of Eustache Deschamps on the 'natural music' of the sound of poetry in his *Art de dictier* indicate that the musical qualities of medieval poetry were appreciated in that era. In his comparisons of Chaucer's poems with French works, James I. Wimsatt applies these comments to works of Chaucer, and explains 'natural music' as 'simply the sounds of the words of poetry' (Wimsatt, *Chaucer and His French Contemporaries* 12). Does the association with musical sounds lead us to find a passage not merely poetic, but more specifically lyric? If we acknowledge that the sounds and rhythms are not always pleasing, although their effects are present, we may call a passage a 'lyric' but find it unlyrical, just as we acknowledge that a work is 'music' but find it unmusical. A poem called a lyric may not seem lyrical when its music does not seem musical.

There is a more useful analogy in the use of 'sculpture.' A category so widely inclusive might embrace both the beautiful relics of antiquity and garden gnomes. To think only of the medieval period, the term may include exquisite figures of the Virgin and Child, richly decorated chalices, elegant carvings on combs and boxes, jewellery of all kinds, and hideous gargoyles. The themes and sites of some of these works, inside and outside churches, could establish a loose (and misleading) category of 'ecclesiastical' or 'religious' for some of them, so that 'secular' could be applied to those situated elsewhere, with no obvious religious significance. (It is of course difficult to imagine any phenomenon or artifact of the Middle Ages being without religious significance or connotation. A distinction such as 'religious' or 'secular' that was not related to the disposition of the clergy would seem incongruous to people of that time.) The designations could extend to the decorations of capitals and church furniture, some of which display satirical representations of the clergy. From the permitted decorations it is only a short step to the cruder pictorial comment of unsanctioned scratchings on pews and walls. To pursue the analogy with the poems called 'ME lyrics,' there are lyrics to the Virgin composed with the grace and delicacy of the ivory figurines of the same subject, and others to earthly beloveds that express the intense feelings conveyed in the erotic carvings on ivory combs. Some works illustrate church teachings, as did the symbolic decoration of the ecclesiastical vessels; some, easily visible or concealed, tell of corruption in church and state in light-hearted or bitter terms. Other poems have purposes as practical as the spouting gargoyles and similar pretensions to beauty. The scratchings of choristers have their parallels in the scribbles in the margins of manuscripts and the fly-leaves of books. Acephalous and trimmed lyrics may even bear a passing resemblance to damaged statues. The terms 'lyrics' and 'sculpture' include disparate elements, varying in purpose and in the responses aroused in those who examine them. They may be found beautiful, ugly, amusing, elegant, ill-formed, useful, trifling, informative, and any combination of these and many other adjectives. Their qualities seem protean, and grouping them together a procrustean exercise.

An analogy, after all, is no more than that. Auden's warning is pleasingly apt:

> Man is an analogy-drawing animal; that is his great good fortune. His danger is of treating analogies as identities, of saying for instance, 'Poetry should be as much like music as possible.' (52)

Although the figure should not be used too sweepingly, it can yield some insights. The range of poems labelled 'ME lyrics' may well be as wide as that of medieval sculpture, and there are difficulties in making it more narrow. Since it is difficult to adjust the definition, it is worthwhile to try adjusting the term. There are more precise names for poems whose form or context provides reason to use them. Sometimes a poem is clearly a 'song,' 'hymn,' 'carol,' '*virelai*,' 'roundel,' 'lament,' 'pastourelle,' '*chanson de mal mariée*' or '*d'aventure*,' 'mnemonic verse,' or another of such categories. A general term such as 'ME short poem' may at first seem more vague and yet offer more precision, since it can include all the works grouped awkwardly in the category 'ME lyric,' and leave the latter for the works that are lyrical by all standards. Thus 'ME lyric' can include, for example, equivalents (sometimes translations) of troubadour and trouvère lyrics, hymns, and some poems of religious devotion. 'ME short poem' implies qualifications of era and size, but not, for instance, of the poet's emotional state: it allows poems of love to be collected, as in *RobbinsS*, with those of weather prediction and bloodletting. We can extend the category to make it more descriptive. Tables of contents in lyric anthologies suggest many additions, to yield short poems 'of devotion to the Virgin,' 'of the Passion,' 'of joy' or 'of sorrow in love,' 'of medicine,' 'of alchemy.' The contents of *BrownXV*, *RobbinsS*, and *RobbinsH* offer examples. Other extensions and variations would free 'ME lyric' for a narrower range of poems, in general of the kind placed in 'lyric' sections of general ME anthologies, poems which fit the term's connotations. A relatively non-specific term such as 'short poem' could be more illuminating than one that only seems to have more precision.

However, one must question the application of new and different standards to the poems already labelled 'ME lyrics,' because the term is so well established. However there is a precedent for some alteration in the understanding of the term, and a move towards wide range and enhanced precision. Rossell Hope Robbins, in the preface to his collection *Historical Poems of the XIVth and XVth Centuries*, supplies evidence of dissatisfaction with previous usage, in his intention to complete the series of anthologies begun by Carleton Brown, following Brown's principles, but to use, instead of 'lyric,' 'the wider term, "poem"' (**57**: vii). The historical poems use many verse forms found in the other anthologies, and indeed two of these works had already been printed in Brown's selections of religious lyrics of the fourteenth and fifteenth centuries. (*BrownXIV* has 'ȝhit is god a curteys lord' [*4268*]; *BrownXV* has 'Gife hys made domesman' [*906*].)

Examining the definitions and descriptions reveals constants among the characteristics of ME lyrics. E.K. Chambers's essay on 'Some Apects of the Mediæval Lyric' emphasizes the continental origins of the genre, not only in his text but also in the macaronic stanza from 'Dum ludis floribus' [*694.5*] printed with its title (Chambers and Sidgwick, **18**: 257–96). Brown and Robbins do not dwell on details of definition in their editions: rather they explain their choices of poems and describe the works. Their series first mentions definition in Robbins's remark (in the preface to *RobbinsS*) that he has 'accepted Brown's definition of a lyric as any short poem' (**51**: v). Similarly, R.T. Davies states in the 'Introduction' to his anthology that '[b]y a "lyric" is meant simply a shorter poem' (**61**: 46). Other editors, like Brown, concentrate on the poems and the manner of presentation. Some, such as G.L. Brook, **42**, and Maxwell S. Luria and Richard L. Hoffman, **79**, offer reasons for their selections. The term is not a contemporary one – the fact is often recorded – and this may seem reason enough not to linger on a definition. Robert D. Stevick, for example, states that

> these Middle English poems came to be referred to as "lyrics" only by modern convention, and not because of direct continuity with postmedieval literary works known by that same term. The Elizabethan notion of lyrics as poetry composed to be sung and the modern notion of lyrics as expressing intensely personal emotions can be seriously confusing in this connection and are best dismissed during one's initial approach to the poems presented in this collection (**103**: x).

In contrast, Richard Leighton Greene begins the second edition of *The Early English Carols* with a specialized exploration of 'The Meaning of "Carol"' (**86**: xxi–xxxiii).

General and particular examinations of the ME lyrics are illuminating, but it can be misleading and dangerous to use the methods or conclusions of one kind of exploration for the other. In the 'Introduction' to his collection of ME lyrics, Theodore Silverstein explores the lyric briefly, before applying his statements to some of the texts. He finds the lyric 'as it were, short, sweet and meaningful,' and later elaborates on the meaning of brevity in the lyric (**73**: 4, 5–8). Silverstein's adjectives fix his notion of the lyric, but they cannot be accepted without equivocation as broad terms, although they are entirely fitting for particular cases. The path from the general term 'lyric' to the specific 'ME lyric' is an uncertain one.

Many poems that correspond to some or all of Silverstein's specifications are caught in the driftnet category 'ME lyric.' 'Al nist by [þe] rose rose' [*194*] conveys intense emotions of sweet significance in a few lines, engaging the reader so that the poem cannot be easily forgotten. 'Glade us maiden moder milde' [*912*] briefly expresses intense praise and devotion in prayer to the Virgin. Lyrics such as these clearly illustrate Silverstein's idea, but others offer reasons to doubt every part of even that concise description.

The use of an adjective such as 'short' inevitably implies comparison, and hints at the intensity that can accompany brevity. Some ME lyrics are compressed to a quatrain, for example 'Nou goth þe sonne under wode' [*2320*], or even to a couplet, such as 'The ax was sharpe the stokke was hard' [*3306*]. Others are written in more expansive fashion. 'A Luue Ron' [*66*] of Friar Thomas de Hales extends to 208 lines, and *'Le regret de Maximian'* ['Herkneþ to mi ron,' *1115*] to 273, in the transcriptions of *BrownXIII*. There are other poems of more than 150 lines, including some of the historical works collected by Robbins for the anthology that 'completes the assembly in modern editions of the best of the Middle English lyrics' (**57**: vii). Yet works classified as or even related to ME lyrics are conspicuously shorter than such contemporaries as *Sir Gawain and the Green Knight*, *The Canterbury Tales*, or *Piers Plowman*. Although 'short' may seem of limited utility, we should retain it, but remember its relativity, subjectivity, and lack of precision.

The terse couplet on the year 1391, 'The ax was sharpe, the stokke was hard / In the xiiii yere of kyng Richarde' is short and meaningful, but far from sweet. Its quality of startling grimness precludes sweetness: the flavour is bitter. Some lyrics of religious and secular love disclose lightness, joy, and delight, and so sweetness. The lullaby carols of the Nativity intimate tenderness, even when they anticipate the sorrows of the Crucifixion. Many religious lyrics tell of suffering and regret, as do those of unhappy secular love – any experience akin to taste is sharp or bitter. There are delight and joy in 'The smylyng mouth and laughing eyen gray' [*3465*], the roundel associated with Charles d'Orléans, but the sweetness of love is often soured by the prospect of sorrow or rejection, as in 'Wiþ longyng y am lad' [*4194*]. The sharpness in some lyrics of earthly or religious devotion supplies their meaningful quality, to make them memorable, as lines of unalloyed sweetness cannot be. Lyrics of death may impart a message of *memento mori* through shock and disgust. When lyrics have a flavour, it is not always sweet, but its intensity affects the intensity of meaning.

Well-known (i.e. often anthologized) poems, such as 'Nou goth þe sonne under wode,' 'Al nist by [þe] rose rose,' 'The ax was sharpe the stokke was hard,' 'Gold & al þis werdis wyn' [*1002*], 'Wen þe turuf is þi tuur' [*4044*], and 'I syng of a myden þ^t is makeles' [*1367*], engage the reader's mind and emotions. Sweetness is sometimes expressed, but not only sweetness. Humour in the lyrics is often cruel, as in some poems of betrayed girls, and in the fabliau style of 'Old Hogyn' [*1222*]. Blander offerings, and there are many of these, convey familiar thoughts in unimaginative terms; the more dramatic and surprising works seize the reader's attention. The hackneyed poems are now generally printed only in exhaustive thematic studies that present all available works on a particular subject, such as those of Wehrle, **177**, and McGarry, **195**. Engaging freshness, clarity, and novelty supply the flavour and meaningful qualities found in the most effective (hence most anthologized) lyrics. There are examples in the simultaneously shocking yet comforting notion of taking shelter within the wounded skin of Christ, in 'Gold and al þis werdis wyn'; in the startling juxtaposition of courtly style and macabre description in 'Wen þe turuf is þi tuur'; and in the sophistication of apparent artlessness in 'I syng of a myden.'

The flavour of the lyrics makes them meaningful and memorable, and 'the best of the Middle English lyrics' are undoubtedly memorable. They offer poetry in its most compressed form, to declare poets' strongest feelings. Any judgement about a poem's qualities is inexorably linked to an opinion of that poem. Works found mediocre and uninteresting will seem none of short, sweet, or meaningful. Any that seem tedious, flat, and lacking in meaning will not appear lyrical. Poems recalled with pleasure or distaste are those that seem conspicuously 'good' or 'bad' – notoriously subjective terms. Many poems called ME lyrics evoke slight interest; they are repetitive and unimaginative, not meaningful and hence not memorable. These are not likely to appear in collections of 'the best of the Middle English lyrics.' But if they seem not to be short, sweet, meaningful, or lyrical in any sense, are they then not lyrics either?

In spite of cavilling and qualification – Silverstein himself suggests much qualification – 'as it were, short, sweet and meaningful' is a useful description, and offers avenues for exploration. Its lack of specificity is shown in the possibilities for applying it to things as diverse as fireworks or a melody; a letter, an invitation, or a compliment; a kiss, a giggle, a wink, or a sigh; a pun, an innuendo, an aphorism, or a slogan; a jury's verdict or a pathologist's report. It could refer to things that are not necessarily commendable: a retort and revenge spring to mind. The disparate range of interpretations mirrors the assortment of works called 'ME lyrics.' There is often an appeal to the senses, as in the connection with taste. The terms can imply the absence as well as the presence of the qualities, as in sorrowful lyrics of the loss of love's sweetness. Of the three terms, 'meaningful' may be the most important, but it will inevitably be applied as subjectively and imprecisely as the others. In such a context, 'as it were' has unprecedented significance. We may add 'memorable' to the defining terms, and confirm the elasticity and the elusive, evasive nature of the definition, summarized in Elder Olson's advice that

> it is futile to attempt a definition of lyric, if we mean by definition a statement of the nature or essence of something; for things of different natures cannot have one nature or definition. (66).

The attempt may be futile: that is no reason to avoid exploration of the form, in other languages as well as ME. There is greater unity in Latin lyrics, and in those of the troubadours and trouvères, than in the ME lyric. A study of these genres reveals many common characteristics and qualities we can recognize in the lyric in ME. There are lyrics of love in sacred and worldly, courtly and earthy forms, in all the languages of continental Europe. Their influences are seen in ME hymns that translate Latin hymns, in lyrics of adoration of the Virgin or a distant lady, in lyrics that use the form and essence of pastourelle and *tenso*. There are also continuing influences of OE, in mood and wit, and in alliterative and metrical effects, observed for example by Oakden, **163**, Heningham, **226**, Dronke, **935**, and Lerer, **1021**.

The term 'ME lyric' is vague, and a definition born of exasperation, 'a short ME poem that does not fit into any other defined genre,' may sometimes seem as apt as any other. It is legitimate to exclude epic, drama, and narrative, but aspects of the last two may appear, as in lyrics that use a dialogue form or chart the course of love. ('De Clerico et Puella' [*2236*] is a dialogue that implies a narrative; lyrics of betrayed maidens, such as 'As I went on Yole day in oure prosession' [*377*], tell the story of their seduction.) It is futile to question keeping some poems caught in the net of 'ME lyrics,' since the category is already established in canonical anthologies and criticism. Poems with no apparent musical qualities or appeal to any senses may and must be classified with others that clearly display those characteristics. Among the unlyrical lyrics are the works gathered by Robbins as 'Practical Verse' (**51**: 58–84). The diversity of the *Secular Lyrics* reveals scope for altering either the definition or the category, and may explain the title *Historical Poems* for the last anthology in the series Robbins and Brown present. Acceptance of the term 'ME lyric,' as it is used, with all its implications, is unavoidable, but it should be considered carefully.

An approach that indicates the limits of general description and offers an alternative is that of Ann S. Haskell, who looks at ME lyrics before she examines Chaucer's lyrics. She shows the inadequacy of applying general definitions of the lyric to ME works, and proposes distinguishing characteristics of the poems she will discuss as 'lyrics.' These works are

> with greater frequency than other medieval poetry, short; they generally have a tighter metrical pattern than, say, the romance; they are more frequently stanzaic than longer, narrative medieval poems; their rhyme scheme is more complex, in general, than that of narrative or dramatic poetry (although both the Wakefield master's works and the *Troilus* are exceptions which immediately present themselves); and they are frequently celebratory or plaintive, though they can be didactic or practical. Most medieval lyrics are not narrative, though they may contain skeletal plots; when narrative progression does occur in the lyric, it is usually as an objective entity for subjective reaction. In short, there is no quality of the medieval lyric that can be isolated as peculiar to that genre; nor do the characteristics enumerated here occur in predictable constellations. The best we can safely conclude is that they will always exhibit some cluster of the characteristics in this group. (**577**: 4)

Haskell's observations introduce the cluster of characteristics and the inconsistency in the features seen in a range of lyrics. She also alludes to lyrical sections in other works, particularly in medieval drama and in *Troilus and Criseyde*; some of these have been detached from their original context, and may be called isolable lyrics.

Another quality is to be added to Haskell's cluster. This, proposed by Burrow, is 'the most characteristic *axis* of lyric poetry: the "I" addressing the "you."' Like the attributes Haskell lists, this axis exists in other poems – indeed in most successful acts of communication – but the 'I' of lyrics differs from that of other genres. Burrow distinguishes the lyric 'I' from the poet, since this persona speaks 'not for an individual but for a type,' and is 'to be understood not as the poet himself, nor as any other individual speaker.' Thus the lyric 'I' offers thoughts that the reader might appropriate, 'as a lover, a penitent sinner, or a devotee of the Virgin' (**777**: 61). We may extend Burrow's idea to contrast the lyric 'I,' who addresses a singular, reading 'you,' with the 'I' of epic or romance, who may address a plural, listening 'you.' The lyric 'I' may impart a single significant, perhaps intimate, thought to one who seems to be alone, whereas the other 'I' tells of a train of events, relevant but not equally important parts of a larger whole, in a work intended for an audience, in public, rather than for private, individual attention. (Exceptions are inevitable – many carols and political works produce the effect of plural address by beginning with some variation of the 'Lysteneth lordings' formula.) Even when the pronoun 'I' does not appear in a lyric, there is an impression of an addressing voice and the need for a reader or listener, exemplified in the couplet of number maxims, 'Kepe well x And flee fro vii; / Rule well v And come to hevyn' [*1817*]. This impression, and the intimacy that attends it, may be the most constant of the characteristics in any cluster that marks the lyric. Identification of such qualities is the most useful way to describe the genre in general and indicate features to be examined in particular cases.

Definition rather than description is possible for individual types of lyric.

Greene's exploration of the carol, already mentioned, depends on his definition of the form as 'a song on any subject, composed of uniform stanzas and provided with a burden' (**86**: xxxii–xxxiii). He derives it from discussions of previous suggestions, and shows its application to many songs, together with reasons for occasionally rejecting works formerly designated carols, such as 'I syng of a myden' [*1367*], which has no burden. Moving from the definition, he investigates further, to include comparisons with related forms in ME and in other languages. The definition accommodates numerous forms and poems, and includes religious and secular works. There is similarly detailed examination of a restricted area in Martin Camargo's study of the love epistle, **731**, and Margit Sichert's of the pastourelle in ME, **837**. Such limited examinations can establish and employ definitions in ways that more general surveys cannot, and can demonstrate effects of variation as well as conformity, when characteristics are appropriated for particular effects. These characteristics can become salient features used for identification, rather than the vaguer listings of a cluster of possiblities. For instance, the rural encounter of a wanderer and a keeper of sheep signals the pastourelle, with its characteristic idioms, characters, and expected endings to the story. The overturning of such expectations contributes to the pleasure of surprises in 'Robene and Makyne' [*2831*], and the freshness in the lyric of the Five Joys of the Virgin, 'Ase y me rod þis ender day / by grene wode to seche play' [*359*], which so closely resembles the song of the 'litel mai,' with the refrain 'Nou springes the sprai' [*360*]. The most specific investigations of the lyric are those of individual poems. These may yield sharply differing interpretations of aspects of particular works, as in examinations of the 'Corpus Christi Carol' [*1132*], 'How Christ shall come' [*1353*],'The Maid of the Moor' [*2037.5*], and 'Svmer is icumen in' [*3223*].

The findings from broad description and narrow investigation provide information that contributes in different ways to the understanding of poems already accepted as ME lyrics. It is difficult to identify qualities that are universally found and also to justify the inclusion of some poems in the category. The designation 'ME short poem' would be safer, and could be made more precise by the addition of an adjective or phrase, whereas the application of 'ME lyric' to all must seem dubious, even if we allow for its not having been used during the Middle Ages, and try to ignore the connotations of other eras.

COLLECTIONS OF LYRICS

The doubts about definition beget doubts about the lyrics chosen for collections. Silverstein's comment, 'No man likes another man's anthology, however he may dote upon his own' (**73**: 1), has some force. If 'ME lyric' really means no more than a short poem, then brevity may seem to be the only characteristic shared by all poems in a collection, as noted by Julia Boffey (**947**), although their presence in it obviously depends on an editor's idea of a ME lyric. There are no doubts about gathering poems that closely resemble, even translate, the formal lyric poetry of romance languages. Verses of love, of religious devotion, carols and meditations: all are readily seen as ME lyrics. It is not as easy to place them with all the poems included in *RobbinsS*, **51**, as 'Practical Verse' (58–84) and 'Occasional Verse' (85–119). The poems resemble each other, but not in all ways. How are decisions made about which poems merit a place in modern lyric collections?

Any anthologist's selection of the lyrics liked best or thought worthy of preservation – these are almost synonymous – leads to those that have made the sharpest impression. The editors' prefaces sometimes record their guiding principles, the reasons and purposes behind the selection not only of complete poems, but of parts of poems. The intentions of those who first recorded the lyrics are rarely available, and the survival of many lyrics seems to owe much to chance.

The first collectors of texts were compilers of medieval manuscripts, whose intentions have sometimes been subverted by those who added lyrics to margins, fly-leaves, and the backs of pages, in contexts which may suggest reasons for their presence. Scraps of verse, unconnected with their context, may mean no more than a scribe 'intent on beguiling the tedium of his clerical duties' (Cawley, **289**: 142) or a blank space that has offered 'an invitation irresistible to a light-hearted scribe' (Sisam, **480**: 246). The tantalizing song 'Bryd one brere' [*521*] has survived with its music, on the back of a papal bull sent by Innocent III. The choice of this site may show that the scribe was 'calculated and practical and far-sighted,' in the use of a document 'which an undying institution has reason to keep with care' (Saltmarsh, **190**: 11). Each scribe has preserved a poem; the third seems most purposeful.

The compiler's taste and the availability of materials inevitably influence a manuscript's contents, and there are signs of purpose in manuscripts compiled by a single individual or individuals in a particular place. Richard Hill gathered items he thought important in his commonplace book: records of his children's births, recipes, and proverbs are among the literary works. Entries in the Findern MS were made in one place, by various hands, over many years. Those entries are 'illustrative of what people concerned with the reading of English poetry thought valuable for preservation'; as an unintended benefit, they also 'provide a modern reader with a representative anthology of the named Middle English poets' (Robbins, **54**: 612). More coherent collections include assemblies of sermons containing lyrics, such as the *Fasciculus morum*. Unifying purpose is clear in James Ryman's carols, the Red Book of Ossory, and John Grimestone's sermon lyrics. Revard, **787**, and Stemmler, **963**, detect structure in Harley MS 2253, but interpret it differently. Rosemary Woolf summarizes fifteenth-century manuscripts with lyrics as being

> roughly of three kinds: firstly, poetical collections, the work (or poems thought to be the work) of poets known and esteemed, Chaucer, Lydgate, and Hoccleve; secondly, manuscripts designed for the person who would own only one volume, and which therefore included a miscellany of romances, lyrics, didactic treatises, etc. (the Thornton Manuscript is a well-known example of this kind); thirdly, manuscripts which were produced by religious orders, particularly the Carthusians. As an appendix to these should be included the manuscripts of any kind which might contain one or two lyrics as a 'fill-up', to prevent the waste of leaving expensive parchment blank. (**522**: 359)

The collector of a poem always acts as a reader and an editor, and copying a poem may be an idiosyncratic process of uninhibited rewriting or translation. A scribe may work from memory or from an incomplete copy, sometimes in a dialect or a language not his own; he may wish to remove, rearrange, or interpolate passages as he writes. The extraction of the *Canticus Troilii*, from *Troilus and Criseyde*, and its use in different forms and settings is but one example of the last process. *SIMEV* presents 'Gif no luve is o God quaht feill I so' [*1422.1*], George Bannatyne's Scots transcription of the passage. Records such as those Bannatyne left in his collection of literature he wanted to preserve, are regrettably rare. A poem's manuscript context reveals many possibilities for its treatment and for variations in interpretation. Boffey, **795**, illustrates some of these possibilities, in particular the effects on *'De Amico ad Amicam'* [*16*] and *'Responsio'* [*19*], of the clerkly and courtly contexts of MSS Harley 3362 and Cambridge University Library Gg.4.27.

Modern publications offer transcribed texts or show the scribe's pattern by presenting facsimiles. For example, the Findern MS is available in a transcription edited by Robbins, **54**, and in a facsimile prepared by Beadle and Owen, **84**. Modern collectors may declare their purposes and methods, and more often gather lyrics from several sources than from only one manuscript. Editors may present works with a particular theme, such as Wright's collections of political works, **1**, **2**, **3**, and Patterson's of penitential lyrics, **24**. Some editions supply lyrics of particular periods, as in Brown's anthologies of lyrics of the thirteenth, fourteenth, and fifteenth centuries, **36**, **31**, **39**. Some collections gather poems from a particular place, for example Person's of lyrics in Cambridge manuscripts, **53**. Others present the works of a particular author, for instance Zupitza's edition of Ryman's works, **10**. Many editions combine categories, to offer a selection of works from a particular source, such as Brook's, **42**, of ME and macaronic lyrics in Harley 2253. A particular case of specialization is Murray's edition of 'Erthe upon Erthe,' **23**, which includes versions of that poem from 24 manuscripts.

The reasons collectors offer for their choices can be of greater interest than their selections. F.J. Furnivall campaigned energetically to save early literature and castigated anyone who did not share his enthusiasm. His purpose was 'not so much in mere antiquarianism or his interest in language as in discovering the social life of the past.' His work for the EETS included editing 39 volumes, each with a foreword and text 'leavened . . . with the peculiar impish, insinuating, appealing charm of his personality' (White 65, 69). Among these are editions of *Political, Religious, and Love Poems*, **4**, *Hymns to the Virgin and Christ* . . ., **5**, and the second volume of *Minor Poems of the Vernon MS*, **13**. Robbins regrets that ME criticism has passed from the hands of 'the distinguished and talented amateurs of the nineteenth century,' such as Furnivall and other founders of the EETS, 'to the footnoting professionals of today' (Robbins, **86r**: 265). More recent editors can use methods unavailable to Furnivall and his colleagues, and some early editions are now relished more for their forewords than for their texts. However, Wright's collections of political poems have not been superseded, since they offer a wide range of works of that genre in the languages of the time.

Brown, Robbins, Greene, and Brook have been the most influential editors of lyrics in the twentieth century, and their editions are accepted as standard forms of most texts they print. Luria and Hoffman, Silverstein, Stevick, and Davies, who have prepared anthologies for teaching purposes, present few lyrics not printed in one or more of the canonical collections, which they recommend as sources of first resort for further study. (Only seven of the 245 lyrics presented by Luria and Hoffman, **79**, are not represented in the Brown, Robbins, Greene, or Brook collections; Silverstein, **73**, presents 21 such lyrics in 144; Stevick, **62**, **103**, four in 100; Davies, **61**, 46 in 187. These lyrics include works of Chaucer – specifically excluded from the canonical collections – Scots works, and many printed by Robbins in his contributions to journals.) In 1965, Robbins confidently identifies '[t]he main body of Middle English lyrics' as Brown's, Greene's, and his own collections; he categorizes those of Davies, Gray, and Sisam as 'popular anthologies,' drawn from the main body (**479**: 35).

Ideas of the lyric and the grounds for selection presented by Brown, Robbins, and Greene are implied in other works. Brown and Robbins, like Bannatyne, aimed to assemble works worthy of preservation. Robbins's remarks, in the preface to the first edition of his *Secular Lyrics*, **51**, summarize his views and differences from Brown's. He has

> accepted Brown's definition of a lyric as any short poem, but departed from the general rules by which he excluded all poems by well-known authors (Chaucer, Lydgate, Hoccleve); poems of low literary value; and poems already printed in good and accessible editions (such as *The Early English Text Society*) . . . [He has] tried to include poems which would illustrate, irrespective of poetic merit, all the various types of Middle English secular lyrics; all lyrics outstanding either for their literary value or for the tendencies they represent, even if they have been previously printed; the lyrics most current in Middle English – the standard of currency being the number of texts preserved – irrespective of their appeal as literature to the modern reader; and finally, a few lyrics by known authors (except Chaucer), so as to permit a comparative survey in the compass of one volume. (**51**: v–vi)

Robbins alludes to most of the limiting factors that face the compiler of an anthology of ME lyrics. The first is definition, and he permits a very elastic form. The works of well-known authors are already available. Brown sees no need to print them again, but Robbins includes works for comparison. The two editors have different ideas of literary value, implying appeal to the modern reader and subjective judgement. More enlightening is the preface to Robbins's collection of *Historical Poems*, written in 1958, which begins:

> *Historical Poems of the XIVth and XVth Centuries* now completes the assembly in modern editions of the best of the Middle English lyrics, begun in 1924 by Carleton Brown and continued in his anthologies of 1932 and 1939, and in my own *Secular Lyrics of the XIVth and XVth Centuries* of 1952. In general, it follows the principles established in these earlier collections; however, 'lyric' has been replaced by the wider term, 'poem.' (**57**: vii)

The change is not in definition, but rather in the term defined. Robbins places his anthology in the series begun by Brown, (indeed includes works already printed), but speaks of 'poems,' without specifying length, and hints at the intractable nature of definition. McFarlane's review challenges Robbins's title, as 'misleading,' since it implies chronicle and narrative poems, without indicating language or length, but acknowledges that the preface 'makes clear what his title obscures' (**57r**: 58).

Greene's intention, stated in the preface to the first edition, **37**, of his *Early English Carols*, and reprinted in the second, **86**, is to assemble

> all those lyrics extant and accessible in manuscript or printed sources of date earlier than 1550 to which, in the editor's judgement, the term 'carol' can properly be applied. (**86**: xi)

Here 'lyric' is taken for granted, but the editor applies his judgement to a part of the category: 'those lyrics which bear, in their regularly repeated burdens, the mark of their descent from the dancing circle of the carole' (**86**: xxxiii).

Brook's edition of *The Harley Lyrics*, 'does not include the political songs, but contains all the other short poems which can properly be described as lyrics' (**42**: 2). This collection makes the ME and macaronic lyrics containing ME easily accessible. Brook's purpose is at once more specialized and selective yet wider than that of the other editors. He has examined one manuscript, and emphasized one language and genre, but imposed no qualification of literary merit or author.

The selection of the form of the text is as important as that of the poems. Recently published editions vary in more than footnotes or endnotes, presence or absence of titles, marginal glosses, translation, paraphrase, or other aids for the reader. Many editors offer the text as they find it in the manuscript version selected, and some record variants in other sources. They generally supply punctuation and arrangement of the lines, and transcribe the lyrics in a range of dialects, with individual preference in the use of ME characters *wynn*, *thorn*, and *yogh*. This is the style of the editions prepared by Brown, Robbins, and Greene. However, some collections prepared for teaching purposes, in particular those of Luria and Hoffman, **79**, Stevick, **62**, **103**, and Duncan, **104**, present the poems in a standard linguistic form. Luria and Hoffman substitute 'genuine but recognizable Middle English spellings for unrecognizable or grotesque ones' (**79**: x); both Stevick and Duncan use 'the form of English written in London at about 1400' (**103**: xxxv). Although the changes may seem sweeping, the normalization 'does not change the words and it affects very little the basis for recognizing the meter,' as Stevick demonstrates in two readings of 'Murie a tyme I telle in May' [*2162*] (**103**: xliv). Alterations of this kind are an overt form of *mouvance*, a process already in operation in every transcription of a text, since the offices of scribe and editor cannot be separated. Such *mouvance* is noted by Roy Rosenstein, in his observations of the multiplication of unintended variations in editions of the songs of Jaufre Rudel. Thus each modern editor may well offer, not simply a modern transcription of a poem, in diplomatic or other form, but 'a new post-medieval variation on each medieval version of each' (Rosenstein 164).

In summary, the editors of modern collections may declare their purposes to provide texts not otherwise available; to prepare better texts; to gather texts associated with a particular topic, time or place; to include or exclude texts on grounds of authorship, literary merit, length, or other qualifications. Any or all of these may seem fitting. The assured pronouncement that 'for all practical purposes, the entire domain of ME verse has been exhaustively surveyed,' made by Robbins in 1968, seems premature (**519**: 15), although fewer poems have been recently discovered than in the time prior to his statement. O.S. Pickering, for example, has published works formerly overlooked, **909**, **910**, and detected verse in material previously read as prose, **908**. The first transcriptions of such discoveries generally appear in journal articles. If the poems conform to the criteria of those who gather anthologies, they later join more familiar works in those collections. For example Bennett and Smithers, **65**, Greene, **86**, and Gray, **81**, **102**, present some works that have not been listed in *IMEV* or *SIMEV*, although the poems will no doubt be noted in the *New Index of Middle English Verse*, now being prepared by Julia Boffey and A.S.G. Edwards.

More recent editors do not propose replacement of the editions Robbins described as 'the main body' of ME lyrics. Instead, they seek to address their readers' particular needs. These needs include standard forms for teaching purposes, new editions and facsimiles of individual manuscripts, and editions of lyrics of particular genres. Among teaching texts are Duncan's collection, **104**, of lyrics of the period 1200 to 1400, divided according to topic, and Gray's collection of religious lyrics, **81**, **102**, arranged to form a 'Scheme of Redemption' (**81**, **102**: xi). Gray has also gathered a wider range of works, including lyrics, for *The Oxford Book of Late Medieval Verse and Prose*, **91**. Collections restricted by source, authorship, or genre include *The Welles Anthology: MS Rawlinson C. 813*, edited by Jansen and Jordan, **98**; *Women's Writings in Middle English*, by Barratt, **100**; and *Medieval English Songs*, by Dobson and Harrison, **87**.

Trends in presentation of editions are towards clarity and ease of use by the reader. They include the provision of notes and explanatory material in introductions and appendices. The editor's frank statement of intentions and the reasons for selection can be very enlightening. All these tendencies are welcome, as are various means by which scholars can study either the manuscript or a reproduction. Facsimiles, microfilms, and electronic forms of the text allow close study but protect fragile documents, and help scholars at a distance from the texts, although no form has yet offered a completely satisfactory substitute for study of the manuscript itself.

TRENDS IN CRITICISM

A brief review of lyric criticism, in snapshots of works presented at the end of the nineteenth century and in the first and last decades of the twentieth, reveals changes in matter and manner. There is an increasing appreciation of the poems as works of aesthetic worth and as sources of comment on their times. Although some critical preoccupations are constant, there are differences in and additions to methods employed. The greater volume of work is immediately obvious, and similar observations can be applied to other fields of scholarship, and related to increasing access to tertiary education, more critical material in many forms, and pressures to publish. Factors that affect lyric criticism more specifically include availability of manuscripts and methods for examining them; and the critical possibilities of areas such as psychological, cultural, and gender studies.

The three nineteenth-century critical works, **105–7**, illustrate significant fields in lyric scholarship: criticism of a particular lyric, identification of previously undetected poems, and comparative study. The first, $\epsilon.\tau.\kappa.$'s note, **105**, recognizes a variation of the 'Corpus Christi Carol' [*1132*], and elicits responses from Sidgwick, **110**, and later Gilchrist, **125**. Thompson's record of scribbled lyrics, **106**, anticipates similar discoveries. Ten Brink's general criticism, **107**, relates medieval French and English poems. Preparation of editions, often of individual manuscripts, is of paramount importance, and editors vary in the style and depth of explanatory material they provide. In the late nineteenth and early twentieth centuries many editions are published as books by EETS, or as long articles in German journals, by scholars writing in English and German. (I have annotated the longer editions in journals with those published as books, but include shorter editions with annotations of general critical works.) Shorter journal articles announce discoveries of fewer poems, such as those of Heuser, **108**, **114–15**, Hammond, **112**, **123**, McBryde, **116**, McCracken, **117**, Garrett, **120–1**, and Williams, **124**. Heuser also investigates the *O and I* refrain, **109**, and hymns to St Katherine, **114**. Taylor observes medieval drama, relating it to the *planctus Mariae*, at **111**, and to the religious lyric, at **118**. Some critical works assume prior knowledge of the field, and present references and quotations that are brief and occasionally cryptic. This leads to particular difficulties when the critic offers a free rendering of material, from within a poem not identified by its opening lines. No standardized, comprehensive form of reference to individual works is available before the indexes prepared by Brown, Robbins, and Cutler: *RMERV* (1916–20), *IMEV* (1943), and *SIMEV* (1965). Many early scholars refer to editions of Wright, **1**, **2**, **3**, Furnivall, **4**, **5**, **13**, Morris, **6**, Flügel, **7**, **8**, **15**, Fehr, **11**, **12**, **14**, Horstmann, **9**, Zupitza, **10**, Heuser, **16**, Kail, **17**, Chambers and Sidgwick, **18**, Dyboski, **19**, and Padelford and Benham, **20**. Present-day writers generally cite more recent editions such as those of Brown **31**, **36**, **39**, **48**, Robbins, **51**, **55**, **57**, Greene, **37**, **86**, and Brook, **42**. It is surprising and disappointing to find that some critics use only this method, without reference to *IMEV* and *SIMEV*, and the practice can cause confusion when similar poems are not clearly distinguished. It is to be hoped that the *New Index of Middle English Verse* will be extensively used.

In contrast, the last decade of the twentieth century offers few new editions, and only three are devoted to the ME lyric: Gray, **102** (a reprint of **81**), Stevick, **103** (a revision of **62**), and Duncan, **104**. They have full, clear notes, and are intended for student use. The edition of MS Rawlinson C.813, by Jansen and Jordan, **98**, presents other material as well as lyrics. There are some lyrics in more general collections by Conlee, **97**, Kerrigan, **99**, Barratt, **100**, and Burrow and Turville-Petre, **101**. Interests of the first three of these adumbrate critical preoccupations of the period. Conlee has collected debate poetry, and Kerrigan and Barratt works about and by women. There are recently discovered or revised lyric texts in works of Barratt, **931**, Brehe, **932**, Louis, **955**, Breeze, **968**, Duncan, **971**, Hargreaves, **976**, Means, **978**, Pickering, **981**, Willmott, **1004**, and Griffiths, **1006**. McNamer, **958**, proposes new readings of texts in the Findern Anthology; Martine Braekman, **987**, finds a new source for a poem in Rawlinson C.813.

Feminist criticism and interest in poetry of dispute join established critical interests. Studies are full and detailed, but the range of interests is wide, and few common threads can be discerned. Two monographs of specialized lyric criticism are those of Camargo, **949**, on the ME love epistle, and Sichert, **961**, on the ME pastourelle. There are references to ME lyrics in more general works by Astell, **929**, Reed, **941**, Rubin, **960**, and Margherita, **1000**.

Much of the critical material comes from collections of conference papers and *festschriften*. *Studies in The Vernon Manuscript*, ed. Pearsall, includes Burrow, **933**, Marx, **940**, and Thompson, **943**. *Chaucer's England: Literature in Historical Context*, ed. Hanawalt, contributes Green, **975**, and Orme, **979**.

Literature and Religion in the Later Middle Ages: Philological Studies in Honor of Siegfried Wenzel has Newhauser, **1009**, and Reichl, **1013**. Other such papers are Allen, **928**, Axton, **930**, Deyermond, **934**, Dronke, **935**, Stevens, **942**, Waldron, **944**, Boffey, **947**, Boffey and Meale, **948**, Davenport, **950**, Whaley, **966**, Wimsatt, **967**, Frese, **974**, McClellan, **977**, Saint Paul, **982**, Whiteford, **995**, Duncan, **999**, and Schwetman, **1003**.

Some scholars investigate fundamental aspects of the lyric. Dronke, **935**, addresses the ME lyric's continuity with OE verse, Kohl, **939**, the nature and purpose of the religious lyric, and Stevens, **942**, the sound of verse. Several critics explore debate, dispute, and dialogue: Reed, **941**, attends to the area as a whole, Sichert, **961**, to the pastourelle. Those who examine particular examples include Marx, **940**, Hinton, **953**, Lambdin, **954**, Thompson, **965**, Fein, **972**, McClellan, **977**, Wentersdorf, **984**, and Whiteford, **995**. Critics whose work can be loosely grouped as feminist are Astell, **929**, Barratt, **931**, Deyermond, **934**, Hinton, **953**, Lambdin, **954**, McNamer, **958**, Stanbury, **962**, Donaldson, **970**, Saint Paul, **982**, Breeze, **998**, and Margherita, **1000**. Those who find political and social comment (with several allusions to the motif of the gallant) are Brehe, **932**, Wilson, **945**, **1005**, Boffey and Meale, **948**, Green, **952**, **975**, Louis, **955**, Orme, **979**, Parker, **980**, Boffey, **985**, Scase, **1002**, and Wilson, **1005**. In addition to the brief references elsewhere, there are fuller discussions of carols by Whaley, **966**, Breeze, **989**, and Griffiths, **1006**. Frese, **974**, and Parker, **980**, explicate the 'Corpus Christi Carol' [*1132*]. Aspects of alliterative works are considered by Brehe, **932**, Fein, **972** (who also writes of 'The Four Leues of the Trewlufe' [*1453*] at **936**), Pickering, **981**, and Waldron, **994**. Lyrics used in preaching are examined by Willmott, **1004**, Millet, **1008**, and Newhauser, **1009**, who discusses a Franciscan manuscript, as does Reichl, **1013**.

Detailed inspections of manuscripts assist the study of the ME lyric. There is particular interest in the Vernon MS, and its sister, the Simeon. Aspects of Vernon lyrics are discussed by Burrow, **933**, Marx, **940**, Thompson, **943**, and Waldron, **994**. Wilson, **945**, **1005**, investigates Rawlinson C.813, its first owner, Humphry Wellys, and some of its verses, especially 'The Testament of the Bucke' [*368*]; Orme, **979**, writes of the motif of hunting expressed in this poem. Boffey, **946**, and Boffey and Meale, **948**, reflect on the composition and production of early books. At **947**, Boffey demonstrates effects of context on interpretation of texts. Taylor, **964**, questions the existence of minstrel manuscripts.

Comparison of criticism in the two historical periods indicates changes in approach, from the observation of larger fields of lyric study to that of defined areas such as particular issues and poems. Examination of manuscripts continues to reveal more texts, but whereas earlier works concentrate on the supply of texts, later criticism deals more with details of the poems and related issues. The latter involve aspects of psychological, myth, cultural and gender criticism, hardly considered before such studies as Davidson, **634**, Peck, **642**, Dronke, **649**, Hill, **692**, and Hanson-Smith, **712**. Although more recent critical works are more specialized, they address a wider range of readers, whose first interests may not be exclusively literary. The number of essays published in bound collections indicates the specialized nature of lyric study. Literary or linguistic aspects of the poems may be topics for discussion at specialized conferences or for contributions to *festschriften* for scholars with a particular interest in lyrics. On the other hand, the articles in general, rather than

General Introduction 21

medievalist, scholarly journals tend to reflect current critical trends, and to involve the lyrics as illustrations of those trends. This is shown by a comparison of papers published in *Studies in The Vernon Manuscript*, including Burrow, **933**, Marx, **940**, and Thompson, **943**, with journal articles such as Stanbury, **962**, **1022**, Moffat, **993**, and Lerer, **1021**, which explore issues of gender and cultural studies as well as textual matters. The wider interest offers fresh insights into the lyrics, and is a counter to the impression that they are merely obscure scraps of little importance.

The constants in lyric criticism – the study of texts and their significance in medieval society; the examination of whole manuscripts or individual lyrics, words or phrases; the relation of words and music – must remain the most stimulating preoccupations. New insights are encouraged by developing critical theories. Examination of manuscripts and early printed books and awareness of the importance of context, augmented by palaeographic and linguistic research, contribute much to the study of lyrics, to knowledge of conditions of copying, and transmission of texts. The benefits of interdisciplinary studies will include insights gained from further scientific investigation of the texts, to extend information on the age and sources of materials used, and the conditions of their storage.

INDIVIDUAL SCHOLARS

As already stated, Brown, Robbins, Greene, Brook, Stevens, and Gray have been the most authoritative twentieth-century editors of bound collections with significant introductions and notes. Editions of smaller numbers of poems have generally been published in journal articles, for example by Bowers, Bühler, Scattergood, Edwards, Pickering, Heffernan, Wilson, and Wenzel, and also frequently by Robbins. Davies, Stevick, Stemmler, Silverstein, Luria and Hoffman, Gray, and Duncan have prepared collections particularly intended for pedagogical purposes.

Brown and Robbins are the most influential scholars. Their editions are established authorities, especially for teaching editions, and *IMEV* has proved indispensable. Brown, in *RMERV*, compiled the first comprehensive listing of religious verse, and his collections of lyrics of the thirteenth, fourteenth, and fifteenth centuries supply standard forms and notes. Robbins, in his collections, in the compilation with Brown of *IMEV* and, with Cutler, of *SIMEV*, and in numerous journal articles, has contributed a greater volume of information to the study of ME lyrics than any other scholar, and stimulated much discussion. Brown's first interest is in religious verse, as *BrownXIV* and *BrownXV*, and the greater part of *BrownXIII* attest, but Robbins has also gathered a variety of secular verse. The contributions collected for his *festschrift* demonstrate the compass of his interests; several of these are annotated in this bibliography (**604**, **606**, **610**, **612**, **623**, and **628**). His pursuit and acceptance of the very wide range of short ME poems has probably ensured that all such poems, on any subject and in any style, fall into the category 'ME lyrics,' although (as we have seen) he eventually preferred the less specific 'poem.' His extensive listings of poems, to cite every member of any group, sets a precedent for much lyric scholarship. This method places a few poems in the foreground, but includes comparisons and references to many others, often simply through lists of *IMEV* numbers, supplied in footnotes. It is strikingly exemplified in **537**, 'A

Refrain-Poem from N.L.W. Peniarth MS. 395,' an article on 'Who-so kon suffre and hald hym still' [*4121*]. Here Robbins alludes briefly to more than 60 other poems to explain its background, and would perhaps have mentioned more had he not thought the relevant works of Lydgate 'too numerous to list' (48). The style can be recognized in the work of other critics, for example, in articles by Boffey, **795**, Jauss, **805**, and Boffey and Meale, **948**. His influence will no doubt be observed in the forthcoming *New Index of Middle English Verse* and in a collection of essays on the Harley lyrics, begun under his direction, now being edited by Susanna Greer Fein.

Other scholars have pursued specialized areas of lyric criticism. Greene has defined and collected carols. Brook has concentrated on lyrics of MS Harley 2253, the medieval collection about which most has been written. Bowers has contributed transcriptions from manuscripts. Bühler has printed numerous manuscript entries, in particular those in early printed books. Wenzel has collected and commented on many sermon lyrics. Stevens has transcribed early Tudor songs and carols, and focused much attention on musical aspects of the works. Heffernan concentrates on religious lyrics. The editors of pedagogical works have provided notes and classifications, and sometimes used standardized linguistic forms in their texts.

The most significant books of criticism of ME lyrics are generally specialized. Greene, **37**, **86**, provides general and specific study of the carol in his introductory chapters and notes, with a smaller selection from this work, **59**. Woolf, **522**, and Gray, **575**, present comprehensive examinations of the religious lyric. Luria and Hoffman, **79**, describe Woolf's chronological study as the 'most distinguished book on the Middle English lyric' (352). Gray's perceptive investigation is thematic rather than chronological. Wenzel writes extensively on lyrics of sermons, in particular at **701** and **882**. Rogers, **585**, offers a study of six religious lyrics. Most books of criticism of the secular lyric have made a slighter impression, but exceptions include the studies of Stevens, **438**, and Boffey, **848**. Stevens presents a discerning examination of the Tudor court, its music and song. Boffey judiciously assesses the evidence of manuscripts of courtly love lyrics and the conclusions to be drawn safely. Reiss, **583**, supplies detailed individual accounts of 25 lyrics in his collection of critical studies; responses to these include Robbins's disagreement, **517**. Books that range more widely over other European languages and genres include those of Dronke, **472**, **509**, Kane, **292**, and Diehl, **850**. Moore's general study of the secular lyric, **297**, conveys a disappointing effect of distaste for the poems, which is absent from his other works. Ransom's arguments, **857**, on parody in the Harley lyrics, seem forced, as are some ideas advanced by Oliver, **549**. Jeffrey's extensive expositions of the influences of the friars **569**, **639**, have provoked equivocal response.

Perhaps the fragmented nature of the genre and the brevity of the lyrics make the shorter, more specialized essay form most suitable for their criticism. It is the form most often used, and the following examples are among the most informative. Introductions to general and specific aspects of the ME lyric include those of Gray, **544**, Woolf, **559**, Salter, **598**, Stevens, **788**, and (in German) of Wolpers, **703–4**. Saltmarsh, **190**, conveys the excitement of the discovery of two songs with music. Robbins edits many lyrics, and classifies newly-found works, as in his articles on 'Popular Prayers,' **217**, and 'Private Prayers,' **218**. Spitzer, **303**, offers detailed, lucid explication of three well-known lyrics. Frankis, **365**, traces the motif of the lover's dream in lyrics of several languages and periods. Among expositions of aspects of medieval piety, Woolf, **446**, explains the allegory of Christ, the lover-knight, and Gray, **451**, the cult of the Five Wounds of Our Lord. Haskell, **577**, distinguishes the terms 'lyric' and 'lyrical.' Robbins, **744**, applies general principles to the specialized topic of court verse. Rogers, **658**, Stevens, **771**, and Copeland, **825**, examine permutations of translation into ME verse. Many critics consider influences on the ME lyrics. Osberg, **671**, traces effects of alliterative prose, and Wimsatt, **680**, **842**, those of the Song of Songs. Burrow, **709**, deals with poems that have no context, but Croft, **754**, Boffey, **795**, and Wenzel, **861**, demonstrate the significance and possibilities of context. Dronke, **935**, and Lerer, **1021**, investigate the continuity of OE and ME lyric forms. Matonis, **582**, **763**, **907**, writes in great detail on alliterative verse and Celtic influences, particularly in the Harley lyrics. The many contributions of Breeze, **885**, **902**, **915**, **968–9**, **988–91**, **997–8**, enrich the study of Celtic relationships and of particular words. Duncan, **971**, **1015**, offers plausible reconstructions of texts, as well as an anthology, **104**. In all aspects of lyric criticism, the direction of progress has been from general examinations towards investigation of more specialized topics.

INDIVIDUAL LYRICS

There can be no surprise in finding that the most challenging lyrics produce the most stimulating criticism.

There is much variation in explications of 'The Maid of the Moor' [*2037.5*]. Robertson, **298**, reads the poem as an allegory, and the Maid as the Virgin, arguments rejected by Donaldson, **414**. Tillyard, **304**, answered by Schoeck, **301**, suggests that the Maid may be an ascetic, perhaps Mary Magdalene. For different reasons, Harris, **567**, relates the poem to European traditions of Mary Magdalene. In another line of thought, Greene, **314**, proposes that the poem is secular, extending his interpretation at **484**, in answer to Curry, **459**, who finds a connection with 'The last tyme I the wel woke' [*3409*]. Speirs, **385**, sees connections with nature and the dance. Mason, **405**, comments on the sophisticated use of formula. Manzalaoui, **477**, observes parallels to a passage in the Apocrypha. Reiss, **583**, supplies a structural and stylistic analysis. Wenzel, **627**, finds traces of the work in a contemporary witness (intimating that it is a secular carol and the Maid a sprite) and, at **817**, in a macaronic poem; from these findings he infers that the poem spread beyond Ireland. Comparisons with other Rawlinson lyrics suggest to Burrow, **709**, that the song is secular. Stevens, **788**, thinks it is a dance song; at **880**, he relates it to the Latin 'Peperit virgo' of the Red Book of Ossory. Fowler, **827**, is another who perceives references to Mary Magdalene; he compares ballads of her legendary life and the carol 'I saw three ships come sailing in.' In the most recent contribution, Duncan, **1015**, supplies a reconstruction of the work, with his ideas of its performance, and assesses versions provided by Sisam, **30**, Robbins, *RobbinsS*, **51**, Sisam and Sisam, **69**, Dobson, **87**, and Greene, **314**. Duncan recalls Robertson's thoughts in his conclusion that the poem is 'sophisticated Christian allegory,' rather than a dance song; he observes 'its curious combination of simplicity and enigmatic allure' (162).

A similarly enigmatic work is the 'Corpus Christi Carol' [*1132*], which has also attracted many interpretations but remains tantalizingly elusive. Its preservation in Richard Hill's commonplace book, edited by Dyboski, **19**, has provided a context of some influence on those who have examined the carol. It is seen as an allegory of the Eucharist by Davies, **61**, and by Gilchrist, **125** (answering a question posed by ε.τ.κ., **105**), who also detects Arthurian allusions. Berry, **345**, **387**, examines later versions of the work, in particular James Hogg's, and differs in some respects from Gilchrist: he finds Hill's version a religious poem and Hogg's secular. Speirs, **385**, also traces the carol's descendants. Greene, **418**, offers a very full account, which relates the poem to heraldic symbolism and to Henry VIII's divorce from Catherine of Aragon in order to marry Anne Boleyn; at **461**, he also considers implications of the Hogg version, and answers Davies, **61**, and Manning, **443**. Greene summarizes comments on the work at **418**, and in his *Early English Carols*, particularly in the second edition, **86**, as does Gray, **575**. Bradford, **543**, finds both Christian and Celtic imagery. Peck, **642**, examines medieval perspectives on metaphor demonstrated there. Fowler, **827**, sees a pietà tableau, Frese, **974**, a trace of a *lai* of Marie de France, Parker, **980**, an allegorical puzzle and an allusion to Henry VIII's Act of Supremacy. Boklund-Lagopoulou, **986**, relates its form to folksong and ballad. The explications are fascinating, imaginative, and contradictory. Eventually the most convincing comments are those of Stevens, **788**, on the capacity of such lyrics to 'go on teasing us for ever with their enigmatic power' (275), and of Brewer, **796**, on the 'strange images of sorrow and beauty' and 'haunting power' (55).

Another lyric that has provoked contradictory responses is 'Westron wynde when wylle thou blow' [*3899.3*]. Davies, **61**, and Stevens, **438**, note that three masses were written to its music. Bateson, **276**, sees a merging of the human and the natural, with Christ invoked as a fertility spirit. In an exchange of views published in *The Explicator*, 1955–63, Gierasch, **355**, Sweeney, **363**, Henry, **379**, Lewis, **366**, and Griffith, **452**, offer spiritual and carnal explanations for the passionate cry, which the last compares to the blues. Dronke, **649**, finds a trace of the lyric in a more recent ballad, and places it in the context of works in other European languages of the period. Frey, **652**, **711**, investigates problems of interpretation and editing revealed in the poem's structure. Short and Williams, **674**, take a similar course, looking in particular at the scope for punctuation, which is absent from the manuscript. Chu-chin Sun, **797**, relates the poem to Chinese lyric style. Again, there are no certain answers, beyond the unquestionable power of the lyric to engage the attention of those who hear and read it, and experience the force of its words.

The fifteenth-century lyric, 'I syng of a myden' [*1367*] has been praised for the beauty, poise, and delicacy of its images, and compared, in particular, to a thirteenth-century work, 'Nu þis fules singet hand maket hure blisse' [*2366*], thought to be its source, an observation made first by Greg, **122**. The poem is frequently included in collections, and there is detailed comment in *BrownXV*, **39**, and Davies, **61**. Luria and Hoffman, **79**, present extracts from remarks of five critics, as noted in the annotation for this work. Spitzer, **303**, Woolf, **522**, Jemielity, **532**, Reiss, **583**, and Medcalf, **764**, explicate the poem with varying emphases. Mason, **405**, considers its use of conventions of simplicity. Manning, **420**, examines implications of *makeles*, and is answered by Halliburton, **511**, and Moran, **595**. Raw, **422**, investigates the imagery, and compares the earlier poem, as do Copley, **429**, Wolpers, **521**, Brewer, **796**, and MacDonald, **906**. Reiss, **551**, observes number symbolism. Fletcher, **685**, finds an echo in a sermon lyric.

Two ME lyrics of deceptively slight appearance exemplify the richness of the genre. 'Foweles in the frith' [*864*] conveys mysterious sorrow, understood in various ways. It is investigated especially by Reiss, **478**, **583**, Luisi, **498**, Chickering, **562**, Osberg, **856**, Weiss, **860**, and Moser, **893**. Sister Mary Jeremy, **497**, and Revard, **698**, note textual details. The secular and religious elements observed in the brief, evocative work allow abundant diversity in individual readings. There is similar lavishness in the imagery of 'Nou goth þe sonne under wode' [*2320*], the ME quatrain in St Edmund Rich's *Speculum Ecclesie*, entitled 'Sunset on Calvary' by Brown, **36**. Particular details among its ambiguities are amplified by Cutler, **250**, Thayer, **320**, Manning, **404**, Lockwood, **435**, Reiss, **478**, **583**, Burrow, **777**, Allen, **821**, Innes, **853**, and Weiss, **860**. The densely suggestive imagery of both lyrics has ensured that they are often chosen for collections to represent the most beautiful and moving of the ME lyrics.

Most has been written of 'Svmer is icumen in' [*3223*], because its music, date, language, provenance, the accompanying Latin poem, '*Perspice christicola*,' and the word *uerteþ* have attracted the notice of scholars in many fields. Comments embracing aspects of text and music have been made by Chambers and Sidgwick, **18**, Moore, **297**, Manning, **394**, Sikora, **466**, Reiss, **583**, Helterman, **593**, Travis, **625**, Wolpers, **704**, Booth, **708**, Obst, **810**, and Fulton, **828**. There are brief allusions in Allen, **821**, Albright, **844**, and Stemmler, **912**. The date has been considered by Bukofzer, **244**, Hoepfner, **249**, Pirotta, **263**, Schofield, **265**, and Handschin, **268**. *Uerteþ* has been pursued by Silverstein, **73**, Ericson, **207**, Huntington Brown, **243**, Hoepfner, **245–6**, and Fain, **291**, more briefly by Reiss, **583**, and, in greatest depth, by Platzer, **1012**.

Interest has been focused on some manuscript collections of lyrics, including the Rawlinson, Vernon and Simeon, and Welles poems, and in particular on the Harley lyrics. The last term refers to the ME and macaronic lyrics in Harley MS 2253, which also preserves works in Latin and French, and especially to the 32 works, mostly lyrics of religious and secular love, edited by Brook, **42**. The structure of the whole manuscript has been examined by Revard, **787**, and Stemmler, **963**. Matonis, **582**, **763**, and particularly at **907**, examines the language and Celtic influences seen in the texts. Scholars have written of the puzzling 'Man in the Moon' [*2066*], of the monitory 'Earth upon Earth' [*3939*], and of the political poems (not edited by Brook) in particular the satires on 'The Consistory Courts' [*2287*] and 'The Retinues of the Great' [*2649*], but there has been most interest in the lyrics of secular love.

The Harley love lyrics offer freshness, sophistication, and ample scope for interpretation. These poems present a range of styles; their novel use of conventional techniques and phrases achieves unconventional effects, both beautiful and grotesque. Some critics have read the exaggerated and bizarre descriptions as irony and parody, especially in 'The Fair Maid of Ribblesdale' [*2207*], observed by Brewer, **351**, Burton, **752**, Jauss, **805**, Ransom, **857**, and Glasscoe, **869**. Different opinions are tendered by Jones, **875**, about the Fair Maid, and by Stemmler, **839**, who also writes of 'Annot and John' [*1394*], and finds no trace of parody in either poem. Degginger, **330**, and Duncan, **971**, demonstrate plausible reconstructions of 'A wayle whyt ase walles bon' [*105*]. The line 'Al that gren me graueth grene' in 'Wynter wakeneþ al my care' [*4177*] has been explained by Brown, **31**, Sisam and Sisam, **69**, Reed, **159**, Speirs, **385**, Manning, **443**, Shannon, **621**, Scattergood, **645**, and Harrington, **872**. The love song 'Blow, Northerne Wynd' [*1395*], often appears in collections; criticism of the poem includes that of Brown, **36**, Greene, **37**, Brook, **42**, Davies, **61**,

Stevick, **62**, **103**, Bennett and Smithers, **65**, Sisam and Sisam, **69**, Spitzer, **303**, Brewer, **351**, Einarsson, **432**, and Crampton, **732**.

Within the disparate assortment of lyrics that are most fascinating to their readers, only one characteristic seems constant – a tantalizing quality that evades simple explanation. Wenzel, **861**, confidently pronounced the mysterious work 'I sayh hym wiþ fless al bi-sprad' [*1353*] '*not a lyrical "poem" at all,*' but such finality seems elusive in other cases. This elusiveness is undoubtedly significant in the charm of the lyrics that have gained most attention.

THE ISOLABLE LYRICS

The lyrics called 'isolable' are an unusually enigmatic part of a genre that is already enigmatic. They are discrete passages that are separable from a larger work, the poem or play of which they form a part. The lyrics may be established poems, with a life of their own, inserted by the author of the larger work, or they may be identified after composition as formed sections that can be extracted and used, either alone or in combination with other poems. As a paradigm, we may take 'Now welcome somer with thy sonne softe' [*2375*], the roundel within *The Parliament of Fowls* [*3412*] that demonstrates unexceptionable criteria for recognition of an isolable lyric.

> "Now welcome, somer, with thy sonne softe,
> That has thes wintres wedres overshake,
> And driven away the longe nyghtes blake!
>
> "Saynt Valentyn, that art ful hy on-lofte,
> Thus syngen smale foules for thy sake:
> [Now welcome, somer, with thy sonne softe,
> That hast thes wintres wedres overshake.]
>
> "Wel han they cause for to gladen ofte,
> Sith ech of hem recovered hath hys make,
> Ful blissful mowe they synge when they wake:
> [Now welcome, somer, with thy sonne softe,
> That hast thes wintres wedred overshake,
> And driven away the longe nyghtes blake!"]
>
> (lines 680–92, *Riverside*)

The passage displays most of the distinguishing marks of the isolable lyric. It is clearly identified within the work from which it can be isolated, and introduced when the narrator tells us:

> But fyrst were chosen foules for to synge,
> As yer by yer was alwey hir usaunce
> To synge a roundel at here departynge,
> To don Nature honour and plesaunce.
> The note, I trowe, imaked was in Fraunce,
> The wordes were swiche as ye may heer fynde,
> The nexte vers, as I now have in mynde. (lines 673–9)

The form of the roundel is conspicuously different from that of the body of *The Parliament of Fowls*. There is a change of speaker: although the birds who sing are not specified, there is a clear break from the speech of the narrator. This is shown, with some variation, in the manuscripts. The song is presented in full only in Cambridge University Library Gg.4.27, and as a stanza (lacking one line) in Digby 181. Other witnesses have fewer lines, and vary in setting the roundel apart from the rest of the poem. Modern editorial practice, admittedly an artificial kind of evidence, places it within quotation marks, in a different stanza form. The lines also have an entry and number in *IMEV*, a bureaucratic proof of existence, rather like a passport, nevertheless a useful and relatively impartial standard to identify poems and their sources, and to establish them as discrete entities, independent of their surroundings.

These are the criteria available to show lyrics that are truly isolable. They should be formed structures, clearly distinguishable from the work around them by a difference in any of the following, alone or in combination: metre, rhyme scheme, stanza form, topic, or speaker. There may also be a change from speech to song. There should be a distinct beginning and ending, and it should be possible to extract an isolable lyric without affecting its coherence. 'Now welcome somer' satisfies all of these criteria. Some other works that have been described as isolable lyrics satisfy only some of the criteria, and some do not seem to satisfy enough.

The resemblance of passages in medieval drama to other works, especially the lyrics, has frequently been remarked. The observations of Taylor, **111**, and his cautious findings make a helpful precursor to considerations of isolable lyrics in medieval plays. Writing of 'The English "Planctus Mariae,"' he relates laments written in non-dramatic lyric form to the *planctus* of medieval drama. He finds many common factors of motif and expression, to conclude that the correspondences 'at least suggest that the dramatic are, in certain cases, drawn from the non-dramatic' (623), and that in many cases the *planctus* could be removed. His examination, **118**, of 'The Relation of the English Corpus Christi Play to the Middle English Religious Lyric,' extends the observations to a wider range of themes. These include many prayers, the 'Testament of Christ,' 'Hail Jesus,' Hail Mary,' 'Complaints of an Old Man,' 'Christmas,' and 'Ubi Sunt.' Taylor assesses 'to what extent the plays are indebted to the antecedent and contemporaneous religious lyric in Middle English' (15). Using detailed comparisons, he shows that thoughts and phrases in passages of the plays echo the lyrics. Similarly, Keiser, **854**, recognizes the *planctus Mariae* as 'most often a free-standing lyric poem,' but also to be found 'imbedded in a dramatization or a narrative of the Passion' (168). We may agree with Reed, **135**, that songs from other sources are added to the mystery plays when we find such stage directions as 'Here shall enter a ship with a merry song,' 'Et tunc cantant,' 'Tunc cantant angeli Te Deum' (79–80), and with his description of some passages as 'lyrical in their subjective spirit,' although we may not necessarily accept that they are 'short poems' (81). Osberg, **767**, includes 29 isolable lyrics from the text of *Corpus Christi* plays in his 'Hand-list of Short Alliterating Metrical Poems in Middle English.'

The term 'isolable' is used freely by Pearson, **196**, when she writes of passages in the mystery plays, and concentrates on

> isolable lyrics proper, which consist of lyrics forced into the play for their own sake, and left with scarcely any connecting material; [and] the lyrics with dramatic significance, but which can well stand alone without their setting. (228)

She states that her numerous examples have 'the primary requirement of lyric verse, the unity in emotional attitude' (229). There are speeches, complete or incomplete, but among them are some passages that are spoken by more than one character, some that are addressed to more than one listener, and many that deal with more than one topic. Few could be called isolable as confidently as can 'Now welcome somer.' A limiting factor shared by many of Pearson's examples is specificity to their speakers, demonstrated in references that associate speeches and characters, and argue against the passages' being isolable for use in another setting, since the characters' attitudes and identities seem to persist in the new location. For example, although men, as well as angels, may wish to offer praise to God, the song cited by Pearson, from the Towneley play, *The Creation*, includes the lines

> Lord, thou art full mych of myght,
> that has maide lucifer so bright;
> we loue the, lord, bright ar we,
> bot none of vs so bright as he (lines 67–70)

that attach the speech to the angelic being who speaks. An equivalent passage in the York play (stanzas 6 and 10 of *The Creation and the Fall of Lucifer*) is similarly specific. In addition, its emotional unity is marred by the interruptions of Lucifer and a cherub, which come between the words of the first seraph and responses of other angels (lines 41–8, 73–80). On the other hand, Abraham's speech from the Coventry *Abraham and Isaac* has some claim to being considered isolable, since it could be extracted to express praise and the wish to live a godly life:

> Most myghty maker*e* of Sunne and of mone
> Kyng of kyng*ys and* lord ou*er* all
> All myghty god in hevyn trone
> I þ*e* honowr*e and* evyr mor*e* xal
> My lord my god to þ*e* I kall
> wi*th* herty wyll lord þ*e* pray
> In synfull lyff lete me nevyr fall
> but lete me leve to þ*i* pay. (lines 1–8)

Pearson presents four examples of Gabriel's greeting from Annunciation plays. These could be considered variations on the theme of other 'Hail Mary' lyrics, found in many other sources. They are also integral to the play, indeed inevitable, as are other passages that resemble the songs *Nunc dimittis* and *Magnificat* in the liturgy. The presence of these speeches cannot be considered remarkable or contrived, nor could the passages be thought to be 'forced into the play for their own sake.'

Isolable lyrics are comparable to songs in Shakespeare's plays, which seem sometimes to have a life of their own and to be freely isolable from their context. 'When daisies pied and violets blue,' for example, was performed in both *Love's Labour's Lost* and *As You Like It*; stage directions, such as 'Marina sings' (*Pericles*: V.i), indicate a song neither noted nor remembered, and perhaps not specified either. There is still more variation in present-day Shakespearian productions. Songs may be said or sung, perhaps not at the times prescribed in the stage directions, with or without musical accompaniment, sometimes by the characters specified, sometimes by others; frequently they are not performed at all. This is *ex post facto* evidence again, but also a demonstration of the freedom with which some songs may be used, perhaps with scant reference to the original context, in non-specific ways, in short a demonstration that they are genuinely isolable. In contrast, although particular Shakespearian speeches have become famous and are frequently performed out of their context, we still think of *Hamlet's* soliloquies, *Portia's* speech about mercy, and *Mark Antony's* address. Even in discrete performances, they are still associated with their speakers, and need some form of introduction for a full appreciation of the lines. They cannot be isolated as can 'Tell me where is Fancy bred,' 'Under the greenwood tree,' or 'Take, O, take those lips away.' Comparison with Shakespeare's songs and speeches offers another criterion for identification of an isolable lyric. Isolable entities can be detached without loss to their integrity, whereas other passages, although they may be appreciated and performed for their characteristics of beauty or ideas, remain parts of a larger whole, and evoke a particular speaker and situation. Although many examples of isolable works have been songs, this is coincidence rather than a criterion of isolability. It is more pertinent that they offer oblique rather then direct comment on their settings, and that this comment may be transferred to other speakers and contexts.

If passages do not answer these criteria, then we should regard them simply as parts of larger works which echo a style or motif for a particular effect, as for example the words of Flesh, in the Digby play, *Mary Magdalene*:

> now þe lady lechery, yow must don your attendans,
> for yow be flower fayrest of femynyte:
> yow xal go desyyr servyse, and byn at hur attendavns,
> for ye xal sonest enter the beral of bewte. (lines 422–5)

These lines suggest to Robbins, **744**, 'a hint of parody of a courtly love lyric' (227), but they cannot be fully appreciated without an understanding of their setting. There are many lyrical passages in Chaucer's works, but we should be cautious about classifying sections as isolable lyrics, although we can be confident about 'Nou welcome somer,' the balade 'Hyd, Absolon, thy gilte tresses clere' in *The Legend of Good Women* [*100*], and possibly the envoys which conclude some short poems such as 'Truth' [*809*], 'Lak of Stedfastness' [*3190*], and the 'Complaint to his Empty Purse' [*3787*]. Moore, **295**, details Chaucer's use of interpolated lyric and compares the work of other poets such as Jehan Renart.

A section regarded as isolable both by medieval scribes and modern editors is the 'Ubi sount qui ante nos fuerount' passage of 'The Sayings of St Bernard' [*3310*], which is written differently in the six manuscripts that contain the poem, and seems in at least one of them, Digby 86, to be a separate work (see Cross, **391**). It has been selected by many editors as a lyric, and is printed in several anthologies, including *BrownXIII*, **36**, Dickins and Wilson, **47**, Davies, **62**, Stevick, **62**, **103**, Sisam and Sisam, **69**, and Silverstein, **73**. Two other passages clearly intended for extraction are 'Harus in cyue' and 'Harus in a sewe,' the recipes noted by Ross, **189**: 369–70 (the former in the *Liber Cure Cocorum* [*2361*] and the latter derived from *Sir Gawain and the Green Knight* [*3144*]). Although these are not as lyrical as the other lines mentioned, they resemble the verse of instruction selected in *RobbinsS*.

There are engaging possibilities in the use of isolable poems in other settings and in varied combinations. Boffey, **947**, describing the incorporation of passages and allusions to them within other poems, looks at the process 'by which one poem answers, anticipates, or spawns another' (131), and finds significance in 'the nature of some texts, both verse and prose, in which particular portions were expressly designed to be extracted' (135–6). She considers the contexts of various isolable lyrics, including plays, sermons, and *Troilus and Criseyde*, and the effects of changes in surroundings. The changes in meaning may be marked, as in a 'Lydgatian lyric in the Bannatyne manuscript ["Quhat meneth this Quhat is this windir vre," *3911.5*], which is comprised of stanzas from *The Complaint of the Black Knight* [*1507*]: here, reordered and without their narrative framework, the stanzas are given a distinctly antifeminist thrust' (137).

Some medieval writers, with more imagination and fewer inhibitions than their fellows, arranged stanzas written by more than one poet to form centos. One of these is 'The Tongue' ['Ther is no more dredfull pestilens,' *3535*], described in *IMEV* as 'a composite poem incorporating three stanzas from Lydgate's *Fall of Princes* (I. ch. xiii) and three stanzas from Chaucer's *Troilus and Criseyde* (III. 260–80).' Indeed *Troilus and Criseyde* [*3327*] has seemed to any who wished to extract passages as 'fair game' (Robbins, 'The Lyrics,' in Rowland, *Companion*, 315). The *Canticus Troilii*, in particular, appears in many collections and forms; the version cited in *SIMEV* is Bannatyne's Scots transcription of the 'Song of Troyelus,' 'Gif no luve is o God quaht feill I so' [*1422.1*]. At our remove from the original, we may see the extraction and formation of a cento as an imaginative and creative process, but unlike the original composition of the poem. The composer of the cento has seen different opportunities in the original poet's work, and made modifications to emphasize or express a particular thought, not inevitably a thought of the first poet. The second artist is the composer of a collage rather than a poem.

We must recall the milieu of composition of the centos, the second-order creations, and bear in mind that creativity itself was not esteemed in the Middle Ages as it is in the present day. The frequent references to 'myn auctour,' just as likely to be a fiction as any other part of the work, imply a mistrust of originality as intense as any current suspicion of plagiarism. Copyright was not an issue, and citation of an author could lend respectability to original thoughts. In such circumstances, rearrangement of another's stanzas appears unremarkable, and unlikely to arouse the furore of the discovery of such an action today. We may remember Sir John Paston's wish for his copy of *The Temple of Glas* to use in his own love letters. It seems acceptable, in the familiar analogy of the rearrangement of genetic material, to treat the stanzas as beads to be arranged on a string, or, in another clothing metaphor, as a length of fabric in the hands of various designers. The colours and texture are already determined, but each designer makes an individual contribution to another creation. A successful style may be imitated, perhaps in another fabric, sometimes even with a bogus label, akin to 'quod Chaucier,' a gesture towards acknowledgement of the idea and an attempt to acquire some of its author's respectability.

Although we may think of rather plodding poetical collages simply as reworkings or imitations, should we regard an integrated and elegantly linked work as a new composition? If so, then who is the author? There is no difficulty in seeing a poem in the Welles Anthology, 'Loo he that ys all holly you₃ soo free' [*1926.5*] as a rearrangement. It adapts lines spoken by Troilus, Criseyde, and Pandarus to make a love letter, and the editors, Jansen and Jordan, **98**, describe the compiler as 'guilty of some clumsiness' (195). Other poems in the same collection have been adapted from works of Stephen Hawes, and some modifications supply commentary on metrical changes since their composition (18–20). Those works seem rather less inspired, but the compiler of 'The Tongue' shows imagination in the felicitous arrangement of Lydgate's and Chaucer's stanzas. Sarah Wilson, **411**, observes rearrangements in manuscript versions of 'Luf es lyf þᵗ lastes ay it in Criste es feste' [*2007*], including the insertion of another lyric, 'Ihesu god sone of mageste' [*1715*], within the copy in Longleat MS 29, and the division of the long poem in Lambeth 853 'into three separate lyrics, each concluded by "Amen"' (337).

On a smaller scale, individual lines, such as quotations from earlier political works, are sometimes used with different emphasis, possibly to make the audience recollect and revise earlier opinions. Arens, **914**, notes that the poem 'On English Commercial Policy' ['Goo forth lybell and mekly schew thy face,' *921*] presents 'whole lines of verse . . . copied from the "Libel [of English Policy]"' (178), composed some 25 years before. 'On English Commercial Policy' offers an abstract of the 'Libel' ['The trewe processe of Englysch polycy,' *3491*], but another perspective on foreign policy, 'in favour of a commonweal seen from the viewpoint of domestic affairs' (179), rather than the earlier representation of views of 'a clearly factional interest, namely that of the merchant class' (178). A celebrated case of development that goes beyond mere reworking is the composition of 'I syng of a myden' [*1367*], first related to 'Nu þis fules singet hand maket hure blisse' [*2366*] by Greg, **122**. There are more recent instances of alteration of emphasis and interpretation in the practices of modern editors, particularly when they attach titles to the poems they present. A striking example of reinterpretation is that of the Findern Anthology, first edited by Robbins, **54**, who reads many of the love lyrics as conventional lovers' complaints, in the male voice. In contrast, Hanson-Smith, **712**, and McNamer, **958**, characterize them as the work of women, writing openly and earnestly, often of the pain of separation from their husbands. Thus a poem, 'Where y haue chosyn stedefast woll y be' [*4059*], described by Robbins, **54**, as 'To his Mistress' (613), is seen as 'A Woman Affirms her Marriage Vow' by McNamer (303).

How should we think of the idea of 'isolable lyrics'? Is it a useful classification or merely a latter-day perspective on an unremarkable phenomenon of the Middle Ages? Should we distinguish, for instance, between isolable passages in medieval plays which appear to have been taken from other sources, and those that recent critics think *could* be taken to another setting? Is the idea of taking stanzas from one poem to another simply a pleasing diversion, or is it a creative way of seeing the original, to produce a cento, a catenulate collage? Should we imagine that knowledge of such an occurrence would induce proprietorial anxiety in the original poet? Is the appropriation of lines or stanzas to be considered only an extension of the use of popular motifs or phrases?

Current preconceptions do not apply. Plagiarism is an alien concept to a time when poets invented authorities and scribes were unrestrained in their copying, so that they freely added, subtracted, annotated, expanded, and extracted. Rearrangement could create a new poem or a different emphasis, and appears to be an imaginative and permissible way of using material, not likely to provoke the outcry that attends such behaviour now. Present-day inspection of longer poems, as in Pearson's study, in search of isolable sections, is dubious and unlike the observation of interaction between various poets and their works. Whereas the recognition of creative use of lines and stanzas is little more than that of motif and theme, the isolation of passages without medieval precedent strikes a false note.

THE MUNDANE LYRICS

Among works gathered as 'ME short poems' or, more often as 'ME lyrics,' are some that do not conform to criteria of lyricality for poems of any other language or period. These are poems of mundane life, mnemonic reminders, verses of practical instruction, of proverbial wisdom, of political comment: lyrics only by the elastic standards of criticism of ME lyrics. The difficulty lies less in calling these ugly ducklings 'lyrics' than in deciding what else to call them. It is hard to imagine that 'Al nist by [þe] rose rose' [*194*] and 'XXX^{ti} days hath novembre' [*3571*] are both lyric quatrains, and almost depressing to realize that the latter is the most widely known of all poems called ME lyrics. The mundane verse of days in the months has been known and used by innumerable people, few of whom have thought of it as a ME lyric. There are benefits to be gained from studying the mundane lyrics, which pass on ideas of medieval life in the attitudes they convey and the knowledge they preserve. They keep the thoughts of a society in which many people could not read or write. These works, with few poetical devices beyond relentless rhyme and rhythm, were not treasured for beauty, but rather retained for utility, to transmit cultural patterns as the learned basis for actions that eventually seem to be reflexes. They echo the rhythms of everyday speech: did they mimic, or indeed induce the rhythms of thought in those who use them?

The mundane verses educate, not only in formal matters of prayers, the Ten Commandments and the Creed, the calendar, saints' days, ways to find Easter, and rules of grammar. There is more subtle, pervasive education, in verses of behaviour and attitudes, in proverbial scraps and saws handed on by family and friends. The range is wide, with poems to deal with most aspects of the life of body and soul, to state and reinforce expectations of society, to offer predictions and guidance for mortal life and aid the transition to an immortal one. In uncertain times, there is reassuring stability in verses that recall the ceremonies of the church and show patterns in the natural world.

'By thys fyr I warme my handys' [*579*] confidently prescribes the occupations for each month of the year in an ordered, unchanging world, and the obligations to kill swine at Martinmas and drink red wine at Christmas. Humanity is always helpless to control the climate or ensure that the world will not change, but the almanac verses offer a kind of comfort in predictions of the seasons to be expected, according to weather on significant days, or the day of Christmas or New Year's Day. They tell of climate, crops, trade, and sickness, with predictions for children born on Christmas Day. Anyone who compared the Christmas Day prognostications of 'Now hathe ye harde bothe olde & yonge' [*2323.4*] and 'Lordynges I warne yow al beforne' [*1989*] would find disconcerting variations, according to the manuscript consulted. There are further differences from the 'Prognostications of Esdras' or Ezekiel, 'Ye mene that wysdome will lerne' [*4253*], reckoned from New Year's Day, and thus from the same day of the week. Any prophet could safely predict that winters would be wet, princes would wage war, winds would blow hot and cold, people and animals would die from diseases, and women with child would swoon: a versified statement lends a veneer of authority. The weather on St Paul's and St Swithin's Days were used for predictions, as in 'Giff sanct Paullis day be fair and cleir' [*1423*] and 'In the daye of Seynte Svythone' [*1545*]. 'Maysters that was of craftes seere' [*2131*] lists lucky and unlucky days of the year, in particular the favourable or dangerous days on which to be bled or take medicine. For anyone needing more precise instructions, '*Nota* for the Days of the Moone,' ['God made Adam the fyrst day of þe moone,' *956*], specifies conduct for each day of a month of 30 days, generally based on events recorded in the OT.

Other such instructions and warnings come in gnomic maxims and proverbs, or more comprehensive accounts. 'Veynes þer be XXX^{ti} and two' [*3848*] presents details of bloodletting; there are explications of the humours in 'Sluggy & slowe in spetynge much' [*3157*] and 'Of yiftis large in love hathe gret delite' [*2624*]. Lydgate offers ideas of diet and other advice in 'For helth of body couer for colde thyn hede' [*824*]; other writers advocate temperance in 'Phebus fonde first the craft of medicine' [*2751*] and the use of leeks in 'Juce of lekes with gotes galle' [*1810*]. Secrets of preparing the Philosopher's Stone are imparted in 'Of spayn take the clere light' [*2656*], and of buying land wisely in 'Who so wylle be ware of purchassyng' [*4148*]. Robbins includes all of these works in *RobbinsS*, **51**, **55**.

Poems of women seem lyrical or mundane, and disclose as much of the poets as of their subjects. The works stress the poles of medieval attitudes towards women, the Eva-Ave dichotomy of Eve's corruptibility and frailty opposed to Mary's purity and perfection. Many women of lyrics are described in stock similes to conform to one of these patterns – shrewish and faithless or impossibly beautiful and virtuous. Some poets' play with secular stereotypes creates refreshing vitality to engage the reader's imagination. This is seen in the amusing absurdities of 'The Fair Maid of Ribblesdale' [*2207*] and the animated details of the sketch offered by Charles d'Orléans, in 'The smyling mouth and laughing eyen gray' [*3465*]. Some verses offer light-hearted advice to men to beware of marriage, as in 'I winked I winked when I a woman toke' [*1392*], and 'What why dedist þou wynk whan þou a wyf toke' [*3919*]. There is a malicious, clerkly edge to the song 'When nettuls in wynter bryng forth rosys red' [*3999*] and in the subversive burden 'of all creatures women be best: / Cuius contrarium verum est,' in a lyric of women's virtues, 'In euery place ye may well see' [*1485*]. The debate of 'The Thrush and the Nightingale' [*3222*] offers only the Virgin's existence to justify that of all other women. Such lyrics elegantly and neatly reinforce attitudes already formed. To see how those are formed we should probably look at humbler, harsher saws such as the proverbial tags 'A wylde beest a man may tame / A womanes tunge will never be lame' [*106.5*] and 'A nyce wyfe A backe dore / Makyth oftyn tymes a ryche man pore' [*81.5*]. The scarcity of verses of happiness with women offers a regrettable comment on attitudes towards them.

The mundane lyrics prompt two questions. The first concerns the poems themselves: why was the information recorded in this way? The second concerns Robbins, who collected most of these poems and similar verses, in his *Secular Lyrics*, **51**, **55**. Why did he place them there, when they are so unlike contemporary lyrics in other European languages?

The anwer to the first question is in the society that gathered and stored the information. It existed when reading and writing were at first not widespread, when the written (and later the printed) work might be mistrusted as readily as it might be revered, when some members of the clergy, and many people holding public office could not read and saw no need to do so. The mnemonic verses offer an easy, effective way to store and transmit information, as we see in apparently similar poems that exploit or ignore the accomplishment of reading. 'VIIJ ys my love ʒif IX go before' [*717*] is cited in *RobbinsS* (at no. 82) as:

> In 8 is alle my loue
> & 9 be y-sette byfore   ⎱ IH̄C
> So 8 be y-closed aboue
> Thane 3 is good therefore

The verse demands a reader's knowledge of letters and their place in the alphabet, together with significant numbers and a contracted spelling of the name of Jesus, in Greek. 'Kepe well x & flee from sevyn' [*1817*] (no. 83 in *RobbinsS*), on the other hand, draws on information instilled in a listener's mind, to emphasize its lessons with conspicuous rhyme and rhythm and the force of numbers which have already gained powerful associations:

> Kepe well x And flee fro vii;
> Rule well v And come to hevyn.

This tag neatly clinches all that has been learned of the Ten Commandments, Seven Deadly Sins, and Five Wits, and their importance for the next life as well as this. The descendants of such verses are advertising slogans and mnemonic scraps, with little artistic merit, but considerable effect. Wenzel, **664**, offers 'Winston tastes good, like a cigarette should' as a counterpart of medieval sermon tags. Similar slogans are 'The family that prays together stays together,' and 'First the foot and then the head / That's the way to make a bed.'

Verse augments the effect of ritual. This encourages piety and adds authority to ordered scraps of information and instruction that come rapidly to mind, such as charms and spells, and short prayers and meditations. Patterned repetition and recitation resemble the ritual chanting of the Latin mass, heard by many but understood by few. A common factor of the mnemonic verse is the impression of an authoritative speaking voice addressing an attentive listener. These are works for a listening audience rather than a single reader, in a situation unlike the intimacy of unquestionably lyrical verses. The tags could be implanted in the memory before being consciously comprehended, rather than reasoned and understood from knowledge already gained. By such methods, fundamental attitudes can be fixed. It resembles children's learning of multiplication tables by uncomprehending recitation: the lines are repeated without thought, when they have no meaning, until they can be retrieved without thought, when the words have gained meaning to become stored knowledge. Knowledge absorbed before it is understood has acceptance rarely granted to any that must be understood before it is learned.

It is easy to see reasons for having mnemonic short poems, and to enjoy the insights into medieval learning and attitudes imparted by proverbial tags.

Similarly it is easy to understand Robbins's interest in all the verses in his collection. As he states in the second edition of *RobbinS*, **55**, the poems 'deal with the realities of the daily life of the period,' and 'were meant for daily use.' They are clearly 'free from the pretensions and fakery which often come with more highly developed art.' He enjoyed in the best of them (which of course need not mean the most mundane) 'a natural and unaffected charm, a quality which much of the poetry of later centuries has lost' (lv). It may seem strange, however, to find mundane scraps, book-plate verses, charms, recipes, and secrets of the Philosopher's Stone in the same volume as poems that are lyrical by any standards. How can we place instructions for washing clothes or making medicines and sauces with poems that correspond to troubadour and trouvère verse, that express emotions, and impart beauty and passion to their audience? The short answer is that we cannot and should not try. It is better to change the terms, and put the anomalous poems into a group that suits them. The ME short poems of mundane life have value, but not necessarily artistic value. Rather, they are precious indicators of the mores of medieval culture. There is another question, but it has no answer: would Robbins have preferred a title such as 'ME Secular Poems' if he had prepared a third edition of *RobbinsS* after concluding the series of lyric editions with *Historical Poems of the XIVth and XVth Centuries*?

CONCLUSIONS

The lyrics may seem to be a disparate group of insignificant pieces, not as serious as longer works, but that impression is a misrepresentation. In these poems, sometimes only scraps, are distillations of emotion and capsules of knowledge, offerings of devotion or opinion, some slight, but some enduring.

The rich texture of lyric imagery counters any idea of flimsiness. In his remarks on 'I syng of a myden' [*1367*], Brewer, **796**, alludes to 'an astonishing weight of significance lightly carried' (52), and the observation applies to many other poems. The weight is that of cultural significance. It can be traced to the Latin love lyric, in pieces that are unquestionably short, but not trivial. The Latin lyric's gift includes metre and motif, and the compression of complex messages into brief, striking conceits; it endures, with different accents, in all the European languages, in poems of religious and secular love. Some themes recur – unceasing devotion; simultaneous love and hatred of the beloved; becoming a bird to court a mistress; the world of nature as a mirror of the lover's mood. ME lyrics written after the Latin, troubadour, and trouvère lyrics may evoke the weeping of courtly lovers or the essence of the pastourelle, with varying local expressions and mood. Some ME versions of this heritage have only colourless recitations of clichés, but others present fresh variations on old themes, delicately fashioned structures of seemingly artless works, exposure of the absurdities of description in a tendency to parody, the use of familiar themes for surprising purposes. The poet may glance at inherited themes in expressions that seem cryptic and even incomplete, because they imply thoughts he felt no need to state. The concentration of material in a brief, pregnant whole is characteristic of lyrics in every language: the weight they carry argues against triviality of matter in an apparently slight form.

How should we observe and value the lyrics? Kane's advice, **579**, on the study of the secular lyrics is instructive. Although he writes of difficulties, deceptive appearances, and the wariness of those who consider the poems, he offers advice for lyric scholars, emphasizing literary history, philology, and acquaintance with the languages in which many lyric forms originated. Dronke, **935**, and Lerer, **1021**, among others, stress the relation and continuity of OE forms. Scrutiny of equivalents in other languages reveals similarities and differences in forms, styles, and attitudes, seen in comparative studies of such forms as the carol and pastourelle. Study of the musical accompaniment of some lyrics offers still more information. Contributions of Stevens, in particular **788**, **789**, and **942**, show the intimate connections of sounds, rhythms, and speech, to reveal more of songs in their first setting and their relation to other verse and speech. Context study and palaeographical insights, noted by many critics, demonstrate the worth of manuscript study and awareness that every scribe was an editor. Comparisons of edited texts disclose the converse, that every editor is a scribe, noted by Rosenstein in his observations of recent *mouvance*.

The scholar's first need is for texts, in original or suitably edited form, with the understanding that 'suitably edited' is a relative term. The form of an edition is governed by the needs, for instance, of an undergraduate for a standardized dialect with easily accessible notes, to encourage further study, or of a scholar for a facsimile or the opportunity to handle a manuscript. As for criticism, the first priority, after enlightening thought, must be accuracy and clarity in references.

The last wish is not new; it was expressed with feeling in a letter to *Notes and Queries* 9 (1854), by τ, who had experienced 'much loss of time from incorrect and imperfect references, not to mention complete disappointment in many instances' (282). Those experiences are now fortunately rare, but lyrics present particular problems to writer and reader. First lines may vary sharply from one manuscript to another, so that first words of different versions begin with letters widely separated in the alphabet and thus in *IMEV* or *SIMEV*. Confusion is exacerbated in indexes prepared by systems based on ME words without reference to the MnE word they represent. (The latter problem is anticipated in *IMEV* and *SIMEV*, which gather forms that represent the same word although they may not immediately appear to be closely related.) The use of burdens in an index adds another variable and possibility for confusion unless burden and first line are clearly distinguished, as in the many indexes that set burdens in italics.

Titles may be helpful, as shown by two pairs of Harley lyrics with very similar first lines. It is simpler to use Brook's titles 'Annot and John' and 'Blow, Northerne Wynd,' rather than 'Ichot a burde in a boure ase beryl so bryht' [*1394*] and 'Ichot a burde in boure bryht' [*1395*]; and 'The Way of Woman's Love' and 'The Way of Christ's Love,' rather than 'Lutel wot hit anymon / Hou derne loue may stonde' [*1921*] and 'Lytel wotyt onyman hu derne loue was funde' [*1923*]. Some poems are so often mentioned by title that the titles are more easily recogized than the first lines. Among such works are 'The Maid of the Moor' [*2037.5*], 'The Fair Maid of Ribblesdale' [*2207*], and the 'Corpus Christi Carol' [*1132*]. The last of these would be particularly difficult to identify from its burden, since so many begin 'Lullay.'

Unfortunately, titles are frequently less informative. Vague labels, such as 'A Spring Song,' 'To his Mistress,' or 'A Song of Love,' offer minimal details of the topic and none of the first line. Different editors may use the same title for different poems, a further disadvantage. Another complication is introduced when different editors call the same poem by different names. Thus 'Blow, Northerne Wynd' is used by Brook, **42**, Sisam and Sisam, **69**, and Silverstein, **73**, but Brown, in *BrownXIII*, **36**, calls the poem 'The Loveliest Lady in Land' and Davies, **61**, names it 'Love for a beautiful lady.' Thus titles should generally be avoided, unless they can prevent confusion, or are well established in critical discourse: first lines and *IMEV* or *SIMEV* numbers offer safer identification.

J.M. Willeumier-Schalij concisely states the problems of indexing, with proposals for solving them, and generally moves towards an effect similar to that of *IMEV* and *SIMEV*. A departure from the methods of those works is to ignore exclamations such as *o*, *a*, *heu* and their variations, as well as any 'article, demonstrative pronoun, and possessive pronoun at the beginning of the line ... except when these pronouns are used substantively' (Willeumier-Schalij 16). Listing the verse according to the next word after an exclamation could alter alphabetical placement, and so make an undesirable change. The suggestion to quote no fewer than three lines of a song, however, is a welcome innovation.

Many first impressions of the ME lyrics have some basis. The poems are small and disparate; it is hard to recognize any coherent body of characteristics; the very term may be misleading. More information could be supplied by using 'ME short poem' with a distinguishing adjective, and saving 'ME lyric' for those poems easily seen as lyrical, with aesthetic worth. There are many reasons, though, not to dismiss the poems in the driftnet of 'ME lyric,' but rather to retain, examine, and cherish them, for their individual characteristics and for what they reveal of those who knew them first.

Annotations of Editions

This section includes bound collections of poems, gathered for preservation or teaching, and some lengthy journal articles that are editions of a particular manuscript and are frequently cited. Most of the editions annotated here were published in the twentieth century, but some earlier works are included because many references are made to them. Many ME lyrics first appear in print in brief journal articles, often with critical commentary in addition to the texts; such articles are treated in this bibliography with the critical works and are listed at the end of this section. Because the poems are so widely scattered, it has not been practicable to annotate every edition of every manuscript in which they occur, or to annotate every section of lyrics in general collections. The italicized numbers following each annotation are the numbers given in *IMEV*, *SIMEV*, or the Temporary Index of First Lines not noted in *IMEV* or *SIMEV*. In annotations of editions of wider scope, only the numbers of ME short poems are listed.

1 Wright, Thomas, ed. and tr. *The Political Songs of England, from the Reign of John to that of Edward II.* London: Camden Society, 1839.

Gives poems of political comment from the reigns of John (1–18), Henry III (19–127), Edward I (128–240), and Edward II (241–345); an 'Appendix' containing extracts from Peter Langtoft's Chronicle (in Anglo-Norman and English) (273–323) and a 'Poem on the Evil Times of Edward II,' or 'The Simonie' [*4165*]; and 'Notes' (347–402). The range of languages used in the poems shows how thoughts were expressed, as 'the clerk (or scholar) with his Latin, the courtier with his Anglo-Norman, and the people with their good old English, came forward in turns upon the scene' (ix). Wright presents each poem with a headnote to explain its historical setting and a prose translation at the foot of the page.

205, 310, 313, 814, 841, 848, 1320.5, 1638, 1857, 1889, 1894, 1974, 2287, 2649, 2686, 2754, 2787, 3155, 3352, 4144, 4165.

2 ———, ed. *Political Poems and Songs Relating to English History, Composed During the Period from the Accession of Edward III to that of Richard III.* Rolls Series. Vol. 1 London: Longman, 1859. 2 vols. 1859–61.

Presents 45 poems, edited from the original manuscripts, including some in Latin and French, and traces political comment on the times, 'between what may be considered, properly speaking, as the feudal age, and the commencement of our modern history' (ix). This volume covers the reigns of Edward III and Richard II. In his 'Introduction' (ix–civ) Wright first comments briefly on the historical period; he notes the use of various languages in England, as AN disappeared and Latin and English were used by those who were educated, especially the clergy. He offers a comprehensive description of each poem, relating it to the historical context and circumstances of composition. He translates two French poems, 'The Vows of the Heron' (1–25), and 'On the Truce between England and France, 1394' (by Eustache Deschamps) (300–3), with explanatory notes. When a work has several sources, Wright notes manuscript variations in footnotes.

5, 296.3, 585, 709, 987, 1401, 2149, 2189, 2663, 2777, 3080, 3081, 3113, 3117, 3260, 3448, 3529, 3796, 3899, 4268.

3 ——, ed. *Political Poems and Songs Relating to English History, Composed During the Period from the Accession of Edward III to that of Richard III.* Rolls Series. Vol. 2. London: Longman, 1861. 2 vols. 1859–61.

Continues the work of Wright's first volume, **2**, but omits 'poems which have previously been printed in works generally known and easy of access,' rather than re-editing them to present all political and historical works of the period. The first works are Gower's 'Complimentary Verses on King Henry IV,' composed in Latin, and his address to the king, 'O worthi noble kyng Henry the ferthe' [*2587*]. The last are 'On the Recovery of the Throne by Edward IV' ['Remembyr with reuerens the Maker of mankynde,' *2808*] and 'On England's Commercial Policy' ['Goo forth lybell and mekly schew thy face,' *921*]. In his detailed introduction (vii–lxxii), Wright describes each poem, in relation to the events of the period, with particular attention to poems concerning Wyclif, the Lollards, and the friars; the English claim to the throne of France; and the intriguing and warfare between the parties of York and Lancaster. He also notes the commercial context and effects of England's foreign policies. Wright includes a 'Glossary and Index of Medieval Latin Words' (291–7) and a 'Glossary and Index of Obsolete English Words' (301–41).

544, 811, 818, 871, 884, 921, 1224, 1497, 1555, 1653.5, 1926, 2010, 2156, 2211, 2317, 2335, 2338, 2587, 2808, 3173, 3213, 3455, 3491, 3682, 3720, 3756, 3782.5, 3808, 3929, 4007, 4098.3, 4255, 4261.

4 Furnivall, Frederick J., ed. *Political, Religious, and Love Poems.* EETS 15. London: Kegan Paul, 1866.

The collection is 'somewhat of a medley' (ix), with poems taken chiefly from MSS Lambeth 306 and Harley 7322. Furnivall discusses the preparation of the texts in 'Forewords' (ix–xix) and 'Afterwords' (309–11), and includes notes 'On the Date of Lydgate's "Horse, Goose, and Sheep" ['Controuersies plees and al discord,' *658*]' by Max Förster (xix–xx), and on 'The Stacyons of Rome ['He þat wyll hys sowle leche,' *1172*]' by W.M. Rossetti (xxi–xlv).

33.8, 83, 101, 102, 155, 172, 187, 221, 373, 404, 502, 592, 658, 700, 798, 819, 827.5, 850, 868, 897, 1086, 1131, 1137, 1172, 1217, 1267, 1269, 1290, 1294, 1460, 1463, 1466, 1523, 1555, 1585, 1615, 1634, 1639, 1732, 1780, 1789, 1822, 1847, 1958, 2008, 2014, 2074, 2133, 2141, 2155, 2157, 2167, 2227, 2247, 2382, 2383, 2397, 2625, 2646, 2695, 2786, 2789, 3106, 3127, 3219, 3228, 3278, 3291, 3325, 3332, 3353, 3357, 3411, 3422, 3506, 3546, 3610, 3612, 3644, 3647.5, 3680, 3734, 3845, 3858, 3880, 3907, 4033, 4045, 4062, 4088, 4107, 4148, 4208, 4224, 4259, 4273.

5 ——, ed. *Hymns to the Virgin and Christ, The Parliament of Devils, and other Religious Poems, Chiefly from the Archbishop of Canterbury's Lambeth MS. No. 853.* EETS 24. London: Kegan Paul, 1867. New York: Kraus, 1973.

After listing the contents of the manuscript (xiii–xiv), Furnivall provides notes on some poems (xv–xvi) and prints 21 of the texts, with occasional variation from the order of the manuscript. He prints another text of 'I warne vche leod þat liueþ on londe' [*1379*] for comparison.

349, 547, 560, 744, 880, 1028, 1032, 1259, 1379, 1454, 1511, 1570, 1727, 1769, 1781, 1823, 2007, 2040, 3225, 3308, 3533, 3985, 3992, 4160, 4189.

6 Morris, Richard, ed. *An Old English Miscellany: Containing a Bestiary, Kentish Sermons, Proverbs of Alfred, Religious Poems of the Thirteenth Century, from Manuscripts in the British Museum, Bodleian Library, Jesus College Library, etc.* EETS 49. London: Trübner, 1872. New York: Kraus, 1988.

A variety of works in ME verse and prose, 'of a religious or didactic nature' (vii), including some printed as parallel texts to display variations in manuscript sources. Morris provides paraphrases in marginal notes and a comprehensive 'Glossarial Index' (233–308). In three appendices, he prints *Liber Fisiologus a Thetbaldo Italico Compositus* (201–9), the Latin source of the Bestiary [*3413*]; 'The XI Pains of Hell' ['þe sononday is godis own chosen day,' *3481*] (210–22); and 'The Visions of Seynt Poul, etc.' ['Lustneþ lordynges leof and dere,' *1898*] (223–32).

66, 233, 433, 695, 877, 1091, 1272, 1407, 1441, 1833, 1839, 1898, 1948, 2070, 2284.5, 2645, 2687, 3221, 3413, 3474, 3481, 3517, 3607, 3684, 3704, 3828, 3873, 3967, 4016, 4047, 4051, 4085, 4162.

7 Flügel, Ewald. 'Liedersammlungen des XVI Jahrhunders, besonders aus der Zeit Heinrich's VIII. I.' *Anglia* 12 (1889): 225–71.

In the first part of this series [see also **8, 15, 20**], Flügel prints the songs of two sixteenth-century manuscripts, Add. 31922 and Royal Appendix 58, and summarizes the publishing history of the works. He cites many attributions of authorship, some of them not endorsed in *IMEV* and *SIMEV*. The authors named in MS Add. 31922 are Henry VIII, William Cornish, Thomas Fardyng, Dr Cooper, ffluyd, Rysbye, and Pygott. Those named in MS Royal Appendix 58 are Cornish, Parker (monk of Stratford), Cooper, and Raff Drake.

MS Add. 31922: *13.8, 14.5, 98.5, 112.5, 120.4, 120,5, 120.6, 134.5, 135.5, 159.5, 266.5, 302.5, 409.5, 675.5, 676.5, 688.8, 765.5, 1214.7, 1303.5, 1328.8, 1329.5, 1414.8, 1420.5, 1504.5, 1866.5, 2025.5, 2028.5, 2034.5, 2250.5, 2261.4, 2271.2, 2272.5, 2531.5, 2737.5, 2766.8, 3193.5, 3199.8, 3405.5, 3438.3, 3486.5, 3487.5, 3635.5, 3706.5, 3706.7, 3800.5, 4058.3, 4068.6, 4070.5, 4143.3, 4143.5, 4143.8, 4201.3, 4213.5.*
MS Royal, Appendix 58: *13.8, 14.5, 263.3, 558.5, 688.8, 835.5, 870.5, 1414.8, 1540.5, 1824.8, 2255.3, 2272, 2308.5, 2532.3, 2794.4, 3144.5, 3199.8, 3413.3, 3498.5, 3595.6, 3627, 3703.5, 3706.8, 3758.5, 3899.3, 3947.6.*

8 ———. 'Liedersammlungen des XVI. Jahrhunderts, besonders aus der Zeit Heinrich's VIII. II.' *Anglia* 12 (1889): 585–97.

In the second part of the series [see also **7, 15, 20**], Flügel prints two Christmas carols printed by Wynkyn de Worde (1521), Douce Fragment 94v.; two Christmas carols (undated), Douce Fragment 94; and Bassus, a collection of songs written in four parts. Flügel attributes some of the songs in Bassus to Cornish, Pygot, Ashwell, Taverner, Gwynneth, Dr Fairfax, Dr Cooper, and Jones. [One attribution (that of 'Pleasure yt ys/ to here Iwys,' [2757.5], 'probably by William Cornish') is confirmed by *SIMEV*.]

Fragment of Christmas Carols, Wynkyn de Worde, 1521, Douce Fragment 94v: *418, 3313.*
Christmas Carols, Douce Fragment 94: *905.5, 1575.5.*
Bassus: *66.5, 87.5, 558.3, 1448.5, 1485.5, 2182.6, 2245.6, 2757.5, 3163.5, 3632.3, 3706.4, 3863.5, 4094.3, 4098.6, 4265.5.*

9 Horstmann, Carl, ed. *The Minor Poems of the Vernon MS*. Part 1. EETS 98. London: Kegan Paul, 1892. New York: Kraus, 1976.

Prints the texts of 38 of the minor poems of the Vernon MS, with marginal notes by Furnivall. [For other poems from the Vernon MS see **13**.]

639, 701, 775, 937, 965, 974, 975, 1030, 1031, 1057, 1060, 1122, 1372, 1512, 1602, 1653, 1684, 1752, 1759, 1781, 1869, 1898, 1959, 1967, 1969, 1970, 1984, 2038, 2110, 2116, 2118, 2157, 3194, 3231, 3247, 3270, 3883, 4145, 4250.

10 Zupitza, J. 'Die Gedichte des Franziskaners Jakob Ryman.' *Archiv* 89 (1892): 157–338.

Zupitza presents James Ryman's works from Cambridge University Library MS Ee.1.12, with editorial numbering, capitalization, and punctuation. The works include carols of the Annunciation and the Nativity, and of praise to Christ, Mary, the Trinity, and St Francis.

67, 115, 278, 279, 280, 282, 283, 328, 398, 434, 449, 486, 488, 489, 492, 546, 597, 613, 617, 618, 619, 641, 731, 781, 785, 815, 879, 1042, 1043, 1049, 1072, 1074, 1076, 1080, 1124, 1125, 1231, 1298, 1328, 1434, 1542, 1802, 2087, 2122, 2193, 2310, 2313, 2332, 2367, 2402, 2404, 2405, 2408, 2414, 2415, 2417, 2418, 2419, 2426, 2429, 2430, 2431, 2432, 2434, 2435, 2448, 2454, 2460, 2462, 2466, 2467, 2476, 2477, 2480, 2484, 2505, 2506, 2530, 2535, 2539, 2540, 2542, 2543, 2544, 2545, 2552, 2554, 2555, 2559, 2561, 2562, 2563, 2575, 2578, 2582, 2603, 2690, 2691, 2745, 2779, 2801, 2807, 3072, 3076, 3092, 3093, 3094, 3095, 3096, 3097, 3123, 3136, 3148, 3149, 3152, 3267, 3272, 3284, 3303, 3304, 3328, 3331, 3332, 3333, 3334, 3374, 3378, 3379, 3390, 3417, 3450, 3467, 3468, 3469, 3470, 3530, 3583, 3585, 3620, 3667, 3710, 3724, 3725, 3726, 3728, 3751, 3775, 3779, 3837, 3930, 3944, 4166, 4197.

11 Fehr, Bernhard. 'Die Lieder der Hs. Add. 5665 (Ritson's Folio-Ms.).' *Archiv* 106 (1901): 262–85.

An edition of the manuscript formerly owned by Joseph Ritson. Fehr describes the manuscript and its contents – religious songs in Latin and English, and a variety of secular lyrics. Most translations of hymns from Latin to English were made during the reign of Henry VIII, but many of these are from the periods of Henry VII and Edward IV. Among the religious works are hymns of saints, events of the Nativity, Marian lyrics, and songs of God's grace and wish to redeem the world. The secular works include songs of love, and of political and social comment on the times. Fehr lists 98 English works in the manuscript, noting those that have already been printed and the non-lyrical items. He prints the lyrics that have not formerly been published.

18, 31, 113.5, 263.5, 263.8, 474.5, 507, 581, 680, 681, 753.8, 887, 918, 962, 1212, 1214.5, 1234, 1303.3, 1322, 1578, 1589.5, 1710, 1738, 2044, 2053, 2244.6, 2277.5, 2323.8, 2370, 2377, 2388, 2393.5, 2409, 2453, 2533, 2636, 2731, 3168.4, 3382, 3587, 3652, 3677.5, 3737, 3776, 3832.5, 3950, 3975, 3988, 4077, 4283.5.

12 ———. 'Die Lieder des Fairfax Ms. (Add. 5465 Brit. Mus.).' *Archiv* 106 (1901): 48–70.

Describes the manuscript, noting the religious, love and political lyrics found in it, before printing the poems, with ascriptions.

.2, 1, 13, 146.5, 155.5, 364, 456.5, 490.5, 497, 506.5, 557.5, 649.5, 675.8, 1326, 1328.5, 1339.5, 1450, 1636.5, 1731, 1866.8, 1999.5, 2007.5, 2028.8, 2200.3, 2277, 2364, 2394.5, 2530.5, 2547.5, 2832.2, 3131, 3162.5, 3193.5, 3206.5, 3270.5, 3437, 3597, 3724.5, 3750, 3751.3, 3845, 3903.8, 3927.3, 3927.5, 4098.6, 4184, 4281.5.

13 Furnivall, F.J., ed. *The Minor Poems of the Vernon MS.* Part 2 (with a few from the Digby MSS. 2 and 86). EETS 117. London: Kegan Paul, 1901. New York: Kraus, 1987.

Supplies texts of 46 poems of the Vernon MS and 'Various Readings to the Vernon MS' (747–52). An appendix provides nine poems from Digby MSS. 2 and 86, and another leaf (753–86). [For other poems from the Vernon MS see **9**. Part 3 of the edition, 'the Introduction and Glossary, by Miss F. Lejeune,' is announced on the title page, but has not been traced.]

Annotations of Editions 43

5, 167, 247, 374, 419, 562, 563, 583, 606, 678, 872, 1066, 1081, 1229, 1365, 1369, 1379, 1402, 1443, 1448, 1455, 1532, 1596, 1695, 1718, 1840, 1887, 1962, 2108, 2280, 2293, 2302, 2605, 2607, 2718, 2790, 2865, 3211, 3233, 3238, 3310, 3419, 3420, 3501, 3553, 3760, 3925, 3996, 4135, 4157, 4158, 4268, 4276.

14   Fehr, Bernhard. 'Die Lieder der Hs. Sloane 2593.' *Archiv* 109 (1902): 33–72.

Describes the manuscript and its songs, mostly religious lyrics of the fifteenth century. Some urge people turn to God from the punishments of rising costs, pestilence, starvation, and plague. The cheerful Christmas songs resemble folk-songs, and express almost childlike good humour, even when referring to the killing of the children in Bethlehem and to the Passion. Descriptions of Christ's sufferings emphasize the cruelty of the Jews; they express love and pity for the Saviour and hatred of those who put him to death. The Marian and Christmas songs depict Mary as the personification of female beauty. Fehr summarizes the topics: religious songs of Mary, Christmas, and the Passion; religious legends; and secular songs similar to folk-songs. He explains various concepts in the lyrics, and comments on the history of publication of the songs. He prints the texts, with corrections and additions to previous articles.

20, 72, 80, 117, 118, 354, 356, 361, 377, 378, 454, 527, 562, 725, 739, 1020, 1230, 1268, 1299, 1302, 1303, 1351, 1367, 1417, 1433, 1522, 1568, 1574, 1575, 1627, 1650, 1662, 1739, 1785, 1892, 1896, 1914, 1938, 2061, 2103, 2111, 2113, 2339, 2364, 2384, 2675, 2730, 2747, 2771, 3034, 3058, 3070, 3085, 3329, 3343, 3347, 3472, 3526, 3537, 3566, 3645.8, *3700.5, 3707, 3733, 3864, 3877, 3920, 3959, 4219, 4279, 4281.

15   Flügel, Ewald. 'Liedersammlungen des XVI Jahrhunderts, besonders aus der Zeit Heinrichs VIII. III.' *Anglia* 26 (1903): 94–285.

The third article in this series [see also **7**, **8**, **20**] presents the songs of MS Balliol 354 and notes the numerous other entries in the manuscript.

20, 22, 39.5, 65, 103, 108.5, 112, 236, 294, 324, 343, 346, 350, 354, 374, 375, 376, 418, 425, 465.5, 470, 506, 548, 552.5, 597.5, 608, 675.5, 678.5, 704, 755, 769, 825, 878, 889, 890, 895, 898, 903, 916, 977, 1032, 1055, 1132, 1136.5, 1149.5, 1151, 1163, 1194.5, 1198, 1222, 1226, 1259, 1286, 1314, 1350, 1354.5, 1362, 1363, 1383, 1386, 1399, 1412, 1444, 1445.5, 1454, 1471, 1485, 1575, 1587, 1601, 1609, 1653, 1817, 1866, 1873, 1891, 1892, 1914, 1919, 1920, 1933.5, 1941, 1957, 2053, 2060, 2072.6, 2090, 2097, 2098, 2183.5, 2346, 2358.5, 2385, 2410, 2511, 2525, 2586, 2678, 2681, 2732, 2771, 3074, 3087, 3161, 3171, 3307, 3313, 3318, 3424, 3438.6, 3460, 3473, 3527, 3553.3, 3574, 3575, 3603, 3627, 3635, 3669, 3706.2, 3720, 3736, 3776, 3792.5, 3820, 3835, 3852, 3922, 3930, 3969, 3975, 3999, 4012, 4023, 4044.3, 4049.2, 4137, 4148, 4176.5, 4181, 4246, 4263.3.

16   Heuser, W. *Die Kildare-Gedichte: Die Ältesten mittelenglischen Denkmäler in Anglo-Irischer Überlieferung.* Bonner Beiträge zur Anglistik 14. 1904. Darmstadt: Wissenschaftliche Buchgesellschaft, 1965.

Presents detailed information on the linguistics, dialects, and provenance of the Kildare Poems [MS Harley 913] and prints the texts, noting other sources of the poems. Heuser's first concern is linguistic, and he seeks (by using evidence from the poems) to prove the past existence in southern Ireland of an Irish-English dialect, with words of Celtic origin.

214, 705, 718, 762, 1078, 1638, 1776, 1820, 1940, 1943, 1978, 2003, 2024, 2025, 2042, 2081, 2270, 2344, 3110, 3126, 3234, 3365, 3366, 3367, 3400, 3685, 3812, 3939, 4088, 4144, 7141, 7376, 7407, 7409, 7432, 7469, 7483.

17 Kail, J., ed. *Twenty-Six Political and Other Poems (Including 'Petty Job') from the Oxford MSS. Digby 102 and Douce 322*. EETS 124. London: Kegan Paul, 1904. New York: Kraus, 1973.

Most of the 24 Digby poems have 'the same religious character,' and are probably the work of the same author. They caution against folly and praise virtue, 'always setting a great value on the works of a man, but none on his words' (vi); they recommend righteousness for its expected rewards. Their political comment shows the Commons as 'the most important of all estates,' and condemns injustice and defends 'truth, and . . . the suppression of falsehood' (viii). The poet does not criticize church doctrine, and was 'probably an abbot or a prior,' who 'occupied a seat in parliament, and voted with the Commons' (ix). His political views imply the South or South Midlands, and his dialect the Western or Southwestern Midlands. From allusions to plague and political events Kail conjectures dates, finding that 'the first poem is not to be dated before January 1400' (xi). Historical allusions explain the poems' contexts, and suggest a chronological order; the eighteenth poem, for instance, refers to events of 1421. The *Pety Job* ['Lyef lord my soule thow spare,' *1854*], is, 'like the *Lessons of the Dirige* ['Almy3ty god lord me spare,' *251*], a paraphrase of the *Lamentations of Job*' (xxii). Although a headnote assigns it to Richard of Hampole, it does not belong 'to his time nor to his dialect' (xxiii).

251, 411, 561, 697, 817, 910, 911, 1389, 1475, 1508, 1845, 1854, 1939, 2048, 2054, 2088, 2091, 2763, 3279, 3381, 3484, 3564, 3608, 3924, 4070, 4109.

18 Chambers, E.K. and F. Sidgwick, eds. *Early English Lyrics: Amorous, Divine, Moral and Trivial*. London: Bullen, 1907.

Presents 152 lyrics in the categories indicated, a few of them sixteenth-century pieces and some extracted from longer poems or plays. In 'Some Aspects of Mediæval Lyric' (259–96) Chambers describes the history of the lyric, particularly considering French influences on the love lyrics, and illustrates his remarks with quotations from *chansons courtois* and *chansons populaires*. The influence of 'Anglo-Saxon melancholy' (284) and of the Latin hymns is more significant in the religious lyrics. Most of the few known authors are religious: Chambers notes Richard Rolle, Michael Kildare, Thomas de Hales, William of Shoreham, William of Nassington, John Audelay, and James Ryman, most of them Franciscans, with a 'tradition of religious minstrelsy' (292). Many of the collection are carols, showing the influence of folk songs and dances. The manuscript sources of the texts are listed and described (299–312), with references to their printed forms (313–25) and notes on the poems (326–78).

16, 19, 63, 66.5, 72, 76, 100, 111, 112, 117, 163, 210, 267, 340, 354, 361, 375, 377, 409.5, 418, 454, 463, 467, 506.5, 515, 543, 549, 554.5, 558.5, 642.5, 704, 707, 729.5, 739, 809, 825, 864, 903, 999, 1004, 1132, 1194.5, 1195, 1219, 1225, 1226, 1268, 1299, 1303.3, 1311, 1313, 1314, 1327, 1351, 1367, 1414.8, 1433, 1454, 1463, 1468, 1471, 1620.5, 1861, 1866, 1866.5, 1893, 1896, 1957, 2025, 2029, 2031, 2034.5, 2039, 2103, 2138, 2163, 2224, 2236, 2243, 2250.8, 2262, 2342, 2359, 2375, 2381, 2418, 2645, 2687, 2733, 2737.5, 2757.5, 2771, 2832, 2995, 3085, 3097.6, 3171, 3190, 3223, 3259, 3310, 3313, 3344, 3348, 3405.5, 3411, 3413.3, 3434, 3438, 3460, 3536, 3537, 3574, 3596, 3597, 3603, 3627, 3635.5, 3658, 3706.4, 3737, 3782, 3787, 3820, 3877, 3879, 3899.3, 3932, 4023, 4037, 4065, 4068.6, 4070.5, 4098.6, 4177, 4189, 4219, 4236, 4277, 4278, 4282, 7140, 7171, 7493.

19 Dyboski, Roman, ed. *Songs, Carols, and other Miscellaneous Poems, from the Balliol MS 354, Richard Hill's Commonplace-Book*. EETS ES 101. London: Kegan Paul, 1908 (*for* 1907). New York: Kraus, 1973.

The book is a collection of items Richard Hill wished to preserve, including family records and passages of verse and prose. Dyboski's edition presents a selection of 114 poems, chiefly in ME, with some in Latin. After an account of the manuscript and events of Hill's life noted in it, Dyboski explains his divisions of the poetry, with general descriptions of the sections and particular comments on some individual works. 'Sacred Songs and Carols' (1–50) include carols of the Annunciation, praise of Mary, Christmas, Epiphany, the saints, and some moral songs. The 'Religious Poems and Prayers in Verse' (51–71) are 'of Lydgate's school and epoch, all of them rather uniformly typical in contents as well as in form' (xxi). The 'Didactic, Moral and Allegorical Poems' (72–94) stress 'the mutability of Fortune, the idea of *death* and the vanity of all earthly things' (xxiv). 'Historical Poems' (95–102) comment on dramatic events through complaints of princesses, and include Dunbar's 'Praise of London' [*1933.5*]. Although most of the 'Ballads and Worldly Songs' (103–28) are humorous, the first is the 'Corpus Christi Carol' [*1132*], which reminds Dyboski 'most strikingly of some features of the Holy Grail legend' (xxvi). The poetical works conclude with a diverse collection of 'Proverbs, Verse-rules and Moral Sentences' (128–41). Dyboski explains his exclusion of some parts of the manuscript (xxviii–xxxii), and prints a 'Table of Contents' (xxxiv–lix). He supplies 'Notes' (169–90) on the poems printed, and a 'Glossary.'

20, 22, 37.5, 39.5, 65, 103, 108.5, 112, 294, 324, 343, 346, 350, 354, 374, 375, 418, 425, 465.5, 470, 506, 548, 552.5, 608, 675.5, 687.5, 704, 755, 769, 825, 878, 889, 890, 895, 898, 903, 916, 977, 1032, 1055, 1088.5, 1132, 1136.5, 1142.5, 1149.5, 1162.8, 1163, 1194.5, 1198, 1206.9, 1222, 1226, 1286, 1314, 1350, 1354, 1362, 1363, 1383, 1386, 1412, 1444, 1445.5, 1454, 1471, 1485, 1488, 1575, 1587, 1601, 1609, 1817, 1866, 1873, 1892, 1914, 1933.5, 1941, 1957, 2053, 2060, 2076, 2090, 2097, 2098, 2183.5, 2293.8, 2346, 2385, 2410, 2511, 2525, 2586, 2678, 2681, 2732, 2771, 3074, 3161, 3171, 3199.3, 3307, 3313, 3424, 3460, 3473, 3527, 3553.5, 3574, 3575, 3603, 3627, 3635, 3669, 3706.2, 3720, 3736, 3776, 3792.5, 3820, 3835, 3852, 3922, 3969, 3975, 3999, 4012, 4023, 4044.3, 4049.2, 4079.3, 4079.6, 4137, 4148, 4176.5, 4181, 4263.3.

20 Padelford, Frederick Morgan, and Allen R. Benham. 'Liedersammlungen des XVI. Jahrhunderts, besonders aus der Zeit Heinrichs VIII. IV.' *Anglia* 31 (1908): 309–97.

The fourth article in this series [see also **7**, **8**, **15**] presents the English songs of MS Rawlinson C. 813 [now Bodleian 12653], most of them previously unprinted. Padelford anticipates 'historical and critical notes . . . in some subsequent number of this journal' (310). [See Bolle, **127**.]

79.5, 159.8, 172, 340.5, 366, 368, 430, 642.5, 649, 729, 767, 1017.5, 1180, 1328.7, 1329, 1349.5, 1450.5, 1768, 1841.5, 1926.5, 2228, 2245.1, 2261.8, 2271.6, 2409.5, 2421, 2439.5, 2482.5, 2496, 2498, 2500.5, 2529, 2532, 2532.5, 2547, 2552.5, 2560.5, 2757.3, 2821, 2822, 2827.5, 3098.3, 3228.5, 3713.5, 3785.5, 3804, 3917.8, 3962.5, 4020.3, 4190, 4210.

21 Reed, Edward Bliss. 'The Sixteenth Century Lyrics in Add. MS. 18,752.' *Anglia* 33 (1910): 344–69.

After a description of this work 'of manuscript and print' (344), which offers writing of the fourteenth, fifteenth, and sixteenth centuries, Reed prints the twenty-eight lyrics, formerly called 'English sonnets,' which he assigns to the sixteenth century, in the reign of Henry VIII.

681.5, 1356.8, 1414.8, 1864.5, 2195.5, 2245.3, 2245.6, 2249, 2255.6, 2307.5, 2619.5, 2736.6, 2736.8, 2753.5, 3880.6, 7129, 7365, 7371, 7383, 7394, 7398, 7423, 7446, 7460, 7497, 7508, 7552, 7600.

22 Rickert, Edith, ed. *Ancient English Christmas Carols 1400–1700.* London: Chatto, 1910.

The collection is arranged as 'Carols of the Nativity' (3–130), with appendices of 'Latin, Anglo-Norman, and French carols' (131–138) and 'Carols not related to Christmas'

(139–48); 'Carols of the Divine Mystery' (159–216); and 'Carols of Yuletide Festivity' (217–68). There are appendices of 'Christmas Hymns and Other Lyrics' (269–86) and 'Modern Carols in the Medieval Manner' (287–98), and some traditional works. The texts are presented in standardized, modernized form. Rickert supplies an introduction (xiii–xxviii), briefly describing the origins and evolution of carols, with notes on some individual carols (149–56, 299–302) and a glossary of foreign phrases (303–10).

18, 20, 21, 22, 54.5, 61, 63, 66.5, 76, 78, 88, 103, 112, 117, 118, 236, 343, 354, 361, 378, 418, 436, 454, 463, 507, 527, 549, 581, 608, 681, 753, 825, 878, 887, 889, 890, 905.5, 916, 918, 997, 998, 1004, 1132, 1195, 1198, 1212, 1225, 1226, 1230, 1322, 1351, 1352, 1363, 1367, 1383, 1448.5, 1471, 1575, 1575, 1575.5, 1601, 1650, 1662, 1738, 1866, 1873, 1892, 1893, 1984.5, 2044, 2097, 2103, 2113, 2250, 2315, 2332, 2333, 2339, 2342, 2346, 2377, 2384, 2388, 2400, 2551.8, 2586, 2665, 2665, 2675, 2681, 2730, 2732, 2733, 2995, 3058, 3070, 3161, 3313, 3313, 3314, 3315, 3329, 3343, 3344, 3347, 3385, 3438, 3438.3, 3457, 3460, 3472, 3473, 3527, 3536, 3574, 3596, 3597, 3603, 3619, 3627, 3630, 3638, 3643, 3669, 3674, 3735, 3736, 3776, 3822, 3877, 3932, 3932, 3950, 4012, 4065, 4094.3, 7063, 7305, 7321, 7422.

23 Murray, Hilda M.R., ed. *The Middle English Poem, Erthe upon Erthe, Printed from Twenty-Four Manuscripts.* EETS 141. London: Kegan Paul, 1911.

The poem belongs to 'the same class of literature as the English versions of the *Soul and Body* poems' (ix). The A version ['When erþ haþ erþ i-wonne wiþ wow,' *3939*; 'Herde maket halle,' *703*], apparently representing 'a thirteenth or fourteenth-century type of the poem,' is found in MSS Harley 2253 and 913. The B version ['Erth owte of erth is wondyrly wroght,' *704*; 'Whan lyf is most louyd & deþ ys most hatid,' *3985*], a fifteenth-century type, is in eighteen texts, 'dating from the fifteenth to the seventeenth century.' The C version ['Erthe vpon erthe is waxin and wrought,' *705*], in 'a single fifteenth-century MS. (Cambridge University Library, Ii, 4. 9)' (x), combines A and B and 'several independent stanzas' (xxv). Murray compares the versions, tracing transcription of the poem and noting changes in the language. Although there are Latin and French translations, its origin is thought to be English. English, rather than Latin, is the language of epitaphs that use the text, and 'play on the word *earth*, which is the most essential feature of the poem' (xxx), is less effective in other languages. In support of the English origin, Murray shows similarities with other poems, in particular with Body and Soul dialogues. After the texts (1–34), she supplies 'Notes' (35–40), including analogues (39–40). 'Appendix I' (41–6) supplies '*Erthe* poems, in Latin, French, and English . . . discovered too late for inclusion in the text' (41). 'Appendix II' (47–8) offers two more versions of the B text.

703, 704, 705, 1461, 1932, 2192, 2684.5, 3517, 3939, 3940, 3967, 3985, 4129.

24 Patterson, Frank Allen. *The Middle English Penitential Lyric: A Study and Collection of Early Religious Verse.* New York: Columbia UP, 1911.

The essential requirement of the lyric is the unity of emotion. Patterson's classification depends on internal character, rather than external features of the poems, and he considers the influence of mysticism. The English religious lyrics may be grouped as poems of purification or of divine love-longing, and Patterson's study concerns penitential poems, in the first group. He explains the sacrament of penance, and uses confession and contrition as the main divisions in his classification of the lyrics presented. He divides them further into liturgical or non-liturgical poems, with other divisions, according to genre and the one addressed, particularly in the poems expressing contrition,. The Latin influence on the English lyrics came 'invariably through the liturgy' (25) rather than from sacred and devotional Latin poetry or hymns, and this influence suggested their subject matter. The relation to mysticism, 'plain, direct, fervent,' is seen in the penitential lyric 'simple in every aspect' (26), with practical purposes and direct methods. Friars and monks, who wrote most vernacular religious lyrics, drew on familiar material, best suited to their needs. The works of St Edmund, Richard Rolle, St Anselm, St Thomas Aquinas, and St Bernard affected lyrics, but not always directly. The songs of Northern France, particularly the *chanson d'amour* and *chanson à personnages*, affected the lyrics in spirit and style, as illustrated in several examples. Patterson describes the composition of *serventois*, closely related to the *ballade*, in the *puys*. Although some English poems translate French religious works, most lyrics influenced by the *chanson* have 'a spirit of sincerity and a freedom from restraint and literary convention which forbid our thinking that they can be . . . an imitation at all' (44). The effects of French secular verse are on external form, with is 'hardly an echo [of French religious poetry] in English lyric verse' (45). Patterson presents 69 lyrics, including some extracted from the *Lay Folk's Mass Book* and paraphrases. He supplies notes, with attention to the provenance of the individual lyrics (157–98), and a bibliography (198–203).

374, 375, 376, 643, 664, 708, 775, 918, 951, 968, 975, 1030, 1054, 1066, 1081, 1216, 1323, 1324, 1340, 1369, 1372, 1407, 1444, 1511, 1532, 1617, 1674, 1678, 1684, 1692, 1704, 1727, 1732, 1759, 1780, 1833, 1839, 1952, 1963, 1967, 1968, 1970, 2110, 2116, 2118, 2119, 2125, 2220, 2293, 2316, 2359, 2385, 2645, 2687, 2702, 2703, 2892, 2988, 2995, 3160, 3228, 3231, 3507, 3533, 3774, 4077, 4276.

25 **Padelford, Frederick Morgan.** 'English Songs in Manuscript Selden B. 26.' *Anglia* 36 (1912): 79–115.

A group of miscellaneous manuscripts, with 'carols, moral songs, and drinking songs' (79), in Southern dialect, copied by several hands, probably in a monastery. Padelford assigns hands and music to the songs, and differs in some respects from Nicholson [*Early Bodleian Music* (London: Novello, 1901; Amsterdam: Knuf, 1966; Farnborough: Gregg, 1967)]. He prints the text, with variants, after a discussion of the various hands and the date of the manuscript. Taking account of historical events (such as the Battle of Agincourt) he concludes that the date is 'not prior to 1570–1575' (85).

18, 21, 81, 93, 111, 353, 354, 753, 795, 909, 1004, 1036, 1230, 1234, 1430, 1473, 1931, 2053, 2377, 2716, 2734, 3259, 3283, 3385, 3434, 3619, 3638, 3659, 3674, 3879, 4229.

26 **Cook, Albert Stanburrough, ed.** *A Literary Middle English Reader.* Boston: Ginn, 1915.

Presents selections of verse and prose, after brief introductions entitled 'The Literature' (xiii–xvii) and 'The Language' (xviii–xxv). Cook includes lyrics in 'Illustrations of Life and Manners' (361–88) and 'Lyrics' (406–75).

5, 66, 100, 359, 404, 515, 598, 704, 709, 762, 809, 1132, 1292, 1299, 1362, 1365, 1367, 1395, 1463, 1468, 1649, 1861, 2157, 2233, 2236, 2375, 2381, 2645, 2663, 2744, 2777, 2988, 3031, 3058, 3211, 3223, 3310, 3327, 3415, 3460, 3491, 3596, 3787, 3932, 4037, 4098.3, 4194, 4282.

27 **Förster, Max.** 'Kleinere mittelenglische Texte.' *Anglia* 42 (1918): 145–224.

An edition of shorter ME texts prepared to address the problems of a lack of access for German scholars to English libraries and a dwindling interest in manuscript study. Förster stresses the importance of historical philological studies. He offers a range of short texts, including some prose works, Lydgate's 'Dietary' ['For helth of body couer for cold thyn hede,' *824*], proverbs, sets of questions and answers, riddles, and various ME lyrics. He provides comprehensive notes on each work, and concludes with a short glossary.

445, 824, 1174.5, 1396, 1422, 2110, 2119, 2162, 2619, 3087, 3273, 3572, 3651, 3792.5, 3969, 3998, 4111, 4184.

28 Hall, Joseph, ed. *Selections from Early Middle English 1130–1250.* Vol. 1: Texts. Vol. 2: Notes. Oxford: Clarendon, 1920.

An edition of early ME verse and prose, including some shorter poems, presenting the works as in the manuscripts, sometimes with variant texts. Hall supplies footnotes on the manuscripts in Vol. 1 and more extensive notes on the individual texts in Vol. 2.

433, 598, 631, 1272, 2070, 2988, 3031, 3413, 4098.

29 Day, Mabel, ed. *The Wheatley Manuscript: A Collection of Middle English Verse and Prose Contained in a MS now in the British Museum Add. MSS. 39574.* EETS 155. London: Oxford UP, 1921 (*for* 1917). New York: Kraus, 1971.

The fifteenth-century manuscript has 11 religious works in verse, and three prose works. In the preface, Day describes the manuscript, with notes on its contents (vii–xxxii). Following the text (1–100), which includes prayers, psalms, meditations, and instructive pieces, she provides notes on particular words and passages (101–18), and a glossary (119–24).

253, 528, 985, 1038, 1761, 2101, 2119, 2924, 3533, 3612, 3755.

30 Sisam, Kenneth, ed. *Fourteenth Century Verse and Prose.* Oxford: Clarendon, 1921; numerous reprints.

Includes short poems in the sections 'Political Pieces' (151–61) and 'Miscellaneous Pieces in Verse' (162–70), with an introduction to each section and notes on some individual poems (253–8). There is a general introduction (ix–xliii), select bibliography (xlvi–ii), 'A Middle English Vocabulary' by J.R.R. Tolkien (293–454), and an index of names (455–60).

5, 360, 515, 585, 1008, 1290, 1649, 1847, 1861, 2037.5, 3080, 3227, 3306.

31 Brown, Carleton, ed. *Religious Lyrics of the XIVth Century.* Oxford: Clarendon, 1924. [*BrownXIV*]

The first of Brown's collections of ME lyrics [see also **36, 39, 48**] with the aims 'to publish hitherto unprinted material; to offer better texts of poems already printed from inferior MSS; to give trustworthy texts of poems that have been printed inaccurately; to bring together texts that are found in scattered and often inaccessible publications; above all, to represent the lyrical development of the century' (xi). It is difficult to date the poems precisely; those included have been found in fourteenth-century manuscripts, but may have been composed earlier. The 135 lyrics are arranged chronologically, in the following sections: 'of the Beginning of the Century' (1–3); 'from Harley 2253' (3–14); 'by Friar William Herebert' (15–28); 'before 1350' (29–50), 'collected by Bishop Sheppey' (51–5); 'of the mid-century' (56–68); 'from the Commonplace Book of John Grimestone' (69–92); 'of the School of Richard Rolle' (93–108); 'from about 1375' (109–24); 'Vernon Series' (125–207);'of the end of the century' (208–40). Brown supplies a title to each lyric. He provides a general introduction (xi–xxii) and specific notes on many of the lyrics (241–88), followed by a glossary (289–358). There is no index of first lines. The text preserves most manuscript forms, including *thorn* and *yogh*, but expands contractions and supplies some words and letters. Punctuation is editorial. [Second edn. 1952, rev. Smithers, **48**.]

14, 29, 94, 101, 190, 196, 352, 353, 359, 374, 420, 441, 561, 562, 563, 583, 600, 606, 611, 640, 643, 678, 759, 775, 776, 779, 780, 872, 994, 1002, 1024, 1027, 1029, 1030, 1034.5,

1053, 1054, 1082, 1179, 1213, 1216, 1232, 1235, 1274, 1311, 1353, 1379, 1402, 1443, 1448, 1455, 1460, 1472, 1532, 1596, 1663, 1678, 1684, 1699, 1708, 1715, 1742, 1747, 1749, 1752, 1761, 1775, 1781, 1818, 1832, 1847, 1930, 1940, 1943, 1978, 2007, 2012, 2023, 2024, 2025, 2034, 2036, 2042, 2080, 2107, 2108, 2119, 2150, 2155, 2159, 2240, 2241, 2260, 2273, 2280, 2302, 2359, 2607, 2684, 3109, 3132, 3135, 3212, 3230, 3233, 3236, 3245, 3371, 3405, 3408, 3420, 3462, 3565, 3676, 3691, 3700, 3730, 3825, 3826, 3862, 3872, 3906, 3921, 3925, 3996, 4088, 4135, 4157, 4158, 4159, 4160, 4177, 4200, 4239, 4263, 4268.

———— Review by F. Sidgwick, *Review of English Studies* 1 (1925): 116–18. Supplies a general description of the range of lyrics, notes and apparatus, and remarks on the persistence of some phrases of the lyrics in other works.

———— Review by Karl Young, *Modern Language Notes* 39 (1924): 419–24. Relates Brown's collections of lyrics to his compilation of *RMERV*, and notes the superiority of the readings to those found elsewhere. He expresses admiration for Brown's achievement, and hopes for 'an index of first lines, and a slightly more considerate glossary' (424) in later editions.

32 Sampson, George, ed. *The Cambridge Book of Prose and Verse: In Illustration of English Literature from the Beginnings to the Cycles of Romance.* Cambridge: Cambridge UP, 1924.

Intended to illustrate the first volume of *The Cambridge History of English Literature*. It includes lyrics in the sections 'Early Transition English' (172–205), 'Later Transition English: Legendaries and Chronicles' (340–66), and 'Later Transition English: Songs, Satires, Stories' (367–432). Sampson provides a general introduction (xix–xxxviii), and an appendix on changes to the language, grammar, pronunciation and spelling, vocabulary, and dialects (433–8).

66, 105, 359, 515, 709, 1320.5, 1365, 1367, 1395, 1407, 1861, 1894, 1921, 1922, 2039, 2164, 2287, 2645, 2988, 3155, 3211, 3221, 3223, 3236, 3310, 3963, 4037, 4177, 4194.

33 Patterson, Frank A. 'Hymnal from MS Additional 34,193 British Museum.' *Medieval Studies in Memory of Gertrude Schoepperle Loomis.* Paris: Champion; New York: Columbia UP, 1927. Geneva: Slatkine, 1974. 443–88.

Prints and briefly describes the text of a hymnal of 22 hymns, in the form of Latin stanzas of four lines, followed by an English version of six lines.

487, 625, 642, 732, 881, 996, 999, 1000, 1868, 2327, 2362, 2387, 2403, 2433, 2499, 2664, 2728, 3077, 3359, 3668, 3679.

34 Dearmer, Percy, R. Vaughan Williams, and Martin Shaw, eds. *The Oxford Book of Carols.* London: Oxford UP, 1928; numerous reprints.

A collection of 197 carols with music, most presented in MnE, arranged according to season. Twenty-two are English carols of the fourteenth and fifteenth centuries. The 'Preface' (v–xix) describes carols as 'songs with a religious impulse that are simple, hilarious, popular, and modern,' with literature and music 'rich in true folk-poetry,' remaining 'fresh and buoyant even when the subject is a grave one' (v). The editors offer a brief history of the carol, relating it to forms of dance and its appearance in other European languages, and showing its progress from the Middle Ages to the twentieth century.

18, 20, 21, 63, 112, 117, 681, 753, 1351, 1367, 1471, 1866, 2339, 2551.8, 2733, 3627, 3635, 3737, 3877, 3932.

35 Adamson, Margot Robert. *A Treasury of Middle English Verse: Selected and Rendered into Modern English.* London: Dent, 1930.

In her introduction, Adamson compares her collection to that of George Bannantyne. She has rendered the poems in MnE, '[w]ith the utmost fidelity to sense, rhyme and rhythm . . . so that they may be read easily as poems, without a glossary or notes' (ix), and has supplied titles for the works. She has generally selected shorter lyrics.

72, 105, 254, 322, 359, 360, 583, 657, 695, 704, 762, 769, 868, 893, 1008, 1029, 1032, 1091, 1116, 1225, 1234, 1290, 1314, 1353, 1356, 1376, 1402, 1407, 1448, 1509, 1532, 1657, 1727, 1789, 1847, 1952, 2012, 2044, 2082, 2100, 2119, 2148, 2155, 2182, 2244, 2245, 2255, 2260, 2273, 2302, 2302, 2342, 2359, 2381, 2514, 2619, 2619.5, 3058, 3080, 3087, 3180, 3212, 3221, 3225, 3225.5, 3343, 3460, 3533, 3603, 3630, 3700, 3734, 3759, 3782, 3835, 3852, 3873, 3880, 3964, 4037, 4085, 4159, 4184, 4189, 4194, 4236, 7454, 7526.

36 Brown, Carleton, ed. *English Lyrics of the XIIIth Century.* Oxford: Clarendon, 1932. Numerous reprints. [*BrownXIII*]

A collection of 91 religious and secular lyrics, grouped according to manuscript source. In his comprehensive general introduction (x–xlii), Brown alludes to '[þe]h þet hi can wittes fule-wis' [*3512*], 'the earliest example of a secular lyric' (xii), which is 'wholly distinct from folk poetry' (xiii). He explores the relation between music and lyric, and the purpose of some works, such as religious poems 'inspired by an impulse more didactic than lyrical' (xvi), and makes specific comment on manuscripts from which the lyrics are taken. He provides a title for each lyric, and in several cases presents two or three versions. There are notes on many individual lyrics (165–237), a glossary (239–307), an index of persons and places (308–9) and an index of first lines (310–12). The characters *eth, yogh, thorn,* and *wynn* have been retained in the text, but 'blunders of scribes' (xliii) have been corrected. Punctuation is editorial. [The book has been extensively reviewed and a number of articles refer to it, some suggesting emendations. See Subject Index, *s.v. BrownXIII*.]

66, 293, 322, 360, 515, 519, 613, 695, 708, 740, 864, 885, 888, 912, 968, 968, 1066, 1115, 1129, 1233, 1365, 1394, 1395, 1407, 1422, 1504, 1617, 1649, 1697, 1705, 1833, 1836, 1839, 1861, 1921, 1922, 1949, 1974, 1977, 2005, 2009, 2037, 2039, 2051, 2066, 2070, 2163, 2166, 2220, 2236, 2286, 2291, 2293, 2320, 2336, 2366, 2369, 2604, 2645, 2687, 2992, 2995, 3078, 3155, 3211, 3216.5, 3221, 3222, 3223, 3236, 3310, 3432, 3517, 3696, 3873, 3874, 3939, 3961, 3963, 3964, 3965, 3967, 3968, 3969, 3998, 4016, 4037, 4044, 4141, 4170, 4194, 4211, 4221, 4223.

———— Review by G.L. Brook, *Medium Ævum* 2 (1933): 88–92. Although there are 'many valuable contributions to learning' (91) in the notes and introduction, 'no part of the book is wholly free from signs of hasty workmanship' (90), nevertheless it must be 'of great value to those who have sufficient training to be able to dispense with its linguistic apparatus' (92). Brook's criticisms relate chiefly to manuscripts and the glossary. He includes a number of suggestions for emendations.

———— Review, *TLS*, 12 Jan. 1933: 20. 'Professor Brown has collated all his texts afresh, and his notes make a distinct advance in the interpretation of the poems.' The reviewer has reservations about the glossary and etymological material. The reviewer notes the anthology's scope; comments particularly on 'Annot and John' [*1394*], 'Lenten ys come wiþ loue to toune' [*1861*] and 'Hwenne so wil wit ofer-stieð' [*4016*]; and expresses concern about references to ON and the use of accents.

———— Review by W.W. Greg, *Review of English Studies* 10 (1934): 212–15. In spite of occasional reservations about the anthology, Greg considers it 'a work of research that will be a permanent delight to scholars' (212). He finds 'obstacles between the thirteenth century and the twentieth' generally 'much less in the language than in the spelling'; thus

the use of 'rational spelling . . . with a somewhat freer use of emendation' would provide 'a further service to the study of English literature' (215).
[Malone comments on the work, **186, 211**; Menner offers comments and suggestions for *BrownXIII* and *BrownXIV*, **229**.]

37 Greene, Richard Leighton, ed. *The Early English Carols.* Oxford: Clarendon, 1935.

A collection of 474 carols, some in several versions, with an appendix of 8 fragments that are probably in carol form. The texts are arranged thematically; religious works deal with 'Advent, the Nativity, the feasts of the Twelve Days, the Purification . . . the infant Christ and His mother . . . the Passion, including *planctus Mariae* . . . the Virgin, including those [carols] on the Annunciation . . . the Trinity, God the Father, and Christ, including appeals of Christ to mankind . . . the Saints . . . the Mass and the Eucharist . . . religious and moral counsel . . . doomsday and mortality' (ix); these are followed by satirical, political, amorous, and humorous carols. In his introduction, Greene discusses 'The Carol as a *Genre*' (xiii–xxviii), 'The Carol as Dance-Song' (xxix–lix), 'The Latin Background of the Carol' (lx–xcii), 'The Carol as Popular Song' (xciii–cx), 'The Carol and Popular Religion' (cxi–cxxii), and 'The Burdens of the Carols' (cxxxiii–cxlv). The genre is distinguished from others by its burden, which precedes the first stanza and is repeated after that and all others. The arrangement implies a leader and chorus, and the round dance from which it developed, related to the *chanson à danser* and *ballata*. Many religious carols are of clerical origin, revealed in the idiom of Latin lines included in the macaronic verse and resemblances to proses of the Mass, antiphons, and *catilenae*. Carols might also be popular songs, and some were used and adapted for spiritual purposes, especially by Franciscans, in their itinerant preaching. The Franciscans also composed many original carols. Their poets included Thomas de Hales, William Herebert, James Ryman, and John Grimestone; the Augustinian John Audelay was also a disciple of St Francis. The friars' interest in carols may be related to the devotion of St Francis to the Christ-Child and the Nativity, since so many carols involve Christmas and related seasons. Greene's introduction is copiously illustrated with examples taken from carols in the collection and related works in various languages. There are notes on the individual carols after the texts and appendix.

17, 18, 20, 21, 22, 29, 30, 31, 34, 44, 54.5, 61, 63, 65, 67, 72, 76, 78, 80, 81, 87.5, 88, 93, 102.3, 103, 107, 111, 112, 113, 115, 116, 118, 150, 163, 210, 225, 226, 236, 261, 278, 279, 280, 281, 282, 283, 294, 298, 304, 320, 328, 340, 343, 352, 354, 358, 360, 375, 376, 377, 377.5, 398, 405, 409.5, 418, 425, 436, 449, 463, 470, 488, 489, 490.5, 503, 507, 527, 535, 536, 543, 546, 548, 549, 581, 597, 601, 608, 610, 641, 651, 667, 672.4, 680, 681, 693, 731, 739, 743, 753, 755, 781, 782, 785, 792, 813.6, 822, 825, 831, 838, 840, 858, 878, 887, 889, 890, 893, 895, 903, 905.5, 916, 918, 933, 962, 972, 997, 998, 1004, 1020, 1042, 1043, 1072, 1074, 1080, 1119, 1124, 1125, 1132, 1195, 1198, 1212, 1219, 1226, 1226, 1230, 1234, 1263, 1268, 1280, 1298, 1303.5, 1315, 1322, 1327, 1328, 1330, 1350, 1351, 1352, 1362, 1363, 1364, 1380, 1383, 1386, 1395, 1399, 1412, 1415, 1433, 1434, 1444, 1450, 1468, 1471, 1473, 1484, 1485, 1492, 1522, 1524, 1568, 1574, 1575, 1575.5, 1578, 1587, 1588, 1595, 1601, 1605.5, 1609, 1627, 1630, 1633, 1641.5, 1650, 1662, 1704, 1710, 1738, 1739, 1744, 1785, 1802, 1824.8, 1849, 1873, 1892, 1893, 1896, 1900, 1914, 1931, 1938, 1966, 1984.5, 2007.5, 2024, 2036, 2039.5, 2041, 2044, 2050, 2053, 2061, 2076, 2086, 2087, 2090, 2097, 2098, 2098, 2103, 2109, 2111, 2113, 2122, 2173, 2185, 2217.5, 2231.5, 2250, 2281.5, 2310, 2315, 2332, 2332, 2333, 2334, 2339, 2343, 2346, 2358.5, 2367, 2370, 2377, 2384, 2388, 2392.5, 2394.5, 2396, 2400, 2404, 2405, 2409, 2416, 2417, 2418, 2419, 2426, 2430, 2431, 2432, 2435, 2443, 2448, 2453, 2460, 2462, 2467, 2476, 2480, 2485, 2501, 2506, 2508, 2511, 2527, 2530, 2533, 2534, 2540, 2542, 2544, 2545, 2551.8, 2554, 2555, 2559, 2561, 2563, 2575, 2577.3, 2578, 2586, 2603, 2618, 2636, 2645, 2652.5, 2654, 2665, 2681, 2690, 2691, 2716, 2730, 2731, 2732, 2733, 2735, 2745, 2747, 2771, 2801, 3034, 3057, 3070, 3085, 3097.6,

3098, 3112, 3118.5, 3119.5, 3123, 3127, 3136, 3144.5, 3148, 3152, 3161, 3171, 3179, 3180, 3206.5, 3214, 3235, 3244, 3267, 3271, 3272, 3283, 3284, 3297, 3303, 3304, 3308, 3312, 3313, 3314, 3315, 3329, 3332, 3333, 3334, 3343, 3344, 3346, 3347, 3378, 3379, 3382, 3385, 3405, 3409, 3418, 3424, 3438, 3438.8, 3443.5, 3450, 3457, 3460, 3467, 3468, 3469, 3470, 3471, 3472, 3473, 3515, 3525, 3526, 3527, 3536, 3537, 3550, 3566, 3574, 3575, 3583, 3593, 3594, 3595, 3596, 3597, 3603, 3609, 3619, 3620, 3627, 3630, 3635, 3638, 3643, 3645.8, 3652, 3654, 3658, 3659, 3667, 3669, 3674, 3691, 3700.5, 3706.5, 3707, 3710, 3724, 3725, 3726, 3728, 3733, 3736, 3737, 3742, 3750, 3751, 3775, 3776, 3779, 3820, 3822, 3835, 3836.5, 3837, 3845, 3852, 3864, 3876, 3877, 3920, 3927, 3929, 3930, 3932, 3944, 3950, 3959, 3975, 3988, 3999, 4001, 4012, 4023, 4065, 4068.6, 4077, 4078, 4163, 4189, 4197, 4198, 4218, 4219, 4229, 4241, 4256.3, 4278, 4279, 4281, 4285, 7422.

——— Review by Carleton Brown, *Modern Language Notes* 52 (1937): 125–9. Questions Greene's criteria for selection, particularly the burden and its place before or after the stanzas of the works, chiefly because of the range of material thus included in the collection. Brown finds that insistence on the burden makes 'a shibboleth of what is in many instances a formal rather than an essential criterion' (127). He commends Greene's attempt 'to fix boundaries' (128) although it is made by considering metrical form rather than general usage. Brown concludes with a list of different manuscript readings. [Some of these were incorporated into the second edition.]
——— Review by G.H. Gerould, *Speculum* 11 (1936): 298–300. Approves Greene's definition of the genre of the carol and the collection of works corresponding to it. Gerould considers Greene's methods and summarizes his discussions of the origins of carols. He notes some points of difference on the ballad stanza, but concludes that the book is 'a notable monument of American scholarship' (300).
——— Review by Bruce Pattinson, *Modern Language Review*, 32 (1937): 453–5. Welcomes Greene's comprehensive study, with its explanation of the genre and discussion of its relation to other forms of lyric and to the dance. Pattinson is interested in the 'persistent triangle' of dance, music and poetry, a theme on which he expands, and finds, as the book's only fault, that 'its point of view is too exclusively literary' (453).

38 Comper, Frances M.M., ed. *Spiritual Songs: From English MSS of Fourteenth to Sixteenth Centuries.* London: Society for Promoting Christian Knowledge: New York Macmillan, 1936.

A collection of 112 religious songs, in modernized form 'to render them acceptable to modern ears' (xx). In her Introduction (xi–xxii), Comper describes the themes of love, the Passion, and suffering, as they were presented in the medieval church and in these lyrics, referring in particular to the work and influence of Anselm, Richard Rolle, John Audelay, James Ryman, William Herebert, Bernard of Clairvaux, Augustine, and Bonaventure. She divides the poems into the following sections: 'The Incarnation' (1–14); 'The Nativity' (15–69); 'Theme of the Passion' (71–171); 'Orisons to the Holy Trinity and to Our Lady and Saint John' (173–238); and 'Eucharist and Mass' (239–51). Comper supplies a list of the manuscripts consulted (253–4), with notes on the manuscripts (255–64) and the authors (265–79).

14, 21, 22, 110, 117, 196, 246, 298, 352, 361, 378, 412, 502, 536, 548, 611, 643, 664, 693, 755, 775, 782, 825, 831, 975, 1001, 1053, 1066, 1125, 1132, 1328, 1365, 1367, 1369, 1372, 1383, 1460, 1463, 1627, 1663, 1674, 1678, 1684, 1699, 1715, 1731, 1739, 1741, 1752, 1757, 1759, 1761, 1841, 1847, 1930, 1950.5, 1967, 2012, 2017.5, 2024, 2076, 2080, 2111, 2238, 2250, 2270, 2273, 2385, 2432, 2477, 2505, 2582, 2645, 2681, 2684, 3092, 3093, 3094, 3095, 3096, 3097, 3131, 3161, 3211, 3221, 3416, 3424, 3472, 3530, 3574, 3575, 3583, 3597, 3603, 3627, 3669, 3691, 3732, 3776, 3825, 3826, 3845, 3920, 3963, 4023, 4056, 4076, 4189, 7488, 7594.

39 Brown, Carleton, ed. *Religious Lyrics of the XVth Century*. Oxford: Clarendon, 1939. [*BrownXV*]

Completes Brown's collections of ME lyrics [see also **31, 36**]. It contains 192 poems, most of them anonymous and many previously unprinted, arranged according to subject rather than manuscript or chronological order. The work reflects 'the prevailing taste and interest of the period instead of the literary accomplishment of a few' (xix), and includes carols, which were characteristic of the century. The lyrics continue the themes of fourteenth-century poems, but in contrasting styles, with popular and theological lyrics and some dramatic monologues. There is a softening of attitudes towards death in some lyrics on mortality. The lyrics are arranged as follows: 'Dialogues between the Blessed Virgin and Child' (1–7); 'Marian Laments' (8–22); 'Songs and Prayers to the Blessed Virgin' (22–78); 'Hymns to the Trinity' (79–83); 'Hymns to God the Father, Creator' (84–103); 'Songs of the Annunciation' (103–9); 'Songs of the Nativity' (109–21); 'Songs for the Epiphany' (122–31); 'Hymns and Songs of the Passion' (131–50); 'Appeals to Man from the Cross' (151–62), 'Complaints of Christ' (162–77), 'Easter Songs' (177–80); 'Songs of the Eucharist' (180–3); 'The Mysteries of the Faith' (184–8); 'Occasional Prayers and Songs' (188–202); 'Prayers to the Guardian Angel' (202–5); 'Two Prayers by Lydgate against the Pestilence' (206–10); 'Songs of Penitence' (210–36); 'Songs of Mortality' (236–62); 'Songs of the Decadence of Virtue' (262–72); 'Songs against Vices' (273–8); and 'Proverbs and Moral Sentences' (279–91). Brown supplies notes on individual lyrics (293–351), a glossary (352–89), and an index of first lines (390–4).

2, 12, 22, 37, 61, 78, 117, 181, 183, 236, 240, 241, 253, 254, 298, 340, 349, 354, 364, 373, 378, 404, 452, 454, 465, 497, 532, 534, 550, 610, 648, 651, 664, 707, 725, 742, 769, 773, 774, 880, 896, 906, 909, 927, 933, 952, 985, 1001, 1005, 1026, 1032, 1033, 1039, 1044, 1046, 1048, 1051, 1073, 1077, 1079, 1119, 1234, 1254, 1264, 1308, 1310, 1318, 1340, 1341, 1355, 1359, 1367, 1387, 1415, 1456, 1473, 1488, 1489, 1627, 1659, 1680, 1687, 1693, 1700, 1701, 1720, 1723, 1727, 1734, 1735, 1748, 1785, 1787, 1804, 1830, 1841, 1846, 1871, 1892, 1899, 1936, 1971, 1982, 2057, 2073, 2101, 2115, 2136, 2154, 2171, 2192, 2202, 2269, 2272, 2334, 2345, 2357, 2390, 2401, 2411, 2442, 2459, 2461, 2471, 2472, 2474, 2483, 2486, 2504, 2519, 2528, 2546, 2549, 2557, 2560, 2576, 2610, 2619, 2719, 2730, 2738, 2789, 2792, 2799, 2800, 2802, 2824, 2924, 3070, 3071, 3083, 3151, 3225, 3240, 3283, 3297, 3329, 3385, 3391, 3410, 3483, 3504, 3522, 3538, 3543, 3567, 3597, 3628, 3660, 3673, 3692, 3695, 3719, 3727, 3805, 3812, 3821, 3827, 3836, 3844, 3859, 3892, 3904, 3909, 3931, 3948, 4001, 4065, 4083, 4163, 4181, 4189, 4220.

———— Review by Richard L. Greene, *Modern Language Notes* 55 (1940): 308–10. Finds the book 'entirely worthy to stand beside its two distinguished predecessors' (308) and welcomes some changes in the grouping of texts 'according to their subject matter instead of by their manuscripts or their uncertain chronological order' (308–9). Greene notes only a few disappointments, chiefly concerning the lack of identification of carols and a typographical problem, among 'a wealth of editorial as well as poetical merits' (309).

———— Review by Henry A. Person, *Modern Language Quarterly* 1 (1940): 243–5. Relates the volume to its predecessors and finds it 'an inspiration and a model to future editors of Middle English texts' (245). He commends Brown's accuracy and ingenuity in editing, noting a few questionable readings.

———— Review by G.L. Brook, *Medium Ævum* 10 (1941): 26–8. Questions the intention to omit so many fifteenth-century lyrics 'easily accessible elsewhere' since 'the inevitable result has been to rob the collection of most of the best,' so that it appeals 'to the literary historian rather than to the lover of literature' (26). Although he welcomes publication of the book, Brook finds that 'accuracy of the texts cannot be taken for granted' (28), and he suggests some emendations.

40 Funke, Otto, ed. *A Middle English Reader (texts from the 12th to the 14th c.)* Bibliotheca Anglicana (Texts and Studies) 7. Bern: Francke, 1944.

Includes four examples of 'Lyrical Poetry' (47–51), in the 'Specimens of Middle English Poetry' (33–60). Funke takes the texts from *BrownXIII*, **36** ['Lenten ys come wiþ loue to toune,' *1861*; 'Svmer is icumen in,' *3223*] and *BrownXIV*, **31** ['Ase y me rod þis ender day/by grene wode to seche play,' *359*; 'Wynter wakeneþ al my care,' *4177*], and refers to Brown's notes. A glossary is published separately.

359, 1861, 3223, 4177.

41 Muir, Kenneth. 'Unpublished Poems in the Devonshire MS.' *Proceedings of the Leeds Philosophical and Literary Society* (Literary and Historical Section) 6 (1944–7): 253–82.

Examines unpublished poems from the Devonshire MS (MS Add. 17492) chiefly to determine which of them could be the work of Wyatt. Muir identifies some small groups of these, as well as works of other poets, some of them perhaps written by Lord Thomas Howard, who was imprisoned for his marriage to Lady Margaret Douglas. [The few poems entered in *IMEV* or *SIMEV*, and the sequence which may represent verse correspondence between Lord Thomas Howard and Lady Margaret Douglas, are listed.]

232, 666, 848.5, 1086, 1409.3, 1418.5, 2577.5, 3670, 4201.6, 4217.6, 7051, 7229, 7385, 7556, 7589, 7611.

42 Brook, G.L., ed. *The Harley Lyrics: The Middle English Lyrics of MS Harley 2253.* Old and Middle English Texts. General Editor G.L. Brook. Manchester: Manchester UP, 1948. [2nd edn. 1956. 3rd edn. 1964. 4th edn. 1968.]

Brook prints the texts of ME and macaronic lyrics of MS Harley 2253 (29–72), with an introduction (1–26), bibliography (27–8), notes on individual lyrics (73–88), a ME glossary (89–122), an Anglo-Norman glossary (123–4), index of proper names (125), and index of first lines (126). The introduction describes the manuscript and its contents, referring to the date and orthography (1–4), and provides a general introduction to the secular lyrics (4–8), the conventions of courtly love (8–14), and the religious lyrics (14–17). The section on metre (18–20) deals particularly with the line, stanza forms, and alliteration. Brook concludes the introduction by considering the lyrics as literature (20–6). He supplies a title for each lyric. [These are frequently used in other critical material, and generally in this bibliography.]

The second edition supplies a fuller bibliography (127–31), but is essentially unchanged from the first. Following Smithers, **273**, Brook adopts the reading *sully* rather than *fully* in 'The Three Foes of Man' [*2166*] and 'Blow, Northerne Wynd' [*1395*].

The third edition differs significantly only in additions to the bibliography (127–31).

In the fourth edition changes have been made to the notes on 'The Meeting in the Wood' [*1449*] and 'The Fair Maid of Ribblesdale' [*2207*] following Bennett and Smithers, **65**.

105, 359, 515, 694.5, 968, 1216, 1365, 1394, 1395, 1395, 1407, 1449, 1504, 1678, 1705, 1861, 1921, 1922, 2039, 2066, 2166, 2207, 2236, 2359, 2604, 3211, 3236, 3874, 3939, 3963, 4037, 4177, 4194.

——— Review by R.J. Schoeck, *Modern Language Notes* 66 (1951): 404–7. Examines Brook's edition in relation to Brown's, *BrownXIII*, **36**, and Böddeker's [*Altenglische Dichtungen des MS. Harl. 2253* (Berlin, 1878)], and considers comments on *BrownXIII* made by Malone, **186**, and Menner, **229**. He finds Brook's ME glossary 'far richer' (405) than Brown's, but is somewhat disappointed by the 'chiefly textual' (406) notes supplied by Brook, although he acknowledges their soundness. Schoeck makes suggestions for additions to the bibliography, but finds the work 'a welcome addition to any medieval shelf' (407).

43 Loomis, Roger Sherman, and Rudolph Willard, eds. *Medieval English Verse and Prose in Modernized Versions.* New York: Appleton, 1948.

The anthology includes lyrics of the thirteenth and fifteenth centuries, modernized by several translators. Some of the earlier poems have the titles supplied in *BrownXIII*, **36**.

37, 66, 360, 515, 1132, 1198, 1299, 1367, 1836, 3058, 3078, 3314, 3932, 3969, 4044.

44 Kreuzer, James R. 'Thomas Brampton's Metrical Paraphrase of the Seven Penitential Psalms: A Diplomatic Edition of the Version in MS Pepys 1584 and MS Cambridge University Ff 2.38 with Variant Readings from All Known Manuscripts.' *Traditio* 7 (1949–51): 359–403.

The six manuscripts which contain the *Metrical Paraphrases of the Seven Penitential Psalms* can be related in two groups of three. Kreuzer postulates lines of descent from MS Sloane 1853 and MS Cambridge University Ff.2.38, and presents sample readings in confirmation. John Alcock and Thomas Brampton have been suggested as author of the work. Kreuzer supplies a detailed description of the poem ['As I me lay aloone in bed,' *355*; 'In wynter whan the wedir was cold,' *1591*], and relates the paraphrases of Pss. 6, 32, 38, 51, 102, 130, and 143 to the poet's use of the Vulgate, noting his interpretations and personal references in the introductory stanzas which deal with 'illness and an awareness of his sins' (366). The poet's treatment of the Bible is 'essentially literal,' with some 'christological, allegorical, and tropological interpretations' (368). Kreuzer provides a chart listing those passages before presenting a diplomatic edition, with variations and passages from the psalms in footnotes.

355, 1591.

45 Frost, William. *The Age of Chaucer.* English Masterpieces. Gen. ed. Maynard Mack. Englewood Cliffs, NJ: Prentice, 1950. 2nd edn. 1961

Frost gives most consideration to Chaucer's works and *Sir Gawain and the Green Knight* [*3144*] (in verse translation) but includes nine 'Anonymous Lyrics' (413–21), presented with glosses at the foot of the page. The introduction provides 'A Note on Language and Versification' (24–8).

117, 1132, 1367, 1861, 2645, 3223, 3310, 3899.3, 4177.

46 Robbins, Rossell Hope. 'The Poems of Humfrey Newton, Esquire, 1466–1536.' *PMLA* 65 (1950): 249–81.

Humfrey Newton's commonplace book (MS Bodleian Lat. Misc. c 66, *olim* Capesthorne MS) is a secondary source of Cheshire words and usages, and 'an indication of the literary interests of the provincial reading public of about 1500' (249). Robbins gives an account of the biographical data available, which make Newton 'a welcome addition to the limited roster of known authors of the late fifteenth century' (249). The manuscript has suffered damage, but Robbins prints the poems, with editorial punctuation and comment. Newton composed sixteen poems, most of them epistles of love, and including five acrostics. The others are 'well-known texts' (257), including a 'Prophecy' ['When feithe fayles in prestys sawes,' *3943*], Richard de Caistre's hymn ['Ihesu lord þat madist me,' *1727*], 'Twelve points for purchasers of land to look to' ['Who so wylle be ware of purchassyng,' *4148*], and Lydgate's first 'Nightingale' poem ['Go lityll quayere And swyft thy prynses dresse,' *931*, listed here as *871*]. One poem, 'On clife þat castell so knetered' [*2682*], is written 'in three-stress alliterative cross-rimed quatrains, and its vocabulary is that of the poems of the alliterative "revival" ' (258). Some phrases suggest a close connection with *Sir Gawain and the Green Knight* [*3144*]. [See Robbins, **240**]. The works offer the range to be expected in a commonplace book, and include 'genealogical and historical notes, copies of legal forms and rentals . . . a fourteen-page tract on urine, some Latin prayers and verse, recipes, and a three-page "Vision in a Traunce" by John Newton of Congleton in 1492' (256–7). Robbins compares favourite lines in the work of Newton and the Rawlinson poet, concluding that Newton 'shows himself a typical product of the times' (281).

137, 481, 556, 572, 735, 737, 768, 855, 926, 931, 1187, 1344, 1727, 2217, 2263, 2281, 2597, 2682, 2760, 3793, 3943, 4057, 4148.

47 Dickins, Bruce and R.M. Wilson, eds. *Early Middle English Texts.* London: Bowes, 1951. Rev. edn. 1952.

The authors give texts of the lyrics (118–35) with an introductory article (117–18), and notes (224–39) on dialect, inflexions, sounds, orthography, and passages needing explanation.

66, 864, 1395, 1974, 2066, 2163, 2236, 2293, 2645, 3078, 3211, 3223, 3310, 3857.5, 4037, 4044.

——— Review by D.S. Brewer, *Medium Ævum* 22 (1953): 119–23. Assesses the book as 'on the whole well-balanced.' Brewer finds 'its chief merit' is 'the discerning and informed judgement implied in the choice of text,' but its 'one general defect' is 'scrappiness' (120), caused by the brevity of the selections. The notes are 'often helpful, but . . . not without flaws' (121).

48 Brown, Carleton, ed. *Religious Lyrics of the XIVth Century.* Second edn., rev. G.V. Smithers. Oxford: Clarendon, 1952. [*BrownXIV*]

The text of this edition is essentially unchanged from that of the first, **31**, but Smithers adds a short preface (v), mentioning changes in the notes, 'arising chiefly out of the interpretation of the text' (v), and the revision of the glossary (289–365). Changes are found in the notes for the following: 'Ase y me rod þis ender day' [*359*]; 'Frenschipe faileþ & fullich fadeþ' [*872*]; 'Heȝe louerd þou here my bone' [*1216*]; 'I wolde witen of sum wys wiht' [*1402*]; 'Ilk a wys wiht scholde wake' [*1443*]; 'In a tabernacle of a toure' [*1460*]; 'Ihesu þat al þis world haþ wroȝt' [*1749*]; 'Loke man to iesu crist hi neiled an þe rode' [*1940*]; 'Loke to þi louerd man þar hanget he a-rode' [*1943*]; 'Mayde and moder mylde' [*2034*]; 'þe siker soþe who so seys' [*3462*]; 'Whan adam delf & eve span spir if þ^u wil spede' [*3921*]; 'Wyth was hys nakede brest and red of blod hys syde' [*4088*]. [The corresponding numbers of the lyrics in *BrownXIV* are 11, 104, 6, 106, 116, 132, 35, 2A, 2B, 33, 27, 81, 1.]

——— Review by S.S. Hussey, *Modern Language Review* 48 (1953): 497. Notes a few alterations from the first edition, and in general finds the revision 'a careful and conscientious piece of scholarship which should ensure that the collection retains its place as a standard work.'

49 Kaiser, Rolf. *Medieval English: An Old English and Middle English Anthology.* [First edn. *Altenglische und mittelenglische Anthologie,* 1954. 2nd edn. 1955.] 3rd edn. Berlin: Privately published, Rolf Kaiser, 1958.

A wide selection of poetry and prose in OE and ME, including lyrics, prepared for student use.

5, 16, 19, 29, 66, 99, 105, 117, 161, 180, 194, 196, 205, 267, 269, 322, 360, 375, 377, 469, 515, 549, 585, 671, 696, 703, 704, 705, 762, 813, 824, 864, 935, 961, 979, 1078, 1091, 1213,

1216, 1272, 1297, 1362, 1365, 1394, 1395, 1399, 1402, 1422, 1460, 1463, 1485, 1495, 1504, 1588, 1669, 1796, 1849, 1861, 1889, 1921, 1922, 1974, 2012, 2025, 2037.5, 2039, 2066, 2078, 2149, 2163, 2236, 2270, 2290, 2293, 2302, 2315, 2320, 2359, 2381, 2437, 2444, 2446, 2645, 2742, 2747, 2777, 2787, 2817, 3080, 3117, 3155, 3201, 3209, 3211, 3219, 3221, 3223, 3227, 3260, 3310, 3418, 3517, 3526, 3700, 3701, 3782, 3801, 3809, 3939, 3940, 3963, 3967, 3969, 3999, 4037, 4085, 4129, 4143, 4165, 4194, 4211, 4256.8, 4268, 4279.

50 Mossé, Fernand. *A Handbook of Middle English.* Tr. James A. Walker. Baltimore: Johns Hopkins UP, 1952.

As well as six short poems in 'Lyric Poetry' (200–10), Mossé cites Chaucer's *Legend of Good Women* [*100*] as an example of lyricism, and includes Minot's 'Song of Edward' ['Edward oure cumly king,' *709*] with poetry of the fourteenth century. He provides general comment on the influence of Eleanor of Aquitaine and the Provençal background to the ME lyrics, with a bibliography of editions and criticism (200-1), and prefaces each poem with a short commentary.

66, 100, 709, 1395, 1649, 2320, 3223, 4037.

51 Robbins, Rossell Hope, ed. *Secular Lyrics of the XIVth and XVth Centuries.* Oxford: Clarendon, 1952. [*RobbinsS*]

The collection presents, 'among the 212 items from 114 manuscripts, 57 poems not heretofore published, and 17 poems from hitherto unpublished variants' (v), with additional poems in the Introduction and Notes. Only 17 works are from the fourteenth century. The poems illustrate all types of ME secular lyrics, grouped as 'Popular Songs' (1–57), 'Practical Verse' (58–84), 'Occasional Verse' (85–119), and 'Courtly Love Lyrics' (120–226). These groups are further divided by theme, style, and author. There are Notes (227–90), a Glossary (291–326), and an Index of First Lines (327–31). Each lyric has a title, and the Notes record its number in *IMEV*. [This number is occasionally altered in *SIMEV*, always in the case of acephalous lyrics.] Secular lyrics of the period are greatly outnumbered by religious verses, because 'all problems and conflicts had a religious frame of reference' (xvii). Sources of the lyrics chosen include Aureate Collections (xxiii–vi), Minstrel Collections (xxvi–vii), Song Books (xxvii–viii), Commonplace Books (xxviii–xxx), Fly-leaf Poems (xxx–xxxiii). Courtly and popular poems reflect 'the stratification of medieval society' (xxxiii). Robbins summarizes sources and forms of the poems, and writes of the simplicity of their metrical forms (xlviii–ix), class division and standardization of the forms (l–li), and the unimportance of French influence (li–iv). [2nd edn. 1955, **55**.]

4, 33, 138, 139, 145, 146, 150, 152, 194, 210, 225, 237, 267, 295.5, 344, 366, 377, 380, 383, 436, 438, 521, 549, 559, 579, 590, 674, 717, 724, 734, 751, 752, 754, 763, 766, 767, 783, 795, 813, 824, 869, 870, 903, 922, 925, 926, 929, 932, 1007, 1008, 1010, 1018, 1120, 1121, 1151, 1163, 1165, 1182, 1195, 1199, 1201, 1206, 1207, 1222, 1225, 1238, 1240, 1241, 1278, 1280, 1293.5, 1297, 1299, 1302, 1303, 1305, 1314, 1330, 1331, 1333, 1334, 1344, 1396, 1417, 1423, 1452, 1468, 1480, 1485, 1502, 1510, 1593, 1608, 1609, 1622, 1652, 1768, 1810, 1817, 1829, 1849, 1866, 1905, 1929, 1938, 1944, 2016, 2017, 2037.5, 2082, 2131, 2135, 2141, 2161, 2162, 2178, 2182, 2185, 2188, 2214, 2231, 2232, 2243, 2245, 2254, 2257, 2267, 2293.5, 2311, 2318, 2343, 2364, 2381, 2386, 2421, 2437, 2475, 2478, 2491, 2494, 2517, 2518, 2547, 2567, 2580, 2594, 2622, 2624, 2634, 2640, 2654, 2656, 2675, 2742, 2747, 2751, 2903, 3157, 3162, 3174, 3209, 3227, 3259, 3291, 3313, 3314, 3324, 3328, 3376, 3409, 3418, 3422, 3438, 3465, 3533.5, 3534, 3571, 3572, 3580, 3594, 3604, 3613, 3637, 3722, 3735, 3771, 3782, 3785, 3807, 3809, 3831, 3832, 3848, 3864, 3879, 3881, 3895, 3898, 3911, 3919, 3999, 4092, 4096, 4104, 4126, 4148, 4182, 4199, 4206, 4209, 4256.8, 4279.
Poems cited in full in the Introduction:
445, 827.5, 1151, 1312, 1421, 1798, 2757, 2824, 3849.5, 3899.3, 4260.

Poems cited in full in Notes:
496, 588, 823, 956, 993, 1279, 1354, 1392, 1410, 1793, 3943, 4058.8, 4138.

——— Review by A.A. Prins, *English Studies* 34 (1953): 32–3. Welcomes Robbins's 'admirable introduction' (32) and the choice of poems.

——— Review by Phyllis Hodgson, *Modern Language Review* 48 (1953): 329–30. Records the pleasure and disappointment of being able to compare Robbins's collection with Brown's of religious lyrics [**31, 39, 48**]. Although the presentation is pleasing, she is disappointed by 'the comparative paucity and poverty of the material' (329). Hodgson finds the introduction instructive and lucid, and the glossary and notes comprehensive. She gains most enjoyment in 'the Popular Songs gleaned from Minstrels' Collections, commonplace books, fly-leaves and scraps of vellum accidentally preserved' (329).

——— Review by Kenneth G. Wilson, *Modern Language Quarterly* 15 (1954): 372–3. Notes Robbins's departure from the purposes and selection of text observed in Brown's anthologies, and considers in particular Robbins's resolution of the needs of the general and specialist reader. Wilson is generally pleased with the accuracy and presentation of the texts, but he prefers a rather different interpretation of no. 199 ['Fair fresshest erthly creature,' *754*]. He concludes that the work is 'a valuable book, but could have been either a far more useful one for the scholar, or a far more interesting and representative one for the general reader,' if Robbins had 'chosen one audience or the other' (373).

52 Stevens, John, ed. *Mediæval Carols*. Musica Britannica 4. London: Royal Musical Association, Stainer, 1952. 2nd edn. 1958. 98 vols. to date. 1951–.

The collection includes 118 religious and secular carols, in English and Latin, with an appendix of 16. In his introduction (xiii–v), Stevens distinguishes 'at least three kinds of carols – those intended to "improve" the minds of the congregation, those which reflect the more instructed piety of composers and singers, and those which by their brilliance directly enhance the splendour of their ceremonial setting' (xiv). He includes notes on the individual carols (117–24), descriptions of the manuscripts (125), an analytical index and concordance (126–39), a glossary (140–1), a table of Latin lines (141–2), and translations of the Latin carols (143–5).

18, 21, 31, 54.5, 81, 88, 93, 111, 182, 187.5, 340, 352, 353, 354, 507, 581, 680, 681, 753, 772.5, 795, 887, 889, 918, 962, 1030.5, 1036, 1070.5, 1212, 1220.5, 1230, 1234, 1315, 3220, 3520, 1363.5, 1405.5, 1471, 1473, 1578, 1651.5, 1710, 1738, 1931, 2044, 2185, 2053, 2315, 2370, 2377, 2388, 2409, 2453, 2476, 2533, 2612, 2636, 2665, 2674.5, 2716, 2731, 2733, 3283, 3315, 3382, 3385, 3536, 3574, 3595, 3596, 3619, 3638, 3652, 3659, 3674, 3736, 3737, 3776, 3950, 3975, 3988, 4077, 4229, 4229.5, 4283.5.

53 Person, Henry A., ed. *Cambridge Middle English Lyrics*. Seattle: U of Washington P, 1953.

An edition of 70 poems, most of the fifteenth century, 'from MSS in the libraries of several of the colleges of Cambridge University' (iii). Person follows the manuscripts as closely as possible, without altering punctuation or spelling. The works are arranged in religious and secular sections thus: 'Prayers, Songs and Orisons to or about God, Christ, and the Virgin' (1–18); 'Precepts and Admonitory Pieces: Signs of Death' (19); 'Instructive Pieces: Religious, Moral, Ritual' (21–6); 'Parts of the Mass in English Rime' (27–9); 'Reflective, (Exegetical) Poems' (29–30); 'Love Songs and Complaints' (31–8); 'Satirical Pieces' (38–49); 'Wise Sayings' (49–53); and 'Riddles' (53–6). Person describes the manuscripts: Cambridge University Library Dd.5.16, Dd.6.1, Dd.8.2, Ee.4.35, Ff.1.6, Ff.2.38, Ff.5.48, Gg.4.12, Gg.4.32, Hh.4.12, Ii.6.43, Mm.4.41; Corpus Christi College 294, 405; Gonville and Caius College 174/95, 176/97; Emmanuel College 27; Pembroke College 307; St John's College G.28; Trinity College B.2.18, B.14.39, O.1.29, O.2.40, O.2.53, O.9.38, R.3.19 (59–63). He provides comprehensive notes on individual poems (65–85), a bibliography (89–90), an appendix listing Stowe's variations for two poems ['I haue a lady where so she be,' *1300*; 'O Mossie Quince hangyng by youre stalke,' *2524*], and an index of first lines (91–2).

106, 109, 139, 159, 177, 241, 268, *296.6, 317, 383, 469, 580, 604, 655, 726, 806, 826, 853, 1041, 1047, 1062, 1064, 1126, 1218, 1255, 1300, 1331, 1565, 1599, 1730, 1827, 1838, 1924, 2187, 2412, 2507, 2524, 2568, 2624, 2704, 2714, 2746, 2769, 3100, 3170, 3475, 3493, 3672, 3697, 3809, 3866, 3884, 3905, 3946, 3958, 4035, 4046, 4059, 4184, 7076, 7221, 7222, 7511, 7515, 7564.

——— Review by Richard H. Green, *Modern Language Quarterly* 16 (1955): 171. Welcomes the light cast by new texts on 'the interests, techniques, and figurative modes of medieval poetry,' and finds 'interesting and useful pieces' in the miscellany. However, Green regrets vagueness in the definition and limiting of Person's purposes, and in the 'principles of selection [that] underlie the notes and bibliography of this volume, though there is much of value in both.'

54 Robbins, Rossell Hope. 'The Findern Anthology.' *PMLA* 69 (1954): 610–42.

MS Cambridge Ff.1.6, which Robbins calls the 'Findern' MS 'from its place of origin,' presents 'many well-known longer secular poems as well as a large group of short lyric poems' (610). It is a 'polite anthology' compiled 'through the cooperative efforts of itinerant professional scribes and educated women living in the neighborhood' (611). Recurrence of the names of Chaucer and Lydgate, even in the ascription of poems which they did not write, offers 'evidence of their contemporary and later esteem in English letters' (612). Robbins describes the manuscript and lists its 62 items, before proposing an order for the copying of the poems, which have been entered in approximately 28 hands. He provides biographical material about the Finderns and their connections, including records of marriages and houses owned by the family. There are examples of SE London and Derbyshire dialects in the manuscript, which is the only source of some of the lyrics. Robbins prints 13 texts ['Alas what planet was y born vndur,' *159*; 'Continvaunce/Of remembraunce/withowte endyng,' *657*; 'ffor to p[reue]nte/And after repente/hyt wer ffoly,' *853*; 'My whofull herte plonged yn heuynesse,' *2277.8*; 'My woofull hert thus clad in payn,' *2279*; 'O þou fortune why art þou so inconstaunt,' *2568*; 'Sith fortune hathe me set thus nethis wyse,' *3125*; 'Veryly/and truly/I schall nat fayne,' *3849*; 'Welcome be ȝe my souereine,' *3878*; 'What so men seyn/Love is no peyn,' *3917*; 'where y haue chosyn stedefast woll y be,' *4059*; 'Ye aar to blame to sette yowre hert so sore,' *4241.5*; 'Yit wulde I not the causer faryd amysse,' *4272.5*]. Nine poems have not previously been published, and four have been printed, 'somewhat inaccurately, in out-of-the-way books' (632). [Item IX, not listed in *IMEV*, is *4241.5* in *SIMEV*; item L, *IMEV 3613*, is *2277.8* in *SIMEV*; item LII, not listed in *IMEV*, is *4272.5* in *SIMEV*; item LX is listed in *SIMEV* as **586.5*.] [See also Beadle and Owen, **84**; Hanson-Smith, **712**; McNamer, **958**.]

12, 100, 139, 159, 373, 380, 383, 402, 576, *586.5, 653, 657, 666, 734, 828, 853, 854, 919, 1017, 1086, 1331, 1489, 1953, 2202, 2269, 2277.8, 2279, 2317, 2381, 2383, 2401, 2568, 2624, 2662, 2742, 2756, 3125, 3179, 3180, 3361, 3412, 3437, 3535, 3542, 3613, 3670, 3787, 3849, 3878, 3917, 3948, 4059, 4241.5, 4254, 4272.5.

55 Robbins, R.H., ed. *Secular Lyrics of the XIVth and XVth Centuries*. 2nd edn. Oxford: Clarendon, 1955. [*RobbinsS*]

The Introduction differs from that of the first edition, **51**, in supplying updated references such as notes on the *Red Book of Ossory* (xxxvi–vii) and the 'Findern Anthology' (xlvi). There are alterations to Robbins's notes on the following lyrics: 'A dere god haue I deseruyd this' [*4*]; 'As I went on Yole day in oure prosession' [*377*]; 'Grevus ys my sorowe' [*1018*]; 'Have all my hert and be in peys' [*1120*]; 'In erth there ys a lityll thyng' [*1480*]; 'Lett no man cum into this hall' [*1866*]; 'Mercy me graunt off þat I me compleyne' [*2161*]; 'Myn worldly Ioy vpon me rewe' [*2188*]; 'Now ys 30le comyn w^t gentyll chere' [*2343*]; 'Peny is an hardy knyght' [*2747*]; 'Tappster fyll another ale' [*3259*]; and 'The false fox came vnto oure croft' [*3328*]. In other respects the text is little altered from that of the first edition.

———— Review by A.C. Cawley, *Modern Language Review* 52 (1957): 408–9. Questions some aspects of Robbins's choice of poems, since 'he is prepared to accept Carleton Brown's definition of a lyric as "any short poem"' (408), but is generally pleased with the selections and with the introductory material, concluding that the work is 'an important book for every student of the medieval English secular lyric' (409).

56 Baugh, Nita Scudder, ed. *A Worcestershire Miscellany Compiled by John Northwood, c 1400: Edited from British Museum MS. Add. 37,787*. Philadelphia: n.p., 1956.

The manuscript is 'a religious miscellany of prose and verse in Latin and English' (13), compiled by John Northwood, at Bordesley Abbey. The introduction has the sections: 'B.M. Add. 37,787' (13–17); 'Northwood as a Family Name' (17–21); 'Northwood as a Place' (21–3); 'Bordesley Abbey' (24–32); 'Library and Scriptorium' (33); 'Manuscripts at Bordesley' (33–5); 'The Scribe of Add. MS. 37,787' (35–7); 'Relation to the Vernon MS' (37–9); 'A Form of Confession (I)' (39–40); 'The Stacyons of Rome' (VII)' (40–2); 'The Debate of the Body and Soul (VIII)' (42–50); 'Two Songs of Love-Longing' (XI)' (50–4); and 'The Shorter Pieces' (55–62). Shorter pieces include verse confessions (55–7), *Septem Dona Spiritus Sancti* (57–8), liturgical prayers (58–9), the Hours of the Cross (59–60), poems to the Trinity (60–1), and Mary texts (61–2). Baugh presents an account of Phonology (63–85), 'as a basis for any trustworthy judgement as to the dialectical character of the language of the MS' (85), and describes dialect (85–6). She prints the texts (87–154), with notes on some works (155–9), and a glossary (160–5).

310.5, 351, 701, 775, 780, 965, 975, 1202, 1372, 1602, 1747, 1959, 1969, 2119, 3231, 3236, 3238, 3883.

57 Robbins, Rossell Hope, ed. *Historical Poems of the XIVth and XVth Centuries*. New York: Columbia UP, 1959. [*RobbinsH*]

Completes 'the assembly in modern editions of the best of Middle English lyrics' (vii) compiled by Brown, **31, 36, 39, 48,** and Robbins, **51, 55.** In this collection '"lyric" has been replaced by the wider term, "poem"' (vii). Most of the works have 'literary qualities that bear comparison with those of similar collections of religious and secular lyrics,' and the historical and political poems are 'competent, invigorating, and lively' (xvii). Some poems deal with civil and national strife, including the battles of Agincourt, Northampton, Bannockburn, and Otterburn; some comment on contemporary issues including economic policies, Lollardry, the Friars, and Abuses of the Age; others commemorate and advise monarchs, speak for Lancastrians or Yorkists (particulary through imagery of roses), offer prophecies, and pray for peace. Robbins supplies a critical introduction (xvii–xlvii), the texts of 100 poems, arranged according to topic or source (1–242), and notes on the poems (248–391).

5, 72, 113, 161, 205, 320, 356, 372, 455, 500, 585, 605, 700, 762, 817, 818, 822, 849, 871, 884, 892, 899, 906, 910, 920, 921, 936, 941, 1320.5, 1327, 1380, 1450, 1497, 1543, 1544, 1552, 1555, 1620, 1710, 1719, 1772, 1796, 1820, 1857, 1889, 1894, 1926, 1939, 2218, 2228, 2287, 2335, 2338, 2454, 2609, 2649, 2663, 2716, 2727, 2777, 2805, 3080, 3117, 3127, 3133, 3206, 3213, 3260, 3306, 3308, 3322, 3434, 3455, 3457, 3632, 3682, 3697, 3698, 3720, 3742, 3756, 3759, 3838, 3851, 3899, 3929, 3943, 3989, 4008, 4018, 4029, 4056.8, 4062, 4066, 4236, 4257, 4261, 4268.

Annotations of Editions 61

———— Review by R.M. Wilson, *Modern Language Review* 55 (1960): 429. Finds the collection an 'excellent selection from the shorter political poems' of the period, each with 'its own particular interest.' The introduction characterizes the poetry and its contribution to knowledge. The glossary 'has been competently compiled and is reasonably full.' Wilson's few points of disagreement are 'suggestions . . . easily enough made with the help of the material supplied by the editor . . . and only help to emphasize the general excellence of his edition.'

———— Review by K.B. McFarlane, *Medium Ævum* 30 (1961): 57–9. Takes issue with the title of the collection, since the poems are 'political and social,' rather than 'historical,' and it does not show that all the poems are in English. McFarlane finds the order of printing the poems 'extraordinarily inconvenient.' (58), with flaws in the transcription and in historical judgements.

———— Review by Ethel Seaton, *Review of English Studies*, NS 13 (1962): 400–1. Regrets the need to exclude some political poems of more than 150 lines, but generally finds the work an 'excellently edited book,' with 'copious and widely informative notes [that] hold the balance between the literary, historical, and economic interests' (401).

———— Review by A.A. Prins, *English Studies* 45 (1964): 53–4. Records Robbins's methods of selection and finds that 'the anthologist has rendered literary scholars a great service' (53). Most poems are 'vigorous, interesting and lively,' although they differ from the secular or religious verse of other anthologies in the series. The introductions are necessary and the anthology is 'a worthy successor to the earlier volumes' (54).

58 ————, ed. *Early English Christmas Carols.* New York: Columbia UP, 1961.

Presents 30 carols for the Christmas season, with music, and the text transcribed in modified MnE form. Robbins provides a general 'Introduction' (1–6), which distinguishes medieval carols from hymns and other religious songs, and accounts for them as processional antiphons rather than as works derived from the French *carole* dance. He adds a short note to the text of each carol, with comments on its origin and any unusual words, and makes suggestions for performance.

18, 21, 54.5, 88, 93, 352, 354, 507, 581, 681, 753, 889, 1004, 1030.5, 1036, 1070.5, 1352, 2315, 2377, 2551.8, 2733, 3283, 3315, 3385, 3536, 3596, 3638, 3736, 3737.

———— Review by Richard L. Greene, *Renaissance News* 15 (1962): 224–7. Welcomes the presentation of this volume, 'intended less for scholars than for the discriminating general public.' Greene finds the selection 'judicious' (224), and the notes 'generally correct and well phrased.' He notes some inaccuracies in the commentaries and introduction, and rejects Robbins's theory of the origin of the carol in liturgical processions rather than a relation to the *carole*. In spite of various points of difference, Greene suggests that the book 'should win the attention and thanks of a new audience and create new connoisseurs of the carol' (227).

———— Review by Winifred A. Maynard, *English Studies* 44 (1963): 364–7. Traces the course of the opposed theories of the origin of the carol. After discussion of their merits, Maynard suggests that they should not be seen as 'mutually exclusive.' She examines the edition as one for singers, expressing some regret that occasionally 'fidelity to fine points of rhythm has been subjugated to the need for clarity' (366). She suggests a paperback edition of the carols for singers, since the work can otherwise have 'only a limited effect,' although 'it provides an attractive selection of authentic carols, well-edited and set out for singing' (367).

59 Greene, Richard Leighton, ed. *A Selection of English Carols.* Oxford: Clarendon, 1962.

Offers 'a representative selection' of 100 carols, 'in part an abridgement' (v) of *The Early English Carols*, **37**, with 'Introduction' (1–52), notes on 'Manuscripts and Printed

Sources' (170–85), and 'Texts' (186–263). Greene defines the carol as 'a poem for singing, on whatever subject, in uniform stanzas and provided with a burden, a choral element, which is sung at the beginning of the piece and repeated after each stanza' (1). He associates the word with the OF *carole*, a round dance, rather than a hymn (as proposed by Sahlin, **232**, and Robbins, **407**), and contrasts the carol's popularity with the lay public with the disapproval of church authorities. Nicholas Bozon, William Herebert, John Grimestone, and Richard de Ledrede were prominent among Franciscans who composed pious verses to use with carol tunes. Greene instances the 'Boar's Head Carol' ['The borys hede that we bryng here,' *3315*], the 'Corpus Christi Carol' [*1132*], 'When cryst was born of mary fre' [*3932*], and 'A chyld ys borne e-wys' [*30*] among the few carols that have survived unchanged. He distinguishes between the carol and the narrative ballad on grounds of 'method of transmission, narrative quality, and metrical form' (25). Some carols associated with Christmas use the symbolism of holly and ivy. Macaronic carols maintain 'a continuous sense in a patterned alternation of the two languages' (35), and thus differ from translations. No carol is undoubtedly 'a full translation of a Latin hymn' (36), but the influence of Latin hymns, exemplified in the compositions of Adam of St Victor and St Bernard of Clairvaux, is significant. This influence can be seen in the verses of James Ryman, one of few authors who can confidently be named; John Audelay and John Lydgate are others.

18, 187.5, 21, 22, 29, 30, 44, 72, 80, 112, 163, 190, 225, 298, 320, 340, 360, 375, 377, 409.5, 470, 488, 503, 549, 601, 772.5, 782, 903, 1030.5, 1070, 1132, 1198, 1219, 1226, 1234, 1280, 1322, 1330, 1351, 1362, 1363.5, 1395, 1399, 1415, 1433, 1471, 1485, 1522, 1650, 1651, 1849, 1866, 1873, 1892, 1914, 2024, 2086, 2098, 2113, 2332, 2339, 2343, 2346, 2377, 2432, 2674.5, 2681, 2716, 2733, 3235, 3313, 3315, 3343, 3385, 3434, 3438, 3457, 3460, 3525, 3527, 3536, 3537, 3566, 3583, 3627, 3643, 3654, 3674, 3736, 3776, 3820, 3822, 3877, 3959, 3971, 4197, 4219, 4229.5, 4279.

────── Review by Basil Cottle, *Review of English Studies* NS 14 (1963): 277–9. Perceives the introduction to be 'authoritative and fascinating' (277), while discerning some misprints and 'vagaries among the proper names' (278). Cottle supplies a list of words to be added to the glossary, concluding that the additions would make the book 'admirable for university student or general reader; its criticism and its historical matter are attractive and stimulating' (279).

────── Review by Rossell Hope Robbins, *Speculum* 38 (1963): 484–7. Expresses Robbins's continuing opposition to Greene's view on the origin of the carol in dance song. He finds that in Greene's study of the manuscripts 'the true measure of his scholarship is best displayed' (486), and admires the notes, comparing them with those of the earlier edition, **37**. Robbins provides a list of errata, but concludes that the work is 'a good book . . . compact and inexpensive and will rapidly become the standard text for university students' (487).

────── Review by D.S. Brewer, *English Studies* 51 (1970): 60–1. Welcomes 'such a delightful collection of medieval poetry so admirably edited.' For Brewer, Greene's refutation of Robbins's thesis on the origin of the carol is 'entirely convincing' (60), but he notes some points of disagreement with Greene's comments on minstrels and the musical performances of carols. He explains Greene's adaptation of **37**, and the rewriting of its introduction, and notes a few flaws.

60 **Bowers, R.H**, ed. *Three Middle English Religious Poems*. University of Florida Monographs: Humanities 12. Gainesville, FL: U of Florida P, 1963.

The three poems, previously unpublished, consider the 'great eschatological topics of the Passion and of the Last Judgement' (6). They are 'Here begynnes a new lessoun' [*1189*], in BL Royal 17 c.xvii; 'Also take hede to þis insawmpyl here' [*269*], in BL Add. 37,049; and 'Of alle þe ioys þat in þis worlde may be' [*2613*], in Cambridge University Library Dd.11.89. After bibliographical details of each poem and brief descriptions of the manuscripts, Bowers discusses 'Form and Subject Matter' (3–18). He summarizes each poem: *1189* includes events of the Resurrection, Ascension and Pentecost, and the Blessed Virgin Mary's role as Mediatrix; *269* compares the lure of the penitent to Christ to recalling a hawk, and describes the penitent's self-crucifixion; *2613* advocates meditation on the Passion, with topics for consideration. Since their purpose is 'to stimulate the indifferent to repentance and a renewal of Christian piety,' they can be considered 'homiletic or pastoral . . . designed to save men's souls' (5). They seem to be the work of clerical authors. Bowers explains the changing emphasis in perceptions of the Passion and Last Judgement as the fourteenth century progressed, 'from judgement to redemption, from justice to mercy,' changing the concept of 'Jesus as stern judge' to that of 'Jesus as the loving redeemer' (7). He traces the treatment of such concepts in religious drama and the 'sensibility of devotion to the Passion, or Christocentric piety' (9). Traditions that marked these changes were 'the gradual elevation of the Blessed Virgin Mary to the role of mediator for sinful man,' and 'the allegory of the Four Daughters of God' (10).

269, 1189, 2613.

61 Davies, R.T., ed. *Medieval English Lyrics: A Critical Anthology.* London: Faber, 1963; Evanston, IL: Northwestern UP, 1964.

A collection of 187 lyrics, in which a 'lyric' means 'simply a shorter poem' (46). The poems are arranged chronologically, from St Godric's hymn 'Seinte marie clane uirgine' [*2988*] of the twelfth century to Wyatt's poems of the earlier sixteenth. Davies supplies titles, modern punctuation and capitals, some modification of spelling and characters, but few emendations and 'no alteration that could affect rhythm' (49). The general introduction (13–49) offers 'a short, selective history of the medieval English lyric' (13). Davies explains resonances with poems of other times, and describes the range of the lyrics, 'written by a diversity of people in the course of four centuries' (14), covering many aspects of life and warmly expressing love in both religious and secular poems. Comparing the lyrics with their Latin equivalents, he finds that some are 'peculiarly English and peculiarly good' (23). Among Franciscans who had an important part in the translation of Latin poems and adaptation of secular works were William Herebert, James Ryman, John Grimestone, and Richard de Ledrede. The 'highly conventional character of medieval religious poetry' (25) is also seen in secular works of Chaucer and Charles d'Orléans and in the Harley lyrics. Chaucer and Dunbar show versatility in rhetorical, colloquial, or vulgar verse. Few lyrics have been preserved with music, but in general '"literary" and "musical" lyrics are not very dissimilar' (28). The poems have survived in many ways, with 'a certain element of good fortune in their preservation' (30).

Although most secular lyrics are in the styles of troubadour verse, they also show 'native English characteristics' (32) such as alliteration, homely language, descriptive details, rhythm, and the burden. Chaucer's verse offers 'the earliest, consistently accomplished instances of the characteristic English verse line' (34). Davies comments on the carols, their associations with dancing and possible use as processional hymns (35–6). Many more religious than secular lyrics have survived, in a variety of forms, some showing 'restraint and spareness' and 'significant simplicity,' even in the treatment of moving themes and exposition of aspects of 'the tradition of Latin learning' (37). Many works of the late fourteenth and fifteenth centuries are part of the 'religious poetry of pathos and passion,' which concentrates on love and suffering, with the 'warmth and passionate eagerness' (38) particularly associated with Richard Rolle.

The influence of Latin verse is strong in genre, rhythm, and stanza form. Some poems are translations; some have Latin lines or phrases. Prophetic lullabies 'in which the Passion is foretold' are found 'first in the fourteenth century in English' (40). Latin genres include drinking songs and poems of complaint and contempt of the world, developing to 'a disproportionate and morbid concern with death' (41). Poems that satirize women show Latin and French influences. Although 'forms of lyric poetry that are peculiarly French seem to have had only a limited effect in England' (43), some French forms are found, such as the *chanson d'aventure* (including the pastourelle), the *ballade*, and the *rondeau* or roundel, probably introduced by Chaucer and used by Wyatt and Hoccleve. Many macaronic poems use ME, Latin, and French. The cult of courtly love had aspects of secular and religious love. Davies comments briefly on the ballad (45), but includes only 'Judas' ['Hit wes upon a scereþorsday þat vre louerd aros,' *1649*].

12, 16, 22, 37, 100, 105, 117, 145, 161, 205, 237, 241, 267, 285, 340, 352, 359, 360, 377, 409.5, 420, 441, 497, 515, 543, 549, 551, 611, 648, 657, 664, 688.3, 693, 704, 708, 739, 769, 809, 813, 816, 864, 888, 903, 909, 925, 927, 932.5, 998, 1002, 1008, 1018, 1077, 1082.5, 1132, 1170, 1194.5, 1207, 1226, 1226, 1274, 1299, 1302, 1303, 1327, 1333, 1351, 1359, 1365, 1367, 1370.5, 1395, 1399, 1402, 1433, 1444, 1450, 1450.5, 1460, 1470, 1485, 1488, 1527, 1588, 1640, 1649, 1650, 1684, 1699, 1710, 1727, 1729, 1761, 1787, 1836, 1849, 1861, 1865, 1866, 1944, 2025, 2031, 2037.5, 2057, 2066, 2082, 2086, 2107, 2150, 2163, 2217, 2231.5, 2236, 2240, 2243, 2254, 2270, 2320, 2336, 2359, 2375, 2381, 2507, 2517, 2518, 2550, 2551.8, 2619, 2640, 2645, 2663, 2716, 2733, 2742, 2757.5, 2988, 3142, 3155, 3211, 3212, 3223, 3227, 3235, 3243.3, 3310, 3313, 3343, 3354.5, 3391, 3438, 3656, 3691, 3695, 3700, 3776, 3782, 3787, 3812, 3822, 3832, 3837, 3872, 3899.3, 3906, 3921, 3964, 3996, 3998, 3999, 4037, 4159, 4160, 4185, 4197, 4200, 4229.5, 4263, 4272.5, 4282, 7074, 7238, 7415, 7585, 7586.

———— Review by R.M. Wilson, *Modern Language Review* 59 (1964): 254–5. Finds a few questionable aspects, but generally commends the edition as 'a well-chosen and well-edited selection . . . at once scholarly and popular . . . that provides a good introduction to what is perhaps the most modern in spirit of all medieval literature' (255).

———— Review by Celia Sisam, *Review of English Studies* NS 16 (1965): 59–61. Is generally pleased with the 'tact and good sense' used by Davies in his modifications of medieval spelling, and with the 'careful and reliable texts,' and the 'accurate and well judged' glosses and translations. Sisam corrects a few 'slips in the glossing' (60), but praises the introduction and references in this 'readable and well-presented anthology' (61).

———— Review by Rosemary Woolf, *Medium Ævum* 34 (1965): 154–7. Offers comparisons with the anthology of Chambers and Sidgwick, **18**, and notes many points of difference, most of them related to the different definitions of 'lyric' accepted by the editors. Woolf questions Davies's application of titles to the poems, and has some doubts about the lack of order in the anthology, a problem related to the assignment of dates to the texts. As she proposes some emendations, she admits that it is 'easy to suggest editorial methods when not making an edition.' Woolf acknowledges the difficulties of dealing with ME lyrics, and praises Davies's 'patient thought and scholarship' (156) and merits of the helpful introduction and accurate glosses. She concludes that the anthology is 'sound and pleasant' (157), and includes some notes on particular poems.

62 Stevick, Robert D., ed. *One Hundred Middle English Lyrics*. The Library of Literature. Gen. eds. John Henry Raleigh and Ian Watt. Indianapolis IN: Bobbs, 1964.

A collection of lyrics, with some 'Selected Fragments' (174–5), included as 'facts of literary history, although . . . not . . . in the strict historical sense of being exact transcripts of extant documents' (xii). The chronological arrangement illustrates the development and characteristics of ME lyric tradition, from the twelfth to the fifteenth century. The degree of sophistication of some early lyrics suggests the influence of other languages or a process of development in stages which have not been preserved. To avoid both the need for every potential reader 'to serve an apprenticeship to the trade of philology' (x) and the problems of translation of ME lyrics into MnE, Stevick presents the texts 'in a single Middle English written dialect' which is normalized 'to the emerging literary dialect of Chaucer and his contemporaries of the London–East Midland region at about 1400' (xi). [See also **424**.] He omits 'descriptive and classificatory comments and appreciative remarks' together with 'explications, critical analyses, and assessments of the poems,' which would 'tend to fix the editor's interpretations' (xiv). Instead he supplies sources of texts, offers glosses of 'hard' and specialized words with the poems, and provides a glossary (177–83) for words that are 'less difficult or more common' (xv). A linguistic section (xvi–xxviii), for 'less experienced readers of Middle English' (xvi) and their mentors, deals with the language and principles of normalization. Stevick discusses personal pronouns, nouns, adjectives and verbs, phonological changes, and metrical features. [2nd edn. 1994, **103**.]

14, 29, 72, 117, 146, 194, 210, 274, 320, 359, 360, 364, 375, 376, 378, 383, 445, 515, 521.5, 549, 754, 769, 864, 869, 891, 922, 925, 927, 932, 945.5, 1008, 1125, 1129, 1132, 1142, 1254, 1276.8, 1280, 1298, 1303, 1331, 1333, 1367, 1387, 1395, 1460, 1463, 1468, 1568, 1609, 1849, 1861, 1866, 1871.5, 1914, 1921, 1922, 1978, 2023, 2025, 2037.5, 2070, 2119, 2162, 2163, 2164, 2231, 2243, 2261.2, 2284.5, 2288, 2320, 2343, 2359, 2366, 2381, 2504, 2507, 2527, 2645, 2687, 2716, 2782, 3078, 3122, 3162, 3211, 3223, 3242.5, 3271, 3284, 3310, 3344, 3408, 3525, 3595, 3857.5, 3939, 3959, 3961, 3965, 3968, 3969, 3996, 4037, 4044, 4141, 4177, 4185, 4189, 4198, 4279, 7106, 7217, 7503, 7507.

63 Stone, Brian, ed. and tr. *Medieval English Verse.* Harmondsworth: Penguin, 1964. Rev. 1971.

Presents 96 poems in MnE verse translation, including many lyrics. After a general historical and literary 'Introduction' (12–22), Stone prints the poems in sections according to subject, each with a more specific introduction to the topic and the works offered. His divisions include 'Poems of the Nativity' (23–32); 'Poems on the Passion' (33–41); 'Poems of Adoration' (42–59); 'Poems of Sin and Death' (60–9); 'Miscellaneous Religious Poems' (70–81); 'Selections from the Bestiary' (89–94); 'Miscellaneous Secular Poems' (95–109); 'Political Poems' (110–17); and 'The Harley Lyrics' (175–212).

5, 29, 66, 72, 105, 117, 194, 196, 225, 353, 360, 515, 543, 631, 968, 1008, 1129, 1216, 1279, 1299, 1302, 1303, 1365, 1367, 1394, 1449, 1504, 1649, 1705, 1839, 1847, 1861, 1893, 1921, 1922, 1943, 1974, 1978, 2006, 2007, 2009, 2036, 2037.5, 2042, 2070, 2163, 2166, 2207, 2236, 2241, 2293, 2320, 2336, 2359, 2366, 2622, 2645, 2695, 2739, 2771, 2992, 2995, 3078, 3080, 3155, 3211, 3219, 3222, 3227, 3310, 3353, 3411, 3533, 3594, 3691, 3696, 3707, 3836, 3858, 3874, 3895, 3963, 3998, 4037, 4044, 4088, 4177, 4194.

64 Ker, N.R., ed. *Facsimile of British Museum MS. Harley 2253.* EETS 255. London: Oxford UP, 1965 (*for* 1964).

This edition, the centenary volume of the Early English Text Society, contains facsimiles of MSS Harley 2253 ff. 49–140^v, 1^v and 142, and Royal 12 C.xii, ff 68^v and 76^v. Ker's introduction lists the contents, including English, Latin, and French verse and prose (ix–xvi) and describes the manuscript (xvi–xx). He comments on the hand and origin of Royal 12 C.xii (xx–xxi) and on the date and origin of Harley 2253 (xxi–iii).

English verse contents of MS Harley 2253: *105, 166, 185, 205, 357, 515, 694.5, 968, 1104, 1115, 1196, 1216, 1320.5, 1365, 1394, 1395, 1407, 1449, 1461, 1504, 1678, 1705, 1747, 1861, 1889, 1894, 1921, 1922, 1974, 2039, 2066, 2078, 2166, 2207, 2236, 2287, 2359, 2604, 2649, 3155, 3211, 3236, 3310, 3874, 3939, 3963, 4037, 4177, 4194.*

65 **Bennett, J.A.W., and G.V. Smithers, eds.** *Early Middle English Verse and Prose.* Glossary, Norman Davis. Oxford: Clarendon, 1966. 2nd edn. 1968. Repr. (with corrections and additions) 1974.

The editors provide a general introduction to literature of the period (xi–lxi), with 'Lyrics' (108–35) and notes on individual works (316–36), in which they discuss provenance, dialect, and matters of particular interest. The lyrics selected exemplify secular and religious song, and illustrate the influence of European styles on ME works. Some secular songs have survived with music, and others were parts of dance songs. The religious works represent 'the chief themes of the century's outpourings of devotional verse' (110).

105, 864, 1142, 1395, 1449, 1504, 2066, 2163, 2207, 2236, 2288, 2293, 2320, 2366, 2645, 3223, 3236, 3963, 4037, 4044, 4194, 7013, 7286.

———— Review by R.M. Wilson, *Modern Language Review* 63 (1968): 453–4. Has high praise for the glossary, 'which succeeds admirably' (454). Although Wilson approves of the selection of most texts, he deems inclusion of some of the lyrics 'hardly worthwhile' (453).

66 **Haskell, Ann S., ed.** *A Middle English Anthology.* Garden City, NY: Anchor-Doubleday, 1969.

This collection was prepared for teaching purposes, 'with frank subjectivity.' Haskell modernizes medieval characters, and supplies 'punctuation, capitalization, and accent marks where they seem necessary' (xi). She presents 14 lyrics, with marginal glosses and footnotes, and provides a bibliography (527–8). There are three appendices: 'The Rules of Courtly Love' (513–14), 'The Significance of Numbers' (515–17), and 'The Planets' (518–21).

360, 559, 864, 1132, 1226, 1367, 1849, 1914, 2320, 2716, 3223, 3227, 3310, 3939.

67 **Allison, Alexander W., et al., eds.** *The Norton Anthology of Poetry.* New York: Norton, 1970. 2nd edn. 1975. 3rd edn. 1983.

There is some modernization of texts of ME verses in this anthology, and an essay on 'Versification,' by Jon Stallworthy (1403–22).

117, 375, 377, 456.5, 515, 554.5, 688.3, 729.5, 809, 1132, 1194, 1299, 1303, 1367, 1370.5, 2029, 2031, 2231.5, 2320, 2669, 2733, 3223, 3310, 3465, 3627, 3787, 3899.3, 4282, 7605.

68 **Robertson, D.W., Jr., ed.** *The Literature of Medieval England.* New York: McGraw, 1970.

The collection is intended to introduce the general reader to medieval literature of the British Isles, and presents most texts in translation. 'Middle English Literature: Songs and Short Poems' (345–65) stresses that one should not expect 'the spontaneous expression of feeling to be found in romantic and post romantic lyrics' and that 'in fact, it is better not to call them lyrics at all except to mean "words for a song" in those instances where the poems were set to music' (346). Robertson includes music for 'Foweles in the frith' [*864*], 'Gabriel fram evene king' [*888*], 'Mirie it is while sumer ilast' [*2163*], and 'Svmer is icumen in' [*3223*].

377, 515, 809, 864, 888, 1367, 1454, 1847, 2031, 2034.5, 2037.5, 2163, 2320, 2645, 3155, 3190, 3223, 3348, 3825, 4177.

69 **Sisam, Celia, and Kenneth Sisam, eds.** *The Oxford Book of Medieval English Verse.* Oxford: Clarendon, 1970.

A collection designed 'to show the range of interest offered by medieval verse' (ix), including poems of many kinds. There are more secular works than religious, because

Annotations of Editions

they offer greater variety. The editors arrange the poems 'as a medieval anthologist might have done' (x), with 'juxtaposition of themes, profane and religious, trivial and profound, comic and grave' (xi), and use a chronological order, as far as this can be determined. They supply titles and glosses with the texts. The 'Textual Notes' (568–608) include sources in manuscripts and standard editions.

5, 21, 29, 33, 34, 36, 66, 68, 72, 91, 100, 105, 110, 117, 120, 143, 150, 161, 163, 190.3, 196, 210, 225, 298, 302, 322, 360, 375, 377, 418, 433, 445, 465.5, 515, 519, 521, 543, 549, 559, 579, 597.5, 611, 672.3, 693, 708, 761, 762, 769, 809, 813, 831, 864, 888, 903, 925, 991, 1008, 1014.5, 1029, 1066, 1078, 1091, 1116, 1121, 1132, 1142, 1194.5, 1198, 1199, 1201, 1207, 1225, 1226, 1251, 1254, 1265, 1269, 1280, 1299, 1301, 1303, 1303, 1305, 1311, 1314, 1320.5, 1327, 1330, 1344, 1353, 1358, 1362, 1365, 1367, 1384, 1387, 1389.5, 1394, 1395, 1399, 1402, 1415, 1422, 1433, 1448, 1449, 1454, 1459, 1463, 1468, 1549, 1568, 1589, 1597, 1608, 1609, 1622, 1631.3, 1634.5, 1649, 1650, 1684, 1793.9, 1796, 1798, 1817, 1820, 1822, 1829, 1836, 1847, 1851, 1857, 1861, 1865, 1866, 1893, 1896, 1921, 1930, 1944, 1977, 1978, 2007, 2009, 2012, 2025, 2026, 2037.5, 2039.3, 2066, 2078, 2107, 2125, 2138, 2141, 2148, 2158, 2163, 2164, 2229, 2236, 2241, 2243, 2288, 2320, 2335, 2343, 2359, 2375, 2381, 2504, 2622, 2645, 2675, 2691.5, 2716, 2742, 2754, 2777, 2794.6, 2892, 2903, 2988, 3058, 3078, 3080, 3155, 3167, 3174, 3180, 3209, 3211, 3212, 3221, 3223, 3227, 3236, 3259, 3260, 3284, 3306, 3310, 3313, 3318.7, 3324, 3327, 3328, 3352, 3353, 3408, 3411, 3418, 3434, 3437, 3438, 3439.5, 3449, 3460, 3464.5, 3472, 3504, 3513, 3525, 3533, 3536, 3537, 3538, 3546, 3552, 3580, 3596, 3603, 3627, 3691, 3697, 3706.2, 3782, 3787, 3812, 3815.5, 3818, 3819, 3820, 3857.5, 3859.5, 3893, 3895, 3896, 3897.5, 3898, 3906, 3914, 3918.5, 3919, 3921, 3922, 3927.6, 3939, 3959, 3963, 3964, 3969, 3996, 3998, 4019, 4023, 4037, 4079, 4088, 4104, 4135.5, 4176.5, 4177, 4180.6, 4181, 4185, 4189, 4194, 4197, 4256.8, 4268, 4279, 4282, 7107, 7243, 7573.

———— Review by Rossell Hope Robbins, *Notes and Queries* 217 (1972): 387–8. Doubts that 'this anthology will be surpassed' as 'a loving monument to Middle English poetry,' and applauds the 'very modest editorial apparatus' which leaves 'the stage to the poems themselves.' Robbins offers examples of the regularization of language, and notes that the 'resultant "late Sisam" dialect is perhaps the easiest means of making orthographically difficult and grammatically confusing texts generally available' (387). He comments on a number of readings, with some regret for the brevity in the notes demanded by the format, and offers suggestions for additions. He concludes that it is 'a very pleasant, unpretentiously assured volume; very inexpensive, very elegant, very scholarly, very useful' (388).

———— Review by Susie I. Tucker, *Medium Ævum* 41 (1972): 72–4. Summarizes the range of this 'book for lovers of mediæval poetry' (72), to reveal 'our ancestors, working, fasting, boozing, hunting or poaching, making love, keeping Christmas, reflecting on the economic or political ills of life, fighting, repenting' (73), and to offer much enlightenment in the brief 'snatches' of verse. Most of the critical material is adequate and the whole is 'a richly representative collection' (74).

———— Review by Kari Sajavaara, *English Studies* 55 (1974): 389–91. Finds the book 'delightful and exciting' (389), and welcomes the selection of verse and the happy juxtaposition of a variety of forms. Sajavaara describes procedures for the selection and normalization, expressing general satisfaction with the latter, but some regret that more detailed explanations were not supplied for changes not considered substantial.

70   Stemmler, Theo, ed. *Medieval English Love-Lyrics.* Tübingen: Niemeyer, 1970.

The 112 lyrics in the anthology offer 'typical specimens of popular, courtly, satiric and – not least of all – ribald poetry'. It presents 'all medieval English love-poems from Anglo-Saxon times to the end of the fourteenth century' (v), and 44 of the fifteenth century. Stemmler presents the poems in chronological order, with Italian or French originals of ME poems, textual sources (114–15), and a bibliography (116–20). He includes passages from Chaucer's *Troilus and Criseyde* [*3327*], *The Book of the Duchess* [*1306*], and *The Legend of Good Women* [*100*].

100, 105, 133, 144, 150, 159, 179, 194, 225, 360, 371, 377, 438, 445, 515, 521, 650, 656, 684, 694.5, 734.5, 864, 891, 926, 960, 1008, 1010, 1121, 1142, 1222, 1265, 1279, 1280, 1302, 1306, 1330, 1331, 1333, 1344, 1388, 1394, 1395, 1449, 1504, 1510, 1531, 1768, 1799, 1849, 1861, 1921, 2005, 2009, 2029, 2031, 2135, 2141, 2176, 2185, 2232, 2236, 2243, 2262.5, 2288, 2375, 2412, 2421, 2437, 2494, 2518, 2524, 2622, 2640, 2654, 3164, 3167.3, 3174, 3327, 3409, 3414, 3418, 3512, 3534, 3542, 3594, 3645, 3698, 3795, 3832, 3859.5, 3874, 3899.6, 3900.5, 3902.5, 4014, 4037, 4194, 4209, 4282.

71 Tydeman, William, ed. *English Poetry 1400–1580.* The Poetry Bookshelf. Gen. ed. James Reeves. London: Heinemann, 1970.

A selection of verse that includes anonymous religious and secular lyrics and works of poets such as Lydgate, Skelton, and Wyatt. The 'Introduction' (1–20) surveys years when English poetry assumed 'its moral seriousness, its ability to argue a case or move a listener, its wit, its colloquial strength,' and its ability to fuse discoveries from the classics with 'the brasher native traditions' (1), thus enabling the work of Elizabethan poets. Tydeman explains the use of aureate language and the importance of rhetoric, and describes metrical patterns used by Chaucer, Lydgate, Wyatt, Surrey, and their successors. He contrasts twentieth-century notions with earlier expectations that 'the poet usually effaces his personality . . . or assimilates his own experiences into the general human pattern' (12). Tydeman finds no discontinuity between poetry of the late medieval and early Tudor periods, and traces the use of older traditions by Renaissance poets.

37, 117, 298, 377, 506.5, 729.5, 769, 1132, 1194.5, 1222, 1264, 1299, 1303, 1328.5, 1330, 1367, 1454, 1470, 1507, 1656, 1892, 2231.5, 2243, 2518, 2538, 2550, 2574, 2590, 2591, 2756.5, 3058, 3265.5, 3302.5, 3759, 3782, 3832.5, 3864, 3899.3, 3903.5, 3949, 3999, 4004, 4279.

72 Owen, Lewis J., and Nancy H. Owen, eds. *Middle English Poetry: An Anthology.* Indianapolis: Bobbs, 1971.

The collection is prepared for teaching purposes, and is divided into representative sections illustrating various genres. 'Lyric Poetry' (3–26) follows the 'General Introduction' (xiii–ix). 'The Thrush and the Nightingale' ['Somer is comen wiþ loue to toune,' *3222*], is presented as a beast debate (272–81) in the section on 'Beast Literature.' The poems are arranged chronologically, with glosses at the foot of each page. Detailed commentaries for the individual lyrics follow the texts (339–66).

84, 377, 515, 688,3, 864, 1082.5, 1132, 1302, 1367, 2012, 2024, 2320, 2359, 2831.6, 3223, 3436, 4044, 3222.

———Review by M.C. Seymour, *English Studies* 55 (1974): 65–6. Finds that 'it is difficult to justify another' anthology of ME poetry, and that this is 'too naive for serious use and too ambitious for elementary use' (65).

73 Silverstein, Theodore, ed. *English Lyrics before 1500.* York Medieval Texts. Gen. eds. Elizabeth Salter and Derek Pearsall. London: Arnold; Evanston, IL: Northwestern UP, 1971.

Presents 144 lyrics, each preceded by a head note. The works are arranged according to subject and time of composition: 'Religious and Moral Poems of the Thirteenth Century' (12–36); 'Secular Poems of the Thirteenth Century' (37–41); 'Religious and Moral Poems of the Fourteenth Century' (42–81); 'Secular Poems of the Fourteenth

Century' (82–98); 'Religious and Moral Poems of the Fifteenth Century' (99–126); and 'Secular Poems of the Fifteenth Century' (127–63). The 'Introduction' (1–9) sets out Silverstein's reasons for selecting some poems and omitting others, in an anthology that tries 'in little space to be as comprehensive as it can,' before addressing the question of 'what a lyric poem is and in what sense or senses the poems set before us here are lyrics' (1). Silverstein deals with these matters first by comparison with the lyrics of ancient Greece, then moves towards a definition through 'historical criticism' (2) and 'time and milieu.' He finds the lyric 'short, sweet and meaningful' (4), and explores, in particular, the notion of brevity in the lyric's 'length, concentration, abstraction, form of statement' (8). He provides a list of 'Books for Consultation and Further Reading' (10–11) and a Glossary (164–79).

37, 112, 117, 137, 146, 190, 194, 237, 267, 293, 353, 360, 377, 412.5, 420, 495, 515, 521, 549, 565, 572, 693, 695, 708, 717, 769, 864, 903, 906, 922, 925, 926, 927, 1002, 1004, 1008, 1010, 1054, 1125, 1201, 1207, 1264, 1299, 1302, 1303, 1311, 1312, 1333, 1354, 1365, 1367, 1395, 1422, 1460, 1697, 1787, 1822, 1832, 1849, 1861, 1921, 1922, 1935, 1938, 1977, 1978, 2005, 2016, 2017, 2025, 2037.5, 2039, 2047, 2086, 2114, 2135, 2136, 2141, 2163, 2182, 2231, 2236, 2241, 2243, 2245, 2254, 2273, 2298, 2320, 2343, 2359, 2494, 2511, 2557, 2560, 2567, 2580, 2596, 2645, 2682, 2684, 2730, 2787, 2789, 3078, 3133, 3209, 3211, 3212, 3221, 3223, 3227, 3275, 3310, 3314, 3408, 3533.5, 3552, 3571, 3691, 3771, 3802, 3822, 3844, 3863, 3891, 3898, 3906, 3911, 3917, 3921, 3963, 3965, 3996, 3999, 4037, 4044, 4177, 4189, 4199, 4207, 4239, 4256, 4263, 7005.

———Review by M.C. Seymour, *English Studies* 55 (1974): 65–6. Regrets some omissions from the introduction and prefaces, and discounts some glosses. Seymour finds the texts 'clean . . . seriously and for the most part sensibly edited,' yet decides that 'if one uses this anthology in the classroom, one will have to do much of the editor's work oneself' (66).

74 Wilhelm, James J., tr. and ed. *Medieval Song: An Anthology of Hymns and Lyrics.* London: Allen, 1971.

Prints texts of 230 songs, with MnE translations from the Latin, Provençal, Italian, OF, German, and OE, and original texts of some lyrics. The ME and Scottish songs are presented with some normalized spelling. Wilhelm offers a short introduction to the 'Songs of Great Britain' (337–9), briefly dealing with paradox, puns, and ambiguity, and the relation of the songs to ballads.

120, 194, 515, 864, 1120, 1299, 1303, 1367, 1399, 1861, 2037.5, 2066.5, 2320, 2645, 3078, 3162, 3190, 3223, 3899.3, 4044.

75 Gardner, Helen, ed. *The New Oxford Book of English Verse 1250–1950.* Oxford: Clarendon, 1972.

Presents ME texts with some modernizing of the spelling, and includes extracts from longer poems such as *Troilus and Criseyde* [*3327*], the *Legend of Good Women* [*100*], the *Canterbury Tales* [*4019*], and *Piers Plowman* [*1459*].

100, 117, 377, 688.3, 729.5, 1008, 1132, 1299, 1367, 1370.5, 1463, 1847, 2037, 2243, 2645, 2756.5, 3223, 3327, 3405.5, 3460, 3899.3, 4019, 7493.

76 Dunn, Charles W., and Edward J. Byrnes, eds. *Middle English Literature.* New York: Harcourt, 1973.

An anthology of ME and Scots verse and prose, prepared for teaching, with some modifications of spelling, capitalization, and punctuation, marginal glosses and some modernizations on facing pages. An introduction precedes each item. The works are arranged chronologically, and a table classifies them according to audience and genre (x–xi), with twelve works designated as lyrics. Another, 'Skottes out of Berwik and of Abirdene' [*3080*], is described as 'Minot's violent political lyric' (7). The general introduction (3–33) considers literature and language of the period. The works have titles and are arranged in sections that deal with the Twelfth (36–103), Thirteenth (106–92), and Early Fourteenth (194–236) Centuries, the Age of Chaucer (238–503), the Fifteenth Century (506–21), and the Scottish Renaissance (524–50). There are linguistic appendices (551–9) and a bibliography (560–4).

66, 359, 360, 515, 688.3, 694.5, 1272, 1367, 1861, 2820.5, 3080, 3227, 4037.

77 Trapp, J.B., ed. *The Oxford Anthology of English Literature*. Vol. 1. The Middle Ages through the Eighteenth Century. Medieval English Literature. Gen. eds. Frank Kermode and John Hollander. New York: Oxford UP, 1973.

A general introduction (3–18) offers a critical and historical background to a collection of OE and ME works. Trapp presents 17 lyrics (413–25), with an introduction (411–13) and footnotes on individual lyrics. In theme and imagery he finds the ME lyrics conventional rather than individual or emotional, with 'little metrical subtlety or range' (411); few have music. Most offer 'a bare announcement of experience,' but do not explore it. The poems are 'simple, but not sensuous and passionate,' and do not offer 'conceit or surprise and originality' (412). Many religious works were composed as meditations, but carols were to be sung.

117, 360, 515, 549, 611, 1132, 1303, 1311, 1330, 1367, 1861, 2037.5, 2254, 2716, 3223, 3899.3, 3998.

78 Greene, Richard Leighton. *The Lyrics of the Red Book of Ossory*. Medium Ævum Monographs NS 5. Oxford: Society for the Study of Mediæval Languages and Literature, Blackwell, 1974.

The Red Book has 'sixty Latin poems, to some of which are prefixed scraps of Old French and Middle English verse' (ii), to indicate the airs to which they should be sung. Greene prints the works, with an introduction to describe the book and its history. The lyrics were written by Richard de Ledrede, an English Franciscan and bishop of Ossory from 1317 to 1360, for the cathedral clergy, to prevent the pollution of their consecrated throats and mouths with secular works. The singers were to find tunes for his words. The poems are arranged according to the themes of the Nativity, Easter, the Annunciation, and 'diverse devotional subjects' (v). Greene comments on the ME works, mostly in the form of burdens and fragments, and summarizes criticism of the most celebrated, 'The Maid of the Moor' ['Maiden in the mor lay,' *2037.5*]. ME lines, 'Gayneth me no garlond of greene' [*891*], precede a song concerning the willow, 'the badge of the forsaken lover of either sex' (xvi), and the Latin lyric resembles the English words in rhyme and metre; other lyrics show similar correspondences. Greene explores notions of the word *chevaldour*, and compares Dunbar's use of *chevalour*. The Red Book offers poems in a variety of metres, and shows 'how many differing verse-forms Richard de Ledrede handled with apparently equal ease in this single garland of songs for practical devotional use' (xxx).

684, 891, 1120.5, 1123, 1214.4, 1265, 2037.5, 3118.6.

79 Luria, Maxwell S., and Richard L. Hoffman, eds. *Middle English Lyrics: Authoritative Texts, Critical and Historical Backgrounds, Perspectives on Six Poems.* Norton Critical Editions. New York: Norton, 1974.

A collection of 245 lyrics, intended to offer 'a literary feast as well as a scholarly anthology,' (x). The authors offer standardized language and punctuation, with

Annotations of Editions 71

marginal glosses but no titles. They avoid a division into 'religious' and 'secular,' because this 'more justly expresses modern culture than medieval' (xi). The sections are 'Worldes bliss' (1–15); 'All for love' (16–76); 'I have a gentil cok' (77–91); 'Swete Jhesu' (92–108); 'Thirty dayes hath November' (109–32); 'Make we mery' (133–46); 'And all was for an appil' (147–69); 'A God and yet a man?' (190–222); and 'When the turuf is thy tour' (223–31). 'Critical and Historical Backgrounds' are supplied in extracts from the works of Dronke, **509** (243–66); Manning, **486** (266–80); Oliver, **549** (280–90); and Woolf, **522** (290–308). 'Perspectives on Six Poems' present views on particular lyrics: Moore, **297** (311–13) on 'Svmer is icumen in' [*3223*]; Woolf, **540** (313–17) on 'In a fryht as y con fere fremede' [*1449*]; Reiss, **478** (317–21) on 'Now goth þe sonne under wod' [*2320*] and 'Foweles in the frith' [*864*]; Robertson, **298** (321), Donaldson, **414** (322–3), Speirs, **385** (323–4), and Dronke **509** (324–5) on 'Maiden in the mor lay' [*2037.5*]; Jemielity, **532** (325–30), Manning, **420** (330–6), Halliburton, **511** (337–42), and Spitzer, **303** (342–9) on 'I syng of a myden þ^t is makeles' [*1367*].

12, 37, 63, 94, 105, 110, 113, 117, 146, 150, 194, 196, 210, 225, 237, 266, 298, 353, 359, 360, 374, 377, 420, 436, 438, 441, 465, 497, 515, 521, 549, 559, 579, 583, 600, 643, 717, 769, 795, 809, 813, 864, 903, 925, 926, 939, 968, 1002, 1008, 1010, 1054, 1073, 1121, 1132, 1151, 1163, 1179, 1182, 1195, 1199, 1201, 1207, 1213, 1216, 1222, 1225, 1232, 1235, 1240, 1274, 1278, 1280, 1297, 1299, 1302, 1303, 1308, 1314, 1330, 1333, 1334, 1359, 1365, 1367, 1387, 1394, 1395, 1396, 1407, 1417, 1422, 1423, 1449, 1460, 1468, 1485, 1502, 1504, 1527, 1608, 1609, 1622, 1649, 1678, 1705, 1742, 1768, 1810, 1817, 1818, 1829, 1836, 1849, 1861, 1866, 1892, 1921, 1922, 1938, 1978, 2009, 2012, 2023, 2024, 2037.5, 2039, 2066, 2070, 2082, 2107, 2135, 2150, 2155, 2163, 2166, 2185, 2207, 2231, 2236, 2240, 2241, 2243, 2260, 2293, 2302, 2320, 2343, 2359, 2369, 2381, 2421, 2437, 2494, 2518, 2604, 2622, 2623.3, 2654, 2675, 2742, 2747, 2751, 2756, 2831, 2903, 3078, 3109, 3135, 3157, 3171, 3174, 3190, 3209, 3211, 3212, 3221, 3222, 3223, 3227, 3236, 3245, 3259, 3310, 3313, 3314, 3328, 3348, 3405, 3408, 3409, 3410, 3418, 3438, 3465, 3525, 3565, 3571, 3572, 3594, 3613, 3628, 3676, 3700, 3722, 3735, 3771, 3782, 3787, 3825, 3832, 3836, 3862, 3864, 3872, 3873, 3874, 3879, 3895, 3898, 3906, 3911, 3919, 3939, 3963, 3998, 3999, 4016, 4037, 4044, 4083, 4092, 4096, 4159, 4177, 4194, 4197, 4199, 4221, 4223, 4239, 4256.8, 4263, 4268, 4279.

——— Review by R.T. Davies, *Yearbook of English Studies* 7 (1977): 196–8. Expresses regret that emendations were made silently, but finds the glosses 'generally full and good' and conveniently sited, although they give 'a work-a-day look.' Davies is concerned about the inclusion of extracts of critical material for some poems, but the lack of introduction and individual annotations. As a result, 'over two hundred poems have no specific commentary,' and 'some general topics relevant to some or all of them receive little or no attention' (197). He enjoys the arrangement of poems, in divisions that are 'perhaps a bit whimsical' (198).

80 Reichl, Karl. *Religiöse Dichtung im Englischen Hochmittelalter: Untersuchung und Edition der Handschrift B.14.39 des Trinity College in Cambridge.* Munich: Münchener Universitäts-Schriften, 1974.

Not seen.

81 Gray, Douglas, ed. *A Selection of Religious Lyrics.* Oxford: Clarendon, 1975.

The general introduction (vii–xii) surveys the topics and styles of medieval English religious lyric verse. Gray compares and contrasts lyrics of this period with those that precede and follow them, and finds that '[s]implicity and unaffectedness are the characteristic features of the style' (ix), although the range of mood and tone may be surprisingly wide. He presents examples to illustrate the variety of thoughts and purposes of the lyrics, and sets them within the context of European traditions of piety. There is a bibliography (xiii–vi), and a list of manuscripts and locations (xix–xi).

The collection of lyrics (1–97) is divided as follows: 'The Fall. The Promise of Redemption' (1–2); 'Annunciation and Nativity' (3–15); 'The Passion of Christ' (15–17); 'Mary at the Foot of the Cross' (18–25); 'Complaints of Christ' (25–31); 'The Memory of Christ's Passion' (31–5); 'The Triumph of Christ' (35–8); 'Christ's Love for Sinful Man' (39–47); 'Songs of Love-longing' (47–9); 'Prayers to Christ' (51–7); 'Prayers and Poems to the Virgin Mary' (57–73); 'Prayers to Saints and the Guardian Angel' (73–7); 'Mysteries of the Faith' (77); 'Christian Hope and Joy' (78–80); 'Penitence and the Christian Life' (80–3); 'The Frail Life of Man. The Last Things' (83–95); 'The Pilgrim's Final Rest' (95–7). The texts are followed by comprehensive notes on the individual lyrics (98–156), a glossary (157–70), a list of Latin words and phrases (171) and an index of first lines (172–4). [Repr. 1992, see **102**.]

37, 94, 112, 114, 117, 143, 158.3, 233, 420, 456, 496, 497, 611, 707, 769, 834, 940, 995.3, 1002, 1032, 1041.5, 1049, 1064, 1077, 1145.5, 1244, 1254, 1351, 1353, 1365, 1367, 1387, 1402, 1454, 1460, 1463, 1571, 1664.5, 1684, 1699, 1700.5, 1703, 1708, 1727, 1729, 1733, 1735, 1747, 1758.5, 1786.5, 1787, 1818, 1836, 1847, 1930, 1965, 1978, 2024, 2025, 2150, 2241, 2273, 2320, 2342, 2385, 2393, 2414, 2415, 2471, 2478.8, 2504, 2528, 2551.8, 2556, 2619, 2644, 2645, 2684, 2733, 2757.5, 2988, 2993, 3211, 3212, 3225, 3228.3, 3236, 3339, 3357, 3359, 3433, 3460, 3477.6, 3536, 3753, 3812, 3906, 3939, 3964, 3985, 4044, 4045, 4088, 4159, 4160, 4189, 4263, 7594.

———— Review by R.T. Davies, *Review of English Studies* NS 28 (1977): 204–6. Suggests 'some disproportion' (205) in the lengths of introduction and bibliography, and of text and notes, and proposes 'a little pruning' (206) of some material in the notes. Although the glossary is 'generally very good' (205), Davies notes some omissions, with scope for more extensive reference to music.

———— Review by Derek Pearsall, *Modern Language Review* 73 (1978): 153–4. Commends the 'skill and tact' with which Gray provides an admirable selection of 'authoritative texts and . . . the necessary help for the modern reader and student.' The arrangement of the texts is 'the most important innovation' (153). Some notes also supply 'compact little introductions to particular subjects' (154).

82 Spearing, A.C., and J.E. Spearing, eds. *Poetry of the Age of Chaucer.* London: Arnold, 1975.

Chaucer's 'overwhelming predominance' (1) tends to obscure the work of his contemporaries. The editors seek to restore balance in this collection of works infrequently published and poems by Chaucer that are 'not conventional choices as prescribed texts' (2). There is a comprehensive 'General Introduction' (1–40) and specific introductions to the works presented. 'Short Poems' (194–221) has detailed introductions to the seven poems (194–201) that are 'not "lyrics" in the Romantic and post-Romantic sense of the word.' They are printed with texts and notes on facing pages. The poems have been chosen 'balancing merit with as wide a typicality as possible' (194).

809, 1460, 1861, 2025, 2031, 3227, 3782.

83 Stevens, John, ed. *Early Tudor Songs and Carols.* Musica Britannica 36. London: Royal Musical Association: Stainer, 1975. 98 vols. to date. 1951–.

Transcribes songs of the Fayrfax MS (BL Add. 5465) and the Ritson MS (BL Add. 5665). In his 'Introduction' (xv–xix), Stevens describes and comments on the manuscripts, and notes the range of compositions. The Fayrfax repertoire is 'far from being uniform, let alone monotonous.' It has solemn and satirical courtly love songs, and is 'in every respect a professional production' (xvi). The religious songs reveal 'the strength and persistence of late medieval piety . . . both in literature and music' (xvii). In contrast, the Ritson MS is composite rather than homogeneous, with professional and amateur entries. After setting out his procedure in an 'Editorial Note' (xxii–xxiii),

Annotations of Editions 73

and printing pages from the manuscripts (xxiv–xxvii), Stevens transcribes 20 of the Ritson songs (1–23) and 47 of the Fayrfax (24–152). He supplies 'Notes on the Textual Commentary' (154) and 'Textual Commentary' (155–67) on individual works.

.2, 1, 13, 113.5, 146.5, 155.5, 263.5, 263.8, 364, 456.5, 474.5, 490.5, 497, 506.5, 557.5, 649.5, 675.8, 753.8, 1214.5, 1273.3, 1303.3, 1327, 1328.5, 1339.5, 1450, 1589.5, 1636.5, 1731, 1866.8, 1999.5, 2007.5, 2028.8, 2200.3, 2244.6, 2277, 2277.5, 2323.8, 2364, 2393.5, 2394.5, 2530.5, 2547.5, 2737.5, 2832.2, 3131, 3162.5, 3168.4, 3193.5, 3206.5, 3270.5, 3297.3, 3297.5, 3318.4, 3376.5, 3437, 3597, 3677.5, 3724.5, 3750, 3751.3, 3832.5, 3845, 3903.8, 4098.6, 4184, 4281.5, 4283.5.

84 Beadle, Richard, and A.E.B. Owen, introd. *The Findern Manuscript: Cambridge University Library MS. Ff.I.6.* London: Scolar, 1977.

A facsimile, with an introduction on the history of the Finderns and the manuscript, offering conjecture on the circumstances in which various hands entered the 62 works. The manuscript is 'immediately conspicuous as an anthology of secular and "courtly" verse.' Many poems not found elsewhere are probably compilers' original compositions, 'to some extent distinguishable from the courtly lyrics contributed by the main hands, and copied from other manuscripts' (xii). Beadle and Owen consider it not to be a professional production, but rather one produced 'by and for the use of the Findern family and their associates,' and 'an early and well-defined example of the prolonged and distinctive influence which the country house and its *milieu* were to have on English culture from the mid-fifteenth century onwards' (xiv).

12, 100, 139, 159, 373, 380, 383, 402, 576, 586.5, 653, 657, 666, 734, 828, 853, 854, 919, 1017, 1086, 1331, 1489, 1953, 2202, 2269, 2277, 2279, 2317, 2381, 2383, 2401, 2568, 2624, 2662, 2742, 2756, 3125, 3179, 3180, 3361, 3412, 3437, 3535, 3542, 3613, 3670, 3787, 3849, 3878, 3917, 3948, 4059, 4241.5, 4254, 4272.5.

85 Burrow, John, ed. *English Verse 1300–1500.* Longman Annotated Anthologies of English Verse 1. Gen. ed. Alistair Fowler. London: Longman, 1977.

Presents poems from 'the non-dramatic verse of two centuries' (xxiv). In his general 'Introduction' (xv–xxvii), Burrow compares and contrasts alliterative verse, represented by extracts from longer poems, and describes courtly makers whose work is included, in particular Chaucer, Gower, Hoccleve, Lydgate, Charles d'Orléans, Henryson, and Dunbar. The courtly poets present some features familiar to a modern reader, in their 'distinctive personal tone,' with 'control of diction and syntax' (xvii), and their attention to style, subject and context. 'Outside this tradition' the modern reader may seem to be 'in a less familiar world,' although anonymous works in many ways resemble the courtly verse. Burrow comments on devices of metre and style and investigates poems which might 'invite the label "folk poetry"' (xxiii); he notes the importance of the context in which poems are found. He presents the works with some normalization and modernization of spelling, and a note on 'Pronunciation' (xxvi–xxvii). There are introductory notes at the beginning of each section of poems, generally grouped by author or manuscript, with further notes on particular points following each poem. A 'Chronological Table' (xii–xiv) lists literary and other events during the period.

100, 117, 124, 194, 285, 296.3, 377, 688.3, 769, 809, 1002, 1008, 1132, 1303, 1308, 1367, 1370.5, 1402, 1459, 1599.5, 1865, 1978, 2025, 2031, 2037.5, 2203, 2243, 2550, 2622, 2632.5, 2662, 2739, 2744, 2831.6, 3058, 3137, 3144, 3209, 3327, 3434, 3445.5, 3703, 3747, 3845.5, 3868, 4019, 4282, 4284.

―――― Review by E.G. Stanley, *Notes and Queries* 222 (1977): 563–4. Is pleased to see that the book 'is more than an exercise of filling up so much space by re-using other people's learning' (563), but finds that '[c]omments and notes are too often less good' than expected. Stanley cites some of Burrow's glosses in the selection of lyrics among the notes 'too heavy with the factual information familiar to medievalists, but not always necessary in what by being a *florilegium* looks as if intended for beginners' (564).

86   Greene, Richard Leighton, ed. *The Early English Carols.* 2nd edn. Oxford: Clarendon, 1977.

Presents some revisions of the first edition, **37**, with a larger collection of carols and additional introductory material. 'The Carol as a Genre' (xxi–xlii) includes a section 'The Carol at Feasts and Banquets' (xxxviii–xlii). 'The Carol surviving the Dance' is omitted from 'The Carol as Dance-Song.' 'The "Christmas Carol"' (clvii–clix) is added to 'The Carol and Popular Religion' (cxxxix–clix). Greene adds some carols to the collection, and omits three.

Carols added: *182, 187.5, 772.5, 892, 1030.5, 1070, 1220.5, 1270.2, 1405.5, 1622, 1651, 1793.6, 2232, 2271.2, 2293.5, 2306.5, 2349.5, 2494, 2526, 2635.5, 2727, 3199.8, 3328.5, 3443.5, 3552, 3635.5, 3810.3, 4229.5, 4242.5, 4283.5, 7142, 7386, 7439, 7478.*

———— Review by R.T. Davies, *Notes and Queries* 223 (1978): 163–5. Compares the second edition with the first, and examines changes and Greene's reasons for retaining his definition of the carol. The definition has not been affected by Robbins's contention that the carol has developed from liturgical processions rather than dancing. Although the introduction has been re-ordered, it corresponds closely to those of the first edition and Greene's *A Selection of English Carols.* Davies notes additions to and omissions from the texts of those volumes. He has occasional reservations about Greene's comments, but generally commends the accuracy of the book.

———— Review by John Stevens, *Medium Ævum* 37 (1978) 337–9. Welcomes the re-working of Greene's first edition, the additions to the introduction and text, the checking of sources, and retention of the original scheme of numbering. Stevens comments on some musical objections to Greene's application of his definition of the carol, with consequent omission of some works found in the first edition. He discusses Greene's case for this definition, and his amplification of the introductory material. Stevens enjoys the notes, and finds the work 'a model of what such an edition should be' (339).

———— Review by Rossell Hope Robbins, *Review* 1 (1979): 265–73. Considers Greene's contribution to the study of the carol, and his engagement with other critics, including views of the origin and purpose of the genre. Robbins admires Greene's reliance on manuscript study. He finds the notes in this edition very valuable, and records changes of particular interest, concluding that 'the absence of errors in this huge volume' is 'truly amazing' (272).

87   Dobson, E.J., and F.Ll. Harrison, eds. *Medieval English Songs.* London: Faber, 1979.

An edition of 33 songs, the work of a philologist [Dobson] and a musicologist [Harrison], who collaborate to produce 'texts of music and words which shall fit each other and be singable as . . . the original authors and composers intended them to be sung' (15). The editors feel free 'to emend the transmitted text of the words and, less often, of the music when it seemed to be defective' (11). They choose only works for which words and music have been preserved, sometimes with music of Latin or French origin, rather than English. Dobson provides an 'Introduction to the Texts' (15–51); 'Texts and Textual Commentary' (103–223); and two appendices, 'Pronunciation Tables (317–21) and 'Translations of Texts' (323–9). Harrison supplies an 'Introduction to the Music' (55–98); 'Music' (227–91); 'Musical Commentary' (295–312); and an appendix, 'Notes on Performance' (331). When the English song is a *contrafactum* of one in another language, as 'Ar ne kuthe ich sorghe non nu iche mot manen min mon' [*322*] is of 'Eyns ne soy ke pleynte fu' (to which the 'Planctus ante nescia' of Godefroy of

St Victor is supplied as an *addendum*), the editors print both works; they provide alternative music for some songs. The earliest works are St Godric's twelfth-century hymns; the latest are songs from Cambridge University Library Add. 5943 and Bodleian Douce 381, of the early fifteenth century. Dobson provides details of the composition and history of ownership of these manuscripts. He notes several points of difference with Greene, **37, 59, 86**; Brown, **36, 39**; and Davies, **61**. Most of Dobson's textual emendations are adjustments to metre, chiefly by addition or elision of unstressed *e*, although he adds an entire stanza to 'Danger me haþ vnskylfuly' [*670*]. He supplies extensive notes on the history, metre, and language of individual poems with the texts, including variants from all available sources.

322, 352, 453, 521, 598, 662, 670, 687.3, 708, 864, 888, 1311, 1312, 1347, 1697, 2037.5, 2070, 2138, 2163, 2231, 2687, 2738, 2988, 3031, 3211, 3216.5, 3223, 3432, 3662, 3806, 3893, 4199, 4221, 4223, 7322.

——— Review by J.A. Dutka, *Studia Neophilologica* 56 (1984): 233. Commends the collaboration of scholars of medieval literature and music, but prefers the approach of Harrison to that of Dobson, since the latter's contribution tends to 'protestation rather than elucidation,' with circularity in the arguments for emendation. Although the book is 'a challenging addition' to knowledge, its format is 'an irritant' and some references seem not to be up-to-date.

——— Review by Thomas Duncan, *Medium Ævum* 50 (1981): 338–41. Examines Dobson's emendation of the texts, and notes some circularity in the justification, although he finds the achievement a 'masterly demonstration, lyric by lyric, of what an expert and imaginative scholar can do to rescue lyrics which have been left "lame and deformed."' This involves 'no little conjecture,' but the arguments are 'often convincing' (340). Although the presentation is 'an important new departure in the editing of ME lyrics,' Duncan suggests that the musical settings could be published separately to save expense.

——— Review by Helen Cooper, *Review of English Studies* NS 33 (1982): 69–71. Admires the courage and detail of Dobson's explanations of his methods, without expressing agreement with all his conclusions. The specialist and the performer will be able to use the book's wealth of information, and Cooper applauds the 'clarity of exposition in the introductions to both texts and music,' although she would like 'more supporting matter in the way of bibliography and index.' The authors' interpretations form 'part of the continuing debate about these songs' (71).

88 Norton-Smith, John, introd. *Bodleian Library MS Fairfax 16.* London: Scolar, 1979.

In his introduction to a facsimile of the manuscript, Norton-Smith describes the work, assesses its literary and historical significance, and supplies the history of its ownership. The manuscript includes ballads, complaints, letters, and lyrical poems, some attributed to Chaucer, Clanvowe, Hoccleve, Roos, Lydgate, Charles d'Orléans, and William de la Pole, Duke of Suffolk. Norton-Smith does not accept the attributions to Suffolk, made by MacCracken, **129**. There are also longer compositions by Chaucer and Lydgate.

100, 239, 296, 370, 509, 666, 674, 803, 809, 851, 913, 991, 1086, 1306, 1388, 1507, 1826, 2029, 2178, 2182, 2218, 2230, 2251, 2262, 2295, 2349, 2350, 2407, 2479, 2488, 2567, 2583, 2595, 2756, 2823, 3190, 3361, 3412, 3488, 3504, 3542, 3656, 3661, 3670, 3746, 3747, 3752, 3787, 3854, 3860, 3913, 3915, 4043, 4186, 4230.

88a Robinson, Pamela, introd. *Manuscript Tanner 346: A Facsimile, Bodleian Library Oxford University.* Variorum Edition of the Works of Geoffrey Chaucer. Norman, OK: Pilgrim, 1980.

An anthology of poetry of courtly love, composed by Chaucer, Clanvowe, Hoccleve, Lydgate, and anonymous poets. Robinson lists the contents of the manuscript, and notes modern editions of each work (xvii–xix). She describes the manuscript through consideration of the following: 'Date' (xix), 'Foliation and Collation' (xix–xx), 'Ruling' (xx), 'Layout and Presentation of the Texts' (xx–xxi), 'Handwriting' (xxi–xxii), 'Abbreviations' (xxii), 'Punctuation' (xxii), 'Corrections and Annotations' (xxii–xxiii), 'Decoration' (xxiii–xxiv), 'Binding' (xxiv), and 'History' (xxiv–xxvii), and concludes her introduction with a 'Bibliography' (xxvii–xxviii).

100, 402, 666, 828, 851, 913, 1306, 1507, 2479, 2756, 3361, 3412, 3542, 3670.

88b   Wilson, Edward, and Iain Fenlon, introd. *The Winchester Anthology: A Facsimile of British Library Additional Manuscript 60577 with an Introduction and List of Contents by Edward Wilson and an Account of the Music by Iain Fenlon.* Cambridge: Brewer, 1981.

Wilson's 'Introduction' (1–16) offers a detailed description of the manuscript, dealing in particular with 'Dimensions and Material' (1–2), 'Foliation and Quiring' (2–4), 'Handwriting' (4–5), 'Layout and Presentation' (5–7), 'Binding' (7–8), 'Date' (8–9), 'Place of Production' (9–10), and 'Owners' (10–13). He provides details of the lives of two early owners, 'a man called Brinstan and a monk of St Swithun's Priory, John Buryton, to whom Brinstan sold it' (10), and concludes that the principal scribe was 'a monk of St Swithun's Priory, Winchester' (13), probably a schoolmaster, whose compilation was influenced by Italian humanism, and the traditions of the Burgundian court. Most of the manuscript's contents are in English or Latin. Wilson lists these (18–36), with an explanatory note (17), and a 'First Line Index of English Verse and Songs' (37–8). [See also **819** for a correction to the list.] He appends 'An Outline Description of British Library Harley MS. 172' (39–40), which is also the work of the principal scribe of the Winchester Anthology. In 'The Music' (41–7) Fenton describes the musical works in the manuscript and methods used for the entries and relates these to contemporary compositions, in particular those of the Fayrfax MS, considering in particular the effect of the introduction of printing. [Cf. Wilson, **746**.] The musical works were 'most probably copied by William Way' (43), who was known to own the Winchester Anthology, and Fenton supplies details of Way's life and possible use of the manuscript.

Winchester Anthology: *35.5, 906, 935, 1145.5, 1459, 1825, 1872, 2056, 2547.5, 2627, 2676, 2683, 3168.4, 3297.5, 3436, 3895, 4049.6, 4184, 4215, 7006, 7014, 7066, 7072, 7081, 7110, 7119, 7146, 7155, 7188, 7202, 7212, 7213, 7237, 7241, 7261, 7285, 7308, 7311, 7318, 7343, 7397, 7433, 7434, 7437, 7438, 7465, 7494, 7496, 7559, 7566, 7579, 7587, 7595, 7608, 7622, 7646.*
Harley 172: *199, 854, 1168, 1540, 3121.*

89   Turville-Petre, Thorlac, ed. 'An Anthology of Medieval Poems and Drama.' *Medieval Literature: Chaucer and the Alliterative Tradition.* Ed. Boris Ford. Harmondsworth: Penguin, 1982. 387–602. Vol. 1 of The New Pelican Guide to English Literature. 9 vols. 1982–3.

A selection intended to illustrate essays in the volume and 'give the reader . . . the opportunity to enjoy some of the literature itself.' Turville-Petre includes less familiar works, and has chosen poems from the fourteenth and fifteenth centuries, selecting from 'the three main genres of medieval verse: narrative, drama and lyric' (389). He provides introductory notes on pronunciation and metre (391–2), and end notes on manuscript variations on some works, but provides most information on the texts through footnotes. The lyrics include examples from the Harley and Sloane collections.

117, 515, 611, 1221, 1299, 1303, 1367, 1861, 2640, 2675, 2747, 3227, 3472, 3864, 3889, 4037, 4279.

90 Garbáty, Thomas J., ed. *Medieval English Literature.* Lexington, MA: Heath, 1984.

The collection has sections on 'The Lyric' (631–74), and on 'The Ballad' (479–535), which includes 'Judas' ['Hit wes upon a scereþorsday þat vre louerd aros,' *1649*] and 'Saint Stephen and Herod' ['Seynt Steuen was a clerk in kin herowdis halle,' *3058*]. In his 'General Introduction: Aspects of Medieval English Literature' (1–39) Garbáty summarizes influences on the development of ME language and literature, particularly the Norman invasion and the church. He shows what may be inferred of the society from its literature. Discussing close connections between religious and secular songs, he explains the role of the friars in the composition and adaptation of lyrics for religious purposes. He divides the 23 lyrics chronologically, and supplies individual introductions, marginal notes on particular words, and footnotes. In appendices, he shows several schemes of arrangement for the works, incidentally demonstrating the range of topics considered in the lyrics. 'Appendix A' (961–3) is set out according to chronology and genre. Appendix 'B' (964–6) is arranged by dialect. In Appendix 'C' (967–70) poems are divided according to mode, including courtly, popular, and religious categories, with some lyrics in each, and some in more than one. Appendix 'D' (971–4) is arranged by theme and motif, including lyrics with works in various other genres.

105, 194, 225, 377, 515, 708, 864, 1008, 1367, 1394, 1622, 1649, 1849, 1861, 2037.5, 2066, 2161, 2163, 2238, 2359, 3058, 3223, 3227, 3409, 4037.

91 Gray, Douglas, ed. *The Oxford Book of Late Medieval Verse and Prose.* Oxford: Clarendon, 1985.

An anthology of 'works written in English from about 1400 . . . to about 1520' (iii). The division of the contents allows the inclusion of lyrics in other sections as well as 'Lyrics' (160–79). Thus there are political poems in 'The Mutability of Worldly Changes – and Many More Diversities of Many Wonderful Things' (1–32); mnemonic lyrics in 'The Nature of Things: Science and Instruction' (130–50); and riddles in 'Nifles, Trifles, and Merry Jests' (368–81). Gray supplies a general introduction (xi–xxi), relating English work of the period to that of Scotland and continental Europe, and more specific introductions at the beginning of each section. Norman Davis has contributed 'Notes on Grammar and Spelling in the Fifteenth Century' (415–508).

117, 144, 303, 377, 409.5, 579, 597.5, 624, 769, 925, 1132, 1313, 1352, 1364, 1367, 1399, 1549, 1622, 1920, 2148, 2243, 2250, 2338, 2733, 3199.8, 3213, 3405.5, 3443.5, 3536, 3571, 3759, 3890, 3899.3, 3986, 4284, 7221.

———Review by A.V.C.S[chmidt], *Medium Ævum* 57 (1988): 115–18. Finds that the book shows 'pleasant things . . . not just the morbidity and didacticism that have commonly been taken to characterize the work of this century' (116), accomplished by Gray's innovative selection and arrangement of the material, to reveal 'a fascinating age rich in contrasts and contradictions' (118).

———Review by Siegfried Wenzel, *Notes and Queries* 232 (1987): 64–5. Suggests that the book 'may be more aptly called a historical or even cultural reader,' and applauds the wide range of the selection that includes 'matters of daily life' (64) as well as literary, philosophical, religious, and scientific texts. Wenzel commends the maintenance of the volume's 'high scholarly standard' (65).

91a Fletcher, Bradford Y., introd. *Manuscript Trinity R.3.19, Trinity College Cambridge: A Facsimile.* The Facsimile Series of the works of Geoffrey Chaucer. Vol. 5. Norman, OK: Pilgrim, 1987.

The range of items in the manuscript displays 'a taste that may perhaps most safely be called eclectic'; Fletcher proposes to avoid 'overemphasizing the dreadfulness of what dull verse is here' since 'the more stilted side of John Lydgate' is leavened by 'sprightly misogynic poems,' some 'genuinely masterful efforts' and 'fascinating conceits,' and 'the overwhelmingly Chaucerian nature of the collection' which is 'heavily secular,' with a 'tendency toward rhetorical formality' (xv). In his 'Introduction' (xv–xl), Fletcher lists 'Contents of the Manuscript' (xv–xx); he considers 'Collation and Foliation' (xx–xxii); 'Paper,' including details of 12 watermarks (xxii–xxvi); and 'Handwriting,' identifying and describing the work of a main hand, three subsidiary hands, and John Stow (xxvi–xxix). In comments on 'Accuracy and Evidence of Correction' (xxix), he attends particularly to the efforts of hand A 'to correct Caxton's notoriously bad text, restoring the sense and often the wording of the best manuscripts' of *The Monk's Tale*, and to later traces of emendations by unidentified readers and by Stow. Evidence of 'Date' (xxix) comes from the paper and the text, and suggests 'the second half of the 1470s' as the terminus a quo. Fletcher summarizes the history of the manuscript in 'Provenance and Influence' (xxix–xxxi), and supplies a 'Bibliography' (xxxi), and illustrations of the manuscript (xxxiii–xl).

55, 71, 100, 190.5, 267, 437, 590, 671, 928.5, 935, 1086, 1172.5, 1238, 1300, 1528, 1562, 1592, 1838, 1944, 2128, 2148, 2311, 2384.8, 2464, 2478.5, 2511, 2524, 2541, 2588.5, 2624, 2625, 2661, 2756, 2767, 2784, 3197, 2580, 3412, 3493, 3502, 3761, 3807, 3983, 4005, 4178, 4205, 4231.9.

92   Gretsch, Mechthild. '*The Fair Maid of Ribblesdale*: Text und Kommentar.' *Anglia* 105 (1987): 285–341.

Acknowledges that the secular lyrics of MS Harley 2253 are a high point of ME lyric poetry before Chaucer, and intends to compensate for any impression created by critical commentary that they are difficult poems. Gretsch presents a critical edition of 'The Fair Maid of Ribblesdale' [*2207*], and supplies a line-by-line commentary, considering previous scholarship, clarifying philological and factual matters, and a metrical analysis. She offers an annotated bibliography of editions of and commentaries on the poem (285–7) before presenting the text (291–6), with a translation into German (294–6). The transcription preserves the orthography of the manuscript and Gretsch notes other editors' emendations in footnotes. She comments on the catalogue of beauty in the poem, relating the description of the Fair Maid to the ME ideal of beauty and to the possibility that the poet is exaggerating to parody the conventions of *descriptio pulchritudinis*, as suggested by several critics. Gretsch argues for nuances of individuality in the description, although the poet conforms to an established formula. The commentary (301–31) provides detailed explication of words and phrases, with linguistic commentary and some translation. She concludes with metrical commentary (332–41), which includes details of the structure of the verses, rhythm, cadence, alliteration, rhyme, and the original dialect, and argues that the poem shows metrical consistency.

2207.

93   Moffat, Douglas, ed. *The Soul's Address to the Body: The Worcester Fragments.* East Lansing, MI: Colleagues, 1987.

A comprehensive edition of 'fragments which remain of the *Soul's Address to the Body (SA)* ['*. . . on earde/and alle þeo i-sceaftan þe to him to sculen,' *2684.5*] . . . found on folios 63^v–66^v of Worcester Cathedral MS. F.174, currently located in the Chapter Library of Worcester Cathedral' (1). Moffat considers 'The Manuscript' (1–6); its 'Physical Characteristics' (1–2); 'The Scribe' (2–3), of the 'tremulous hand'; its 'History' (3–6), and a possible rearrangement of leaves. He inspects the 'Language' (7–25), to examine 'Phonology' (7–11), including vowels, consonant, and non-alphabetic signs, and 'Grammar' (11–25). Scrutiny of grammatical forms reveals that 'the scribe was neither a mirror copyist nor a wholesale "translator" of his exemplar.' Instead, he

Annotations of Editions

preserves some archaic spellings but tends towards 'regularization of certain phonological and lexical features' (21), and may substitute such words as '*steel* for *isen* and *euere* for *symle*' (22). Exploring 'Prosody' (25–33), Moffat compares varying combinations of rhyming and alliteration in the lines of the fragments. He confirms that the work is 'a prosodical hybrid,' and attempts 'to examine the verse of *SA* as its writer might have perceived it.' For this purpose he submits several lines to an accentual scansion to demonstrate the use of 'traditional OE rhythms – falling, rising, or clashing' (27), although the work is closer to fourteenth-century alliterative works. A study of 'Style' (33–9) shows the author as not 'quite so artless . . . as it might at first appear' (33) in his use of rhetorical figures and balanced composition. Inspection of 'Sources and Structure' (39–51) reveals a tradition of prose and verse works on the body and soul. There are correspondences with *SA* in the fourth homily of the *Vercelli Book*, 'The Grave' ['ðe wes bold ӡebyld er þu i-boren were,' *3497*], 'þene latemeste dai wenne we sulen farren' [*3517*], 'Als I lay in a winteris nyt' [*351*], and 'In a þestri stude y stod' [*1461*], as well as thematic parallels with body and soul debates in English and other languages. Consideration of the usual pattern of such works, particularly the place of an *ubi sunt* passage, adds weight to the argument for repositioning manuscript leaves. It is possible that a leaf is missing, although more attention to the Last Judgement and a righteous soul seems unlikely. 'The Text' of Fragments A–G (59–81) has textual notes at the foot of the page, followed by 'Explanatory Notes' (83–108), a 'Glossary' (109–24) and 'Bibliography' (125–33).

351, 1461, *2684.5, 3497, 3517.

───── Review by Clare A. Lees, *Medium Ævum* 58 (1989): 150–1. Welcomes Moffat's recreation of 'a coherent text' (150) and his sensible caution in the reassessment of primary material. Lees expects the text to be 'the standard reference work,' and praises the revelation of its vitality, although she feels that 'a bolder reconstruction would have offered more insight into the poem' (151).

94   Paden, William D., tr. and ed. *The Medieval Pastourelle.* 2 vols. Garland Library of Medieval Literature, Series A 34, 35. New York: Garland, 1987.

An edition of classical medieval pastourelles, 'in which the narrator tells of his encounter with a shepherdess and of his attempt, successful or not, to seduce her' (ix). Paden presents poems from the twelfth to the fifteenth centuries with MnE translation on facing pages; he includes 210 works in medieval European languages, together with Chinese and Latin antecedents. He supplies 'Notes' on the individual poems (531–662), a 'Cross-Index to the Editions by Audiau and Bartsch' (663), and indexes of 'Manuscripts' (665–73), 'Proper Names' (675–83), 'Languages' (685), 'Authors' (687–8), and 'First Lines and Titles' (689–93). His general 'Introduction' (ix–xiii) sets out characteristics of the pastourelle, to indicate individual variations in the pattern of pastoral mode, cast of characters, plot, rhetoric, and point of view. He includes a comprehensive 'Bibliography' (xvii–xxxvii). The ME works are numbers 126, 170, and 171: 'Als i me rod this endre dai/ O mi [pleyinge]' [*360*]; 'As I stod on a day me self under a tre' [*371*]; and 'In a fryht as y con fere fremede' [*1449*].

360, 371, 1449.

94a   Reimer, Stephen R., ed. *The Works of William Herebert, OFM.* Studies and Texts 81. Toronto: Pontifical Institute of Mediaeval Studies, 1987.

Presents the Latin sermons and ME lyrics of Herebert's 'Commonplace Book,' BL MS Add. 46919. Reimer's 'Introduction' (1–25) offers information about Herebert's life and work, particularly as lector in the Franciscan convent at Oxford and his possible acquaintance with other scholars there; he also considers critical commentary on Herebert's writings, chiefly on the sermons. He describes the manuscript, listing its contents and assessing the balance of compositions in Latin, ME, AN, and French; most poems in the latter two languages are the work of Nicholas Bozon. Most of Herebert's ME lyrics translate Latin hymns and antiphons, and of the 23 works, only two ['þys nome ys also on honikomb þat ȝyfþous sauour and swetnesse,' *3622.6*; 'þou wommon boute vere,' *3700*] have no direct source. Reimer cites the sources of the other poems in the notes he provides with the lyrics. In the introduction he comments on Herebert's methods and purposes in his translations, and proposes that their 'seeming awkwardness' (19) is not surprising if 'we consider that Herebert was more concerned with didactic and evangelical usefulness than with poetic composition' (19–20), showing 'the obvious advantages of such literalness' (20). He also considers previous criticism of the lyrics, in particular that concerned with questions of authorship and the possibility that the lyrics were intended to be sung or to be used in sermons. Reimer favours the latter idea and notes that 'the poems in general make an affective appeal, intended to produce in the hearers contrition and penitence,' with a focus on 'the Infancy and Passion of Christ, both emotionally appealing aspects of Christ's life.' Recurrent themes include Christ's Cross and Blood, and his portrayal as King and Judge; the Blessed Virgin is 'a focal point for emotional response' (22). Similarly emotional recurrent images include those of light and fire. Reimer concludes with remarks on Herebert's prosody and use of the dialect of the South-West Midlands.

269.5, 600, 643, 861, 1054, 1213, 1232, 1235, 1742, 1821, 1903, 1968, 2241, 2963, 3135, 3405, 3632.6, 3676, 3700, 3872, 3906, 3909.4.

94b James, Thomas Beaumont, and John Simons, ed. *The Poems of Laurence Minot 1333–1352.* Exeter Medieval Texts and Studies. Gen. eds. Marion Glasscoe and M.J. Swanton. Exeter: University of Exeter, 1989.

Presents an edition of 11 poems of Laurence Minot, 'to facilitate access to this unique figure' and 'to demonstrate the value of collaborative enterprise in teaching and scholarship which seeks to open up medieval culture as an interdisciplinary field,' to remove 'barriers which now traditionally separate . . . the literary critic and the historian' (1). The editors deal first with 'Editions' (1–5), in particular those of Joseph Ritson and Joseph Hall. In 'The Manuscript' (5–8), they describe Cotton Galba E.ix, which 'mixes the secular with the religious and the chivalric with the pious' (6), and includes Minot's poetry with romances and pietistic, political, and historical works. They consider the poems' social context and what is known of Minot's life in 'The Poet and the Court of Edward III' (8–11). In 'Style and Content' (12–18), they relate the poems to events of the Anglo-Scottish and Hundred Years Wars, noting resemblances to ME romance, particularly in the contrasts between Edward III and Philip of Valois; they draw comparisons with works of Jean Froissart. A 'Chronological Table' (19–22), 'Location Map' (23), and table of 'Capet/Valois Descent and Claimants to the Throne of France' (24) illuminate the historical context of the poems. 'The Poems' (26–56), in the order of the manuscript, with 'Notes' (57–68) follow. There are three appendices. Those on 'The Vows of the Heron' (69–83) and contemporary Latin poems (84–99) supply prose translations of the works, with notes. The third is a 'Brief Table of Contents of Cotton Galba E.ix' (100). There is a 'Select Bibliography' (101–3).

585, 709, 987, 1401, 2149, 2189, 3080, 3117, 3796, 3801, 3899.

95 Jansen, Johannes Petrus Maria, ed. *The 'Suffolk' Poems: An Edition of the Love Lyrics in Fairfax 16 Attributed to William de la Pole.* Groningen, 1989.

Not seen.

96   Turville-Petre, Thorlac. *Alliterative Poetry of the Later Middle Ages: An Anthology.* Routledge Medieval English Texts. Gen. ed. Malcolm Andrew. London: Routledge, 1989.

The collection includes a number of lyrics and short poems, with extracts from longer alliterative works. In the 'Introduction' (1–8), Turville-Petre states his purposes 'to present a number of less well-known Middle English alliterative poems that have been overshadowed,' and 'to illustrate the great range and variety of alliterative verse' (1). Here he demonstrates the genre's descriptive possibilities and its use for instruction as well as entertainment, with general remarks on 'Dates and Places' (2–3), 'Authors and Audiences' (4), 'The Metre' (5–7), and 'Editorial Procedures' (7–8). He supplies the texts with general headnotes and comprehensive footnotes. They include nine Harley lyrics (9–37), some expressing 'social comment or satire' and others 'witty and often surprising poems of love' (10); 'The Pistill of Susan' [*3553*] (120–39); 'Somer Soneday' [*3838*] (140–7); and 'The Three Dead Kings' [*2677*] (148–57).

1320.5, 1394, 1449, 1974, 2066, 2287, 2649, 2677, 3553, 3838, 3874, 3989.

97   Conlee, John W., ed. *Middle English Debate Poetry: A Critical Anthology.* East Lansing, MI: Colleagues, 1991.

The 'Introduction' (xi–xxxvii) offers 'broad historical and literary contexts for the study of these poems' (x), which cover a wide range of disputes between complementary pairs of entities, 'concrete or conceptual, animate or inanimate' (xi). Conlee describes the genre's antecedents in Latin allegorical debate poems, and traces its progress to such fields as flytings, parliamentary debates and the pastourelle; he explains the wide range of poems which belong to the genre, and refers to related works as well as to the texts he prints. He divides the texts into 'Body and Soul' (3–62), 'Alliterative Debates' (63–165), 'Didactic and Satiric Disputations' (167–235), 'Bird Debates' (237–93), and 'Middle English Pastourelles' (295–312). Within these sections, he provides detailed headnotes for each text, and lists manuscript sources and printed editions, noting variations and points of interest at the foot of the page.

167, 295.5, 351, 371, 560, 603, 995.4, 1449, 1452, 1461, 1475, 1503.5, 1506, 1556, 1563, 1887, 2336, 3137, 3222, 3361, 3461, 3482, 3497, 3713.5, 7268.

98   Jansen, Sharon L., and Kathleen H. Jordan. *The Welles Anthology MS Rawlinson C. 813: A Critical Edition.* MRTS 75. Binghamton, NY: CMRTS, State U of New York at Binghamton 1991.

This edition presents not only the secular lyrics (printed by Padelford and Benham, **20**), but also 'a few medical recipes, a ribald paragraph or two, and a portion of Skelton's "Why come ye nat to court?" [*813.3*],' together with 'six political prophecies that occupy the last quarter of the manuscript,' previously 'largely ignored' (xiii). In the 'Introduction' (xiii–xvii), the editors briefly summarize critical comment on the manuscript and list its contents, with more detailed chapters on particular topics. 'The Anthology' (1–16) considers 'The Compilers' (1–7), with biographical information on Humphrey Welles and William Coffin, related to contemporary events. 'The Compilation' (7–16) offers conclusions about 'Dating' (7–9), 'Associations' (9–13), and 'Accomplishments' (13–16) of the manuscript, to explain its importance as 'something of a rarity, one of only three large collections of late Middle English secular lyrics' (13), and to compare it with Humfrey Newton's commonplace book and the Findern anthology. 'Lyrics in the Welles Anthology' (17–35) investigates 'Rhyme and Meter' (17–21), 'Subject and Form' (21–32), and 'Arrangement of the Lyrics' (33–5). The lyrics are grouped, rather than gathered haphazardly, and include didactic works, love poetry, satirical antifeminist poems, pastourelles, and ballads. Among the love poems are many courtly works, including some that borrow from works of Chaucer and Hawes. All are arranged according to form and content. The political prophecies are studied in 'Prophecies in the Welles Anthology' (37–55), and shown to be avenues of expression for criticism of church and state. Welles's gathering of these texts hints at his own opinions; the striking out of the word 'pope' in several places 'surely is a witness to Welles's sensitivity to the political climate' (53). 'The Welles Manuscript' (57–65) provides a description and history of the manuscript, including the materials, pagination, collation, hands (recognizing three), the unlikely possibility that individual quires circulated independently, and what is known of ownership. The editors explain their 'Editorial Procedures' (67–72), and present 'The Texts' (85–298) of 65 works, with notes. They provide appendices on 'Notations in the Manuscript' (299), 'Borrowings from *The Pastime of Pleasure* and *The Comfort of Lovers*' (300–3), and 'Borrowings from Chaucer and Lydgate' (303–4), and a 'Glossary' (304–8).

79.5, 159.8, 172, 340.5, 366, 368, 430, 642.5, 649, 729, 767, 813.3, 1017.5, 1180, 1253.5, 1328.7, 1329, 1349.5, 1450.5, 1768, 1841.5, 1926.5, 2228, 2245.1, 2261.8, 2271.6, 2409.5, 2421, 2439.5, 2482.5, 2496, 2498, 2500.5, 2529, 2532, 2532.5, 2547, 2552.5, 2560.5, 2613.5, 2757.3, 2822, 2827.5, 3098.3, 3228.5, 3713.5, 3785.5, 3804, 3889.5, 3917.8, 3962.5, 4008, 4020.3, 4096, 4190, 4210.

——— Review by Edward Wilson, *Review of English Studies* NS 44 (1993): 246–9. Records many points of disagreement with the editors, concerning the hands of the manuscript, details of the account of Welles's life, and various readings. Wilson's checks of the transcription found 'that the text of the prophecies was reasonably good, but that of the non-prophetic items was notably less accurate' (248).

99 Kerrigan, John, ed. *Motives of Woe: Shakespeare and 'Female Complaint.' A Critical Anthology.* Oxford: Clarendon, 1991.

Sets the text 'on which this anthology centres, Shakespeare's *A Louers Complaint*' (1) in the context of poems that preceded and followed it. Kerrigan prints seven ME lyrics and Chaucer's *Anelida and Arcite* [*3670*], and alludes briefly in the 'Introduction' (1–83) to other medieval works. Examples include some *chansons d'aventure*, and musical versions extend to 'the troubadour *planh* and early *planctus Beatae Virginis Mariae*' (61). Kerrigan's headnote to the 'Medieval Lyrics' (87–97) summarizes the range of themes. 'Als i me rod this endre dai/O mi [pleyinge]' [*360*], 'Y louede a child of this cuntrie' [*1330*], and 'þis endyr day I mete a clerke' [*3594*] present the betrayed maiden, the first two sympathetically, the last mockingly. Lydgate's 'A Balade, Sayde by a Gentilwomman . . .' ['Allas I wooful creature,' *154*] expresses 'frustrations of a would-be wooer.' '*Canticus Amoris*' ['In a tabernacle of a toure,' *1460*], of the Virgin, resembles lover's complaint 'in its description of a figure who implores the human soul with a refrain drawn from the Song of Solomon.' Two lyrics from the Findern MS, 'What so men seyn' [*3917*] and 'My woofull herte thus clad in payn' [*2279*] may be the work of female authors.

154, 360, 1330, 1460, 2279, 3594, 3670, 3917.

100 Barratt, Alexandra, ed. *Women's Writings in Middle English.* Longman Annotated Texts. Gen. eds. Charlotte Brewer, H.R. Woudhuysen and Daniel Karlin. London: Longman, 1992.

A collection of works in verse and prose, chosen 'both for their intrinsic interest and for their representative nature' (xv). Barratt provides a general 'Introduction' (1–23), which includes several 'anonymous fragments with female personae' (18) in 'Anonymous Texts and Poetry' (16–21). *The Faits and the Passion of Our Lord Jesu Christ* (207–18) concludes with a quatrain of precepts, 'Siʒe and sorwe depeli' [*3102*]. A love letter written by Margery Brews (251–3) includes her verse, 'And yf ye commande me to kepe me true wherever I go' [*303*]. Most lyric verse is in 'Fifteenth- and early sixteenth-century poems' (262–300). Barratt offers an explanatory headnote to each section, with additional information in footnotes to individual texts.

303, 445, 481, 733.1, 768, 1008, 1018, 1046, 1132, 1142, 1170, 1265, 1279, 1389.5, 2179, 2279, 2279, 2393.5, 2551.8, 2821, 3228.5, 3418, 3878, 3900.5, 3917, 4272.5, 4281.5, 7159, 7286.

101   Burrow, J.A., and Thorlac Turville-Petre. *A Book of Middle English.* Oxford: Blackwell, 1992.

Offers an extensive general introduction to the language of the period and a selection of texts, including 'Lyrics' (233–48). The 14 lyrics are divided according to their sources, and each section is introduced by a headnote which describes the poems and supplies further references to criticism and editions. There are six 'Rawlinson Lyrics' (233–6), taken from MS Rawlinson D 913, four 'Harley Lyrics' (236–43), from Harley 2253, and four 'Grimestone Lyrics' (243–8), from the anthology of John Grimestone, Advocates 18.7.21.

179, 194, 515, 1008, 1274, 1861, 2023, 2037.5, 2236, 2622, 3825, 3898, 4037, 4263.

———— Review by Nicolas Jacobs, *Review of English Studies* NS 45 (1994): 545–6. Acknowledges the lack of 'scholarly equipment' assumed by earlier authors of anthologies of this kind, and finds that this book's virtues give it 'a good chance of arresting the decline of the subject' (546). With a few reservations, Jacobs generally applauds the selection of texts and the 'full and lucid' (547) linguistic introduction.

102 Gray, Douglas, ed. *English Medieval Religious Lyrics.* Exeter Medieval English Texts and Studies. Gen. eds. Marion Glasscoe and M.J. Swanton. Exeter: U of Exeter P, 1992.

A reprint of Gray's *A Selection of Religious Lyrics*, **81**.

103   Stevick, Robert D., ed. *One Hundred Middle English Lyrics.* Rev. ed. Urbana IL: U of Chicago P, 1994.

The poems chosen are those of the 1964 edition, **62**, with the addition of more recently available information such as manuscript sources, *SIMEV* numbers, and glosses. Introductory material has been extensively revised and expanded. 'General Background to the Lyrics' (x–xii) deals with origins, traditions and sources, and contrasts 'Elizabethan notions of lyrics as poetry composed to be sung and the modern notion of lyrics as expressing intensely personal emotions' (x) with the ME lyrics. 'The Scope and Purpose of This Edition' (xiii–xviii) explains Stevick's system of regularization of text and his reasons for omitting titles and editorial comments. 'Criticism of Middle English Lyrics' (xviii–xxxiii) examines background and critical material available, listed in the 'Selected Bibliography' (177–82). 'The Language of the Texts' (xxxiv–xlv) describes linguistic variations, parts of speech, phonology, and morphology, comparing and contrasting MnE equivalents. 'Some Features of Form and Style' (xlv–l) illustrates metre, rhyme, stanza forms, and stress patterns from the texts. In an 'Appendix' (li-lii) 'transcriptions of two thirteenth-century copies of part of a preaching text' (li) demonstrate the variations found in prose texts that are 'as near to being the same as one is likely to encounter in Middle English' (lii).

———— Review by David Parker, *Chaucer Yearbook* 3 (1996): 228–30. Welcomes this edition of 'the *only* true student text exclusively devoted to Middle English lyrics,' and praises Stevick's 'particular sort of normalization' (228) and presentation. Although he notes a few flaws, Parker is generally enthusiastic about the book as an introductory text with 'enduring appeal' (230).

104 Duncan, Thomas G., ed. *Medieval English Lyrics 1200–1400*. Harmondsworth: Penguin, 1995.

An anthology of 132 poems, that includes 'all pre-Chaucerian love lyrics,' with those of love and devotion arranged 'according to genre and theme,' and penitental, moral, and miscellaneous works ordered chronologically. Duncan presents the works 'in a readily readable form,' in language 'normalized in accordance with the grammar and spelling of late fourteenth-century London English' (xiii). He supplies extensive marginal glosses and a 'Commentary' (181–250) on individual works. In the 'Introduction' (xviii–xlviii) he traces the development of ME lyric forms and themes, contrasts the work of troubadours, and relates ME poems to OE and French influences, in particular the idea of ennobling love and service offered to a lady rather than to a feudal lord. He shows the use and manipulation of convention in lively verse, and compares the treatment of *chansons d'aventure* and pastourelles. Themes of penitential and moral lyrics are closely related to OE traditions, but they find 'direct and personal expression' (xxvi) in more vivid and touching ways, as in sorrowful lullabies. Chaucer's lyrics show 'poise, imagination and control' (xxviii); Duncan finds them the finest of all the lyrics. As the emphasis in doctrines of salvation changes from heroic to loving interpretations, devotional lyrics express tenderness and compassion, sometimes with great restraint and concentration on a particular image or paradox. The language is simple, but the literary skill, and an 'absence of any display of ecstasy or agony,' enhance 'the direct sincerity of the speaking voice, whether it be that of Christ or the sinner' (xxxii). When the lyrics use language and conventions of secular love poems, such as the *reverdie* or the style of *chanson d'aventure*, they achieve different effects. The declaration of 'unjust imprisonment, exploitations and impoverishment, bribery and corruption, and even noise pollution' (xxxv) are 'readily accessible to the modern reader' (xxxiv). Techniques that allow the vivid expression of the poets' thoughts include forceful alliteration, engaging vitality, the appeal of music, and subtle innuendo. Sections on 'Lyric Stanza and Metre' (xxxvii–xliii), 'Guidance on Metrical Reading' (xliii–xlv), 'Middle English: Manuscripts and Language' (xlv–xlvii), and a 'Pronunciation Guide' (xlvii–xlviii) conclude the introduction. The texts are divided into 'Love Lyrics' (1–46), 'Penitential and Moral Lyrics' (47–92), 'Devotional Lyrics' (93–145), and 'Miscellaneous Lyrics' (147–179). There are appendices on 'Music and Metre' (251–3) and 'The Syllabic Analysis of Middle English Verse' (254–7).

94, 105, 117, 143, 161, 179, 194, 322, 352, 360, 371, 377, 515, 521, 611, 650, 695, 708, 739, 809, 864, 888, 1002, 1008, 1216, 1265, 1274, 1299, 1302, 1303, 1320.5, 1351, 1365, 1367, 1388, 1394, 1395, 1402, 1422, 1422.1, 1433, 1449, 1463, 1504, 1649, 1697, 1699, 1747, 1822, 1836, 1839, 1847, 1861, 1921, 1930, 1978, 2009, 2012, 2023, 2024, 2025, 2029, 2031, 2037.5, 2066, 2070, 2163, 2166, 2207, 2236, 2240, 2273, 2288, 2293, 2320, 2359, 2366, 2375, 2622, 2645, 2649, 2675, 2687, 3058, 3078, 3080, 3164, 3167.3, 3211, 3212, 3221, 3223, 3227, 3236, 3310, 3327, 3348, 3408, 3432, 3512, 3661, 3691, 3697, 3787, 3864, 3874, 3898, 3906, 3939, 3959, 3963, 3964, 3967, 3969, 3996, 3998, 4037, 4044, 4087, 4088, 4159, 4177, 4194, 4221, 4223, 4239, 4256.8, 4263, 4279, 4282.

Other Works that Supply Editions of Lyrics

The following are annotated with the works of criticism. Most are articles in which lyrics are first printed and introduced to the critical discourse. Many of these poems have subsequently been included in collections, but in some cases the works listed here remain the only printed source of the texts. In a few cases they do not supply all the texts to which their authors refer. For instance some works, largely concerned with the criticism of a particular aspect of the lyric or other genre, list many examples, but provide only the texts of poems which have not been published elsewhere; these include Sandison's study

Annotations of Editions 85

of the *chanson d'aventure*, **139**, Stevens's of court lyrics, **438**, and Wenzel's of sermon lyrics, **701**, **882**.

106, 108, 113, 114, 115, 116, 120, 121, 122, 123, 124, 126, 128, 129, 131, 136, 139, 143, 145, 150, 152, 157, 160, 167, 173, 176, 179, 180, 181, 182, 183, 184, 185, 189, 190, 193, 194, 200, 201, 206, 208, 209, 214, 216, 217, 218, 219, 221, 222, 228, 231, 235, 237, 240, 241, 254, 266, 267, 281, 285, 286, 287, 288, 293, 294, 302, 305, 306, 308, 309, 310, 311, 315, 324, 328, 330, 335, 336, 337, 339, 340, 341, 342, 343, 344, 346, 347, 348, 349, 350, 353, 354, 356, 359, 360, 361, 364, 370, 371, 374, 383, 384, 388, 398, 399, 409, 410, 411, 412, 413, 416, 421, 438, 447, 448, 451, 454, 457, 462, 465, 470, 471, 475, 476, 482, 490, 493, 494, 501, 505, 507, 512, 513, 516, 518, 523, 524, 528, 529, 534, 537, 538, 541, 545, 547, 555, 557, 558, 561, 564, 572, 576, 580, 581, 584, 587, 589, 591, 596, 597, 601, 615, 618, 629, 632, 636, 647, 651, 661, 668, 679, 684, 691, 696, 701, 714, 727, 730, 735, 739, 740, 741, 746, 747, 748, 750, 754, 756, 758, 759, 761, 762, 769, 771, 773, 776, 778, 780, 782, 784, 785, 790, 793, 802, 804, 818, 820, 822, 826, 838, 841, 846, 847, 849, 855, 859, 861, 878, 882, 884, 886, 891, 892, 894, 897, 901, 903, 905, 908, 909, 913, 919, 924, 927, 931, 932, 955, 956, 958, 968, 971, 976, 978, 981, 1004, 1006, 1009, 1015, 1016, 1017.

Annotations of Critical Works

The works annotated here offer critical comment on ME lyrics, including some comments in more general and comparative studies. Among these are works in which lyrics are printed for the first time or presented in new readings, as listed above and marked '[Edition]'. A list after each annotation cites the numbers of the poems mentioned, taken from *IMEV*, *SIMEV*, and the temporary index. Some critics include numerous brief references to other poems to enhance their comments on the lyrics, for instance to trace themes and motifs in a range of other works, and supply a detailed background. (Robbins, for example, includes many short quotations and concise allusions as he sets the context in which he considers particular lyrics.) Some works that are not lyrics are also included in the lists, since there are many comparisons with such poems as *Canterbury Tales*, *Troilus and Criseyde*, *Sir Gawain and the Green Knight*, and *Piers Plowman*. For these reasons, the list of numbers may seem longer and more diverse than the title of the work annotated and the text of the annotation at first suggest, and the list is not intended to show the emphasis placed on each work mentioned.

105 κ., ε.τ. 'Christmas Carol.' *Notes and Queries* 3rd Series 2 (1862): 103.

Describes a carol in ballad form, 'Over yonder's a park, which is newly begun' [*7422*], sung in North Staffordshire, and seeks information about the work, which is related to the 'Corpus Christi Carol' [*1132*].

1132, 7422.

106 Thompson, E.M. 'Scraps from Middle-English MSS.' *Englische Studien* 1 (1877): 214–15. [Edition.]

Among entries scribbled on f.5 of Cathedral Library, Sarum MS 126, by Thomas Cyrcetur, canon residentiary, are two lyrics ['Pryde wraþ and enuye,' *2776*; 'þy lord of heuene loue wel,' *3731*], and versions of the Apostles' Creed and the Lord's Prayer ['Hure wader þat is in euene,' *2710*], written in prose form. Thompson prints the poems, without comment.

2710, 2776, 3731.

107 Ten Brink, Bernhard. *Early English Literature (to Wiclif)*. Tr. H.M. Kennedy. Bohn's Standard Library. London: Bell, 1883. 302–24.

The lyric is a point of contact for religious and secular poetry. In the Middle Ages it was created by wandering scholars who 'knew life as well as the schools' (303). Ten Brink describes the background of these clerks, including their familiarity with Latin, French, and ME. He also considers the influence of folk-song and lyrics of various languages on the ME lyric, and contrasts the work of French and English poets, illustrating his discussions with many examples, generally rendered in MnE verse and prose. He compares the debate and dialogue forms, and deals briefly with the proverbs of Hendyng. Gleemen and clergy fostered political and satirical lyrical poetry. Ten Brink supplies examples, most of them in translation, and explains the historical background, with particular reference to clerical satire and works of Adam Davey and Laurence Minot. He notes details, in brief references, of the rhyming and metrical form of lyrics, including *estrif, ryme couée, romanze, versus tripartitus caudatus, ryme plate, planh,* and *descort*.

105, 515, 585, 694.5, 709, 987, 1320.5, 1394, 1401, 1504, 1638, 1857, 1861, 1921, 1922, 1974, 2189, 2236, 2287, 2539, 3080, 3117, 3155, 3221, 3222, 3223, 3801, 3899, 3963, 4037, 4085, 4144, 4177.

108 Heuser, W. 'Ave Maria.' *Anglia* 27 (1904): 320–30. [Edition.]

Prints a previously unpublished poem, 'Hayle mayden of maydyns thorʒt worde consaywyng' [*1059*]. This has a rhyme scheme unique in its time, and begins each stanza with the ME word corresponding to the Latin word beside it. Heuser also prints similar Latin and AN works and two English poems on the Angelic Salutation, 'Heil marie ful of grace' [*1062*] and 'Heil & holi ay be þi name' [*1024*], all preserved in Cambridge University Library manuscripts.

1024, 1059, 1062.

109 ———. 'With an O and an I.' *Anglia* 27 (1904): 283–319.

Considers works that use variations of the *O and I* refrain. Heuser prints the Northern Verses on the Four Evangelists, 'Luke in his lesson leres to me' [*2021*], made of four poems in the voices of the Evangelists. The first three relate episodes in Christ's life; the fourth, in John's voice, offers a philosophical conclusion. The work has a unique epic-lyric character, with consistent characteristics of speech and rhyme, including Northern forms, the use of *scho*, and a debt to the Northern Homily Cycle. Explanations of the refrain include *ay and o*, 'always and forever.' Heuser considers this possibility and variations such as *With I and E, With E and I,* and *With E and O*. Although *ay and o* and *euer and oo* or *ay* appear in earlier works, including some in Harley MS 2253, the *O and I* refrain is not generally seen before the later medieval period. Heuser prints several poems with the refrain and variations, including two where other lines are in Latin, with linguistic comments. The origin is generally Northern, although two, 'As þou for holy churche riʒt' [*412*] and 'Godys sone þat was so fre' [*1001*], apparently closest to the original form, seem Southern, which could explain some unexpected sounds in the Northern poems. In a postscript Heuser prints other poems, in English and Latin, observed more recently, as evidence of the origin of the refrain in hymns of Jesus.

322, 412, 539, 701, 876, 1001, 1921, 1922, 2021, 2663, 3921, 4002.

110 Sidgwick, F. 'A Christmas Carol.' *Notes and Queries* 10th Series 4 (1905): 181–2.

A reply to the query of ϵ.τ. κ., **105**, about the ballad 'Over yonder's a park, which is newly begun' [*7422*]. Sidgwick notes its relationship to the 'Corpus Christi Carol' [*1132*]. In the ballad, the second and fourth line of each stanza are 'All bells in Paradise I heard them a-ring' and 'And I love sweet Jesus above all things'; the 'lullay' burden is omitted. [For other traditional versions, see Greene, **86,** nos. 322, B, C, D, E.]

1132, 7422.

111 Taylor, George C. 'The English "Planctus Mariae."' *Modern Philology* 4 (1906–7): 605–37.

An investigation of non-dramatic and dramatic planctus in English, through examination of the relationships of non-dramatic forms to each other, and of dramatic forms to 'those portions of the miracle-plays which contain the laments of Mary for Christ' (606). The non-dramatic poems include complaints and meditations. Some of them, particularly those in debate form, are 'highly dramatic and . . . closely akin to the drama as a form' (607). As examples of the dramatic form, Taylor cites numerous extracts from the York, Towneley, Chester, Hegge, and Digby plays. He demonstrates the general relations of forms of planctus through a 'Table of Motives' (614–15), with specific comparisons of non-dramatic passages. Later he relates non-dramatic and dramatic examples through connections of structure and phrases, some of which occur in prose translations of Bonaventure's *Meditations*, including Richard Rolle's. The Digby play *The Burial of Christ* shows 'the highest development of the dramatic planctus in English.' In discerning agreements between the works, Taylor warns that 'direct relationships between such highly conventionalized forms of literature' can only be established when there are 'peculiar agreements of phrase or peculiar agreements of arrangement and order of motives' (628). He finds agreement of the Digby planctus and several non-dramatic forms. It is generally difficult to relate dramatic forms to independent works, but possible in the Hegge play of the *Resurrection*. Only the Digby play shows 'the actual development of a planctus into a play,' and 'would not be a play without the planctus' (636). However, no play offers proof that 'the planctus is, in the English passion-play, the original portion from which the rest of the play was expanded' (637).

248, 404, 548, 771, 1718, 1869, 1899, 2111, 2619, 2428, 2718, 3131, 3208, 3211, 3750, 4023, 4189, 7001, 7002, 7008, 7009, 7010, 7020, 7034, 7035, 7047, 7048, 7052, 7453, 7583.

112 Hammond, Eleanor Prescott. 'Ashmole 59 and other Shirley Manuscripts.' *Anglia* 30 (1907): 320–48.

Among the contents of Shirley manuscripts she describes, Hammond lists and prints a bookplate-stanza, 'Yee that deyre in herte and have pleasaunce' [*4260*], which is found in several sites.

4260.

113 ———. 'The Lover's Mass.' *JEGP* 7 (1907–8): 95–104. [Edition.]

There is disagreement about ascription of the work, 'Wyth all myn Hool Herte entere' [*4186*], to Lydgate; Hammond finds external and internal evidence 'very strongly in the other direction' (95). Only 'the substantial agreement of a part of the Epistle in Prose, concluding the Mass, with several stanzas of the prologue to the third book of the *Falls of Princes* [*1168*]' (96) suggests any connection. However, one work may be 'indebted to the other for the idea,' or both may be derived from a passage of Boccaccio's *De Casibus*, 'the ultimate original of Lydgate's lines' (97). Hammond prints the text, from MS Fairfax 16 [Bodleian 3896].

1168, 4186.

114 Heuser, W. 'Die Katherinenhymne des Ricardus Spaldyng und eine Marienhymne derselben Perganmentrolle.' *Anglia* 30 (1907): 523–48. [Edition.]

Describes the manuscript, Bodley Rolls 22 [Summary Catalogue 30445], and provides detailed commmentary on the hymns to St Katherine ['Katereyn þe curteys of all þat I knowe,' *1813*] and the Five Joys of Mary ['Myldeste of moode & mekyst of maydyns alle,' *2171*]. Acrostics reveal the scribe of the former as Richard Spalding, and of the latter as a less imaginative clerk of Pipewell. Heuser compares several versions of the Katherine legends, and finds that this version resembles a poem of St John the Evangelist ['Of all mankynde þat he made þat maste es of myghte,' *2608*] in its versification. He supplies general comment on the long line and alliterative verse in ME poetry, and takes particular examples from the hymn to St Katherine. [See Holthausen, **168, 185**.]

1813, 2171, 2608.

115 ———. 'Fragmente von Unbekannten Spielsmannsliedern des 14. Jahrhunderts, aus MS. Rawl. D. 913.' *Anglia* 30 (1907): 173–9. [Edition.]

The manuscript provides a minstrel's notes on dancing, drinking, and love songs, in ME and OF. Heuser prints the songs, with comment on the dialect, which suggests a southeastern provenance and the work of a bilingual scribe, and a date in the first half of the fourteenth century.

179, 194, 1008, 1301.5, 2037.5, 2288.5, 2622, 3361.3, 4256.8.

116 McBryde, J.M., Jr. 'Charms for Thieves.' *Modern Language Notes* 22 (1907): 168–70. [Edition.]

Prints one Latin and seven ME charms, including two found in seventeenth-century manuscripts, all involving immobilization of thieves and enemies. Important motifs in the charms are the thieves crucified at Christ's Crucifixion, and the stopping of the River Jordan and the Red Sea; the latter idea was also a part of charms used to stanch a flow of blood. [See Bühler, **388**; Gray, **610**; Smallwood, **927**.]

412.5, 993, 1199, 7414, 7441.

117 MacCracken, Henry Noble. 'The Earl of Warwick's *Virelai*.' *PMLA* 22 (1907): 597–60.

MacCracken supplies an edition of a *virelai*, 'I can not half þe woo compleyne' [*1288*], written by Richard Beauchamp, Earl of Warwick, for his second wife, Isabella, and an account of Warwick's life, including some chivalric episodes.

1288.

118 Taylor, George C. 'The Relation of the English Corpus Christi Play to the Middle English Religious Lyric.' *Modern Philology* 5 (1907–8): 1–37.

Compares the plays with 'any verse which ... seemed in any sense to belong to the lyric categories,' thus including prayers and didactic works. Taylor contends that many prayers were used as 'ready-made lyrics by the play-writers and adapted to dramatic purposes' (3). He cites in particular 'the prayer of a repentant sinner, lamenting his past offences'; those 'in which the bodily wounds of Jesus are recounted in detail as cause for lamentation' (4); and the 'Hail' prayers addressed to Jesus and to Mary, 'the development of one line in the annunciation-lyrics, spoken by Gabriel, "Hail Mary"' (5). Although there are many ME Christmas songs, the plays seem only to have 'a few fragments of what may once have been Christmas lyrics' (7). '*The Testament of Christ*, termed variously the *Lament of the Redeemer*, *Christ's Charter*, and *Christ's Complaint*' (8), like the repentance of an old man, is essentially dramatic monologue, so that treatment of the theme hardly differs in drama and independent poems. Taylor doubts that this form or the planctus could be the origin of the passion play [cf. **111**.] Some plays' resurrection lyrics may have been inspired by independent lyrics rather than hymns or liturgical drama. The mutability and brevity of life are often mentioned, as in *ubi sunt* lyrics, with similar allusions in the plays. Judgement plays may be compared with Christ's *Testament*, *The Pricke of Conscience* [*3428*], and *The Dance of Death*. Taylor prints passages from plays and lyrics, for comparison, in an 'Appendix' (16–38), and provides numerous examples in footnotes.

66, 112, 739, 765.3, 820.8, 1032, 1119, 1268, 1491, 1650, 1705, 1731, 2007, 2098, 3233, 3428, 3460, 3596, 3658, 3707, 3812, 3877, 3883, 7134, 7181, 7581.

119 Onions, C. Talbut. 'A Thirteenth-Century Paternoster by an Anglo-French Scribe.' *Modern Language Review* 3 (1908): 69–71.

An explication of the ME Paternoster, 'Hure wader þat is in euene' [*2710*], written 'in a late thirteenth-century hand (MS. No. 82, fol. 271 b, Cathedral Library of Sarum).' [See Thompson, **106**.] Variations in spelling suggest an Anglo-French scribe, 'of French birth or who had had an entirely French education, and was consequently imperfectly acquainted with the grammar and vocabulary of English' (69). Onions provides notes on the unusual forms, and prints a restoration contributed by Skeat, which sets out the poem in metrical form.

2710.

120   Garrett, Robert Max. 'A Satire Against Women.' *Anglia* 32 (1909): 358. [Edition.]

Prints three stanzas of the satirical poem 'When nettuls in wynter bryng forth rosys red' [*3999*], 'written on the back leaf of a copy of Trevisa's Translation of Bartholomew Anglicus, printed by Wynkin de Worde 1495.' This version differs from the form supplied by Flügel, **15**, from MS Balliol 354. [See Utley, **253**.]

3999.

121   ———. 'De Arte Lacrimandi.' *Anglia* 32 (1909): 269–94. [Edition.]

An edition of the poem 'Now late me thought I wolde begynn' [*2347*], preserved in Harley 2274, 'a collection of various medical treatises written in Latin and English,' where it is written 'on paper, in a fine hand.' The refrain of each stanza is 'of the type "Therfor to wepe come lerne att me" or its variants'; it is generally 'an organic part of the stanza,' although sometimes 'at the sacrifice of perfect sense' (269). There are alliteration and internal rhyme, but without a particular pattern. Final *e* is generally silent, and *y* frequently used in place of *e* when the syllable is unstressed. Garrett prints the poem, subtitled 'Prosopopæia B. Virg*in*ie,' and finds the action 'remarkably vivid,' with 'certain passages possessing real dramatic fire' (270).

2347.

122   Greg, W.W. '"I Sing of a Maiden that is Makeles."' *Modern Philology* 7 (1909): 165–8. [Edition.]

The lyric, 'Nu þis fules singet hand maket hure blis' [*2366*], in the thirteenth-century MS Trinity College Cambridge B.14.39, includes 'the whole of the non-repetitional setting of the fifteenth-century carol 'I sing of a myden þ^t is makeles' [*1367*]. Although the work appears 'in substantially the same form,' it is combined 'with quite different material' (165). Greg prints the two poems, with notes, using Sloane 2593 as a source for the carol, and explores possible relationships between the poems. There may be no direct connection between the two; or the fifteenth-century work may be 'an old traditional song . . . utilized by the more sophisticated thirteenth-century writer.' A third possibility is that 'the two rather striking couplets of the not very remarkable thirteenth-century poem were at a later date deliberately combined with three other couplets, equally striking but of an altogether different type, to form what is as it stands in the thirteenth-century manuscript a supremely artistic whole' (165–6).

1367, 2366.

123   Hammond, Eleanor Prescott. 'Lament of a Prisoner against Fortune.' *Anglia* 32 (1909): 481–90. [Edition.]

There are copies of the poem, 'Fortune alas alas what haue I gylt' [*860*], in three BL manuscripts, Harley 2251, Add. 34360, and Harley 7333. Hammond prints the last of

Annotations of Critical Works 91

these, with comments on the authorship of the work, which has been attributed to Chaucer, Lydgate, and Hoccleve. [See also Green, **654**.]

860.

124 Williams, O.J. 'Another Welsh Phonetic Copy of the Early English Hymn to the Virgin from a British Museum MS. No. 14866.' *Anglia* 32 (1909): 295–300. [Edition.]

Williams prints a Welsh phonetic version of a Hymn to the Virgin, 'O meichti ladi owr leding tw haf' [*2514*], 'first printed by F.J. Furnivall in Appendix II to the Transactions of the Philological Society, 1880–1, Part I, from two MSS. of the Hengwrt Collection, Nos. 479 and 294, with Notes on the phonetic copy by A.J. Ellis' (299). The work was sung by Ieuan ap Hywel Swrdwal. Williams comments on the Welsh vowel *y* and variations in the poem, indicating that both a clear and an obscure sound are intended for it. [See Bell, **131**; Davies, **133**.]

2514.

125 Gilchrist, Annie G. 'Over Yonder's a Park.' *Journal of the Folk-Song Society* 4 (1910–13): 52–66.

Summarizes comments of ε.τ.κ., **105**, and Sidgwick, **18**, on 'Over yonder's a park which is newly begun' [*7422*], a traditional variant of 'The Corpus Christi Carol' [*1132*], and prints the texts. Gilchrist elaborates her marginal notes on the poems to relate symbolism to the Eucharist and the legend of the Holy Grail. Thus she reads in *1132*, 'The bed is the altar = sepulchre; the knight is Christ, daily sacrificed in the Eucharist; the stone inscribed *Corpus Christi* is the paten.' In *7422*, '[t]he bed is the altar-sepulchre (or cross); the sacred body is laid upon it; the stone is still present, though the meaning has become obscured . . . the faithful hound [is] to stand for Joseph of Arimathæa, gathering the sacred drops in his vessel, either at the foot of the cross, or . . . after the body has been placed in the sepulchre; the hound thus seems to be a variation of the chalice-symbol' (55). She describes the falcon refrain as originally secular. The Weeping May is, in *1132* a Damsel of the Grail, 'whose office is to weep' (56), and in *7422* the Virgin, following 'the new interpretation of the wounded knight' (57). The bells of Paradise in the traditional carol allude to transubstantiation, the sacring bell, and bells of the Grail legend. Gilchrist also explicates the significance of the orchard, hall, bed, knight, park, the symbolism of red, the hound, and the thorn, associated with the staff brought by Joseph of Arimathea to Glastonbury. A parallel to the structure of incremental repetition in *1132* is found in the folk-rhyme, 'The Key of the Kingdom.'

1132, 7422.

126 Root, Robert K. 'Poems from the Garrett MS.' *Englische Studien* 41 (1910): 360–79. [Edition.]

Describes a manuscript deposited by Robert Garrett in the library of Princeton University. Most of the contents are in prose, but there are four verse pieces: *The Trental of St Gregory* [*1653*] and three lyrics. These are called, in the manuscript: 'þe songe of saing þe best' ['The grete god full of grace,' *3371*], 'þe songe of þonkynge god of al' ['Bi a wey wandryng as I went,' *562*], and 'þe songe of amendis makinge' ['Bi a wode as I gone ride,' *563*]. Root lists other sources of the lyrics, including the Vernon MS, and comments on manuscript variations.

562, 563, 1653, 3371.

127 Bolle, Wilhelm. 'Zur Lyrik der Rawlinson-Hs. C. 813.' *Anglia* 34 (1911): 273–307.

Scrutinizes the edition prepared by Padelford and Benham, **20**, with general and particular comment on matters including the hands (Bolle favours three, rather than two), dating, genres, and metre. Bolle provides an extensive account of borrowings, including those from Chaucer, Hawes, and Lydgate, and sets out various passages in parallel columns, noting similarities to works in the Bannatyne MS. In conclusion he presents suggested emendations (300–7) .

79.5, 146, 172, 340.5, 366, 368, 430, 642.5, 649, 729, 767, 851, 1017.5, 1180, 1328.7, 1329, 1349.5, 1450.5, 1540, 1768, 1841.5, 1926.5, 2092, 2228, 2245.1, 2261.8, 2271.6, 2409.5, 2421, 2439.5, 2482.5, 2498, 2500.5, 2529, 2532, 2532.5, 2547, 2552.5, 2560.5, 2757.3, 2784, 2821, 2822, 2827.5, 3098.3, 3228.5, 3327, 3412, 3713.5, 3785.5, 3804, 3917.8, 3962.5, 4004, 4019, 4020.3, 4190, 4210.

128 Garrett, Robert Max. 'Middle English Rimed Medical Treatise.' *Anglia* 34 (1911): 163–93. [Edition.]

Prints the two medical treatises preserved in BL Add. MS 17,866, 'in a text so different [from that of a Stockholm manuscript] that it would be impossible to print merely a list of variants' from texts previously printed. The text has a medico-botanical poem, followed by prescriptions, the reverse of the Stockholm order; Garrett lists points of difference and correspondence in the two manuscripts. The first poem, 'Of erbis xxiij/I wyl þe telle by and by' [*2627*], deals with herbs, in particular betony. The second, 'Iff a man or woman more or less' [*1408*], offers discrete recipes for various conditions. The text shows 'many traces of northern dialect, but is not consistent' (163). [See Powell, **894**.]

1408, 2627.

129 MacCracken, Henry Noble. 'An English Friend of Charles of Orléans.' *PMLA* 26 (1911): 142–80. [Edition.]

As well as poems written by Charles d'Orléans, MS Bibliothèque Nationale fr. 25248 preserves some 'English pieces by an English hand' (142). The same hand is that of two roundels in English in Royal 16 F.ii, 'no doubt derived from the court of Burgundy' (142). The poems may have been written by an English friend, possibly William de la Pole, Duke of Suffolk, who was the guardian of Orléans for four years. MacCracken considers the poems 'not bad of their kind,' and the themes they treat are 'precisely those of Orléans' poems.' They include 'fidelity in love, the piteous state of the absent, the pain and joy of the lover under the commands of Bel Acueil, the woes of love, the perplexity of the lover's life' (146). His evidence is external and internal, and includes the interest in literature of Suffolk and his circle, and the style of Suffolk's letters and verse. MacCracken concludes that 'the translator of Orléans in MS Harley 682 and the author of the *Complaint against Hope* in MS Fairfax 16' are 'one man . . . not a humble poet, but a man of position . . . The tone is that of a lordly lover, not the sickeningly humble imaginary slave of love in Lydgate's verse' (148–9). Some poems seem covert references 'to political misunderstandings' (149) not poems of love. Rhyme, style, and structure show resemblances between the Harley and Fairfax poems. MacCracken prints 38 poems he ascribes to Suffolk: seven French poems from Trinity College Cambridge R.3.20 (151–5), 20 English poems from Fairfax 16 [Bodleian 3896] (155–74), 11 English poems in French manuscripts of Orléans [all ascribed in *IMEV* to Orléans] (174–8), and two 'Poems in Suffolk's Manner' (179–80).

Poems from MS Fairfax 16: *296, 509, 1826, 2178, 2182, 2230, 2295, 2349, 2350, 2407, 2488, 2567, 2583, 2595, 2823, 3488, 3752, 3860, 3913, 3915.*

English Poems in French Manuscripts of Orléans: from Grenoble MS: *134, 158, 844, 922, 2176, 3162, 4014, 4256*; from MS Royal 16 F. ii: *2246, 2289*.
Poems in Suffolk's Manner: *12, 1237*.

130 Müller, Alexander. *Mittelenglische geistliche und weltliche Lyrik des XIII Jahrhunderts (mit Ausschluss der politischen Lieder) nach Motiven und Formen.* Studien zur englischen Philologie 45. Ed. Lorenz Morsbach. Halle an der Salle, 1911. Tübingen: Niemeyer, 1973.

Begins this detailed study of ME lyrical poetry (excluding political songs) with a summary of previous scholarship, and scrutinizes 78 lyrics of the thirteenth century according to motif and form. Müller lists printed sources and criticism (ix–xi); he provides a chronological account of the manuscripts (6–8), and lists the poems (8–11). He groups the religious lyrics according to content: of Mary, of Jesus, and of devotion. Those addressed to Mary and Jesus are generally praise or pleas. The lyrics of devotion stress the false and transitory nature of the world; they are impersonal, unlike those of Mary and Jesus, which emphasize the poet's individuality. Müller explains aspects of style, including rhetorical figures, metrical form, rhyme schemes, and metre. After this general study he describes each lyric, with critical opinion, motifs, metrical form, use of alliteration, and rhyme scheme in the individual analysis, using a chronological arrangement. He considers St Godric's hymns ['Crist and saint marie swa on scamel me iledde,' *598*; 'Seinte marie clane uirgine,' *2988*; 'Sainte Nicolaes godes druð,' *3031*], and precursor works in lyrical prose (43–57); the lyrics written before *c.* 1250 (57–84); and those written before *c.*1310 (84–133). The examination of individual secular lyrics has a similar chronological scheme, separating those written before 1250 (134–6), and those before *c.* 1310 (136–55), with a summary (155–8). Müller notes similarities in the religious and secular lyrics. These include resemblances in the praise of Mary, Jesus, and God and that of the earthly beloved, and in regrets for sin and wasted life in lovers' complaints. Nature is of great importance, especially in setting the mood of secular lyrics.

66, 105, 322, 359, 515, 598, 631, 695, 705, 708, 718, 877, 888, 968, 1066, 1078, 1091, 1115, 1216, 1233, 1365, 1394, 1395, 1407, 1449, 1504, 1617, 1678, 1697, 1705, 1747, 1820, 1833, 1839, 1861, 1921, 1922, 1943, 1948, 2003, 2025, 2039, 2066, 2070, 2166, 2207, 2220, 2236, *2284.5, 2293, 2359, 2604, 2645, 2687, 2988, 2992, 3031, 3211, 3222, 3223, 3234, 3236, 3310, 3432, 3517, 3873, 3874, 3963, 3967, 4037, 4047, 4051, 4177, 4194, 4223.

131 Bell, H. Idris. 'Welsh Phonetic Copy of the Early English Hymn to the Virgin.' *Anglia* 36 (1912): 116–21. [Edition.]

Another printing of the hymn 'O meichti ladi owr leding tw haf' [*2514*], prepared to correct inaccuracies Bell discerns in the version printed by Williams, **124**. Bell provides the punctuation, capitals, metrical arrangement, etc. of the original, noting alterations made by the scribe and some variant readings supplied by Davies. [See Davies, **133**.]

2514.

132 Brown, Carleton. 'The "Pride of life" and the "Twelve abuses."' *Archiv* 128 (1912): 72–8.

Investigates the source of 'the lament upon prevailing evil conditions voiced by Episcopus,' in 'the early Morality, the *Pride of Life* ['Pees and horkynt hal ifer,' *2741*]' (72). Brown notes ME and Latin catalogues of abuses of the age that list twelve, ten, or nine abuses. A metrical variation of the Twelve Abuses of the Age, 'Gifte hys made domesman' [*906*], is the source of the lament; it is found in MSS Worcester Cathedral, F.154 and Ashmolean 750, which vary to some extent. Brown's examination of rhyme words and arrangement shows that although neither variant is 'as old as the text of the *Pride of Life*' (76), they have the original form of the lament and demonstrate that 'the verbal relation between the Worcester-Ashmole lines and the *Pride of Life* is so close that it clears up certain doubtful readings in the text of the latter' (77).

906, 920, 2741, 4051.

133   Davies, J. Glyn. 'Metrical Analysis of the BM Text.' *Anglia* 36 (1912): 121–6.

Supplies a metrical analysis of the Welsh poem 'O meichti ladi owr leding tw haf' [*2514*] published by Bell, **131**. Davies presents a detailed description of the rhyming, scansion, and alliteration of the poem, noting the two kinds of strophes used in the *Englyn unodl union* (the first seven stanzas) and the *Tawddgyrch Cadwynog*, where both strophes have '*cynghanedd*, the generic term for alliteration, or internal rhyme, or both combined' (121). [See Williams, **124**.]

2514.

134   Padelford, Frederick Morgan. 'MS Rawlinson C. 813 Again.' *Anglia* 35 (1912): 178–86.

A reply to Bolle's comments, **127**, on Padelford's transcription of the manuscript, **20**. Padelford asserts that he did not attempt 'to emend the mistakes of the scribe,' since he intended to prepare notes with such emendations later. He acknowledges 'a good many valid corrections' (178), and comments on individual readings that seem 'questionable or altogether wrong, or that do . . . [his] work an injustice' (179). After reconsideration, he is 'still of the opinion that there are two hands, and not three' (186).

79.5, 172, 340.5, 368, 430, 642.5, 729, 1017.5, 1180, 1349.5, 1450.5, 1926.5, 2228, 2261.8, 2271.6, 2409.5, 2496, 2500.5, 2529, 2532, 2532.5, 2560.5, 2757.3, 2822, 3098.3, 3228.5, 3785.5, 3917.8, 4020.3, 4190, 4210.

135   Reed, Edward Bliss. *English Lyrical Poetry: From Its Origins to the Present Time.* New Haven: Yale UP; London: Oxford UP, 1912.

In his introductory chapter, Reed offers a general discussion, to establish definitive features of the lyric genre. He deals specifically with the ME lyric in the second chapter (22–98). Here he describes the French lyric forms *chanson courtoise, chanson d'amour*, and *poesie populaire*, and prints examples of the French forms, with English translations, noting their influence on English poems. Reed writes of the aube, pastourelle, *débat, ballade, chanson de toile, rondet, rondet de carole, rondel, roundeau, triolet*, and *Noël*; he comments in particular on lyrics written to the Virgin. Among his many examples are some taken from mystery plays.

22, 61, 66, 100, 105, 113.5, 124, 179, 205, 299, 359, 360, 456.5, 515, 631, 681, 694.5, 708, 729.5, 753.8, 809, 864, 903, 925, 1008, 1030, 1162, 1272, 1301.5, 1306, 1319, 1365, 1367, 1394, 1395, 1405.5, 1534, 1678, 1839, 1861, 1889, 1914, 1921, 1922, 2037.5, 2149, 2163, 2189, 2207, 2220, 2229, 2231.5, 2231.5, 2236, 2243, 2270, 2375, 2645, 2687, 2716, 3080, 3155, 3190, 3223, 3236, 3270.5, 3297.3, 3414, 3536, 3542, 3627, 3645, 3722, 3782, 3903.5, 4037, 4177, 4194, 4256.8, 4279, 7342.

136   Skeat, Walter W. '"Elegy on the Death of King Edward I"': From a New MS.' *Modern Language Review* 7 (1912): 149–52. [Edition.]

Supplies the elegy 'Alle þat beoþ of huert trewe' [*205*] transcribed as it is found, in three fragments, in Cambridge University Library MS. 4407 (19). The ME work loosely translates 'a French Elegy of the same date (1307)' (149). Skeat comments on the text, suggesting additions and correcting earlier transcriptions. Another fragment has scraps of a poem 'In þis werd þat hys so wicke' [*1580*], which he considers 'of no merit' (150), except for the presence of 'the extremely rare word "flicke"' (151). [Cf. Smithers, **897**.] A last fragment, 'Ihesu crist godis sone of heuene' [*1669*] offers 'another MS. authority for the commencement of the *Proverbs of Hendyng*' (151), which most closely resembles the version of Harley MS 2253.

205, *2685.5, 1669.

137   Dudley, Louise. '"The Grave."' *Modern Philology* 11 (1913): 429–44.

Dudley summarizes criticism of the lyric with the title 'The Grave' ['ðe wes bold ȝebyld er þu i-boren were,' *3497*], but does not accept that it is either a fragment or a speech made by a soul to its body. Citing differences as well as similarities in 'The Grave' and the Worcester 'Fragments,' she suggests that *3497* may be the source rather than a part of the 'Fragments.' She stresses the difference in tone between the poem and speeches of a soul, and finds no evidence of damage to the manuscript to suggest that the work is incomplete. Dudley concludes that '[i]f the poem is complete . . . it is clear that it does not belong to the class of body and soul poems, but to the even more popular class of death and grave literature' (442). [See Moffat, **93**.]

3497.

138   Rhys, Ernest. *Lyric Poetry*. The Channels of English Literature. Ed. Oliphant Smeaton. London: Dent, 1913.

This general study of the lyric in English traces the development of lyric poetry from OE forms, and alludes briefly to many examples in 'The New Poetry' (31–9), 'The Harleian Anthology' (40–7), and 'The Transition' (48–57). Rhys notes the influence of Latin and French forms, and the importance of the caesura, in tracing 'the development of the old rhythm into the modulated verse-forms' (36). He cites the works of Robert Grosseteste, Robert Manning, Robert of Gloucester, Robert of Brunne, Richard Rolle, Thomas de Hales, and William of Shoreham, and refers to the lyrics of the Vernon and Harley MSS.

105, 354, 515, 704, 1030, 1122, 1225, 1226, 1252, 1395, 1596, 1914, 1921, 2025, 2078, 2163, 2164, 2236, 3199, 3270, 3883, 3992, 4177, 4194.

139   Sandison, Helen Estabrook. *The 'Chanson d'Aventure' in Middle English*. Bryn Mawr Monographs 12. Bryn Mawr, PA: Bryn Mawr College, 1913. [Edition.]

In English, the *chanson d'aventure* follows convention in 'the designation of hour and season, the appearance of the solitary poet "wandering by the way", the announcement of his mood and his motive for being abroad, and the tale of his unexpected encounter with some frequenter of field or forest' (25). The narrative has dramatic and lyric elements, 'set within a framework in which the poet appears as narrator' (43), but English poets worked within their tradition rather than 'slavishly translating or imitating particular foreign models' (44). The themes of the *chanson d'aventure* in England are amorous, religious, didactic, and miscellaneous. The first two appear in varying proportions, in the fourteenth, fifteenth, and sixteenth centuries, and resemble love songs, with more monologues of Mary than of her Son, in *planctus Mariae* and *planctus Christi*. The poet's preface rarely suggests a human encounter; occasionally he listens to birds who sing of or represent religious figures, or overhears dialogues between Mary and Christ, frequently carols in lullaby form. Didactic *chansons d'aventure* are plentiful in the fifteenth century. Their themes do not express personal feeling and are stated in monologues, dialogues, formal debates, or the '"spekyng" of a company of clerks' (82), with no fixed relation between form and theme. The didactic poet's cry is 'far indeed from the lyric cry' (88). The 'miscellaneous' category includes 'adventure-lyrics of political, satiric, or occasional nature' (88). They appear later, and are *chansons dramatiques*, faithful to the traditions of *chansons d'aventure*. Sandison describes the work of the *jongleurs*, trouvères, and the poets who followed them. She cites many examples, including French, English, and Scottish pastourelles, and *chansons des femmes mal mariées*, and comments on all aspects of the *chanson d'aventure*. She prints several poems, and provides a register of ME *chansons d'aventure* and other poems cited.

Amorous: *340.5, 360, 370, 371, 558.5, 835.5, 1214.5, 1449, 1449.5, 1506, 1527, 1540.5, 1549, 1589.5, 2207, 2295, 3595, 3596.6, 3635.5, 3713.5, 3832.5, 3836.5, 3860, 3946.5, 7071, 7098, 7099, 7124, 7152, 7163, 7254, 7257, 7259, 7263, 7266, 7268, 7275, 7370, 7380, 7468, 7565, 7599.*
Religious: *112, 298, 343, 352, 357, 359, 361, 364, 378, 404, 407, 447, 1447, 1463, 1503.5, 1532, 1678, 1841, 2018, 2359, 3822, 7063, 7120, 7267, 7591.*
Didactic: *277, 341, 245, 346, 349, 356, 369, 373, 374, 375, 419, 560, 561, 562, 563, 583, 1319, 1355, 1446, 1448, 1453, 1454, 1456, 1475, 1598, 1842, 2678, 3715, 3797, 3820, 3942, 4025, 7153, 7154, 7306, 7571, 7597.*
Miscellaneous: *350, 362, 363, 368, 377, 379, 418, 558.3, 559, 700, 1317, 1450, 1452, 1505, 2226.5, 3720, 7096, 7260, 7600.*

140 Schelling, Felix E. *The English Lyric*. 1913. Port Washington, NY: Kennikat, 1967.

Lyric poetry is linked to song, and needs 'devices of language which ally human speech to music' (2). The lyric is 'personal and subjective, concerned with the poet himself, his thoughts, emotions, and sentiments' (3), distinguished from the epigram in being 'emotional, poetic and unconscious' (7). The medieval lyric may be traced from the poetry of troubadours. Schelling provides religious and secular examples in his general survey, 'The Medieval Lyric' (9–30).

66, 436, 515, 549, 704, 1132, 1226, 1314, 1866, 2034.5, 2037.5, 2207, 2236, 2645, 2831, 3310, 3313, 3223.

141 Spalding, Mary Caroline. *The Middle English Charters of Christ*. Bryn Mawr College Monograph 15. Bryn Mawr, 1914.

Not seen.

142 Baum, Paull Franklin. 'The English Ballad of Judas Iscariot.' *PMLA* 31 (1916): 181–9.

Describes 'Judas' ['Hit wes upon a sereþorsday þat ure louerd aros,' *1649*], the earliest recorded ballad in English, and suggests origins much earlier than the thirteenth century. Baum relates the story of Judas's motivation for selling Jesus to other sources. In a Wendish folk-song Judas loses the thirty pieces of silver by gambling; a fragment in the apocryphal Coptic *Gospels of the Twelve Apostles* blames the evil influence of his insatiably avaricious wife. The stories have various differences, but each assigns Judas' burden of guilt 'to a woman, his sister or wife.' Baum inclines to the idea of 'some kind of relationship, devious and distant enough' (186), between the English ballad and the Coptic fragment, and suggests 'folk-lore ramifications' for the Wendish ballad, and its conclusion of 'Judas's hanging on the fir and aspen' (189).

1649.

143 Brown, Carleton. 'Dialogue between a Clerk and a Husbandman.' *Modern Language Notes* 33 (1918): 415–17. [Edition.]

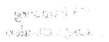

Presents 'As I cowthe walke because of recreacioun' [*344*], a debate on love between a Clerk and a Husbandman, from BL MS Add. 38666. The clerk's stanzas are 'very obviously modelled upon the well-known *Quia amore langueo* lyrics ['In a tabernacle of a toure,' *1460*; 'In a valey of þis restles mynde,' *1463*] in which the Blessed Virgin or Christ pleads for the love of man,' which have the same refrain. This is balanced by the Husbandman's 'Turn up hyr haltur and let her go,' used elsewhere with similar effect ['That ilke man wole lerne wel,' *3279*]. Brown shows the humorous effect of alternation of the refrains, and suggests that perhaps 'the earlier "Turne up hur haltur" poem was set to the tune of "*Quia amore langueo*" and . . . intended as a parody' (415). He prints the poem, noting his editorial procedure.

344.

144   Förster, Max. 'Zu den "Kleineren ME. Texten". (Anglia 42, 145 ff.).' *Anglia* 43 (1919): 191–4.

Adds further critical information to the edition of shorter ME texts, **27**, particularly of the sermon lyric 'Atte wrastlynge mi lemman i ches' [*445*]; the warnings 'If man him biðocte' [*1422*], 'Wanne i ðenke ðinges ðre' [*3969*] and 'Wanne mine eyhnen misten' [*3998*]; and 'Wyteth now all þat ben here' [*4184*], one of the Charters of Christ.

445, 1422, 3969, 3998, 4184.

145   Holthausen, F. 'Der mittelenglische Streit zwischen Drossel und Nachtigall.' *Anglia* 43 (1919): 52–60. [Edition.]

The first critical edition of 'The Thrush and the Nightingale' ['Somer is comen wiþ loue to toune,' *3222*]. Holthausen relies chiefly on Digby MS 86, which has 192 stanzas, a better and more complete text than that of the Auchinleck MS, with only 75 stanzas. He summarizes the poem's history of publication, and prints the text, with variations (53–9), and notes (59–60).

3222.

146   Audiau, Jean. *Les Troubadours et l'Angleterre: Contribution à l'Etude des Poètes Anglais de l'Amour au Moyen-Age (XIIe et XIVe Siècles)*. Tulle: Juglard, 1920. 2nd edn. Paris: Vrin, 1927.

Troubadour influences may be discerned in love lyrics of the fourteenth century, particularly in those connected with Eleanour of Aquitaine and Richard I. Describing their influence on poets before Chaucer and Gower, Audiau refers frequently to works in MS Harley 2253. He compares the treatment by English poets and troubadours of common themes, including the beginning of spring after the confinement of winter, the coming of dawn to end the poet's dreams of his lady, the suffering of the lover, and the wounding beauty of the beloved. He considers Chaucer and Gower imitators of the troubadours.

105, 515, 1394, 1395, 2207, 2236, 3291, 3963, 4037, 4194.

147   Baskerville, Charles Read. 'Dramatic Aspects of Medieval Folk Festivals in England.' *Studies in Philology* 17 (1920): 19–87.

Includes brief references to lyrics in descriptions of dramatic aspects of folk festivals such as May Day. Baskerville also mentions songs of wooing and of politics.

835.5, 1889, 2163, 3221, 3223, 7148, 7193.

148   ——. 'English Songs on the Night Visit.' *PMLA* 36 (1921): 565–614.

Themes of these songs include 'Open the door' and 'Go from my window.' The aube developed before other songs of 'phases of a lover's secret visit to his lady at night' (565), and was more widespread, because it offered 'the dramatic moment for the expression of lyric passion' (570). There are aubes and references to them in various longer poems; Baskerville cites examples, including Chaucer's *Troilus and Criseyde* [*3327*] and several Scottish works. Birds, particularly the nightingale and the cock which sings at dawn, are frequently mentioned. Some songs were adapted by the Bishop of Ossory for religious purposes. Baskerville finds the works 'lyric rather than narrative . . . [with their] origin in a lyric, probably a carol, describing a phase of primitive wooing' (614). He relates the songs to the lover's visiting of the girl before marriage, at a time when marriage could be cancelled, 'an aspect of primitive social life' (614). [See Colaco, **863**.]

488.5, 683, 684, 913, 1214.5, 1299, 1450, 1842.5, 3327, 4165.5, 4284.3, 7105, 7201, 7294, 7568.

149   Phillips, William J. *Carols: Their Origin, Music, and Connection with Mystery-Plays.* London: Routledge, 1921. Westport CT: Greenwood, 1970.

A general study of carols, with particular sections on 'Carols of the Virgin Mary' (26–30); 'The Narrative or Story-telling Carols' (31–52); 'Carols of Nature' (53–5), including 'Trees' (56–62); and 'Spring Carols' (63–7). Among those associated with Christmas are 'Lullabies and Cradle-songs' (68–78); 'The Wassails' (95–104); 'Angels and Shepherds' (105–9); 'Epiphany' (110–16); 'Welcome' (117–21); and 'Farewell to Christmas' (122–4). There are carols of 'The Childhood of Christ' (79–89) and 'Numeral Carols' (90–4). The first carols were sung in Grecia; they were associated with dancing (12–15) and mystery-plays (16–25). Phillips's examples extend to the twentieth century.

18, 112, 354, 681, 715, 1225, 1226, 1352, 1367, 2332, 2333, 2551.8, 3058, 3223, 3313, 3347, 3460, 3536, 3627, 3736, 3877, 7063, 7171, 7321.

150   Farnham, Willard. 'The Dayes of the Mone.' *Studies in Philology* 20 (1923): 70–82. [Edition.]

'He þat wol herkyn of wit' [*1171*], a 'homely rhyme' in MS Harley 2320, concerns events influenced by the moon: 'blood-letting, buying and selling, setting of houses, journeying, fleeing from enemies, dreaming, finding of lost possessions, and of course being born' (70). The information is simplified and presented in verse, for practical use by unlearned people. Chaucer frequently refers to the use of such knowledge. Farnham prints the text, which supplies information for 30 days, 'from the actual appearance of one new moon to the next, used by almanac makers in marking the moon's cycle' (73).

1171.

151   Rankin, J.W. 'The Hymns of St. Godric.' *PMLA* 38 (1923): 699–711.

Relates the life of St Godric, as described by Reginald of Coldingham, before examining his compositions. Rankin uses a metrical analysis to see if these resemble OE forms, imitate 'foreign verse forms – French, Provençal, Welsh, or Latin,' or are 'a simple native product' (703). Translation seems unlikely since Godric was uneducated, and the songs, communicated to him in visions, concern personal matters. They are unlike most other genres, but resemble Latin hymns in some ways and have a few Romance words. Rankin sets out the poems, 'Crist and saint marie swa on scamel me iledde' [*598*], 'Seinte marie leuedi brist' [*2988*], and 'Sainte Nicolaes godes druð' [*3031*], in four-beat lines, and finds Godric's works most like AS charms or incantations, representing 'native popular verse uninfluenced by any foreign models' (710).

598, 2988, 3031.

152 Hammond, Eleanor Prescott. '"How a Lover Praiseth His Lady."' *Modern Philology* 21 (1924): 379–95. [Edition.]

'When the son the laumpe of heuen ful lyght' [*4043*], is in a commonplace book, Bodleian MS Fairfax 16. The lover describes the lady formally, in a conventionally formal setting, but the poem has 'a clumsy vigor and freshness' (380). The poet offers 'a not uninteresting example, in that transitional period, of earlier formulas mixed with newer perception, of the awakening of the eye and the deafness of the ear' (380). Some allusions suggest a medical background, and Chaucer's influence is seen. Hammond notes many miswritings – 'an unusually long list of turpitudes for the Fairfax scribe' (382). The poet uses two-thirds of the poem for a description of the lady, asserting her perfection and conformation to the golden mean. Hammond compares the poem with others, particularly of Chaucer, and prints the work, 'the interest of which lies in the clumsy attempt of a partly aroused individuality to work with stiffened material' (384).

4043.

153 Brown, Beatrice Daw. 'The Source of a Fourteenth Century Lyric.' *Modern Language Notes* 40 (1925): 318–9.

Carleton Brown, in *Brown XIV*, **31**, describes 'Ihesu doþ him by mene' [*1699*] as 'a distinctly fresh treatment of the old theme of Christ's appeal to man' (xxi), and supplies the title 'Jesus Pleads with the Worldling.' Beatrice Daw Brown considers it 'a sympathetic translation of a passage attributed to St. Bernard in the *Legenda Aurea*' (318). She quotes the passage, and concludes that '[t]he English poet has rendered his original faithfully in essentials but has wrought of the prose material a metrical unit so complete and of such distinctive character as to justify, in all but fact, Professor Brown's comment' (318–19).

1699.

154 Dodds, Madeleine Hope. 'Northern Minstrels and Folk Drama.' *Archeologia Aeliana* 4th Series 1 (1925): 121–46.

Tells of the custom of bringing Raby stags to Durham, to be 'offered at the shrine of St. Cuthbert' and 'afterwards removed to the prior of Durham's kitchen' (132). Dodds describes the decline of the practice, after a battle between the monks and Lord Neville's men in 1290. There were efforts to restore it in 1331, when Lord Neville's son 'brought a writ of novel disseisin' against the prior, in an attempt to revive the custom of presenting a stag as rent, on 4th September, the Feast of the Translation of St Cuthbert. The prior cited the lyric 'Wel and wa sal ys hornes blaw' [*3857.5*] sung 'after the death of lord Neville's great-grandfather, Robert de Neville, who died c. 1280,' as proof that 'the offering had once been made on Holy Rood day (September 14th)' (133).

3857.5.

155 Robbins, Harry Wolcott. 'An English Version of St. Edmund's *Speculum*, ascribed to Richard Rolle.' *PMLA* 40 (1925): 240–51.

Presents the text of an English version of the *Speculum Ecclesie* of Edmund Rich, Archbishop of Canterbury, in Cambridge University MS Ii.6.40. Prose translations are preserved in twelve manuscripts, and this is 'unique in ascribing the treatise to Richard Rolle' (241). The lyric 'Nou goth þe sonne under wode' [*2320*] is found in the 'Contemplacion bifor mydday.'

2320.

156 Kittredge, G.L. 'Note on a Lying Song.' *Journal of American Folk-Lore* 39 (1926): 195–9.

The lying song 'I sawe a doge sethyng sowse' [*1350*], copied by Richard Hill, and perhaps the ancestor of the sixteenth-century 'Martin Said to his Man,' has a refrain that mentions the whetstone, used to signify a liar.

1350.

157 Brett, Cyril. 'Two Newly Found Middle English Texts.' *Modern Language Review* 22 (1927): 73–5. [Edition.]

Prints a prayer, 'Mercy Marie maydene clene' [*2160*], a quatrain from 'the back of a late fourteenth-century Latin grant of lands by Robert de Ward, lord of Kingsley, to Robert Fitzrobert of Lascawe of Thornbury in the vill of Thornbury, temp. Edward III' (75).

2160.

158 Brown, Carleton. 'Texts and the Man.' *Bulletin of Modern Humanities Research Association* 2 (1928): 97–111.

Explores the classification of 'humanistic' studies and the work of the philologist, palaeographer, and bibliographer, stressing the scientific methods employed in study of the humanities. It is difficult to find biographical information about medieval authors, but there are manuscripts of sermons preached by Dominican and Franciscan friars, where lyrics were used by the preacher, 'to gain the attention of his audience' (107), as preaching texts, and to convey homiletic messages. Brown's study of the friars and their texts illustrates his contention that '[t]he final goal of our research should be not only to discover the texts but to reveal the men who wrote them' (110).

445, 522, 1405, 3998, 4211.

159 Reed, Edward Bliss. '"Wynter Wakeneth Al My Care."' *Modern Language Notes* 43 (1928): 81–4.

Prints the poem 'Wynter wakeneþ al my care' [*4177,*] using the punctuation of *Brown XIV*, **31**. Reed seeks to explain the first line of the third stanza 'al that gren me graueth gren,' and summarizes comments made in other editions of the work. He disagrees with Brown's suggestion that it is based on John 12: 24, 25, and proposes that the poet sees 'hideous winter confounding the beauty of summer – stripping the branches and turning the green into the sere and yellow leaf' (83). The word 'green' appears as the northern *gren* in this line, but elsewhere in the manuscript (Harley 2253) as *grene*. [See also Sisam and Sisam, **69**; Speirs, **385**; Manning, **443**; Shannon, **621**; Scattergood, **645**; Harrington, **872**.]

4177.

160 Brown, Carleton. 'Somer Soneday.' *Studies in English Philology: A Miscellany in Honor of Frederick Klaeber*. Ed. Kemp Malone and Martin B. Ruud. Minneapolis: U of Minnesota P, 1929. 362–74. [Edition.]

'[O]pon a somer soneday se I þe sonne' [*3838*] is 'the last of several poems written by the same hand at the end of the Laud MS' (367). Brown prints the work, with comments on verse form, linguistic forms, date and provenance, and possible contemporary references. Evidence of its composition in the West Midlands in the fourteenth century implies reference to Edward II, rather than Richard II. It resembles *Golagrus and Gawane* [*1576*], *Morte Arthure* [*2322*], and the 'Awntyrs of Arthure' [*1566*] in allusions to Lady Fortune and her wheel, 'one of the most familiar [figures] in medieval literature'

(373), and the 'Pistill of Susan' [*3553*] in the structure of stanzas. The first line is like that of *Piers Plowman* [*1459*], but 'the reminiscence would now seem to have been on the part of Langland, rather than of the author of *Somer Soneday*' (374).

1459, 1567, 2322, 3553, 3838.

161   Seymour, St John D. *Anglo-Irish Literature 1200–1582*. Cambridge: Cambridge UP, 1929.

Surveys non-Celtic literature, particularly that composed in Ireland, rather than merely copied there. Seymour considers religious (52–76), secular (77–102), and satirical poems (103–117), and modifies the language in quotations, but retains some medieval forms. He deals chiefly with MS Harley 913 [cf. Heuser, **16**], especially poems of Friar Michael of Kildare, thought to be the author of 'Swet ihc̄ hend and fre' [*3234*] and an influence on other works. Seymour comments in detail on 'Loke to þi louerd man þar hanget he a-rode' [*1943*], 'Now ihc̄ for derworþ blode' [*2344*], 'þe grace of godde and holi chirche' [*3365*], 'þe grace of god ful of miȝt' [*3366*], 'þe grace of ihū fulle of miȝte' [*3367*], and 'þe king of heuen mid us be' [*3400*]. He also writes of the Red Book of Ossory, and its religious songs in Latin, composed by Richard de Ledrede, Bishop of Ossory, 1317–1360; secular songs are among the book's fragments. Seymour offers a full account of 'A Song on the Times' [*4144*], and compares it to *3234, 3365,* and *3400*. Poems with more claim to be called lyrics, 'Elde makiþ me geld' [*718*], 'King conseilles/Bissop loreles' [*1820*], 'Lollai lollai litel child whi wepistou so sore' [*2025*], and 'Erthe upon Erthe' [*3939*], may have been copied rather than composed in Ireland. Seymour prints a ballad on the death of Peter or Piers de Bermingham and comments on another, which warns the young men of Waterford against the le Poers or Powers family. Harley 913 has a short poem in OF, '*Proverbia Comitis Demonie*,' apparently referring to the first earl of Desmond, and the ME 'A Rhyme-Beginning Fragment' [*2003*], perhaps influenced by it. Seymour prints and comments on 'The Land of Cockaygne' [*762*] and 'Hail, St Michael, with the long spear' [*1078*].

2573, 674, 684, 762, 891, 1008, 1078, 1120.5, 1123, 1214.4, 1265, 1638, 1943, 2003, 2344, 2663, 3126, 3234, 3365, 3366, 3367, 3400, 4144, 4280.

162   Brunner, Karl, and Karl Hammerle. 'With an O and an J.' *Anglia* 54 (1930): 288–93.

Brunner supplements the collection of verses presented by Heuser, **109**, by printing two poems with 'O and J' refrains, and Hammerle offers an interpretation of the refrain. The poems are in Cambridge University Library MS Gg.I.32; Brunner describes this fifteenth-century manuscript and similarities in the poems that link them to works printed by Heuser. 'Thyke man qware off thou art wrought' [*3567*], is religious; 'Salamon sat & sayde many soth sawes' [*3069*] is secular; both are didactic. He offers a generally diplomatic transcription, expanding abbreviations, correcting errors, and rationalizing the use of *y* in the manuscript to use þ where appropriate. Linguistic indicators suggest a South or Midlands provenance for *3567* and North-western Midlands for *3069*. Hammerle finds a distinct group of 'O and J' poems of invective against mendicants, and describes the conflict involving friars. Some 'fighting songs' had an 'O and J' refrain, which Hammerle links to an untranslatable exclamation of Latin origin and to the exclamations 'Ho' and 'Hi' in English works. The emotive character may be restrained in religious poems, and may have been derived from 'A and O' formulae in Latin hymns. [See Heuser, **109**; Smith, **302**; Mustanoja, **355**; Greene, **434**; Rigg, **516**; Osberg, **722**; Laing and McIntosh, **780**; Revard, **849**; Grennen, **890**.]

3069, 3567.

163 Oakden, J.P. *Alliterative Poetry in Middle English: The Dialectal and Metrical Survey.* Publications of the University of Manchester 205. English Series 19. Manchester: Manchester UP, 1930.

A general dialectal and metrical survey of ME alliterative poetry, with many illustrations, some taken from ME lyrics, including references to the Harley lyrics and hymns of St Godric. Oakden considers many aspects of the alliterative long line, the use of alliteration in the various ME dialects, and the relation of alliteration in OE and ME. [See **187**.]

60, 351, 371, 428, 433, 471, 598, 631, 663, 696, 718, 1453, 1608.5, 1653.5, 1887, 1924, 2093.3, 2244, 2287, 2678, 2684.5, 2988, 3031, 3227, 3497, 3718, 3782.5, 3793, 3819, 3896, 4155, 4162.

164 Jones, William Powell. *The Pastourelle. A Study of the Origins and Tradition of a Lyric Type.* Cambridge, MA: Harvard UP, 1931. New York: Octagon, 1973.

A general study of the European pastourelle, especially the French folk-song, which is 'dramatic in character, not epic if compared with the Scandinavian *vise* or with the English and Scottish popular ballad' (35). Jones compares French and Scottish pastourelles, with comment on some works in the *Bannatyne MS*, and speculates on the origin of Henryson's 'Robene and Makyne' [*2831*]. He defines the pastourelle as 'essentially a theme: a gallant of high degree meets a country girl in the open, makes love to her, and is in the end repulsed' (193).

2831, 7268.

165 Baldwin, Charles Sears. *Three Medieval Centuries of Literature in England 1100–1400.* Boston: Little, 1932.

'The more we admire a lyric, the less likely we are to associate it with its time or its place' (142). Latin hymns are the 'outstanding medieval achievement in lyric and the most pervasive influence' (143) discerned in the metre of ME verse. In 'The Medieval Lyric,' (142–56), Baldwin describes the work of troubadours, and illustrates his remarks on historical and courtly lyrics, the balade and roundel, *memento mori*, and *ubi sunt*.

515, 1861, 2375, 2684, 3135, 3223, 3405.

166 Brook, G.L. 'Collation of the Text of the English Lyrics of MS. Harley 2253.' *Leeds Studies in English and Kindred Languages* 1 (1932): 28–30.

Collates the text of Böddeker's edition [*Altenglische Dichtungen des MS. Harl. 2253* (Berlin, 1878)] with rotographs of the manuscript. Brook deals with Böddeker's spelling and capitalization in the manuscript, and notes information in the footnotes that suggests he 'had not access to the MS. during the later stages of the preparation of his edition' (28).

105, 205, 359, 515, 968, 1216, 1320.5, 1394, 1395, 1449, 1504, 1705, 1747, 1861, 1889, 1894, 1921, 1922, 1974, 2039, 2066, 2166, 2207, 2236, 2287, 2359, 2604, 2649, 3155, 3211, 3236, 3310, 3874, 3963, 4037, 4194.

167 Brown, Beatrice Daw. 'Religious Lyrics in MS. Don. c. 13.' *Bodleian Quarterly Record* 7 (1932): 1–7. [Edition.]

Presents two texts, not previously printed, with comments. 'I herd an harping on a hille as I lay vnder lynde' [*1320*], a 'pious *chanson d'aventure*' (3), refers to 'symbolic initials M, I, X, and C,' resembling 'Thynke man qware off thou art wrought' [*3567*], in the same manuscript, in the use of 'a 6-line stanza with O and I refrain,' although one cannot 'assert either to be the imitator' (4). 'Ihesu my lefe Ihesu my loue' [*1733*], which exhibits 'close verbal relationship . . . with authentic poetic work of Richard Rolle' (4), 'may be proposed for admission to the canon' (7).

110, 406, 1053, 1320, 1733, 3232, 3567.

168 Holthausen, Ferdinand. 'Zu mittelenglischen Dichtungen.' *Anglia* 56 (1932): 58–68.

Presents corrections to Heuser's readings, **114**, of Richard Spalding's hymn on St Katherine of Alexandria ['Katereyn þe curteys of all þat I knowe,' *1813*] and another on the Five Joys of Mary ['Myldeste of moode & mekyst of maydyns alle,' *2171*]. Holthausen intends to issue a new critical publication when he has received a collation of the manuscript. [See **185**.]

1813, 2171.

169 Le May, Sister Marie de Lourdes. *The Allegory of the Christ-Knight in English Literature.* Diss. Catholic U of America, 1932. Washington, DC: Catholic U of America, 1932.

'The Emergence of the Allegory of Christ as Knight of the Early Romances' introduces the allegory through a passage in *Ancrene Riwle* (1–12), with further references to the 'Luue Ron' [*66*] of Thomas de Hales and 'When y se blosmes springe' [*3963*], in exploration of the relation of spiritual and secular lyrics. 'Christ as Knight in the Lyric' (53–75) deals with lyrics of the Passion and Redemption and with carols. Le May relates these lyrics to passages in mystery plays, and examines the influences of *amour courtois* literature and the Song of Songs. She compares versions of some carols, commenting particularly on the 'Corpus Christi Carol' [*1132*] as an allegorization of 'The Bleeding Knight.' The lyrics show Christ as a king and knight, and paradoxically as a helpless infant in the Nativity poems. [See also Woolf, **446**.]

688.3, 1132, 1143, 1274, 1353, 1460, 1463, 2342, 2481, 2732, 3599, 3627, 3734, 3883, 3906.

170 Onions, C.T. 'Middle English *alod, olod.*' *Medium Ævum* 1 (1932): 206–8.

Alod appears in the Townely Play of Noah ['*Ego sum alpha et o,*' *715*], glossed as 'requited.' Brown, *BrownXIV*, **31**, glosses *olod* in 'When adam delf & eue span spir if þᵘ wil spede' [*3921*], as 'obtained, seized.' Onions observes a resemblance to *'aloddin,* belonging to Cumberland and Westmorland' (206), with 'lost' as one of its senses. He suggests a Norse origin, related to descriptions for worn cloth and animals fit only for slaughter, and possibilities for the derivation of the ME word. Thus he glosses the words 'generally by "wasted, dissipated, destroyed"' (207).

715, 3921.

171 Brook, G.L. 'The Original Dialects of the Harley Lyrics.' *Leeds Studies in English and Kindred Languages* 2 (1933): 38–61.

The lyrics of MS Harley 2253 are written in a single hand, probably by a scribe from the West Midlands, and the prevailing dialect has 'marked West Midland features.' Inconsistent forms suggest that 'some or all of the lyrics were not composed by the scribe of the Harley MS., but were copied by him from MSS. written in other dialects' (38). Brook explores aspects of the dialect, noting characteristics that point to sound changes, revealed by patterns of rhyme, vocabulary, allusions and subjects, evidence from variants, and position in the manuscript. On these bases he assigns most lyrics to

Northerly, Midland, and Southerly dialect groups, with additional classification within these broad divisions. The Northerly poems are: 'A Wayle Whyt ase Whalles Bon' [*105*], 'God þat Al þis Myhtes May' [*968*], 'The Song of the Husbandman' [*1320.5*], 'I Syke when Y Singe' [*1365*], 'Annot and John' [*1394*], 'Blessed Be þou, Leuedy' [*1407*], 'The Meeting in the Wood' [*1449*], 'Advice to Women' [*1504*], 'Iesu Crist, Heouene Kyng' [*1678*], 'Iesu, for þi Muchele Miht' [*1705*], 'The Way of Woman's Love' [*1921*], 'The Fair Maid of Ribblesdale' [*2207*], 'De Clerico et Puella' [*2236*], 'Satire on the Retinues of the Great' [*2649*], and 'A Winter Song' [*4177*]. Midland poems are: 'An Elegy on the Death of Edward I' [*205*], 'The Five Joys of the Virgin' [*359*], 'Alysoun' [*515*], 'An Old Man's Prayer' [*1216*], 'Blow, Northerne Wynd' [*1395*], 'Iesu suete is þe loue of þe' [*1747*], 'The Execution of Sir Simon Fraser' [*1889*], 'The Way of Christ's Love' [*1922*], 'The Three Foes of Man' [*2166*], 'Satire on the Consistory Courts' [*2287*], 'An Autumn Song' [*2359*], 'The Labourers in the Vineyard' [*2604*], 'Dialogue between the Virgin and Christ on the Cross' [*3211*], 'The Sayings of St Bernard' [*3310*]. The Southerly works are: 'The Song of the Flemish Insurrection' [*1894*], 'A Prayer for Deliverance' [*2039*], 'The Man in the Moon' [*2066*], 'The Song of the Battle of Lewes' [*3155*], 'A Spring Song on the Passion' [*3963*], 'The Poet's Repentance' [*3874*]. Brook finds no evidence for the original dialect of 'The Lover's Complaint' [*4194*], and slight evidence for those of *515*, 'On the Follies of Fashion' [*1974*], 'Suete Iesu, King of Blysse' [*3236*], *3963* and 'When þe Nyhtegale Singes' [*4037*]. He uses [but does not explain] the classification of Böddeker [*Altenglische Dichtungen des MS Harl. 2253* (Berlin, 1878)], together with Schlüter's comments on dialect ['Über die Sprache und Metrik der mittelenglischen weltlichen und geistlichen lyrischen Lieder des MS. Harl. 2253,' *Archiv* 71 (1884): 153–84, 357–88].

105, 205, 359, 515, 968, 1216, 1320.5, 1365, 1394, 1395, 1407, 1449, 1504, 1678, 1705, 1747, 1861, 1889, 1894, 1921, 1922, 1974, 2039, 2066, 2166, 2207, 2236, 2287, 2359, 2604, 2649, 3155, 3211, 3236, 3310, 3874, 3963, 4037, 4177, 4194.

172 Collins, Fletcher. 'The Kinges Note: *The Miller's Tale*, line 31.' *Speculum* 8 (1933): 195–7.

The song sung by Nicholas in the *Miller's Tale* may have been 'not a secular, profane ditty, but a sequence, a hymn, popular in fourteenth-century England' (195). Collins proposes that the king is St Edmund, king and martyr, and cites a carol for St Edmund's Day, 'Heil wrth þou King of Englis erde' [*1085*], to show the popularity of the saint who 'in Chaucer's time was just beginning to give place to St George as England's patron saint' (196).

1085, 4019.

173 Greene, Richard L. 'A Middle English "Timor Mortis" Poem.' *Modern Language Review* 28 (1933): 234–8. [Edition.]

Considers two versions of '*Timor mortis conturbat me*/This is my song in my olde age' [*3743*], a fifteenth-century example of the ME lyrics based on 'the phrase from the Office of the Dead, "Timor mortis conturbat me"' (234). The texts are in MSS Longleat 29 and Porkington 10; they differ chiefly in the order of stanzas, and have some verbal variations. Greene prints the Longleat version, which is slightly superior in literary and metrical respects; neither version is likely to have been copied by or for the poet. The fourth stanza preserves the names of two popular songs, one English and the other French. Greene's notes record significant differences in the versions, and comment on the term *stage* as 'a step or station on the rim of Fortune's wheel' and on the phrase *Peccantem me cotidie*. Both the latter phrase and *Timor mortis conturbat me* are erroneously attributed to Job because of their proximity to 'an extract from Job xvii which forms Lectio VII in the third Nocturne of the *Officium Mortuorum* in the Sarum Breviary' (238).

3743.

174 Kar, G. *Thoughts on the Mediæval Lyric.* Oxford: Blackwell, 1933.

'The Middle English Religious Lyric' (17–28), a brief survey, sees ME lyrics as ancestors of metaphysical lyrics and nineteenth-century Anglo-Catholic lyrics, and offers examples of sad poems that deplore the vanity of human life. Kar compares ME works with Ecclesiastes, the Psalms, and patristic works, and notes resemblances to passages in *The Wanderer*. He finds that the ME religious poet 'borrows more than he lends,' chiefly from the 'Latin hymnodists and Fathers' (22), exemplified in passages based on writings of Augustine and Venantius Fortunatus. However originality can be found in 'the alliance boldly sought between the Christian mysteries and chivalry' (24), whereas religious carols resemble those of twelfth-century France. Kar cites Latin and French examples, and compares English verse to show that it borrows 'with intention . . . to pay back in full and with extra values of poetic realism' (27). Other chapters deal with 'Cupid's Biography' (1–3); 'Dante: Vita Nuova' (4–10); 'Marcabru, or Troubadour Realism' (11–16); 'Chaucer and the Troubadours' (29–37); 'Bernart of Ventadour, or Troubadour Idealism' (38–54); 'Amorous Gower' (55–63); and 'Troubadour Melodies and Indian Ragas' (64–7). Kar supplies an Appendix (68–98) of Provençal lyrics, with translations.

66.5, 359, 903, 1455, 1460, 1866, 2039, 2995, 3405, 3411, 3597, 3658, 3700, 4088, 4177.

175 Owst, G.R. *Literature and Pulpit in Medieval England: A Neglected Chapter in the History of English Letters and of the English People.* Cambridge: Cambridge UP, 1933. 2nd edn. Oxford: Blackwell, 1961.

A general study of the sermon in medieval life, acknowledging its 'prominent part in the entertainment as well as the education of the people' (1). Owst shows the interaction of sermons with other literature, including sermon lyrics, and echoes of sermon themes and idioms in such genres as political songs and satirical verse. He deals with these themes in 'Introductory Influences, Linguistic, Romantic and Realistic' (1–55); 'Scripture and Allegory' (56–109); 'Fiction and Instruction in the Sermon *Exempla*' (149–209); and 'The Preaching of Satire and Complaint,' Part 1 (210–86), Part 2 (287–374), and Part 3 (375–470). In 'Sermon and Drama' (471–547) he considers the close connection between sermons and the religious plays of the period. In 'A Literary Echo of the Social Gospel' (548–93) he relates the sermon to comment in such works as *Piers Plowman* [*1459*] and *Pricke of Conscience* [*3428*].

5, 427.5, 457, 635.5, 715, 716, 778, 1091, 1193, 1273, 1320.5, 1337, 1459, 1796, 1857, 1934, 1974, 2235, 2287, 2300.6, 2649, 2743.5, 3218.5, 3428, 3477, 3799.6, 3903.5, 3921, 4019, 4079, 4085, 4144, 4250.

176 Rickert, Edith. 'Verses found at Coughton Court.' *Modern Philology* 31 (1933): 198–9. [Edition.]

Prints verses beginning 'Fare well fare well/All fresh all chere' [*763.5*] written in 'a hand possibly of the late fifteenth or early sixteenth century' (198), on the membrane of a court roll found at Coughton Court, Warwickshire.

763.5.

177 Wehrle, William O. *The Macaronic Hymn Tradition in Medieval English Literature.* Diss. Catholic U of America, 1933. Washington, DC: Catholic U of America, 1933. Ann Arbor, MI: University Microfilms, 1977. AA 60185508.

The chronological study deals in great detail with macaronic hymns and lyrics, from the OE period to the fifteenth century, when they were most numerous, and divides the poems into 13 types. Most works are anonymous, but many were written by Lydgate and Ryman, and Wehrle devotes a chapter to these (129–65). Of the various themes, most are connected with the Nativity and related feasts and circumstances, particularly with the Virgin Mary. English, Latin, and AN are used, with most poems written in arrangements of English and Latin. Wehrle concludes his study at the end of the fifteenth century, since later macaronic works, such as those of Dunbar, do not differ in style or topic.

16, 18, 19, 20, 22, 78, 93, 103, 116, 118, 340, 343, 357, 378, 454, 463, 489, 527, 597, 613, 614, 678, 680, 694.5, 753, 755, 775, 785, 795, 871, 878, 893, 895, 897, 909, 947, 997, 1028, 1032, 1042, 1043, 1045, 1056, 1444, 1471, 1485, 1488, 1542, 1555, 1578, 1738, 1857, 1892, 2039, 2098, 2103, 2113, 2193, 2313, 2377, 2402, 2416, 2429, 2443, 2480, 2561, 2563, 2570, 2586, 2645, 2665, 2675, 2778, 2787, 2800, 2801, 2802, 2833, 2995, 3070, 3072, 3074, 3113, 3122, 3225, 3260, 3261, 3307, 3314, 3334, 3390, 3405, 3438, 3536, 3620, 3630, 3638, 3669, 3710, 3728, 3775, 3776, 3837, 3872, 3950, 4012, 4077, 4166, 4229.

178   Maynard, Theodore. *The Connection between the Ballade, Chaucer's Modification of It, Rime Royal, and the Spenserian Stanza.* Washington: Catholic U of America, 1934. Folcroft, PA: Folcroft Library Editions, 1973.

Influences in Chaucer's literary background include ME verse forms. Maynard cites the 'Canute Song' ['Merie singen þe munaches binnen Ely,' *2164*], a hymn of St Godric, 'Seinte marie clane uirgine' [*2988*], and a verse Paternoster, 'Vre feder þ^t in heuone is þ^t is al soðful iwis' [*2709*].

2164, 2709, 2988.

179   Thomson, S. Harrison. 'A XIIIth Century *Oure Fader* in a Pavia MS.' *Modern Language Notes* 49 (1934): 235–7. [Edition.]

Among entries in English in MS 69 of the Biblioteca Universitaria in Pavia is 'a thirteenth-century English Lord's Prayer, written in neat small chancery hand.' Thompson prints the text, 'Vre fader in heuene y-halȝed be þy name' [*2704*], noting that it is the work of two hands, 'the second certainly contemporary' (236). English is also used in a passage on matrimony, in the Latin tractate '*De Virtutibus et Viciis,* ascribed to Grosseteste,' where details of consanguinity seemed 'to demand the use of vernacular terms,' supplied in English. Thomson infers a reference to William of Leicester which suggests that the treatise is intended 'for the parish clergy of the diocese of Leicester' (237), and speculates on the movement of the manuscript to Italy 'either in the possession of a wandering English student or a returning Italian' (235).

2704.

180   Brunner, Karl. 'Ein typisches Bussgedicht aus dem Fünfzehnten Jahrhundert.' *Anglia* 59 (1935): 322–7. [Edition.]

Presents an almost unknown penitential poem, typical in format and content. The poem 'Blessid god souereyn goodness' [*532*] is preserved in two fifteenth-century manuscripts, San Marino, Huntington Library HM 501 (H) and Cambridge University Library Gg.4.31 (C), in which it has the title 'A goodly Preaer.' Brunner uses the H text, which is generally superior, adding some missing letters from C. The poem is a private prayer, in keeping with the trend to ascetic thought of the fifteenth century which equates tribulations on earth to penance for all kinds of sin. Brunner prints the poem, noting differences in the texts.

532.

Annotations of Critical Works

181 ———. 'Mittelenglische Marienstunden.' *Englische Studien* 70 (1935–6): 106–9. [Edition.]

Offers a brief general introduction to the genre of poems dealing with life events of Mary, her Joys and Sorrows. Early poems of this kind tended to follow the portrayal of Christ's sufferings, but gradually poems dealing with the Sorrows of Mary were composed. Brunner compares 'The Houris of oure Ladyis dollouris' ['Quhat dollour persit our ladyis hert,' *3904*] with *Patris sapientiae* of the life of Christ, and finds close similarities. He describes the manuscript, BL Arundel 285, and prints the text, noting that the writer appears to have been English.

3904.

182 ———. 'Mittelenglische Todesgedichte.' *Archiv* 167 (1935): 20–35. [Edition.]

Death and related topics such as eternal damnation, the pains of hell, and the transitory nature of earthly happiness were frequently themes of medieval sermons. Three aspects were stressed: the universal possibility of death at any time, represented in the Dance of Death; the body's decay and loss of earthly spendour; and the deaths of famous people of earlier times, expressed in the *ubi sunt* motif. Brunner presents previously unpublished poems, with comments on the works and their sources. The *vado mori* distichs reveal death's universal power, including one on death's attack on a knight, a king, and a bishop, 'I Wende to dede a kyng y-wys' [*1387*]. Two related dialogues are set before God's throne, between the soul of a dying person, Death, the devil, a guardian angel, the Blessed Virgin, Christ, and God, 'O hope in nede þᵘ helpe me' [*2463*] and 'Lady for þi sonne sake' [*1834*]. The Barlaam and Josaphat parable, found in many churches, offers an allegory of human life. Brunner describes 'A man pursued by a unicorn,' an illustrated poem, 'Beholde here as þou may se/A man standyng in a tree' [*491*]. The poem 'O ȝe al whilk þᵗ by me cummes and gothe' [*2589*] is not of the Dance of Death, but rather the coming of death, evoked in the *ubi sunt* motif; it has connections with the picture, the Dance of Makabre, in St Paul's in London, showing that this must have been known in northern England when the manuscript originated. The first lines of 'A disputacion betwyx þe body and wormes' [*1563*] recall epidemics of plague and images of decay often used in sermons and paintings.

491, 1387, 1563, 1834, 2363, 2589, 3262.5.

183 ———. 'Zwei Gedichte aus der Handschrifte Trinity College, Cambridge 323 (B.14.39). *Englische Studien* 70 (1935–6): 221–43. [Edition.]

Summarizes the contents of the manuscript, which were entered by several different writers; most pieces are in English, but there are verse and prose works in French and Latin. Brunner outlines the history of scholarship concerning the manuscript, and prints two poems not previously printed. The latter are 'Ic ou rede ye sitten stille/& herknet wel wid god wille' [*1405*], and 'Louerd asse þu ard god ever buten hende' [*1946*], a narrative of OT events including the Fall of the Angels and the story of Adam and Eve, and of the life of Christ. He describes the metre and rhyme scheme of each poem, and concludes that the transcriber of *1405* was not its author, but linguistically close, and that the poem originated in south-west England.

293, 912, 1405, 1836, 1924, 1946, 2366, 2369, 2687, 3078, 3696, 4141.

184 Hammerle, Karl. 'Verstreute me. und frühne. Lyrik.' *Archiv* 166 (1935) 195–204. [Edition.]

Provides notes on some scattered ME lyrics. Two of these, '*Throw hys hond wyth hammur knak þai mad a gresely wound' [**3719.5*] and 'While þᵘ hast gode & getest gode for gode þᵗ migȝt beholde' [*4083*], are 'O and I' poems. 'Saynt George of kyngryk of Capidous so clere' [*2902*], a Northern poem of the Hours of St George, sets out prayers to St George for a young knight for each of the canonical hours. The date, St Michael's Day, in the sixteenth century of the reign of Henry VII, 29 September, 1500, accompanies a macaronic poem of a schoolboy's grief, 'On days when I am callit to þe scole/*de matre et matertera*' [*2683*], and a worldly carol of Christmas 'Now ys ȝole comyn wᵗ gentyll chere' [*2343*]. Hammerle describes the manuscripts in which the poems are found and prints the texts, with comments on the language and style.

2343, 2683, 2902, *3719.5, 4083, 4116.

185 Holthausen, Ferdinand. 'Ein mittelenglisches Gedicht über die fünf Freuden Marias.' *Anglia* 59 (1935): 319–21. [Edition.]

An edition of the hymn on the Five Joys of Mary ['Myldeste of moode & mekyst of maydyns alle,' *2171*], previously edited by Heuser, **114**. Holthausen adds to his earlier comments, **168**, and provides further information on the acrostics in the poem, MARIA and PIPWEL, which indicates the Cistercian monastery at Pipewell in Northamptonshire.

2171.

186 Malone, Kemp. 'Notes on the Middle English Lyrics.' *ELH* 2 (1935): 58–65.

Offers short notes on and suggestions for emendations in 50 of the lyrics in *Brown XIII*, **36**.

66, 293, 322, 515, 519, 631, 695, 708, 885, 888, 968, 1115, 1233, 1394, 1407, 1504, 1617, 1697, 1705, 1833, 1839, 1861, 1921, 1922, 1974, 2005, 2009, 2066, 2166, 2236, 2336, 2366, 2604, 2992, 3078, 3211, *3216.5, 3221, 3222, 3310, 3432, 3517, 3874, 3986, 3998, 4016, 4044, 4194, 4221, 4223.

187 Oakden, J.P., with Elizabeth R. Innes. *Alliterative Poetry in Middle English: A Survey of the Traditions.* Publications of the University of Manchester 236. English Series 22. Manchester: Manchester UP, 1935.

A companion to Oakden's earlier work, **163**, dealing in detail with the ME alliterative poems as literature, again illustrated with numerous examples, including ME lyrics.

60, 371, 433, 598, 663, 696, 1453, 1924, 2093, 2678, 2988, 3031, 3227, 3718, 3838, 3896, 4162.

188 Raby, F.J.E. 'A Middle English Paraphrase of John of Hovenden's "Philomena" and the Text of his "Viola."' *Modern Language Review* 30 (1935): 339–43.

Identifies 'Heyl be þᵘ sone of þe fader aboue' [*1034*] as 'a translation, or, perhaps more correctly, a paraphrase of a very famous Latin poem, the *Philomena* of John of Hovenden' (339), not influenced by the work of Richard Rolle. Hovenden influenced fourteeth-century ME works by being 'a link between the Bernadine-Franciscan movement and the great English mystical movement of the fourteenth century,' and Rolle clearly knew his work. Raby presents three stanzas of Hovenden's poem, with corresponding ME stanzas, to show that the translator follows the Latin order, but in a free rendering, 'sometimes expanded, more often compressed' (340). He also prints Hovenden's *Viola*, 'a rhapsody [in Latin] in praise of the Blessed Virgin' (341).

1034.

189 Ross, A.S.C. 'The Middle English Poem on the Names of a Hare.' *Proceedings of the Leeds Philosophical and Literary Society (Literary and Historical Section)* 3 (1935): 347–77. [Edition.]

The poem 'þe mon that þe hare i-met' [*3421*] written in a hand of the thirteenth century, in Bodleian MS Digby 86, explains 'a ritual to be observed on meeting a hare,' together with '77 terms of abuse which are to be applied to it' (348). Ross prints the poem (350–1), with a philological commentary on unique terms, many of which are illuminated by MnE dialect. He classifies the names as follows: those meaning hare; generally abusive terms; those obviously related to the hare's characteristics of physical and moral nature, its haunts and food, and analogies, which generally compare it to a cat; those related to characteristics not immediately obvious; and names with significance in folklore. He explains these names and other words of philological interest in detail, and describes two methods of cooking the hare: *in ciue*, from instructions in the *Liber Cure Cocorum* [*2361*], and *in bred*, from references in *Sir Gawain and the Green Knight* [*3144*], *Morte Arthure* [*2322*], *The Squire of Low Degree* [*1644*], and 'The Awntyrs off Arthure at the Terne Wathelyne' [*1566*]. As an appendix he supplies, with a translation, Dafydd ap Gwilym's 'Cywydd yr Ysgyfarnog,' a poem similar to *3421*, written 'To the hare which frightened Morfudd who had gone to the grove to keep an appointment with the poet.'

1566, 1644, 2322, 2361, 3144, 3421.

190 Saltmarsh, John. 'Two Medieval Love-Songs set to Music.' *Antiquaries Journal* 15 (1935): 1–21. [Edition.]

Each song has been preserved on the back of an official document. 'Bryd one brere' [*521*] is on a Papal Bull, 'of Pope Innocent III dated 1199' (2); 'Alone, I lyue, alone and sore I syghe for one' [*IMEV 266*; *SIMEV* burden to *2293.5*] on 'the draft findings of an inquiry into a riot, held in the summer of 1457' (12).

The former document, Cambridge, King's College Muniments, 2 W.32, from the Priory of St James, by Exeter, presents the lyric in unpunctuated prose. Saltmarsh supplies it in three stanzas of four lines, with punctuation and corrections, together with a MnE version. Manuscript associations, ink, and language imply that the song was composed in the thirteenth century and copied in the fourteenth, when 'the character of the handwriting suggests the first thirty years of the century' (7). Saltmarsh finds a directness, as in the Harley lyric 'Alysoun' [*515*], but not the conventions of love employed by Chaucer and Charles d'Orléans. He speculates that the scribe may have been a monk sent from a northern Cluniac house, who worked on legal records and copied the song on to a document which would be preserved. F.McD.C. Turner comments on the music of the song (19–20) and transcribes it (20).

The latter document, London, Public Records Office, E. 163/22/1, was 'formerly in the King's Remembrancer's department of the Exchequer' (12). After a literal transcript, Saltmarsh prints the second song, arranged in seven stanzas, with punctuation, refrain, and catchwords. The hand suggests a date of about 1530, and an Exchequer clerk as scribe. Saltmarsh prints two other lyrics from Exchequer documents ['Is it not sure a deadly pain, *1620.5*; 'Tho that ye cannot Redresse,' an Elizabethan lyric] and comments that '[o]fficials of the Exchequer enjoyed peculiar opportunities of culture' (14). E.J. Dent transcribes and comments on the music of *266/2293.5* (20–1).

266/2293.5, 515, 521, 1620.5, 2243, 4282.

191 South, Helen Pennock. '"The Question of Halsam."' *PMLA* 50 (1935): 362–71.

Two lyrics, 'The worlde so wyde th'aire so remuable' [*3504*] and 'The more I goo the ferther I am behinde' [*3437*], found alone or together in several manuscripts, are ascribed to Halsham, in BL Add. MS 34360 and by Caxton. South prints them from Bodley 3896

215 Renwick, W.L., and Harold Orton. *The Beginnings of English Literature to Skelton 1509.* Introductions to English Literature. Gen. ed. Bonamy Dobrée. London: Cresset, 1939. 2nd edn. 1952. 3rd edn. rev. Martyn F. Wakelin. London: Cresset, 1966.

A general survey of English and Scottish literature to Skelton, with brief references to 'Nou goth þe sonne under wode' [*2320*] and '* . . . ȝoure seruand madame' [**4284.3*] and to general categories of religious lyrics. There is a bibliography on 'Lyrical Poetry,' with references to Latin and French works (377–9).

*2320, *4284.3.*

216 Robbins, Rossell Hope. 'English Almanacks of the Fifteenth Century.' *Philological Quarterly* 18 (1939): 321–31. [Edition.]

Relates predictions of the almanac poems of the fifteenth century to those of the sixteenth and nineteenth. Robbins prints an example of the 'Prognostications of Esdras' ['Tell we now of þᵗ ȝere,' *3265*], based on the week day of New Year's Day, and refers briefly to predictions of weather, ways to find Easter, and mnemonic verses on the seasons and lengths of the months.

29, 426, 1545, 2750, 3265, 3571.

217 ———. 'Popular Prayers in Middle English Verse.' *Modern Philology* 36 (1939): 337–50. [Edition.]

The prayers are short, popular works, 'often scribbled on flyleaves or in other unimportant positions in various manuscripts' (337). Of the prayers he prints, Robbins classifies any clearly not included in a manuscript by the scribe as either 'a popular and widely known piece' or as 'a literary attempt on the part of the owner of the manuscript' (340). He prints 30 short prayers, most of one stanza and some simply couplets. Several appear in more than one version, and some are included as tags in longer prayers, both facts suggesting oral transmission. He concludes that such prayers were for 'any man or woman, who would not normally use a prayer book, to say on going to bed, on passing a crucifix, or during service in church' (344–5).

936, 942, 955, 980, 981, 1467, 1586, 1600, 1640, 1687, 1703, 1706, 1711, 1720, 1723, 1724, 1728, 1729, 1737, 1960, 1965, 1971, 2099, 2114, 2174, 2303, 2258, 3075.

218 ———. 'Private Prayers in Middle English Verse.' *Studies in Philology* 36 (1939): 466–75. [Edition.]

Private prayers are among 'those manifestations of extra-liturgical piety which are appended to Books of Hours or recorded in private prayer books,' to supply 'personal and intimate prayers expressed in the mother tongue' (466). Robbins notes the sources and their occurrence in collections of lyrics; he mentions numerous analogues, and prints six of the prayers. The most popular is Richard de Caistre's hymn ['Ihesu lord þat madist me,' *1727*], found in at least 18 manuscripts. The 'Arma Christi' or 'Arms of Christ' ['O vernacule I honoure him and the,' *2577*], a meditation on the crucifixion, is preserved in two devotional manuals and a Book of Hours [see **219, 220**]. Robbins discerns the influence of mysticism in private prayers, with 'no exaggerated reverence for the Mother of God' (473) and 'very little praise of the saints' (474), to produce an effect of 'perfect Christian sanity' (475).

241, 914, 1372, 1703, 1727, 1761, 2119, 2577, 3238.

219 ———. 'Punctuation Poems – A Further Note.' *Review of English Studies* 15 (1939): 206–7. [Edition.]

After adding to Kreuzer's note, **208**, on poems 'capable of bearing two interpretations, depending on whatever punctuation is given by the reader' (206), Robbins offers a medieval poem, 'In women is rest peas and pacience' [*1593*], with 'an attack, veiled or otherwise, on women' (206), and two seventeeth-century poems.

1593.

220 ———. 'The "Arma Christi" Rolls.' *Modern Language Review* 34 (1939): 415–21.

The 'Arma Christi' or 'The Arms of the Passion' ['O vernacule I honoure him and the,' *2577*] survives in at least 15 manuscripts, of which seven are rolls, and in some other small books. The stanzas describe the instruments of the crucifixion, and are generally illustrated with coloured drawings. Prayers precede and follow the text and offer indulgences. Robbins suggests that the rolls were used by the clergy to inspire the prayers of congregations, many of whom were unable to read, and that the books were for the private devotions of the literate. The indulgence does not mention saying prayers, and thus the 'Arma Christi' may be considered 'not a verbal . . . but a pictorial aid to meditation and piety' (418). A friar or priest would display the rolls in church, and 'worshippers would gain the indulgence by gazing at the roll, and while listening to the priest read the descriptions of the instruments, repeating the Pater noster' (240).

1632, 2442, 2577.

221 ———. 'The Gurney Series of Religious Lyrics.' *PMLA* 54 (1939): 369–90. [Edition.]

Robbins describes the 14 religious lyrics of the Gurney Series [now Egerton MS 3245], and prints 12 of them, noting their provenance and dialect, and relating them to other works of the period. He discusses 'the important position which vernacular prayers played in the religious life of the later Middle Ages,' referring to various manuscripts intended 'for use during public or private worship in the church, and by extension in the home' (388), to set the manuscript in the context of 'material for devotion and worship' (390).

**196.5*, 246, 271, 615, 790, 1368, 1691, 1729, 1761, 1781, 1951, 2035, 3557, 3769.8, 3882.*

222 Schulz, H.C. 'Middle English Texts from the "Bement" Manuscript.' *Huntington Library Quarterly* 3 (1939): 443–65. [Edition.]

The 'Bement' Manuscript, HM 142, has a 'twin' in Longleat 30, with which Schulz makes points of comparison. He offers a full description of the manuscript, incuding damage and variations of a careless scribe, T. Werkens, and prints six works previously unpublished ['*Kyrieleyson* have mercy good lorde,' *1831*; 'Marie Modur wel þe bee,' *2118*; 'Now Criste Iesu soþfast preest and kynge,' *2306*; 'O Ihū cryste of euerlastynge swettnes,' *2469*; 'O Ihū þat madest þe heuenes clere,' *2473*; and a prose prayer]. He describes the manuscript's history and suggests 1467 as the *terminus ad quem*.

896, 914, 1045, 1721, 1727, 1748, 1761, 1831, 1961, 2118, 2119, 2306, 2352, 2469, 2473, 2577, 2711.

223 Wilson, R.M. *Early Middle English Literature*. Methuen's Old English Library. London: Methuen, 1939. 2nd edn. 1951. 3rd edn. 1968.

['Lyric Poetry' (250–74) is uniform in the three editions.] Little in the ME lyric seems to have developed from OE, but 'there can be no doubt of its close connexion with the contemporary French lyric and with the Latin accentual poetry' (251), through courtly and commercial influences. The *carole* made an important contribution. Canute or

St Godric may have composed the earliest ME lyric. More religious than secular lyrics have survived; secular works were both used and condemned by the clergy. Survival was often a matter of chance. Constant themes, in English and French lyrics, are '[l]ove and the coming of spring, the song of the nightingale and the pangs of the forlorn lover' (260); Wilson provides examples, but he finds only one comic lyric, 'The Man in the Moon' [*2066*]. Religious lyrics are influenced by Latin works; some are translations and some macaronic. Themes include praise of Christ and the Virgin and contempt for the world. Some religious songs use tunes of secular works. Few surviving poems deal with political events. These are related to ballads; Wilson cites the *Song of Lewes* [*3155*] and the fragment 'Wel and wa sal ys hornes blaw' [*3857.5*]. The lyrics' maturity of technique is 'one of the most surprising things about Middle English literature' (274).

66, 445, 515, 1252, 1335, 1365, 1395, 1649, 1844.5, 1861, 2009, 2164, 2320, 3155, 3211, 3223, 3310, 3857.5, 3918.5, 3923.5, 4037.

224   Brown, Carleton. 'The Temptation and Fall.' *TLS* 6 Jan. 1940: 7.

This letter comments on a review of *Brown XV*, **39**, (*TLS*, 28 Oct. 1939). Brown writes of the sophistication of the idea of *felix culpa*, expressed in the lyric 'Adam lay I-bowndyn, bowndyn in a bond' [*117*]. He corrects the designation 'not heretofore printed,' for the lyric 'Ha cruell deeth contrarious to creatures in kynde' [*2*], 'overlooking the fact that Dr. MacCracken had included these verses as an "Epilogue" to the text of the apocryphal "Story of Asneth" (*Journal of English and Germanic Philology* IX, 223–262).'

2, 117.

225   Greene, Richard L. 'The Traditional Survival of Two Medieval Carols.' *ELH* 7 (1940): 223–38.

Compares the preservation of ballads with that of lyric carols, in particular that of two carols entitled 'Sweet Jesus' ['A chyld ys borne e-wys,' *30*] and 'Gloria Tibi Domine' ['A babe is born our blysse to brynge,' *22*]. Greene prints these, noting variations that are 'unmistakable signs that the carol has been subjected to popular oral tradition,' and that exemplify 'the usual treatment of obsolete words by folk-singers' (230). He comments that 'until the late eighteenth century at least, the popular religious lyric, as well as the popular narrative ballad, was preserved and transmitted by careful if not learned scribes as well as by the folk-singers' memories and the garlands and single-sheets of the penny press' (238).

22, 30.

226   Heningham, Eleanor K. 'Old English Precursors of *The Worcester Fragments.*' *PMLA* 55 (1940): 291–307.

Examines the 'Address of the Soul to the Body' ['* . . . on earde,' **2684.5*] and its prologue 'Sanctus beda was iboren her on bretone mid us' [*3074.3*], to show that the Worcester Fragments are at 'a central point in a series of documents *in English* which shows a direct line of influence extending from before the Conquest into the lyric poetry of the thirteenth century' (291). Heningham outlines the content of the 'Address,' and relates it to thirteenth-century lyrics, in particular 'þene latemest dai wenne we sulen farren' [*3517*], which she finds 'little more than a condensed version of *The Worcester Fragments*' (293). She notes the close relationship to OE works, in style and theme, and compares passages with sermons of Ælfric and versions of the Body and Soul legend, including those of the Blickling Homilies and homilies of the Vercelli Book. Comparisons show that 'even while he followed the outline of the primitive Body and Soul *exemplum* so closely, the author of *The Worcester Fragments* completely transformed it' (298). Although his sources include

Latin sermons, the poet used English material. In effect, 'prominent lines are taken over almost without change from . . . *The Grave* [*3497*]' (304), and some 'seem to have come ready made from Old English poetry' (305). [See Dudley, **137**; Moffat, **93**.]

2336, *2684.5, 3074.3, 3497, 3517, 3939, 3998.

227 [Creek] Immaculate, Sister Mary. 'A Note on "A Song of the Five Joys."' *Modern Language Notes* 55 (1940): 249–54.

Suggests grammatical and theological reasons for emending Brown's notes [*BrownXIV*, **31**, 246] on the sixth stanza of 'Ase y me rod þis ender day/by grene wode to seche play' [*359*], in particular the note on line 33, which Brown reads as 'When God was born according to "law" or "in due form"' (249). The emendation turns on rendering 'lay' as 'light' rather than 'law,' and 'þoro' as 'complete' or 'entire' rather than 'due.' Thus the stanza may be interpreted: 'The second joy of that maid was on Christmas *day*, when God was born in full light, and brought light to us: the star was seen before the day – the shepherds bear it witness' (254).

359.

228 Meech, Sandford B. 'A Collection of Proverbs in Rawlinson MS D 328.' *Modern Philology* 38 (1940): 113–32. [Edition.]

The manuscript is 'an *omnium gatherum* originally owned by Walter Pollard, who lived as a citizen of Plymouth in the reigns of Henry VI and Edward IV' (113). Its 83 proverbs and aphorisms are supplied in Latin and English versions, and include some in rhyming form. Meech prints the proverbs, and offers notes and comparisons with other similar collections.

465.5, 1137.5, 1354, 1634.5, 1793.9, 3087, 3372.5, 344.5, 3922, 4034.6, 4049.2, 4079.3, 4079.6, 4176.5.

229 Menner, Robert J. 'Notes on Middle English Lyrics.' *Modern Language Notes* 55 (1940): 243–9.

Brief notes on eight lyrics from *Brown XIII*, **36**, and six from *Brown XIV*, **31**. [Smithers refers to Menner's suggestions in the notes to the 2nd edn. of *Brown XIV*, **48**.]

Brown XIII: 66, 322, 1394, 1974, 2070, 2166, *3216.5, 4223.
Brown XIV: 196, 872, 1402, 3135, 3462, 3921.

230 Robbins, Rossell Hope. 'The Authors of the Middle English Religious Lyrics.' *JEGP* 39 (1940): 230–8.

As well as 'the popular sentiment which pictures the Friars Minor as the singing fools of Our Lord' (231), evidence suggests that most religious lyrics composed before the middle of the fourteenth century were written by friars, frequently Franciscans, who were preachers and mystics, with ideals 'not hostile to poetry' (233). This is shown directly in collections of sermon materials, friars' manuscripts of poems and *exempla*, hymns, and carols, many of which were prepared by Franciscans. There is also negative evidence that 'there are comparatively very few MSS in this early period known to have been written by monks or secular clergy' (237). Robbins estimates that about 357 such poems were composed by the middle of the fourteenth century; he links 230 of these with the Franciscans. Franciscan influence declined in the period after 1350 and the Black Death, as did their production of poetry, an estimated decline from 66 per cent to 15 per cent. Robbins supplies numerous brief references, most of them in footnotes, and quotes three poems: 'And we wynd writen of ane hermite' [*314*], 'No more will i wiked be' [*2293*], and 'Stond wel moder ounder rode' [*3211*].

314, 419, 519, 560, 594, 606, 1115, 1365, 1461, 1669, 1832, 1935, 2078, 2293, 2302, 2584, 3133, 3147, 3211, 3212, 3234, 3236, 3254, 3310, 3420, 3887, 3939, 4157.

231 ———. 'Two Fourteenth-Century Mystical Poems.' *Modern Language Review* 35 (1940): 320–9. [Edition.]

Prints two mystical poems written by the same scribe, with detailed comments on the dialects of the two works – one Northern, 'A Ihū þow sched þi blode' [*8*], and one Midland, 'Iesu suete is þe loue of þe' [*1747*]. Robbins explains the orthography of the two pieces, suggests reasons for some variant readings of the second, and relates the first to similar poems, 'to bring into prominence the common stock of all these Passion meditations' (327).

8, 11, 1691, 1693, 1709, 1732, 1747, 1748, 1753, 1779, 1780, 3238.

232 Sahlin, Margit Rigmor. *Etude sur la carole médiévale: l'origine du mot et ses rapports avec l'église.* Uppsala: Almqvist, 1940.

Not seen. [For support for Sahlin's arguments see Miller, **279**, and Robbins, **407**.]

233 Rees, Elinor. 'Provençal Elements in the English Vernacular Lyrics of Manuscript Harley 2253.' *Stanford Studies in Language and Literature* 1941: 81–95.

Finds that 'most if not all' of the ME lyrics in Harley 2253 reveal 'evidence of Provençal influence that must have come to England either directly or through the medium of Old French' (81). Four of 40 vernacular poems have elements of the *chanson d'aventure*. There are aspects of Provençal notions of love in lyrics of religious or secular love-longing. The conventions of courtly love, the poet's madness and pain, and the lady's cruelty and beauty, are evident in the Harley lyrics; they preserve troubadour traditions. Among 'troubadour commonplaces' are 'conventional opening and closing prayers, the poet's call for attention, and his announcement of his subject' (89). The natural setting emphasizes or contrasts with the poet's mood, frequently through references to birds in the Provençal and English poems. The ME lyrics of Harley 2253 surprise 'by their utter unlikeness to Anglo-Saxon poetry, and by their amazing similarity to and subtle difference from the continental verse that inspired them' (95).

105, 359, 515, 1394, 1395, 1407, 1504, 1678, 1747, 1861, 1921, 2207, 2236, 2359, 2366, 3221, 3963, 4037, 4177, 4194.

234 Bukofzer, Manfred F. 'An Unknown Chansonnier of the 15th Century.' *The Musical Quarterly* 28 (1942): 14–49.

Describes the Mellon Chansonnier and its compositions. Its physical appearance suggests 'one of the Burgundian centers of music copying' and 'a date around 1480' (16). It has compositions in French, Italian, Spanish, Latin, and English; the use of these languages 'clearly reflects the international atmosphere of the Burgundian court' (27). Bukofzer comments in particular on 'Alas alas Alas is my chief song' [*138*], 'Myn hertis lust sterre of my confort' [*2183*], and 'So ys emprented in my remembrance' [*3165*]. [Cf. Menner, **252**.] He prints the music of *138*, with commentary, compares it to 'Alas departing is ground of woe' [*146*], and doubtfully ascribes it to Walter Frye. He is more confident in ascribing *3165*, and also considers Frye the composer of the French roundeau 'Tout a par moy.'

138, 146, 2183, 3165

235 Robbins, Rossell Hope. 'Levation Prayers in Middle English Verse.' *Modern Philology* 40 (1942–43): 131–46. [Edition.]

Refers to 15 vernacular verse prayers offered by pious laity at the elevation of the Host. Robbins lists their sources, and prints the texts, with critical commentary, of some previously unpublished ['Hayle Iesu Godys Sone in forme of bred,' *1052*; 'Heyle my lord in wom ich leue,' *1071*; 'I þe honoure wiþ al my miht,' *1372*; two versions of 'Ihesu lord welcom þow be,' *1729*; 'O merciful ihū for merci to the i crie,' *2512*; 'Welcome lord in forme of bred,' *3882*]. They are 'of one pattern.' They invoke Christ, often emphasizing the word 'Bread,' and offer grounds for 'the petition (against sudden death), and the aspiration (for final bliss)' (139). The prayers are 'primarily a native growth' (133), independent of Latin originals. Robbins compares the ME poems with similar works in Latin and French, and quotes other short vernacular prayers and charms, noting their place in everyday life and in vernacular church services. [Cf. Rubin, **960**.]

942, 1052, 1071, 1323, 1368, 1372, 1487, 1729, 1734, 2174, 2512, 3507, 3882, 3883, 3884, 4052, 4149, 4246.

236 ———. 'The Burden in Carols.' *Modern Language Notes* 57 (1942): 16–22.

Expands Greene's comments on performance of the burden of carols in BL Add. 5665 (the Ritson MS). Robbins suggests emendations to Greene's editing, **37**, of the carols 'And by a chapell as y Came' [*298*], 'Bi thi burthe þᵘ blessed lord' [*581*], 'There blows a colde wynd todaye todaye' [*3525*], and 'When Fortune list yewe here assent' [*3948*]. He proposes to consider *3948* a rondel, and lists every occurrence of this form in ME verse. He does not classify *3525* as a carol, but adds seven others to the corpus of carols: 'All heyle Mary and well you be' [*182*], 'Gabriel of hyȝe degre' [*889*], 'Galawnt pride thy father is dede' [*892*], 'I muste go walke þe woed so wyld' [*1333*], 'It fell ageyns the next nyght' [*1622*], 'O lorde so swett ser Iohn dothe kys' [*2494*], and 'Our shyp is launched from the grounde' [*2727*].

182, 298, 581, 889, 892, 1333, 1622, 2494, 2727, 3525, 3948.

237 ———. 'Two Middle English Satiric Love Epistles.' *Modern Language Review* 37 (1942): 415–21. [Edition.]

MS Rawlinson poet. 36, in the Bodleian Library, Oxford (Summary Catalogue 14530) is unusual in containing both religious and secular works. Robbins describes it, listing the contents, and prints two satiric verse epistles, 'O fresche floure most plesant of pryse' [*2437*] and 'Vnto you most froward þis lettre I write' [*3832*], comparing them to similar works. He lists, in footnotes, many examples of love epistles in ME verse. The poet of the manuscript writes love epistles that are both typical and variant, and the satiric verses offer 'a welcome antidote to the general run of the courtly love poetry of the latter part of the century' (421).

333, 1121, 1334, 1395, 1446, 1510, 1652, 1957, 1982, 2237, 2437, 2640, 3065, 3180, 3832, 3879, 4209.

238 Alspach, Russell K. *Irish Poetry from the English Invasion to 1798*. Philadelphia, PA: U of Pennsylvania P, 1943. 2nd edn. 1959.

In 'From the Invasion to 1400' (12–25), Alspach surveys poems written in English in Ireland after the invasion, concentrating on those of Irish composition. He describes Harley 913, a fourteenth-century manuscript with 'prose and verse in English, French, and Latin' (12), written at the Franciscan abbey at Kildare, where some poems were copied and some composed. He tells the manuscript's history, and comments on 'Swet ihc̄ hend and fre' [*3234*], by Friar Michael Kildare, 'The Land of Cockaygne' ['Fur in see bi west Spaygne,' *762*], 'A Satire on the People of Kildare' ['Heil seint Michel wiþ þe lange sper,' *1078*], 'A Song of the Times' ['Whose þenchiþ vp þis carful lif,' *4144*], and 'A Rhyme-Beginning Fragment' ['Loue hauith me broȝt in liþir þoȝt,' *2003*]. [Heuser, **16**, edits the Kildare poems.] Alspach refers to poems in the Loscombe and Croker MSS, particularly 'The Virtues of Herbs' ['To God that is owre best leche,' *3754*]. He prints a poem from the Augustinian priory of Lanthony 'Allas allas vey yuel y sped' [*143*] and 'Gode sire pray ich þe' [*1008*], and a stanza in Rawlinson D. 913, which is perhaps 'the earliest English dance-song extant' (23), and was used by W.B. Yeats. Alspach alludes to fragments in the Red Book of Ossory, 'Hay now the cheualdores' [*1214.4*] and 'Hou shold y with that olde man' [*1265*], and to a poem of warning copied from Harley 913 to Lansdowne 418: 'Yung men of Waterford lernith now to plei' [*4280*].

143, 762, 1008, 1078, 1214.4, 1265, 2003, 3126, 3234, 3754, 4144, 4280.

239 Meroney, Howard. '"Man Must Fight Three Foes."' *Modern Language Notes* 58 (1943): 109–13.

Meroney adds copious notes and emendations to Brown's notes, in *BrownXIII*, **36**, on 'Middelerd for mon wes mad' [*2166*]. He refers to the comments by Menner, **229**, Wells, and Böddeker, and suggests numerous interpretations of meaning and punctuation.

2166.

240 Robbins, Rossell Hope. 'A Gawain Epigone.' *Modern Language Notes* 58 (1943): 361–6. [Edition.]

A poem, 'On clife þat castell so kneterred' [*2682*], in Humfrey Newton's Capesthorne MS [Bodleian Lat. Misc. c 66, see **46**] differs from others, in being written in 'alliterative cross-rimed quatrains' (361). It begins with a description of a castle, then speaks of the approach of summer and a love adventure. Robbins describes the meaning as 'obscure and disjointed' (361), and suggests that 'the three sections are independent of each other' (362). He prints the poem with a glossary, and comments on the vocabulary, that of 'poems of the alliterative "revival"' (365), with particular attention to phrases that resemble those of *Sir Gawain and the Green Knight* [*3144*] and connections with the alliterative tradition. [See Cutler, **313**.]

2682.

241 ———. 'Two New Carols.' *Modern Language Notes* 58 (1943): 39–42. [Edition.]

Prints two carols, found in Hunterian MS 83, 'Gabryell of hyȝe degre' [*889*], f. iiib, and 'All heyle Mary and well you be' [*182*], f. 21a. They are written in spaces in John of Trevisa's translation of Higden's *Polychronicon*, in a hand of the late fifteenth century, and it is noteworthy that 'the texts are provided with music' (40). Although *182* is unique, *889* is found in two other sources, but without music. Robbins compares the text with versions in Bodleian 29734 and Balliol 354.

182, 889.

242 Warren, Robert Penn. 'Pure and Impure Poetry.' [A Mesure lecture, given at Princeton, 1942.] *Kenyon Review* 5 (1943): 228–54.

The 'apparent innocence and simple lyric cry' of 'Westron wynde when wylle thou blow' [*3899.3*] should place it in 'any anthology of "pure poetry"' (233). The lover cries for relief, in 'the sympathetic manifestation of nature,' by 'the fulfillment of grief' (233), and in 'the excitement and fulfillment of love itself.' The first two thoughts are 'romantic and general,' and the third 'realistic and specific.' Since he is faithful to the beloved and to love, the work is 'not a celebration of carnality' (234). The poem's tension is 'between prosisms and poeticisms' (250).

3899.3.

243   Brown, Huntington. 'Sumer Is Icumen In.' *Explicator* 3.3 (1944–5): item 34.

Disagrees with Hoepfner, **245**, that *verteth* in 'Svmer is icumen in' [*3223*] indicates the cavorting of the deer. Brown finds a 'much livelier' interpretation in 'the economy of "verteth" in the sense "farteth"' rather than 'a mere synonym of "sterteth,"' and sees this sense as 'wholly in keeping with the homespun mood of the context,' and the poem's dialect, which is 'if anything, southerly.' This 'normal, native signification' (33) would have to be put out of a thirteenth-century mind before a thought of *vert* as 'turn' or 'harbour in the green' could take its place; and the 'absence of any recorded occurrences of "vert" for "fart" would in no way impair the probability . . . of its early currency' (34).

3223

244   Bukofzer, Manfred F. 'Sumer Is Icumen In': A Revision. U of California Publications in Music 2 (1944): 79–113.

There is new evidence to revise the dating of 'Svmer is icumen in' [*3223*]. Bukofzer describes this in the following: 'Reëxamination of Previous Evidence' (79–82); 'The Present Notation of the Rota' (83–5); 'The original State of the Notation' (86–8); 'The Notation of Bodleian Library MS Hatton 30' (89–93); 'The Index of the Winchester Codex' (94–5); 'Internal Evidence' (96–102); 'Philological Considerations' (103); 'Musical Considerations' (104–6); 'Walter Odington' (107–8); and 'The Rota as a Composition of the Fourteenth Century' (109–10). An appendix provides the original form of the music (111–14). The earlier evidence relates to Madden's conclusions that the rota was written at Reading, *c*. 1240, and its relation to a poem, ascribed to Walter Map, in the same manuscript, Harley 978. Inspection of the mensural notation sets 'a *terminus ante quem non* of *ca*. 1280' (85), confirmed by comparison with Bodleian Hatton 30. The use of duple time and absence of semibreves suggest a date *c*. 1310 and not much later than *c*. 1325. The Winchester codex was coeval. Internal evidence points to *c*. 1310, and philological considerations suggest a southern provenance. Although other items in the manuscript show that its compiler was 'preoccupied with sacred music,' the rhythm and cuckoo's call are 'obtrusively secular' (105). Bukofzer describes alterations to 'an innocent ternary rhythm' (105) and erasure of cuckoo calls, although 'the robust duple rhythm and the angular melody of the original version are conceived with a home-grown freshness that should caution us against declaring the secular version inferior' (106). The Summer-canon is thought to be music of the fourteenth century, which may be compared with a French canon, 'Talent m'est pris de chanter comme le coccu' and a German parody 'Der Summer kumt.'

3223.

——— Review by R.B., *Music and Letters* 26 (1945): 113–15. Summarizes musical scholarship on the lyric to gauge the effect of Bukofzer's findings. The reviewer welcomes Bukofzer's contribution, and assesses it as 'a suggestion that further investigation may even yet be called for.' In that event 'congratulations will be due to this remarkable scholar on having stimulated such an inquiry, whether its conclusions confirm or refute his own' (115).

245   Hoepfner, Theodore C. 'Sumer Is Icumen In.' *Explicator* 3.3 (1944–5): item 18.

Rejects 'currently accepted translations of "verteth" as "breaks wind"' or '"harbors in the green" that 'contradict the sense parallelism which is a distinctive feature of the lyric ['Svmer is icumen in,' *3223*]' (19). It is 'no bit of folk naiveté, but a work of sophisticated skill,' where *sterteth* and *verteth* are related in reference to movement, with modern equivalents such as 'capers, gambols, frisks, cavorts and prances,' and with *verteth* 'derived from the Latin "vertere", to turn' (19). Hoepfner refers to other critics, and acknowledges (but does not favour) the possibility that the word is 'a south-of-England variant of "farteth", so far as its spelling is concerned' (20).

3223

246 ———. 'Sumer is Icumen In.' *Explicator* 3.8 (1944–5): item 59.

Answers Brown, **243**, in reply to Hoepfner, **245**, on *verteth* in 'Svmer is icumen in' [*3223*], **245**. Hoepfner challenges six assumptions he considers 'unwarranted.'

3223.

247 Chambers, E.K. *English Literature at the Close of the Middle Ages.* Oxford: Clarendon, 1945. Vol. 2, Part 2 of *The Oxford History of English Literature.* Ed. F.P. Wilson and Bonamy Dobrée. 13 vols. to date. 1945–.

The origin of the carol is French, from *carole*, a dance-song with a refrain, resembling the pastourelle and *chanson de toile*. Chambers relates these forms to pagan and liturgical rites and to English carols, with examples from collections including MS Harley 2253 and the Red Book of Ossory. The refrain is found consistently, linked by rhyme to other stanzas, and suggesting the presence of a leader and other singers. Many writers of religious carols were Franciscans, in particular Thomas de Hales, Nicholas Bozon, William Herebert, John Grimestone, Richard de Ledrede, and James Ryman. John Audelay, an Augustinian, composed many carols, but is 'rather remote from the main tradition' (94). John Lydgate was the best writer of monitory verses. Most carols were intended for use at Christmas, and those for the Virgin and the Annunciation may be grouped with these. Some carols commemorated the saints and other feasts, and there were humorous, monitory, and historical secular works. Chambers summarizes the various carol forms and the importance of the refrain, with frequent reference to Greene, **37**. The theme of *planctus* appears in many carols of the Passion and Crucifixion, and influences lullaby carols of the Virgin and Child. An *incipit* for the latter may resemble the *chanson d'aventure*. The courtly, aureate language, sometimes with ingenious acrostics and Latinate structures, distinguishes religious poetry of the fifteenth century. Chambers cites numerous examples.

21, 29, 44, 117, 295, 298, 352, 360, 375, 413, 445, 497, 515, 684, 693, 769, 778, 822, 894, 1008, 1120.5, 1132, 1162, 1265, 1314, 1367, 1395, 1555, 1755, 1892, 1921, 1922, 1957, 2025, 2037, 2039.3, 2111, 2153, 2164, 2192, 2228, 2747, 2886, 3144, 3434, 3536, 3596, 3597, 3691, 3759, 3879, 4186, 4189.

248 Kenyon, John S. 'Sumer Is Icumen In.' *Explicator* 3.5 (1944–5): item 40.

In his comments on 'Svmer is icumen in' [*3223*], Kenyon corroborates Ericson's notes on *verteth*, **207**, and refers to those of Hoepfner, **245**, and Brown, **243**. He cites an assertion of 'no other Romance loan words in the poem' and the *NED*'s 'earliest record in English of the rare Latin verb *vert* . . . more than three hundred years later than the "Cuckoo Song" . . . in Scottish, not southern English.' He finds the Meredith reference [cited by Ericson] 'a figment of Meredith's imagination.'

3223.

249 [Withdrawn.]

250 Cutler, John L. 'Nou Goth Sonne Under Wod.' *Explicator* 4.1 (1945): item 7.

Expands comments on technique and imagery of 'Nou goth þe sonne under wode' [*2320*] made in *BrownXIII*, **36**, 'to show that Professor Brown's epithet "perfection" is indeed well

251 Löfvenberg, M.T. 'An Etymological Note.' *Studia Neophilologica* 17 (1945): 259–64.

Suggests that ME *chete*, in the phrase *al hende ase hauk in chete,* in 'Weping haueþ myn wonges wet' [*3874*], is the only trace in literature of OE *cȳte, cēte*. Löfvenberg does not specify a meaning for *chete,* but relates it to words for 'hut.' [See Arngart, **255**.]

3874.

252 Menner, Robert J. 'Three Fragmentary English Ballades in the Mellon Chansonnier.' *Modern Language Quarterly* 6 (1945): 381–7.

Interprets English songs in the Mellon *chansonnier* ['Alas alas Alas is my chief song,' *13*; 'Myn hertis lust sterre of my confort,' *2183*; 'So ys emprented in my remembrance,' *3165*], and refers to the work of Bukofzer, **234**. These were copied by a French scribe, 'obviously unfamiliar with English' (381). Menner offers explanations for difficulties and errors of sound and sense, and presents intelligible forms of the works.

138, 2183, 3165.

253 Utley, Francis Lee. 'When Nettles in Winter Bring Forth Roses Red.' *PMLA* 60 (1945): 346–55.

This exposition of three manuscript versions of the lying-song 'When nettuls in wynter bryng forth rosys red' [*3999*] satirizing women and religion, in Bodleian 29734 (A), Balliol 354 (B), and BL Printed Book IB 55242 (C), illuminates variants in the sources and argues for the priority of C. Although C is somewhat careless, Utley calls it 'the best representative of the original' (352), but not the original itself, which he assumes to have been written 'by a consistent artist, probably of the early fifteenth century' (353). The scribe of B seems to be 'a talented interpolator and corrector' (350). That of A is 'a conscious reviser' (352), perhaps a Franciscan friar who liked the carol form, who added a burden to 'this unmusical poem' (353), whose text shows eccentricities, 'a few vivid editorial touches,' and 'some serious misreadings' (354). Utley interprets this nonsense poem, with explanations of variant readings, and a reference to the Blood of Hayles.

3999.

254 ———. 'The Choristers' Lament.' *Speculum* 21 (1946): 194–202. [Edition.]

Prints the 'Lament of the Monk' or 'Choristers' Lament' ['Vncomly in cloystre i coure ful of care,' *3819*], found in MS Arundel 292. Utley supplies a translation and comment on aspects of musical and philological interest, a description of the manuscript, and a list of other entries. There are three speakers – Walter, William, and the French choir master. Utley conjectures on the identity of 'the "I" of the opening lines' and 'the exact contrast between the musical roles of Walter and William.' The poem offers 'a vivid and valuable picture, composed by a competent artist, of the struggles of a young fourteenth-century monk with his French music-master and his lesson in solmisation' (195).

3819.

255 Arngart, O. '"Al hende ase hak in chete": A Note on a Middle English alliterative Poem.' *English Studies* 28 (1947): 77–9.

Rejects Böddeker's rendering [*Altenglische Dichtungen des MS. Harl. 2253*, 152] of *hende ase hak in chete*, in line 28 of 'Weping haueþ myn wonges wet' [*3874*] as a reference to 'crayfish' or 'hake.' However Arngart accepts Brown's idea, *BrownXIII*, **36**, of *hauk* for *hak*, and 'cottage' or 'chamber' for *chete*, and supports this by comparison with a passage from *Pearl* [*2744*] that includes the phrase *as hende as hawk in halle*. An ironic interpretation of the phrase suggests the contrast between the courtly connotations of *hende* and the wildness of the hawk, so that it can be thought to mean 'not noble or gentle at all' (78). The line from *3874* can be considered 'a deliberate travesty with ironic intention of an alliterating expression which in its proper context had a courtly meaning quite opposed to the meaning it bears in the Harley lyric' (79). [See Löfvenberg, **251**.]

2744, 3874.

256 Fain, John Tyree. 'Holly and Ivy.' *Southern Folklore Quarterly* 11 (1947): 251–5.

The prevailing motif of Holly and Ivy poems is 'the ungallant treatment of Ivy, a woman, by Holly, a man' (251), when Holly and his singing, dancing men refuse entry to Ivy and her weeping women. Greene, **37**, links this to first-footing customs which forbade women to enter first on Christmas and New Year's mornings. Fain connects the poems with the 'ritual seasonal struggle' (252), where Ivy represents winter and Holly summer. He refers to 'Holy berith beris rede ynowgh' [*1226*] and cites examples from Russia, Greece, India, and Sweden.

1226.

257 Meroney, Howard. 'Line-Notes on the Early English Lyric.' *Modern Language Notes* 62 (1947): 184–7.

The notes supply Meroney's explanations and emendations for fourteen lyrics in *BrownXIII*, **36**, adding to the comments made by reviewers of the work in *TLS*, *Medium Ævum*, and *Review of English Studies*, and by Malone, **186**, and Menner, **229**.

293, 631, 1066, 1115, 1395, 1697, 1974, 2066, 2070, 2166, 2220, 2992, 3211, 3517, 3998

258 Moore, Arthur K. 'Mixed Tradition in the Carols of Holly and Ivy.' *Modern Language Notes* 62 (1947): 554–6.

Moore does not cite any specific lyric, but explains beliefs associated with holly and ivy, and hence with the carols. Ivy has (inferior) feminine associations, and holly is generally considered masculine, although there are also traditions of male (prickly) and female (smooth) holly. Holly's dioecious nature accounts for its use to represent the sexes, and may point ultimately, to fertilization rites, in which male and female kinds of holly were used symbolically.

259 Riddenhough, Geoffrey B. 'Bad Will towards Men: Ill-Tempered Christmas Carols.' *Queen's Quarterly* 54 (1947): 500–6.

The survey deals chiefly with post-medieval works, but includes brief references to 'certain stock figures that arouse the carollers' resentment: Adam, the Jews, King Herod.' The carols represent Adam as 'more fool than knave,' since 'his transgression meant in the long run an increase in human happiness' (500), as shown in 'Adam lay I-bowndyn bowndyn in a bond' [*117*].

117, 1785.

260 Adams, Robert P. 'Pre-Renaissance Courtly Propaganda for Peace in English Literature.' *Papers of the Michigan Academy of Science, Arts, and Letters* 32 (1948 for 1946): 431–46.

Examines 'dominant medieval ideas on war and peace,' and the possibility that there was in pre-Renaissance literature 'a tradition of pacifism [that] preceded and paved the way for the work of the London Reformers' (439). Much writing expressed the current views of the king. In *De Regimine Principium* [*2229*] Hoccleve advocates peace with France to avoid the havoc of war. However, in his 'Address to Sir John Oldcastle' ['The laddre of heuene I meene charitee,' *3407*] he exhorts Oldcastle 'to be a true knight and attend to the main business of chivalry – war' (443). The author of 'The Libel of English Policy' ['The trewe processe of Englysch polycye,' *3491*] anticipates Renaissance views on expansion, and sees attainment of peace as 'almost entirely an economic problem, whose solution depended, not on the intervention of the Church, but on the practical efforts of bourgeois merchants seeking stable markets' (444). Lydgate's writing, in 'A Praise of Peace' ['Mercy and Trowthe met on a high monteyne,' *2156*], suggests the unpopularity of mismanagement of war. George Ashby's 'Active Policy of a Prince' ['Maisters Gower Chaucer and Lydgate,' *2130*] reflects court policy, to urge princes to cultivate the arts of peace, as 'usually a wise expedient' (445). Thus courtly writings show 'no consistent expression of a vigorous, emergent pacifism,' but rather 'a progressive weakening and diluting of medieval international idealism,' with no evidence that 'a pre-Renaissance literary tradition of philosophic pacificism preceded and prepared the way for the profound and imaginatively penetrating social criticism developed in the early sixteenth century' (446).

130, 2156, 2229, 3407, 3491.

261 Brown, Calvin S. *Music and Literature: A Comparison of the Arts.* Athens, GA: U of Georgia P, 1948.

Although 'we cannot say that music has wrought any real change in literature as a whole' (219), the converse does not hold. Brown replies to Ernest Newman's comment on 'The Small Poem in Music,' [*A Musical Motley* (New York: Knopf, 1925): 40–53] that 'music has, in general, nothing corresponding to the perfect small lyric' (222). He cites, in modernized style, the lyric 'Westron wynde when wylle thou blow' [*3899.3*].

3899.3.

262 Onions, C.T. 'Two Notes on Middle English Texts.' *Medium Ævum* 17 (1948): 32–3.

In the note 'Now Springs the Spray' (32–3), Onions proposes that *nou* in 'Als i me rod this endre dai' [*360*] should be considered a conjunction. He translates the three lines of the refrain: '"Now that the shoots are sprouting (i.e. now that spring is here), I am so sick for love that I cannot sleep"' (33). A similar use of *nou* may be found in 'Nou goth þe sonne under wode' [*2320*].

360, 2320.

263 Pirotta, Nino. 'On the Problem of "Sumer is Icumen In."' *Musica Disciplina* 2 (1948): 205–16.

Responds to studies of Bukofzer, **244**, and Schofield, **265**, on the date and provenance of 'Svmer is icumen in' [*3223*]. Pirotta hesitates to find in favour of either, and seeks rather to show that divergences are not 'as great and irreconcilable as they appear to be at first sight' (207). To this end, he cites observations from musical palaeography, concerned with mensural notation and binary rhythm in the *rota*, and suggests that it was 'not the only example of binary rhythm in England at the end of the 13th century.' He seeks to eliminate 'reasons which may have compelled Bukofzer to ascribe to our *rota* a date as late as 1310' (211), and to propose that it is secular and may be dated 'from the early epoch of mensural notation in England: that is, from the last two decades of the 13th century' (212). His argument favours performance as a circular rather than a crab canon, through comparison with the *rondellus* and *chace*, and suggests that it may have been known 'in England and in other countries' (214). The setting for six voices fits 'the preference by the English composers for the full sonority produced by a great number of voices.' This exceeds 'all that we know of the English polyphony of this epoch' (215), but there is an analogy with the Italian *cacce* for three voices, and the setting of *3223* may be considered 'an amplification of the usual scheme of the motet for three voices' (216).

3223.

264 Sabol, Andrew J. 'An English Source for One of More's Latin Epigrams.' *Modern Language Notes* 63 (1948): 542.

Notes that the '*Benedicite* what dremyd I this nyȝt' [*506.5*], is an English version of Thomas More's epigram 'In amicam foedifragam iocosvm, versum e contione anglica.'

506.5.

265 Schofield, B. 'The Provenance and Date of "Sumer is Icumen in."' *Music Review* 9 (1948): 81–6.

Replies to Bukofzer, **244**, on 'Svmer is icumen in' [*3223*], and to his doubt about the assignment of date and provenance for Harley MS 978 of *c*. 1240 and Reading Abbey, and proposal of *c*. 1310 at Winchester. Reading Abbey was accepted because a calendar 'which must certainly have been compiled for that house' (81) is on the verso of the last page of the music for the *rota*, suggesting that it was already at Reading when the calendar was compiled. Bukofzer has based some of his findings on a list of musical compositions at the end of the manuscript, which he calls 'the Winchester codex,' although he does not posit 'sufficient evidence to regard "Sumer is icumen in" as a Winchester *rota*' (82). Schofield corrects errors in transcription of the list, and identifies three persons named there as monks of Reading Abbey in the second half of the thirteenth century. They are R. de Burgate, named as 'R. De Burg.'; W. de Winton, 'W. de Wint.,' who had owned the collection of music; and W. de Wicumbe, shown as 'W. de Wic.' or 'Wicb.,' who copied and perhaps composed music. Thus the contents listed in the manuscript are those of 'a Reading and not a Winchester codex.' The connections of Harley 978 are established by its Reading calendar, with obits of Reading officials, material written at Reading, and reference to a Reading manuscript. The only other possibility Schofield admits is the Leominster cell of Reading, 'in which case it might just as likely have been written by a Reading monk' (85). Comparisons of obits on the calendar and those of Vespasian EV reveal similarities strong enough to suggest a contemporary or even the same hand. Although the date could 'be advanced to 1260 . . . it is most unlikely to have been written many years later' (86).

3223.

266 Taylor, F. Sherwood. 'The Argument of Morien and Merlin: An English Alchemical Poem.' *Chymia* 1 (1948): 23–35. [Edition.]

The dialogue between Morien and his son Merlin, 'As the Child Merlin sat on hys fathers knee' [*407.6*], imparts secrets for making the Philosopher's Stone, based on 'the alchemical doctrine that from the "one thing" are made the male and female who bring forth the fruit of the stone' and that of 'the *pneuma*, the philosophic mercury that gives life to everything' (24). The description offers an allegory of human generation and growth, as do other alchemical processes. Some words used are anagrams, unique to this alchemical text; most are explained in marginal annotations. Others, still unknown, 'have the air of being corrupted Arabic or Syriac terms' (25).

Taylor prints the text, preserving 'the original's lack of punctuation and also its orthograph' (26).

407.6.

267 Bowers, R.H. 'Middle-English Poems by Mydwynter.' *Modern Language Notes* 64 (1949): 454–61. [Edition.]

Prints two religious poems by Johannes Mydwynter from MS Harley 2383, 'Man in Heuyn hyt ys mery to dwll' [*2063*] and 'Man þenke here on ofte tyme' [*2079*]. Bowers describes the manuscript, noting its date and provenance, and provides a diplomatic transcription of the text, which is 'presumably apograph rather then holograph' (455). [See Johnston, **403**.]

2063, 2079.

268 Handschin, Jacques. 'The Summer Canon and its Background.' *Musica Disciplina* 3 (1949): 55–94.

Examines contents of the manuscript in which 'Svmer is icumen in' [*3223*] and its music are found, in particular the musical sections. Handschin's exploration of possible clues to the date and provenance responds to views of Bukofzer, **244**, and Schofield, **265**, and includes a detailed account of the Latin compositions, with extensive comment on their musical notation and the possibility of using the presence of binary rhythm to date the compositions. He finds difficulties in setting *3223* into the historical process, because there are gaps in our historical knowledge, 'most of all in the domain from which the Summer canon comes, i.e. that of non-learned secular music' (78). The lyric exemplifies 'the English tendency . . . toward massive vocal sonority' (79). Comparison with other works suggests that the middle of the thirteenth century should be considered for its composition, because 'measured notation appears here in a primitive stage' (82). Handschin discusses the significance of the term *rota* and concludes that the canon was 'neither provided with a convenient close nor designed for being sung as a circular one' (87). It may indicate a connection to the English *rondellus* and French *rondeau*. He concludes with a note on the lost Reading collection (88–94).

3223.

269 [Finnegan] Jeremy, Sister Mary. 'A Triptych for Passiontide.' *Orate Fratres* 23 (1949): 200–2.

The lyric 'Ihesus doþ him by mene' [*1699*], with the title 'Jesus Pleads with the Worldling' in *BrownXIV*, **31**, is Christ's reproach to a fashionably dressed young man. Sister Mary Jeremy includes a version of the poem in MnE.

1699.

270 Menner, Robert J. 'The Man in the Moon and Hedging.' *JEGP* 48 (1949): 1–14.

Revises notes in *Brown XIII*, **36**, on 'The Man in the Moon' [*2066*]. Menner refers to particular passages concerning the hedge, the peasant's employment, hedging practices, the pledge to the hayward, and the comparison with a magpie, specifically considering the word *amarscled* and its interpretation by Meroney, **257**.

2066.

271 Moore, Arthur K. 'Middle English Verse Epistles.' *Modern Language Review* 44 (1949): 86–7.

The love epistle is 'one of the artificial forms cultivated by the courtly versifiers of the fifteenth century' (86). Moore suggests adding to the known corpus three lyrics of MS Rawlinson C 813, 'Entierly belouyd & most yn my mynde' [*729*], 'Hevy thoughtes & longe depe sykyng' [*1180*], and 'O loue most dere o loue most nere my harte' [*2496*]; one from Lambeth 206 ['That pasaunte Goddnes the Rote of all vertve,' *3291*]; and two letters intercalated into *Troilus and Criseyde* [*3327*] (lines 1317–1421, 1590–1631). Love epistles may be traced ultimately to Ovid. The formula 'Go little bil' seems 'a mere refinement of a very old convention, the "Go little book" envoy' (402), of which Moore offers several French examples. [See Schoeck, **317**; Camargo, **949**.]

729, 868, 927, 1180, 1329, 1789, 2496, 2547, 3291.

272 ———. '"Somer" and "Lenten" as Terms for Spring.' *Notes and Queries* 194 (1949): 82–3.

Spring was not used until the sixteenth century to denote 'the interval between the vernal equinox and the summer solstice' (82). *Somer* generally conveys 'the sense of spring, although the term may comprehend the entire period between February and the autumnal equinox' (83); it replaces the term *lenten*, which referred to the fast of Lent. St Valentine's Day was associated with spring, but because of the error in the Julian calendar, the season was already advanced on February 14. Moore cites two examples of formulaic opening in the *reverdie*: 'Lenten ys come wiþ loue to toune' [*1861*] and 'Somer is comen wiþ loue to toune' [*3222*]. He notes the resemblance to 'Svmer is icumen in' [*3223*]. [See Stobo, **811**.]

1861, 3222, 3223.

273 Smithers, G.V. 'Ten Cruces in Middle English Texts.' *English and Germanic Studies* [now *English Philological Studies*] 3 (1949–50): 68–81.

Notes 5 and 6 (81) refer to a word in two Harley lyrics, 'Blow, Northerne Wynd' [*1395*] (line 6) and 'The Three Foes of Man' [*2166*] (line 57). Böddeker [*Altenglische Dichtungen des MS. Harl. 2253*], Brown, *BrownXIII*, **36**, and Brook, **42**, supply *fully*. Smithers reads the word as '*sully*, here used as an adverb (literally "marvellously", i.e. "exceedingly")' (81). *Sully* was written with a long *s*, and 'the stroke which all three editors have interpreted as the bar of an *f* is really a preliminary tick to the first minim of the *u*' (81). [Brook has adopted this reading for subsequent editions of *The Harley Lyrics*, but *IMEV* and *SIMEV* have *fully*.]

1395, 2166.

274 Williams, Margaret. *Glee-Wood: Passages from Middle English Literature from the Eleventh Century to the Fifteenth*. New York: Sheed, 1949. New York: Greenwood, 1968.

Offers general commentary on ME literature, with MnE translations of some passages. Lyrics are included in the chapters 'Scholars at Large' (219–54) and 'Behind the Signs' (419–68).

196, 298, 352, 598, 1008, 1132, 1290, 1299, 1365, 1367, 1395, 1460, 1463, 1861, 1977, 2007, 2024, 2066, 2270, 2320, 2504, 2645, 2787, 2988, 3031, 3080, 3227, 3691, 3891, 3906.

275 Anderson, George K. *Old and Middle English Literature from the Beginnings to 1485*. Oxford: Oxford UP, 1950. New York: Collier, 1966. Vol. 1 of *A History of English Literature*. Gen. ed. Hardin Craig.

A general study, with a section (202–10) on the ME lyric. Anderson describes religious and secular lyrics, relating them to earlier forms, and listing numerous examples.

66, 515, 606, 639, 640, 643, 1132, 1272, 1394, 1596, 1678, 1747, 1861, 1922, 2009, 2081, 2108, 2236, 2302, 2667, 2790, 3223, 3236, 3238, 3420, 3743, 3760, 3819, 3826, 3827, 3921, 3963, 4037, 4077, 4107, 4157, 4177.

276   Bateson, F.W. *English Poetry: A Critical Introduction.* London: Longmans 1950.

Although poetry is meaning, 'poetic meaning is not the only kind of meaning' (57). Bateson considers that the content of poetry is 'best defined as *human nature in its social relations*' (58), and that a poet expresses generally oppositions of conflicting social attitudes. The poem 'Westron wynde when wylle thou blow' [*3899.3*] shows oppositions 'at a less abstract level.' The 'parallelism of form' in prayers for rain and the lover's return 'overcomes the contrast of content' (59), and suggests the lover's involvement 'in the natural cycle of the seasons' (60); Christ has 'the rôle of a fertility spirit.' The poem deals with 'non-human processes of growth and . . . human self-fulfilment in sexual love' (60).

3899.3.

277   Baugh, Albert C., ed. *A Literary History of England.* Book 1. The Middle Ages. Ed. Kemp Malone and Albert C. Baugh. London: Routledge, 1950. [New York: Appleton, 1948.] 2nd edn. 1967.

Considers lyrical forms in 'The Lyric' (208–24). Religious lyrics originate in 'an ecclesiatical and literary tradition which knows no national boundaries' (209), whereas secular works may have roots in French, Provençal, Latin, or folk and minstrel songs, although the French influence seems negligible. The authors survey French and Provençal forms, including *chansons*, *aube*, pastourelle, *rondet*, and *ballette*, to contrast the cold analysis of emotion in *chanson courtois* and its frank expression in ME lyric, particularly in those associating love with spring. Most preserved lyrics are 'religious or moral' (215); they may be touching, imaginative, and occasionally startling. Many works are addressed to the Virgin, offering praise and describing her life. Some poems of her joys and sorrows use secular forms; similar poems of love and praise are addressed to Christ. Many lyrics warn of death's coming; others focus on Christ's appeal to mankind. Carols of Christmas and Epiphany became popular in the fifteenth century, and there are political, 'humorous, satirical and convivial songs' (222). Most lyrics are anonymous, and probably the work of clerks; they grow more literary in the later fourteenth and fifteenth centuries.

12, 210, 352, 360, 515, 704, 769, 864, 1395, 1463, 1575, 1747, 1866, 2025, 2163, 2207, 2645, 3155, 3221, 3223, 3242.5, 3259, 3285, 3305, 3310, 3700, 3963, 4177, 4189, 4194.

278   Mabbott, T.O. 'The Text of the English Xylographic Poem on the Seven Virtues.' *Modern Language Notes* 65 (1950): 545.

Because the broadside that preserves this poem, '*[As] her am I sent by diuine prouidence*' [**338.5*] is 'neither a manuscript nor a typographic incunable,' it has been 'somewhat neglected.' From a photostat, Mabbott makes four 'corrections or additions to the reading of the text as given by [W.L.] Schreiber,' in *Handbuch der Holz- und Metallschnitte*, VI (Leipzig, 1928), 51 ff.

**338.5.*

279   Miller, Catharine K. 'The Early English Carol.' *Renaissance News* 3 (1950): 61–4.

The Ritson MS (BL Add. 5665) includes 44 carols of a choir repertory. This lends support to the view of Sahlin, **232**, that the carol was 'an ornament of the processional rites of the Catholic Church' (63), through its use of dance-songs, which were probably adapted by the Franciscans. The carols became popular processional litanies. Musical references that strengthen Sahlin's conclusion include the frequent occurrence of carols in manuscripts with other processional works, the marking of carols on rubrics for particular feasts, textual and musical quotations from the liturgy in carols, and the classification of carols as *conducti*. Miller offers as an example the setting of a *Te Deum*, 'O blesse god in trinite' [*2388*].

2388.

280   Moore, Arthur K. 'The Form and Content of the *Notbrowne Mayde*.' *Modern Language Notes* 65 (1950): 11–16.

The *Notbrowne Mayde* ['Be it right or wrong,' *467*] avoids 'the tedious preciosity of *vers de société* and the boisterous directness of popular song' (11) of other fifteenth-century verse. Moore briefly surveys previous criticism of the work, including conjecture that its source was German or Latin. The poem is a debate, concerning 'the worth of womankind' (15). The stanza form is 'hardly more than modified common measure,' and 'the culmination of a prosodic tendency manifest in English verse no later than the first decade of the fourteenth century and possibly earlier' (12). Moore cites examples that resemble it in the use of internal rhyme, including a Latin form, the Harley lyric 'De Clerico et Puella' [*2236*], Dunbar's 'Of the lady solistaris at court' [*3556.5*], 'Masteres Anne/I ame your man' [*2195*], and two Child ballads.

467, 2195, 2236, 3556.5

281   Robbins, Rossell Hope. 'The Fraternity of Drinkers.' *Studies in Philology* 47 (1950): 35–41. [Edition.]

A fifteenth-century satirical burlesque, 'Jhesu lord owr heavenly kyng' [*1726*], describes the founding of 'an imaginary "order" of tipplers.' Its narrator proposes a hospice and alms house to receive 'drunken debtors, habitual drunkards . . . and those with troublesome wives'; sets the fees, drinking style and habit; and prescribes the telling of merry tales. Robbins relates the poem to similar works and contrasts one on the founding of the Carthusian order, 'At þe begynnyng of þe chartirhows god did schewe' [*435*]. He prints the poem, with notes, and suggests 'a vaguely southern area' (36) for its dialect.

435, 1362, 1726, 1852, 3845.5.

282   Sitwell, Gerard. 'A Fourteenth-Century English Poem on Ecclesiastes.' *Dominican Studies* 3 (1950): 285–90.

'I wolde witen of sum wys wiht' [*1402*] is found in two manuscripts, Bodleian 3938 (the Vernon MS) and BL Add. 22283. Sitwell summarizes its themes of questions on the nature of the world, man's place there, and his relation to God. These are generally stated with allusions suggesting 'that the author almost certainly had his text of Ecclesiastes fresh in mind, if not by his elbow.' The 'apparent agnosticism' of the fourth stanza's question, 'Who knows what shall become of man when he shall die?' (287), is tempered by consideration of the spirit's return to God. In the fifth stanza, of death, the common fate of men and beasts, the poet did not interpret the relevant passages of Ecclesiastes 'in keeping with orthodox theology,' but rather 'deliberately gave up any attempt to find a solution' (288). This implies theological controversy, and the impossibility of knowing God's secrets. The poet may have been considering Thomas Bradwardine's *De causa Dei contra Pelagium*, which discusses 'the relation of God's foreknowledge to man's free-will' (289) and caused controversy noted in Chaucer's *Nun's Priest's Tale*. The lines 'Whar-to wilne we forte knowe/The poyntes of Godes privete' may allude directly to this matter.

1402.

283 Stevens, John. 'Carols and Court Songs of the Early Tudor Period.' *Proceedings of the Royal Musical Association* 77 (1950–1): 51–62.

First describes the place of the carol, a song with uniform stanzas and a burden, which is 'by far the most important' (51) among the song-forms of medieval England. The Fayrfax book (BL MS Add. 5465) and Henry VIII's Book (BL MS Add. 31922) contain early Tudor songs, many of which are carols. Stevens supplies a more detailed account of the court-song, showing its place and function in the life of the court, when music was 'functional rather than expressive,' and 'part of worship, part of ceremony, part of an allegorical entertainment or a moral play' (53). He explains the 'markedly subordinate position' (54) of music within the ceremonies and entertainments of the court, including tournaments, royal entries, and processions, May games, banquets, and diplomatic meetings such as the Field of the Cloth of Gold. Because such music was intended 'to assist the display' (56) it was more often instrumental than sung, and performed by professional, rather than amateur musicians. There was also music 'for diversion on numerous more private occasions,' where 'professional recitals . . . were given, especially by foreign *virtuosi*' (57). In spite of the interest of Henry VIII and others, there is scant evidence that 'the arts of composition or of instrumental chamber-music flourished among amateurs' (58). Singing was popular, but it does not seem that 'written part-songs were much sought after by amateurs at the turn of the century' (59), and the 'black-and-red notation [of court-songs] demands trained musicians' (60). The song books have a wide range of music, suitable for many occasions.

120.4, 134.5, 302.5, 558.5, 1327, 1333, 2028.5, 2034.5, 2394.5, 3131, 3438.3.

284 Wolpers, Theodor. 'Geschichte der englischen Marienlyrik im Mittelalter.' *Anglia* 69 (1950): 3–84.

A comprehensive account of ME Marian lyrics, copiously illustrated, in which Wolpers explores their development from Latin hymns and related poems. He relates their history to that of prayer and theology, and to the style of religious and secular poetry, considering the evolution of attitudes towards Mary and motifs of prayer and lyrics. He traces the significance and meaning of titles such as 'Star of the Sea,' and changes in ideas of Mary's role as mediator, helper, and Queen of Heaven. Godric's hymn, 'Seinte marie clane uirgine' [*2988*], of the twelfth century, is among the earliest Marian lyrics; Wolpers compares it to earlier, mystical Latin works, and ME works in verse and prose. His account of lyrics of the thirteenth and fourteenth centuries follows a similar plan, beginning with a description of religious feelings, stressing the work of St Francis and Franciscan piety, in which the Virgin is seen as a human mother rather than ruler of Heaven. These themes spread in England, competing with the troubadours' courtly secular poetry, but directed towards all the people rather than a small courtly circle. Some Marian lyrics are macaronic, with lines in ME and Latin. As courtly and popular expressions were used in both secular and religious poetry, Mary was addressed and described as a noble lady; nobility and beauty are discerned even in themes of the Passion. Motifs include planctus, the joys of Mary, and love. Love is described in secular and spiritual terms, emphasized when the theme of *contemptus mundi* is used to compare heavenly and earthly love, as in 'Off alle floures feirest fall on' [*2607*], a Vernon lyric. Richard Rolle and Franciscan sentiments influenced Marian poems of the fourteenth century, in which Mary seems an earthly woman, to be approached trustingly, rather than a noble lady. This approach differs from the cult of Mary in the fifteenth century, which hardly mentions love towards her. Repentance and fear are rare, and almost disappear from Marian poems of the period; the lyrics of prayer and intercession show the influence of the fourteenth-century court style. Wolpers illustrates style and motif in Chaucer's and Lydgate's Marian works, before explicating style, concepts, and motifs in popular Marian poetry of the fourteenth and fifteenth century, particularly in lullaby poems, and the religious style of the fifteenth century. He concludes by considering symbols of the lyrics, especially the star, sun, and flowers.

22, 99, 181, 239, 293, 352, 359, 361, 364, 404, 420, 447, 462, 465, 488, 490, 533, 583, 598, 631, 708, 742, 896, 912, 927, 1026, 1027, 1029, 1030, 1031, 1032, 1034.5, 1037, 1039, 1044, 1045, 1046, 1048, 1054, 1056, 1057, 1060, 1073, 1077, 1080, 1081, 1083, 1122, 1232, 1254, 1395, 1407, 1460, 1804, 1833, 1839, 1930, 1974, 2025, 2038, 2092, 2107, 2118, 2154, 2171, 2202, 2220, 2221, 2320, 2359, 2366, 2398, 2459, 2461, 2556, 2557, 2565, 2570, 2607, 2619, 2645, 2688, 2791, 2800, 2988, 2992, 2995, 3065, 3211, 3222, 3236, 3245, 3391, 3412, 3565, 3627, 3673, 3692, 3821, 4019, 4099.

285 Bowers, R.H. 'Middle-English Verses on the Appearance of Christ.' *Anglia* 70 (1951): 430–3. [Edition.]

An acephalous poem, '*If þai do so he wil þaim safe/as walnot barke his hare' [*1426.8] in BL Add. MS 37,049, offers an analogue to the description of Jesus in the *Cursor Mundi*. Bowers presents a diplomatic transcription with explanatory footnotes. [See Ross, **383**.]

*1426.8.

286 ———. 'Palden's Middle-English Prayer.' *Notes and Queries* 196 (1951): 134. [Edition.]

A prayer 'Iesu that all thys worlde hathe wroght' [*1750*] is 'a hitherto unprinted Middle-English poem of the fifteenth century from the British Museum Royal MS 2 B x fol. 1^r by an unidentified author named Palden.' It is 'a clumsy mixture of verse and prose,' with 'very light pointing and only one symbol: a virgule which evidently serves both to indicate a pause and a full stop.'

1750.

287 ———. 'The Middle English "Oon Sleth Deere with an Hooked Arwe."' *Southern Folklore Quarterly* 15 (1951): 249–50. [Edition.]

The poem 'Oon sleyth the deer wythe an hookid arwe' [*2696*], preserved uniquely in MS Harley 2202, may be of the late fifteenth or early sixteenth century. The imagery of the first stanza, 'from the area of hunting and fishing,' is 'vivid and apposite,' but images of the second stanza are 'trite and hackneyed,' and the third stanza is 'mediocre and unimaginative' (249). Bowers prints the poem 'with editorial pointing and capitalization' (249).

2696.

288 Bühler, Curt F. 'A Middle English Versified Prayer to the Trinity.' *Modern Language Notes* 66 (1951): 312–13. [Edition.]

A manuscript of Nicholas Love's ME translation of the *Meditationes vitae Christi* is another source for a versified prayer to the Trinity, which is also found in Lincoln Cathedral 91 and the Gurney MSS. Bühler prints 'Almighty god in trinite' [*246*], and compares it with the other sources.

246.

289 Cawley, A.C. 'A York Fragment of Middle English Secular Lyric.' *Speculum* 26 (1951): 142–4.

'Vnder a law as I me lay' [*3820.5*], a 'lyrical waif' in the form of a 'scrap of Middle English secular lyric,' has been found in *Acta Capitularia, 1410–29*, fol. 13a. It is in the hand of the probate of a will written above it, and was apparently written by 'a chapter clerk intent on beguiling the tedium of his clerical duties' (142). Cawley relates the lines to 'a *chanson d'aventure* of the *chanson dramatique* type' (142), and finds the closest parallel in 'This other day/I hard a may/Ryght peteusly complayne' [*3635.5*]. The poem may well have resembled 'Als i me rod this endre dai/O mi [pleyinge]' [*360*]. The exclamation *wela hay* in line 3 is of philological interest; it is 'a variant of the familiar *welaway*' (143). [Cf. Mustanoja, **357**.]

360, 3635.5, 3820.5.

290 Donaldson, E. Talbot. 'Idiom of Popular Poetry in the Miller's Tale.' *English Institute Essays*. Ed. A.S. Downer. New York: Columbia UP, 1951. 116–40. Repr. in *Explication as Criticism: Selected Essays from the English Institute 1941–52*. Ed. W.K. Wimsatt, Jr. 1963. New York: Columbia UP. 27–51. Repr. in *Chaucer and His Contemporaries: Essays on Medieval Literature and Thought*. Ed. Helaine Newstead. Greenwich, CT: Fawcett, 1968. 174–89. Repr. in *Speaking of Chaucer*. E. Talbot Donaldson. London: University of London, Athlone, 1970. 13–29 [cited].

Terms from the diction of lyrics are used to describe *derne love*, which is associated with Nicholas, with details of Alison's and Absolon's appearance and clothes, and with Absolon's love-longing. Donaldson relates these descriptions to similar expressions in the Harley lyrics, although he concedes that 'to suggest that Chaucer had the Harley lyrics in mind . . . seems too large an economy' (25).

105, 515, 1394, 1395, 1921, 2166, 2207, 2236, 3874, 4194.

291 Fain, John Tyree. 'Meredith and the "Cuckoo Song."' *Modern Language Notes* 66 (1951): 324–6.

Fain's interpretation of a parody of 'Svmer is icumen in' [*3223*] in George Meredith's *The Ordeal of Richard Feverel* differs from Ericson's, **207**. Fain concludes that 'it seems clear enough that when Richard sings out "Hippy verteth" he means "Hippy fartheth"' (325), rather than Ericson's application of 'the word *verting* to Richard's action.' He also thinks that the parody is the work of 'Adrian, the Wise Youth' (326), not Richard. [See also Brown, **243**; Hoepfner, **245**, **246**; Kenyon, **248**.]

3223.

292 Kane, George. *Middle English Literature: A Critical Study of the Romances, the Religious Lyrics, and Piers Plowman*. Methuen's Old English Library. Gen. eds. A.H. Smith, F. Norman. London: Methuen, 1951.

Examines problems of reading the ME religious lyrics and the modern reader's appreciation of the poems. Kane describes the lyrics systematically, dealing with their moral and devotional functions, and the ways of achieving these effects. He cites numerous examples to show how the poems express advice and emotion, and compares their effectiveness for the modern reader with the effect expected on their intended audience. Occasionally he draws comparisons with later poems, for example 'With fauoure in hir face ferr passyng my Reason' [*4189*] and '*Regina celi* and Lady *letare*' [*2800*] with Hopkins's 'Goldengrove' (118–21). Kane considers prayers and lyrics of death, devotional and meditative verse, and carols, to evaluate their effectiveness and examine techniques. He concludes that, when a religious lyric is a good poem, '[t]he religious emotion must coincide and identify itself with a creative excitement' (138). When he examines the lyrics for transformation of material, by '"literary" treatment,' by 'the play of the poet's fancy,' or, rarely, 'from a pure poetic conception of the subject' (150), he seldom finds such effectiveness. This applies especially to the carols, few of which exceed 'the level of light and fluent verse' (176).

14, 37, 63, 66, 76, 94, 110, 112, 117, 181, 298, 340, 361, 372, 404, 420, 441, 463, 470, 497, 548, 562, 563, 583, 610, 631, 872, 880, 998, 1001, 1002, 1024, 1029, 1029, 1053, 1073, 1119, 1132, 1308, 1311, 1318, 1351, 1353, 1365, 1367, 1379, 1402, 1422, 1448, 1455, 1460, 1463, 1472, 1596, 1649, 1663, 1684, 1700, 1701, 1715, 1735, 1748, 1775, 1836, 1841, 1899, 1914, 1930, 1930, 1943, 1977, 2007, 2012, 2023, 2036, 2042, 2051, 2103, 2107, 2136, 2159, 2171, 2240, 2260, 2273, 2302, 2320, 2366, 2401, 2441, 2461, 2471, 2483, 2483, 2486, 2528, 2576, 2684, 2733, 2800, 3132, 3211, 3212, 3230, 3236, 3245, 3283, 3310, 3420, 3517, 3565, 3597, 3603, 3627, 3628, 3641, 3691, 3692, 3696, 3730, 3825, 3826, 3852, 3862, 3904, 3921, 3939, 3996, 3998, 4023, 4088, 4135, 4157, 4158, 4159, 4170, 4189, 4263, 4268.

293 ———. 'The Middle English Verse in MS Wellcome 1493.' *London Mediæval Studies* 2 (1951): 50–67. [Edition.]

Describes the manuscript, its contents, and the five hands responsible for the entries, and comments on the date of the non-medical contents before describing the ME verses. These are: 'Moral Stanzas' ['Bi sapience tempre þy courage,' *576*]; 'De Veritate & Consciencia' ['Summe maner mater wolde I fayne meve,' *3173.5*]; and 'Erthe upon Erthe' ['Whan lyf is most louyd & deþ ys most hatid,' *3985*]. In style and content the first two do not suggest the work of the same poet. Examination of 'De Veritate' and of an additional stanza inserted later in the manuscript implies 'a most human and somewhat pathetic figure . . . a religious . . . probably a monastic librarian, who had read *Piers Plowman* [*1459*] . . . aware of the shortcomings of his age as of his own monastic house, who aspired to the composition of poetry . . . but whose endowments were unequal to the task' (58). The position of 'Erthe upon Erthe' on the last leaf, which is 'often given over to *trivia*' implies a wish to warn readers who were not serious, and might have turned there first 'in the hope of a diversion' (60). Kane prints diplomatic texts of the works, with comments on the language.

576, 1459, 3173.5, 3985.

294 Kreuzer, James R. 'Richard Maidstone's Version of the Fifty-First Psalm.' *Modern Language Notes* 65 (1951): 224–31. [Edition.]

Richard Maidstone's metrical version of Ps. 51, 'Mercy god of my mysdede' [*2157*], is found independently of the other six *Penitential Psalms*. Kreuzer notes the manuscript sources, and corrects some erroneous listings in *RMERV* and *IMEV*. He presents the text with some linguistic comment. The presence of Midland, Southern, Northern, and Kentish forms suggests that 'the scribe was using as his source an impure form whose basic dialect differed from his own' (226).

2157.

295 Moore, Arthur K. 'Chaucer's Use of Lyric as an Ornament of Style.' *Comparative Literature* 3 (1951): 32–46.

Interpolation of lyrics within longer poems was sometimes a device of amplification. Chaucer's use was generally 'superbly functional' (32). Moore compares lyrical ornament to the *satura* and to the songs and lyrics of English mystery plays. As one can see in the *Coventry Pageant of the Shearman and Taylors* [*3477*], many of the latter 'seem to have no special pertinence of any kind, while others serve mainly to effect transition' (34). He cites *Roman de la Rose*/*Guillaume de Dole* by Jehan Renart as 'an invaluable repository of medieval song' (36). In contrast to Jehan's blending of song and narrative, some ME romances contain lyrics that are decorative rather than appropriate, as seen in *King Alisaunder* [*683*] and *Richard Coer de Lyon* [*1979*]. Moore offers examples from Machaut and Froissart before turning to works of Chaucer and Lydgate, with detailed comment on the *Parliament of Fowls* [*3412*], *Legend of Good Women* [*100*], *Troilus and*

Criseyde [*3327*], and briefer references to *Canterbury Tales* [*4019*], *Fall of Princes* [*1168*], *Temple of Glas* [*851*], and *Pilgrimage of the Life of Man*. Other poets use similar interpolations, but 'Chaucer alone in mediaeval England definitely understood the proper use of the lyric as an ornament of style' (46).

100, 683, 1168, 1306, 1979, 2254, 2375, 3327, 3412, 3477, 4019.

296 ――――. 'Some Implications of the Middle English *Craft of Lovers*.' *Neophilologus* 35 (1951): 231–8.

'The Craft of Lovers' ['To moralise ⟨a similitude⟩ who list these ballets sewe,' *3761*] stands as 'a reaction against insipid courtly verse filled with denatured *amour courtois* and allegorical conceits' (231). It is not likely to be the work of Chaucer or Lydgate, as previously suggested. Moore compares it with verse which employs 'the devices of courtly panegyric ironically' (232) against forms and attitudes of *vers de société*. His explication of the dialogue between Cupido and Diana shows that 'the odd stanzas, assigned to the man, represent the much-inflated courtly style,' whereas 'the woman's acute rejoinders, which are not "aureated," fill the even ones.' The poem offers 'a keen analysis of courtly supplication' which rejects 'that artificial system of love which in the fifteenth century was, like chivalry, largely anachronistic' (234). Diana is won, 'not by that part of Cupido's speech which resembles the conventional complaint, but by that part which honestly reveals a natural passion,' the Ovidian element. Thus the poem stands against both courtly love and aureate diction, 'two central pillars of fifteenth-century literary practice' (237). [Cf. Wilson, **343**; Robbins, **336**.]

3761.

297 ――――. *The Secular Lyric in Middle English*. Lexington: U of Kentucky P, 1951.

Although early lyric poets dealt 'almost exclusively' (76) with religious or secular love, relatively few secular lyrics have been recorded. In 'Lyric Development' (1–40) Moore deals with orthodox opinion of and influences on ME lyrics. He compares definitions of the lyric that characterize it as 'amplified exclamation in verse . . . ideally marked by freedom of the emotions and liveliness of the imagination' (6). He also compares similar songs of other cultures, and discusses the relation to music. In 'The Harleian Love Lyrics' (41–75), Moore explores the relations of ME, AN, and Provençal forms, and cites examples. He writes in detail of some individual poems, most of them from MS Harley 2253. These include 'Alysoun' [*515*], which he finds successful; 'The Way of Woman's Love' [*1921*]; 'The Fair Maid of Ribblesdale' [*2207*], 'a disguised catalogue' (70); 'De Clerico et Puella' [*2236*]; 'The Poet's Repentance' [*3874*]; and 'Svmer is icumen in' [*3223*, from Harley 978]. His conclusion is that the Harleian lyrics are 'relatively free of artificiality' (75). Moore examines occasional verse in 'Songs of Satire and Protest' (76–99), generally written between 1250 and 1350, 'between the *Song of Lewes* [*3155*] and the battle songs of Laurence Minot' (76). Although he deems Minot 'a mean-spirited man of narrow sympathies and cankered prejudices' (94), he concedes that 'spontaneous and vigorous relics of political and social strife, though uncontrolled, frequently achieve a rough eloquence and occasionally a passage of real power and beauty' (100). In 'Art Lyric: A Preliminary,' Moore describes effects of French forms, to contend that after the loss of their inspiration, 'polite lyric was in the time of Chaucer and after seldom meritorious' (101). His consideration of work of Chaucer, Machaut, and Deschamps, with examples of forms of lyric, leads him to decide that '[s]aving the sonnet . . . no strictly fixed genre has ever caught on with English writers' (119). In 'The Chaucerian Lyric Mode' (124–54), he examines works of Chaucer, Lydgate, Hoccleve, Charles d'Orléans, and William de la Pole, Duke of Suffolk, and discerns no trace of the twelfth century's sincerity in work of the fifteenth. 'The Debris of the Transition' conceit has viability and meaning whenever a poet breathes life into it, from Chaucer down to William Meredith' (372).

926, 929, 932, 3327, 4004.

318 Spitzer, Leo. 'Emendations Proposed to *De Amico ad Amicam* and *Responcio*.' *Modern Language Notes* 67 (1952): 150–5.

The two macaronic poems, '*A celuy que pluys eyme en mounde*/Of alle tho that I have found/*Carissima*' [*16*], and '*A soun treschere et special*/ffer and ner and oueral/In mundo' [*19*], are preserved in MS Cambridge Gg.iv.27. Spitzer proposes to emend 'terse comments of the editors' (150), Chambers and Sidgwick, **18**, particularly those on the French lines. He concludes that the poems 'have been conceived, consciously and with some sophistication, on three separate linguistic levels every one of which has its special climate: The English – that of genuine feeling, the French – of conventional courtesy, the Latin – of epigrammatic terseness' (152). [See also Boffey, **795**.]

16, 19.

319 Telfer, J.M. 'The Evolution of a Mediaeval Theme.' *Durham University Journal* NS 45 (1952): 25–34.

Examines the nightingale, its song and symbolic place in literature, beginning with Pliny's account in *Naturalis Historia*. It may be linked with Procne's lament or joyful song in Latin verse. In Provençal songs the troubadour may associate the nightingale either with his song or his silence. In Northern French lyrics it is 'the symbol of love' (26), an oracle, messenger, or even the lover. It is essential in many legends; Tristan can imitate its song, and Sigurd can understand it. The story of the nightingale sent by a lady to the knight she loves is mentioned in *The Owl and the Nightingale* [*1384*]. The nightingale defends women in love in various debates, with the thrush ['Somer is comen wiþ loue to toune,' *3222*], the cuckoo ['The God of loue A benedicte,' *3361*], the merle ['In May as that Aurora did upspring,' *1503.5*], and a clerk ['In a mornyng of May as I lay slepyng,' *1452*]. Bestiaries mention its death and song, and draw a 'parallel between the nightingale and the soul' (31). In bestiaries of love it has courtly significance, symbolizing the lover; later it represents the pious soul. Lydgate's nightingale poems ['Go lityll quayere And swyft thy prunses dresse,' *931*; 'In Iune whan Titan was in Crabbes hede,' *1498*] draw on the associations, and show the nightingale as a symbol for Christ.

931, 1384, 1452, 1498, 1503.5, 3222, 3361.

320 Thayer, C.G. 'Nou Goth Sonne Under Wod.' *Explicator* 11.4 (1952): item 25.

Rode in 'thi faire Rode,' in the second line of 'Nou goth þe sonne under wode' [*2320*], may mean 'cross' as well as 'face,' to create 'a pun which is particularly distinguished for its emotional connotations and for its poetic sophistication.' Thus 'pathos is heightened and we have new poetic implications.' The Cross becomes 'Mary's Cross,' and so the poet's pity is directed to Mary, 'through her relationship to the Cross,' and also 'toward the Cross itself.'

2320.

321 Wilson, R.M. *The Lost Literature of Medieval England*. Methuen's Old English Library. Gen. eds. A.H. Smith and F. Norman. London: Methuen, 1952. 2nd edn. 1970.

Considers literature known by its traces, including 'Lyrical Poetry' (171–91) and 'Political and Satirical Poetry' (192–214). Cnut's verses on the monks of Ely ['Merie singen þe munaches binnen Ely,' *2164*] may be the first lyric in English. Thomas of Bayeux and St Godric of Finchal are early lyrical poets who composed religious verse, and there were secular lyrical poets. Religious references to secular verse include a Cistercian rhyming toast ['Loke nu frere,' *1940.5*], the condemnation of love songs, and their use in sermons. Lines and stanzas are quoted 'in Latin chronicles, in works of edification, whether Latin or English, and even in sermons' (176). In fact 'any blank piece of vellum seems to have been regarded as a suitable place for the recording of a verse or stanza' (177). Wilson cites numerous examples of such findings; he refers in particular to the evidence of the stanza 'Wel and wa sal ys hornes blaw' [*3857.5*] in the lawsuit brought by Lord Neville of Raby against the prior and convent of Durham (186–7). The *Red Book of Ossory* has 'all that has remained of some half-dozen English lyrics' (187), among Latin pieces composed 'by the bishop of Ossory, perhaps Richard de Lesdrede (1318–60), in order to displace certain "popular and secular songs"' (187). There are references to popular songs in longer works, including those of Chaucer, Henryson, and Dunbar.

Numerous works of political and social comment have survived, including poems referring to individuals, such as John Ball ['John Ball Saint Mary priest,' *1791*] and Henry Percy ['Henry haitspours haith a halt,' *1185*]; and to events, including the Kentish insurrection ['God be oure gyde,' *941*] and wars against the Scots ['Piket hym and diket hym, *2754*; 'Tprut Scot riueling,' *3799.3*]. Wilson cites many examples.

The second edition expands the scope of the first, by adding and commenting on more examples of lyrics in all categories. Wilson prints as separate poems the sections of two lyrics ['Ne saltou neuer leuedi,' *2288*; 'Ye Sir [þat is] idronken,' *4256.8*] previously considered complete poems.

179, 194, 445, 466, 521, 521.5, 556.5, 684, 734.5, 814, 848, 900, 941, 945.5, 1010, 1121, 1123, 1142, 1147.9, 1185, 1214.4, 1252, 1265, 1301.5, 1305, 1335, 1377, 1389.5, 1445, 1791, 1798, 1799, 1844.5, 1922, 1925, 1934, 1940.5, 1941.8, 2039.3, 2164, 2261.2, 2288, 2288.5, 2541.5, 2622, 2754, 2774, 2782, 2988, 3031, 3306, 3318.7, 3361.3, 3515.5, 3558.5, 3595, 3799.3, 3857.5, 3898, 3918.5, 3923.5, 4088, 4185.5, 4206, 4256.8, 4280, 7133, 7168, 7578.

Poems added to the second edition: *152, 231.5, 274, 598, 664.3, 730, 811, 851.3, 1120.5, 1140, 1142, 1163.5, 1201, 1301, 1393.5, 1445.6, 1531.5, 1589.5, 1944.5, 2012.3, 2086, 2141, 2162, 2231.8, 2261.6, 2289.3, 2323.3, 2437.5, 2541.5, 2797.5, 3098.5, 3104.5, 3131.5, 3167.3, 3306, 3439.5, 3721.5, 3808.5, 3820.5, 3859.5, 3899.3, 3899.6, 3900.5, 3902.5, 4284.3, 7057, 7079, 7435.*

——— Review of the first edition by Dorothy Everett, *Medium Ævum* 22 (1953): 31–4. Compares Wilson's work with earlier explorations by R.W. Chambers, and suggests that a radical reassessment of the OE period would follow if we were able to recover the literature that has been lost. Everett accepts the notion of firm establishment of the lyric early in the twelfth century, but finds some of Wilson's other conclusions 'dubious, at least in the form in which they are expressed' (32). Most of these are in the last chapter, and 'the rest of the book is conveniently arranged and much of it is interesting and thought-provoking' (34).

——— Review of the second edition by Norman Davis, *Review of English Studies* NS 22 (1971): 322–4. Welcomes the new edition, 'not only brought up to date in its references but thoroughly revised in many details of writing and arrangement' (322). Davis has some quibbles about lyrics included or omitted, but generally finds the book 'the fruit of wonderfully wide reading' and 'a great improvement' (324.)

322   Bazire, Joyce. '"The Fox and the Goose."' *English Studies* 34 (1953): 163–4.

In line 8 of 'The Fox and the Goose' ['It fell ageyns the next nyght,' *1622*], the expression *macke . . . yowre berde* conveys the fox's intention to outwit the geese. Bazire differs from *RobbinsS*, **51**, in reading *berde* rather than *lerde*, and from Bowers, **311**, in interpreting this as 'delude' rather than 'despoil.' She finds a different meaning for *will* in line 24, to read the line as '"While they are lying down"', that is, the whelps need bones to pick to keep them quiet in the lair' (164).

1622.

323 Kurvinen, Auvo. 'MS Porkington 10: Description with Extract.' *Neuphololologische Mitteilungen* 54 (1953): 33–67.

A detailed description of the manuscript and its varied contents, with extracts of many of the works, some of which are in prose. Kurvinen refers to edited sources of the works, and provides a glossary (65–7). The poems present a wide range of religious and secular works.

4, 22, 298, 324, 341, 349, 369, 479, 559, 560, 704, 977, 1116, 1120, 1241, 1641, 1785, 1852, 1897, 1932, 1957, 2018, 2610, 3289, 3314, 3330, 3363, 3743, 4001, 4029.

324 Robbins, Rossell Hope. '"Consilium domini in eternum manet" (Harley MS. 2252).' *Studia Neophilologica* 26 (1953–4): 58–64. [Edition.]

The poem 'O Mortall Man By grete exaltacion' [*2521*], found in the commonplace book of John Colyn, 'wealthy textile dealer and citizen of London in the early sixteenth century,' offers 'moral admonitions to a man of substance' (58). It is written twice in the commonplace book, and Robbins notes variations in the two copies. He describes the varied religious and secular contents of the book: romances, poems on current events, poems of instruction, prognostication, medical recipes, and a few love poems. After comparing the book briefly with similar works, to display connections between literature of the fifteenth and sixteenth centuries, Robbins prints the poem (61–4). The first four stanzas advise 'an acknowledgedly rich man on the canny conduct of business affairs.' The next six present moral precepts concerning duty to God. The last is 'a "Consider" anaphora that death will spare no one' (60)

432, 824, 1411, 1944, 1989, 2142, 2224, 2518, 2521, 2522, 2549.5, 3087, 3172, 4253.

325 Vincent, Sister Mary. '*PEARL*, 382: *mare reȝ mysse*?' *Modern Language Notes* 68 (1953): 528–31.

Cites the use of *rese* in two versions of 'God þat al þis myhtes may' [*968*] to support the contention that line 382 of *Pearl* [*2744*] reads *mare reȝ mysse*, rather than *marereȝ mysse*.

968, 2744.

326 Bowers, R.H. 'A Middle-English Diatribe against Backbiting.' *Modern Language Notes* 69 (1954): 160–3.

An attack on backbiters, 'Seynt Bernard seiþ and soo seye I' [*2864*] is preserved 'in a fifteenth century anonymous fair copy' in BL MS Royal 18 A.x. Bowers prints it, with expansion of 'obvious abbreviations' and 'a modicum of pointing' (160).

2864.

327 ———. 'The Middle English "The Insects and the Miller."' *Notes and Queries* 199 (1954): 187–8.

Bowers offers 'several glossarial notes – especially on the Latin words' (187), for *RobbinsS*, **51**, of 'The krycket & þe greshope wentyn here to fyȝht' [*3324*].

3324.

328 Bühler, Curt F. 'A Satirical Poem of the Tudor Period.' *Libri Impressi cum Notis Manuscriptis VI.' Anglia* 72 (1954): 419–22. Repr. in *Early Books and Manuscripts: Forty Years of Research by Curt F. Bühler*. New York: The Grolier Club and the Pierpont Morgan Library, 1973. 624–7. [Edition.]

The sixth of Bühler's notes on manuscript entries in early printed books concerns a satirical poem, 'O pereles Prynce of Peace/And Lord of Lordes all' [*2536.5*]. This is written 'on the verso of the first (blank) folio in the copy of Caxton's *The Life of St Winifred* belonging to the Pierpont Morgan Library,' and describes 'what a graceless age it was wrote in' (419). Errors in transcription and an absence of Protestant attitudes suggest that the text is a copy rather than an original, and that the spirit of the poem is 'rather that of the typical fifteenth-century complaint on the state of morality amongst the laity and the clergy' (420). Forms of characters and pronouns also hint at the fifteenth century. Bühler prints the poem with expanded contractions, and editorial punctuation and capitalization, with endnotes on particular words.

2536.5.

329 Copley, J. 'The 15th-Century Carol and Christmas.' *Notes and Queries* 199 (1954): 242–3.

Examination of the collections of carols made by Greene, **37**, and Stevens, **52**, leads Copley to conclude that the carols associated with Christmas make up a high proportion of the total, many more than had been estimated by Chambers, **247**. [Does not cite any specific carol.]

330 Degginger, Stuart H.L. '"A Wayle Whyt Ase Whalles Bon" – Reconstructed.' *JEGP* 53 (1954): 84–90. [Edition.]

There is generally more unity shown in ME lyrics than in those of the troubadours. However, 'A wayle whyt ase whalles bon' [*105*], as edited by Brook, **42**, is 'both formally irregular and substantially confusing' (84). Degginger prints it in this form, to explain the anomalies and difficulties he finds there, and proposes explanations based on the possibility of mistakes in copying to Harley MS 2253. He proposes that a 'single page . . . was notated on one side, the *recto*, giving the music for the poem proper, the text of the two final stanzas, then the music and text of a refrain . . . On the *verso* the rest of the poem was then continued without musical notation.' Then the scribe began his transcription, 'inadvertently with the text of the *verso*,' so that he 'thus disarranged the order of the stanzas' (88). On this basis Degginger prints the poem with a refrain, reordering the stanzas to begin with the seventh, so that 'not only is the *concatenatio* re-established more or less in all stanza-links, but the sense of the whole poem is also immeasurably improved' (88), and seen to be a '*rotruenge* or *chanson à refrain*' (90). The sequence of 'a lilting refrain, expansiveness (stanza I), contrast (II), descriptiveness (III), satire (V), mock sadness (VI), mock courtliness (VII), ending in outright mockery (VIII),' produces 'not a courtly lyric at all but a parody' (90). [See also Duncan, **971**.]

105.

331 Friend, Albert C. 'Fourteenth-Century Couplets of English Verse.' *PMLA* 69 (1954): 984.

Three fragments of English verse under Latin headings are to be found in MS Arras Bibliothèque de la Ville 184 (254), written *c*. 1400. The last, headed 'song of joy,' is the opening of a 'A Song of Love to the Blessed Virgin,' which begins 'Off alle floures feirest fall on/And þat is Marie Moder fre' [*2607*]. Friend conjectures that other couplets of 'the song of love and . . . the song of sorrow may also be the initial lines of longer lost poems.'

2607.

332 Greene, Richard L. '"The Port of Peace": Not Death but God.' *Modern Language Notes* 69 (1954): 307–9.

Brown gave the title 'Death, the Port of Peace' to the lyric 'Howe cometh al ye That ben y-brought' [*1254*], and commented that in it 'we recognize clearly the spirit of the Renaissance' [*BrownXV*, **39**: xxxix]. Reviewers of *BrownXV* have admired the poem and generally agreed with this interpretation. Greene notes that the work is 'a translation and slight expansion of the opening lines of Meter 10 in Book III of Boethius's *Consolation of Philosophy*' (308), from a translation made in 1410, by John Walton, of Oseney Abbey. Although this stanza does not depend on Chaucer's translation, Greene supplies Chaucer's 'Glose.' The lyric is thus not one on mortality; rather 'we must acknowledge its context and date and grant to its substance the highest degree of earlier medieval currency and of acceptance as Christian orthodoxy' (309). [See *TLS* Oct. 28 1939: 628; Greene, *Modern Language Notes* 55 (1940): 309; for a different view see also Greg, *Review of English Studies* NS 16 (1940): 198.]

1254.

333 Hatto, A.T. 'The Lime-Tree and Early German, Goliard and English Lyric Poetry.' *Modern Language Review* 49 (1954): 193–209.

Trees are frequently mentioned in love poetry, usually as places for lovers' meetings. The lime-tree appears in many medieval English and German works. Hatto notes connections 'between *leaf* and *linde*, and . . . *love*' (196) and Lent, and cites examples from ME poems. In ME, as in MHG, '*linde* had the generic meaning of "tree", not "lime-tree"' (200). The lime had stronger erotic significance in German symbolism, and this extends to Slavonic languages.

1459, 1504, 1861, 4019.

334 Hodgart, M.J.C. 'Medieval Lyrics and the Ballads.' *The Age of Chaucer*. Harmondsworth: Penguin, 1954. 157–64. Vol. 1 of *The Pelican Guide to English Literature*. Ed. Boris Ford. 7 vols. 1954–61.

Describes the lyric as 'a poem set to music,' and the ME lyric as 'a poor relation of the splendid Continental art-form' (157). Hodgart alludes briefly to various lyrics, to show *ubi sunt* and its variations as important themes of the religious works, and to demonstrate the inspiration of troubadour forms and ideas in the secular poems. The fifteenth-century carol is the 'most original and fruitful development of the English lyric' (161). The ballads are narrative songs, bearing 'the stamp of folklore' (162), and include 'Judas' [*1649*].

66, 117, 360, 1008, 1132, 1367, 1649, 1861, 2375, 2551.8, 2831, 3223, 3310, 3536, 3845.5.

335 Robbins, Rossell Hope. 'A Late Fifteenth-Century Love Lyric.' *Modern Language Notes* 69 (1954): 153–60. [Edition.]

'Thoythis fre þat lykis me' [*3707.8*], a late fifteenth-century love lyric, 'written as prose on the end flyleaves of an early fifteenth-century copy of a *Pricke of Conscience*, MS 157 (D.4.11) of Trinity College, Dublin' (153), has two instances of Southern inflexion, but generally suggests a Middle Scots dialect. Robbins prints it in quatrains with punctuation, and indicates the ends of lines in the original. He comments on dialect, vocabulary and style, with examples of 'stock poetic diction' (159). His comparisons with similar forms are brief allusions to numerous other lyrics, including some in Rawlinson C.813 and Bannatyne MSS, to show that 'by the late fifteenth century a Northern gentleman composes a love lyric in the accepted fashion of his day' (160).

137, 366, 767, 812, 1068, 1086, 1160, 1283, 1330, 1344, 1678, 2015, 2245, 2303, 2381, 2421, 2517, 2517, 2597, 3196, 3291, 3418, 3707.8, 4200.

336 ———. 'A Love Epistle by "Chaucer."' *Modern Language Review* 49 (1954): 289–92. [Edition.]

A love epistle in Trinity College Cambridge MS 599 (R.3.19), headed 'Chaucer,' has stanzas (3, 4, 5, and 10) from 'The Craft of Lovers' [*3761*]. Spoken by the wooer (Cupido), they provide 'a general narrative rather than a dialogue content' (290); without Diana's reply, they do not produce an effect of parody. [Cf. Moore, **296**.] Robbins resolves confusion about its authorship as 'not by Chaucer – nor by Lydgate either' (289). Its nature too has been in doubt; the first lines caused Brown to list it in *RMERV* as 'An orison to the B.V.' but it is not a religious work. The poem is 'carefully written in a chain of similar aureate love lyrics' (290). Robbins prints it, with editorial punctuation. [See also **657**; Wilson, **343**; Kooper, **892**.]

1838, 3761.

337 ———. 'A Song for Victory in France. (1492)' *Neuphilologische Mitteilungen* 55 (1954): 289–93. [Edition.]

At the end of the *Historia Regis Henrici Septimi*, by Bernard André, in MS Cotton Domitianus xviii, is the song 'And save thys flowre wyche ys oure kyng' [*306.8*], described as 'a short English adulation for the success of Henry's invasion of France in 1492' (290). Robbins explains the historical background to its composition and compares it with other poems that use rose imagery, including political carols ['I loue a flour of swete odour,' *1327*; 'In a gloryus garden grene,' *1450*], and the early sixteenth-century ballad 'The Rose of England.' He prints the poem, 'for the first time, as it appears in the MS' (293), with editorial punctuation.

306.8, 1327, 1450.

338 ———. 'An Unkind Mistress (Lambeth MS. 432).' *Modern Language Notes* 69 (1954): 552–8.

A stanza in MS Lambeth 432, 'O ye prynces þat prechyd hase my hert' [*2599*], was at first identified as 'Moral Admonitions' and so described in *IMEV*, but is a lover's complaint. Robbins finds it 'a typical routine performance of some amateur author putting together the clichéd poetic formulas of his age, and it demonstrates the interplay of sensuous phraseology in secular and religious lyrics which in quite a few examples makes identification dubious' (553). He expands this in a detailed comparison of clichés used in love lyrics, with Appeals of Christ to Man, and cites numerous examples in brief references. In the love lyrics the clichés are '[t]he unkindness of his mistress,' '[l]ove's piercing of the heart and the smart of the wound,' and '[t]he poet's complete and undemanding devotion' (554). Corresponding to these are '[t]he unkindness of man,' '[l]ove's piercing the heart and the smart of the wound' (with a similar metaphor in the *Stabat Mater* laments), and 'Christ's complete and undemanding devotion' (555–6). There is a striking illustration in 'two lyrics of the fifteenth century, which, for eight lines, are identical' (556). One of these, 'Have all my hert and be in peys' [*1120*], is secular, whereas 'Trewloue trewe on you I truste' [*3805*], is religious. Robbins quotes the lines, with other examples from 'those poems which lack sufficient direct evidence to classify them as religious or secular' (557).

152, 352, 366, 380, 456, 479, 495, 588, 831, 925, 927, 1018, 1120, 1310, 1311, 1328, 1331, 1700, 1715, 1735, 1761, 1781, 1838, 1841, 2080, 2245, 2412, 2502, 2504, 2567, 2599, 2618, 2687, 2824, 3071, 3179, 3228, 3238, 3414, 3498, 3543, 3611, 3612, 3704, 3760, 3785, 3805, 3825, 3826, 3827, 3835, 3836, 3845, 4056.

339 ———. 'Five Middle English Verse Prayers from Lambeth MS. 541.' *Neophilologus* 38 (1954): 36–41. [Edition.]

The prayers, 'Ffrom all mysrewle in ȝowthe exercisyd by me' [*874*], 'Jesu lythe my sowle with þi grace' [*1719.5*, transferred from *1666*], 'Ihesu my louer and my delite' [*1736*], 'Lorde be þᵘ my kepere' [*1947*], and 'The ryȝth wey to heuen Ihesu þᵘ me shewe' [*3454*], were added to the manuscript in 'a late fifteenth-century hand' (37). Four of these, *874*, *3454*, *1947*, and *1719.5*, paraphrase verses from the Psalter; Robbins incorporates the psalm references in the texts, and compares the prayers to similar works. The rubrics for *874* and *3454* are unique in identifying prayers 'for Ianiver*e* p*er*sonis' and 'for may p*er*sonis.' The last prayer, *1736*, is remarkable 'for its invocation of the "11,000 Virgins" for chastity' (38). Robbins presents the texts as they appear in the manuscript, with editorial punctuation and references to the Psalter. [Cf. **218**.]

874, 1719.5, 1736, 1947, 3454.

340 ———. 'Middle English Versions of "*Criste Qui Lux es et Dies.*"' *Harvard Theological Review* 47 (1954): 55–63. [Edition.]

The popularity of the Latin hymn '*Criste qui lux es et dies*' is demonstrated by the survival of eight versions in ME verse. Robbins lists variants and their sources in manuscripts and editions, with dates. All of these are of the fifteenth century except for the version in the Bannatyne MS, '*Criste qui lux es et dies*/O Iesu crist þe verray lycht' [*612*]. The earliest translation is an AS gloss in the Durham Hymnal. The Latin hymn was connected with St Ambrose, and is mentioned in the sixth century. Robbins supplies the hymn's history and prints two translations, in Harley MSS 1260 ['Cryst that day ert and lyght,' *620.5*] and 665 ['Cryst þᵗ art boþe lygt & day,' *616*], with punctuation and comments in footnotes. He compares the eight versions, commenting particularly on those of Lydgate and Ryman, and speculating on their use in the liturgy. Statistics reveal that 'of the 1900 or so religious lyrics in Middle English, nearly 200 are either direct translations or very close paraphrases of Latin hymns' (63).

612, 614, 615, 616, 617, 618, 619, 620.5.

341 ———. 'The World Upside Down: A Middle English Amphibole.' *Anglia* 72 (1954): 385–9. [Edition.]

A poem written in a fragment in Bodleian Library MS Eng. poet. b. 4 takes 'an oblique or satiric approach' to the theme of the Abuses of the Age, by assuming that 'wickedness is a thing of the past, and now everything in England is right as right could be.' It adds, in a refrain, 'that "stability is assured, especially in matters of apparel"' (385). Robbins prints the work, 'Religous pepille leuyn in holyness' [*2805*], and compares 'Fulfylled ys þe profe[s]ly for ay' [*884*]. He concludes that 'techniques which distinguish this amphibole are the catalogue of impossibilities and the destroying refrain and last stanza' (388). Other poems show some of the devices. He cites examples of the use of impossibilities ['Herkyn to my tale I schall to yow schew,' *1116*; 'The mone in the mornyng merely rose,' *3435*; 'When feithe fayles in prestys sawes,' *3943*; 'When nettuls in wynter bryng forth rosys red,' *3999*], the destroying refrain ['In euery place ye may well see,' *1485*], and some 'less cynical' but 'more apocalyptic jeremiads ['As i me lend to a lond,' *356*; 'Now pride ys yn pris,' *2356*; 'Vertues & good lyuinge is cleped ypocrisie,' *3851*; 'Wold god þᵗ men myȝt sene' *4236*]. By introducing irony, 'The World Upside Down' [*2805*] suggests 'a fin de siécle worldliness, the hallmark of a period's closing years' (389).

356, 884, 1116, 1485, 2356, 2805, 3435, 3851, 3843, 3999, 4236.

342 Wilson, Kenneth G. 'Five Fugitive Pieces of Fifteenth-Century Secular Verse.' *Modern Language Notes* 69 (1954): 18–22. [Edition.]

These brief poems, written in blank spaces in older manuscripts, are of love. Three, perhaps four, are lyrics in rhyme royal; the fifth is a didactic quatrain. Wilson prints them, with titles and comments. 'Come Death' ['O dethe whylum dysplesant to nature,' *2412*], in Pembroke College, Cambridge 307, is a conventional plea to Death. 'Thanks, Gentle Fortune' ['O gentyll fortune I thonke yowe I wys,' *2440*], from Trinity College, Cambridge 652, fits convention in praising the lady and in apostrophizing Fortune. The acrostic 'Katyryn' ['Kavser of my goy helthe and comford,' *588*], in Trinity College, Cambridge 257, may address 'a living lady, not a saint' (20). 'Advice to Lovers' ['He that wilbe a lover in euery wise,' *1170*], from Royal 18 A.vi, is 'cynically practical' (21) in listing qualities 'so necessary for success in love' (21). The quatrain 'Where I Love' ['Where I loue rigth wele,' *4060*] in Trinity College, Cambridge 263, uses a kind of incremental repetition to express a fine distinction between lust and love' (22).

588, 1170, 2412, 2440, 4060.

343 ———. 'Five Unpublished Secular Love Poems from MS Trinity College Cambridge 599.' *Anglia* 72 (1954): 400–18. [Edition.]

None of these previously unpublished poems is 'good poetry,' but the works are 'of considerable interest' (401), in historical and linguistic senses. They are anonymous love lyrics, with 'neither internal nor external evidence of authorship' (401). Wilson provides a title for each and explores points of interest in footnotes, commenting that the poems are 'traditional, employing the rime royal stanza in a fashion sometimes brutally exact, sometimes metrically undisciplined.' He notes that the 'extremely prolix' work, the 'Lover's Book' ['O Lady myne to whom thys boke I sende,' *2478.5*] 'illustrates almost every facet of the traditional complaint,' and 'To the Floure of Formosyte' ['O beauteous braunche floure of formosyte,' *2384.8*] has 'exceptionally extravagant aureate diction' and 'nearly systematic use of alliteration.' Wilson simply prints the texts of the other poems, with manuscript spelling, expanded contractions and abbreviations, and editorial punctuation and capitalization, since extended discussion would be 'bootless' (401). 'A Lover's Appeal' ['Lady of pite for þy sorowes þ^t þ^u haddest,' *1838*] (415–18), signed 'Chaucer,' has stanzas in common with 'The Craft of Lovers' [*3761*]. [See Moore, **296**; Robbins, **336**.] The remaining poems are 'Help Me to Weep' ['O ye all that ben or haue byn in dyssease,' *2588.5*] (404–5) and 'Let Pyte Comfort Your Daungernesse' ['All lust and lyking I begyn to leue,' *190.5*] (405–6).

190.5, 1838, 2384.8, 2478.5, 2588.5.

344 ———. '*The Lay of Sorrow* and *The Lufaris Complaynt*: An Edition.' *Speculum* 29 (1954): 708–24. [Edition.]

The poems are in MS. Arch. Selden B.24 (Bodleian 3354), and their Scottish characteristics 'may be purely scribal in origin' (709). Stanzaic similarity suggests a close relationship between 'The Lay of Sorrow' ['Befor my deth this lay of sorow I sing,' *482*] and 'The Lufaris Complaint' ['Be cause that teres waymenting and playnte,' *564*] (the titles supplied by Wilson). 'The Lay of Sorrow' resembles works of Dunbar in aspects of rhyme and line length, and both poems use the basic stanza of nine decasyllabic lines of 'The Golden Targe' [*2820.5*]. Wilson offers a detailed analysis of the stanza forms and variations. The lyrics are probably 'from the same unknown original manuscript,' perhaps works of one author, although 'The Lufaris Complaynt' is 'far less polished.' They have 'historical and intrinsic interest,' and illustrate trends. 'The Lufaris Complaynt' is conventional in treatment, diction, figures, and matter. 'The Lay of Sorrow' uses conventions, 'but goes beyond them' (711), and succeeds where the other poem fails. Wilson's account of 'The Lufaris Complaynt' emphasizes its allusive nature. The poet's consciousness of writing makes it 'a work of study' which attempts 'realistic description of emotional upheaval' (713). The speaker of 'The Lay of Sorrow,' a woman lamenting the loss of her lover, addresses God, her lover, and then '*all* men, bewailing the lot of women' (714). She expresses many emotions, but, after apologizing, concludes that 'lamenting is of no help whatsoever to the heart torn by lovesickness,' and farewells her lover in a lay of death. The dedication with which the poem concludes creates a surprising effect, since 'the woeful lady has seemed very real' (715). The poem has vivid, original figures and diction, and successfully executes the complex metrical pattern. Wilson prints the poems, with additional notes for 'The Lay of Sorrow.'

482, 564.

345   Berry, Francis. 'A Medieval Poem and its Secularized Derivative.' *Essays in Criticism* 5 (1955): 299–314.

Compares the version of the 'Corpus Christi Carol' [*1132*] in Richard Hill's Commonplace Book with 'The *Herone* flewe eist, the *Herone* flewe west' [*7422*], cited in 1820 by James Hogg. Berry's analysis explains differences in 'kind and function,' to reveal the strengths of *1132*. This is a carol with a refrain; it has the rhythmic power of a dance, emphasized by alliteration and anaphora; except in the first and last stanzas, the lines are balanced about a caesura. In contrast, the Hogg version has lost the refrain and stanza structure, to become 'continuous narrative verse' (302), in which alliteration and repetition seem merely accidental. Most of the few adjectives of *1132* are of colour; those of Hogg's poem contribute to the reader's 'suitable emotion' (305) towards the scene he describes. Hogg's poem is 'the "Hill" version after four hundred years of oral transmission, published by Hogg some seventy years before the "Hill" version was discovered' (305–6). The Hill version is religious, with meaning that is difficult to discern; the Hogg version is secular and meaningless. Although other versions imply that the Hill poem is a carol of Christmas, Berry relates it to the Passion. He finds Gilchrist, **125**, on Arthurian interpretation, 'secondarily correct but primarily wrong (accepting as the real subject of the poem *Christus mortuus*) . . . because Jesus poetically *includes* these figures of Himself,' although 'the reverse does not hold.' Thus the knight of Hill's version is Christ and so includes Arthur, King Pellam, or Amfortas, 'but the lesser does not include the greater' (308). Berry confirms Edith C. Batho's identification [*The Ettrick Shepherd* (Cambridge: Cambridge UP, 1927)] of *1132* as a carol of the Passion, through its resemblances to the Good Friday gospel in John 28 and 29, and to enclosure of the Sacrament in a sepulchre on Good Friday. He comments on the narrow, intense experience of spoken rather than written language, and the modern thinning of language, with the result that man's harmony with nature, discerned in the Hill version, is lost in versions such as Hogg's.

1132, 7422.

346   Bowers, R.H. 'A Middle English Mnemonic Poem on Usury.' *Mediaeval Studies* 17 (1955): 226–32. [Edition.]

Since practices of usury were frequently condemned by homilists, 'it is surprising that not more mnemonic versifications of such admonitions . . . have survived in the vernacular,' since such verse played 'an important role in mediaeval England' (227). The poem 'Okure þrowe crafte of okerrers' [*2671*], with a stanza for each of twelve methods of usury, is preserved in BL MS Egerton 2810. It is of the mid-fifteenth century, and some Northern forms, suggest that the author was 'a Yorkshireman or a Scot.' It has characteristics typical of mnemonic verse: 'cramped syntax, ambiguity of reference in personal pronouns, restricted and iterated vocabulary, and emphasis on exposition from a practical point of view.' Bowers prints the poem and a prose text from Harley 45, 'a useful parallel' which has 'a less involved grammatical structure.' His transcriptions 'silently expand obvious abbreviations and introduce modern capitalization and punctuation' (228). He makes no comment on the prose text, but adds footnotes to the poem.

2671.

347 ——. 'A Middle-English Poem on the Seven Gifts of the Holy Ghost.' *Modern Language Notes* 70 (1955): 249–52. [Edition.]

Isaiah 11. 2–3 is the source of 'the medieval figura of the seven gifts of the Holy Ghost as protection against sin' (249), which is found in several fourteenth-century English versions. Bowers offers 'Alle þᵗ well a stownde dwelle' [*215*], previously unprinted, 'preserved in fifteenth-century apograph fair copy in Cambridge University Library MS Ii.iv.9.' His transcription 'silently expands unmistakable abbreviations and introduces editorial punctuation' (250).

215.

348 ——. 'A Middle English "Rake's Progress" Poem.' *Modern Language Notes* 70 (1955): 396–8. [Edition.]

The 'exceedingly coarse' verses 'Burgeys thou hast so blowen atte the Cole' [*551*], uniquely preserved in MS Harley 7578, demonstrate the poet's sense of humour' and 'pose some minor problems in ME lexicography' (396). For these reasons, Bowers prints them, with punctuation and capitalization, and adds footnotes on particular senses of various words. [See Robbins, **370**.]

551.

349 ——. 'Three Middle English Poems on the Apostles' Creed.' *PMLA* 70 (1955): 210–22. [Edition.]

Doctrinal commentary on and formulation of the Apostles' Creed and the careers of the Apostles were 'themes of pleasure and curiosity to the medieval hagiographer and poet' (210). Bowers briefly surveys such works and prints 'three hitherto unprinted ME didactic poems, all preserved uniquely in fifteenth-century fair copies, on "How the Apostles made the Creed"' (212). He finds the poem, 'I trow in god fader of myghte þᵗ all has wroghte' [*1374*] in MS Corpus Christi College, Oxford 155, 'of little interest.' That of BL Add. 39,996 (*olim* Philipps 9803), 'And þen þe apostles togeder went' [*311*], is 'more ample ... but it exhibits mediocre poetic talent' (212). 'Or Crist into clouds gan flueȝ vp so swiftly' [*2700*], in BL Add. 32,578, by Robert Farnelay, is 'of considerable interest, for the author writes with imagination and a feeling for language' (213), with 'thirteen well-cast stanzas ... containing alliteration and internal assonance'; it represents 'the process of the gradual triumph of rime over the native alliterative style' (213). The themes of the formulation of the Creed and the Apostles' careers are fused, and the work ends in 'a brilliant apostrophe to Mary' (213). Bowers provides brief descriptions of the manuscripts and prints the texts, with explanations in footnotes.

311, 1374, 2700.

350 ——. 'When Cuckow Time Cometh Oft So Soon: A Middle-English Animal Prophecy (Lansdowne MS 762, fol. 767, fol. 59–61).' *Anglia* 73 (1955): 292–8. [Edition.]

The title Bowers supplies comes from a line which serves as a refrain to 'The hedgehoge will the cookcok fed' [*3375*], although there is no stanzaic structure in this prophecy of 141 lines. He prints the poem, 'with modern capitals, a modicum of punctuation and expansion of obvious abbreviation' (292), and with end-notes, from the unique text in Lansdowne 762. Although there are no obvious political allusions, 'it would be presumptuous to argue that the piece has no political inspiration' (293). The closing lines, 'beyond the conventional pious endings of many Middle-English poems ... argue that the author may have been a cleric' (293).

3375.

351 **Brewer, D.S.** 'The Ideal of Feminine Beauty in Medieval Literature, especially "Harley Lyrics", Chaucer, and some Elizabethans.' *Modern Language Review* 50 (1955): 257–69.

Examines traditions of formal description of heroines, including conventional comparisons and the effects of variations. Matthew of Vendôme's description of Helen of Troy sets the medieval pattern, with little variation from the classical model. Geoffrey of Vinsauf offers more detail in the same style. Examples are taught in the schools, and the conventions influence descriptions in several Harley lyrics. Brewer notes the luminous 'Fair Maid of Ribblesdale' [*2207*], and the comparisons with whalebone in this lyric and in 'A wayle whyt ase whalles bon' [*105*]. Likening the lady's neck to that of a swan adds 'a certain grotesque charm' (260) to *2207*; her jewelled girdle shows the influence of *Roman de la Rose*. The treatment is learned and courtly, but the lyrics also have 'a certain rusticity, and occasional slightly absurd *naïveté*.' Brewer questions Chambers's comments, **18**, on the Fair Maid (261). 'Blow Northerne Wynd' [*1395*] and 'Alysoun' [*515*] conform to traditions, but their variations add freshness, especially to the latter poem; they distinguish 'vernacular poetry from that of the learned, though often grosser tongue.' Since beauty is associated with goodness, and love is 'a moral emotion for the later medieval courtly writers . . . the heroine herself becomes more precious' (262). Chaucer sometimes exploits the traditions, which survive in works of Shakespeare and Donne.

105, 515, 1306, 1395, 2207, 3327, 4019.

352 **Bühler, Curt F.** 'Two Renaissance Epitaphs.' *Renaissance News* 8 (1955): 9–11.

Some lines on giving, in an epitaph, 'As I was so be ye' [*374.5*], found at St Olaf's Church, London, are incorporated into the epitaph for Edward de Courtenay, the 'blind Earl' of Devon, and his wife Maud. They are also, inexplicably, in a form that suggests his wife's name is Kate.

374.5.

353 **Cutler, John L.** 'A Middle English Acrostic.' *Modern Language Notes* 70 (1955): 87–9. [Edition.]

ME acrostics deal with both religious and secular themes. Cutler list 17 such poems, with brief comment. He prints one, of 'the *memento mori* tradition' (89), not previously noted as an acrostic, with a full critical appreciation. It is 'A Mirror for Young Ladies at their Toilet' ['Maist thou now be glade with all thi fresshe aray,' *2136*]. With two emendations of the text of *Brown XV*, **39**, it spells MORS SOLVIT OMNIA. The acrostic motto powerfully reinforces the theme of Death, admonishing the young and frivolous, so that 'a form likely to result merely in ingenuity becomes the vehicle of eloquent statement' (89).

158, 456, 481, 588, 737, 1024, 1026, 1570.5, 1634, 1813, 1874, 2136, 2171, 2190, 2217, 2233, 2479.

354 **Frankis, P.J.** 'Some Late Middle English Lyrics in the Bodleian Library.' *Anglia* 73 (1955): 299–304. [Edition.]

Two fifteenth-century lyrics, 'Lett lowe to lowe go kyndly and sowfte' [*1864.5*] and 'O paineful hart in peiyns syȝht' [*2535.5*] in Bodleian MS 13679 [Rawlinson D.913], have been 'almost unnoticed' (299). Frankis prints them with commentary, and notes possible connections with Scots poems in Hunterian 230 and a fragment in Selden B.24 ['. . . ȝoure seruand madame,' **4284.3*], which he reconstructs in a form that 'may perhaps have been a carol' (301) and 'must be the earliest known version of what was to become a very popular sixteenth century song' (302), 'Go from my window.' [See Baskerville,

148.] The literary relationships of poems in Rawlinson C.813 and Porkington 10, fragments in the Chapter Library of Canterbury Cathedral, Hunterian 230, and the *Mellon Chansonnier* in Yale University Library [see Bukofzer, **234**] lead Frankis to conclude that 'a poet would freely borrow and appropriate any existing stanza which happened to suit his purpose.' Thus the verse of later poets such as Skelton and Wyatt may be seen 'to have sprung in part from medieval English sources and not simply to have been transplanted from the Mediterranean hot-house of Renascence culture' (304).

1349.5, 1864.5, 2245.1, 2318, 2478, 2532.5, 2535.5, 2536, 3165, *4284.3.

355 Gierasch, Walter. 'O Western Wind, When Wilt Thou Blow?' *Explicator* 14.7 (1955): item 43.

To supplement and corroborate Sweeney's explication, **363**, of 'Westron wynde when wylle thou blow' [*3899.3*], Gierasch cites Robert Graves's reference to Eros, the son of Iris and the West Wind, and biblical instances of 'small rain,' which represent 'the goodness and gentleness of fruition.' These ideas help to confirm 'a symbolic longing for the renewal of love.'

3899.3.

356 Long, Mary McDonald. 'Undetected Verse in Mirk's *Festial*.' *Modern Language Notes* 70 (1955): 13–15. [Edition.]

Some 'scraps of undetected verse, printed as prose' begin or end sermons in John Mirk's prose *Festial*, in MS Bodleian 17680 (Gough Eccl. Top. 4). They generally take the form of a prayer, to be 'more easily remembered by the congregation' (13). Long prints the lines, arranged as verse, noting the 'tortured construction to which Mirk resorted for the sake of his rime' (14). Although many passages 'might be dismissed as rimed prose' (14), a dialogue in Sermon 53 is 'the only one in medieval English verse that is based on the Assumption of the Blessed Virgin and is worthy of being accorded recognition among the religious poetry of the fifteenth century' (15).

956.5, 7011, 7051, 7107, 7544, 7545, 7554.

357 Mustanoja, Tauno F. 'Middle English with an O and an I: With a Note on Two Shakespearean "O-I Puns."' *Neuphilologische Mitteilungen* 56 (1955): 161–73.

The ME refrain *with an O and an I* and variants *A-I, U-I, I-E,* and *O-U* may be related to similar elements in Latin and vernacular poems, to *hey-ho,* and *hey nonino.* Mustanoja notes the hymn 'Godys sone þat was so fre' [*1001*] and 'The False Fox' ['The false fox came vnto oure croft,' *3328*], and traces patterns of varied repetition with alternating vowel gradation and quality, leading to examples from *As You Like It.* 'A Note on Two Shakespearean Puns on *O* and *I*' provides detailed analysis of sequences of word-play in *Romeo and Juliet* and *Midsummer Night's Dream.* [Cf. Cawley, **289**.]

1001, 3228.

358 Ringler, William. 'A Bibliography and First-Line Index of English Verse Printed Through 1500: A Supplement to Brown and Robbins' "Index of Middle English Verse."' *Papers of the Bibliographical Society of America* 49 (1955): 153–80.

An index intended as a supplement to *IMEV*, to list 'all items of English verse that appeared in print through the year 1500' (153). Ringler aims to extend the knowledge of previously unrecorded ME poems and to supply 'a conspectus of the English taste in poetry during the last quarter of the fifteenth century' (154). He supplies a bibliography of the books containing verse, and a first-line index of verse items, and concludes with 'a concordance of *Short-Title Catalogue* and Duff number' (156), showing works he has examined, as an aid to further explorations in this field.

33, 33.5, 42.5, 168, 233, 263, 272.5, 286.5, 316.6, 324, 520, 524, 527.5, 540, 554.3, 658, 731.5, 761, 809, 824, 841, 851, 854, 913, 920, 927.5, 991, 1168, 1192, 1242, 1243, 1244, 1245, 1246, 1247, 1248, 1249, 1296, 1324, 1342, 1470.5, 1491, 1596.5, 1618, 1619, 1629, 1719, 1725, 1915, 1919, 1920, 1933, 1934, 1993, 2039.3, 2119, 2167, 2233, 2233.5, 2262, 2264, 2361.5, 2428, 2574, 2662, 2663.5, 2664.5, 2711.5, 2754, 2784, 3074, 3145, 3252, 3327, 3372.1, 3412, 3446, 3496.6, 3503, 3521.5, 3540, 3542, 3584, 3651, 3651, 3661, 3670, 3747, 3787, 3818, 3830.5, 3928, 3955, 3986, 4005, 4019, 4064, 4101, 4106, 4106.5, 4109.5, 4187.8.

359 Robbins, Rossell Hope. 'A Middle English Diatribe against Philip of Burgundy.' *Neophilologus* 39 (1955): 131–46. [Edition.]

MS Rome, English College 1306 preserves in full 'A songe made of the duc of Bourgone' ['Thow Phellipe foundour of new falshede,' *3682*], the ME poem 'of scorn against Philip, Duke of Burgundy and Flanders, on his retreat from a siege of Calais in 1436' (131). Robbins describes the manuscript, lists its contents, and records its history before explaining the historical background of the poem, which he prints with editorial punctuation and notes. The work is one of the 'English counterparts to the continental *sirventes*' (140), which Robbins places in the tradition of personal abuse. He cites other examples that are directed against the friars ['Allas what schul we freris do,' *161*; 'Freers freers wo ȝe be *ministri malorum*,' *871*; 'þou þᵗ sellest þe worde of god,' *3697*], gallants ['Galawnt pride thy father is dede,' *892*; 'Ye prowd galanttes hertlesse,' *4255*], women ['O wicket wemen wilfull and variable,' *2580*], the lecherous ['Burgeys thou hast so blowen atte the Cole,' *551*], and ridiculed lovers ['O fresche floure most plesant of pryse,' *2437*; 'O Mossie Quince hangynge by youre stalke,' *2524*]. He expands the references to military and political enemies of England by describing and quoting from some works. Those abused include the Scots ['And swa mai men kenne,' *310*; 'For boule bred in his boke,' *814*; 'For thar wer thai bal bred,' *848*; 'Longe berde herteles,' *1934*; 'On grene/That kynered kene,' *2686*; 'Skottes out of Berwik and of Abirdene,' *3080*; 'Sir Dauid þe Bruse was at distance,' *3117*], the French ['In Iuyli whan the sonne shone shene,' *1497*; *3682*; 'War þis winter oway wele wald I wene,' *3899*], and the Flemings ['Off stryvys new and fraudulent falsenesse,' *2657*; 'When ye fflemyng wer fressh florisshed in youre flouris,' *4056.8*, formerly entered as *4034*]. Laurence Minot wrote against the Scots [*3080, 3117*] and French [*3899*]. The poems have similarities, and Robbins cites several lines in which *3682* resembles *1497, 2657,* and *4056.8* (142–3). He notes parallels with prose sources of events in *An English Chronicle, St Remy, Chronicles of London,* and English and Latin *Brut* chronicles, and extends the comparisons to Shakespeare's use of Hall's and Holinshed's *Chronicles.*

161, 310, 551, 576, 653, 814, 824, 848, 854, 871, 892, 919, 1497, 1874, 1934, 1944, 2437, 2524, 2574, 2580, 2591, 2657, 2686, 3080, 3117, 3682, 3697, 3799, 3899, 3910.5, 3955, 4034, 4230, 4255.

360 ———. 'An Epitaph for Duke Humphrey (1447).' *Neuphilologische Mitteilungen* 56 (1955): 241–9. [Edition.]

Some critics have attributed to Lydgate an epitaph for the murdered Humphrey, Duke of Gloucester, 'Soueraynelmmortal euerlastyng god' [*3206*], found in BL MSS Harley 2251 and Add. 34360. Robbins summarizes the scholarship and the differing views on this attribution. MacCracken rejected Lydgate's authorship after applying a rhyme test [*John Lydgate: The Minor Poems*, 1: xi]. Critical opinion of the work is generally unfavourable, and Robbins presents it 'so that scholars can examine an uninspired formal political poem, the equivalent of the mid fifteenth-century dull, aureate effusions to the Virgin and the catalogues of physical charms' (242–3). Robbins contrasts lines in Lydgate's *Fall of Princes* [*1168*] which praise Humphrey. He proposes as the author 'some chaplain or secretary in Gloucester's train, who accompanied the corpse to St. Alban's' (248), and compares the epitaph to similar works of the period.

5, 92, 444, 490, 520, 769, 1168, 2588, 3206, 3431, 3632, 3808, 4026.

361 ———. 'God Amende Wykkyd Cownscell (1464).' *Neuphilologische Mitteilungen* 56 (1955): 94–102. [Edition.]

'God Amende Wykkyd Cownscell,' ['As I walkyd my self alone,' *372*], printed for the first time by Robbins, presents a view of Henry VI which is 'similar in outline to that accepted by the late Tudor and Elizabethan chroniclers, and, through Shakespeare's adaptations, by many Englishmen today' (94–5). The poem is the complaint of Henry VI, who mourns the loss of his power. It is not hostile in tone to the king; rather 'the blame falls on his queen, Margaret of Anjou' (99). The marriage and its consequences are similarly deplored in the *Brut*, and by Hall, Fabyan, Stow, and Holinshed. The poem is in *chanson d'aventure* form, with conventional imagery. The refrain recurs irregularly, making it 'a moralising lament on the uncertainty of worldly greatness, a stock theme of Middle English didactic verse' (101). The work is part of a literary tradition of the fall of princes. Robbins illustrates resemblances to a Latin elegy of Abbot Whethamstede and to poems on Edward II ['[O]pon a somer soneday,' *3838*], Edward III ['A dere god what may this be,' *5*], and Edward IV ['Where is this Prynce that conquered his right,' *4062*].

5, 372, 3838, 4062.

362 ———. 'On Dating a Middle English Moral Poem.' *Modern Language Notes* 70 (1955): 473–6.

Most poems describing Abuses of the Age or Evils of the Times come from 'a list in a Latin tract, ascribed variously to Cyprian, Augustine or Origen' (473). They are similar in content, whether written in the thirteenth, fourteenth, or fifteenth centuries, with themes that include 'might making right and . . . rich men plundering' (473), 'love turned to lust,' and 'feigned friends or crooked lawyers' (474). It is usually difficult to determine the date of composition, because 'the sentiments are so hackneyed and conventionalized' (474). Robbins notes two exceptions, which he dates from historical references. 'This holy tyme make ȝow clene' [*3608*], is in a series in MS Digby 102. It condemns 'those who clip money, use false weights and measures, "storble" the rights of the poor, and take bribes and pervert the law' (474), all matters discussed in the Parliament that assembled near Easter, 1410. Reference to *Gregory's Chronicle*, which records 'the shocking story of a thief turned state informer' (475), suggests 1456 for 'The bysom ledys the blynde' ['Fulfylled ys profe[s]ly for ay,' *884*]. These instances, and brief references to other poems, show the value of considering the historical background of ME poems to avoid 'lumping together thirteenth- and fifteenth-century materials and . . . ignoring the growth and development of medieval literature over a changing two hundred years' (476).

72, 884, 906, 1857, 1871, 2167, 2356, 3133, 3522, 3608, 3851, 4180.

363 Sweeney, Patric M. 'O Western Wind, When Wilt Thou Blow?' *Explicator* 14.6 (1955): item 6.

In 'Westron wynde when wylle thou blow' [*3899.3*], the lover does not curse, but cries to Christ, conqueror of death. Just as the earth will come to life when the wind blows from the west, so 'he will come to life only when the dead woman returns, and her love, like rain, renews him.' He does not speak of sexual pleasure, but rather of 'the moment when he most protected his love, both the woman and her emotion, from the change that destroys both, and when he himself was protected from the change, by his bed, his room, and darkness.' [See Gierasch, **355**.]

3899.3.

364 Bowers, R.H. 'A Middle English Mnemonic Plague Tract.' *Southern Folklore Quarterly* 20 (1956): 118–25. [Edition.]

An anonymous versified ME translation of a Latin treatise on bubonic plague, 'Her begynys A tretis fyne' [*1190*], considers therapeutic techniques 'of venesection or cupping' (118), with some medical recipes, but no reference to magic or charms. Such mnemonic, functional, didactic verse may seem crude and clumsy: 'crude, because it versifies data which would be presented in prose in a more scientific age; clumsy, because its maker must retain the accuracy of such items as medical recipes' (119). Bowers prints the poem, written in a fifteenth-century hand in Egerton MS 1624, with 'editorial punctuation, capitalization and silent expansion of obvious abbreviations' (119), and end notes on matters of philological and medical interest.

1190.

365 Frankis, P.J. 'The Erotic Dream in Medieval English Lyrics.' *Neuphilologische Mitteilungen* 57 (1956): 228–37.

Three poems in MS Rawlinson C.813 ['As I myselfe lay thus endr3 nyght,' *366*; 'In a goodly nyght as yn my bede I laye,' *1450.5*; 'Late on a nyght as I lay slepyng,' *1841.5*] deal with the erotic dream and disappointment on waking; *366* is also a love epistle. Their impression of experience is 'a very rare quality in the late medieval English lyric' (229). In the exploration of the possibilities that they are 'a more or less unique record of actual experience' (229), or part of an established convention, Frankis compares the poems with religious dream lyrics, where the poet is 'a mere spectator' (230), not an active participant, and traces dreaming and disillusionment in Latin, French, and German verse. He refers to poems in fifteenth-century manuscripts ['Syn that y absent am thus from yow fare,' *3140*; 'That pasaunte Goddnes the Rote of all vertve,' *3291*; 'Thoythis fre þat lykis me,' *3707.8*]; and the Bannatyne MS ['O maistres myn til 3ou I me commend,' *2517*, 'Lait lait on sleip as I wes laid,' *7300*]. The last lyrics anticipate Wyatt's 'They Flee from Me.' A similar phrase in each, 'to describe the disillusionment of waking' (236), suggests a conventional theme, 'presumably derived from French verse' (237).

366, 1450.5, 1841.5, 2517, 3140, 3291, 3707.8, 7300.

366 Lewis, Arthur O., Jr. 'O Western Wind, When Wilt Thou Blow?' *Explicator* 15.5 (1956): item 28.

Rejects previous explications of 'Westron wynde when wylle thou blow' [*3899.3*], in particular Sweeney's 'highly Christian contention,' **363**. Lewis argues that '[t]he charm and beauty of the quatrain lie almost wholly in its simplicity.' The speaker, 'a man not happy in his present situation,' longs for the return of spring, then 'by the traditional association of spring and lovemaking,' to be in bed with his beloved. [See Henry, **379**.]

3899.3.

367 Malone, Kemp. 'Further Notes on Middle English Lyrics.' *ELH* 23 (1956): 1–13.

Offers emendations and corrections for lyrics in *BrownXIV*, **48**, revised by Smithers, and compares Smithers's interpretations with those of Brown, in *BrownXIV*, **31**.

353, 372, 562, 563, 583, 678, 780, 872, 1216, 1379, 1402, 1455, 1596, 1708, 1715, 1742, 1940, 2007, 2080, 2108, 2273, 3236, 3245, 3405, 3420, 3462, 3565, 3925, 3996, 4157, 4158, 4160, 4268.

368 Raymo, Robert R. 'Mors Solvit Omnia.' *Modern Language Notes* 71 (1956): 249.

A source for the Latin proverb, *Mors Solvit Omnia*, in the acrostic poem, 'A Mirror for Young Ladies at their Toilet,' ['Maist thou now be glade with all thi fresshe aray,' *2136*], considered by Cutler, **353**. It may be found, 'with the substitution of *cuncta* for *omnia*, in Nigel de Longehamps' *Speculum Stultorum*,' in the tale of two cows, Brunetta and Bicornis.

2136.

369 Robbins, Rossell Hope. 'A Political Action Poem, 1463.' *Modern Language Notes* 71 (1956): 245–8.

The Libelle of Englyshe Polycye ['The trewe processe of Englysch polycye,' *3491*], addressed in three versions to lords of the Privy Council, three unnamed lords and Archbishop Chicele, and intended 'to formulate England's trade policies' (245), deals with the woollen trade. A later poem ['Goo forth lybell and mekly schew thy face,' *921*] uses and parallels some lines of the *Libelle*, 'but omits the illustrations and digressions of the earlier work, and introduces many new concepts.' This 'vigorous demand for political action' is addressed to 'the factors of cloth and wool' (245), demanding changes and deploring dishonest exploitation. Eventually 'the specific demands for regulation of the woolen trade and protection of the workers presented in the poem were accepted into law' (247). Robbins compares passages from the poem with the legislation, and points to the poem 'as the successful lobbying of a medieval pressure group' (248).

921, 3491.

370 ———. 'A Warning against Lechery.' *Philological Quarterly* 35 (1956): 90–5. [Edition.]

A reply to Bowers, **348**, in which Robbins prints the poem he styles 'A Warning against Lechery' ['Burgeys thou hast so blowen atte the Cole,' *551*], and notes many different interpretations. He compares the poem with various other warnings. These include a tag from the *Fasciculus Morum* ['Whoso levyth in flescly wylle,' *4134*], a Vernon lyric ['Bi west vnder a wylde wode syde,' *583*], and two recommending spiritual thoughts to overcome sin ['Ihū for þyn precius blode,' *1708*; 'Wyth bodylye ffode Encreasyng in quantitee,' *4187*]. Others, written after the middle of the fifteenth century, emphasize the inconvenience caused by bad action and have 'never an allusion to the soul' (91). Robbins cites two examples of the last type ['O Mortall Man By grete exaltacion,' *2521*; 'Ye that ar comons obey yovr kynge and lorde,' *4257*].

231, 551, 583, 1708, 2521, 3129, 4134, 4187, 4257.

371 ———. 'The Five Dogs of London.' *PMLA* 71 (1956): 264–8. [Edition.]

The poem, 'My mayster ys cruell and can no curtesye' [*2262.3*], a 'lively piece of political verse,' in Trinity College, Dublin MS 516 (E.5.10), comments on events of 1456 and shows 'an astute Lancastrian taking advantage of a serious riot, ostensibly non-political, to attempt to win over the Londoners, traditionally supporters of the Yorkists' (264). The five dogs of the poem represent five men who were hanged, and 'complain that they have been punished for their master' (266). It is not possible to document any coincidence of the names of the dogs with those of mercers or apprentices hanged after the riot against Italian merchants. The poem seems 'a Lancastrian gibe to divide the Duke of York from his supporters,' and to have the moral: 'do not support York ... uphold King Henry VI' (266). Robbins prints the poem, with editorial punctuation and footnotes on points of interest, including *IMEV* numbers of Lancastrian and Yorkist poems.

455, 700, 899, 936, 1380, 1544, 2262.3, 2454, 2609, 2727, 2808, 3127, 3742, 3756.

372   Schlauch, Margaret. *English Medieval Literature and its Social Functions.* Warsaw: Polish Scientific; London: Oxford UP, 1956. New York: Cooper Square, 1971.

Briefly surveys lyric modes, generally as a source of influence on the 'Owl and the Nightingale' [*1384*]. Schlauch cites 'Nou goth þe sonne under wode' [*2320*] as a religious lyric, noting the force achieved by 'the choice of images and economy in lyrical expression' (162).

1384, 2320, 3222.

373   Seaton, Ethel. '"The Devonshire Manuscript" and its Medieval Fragments.' *Review of English Studies* NS 7 (1956): 55–6.

The last poems in the Devonshire MS [BL Add. 17492] are 'all fragments from poems of earlier periods' (55), most arranged from works of Chaucer, Hoccleve, and Roos.

666, 1409.3, 1418.5, 1609.5, 3760, 4217.6.

374   Bowers, R.H. 'Versus Compositi de Roger Belers.' *JEGP* 56 (1957): 440–2. [Edition.]

Macaronic verses '*Miles Rogerus* by ten mile wons he to neer us' [*2172*], 'impugn the reputation of Sir Roger [Belers]' (441), a Lancastrian partisan, 'prominent Leicestershire politician and baron of the exchequer under Edward II,' who was murdered 'as the result of a local feud' (440). Bowers prints *2172* with expanded abbreviations, punctuation, a translation, and endnotes.

2172.

375   Bühler, Curt F. 'The Verses in Lambeth Manuscript 265.' *Modern Language Notes* 72 (1957): 4–6.

The manuscript has 'the text also found in the first dated book to be printed in England (*The Dictes and Sayings of the Philosophers*)' (4). A dedicatory stanza ['This booke late translate here in syght,' *3581*] has been ascribed to Antony, Earl Rivers. Bühler also cites two nineteenth-century occurrences of the verse. He prints this verse and verses in another hand written at the end of the *Dictes*, concluding with the initials TER ['Yone that haue redd the contentes of thys booke,' *4273.8*], for which he suggests a date of early in the sixteenth century.

3581, 4273.8.

376   Cutts, John P. 'The Second Coventry Carol and a Note on *The Maydes Metamorphosis.*' *Renaissance News* 10 (1957): 3–8.

Although Thomas Sharp's copying of the women's carol ['O sisters too/how may we do,' *2551.8*] in *The Pageant of the Shearmen and Taylors* is accurate, the shepherds' song ['Abowt the fyld thei pyped ful right,' *112*] has 'corrupt readings and inconsistencies' (4). Cutts suggests a reference to the latter as 'the source of a hitherto unexplained song snatch' (4) sung by Mopso in *The Maydes Metamorphosis*, which may indicate the playwright's connection with Coventry. He prints the music of the shepherds' carol, with detailed comment. [See Greene, **377**.]

112, 2251.8.

Annotations of Critical Works 161

377 Greene, Richard L. 'The Second Coventry Carol: A Correction.' *Renaissance News* 10 (1957): 142.

Differs from Cutts, **376**, concerning 'Abowt the fyld thei pyped ful right' [*112*]. Greene contends that Mopso's song in *The Mayde's Metamorphosis* may be related to the burden 'Tyrle, tyrlo . . .' of a variant of *112*, rather than to the shepherds' song in the Coventry play.

112.

378 Hanham, Alison. 'The Musical Studies of a Fifteenth-Century Wool Merchant.' *Review of English Studies* NS 7 (1957): 270–4.

Accounts for music and dancing lessons, taken in Calais by George Cely, offer 'a remarkable picture of the musical interests of a young man of middle-class family, and an indication of some of the gaiety which caused Sir John Paston to describe Calais at this time as "a merry town" ' (270). The records include the names of seven songs (four in English), taught by the harper Thomas Rede, and 'one piece of ungrammatical doggerel which appears in George Cely's writing' ['To sorow in the morning,' *3768.2*], which expresses 'improving sentiments' (*274*).

925, 2183, 2437.5, 2657.5, 3768.2.

379 Henry, Nat. 'O Western Wind, When Wilt Thow Blow?' *Explicator* 16.1 (1957): item 5.

Agrees generally with Lewis, **366**, in his comments on 'Westron wynde when wylle thou blow' [*3899.3*], but asserts that the speaker wishing for rain is 'the stay-at-home woman longing for the weather change that will bring her man home to her bed.'

3899.3.

380 Holland, Norman. 'Ich Am of Irlaunde.' *Explicator* 15.9 (1957): item 55.

The image of dancing in 'Gode sire pray ich þe' [*1008*] signifies marriage, and 'the speaker's invitation to dance is also a covert invitation to wed.' The relation of body and soul is implied in that of 'body and pattern in a dance' and of 'Irlaunde' and 'the holy land of Ireland.' A spiritual invitation, for the sake of Christian love, is added to the physical dance, and 'the dancer and her partner must . . . meet at both levels.'

1008.

381 Johnston, G.K.W. 'A Prayer of the Five Joys.' *Notes and Queries* 202 (1957): 508.

The word *tuet* in line 58 of 'Seinte marie leuedi brist' [*2992*], 'leuedi, tuet *th*ov me mi bene,' has been glossed in *BrownXIII*, **36**, as 'urge, present urgently,' and emended to *cuet*, from OE *cwethan* 'declare,' by Malone, **186**. Johnson proposes the reading '*tute* th*ou* me mi bene, 'grant me my request,' from the association of *tithe* with *bene* and *bone*.

2992.

382 Robbins, Rossell Hope. 'Friar Herebert and the Carol.' *Anglia* 75 (1957): 194–8.

The Franciscans were first to develop the carol for religious purposes, with William Herebert's and John Grimestone's works found in fifteenth-century portable collections. Herebert's carols are based on Latin processional hymns rather than 'nebulous Middle English dance songs' (195). Robbins notes some of Herebert's translations from the Latin and the AN of Nicholas Bozon, and compares Grimestone's freer rendering of the

Good Friday *Improperia*. The Latin processional hymns may have been 'decisive in sparking the growth of the English carol' (198).

110, 497, 610, 1321, 1841, 2080, 2240, 2241, 2689, 3135, 3872.

383 Ross, Thomas W. 'Five Fifteenth-Century "Emblem" Verses from Brit. Mus. Addit. MS. 37049.' *Speculum* 32 (1957): 274–82. [Edition.]

The manuscript contains, in 'an odd assortment of late medieval writings' (275), five antecedents of seventeenth-century emblem verse. 'The Heart' ['O man vnkynde,' *2504*], 'The Harper' ['Allas ful warly for wo may I synge,' *149*], and 'The Invitation' ['Cum folow me my frendes vnto helle,' *637*] are represented graphically. 'The Portrait' [**If þai do so he wil þaim safe,*' **1426.8*] and 'The Falcon' ['Also take hede to þis insawmpyl here,' *269*] could be similarly illustrated, and probably were, in other versions which have not been preserved. Ross describes and prints the poems and drawings, both of which 'communicate their ideas with a fair amount of crude power' (275). The drawing which accompanies 'The Heart' supplies a calculation of the number of drops of blood issuing from wounds in Christ's heart. For 'The Invitation,' the demons are 'inexpertly delineated but reveal a startling amount of almost uncontrolled emotionality in the artist' (276). Since the ink of the poetry resembles that used for the drawings, 'it may be that the same Carthusian monk *scripsit atque pinxit*' (276). [See Bowers, **285**.]

149, 269, 637, *1426.8, 2504.

384 ———. 'On the Evil Times of Edward II. A New Version from MS Bodley 48.' *Anglia* 75 (1957): 173–93. [Edition.]

The Bodleian source supplements the existing editions prepared from versions in National Library of Scotland 19.2.1 (Auchinleck MS) and Peterhouse, Cambridge 104. The latter have been listed as 'Why werre and wrake in londe' [*4165*], whereas the Bodleian poem has a different incipit 'Lordyngis leue & dere listneþ to me a stounde' [*1992*]. Internal evidence used to date the poem in 'the middle or last years of the reign of Edward II' includes references to '[c]harges against the Knights Templar, complaints against high prices, [and] pious fear that the unusual cold and dearth were . . . manifestations of God's wrath' (174). Ross finds it a poem of complaint rather than a satire or political poem, since the 'bitter iteration of abuses' deals unsystematically with all classes of society, and concludes with general matters such as 'high prices, plague, and the absence of piety in Englishmen' (175). The manuscript was probably written early in the fifteenth century, but it is likely that the poem was composed a century earlier. Although the dialect of the manuscript seems to be East Midland, it may be possible to localize the writer's dialect 'somewhat farther west.' Ross prints the poem, with footnotes on points of interest, and augments some sections from the other manuscripts. He records details of differences in the length of the texts, noting that 'the Bodleian MS includes 114 lines not found in either of the other versions; that it is 414 lines in length, compared with 467 lines in the Auchinleck MS and 468 in the Peterhouse MS; and that both of these latter are defective in other ways' (176). When the texts differ markedly, he cites the other versions in the notes.

1992, 4165.

385 Speirs, John. *Medieval English Poetry: The Non-Chaucerian Tradition.* London: Faber, 1957.

Most surviving lyrics are in 'about half a dozen outstanding MSS collections' which Speirs considers in 'Carols and Other Songs and Lyrics' (45–96); the heaviest losses are in 'indigenous song verse' (45). Many Christian lyrics are preserved, including traditional carols, kept because they were '*made* Christian' (46). Religious and secular works have much in common, and those poems distinguished as 'good' are those 'still effective,' because they are experienced by, and seem 'contemporary with the reader' (47). Speirs favours sensitive editing of the texts. He discusses the association of music and dance with the lyrics, and the influence of French, Latin, and Provençal forms. The association of lyrics with nature and the seasons is exemplified in 'Alysoun' [*515*], 'Lenten ys come wiþ loue to toune' [*1861*], and 'Wynter wakeneþ al my care' [*4177*]. 'At a sprynge wel vnder a þorn' [*420*], 'Gode sire pray ich þe' [*1008*], 'Maiden in the mor lay' [*2037.5*], and 'Of euerykune tre' [*2622*] illustrate connections with dance and nature, and lead to Marian hymns with similar imagery, particularly of roses. Speirs describes carols of the Nativity and lyrics on Christ's death, and traces descendants of the 'Corpus Christi Carol' [*1132*]. There are 'profane songs expressive of the jollity of the folk' (82), not to be confused with those of Yule, such as carols of the Boar's Head, and of Holly and Ivy. Melancholy songs deal with the theme of *ubi sunt*. Comedy is found in 'The Man in the Moon' [*2066*] and 'Swarte smekyd smethes smateryd wythe smoke' [*3227*]. Speirs relates the lyrics to works of other poets, noting connections with Chaucer, post-Chaucerian poets, and Dunbar, leading to Wyatt, and 'to Donne and the seventeenth-century poets' (95).

117, 377, 429, 515, 903, 1008, 1132, 1226, 1367, 1463, 1861, 1893, 2025, 2037.5, 2066, 2622, 2645, 3227, 3310, 3313, 3315, 3460, 3603, 4177.

386 Bennett, Josephine Waters. 'The Mediaeval Loveday.' *Speculum* 33 (1958): 351–70.

There are references to the loveday in 'literary, legal, and historical records of mediaeval England' (351). Bennett describes the background and context of some of these. She adds to the work of Bowers, **307**, on 'And þerfor ȝe lordingis þ^t louedays wile holde' [*312*], concerning lovedays, and comments on a poem of instruction in Freemasonry, 'Whose wol boþe wel rede and loke' [*4149*], which suggests holding lovedays on Sunday. [See also Heffernan, **636**.]

312, 4149.

387 Berry, Francis. *Poets' Grammar: Person, Time and Mood in Poetry*. London: Routledge, 1958.

'Introductory' (1–12) explains Berry's treatment of 'a few grammatical forms and inflexions as they function in the work of some English poets and dramatists' (1). 'The Grammar of Two Poems' (20–35), in 'Tense in Medieval Pageant and Poem' (13–35), repeats arguments of **345**, on the 'Corpus Christi Carol' [*1132*], in versions of Richard Hill and James Hogg. Berry supplies an appendix (178–82), and prints variants in the Staffordshire and Derbyshire versions of Hogg's poem [*7422*].

1132, 7422.

388 Bühler, Curt F. 'Middle English Verses against Thieves.' *Speculum* 33 (1958): 371–2. [Edition.]

Two charms, 'Lord god in Trinite' [*1952.5*] and 'Wo-so wol this oureson saie' [*4151.8*], seemed to be part of a metrical herbal, 'Of erbis xxiij' [*2627*] in MS BL Sloane 2457. The former was written as prose, and the loss of couplets in the first lines may show 'that the charm is of much earlier composition than the date of this manuscript and that it has suffered from the inaccuracies of more than one scribe' (371). The latter precedes 'a very long Latin prayer, invoking in addition to the Virgin Mary, God the Father, and St John, some "powers" unknown to traditional Christian belief (i.e., Iskiros, Otheos, Athanatos, On, Nic, etc.)' (372). [See Vann, **410**.]

1952.5, 2627, 4151.8.

389 Copley, J. 'John Audelay's Carols and Music.' *English Studies* 39 (1958): 207–12.

His collection of carols suggests that Audelay wished 'to reform the taste of the day rather than to illustrate it' (208). This is shown in the inclusion of carols (to saints) that are not found elsewhere. The carols are to be sung at Christmas, but references to other religious occasions and moral counsel suggest that Audelay tries to stress 'the high seriousness of the festival of Christmas rather than its joyful tidings' (208–9). He does not alter the fifteenth-century pattern of stanza and burden, and most carols could be fitted to known music, but some, such as 'þis flour is faire & fresche of heue' [*3603*] seem more literary than musical. Copley compares Audelay's carols with similar works, and notes the use of *redis* rather than *syng* in similar stanzas of two of three carols ['A hole confessoure þ^u were hone,' *44*; 'Als þ^u ware marter & mayd clene,' *413*; 'fore he is ful ʒong tender of age,' *822*], demonstrating that 'here the music is at some distance from his mind' (212).

21, 44, 328, 413, 536, 753, 822, 858, 895, 1211, 2716, 3457, 3526, 3603.

390 ———. 'Two Notes on Early English Carols.' *Notes and Queries* 203 (1958): 239–40.

'A Second Carol of Agincourt' (239) examines 'Worschip of vertu ys þe mede' [*4229.5*], a didactic carol to celebrate St George's Day, to identify St George with Henry V, and to recall the Battle of Agincourt. In 'Carol and Cantilena' (239–40) Copley illustrates differences in the stanza pattern of Latin cantilenae and related English carols, and effects of the musical settings. In the English carols, the words 'mirror an older tradition than their earliest musical settings,' not seen in the cantilenae. This happens because of the wish of Church authorities to break connections with 'some sort of secular round dance with pagan associations' (240).

4229.5.

391 Cross, J.E. 'The *Sayings of St Bernard* and *Ubi sount qui ante nos fueront*.' *Review of English Studies* NS 9 (1958): 1–7.

Seeks to establish whether there are two poems, or whether the *ubi sunt* verses simply conclude 'the *Sayings of St Bernard* [*3310*], a longer poem in the same verse-form.' In four of six manuscripts that preserve the *ubi sunt* verses they seem to be a part of the *Sayings*. In Digby 86 'they follow the *Sayings* though they appear to be divided from it by the Latin title' (1). They seem to be separate only in the Auchinleck MS, but they follow a gap of perhaps five folios that could have contained the *Sayings*. Comparisons indicate that the Digby version probably represents 'the original extent of the poem(s)' and offers 'a fair representative of the archetype' (2). The *ubi sunt* verses and the *Sayings* echo a prose tract, *Meditationes piissimae de conditione humana*, usually attributed to St Bernard, but with some variations and obscurities, which Cross notes in detail. The sentiments of the *ubi sunt* poem are found elsewhere, but there are clear similarities to the *Meditationes*; the apparently abrupt ending of the *Sayings* is explained as 'a locking verse,' which looks back to preceding admonitions and also to 'the succession of "ubi sunt" questions which follow' (5). The Latin phrase in Digby 86 should be seen as an error of the scribe, rather than 'a title dividing the "ubi sunt" verses from the others in the *Sayings*' (6), although he may have included it to recall the theme. Cross finds that the inclusion is unique, so that 'the "ubi sunt" verses should henceforth be printed . . . as an extract from the *Sayings of St Bernard*' (7).

3310, 4160.

392 Friedman, Albert B. 'The Late Mediæval Ballade and the Origin of Broadside Balladry.' *Medium Ævum* 27 (1958): 95–110

Explores the relation of the ballad and the ME ballade, French *balade* and *ballette*, Provençal *balada*, and Italian *ballata*, with emphasis on the ballade, which is used, with variations, by Chaucer, Hoccleve, Lydgate, and some Middle Scots poets. The ME ballade was less popular than the *balade* had been in France; its rhyme scheme was restrictive, and English poets did not vary the metre and stanza form as did the French. Many ME ballades lack the envoy, which French masters thought 'an optional flourish' (101). French *balades* had three stanzas, unless they were double or triple *balades*, but the number was not fixed in English works. English poems were united by the refrain, as the French were by the rhyme scheme. When the refrain was lost, the term 'ballade' came to refer to any poem in rhyme royal or the ballade octave. Thus 'the pseudo-ballade was merely the English counterpart of the double or triple *balade*' (102), as in most Vernon and Simeon religious lyrics and many secular works. When carols are excepted, rhyme royal lyrics account for 'over 29 per cent of the remaining poems,' and those 'in the ballade octave . . . for over 28 per cent' (103). The term *ballade* is used loosely, even for poems with a single stanza. Since political pseudo-ballades must have appeared on broadsheet, Friedman argues that '"ballad" for broadside verse in general first came into use' (107) in this way. He instances Skelton's public poems as such works, with 'libels' and 'litel treatyses' as 'next of kin typographically to the broadsides.' The earliest of these were not sung, 'since the extant examples are not singable' (109). Although some courtly verse was published there, doggerel became 'standard on broadsides' (110).

4, 100, 285, 590, 869, 1168, 1378, 1822.5, 2031, 2192, 2229, 2262, 2451.5, 2517, 2578.5, 2634, 2803.5, 3154.5, 3348, 3448, 3542, 3625, 3655, 3661, 3747, 3759, 4004.

393 Hussey, Maurice. 'The Petitions of the Paternoster in Mediæval English Literature.' *Medium Ævum* 27 (1958): 8–16.

The divine origin and adaptability of the Paternoster assured its importance in the medieval church, as a charm and a source of homiletic material in its seven petitions. The latter are related to the beatitudes, gifts of the Holy Ghost, deadly sins, and to the planets and days of the week. There are numerous commentaries in sermons and for 'the intelligent private suppliant' (10). Hussey notes translations of the prayer into English verse, including one printed by Thomson, **179**, 'Vre fader in heuene y-halȝed be þy name' [*2704*], and another noted by Onions, **119**, 'Hure wader þat is in euene' [*2710*]. There are numerous contemporary literary references to the prayer, and it was the basis of complex pictorial expositions of aspects of the Christian life.

1459, 2704, 2710, 3182.

394 Manning, Stephen. 'Sumer Is Icumen In.' *Explicator* 18.1 (1958): item 2.

'Svmer is icumen in' [*3223*] is 'not completely objective,' since the cuckoo is directly addressed, and the speaker's delight and wish for an eternal spring are expressed. The structure is triple, 'in that the exultation in spring moves from the vegetable to the animal to the human level,' but twofold in the relationship between the speaker and the cuckoo. The poet's presentation of 'so personal a wish in such objective terms . . . is an indication of his art.'

3223.

395 Moran, Jo Ann Hoeppner. *The Growth of English Schooling 1340–1548: Learning, Literacy, and Laicization in Pre-Reformation York Diocese.* Princeton, NJ: Princeton UP, 1958.

The books, made of wood, horn and paper, used by the youngest children in elementary reading schools, are described in the verses of instruction that they used. Moran describes methods of teaching and the books, and notes some of the verses.

33, 1523, 7633.

396 Routley, Erik. *The English Carol.* London: Jenkins, 1958.

Summarizing definitions of the carol, Routley emphasizes its popular qualities, burden, and connection with the dance. He refers in particular to Greene, **37**, and Dearmer, **34**, and offers examples of religious and secular carols, to illustrate resemblances in stanza form and tune. 'The Ballad Carol' (43–80) traces connections with folk-song, particularly in the noel, ballad carols, and legendary carols.

18, 21, 546, 581, 681, 753, 960.1, 1132, 1195, 1225, 1226, 1350, 2716, 3097.6, 3313, 3315, 3536, 3596, 3627, 3877, 3999, 7063.

397 Brice, Douglas. 'The Folk Carol.' *The Month* NS 22 (1959): 266–78.

Distinguishes between ballads and carols, with a brief survey of scholarship and a history of the carol and its relation to folk music. Brice considers the carol 'a gipsy folk song' (272), with its origin in 'the bright and genial spirituality of the Franciscan friary' (273), having many connections with Mystery Plays. He alludes briefly to various carols, with comments on those included in the Mysteries, such as 'Abowt the fyld thei pyped ful right' [*112*], and extends his discussion to carols of the nineteenth and twentieth centuries.

112.

398 Bühler, Curt F. 'A Tudor "Crosse Rowe."' *Libri Impressi cum Notis Manuscriptis IX.'* *JEGP* 58 (1959): 248–50. Repr. in *Early Books and Manuscripts: Forty Years of Research by Curt F. Bühler.* New York: The Grolier Club and the Pierpont Morgan Library, 1973. 634–6 [cited]. [Edition.]

The poem is added to a '"Sammelband" . . . printed in Cologne in the fifteenth century and located in the British Museum,' in a hand that suggests that 'the text was written into the incunabulum before 1501,' although the alliterative style of the work 'implies an origin of no later than the fifteenth century' (634). Although the Cross Row's ribald character could have excluded it from literary manuscripts, this glimpse of 'the sort of humor which appealed to the average reader of that day' carries 'an importance quite out of proportion to its literary value' (635). Bühler prints the alphabetical poem, 'A for Alyn Mallson þat was armyde in a matt' [*0.1*] with its traditional heading beginning 'Crystes crosse be my spede,' and annotates points of interest.

0.1.

399 Cooling, June. 'An Unpublished Middle English Prologue.' *Review of English Studies* NS 10 (1959): 172–3. [Edition.]

Prints a poem, the prologue of a play, 'Pes lordyngs I prai ӡow pes' [*2741.5*], from 'the dorse of Durham Dean and Chapter MS. Archid. Dunelm. 60' (172). The hand is of the fifteenth century, although the document is dated 1359, and was presumably written by a monk. The dialect is Northern. Cooling supplies the poem and suggests a possible transposition of the lines 31–3.

2741.5.

400 Copley, J. 'A Popular Fifteenth-Century Carol.' *Notes and Queries* 204 (1959): 387–9.

The musical setting of the carol 'Wonder Tidings' ['A babe is born of hey nature,' *21*] suggests that it is to be sung in two parts, by soloists, rather than by 'the company' or 'a choir,' as suggested in *The Oxford Book of Carols*, **34**. Copley examines three versions of the carol, in MSS Trinity College, Cambridge 1230 and Bodleian Arch. Selden B.26, and in John Audelay's collection, to show the relation of burden to stanzas and the voices for which they were intended, 'not in terms of the older round dance, with simple chorus and solo alternation' (389).

21.

401 Frankis, P.J. 'Two Minor French Lyric Forms in English.' *Neuphilologische Mitteilungen* 60 (1959): 66–71.

The aube and Bele Aeliz forms are rarely found in English verse. 'This day day dawes,' the burden to 'In a gloryus garden grene' *[1450]*, is a surviving *aube*, and there are similar forms in Scottish and Danish verse. There are essentials of the Bele Aeliz poems in 'In Aprell and in May' *[1470]*, of a miller's maid, Bessy Bunting, a song related to 'A wayle whyt ase whalles bon,' *[105]*, which mentions a bunting.

105, 1450, 1470.

402 Friedman, Albert B. 'Medieval Popular Satire in Matthew Paris.' *Modern Language Notes* 74 (1959): 673–8.

Two songs in the *Historia Anglorum* of Matthew Paris have been ascribed to the Earl of Leicester's Flemish mercenaries; the better known is 'Hoppe hoppe Wilekin hoppe Wilekin' *[1252]*. Friedman summarizes critical opinions about the poem. He posits that it is 'definitely English and not really sung by Flemings,' but composed instead 'by partisans of Henry II, though framed in such a way as to appear to come from Leicester's mercenaries' (674), to hint at 'an exultant boast imputed to the enemy' (675), as 'a satirical attack on the Flemings' (676). A name ending in -*kyn* may sound Flemish, and the course of the wool trade generated ill feeling against Flemings. The second song, 'I ne mai a liue' *[1335]*, derides St Benedict and St Ive, and is apparently sung by a Norman follower of Geoffrey de Mandeville about the sacking of Ramsey Abbey and its branch house. Paris emphasizes that the saints 'did not allow the taunt to go unpunished,' and that Mandeville 'met his end while standing on land belonging to Ramsey Abbey' (678).

1252, 1335, 2832.2.

403 Johnston, G.K.W. 'The Interpretation of Poems by Mydwynter.' *Notes and Queries* 204 (1959): 244–5.

Explicates some difficulties in two poems in Harley MS 2383, on Heaven ['Man in Heuyn hyt ys mery to dwll,' *2063*] and Purgatory ['Man þenke here on ofte tyme,' *2079*]. They are attributed to 'Johannes Mydwynter' and edited by Bowers, **267**.

2063, 2079.

404 Manning, Stephen. 'Nou goth Sonne vnder wod.' *Modern Language Notes* 74 (1959): 578–81.

The details of symbol and setting evoked in 'Nou goth þe sonne under wode' *[2320]* deepen the 'simple surface emotion aroused by the Crucifixion' (578). Manning comments on previous criticism of the lyric [*BrownXIII*, **36**; Cutler, **250**; Kane, **292**; Thayer, **320**]. He discusses the poem's two scenes, their imagery and symbolism, relating the work to the Latin *Stabat Mater Dolorosa*, to an English version of the sequence *Stabat iuxta Christi Crucem* ['Iesu cristes milde moder,' *1697*], and to comments of Philippe of Harvengt and John Halgrinus (*Patrologia Latina* 203: 224–5 and 206: 84–6). The sun/son imagery and word-play, and the association of red with the sunset and love evoke 'the grief and love which Mary felt for her dying Son' (581).

1697, 2320.

Philadelphia: U of Pennsylvania P. 1961. 285–98. Repr. in *Early Books and Manuscripts: Forty Years of Research by Curt F. Bühler*. New York: The Grolier Club and the Pierpont Morgan Library, 1973. 544–54.

The manuscript, Bühler 21, has short poems, medical recipes, a calendar with tables, and herbal and medical treatises in verse and prose. The Metrical Herbal [*2627*] has a different incipit ['These lechys for seke mannys sake'] from that cited in *IMEV* ['Of erbis xxiij/I wyl þe telle by and by'], as does the Metrical Medical Treatise [*1408*, listed as 'Iff a man or womman more or less/In his hede haue grett etc.']. Bühler notes unique features of the texts in the manuscript, and prints extracts from the treatises, showing how they differ from other sources.

1163, 1328.3, 1408, 2627, 3079.8, 3754.

428 ———. 'The New Morgan Manuscript of *Titus and Vespasian*.' *PMLA* 76 (1961): 20–4 [cited]. Repr. in *Early Books and Manuscripts: Forty Years of Research by Curt F. Bühler*. New York: The Grolier Club and the Pierpont Morgan Library, 1973. 533–43.

Comments on a manuscript of *Titus and Vespasian* held at the Pierpont Morgan Library. Bühler notes three stanzas, 'He that in youthe no care will take' [*1105.5*], 'Bewty is subiect vnto age' [*7079*], 'The ape the lyon the foxe the ase' [*7479*], in three different sixteenth-century hands, '(all carefully written) as marginalia' (22).

1150.5, 7079, 7479.

429 Copley, J. '"I Syng of a Myden."' *Notes and Queries* 207 (1962): 134–7.

The lyric 'I Syng of a myden þᵗ is makeles' [*1367*] has many verbal echoes. Copley traces these, and compares the poet's sources and effects, in particular the developments from 'Nu þis fules singet hand maket hure blisse' [*2366*] and earlier uses of the images of *1367*. Although there are echoes, the poet omits 'purposeless repetition' of some earlier verse, to achieve 'comprehensive simplicity' (136) and originality in using 'basic images of medieval lyric poetry' (137).

93, 515, 888, 1299, 1303, 1367, 1471, 1472, 1931, 2061, 2107, 2339, 2366, 2405, 3222, 3332, 3472, 3603, 3674, 4037.

430 Curry, Jane L. '"Silver White."' *Notes and Queries* 207 (1962): 410.

'Seluer white,' in 'At the northe end of seluer whyte' [*438*], may be 'simply a bed-sheet,' rather than the 'place of assignation,' as suggested by Robbins, *RobbinsS*, **51**.

438.

431 Dronke, Peter. 'The Rawlinson Lyrics.' *Notes and Queries* 206 (1961): 245–6.

Examination under ultraviolet light has enabled Dronke to discern 'many new words and lines, as well as some corrections and some conjectures' (245) in hitherto illegible lines in the Rawlinson lyrics. He contributes new readings for 'Al gold Ionet is þin her' [*179*], 'Al nist by [þe] rose rose' [*194*], 'Of euerykune tre' [*2622*], 'Wer þer ouþer in þis toun' [*3898*], 'Ye Sir [þat is] idronken' [*4256.8*], and a French lyric.

179, 194, 2622, 3898, 4256.8.

432 Einarsson, Stefán. 'A Burde of Blod ant of Bon.' *Modern Language Notes* 76 (1961): 852–5.

Interprets the reference to blood and bone, in 'Blow, Northerne Wynd' [*1395*], as one to family relationship. Einarsson cites corresponding terms in Altaic, German, and

Annotations of Critical Works 175

Icelandic languages, which express relationships in terms of the skeleton or body, rather than the image of a family tree. He notes stories of recovery of bodies from bones. Although qualities of blood, as 'fine, royal, blue, or tainted,' may be used to make eugenic judgements in western societies, Siberian tribes speak of bones or legs, which may be called 'white or black, hard or brittle.' Thus the phrase in the ME lyric comes from 'the sphere of words dealing specifically with family relationship' (855).

1395.

433 Gray, Douglas. 'A Middle English Epitaph.' *Notes and Queries* 206 (1961): 132–5.

'Farewell, this World is but a Cherry Fair' ['Farewell this world I take my leue for-euer,' *769*] is an example of the verse epitaph. The last stanza and variations are found at St Michael's, Crooked Lane, London; Romford, Essex; Northleach, Gloucestershire; Baldock, Hertfordshire; St Martin's, Ludgate Hill, London; Royston, Hertfordshire; and Maldon, Essex. Gray comments on the poem and variants, and on other verse epitaphs, including those of some public figures. He finds their 'sentiments trite, the language awkward, the metre limping,' but '[t]he solemnity and sombre force of *Farewell My Friends* gives it a special place of honour' (135).

765, 769.

434 Greene, R.L. 'A Middle English Love Poem and the "O-and-I" Refrain-Phrase.' *Medium Ævum* 30 (1961): 170–5.

The single stanza of the informal lyric 'Sche þat I loue alle þermoost & loþist to begile ' [*3098.5*], found 'on the back of a fly-leaf, f. 129v, of Huntington Library MS. HM 503, along with some idle jottings in Latin,' may not be complete, but it permits this reading. Greene prints the poem, and briefly describes the manuscript, a Wycliffite prose tract. The fifth line begins 'Wiþ and Y and an O,' a variant of the 'O and I' refrain. Greene lists ME works with this refrain, noting that it was imitated in two Latin poems, and summarizes critical opinion. He relates the refrain to lines in Dante's *Inferno*, Canto XXIV, 97–102, where rapid strokes for writing the two letters emphasize speed of an action. The phrase then suggests '"with two strokes of the pen" or "very quickly or surely"' (174), appropriate to many of the contexts. Association with promptness, force, and the scriptorium is apt for 'the work of clerics familiar with the mechanics of writing,' so that the refrain can 'without strain be understood as meaning "Indeed and without delay"' (175).

412, 701, 1001, 1320, 2021, 2663, 3069, 3098.5, 2263, 3567, 3921.

435 Lockwood, W.B. 'A Note on the Middle English "Sunset on Calvary."' *Zeitschrift für Anglistik und Amerikanistik* 9 (1961): 410–12.

The first line, 'Nou goth þe sonne under wode' [*2320*], may mean 'effectively nothing more than "now the sun is setting,"' from 'disinclination to refer to the setting sun in so many words' (410). Lockwood cites examples of Lusatian, Old Saxon, and North Germanic phrases, including some now used in the Faroes, Germany, and Iceland, and suggests that 'the English expression . . . may be a borrowing from Norse – though of course the reverse is not excluded' (411).

2320.

436 Maxwell, J.C. 'Note on a Harley Lyric.' *Notes and Queries* 206 (1961): 167–8.

Proposes the deletion of 'swyþe' in the line 'swannes swyre swyþe wel ysette,' in 'The Fair Maid of Ribblesdale' [*2207*], 'as a dittographic error' (168).

2207.

German scholarship' (505). Robbins sets Stemmler's work in its context of other studies, to expand discussion of the date and provenance of the manuscript; to consider other occurrences of Harley poems or individual lines from them; and to answer the question 'What really needs to be done with Harley 2253?' (509).

445 ———. 'Zur Datierung des MS. Harley 2253.' *Anglia* 80 (1962): 111–18.

Evidence for revised dating of the manuscript implies that previous findings are erroneous, and that it could not have been copied earlier than 1340. Reference to prophecies of Thomas of Erceldoune, concerning the Battle of Bannockburn, in 1314, furnished the previously accepted date of 1320, but J.A. Gibson ['The Lyrical Poems of the Harl. MS 2253,' MA diss., London University, 1914] demonstrated that the latest political poem told of Edward III, who left for the Hundred Years War in 1338. Other evidence concerns writings of Nicholas Bozon, in particular the legend of St Elizabeth of Hungary. Most of the secular poems were composed at the beginning of the Alliterative Revival. Stemmler's stylistic examination, especially of stanza form and rhyme scheme, suggests that poems with less alliteration were composed in the last half of the thirteenth century, and more alliterative verse after 1320.

205, 1320.5, 1449, 1889, 1894, 1974, 2649, 3155.

446 Woolf, Rosemary. 'The Theme of Christ the Lover-Knight in Medieval English Literature.' *Review of English Studies* NS 13 (1962): 1–16 [cited]. Repr. in *Art and Doctrine: Essays on Medieval Literature. Rosemary Woolf.* Ed. Heather O'Donoghue. London: Hambledon, 1986. 99–117.

The allegory of 'the knight who dies for the sake of his lady,' in preaching books, exempla, and poetic works, fits the 'dominant idea of medieval piety, that Christ endured the torments of the Passion in order to win man's love' (1). It develops from the story of winning back an unfaithful wife, and from images of arming a knight and keeping, as a treasure, his blood-stained shirt and armour. The knight's horse has its analogy in the Cross.

143, 498, 1274, 1301, 1930, 2150.

447 Bowers, R.H. 'A Middle-English Anti-Mendicant Squib.' *English Language Notes* 1 (1963–4): 163–4. [Edition.]

With 'no great pleasure,' Bowers prints 'He that harborythe a ffrere harborythe fesyke' [*1148*], scribbled 'on the verso of the binder's waste initial folio of Harley MS 2252.' Although the friars 'have surely suffered enough,' it seems 'of sufficient literary adroitness to merit publication' (163)

1148.

448 Bühler, Curt F. 'Middle English Apophthegms in a Caxton Volume': *Libri Impressi cum Notis Manuscriptis X. English Language Notes* 1 (1963–4): 81–4 [cited]. Repr. in *Early Books and Manuscripts: Forty Years of Research by Curt F. Bühler.* New York: The Grolier Club and the Pierpont Morgan Library, 1973. 637–40. [Edition.]

Verses in a volume 'composed of two of Caxton's French publications' may have been 'simply copied into it from the so-called "Boke of St. Albans"' (81), but both may have a common source. Bühler prints 'Who that mannyth hym with his kynne' [*4106.5*], to make them available 'either as texts predating the familiar early-printed versions or as an illustration of the free and easy manner in which the scribes were wont to treat their sources' (84). The presence of English notes in French incunabula may suggest that 'when Caxton moved his press to Westminster in 1476, he brought with him from Bruges the still unsold stock of his publications' (84). [See Keiser, **1019**.]

324, 761, 3818, 4101, 4106, 4106.5.

449   Fifield, Merle. 'Thirteenth-Century Lyrics and the Alliterative Tradition.' *JEGP* 62 (1963): 111–18.

A statistical analysis of the recurrence of alliterative phrases from OE, tracing frequency in the lyrics of the thirteenth, fourteenth, and fifteenth centuries. Fifield looks in particular at lyrics of MS Harley 2253, and at distribution in religious and secular lyrics of the fourteenth century. She relates some phrases to German and Norse cognates, and suggests borrowings from French. The thirteenth-century lyrics preserve OE phrases and contribute to the continuing expansion of alliteration, found more in the Harley lyrics than in others of the fourteenth century, and more in religious than secular lyrics of the fifteenth century. She does not cite specific lyrics.

450   Frankis, P.J. 'Flemish Words in a Fifteenth-Century English Poem.' *Notes and Queries* 208 (1963): 12–13.

'Mockery of the Flemings' ['When ye fflemyng wer fressh florissked in youre flouris,' *4056.8*], in a prose *Brut*, is in 'vigorous and colloquial' style, with 'several technical military terms' (12), including the Flemish *weth*, *hounsculles*, *kettill-hattes*, *pykes*, *godendgaghes*, *messes* & *meskins*, *camp*, and *quadrenramp*. Frankis classifies these as Middle Dutch, and supplies linguistic notes. Although '[i]t is quite likely that most readers of *The Brut* in fifteenth-century England would not have understood these Flemish words . . . the abusive tone of the poem is clear' (13).

4056.8.

451   Gray, Douglas. 'The Five Wounds of Our Lord.' *Notes and Queries* 10 (1963): 50–1, 82–9, 126–34, 163–8. [Edition.]

The cult of the Five Wounds of Our Lord was part of the 'strongly affective and Christocentric type of piety' that began in the eleventh century. Its 'heightened sense of tenderness and pathos' dwelt on 'the Humanity of Christ and especially on the details of his Passion.' It inspired moving works of art and literature, but was 'sometimes distasteful, sometimes plainly dull, in its insistence on the physical aspect of the Passion' (84). Gray prints an illustrated poem on the Five Wounds, 'Gracyous lord for thy bytter passyon' [*1011*], from Douce MS 1, and places it in the tradition. The cult included charms, prayers, and social customs, with depictions of the Five Wounds and the fifteenth-century Blazon of the Five Wounds. It is related to devotion to the Sacred Heart and Precious Blood. The poetic works show the wounds as remedies against sins, a refuge, and wells or fountains, and attribute specific functions to each wound. Gray's examples show the relation to occasions of shedding of Christ's blood, prefiguring of the wounds in the OT, stigmatization, and traditions of English hymn writing. The illustrations provide 'a sensible object of piety for the eye of some devout beholder to rest on in the work of meditation' (168).

44, 631, 644, 1002, 1011, 1270, 1378, 1463, 1498, 1687, 1706, 1711, 1943, 1961.5, 2081, 2312, 2428, 2464, 2504, 3072, 3144, 3212, 3845.

452   Griffith, Richard R. 'Westron Wynde When Wyll Thow Blow.' *Explicator* 21.9 (1963): item 69.

Adds to earlier explications of 'Westron wynde when wylle thou blowe' [*3899.3*]. Griffith reads *can* as a variant of *gan*, so that 'the speaker, far from requesting rain, declares that the showers – the first token of spring – have already appeared, and longs for the warm breezes and fair weather which should follow.' His wish to be in bed again hints that he left it recently, in the morning. The poem is 'an analogue to the blues . . . most malevolent when one wakes to a rainy day and an empty bed.' The lovers seem not to be married, and perhaps meet only 'in garden or greenwood, which would explain neatly the plea for better weather.' The poem's intensity may imply the mistress's death and the lover's hope 'to find spring a restorer of meaning to life.' He utters 'the spontaneous surface outcry of a profoundly troubled heart finding even the weather against him.'

3899.3.

453   Reiss, Edmund. 'Chaucer's Friar and the Man in the Moon.' *JEGP* 62 (1963): 481–5.

The name 'Huberd' for the Friar in Chaucer's *Canterbury Tales* can be related to 'The Man in the Moon' [*2066*], where the man, who is called 'Hubert' and resembles a grey friar, is shown as a thief. The Man in the Moon is also identified with Judas and Cain, and the latter is 'strikingly seen in a fourteenth-century poem called both "The Orders of Cain" and "Against the Friars" ['Preste ne monke ne ȝiy chanoun,' *2777*]' (484). The name and its associations reveal the Friar's evil nature and 'the incongruity of the praise Chaucer gives him throughout the description' (485).

2066, 2777.

454   Robbins, Rossell Hope. 'An English Nativity Song from a Latin Processional.' *American Notes & Queries* 2 (1963–4): 147–8. [Edition.]

On a flyleaf of a fifteenth-century Latin processional, MS Harley 2942, are found a Nativity song, 'Now let vs be mery bothe all and some' [*2348*], and a hymn to the Virgin, ['Such a lady seke I neuer non,' *3220*]. Robbins prints the song, perhaps a carol without a burden, in three macaronic quatrains, and proposes three possible burdens, from 'Now in Betheleme that holy place' [*2332*], 'Lett no man cum into this hall' [*1866*], and 'Now forto syng I holde it best' [*2310*].

1866, 2310, 2332, 2348, 3220.

455   ———. 'Good Gossips Reunited.' *British Museum Quarterly* 27 (1963–4): 12–14.

Among ale-wives' tales that poke fun at women 'for their proclivity for deep drinking' (12), only one, 'I shall you tell a full good sport' [*1362*] has been found in carol form. It is from MS Cotton Titus A.xxvi, and was formerly thought to be acephalous. Its six missing stanzas have been found in Cotton Vitellius D.xii. The complete poem now begins 'Now shall youe her a tale fore youre dysport' [*2358.5*]. The manuscripts are also connected by the presence of portions of a *Siege of Rhodes*, in the same hand as the ale-wives' poem.

1362, 2358.5.

456   ———. 'Isabel: A Riddling Mistress.' *English Language Notes* 1 (1963–4): 1–4.

Among acrostic love lyrics of the fifteenth century is 'the anagram headed "Devenayle par Pycard," ["Take þe sevenþ in ordre sette," *3256*] forming the concluding stanza (in one MS. only) of a pseudo-Lydgatian love poem' (1). Robbins does not offer a solution for this puzzle, but presents some for verses concealing names in words or numbers, and lists others in footnotes.

158, 481, 597.5, 717, 735, 737, 1024, 1026, 1063, 1187, 1813, 2136, 2217, 2223, 2479, 3228, 3256.

457 Bühler, Curt F. 'A Middle-English Stanza on "The Commonwealth and the Need for Wisdom."' *English Language Notes* 2 (1964–5): 4–5. [Edition.]

John Walton's metrical translation of *De consolatione philosophiae* of Boethius is the source of isolated stanzas described in *IMEV* as 'On the Evils of Prosperity' ['Ryght as pouerte causeth sobreness,' *2820*]. Bühler prints a similar stanza, 'fformynge in me the maner of my lyffe' [*856.5*], from MS Bühler 17; this has a Latin preface from Liber I, Prosa IV of Boethius, and explains a reference to an aphorism of Plato.

856.5, 2820.

458 ———. 'Prayers and Charms in Certain Middle English Scrolls.' *Speculum* 39 (1964): 270–8 [cited]. Repr. in *Early Books and Manuscripts: Forty Years of Research by Curt F. Bühler*. New York: The Grolier Club and the Pierpont Morgan Library, 1973. 564–75.

Autobiographical details in 'Noghte to lyke þow me to lake' [*2300.3*] which concludes MS Glazier 39, establish the scribe as 'a certain Percival, born in Rudby in Cleveland . . . who had entered the Premonstratensian order on Halloween . . . and had become a canon of Coversham Abbey . . . by the time the scroll was written . . . after 1484' (278). This is clear from references to Pope Innocent VIII and Charles VIII of France. The dialect is of the North-Eastern Midlands.

2300.3.

459 Curry, Jane L. 'Waking the Well.' *English Language Notes* 2 (1964–5): 1–4.

Greene, **314**, relates 'The Maid of the Moor' [*2037.5*] to 'The Betrayed Maiden's Lament' ['The last tyme I the wel woke' [*3409*]. He wonders 'whether the maiden may be under a spell or weaving one,' and comments on 'the persistent pagan custom of merrymaking by holy wells' (1). Curry proposes that the betrayed maiden came to the well to keep a 'wake' by the well, intending to disturb it to divine 'the identity of her lover-to-be,' and had 'a prompt and violent answer' (3) when Sir John caught her with his crook. The other maiden remains more magical and elusive.

2037.5, 3409.

460 Greene, Richard Leighton. '"If I Sing, Tie Up Your Cows."' *Notes and Queries* 209 (1964): 88–9.

Corrrects Robbins's gloss of *tey vp ȝour ky!* 'tune up your instruments' [*RobbinsS*, **51**, 228] to 'tie up your cows' (89). Greene interprets the speaker of 'If I synge ȝe wyl me lakke' [*1417*] as 'one of a company at a dinner or other occasion at which a song is required of everyone' (88), who says 'if I sing the cows will think that they are being called and will come.' The allusion to fixing another time suggests 'that the master of ceremonies excuse him from his forfeit' (89).

1417, 1866, 2343.

461 ———. 'The Burden and the Scottish Variant of the Corpus Christi Carol.' *Medium Ævum* 33 (1964): 53–60.

Adds to **418**, which identifies the falcon of the 'Corpus Christi Carol' [*1132*] with Anne Boleyn. Greene answers Davies, **61**, and Manning, **443**, whose interpretations differ. He reads *lulley, lulley* in the burden as a reference to 'an amatory rather than a religious situation,' and cites the phrase in poems of betrayed women or 'a taunting of the lover whose mistress has slipped away' (54); thus it is fitting 'in a couplet which refers to a stolen mate.' Allusions in Skelton's 'Why Come Ye Not to Court' [*813.3*] supply further instances of heraldic imagery to stand for the Boleyn family, Henry VIII, and Cardinal Wolsey, and so convey messages 'as plain to a Tudor courtier as the meaning of the burden of "Corpus Christi" itself' (55). Such messages are confirmed in knowledge of falconry and Catherine's love of the sport. Greene's exposition of *purpill and pall* reveals connotations of 'secular royalty or nobility or great wealth,' and argues that it cannot 'be forced into a liturgical reference' (57). The *orchard brown* is most likely a shaded garden, the *hall* a queen's residence rather than a church. A folk-rhyme cited by James Hogg, in 'Sir David Graeme' and 'The Bridal of Polmood' sheds further light. In 'The Bridal of Polmood' James IV's infidelities are revealed when William Moray sings of 'The Heron' to the king, whom he does not recognize, and to his queen, Margaret, who pretends not to understand its meaning. In the allusions in his tale, which is set 'about twenty-five years earlier than the date of the manuscript copy of "Corpus Christi,"' Hogg deals with 'the strange rich world of the secular ballads' (60), rather than with religious allegory.

358, 813.3, 1132, 1367, 2231.5, 3445, 3782, 4160.

462 ———. 'Wyatt's "I Am as I Am" in Carol-Form.' *Review of English Studies* NS 15 (1964): 175–80. [Edition.]

The poem is in this form on a flyleaf of University of Pennsylvania MS, Latin 35, and varies from other versions of Wyatt's poem ['I ham as I ham and so will I be,' *1270.2*]. Greene prints the carol, opposite the version of BL Add. 17492, which has no burden. He supplies the burden and first stanza of two other carols that are ascribed to Wyatt ['For as ye lyst my wyll ys bent,' *813.6*; 'My yeris be yong even as ye see,' *2281.5*], noting significant variants in manuscript sources. For *813.6* it is impossible to discern which is the earlier version, and establish whether this is 'a case of a carol-burden's being added to an already existing lyric . . . or . . . a carol [that] has had its burden removed' (178–9). Evidence suggests that the Pennsylvania version of *1270.2* is earlier, 'a carol (anonymous as far as we know) which Wyatt appropriated and expanded into a longer poem, eliminating both the burden and the "envoy"' (179). There is no evidence that Wyatt was a musician.

813.6, 1270.2, 2281.5.

463 Hill, Betty. 'The "Luue-Ron" and Thomas de Hales.' *Modern Language Review* 59 (1964): 321–30.

The 'Luue Ron' ['A Mayde Cristes me bit yorne,' *66*], composed by the Franciscan Thomas de Hales 'at the urgent request of a maiden dedicated to God,' blends the themes *contemptus mundi* and *sponsa Christi*. After showing 'the transitory nature of earthly love and lovers,' the poem contrasts 'Christ's sovereignty, the durability and rewards of His love' (321) as the maiden's betrothed. The maiden must unroll the roll on which the lyric is written, learn it by heart, sing it sweetly, and teach it faithfully to others. This may be the first reference to a vernacular religious text on a roll, and Franciscans may have used this minstrels' way of carrying verse sermons, since no manuscript book for itinerant preachers of the thirteenth century has survived. The 'Luue Ron' is Thomas de Hales's only known English work, and was probably composed between 1225 and 1272. Hill cites records of his life and his associates, in particular Adam de Madderley.

66.

464 Moore, Arthur K. 'Lyric Voices and Ethical Proofs.' *Journal of Aesthetics and Art Criticism* 23 (1964–5): 429–39.

Investigates the lyric's 'largely unrestricted privilege of verbalizing any experience, however improbable or trivial, without directly appealing to any value or set of values approved by custom' (429). Moore begins by considering medieval lyrics, which 'usually appeal directly to approved social and religious sympathies' (430), with religious lyrics endorsed by their subjects, and courtly lyrics endorsed by 'the pretended usefulness of the pieces to the conduct of courtly love' (431). The voice of a medieval lyric may be that of the poet, 'but it is most evidently that of a well-defined social or religious predicament' (431). He does not cite specific lyrics.

465 Robbins, Rossell Hope. 'Wall Verses at Launceston Priory.' *Archiv* 200 (1964): 338–43. [Edition.]

Moralizing proverbs in verse form, inscribed on the walls of the hall of Launceston Priory, are preserved in 'a near-contemporary manuscript, Bodley MS.315 (SC. 2712)' (339). Robbins prints them with other sources for the proverbs. The verses offer 'appropriate counsel for the various categories of permanent officials and senior servants who would be seated together at each *tabula* . . . and the corrodians or pensioners and lay administrators.' A Latin stanza, urging almsgiving 'might have looked down on the high table of the guest hall' (341). The building was pillaged for its masonry after the Dissolution, and it is 'a curious quirk of history that this detailed information about the interior of Launceston Priory has survived by means of vellum long after the building itself has disappeared' (343). Robbins includes numerous brief references to other verses for display and to other occurrences of the Launceston Priory verses.

192, 237, 321, 444, 500, 520, 671, 691, 704, 730, 765, 798, 854, 1156, 1160, 1206, 1207, 1349, 1619, 1929, 2152, 2464, 2511, 2577, 2592, 2785, 2811, 3088, 3206, 3273, 3274, 3275, 3400, 3431, 3482, 3632, 3793, 3808, 3886, 4039, 4102, 4129, 4135.5, 4137, 4203.

466 Sikora, Ruta. 'The Structural Simplicity of the Early Middle English Lyric: Three Examples.' *Kwartalnik Neofilologiczny* 11 (1964): 233–42.

Simplicity in the ME lyric comes from 'neatly organized metrical and grammatical features' (233), rather than plainness and lack of technical devices. Sikora analyses grammatical and metrical structures in 'Foweles in the frith' [*864*], 'Svmer is icumen in' [*3223*], and 'Leuedi ic þenke þe wid herte suiþe milde' [*1836*], to show patterns of parallelism, rhyme, alliteration, repetition, and mood in their construction.

864, 1836, 3223.

467 Stemmler, Theo. 'Interpretation des Mittelenglischen Gedichts *God þat al þis myhtes may.*' *Anglia* 82 (1964): 58–75.

The penitential lyric 'God þat al þis myhtes may' [*968*] exemplifies the poetry and thinking of the late Middle Ages. Symmetry of the rhymes in the first and seventh stanzas emphasizes its ordered structure and shows that the arrangement is invariable, with three pairs of linked stanzas and a concluding stanza. Stemmler describes the structure, stressing the use of apostrophe and paradox, and the implications of number symbolism, particularly involving the number seven and its products. Of the seven deadly sins, most attention is paid to pride and its branches, balanced by the seven virtues. The number seven is also related to the petitions of the Lord's Prayer. The motif of good and bad works recurs, as the poet addresses God and reflects on the paradoxes of his power and mortality. The sequence of thoughts is playful rather than logical.

968.

468 ———. 'Zur Verfasserfrage der Charles d'Orléans Zugeschriebenen englische Gedichte.' *Anglia* 82 (1964): 458–73.

Investigates the authorship of ME poems attributed to Charles d'Orléans. Stemmler's survey of criticism of verse in MS Harley 682 concentrates on that of MacCracken, **129,** who attributed the poems to the Duke of Suffolk, and of Steele [ed., with Mabel Day, *The English Poems of Charles d'Orléans*]. Suffolk was Charles's best known visitor, but not the only one, and any English visitor could have contributed the works. Stemmler rejects the premise on which MacCracken's belief that Suffolk wrote the Fairfax poems is based. He agrees with Steele that the poems are adaptations rather than translations of Charles's French works, but not that they are 'author's corrections.' Adaptations of and sequels to another poet's work were not rare, and Charles's name could have been used for poetic reasons rather than to establish or disguise authorship. Stemmler presents examples of three kinds of evidence against Steele's theory: from comparisons of words, forms, and styles used in the French and English. Literal comparisons suggest that the ME works are not translations; they have syntactic and conceptual differences rather than misunderstandings. Charles was fluent in English and Suffolk in French. The French and English poems differ in form. Of 81 English ballades, 40 have no French originals. There are differences in numbers of stanzas, rhyme schemes, and *envoi*; only seven of the ME ballades have no *envoi*, but 18 of the French works have none. The *chansons* differ in rhyme scheme, and Stemmler considers that Charles would have retained his scheme in translation. He accepts that Charles wrote two *chansons* ['Myn hert hath sent glad hope in hys message,' *2176*; 'When shal thow come glad hope from your vyage,' *4014*] and four macaronic poems. Comparisons of style suggest that the Harley poems had one editor or author, conforming to English traditions of alliteration and description, with elements of travesty and irony not to be expected of Charles. Stemmler concludes that the poet was neither Charles nor Suffolk; that he was English, with good, not perfect, French; that he translated for Charles, and composed poems himself. The use of tags implies a professional minstrel rather than an aristocrat.

165, 309, 553, 567, 867, 1339, 1404, 1413, 2176, 2184, 2203, 2309, 2378, 2379, 2564, 2567, 4014, 4024.

469 Abel, Patricia. 'The Cleric, the Kitchie Boy and the Returned Sailor.' *Philological Quarterly* 44 (1965): 552–5.

'De Clerico et Puella' [*2236*] is unusual; although it has obvious connections 'with the convention of love complaint and spring song . . . it is not a subjective lyric, but a conversation between two people' (552). Their speech patterns characterize them, in the clerk's courtly language and the girl's direct, colloqual idiom. Narrative is presented through the clerk's persuasion and the girl's indignation which becomes enthusiasm. The change seems more clear and motivated when the figures are seen 'not as the Cleric and Puella only, but the Returned Sailor and the pretty fair Miss, or . . . the Kitchie Boy and the Merchant's Daughter' (552–3). Their dialogue is a reunion after a long parting, and a test of the girl's faithfulness to the lover she does not at first recognize. If this motif is being used 'it is probably the most artistic handling of it that has survived' (555).

2236.

470 Brewer, D.S. 'An Unpublished Late Alliterative Poem.' *English Philological Studies* 9 (1965): 84–8. [Edition.]

Presents 'Ielosy' ['In soumer seson, as soune as the sonne,' *7266*], a poem of 'very modest literary merit.' It is an alliterative work of the sixteenth century from the Blage MS (D.2.7) of Trinity College, Dublin, which has 'the sort of poems that Wyatt and his circle composed and enjoyed' (84). Brewer notes the imitation of the first line of *Piers Plowman* [*1459*] and resemblances to other works. He transcribes the poem, with punctuation and capitalization, and comments on various points, including the reference to Kent, but finds that '[t]he relationship between the meeting with Cupid and the allegorical description of Jealousy is not at all clear' (85)

1333, 1459, 7266.

471 Bühler, Curt F. 'Owners' Jingles in Early Printed Books: *Libri Impressi cum Notis Manuscriptis XI.*' *Studies in Philology* 62 (1965): 647–53 [cited]. Repr. in *Early Books and Manuscripts: Forty Years of Research by Curt F. Bühler*. New York: The Grolier Club and the Pierpont Morgan Library, 1973. 641–6. [Edition.]

Among jottings found 'in the margins and blank portions of leaves' (647), Bühler presents some verses in English, one of which [A scholer must in youth bee taughte,' *7018*] translates a Latin stanza. They include an apology for the scribe's poor writing, blamed on his pen ['Thomas Albone is my name,' *3662.5*], and advice, such as a poem against hasty speech ['Yffe anye man aske a question of the,' *1409.5*] and one in favour of courtesy ['Here maist thou learne thyselfe how to be-haue,' *7199*].

1409.5, 1489.5, 3662.5, 3976.5, 7018, 7199, 7533.

472 Dronke, Peter. *Problems and Interpretations.* Oxford: Clarendon, 1965. Vol. 1 of *Medieval Latin and the Rise of European Love-Lyric.* 2 vols.

Considering the lyric in Latin and other European languages, Dronke writes of the Harley lyrics (112–25), in 'The Ideas and the Poets: Illustrations' (98–162). He distinguishes between ME lyrics and those of the troubadours and trouvères, and cites ME examples more closely related to the Mozarabic *kharja* and the early German lyric. In the latter poems 'a dramatic situation and a complex state of feelings are evoked in a few lines, by words of the greatest forthrightness and simplicity,' and in 'swift, sometimes humorous, transitions of thought' (114). Repetition is used in English and German songs in ways 'far simpler than those of *rondeau* or *virelai*' (116), yet in 'a language that is homely, not elegant' (117); subtle ideas of courtly love are conveyed, especially in the Harley lyrics. Dronke compares 'incongruities between an exalted and a down-to-earth language of love' (117) to the language of *The Miller's Tale* [*4019*], and demonstrates aspects of English style in some Harley poems. 'Annot and John' [*1394*] exemplifies elaborate description; the beloved is 'joyfully blessed by Christ when she gives her favours in *derne dedis*' (122–3). 'Alysoun' [*515*] indicates that 'the beloved is her lover's destiny' (121); although the language is 'almost comic in its homely, quacking sounds, we are confronted with one of the profoundest enigmas of *amour courtois*' (122). 'Wiþ longyng y am lad' [*4194*] conveys '[t]he *whole* of heaven in one night with the beloved . . . the notion of pleroma' (122–3). The descriptions of 'The Fair Maid of Ribblesdale' [*2207*] 'give intimations of a celestial power' (123). 'Blow, Northerne Wynd' [*1395*] recalls 'the earliest surviving medieval Latin song of *amour courtois*: "Deus amet puellam"' (124) in its refrain, where 'the words that summon the highest veneration of the beloved are fused with the words of elemental longing for her' (125).

179, 515, 1142, 1394, 1395, 2207, 2622, 3512, 4019, 4194.

473 Hardy, Adelaide. 'Nicholas Bozon and a Middle English Complaint.' *Notes and Queries* 210 (1965): 90–1.

Notes the possibility that 'Whose þenchiþ vp þis carful lif' [*4144*] has its source in the AN *Contes Moralisés*, 'compiled by the Franciscan Nicholas Bozon probably soon after 1320.' The poem is found in the Franciscan MS Harley 913, and is 'a complaint against the oppression of the innocent and defenceless in which a fable of a lion, fox, wolf and ass is used to illustrate the evils of bribery,' (90). Bozon does not speak of bribery, but finds that nature induces the wolf to kiss the sheep, and the fox to require penance from the goose, after confession. Similarities in the works include the reason for the wolf's acquittal, and verbal parallels, in the sage eaten by the ass and the adjective *dogged* for the wolf. Criticism of the clergy is more direct in the *conte*, but the complaint shows 'the prevalence of "Couetise."' The poet develops the theme of *contemptus mundi*, and urges deeds of charity, 'exhorting his listeners to honour God and "Holi Chirch" and give to the needy poor,' intending to encourage 'spiritual enlightenment not social reform' (91).

4144.

474   **Hatto, Arthur T., ed.** *Eos: An Enquiry into the Theme of Lovers' Meetings and Partings at Dawn in Poetry.* The Hague: Mouton, 1965.

Has many references to particular ME lyrics on this theme and to passages from longer works. Hatto surveys poetry of the dawn in many languages, with chapters on 'The "Origins" of Dawn Poetry' (47–68); 'Mythology' (69–72); 'The Crystallization and Diffusion of some Dawn Themes' (73–86); 'Religion' (87–96); and 'Mime and Drama' (97–102). Sections dealing with particular languages follow; these are the work of various authors, and include T.J.B Spencer's contribution, 'English (English, Scots, Anglo-Irish and American)' (505–53). Spencer explores the relation between religious and secular songs, including the use of secular tunes for religious works. He traces references (in poems of various eras) to popular themes such as bird song, the appearance of the sky, and warnings of the watchman (505–31), and prints 16 examples of dawn poems in English (532–53). Hatto supplies an appendix on 'Imagery and Symbolism' (771–819). This includes references to trees, signs of the dawn, and various birds: the cock (787–92), nightingale (792–800), cuckoo (800–8), swallow (808–10), lark (810–12), and crow (812–15).

683, 913, 1299, 1450, 2007, 2516, 2662, 3327, 3329, 4019, 7201.

475   **Ker, N.R.** 'Middle English Verses and a Latin Letter in a Manuscript at Stanbrook Abbey.' *Medium Ævum* 34 (1965): 230–3. [Edition.]

Additions to a manuscript at Stanbrook Abbey, containing 'for the most part the homilies of Haymo on the gospels for Sundays through the year' (230), include 'English verses, divisible, but not divided into seven stanzas' (231) of 'Ion Clerke of toryton I dar avow' [*1793.6*], and a lullaby song of the Virgin to the Christ Child, 'Ʒe ben my fader my creacion' [*4242.5*].

1793.6, 4242.5.

476   **Lass, Roger.** 'Three Middle English Cautionary Lyrics, from a Yale University MS.' *Anglia* 88 (1965): 172–5. [Edition.]

The lyrics are in a miscellany for 'a country gentleman of some education, with a lively concern for the technicalities of farming, hunting and astronomy, as well as a gastronomic taste worthy of Chaucer's Franklin,' (173). The first 'Ryght as pouerte causeth sobrenesse' [*2820*], has 'neatness and control of diction.' [See also Bühler, **457**.] The second 'The wyse man his sone for bede' [*80280*], has a rare 'verbal freshness' (172). The third is an incomplete gnomic fragment of 'Now to speke will I noght spare' [*2371*]. Lass prints them, with comments and comparisons with versions of *2820* found in the Bannatyne MS and Bodleian 3554.

2371, 2820, 7507.

477   **Manzalaoui, Mahmoud.** '"Maiden in the Mor Lay" and the Apocrypha.' *Notes and Queries* 210 (1965): 91–2.

Parallels to the situation of 'Maiden in the mor lay' [*2037.5*] are found in a passage in 2 Esd. 9, where 'the angel Uriel commands the Prophet to go out into a field of flowers, and live there for a week, eating nothing but the flowers, and drinking no wine' (92). The resemblance may suggest that 'both Esdras and the Maiden of the poem are types of the soul in expectancy, in a stage of purification prior to the vision of Divine Truth' (92).

2037.5.

478   **Reiss, Edmund.** 'A Critical Approach to the Middle English Lyric.' *College English* 27 (1965–6): 373–9.

Surveys scholarly editions and comment on the ME lyric, and notes comparisons with Latin and continental vernacular lyrics. Reiss asserts that English lyric, which is 'not especially courtly but – by and large homely, moralistic, sometimes didactic, sometimes bawdy, and mostly lacking in intricacies of verse technique – is rather in what has been called the bourgeois tradition' (374). He examines the thirteenth-century lyrics, 'Sunset on Calvary' ['Nou goth þe sonne under wode,' *2320*], 'Foweles in the frith' [*864*], and 'Wel and wa sal ys hornes blaw' [*3857.5*], and compares 'Westron wynde when wylle thou blow' [*3899.3*]. Through implications of diction and metrical structure, he shows that 'Middle English lyrics are worth analyzing and that they can and should be looked at as responsible poetry' (379).

864, 2320, 3857.5, 3899.3.

479 Robbins, Rossell Hope. 'Middle English Lyrics: Handlist of New Texts.' *Anglia* 83 (1965): 35–47.

Adds 106 entries to the 'main body of Middle English lyrics' (35), listing first lines and numbers as in *SIMEV*. Robbins divides them under the headings: 'Religious Lyrics' (36–41), written to the Deity, Christ, the Virgin and the saints, with lyrics inserted into a 'prose translation of de Guileville's *Pèlerinage de l'Ame* in the MS. at the Victoria Public Library, Melbourne' (40); 'Moral and Didactic Lyrics' (41–3); 'Secular Lyrics,' love lyrics and trivial lyrics (43–5); and 'Scraps and Scribbles' (45–7), including some found by inspection using ultra-violet light. He lists the sources of the lyrics and notes critical references, in the style of *IMEV* and *SIMEV*.

34.5, 35.5, 120.2, 135.3, 143.5, 158.3, 231.5, 265.5, 270, 317.5, 378.5, 454.5, 502.5, 528.5, 550.5, 553.5, 711.5, 754.5, 790.5, 853.2, 854.5, 870.8, 871.5, 995.2, 995.3, 995.4, 1011.8, 1041.3, 1041.5, 1151.5, 1176.5, 1249.5, 1295.8, 1322.5, 1344.5, 1355.5, 1376.5, 1393.5, 1414.5, 1422.5, 1455.5, 1489.5, 1490.5, 1531.5, 1561.5, 1570.8, 1580.5, 1596.8, 1637.8, 1700.5, 1709.5, 1732.5, 1739.5, 1758.5, 1779.5, 1808.5, 1817.5, 1838.5, 1856.5, 1929.5, 2033.5, 2124.5, 2153.5, 2195.3, 2271.4, 2323.3, 2384.5, 2412.5, 2420.5, 2440.5, 2478.8, 2533.5, 2635.5, 2723.5, 2806.5, 2820.3, 3131.5, 3167.3, 3200.5, 3238.3, 3306.3, 3318.2, 3328.5, 3416.5, 3439.5, 3461.8, 3477.6, 3483.5, 3530.5, 3538.5, 3559.5, 3598.5, 3721.8, 3808.5, 3899.6, 3900.5, 3902.5, 3941.5, 4014.5, 4073.5, 4098.8, 4126.5, 4162.5, 4227.5, 4242.5.

480 Sisam, Celia. '"Ne Saltou Neuer, Leuedi."' *Notes and Queries* 210 (1965): 245–6.

The ten lines of 'Ne saltou neuer leuedi Tuynklen wyt þin eyen' [*2288*] make 'no satisfactory sense as a single poem,' and so Sisam proposes that 'Robert, the scribe, has here recorded three unrelated scraps of song' (245). In a space after the *Expositio Donati*, which offers 'an invitation irresistible to a light-hearted scribe . . . he wrote two separate and well known Latin *explicit* tags, and then such Middle English verses as occurred to him,' and '[f]inally he crowded in his name and address' (246). The irregular spacing of the lines suggests 'that he wrote down haphazardly scraps of song that he remembered, until he had no room left. His English verses are no more likely to be one poem than his two Latin verses' (246). [See Burton, **751**.]

2288.

481 Smithers, G.V. 'Some Textual Problems in Religious Lyrics of the Fourteenth Century.' *English Philological Studies* 9 (1965): 89–96.

A reply to Malone's discussion, **367**, of 'detailed textual problems' in Smithers's edition of *Brown XIV*, **48**. Smithers wishes to demonstrate 'dubious, misleading, or erroneous views' that might 'escape detection by other readers if they are allowed to go unrefuted.'

prayer,' *3443.5*]. Robbins prints them, with comments, briefly noting resemblances in similar works. [See Croft, **754.**]

377, 434, 1344.5, 1471, 1738, 2332, 2494, 2635.5, 3328.5, 3332, 3443.5, 3467, 3585.

491   Stevick, Robert D. 'The Criticism of Middle English Lyrics.' *Modern Philology* 64 (1966): 103–17.

Surveys treatment and current neglect of ME lyrics. Stevick disapproves of 'all-or-none patristic interpretation' (103), and asserts that Moore's hypothesis, **297**, of lyric impulses offers 'fiction when we would have criticism' (105). Kane, **292**, considers special problems of ME lyrics, and Stevick develops his remarks on 'Louerd þu clepest me' [*1978*] to examine the 'poem's structure and execution' (106), extending this work to consideration of Manning, **443**. An important aspect of criticism is choice of text; Stevick illustrates difficulties of selecting and reading from closely related versions. He finds the suggestion that 'texts be tinkered with until they resemble our ideal version of the poem, or that we criticize the ideal rather than the real texts, invites the response, "That way madness lies"' (111). Stylistics demand attention; Stevick expands on structural characteristics in 'the best of the (anonymous) lyrics' (113). Stanza form, stresses (four), lines as syntactic units, and relation to grammatical constructions, make 'the verse norm of traditional Middle English lyrics . . . conducive to assertions and questions confined to small multiples of major syntactic unit lines organized by rhyme' (115). Reasons for neglect include 'uncertainty about how to deal directly with the poems . . . instead of the (anonymous) poets, how to treat the texts as texts rather than as relics . . . how to analyze the structuring of expression . . . more deeply than for tropes, rhyme schemes, and metrical feet' (117).

360, 375, 515, 704, 769, 1367, 1370.5, 1460, 1463, 1921, 1978, 2163, 2320, 2504, 2507, 2645, 3223, 3310, 3874, 3899.3, 3939, 4181, 4185.

492   Virginia, Sister Marie. 'William of Shoreham's "A Song to Mary," Stanza 10.' *Explicator* 25.2 (1966): item 16.

Explains the line 'Thou art Emaus, the riche castel' in William of Shoreham's 'Marye mayde mylde and fre' [*2107*], in answer to Davies, **61**. The image 'Castle of Emmaus' links the associations of Mary as a castle 'adorned with all virtues,' fortified and raised above all, with those of Emmaus, the resting-place of Christ, where he revealed himself to disciples [Luke 24: 13ff.]. Thus Mary can be 'the house or castle of Emmaus, where all who seek Christ find him and through whom he reveals his identity as Christ (and therefore King) to the world.' Another possible reading of the line is 'Thou art Emmaus, (Thou art also) the rich castle.'

2107.

493   Bowers, Robert H. 'A Middle English Poem on the Nine Virtues.' *Southern Folklore Quarterly* 31 (1967): 37–47. [Edition.]

Prints, with notes and glosses, 'a hitherto unpublished anonymous ME didactic poem of the fifteenth century, 'Alle þᵗ loue to here þis lessoun [*212*]. This shows Jesus 'as a moral teacher expounding nine virtues to a nameless pupil, a "good trewe Christian"' (37). Bowers compares the poem, which is found in MS Cambridge University Library Dd.1.1, to similar works. He explains the system of virtues, developed from Ciceronian and Pauline concepts, which shows them to be 'specific remedies for the seven deadly sins' (38).

212, 2186, 3571.

494 ———. 'Middle English Verses on the Founding of the Carthusian Order.' *Speculum* 42 (1967): 710–13. [Edition.]

'At þe begynnyng of þe chartirhows god did schewe' [*435*] recalls 'in nostalgic vein . . . the supposedly pristine purity of the austere founding fathers' of the Carthusians. Bowers finds a crux in line 24, where '[i]nstead of the traditional seven founders our author cites but six . . . namely, Bruno, Hugh, Anoelius, Basilius, Bridius, and Bovo, although the illustrations . . . clearly present seven persons making their supplication to the Bishop of Grenoble, and on l.8 our author refers to St Bruno and his "sex felowes"' (710). Bowers's transcription provides 'modern capitalization and pointing, and indicates expansion of abbreviations with italics' (711).

435.

495 Evans, W.O. '"Cortaysye" in Middle English.' *Mediaeval Studies* 29 (1967): 143–57.

In the exploration of the range of concepts associated with *cortaysye* in ME literature, Evans draws on two lyrics among many examples. In 'The Bird with Four Feathers' ['By a forest syde walkyng as I went,' *561*], the bird rejects the notion of *cortaysye* as beauty, and 'by implication replaces it with Christian virtue' (151). The Vernon lyric 'Mercy Passes All Things' ['Bi west vnder a wylde wode syde,' *583*] presents the idea of 'good life in a religious sense,' with 'pleasure of a spiritual nature, free from sin, compared with fleshly excesses' (155).

561, 583.

496 Gray, Douglas. 'A Middle English Verse at Warkworth.' *Notes and Queries* 212 (1967): 131–2.

A 'fragmentary inscription' preserved in the church at Warkworth is 'almost identical with the popular Middle English verse prayer' (131) 'Ihū for thy holy name' [*1703*]. Gray speculates, without confidence, that it 'might possibly have been worked into a longer poem on the Five Wounds,' and offers examples of the 'functional use of devotional verses as inscriptions' (131).

1703.

497 [Finnegan] Jeremy, Sister Mary. '*Mon* in "Foweles in the Frith."' *English Language Notes* 5 (1967–8): 80–1.

Proposes to read *mon* in line 3 ['And I mon waxe wod'] of the lyric 'Foweles in the frith' [*864*] not as a verb (with the sense 'And I must go mad,' as suggested by Brown, **36**, and Davies, **61**), but as 'the noun *man* in apposition with *I*' (80), to yield 'And I, man, am going mad' (81). There are analogies in 'Allas I wooful creature' [*154*], 'Vnto the rial egles excellence/I humble Clerc, with all hertes humblesse' [*3831*], and 'I patrik larrons of spittale feyld' [*1338.5*].

154, 864, 1338.5, 3831.

498 Luisi, David. 'Foweles in the Frith.' *Explicator* 25.6 (1967): item 47.

Any disjointedness of the two couplets of 'Foweles in the frith' [*864*] is 'only apparent, for all the lines substantiate a basic medieval assumption which renders the poem intelligible.' As he thinks of the order that should obtain in Nature, 'the poet is as certain that he must become mad on account of the deliberate excess of his sorrow as he is that the "foweles" and the "fisses," each in its proper habitat, must instinctively adhere to the order designed for their well-being.'

864.

499 Revard, Carter. 'The Lecher, the Legal Eagle, and the Papelard Priest: Middle English Confessional Satires in MS. Harley 2253 and Elsewhere.' *His Firm Estate: Essays in Honor of Franklin James Eikenberry.* Monograph Series, University of Tulsa, Department of English 2. Tulsa, OK: U of Tulsa, 1967. 54–71.

Examines 'The Papelard Priest' ['Of Alle þe witti men and wise I warn Alle i þe wache,' *2614.5*], in Add. MS 45896, and 'A Satire on the Consistory Courts' ['Ne mai no lewed libben in londe,' *2287*] and 'The Man in the Moon' ['Mon in þe mone stonde and strit,' *2066*] in Harley 2253. Revard sees the poems as *yeddyng*, dramatic monologue, and confessional satire, and finds that all terms fit *2614.5*, whereas the latter two and possibly the first terms apply to the other poems. Internal evidence hints that *2614.5* was made 'for (and likely by) a friar,' since it links 'mockery of secular clergy with praise of friars' (56). Revard places it with the few ME dramatic monologues that prove the existence of confessional satire, with a speaker whose shortcomings are 'the central comic revelation,' who unintentionally confesses that he is 'in some part a knave and in large part a fool,' (57). He shows, by paraphrasing the poem as words of a peasant who offers legal advice to the Man in the Moon, but loses patience when the Man will not come down to him, that the speaker of *2066* is 'a would-be Legal Eagle whose squawks reveal him to be a barnyard cockerel' (58). Revard suggests 'A Sinner in the Archdeacon's Court' rather than Thomas Wright's title for *2287*. The speaker is an unlettered 'household retainer,' but also 'a prompt, skilful, courteous servant' (62). His name in the Archdeacon's book discloses an accusation of lechery; although he claims to be slandered, his words are 'strong evidence of his guilt' (66). Thus the poem satirizes 'complaining sinners' rather than 'the church-courts' treatment of sinners' (67). The Lecher is 'sour, a vindictive, hangdog, self-justifying type,' but the Papelard Priest [*2614.5*] is 'stupidly well-meaning, convinced of his own hopeless incapacity, yet with a mindless ignorance of how immoral he is' (67). Revard does not interpret the poem, but notes the 'fine use of sound-effects' (68). The characters could be a source of 'the Canterbury Pilgrims' (69).

1320.5, 1459, 1894, 2066, 2287, 2614.5, 2649, 4019.

500 Riddy, Felicity. 'The Provenance of *Quia Amore Langueo*.' *Review of English Studies* NS 18 (1967): 429–33.

'In a tabernacle of a toure' [*1460*] survives 'in more or less complete versions, in eight fifteenth-century manuscripts (a ninth preserves a single stanza as a fragment)' (429). Rhymes, words and usage suggest the original composition 'in a north-midland dialect' (430), rather than Brown's claim, *BrownXIV*, **31**, that the version of MS Bodley Douce 322 represents its original form. As '[t]he nearest an editor could hope to get to the original text,' Riddy proposes BL Add. 37049 for stanzas 1–7 and 11, with 9, 10, and 12 from Douce 322, 'possibly altering the accidentals to conform . . . and correcting both in the light of the other manuscripts' (433).

1460.

501 Rigg, A.G. 'The Letter "C" and the Date of Easter.' *English Language Notes* 5 (1967–8): 1–5. [Edition.]

The mnemonic lyric 'In March after þe fyrst C' [*1502*], has instructions for finding the date of Easter. These are based on a system in which 'the days of the year were given letters in such a way that the letters A-G correspond to 1-7 January (thus 8 January = A, etc.)' (1), so that 'the first "C" in March must always be the 7th (as in Leap Years 29 February is given the same letter as 28 February)' (2). The date of Easter can be calculated from a calendar with the Golden Numbers of the Metonian cycle. This explanation refutes the *MED* definition of *C* as 'the dominical letter representing the third Sunday of the year, the tenth Sunday, the seventeenth, etc.' (1). Rigg prints the poem, notes its occurrence in 16 manuscripts, and compares variants.

1502.

502 Rowland, Beryl. 'Forgotten Metaphor in Three Popular Children's Rhymes.' *Southern Folklore Quarterly* 31 (1967): 12–19.

Implied meanings in the erotic carol about Kitt Lostkey, 'Kytt hathe lost hur key' [*1824.8*] resemble those of the rhyme of Lucy Locket and her pocket.

1824.8.

503 Sajavaara, Kari. 'The Relationship of the Vernon and Simeon Manuscripts.' *Neuphilologische Mitteilungen* 68 (1967): 428–40.

Attempts to explain and reconcile evidence of comparative studies of the manuscripts, including possibilities that one is a copy of the other or that the two have a common exemplar. Sajavaara summarizes critical opinions and suggests reasons for some differences. Two lyrics found in the Simeon MS (BL Add. 22283), 'Who-so loueth endeles rest' [*4135*] and 'I þonke þe lord god ful of miht' [*1369*], are not in the Vernon (Bodleian Library, English Poetry a.1). Two stanzas of 'Whon grein of whete is caste to grounde' [*3952*] are defective in the Vernon MS. [See also Burrow **933**; Thompson, **943**.]

1369, 3952, 4135.

504 Salter, Elizabeth. 'Piers Plowman and "The Simonie."' *Archiv* 203 (1967): 241–54.

Seeks, by tracing similarities of matter and style, to show influence of 'The Simonie' [*4165*] on Langland's composition of *Piers Plowman* [*1459*], and to establish that he could have read the poem, perhaps in both the Auchinleck MS and Peterhouse, Cambridge 104. Salter proposes numerous examples of correspondences of metre and alliteration and echoes of phrase and syntax. She suggests that if Langland had been aware of a need to fit his verse for a public in areas extended beyond the West Midlands, he could have found 'in poems such as *The Simonie* something to his purpose,' and for 'a more flexible and permissive alliterative range . . . *The Simonie* . . . might have shown him a way' (247). There are significant similarities in the characterization of abstract concepts and people in both poems. [See also Embree and Urquhart, **887**; Finlayson, **918**.]

1320.5, 1459, 3989, 4165.

505 Scattergood, V.J. 'An Unpublished Middle English Poem.' *Archiv* 203 (1967): 277–82. [Edition.]

The poem, 'ffro this worlde be gynyng' [*7158*], preserved on 'the back of Bicester Priory Bursar's Accounts Roll for 17–18 Edward III, Michelmas to Michelmas' (277), is 'a rudimentary historical and topographical description of Rome' (278). It resembles *The Stacions of Rome* [*1172*], with which it is found. Both works draw on earlier sources of information for pilgrims. Scattergood prints the text, with editorial lineation and punctuation; he provides notes on variations from *1172* and other points of interest. The poem's language implies that its author was 'probably from the North East Midland dialect area, but his forms occur alongside the more Southern forms of the copyists.' The introduction of matters not pursued suggests that the poem was 'conceived as a longer and more ambitious work than achieves completion' (279).

1172, 7158.

506 Thornley, Eva M. 'The Middle English Penitential Lyric and Hoccleve's Autobiographical Poetry.' *Neuphilologische Mitteilungen* 68 (1967): 295–321.

In a study of Hoccleve's autobiographical poetry, especially of *La Male Regle* [*2538*], Thornley shows the literary potentiality and status of the penitential lyric. *La Male*

Regle is such a lyric, 'remarkable in virtue of the ingenuity with which it conforms to, parodies and transcends this genre' (296). She describes the genre, related to themes of mortality and Penance, intended to assist the laity 'in the examination of conscience before auricular confession' (296–7), or 'to fulfil the function of homily' (297), as *exempla*. The latter are written in the first person, occasionally after the poet's encounter with the penitent, in the style of *chanson d'aventure*. In *La Male Regle*, Hoccleve, as penitent, addresses the god of health, with medical references, confessing as he would to the Christian Deity. Thornley notes many illustrations of parallels in pentitential lyrics and other works, and concludes that *La Male Regle* represents 'an ingenious merging of three traditions – the poem pleading for money, the parody of Christianity apparent in certain conventions of courtly love, and the penitential lyric' (321). His use of the last tradition indicates Hoccleve's assumption that it was well established and so would be understood by his audience.

349, 374, 561, 776, 778, 906, 951, 961, 1115, 1871, 2359, 2538, 3231, 4135, 4158.

507 Zettersten, Arne. 'The Middle English Lyrics in the Wellcome Library.' *Neuphilologische Mitteilungen* 68 (1967):288–94. [Edition.]

Lists the lyrics in manuscripts in the Wellcome Historical Medical Library. Zettersten supplies the history, since 1854, of the Loscombe MS (London, Wellcome Historical Library 406), and prints 'The Poem of the Three Worthies' ['I Julius cesar your high emperour,' *1322.5*.]

113.8, 576, 624, 824, 1293, 1322.5, 1703, 1905, 2323.5, 3173.5, 3422, 3721.8, 3754, 3848, 3985, 4181.

508 Buckley, Vincent. *Poetry and the Sacred*. London: Chatto, 1968.

A general account of 'the variety of modes and directions which the religious impulse in literature may take' (3). As he explores the 'interesting and baffling question in what sense are we to call this or that medieval poem a religious one' (25), Buckley discusses ironies of the *Canterbury Tales* [*4019*]; he examines aspects of the lyrics, including carols, and some of Dunbar's works.

688.3, 1367, 1370.5, 1460, 4019.

509 Dronke, Peter. *The Medieval Lyric*. Hutchinson University Library: Modern Languages and Literature. Literature ed. J.M. Cohen. London: Hutchinson, 1968.

The subject is 'the contents of the *chansonniers* or *Liederhandschriften* of the Middle Ages'; 'lyrical' means 'whatever belongs to, or essentially resembles, what is contained in these' (10). Dronke writes of lyrics of France, Italy, England, Spain, Portugal, Germany, and the Low Countries, and offers numerous detailed illustrations. He considers early ME religious lyrics (63–70); ME love lyrics, comparing them to Galician love-songs (144–51); and 'The Maid of the Moor' [*2037.5*] as a dance-song (195–6). Through examination of the imagery of religious lyrics, such as St Godric's hymn to St Nicholas ['Sainte Nicolaes godes druð,' *3031*], and comparison of lyrics of the Passion ['Nou goth þe sonne under wode,' *2320*; 'Wyth was hys naked brest and red of blod hys syde,' *4088*] and their Latin equivalents, Dronke shows that in 'the finest early English lyrics, even very complex thoughts and images can be unfolded with the same vivid and personal lucidity' (66). There is great 'freedom of invention' (67), exemplified in 'Judas' [*1649*]. The themes include mortality, devotion to the Virgin, and 'mystical aspiration towards union with Christ' (70). In English and Galician love-songs 'the same underlying innocence' (144) is expressed differently. The English songs tell of sorrow or joy, sometimes with 'a conscious echo of popular balladry' (146). Commonplaces of love poetry 'could still be treated in plain English freshly and directly' (147).

420, 521, 593, 864, 1002, 1365, 1649, 2037.5, 2161, 2320, 3031, 3167.3, 3216.5, 3512, 4044, 4088, 4194.

——— Review by T.P. Dunning, *Review of English Studies* NS 20 (1969): 474–7. Although he regrets the absence of Irish and Welsh lyrics, Dunning finds that Dronke, '[w]ithin his staged limits . . . does bring the medieval lyric tradition to vigorous life . . . by a novel and effective *dispositio* of his material.' Dunning's reactions to Dronke's treatment of various lyrics include exasperation with 'over-elaborate' analysis of 'the beautiful and tightly compressed' ME 'Sunset on Calvary'; delight at 'perceptive comments' (476) as on the ME mortality lyrics; and excitement about the 'brilliant conjecture that the lovely English "Maiden in the mor" represents a mime.' He was 'continually engaged' by this 'superb introduction to the Romance and Germanic medieval lyric' (477).

510 Gray, Douglas. 'Two Middle English Quatrains and Robert Holcot.' *Notes and Queries* 213 (1968): 125.

Provides sources for 'At þis ȝate þe laghe is sette' [*442*] and variations. The exemplum is 'told by Robert Holcot in a discussion of hospitality in . . . his commentary on the Book of Wisdom.'

442.

511 Halliburton, David G. 'The Myden Makeles.' *Papers on Language and Literature* 4 (1968): 115–20.

Rejects the proposals of Speirs, **385**, and Manning, **443**, that *makeles* refers primarily to Mary's lack of a sexual mate. Halliburton stresses that her peerlessness, developed throughout the poem, in 'choosing the King of Kings as her son' is the source of her matchlessness: 'the wonder is that this son is the Son of God' (117). Comparisons with 'Nu þis fules singet hand maket hure blisse' [*2366*], considered the source of 'I syng of a myden þ^t is makeles' [*1367*], suggest that it is not 'the oddity of her sexual state which is the basis of the mother's supremacy among women, but . . . her having been chosen for the divine purpose' (117–18). He finds the poem traditional, and cites Raw's comment, **422**, that its imagery is 'uniformly conventional' (118). Mary's marriage should not be dismissed, since declaring Mary '*without a mate* is perilously close to declaring her *without Joseph*' (119). The word *makeles* invites exploration and possibilities for punning, but Halliburton does not endorse Manning's proposal of a macaronic pun with *sine macula*. The lyric dramatizes the paradox of Mary's being maiden and mother, to show her as 'without equal for what she did *and* for what happened to her' (120).

708, 1367, 2366.

512 Hirsh, John C. 'Two English Devotional Poems of the Fifteenth Century.' *Notes and Queries* 213 (1968): 4–10. [Edition.]

The printing of an *Arma Christi* poem, 'of brief devotional stanzas on the instruments of torture and comfort used in the Passion' ['O glorius god redemer of mankynde,' *2442*; 'O vernacule I honoure him and the,' *2577*], and 'The nowmer of Ihū cristes wowndes' [*3443*], 'on the drops of blood Christ shed' (4), completes the transcription of poetic writings in the devotional prayer book MS Douce 1. [See also Gray, **451**.] Hirsch describes the manuscript and the *Arma Christi* genre, in which 'instruments that were used to degrade the Saviour were transformed into objects of veneration by reason of the new ideals of Christianity' (7). Meditation on these was linked to the belief that 'in the passion Christ had showed his love for mankind,' and to belief 'in a loving, not merely a victorious, saviour' (8). Such poems were to deepen rather than induce devotion, and references to arms, wounds, and blood were found in the decoration of churches and pilgrims' clothing. Estimates of the number of drops of blood Christ shed vary; 5,475 is suggested here. Prayers of SS Sebastian and Roche, both associated with protection from plague, follow the ME poems.

2442, 2577, 3443.

513   Hodder, Karen. 'Two Unpublished Middle English Carol-Fragments.' *Archiv* 205 (1968): 378–83. [Edition.]

The fragments are sections of a Christmas carol ['In Bedleem in that fair cete,' *1471*], and of a Passion carol related to 'Maiden & moder cum & se' [*2036*] and 'Mary moder cum & se [*2111*]. They have been added to BL MS Add. 31042, a Thornton manuscript, in 'a slightly different colour from that of the text before and after' (382), and in a hand unlike that of Thornton or John Nettleton. The scribe may not have intended to complete them, or perhaps could not remember more; they may never have been 'more than pious handwriting exercises' (383).

1471, 2036, 2111, 3457.

514   Mitsui, Tōru. 'Notes on the Stanzaic Division and the Metre of "Judas."' *Studies in English Literature* [English Literary Society of Japan, University of Tokyo] 44 (1968): 209–20.

The transcriptions by Child and Skeat have influenced texts of 'Judas' [*1649*]; Mitsui summarizes the history of transcription and division of the stanzas. There is a difficulty in interpretation of the sign '.ii.,' which Sisam, **30**, renders as '*bis*.' Mitsui suggests that it refers to the music rather than the words of the ballad, and means that 'the melody which accompanies the second line of a triplet is repeated as the third line,' which perhaps implies that the text was taken 'from actual singing' (211). Variations in possible pronunciation of the language, especially of *e*, and 'the general opinion' of pronunciation 'with considerable flexibility' (213) lead Mitsui to examine musical analysis of 'Judas' based on the demands of triple and common metre, with several comparisons with other ballads, and to conclude by printing the text in quatrains, noting the stresses and the three occurrences of '.ii.' (218–19).

1649.

515   Reiss, Edmund. 'Reply: Concerning Literary Meaning.' *College English* 30 (1968-9): 76–8.

Refutes Robbins's comments, **517**, on 'Wel and wa sal ys hornes blaw' [*3857.5*], in reply to **478**, by discussing a poem's meaning, relation to historical circumstances, and interpretations made by the author or others, writing contemporaneously or later. [See also Dodds, **154**; Wilson, **321**.]

3857.5.

516   Rigg, A.G. *A Glastonbury Miscellany of the Fifteenth Century: A Descriptive Index of Trinity College, Cambridge, MS O.9.38.* London: Oxford UP, 1968. [Edition.]

The manuscript is a commonplace book, which Rigg has edited as a dissertation. The Descriptive Index has an Introduction, which describes 'the appearance of the manuscript, its history, language, literary interest, etc.' (v), followed by the Index itself, with extracts, a description, and bibliographical information for each poem. In 'Literary Interest of the Manuscript' (24–35), Rigg considers commonplace books in general, and this manuscript in particular. He concludes that its compiler he had 'a high degree of literacy,' and was 'a scribe of moderate competence,' with 'a great liking for satire' (31).

He also discusses humorous items in the manuscript: burlesque, parody, and paradox. As well as English poems and proverbs, there are some prose stories and Latin verses, some of which have English inclusions, such as an 'O and I' refrain. There are appendices of 'Texts (mainly associated with Glastonbury Abbey)' (100–39) and 'Later Additions to the MS' (140–6), including some texts.

199, 240, 561, 562, 1454, 1502, 1703, 1944, 2519, 3170, 3416.5, 3420, 3424, 3715, 4014.5, 4083, 4090, 4102, 4106, 4146, 4189, 4202, 7195, 7444, 7626.

———Review by Bruce Harbert, *Medium Ævum* 89 (1970): 374–5. The idea of the 'descriptive index,' Rigg's own, 'will surely be welcomed enthusiastically,' as 'a symptom of the trend in mediaeval studies towards seeing manuscripts as a whole' (374). Harbert is very pleased by Rigg's inclusions and wishes for more details of some matters. He hopes that 'others who are making studies of complete manuscripts will follow Dr. Rigg's example and publish their material in a similar form' (375).

517 Robbins, Rossell Hope. 'A Highly Critical Approach to the Middle English Lyric.' *College English* 30 (1968–9): 74–5.

A reply to Reiss **478**, on interpretation of 'Wel and wa sal ys hornes blawe' [*3857.5*]. Robbins's reading is historical, and rejects the idea that the poem laments a dead horn blower and addresses the Cross. It refers rather to mourning and horn blowing on Holy Rood Day (14th September), after the death of Lord Robert de Neville, about 1282. [See also Dodds, **154**; Wilson, **321**; Reiss, **515**.]

1844.5, 2830.5, 3857.5.

518 ———. 'A Middle English Prayer to St. Mary Magdalen.' *Traditio* 24 (1968): 458–64. [Edition.]

The fourteenth-century 'Seint marie magdalene lady ffair and brithg' [*2993*], is the ME member of the European corpus of hymns and prayers to St Mary Magdalene. Robbins prints it, with the accompanying Latin collect and rubric for a pardon, but finds that it relates 'only vaguely to the European Latin tradition' (459), as does Osbern Bokenham's *Life* of the saint. Robbins notes other English and Latin references to St Mary Magdalene in English manuscripts, including some in sixteenth-century hands. He lists *IMEV* and *SIMEV* numbers of ME verse prayers to saints, and prints previously unpublished prayers to All Saints ['O ƺe holy Angeles in ƺoure Ordres nyne,' *2593*] and to St Sebastian ['Blessid Sebastian goddis martir and knyght,' *537*].

413, 528, 529, 531, 537, 538, 854.5, 894, 914, 915, 1038.5, 1048.8, 1049, 1050, 1058, 1078.5, 1084, 1085, 1233, 1808.5, 1813, 1814, 2399, 2443, 2445, 2513, 2566, 2593, 2606, 2659.3, 2659.6, 2812, 2892, 2902, 2993, 3027, 3031, 3072, 3115, 3244, 3669, 3671, 4243.

519 ———. 'Mirth in Manuscripts.' *Essays and Studies* 21 (1968): 1–28.

Encourages the study of ME manuscripts for the pleasure of discoveries to be made there. Robbins mentions some discoveries he has most enjoyed, many of them ME lyrics, but he wishes chiefly to motivate the study of ME prose, since 'for all practical purposes, the entire domain of ME verse has been exhaustively surveyed' (15).

152, 561, 597.5, 870.8, 995.3, 1322.5, 1589.5, 2261.6, 2320, 3167.3, 3439.5, 3461.8, 40286.

520 Scattergood, V.J. 'The Political Context, Date and Composition of *The Sayings of the Four Philosophers*.' *Medium Ævum* 37 (1968): 157–65.

Two versions of '*Len puet fere et defere*' [*1857*], this 'deeply felt political complaint against royal excesses by a supporter of the barons' (157), are preserved in

MSS Advocates 19.2.1 (*A*) and St John's College, Cambridge 112 (*J*). Scattergood compares the two, and finds that *J* refers to events in the reign of Edward I, and that *A* is a condensed revision, which refers to the reign of Edward II; each poem considers the theme of degeneracy. He relates political allusions to contemporary matters, in particular to Edward II's breaking of Ordinances (a parallel to Edward I's breaking of the Provisions of Oxford), his dependence on Piers Gaveston, and the hatred of aliens in England.

1857.

521 Wolpers, Theodor. 'Zum Andachtsbild in der Mittelenglischen Religiösen Lyrik.' *Chaucer und seine Zeit: Symposion für Walter F. Schirmer.* Ed. Arno Esch. Buchreihe der Anglia Zeitschrift für Englische Philologie 14. Ed. Helmut Gneuss, et al. Tübingen: Niemeyer, 1968. 293–336.

Surveys changes in imagery in the religious lyric, and the influences of courtly poetry and liturgical hymns. Liturgical works emphasize the distance between God and man, and the reader is an observer. In the lyrics there is a tendency towards pious contemplation of human characteristics of Christ and Mary, to inspire loving emotions. The lyrics can be seen as devotional objects; their tone becomes more moralizing in the fourteenth and fifteenth centuries, and they are never as complex and introspective as metaphysical works. Wolpers offers many examples of changes in imagery, such as 'star of the sea' and courtly floral images in hymns to the Virgin; he describes lyrical and iconic imagery in 'I syng of a myden $þ^t$ is makeles' [*1367*]. Lyrics of Christ the lover-knight combine the language of courtly love with biblical imagery. Manipulation of the reader's emotion and involvement, to invite meditation on particular images, assists the movement from narrative to icon. Changes in the presentation of images, in narrative and metaphorical details, link the author and the reader, and so encourage meditation. Significant motifs include the crucified figure, Mary's lament, the Pietà, Nativity, the Five Wounds, and Christ's heart. Connections with aspects of salvation and images from visual arts involve the reader directly, to place emphasis on immediacy and the moment. Wolpers details changes in imagery from the Latin originals of Passion poems, such as images of flowing blood to the motif of the Five Wounds, with examples from John Grimestone's book of sermons. He provides close analysis of 'When y se blosmes springe' [*3963*] and 'I syke when y singe' [*1365*], and compares the effects of variations. Other poems of the Passion illustrate particular details and the transformation from narrative to icon; they include emblem poems and laments of Mary. The process is related to the presentation of events as particular moments, and this must be considered as well as literary rhetoric.

110, 143, 207, 239, 404, 461, 495, 497, 550, 631, 648, 1001, 1030, 1274, 1318, 1365, 1367, 1460, 1787, 1930, 1940, 1943, 1977, 2042, 2051, 2107, 2150, 2320, 2347, 2471, 2504, 2607, 2619, 2645, 2687, 2988, 2995, 3109, 3543, 3825, 3826, 3827, 3904, 3963, 3965, 3968, 4088, 4141, 4263.

522 Woolf, Rosemary. *The English Religious Lyric in the Middle Ages.* Oxford: Clarendon, 1968.

A comprehensive critical survey, arranged historically, with sections devoted to lyrics of the thirteenth and fourteenth centuries (19–179), and of the fifteenth century (183–371), followed by appendices. The 'Introduction' (1–15) characterizes the works as 'short, religious, meditative poems,' that have 'by recent convention been described as lyrics, although the term "lyric" was not known to their authors' (1). It shows their relation to secular forms and Latin devotional works. The poems were generally not sung, and most were anonymous, unlike the metaphysical meditative poetry of the seventeenth century.

Examination of thirteenth- and fourteenth-century lyrics begins with those 'On the Passion' (19–66), where lack of a native lyric tradition at first produced works close to the Latin sources, with 'mnemonic brevity and a bare listing of detail' (28). Woolf describes lyrics for meditation and sermons, linking some with Latin and French works. The theme of Christ, the lover-knight, is related to that of the bridegroom. The 'Lyrics on Death' (67–113) fix the meditator's mind on processes of death and burial, rather than the moment of death. Their gruesome and revolting images are intended to provoke fear, as lyrics of the Passion are meant to provoke love. Lyrics of death are closely related to the sermon; they stress the transience of life, but their theme is *ubi sunt* rather than *carpe diem*. Some list the Signs of Death, which may be related to advice to the living, as in verses in the *Fasciculus Morum*. Such admonitions are in many collections, including John Grimestone's preaching book. Some are spoken by the corpse to passers-by; the most powerful are the Body and Soul debates; a related theme is the complaint of old age. 'Lyrics on the Virgin and her Joys' (114–58) are those 'that praise the Virgin and implore her mercy . . . semiliturgical celebrations of the Virgin's five joys,' and those, 'mainly lullabies – in which the Virgin is associated with the Christ-Child' (114). Most are in the second group, and many are in carol form. Marian piety was already established in England, and encouraged in the twelfth century by observance of the feast of the Immaculate Conception and devotion to Mary as the second Eve. Attention is paid to the paradoxes of Mary as mother and daughter of God, but most praise is offered 'in human terms, for her beauty, her nobility, and her mercy' (134), and by enumerating the Five Joys. The tender Nativity lyrics contrast with stylized illustrations of the scene. Most of these stress the hardship and poverty of the Nativity; some lullaby carols anticipate the Crucifixion, resembling lyrics of the Passion. In 'The Lyrics of Richard Rolle and the Mystical School' (159–79) Woolf surveys mystical poetry of the period, relating it to works of St Bernard and St Augustine, and showing the effects of Rolle's distinctive style. The themes of love and the Holy Name recur in these poems, which combine 'homeliness with rapture,' to be 'especially moving and aesthetically satisfying' (179).

Woolf considers the development of these and related genres in the fifteenth century. 'Lyrics on the Passion' (183–238) traces the increasingly didactic and affective nature of the works, now often accompanied by a visual image. The *imago pietatis* is characteristic; the theme of Christ's offering his heart may resemble the exchange of hearts in secular love lyrics. Imagery recalls the Song of Songs and the idea of Christ the bridegroom. Woolf relates some lyrics to passages in *Ancrene Wisse* and to *The Revelations of Divine Love* by Julian of Norwich. There are many complaints of Christ on the Cross, where the speaker appears to be an *imago pietatis*; Woolf cites examples by Lydgate and William Herebert, among others. The association with the Christ-knight continues; recurrent themes include the arms of the Passion and the Charter of Christ. Christ is seen as a friend, both courteous and reproachful. Poems of the seven sheddings of blood sometimes relate them to the seven deadly sins. Some first-person meditations consider the five wounds, a few in the style of the school of Rolle. Dunbar describes the Passion in 'vigorous and precise detail' (233). Many 'Lyrics on the Compassion of the Blessed Virgin' (239–73) are third-person narratives rather than first-person addresses; Woolf relates some of the latter to their Latin sources. The themes include the Virgin's dialogues with Christ and St John, and her reproaches of the Jews, death, and the Cross. The Pietà corresponds to the *imago pietatis*, and informs some works, including complaints of the Virgin and first-person meditations. Some meditations are dream visions. 'Lyrics on the Virgin and her Joys' (274–308) probably form 'the largest and also the most ornate and rhetorical section of the religious lyric in the fifteenth century' (274). Some have the style of secular love poetry; others are in liturgical form. Woolf cites numerous examples, showing particular uses of imagery. The joy most celebrated was the Nativity, with many carols for the occasion, including James Ryman's. There are still many 'Lyrics on Death' (309–55), frequently warnings from the dead, the old, the dying, and the proud, with 'a preference for the warning from the female dead' (318). Death is often personified, and the continental themes of the Three Living and the Three Dead and of the Dance of Death appear. The presence of plague may have made it unnecessary to emphasize the horrors of death and burial, so that fifteenth-century poetry is less gruesome than earlier works and '[i]n many ways . . . reticent and discreetly evasive' (311). Such commonplaces as false executors, worms, and decay are still mentioned, with *timor mortis* a recurring theme.

The 'Conclusion' (356–71) summarizes historical trends, and examines copying and circulation. Four factors seem responsible for the lyric's decline: 'the Reformation and the Renaissance . . . the printed book and . . . the use of prose for meditations' (358). Woolf shows that the ME lyric was superseded 'by something alike but different' (371), in metaphysical poetry.

Appendices examine 'The Manuscripts' (373–6); 'Authorship' (377–9); 'The Canon of Richard Rolle's Poetry' (380–2); 'The Carol' (383–8); 'History of the *Imago pietatis*' (389–91); 'History of the Pietà' (392–4); 'Complaints against Swearers' (395–400); 'The History of the Warning from the Dead' (401–4); 'The Prose Dialogue between Body and Soul in Guillaume de Guilleville's *Pèlerinage de l'âme*' (405–6); and 'Some Sixteenth-Century Parodies' (407–11).

14, 16, 18, 22, 52, 66, 99, 103, 112, 117, 143, 158.4, 172, 207, 229, 276.5, 293, 296.6, 340, 351, 352, 353, 358, 359, 375, 377.5, 378, 404, 441, 445, 447, 456, 461, 489, 495, 497, 498, 504, 517.5, 533, 550, 611, 623, 636, 641, 644, 648, 688.3, 693, 702, 703, 708, 718, 769, 776, 789, 797, 846, 880, 888, 894, 895, 912, 927, 931, 994, 1001, 1011, 1026, 1030, 1037, 1040, 1061, 1066, 1074, 1115, 1119, 1122, 1125, 1127, 1140, 1152, 1210.5, 1216, 1254, 1268, 1270, 1274, 1298, 1301, 1309, 1318, 1321, 1365, 1367, 1370.5, 1383, 1402, 1407, 1422, 1455, 1460, 1461, 1463, 1472, 1498, 1563, 1565, 1650, 1692, 1697, 1699, 1700, 1707, 1708, 1714, 1715, 1718, 1727, 1735, 1747, 1749, 1761, 1775, 1779, 1780, 1818, 1833, 1839, 1841, 1847, 1899, 1930, 1931, 1943, 1977, 2007, 2011, 2012, 2017.5, 2023, 2024, 2025, 2036, 2037, 2038, 2042, 2051, 2057, 2070, 2074, 2080, 2081, 2086, 2088, 2107, 2114, 2118, 2136, 2150, 2168, 2171, 2192, 2220, 2240, 2241, 2250, 2255, 2270, 2273, 2300, 2307, 2320, 2336, 2347, 2359, 2366, 2369, 2398, 2405, 2408, 2409, 2411, 2426, 2464, 2468, 2486, 2504, 2507, 2523, 2528, 2530, 2533, 2544, 2551, 2570, 2577, 2579, 2589, 2591, 2596, 2607, 2613, 2619, 2644, 2645, 2677, 2687, 2688, 2714, 2718, 2791, 2803, 2831, 2865, 2992, 2995, 3065, 3071, 3074, 3112, 3121, 3131, 3143, 3161, 3211, 3220, 3221, 3225, 3228, 3230, 3233, 3234, 3236, 3238, 3239, 3242, 3244, 3245, 3251, 3252, 3310, 3318.4, 3330, 3332, 3356, 3365, 3374, 3391, 3419, 3432, 3433, 3438, 3460, 3475, 3499, 3517, 3525, 3536, 3543, 3560.5, 3567, 3574, 3575, 3597, 3603, 3607, 3612, 3627, 3635, 3654, 3671, 3673, 3674, 3678, 3681, 3691, 3692, 3695, 3700, 3701, 3730, 3743, 3750, 3779, 3805, 3821, 3825, 3826, 3828, 3835, 3845, 3846, 3862, 3901, 3902, 3904, 3906, 3907, 3921, 3924, 3939, 3963, 3965, 3969, 3996, 3998, 4023, 4031, 4035, 4044, 4076, 4087, 4088, 4089, 4159, 4160, 4184, 4185, 4189, 4200, 4221, 7025, 7082, 7107, 7317, 7338, 7341, 7436, 7440, 7540, 7588, 7594, 7624.

———— Review by Stephen Manning, *JEGP* 70 (1971): 145–6. 'A thorough, scholarly account of the development of the religious lyric in medieval England' which places the lyrics 'within a larger framework of religious thought' (145). Manning describes Woolf's methods and summarizes her exposition of the differences between medieval lyrics and those of the seventeenth century. He explains the course of the book, and concludes that the study is 'solid, exhaustive, and alert to both historical and literary values' (146).

———— Review by John Stevens, *Medium Ævum* 40 (1971): 72–4. Deems this 'a long and learned book which is sure to become a standard work' (72). Stevens discerns some 'slight distortions' that arise from the reconciliation of Woolf's aim to be comprehensive and her thesis of 'religious lyric as meditative poem' (73), and the implications of that notion. The book has 'great scope and depth' and elucidates characteristics of the lyrics in an 'enormously detailed' work, in which a 'generous wealth of material [is] assembled and discussed.'

523   Baker, D.C. '"Therfor to Wepe, Cum Lerne off Me": A *Planctus* Fragment in MS. Corpus Christi College Oxford F. 261.' *Medium Ævum* 38 (1969): 291–4. [Edition.]

The fragment 'Now late me thought I wolde begynn' [*2347*], previously unpublished, is 'a rather interesting and very individual variant of what was probably a large class of late fifteenth-century *planctus*' (291). Baker edits the poem, comparing versions in MSS Harley 2274, Bodley 2322, and Trinity Dublin D.2.7, vol. i, and comments on previous editions of these works.

2347.

524   Braekman, Willy L., and Peter S. Macaulay. 'The Story of the Cat and the Candle in Middle English Literature.' *Neuphilologische Mitteilungen* 70 (1969): 690–702. [Edition.]

The debate between 'Nurtur' and 'Kynd' tells the story of the Cat and the Candle. Braekman and Macaulay describe the poem, 'Goddis grace is redy bothe erly & late' [*995.4*], and the ingenious trick 'Kynd' uses to show the superiority of 'instinct over education' (691). They print the work with linguistic comments, for example on the Northern form *semand*, and place it in 'the early fifteenth century' when 'standardization of English was nearing completion' (694). It is sophisticated, and 'the display of wit and character, and the narrative art raise it well above the usual level of late medieval English didactic verse' (695). The story is in literature of 'medieval Europe, in India, Central Asia, Northern Africa and in modern Europe'; European versions usually concern 'the famous dispute between King Solomon and the witty peasant Marcolphus' (696). The authors survey the forms, and quote Latin and ME prose versions, and a stanza of a fourteeth-century French fable, noting characteristic details. The debate is apparently 'the only representative in Middle English . . . outside the context of the dialogue of Solomon and Marcolphus' (701–2). [See Scattergood, **557**.]

995.4.

525   Bühler, Curt F. 'At Thy Golg First Eut of the House Vlysse The Saynge Thus.' *Studies in the Renaissance* 6 (1969): 223–35. Repr. in *Early Books and Manuscripts: Forty Years of Research by Curt F. Bühler*. New York: The Grolier Club and the Pierpont Morgan Library, 1973. 518–32 [cited].

Examines 'peculiar English' in 'books of hours for the use of Sarum printed on the continent for sale in England' (518). Bühler finds the prayer 'God be in my hedde & in my understonding' [*940*], and suggests its 'oldest surviving appearance . . . is that on the title page of the Rouen *Horae ad usum Sarum*' (520). Instructive works transformed from French include a stanza of the ten commandments, rendered in two ME forms ['One only god thou shalt loue and worship perfytely,' *2695.5*; 'Thou shalt worshyp one god onely,' *3689.5*]. Mnemonic verses, 'Cir-cum-staunt-ly thre Kings came by nyght,' [*633.5*], are used 'to recall the saints venerated in the several months' (525), by allocating a syllable to each day of the month. This verse emphasizes saints revered in England, but imperfect correspondence has caused some discrepancies. In other verses 'just as frequently attached to the calendar . . . the course of human life was compared to the months of the year, six years of a man's life being allotted to each month' (528–9). This poem, 'The first vj yeres of mannes byrth and aege' [*3347.5*], suggests a life span of 72 years.

633.5, 940, 2695.5, 3347.5, 3689.5.

526   Cottle, Basil. *The Triumph of English 1350–1400*. Blandford History Series. Gen. ed. R.W. Harris. London: Blandford, 1969.

This historical survey allows literature to illuminate the topics: 'The English Language' (15–50); 'Wars' (51–88); 'Domestic Affairs' (89–147); 'Religious Orthodoxy' (148–220); 'Religious Heterodoxy' (221–57); 'Chaucer's Religious Views' (258–76); and 'On Being Alive in the Late Fourteenth Century' (277–302). Against the background of historical and political comment from the *Brut*, *Confessio Amantis*, *Piers Plowman*, and poems of Chaucer, Cottle discusses Laurence Minot's accounts of victories, ballads of wars against the Scots, poems of kings, plagues, and domestic policies. Most religious lyrics (169–93) are anonymous, but often 'so grouped in metre and manner as to suggest common authorship or a "school" of writers' (169), such as that of Richard Rolle. They include works of *memento mori* and Christian virtues, and moving poems 'in which the love of Christ for man is central' (172). Some have Latin analogues, and may be 'exercises, copies, formulae,' prompting disappointment that 'many religious lyrics are not original' (175). Cottle provides examples of treatment of topics including the question '*Is it nothing to you, all ye that pass by?*' (178), meditations on the Cross, the Nativity, love-poems to Mary, and the Passion; he explores 'This World Fares as a Fantasy' ['I wolde witen of sum wys wiht,' *1402*] in detail (188–93). The friars are often mentioned, and more often blamed than praised. Aspects of secular love are recorded with a range of poetic devices. In the poem on Blacksmiths ['Swarte smekyd smethes smateryd wythe smoke,' *3227*], 'the resources of a pounding alliteration are exploited to the full' (300).

5, 100, 110, 194, 196, 295, 352, 353, 374, 441, 563, 583, 606, 663, 960.1, 1064, 1274, 1353, 1401, 1402, 1443, 1448, 1459, 1543, 1596, 1620, 1699, 1761, 1791, 1796, 1818, 1832, 1847, 1930, 2007, 2012, 2024, 2036, 2037.5, 2162, 2167, 2254, 2262, 2302, 2607, 2662, 2663, 2777, 3212, 3227, 3260, 3306, 3371, 3529, 3566, 3691, 3697, 3787, 3898, 3899, 3925, 3996, 4018, 4019, 4157, 4158, 4159, 4163, 4181, 4185, 4239, 4256.8, 4268.

527 Downing, Janay. 'An Unpublished Weather Prognostic in Cambridge University MS Ff. 5.48.' *English Language Notes* 7 (1969–70): 87–9.

Alludes briefly to a verse of weather prophecy, 'When thonder comeþ in Januere' [*4053*], based on the occurrence of thunder in particular months.

4053.

528 Edwards, A.S.G. 'A Fifteenth Century Didactic Poem in British Museum Add. MS. 29729.' *Neuphilologische Mitteilungen* 70 (1969): 702–6. [Edition.]

Prints 'O mortall man masyd w^t pompe and pride' [*2523*], a poem of *contemptus mundi*. This warns that man is meat for worms, and links 'exhortations to repentance with admonitions on the sinfulness and transience of earthly appetites' (703). It is associated with Lydgate, although not ascribed to him, because the manuscript, 'copied by John Stow from a lost codex by John Shirley,' is 'mainly an anthology of poems by Lydgate' (702). Edwards expands contractions, and supplies editorial capitalization and normalization of *j* and *w*.

2523.

529 ———. 'Stanzas on Troy.' *English Language Notes* 7 (1969–70): 246–8. [Edition.]

Prints verses on the legend of Troy, 'Whan that in old tyme by awnsyent antyquety' [*4021*], found 'on the flyleaf of MS McLean 182 in the Fitzwilliam Museum, Cambridge,' in which most other texts are works of Lydgate and Hoccleve. Edwards disagrees with the comment in *IMEV* that the stanzas are in Hoccleve's style. Capitalization and punctuation are editorial, contractions have been expanded, and some letters added, owing to the 'difficulty of the cursive hand' (247).

4021.

530 Hanna, Ralph. 'A Note on a Harley Lyric.' *English Language Notes* 7 (1969–70): 243–6.

Another interpretation of lines 34–7 of 'Middelerd for mon wes mad' [*2166*], which differs from those of Brook, **42**, Menner, **229**, Meroney, **239**, and Malone, **367**. Hanna's reading points to 'scribal mishandling' in an exemplar, and a later scribe's decision for 'the easiest orthographic expedient' (245). His reconstruction suggests the poet's contrasting of lecherous and frigid women, and the conclusion that chastity, although it represents 'frustration and crisis in our world of unrestrained desire . . . is also the first step toward . . . the salvation of one's immortal soul' (246).

2166.

531 Hargreaves, Henry. 'Additional Information for the Brown-Robbins "Index."' *Notes and Queries* 214 (1969): 446–7.

Adds to information in *IMEV* about manuscript sources and similarities for the poems listed at *1605* ['Ipocras this boke made ȝare'], *3422* ['þe man þᵗ wylle of lechecraft lere'], and *4182* ['Wite thou wel that this bok ys leche'].

1605, 3422, 4182.

532 Jemielity, Thomas. '"I Sing of a Maiden": God's Courting of Mary.' *Concerning Poetry* (West Washington State College) 2 (1969): 53–9.

'I syng of a myden þᵗ is makeles' [*1367*], is an 'apparently artless and conventional work . . . replete with liturgical symbols and allusions and very candid about the physical intimacies of Christ's conception in Mary' (53). The work depicts 'the courtly ideals' of Christ, the lover knight, and Mary; they are shown 'as knight and maiden' (54). The emphasis on *chees* stresses Mary's willingness. Reiteration of *He cam* and *stille* implies 'God's repect for the virginity of Mary' (55), her silence and composure. Jemielity contrasts Yeats's accounts of the Annunciation in 'The Mother of God' and the violence of Leda's experience in 'Leda and the Swan.' His detailed reading of the lyric considers the motifs of dew, spray, and flower, and their liturgical use in Advent. The poem conveys 'wonder and a sense of the ineffable . . . delicacy and soft amusement,' and the hesitation in God's approach to 'the physically intimate moment of intercourse and conception' (58).

1367.

533 Keller, Joseph R. 'The Triumph of Vice: A Formal Approach to the Medieval Complaint Against the Times.' *Annuale Medievale* 10 (1969): 120–37.

Most verses deploring evils of the times were general in nature, without specific allegations, even in metaphors. This protected the poet, but 'the artistic cause . . . is rather to be sought in that mode of thought which, especially in the late Middle Ages, detects universals in the particular' (122–3). Keller writes of a kind of complaint where the motif of triumphant vice is 'the controlling image or formal principle' (124), with Latin, Provençal, and English examples. Themes include the coming of the Last Days and the triumph of sin, in specific places and in a world upside down. In such a world, vices and virtues may be confused or interchanged. The English poems are more 'metaphorically exuberant' (135), and some incorporate proverbs and macaronic lines. [See Kinney, **485**; Elliot, **592**.]

583, 592, 696, 1871, 2008, 2145, 2787.

534 Moe, Phyllis. 'A New Text of *Cur Mundus Militat*.' *English Language Notes* 7 (1969–70): 6–9. [Edition.]

The text of 'Whi is þis world biloued þat fals is & veyn' [*4160*] appears in Cleveland, Public Library, MS W q091.92-C468, and is the twelfth of this popular lyric to be found. Moe lists the manuscript's contents and describes the text of the lyric, which was perhaps not written by a professional scribe; she shows how it differs from other sources. She prints the Cleveland version, and notes variant readings.

4160.

535   Muraoka, Yu. 'The Maiden Makeles.' *Eigo Seinen* 115 (1969): 346–8.

Not seen. In Japanese.

1367.

536   Owen, Lewis J. '*The Thrush and the Nightingale*: The Speaker in Lines 94–96.' *English Language Notes* 7 (1969–70): 1–6.

Argues against the assignment of lines 94–6 of 'The Thrush and the Nightingale' ['Somer is comen wiþ loue to toune,' *3222*] to the Nightingale. The scribes of the manuscript sources (Oxford, Bodleian Library, Digby 86 and Edinburgh, National Library, Auchinleck MS) indicate the speakers by large capitals or explicit assignments. In general, the speeches have a regular length. This is presented by Brown, *BrownXIII*, **36**, and by Dickins and Wilson, **47**, as two stanzas of six lines, but these editors specify the Nightingale, so interrupting the pattern. Owen suggests that the Thrush promises to 'expose the irresponsible sentimentalism of the Nightingale' and defies her 'earlier threat of banishment' (5). He finds the next stanza more persuasively assigned to the Nightingale if it responds to the Thrush's challenge to her right to be in the orchard. The change he proposes would cause 'a return in the poem to the unbroken formality of regularly alternating two-stanza speeches' (6).

3222.

537   Robbins, Rossell Hope. 'A Refrain-Poem from N.L.W. Peniarth MS. 395.' *Trivium* 4 (1969): 43–9. [Edition.]

A general account with many specific examples of the refrain poem in ME. In footnote 1 Robbins distinguishes between 'burden,' 'refrain,' and 'refraid,' and proposes that 'refrain' should now denote 'the final line of a stanza that is repeated throughout a poem, with or without minor verbal alterations' (48). He prints a poem from MS Peniarth N.L.W. 395, 'Who-so kon suffre and hald hym still' [*4121*], with comment on resemblances to other poems, referring in detail to poems in 'the Vernon and Simeon sister manuscripts' ['In a Chirch þer I con knel,' *1448*; 'þe man þ^t luste to liuen in ese,' *3420*; 'Whon alle soþes ben souht and seene,' *3925*]. In footnotes, Robbins briefly cites examples of refrain poems, to show general and particular characteristics. His examples include works of Chaucer, Charles d'Orléans, Ryman, Henryson, Kennedy, Dunbar, Skelton, Wyatt, and Lydgate.

4, 121.5, 349, 374, 404, 429, 479, 541.5, 547, 560, 561, 562, 563, 583, 679.8, 688.5, 697, 758, 806.5, 809, 932.5, 1041, 1310, 1379, 1448, 1460, 1463, 1511, 1769, 1842, 1854, 1921, 1922, 2031, 2040, 2088, 2159, 2192, 2277, 2281.5, 2458, 2464, 2522, 2790, 2800, 3072, 3155, 3190, 3225, 3348, 3371, 3420, 3451, 3531, 3533, 3542, 3612, 3656, 3661, 3787, 3798, 3925, 4121, 4157, 4268.

538   ———. 'John Crophill's Ale-Pots.' *Review of English Studies* NS 20 (1969): 182–9. [Edition.]

John Crophill's poem of the cups given him by Friar Thomas Stanfeld ['ffrere tams stanfeld,' *870.8*] is found in his notebook, with medical texts, notes, accounts, and jottings. It differs from others of the ale-wife genre in naming people Crophill knew. Thus it describes 'an actual occurrence, involving an actual occasion, place, and characters,' to add 'a vividness to the poem out of proportion to its literary merits' (189). [See Scattergood, **556**.]

870.8, 981.5, 1362.

539 Weber, Sarah Appleton. *Theology and Poetry in the Middle English Lyric: A Study of Sacred History and Aesthetic Form.* Columbus, OH: Ohio State UP, 1969.

Deals with the relationship of religious lyrics to the liturgy and to events of sacred history, through close readings and theological interpretations of some lyrics, with briefer references to others. The introduction explains the relation of sacred history and the liturgy, to develop the analogy between 'the medieval theologian's understanding of the events of creation and the universe as the language of God – theology its grammar – and the modern linguist's approach to semantics through structure – through phonemic, morphemic and syntactic analysis' (3). The lyrics to which Weber pays closest attention are: on the Annunciation and the Birth of Christ, 'Als i lay vp-on a nith' [*352*] 'Gabriel fram evene king' [*888*], 'I syng of a myden þ^t is makeles' [*1367*], and 'Nu þis fules singet hand maket hure blisse' [*2366*]; on the Crucifixion, 'Iesu cristes milde moder' [*1697*], 'Stond wel moder ounder rode' [*3211*], 'Suete sone reu on me & brest out of þi bondis' [*3245*], 'The milde Lomb i-sprad o rode' [*3432*], and 'Wy haue ȝe no reuthe on my child' [*4159*]; on the Joys of Mary, 'Glade us maiden moder milde' [*912*] and 'Leuedy for þare blisse' [*1833*].

14, 352, 353, 888, 912, 1030, 1367, 1460, 1472, 1697, 1833, 1847, 2023, 2024, 2036, 2366, 3211, 3245, 3432, 4159.

——— Review by R.T. Davies, *Review of English Studies* NS 22 (1971): 324–6. Compares and contrasts Weber's methods with those of Woolf, **522**. Although he has some reservations on cases of special pleading, Davies considers the work a 'stimulating and challenging book [that] appeals to both the intellect and the literary sensibility' (326).

540 Woolf, Rosemary. 'The Construction of *In a Fryht as Y Con Fare Fremede.*' *Medium Ævum* 38 (1969): 55–9 [cited]. Repr. in *Art and Doctrine: Essays on Medieval Literature. Rosemary Woolf.* Ed. Heather O'Donoghue. London: Hambledon, 1986. 125–30.

The Harley lyric 'In a fryht as y con fere fremede' [*1449*] is 'the earliest extant and also the best of the English pastourelles.' Woolf supplies a close reading, to counter the charges of clumsiness and obscurity made by Moore, **297**. An emendation and elucidation of a reference reveal its 'coherent and subtle construction' (55). Woolf relates this to Latin, French, and Provençal pastourelles, to reveal comparisons with the maiden's complaint that she does not wish to relinquish her virginity and be an outcast. The lover's reply recalls the genre of '*chanson de mal mariées*, in which a married woman complains of her life with an aged and jealous husband and longs for her young lover' (57). Emendation in line 40 would make this reply clear. The maiden's capitulation is related to the *chanson des transformations*, a forerunner to the pastourelle.

1265, 1449, 1589.

541 Besserman, Lawrence L., Gail Gilman, and Victor Weinblatt. 'Three Unpublished Middle English Poems from the Commonplace-Book of John Colyns (B. M. MS Harley 2252).' *Neuphilologische Mitteilungen* 71 (1970): 212–38. [Edition.]

Provides a description and catalogue of the manuscript, and prints the three poems: 'O Mortall man call to Remembraunce' [*2522*], a 'metrical meditation upon Psalm 130'

(221); 'When the prime fallythe vppon Sonday' [*4040*]; and 'Ye mene that wysdome will lerne' [*4253*]. The latter two are prognostics, *4040* for weather, according to the day of the Prime, *4253* for events of the following year, according to the day of New Year's Day. The authors comment generally on the linguistic and metrical nature of the poems, and provide footnotes on particular words and phrases.

2522, 4040, 4253.

542   Blake, N.F. 'Wynkyn de Worde and the *Quatrefoil of Love.*' *Archiv* 206 (1970): 189–200.

Describes Wynkyn de Word's edition of 'The Quatrefoil of Love' ['In a mornynge of May when medose schulde sprynge,' *1453*], and its relation to versions in BL MS Add. 31042 and Bodleian Library A.106; it is generally closer to the latter. It is 'a unique early printing of a Northern alliterative poem,' prepared by a reviser, 'a Southerner who carried out his alterations in the late fifteenth or early sixteenth century' (190), but apparently did not understand the stanzaic construction. The reviser adjusted the bob and wheel structures to make four-line stanzas, and altered alliteration and vocabulary. Blake offers detailed accounts of the changes: 'Words misunderstood by the reviser' (196–7); 'Northern words changed for a Southern one of the same meaning' (197); 'Modernization' (198); 'Changes which retain the meaning but are not modernizations' (198); and 'Changes of meaning which are not modernizations' (198). They reveal the reviser's ideas and prejudices, 'a desire to eradicate the Northern dialect forms, to modernize the language, and to make the poem suitable reading matter for a sixteenth-century Londoner (or Southerner)' (199). Later in the century archaisms would have been preserved.

1453.

543   Bradford, Melvin E. 'Come Slowly All Together: A Reading of the "Corpus Christi Carol."' *South Central Bulletin* 30 (1970): 168–71.

An explication of the 'Corpus Christi Carol' [*1132*], with references to previous scholarship. The burden implies a lullaby, 'for pacification of the young, the puzzled, and the distressed.' It 'antedates the text proper and comes from another, a more "secular" poem' (169), which was already an established means of consolation. The problem is bereavement, as intimated in the lament of the first line and the implication that lovers, represented by birds, are separated by the falcon of death. Through the use of Celtic and Christian imagery, the poet has made Christian teaching 'new, "naturalized" according to the habit of the medieval English' (170). Bradford explains eucharistic references and proposes that the orchard corresponds to the Psalmist's Valley of the Shadow. The standing stone, inscribed 'Corpus Christi,' is related to the seal of the tomb and the Grail. He traces the poem's movement 'from sorrow and its cause to ancient, natural responses to such sorrow,' instancing the images of Adonis and the Fisher King, and the 'muted rounding' (170) of the last repetition of the burden.

1132.

544   Gray, Douglas. 'Later Poetry: The Courtly Tradition.' *The Middle Ages.* Ed. W.F. Bolton. History of Literature in the English Language 1. London: Barrie, 1970. Rev. edn. Sphere History of Literature 1. London: Sphere, 1970 [cited]. 10 vols. 1970–5. Rev. 1986–8. 312–70.

Much courtly poetry is the work of known poets, such as Charles d'Orléans, William de la Pole, Duke of Suffolk, Chaucer, Lydgate, Skelton, and Gower. Many noble patrons encouraged poets and collected literary works. The most numerous of these are courtly lyrics of love, including those that praise the poet's lady with variations on the conventions. Some political poems deal with contemporary events, and others are satirical. Lyrics of love and drinking 'often reach a high level of technical achievement' (345); some are 'very close to the world of the fabliaux' (346). Parody, burlesque and nonsense verse are to be found.

3, 549, 925, 929, 941, 1028, 1222, 1256, 1549, 1622, 1849, 2243, 2311, 2338, 2437, 2609, 2813, 3361, 3613, 3759, 3832, 3912, 3999.

545   Hieatt, A. Kent, and Constance Hieatt. '"The Bird with Four Feathers": Numerical Analysis of a Fourteenth-Century Poem.' *Papers on Language and Literature* 6 (1970): 18–38. [Edition.]

Close examination of 'The Bird with Four Feathers' ['By a forest syde walkyng as I went' *561*] reveals complex numerical patterning and symbolism. The authors offer a close analysis of the poem, and compare paintings and other lyrics. They find a symmetrical structure in the work, and note patterns in the subject matter and arrangement of stanzas. They propose a relationship between simultaneous and successive aspects in poetry and painting, and the possibility of representing these aspects in the patterns of the poem. Their findings imply that *561* provides 'historical evidence for supposing that late medieval poets went further in the development of this purely logical possibility [of simultaneity] than had formerly been supposed' (38).

561, 779, 1029, 1030, 1395, 1708, 1748, 2286, 2291, 2390, 2730, 2992, 3347, 3462.

546   Hirsh, John C. 'A Fifteenth-Century Commentary on "Ihesu for Thy Holy Name."' *Notes and Queries* 215 (1970): 44–5.

The prose commentary that follows the devotional poem 'Ihū for thy holy name' [*1703*] explains that the 33 words in it represent the years of Christ's life; that the remembrance of the 5,475 wounds of Christ can gain an indulgence of the same number of years; and that there is a correspondence between lines of the poem and beads of the rosary: 'white for the Holy Name and for heaven; red for the blood of the passion, black for sin and damnation' (45). The poem is found in MS Douce 54.

1703.

547   Monda, Joseph B. '"The Sayings of Saint Bernard" from MS Bodleian Additional E 6.' *Mediaeval Studies* 32 (1970): 299–307. [Edition.]

The poem 'þe blessinge of heuene king' [*3310*] is best known 'for its frequently anthologized "ubi sunt" stanzas' (299), which begin 'Uuere beþ they biforen vs weren.' Monda cites this manuscript's version, previously unpublished, and finds that it seems 'closer to the prototype' than others, because it has not 'apparently been contaminated by a false stanza' (301). He comments on the South-East Midland dialect and variations from other manuscripts, and prints the text, with notes. He expands abbreviations and offers conjectural readings in place of illegible text, with capitalization as in the manuscript, but without punctuation.

3310.

548   Mustanoja, Tauno. 'The Suggestive Use of Christian Names in Middle English Poetry.' *Medieval Literature and Folklore Studies: Essays in Honor of Francis Lee Utley.* Ed. Jerome Mandel and Bruce A. Rosenberg. New Brunswick, NJ: Rutgers UP, 1970. 51–76.

Explores associations of names used in various kinds of poetry and their effects. Among those considered, a form of *Robert*, most often *Robin*, and some 'pet form of Marie' (52) are often used in pastourelles. *Malkin* brings many connotations to its use in other works. *Jankin* implies 'light-hearted and light-headed young people' (61), as do *Alis* and *Alison*; the latter is sometimes used in a pun with *eleyson*. *John* can symbolize 'any man' (56); *Sir John* is a priest; additions to *John* and *Jack* hint at occupation or nature. *Richard* means 'a *rich, hard* man.' *Robert* is 'commonly associated with robbers' (62). Although *Johane* suggests virtue, 'the diminutive form *Janet* tended to be associated with loose sexual attitudes' (72). *Katherine* and its variations have varied associations. Of all religious and biblical names, the symbolic names of *Mary* have most significance.

179, 377, 871, 1091, 1302, 1459, 1468, 1484, 1555, 2107, 2287, 2338, 2494, 2615, 2662, 2831, 3155, 3409, 4019, 7286.

549 Oliver, Raymond. *Poems Without Names: The English Lyric, 1200–1500.* Berkeley: U of California P, 1970.

A general study of ME lyrics, with texts of 86 poems. Oliver deals with 'Theory and Method' (3–10), introducing his contention that the works are 'Public, Practical, Anonymous' (11–40). He finds the poems' intentions are celebration, persuasion, and definition, and frequently returns to this idea. In 'Words and Metaphors' (41–73), he writes of nouns as 'the dominant words in the Middle English poems . . . especially abstract nouns referring to moral, emotional, and existential reality, and . . . social nouns, referring to classes of people' (41). Writing of metaphor he compares the work of more recent poets, as in the chapter on 'The Three Levels of Style' (74–85); he also invites comparison with classical and OE works. In 'Sound and Rhythm' (86–102), he describes effects and the use of figures of sound, metre, syntax and versification. 'Large Structures' (103–23) describes 'larger principles of order . . . repetition, logic, and such external forms as scriptural narrative, allegory, and miscellaneous formulas like the Ten Commandments or the agricultural calendar' (103). The 'Conclusion' (124–40) compares ME works with lyrics in OF, MHG, and Medieval Latin, and briefly describes ideas held in common by ME poets.

37, 93, 117, 194, 298, 320, 377, 515, 549, 579, 657, 740, 795, 864, 871, 925, 994, 1077, 1132, 1179, 1201, 1207, 1254, 1274, 1280, 1303, 1308, 1367, 1387, 1422, 1423, 1467, 1684, 1687, 1787, 1818, 1846, 1866, 1914, 1978, 2034, 2037.5, 2051, 2135, 2163, 2284.5, 2293, 2320, 2504, 2507, 2518, 2622, 2645, 2733, 2742, 3070, 3078, 3209, 3212, 3223, 3227, 3236, 3259, 3310, 3313, 3408, 3536, 3637, 3857.5, 3864, 3909, 3917, 3948, 3964, 3969, 3998, 4044, 4135.5, 4177, 4204, 4220, 4239, 4256.8, 4279.

——— Review by A.S.G. Edwards, *English Studies* 53 (1972): 553–6. Pronounces the book a 'curious' one, 'which tends to fluctuate between tedious banality and unhelpful generalization,' in which Oliver seems to be 'looking, often rather desperately, for something to say' to his general and scholarly audience (553). Edwards deplores Oliver's apparent neglect of important critical opinion and the 'muddled and unhelpful' (555) discussions of detailed and larger structures. However he has some praise for the 'number of very sensible points' Oliver makes in 'the examination of medieval lyric diction.' Since 'such discussions are rare,' the book 'is not a significant contribution to the study of the medieval lyric' (556).

550 Reiss, Edmund. 'Daun Gerveys in the *Miller's Tale*.' *Papers on Language and Literature* 6 (1970): 115–24.

Exploring the character of Gerveys in the *Miller's Tale*, Reiss refers to 'Swarte smekyd smethes smateryd wythe smoke' [*3227*], to show a smith as 'an appropriate guise for the devil' (118).

3227, 4019.

551 ———. 'Number Symbolism and Medieval Literature.' *Studies in Medieval and Renaissance Culture: In Honor of S. Harrison Thomson.* Ed. Paul Maurice Clogan. *Medievalia et Humanistica* NS 1 (1970): 161–74.

A general account of medieval concepts of number symbolism, related to structure and meaning, with examples from references to various works, including lyrics. The significance of the number five informs 'I syng of a myden þ^t is makeles' [*1367*] and 'The Lily with Five Leaves' ['Ful feir flour is þe lilie,' *885*]. In number maxims ['VIIJ ys my love ʒif IX go before,' *717*; 'Kepe well x & flee from sevyn,' *1817*] the numbers are 'not so much symbols as elements in a code' (167).

717, 885, 1306, 1367, 1817, 3144, 4019.

552 ———. 'Religious Commonplaces and Poetic Artistry in the Middle English Lyric.' *Style* 4 (1970): 97–106.

Presents close readings of two lyrics that illustrate 'the theme that most permeates medieval literature . . . the concern for salvation' (97). 'Naueþ my saule bute fur and ys' [**2284.5*] concerns Judgement Day, and so the need and opportunity to repent. 'Gold & al þis werdis wyn' [*1002*], with its grotesque paradoxes, illustrates the poet's wish to reject the world to be with Christ. Reiss supplies detailed analyses of both poems, to show effects of diction, word play, metre, symbolism and parallelism, and discusses the significance of the number eight in *1002*.

1002, *2284.5.

553 ———. 'The Art of the Middle English Lyric: Two Poems on Winter.' *Annuale Mediaevale* 11 (1970): 22–34.

'Mirie it is while sumer ilast' [*2163*] and 'Wynter wakeneþ al my care' [*4177*] express 'a commonplace theme – the individual's response to the coming of winter,' in 'homely language and ordinary versification,' but they demonstrate such lyrics' effectiveness. Reiss analyses the ways they achieve effects that make them 'fresh, meaningful, and compelling works of art' (22), to counter notions of the ME lyric as monotonous and limited; he considers their diction and metrical structure. Although the first poem is perhaps 'but the first stanza of a much longer poem,' it is 'complete and powerful,' and 'meaningful and effective as it stands' (26). The second, *4177*, deals with the themes of mutability, death, and the fate of the soul, and the long last line of each stanza 'climaxes the developing thought' (32).

2163, 3969, 4177.

554 Robbins, Rossell Hope. 'Signs of Death in Middle English.' *Mediaeval Studies* 32 (1970): 282–98.

The Signs of Death have two functions: 'the age-old diagnostic use to ascertain whether a sick man live or die, and the later religious use to warn the dying sinner to repent' (282). Robbins presents prognostics in English prose and in Latin prose and verse, with observations and tests. Homilies list the signs of death, and in one, 'for the Second Sunday after Advent, the world is likened to a senescent man' (288). There are many tags in the *Fasciculus Morum*. Robbins lists 13 sources of the Signs of Death, showing in which each sign is found, and prints some, with manuscript variants and comments on their use; in some cases he shows the relation to Latin sources. In a long footnote, he notes several tags in the *Fasciculus Morum*.

187, 228.5, 230.5, 624, 703, 825.8, 853.8, 1003, 1210.5, 1220, 1422, 1935, 2066.8, 2083, 2190, 2684.5, 3078.5, 3079.3, 3100.5, 3275, 3282, 3567, 3998, 4031, 4033, 4035, 4036.5, 4040.6, 4045, 4046, 4047, 4049.7, 4129.

555 ———. 'Victory at Whitby, A.D. 1451.' *Studies in Philology* 67 (1970): 495–504. [Edition.]

Cites the *Cronica*, from Trinity College, Dublin, MS E.5.10., 'describing an English naval victory over the French at Whitby Haven in November, 1451' (496). After a general description of the manuscript, with a list of its verse contents, Robbins supplies the historical background to the battle. He then describes the 'almost rambling stanzas' of the poem 'Sythen the furste þat were here or may be' [*3143.5*], in which 'unity is imposed by the balancing of various recognized literary genres, like the political prophecy, the catalogue of leaders, advice to rulers, and jingoistic abuse, and by the rhetorical decoration of stanza-linking' (497). He prints the text, with comments, and speculates on the colophon 'Quod Benet.' After summarizing records of John Benet of Harlington, Robbins concludes that he is unlikely to have been the author of the poems he copied.

3143.5.

556 Scattergood, V.J. 'Correspondence.' *Review of English Studies* NS 21 (1970): 337–8.

Adds to the information offered by Robbins, **538**, about John Crophill's notebook. Scattergood prints a poem about Hippocrates, Galen and Socrates ['þis bok heyght yppocras,' *7521*], 'written in Crophill's untidy hand' (337), which may be his version of the poem. A tract on the uses of rosemary ['þe leuys sothyn in wit wyn,' *7492*] is supplied in prose and verse.

7492, 7521.

557 ———. '"The Debate between Nurture and Kynd" – an Unpublished Middle English Poem.' *Notes and Queries* 215 (1970): 244–6. [Edition.]

Describes the poem, 'Goddis grace is redy bothe erly & late' [*995.4*], with comment on linguistic forms, such as *semand* and *semyng*, and finds that it 'draws heavily on proverbial lore for its inspiration.' The story's essentials are in the *Manciple's Tale*, lines 175–82, but Scattergood suggests that the poet drew on Chaucer's source, 'the Duenna's speech from *Le Roman de la Rose* lines 14039–52,' although this 'does not account for all the details' (245). He prints the poem, with notes, and supplies proverbs implied in the text. [See Braekman and Macaulay, **524**.]

995.4.

558 ———. 'Unpublished Middle English Poems from British Museum MS Harley 1706.' *English Philological Studies* 12 (1970): 35–41. [Edition.]

The manuscript was compiled 'for religious and devotional use' (36). Scattergood offers a description and what is known of its compilation and history, which is uncertain after its passing from the possession of Elizabeth Scrope (later Beaumont and Vere). He prints four poems *'Sex obseuanda omni Christiano in extremis'* ['Every man and woman hath grete nede,' *741*], *'Tres virtutes theologice'* ['Byleue in god þat alle haþ wrouȝte,' *505*], *'Quattuor virtutes cardinales'* ['Be ryȝtwys man what euer be-tyde,' *475*], and *'Otto beatitudines'* ['Ihesus seynge peplys comynge hym tylle,' *1746*]. Scattergood capitalizes the texts as in the manuscript, expands contractions, and suggests some emendations, explained in notes.

475, 505, 741, 1746.

559 Woolf, Rosemary. 'Later Poetry: The Popular Tradition.' *The Middle Ages*. Ed. W.F. Bolton. History of Literature in the English Language 1. London: Barrie, 1970.

Rev. edn. Sphere History of Literature 1. London: Sphere, 1970 [cited]. 10 vols. 1970–5. Rev. 1986–8. 263–311.

A general survey of 'romances, lyrics and mystery and morality plays,' which were 'the literature of the unlearned . . . from roughly the thirteenth to the fifteenth century' (263). In England only dance-songs can be reliably recognized as popular lyrics, since other songs, even if they were sung by minstrels, seem to have been composed by learned authors. Woolf's exploration of the terms 'popular' and 'courtly,' reveals complex implications in seemingly artless lyrics. Among works that imply 'a dramatic context' (281) are the *aube*, the *chanson de mal mariée*, the *chanson d'aventure*, the pastourelle, and lyrics of the betrayed maiden and the night visit. In spite of many 'stereotyped thoughts and formulae,' the Harley lyrics 'nevertheless give an impression of freshness,' (288). Woolf provides examples of descriptions of the lady and appeals for her love, and she notes conventions and variations. Lyrics written to the Virgin resemble love lyrics, and some poems on the Passion, Nativity, and Death recall the *aube* and the complaint of the betrayed maiden. Most significant differences between secular and religious lyrics are seen in 'the relationship between the "I" character in the poem and the reader or hearer' (290). The relationship is intimate rather than objective in the religious works, making the lyrics prayers or meditations. Although there are many good Passion lyrics, those on the Nativity are 'fewer, late, and less interestingly varied' (294); some are learned, some are simple, and the best are in lullaby form. Many lyrics emphasize the inevitability of death and 'the inexorable link made between the living and the dead' (298).

105, 194, 359, 360, 515, 1119, 1265, 1394, 1395, 1449, 1450, 1699, 2034.5, 2136, 2207, 2236, 2320, 2591, 2619, 2640, 2677, 3223, 3227, 3597, 3627, 3691, 3899.3, 4035, 4087, 4194.

560 Bessai, Frank. 'A Reading of "The Man in the Moon." ' *Annuale Mediaevale* 12 (1971): 120–2.

'The Man in the Moon' [*2066*] is 'probably not a lyric,' but has 'narrative elements based on the legend of the thief imprisoned in the moon for stealing thorns.' The legend is distorted to make a poem of social change, 'a good sixty years before the Peasants' Rebellion' (120). Bessai's reading describes Hubert's political education and his work as a hedger, with his hedging tool 'potentially the weapon of revolt' (121). The poem's speaker decries Hubert's slowness and passivity, urging him to 'free himself from the maw of manorial oppression,' but he will not be roused 'nor come down from the moon till a new day dawns' (122).

2066.

561 Braekman, Willy L., and Peter S. Macaulay. 'Two Unpublished Middle English Exempla from MS Royal 18 B. XXIII.' *Neuphilologische Mitteilungen* 72 (1971): 97–104. [Edition.]

The *exempla* concern repentance and confession; the second includes passages of verse. The work, 'This vnryghtwys man said is sawe' [*3645.5*], tells of a robber's death, and the struggle between devils and angels; it is attributed to Jacques de Vitry. The authors present the texts, with comments on *exempla* in general and on these in particular, and compare other manuscript sources. Marginal notes found with the second *exemplum* point to the possibility of dramatic presentation 'in the manner of the early morality plays' (101).

3645.5.

562 Chickering, Howell D., Jr. ' "Foweles in þe frith": A Religious Art-Song.' *Philological Quarterly* 50 (1971): 115–20.

Refers to comments on 'Foweles in the frith' [*864*] made by Bennett and Smithers, **65**, Manning, **486**, Reiss, **478**, and Sister Mary Jeremy [Finnegan], **497**, before presenting a musicological reading. The work, which may be a gymel, is 'one of three surviving thirteenth-century examples of the earliest English polyphony in the vernacular' (117); the others are 'Edi beo þu heuene quene' [*708*] and 'Iesu cristes milde moder' [*1697*]. The secular conductus, from which such music was derived, was 'a type of learned religious composition, closely related to the texts and musical practice of sequences, but not itself liturgical music' (119). Chickering prints the music for *864*. His analysis of musical and textual resemblances in the songs hints that *864* is religious rather than secular; aspects of both forms are found in the three songs. A tentative proposal connects 'the appearance of vernacular polyphonic writing with the founding of Franciscan houses in late thirteenth-century England,' and all three songs would fit 'the context of Franciscan piety' (120).

708, 864, 1697.

563 Crowther, J.D.W. 'The Middle English Lyric "Joly Jankyn."'' *Annuale Mediaevale* 12 (1971): 123–5.

The speaker's recollection of the mass in 'As I went on Yole day in oure prosession' [*377*] is 'a deliberate device to highlight the girl's mental distraction,' which enhances parody in the pun of 'eleyson' and 'Alison.' She thinks of the parish clerk Jankyn, 'brother in spirit to Absolon of Chaucer's *Miller's Tale*' (124), who has seduced her and caused her pregnancy. The girl recalls the mass for Christmas Day, and the device juxtaposes the two births, 'one bringing rejoicing and hope for all sinners, the other shame' (125). [See also Mustanoja, **548**.]

377.

564 Erb, Peter C. 'Vernacular Material for Preaching in MS Cambridge University Library Ii.III.8.' *Mediaeval Studies* 33 (1971): 63–84. [Edition.]

The manuscript contains many short vernacular verses among 'sermons, sermon-notes, exempla and other homiletic aids' (64), most of which are in Latin; some of these 'merit consideration more as complete lyrics than mere rhyming lists' (67). Some form divisions within sermons and others incorporate proverbs, riddles, and paradoxes, as in the description of a soul, 'Hit is a marchaund and spendeȝt nouth' [*1625*]. There are translations and expositions of scriptural themes, and variations of passages in the liturgy. Some poems are supplied in Latin and English versions; the exempla have most vernacular material. There are 'abundant examples of lyric laments over a life of sin' (78), but also humorous tales of 'foolish rustics, self-willed women and human foibles' (82), such as one based on the Story of the Three Cocks in the *Gesta Romanorum*. Twenty of the lyrics Erb presents have not been listed in *IMEV* or *SIMEV*.

10, 141, 158.8, 158.9, 457, 514, 607.8, 825.5, 835, 1134, 1406, 1428, 1493.5, 1625, 1803, 2046, 2052, 2085, 3563, 3863, 4056.3, 4091.6, 4094.8, 4193, 4240, 7040, 7041, 7086, 7101, 7144, 7185, 7244, 7246, 7320, 7337, 7372, 7459, 7463, 7472, 7495, 7506, 7513, 7527, 7612, 7640.

565 Gardner, John. *The Alliterative Morte Arthure, The Owl and the Nightingale, and Five Other Middle English Poems in a Modernized Version with Comments on the Poems and Notes.* Carbondale: Southern Illinois UP; London: Feffer, 1971.

Presents free translations of poems, including 'Somer Soneday' ['[O]pon a somer soneday se I þe sonne,' *3838*] and 'The Thrush and the Nightingale' ['Somer is comen wiþ loue to toune,' *3222*]. 'Somer Soneday' is 'the most intricate and ornate of the poems modernized' (263), with complex repetition, and conventions of 'the hunt, the dream vision, the wheel of Fortune scene, and so forth'; the occasion for which it was written is 'a matter of uncertainty' (264). Gardner finds 'The Thrush and the Nightingale' 'illuminates *The Owl and the Nightingale* [*1384*]' (266), and describes it in relation to the latter poem.

1384, 3222, 3838.

566   Gradon, Pamela. *Form and Style in Early English Literature.* London: Methuen, 1971.

A general study of the relationship 'between language and literature in the medieval period' (vii), illustrated with many examples, including lyrics. Comparison of treatment of pastourelle themes in a lyric of the *Carmina Burana* and the Harley lyric 'De Clerico et Puella' [*2236*] shows 'a move in the direction of the particularity of naturalism' (13). The tendency is also seen in the 'Luue Ron' [*66*], which Gradon compares with the OE *Wanderer*. She traces imagery to its sources, in particular to the Song of Songs, in examinations of 'þou wommon boute vere' [*3700*], 'Nou goth þe sonne under wode' [*2320*], 'I syng of a myden þ^t is makeles' [*1367*], Lydgate's 'Midsomer Rose' [*1865*], and 'In a valey of þis restles mynde' [*1463*]. 'Wyth was hys nakede brest and red of blod hys syde' [*4088*] presents realistic details. Gradon examines work of Charles d'Orléans, and finds the style of 'The smylyng mouth and laughing eyen gray' [*3465*] abstract. In contrast, the style of 'Wiþ longyng y am lad' [*4194*], seems 'more direct and passionate' (338). She compares Charles's poems with a Harley lyric, 'Lenten ys come wiþ loue to toune' [*1861*], and uses 'Honure ioy helth and plesance' [*1240*] to show his use of abstract nouns. Gradon demonstrates aureate style in religious lyrics such as William of Shoreham's 'Marye mayde mylde and fre' [*2107*], Lydgate's 'Balade in Commendation of Our Lady' [*99*], and Dunbar's 'Ane ballat of Our Lady' [*1082.5*] and *The Goldyn Targe* [*2820.5*]. She contrasts the last poem with 'Annot and John' [*1394*] and 'Blow, Northerne Wynd' [*1395*]. In summary, she describes the history of styles as 'an increasing sense of naturalism' (385) and a movement towards symbolism, exemplified in *1367*.

66, 99, 1082.5, 1240, 1394, 1395, 1463, 1861, 2107, 2236, 2320, 2820.5, 3465, 3700, 4088, 4194.

567   Harris, Joseph. '"Maiden in the Mor Lay" and the Medieval Magdalene Tradition.' *Journal of Medieval and Renaissance Studies* 1 (1971): 59–87.

Surveys comments on 'Maiden in the mor lay' [*2037.5*], particularly those of Schoeck, **301**, Robertson, **298**, Greene, **314**, and Donaldson, **414**, before questioning the view that Richard de Ledrede intended the Latin poem 'Peperit virgo' to be 'an "antidote" to the popular and secular song "Maiden in the mor lay"' (61). Harris posits rather that the vernacular lines found with Latin verses in the Red Book of Ossory are 'the product of a desultory search for fitting tunes' (62). The juxtaposition of lines shows only that 'a clerk thought the tune of the English song would be suitable for the new Latin poem' (63). He relates the ME lyric to Mary Magdalene's penance, a theme of numerous European ballads, to suggest that the lyric comes from the ballad tradition, and cites French and Scandinavian examples with similar motifs of sufficient food, drink, and bed. For other reasons, Tillyard, **304**, and Speirs, **385**, also identify the moor maiden with Mary Magdalene. Comparison with an Italian song hints that the poem is an art song not a folk work, and was composed by a learned poet, aware of 'his poem's relation to the ballad and of the implications of his changes in imagery, of . . . the Magdalenian background and Marian foreground' (73). Harris describes suggestive images in detail: *seuenistes fulle ant a day* (74–5), *þe chelde water of þe welle-spring* and the implications of imagery of flowers (76–80), *maiden in the mor lay* (80–4), *welle was hire . . .* (84), and the moor (85–6). The conjunction and transformation of Magdelenian and Marian imagery are essential. The lyric expresses, through 'the same kind of miraculous change that the other Mary performed in "mutans nomen Evae," [that] the Magdalene has fled to the sweet lily of chastity and come a maiden home' (87).

2037.5, 2645.

568   Heidtmann, Peter. 'The *Reverdie* Convention and "Lenten is Come with Love to Toune."' *Annuale Mediaevale* 12 (1971): 78–89

A close reading of 'Lenten ys come wiþ loue to toune' [*1861*], as a part of the *reverdie* tradition, the 'poetic celebration of the return of spring' (79). Spring could bring joy in the human mood, or present 'a situation of unfulfilled love . . . and consequently a mood of love-longing . . . which contrasts with the joyous response of the natural world to the season' (79). Heidtmann provides examples of the juxtaposition of moods and the world of nature. 'Foweles in the frith' [*864*] has no specific reference to spring. 'Alysoun' [*515*] belongs to the *reverdie* tradition, but has vitality *'despite* the first four lines which are *merely* conventional' (82). 'The relative proportions of the spring theme and the love-longing motif' in *1861* are 'just the reverse' (83) of those of 'Alysoun.' Analysis relates the poem to others of the genre, and to the speaker's state and the natural world. In the 'poet's artful use of the *reverdie* . . . in juxtaposition with a mood of love-longing,' the poem reveals a disconsolate lover 'whose sexuality has been repulsed' (89).

515, 864, 1861, 3223, 4037.

569   Jeffrey, David L. 'Forms of Spirituality in the Middle English Lyric.'
Imagination and the Spirit: Essays in Literature and the Christian Faith Presented to Clyde S. Kilby. Ed. Charles A. Huttar. Grand Rapids, MI: Eerdmans, 1971. 55–85.

Understanding of the Franciscan influence on ME religious lyrics can be extended by examining methods of the Vaudois or Waldensians, a similar movement for spiritual reform. Jeffrey surveys ME religious lyrics, their occurrence in sermon material and miscellanies, and Franciscan influence, in examples where 'the object of the poem is not only instruction and worship, but *penaunce* and *amendement*' (59). In the eleventh and twelfth centuries such movements were 'principally manifestations of . . . anti-clericism and religious "zealotism"' (62), and so generally considered heretical. Jeffrey describes the Waldensians' use of vernacular poetry to transmit 'scriptural and doctrinal instruction to a basically illiterate (un-Latinate) people' (64). He also considers the use of amatory poetry by monks and religious poetry by jongleurs and troubadours. Waldo and Francis sought 'spiritual regeneration of men,' and employed poetic forms that had 'obvious similarities' but also 'marked and important differences' (69). Jeffrey supplies a history of Francis and the Franciscans, leading to their application of poetic sermons and lyric tags. Secular songs are the basis of many sacred parodies, including those of the Red Book of Ossory, which was begun by the Franciscan Richard de Ledrede. Franciscan poets included Francis himself, Jacopone da Todi, and James Ryman. Jeffrey uses 'Wynter wakeneþ al my care' [*4177*] and Ryman's 'That holy clerke seint Augustyne' [*3272*] to illustrate Franciscan teaching. He finds ME lyrics 'perhaps the most vibrant popular expression of medieval spirituality,' as they serve 'to marry the message of God's love for fallen men to the aesthetic of popular song' (85).

1978, 2034, 3078, 3272, 3779, 4160, 4177.

570   Scattergood, V.J. *Politics and Poetry in the Fifteenth Century.* Blandford History Series. Gen. ed. R.W. Harris. London: Blandford, 1971.

Examines the historical context of fifteenth-century historical and political poetry, to show the benefit of considering historical records and political thought. After the 'Introduction' (9–12), Scattergood presents chapters on 'Political Verse in Medieval

England' (13–34); 'Nationalism and Foreign Affairs' (35–106); 'Domestic Affairs': '1399–1422' (107–36), '1422–1455' (135–72), '1455–1485' (173–217); 'Religion and the Clergy' (218–63); 'English Society I: The Theoretical Basis' (264–97), 'II: Some Aspects of Social Change' (298–349), 'III: Verses of Protest and Revolt' (350–77). Most of the authors are unknown; known poets include John Gower, Thomas Hoccleve, John Lydgate, George Ashby, John Audelay, John Crophill, and Osbern Bokenham. Some of the examples are short and generally classified as lyrics. The range of topics is wide. Political verse was 'essentially public and depended largely for its effectiveness on being brought before the notice of a large number of people' (22); it was sometimes commissioned. The posting of verses on walls and gates implies literacy. The period includes the reigns of Richard II, Henry IV, Henry V, Henry VI, Edward IV, Edward V, Richard III, and Henry VII; some verses comment on their involvement in foreign and domestic wars. The poems address vices of the times; the ideal state; general and particular troubles, and their perpetrators. Initials or badges of political figures are used, rather than names, in poems of roses and those using animal imagery from emblems.

92, 113, 161, 199, 295, 296.3, 299, 316.3, 372, 437, 455, 544, 605, 658, 700, 762, 818, 822, 871, 882, 884, 892, 899, 906, 921, 935, 969, 970, 1147.9, 1157, 1168, 1320.5, 1327, 1380, 1450, 1470.5, 1480, 1497, 1514, 1533, 1534, 1540, 1544, 1555, 1653.5, 1655, 1791, 1796, 1830, 1926, 1929, 1939, 2066, 2082, 2130, 2154, 2156, 2167, 2192, 2200, 2219, 2229, 2262.3, 2338, 2445, 2454, 2464, 2516, 2538, 2587, 2590, 2591, 2609, 2625, 2662, 2716, 2727, 2786, 2804, 2805, 2808, 3115, 3127, 3206, 3213, 3252, 3308, 3402, 3402, 3407, 3455, 3457, 3491, 3529, 3625, 3632, 3655, 3682, 3697, 3718, 3720, 3756, 3759, 3782, 3787, 3799, 3808, 3809, 3859, 3922, 3926, 3928, 3929, 4018, 4019, 4056.8, 4062, 4066, 4070, 4098.3, 4250, 4251, 4257, 4265.

571   Tierney, Frank. 'The Development of the Rondeau in England from its Origin in the Middle Ages to its Revival in the Years Following 1860.' *Revue de l'Université d'Ottawa* 41 (1971): 25–46.

Describes the development of the rondeau, from the 'folk or tribal animistic ritual dance of preliterate primitive cultures' (25), to thirteenth-century French fixed literary forms, to become established as simple and double rondeaux in England in the fifteenth century. Tierney traces use of the form by Chaucer, Hoccleve, Lydgate, and Wyatt, with examples, and notes Chaucer's references in other poems, where it is called the 'rondel' or 'roundel,' and associated with the *ballade* and *virelay*. 'Now welcome somer with thy sonne softe' [*2375*], included in *The Parlement of Fowles* [*3412*], resembles works of Eustache Deschamps, in structure, substance and style. *Merciles Beaute* [*4282*] recalls 'Petrarchan sonnet substance and style' (32). Lydgate's roundel style is like those of Chaucer and Hoccleve, with the addition of a fourteenth line. The next significant user of the form was Wyatt, 'a student of Chaucer,' and familiar with 'lyric forms and commonplaces of Provençal, French, and Italian poetry alike' (38). The influence of French forms is seen in rondeaux such as 'What no, perdy, ye may be sure!' [*7586*]. Tierney concludes by examining the form in poems of the seventeenth, eighteenth, and nineteenth centuries.

100, 2375, 3224, 3412, 3799, 4019, 4282, 7586.

572   Wenzel, Siegfried. 'A Latin Miracle with Middle English Verses.' *Neuphilologische Mitteilungen* 72 (1971): 77–85. [Edition.]

Within a Latin account of a miracle of the Virgin, in Eton College MS 34, are some lines of ME dialogue. They tell of the struggle for the soul of a Parisian goliard, who 'despite his rather loose life and morals never failed to honor the Blessed Virgin by offering her candles and prayers' (77). In sickness, he has a vision of God the Father, Christ, the devil, the Virgin, and an angel; the last three are gathered around his bed. Mary defends him against the devil's claim for his soul; she shows her breast to Christ in her appeal, and he, in turn shows his wounds in an appeal to God. The angel summarizes the vision, and the sinner reforms and recovers. Although the Virgin's appeal by exposing her breast appears in books of devotion, the fine arts, and other accounts of miracles, the story of the goliard seems unique. The practice of using ME verses within a Latin text is not unusual, and Wenzel notes examples from the *Fasciculus Morum* and the *Gesta Romanorum*. He prints the Latin text and ME verses, and translates the words of the characters. [See also Heffernan, **802**.]

835, 1428, 3568.5, 4202, 7214.

573   Brian, Beverley. 'Franciscan Scenes in a Fourteenth-Century Satire.' *Medium Ævum* 4 (1972): 27–31.

Seeks to identify scenes in the satirical poem 'Of thes frer mynours me thenkes moch wonder' [*2663*], which Robbins, **57**, thought referred to 'a series of wall-paintings like those with which the Franciscans decorated their churches.' The poem is an attack delivered by 'a plain, blunt Christian who has no patience with the hauteur and vanity of the friars.' The first scene, thought 'ignorant and disrespectful' by the poet, displays 'Christ hanging on a flowering tree,' (27). Brian suggests a 'specifically Franciscan source,' St Bonaventure's 'treatise called *Lignum Vitae*, a meditation on the life, passion, and glorification of Christ.' The second depicts 'the seraph, surrounded by light and nailed to a cross, who appeared to St. Francis just before he received the stigmata' (28), although the poet sees the figure as Christ with wings. The image thought by the poet to be a deified flying friar is probably 'the levitation of St. Francis in ecstasy.' The next scene depicts a legend of the appearance of Francis in a dream of Pope Gregory; here Francis displays the wound in his side and offers a phial of blood to Pope Gregory. The poet finds that 'the pope is ministering to a friar,' and considers the situation improper. Similarly, he inteprets the appearance of a fiery chariot to friars in a village near Assisi not as a sign of the presence of Francis in spirit, but rather of 'the fiery finish not only of the friars, but of all of those who help them' (29). The poet's knowledge implies a close acquaintance with such wall-paintings; his aim is 'to ridicule the legend as a fabrication of the Franciscans to glorify the order' (30).

2663.

574   Cross, J.E. 'The Virgin's *Quia Amore Langueo*.' *Neuphilologische Mitteilungen* 73 (1972): 37–44.

Cross seeks to motivate and so to dispel 'the "discrepancy" and "confusion,"' found by Woolf, **522**, in 'In a tabernacle of a toure' [*1460*], and also to demonstrate that 'the "cleverness,"' discerned by Kane, **292**, is simply 'normal sequence of thought to the mediaeval mind,' (37). He endorses Riddy's reading of two lines, **500**, rather than the those of *BrownXIV*, **48**, and Davies, **61**. Cross reconciles apparent confusion in addressing the Virgin in terms of love-longing from the Song of Songs by reference to liturgical use, and to the medieval sickness of 'love's illness.' The paradoxical images of her family relationships and of Mary as 'the queen in "pore array"' (40) were familiar, not confusing, to a medieval Christian. The poem recalls the *chanson d'aventure*, described by Sandison, **139**. Its variations from the usual pattern, '*rarity* in its *timing* and in the poet's *musing*,' make it memorable; 'its *uniqueness* . . . in "musing on the moon"' (42) makes it fitting for the Virgin, since the moon and virginity are readily associated. Images recall the wise virgins and the Woman of the Apocalypse. The opening is 'an apt prelude to the plaint of Mary in her exalted position for return of her magnanimous love from her spiritual son' (44).

1460, 3700.

575 **Gray, Douglas.** *Themes and Images in the Medieval English Religious Lyric.* London: Routledge, 1972.

Gray emphasizes 'the way in which a tradition may be *used* by a creative intelligence,' and considers poems 'thematically, rather than chronologically' (ix). He investigates 'The Background' (3–71), 'The Scheme of Redemption' (75–150), and 'The Life of this World' (153–220), before his 'Conclusion' (221–6), and illustrates each chapter with numerous examples.

'The Inherited Tradition' (3–17) stresses the influence of Latin, and takes examples from Lydgate and Herebert. 'Medieval Devotion' (18–30) surveys affective piety; Gray reviews its background, and influential groups and individuals. These include Franciscans, particularly Thomas de Hales, William Herebert, Michael of Kildare, and James Ryman; the Dominicans and Carthusians; Margery Kempe; and recluses such as the monk of Farne, Julian of Norwich, St Godric of Finchdale, Richard Rolle, and Christina of Markyate. In a time of fervent devotion, many ME lyrics achieved 'clarity, simple dignity, and moderation' (30). 'The English Lyrics, I' (31–58) examines the immediate background of religious books, images, prayers and charms, and adaptations from secular sources. Mnemonic properties in lyrics and visual images are valued; some lyrics are *tituli*. Secular and religious works share forms and language. There are courtly lyrics of the Virgin, religious parodies of secular songs, and religious songs written for secular tunes, for instance by Richard de Ledrede. 'The English Lyrics II' (59–71) describes the poems, their forms (prayer and the carol) and styles (humble, aureate, macaronic, and 'wit-poetry'). Most lyrics are affective rather than theological, with 'isolated conceits or paradoxes' (68).

'Christ and the Virgin Mary' (75–94) concentrates on images, including figures from the OT and pagan literature. Christ's humanity, name, and love for mankind are stressed. Lyrics to the Virgin add to established Marian devotion, incorporating figures and symbols, such as the rose. Some of these are 'simply the product of pious ingenuity,' others are 'startlingly successful' (87). Lyrics of 'Annunciation and Nativity' (95–121) characteristically display joy and light. Many, such as 'I syng of a myden þ^t is makeles' [*1367*], explain mysteries of the Incarnation. Some render the relation of mother and child in lullabies; others show that 'the Nativity, although it is a joyful mystery, is set in a world of misery, cold and doubt' (119). Lyrics of 'The Passion' (122–145) concentrate on its torments, and may involve the reader emotionally. Some supply 'a verbal devotional image' (128); some have the form of the 'Charter of Christ.' Images of Christ as knight or nightingale are among the most successful. Instruments of the Passion illustrate *Arma Christi* poems, and lyrics are related to the cults of the Precious Blood of Christ and the Five Wounds. Mary's grief is communicated in laments, dialogues, and lyrics which imply the image of the *pietà*. Christ himself appeals to man in some poems. Lyrics of 'Resurrection and Assumption' (146–50) express triumph in vivid images and splendid diction.

Lyrics of 'The Christian Life' (153–75) show how to live, often in prayers. Some deal with matters of faith, others with charms, spells, and Lady Fortune. Gray summarizes writing about the 'Corpus Christi Carol' [*1132*] (164–7). Old age appears in many lyrics of penitence, leading to the theme of *memento mori*. 'Death and the Last Things' (176–220) are important themes; Gray relates the images and notions to ancient literature. The 'deep sense of mortality' leads sometimes to 'an extreme preoccupation with decay and death' (179). The plague inspired some prayers. *Ubi sunt* and *Proprietates Mortis*, 'Signs of Death,' are significant themes. Versions of 'Erthe upon Erthe' [*3939*] are widespread, sometimes *tituli*, occasionally used in epitaphs. There are laments and warnings from the dead. The most imaginative lyrics gain their power from the combined moods of pessimism, questioning, doubt, and the need for faith. Dunbar's poems of death are intensely powerful. A few lyrics express tenderness and acceptance.

Gray's conclusion summarizes the influence of the lyrics. He finds 'the great religious poets of the seventeenth century' to be 'inheritors of that delicate balance of emotion

French lyrics, but 'the fitting length of lines' is determined by 'sensory, auditory criteria' (115), rather than by counting syllables. The terms 'courtly' and 'popular' have little significance, since knowledge and composition of the lyrics were not rigidly restricted; the 'real distinction' is 'between literary or art poetry, and untutored instinctive or natural verse' (118). There are four styles: plain, early decorated, polished, and aureate. Kane suggests the qualifications needed for anyone embarking on a new study of ME secular lyrics. He predicts the discovery of 'no "poetic tradition" of the kind which existed here [in England] from the sixteenth century onwards,' and 'no formulated conception of the writing of poetry as an activity in the vernacular' (120). Lack of a prose tradition and influences of 'the ascendancy of Latin' and 'the social inferiority of English until the 1370's' (121) are significant factors. Findings of this kind must be based on historical considerations.

100, 467, 2031, 2254, 2421, 2757, 3512, 3542, 3838.

580 Kurvinen, Auvo. 'Mercy and Righteousness.' *Neuphilologische Mitteilungen* 73 (1972): 181–91. [Edition.]

The debate between Mercy and Righteousness, 'Bi a forest as y gan walke' [*560*], has already been described by Kurvinen, **323**, who now presents it with extensive comment on the scribe's language and its mixed Midland character, and compares it with other manuscript versions. She prints the text from MS Porkington 10, with editorial capitalization, punctuation, and division of words, and explains emendations in footnotes.

560.

581 Mason, H.A. '"I Am as I Am."' *Review of English Studies* NS 23 (1972): 304–8. [Edition.]

To supplement the comments of Greene, **462**, on 'I ham as I ham and so will I be' [*1270.2*] (a poem attributed to Wyatt) Mason provides a table of variants and supplies a text. The variants come from MSS Bannatyne; Trinity College, Dublin, D.2.7; BL Add. 17492 [Devonshire]; and University of Pennsylvania, Latin 35. Mason finds some of Bannatyne's readings particularly attractive, and suggests that consideration of this manuscript strengthens 'the claims of the "Devonshire" MS. to be providing the most reliable text of the three longer extant versions' (307).

1270.2.

582 Matonis, A.T.E. 'An Investigation of Celtic Influences on MS Harley 2253.' *Modern Philology* 70 (1972): 91–108.

Critics have considered that important influences on ME poetry include 'Latin-Romance stanza forms, the *amour courtois* theme, and the elaborate imagery of the *Roman de la rose*' (91). Matonis asserts the importance of Celtic influence, which she illustrates in some Harley lyrics, and comments on thematic similarities to OE verse. After summarizing the relation of Irish and Welsh styles to ME verse, Matonis offers detailed descriptions of stanza linking, binding or concatenating alliteration, *aicill*, *saigin*, *breccas*, *trebad*, and *cynghanedd*. She demonstrates their occurrence in 'The Poet's Repentance' [*3874*], 'The Three Foes of Man' [*2166*], 'The Meeting in the Wood' [*1449*], and 'The Song of the Husbandman' [*1320.5*]. Some features imitate Latin, but a Celtic influence can be discerned, as in the Irish reinforcement of Latin syllabic style, which is seen in Latin verse written by Irishmen.

1320.5, 1394, 1449, 2166, 2207, 2236, 3874.

583 Reiss, Edmund. *The Art of the Middle English Lyric: Essays in Criticism.* Athens, GA: U of Georgia P, 1972.

Reiss's introduction (x–xv) is a general survey of the criticism of and attitudes to the ME lyric. After drawing general conclusions about 'artificial and inadequate' (xiii) distinctions between religious and secular lyrics, he considers the poems' complexity and degree of conformity to conventional forms, and relates the work of the artist to that of the mathematician. The critical essays are detailed studies of 25 lyrics: 'Adam lay I-bowndyn bowndyn in a bond [*117*], 'Als i me rod this endre dai' [*360*], 'Alysoun' [*515*], 'Foweles in the frith' [*864*], 'Gold & al þis werdis wyn' [*1002*], 'I sayh hym wiþ fless al bi-sprad' [*1353*], 'I syng of a myden þ^t is makeles' [*1367*], 'I Wende to dede a kyng y-wys' [*1387*], 'Lenten ys come wiþ loue to toune' [*1861*], 'Maiden in the mor lay' [*2037.5*], 'Mirie it is while sumer ilast' [*2163*], '*Naueþ my saule bute fur and ys' [**2284.5*], 'Nou goth þe sonne under wode' [*2320*], 'Svmer is icumen in' [*3223*], 'Swarte smekyd smethes smateryd wythe smoke' [*3227*], 'Vndo þi dore my spuse dere' [*3825*], 'Wel and wa sal ys hornes blaw' [*3857.5*], 'What ys he þys lordling þat cometh vrom þe vyht' [*3906*], 'Erthe upon Erthe' [*3939*], 'Quanne hic se on rode' [*3964*], 'Wanne mine eyhnen misten' [*3998*], 'Wen þe turuf is þi tuur' [*4044*], 'Wynter wakeneþ al my care' [*4177*], 'With fauoure in hir face ferr passyng my Reason' [*4189*], and 'Worldes blys haue god day' [*4221*]. The essays follow the poems' chronological order, and relation to historical context. They offer analysis of 'poetic structure, verse technique, and wordplay,' from 'principles and insights of those present-day linguists interested in stylistics' (xii). Reiss prints the works and lists editions and sources of criticism with his discussions. There are brief references, in essays on other lyrics, to 'Al nist by [þe] rose rose' [*194*], 'Pees maketh plente' [*2742*], 'Westron wynde when wylle thou blow' [*3899.3*], and *4221*.

117, 194, 360, 515, 864, 1002, 1353, 1367, 1387, 1861, 2037.5, 2163, *2284.5, 2320, 2742, 3223, 3227, 3825, 3857.5, 3899.3, 3906, 3939, 3964, 3998, 4044, 4177, 4189, 4221.

——— Review by T.P. Dunning, *Review of English Studies* NS 24 (1973): 467–70. The review includes an examination of Gray, **575**, and Dunning shows that Reiss's work 'valuable in many ways as it is must be regarded on the whole as an example of how indispensable is an introduction of the kind Mr. Gray has now happily supplied' (469). Dunning regrets the absence of reference to the background of the lyrics, and finds comparison 'underlines the laboriousness of Mr. Reiss's analysis,' although the latter is 'useful and stimulating' (470).

——— Review by Ralph W.V. Elliott, *English Studies* 55 (1974): 155–9. The review also examines Gray, **575**, and expresses many comments as comparisons of the two authors' methods. Elliott acknowledges the difficulties of 'microscopic scrutiny' (156) for some ME lyrics and observes that some 'do not stand up well to Professor Reiss's type of close analysis' (158). He commends most of the essays, with few objections to the choice of lyrics, and concludes that the reader 'will gain valuable insight into the medieval lyric poet's art' (159) from Reiss's discussions.

584 Robbins, Rossell Hope. '"Conuertimini": A Middle English Refrain Poem.' *Neuphilologische Mitteilungen* 73 (1972): 353–61. [Edition.]

'The prophete in his prophecye' [*3451*] recalls a passage from the epistle for Ash Wednesday, Joel 2. 12–19. Robbins cites examples of sermons for the day, which advocate penance with fasting, weeping, and mourning. He presents the text of *3451* with notes, and recommends that such poems 'be viewed against the background of the main Vernon-Simeon corpus' (360), to show similarities in *'Conuertimini.'* The poems could have been used in preaching, as 'verse summations of vernacular sermons' (361), and some have lines that imply such use. Although the manuscript was copied by John Benet, it is unlikely that he was the author of the poem.

1379, 1455, 1532, 3420, 3451, 3996, 4135.

Resurrection and the Soldiers' Report, before going on to the Maries at the Sepulchre and their meeting with Christ, the Journey to Emmaus, the Reunion of the Disciples, the Harrowing of Hell and the Ascension.' Pickering describes the poem as 'a religious romance,' with changes in the retelling of a familiar story, to produce 'unusual immediacy, speed and concision,' and sometimes a 'ballad feel' to the work. Limitations in the poet's technique are overcome by his 'vitality and overall achievement as a raconteur,' when he presents 'new twists' (272). Pickering comments on the poem and on the forms of the 'South-East Midland dialect of the fourteenth century' (273) in which it is written. He prints the poem, with modern punctuation, capitalization and word-division, and two emendations demanded by the sense.

173, 212, 312, 1860, 1869, 1907, 2157, 2647, 2685, 4250.

597   Roberts, P.D. 'Some Unpublished Middle English Lyrics and Stanzas in a Victoria Public Library Manuscript.' *English Studies* 54 (1973): 105–18. [Edition.]

A manuscript of a prose adaptation of Guillaume de Guileville's *Pilgrimage of the Life of Man* and *Pilgrimage of the Soul*, held in the State Library of Victoria has, among 24 ME poems, 'nine not found in any of the 15 other *Pilgrimage* MSS extant, while three others, ascribed to Hoccleve, have extra unique stanzas added to them' (105). Roberts notes features used to identify Hoccleve's verse, and lists the poems, printing the anonymous lyrics ['A floure is sprongen þat shall never faile,' *34.5*; 'Blisside be þou holy trinite,' *528.5*; 'Haile festivale day with al honoure,' *1041.3*; 'Honoured be þou lorde of myghte,' *1249.5*; 'In hevene and erth aungell and man,' *1490.5*; 'My soverayne saveoure to þe I calle,' *2271.4*; 'O altitude of alle science,' *2384.5*; 'O glorious feste among al other,' *2440.5*; 'O orient lyghte & kinge eterne,' *2533.5*], and those attributed to Hoccleve ['Honured be þis holy feste day,' *1242*; 'Honured be þu blisful heuene queene,' *1243*; 'Honured be þou holy gost on hie,' *1248*].

34.5, 528.5, 1041.3, 1242, 1243, 1248, 1249.5, 1490.5, 2271.4, 2384.5, 2440.5, 2533.5.

598   Salter, Elizabeth. 'The Mediaeval Lyric.' *The Mediaeval World*. Vol. 2 of *Literature and Western Civilization*. Gen. eds. David Daiches and Anthony Thorlby. London: Aldus, 1973. 445–84. 6 vols. 1972–6.

Surveys the lyric in medieval Europe, where no other genre is 'so comprehensive in range and appeal' (445). Salter shows connections between music and poetry, and traces the influence of Latin hymn traditions, but notes that many ME religious lyrics were not intended to be sung. It is unsatisfactory to distinguish between languages and countries and between religious and secular areas, although contrasts are possible, since the lyric 'covers all parts of medieval life' (456). The presence of bilingual and trilingual poems, as in the Harley lyrics, implies 'a cultured milieu, in touch with courtly and devout literature' (458). Some lyrics show that contacts between religious and secular literature were 'close and mutually beneficial' (459), with examples in seasonal motifs and lyrics of love. In her study of 'The Mediaeval English Religious Lyric' (476–81), Salter examines its relation to Latin verse and the anticipation of some works of George Herbert. She finds in the lyrics that explore religious paradoxes 'a poetry of service, not of self-expression, in which private experience is used, not exploited' (480).

37, 694.5, 769, 1394, 1697, 1921, 1922, 1978, 2070, 2207, 2270, 2320, 2359, 2494, 3236, 3405, 3963, 4044, 4088.

599   Smallwood, T.M. 'The Interpretation of *Somer Soneday*.' *Medium Ævum* 42 (1973): 238–43.

Argues against opinions of Brown, **160**, and *RobbinsH*, **57**, that 'Somer Soneday' ['[O]pon a somer soneday se I þe sonne,' *3838*] is complete and intended for 'the "commemorations of kings", an elegy for Edward II or conceivably . . . for Richard II' (238). Smallwood considers that it is based on the 'Formula of Four' tradition of Wheel of Fortune iconography, which show four kings in varying positions on the wheel, and suggests that a blank space left for a picture was intended for such an illustration. The poem shares some phrases with 'The Awntyrs of Arthure' [*1566*] and *Morte Arthure* [*2322*], and Smallwood suggests that these poems have borrowed from *3838*. The stanza form resembles that of 'Susannah (The Pistill of Susan)' [*3553*] and 'The Quatrefoil of Love' [*1453*]. These poems have 'some striking echoes of the last lines of our text,' and refer to 'the common approach of death to all people, thus corroborating our interpretation' (242) of a universal theme rather than commemoration of an individual. [See also Turville-Petre, **626**.]

1453, 1566, 2322, 3553, 3838.

600   Townsend, Brenda. 'The Word "Pyn" in the Harley Lyric "Ichot a Burde in a Bour ase Beryl so Bryht."' *English Language Notes* 11 (1973–4): 89–91.

Brook, **42**, reads the word *pyn*, in the line 'he is papeiai in pyn þat beteþ me my bale,' as a reference to pain sufferred by the poet of 'Annot and John' [*1394*]. Townsend finds that alliteration associates it with the parrot, and that in each stanza a figure refers to the description of the lady 'by indicating its typical setting'; thus 'the papeiai too would need to be seen in typical surroundings' (89). Since *pyn* can convey 'the sense of a poultry coop,' this sense can fit 'both the pattern of this stanza and of the poem as a whole, while in no way detracting from the function of the parrot, to cure the lover of his sorrow by its song' (90).

1394.

601   Wilson, Edward. *A Descriptive Index of the English Lyrics in John of Grimestone's Preaching Book.* Medium Ævum Monographs NS 2. Society for the Study of Mediæval Languages and Literature. Oxford: Blackwell, 1973. [Edition.]

Lists 246 items in MS Advocates' Library 18.7.21, 'lyrics and tags which a Norfolk Franciscan assembled in 1372,' of which many are 'the daisies and dandelions of fourteenth century poetry' (i). Wilson describes the manuscript, and differs from Robbins, **230**, in proposing that it is in one hand. The preaching notes are mostly in Latin, and have classical and patristic references. Wilson notes the sources of the lyrics, some of which are also found in other manuscripts. He summarizes comments on the language and provenance of the manuscript, which he concludes is of South-West Norfolk. There are subject headings, folio numbers, introductory sentences, and any other printing of each lyric, with the full text if the poem has not been printed before. Wilson also records 'any Latin source or version in the manuscript' (xxi), with bibliographical notes, and references to other indexes and anthologies in which the poems are noted.

7, 23, 33.6, 52.6, 91, 94, 156, 162, 193.8, 197, 221, 222.5, 230.5, 327, 352, 353, 424, 441, 461, 468, 480, 494, 499, 501, 504, 517.5, 554, 593, 602, 607.5, 609, 628, 629, 634, 703, 825.8, 829, 873, 955, 1002, 1061, 1089, 1129, 1139, 1140.5, 1167, 1210.5, 1220, 1262, 1274, 1336, 1337, 1431, 1432, 1436, 1436.5, 1472, 1523, 1606, 1610, 1636, 1714, 1737, 1847, 1864, 1942, 1965, 2006, 2011, 2012, 2023, 2024, 2036, 2066.8, 2074, 2083, 2095, 2155, 2234, 2240, 2258, 2260, 2289.5, 2298, 2341, 2708, 2743.5, 2762, 2817, 3078.5, 3079.3, 3100.5, 3109, 3111, 3245, 3264, 3277, 3356, 3452.8, 3464, 3485, 3500, 3505, 3510.5, 3516.5, 3520, 3562, 3567.6, 3678, 3690, 3691, 3743.6, 3764, 3783, 3825, 3846, 3862, 3862, 3903, 3908, 3969, 4084, 4088, 4110.3, 4150.3, 4159, 4221, 4222, 4225, 4256.5, 4263, 4286, 7028, 7029, 7032, 7039, 7060, 7067, 7078, 7083, 7084, 7085, 7090, 7092, 7102, 7109, 7114, 7115, 7117, 7121, 7122, 7123, 7132, 7139, 7145, 7149, 7150, 7160, 7162, 7166, 7167, 7180, 7182, 7186, 7187, 7190, 7191, 7192, 7207, 7208, 7231, 7236, 7242, 7248, 7249,

7250, 7251, 7253, 7276, 7279, 7280, 7282, 7284, 7287, 7297, 7301, 7302, 7314, 7339, 7362, 7374, 7406, 7412, 7413, 7421, 7424, 7425, 7426, 7430, 7445, 7447, 7449, 7457, 7462, 7464, 7466, 7471, 7473, 7481, 7485, 7487, 7498, 7502, 7509, 7516, 7517, 7519, 7524, 7535, 7537, 7543, 7549, 7560, 7575, 7607, 7609, 7610, 7616, 7617, 7619, 7629, 7632, 7637, 7647, 7648, 7649.

602 Casling, Dennis, and V.J. Scattergood. 'One Aspect of Stanza-Linking.' *Neuphilologische Mitteilungen* 75 (1974): 79–91.

Considers the disintegration of systems of stanza-linking, with examples that include some Harley lyrics and works of Laurence Minot. Casling and Scattergood use the linking pattern to counter the argument of Degginger, **330**, for altering the order of stanzas of 'A wayle whyt ase walles bon' [*105*], and suggest that the order of Harley 2253 is correct. Disruption of the system in 'An Old Man's Prayer' [*1216*] marks a change in emphasis and addressee. Minot uses breaks in the sequence of poems of Edward III's campaigns to emphasize changes in the subjects of his verse.

105, 585, 1216, 2149, 3796.

603 Colledge, Eric [Edmund]. 'A Middle English Christological Poem.' *Essays in Honour of Anton Charles Pegis.* Ed. J. Reginald O'Donnell. Toronto: Pontifical Institute of Mediaeval Studies, 1974. 248–61.

The description in *Brown XIV*, **31**, of 'I sayh hym wiþ fless al bi-sprad' [*1353*], in a sermon by John Sheppey, 'misunderstood the poet's intentions and sadly mutilated his work' (248). The poem's structure has been misinterpreted because the stanzas are 'in a form dictated by the quaternions which inspire it: the four points of the compass, Christ's four manifestations as bridegroom, knight, merchant and pilgrim, and the four riders' (249). Each image is extended after the caesura in long lines, which should be read across the page, rather than as stanzas in double columns. The verse continues the dialogue of the soul and Christ, begun in the preceding part of Sheppey's sermon, which is in Latin prose arranged in columns. Colledge relates *1353* to similar Latin and English compositions. He explores the use of images and symbols, particularly in *þe Wohunge of ure Lauerd*, Bernard's *Sermones de diversis* IV 1, *Quis est hic qui pulsat*, *Ancrene Wisse*, and the Apocalypse. The poet seems learned, familiar with Berengaudus's commentary on the Apocalypse, and a speaker and writer of a South-Eastern dialect, all consistent with what is known of Sheppey's life and work.

1353, 1749, 3238.

604 Dronke, Peter. 'Two Thirteenth-Century Religious Lyrics.' *Chaucer and Middle English Studies in Honour of Rossell Hope Robbins.* Ed. Beryl Rowland. London: Allen, 1974. 392–406 [cited.] Repr. in *The Medieval Poet and His World.* Peter Dronke. Storia e Letteratura Raccolta di Studi e Testi 164. Rome: Stori e Letteratura, 1984. 341–56.

A Latin and an English song show 'poets working towards a new mode of organizing lyrical poetry' (392), by linking form and content in echo and association. Dronke's close readings of the Latin lyric *Furibundi* and the ME 'Somer is comen & winter gon' [*3221*], explore complexities of stanza form and rhyme scheme. The ME lyric resembles the style of the Flemish Hadewijch, 'in her state of longing for divine love' (400), as well as 'all the religious poetry inspired by the Song of Songs' (401), and chivalric romance in allusions to Christ as knight. Its tone progresses to one of bitter satire, 'as dramatic as in *Furibundi*, where the soul identifies herself with the executioners' (401), and becomes frankly didactic in the concluding stanzas, which evoke Mary's sufferings and the image of 'Christ as the deer, slain and dismembered' (402). Imagery of the five wounds and the flow of blood and water stress 'the Christian paradox: the knight's heroic moment is his moment of utter weakness and helplessness.' The pattern of echoes and meaning is 'determined by the texture of the verse, by the play of word and sound' (403).

3221.

605   Evans, Robert. 'A Neglected Fourteenth-Century Religious Lyric.' *Studies in Medieval Culture* 4 (1974): 368–73.

Draws on Manning, **443**, in a close examination of 'How Christ Shall Come' ['I sayh hym wiþ fless al bi-sprad,' *1353*]. Evans discerns three voices: a 'passive and time-bound observer' in the first stanza; 'the divine agent' of the second stanza; and the 'grave, deliberate, impersonal, anonymous' (369) speaker of the monsyllabic second half-lines of the first stanza. These lines belong to earth and to heaven, and comment on the temporal events of stanza one, through the symbolic associations of East with birth and the Incarnation, West with death and the Crucifixion, South with Ecclesia, and North with Synagoga and the World. They look backwards and forwards, 'to completed events in Christ's earthly career, and . . . to the Second Coming,' to link the two stanzas. In first person statements, the speaker of the second stanza refers to the same events, characterizing himself in 'images of dominance and power: the husband taking his wife, the vigorous warrior defeating his enemy, the rich merchant who has ransomed all mankind,' and finally 'a simple pilgrim from an unknown land' (370), the latter in sharp contrast to medieval images of the powerful judge of the Second Coming. The poet reconciles all images and assumes 'no discontinuity in character between Christ . . . on earth and . . . in eternity,' finding 'in Christ the King and Judge those same qualities of love and sacrifice that distinguished him as the Son of Man' (379).

1353.

606   Friedman, Albert B. 'A Carol in Tradition.' *Chaucer and Middle English Studies in Honour of Rossell Hope Robbins*. Ed. Beryl Rowland. London: Allen, 1974. 298–302.

Summarizes opinion on the origin of carols, which are judged processional hymns by Robbins, **407**, and dance songs by Greene, **59**, and considers the significance of oral or written transmission of the texts. Friedman posits the conservative transmission of the folk carol 'as a result of its control by writing and print' (299), and examines the work recorded as 'We happie hirdes men heere' [*7576*] in the Shanne MS and as 'We happy hardmen here' in a Manx version. Comparisons reveal two differences that seem to be 'manuscript miscopying,' whereas others show 'the workings of oral transmission' (301), and seem corruptions.

7576.

607   ———. '"When Adam Delved . . .": Contexts of an Historic Proverb.' *The Learned and the Lewed: Studies in Chaucer and Medieval Literature*. Ed. Larry D. Benson. Harvard English Studies 5. Cambridge, MA: Harvard UP, 1974. 213–30

The proverb is first recorded in English, in a sermon delivered on 13 June 1381, by John Ball, 'a Kentish priest freed by a mob a few days before from prison in Maidstone,' and is noted in 'a recension of Thomas Walsingham's *Chronica Maiora* made sometime in the 1390s' (213). Ball used the proverb to refute the notion that 'the accident of birth should entitle any man to hold others in servitude' (224), but it was interpreted elsewhere to show that since 'all men have a common origin, to boast of one's lineage is arrogant and foolish' (219). Friedman traces the idea of descent from Adam and Eve, and the notion of formation of man from the soil. The couplet appears in many English works, and it (rather than a Latin form) seems the source for versions in vernaculars of northern

Europe. Bishop Brinton and friars such as the Dominican Bromyard preached the idea of common descent before Ball; they recommended acceptance of life on earth to attain happiness in Heaven. Stories of Eve's or Noah's children explain the ordering of the estates. Friedman's latest allusion is to William Morris's *A Dream of John Ball* (1886).

778, 1568, 2153, 2662, 3921, 3922.

608 Gellrich, Jesse M. 'The Parody of Medieval Music in the *Miller's Tale*.' *JEGP* 73 (1974): 176–88.

Examines the contribution of musical allusions to the 'pervasive tone of . . . comic irony' (177) in Chaucer's *Miller's Tale* [*4019*]. In particular, Gellrich notes the implications of Nicholas's singing *Angelus ad virginem*, and compares lines from the ME lyric 'Gabriel fram evene king' [*888*].

888.

609 Gibińska, Marta. 'The Early Middle English Lyrics as compared to the Provençal and Latin Lyrics.' *Kwartalnik Neofilologiszny* 21 (1974): 459–76.

Explores the influence of Latin and Provençal secular love lyrics on their ME counterparts, concentrating on poems of courtly love. Gibińska compares variations on the *reverdie* opening in the three languages, to find the English verse 'heavier' (465), with descriptions of nature that are closer to folk tradition than to the court. Poets in each language emphasize the lover's suffering and longing for his lady's mercy. Although some Provençal and Latin poets express the wish to possess her in sensual terms, ME verses may seem to be more modest, and to lack 'the artificial quality of many similar Provençal songs' (470). Descriptions seem more detailed in ME than in Provençal lyrics, where 'lovers had to keep their love secret in fear of scandalmongers' (471). English descriptions are more conventional than individual, and exclude the lady's psychological traits. Although Provençal poets use the theme of happy love, it is rarely found in ME works. Gibińska finds a pastourelle ['Als i me rod this endre dai,' *360*] and a *tenso* ['Somer is comen wiþ loue to toune,' *3222*] among ME lyrics, and implies that others correspond to the *canso*. She finds more similarities than differences in the poems, but believes that 'English poets showed a taste less sophisticated and less courtly than that of the continental writers' (476).

360, 515, 864, 1394, 1395, 1861, 1921, 2236, 3222, 3223, 4037.

610 Gray, Douglas. 'Notes on some Middle English Charms.' *Chaucer and Middle English Studies in Honour of Rossell Hope Robbins.* Ed. Beryl Rowland. London: Allen, 1974. 56–71.

ME charms, in prose and verse, were used for a range of medical conditions, for humans and animals, and to protect property. Gray explains their social setting and conditions needed for their effectiveness. He notes the derivations of some charms; two to stanch bleeding recall the arrest of the Jordan ['Crist that was in Bedelem born,' *624*] or Red Sea ['Stanche blood stanche blood,' *3209.5*]. 'As þou Lord dyddest stope and staye' [*412.5*] invokes 'three supernatural "stoppings" – God and the Red sea, Joshua and the sun and moon, Jesus and the tempest,' to stop thieves and keep them bound. Such passages are in many literary works, where the charms are shown as 'efficacious symbolic actions,' and 'their language, with its urgent and expressive rhetoric and rhythmical patterns, often seems both to imitate and instigate the magical action' (67). [Cf. Smallwood, **927**.]

412.5, 624, 1182, 1292, 2367, 3209.5, 3709, 3771, 3896, 3975, 7215, 7410.

611 Greene, Richard Leighton. 'A Carol of Anne Boleyn by Wyatt.' *Review of English Studies* NS 25 (1974): 437–9.

The burden, 'Grudge on who list, this is my lott:/Nothing to want if it ware not,' of a poem in carol form ['My yeris be yong even as ye see,' *2281.5*] begins with 'an unmistakable translation of the motto or device used by Anne Boleyn on her servants' liveries for a few months in 1530' (438). The speaker, a young woman, must represent Anne, although Greene proposes that Wyatt, not Anne, is the author. The refrain-phrase, 'If yt ware not,' implies the impediment of Henry VIII's marriage to Queen Catherine. 'The happiest that euer was,' in the second stanza could render 'La Plus Heureuse,' the motto worn by Anne's servants after her marriage. Thus the poem offers 'a striking example of the Tudor lyric which is not a general or fictitious and conventional love song, but which is connected with a real social situation' (439).

2281.5.

612 ———. 'Carols in Tudor Drama.' *Chaucer and Middle English Studies in Honour of Rossell Hope Robbins*. Ed. Beryl Rowland. London: Allen, 1974. 357–65.

Among songs in carol form traced in Tudor works is 'Back and side go bare' ['But yf that I maye have,' *554.5*]. This work is known 'almost universally . . . in the form in which it is sung to open the second act of *Gammer Gurton's Needle*' (364).

554.5.

613 Hallwas, John E. 'I am Iesu, that Cum to Fith.' *Explicator* 32.7 (1974): item 51.

'I am iesu þᵗ cum to fith' [*1274*] first identifies Christ as the lover-knight, who announces his intention to fight and shows 'the spiritual nature of the battle that He is asking to undertake.' The second part of the poem tells 'His reason for expecting to be victorious and asks for the beloved's cooperation in the fight,' when the remedy is grace, 'unto which each Christian must open his heart.' The letters that begin lines 1, 3, 5, and 7 form 'an acrostic which spells IESV,' to make the lyric itself 'a device to identify the speaker, the chivalric champion of the soul.'

1274.

614 ———. 'The Identity of the Speaker in "I am a fol, i can no god."' *Papers on Language and Literature* 10 (1974): 415–17.

Although 'Foolish Love,' (a translation of '*Amor fatuus*'), Furnivall's title for 'I am a fol i can no god' [*1269*], is 'not entirely inappropriate, it is misleading' (414). Hallwas prints the poem and identifies the speaker as Satan, rejecting the possibility that the king who had loved foolishly could be Edward II, in his involvement with Piers Gaveston. Hallwas's identification reveals the poem's meaning and nature as 'the only Middle English lyric that is a Satanic monologue' (417).

1269.

615 Hirsh, John C. 'A Middle English Metrical Version of *The Fifteen Oes* from Bodleian Library MS. Add. B. 66.' *Neuphilologische Mitteilungen* 75 (1974): 98–114. [Edition.]

This version, 'Ihesu crist godis sone of heuene' [*1672*], of the popular meditation has 'an introduction of twelve quatrains, a fifteen-part body of seventy-three, and an epilogue of six lines' (98). Hirsh prints it, with notes and punctuation. Striking similes and images add grotesque details to the account of the Passion; it juxtaposes Christ's majesty and humanity to enhance devotion. His last words serve 'to bridge the gap between the removed and suffering Christ and the devout reader who thus overhears Christ speak, and is so able to visualize his passion more clearly' (102).

1672, 2473.

616 Janofsky, Klaus. 'A View into the Grave: "A Disputacion betwyx þe Body and Wormes" in British Museum MS Add. 37049.' *Texas Arts and Industries University Studies* 7.1 (1974): 137–59.

First compares the 'Disputacion' ['In þe ceson of huge mortalitie,' *1563*] and Marvell's 'To his Coy Mistress.' Janofsky discerns resemblances in the devouring worms and the speakers' assertions of rightness, but differences in the worms' significance and purpose. The 'Disputacion' is a debate poem, and is related to debates of the body and soul. It differs from these in not explicitly alluding to the soul; in speaking of a particular body with her own personality; in ending 'with a serene, almost joyous outlook and expectation of the glorification of the body and eternal bliss' (140); and in its illustrations that imply the fifteenth-century double-tombs. Janofsky describes speech patterns and summarizes the arguments; he notes the central turning point and conclusion, in 'Christian reconciliation and harmony,' from which the worms' literal, allegorical, moral, and anagogical functions can be appreciated. The body and soul never seem to be separate entities; rather the body seems 'an image and . . . expression of a total and uniquely unified personality' (144). The illustrations reinforce the text's messages, but raise questions about 'style, date, provenance, inner relationships with other items in the entire manuscript, and relationship of the poem to contemporary 15th Century reality' (146). Of these matters, Janofsky deals only with implications of the English double-tomb, to suggest that a grave rather than such a tomb is depicted when the lady is shown lying above a decaying corpse, with the prefatory verses,'Take hede vnto my fygure here abowne' [*3252.5*]. Later illustrations represent events of the poem and the body's changing association with the worms. They assist understanding of the text, displaying confrontations and double aspects of 'Beauty and Decay, Glory and Humiliation, Greatness and Insignificance, Life and Death,' revealing 'the elegance and worldly splendor of an individual's [past] existence . . . and the grossness of the flesh revealed in death' (151). Janofsky explains the paradox of *dignitas non moritur*, and relates it to the double-tombs and some funeral processions. The tombs and inscriptions demonstrate medieval characteristics that include 'curiosity, self-detachment, even humor, which permits the individual to see himself or herself both as alive and dead, attractive and repulsive, grossly disfigured and gloriously transfigured' (153). The 'Disputacion' resolves the tension of life and death, whereas the tombs extend it in their messages. In an appendix (158–9), Janofsky discusses lines missing in the manuscript and their effects. [See Malvern, **782**.]

1563, 3252.5.

617 Lasater, Alice E. *Spain to England: A Comparative Study of Arabic, European, and English Literature of the Middle Ages.* Jackson, MS: UP of Mississippi, 1974.

In her study of the literature of the period, Lasater considers the Provençal and French influences seen in ME lyrics, particularly noting verse forms and rhyme schemes.

359, 515, 1395, 1463.

618 Ogilvie-Thomson, S. 'Some Unpublished Verses in Lambeth Palace MS. 559.' *Review of English Studies* NS 25 (1974): 385–95. [Edition.]

Counters Robbins's contention [*IMEV*] that the text beginning 'O god swete lord ihū crist that madest me' [*2451*] is one composite work, and proposes 'six separate items' (385). Ogilvie-Thomson prints these with versions from other manuscripts. Richard de

Caistre's hymn 'Ihesu lord that madist me' [*1727*] is the source of poem I, which she compares with entries in Stonyhurst College XLIII, and Sidney Sussex 80. Poem II is an 'attempt at improvisation . . . on a well-known Latin hymn, "Criste qui lux es et dies" ' (387), compared with the version, 'Cryst þat art [boþe d]ay & lyht'[*615*] in Egerton 3245. Poem III, 'Fader and sun and hali gast' [*780*], addresses the three persons of the Trinity; elsewhere it is not connected with the two poems preceding it in Lambeth 559. Ogilvie-Thomson compares IV, 'Almyghty god fadir of heuene' [*241*], and V, 'Mary of help both day and nyght' [*2121*], with Longleat 29, to show differences from Robbins's description of the Lambeth text. She detects 'signs of a more Northerly provenance' in *2121*, although Lambeth 559 and Longleat 29 are not Northern manuscripts, and finds signs in Lambeth 559 of 'a Southern scribe's misunderstanding' (393). The last lines of VI, 'Emperasse of helle, heven quene' [*7128*], resemble some versions of 'Mary moder well thou be' [*2119*], but Ogilvie-Thomson considers it unique; she prints it in quatrains. Thus the Lambeth text seems 'a devoted transcription of some rough workings, made by a scribe . . . unable to realize that he was in fact copying not a single finished poem, but creative work on six' (395).

241, 615, 775, 1727, 2119, 2121, 2451, 7128.

619 Porter, Peter, and Anthony Thwaite, eds. *The English Poets from Chaucer to Edward Thomas.* London: Secker, 1974.

In 'Anonymous Medieval Lyrics' (17–28) Porter comments on the language and tone of the lyrics, to show the sophistication of poets of the era, who 'valued technical skill with words and ideas,' and 'relished jokes and games with language' (18). He offers illustrations from a range of poems, including some Border ballads. Thwaite, in 'John Skelton (*c*. 1460–1529)' (29–41), relates Skelton's work to the context of his times, and discusses his influence on other poets.

223.5, 497, 729.5, 1132, 1299, 2037.5, 2263.5, 2756.5, 3265.5, 3899.3, 3998, 7605.

620 Scattergood, V.J. 'Revision in some Middle English Political Verses.' *Archiv* 211 (1974): 287–99.

Textual variations that result from deliberate revision rather than unintentional error may be clearly discerned in some political verses, since these works 'usually refer to precise and recognizable contexts and usually embody firm attitudes' (287). Scattergood compares differences produced by alterations to produce different emphasis; adjustments to take account of recent events; omissions; and additions which may make the tone of the poem more or less favourable than other versions. Revision is sometimes extensive, as in 'The Abuses of the Age' ['*Len puet fere et defere,*'*1857*]. Two versions of 'The Lament of the Duchess of Gloucester' ['Thorow owt a pales as I can passe,' *3720*] show a difference in tone. When political verse deals with controversial topics, it may provoke 'violent feelings in a prospective copyist' (299).

841, 921, 1555, 1857, 2192, 3491, 3558.5, 3720.

621 Shannon, Ann. 'The Meaning of *Grein* in "Wynter wakeneþ al my care." ' *Philological Quarterly* 53 (1974): 425–7.

There is a contradiction implied in reading *grein* as 'seed,' since 'one does not plant green seeds, but ripe, dry ones' (425). Shannon summarizes and discusses the emendation of this word in 'Wynter wakeneþ al my care' [*4177*] in *BrownXIV*, **48**, (by reference to John 12: 24–5), and in comments of Speirs, **385**, and Reed, **159**. She proposes 'a homonym of *grein* "seed," a relatively rare word derived from Old Norse, with a variety of specific senses, one of which is "a cutting of a tree" ' (426). This accords with *graven* 'to plant,' and provides 'a visible *grein*, a cutting which is green when one plants it, but soon fades, withers, and dies' (427). This is fitting in a poem of mortality.

4177.

622 Spears, James E. 'The "Boar's Head Carol" and Folk Tradition.' *Folklore* 85 (1974): 194–8.

The 'Boar's Head Carol' ['The boris hed in hondes I brynge,' *3313*] recalls Germanic legends and customs connected with Freyr and Freya, their boars, and the sacrifice of a boar to Freyr, to ask him 'to show favor to the new year' (196). The boar's head in AS literature is a protective symbol; the boar hunt and Christmas festivities appear in *Sir Gawain and the Green Knight* [*3144*]. The roots of the tradition are 'deep and unbroken in the folk cultures of England, Sweden, and Denmark' (197). It persists in the United States 'as a part of its inherited folk culture' (198).

3144, 3313.

623 Stemmler, Theo. 'An Interpretation of *Alysoun*.' *Chaucer and Middle English Studies in Honour of Rossell Hope Robbins.* Ed. Beryl Rowland. London: Allen, 1974. 111–18.

'Alysoun' [*515*] has often been published and enjoyed, but for 'aesthetic properties which so far have never been precisely analysed.' Stemmler aims 'to replace uncritical opinion by reasoned judgement' (111). He discusses the rhyme scheme, spring opening, and metrical and thematic structure; compares 'Alysoun' with other lyrics; and notes that the name continues the tradition of Aëliz in French popular carols and is used by Chaucer. The description of the beloved follows the conventional head to foot style, but has unconventional details, such as colour of eyes and eyebrows. Alliteration emphasizes the symptoms of love-sickness. Thus 'conventions of the Continental courtly love-lyric are modified by means of native literary techniques' and anglicized, with 'complete mastery of rhyme, metre and structure,' to effect '"simple complexity" . . . the reason why *Alysoun* has always been appreciated, but rarely understood' (116).

360, 515, 2207.

624 ———. 'Textologische Probleme mittelenglischen Dichtung.' *Mannheimer Berichte aus Forschung und Lehre* 8 (1974): 245–8.

Not seen.

625 Travis, James. 'The Celtic Derivation of *Somer is Icumen In*.' *Lochlann* 6 (1974): 128–35.

Adds to comments on Celtic characteristics of the music of the Reading Rota, 'Svmer is icumen in' [*3223*], by examining the words, in which Travis finds resemblances to OIr and medieval Welsh verses. Since the themes of the advent of summer and the cuckoo are also found in the verse of France, Italy, and Germany, the lyric, 'far from being unique thematically, represents a genre' (129). The music is in the Welsh style, 'in as many parts as there are voices' (130), but the Rota suggests a note-for-syllable relation. This cannot be maintained with the Latin or ME texts, and the scribe has altered the music to fit. The unworkable result shows that he did not understand the system, and copied rather than composed the music. Travis analyses the words and their relation to the music. He concludes that the song translates a Celtic lyric, which was originally in Welsh or Irish, and that the music is 'an example of medieval Welsh part singing' (134). This suggests that the translator was 'a bilingual Celt,' who conveyed 'not merely the substance of the lyric but its versecraft' (134–5), and no doubt also the music; however 'an English monastic' must have 'perpetrated the mutilation of this music' (135).

3223.

626 Turville-Petre, Thorlac. '"Summer Sunday", "De Tribus Regibus Mortuis", and "The Awntyrs off Arthure": Three Poems in the Thirteen-Line Stanza.' *Review of English Studies* NS 25 (1974): 1–14.

The thirteen-line stanza was the most popular among medieval alliterative poets. Turville-Petre supplies examples of it and similar stanzas, before discussing three poems which have in common 'a description of a hunting expedition which introduces, in a delicately oblique fashion, a vision in which the protagonist is confronted by a personification of death or mutability' (3). He describes the hunting scene and vision of Lady Fortune in 'Somer Soneday' [*3838*], and reviews discussion of the poem's date and the possibility that it refers to Edward II, as suggested by Brown, **160**, and Robbins, **57**. Although 'De Tribus Regibus Mortuis' [*2677*] is found in John Audelay's collection, it differs in 'rhyme scheme, regularity of alliteration, and, most significantly, imaginative power and technical skill,' making it 'safe to say that it is not by the author of the other poems' (7). It is an English version of the 'Three Living and Three Dead' theme. Turville-Petre also considers 'the meeting of Guenevere and Gawain with the ghost of Guenevere's mother' from 'The Awntyrs of Arthure' [*1566*]. The latter poems resemble each other in theme and style, but similarities in the first two are less striking, although they offer 'the only two examples in the *O.E.D.* of the word *wheelwright* to refer to one who *turns* a wheel rather than one who makes a wheel' (12). Similarities reveal that a 'school' of poets expressed similar themes in the stanza. An appendix (12–14) lists 'English Poems of the Fourteenth Century,' 'Poems in John Audelay's Manuscript,' 'Drama,' and 'Scottish Poetry of the Fifteenth and Sixteenth Centuries' that use the thirteen-line stanza. [See also Smallwood, **599**.]

1453, 1566, 1899, 1974, 2481, 2677, 2718, 3415, 3553, 3838.

627 Wenzel, Siegfried. 'The Moor Maiden – A Contemporary View.' *Speculum* 49 (1974): 69–74.

After a brief survey of the 'forest of ingenious and often very speculative interpretations' of the lyric of the Moor Maiden, 'Maiden in the mor lay' [*2037.5*], Wenzel introduces 'a small ray of light . . . a fact that might tell us what a *medieval* witness thought of the poem' (70). There is an allusion in a sermon on 'the moral deterioration of mankind through its history' (70), found in MS F.126 of Worcester Cathedral Library. Here the maid is said to lie 'be wode' rather than 'in the mor,' and the lyric is called a *karole*, which implies a secular song, probably for dancing. The structure of the sermon echoes the song, and hints that the preacher 'took the entire lyric to be about man's primitive state' (73). The maiden is not specifically identified, but she seems likely to be 'a figure of medieval folk-belief, perhaps some woodland or water sprite or *fée*' (74).

2037.5.

628 ———. 'The English Verses in the *Fasciculus Morum*.' *Chaucer and Middle English Studies in Honour of Rossell Hope Robbins*. Ed. Beryl Rowland. London: Allen, 1974. 230–48.

The *Fasciculus Morum* includes many ME verses among 'homiletic material, *exempla*, similes, and *narrationes*' (230), which Wenzel relates to their Latin context. He finds four types: some 'translate the preceding Latin passage'; some are suggested by it; of those 'neither translated nor suggested' (231), some are dispensable, others integral; he supplies examples of each type, noting the relation of each to its context. He compares manuscripts that contain ME items with others that have none, in particular Madrid University Library, Faculty of Law 116^{20}.3, which was 'perhaps copied by a Spanish or Portuguese scribe,' and Pierpont Morgan Library, Morgan 298, 'made by a German Franciscan, Friar Johannes Sintram of Würzburg, who copied the *Fasciculus* at Oxford about 1412' and 'frequently made his own German verse translations of corresponding Latin pieces' (237). The importance of the ME verses is 'not that these items are in English, but that they are in verse,' to lend rhetorical and mnemonic force. Of the verses, some were current, 'while others were made up by the author *ad hoc*' (242). Favourite topics include *memento mori*, the lament of Christ on the Cross, love, and Fortune. Wenzel classifies some English items as 'message verses.' Of the 'strongly proverbial' (243) verses, some are attributed to 'Hendyng,' to imply authority. The compositions suggest 'verbal facility, moral stance, and ready wit' (244). [See also **663**.]

142, 1204, 1321, 1935, 2001, 2002, 2058, 2077, 2283, 2298, 2329, 3282, 3287, 3339, 3408, 3716, 3792.5, 3802, 4020.6, 4143, 4151, 4156.

629 ———. 'Unrecorded Middle-English Verses.' *Anglia* 92 (1974): 55–78. [Edition.]

A handlist of 97 verses, 'either not recorded in *The Index of Middle English Verse* or its *Supplement*, or . . . found in additional manuscripts not yet listed.' Most of these are 'pious pieces of two or four lines used by medieval preachers' (55); 'versified prayers . . . and several translations of liturgical pieces'; together with 'scribal verses' and 'quotations from or allusions to English songs.' Although many have no 'aesthetic splendor,' and reveal little 'about the nature of late medieval poetry' (56), they add to knowledge of the composition and spread of preachers' tags, many of which are directly translated from Latin verses. Wenzel prints the verses in alphabetical order, in the version of the first manuscript listed, and refers to alternative versions.

14, 86.3, 221, 427.5, 541.8, 593.5, 735.3, 811, 830, 834, 847, 994, 1089, 1119, 1140, 1273.5, 1304, 1332, 1422, 1436.5, 1502, 1551, 1975, 1977, 2037.5, 2074, 2078, 2238.5, 2256, 2289.3, 2740, 2817, 2833, 2835, 3081, 3167.3, 3306, 3311, 3322.3, 3397, 3398, 3403, 3405, 3433, 3568.5, 3600, 3640, 3641, 3897.5, 3900.5, 3907, 4020.6, 4033, 4094.8, 7017, 7056, 7059, 7062, 7073, 7077, 7108, 7112, 7113, 7127, 7130, 7147, 7156, 7189, 7206, 7210, 7211, 7219, 7223, 7269, 7289, 7290, 7293, 7296, 7316, 7325, 7351, 7356, 7357, 7364, 7377, 7381, 7382, 7387, 7402, 7408, 7417, 7418, 7452, 7456, 7474, 7476, 7491, 7504, 7505, 7510, 7520, 7532, 7538, 7541, 7542, 7547, 7553, 7561, 7562, 7563, 7567, 7577, 7590, 7592, 7596, 7602, 7613, 7615, 7620, 7623, 7635, 7636, 7639.

630 **Barratt, Alexandra.** 'The Prymer and its Influence on Fifteenth-Century English Passion Lyrics.' *Medium Ævum* 44 (1975): 264–79.

Prymers were popular with the literate laity, as sources of the Passion narrative and offices such as the Hours of the Virgin, the Passion, and the Compassion. They affected the composition of lyrics on the Passion, which were acquiring 'a markedly more intellectual and theological nature than before,' because 'the ability to read had become relatively common among the middle-class laity' (264). Barratt describes the prymers and their contents, and relates them to various lyrics. Thus she reveals resemblances, including those to such images as the *Imago pietatis*, and to themes that include the Five Wounds of Christ and the Seven Words from the Cross. She compares lyrics on these themes by Lydgate, Audelay, Ryman, and others, and traces the treatment of a prayer on the Seven Words and seven deadly sins (attributed to Bede) by Audelay ['O Ihū crist hongyng on cros,' *2468*], and by an anonymous poet ['O lord God O Ihū Crist,' *2486*].

497, 550, 623, 644, 1011, 1125, 1318, 1739, 1787, 2081, 2468, 2486, 2504, 3499, 3904, 4023.

631 Bornstein, Diane. *Mirrors of Courtesy.* Hamden, CT: Archon-Shoe String, 1975.

In her survey of the ideals and customs of chivalry and courtesy, Bornstein refers to John Russell's 'Boke of Kervyng & Nortur' [*1514*]. This manual is set in 'the narrative framework inherited from Chaucer's *Book of the Duchess* [*1306*] and many a French *chanson d'aventure*' (74).

1514.

632 Bradley, S.A.J. 'An Incompletely Noted Variant of the Middle English Lyric "Faith is above Reason" (Index 4181).' *Notes and Queries* 220 (1975): 341–3. [Edition.]

Copenhagen Royal Library MS Thott 4° 110 has four ME lyrics. Bradley corrects inconsistent entries in *IMEV* and *SIMEV* which offer another source for 'Worship wymmen wyne and vnweldy age' [*4230*] and 'Y shall say what ynordynat loue ys' [*1359*], and notes the relationship of *4230* to 'þer ben foure thinges causing gret folye' [*3521*] and 'þer beoþe foure things þat makeþ man a fool' [*3523*]. 'Witt hath wunder that reson ne telle can' [*4181*] is attributed to Reginald Pecock; Thott 110 associates a variant with Nicholas Barkley, the owner of the manuscript, by whom it may have been 'written down, if not actually composed' (342). The poem deals with reason, mysteries, and paradoxes of faith with 'its own pleasing logic and wit,' (343).

1359, 3521, 3523, 4181, 4230.

633 Crowther, J.D.W. ' "The Bargain of Judas." ' *English Language Notes* 13 (1975–6): 245–9.

Describing 'Judas' [*1649*] as 'a masterpiece of ironies' (246), Crowther explores the ironies inherent in Christ's insistence that Judas should go to Jerusalem, and his foreknowledge of all that would occur. The bargain with Pilate establishes 'the kinship of Judas, his mistress, and Pilate: all three are traders in bodies' (247). Christ's 'bartered body becomes the "mete" and promise of the redemption' (248); his divine knowledge prompts the human reaction expressed in his words to Judas and Peter. The poem's power comes from 'the ironic balancing of Christ's human nature against his divine one,' exploiting 'the inextricable tangle of Christ's two natures, and with remarkable economy . . . the tragedy and triumph of Christ's love' (249).

1649.

634 Davidson, Clifford. 'The Love Mythos in the Middle Ages and Renaissance.' *Ball State University Forum* 16 (1975): 3–14.

To establish a love mythos, Davidson examines the notions of courtly love advanced by twentieth-century critics, and compares evidence for ideas and expression of love in poems of the Middle Ages and Renaissance. Men's experience of love is recorded in ways influenced by troubadours and in traditions such as women's songs. Love is 'a way to woe and despair' (6), but also an ennobling and religious experience, as illustrated by Dante, Cavalcanti, Sidney, and Chaucer. It is parodied in the *Lover's Mass* ['Wyth all myn Hool Herte entere,' *4186*] and 'The X Commaundementes of Love' ['Certes fer extendeth my Reason,' *590*]. The initiate's ordeal offers other parallels. Davidson presents a Jungian explanation of the lover's individual and shared experiences, illustrated in medieval lyrics and Wyatt's poems. The lover finds earthly joy in worship of his lady, but often bears the pain of separation. Love may be sanctified and be 'an initiation into life itself' (14).

146, 515, 590, 752, 1240, 2092, 2188, 2207, 2517, 3291, 3785, 4186, 4194.

635 Edwards, A.S.G., and J. Hedley. 'John Stowe, *The Craft of Lovers* and T.C.C. R.3.19.' *Studies in Bibliography* 28 (1975): 265–8.

Comparison of manuscript variations establishes that John Stowe used Trinity College, Cambridge R.3.19 for his edition of 'The Craft of Lovers' ['To moralise ⟨a similitude⟩ who list these ballets sewe,' *3761*]. Stowe's edition has a significant unique reading in line 159 ['CCCCxl & viii yere folowyng']. Here, in a reference to the date 1449, 'CCCC' has been altered to 'CCC,' to fit the note in the margin: 'Chaucer died . 1400.' Stowe based his edition on this manuscript, with 'a few readings from either the Additional [34360] or Harley [2251] manuscripts' (267). The other black letter edition of the poem, Speght's, is based on Stowe's, with a few variants that seem 'reasonable conjectural restorations' (268).

3761.

636 Heffernan, Thomas J. 'A Middle English Poem on Lovedays.' *Chaucer Review* 10 (1975–6): 172–85. [Edition.]

The poem 'And þerfor ȝe lordingis þᵗ louedays wile holde' [*312*], in Latin and English, sets out 'duties of arbitrators and litigants who take part in lovedays' (172). Heffernan describes and lists the contents of Cambridge University Library MS Dd.1.1, with notes on palaeography and language. He traces comments on *loveday* and meanings assigned to the term, by John Webster Spargo [*Speculum* 15 (1940): 36–56] and Bennett, **386**, and concludes that it was an amicable way of settling cases out of court, but no longer efficacious in the late fourteenth century, when it 'had become a burlesque' (175). Early in the fifteenth century public officials were not permitted to be arbiters. The corruption of umpires is condemned by Langland in *Piers Plowman* [*1459*] and satirized by Chaucer through Friar Huberd in the *Canterbury Tales* [*4019*]. Heffernan prints the poem, commenting on its structure and its account of 'the abuses to which the practice of loveday making was susceptible in late fourteenth-century England' (176).

312, 1459, 4019.

637 Hill, Thomas D. 'Parody and Theme in the Middle English "Land of Cockaygne."' *Notes and Queries* 220 (1975): 55–9.

Explores the juxtaposition of the order expected in the earthly lives of the cloistered monks and nuns and the 'radically disordered life in a paradise of sensual delight' (56) described in the 'Land of Cockaygne' ['Fur in see bi west Spaygne,' *762*]. Hill notes the significance of themes of Enoch and Elias, the joys of heaven, flying to God, and the image of the river of milk.

762.

638 Jeffrey, David L. 'Franciscan Spirituality and the Rise of Early English Drama.' *Mosaic* 8 (1975): 17–46.

Examines the involvement with ME drama in the Franciscans' use of popular culture, suggesting that some plays developed from semi-dramatic sermons delivered by the Franciscans. Italian preaching manuscripts which preserve these sermons resemble 'those English homiletical collections in which we find the majority of Middle English lyrics of the dramatic type' (28). Jeffrey illustrates the account of dramatic performances with examples of sermon lyrics, verse sermons and the play *Cayphas*, and instances of association with the Franciscans within several other plays. He suggests a closer connection of the 'vigorous vernacular homiletical tradition' of the Friars Minor to ME religious drama than to that of 'Latin liturgical drama with which it has been so long associated' (46).

180, 1405, 2663, 3211, 7442.

639 ———. *The Early English Lyric and Franciscan Spirituality*. Lincoln, NE: U of Nebraska P, 1975.

Explains the spiritual context of Franciscans' contributions to ME lyrics, and details their use of lyrics and tags. The early chapters, 'Introduction: An Abbreviated History of Approaches' (1–11), 'Spiritual Revolution and Popular Poetry' (12–42), 'Franciscan Spirituality' (43–82), 'Aesthetics and Spirituality' (83–117), and 'The Earliest Lyrics in Italy' (118–68) supply this background to '*Ioculatores Dei* in England' (169–230) and 'Spirituality and Style in the Early English Lyric' (231–68). Appendices deal with 'The *Lamentatio Beate Virginis de Cruce* of Ubertino da Casale' (269–71), 'Music from a Franciscan Sermon Manuscript' (272), and 'The Franciscans after 1350' (273–5). Jeffrey examines the order's preaching methods and handling of secular material, particularly considering influences of St Francis; Peter Waldes or Waldo and the Waldensians; Richard de Ledrede, who compiled the Red Book of Ossory; St Bernardino of Siena; and St Bonaventure. Sources of lyrics include sermons such as John Grimestone's, the *Fasciculus Morum*, and carols of James Ryman. Themes include repentance and contrition, the Nativity and Passion, and identification with Christ and the Virgin; their expression involves emotion, mysticism, and urgency. Jeffrey finds the Francisans' contribution considerable, and proposes that the ME lyric is 'essentially, a Franciscan song' (261). Many lyrics formerly thought secular should be reconsidered to assess their religious content.

29, 66, 110, 117, 162, 282, 283, 293, 352, 398, 433, 434, 441, 445, 498, 613, 621, 641, 660, 670, 678, 695, 776, 796, 798, 815, 888, 940, 968, 1002, 1066, 1074, 1091, 1111, 1125, 1129, 1132, 1143, 1150, 1204, 1216, 1272, 1352, 1353, 1365, 1402, 1407, 1422, 1443, 1461, 1491, 1577, 1684, 1698, 1705, 1775, 1777, 1818, 1822, 1847, 1861, 1902, 1921, 1935, 1943, 1975, 1978, 2001, 2002, 2009, 2012, 2017, 2022, 2025, 2047, 2066, 2070, 2073, 2080, 2087, 2107, 2114, 2128.5, 2155, 2163, 2164, 2166, 2236, 2240, 2241, 2293, 2320, 2340, 2359, 2405, 2476, 2506, 2535, 2543, 2604, 2645, 2684, 2687, 2988, 3072, 3081, 3133, 3135, 3147, 3211, 3222, 3223, 3230, 3233, 3236, 3254, 3272.5, 3275, 3304, 3310, 3339, 3350, 3366, 3405, 3408, 3517, 3583, 3596, 3607, 3684, 3696, 3727.5, 3825, 3906, 3963, 3965, 3967, 4035, 4037, 4141, 4143, 4144, 4151, 4160, 4162, 4177, 4200, 4211, 4223, 4225.5, 4239, 4263.

——— Review by Caroline W. Bynum, *Medievalia et Humanistica* NS 7 (1976): 195–7. Discerns some confusion, which lends 'a disturbing circularity in his argument,' when Jeffrey needs to deal with ambiguity in the phrase 'Franciscan spirituality,' and its potential to mean '(a) religious attitudes that are Franciscan or (b) religious attitudes that are uniquely Franciscan' (195). This leads to further confusion about 'quite how much he has proved' (196) of the Franciscan origin of the ME lyric, although he establishes 'that Franciscan friars played the major role in the development of the earliest vernacular lyric in England, and in the course of the argument he provides many convincing and lovely analyses of medieval poems' (197) in a good book.
——— Review by Edward Wilson, *Review of English Studies* NS 28 (1977): 318–21. Records a number of inaccuracies in transcriptions and references, and '[f]aults of omisssion' that are 'equally serious' (320). Wilson 'sees no profit in discussing the speculations which Mr. Jeffrey has based upon' his presentation and understanding of primary sources, and judges the book 'thoroughly shoddy' (321).

640 Kiernan, Kevin S. 'The Art of the Descending Catalogue, and a Fresh Look at Alisoun.' *Chaucer Review* 10 (1975): 1–16.

Geoffroi de Vinsauf prescribed the medieval convention for description of a beautiful woman, which should begin 'at the top of the head and descend to the toe' (1). Violation and manipulation of the conventional expectations achieve startling effects. Kiernan offers many examples of variations of the convention in ME lyrics, before he proceeds to the celebrated description of Alison in the *Miller's Tale*. He shows the annoying effect of overamplification in 'A Catalogue of Delights' ['With wooful hert & gret mornyng,' *4209*] and the more discriminating use of convention in 'Blow, Northerne Wynd' [*1395*] and 'Alysoun' [*515*]. Other works show the descending catalogue and its variations, including humorous consequences of unexpected descriptions. The results involve the initiated audiences in the poets' acts of creation.

515, 1010, 1395, 1452, 1888, 1916, 2232, 2421, 2437, 2640, 2662, 3203, 3327, 3465, 3832, 4019, 4209.

641 **Meier-Ewart, C.** 'The Anglo-Norman Origin of *Thou Wommon Boute Uere*.' *Anglia* 93 (1975): 424–8.

Shows the similarities between William Herebert's 'þou wommon boute vere' [*3700*] and two AN works, 'Le mel de ceel,' attributed to Bozon, and 'Douce dame pie mere,' both found in BL MS Add. 46919, with Herebert's poems. Meier-Ewart prints the corresponding sections of the poems, to reveal the source of paradoxes explored by Herebert, in 'Le mel de ceel,' and the figure of the charter of Christ, in 'Douce dame pie mere.'

3700.

642 **Peck, Russell.** 'Public Dreams and Private Myths: Perspective in Middle English Literature.' *PMLA* 90 (1975): 461–8.

Examines the effect of perspective on medieval notions of experience by comparing medieval and modern art forms, and recording similarities and differences. Peck considers private and public myths and dreams and effects of their juxtaposition. 'Wel and wa sal ys hornes blaw' [*3857.5*] demonstrates 'the shock – the tension or thrill – of a medieval poem . . . in the bursting of this barrier between private dream and public dream' (462), by evoking the summons to Judgement in the question about the dead bugler. He cites changes in perspective and perception in Chaucer's *Miller's Tale* and *Second Nun's Tale* [*4019*], and compares the imagist poems, 'Spring and All,' by William Carlos Williams and 'Merie singen þe munaches binnen Ely' [*2164*], to discuss implications of the images. Peck relates medieval ideas of cosmology, as expressed by Augustine, Anselm, and Bonaventure, and in the notion of the world as a riddle, and supplies four interpretations of the poem 'Erthe upon Erthe' [*3939*]. Thus he indicates 'something of the range of response we might expect from a medieval "reader"' (465) and the need for 'a peculiarly medieval perspective on time and space.' Medieval perspective is both spacious and intimate. It reveals a mind that 'knows where it is' and 'understands words and knows how to use metaphor' (466), as in the 'Corpus Christi Carol' [*1132*] and in the changing perceptions of 'Nou goth þe sonne under wode' [*2320*]. Peck's last example is from Chaucer's 'Words unto Adam' [*120*]. He concludes that medieval literature deals with myth in its concern with the mind's journey to a sense 'large enough to hold both our public and private dreams within a single purview' (467).

120, 1132, 2164, 2320, 3857.5, 3939, 4019.

643 **Perényi, Erzsébet.** 'The Growth of Medieval English Lyrics: An Analysis of the Secular Pieces of the Harley Collection.' *Studies in English and American*. Vol. 2. Ed. Erzébet Perényi and Tibor Frank. Rev. László Báti and Ian David Hays. Budapest: Department of English, L. Eötvös U., 1975.

Not seen.

644 **Plummer, John F., III.** 'The Poetic Function of Conventional Language in the Middle English Lyric.' *Studies in Philology* 72 (1975): 367–85.

ME lyrics recall songs of troubadours and trouvères in conventional phrases, to effect 'an alteration of the way in which the language of the lyrics carries meaning, or it signifies' (371). Plummer offers examples of clichés, and draws analogies with the writings of Dante on song tradition. The phrases reduce 'the ambiguous to the specific' (374); the conventional phrase is the 'smallest form in the lyric which is satisfyingly significant' (374–5), that is 'a sign token' (375). He briefly illustrates conventional descriptions of the lady's eyebrows, the lover's sorrow, and the bringing of bliss. In a detailed analysis of 'Alysoun' [*515*], he demonstrates symmetry in verbal and stress patterns, rhyme scheme, and topic, in the structure of *pedes, caudae*, and refrain; the pattern of distribution of *ich*; and themes of Spring, Love Service, Joy of Love, and Beauty, relating the thematic analysis to the occurrence of themes of spring and beauty in other lyrics. After noting the conventions of the *Natureingang* and envoy, he concludes that the conventional phrases, 'a stylistic resource' (380), are 'the key source of the formal artistry of the lyric' (385).

105, 360, 515, 521, 864, 1010, 1394, 1395, 1504, 1768, 1861, 2207, 2236, 4037, 4194.

645 Scattergood, V.J. '"Wynter Wakeneth Al My Care . . ." Lines 11–15.' *English Philological Studies* 14 (1975): 59–64.

Lines 11–15 of 'Wynter wakeneþ al my care' [*4177*] have attracted critical comment. Scattergood refers in particular to *BrownXIV* **48**, Reed, **159**, Manning, **443**, and Kenneth and Celia Sisam, **69**, most of whom see an allusion to the decay of life in winter. Linguistic evidence is too ambiguous for a definitive reading, but the poem works 'on a literal level if "Al þat gren me graueþ grene" is taken as a reference to planting winter corn.' It is 'plainly about transitoriness and death' (62), and such poems often concern 'speculations about resurrection' (63). The implications of the poet's hopes for a good harvest from his winter corn and resurrection of his soul suggest that '*gren* should be read as "grain" or "seed" and *graueþ* as "plants" or "buries"' (64).

66, 579, 695, 1115, 1459, 3996, 4177.

646 Stanley, E.G. 'Richard Hyrd (?), "Rote of Resoun Ryht" in MS. Harley 2253.' *Notes and Queries* 220 (1975): 155–7, 413.

Notes that the pun in 'Annot and John' [*1394*], revealing the name of the poet's mistress, cited in *Brown XIII*, **36**, had been observed by Humfrey Wanley (*A Catalogue of the Harleian Collection of Manuscripts . . . in the British Museum*, London 1759, II, sig. [4C2ro/b]). Stanley finds a similar identification in 'Weping haueþ myn wonges wet' [*3874*], and proposes that *hyrd* in the sixth stanza may suggest that the name of Richard is '*Hyrd*, or *le Hyrd*, or *Hird*, or *Herd*, or *Hurd*, without or with final *e*' (157). Stanley comments further in a reply to Revard's suggestion that *hyrt* in line 2 of the Harley poem, 'Ne mai no lewed libben in londe' ['A Satire on the Consistory Courts, *2287*] 'has the same sense' as in *3874*, but is not convinced by Revard, since 'the word comes again (line 56) unambiguously as "court of law"' (413).

1394, 3874.

647 Stemmler, Theo. 'More English Texts from MS. Cambridge University Library Ii.III.8.' *Anglia* 93 (1975): 1–16. [Edition.]

Augments Erb, **564**, by noting misreadings and adding 'an edition of the 49 English texts not discovered or published by Erb' (1). Twenty-five of the sermon lyrics are not noted in *IMEV* or *SIMEV*.

103.5, 197.5, 445, 853.8, 873.5, 1009, 1265.5, 1301, 1311, 1478, 1611, 2077.5, 2602.6, 2811.8, 3246.5, 3292, 3293, 3302, 3690, 3699, 3803, 3901, 4020.6, 4263,

7012, 7023, 7044, 7045, 7058, 7068, 7095, 7103, 7116, 7118, 7131, 7239, 7262, 7330, 7336, 7347, 7348, 7354, 7427, 7431, 7450, 7452, 7480, 7486, 7490, 7512, 7627, 7628.

648 Borroff, Marie. '"It Wern Fowre Letterys of Purposy": A New Interpretation.' *Notes and Queries* 221 (1976): 294–5.

Instead of reading *purposy* as a nonce form of 'purpose,' in 'It wern fowre letterys of purposy' [*1650*], Borroff proposes to interpret it as 'two words, *pur*, i.e. "pure", and *posy*, the latter being used in two obsolete meanings, "poesy" and "emblem"'' (294). Thus the line praises 'the letters of Mary's name as "pure poesy", a poem of joy,' and alludes to 'the treatment of the name in the carol as an emblem or "posy"'' (295). This suggests another, earlier citation for *posy* in *OED*.

1650.

649 Dronke, Peter. 'Learned Lyric and Popular Ballad in the Early Middle Ages.' *Studi Medievali* 3rd Series 17 (1976): 1–40 [cited.] Repr. in *The Medieval Poet and his World*. Peter Dronke. Rome: Storia e Letteratura, 1984. 167–207.

Investigates 'some of the oldest evidence for ballads and related songs in medieval Europe,' in 'direct and indirect testimonies for one characteristic European ballad theme' (1), the return of the ghost of a dead lover. Dronke takes examples from the Song of Songs, and from Latin, Scots, German, Hungarian, Danish, Norse, Irish, Greek, French, and English works, to show the recurrence of motifs in a range of lyrics, songs, lays, and ballads. These include moonlight, the crowing of the cock, and the longings to lie with the ghost and take revenge for the lover's death. A ballad recorded in Birmingham, in 1953, incorporates several of the motifs. A version of this work, 'given by a Dorset farmer in 1905 echoes, almost word for word, the stark longing of the second couplet of *Westron winde* [*3899.3*]' (36). Dronke concludes that much remains to be learned of the origin of European ballads, and 'evidence from the early Middle Ages can no longer be ignored.' This hints at 'bonds that unite learned and literary traditions with popular,' when poets of either tradition draw on materials of the other. Ballads uniformly envisage the woman's role as 'that of the victim' (38), who follows her lover to death. The ballads reveal ambivalent attitudes towards the realm of the dead, in the love or fear of the dead expressed by the living.

3899.3.

650 Fallows, David. 'English Song Repertories of the Mid-Fifteenth Century.' *Proceedings of the Royal Musical Association* 103 (1976–7): 61–79. Repr. in *Songs and Musicians in the Fifteenth Century*. David Fallows. Variorum Collected Studies Series. CS519. I 61–79.

Fallows intends to survey 'the polyphonic secular song repertory in England from about 1430 to 1470,' following the studies of Stevens, **52, 83**. He summarizes insular sources before considering continental manuscripts, in which English songs are sometimes recognized from a scribe's difficulties with his copy text. The investigations follow fixed forms of poetry, particularly the ballade and rondeau. The ballade was hardly used in this period by continental composers, so that any ballades 'that cannot be connected with a particular occasion automatically come under suspicion of being English' (69). Fallows notes several of these, and also some textless music which fits the form. The rondeau was more popular in France, but there is 'more evidence of rondeau settings in England than may hitherto have seemed the case' (71); they seem 'not only thoroughly French but clearly separable from other kinds of song in English' (74). Among these are settings of John Bedynham, preserved in Trent codices, and of Robert Morton who composed at the Burgundian court. Evidence against England's musical isolation includes Skelton's allusions to a rondeau of Binchois. Fallows comments on songs ascribed to Galfridus de Anglia and to Robertus de Anglia in MS Oporto 714, and relates these to English compositions. His summary cites four stylistic strands of song sources: the rondeau; the ballade; another form known only in 'the Ashmole strophic song "Now wolde y fayne sum merthis mak" [*2381*] and the Escorial ballade "Pryncess of youth" [*2782*]'; and some in 'the truly English tradition of free-form songs' (78), with characteristics of the Fayrfax MS. He concludes by warning of gaps in such a survey.

113.5, 135.3, 138, 146, 270, *317.5, 474.5, 753.8, 767, 860, 865.5, 925, 2016, 2017, 2183, 2274, 2277, 2323.8, 2375, 2381, 2393.5, 2475, 2782, 3165, 3259, 3376.5, 3536, 3677.5, 3722, 3879.

651 Fletcher, Alan J. 'Death Lyrics from Two Fifteenth-Century Sermon Manuscripts.' *Notes and Queries* 221 (1976): 341–2. [Edition.]

Vernacular sermons in Bodleian MSS e Museo 180 and Hatton 96 tell of the *Castrum Sapiencie*, 'a castle into which none may enter unless he first construe the significance of three shields that hang in the doorway' (341). The exemplum, of death and judgement, is enforced by three lyrics. 'Thy lyfe it is a law of dethe' [*7546*] renders the Latin verses written over the first shield. The others, 'Wan þat is wyte waxit falou' [*7601*] and 'Wan is heyn turniþ' [*7593*], of old age and signs of death, are 'accretions from an external tradition of death poetry' which present a picture of 'the untolerated old man, dignity gone, and now reduced to a *kombir-flet*' (342).

7546, 7593, 7601.

652 Frey, Charles. 'Interpreting "Western Wind."' *ELH* 43 (1976): 259–78.

Summarizes critical interpretations of 'Westron wynde when wylle thou blow' [*3899.3*], to investigate the association of music and words, and the distortions of modernized and bowdlerized versions. Variation in the position of a question mark, after the first or second line, causes different interpretations, since marks are usually intended 'to determine whether the rain should go away or stay' (261). Less significant is 'the change from "can" as "may" to "can" as "does,"' since the poet invokes the wind 'for the sake of *change*.' One should not try to specify the speaker and context, or 'to posit "my love" as either dead or alive, or as either husband or wife or sweetheart' (263). Frey notes resemblances to similar works, and the relation to folk song, but suggests that the poem is courtly rather than popular, with music written specifically for it. Christ is invoked as 'the active dispenser of time's gains and losses, of company and desolation' (267). Detailed analysis of the structure reveals many internal parallels, so that the 'kinesthetic flux of wind, rain, love, arms, and bed, exemplifies the plangent realism typical of the late northern middle ages' (272), with the wind the factor of greatest significance.

320, 1306, 1395, 3112, 3525, 3899.3.

653 Gibińska, Marta. 'Some Observations on the Themes and Techniques of the Medieval English Religious Love Lyrics.' *English Studies* 57 (1976): 103–14.

The lyrics express emotionally the love of God for man and of man for God. Gibińska offers numerous examples of the treatment of 'earthly and divine love ... secular models taken from the convention of courtly love ... Bernardian symbolism and ... the Passion itself' (104). 'A Luue Ron' [*66*] of Thomas de Hales and lyrics of the School of Richard Rolle contrast the false, transitory nature of earthly love, *cupiditas*, with the sweetness and fire of divine love, *caritas*. Some religious lyrics show their origins in courtly forms. There is Bernardian influence in lyrics of 'love longing and desire for mystical union with God' (108), some with the *sponsus* theme. Important Latin sources for Passion lyrics are

Candet Nudatum Pectus, attributed to Augustine, and *Respice in Faciem Christi*. Some English forms are translations, but in some cases 'the imagery and the language ... make the poems both original and beautiful' (114).

29, 66, 196, 611, 776, 1053, 1311, 1460, 1699, 1715, 1747, 1761, 1781, 1922, 1940, 1943, 2007, 2042, 2051, 2273, 3109, 3565, 3730, 3826, 3961, 3963, 3964, 3965, 3968, 4141.

654 Green, Richard Firth. 'The Authorship of the Lament of a Prisoner Against Fortune.' *Mediaevalia* 2 (1976): 101–9.

Many medieval literary works written in prison were influenced by Boethius, 'the archetypal literary prisoner' (101). Green examines the anonymous 'Lament of a Prisoner Against Fortune' ['Fortune alas alas what haue I gylt,' *860*] for details that could indicate its author. It has been ascribed to John Lydgate, Thomas Usk, George Ashby, and Sir Richard Roos, but the cases are not strong. Associations of manuscripts with John Shirley's *scriptorium* suggest William de la Pole, Duke of Suffolk. Green provides a brief account of Suffolk's political career, and records correspondences between biographical details and lines in the 'Lament,' as well as resemblances to a poem written by Suffolk when he was in a French prison. [See also Hammond, **123**.]

860.

655 Hallwas, John E. 'The Two Versions of "Hi Sike, Al Wan Hi Singe."' *Neuphilologische Mitteilungen* 77 (1976): 360–4.

Versions of 'I syke when y singe' [*1365*] in MSS Digby 2 and Harley 2253 differ significantly in presentation of a Passion meditation, with emphasis on 'the meditator's inner reaction to his visualization of the crucifixion' (360). There are differences in order of stanzas and in references to Mary and St John. The psychological progression is affected, to make the Harley version 'valuable only for displaying the superior poetic achievement of the Digby text' (364).

1365.

656 Pratt, John H. 'The "Scharpe Ax" of Richard II.' *Neuphilologische Mitteilungen* 77 (1976): 80–4.

Two versions of 'The ax was sharpe the stokke was hard' [*3306*], on 'a harsh year of excessive capital punishment during Richard II's rule' (80), nominate the fourth or fourteenth year, which could indicate 1381, and so the Peasants' Revolt and reprisals, or 1391, 'a year of peace and calm' (82). Both versions can refer to 1381: *fourthe* if the *e* is inflectional, so that the line is metrically correct; *fourteenth* if the reference is 'not to the fourteenth year of his sovereignty, but to the fourteenth year of his life' (83), when 'the axe was indeed sharp and royal justice hard' (84).

3306.

657 Robbins, Rossell Hope. 'The Vintner's Son: French Wine in English Bottles.' *Eleanor of Aquitaine, Patron and Politician*. Ed. William W. Kibler. Symposia in the Arts and the Humanities 3. Austin, TX: U of Texas P, 1976. 147–72.

In this survey of the transition from French to English literature in the medieval English court, with particular emphasis on Eleanor and Chaucer, Robbins argues for Chaucer's establishment of his poetic reputation by works written in French. He refers briefly to the English works 'The Craft of Lovers' ['To moralise ⟨a similitude⟩ who list these ballets sewe,' *3761*] and 'The Quatrefoil of Love' ['In a mornynge of May when medose schulde sprynge,' *1453*].

1453, 3761.

658 Rogers, William Elford. 'Middle English Verse Translations: A Model for a General Critical Problem.' *Furman Studies* 25 (1976): 24–46.

'Louerd þu clepest me' [*1978*], which translates a passage of St Augustine's *Confessions*, illustrates the problems of the relation of allusions to their sources and the critic's estimation of the author's intentions and of the value of the poem. Rogers relates his criticism to that of W.K. Wimsatt, Jr. and Monroe C. Beardsley, on 'The Intentional Fallacy' [*The Verbal Icon*], Kane, **292**, Manning, **443**, Oliver, **549**, and E.D. Hirsch [*Validity in Interpretation*]. He considers authorial intentions, the significance of the translated passage, the distinction between content and subject-matter of a poem, and the poetic value of a poem, and finds that 'in a translation-poem the insight into the meaning that is translated gives the poem its independent poetic value' (36). He applies his conclusions more generally, to assess the effect of literary allusions. These theoretical methods allow us to 'discuss sources without introducing certain assumptions about the author and the audience' (42).

1978.

659 Saíz, Próspero. *Personae and Poiesis: The Poet and the Poem in Medieval Love Lyric.* De Proprietatibus Litterarum, Series Minor, 17. Ed. C.H. van Schooneveld. The Hague: Mouton, 1976.

A study of lyrics 'of the imagined event and . . . the imagined state of being' (5), which refers most to Old Provençal, OF, and MHG works, in the genres of *alba*, *aube*, *tageliet*, and pastourelle. Saíz mentions the *alba* in *The Compleynt of Mars* [*913*], the 'Baffled Knight' sub-class of the pastourelle (59–60), and the Harley pastourelle 'In a fryht as y con fere fremede' [*1449*] (67).

913, 1449.

660 Schueler, Donald G. 'The Middle English *Judas*: An Interpretation.' *PMLA* 91 (1976): 840–5.

'Judas' [*1649*], 'the earliest surviving ballad in Middle English,' has been seen as 'a riddle' and 'a fragment, not a finished piece' (841). Schueler explores its dramatic episodes and the shift in focus from Judas to Peter. The narrative work relies on the reader's knowledge and anticipation, and its real concern is 'less to do with Judas than with . . . the universality of the human guilt that brought Christ to the Cross' (842). Judas' climbing to the rock sets up associations, to make him appear 'no worse than most of us, just as, at the end, Peter seems no better.' Sympathy with both disciples implicates the reader in Christ's death. The poem's link between the Last Supper and the thirty pieces of silver is not seen in biblical narratives; it shows that the food 'has cost Jesus his life – his body and blood: he has been sold to buy it' (843). The logic is that of preordained events; the audience's imagination and knowledge supply anything missing in the poem.

1649.

661 Short, Douglas D. 'Aesthetics and Unpleasantness: Classical Rhetoric in the Medieval English Lyric *The Grave*.' *Studia Neophilologica* 48 (1976): 291–9. [Edition.]

A detailed analysis of 'The Grave' ['ðe wes bold ʒebyld er þu i-boren were,' *3497*], to examine the structure that underlies its 'distinctive aesthetic quality.' Short prints the poem, and describes the balance of rhetorical figures, to show that 'the overt didacticism inherent in the death and the grave tradition has in this poem been subsumed by an aesthetic mode characterized by rhetorical manipulation' (292). The metaphor of the grave as a house is a structural device. Words of dwellings and building are manipulated in rhetorical figures throughout the poem, and images of birth are contrasted with thoughts of death. There is another pattern in the use of second person pronouns, to produce in the poem a 'dual focus . . . on the grave and on the auditor' (295). Short examines the rhetorical patterns to reveal the effect of the presentation of the grave as 'the inevitable end of all men,' then as 'a specific plot of ground prepared for the interment of the corpse,' and finally, 'as a finished house' (297). The description of decay moves 'from the neutral to the graphic, from the distasteful to the gruesome' (298), introducing the rejection of the dead 'as the ultimate corporeal horror is realized' (299).

3497, 3517, 4044.

662 Tristram, Philippa. *Figures of Life and Death in Medieval English Literature.* London: Elek, 1976.

Many figures are represented in ME lyrics, including personifications of Nature, Fortune, Death, Youth, the Pride of Life, and Age. After explicating 'The Figures' Context' (1–19), Tristram considers 'Youth and its Mentors' (20–61) and 'Age and its Perspectives' (62–94), before discussing 'Related Views of Temporal Life' (95–151) and 'Mortality and the Grave' (152–83), to conclude with 'Christ and the Triumph of Eternal Life' (184–212). She examines teaching on mortal life and living to attain eternal life, and shows aspects of its stages in many works. 'Erthe upon Erthe,' in its B version ['Erth owte of erth is wondyrly wroght,' *704*], is 'an admonition specific to the Pride of Life' (47), to express *contemptus mundi*. The miseries of Elde may come 'close to humour' (71), in 'From þe tyme þat we were bore' [*880*]. Nature's pattern is stated in the labours of the months, 'By thys fyr I warme my handys' [*579*], 'in which man is identified with her purposes' (99). The debate, 'Holy berith beris rede ynowgh' [*1226*], is the contention between 'Holly, the male principle of life, the independent tree which stands for joy' and 'Ivy, the solemn and possibly kill-joy female, the clinging parasite' (103). In 'A Winter Song' [*4177*] 'themes of Winter, Age and Death become virtually interchangeable,' but 'An Autumn Song' [*2359*] reveals 'the delicate regret of transience' (108) and *memento mori*, although its images soften mortality's horrors 'by suffusing death with autumnal resignation' (127). The *ubi sunt* theme is often expressed, as in the 'Luue Ron' [*66*] of Thomas de Hales. The many warnings of mortality occasionally have 'something approaching a satiric buoyancy' (154), as in 'Wanne mine eyhnen misten' [*3998*], but are more often grim. The celebration of Resurrection in 'On leome is in þis world ilist' [*293*] makes it possible 'to rejoice in the promised resurrection of all mankind' (194).

2, 12, 66, 108, 248, 293, 355, 529, 579, 603, 646, 849, 880, 937, 1115, 1132, 1216, 1226, 1272, 1370.5, 1387, 1459, 1475, 1563, 1591, 1599.5, 1865, 2143.5, 2192, 2228, 2338, 2359, 2551, 2579, 2590, 2591, 2619, 2677, 2716, 2744, 3074.3, 3143, 3310, 3457, 3517, 3531, 3756, 3795, 3798, 3909, 3921, 3992, 3998, 4019, 4044, 4099, 4177.

663 Wenzel, Siegfried. 'The "Gay" Carol and Exemplum.' *Neuphilologische Mitteilungen* 77 (1976): 85–91.

The word *gay*, repeated in the burden of the carol 'Euery day þ^u myʒt lere' [*739*] is interpreted by Greene, **37**, as 'a mere ejaculatory syllable' (85), and by Davies, **61**, as a glance at the foolishly gay. It may recall 'a Latin *exemplum* concerning an overseer or chamberlain named Gayus who . . . is visited by four devils who . . . frighten him literally to death' (87). They perform a carol-like dance, 'alternating a fixed line ("Gay, Gay, tu morieris") with a variable one sung by the *Vorsänger*' (87). This accords with the dates of the exemplum, with references in the works of John Bromyard and Bishop John Sheppey, the *Fasciculus Morum* (*142*), and with a ME version 'Gay gay þou art yhent' [*900*] in a sermon. Details preserved include the devils' song and Gay's words. In the adaptation for the sermon, Gayus has become 'an anomymous medieval playboy who eventually changes his real name to "gay Gay,"' and Gayus seemed to the preacher 'a protagonist of a "gay," that is, carefree and mundane character' (90).

142, 739, 900.

664 ———. 'Vices, Virtues, and Popular Preaching.' *Medieval and Renaissance Studies* 6. Proceedings of the Southeastern Institute of Medieval and Renaissance Studies. Summer 1974. Ed. Dale B.J. Randall. Durham, NC: Duke UP, 1976. 28–54.

After a general survey of the preaching, Wenzel presents an explication of the *Fasciculus Morum*, 'a preacher's aid,' which provides 'a thesaurus which preachers would study and from which they would cull their material' (37). Among its devices are short ME poems or tags used for the memorable emphasis of material, many of which are 'an integral and necessary part of the text' (47). Wenzel's examples of proverbial and doctrinal tags include '"message verses," in which a character within a tale formulates in meter and rhyme whatever needs to be driven home with particular force.' Most verses are 'direct translations of one or two Latin hexameters' (48). Although many vernacular tags are found in Latin handbooks, sermons, and commonplace books of the thirteenth century, there are few in fifteenth-century works, which impart such messages in prose. The delight of earlier preachers 'in Latin and in the vernacular . . . in sprinkling, or peppering, their prose sermons with verses' implies that they recognized 'the mnemonic and rhetorical or persuasive usefulness of such verse items for their audience,' and also experienced 'genuine pleasure in turning out a good verse' (49). [See also **628**.]

142, 1935, 3081, 3254, 3287, 4151.

665 Blake, Norman. *The English Language in Medieval Literature.* Everyman's University Library. London: Dent, 1977.

Examines the relation of the English language to medieval literature and seeks to show how knowledge of the language of that period helps in understanding 'the nature and type of literature written then' (7). Blake uses ME lyrics to illustrate some of his findings. The reference to 'My lefe ys faren in londe' [*2254*] in the *Nun's Priest's Tale* [*4019*] may suggest that 'it was widely known by the 1390s even though it survives only in a manuscript from about 1500' (19), but it need not, since Chaucer was more widely read than many of his readers. His own lyric, 'Adam scryveyne if euer it þee byfalle' [*120*], implies Chaucer's 'concern for the quality of his text and . . . helplessness in the face of faulty copying' (25). Varieties of word-play are exemplified in lyrics, including repetition in 'Erthe upon Erthe' [*3939*], and punning in 'Jentill butler bell amy' [*903*] and 'I have a newe gardyn' [*1302*]. 'O fresche floure most plesant of pryse' [*2437*], a 'fifteenth-century attack on women' (123), and 'The Land of Cockaygne' [*762*] are parodies.

120, 762, 903, 1302, 2254, 2437, 3939, 4019.

666 Fletcher, Alan J. 'A Death Lyric from the Summa Predicantium, MS. Oriel College 10.' *Notes and Queries* 222 (1977): 11–12.

In a space left, 'towards the end of the long chapter on death . . . for the inclusion of a vernacular death lyric' (11), the scribe has written the first six lines of 'Whanne þe ffet coldetȝ' [*4033*] and a contemporary corrector has added the rest of the text. The *Summa Predicantium* is the work of John Bromyard, but he did not compose the lyric, which uses motifs of *Proprietates Mortis*, death's poverty, and *Memorare Novissima*. Other spaces left by the scribe remain unexplained. The change in the lyric, 'from an objective, third person contemplation on death to an immediate second person warning in the last four lines' (12), implies an intention to use it in a sermon.

4033.

667 Hallwas, John E. 'þu Sikest Sore.' *Explicator* 35.3 (1977): 13.

Explores play on *weder is went* in 'þu sikest sore' [*3691*]. This can mean both departure of a sheep and a change in weather, to allude 'to the darkened sky at the Savior's death, which is a testament to His divinity, and to the Lamb of God's release from His earthly bonds.' Thus the line evokes 'the sudden release of the Savior's divine power at the moment of His physical defeat.'

3691.

668 Hargreaves, Henry. '*De Spermate Hominis*: A Middle English Poem on Human Embryology.' *Mediaeval Studies* 39 (1977): 506–10. [Edition.]

A poem in National Library of Scotland Advocates' MS 23.7.11 is a composite of astronomical and astrological material, tables, and recipes, 'stock subject matter for the medieval medical man' (506). The work describes the development and position of the foetus. Hargreaves summarizes medieval notions of fertilization, noting that the poem's first line, 'The sede of man and woman clere as cristal it is' [*7501*], shows that its author did not subscribe to 'the Aristotelian doctrine that only the male contributed seed, while the female provided blood' (508). Rather, the poet follows Giles of Rome on the development of the liver, heart, and brain, 'seats of respectively the Natural, Vital and Animal Spirits' (510). The description of the position of the foetus is more accurate than those of other contemporary sources.

7501.

669 Hirsh, John C. 'Me þingkit.' *Explicator* 35.3 (1977): 11.

The conceit of the poet of 'Me þingkit þou art so loueli' [*2141*] as 'debtor, not a creditor, if he lends his love,' twists conventions of courtly love with 'an intellectual as well as an emotional reaction to the threat of physical separation.'

2141.

670 McIntosh, Angus. 'Some Notes on the Text of the Middle English Poem *De Tribus Regibus Mortuis*.' *Review of English Studies* NS 28 (1977): 385–92.

Provides detailed notes on the text of the alliterative poem 'De tribus regibus mortis' [*2677*] edited by E.K. Whiting [*The Poems of John Audelay*, EETS 184]. McIntosh intends to resolve some difficulties and correct parts of the commentary and glossary. This and the poem preceding it in Whiting's edition are probably the work of the same author, but not that of Audelay. The scribe had 'special difficulty' with the 'highly complex form and the unusual diction' (385). There may have been errors in the copy text, and it was 'almost certainly in a dialect more northerly than his own' (386). McIntosh attends particularly to three problems connected with the poem: 'antecedents and affinities of the very complex conventions of ornamentation'; its thirteen-line stanza and connections with others in this form; and 'its relationship . . . to the acknowledged work of the *Gawain* poet' (386). He provides an appendix on the phrase *to lede bi lagmon* and possible connections with Laȝamon [*295*], to postulate 'a West Midland ME. noun *Lagmon*, referentially identical to *S.E.L*'s [the *South English* Legendary's] *Luttel Man*, but which characterizes the little finger . . . by its position as *last* in the series of four "true" fingers' (391).

295, 2677.

671 Osberg, Richard H. 'The Alliterative Lyric and Thirteenth-Century Devotional Prose.' *JEGP* 76 (1977): 40–54.

The 'structural alliteration' of some ME lyrics has evolved from 'the rhythmical alliteration of certain veins of devotional prose' (40–1), rather than from the long lines of verse of the alliterative revival. Although it is syllabic, lyric alliterative verse has an 'apparent disregard for either strict or consistent meter' (42). Osberg demonstrates correspondences in shared alliterative phrases in examples from prose passages in the St Katherine Group and from alliterative lyrics. He shows the association of similar constructions with some topics, and scans passages of prose with identical patterns of alliteration. In devotional prose he finds 'all the alliterative patterns characteristic of Anglo-Saxon verse and the Middle English alliterative lyric' (50), and examples of rhyme. The relation is seen in thirteenth-century lyrics, in works of the school of Richard Rolle, and in fifteenth-century works where alliteration may or may not coincide with 'regular metrical rhythms' (54).

2, 631, 872, 1310, 2951, 4044, 4162.

672 Pearsall, Derek. *Old English and Middle English Poetry.* London: Routledge, 1977. Vol. 1 of the Routledge History of English Poetry. Gen. ed. R.A. Foakes. 4 vols. 1977–81.

A general study, mainly of 'poetry written before the introduction of printing into England in the 1470s' (x), which attends particularly to 'provenance and audience' (xi) and so to manuscript context. In 'Poetry in the early Middle English period' (85–118) Pearsall considers the use of Latin, ME, and AN; the clerical tradition of writing; friars' miscellanies; poetry of popular instruction; Laȝamon; romance; and chronicle. In 'Some Fourteenth-Century Books and Writers' (119–49), he describes several manuscripts, particularly Harley 2253 (120–32), relating contents of other manuscripts to its political, courtly and non-courtly verse, and considering possible influences on the works. Collections of religious verse include the Prymer, the Vernon MS, and works of William Herebert, Bishop Sheppey of Rochester, John Grimestone, Richard Maidstone, William of Shoreham, and Richard Rolle and his school. 'Court Poetry' (189–222) outlines the interaction of French and English, and the influence of Chaucer, his circle, and Gower, before proceeding to courtly patronage of such poets as Lydgate, Hoccleve, and Roos, and to wider distribution of poetry, for example by John Shirley. Charles d'Orléans influenced English composition during his captivity, and, in the Fairfax poems, 'Chaucerian cadences are often echoed' (218). In 'The Close of the Middle Ages' (223–81) Pearsall describes poetry of the fifteenth century, and finds the time 'a shallow trough rather than an abyss in the history of English poetry' (223). Books and reading are more widely distributed, and there are some libraries which 'only the most exceptional fourteenth-century collections can match' (225). Lydgate and Hoccleve are prolific and versatile. Many religious lyrics of the period have survived, and some authors are known, including Richard de Caistre, James Ryman, John Audelay, and the secular writers 'R. Stokys' and 'Squire Halsham.' Stephen Hawes, Alexander Barclay, and John Skelton are poets of the Transition period, 'between the introduction of printing into England (1476) and the publication of Tottel's *Songs and Sonettes* (1557)' (266). Scots poetry, of Henryson, Dunbar, and Douglas, surpasses English work. Many early sixteenth-century lyrics are 'medieval in most essentials of form and subject' (273). In conclusion Pearsall examines 'tenacity of the medieval tradition' (283), maintained by Wyatt and Spenser, and offers two appendices: 'Technical Terms, mainly metrical' (284–90) and a 'Chronological Table' (291–302).

66, 100, 120, 159.5, 239, 359, 360, 368, 404, 467, 497, 561, 563, 583, 611, 631, 695, 762, 769, 912, 1008, 1078, 1091, 1119, 1237, 1272, 1320.5, 1365, 1388, 1394, 1395, 1402, 1453, 1454, 1460, 1463, 1506, 1540, 1620, 1649, 1653.5, 1747, 1761, 1841, 1889, 1894, 1940, 1943, 1949, 1974, 2007, 2009, 2025, 2029, 2066, 2070, 2108, 2163, 2166, 2236, 2270, 2273, 2287, 2320, 2359, 2401, 2547.3, 2649, 2677, 2737.5, 3078, 3109, 3190, 3211, 3222, 3223, 3226, 3227, 3310, 3445.5, 3491, 3497, 3504, 3517, 3607, 3720, 3747, 3759, 3782.5, 3787, 3827, 3838, 3899.3, 3963, 3967, 3969, 3998, 4043, 4085, 4088, 4177, 4186, 4189, 4256.8, 4263.

673   Schibanoff, Susan. 'Criseyde's "Impossible" *Aubes*.' *JEGP* 76 (1977): 326–33.

The figure *impossibilia* or *adynata* produces an ironic effect in Criseyde's *aubes* to make her vows of constancy to Troilus. The figure would already be familiar to the audience from 'a strikingly different context, that of the popular anti-feminist lying-song.' Schibanoff cites 'When nettuls in wynter bryng forth rosys red' [*3999*] to show that Criseyde's assertions must have seemed 'an almost certain prediction of the opposite course of behaviour' (327).

3327, 3999.

674   Short, Douglas J., and Porter Williams, Jr. '"Westron Wynde": A Problem in Syntax and Interpretation.' *Papers on Language and Literature* 13 (1977): 187–92.

Examines punctuation and its effect on the first lines of 'Westron wynde when wylle thou blow' [*3899.3*]. The first line may be 'a question about a desirable future event, the coming of the west wind,' and the second 'an exclamation about the present undesirable state of the weather.' Both lines together may pose 'a question about the future' (187). The authors survey interpretations, including the suggestion that the second line is a result clause without a conjunction. 'Purposeful ambiguity' (189) is not possible; the manuscript has no punctuation. *Small* when applied to rain suggests an 'association of small, gentle rain with Zephyrus, the warm western wind that ushers in the spring' (190). Evidence from the musical score supports reading the two lines 'as a single syntactical unit' (191). Short and Williams place a question mark after the second line, and regularize the capitalization, but find otherwise that 'the poem as found in the original manuscript can be left to speak for itself.' Thus the last lines echo the first two, and the poet longs for 'the spring breeze, the gentle rain, his love, and his own bed.' The journey is 'a secular one . . . towards home' (192)

3899.3.

675   Smith, Sarah Stanbury. '"Adam Lay I-Bowndyn" and the *Vinculum Amoris*.' *English Language Notes* 15 (1977–8): 98–101.

The image of Adam bound in 'Adam lay I-bowndyn bowndyn in a bond' [*117*] recalls the paradox of *felix culpa* and the *vinculum amoris*, 'the chain of love which binds man to his lady, or in sacred literature, to Christ' (99). Adam was bound because of his sinful love, but Mary, 'the second Eve, offers the corrective to Adam's misdirected love bond'; her crowning comes after Christ's Passion and Resurrection. The last irony is the paradox of freedom, 'to praise God because we are prisoners of His love' (101).

117, 2023.

676   Stemmler, Theo. 'The Vernacular Snatches in the *Red Book of Ossory:* A Textual Case-History.' *Anglia* 95 (1977): 122–9.

Presents the texts of nine incipits of English songs in the *Red Book of Ossory*, with corrections and information additional to that found in *IMEV* and in numerous earlier editions. Stemmler examines, in particular, the editions of J. Graves ['English and Norman Songs of the 14th Century,' *Notes and Queries* 2 (1850): 385–6]; of J.T. Gilbert ['Archives of the See of Ossory,' *Historical MSS Report* 10, Appendix, Part V (London, 1859): 219–65]; and of Greene, **37, 78**. Stemmler traces the origins and development of variations in editors' transcriptions, and presents his revisions. He stresses the importance of 'the discovery even of seemingly slight mistakes' (129) and the preparation of reliable texts.

684, 891, 1120.5, 1123, 1214.4, 1265, 2037.5.

Annotations of Critical Works 253

677 Turville-Petre, Thorlac. *The Alliterative Revival.* Cambridge: Brewer; Totowa, NJ: Rowman, 1977.

Considers aspects of the alliterative style and its place in ME literature, using examples from particular works, generally longer poems, to illustrate the style's features and effects. The influence of the 'short and impressive poem "The Grave" [*3497*]' (9) is seen in 'The Soul's Address to the Body' [*2684.5*], where the poet expands the theme of the grave as the body's house, using 'the alliterative line with a little more freedom than the author of *The Grave*' (10). Poets of the Harley lyrics use alliteration and other devices 'to achieve a number of different effects' (18). Turville-Petre supplies examples of style, alliterative patterns, stanza form, and satire from these poems. He explains uses of the thirteen-line stanza in 'The Quatrefoil of Love' [*1453*], 'The Pistill of Susan' [*3553*] 'Somer Soneday' [*3838*], and '*De Tribus Regibus Mortuis*' [*2677*]. In conclusion, he considers Scottish treatments of alliterative style; its use during Lollard controversies in 'three unattractive works, *Jack Upland* [*3782.5*], *Friar Daw's Reply* [*4098.3*] and *Upland's Rejoinder* [*1653.5*]'; the survival and rediscovery of the verse; and the prospect of 'a second alliterative revival' (128).

*295, 603, 1011.5, 1320.5, 1394, 1541, 1554, 1556, 1583, 1653.5, 1918, 2066, 2166, 2244, 2270, 2287, 2322, 2649, 2677, 2682, *2684.5, 2744, 3117, 3137, 3281.5, 3352, 3497, 3782.5, 3793, 3845.5, 3874, 3989, 4098.3, 4262.*

678 Wilson, Edward. 'A Middle English Manuscript at Coughton Court, Warwickshire, and British Library MS. Harley 4012.' *Notes and Queries* 222 (1977): 295–303.

After detailed descriptions and histories of the two fifteenth-century manuscripts, which share eight items, Wilson considers their ownership. It is likely that Dame Margaret Throckmorton owned the Coughton Court MS, and Dame Anne Wingfield Harley 4012. Wilson provides a brief biography of these ladies, each of whom read devout literature of the kind found in the manuscripts.

497, 854, 1779, 3038, 3207, 3827, 3955.

679 ———. 'An Unpublished Passion Poem in British Library MS. Harley 4012.' *Notes and Queries* 222 (1977): 485–8. [Edition.]

The manuscript may have been compiled for Dame Anne Wingfield, of East Harling in Norfolk, probably in the 1460s. Wilson prints the poem 'Ihesu the sonne of mare myle' [*1779*], 'of twenty stanzas in rhyme royal,' with comment on 'clerkly aureation' (485). He supplies some editorial modifications of abbreviations, punctuation, and word-division, with notes on some lines.

1779.

680 Wimsatt, James I. 'The Canticle of Canticles, Two Latin Poems, and "In a valey of þis restles mynde."' *Modern Philology* 75 (1977–8): 327–45.

Interprets 'In a valey of þis restles mynde' [*1463*] by examining 'the medieval tradition of the Canticle of Canticles, which is the primary source for both the structure of the poem and its imagery' (327). Canticles is seen as a mystical work, and Christ the bridegroom of the soul. Similar readings apply to the Latin lyrics: 'Quis est hic qui pulsat ad ostium?' and 'Dulcis Iesu memoria.' The works are alike, despite differences in 'time of composition . . . place of origin and language . . . length, verse form, point of view, dramatic situation, and incident' (328). The sermons of St Bernard of Clairvaux on Canticles are also relevant. Wimsatt analyses themes and images in the Latin poems. He refers to passages in Canticles and the sermons, and traces the soul's progress 'from meditation to union' (335), before examining this movement in the ME lyric. The latter offers first 'a vivid and moving presentation by Christ of his Passion as an act of love to man ... the basis for Christ's ensuing appeal to the soul to come and rest in the chamber of his side and for the soul's ultimate acquiescence.' Wimsatt's exposition explains the images of the lover as 'brother, humble suitor, bridegroom, and husband of the beloved,' as well as those of 'pursuing hunter and nursing mother' (336). Bernard's interpretations are supplemented by those of Bede and Origen. The imagery is complex, and includes relating the wound in Christ's side not only to the scrip containing the pilgrim's needs, but also to 'the nest of the dove and the marriage chamber' (341). The bridal chamber is a place for contemplation, where the soul may be cleansed and healed. The soul's 'sleep of the contemplative,' which signifies 'the ecstasy of communion with God,' is compared to that of a child at the mother's breast. A tradition of Christ as mother supports images of the wound as 'the breast which feeds the soul with spiritual milk' (343). The English lyric may rank 'with the very best of mystical writings' (345).

1463.

681 Bergner, Heinz. '*Miles*: A Crux in MS. Harley 2253 f.71v.' *Neuphilologische Mitteilungen* 79 (1978): 354–8

Miles, in line 20 of 'Lenten ys come wiþ loue to toune' [*1861*], is a *hapax legomenon* 'now generally accepted to be derived from the Welsh noun *mil* meaning "animal"' (354), but it may have a different meaning. With a change in punctuation this may alter the sense of lines 19–22. Berger examines suggested readings, and rejects *mules*, *myles*, and *meles*, in favour of *males*, with a full stop after *makes*. This makes line 20 ['Males murgeþ huere makes'] 'a graphic generalization of line 19' ['Wowes þis wolde drakes']. Line 21 ['ase strem þat strikeþ stille'] illustrates 22 ['Mody meneþ so doþ mo']. In the latter pair of lines the concept 'lack of vigour and joy,' is integrated in the 'image of the river flowing slowly and that of the man complaining sadly about his fate' (357), consistent with the lines that follow.

1861.

682 Bibby, Cyril. *The Art of the Limerick*. London: Research, 1978.

Detects stanzas with 'the limerick rhyme-scheme with approximations to its rhythm-scheme' in works of Dunbar: 'To a ladye' ['Sweit rois of vertew and of gentilness,' *3243.3*] and stanzas of 'How Dunbar was desyred to be ane freir' ['This nycht befoir the dawing cleir,' *3634.3*]. There is 'a faintly limerick-like quality' (57) in 'Svmer is icumen in' [*3223*], and a closer resemblance in a stanza of the *Bestiary* [*3353*], which begins 'The lion is wonderly strong.'

3223, 3243.3, 3353, 3634.3.

683 Boyer, Raymond. 'The Companions of St. Bruno in Middle English Verses on the Foundation of the Carthusian Order.' *Speculum* 53 (1978): 784–5.

Differs from Bowers, **494**, in his identification of Carthusians named as companions of St Bruno in the poem on the order's origin, 'At þe begynnyng of þe chartirhows god did schewe' [*435*]. Boyer proposes that they were famous holy men of the order, not its founders. Thus 'Saynt Hewe' is Hugh of Avalon; 'Saynt Anoelius' is St Anthelmus; and Bridus is Britius of Auxerre.

435.

684 Braekman, W.L. 'A Middle English Didactic Poem on the Works of Mercy.' *Neuphilologische Mitteilungen* 79 (1978): 145–51. [Edition.]

'Man ʒyf þᵘ wylt here' [*2062*] prescribes seven works of mercy. It is found in MSS BL Harley 3594 and Cambridge University Library Ii.4.9; Braekman's edition is drawn chiefly from the former. He summarizes sources of the teachings before describing the poem's treatment. The *exemplum* to illustrate the third work, of clothing the naked, is the story of St Martin's clothing a beggar; that for the sixth work, of giving hospitality to the homeless, is a story of a woman who shelters a leper. The brief treatment of the seventh work, of burying the dead, implies that it is included only for the sake of completeness. The remaining third of the poem explains that there are more good works to do, but stresses the greater importance of the seven works of the poem, 'since at the Day of Judgement every human being will be asked about his practising them' (147). Braekman prints the poem, noting variations found in the two manuscripts.

2062.

685   Fletcher, Alan J. '"I Sing of a Maiden": A Fifteenth-Century Sermon Reminiscence.' *Notes and Queries* 223 (1978): 107–8, 541.

Notes portions of ME lyrics found within Bodleian MS Barlow 24, a collection of sermons, in Latin, which were assembled by a compiler who gave his name as 'Selk,' in the capitals of divisions in the sermons. Most of the lyrics appear in Selk's funeral sermons, and are concerned with 'age and mortality' (107). A sermon for the Assumption includes a couplet, 'Mayde, wyff and moder whas neuer but ye;/Well may suche a Lady Goddys modyr be,' lines 'commonly sung about the Virgin Mary,' and 'an unmistakable reminiscence of the last two of "I Sing of a Maiden [*1367*]."' The comment demonstrates a wider currency in the fifteenth century 'than its solitary appearance in the Sloane manuscript might suggest' (108). [On p 541, the editors correct a quotation printed on p 108.] [See **800**; Wenzel, **701**; Powell, **786**.]

1367, 2058, 3969, 7065, 7328, 7402.

686   Fletcher, Bradford Y. 'Printer's Copy for Stow's *Chaucer*.' *Studies in Bibliography* 31 (1978): 184–201.

Considers John Stow's part in preparing his 1561 edition of *Chaucer*, in particular the addition of 24 poems to the edition of *c.* 1550, many of which are attributed incorrectly to Chaucer. Examination of Trinity College Cambridge MS R.3.19 reveals that this was often Stow's copy text. The accuracy of the transcription suggests that Stow supervised the work as well as providing manuscripts for the printer. Fletcher discusses the poems individually, with Stow's titles, citing all manuscript sources, and suggesting which was used. He concludes with comments on Stow's accuracy in preparing the print, modifications of spelling, and discriminating choice of manuscript sources.

120, 267, 590, 1300, 1419, 1562, 1592, 1944, 2029, 2128, 2510, 2524, 2661, 2767, 3197, 3348, 3414, 3521, 3523, 3656, 3761, 3914, 3928, 4205.

687   Friedlander, Carolynn VanDyke. 'Early Middle English Accentual Verse.' *Modern Philology* 76 (1978–9): 219–30

The term 'Early ME Accentual Verse' is the 'least inaccurate' (220) designation for a small body of literature, some written before 1050, in a period when writers 'probably did not clearly distinguish poetry from prose' (219). Friedlander explains the metrical and rhyming patterns of OE and Early ME poetry in detail, and labels 'The Grave' ['ðe wes bold ʒebyld er þu i-boren were,' *3497*] and the Worcester fragments as 'accumulations of clichés,' in which 'reiteration of the obvious sometimes makes them grimly effective' (227). Hints of OE tradition in Early ME verse suggest that the poets were 'nostalgic about it' (230).

3497.

688   Giaccherini, Enrico. 'Due liriche amorose del MS Harley 2253.' *Critical Dimensions: English, German and Comparative Literature Essays in Honour of Aurelio Zanco Cuneo.* Ed. Mario Curreli and Alberto Martino. Cuneo: SASTE, 1978. 3–19.

Not seen.

689   Hardman, Philippa. 'A Mediaeval "Library *In Parvo*."' *Medium Ævum* 47 (1978): 262–73.

MS Advocates 19.3.1 is 'a "Library *in parvo*,"' because of 'the catholicity of its contents'; its collection of quires 'arranged and written independently of each other'; and the probability that the booklets were kept 'as separate, unbound volumes' (262). Hardman lists each quire's contents, and records the hands in which the manuscript was written, noting names of the scribes who have signed their work: Recardu*m* Heege and John Hawghton. The hands are of the late fifteenth century; the language implies 'a North Midland provenance' (264). Hardman discusses the work by theme, noting that quires 1 and 6 are anthologies of comic and religious verse.

62, 64, 172, 340, 347, 358, 378, 674, 707, 973, 1032, 1184, 1116, 1446, 1448, 1724, 1772, 1781, 1920, 2157, 2714, 3038, 3087, 3088, 3184, 3435, 3507, 3627, 4053, 4153, 4230.

690   Harvey, Carol J. 'Macaronic Techniques in Anglo-Norman Verse.' *L'Esprit Créateur* 18 (1978): 70–81.

AN literature mirrors a society in which 'English was the language of the "common folk," Anglo-Norman that of the descendants of William the Conqueror and his followers, and Latin the language of religion, law and erudition' (70). Macaronic works combine the languages with varying techniques. Harvey examines works in Latin and AN, and some that use ME with either or both of the other languages. She notes varying patterns of rhyme, in and between the languages, and a tendency to English rhythms. Increasing use of ME shows 'the changing prestige of the three languages,' as it gradually becomes 'the literary language of the country,' while Latin declines. When 'the different registers of the vernaculars offer little contrast,' macaronic verses become 'little more than a literary curiosity' (81).

16, 19, 694.5, 724, 1799, 1857, 2039.

691   Hill, Betty. 'British Library MS. Egerton 613.' *Notes and Queries* 223 (1978): 394–409, 492–501. [Edition.]

Included in the manuscript are five ME poems ['Ic eom eldre þanne ic wes a wintre and a lare,' *1272*; 'I-blessed beo þu lauedi ful of houene Blise,' *1407*; 'Litel uotit eniman ou trewe loue bi-stondet,' *1923*; 'Of on þat is so fayr and briȝt,' *2645*; 'Somer is comen & winter gon' *3221*], an English rhyming proverb ['Leef hen. Whanne hue Leyth,' *7303*], and two macaronic ME and AN poems ['kar bon ostel aurerez,' *7295*; '*Wyd is swete armes*,' *7625*]. Hill's account provides a 'Technical Description' (395–7), 'Contents' (397–404), 'Additions in Other Hands' (405–8), and 'The History of the Manuscript' (408–9), and concludes with an appendix with the text of *Salut et solace par l'amour de Jésu* (492–501), in which the macaronic poems are found.

1272, 1407, 1923, 2645, 3221, 7295, 7303, 7625.

692   Hill, Thomas D. '"Half-Waking, Half-Sleeping": A Tropological Motif in a Middle English Lyric and its European Context.' *Review of English Studies* NS 29 (1978): 50–6.

Explores the motif used in the Marian lyric 'With fauoure in hir face ferr passyng my Reason' [*4189*] for 'a hard-hearted speaker who is eventually moved from his initial indifference to tears.' Hill relates this to Dante's description of himself, to suggest 'a mediate status, *between* that of a sinner who is insensible of or indifferent to his condition and hence "asleep" and that of a Christian in a state of grace who is thus fully "awake"' (51). This recalls Lancelot's torpor in *La Queste de Saint Graal* (described by Malory as *half wakyng and half slepyng*), when he cannot respond to the sight of the Grail and the healing of a knight. There is another echo in the *Speculum Sacerdotale*, in the exemplum of a Flemish clerk's vision of Mary Magdalene, while he is 'half-waking, half-sleeping' (53). In the admonition 'Wake man slepe not rise vp and thynk þat erth thou art' [*3859*], the poet hears a message as he lies 'between sleep and wakefulness.' Augustine's account of the movement from folly to wisdom posits 'a mediate state between these two conditions just as there is a transitional condition between sleep and waking' (54). In *4189* the motif defines 'a specific moment in a man's moral life – the time *between* sin and repentance when a man must choose to awaken or to fall back into the sleep of sin' (56).

3859, 4189.

693 Johnston, Jeanette. 'The Points of Thomas Becket.' *Notes and Queries* 223 (1978): 296–9.

Accounts of the martyrdom of St Thomas Becket, in two carols printed by Greene, **86**, vary in 'the number of points for which he is said to have lost his life' (296). John Audelay's carol, 'ffor on a tewsday thomas was borne' [*838*] suggests 50, whereas 'Lestenytȝ lordingis boþe grete and smale' [*1892*], notes 52, 15, and 50 (or possibly five), according to the manuscript consulted. The points may be 'the items set out by Henry II in the Constitutions of Clarendon of 1164' (297) and at the council of Northampton. Becket granted four points gladly, 'as well as an unspecified number of others,' but not ten. Although the carols give precise numbers, *The South English Legendary* and a Trinity College Dublin manuscript are vague. The life of Herbert of Bosham proposes 16 points, and William of Canterbury's account is similar. This is 'the number accepted in modern historical works' (298). Johnston suggests possibilities to explain scribal misreadings and errors from oral transmission, to find that 'fifteen is the most satisfactory solution' (299).

838, 1892.

694 McIntosh, Angus. 'The Middle English Poem *The Four Foes of Mankind.*' *Neuphilologische Mitteilungen* 70 (1978): 137–44.

Offers detailed comments on the language and text of the poem 'þe siker soþe who so seys' [*3462*], of Northern origin, in a genre 'confined mainly to the West Midlands and parts of the North' (137), and on the unique copy in the Auchinleck MS, which was 'presumably made in London by a scribe whose own orthographic and dialectical characteristics indicate that he probably came from Middlesex' (137–8). McIntosh's remarks cover words used in the North and sometimes the North Midlands; some with wider distribution which do not imply a place of origin; some apparently changed to a Southern form; and some 'which cannot be assumed to have been introduced by the scribe but for which the evidence for use in the north is rather slender' (140).

3462.

695 Palmer, Barbara D. '"To Speke of Wo that is in Mariage": The Marital Arts in Medieval Literature.' *Human Sexuality in the Middle Ages and Renaissance.* Ed. Douglas Radcliff-Umstead. U of Pittsburgh Publications on the Middle Ages and the Renaissance. 4. Pittsburgh, PA: Center for Medieval and Renaissance Studies, 1978. 3–14.

Most legal documents on medieval marriage deal with 'those couples who ended in court' (3). Two lyric categories consider this: 'the *chanson de mal marié*, or husband's lament; and the *chanson de mal mariée*, wife's lament.' Only one of the latter truly defends women against anti-feminist satire, since they are often 'a dialogue between gossips in a tavern which catalogues their husbands' respective shortcomings' (6). The more numerous husbands' laments are usually monologues that list specific complaints, condemn marriage, or stress the need to choose a wife carefully. Palmer has yet to discover a poem that 'records or celebrates domestic bliss' (7).

210, 1459, 3533.5, 3919, 4019, 4279.

696 Pickering, O.S. 'A Middle English Poem on the Eucharist and Other Poems by the Same Author.' *Archiv* 215 (1978): 281–310. [Edition.]

'Alle ʒe mowyn be blyth & glade' [*235*] differs from works of instruction or exhortation on similar subjects, because the poet expresses 'spectacular truths of Christ's redemption of man and transubstantiation on the altar.' The poem's images include Christ as Eucharistic bread, 'a morsel of food, deadly to Satan but beneficial to man' (283), as a doctor, and as Passover lamb, his blood as ointment; the medical imagery is extended to an OT treatment of lepers. Pickering notes similar images of bread and wheat, and compares the metrical structure with that of other works with thirteen-line stanzas. A poem on the 'Festivals of the Church' ['The lord þat is a howsholder,' *3415*] shares the verse-form; resemblances in 'more personal stylistic features such as vocabulary, phrasing and imagery' (288) imply common authorship. There are shared characteristics in the 'Dispute between Mary and the Cross' ['O litel whyle lesteneþ to me/ententyfly so haue ʒe blys,' *2481*; 'Oure ladi freo on Rode treo made hire mone,' *2718*] and 'Whon grein of whete is cast to grounde' [*3952*]. Pickering traces similarities in style and imagery, in particular the 'intense, concise phrasing and the selection of uncommon vocabulary' (293). Analysis of the rhymes indicates a clerical poet, 'working probably in East Anglia and possibly in Norfolk . . . in the mid-fourteenth century.' His audience for *3952* and *235* may have been a congregation, with the latter perhaps 'written for delivery on Easter Day' (297), on the occasion of annual communion; he is 'consciously a poet' (298). Pickering prints *235*, arranging it to bring out its sense and rhyme scheme, with apparatus and 'expanatory notes of considerable length' (299).

235, 1627, 2481, 2681, 2718, 3415, 3583, 3920, 3952.

697 Ransom, Daniel J. '"Annot and John" and the Ploys of Parody.' *Studies in Philology* 75 (1978): 121–41.

Close study of 'Annot and John' [*1394*] shows that it is not only 'a mechanically composed list of gems, flowers, birds, herbs, and people to which a lady is compared' (121). Ransom refers briefly to Brook, **42**, Moore, **297**, and Stone, **63**, and in greater detail to Dronke, **472**, and Stemmler [*Die englischen Liebesgedichte des MS. Harley 2253*, diss. Rheinische Friedrich-Wilhelms-Universität, 1962 (Bonn, 1962)]. Detailed examination reveals incongruities in the many comparisons. The pun that reveals Annot's name, noted for instance in *BrownXIII*, **36**, encourages 'pun-hunting elsewhere in the poem' (128). Ransom explores the possibilities of play on *coynte* and *cunde*, on *gome* as 'game' or 'man,' and in the notion that Annot is as chaste as emerald in the morning. Many inconsistencies in the associations of birds, particularly with lechery and chastity, emphasize the strategy used to achieve 'not an accumulation of complementary similes and metaphors but a pronounced tension in the terms of comparison' (137), with similar tensions in the stanzas on herbs and heroic figures. Contradictory descriptions of Annot show the poet's 'combined enthusiasm and irony' (140). He burlesques 'the form and conventions of courtly love poetry without reducing its subject to mere caricature' (141).

1394, 1485, 3222.

698 Revard, Carter. '"Sulch Sorw I Walke With": Line 4 of "Foweles in the frith."'
Notes and Queries 223 (1978): 200.

The '"beaver-tailed" form of capital *S*' used by thirteenth-century scribes has often been misread as *M*, 'especially when the misreading would yield reasonable sense.' Revard suggests such a misreading in line 4 of 'Foweles in the frith' [*864*], to produce *mulch*, rather than *sulch*. The latter offers 'smoother syntax' and is also 'linguistically regularly derived from OE. swylc.' He makes the alteration and prints the text of the poem.

864.

699 Rowland, Beryl. *Birds with Human Souls: A Guide to Bird Symbolism*. Knoxville, TN: U of Tennessee P, 1978.

Surveys the symbolic use of birds, especially as figures for the soul. Rowland describes many species, in alphabetical order, noting the characteristics ascribed to them, and illustrates her findings with references to literature and folklore. Birds in the lyrics include the bunting ['In Aprell and in May,' *1470*]; cock ['I have a gentil cok,' *1299*]; goose ['There ben women there ben wordis,' *3522.5*]; pheasant ['In a noon tijd of a somers day,' *1454*]; and thrush ['Annot and Iohn' *1394*].

1299, 1394, 1454, 1470, 3522.5.

700 Stemmler, Theo. 'Observations on Some Difficult Passages in the Harley Poems.' *Notes and Queries* 223 (1978): 490–2.

Explains cruces in three Harley poems: 'Lystneþ lordynges a newe song Ich ulle bigynne' [*1889*], 'Alle þat beoþ of huert trewe' [*205*], and 'Annot and Iohn' [*1394*]. Stemmler investigates the phrases *aʒeyn star* and *his þonkes* in *1889*. He considers the faulty rhyme scheme of a stanza of *205*, with suggested emendations and the possibilities of sound changes and implications for other Harley poems. He compares transcriptions and interpretations of the words *sauue/sanne* and *saueþ/saneþ* in *1394*.

205, 1394, 1889.

701 Wenzel, Siegfried. *Verses in Sermons:* Fasciculus Morum *and Its Middle English Poems*. Cambridge, MA: Mediaeval Academy of America, 1978. [Edition.]

The *Fasciculus morum*, a fourteenth-century preachers' handbook, presents sermons that are arranged to deal with the seven vices, their opposing virtues, and related material, including catechetical topics. The sermons are recorded in Latin, for delivery in that language or the vernacular, according to the audience. Included in the text are numerous verses and tags, 'variously mnemonic, rhetorical, or meditative, or simply an outlet for wit and verbal skill' (66). Wenzel supplies a detailed account of the work and its 28 varied manuscripts, and of excerpts and references to the *Fasciculus morum* in other sources. Examination of versions of exempla leads him to place the *terminus a quo* in the early thirteenth century, and to conclude that 'the greatest claim for authoring *Fasciculus morum* belongs to Robert Selk' (39). Some verses render Latin sermon lines exactly or freely; some provide biblical quotations or proverbs; some accompany moralized pictures; others supply headings for the preacher's divisions of his text. Comparison with other sermon manuscripts shows similar use of ME verses within the Latin compositions by their authors, most of them considered to be Franciscan or Dominican friars.

In 'The English Verses of *Fasciculus Morum*,' Wenzel provides details of the 55 ME verses found in the *Fasciculus morum*, discussing their 'Nature, Function, Textual History' (101–14). He demonstrates the range and contexts of the verses, with a table to illustrate their distribution in the various manuscripts (106–7). In an examination of

'The Originality of *Fasciculus morum*' (114–20), he compares similar material, in particular MS Harley 7322, and concludes that 'a good many English verses have come from the very quill of the unknown preacher who compiled this "bundle of virtues"' (121). In 'Preacher's Verses and the English Religious Lyric' (121–32) he compares the verses with other religious lyrics, and considers criticism, particularly that of Woolf, **522**.

37.3, *142*, *191*, *400*, *495*, *498*, *565*, *621*, *704*, *797*, *798*, *994*, *1127*, *1150*, *1204*, *1223*, *1321*, *1490*, *1822*, *1935*, *2001*, *2002*, *2025*, *2058*, *2077*, *2114*, *2190*, *2283*, *2293*, *2298*, *2320*, *2329*, *2340*, *2596*, *2729*, *2775*, *2817*, *2832*, *3081*, *3133*, *3223*, *3254*, *3273*, *3275*, *3281*, *3282*, *3287*, *3339*, *3350*, *3408*, *3433*, *3463*, *3496*, *3518*, *3649*, *3716*, *3802*, *3838*, *3863*, *3907*, *4035*, *4079*, *4134*, *4143*, *4156*, *4174*, *4221*, *4239*, *7091*, *7127*, *7130*, *7194*, *7219*, *7232*, *7247*, *7344*, *7387*, *7417*, *7491*, *7500*, *7538*, *7567*, *7615*.

———Review by Marjorie Rigby, *Review of English Studies* NS 32 (1981): 439–40. Summarizes the content and method of the book, and makes comparisons with Silverstein, **73**, and Woolf, **522**. Rigby comments on 'the category of religious lyric as Rosemary Woolf defined it' and the fitness of some of the verses from the *Fasciculus Morum* to be included in it; she also notes distinctions 'between the sermon-verses and the meditative poems.' She finds Wenzel's work 'a densely paced study, informative and stimulating' (440).

702 Whitfield, D.W. 'A Contemporary Reference in a Fourteenth-Century Carol.' *Notes and Queries* 223 (1978): 203–4.

The record in BL MS Add. 47214 can be used to date the destruction by lightning of the Carmelite friary at Lynn at 6 July, 1363. Reference in the present perfect tense to this incident in the carol 'Thynk man qwerof þ^u art wrout' [*3566*] implies assignment 'to the year 1363 or 1364' (203). Evidence from the manuscript, which had belonged to the Franciscans of Lynn, suggests Franciscan authorship of the carol.

3566.

703 Wolpers, Theodor. 'Geistliche Lyrik in England.' *Europäisches Spätmittelalter*. Ed. Willi Erzgräber et al. *Neues Handbuch der Literaturwissenschaft*. Ed. Klaus von See et al. Vol. 8. Wiesbaden: Akademische Verlagsgesellschaft, 1978. 405–26. 9 vols. 1972–83.

A general historical study of ME religious lyrics with many literary and pictorial examples, and German translations of some texts. Wolpers examines the relationship of lyrics and prayers, and notes parallels with secular poems. He contrasts the distance established between God and the believer in early medieval Latin hymns with the tendency to mystical identification in ME poetry, seen in St Godric's hymn, 'Seinte marie clane uirgine' [*2988*]. Most prayers and sermon lyrics of the thirteenth and fourteenth centuries were anonymous works, with signs of Franciscan piety, delivered by the preachers to a public with no knowledge of Latin or French. These Marian and Passion verses resemble secular verse, and make their subjects seem more human. Wolpers reproduces pictures that accompanied the lyrics and decorated books of devotion. They stress the humanity of Christ and Mary, stir emotions, and encourage meditation. Among the many verses composed at the beginning of the fourteenth century, those of Harley MS 2253 are outstanding. Wolpers considers in particular 'A Prayer for Deliverance' [*2039*], 'A Winter Song' [*4177*], and 'An Autumn Song' [*2359*]. These poems, like miniatures in books of devotion, demonstrate connections between courtly elegance and natural beauty and tender feelings. Preaching lyrics of the late fourteenth and fifteenth centuries resemble emblem poems, for example 'O man vnkynde/hafe in mynde/my paynes smert' [*2504*], spoken by Christ's wounded heart, and images of suffering such as the Pietà. There are severe warnings and reproaches, and commentary on morality and social conditions. The Commonplace Book of John Grimestone, intended only to enforce Christ's message, has no literary importance. The few poems of personal piety of the thirteenth and fourteenth centuries include the 'Luue Ron' [*66*] of Thomas de Hales, and the hymns translated by William Herebert, who employs the image of Christ as knight in 'What ys he þys lorldling þat cometh vrom þe vyht' [*3906*], and explores the Virgin's paradoxical relationships in 'þou wommon boute vere' [*3700*]. Songs of Richard Rolle's school continue monastic, mystical literature in the fourteenth century. Chaucer's Marian lyrics are different in nature. Wolpers notes the change in emphasis, from humanity's address to Christ or Mary to their own request for the human believer's love. Aureate diction in some fifteenth-century poetry may be more conspicuous than religious content, and there is less expression of emotion. It presents Mary in shining images of beauty and virtue, as in Lydgate's poems; in contrast, carols and lullabies depict a human mother. It is remarkable that the finest ME poem, 'I syng of a myden þ^t is makeles' [*1367*], seems independent of the general conventions.

66, 94, 99, 110, 239, 352, 353, 361, 441, 447, 550, 583, 600, 643, 695, 872, 888, 1002, 1031, 1054, 1213, 1216, 1232, 1235, 1274, 1365, 1367, 1448, 1460, 1472, 1699, 1742, 1747, 1781, 1833, 1847, 2007, 2012, 2024, 2033, 2036, 2039, 2070, 2092, 2155, 2240, 2241, 2260, 2320, 2359, 2504, 2507, 2577, 2607, 2619, 2645, 2791, 2992, 3109, 3135, 3211, 3245, 3405, 3627, 3676, 3691, 3700, 3821, 3825, 3826, 3862, 3872, 3906, 3963, 3969, 4019, 4135, 4159, 4177, 4200, 4223, 4263, 4268.

704 ———. 'Weltliche Lyrik in England.' *Europäisches Spätmittelalter*. Ed. Willi Erzgräber et al. *Neues Handbuch der Literaturwissenschaft*. Ed. Klaus von See et al. Vol. 8. Wiesbaden: Akademische Verlagsgesellschaft, 1978. 373–403. 9 vols. 1972–83.

A detailed historical account of secular lyrics, with numerous examples, and German translations of some texts. Wolpers explains poetic effects in the expression of thoughts and emotions in love lyrics of the thirteenth and fourteenth centuries, and the links with folk elements and French styles and motifs. Simplicity of structure is characteristic, even when artful rhetorical means are employed; among others Wolpers cites 'Svmer is icumen in' [*3223*], and Rawlinson and Harley lyrics. He writes at length about the Harley collection, considering its historical importance and varied styles; he stresses the language's connections to that of religious lyrics, even in the declaration of erotic feelings. Popular and courtly poetry of the late fourteenth and fifteenth centuries generally cannot equal the fresh approach of the Rawlinson or the variety of the Harley lyrics. Some popular love poetry imitates the courtly manner in coarsely explicit style, often mocking women and their weaknesses. There are many political and moralistic poems of national and individual matters. They may be written against general and individual enemies, as in the poems of the French and the Scots, 'The Execution of Sir Simon Fraser' [*1889*], and the condemnation of Richard, Earl of Cornwall in 'The Song of the Battle of Lewes' [*3155*]. Laurence Minot's poems present patriotic accounts of battles, to stress English heroism and victory; they include 'The Siege of Calais' [*585*], 'The Battle of Bannockburn' [*3080*], and 'The Battle of Neville's Cross' [*3117*]. There are anonymous works such as 'The Battle of Otterburn' [*1620*] and 'The Battle of Agincourt' [*3213*]. Poems of the Wars of the Roses combine metaphor and allegory, yet remain concrete; they may conceal identities in allusions to heraldic emblems. Satirical songs attack greed, corruption, luxury, and oppression of the poor; Wolpers cites works in ME, Latin, and AN. He considers, among others, poems written against extravagant fashions and of moral advice. Even satires on 'Retinues of the Great' [*2649*] and 'Consistory Courts' [*2287*], and 'The Song of the Husbandman' [*1320.5*], the moralizing works of Harley 2253, seem to be lyrical. Such poems in the fourteenth and fifteenth centuries tend to stress concrete details, and to lack lyrical emotion, as seen in the mockery of the gallant ['Galawnt pride thy father is dede,' *892*].

262   *Annotations of Critical Works*

A song of Edward II, 'Somer Soneday' [*3838*], tells of a meeting in a forest with Fortune. A lament for Edward III, 'A dere God what may this be' [*5*], presents him as an example of royal greatness, and knighthood as the ship of state. Other poems of monarchs include Hoccleve's of the reburial of Richard II, 'Whereas þat land wont was for to be' [*4066*], and Audelay's on Henry VI, 'Fore he is ful ȝong tender of age' [*822*]; each work, in fact, is intended to praise Henry V. John Ball expressed the anger of the oppressed in his sermon on the theme 'Whan adam delffid & eva span/who was than a gentilman' [*3922*]; many other poems were directed against those in authority. Attacks against the mendicant friars include that of Wyclif's supporters, 'Preste ne monke ne ȝiy chanoun' [*2777*]. The power and use of money are satirized in 'London Lickpenny' [*3759*] and poems such as 'Sir Penny' ['In erth there ys a lityll thyng,' *1480*; 'Peny is an hardy knyght,' *2747*; 'Man vpon molde whatsoever þou be,' *2082*]. These works show the coming of an era of capitalism, displayed in Chaucer's *Canterbury Tales* [*4019*] in characters and their tales. The power and prestige of wealthy citizens of London is displayed in some lyrics of the fifteenth century; the city is celebrated by Dunbar, in 'London thou art of townes a per se' [*1933.5*]. The fourteenth and fifteenth centuries produced many cheerful songs for festivities and practical verses for teaching and mnemonic purposes.

5, 72, 105, 179, 205, 210, 225, 377, 436, 438, 515, 521, 549, 579, 585, 694.5, 809, 822, 824, 849, 864, 869, 892, 903, 922, 960.1, 1008, 1195, 1201, 1222, 1240, 1280, 1293.5, 1299, 1302, 1303, 1314, 1320.5, 1333, 1394, 1395, 1417, 1449, 1468, 1480, 1485, 1502, 1504, 1555, 1608, 1609, 1620, 1622, 1791, 1796, 1829, 1849, 1857, 1861, 1866, 1889, 1933.5, 1938, 1974, 2031, 2037.5, 2082, 2135, 2161, 2163, 2166, 2207, 2236, 2243, 2262.3, 2311, 2338, 2343, 2624, 2634, 2649, 2654, 2656, 2663, 2675, 2747, 2756, 2777, 3080, 3117, 3155, 3157, 3162, 3164, 3174, 3190, 3213, 3222, 3223, 3259, 3310, 3313, 3327, 3348, 3409, 3412, 3438, 3445.5, 3465, *3533.5, 3534, 3571, 3572, 3594, 3661, 3682, 3735, 3759, 3771, 3782, 3838, 3848, 3874, 3898, 3919, 3922, 4037, 4056.8, 4066, 4144, 4148, 4194, 4256.8, 4279.

705   Best, Larry G. 'Dissociative Allegory in Medieval Lyrics.' *Encyclia* 56 (1979): 83–90.

The allegory Best calls 'dissociative' is a system running 'parallel to the work of literature but having nothing to do with, or being barely incidental to, the central theme or ideas of the work.' He compares this to illumination of medieval manuscripts that supplies 'decoration for the sake of decoration' (85). There are examples in two lyrics, 'With a garland of thornes kene' [*4185*], in which images of the Passion are seen as remedies against the Deadly Sins, and 'Judas' [*1649*]. The first poem operates 'with a careful interaction between image, symbol, and idea.' This method is seen also in 'Judas,' but with addition of images 'which operate independently of the central meaning of the poem, forming a type of contrapuntal allegory of images associated with the passion of Christ but dissociated from the primary meaning of the poem' (87). Best notes implications of the imagery. He distinguishes between images 'not dissociated but . . . integral to the meaning' and others that contribute 'moral decoration' (88) rather than understanding, to allow allegorical manipulation on two levels.

1649, 4185.

706   Bitterling, Klaus. 'Signs of Death and Other Monitory Snatches from MS. Harley 2247.' *Notes and Queries* 224 (1979): 101–2.

The last sermon in this manuscript is a model sermon for a funeral, embellished with verses, *exempla* showing death as an archer and the keeper of a garden, and a list of the signs of death. The last reveals 'a partial identity' with that in 'the Franciscan *Fasciculus Morum* (102).

4033, 7296, 7402.

707 Boenig, Robert. '"There is no rose": Mysticism and the Medieval English Carol.' *Studia Mystica* 2 (1979): 52–9.

A holistic study, which relates musical, literary, and theological exploration of the carol 'Ther is no rose of swych vertu' [*3536*]. Boenig compares the music to the style of *Ars Nova,* with examples of syncopation, rhythmic counterpoint, and hocket by Gilles Binchois, Guillaume Dufay, and an anonymous composer. He relates literary and theological considerations to the work's diction and structure, derives the notion of a monastic origin, and compares the carol with 'I syng of a myden $þ^t$ is makeles' [*1367*]. The macaronic form sets 'a counterpoint between its English, the language of everyday life, and Latin, the special language heard inside churches' (57). This is echoed in the music, which is syllabic or neumatic for English lines and melismatic for the Latin tags.

1367, 3536.

708 Booth, Mark W. '"Sumer is Icumen In" as a Song.' *Chaucer Review* 14 (1979–80): 158–65.

Because 'Svmer is icumen in' [*3223*] has been explicated as a lyric, it offers 'a good occasion for exploring the significant difference between song and poem' (158). A lyric poem arouses the reader's romantic expectations and perhaps 'fixation upon that moment of inspired experience' at its creation. Booth considers the song and its music, with the words 'sung over each other by up to six voices' (160), as a round. He relates his findings to criticism, including that of Moore, **297,** Manning, **394,** Reiss, **583,** and Chambers and Sidgwick, **18.** Comparison with the Latin 'pious impostor,' *Perspice christicola,* in the same manuscript reveals the ME lyric as 'a genuine song' (161), in the experience of the singer and audience. Its 'most insistent sound is the nonsense sound of *cuccu,*' which is 'part of the magic that lifts us into celebration' (163), the conventional response to a spring song. The metrical structure and repetition of *cuccu* produce a 'strong rocking effect.' Thus 'the *rota* arrangement does no violence to the effective verbal structures of the verse, and even extends and amplifies their effects' (164).

3223.

709 Burrow, J.A. 'Poems without Contexts.' *Essays in Criticism* 29 (1979): 6–32 [cited]. [A paper given on 'Literature and its Context,' at the Conference of University Teachers of English, Southampton, 1978.] Repr. in *Essays on Medieval Culture.* J.A. Burrow. Oxford: Clarendon, 1984. 1–26.

Ten poems in English and two in French survive only in MS Bodleian Rawlinson D. 913. Burrow groups them by their position in the manuscript and subject matter, and deals first with the 'merest scraps: Items 2, 3 and 4' (8) ['þe gode mon on is weie,' *3361.3*; 'Ich aue a mantel i-maket of cloth,' *1301.5*; 'Ne sey neruer such a man a Iordan was,' *2288.5*], each of only one line. Items 1, 10, and 11 are 'clearly concerned . . . with sexual love.' Although the last, 'Al gold Ionet is þin her' [*179*], seems to be simple, more knowledge of its context could alter critical opinion. If it were the work of Chaucer, it would be 'a version of the pastoral, in Chaucer's "small-town" manner' (9). He sees in Item 1, 'Of eueryukune tre' [*2622*], a wooing song for a mistress described with nature-imagery; Speirs, **385,** sees a wooing song for a hawthorn tree. Item 10, 'Al nist by [þe] rose rose' [*194*], is generally read as an allegory of deflowering. Item 5, a French *chanson de mal mariée,* which 'conforms exactly to the pattern of the carol' (13), is interpreted more easily than Item 9, 'Wer þer ouþer in þis toun' [*3898*], in which the text is illegible and obscure. The last poem, a song of drinking, 'Ye Sir [þat is] idronken/dronken ydronken' [*4256.8*], conveys 'an effect of tipsy and slightly incoherent excitement' (16), perhaps for a dance. The most difficult poems are Items 7 and 8 ['Gode sire pray ich þe,' *1008*; 'Maiden in the mor lay,' *2037.5*]. The former, 'Icham of Irlaunde,' seems to be a carol that perhaps identifies Ireland, 'in the make-believe geography of the dance floor, with the area occupied by the soloist at the centre of the ring of carollers' (19). Burrow summarizes readings of *2037.5*, 'The Maid of the Moor,' and suggests that the other Rawlinson poems provide its context and imply a secular poem. He stresses the value of context to indicate the genre of a poem, and points to genre 'as an internal substitute for context' (27).

179, 194, 1008, 1301.5, 2037.5, 2288.5, 2622, 3361.3, 3898, 4256.8.

710 Dronke, Peter. 'The Song of Songs and Medieval Love-Lyric.' *The Bible and Medieval Culture.* Ed. W. Lourdaux and D. Verhelst. Mediaevalia Lovaniensia. Series 1, Studia 7. Louvain: Leuven UP, 1979. 236–62 [cited.] Repr. in *The Medieval Poet and His World.* Peter Dronke. Storia e Lettera Raccolta di Studi e Testi 164. Rome: Storia e Letteratura, 1984. 209–36.

Examines medieval European lyrics influenced by versions of the Song of Songs, and by translations and paraphrases found in literature. Dronke cites the ME lyric 'Als i me rod this endre dai' [*360*] to show that here the girl, 'sick with love like the bride in the Canticle (*quia amore langueo*), both laments and cries out against the lover who has left her' (255).

360.

711 Frey, Charles. 'Transcribing and Editing *Western Wind.*' *Manuscripta* 22 (1979): 108–12.

Explores points of palaeographical and editorial doubt in 'Westron wynde when wylle thou blow' [*3899.3*]. The ninth and twelfth words are generally read *rayne*, but Frey notes differences between them and suggests that the twelfth could be *vayne, wayne,* or *bayne,* creating ambiguity compounded by the interpretation of *can.* The fourth word could be *wyll* or *wylt*; Frey prefers the former. The poem may be closed with an exclamation mark, but Frey proposes 'a period or, better . . . no punctuation.' Editing should show the speaker's wish for 'a change in the weather, just as he or she desires a change from the temper of that poignant loneliness,' and it should present the text 'in such a way as to let its unfettered strength stand forth' (111).

3899.3.

712 Hanson-Smith, Elizabeth. 'A Woman's View of Courtly Love: The Findern Anthology Cambridge University Library MS. Ff.1.6.' *Journal of Women's Studies in Literature* 1 (1979): 179–94.

Unlike Robbins, **54**, Hanson-Smith finds that many of the 24 secular lyrics of the Findern Anthology are 'written from the female perspective, in a woman's persona' (179). In support of her contention she cites 'direct reference to men as the object of love' (180); the unique occurrence of all but four lyrics; the use of Derbyshire dialect for the shorter poems (with Southeastern London dialect for longer poems, probably entered by professional scribes); and the possibility that authorial correction rather than scribal error explains some transcription practices. The lyrics express the limitations of social condition and mobility experienced by women. Their feelings show 'openness and *elan*' (186) towards their lovers, rather than the haughtiness and cruelty often evoked by male poets of courtly love. The motif of Fortune's wheel appears in poems frequently pervaded by 'a profound pessimism or fatalism' (187), with resignation as part of the female perspective. Male figures seem powerful, even in light-hearted references; the lover may be compared to a sovereign, priest, governor, or mentor. Humour, rather than an excuse such as the protection of virtue, is used to reject a lover. Themes in the Findern lyrics are those of other love poetry, but details suggest the female experience of love. [See McNamer, **958**.]

12, 360, 657, 1170, 1331, 2009, 2279, 3878, 3917, 4272.5.

Annotations of Critical Works 265

713 **Hirsh, John C.** '*I Seche a Youthe:* A Late Middle English Lyric.' *English Language Notes* 17 (1979–80): 163–5.

'I seche a þouthe þat eldyth no3t,' [*1356.3*] speaks of the religious life, 'the quest of a *homo viator*, and a simple attestation of the value of the life of a religious – perhaps a friar.' The idea of the paradoxical search is not unique; Hirsh cites other examples of the figure. In *1356.3* a secular search for youth that does not age becomes 'a sacred quest for eternal life' (164). References to need and strife could apply in most times, but one can discern a Lollard belief, that 'certain kinds of "nede" ought not to exist among Christians.' The last apology in this poem of spiritual quest informs the reader 'that he must begin in the present and that the best way to future perfection is to be found in the religious life.' The present tense in the last line emphasizes 'the abiding present and gives directions to the seemingly impossible quest' (165).

1356.3, 1356.5, 1359.

714 ———. 'Prayer and Meditation in Late Medieval England: MS Bodley 789.' *Medium Ævum* 48 (1979): 55–66. [Edition.]

Devotional literature may be affective or admonitory, depending on 'the disposition with which the reader addressed his codex.' Thus some texts in Harley 1706 may be read as instruction or prayers, according to the reader's choice. In Bodley 789, however, 18 articles, in prose and verse, offer 'a reasonably complete religious *vade mecum.*' A meditation 'ascribed to Bonaventure' lists six things the reader must know: 'the fourteen points of truth, the ten commandments, the seven sacraments, the seven works of mercy, the seven virtues, the seven deadly sins.' With a *Speculum Peccatoris*, these complete the first sequence. The next sequence has 'expositions on the Pater Noster, the Ave, the Creed, and the Ten Commandments, and an Art of Dying' (56). Hirsh considers the final series of devotions and prayers in detail. The introductory rubric and prose *ABC of Aristotle* stress the reader's helpless sinfulness, leading to a verse prayer to the Trinity, 'Almyghty god fadir of heuene' [*241*], and a prose accusation of Christ. 'Aware of his own sinfulness, mindful both of Christ's Passion and of his own salvation, and having just praised the Trinity, the reader now confronts the power of the divine, and its exclusiveness' (60), to confirm his wish to be saved and avoid damnation. The next poems are of the seven deadly sins ['Ihesu for þi precius blood,' *1707*] and a warning from a dead man ['Mi leeue lyf þat lyuest in welþe,' *2255*]. The latter's *Explicit* concludes 'not only the grim description of a corpse, but also the sequence of poems and prose texts that lead the devout reader into prayer and meditation' (62). In an appendix, Hirsh lists the poems in ff. 205–14^v of MS Harley 1706, and prints three previously unpublished ['Be ry3twys man what euer be-tyde,' *475*; 'Byleue in god þat alle haþ wrou3te,' *505*; 'Ihesus seynge peplys comynge hym tylle,' *1746*].

241, 469, 475, 505, 880, 1126, 1416, 1707, 1746, 1748, 1815, 2255, 2352, 2770, 3040, 3262, 3685.

715 **Jeffrey, David L.** 'Franciscan Spirituality and the Growth of Vernacular Culture.' *By Things Seen: Reference and Recognition in Medieval Thought*. Ottawa: U of Ottawa P, 1979. 143–60. [A revision of 'Franciscan Spirituality and the Elevation of Popular Culture,' *Annales canadiennes d'Histoire* 9 (1976): 1–18.]

Concludes a discussion of Franciscan theology and its use of aspects of popular culture by noting that 'the medieval vernacular lyric . . . is related by Franciscan aesthetics and spirituality to the social context and spiritual function of dramatic art' (158). Thus it can be related to identification and to redemption, 'not only in the usual theological sense, but in the redemption and elevation of popular culture through a beautiful literary expression' (158–9). Jeffrey illustrates his remarks by reference to 'Wynter wakeneþ al

746 Wilson, Edward. 'Some New Texts of Early Tudor Songs.' *Notes and Queries* 225 (1980): 293–5. [Edition.]

Most of the contents of BL MS Add. 60577 are 'religious, moral or pedagogic,' but seven songs are included among 'distinctively secular and courtly' (293) items. Three works ['O rote of trouth o princess to my pay,' *2547.5*; 'So put un feyre I dare not speke,' *3168.4*; 'That was my woo is nowe my most gladness,' *3297.5*] are also found in the Fayrfax or Ritson manuscripts; the others ['Why dare I not compleyne to my lady,' *7622*; 'Fortune vnfrendly þou art vnto me,' *7155*; 'Whan I wold fayne begynne to pleyne,' *7595*; 'A lady bry3t, fayre and gay,' *7014*] have not been recorded elsewhere. Wilson prints the songs, with notes on the texts.

2547.5, 3168.4, 3297.5, 7014, 7155, 7622, 7595.

747 ———. 'Two Unpublished Fifteenth-Century Poems from Lincoln College, Oxford, MS. Lat. 141.' *Notes and Queries* 225 (1980): 20–6. [Edition.]

Among the medieval items in this manuscript are a 'hitherto unrecorded Shoemaker's Testament . . . and a likewise unrecorded misogynistic carol' (20), which can 'probably be placed on the Cambridgeshire-Norfolk border.' The Shoemaker's Testament, 'Lystyne lordys verament,' [*7310*] may be a mnemonic used to teach the names of the shoemaker's tools, but the suggestion of irony in the burden implies 'the same literary predeliction as is shown by the satiric misogynistic carol which follows it' (21). Solomon is the stock figure of the anti-marital carol, 'Salomon þe wyse he tawt in his lyf' [*7458*], which warns against allowing a wife to rule her husband. Wilson edits and prints the poems, with full explanatory notes.

368, 7310, 7458.

748 Benedikz, B.S. 'Morning Prayer in Staffordshire.' *Occasional Papers in Linguistics and Language Learning* 8 (1981): 33–9. [Edition.]

MS Lichfield 10, 'a handsome, if sadly trimmed copy of the Wycliffite New Testament,' written 'in a clear, well-formed hand of c. 1410' (33), has a devotional poem, 'I þonke þe lord god ful of miht' [*1369*], in 'the space on fol. 124v not used up by the last verses of the Book of Revelation' (34). The manuscript lost its original covers and flyleaves in the most recent binding, and its origin seems to have been in the West Midlands. The poem is found 'in only one other MS, the Simeon MS (now MS BL Add. 22283), which also has strong Midlands connections' (34). Benedikz prints the poem and records significant differences from the Simeon version, in particular the omission of the Simeon scribe's instruction to recite the *Ave Maria* after the second stanza. These changes imply the influence of Wycliffite scriptures and suggest that 'the omissions may represent an exercise in Staffordshire Lollardry' (38).

1369.

749 Bloomfield, Morton W. 'Thomas of Hales' *A Love Rune* (1250–1270): A Christian Didactic Poem.' *Europäische Lehrdichtung: Festschrift für Walter Naumann zum 70. Geburstag.* Ed. Herbert Walz. Darmstadt: Wissenschaftliche Buchgesellschaft, 1981. 49–60.

'A Luue Ron' [*66*] teaches and exhorts 'the glory of chastity' (49). Bloomfield prints the text and describes the rhyme scheme before exploring the thematic structure, which begins with 'a kind of brief *razo*' to explain that 'a maid asks Thomas about a true lover' (54). This and the last three stanzas, addressed to the maiden, frame the poem. Two prose lines that follow the poem pray for the poet's good death, offering 'the sign of a good destination in the next world' and 'a personal reference . . . back to the beginning of the poem.' The themes of the 'inner poem' are *contemptus mundi* (lines 9–89) and *sponsa Christi* (lines 89–184). They contrast human love with that of the true lover, Christ, who is 'always faithful, powerful and always beautiful and attentive.' The maid is 'probably a laywoman,' but could be 'a nun thinking of abandoning her virginity' (55). The first section presents the *ubi sunt* topos (lines 65–72), including the words 'So the schef is of the cleo,' which Bloomfield translates 'As the sheaf is by the sickle' (56–7). In contrast, Christ is a lover whose virtues are 'loyalty, wealth, power, beauty, permanence and love,' whose love is 'pure and always chaste.' Apocalyptic imagery describes Solomon's temple, 'the reward to the true lovers of Christ' (58). The maid's virginity is her greatest treasure. The poem is the didactic, direct address of a teacher to his pupil, and the term 'Rune' implies 'an inner meaning,' here 'the paradoxical secret: that he who truly loves, loves Christ.' The form suggests secret wisdom, with the poem 'enclosed in a frame which must be "opened" to understand but which also must remain closed' (59), as virginity is 'forever held within the frame of desire' (60).

66.

750 Boffey, Julia. 'Two Unnoticed Love-Lyrics from the Early Sixteenth Century.' *Notes and Queries* 226 (1981): 20–1. [Edition.]

Presents text and commentary on a love epistle, 'my owne dere hart I grete you well' [*7373*], and a cryptogram, 'I love goode alle þat ys no fayle' [*7228*], which are found in two BL manuscripts: Harley 4011 and Add. 38666. The name may be explained 'by unsophisticated guesswork as "Alice" ("Alle-ys") or "Goodall" (the lady's surname), or [is] else all too cunningly concealed' (21).

7228, 7373.

751 Burton, T.L. 'Ne Saltou Neuer, Leuedi.' *Explicator* 39.3 (1981): 19–21.

Refutes Sisam's suggestion, **480**, that the lyric ['Ne saltou neuer leuedi Tuynklen wyt þin eyen,' *2288*] consists of three unrelated and possibly corrupted scraps. The lines are the complete monologue 'of a frustrated lover, in which he first threatens to take revenge on his lady for her hard-heartedness, and finally (in his imagination) carries out the threat' (19). In a detailed account of the lines, Burton notes ambiguities and the change from a generalized to a specific threat. The result is a poem that could seem 'a declaration of intended rape,' but is 'wish-fulfilment.' It is 'a male counterpart of the song of the "litel mai" ' of 'Als i me rod this endre dai' [*360*], and rejects 'the courtly love ethic of limitless service without thought for reward' (20). Corruption may be discounted since 'the raggedness of the rhyme and syntax' are consonant with the thoughts of 'a lover whose patience is exhausted' (21).

360, 2288.

752 ———. ' "The Fair Maid of Ribblesdale" and the Problem of Parody.' *Essays in Criticism* 31 (1981): 282–98.

Although it may be difficult to recognize and prove the existence of ME parody, the poet may give internal signals of intention to create it. Burton examines 'The Fair Maid of Ribblesdale' [*2207*] for such signs. He prints the text, with MnE notes from several sources, and compares aspects of the poem with similar details in poems that are assumed not to be parodic. The single place-name 'Ribblesdale,' an area 'of limited extent and wild terrain,' appearing instead of the usual formula of extent, expressed by two names, seems deflationary; it may imply that 'the woman is no beauty' and suggest to the audience that 'this poem is not going to be straightforward' (287). The poet lists unexpected attributes, such as the lady's boldness and the noon-time brightness of her complexion, with surprising details, such as the arching of *both* eyebrows, and the possibility that her nose is 'the cause of the speaker's impending death' (290). There are similarly strange descriptions of her teeth and neck, and estimates of the length of her arms suggest either a gorilla or a midget. Indelicate and irreverent images are associated with the lady's breasts and girdle. The poem does not conform to conventions of expectation, common sense, or delicacy, and has exaggerated, contradictory, inconsequential, equivocal, and blasphemous descriptions. Taken together, 'a small number of blatant internal indicators will suffice to convey the author's intention,' so that the poet's manipulations of convention 'fall into place as part of the parody' (296).

105, 515, 751, 754, 1010, 1216, 1394, 1395, 1449, 1504, 1768, 2031, 2207, 2232, 2236, 2359, 2421, 2437, 2491, 2640, 3144, 3236, 3465, 4019, 4037, 4194, 4209, 4282.

753 Coleman, Janet. *English Literature in History 1350–1400: Medieval Readers and Writers.* London: Hutchinson, 1981.

Considers literature intended 'to instruct, exhort and ultimately, to inspire readers to criticize and eventually reform social practice' (16), and relates the works to historical events. In 'Vernacular literacy and lay education' (18–57), Coleman surveys French and ME texts and their readers, and notes changes in the balance in the use of the languages. She discusses the nature and sources of literacy; the universities, schools, and education; and the influence of bishops and other patrons. The spread of literacy reveals differences in tastes and diction of readers in courtly and middle classes, with romance literature 'drawing heavily on gallicisms,' whereas the 'literature of edification' develops 'a specifically English vocabulary to suit its polemical purposes' (43). Examination of administrative records and imaginative literature conveys an idea of the social structure, and implies 'an extended public for both kinds of writing' (46). The works of Chaucer and Langland, in particular, should be read against the social background. 'The literature of social unrest' (58–156) surveys condemnation of the age, in specifically spiritual, social, and political works, such as *Pierce the Plowman's Crede* ['Crose and curteys Christ thys begynnyng spede,' *663*] and verses of John Ball ['John Ball Saint Mary priest,' *1791*; 'Johan the Muller hath ygrownde smal smal,' *1796*]. The audience of complaint was not likely to be the 'peasantry' or 'immobile rural small freeholder[s],' but rather 'lower echelons of the middle class.' This hints that a middle class can be defined 'in terms of literacy' (63). There is nationalist propaganda against the French, Scots, and papacy, including Minot's poems of Edward III's campaigns. Early complaint verse (including some Harley lyrics) is trilingual; the verse airs themes of injustice and corruption later elaborated by Gower. Some late fourteenth-century complaint condemns war with France, and much of it speaks against the clergy, citing simony at all levels. Some of the verse judges individuals, especially the king's advisers, often in terms of heraldic allusions. 'Memory, preaching and the literature of a society in transition' (157–231) deals with the interaction of oral and written literature, the alliterative revival, and the significance of the Bible and theological writings. Preaching handbooks, such as John Grimestone's, include lyrics and tags to explain Latin teachings. Coleman pays much attention to preaching and Lollardy. In 'Theology, non-scholastic literature and poetry' (232–70) she examines theological dispute outside universities, and compares texts of *Piers Plowman* [*1459*]. She finds that people of the prosperous, enterprising fifteenth century wanted 'a literature that soothed, entertained and comforted, rather than one that disrupted and questioned' (270). Her 'Conclusion' (271–80), stresses the value of comparing literary and historical data. She notes literature's 'social function,' as 'a consciously wrought medium used either to support a contemporary ethic or incite to change,' and stresses that few works were '"mere" entertainment and escapist' (274). Many religious lyrics express affective piety, and the didactic poetry questions commonplaces, to show 'what lay beneath the assumed smooth surface of an age of simple faith' (278). The literature, like the period, was in transition.

5, 296.3, 411, 424, 585, 663, 709, 759, 817, 1034.5, 1162, 1320, 1353, 1459, 1475, 1523, 1749, 1832, 1845, 1894, 2006.8, 2048, 2054, 2149, 2189, 2662, 2684, 3113, 3137, 3212, 3428, 3448, 3899, 4008, 4019, 4029, 4165, 7251, 7276, 7302, 7339, 7543, 7549, 7567.

754 Croft, P.J. 'The "Friar of Order Gray" and the Nun.' *Review of English Studies* NS 23 (1981): 1–16. [Edition.]

Describes a 'small unbound paper bifolium' found by Henry Bradshaw, and designated King's College MS 21B. This contains 'four otherwise unknown late medieval English carols transcribed in three different hands of late fifteenth-century type.' The first two of these, 'Of mary a mayd withowt lesyng [*2635.5*] and 'The ffather of heuyn from aboue' [*3328.5*], have been edited by Robbins, **490**, and Greene, **86**. They are 'conventional hymns employing a *Te Deum* refrain' ascribed to the Franciscan James Ryman. The others, which tell of a friar and a nun [both 'I pray yow maydens euerychone, *1344.5*], are among few recorded ribald carols. The bifolium is complete, not a fragment. Carol 3 is 'an audacious anti-clerical satire' in which the 'simple tale of seduction becomes a parody of the sung liturgy.' It represents 'a sophisticated human reaction to the unremitting piety of Ryman and his kind' (2). Carol 4 is 'innocent of a satirical dimension.' Croft explores carol 3, and corrects the misreadings of *Segnory* to *Bequory*, 'sustaining the musical metaphor' (3), and *depe* to *sepe*, 'normal medieval spelling of Latin *saepe*.' The nun's song, answering the friar's lesson, continues 'the thread of irreverent allusions to the Vulgate which runs through all the carol's Latin phrases' (4). Other playful uses of Latin forms include the allusion to *pungere, tollum* as a 'latinization of the vernacular "thole," ' the macaronic pun in *lapides*, and 'the nun's vernacular *Quoniam*' (5). Casual popular references show that ' "the friar and the nun" had for long a scandalous reputation which outstripped even that more recently enjoyed by "the bishop and the actress" ' (6), and that his reputation is probably implied in Petruchio's song in *The Taming of the Shrew*. The bifolium's possible provenance suggests an association with a book owned by Richard Green (perhaps a chorister at King's College), which was later used in binding a book that belonged to 'Samuel Thoms alias Toms alias Thomas' (12), who gave manuscripts to King's College. Bradshaw's designation of the bifolium as MS 21B may mean that he inserted it in MS 21 'for protection until he could return for a closer examination' (14). The satirical carol may be the original unvulgarized text on the 'friar-and-nun' theme. Croft prints the texts of carols 3 and 4.

2635.5, 3328.5, 3443.5.

755 Fries, Maureen. 'The "Other" Voice: Woman's Song, its Satire and its Transcendence in Late Medieval British Literature.' *Vox Feminae: Studies in Medieval Woman's Song*. Ed. John F. Plummer. Studies in Medieval Culture 15. Medieval Institute Publications. Kalamazoo, MI: Western Michigan U, 1981. 155–78.

Woman's song, as diverse as the Virgin's *planctus* and the pastourelle, is characterized by its Otherness. Its conventions and characteristics differ from those of the male-voiced lyric. The characteristics include concentration on 'a particular beloved man' (unlike the male persona's 'obsession with itself'); cultural distinction of voices through use of 'a vernacular or dialect [for the female] as opposed to a learned tongue [for the male]'; the speaker's absorption in 'experience of the beloved's presence in or absence from her arms'; powerlessness, even when the woman is rhetorically dominant, 'most dramatically illustrated in the *alba*' (159); and occasional capacity for satire, as in the pastourelle. Fries cites examples from ME and Middle Scots poetry, with emphasis on opposed examples of behaviour related to Mary and to Eve, found in *planctus* and carols of betrayed girls. Chaucer manipulates traditions of the *alba* in the *Reeve's Tale* and the *Merchant's Tale* [*4019*], and in *Troilus and Criseyde* [*3327*]. Henryson performs similar manipulation in *The Tale of the Cock and the Fox* [*3703*], 'Robene and Makyne' [*2831*], and Cresseid's 'Complaint' in *The Testament of Cresseid* [*285*], as does Dunbar in 'The tretis of the tua mariit wemen and the wedo' [*3845.5*]. Woman's song is generally other, 'not only to the predominant male voice which utters the real "stuff of courtoisie" but to the pervasive male warrior ethos from which the female persona emerged' (173).

14, 285, 352, 360, 377, 404, 1299, 1460, 1849, 1899, 2036, 2619, 2831, 3327, 3692, 3703, 3845.5, 4019, 4159, 4189.

756 Gray, Douglas. 'A Middle English Illustrated Poem.' *Medieval Studies for J.A.W. Bennett* Aetatis Suae LXX. Ed. P.L. Heyworth. Oxford: Clarendon, 1981. 185–205. [Edition.]

The poem 'Glorieux crosse that with the holy blood' [*914*], based on the Litany, is found in 'a particularly fine example of an illustrated devotional book, the "Beauchamp Hours", now in the Library of the Fitzwilliam Museum' (185). Other sources of the poem include the 'Talbot Hours,' an adaptation in Blairs College, Aberdeen, and MS Cotton Tiberius B.iii. Gray describes the first book, which was probably made for Margaret Beauchamp, and some of its illustrations, and compares other books of hours and devotional literature. He considers, in particular, the arrangement of illustrations and relationship of images and words. In general, the relationship is 'a simple and practical one: the image gives a visual focus for the reader of the words, and the words direct the eye of the worshipper to the image' (187–8). In *914* there is a 'simple pattern of image followed by words' (188), which is 'complementary,' so that 'each part exists in its own right, and illuminates the other' (189). This differs from the 'neatly reciprocal' relationship of the *Arma Christi* ['O vernacule I honoure him and the,' *2577*]. Gray compares versions of *914* and other poems based on the Litany, and prints the poem 'with a minimum of emendation' (194), noting variations in the textual notes. Some words have Northern forms, but the spelling in the Beauchamp, Talbot, and Blairs manuscripts more strikingly reveals their French origin. The scribe's alterations to pronouns (from singular to plural) in the Beauchamp text may suggest a trend 'towards the more general "congregational" form' or 'the more romantic possibility that he made the changes with his patron's wife in mind, so that she might include her spouse with herself in her prayer' (196).

529, 672, 914, 1704, 1831, 2115, 2282, 2577, 3027, 3584.

757 Greenberg, Cheryl. 'Marie Moder, Wel The Be: A Study of the Mnemonic Lyric.' *Neuphilologische Mitteilungen* 82 (1981): 289–94.

The lyric 'Mary moder well thou be' [*2119*] exemplifies penitence and petition. It presents an example 'of how prayer should be offered,' to express 'sorrow for sin and the desire for amendment' (289), and then to pray for the speaker, friends, foes, and those who do good and evil, to ask for all that is needed in life and after death. Its pattern follows 'outlines for prayer in contemporary prose expositions.' The form is mnemonic, and it achieves memorability by 'the use of four-stressed lines in rhyming couplet form' (290). Greenberg demonstrates the importance of the rhyme scheme as an aid to learning by breaking the stanzas, 'so that the couplet forms the single prayer unit' (291). Copying of such a lyric would produce variations in the lines. Greenberg discusses variations of this poem and similar works, and finds that the mnemonic poems form a genre 'clearly distinguishable from the so-called "invocatory" type of the same period' (293), although their petitions allow for a transition to those lyrics. They differ from the devotions of elegant praise to Mary found in the Prymer, but were known to a wider audience.

1030, 2099, 2110, 2118, 2119.

758 Heffernan, Thomas J. 'Four Middle English Religious Lyrics from the Thirteenth Century.' *Mediaeval Studies* 43 (1981): 131–50. [Edition.]

The lyrics are on a vellum bifolium, perhaps used for binding, which Heffernan describes in detail. The first, 'Bird us neure bliþe be' [*550.5*], begins with a version of the 'Three Sorrowful Things' and the entire poem may be an expansion of this theme. The stanzas deal with Christian counsel and charity, God's healing powers, and Mary's role as *mediatrix nostra*. The poem has its resolution in implications of *contemptus mundi*, man's need to 'renounce earth in order to gain heaven.' Although the second lyric fragment, '[I] wote a boure so bricht' [*1393.5*], could be secular or religious, 'the context of the other poems argues for a religious theme' (137). The third, '*Godes boure as tu gane bilde' [**995.2*], is acephalous, and the number of lines lost cannot be estimated. Its first three stanzas are addressed to Mary as *mediatrix*; the remainder of the poem depicts 'events necessary for salvation,' in a way intended 'to stimulate the listener and/or reader to spiritual contemplation' (138). The last poem, a version of 'God þat al þis myhtes may' [*968*], is 'a penitential piece designed to illustrate the all-encompassing mercy of God and man's repeated opportunity for salvation' (138). Heffernan describes metrical and linguistic features of the lyrics in detail, and prints the poems with notes.

550.5, 631, 968, *995.2, 1393.5, 1394, 3939.

759 ———. 'On the Importance of *Schrifte*: A Middle English Poem on Penance.' *Neuphilologische Mitteilungen* 82 (1981): 362–7. [Edition.]

'Lenten is an holy tyme' [*1860*] has been described in *IMEV* as 'a fragment based on the last 92 lines of the *Quadragesima* piece in the *South English Legendary* ["Leynte comeþ þer afterward þ^t six wike i-lasteþ," *1859*]' (362), but Heffernan finds the affiliation mistaken and the error compounded by confusion with 'Lenten ys come wiþ loue to toune' [*1861*] in *SIMEV*. The texts of *1860* and *1859* differ significantly, and 'the addition of another 77 lines to the *SEL* composition would surely represent sufficient amplification to give the two texts a markedly different character.' The author of *1860* may have been 'a mendicant preacher fulfilling his catechetical obligations' (363), by presenting popular homiletic themes for Lent. Heffernan comments on the use of metre, rhyme and alliteration. He suggests that the text 'need not derive from a specific source, but rather is simply yet another representative expression of a much discussed topic in fourteenth-century England.' He prints the poem, which is an example of 'admonitory verses written in homiletic fashion and intended for oral delivery' (365).

1859, 1860, 1861.

760 ———. 'The Affiliation of Houghton MS 1032 and the *Northern Homily Cycle*: A Disclaimer.' *Notes and Queries* 226 (1981): 301–3.

Seeks to establish that the 'fragmentary exemplum of Theobaldus and the Leper in Harvard University, Houghton Library MS 1032' (301–2) is related to 'kindred versions in *Jacob's Well* and the *Alphabet of Tales*' (302), rather than the homiletic exemplum ['Hit was an Erl of muche miht,' *1645*] of the *Northern Homily Cycle.*' *SIMEV* proposes the latter connection, but each story has its source in the exempla of Jacques de Vitry. Heffernan prints a transcription of the exemplum from Houghton 1032.

1645.

761 King, Pamela M. 'Eight English *Memento Mori* Verses from Cadaver Tombs.' *Notes and Queries* 226 (1981): 494–6. [Edition.]

The effigy of the individual on these cadaver tombs depicts the body 'as a shrouded corpse, in a state of putrefaction, or as a skeleton' (494). The tombs' exhortation to penance reveals their purpose of *memento mori* as well as that of recording the donors' names. King prints the poems, only two of which have previously been published ['Here lythe Joh Brigge under this marbil ston,' *1206.6*; 'Here lieth Marmaduke Cunstable of Flaynborght knyght,' *7197*].

1206.6, 1206.7, 7197, 7315, 7335, 7461, 7529, 7621.

762 Lucas, Peter J. 'The Versions by John Shirley, William Gybbe and Another, of the Poem "On the Virtues of the Mass": A Collation.' *Notes and Queries* 226 (1981): 394–8. [Edition.]

Versions of 'St Augustine on the Virtues of the Mass' ['Now herken euery man bothe more and lesse,' *2323*; 'Nowe vnderstonde boþe more and lesse,' *2373*] are found in Trinity College, Cambridge, MS R.3.21 (T) and two Bodleian manuscripts: Ashmole 59 (A) and Rawlinson poet. 118 (R). Version A was written by John Shirley, and version R by William Gybbe. Lucas notes codicological and textual aspects of relevant introductory matter and presents the previously unprinted A and R [both listed at *2373*], 'collating them with each other and with the version T [*2323*], which is already in print' (395). Lucas comments on R's manuscript context, of works on the sanctity of marriage and the need to live virtuously to attain salvation, and on Gybbe's alterations of the text to suit his purpose. He prints A and R side by side, and comments on differences from each other and from T, proposing that Gybbe may have thought the text was 'designed to be readily recalled from memory.' He suggests that variation in the deference felt by scribes in their approaches to texts 'should be taken into account when modern scholars comment, often adversely, on the work of medieval scribes' (398).

1107, 1762, 2052, 2323, 2373.

763 Matonis, A.T.E. 'Middle English Alliterative Poetry.' *So Meny People Longages and Tonges: Philological Essays in Scots and Mediæval English presented to Angus McIntosh.* Ed. Michael Benskin and M.L. Samuels. Edinburgh: Benskin and Samuels, 1981. 341–54.

Indicates 'technical features' of 'the "non-classical," shorter stanzaic alliterative poem' (341), and includes Harley lyrics among examples of the form. Matonis bases her examination on the following: counting and notation of alliterative syllables with secondary metrical stress; metrical ambiguity and variety within a poem; compound or alternating alliteration on syllables with varying stress, thereby accounting for supplementary alliteration; generic alliteration and numerical classification of alliterating syllables; consonantal correspondence or *cynghanedd* [see **582**]. She challenges the notion of regular alliteration of four stressed syllables in shorter stanzaic alliterative poems, to show that frequently lines alliterate 'only three of the four metrically stressed syllables in a line.' To this end she cites numerous examples of 'compound, alternating, and generic alliteration' (347), and records tables of alliterations per line in 10 poems and alliterative patterns in 11. The variations illustrate difficulties experienced in formulation of rules, caused by 'metrical diversity within a poem and within the tradition itself during this period' (350). Matonis uses passages from 'The Satire on the Consistory Courts' [*2287*], 'The Satire on the Retinues of the Great' [*2649*], and Audelay's '*De tribus regibus mortuis*' [*2677*] to illustrate the influence of metrical traditions and alliterative mannerisms. She demonstrates that some descriptive categories may not accommodate 'the variety of alliterative, metrical and stylistic mannerisms present in much of this verse' (352).

295, 1216, 1320.5, 1394, 1449, 2166, 2287, 2322, 2608, 2649, 2677, 2744, 3144, 3445, 3462, 3838, 3874.

764 Medcalf, Stephen. 'On Reading Books from a Half-Alien Culture.' *The Later Middle Ages.* Ed. Stephen Medcalf. London: Methuen, 1981. The Context of English Literature. 1–55.

Explores a modern reader's wish to understand intentions and nuances and to reconcile familiar and unfamiliar aspects of medieval literature. This exploration is exemplified in reading 'I syng of a myden þ^t is makeles' [*1367*], not as translation, but 'more like reading a book of our own age in which certain idioms and words escape us' (9). Medcalf assesses associations, imagery, and shades of meaning, and compares 'Nu þis fules singet hand maket hure blisse' [*2366*], from which *1367* is derived. He examines medieval and twentieth-century ideas of authorship, and the oral nature of medieval literature, which ensures that some lyrics seem 'to carry their own music with them over and above the ordinary music of words' (14). Although the medieval period was one of increasing literacy, private reading need not have meant abandoning 'oral feeling for literature' (15). Poetry could have fitted 'the general situation of the arts,' such as painting, sculpture, or building, as one of the 'craft skills' (18). Medcalf uses examples from the mystery plays, and works of Chaucer, Lydgate, the *Gawain* poet, and Langland, to illustrate his comments on aspects of society, including public and personal piety. He notes that the history of the carols ran parallel to that of the mystery plays. His historical summary begins with the period before 1373, roughly coinciding with 'the long reign of Edward III (1327–77)' (37). This period includes 1497 to *c.*1525, in which '[t]he most powerful writing is a pure, intense crystallization of the Middle Ages' (45–6), when Dunbar, Douglas, and Skelton were writing. It concludes with *c.*1525 to 1549, 'the purging of the Middle Ages' (48), of which Thomas Cranmer's first Book of Common Prayer is the 'typical product' (49). The bibliography (53–5) includes brief comments on the works cited.

117, 285, 693, 925, 991, 1011.5, 1132, 1168, 1367, 1459, 1463, 1842.5, 2178, 2366, 2381, 2464, 2591, 2744, 2831.6, 2832.2, 3137, 3144, 3327, 3412, 3691, 3899.3, 4019.

765 Mooney, Linne R. 'Additions and Emendations to *The Index of Middle English Verse* and its *Supplement.*' *Anglia* 99 (1981): 394–8.

Presents additions and emendations to *IMEV* and *SIMEV* (generally concerned with practical verse) and includes some new entries presented in the format of *SIMEV*.

42.5, 73, 199.3, 292.5, 444, 674, 688, 861.7, 1253, 1396, 1410.5, 1423, 1426.1, 1436.3, 1502, 1545, 1651.8, 1905, 1989, 2323.4, 2624, 2668, 3074.4, 3157, 3265, 3413.6, 3423, 3449, 3479, 3503, 3571, 3572, 3632, 3638.6, 3729.7, 3848, 4040, 4148, 4175, 4175.1, 4253, 4258, 4264.2.

766 Nitecki, Alicia K. 'The Convention of the Old Man's Lament in the *Pardoner's Tale.*' *Chaucer Review* 16 (1981–2): 76–84.

The mimetic use of conventions for portrayal of old age in the *Pardoner's Tale* [*4019*] allows 'new psychological significance.' Chaucer draws on the work of Maxiamus and Innocent III who cite the miseries of age, to warn against pride, and to recall the transience of the world, in their 'descriptions of aging . . . to show the levelling effect which old age has on man' (76). Chaucer's use of lyric elements is seen in the old man's elegaic complaint, which is directly related to meditative lyrics seeking 'the meaning of old age' (77) and most closely linked to 'Herkneþ to mi ron' [*1115*]. Nitecki explores differences in Chaucer's treatment from that of other works, including *Piers Plowman* [*1459*] and *The Parlement of the Thre Ages* [*1556*]. She concludes that the lament is 'no longer merely a lament on old age,' and that the topos is rather 'a trope for the human longing for transcendence' (83).

718, 1115, 1216, 1459, 1556, 2092, 3996, 4019.

767 Osberg, Richard H. 'A Hand-List of Short Alliterating Metrical Poems in Middle English.' *JEGP* 80 (1981): 313–26.

Summarizes patterns of alliteration in ME lyrics to indicate resemblances to OE types and to distinguish between alliterative lyrics and 'those which simply contain alliteration' (314). Osberg supplies tables of frequency of alliterative phrases in lyrics and other literature to show that, although lyricists were 'actively engaged in creating new alliterative language,' the frequent use of some phrases points to 'the dependence on a core vocabulary of alliterative formulae' (315). The list of short alliterative poems that have been edited includes 29 isolable lyrics from the *Corpus Christi* plays.

.1, 2, 4, 5, 20, 33.5, 60, 78, 105, 182, 196.5, 197.8, 354, 371, 374, 429, 515, 521, 541.5, 544, 562, 563, 583, 585, 598, 605, 631, 718, 752, 759, 763, 766, 767, 811, 814, 848, 864, 872, 884, 891, 912.5, 986, 1026, 1031, 1032, 1034.5, 1038.5, 1039, 1044, 1053, 1055, 1075, 1116, 1182, 1186, 1216, 1320, 1320.5, 1352, 1365, 1373.5, 1379, 1394, 1395, 1402, 1443, 1448, 1449, 1450, 1455, 1470.8, 1475, 1504, 1532, 1596, 1608.5, 1628.5, 1715, 1733, 1830, 1848, 1861, 1889, 1926, 1974, 2007, 2009, 2039, 2066, 2073, 2108, 2128.5, 2149, 2159, 2162, 2166, 2189, 2207, 2214, 2215, 2216, 2273, 2280, 2287, 2302, 2308.5, 2384.8, 2470, 2498, 2517, 2526, 2599, 2604, 2607, 2615, 2619.2, 2634, 2649, 2678, 2682, 2684.5, 2686, 2742, 2773, 2781, 2792, 2800, 2811.5, 2902, 2988, 3031, 3069, 3074.3, 3080, 3101, 3104, 3256, 3349, 3352, 3408, 3435, 3438.3, 3462, 3513, 3707.8, 3719, 3730, 3796, 3801, 3819, 3820.5, 3821, 3838, 3873, 3874, 3881, 3896, 3921, 3925, 3929, 3939, 3988, 3996, 4029, 4044, 4083, 4116, 4135, 4162, 4194, 4206, 4268, 7003, 7036, 7037, 7038, 7043, 7049, 7050, 7053, 7135, 7136, 7164, 7170, 7173, 7174, 7178, 7179, 7218, 7230, 7233, 7273, 7274, 7319, 7369, 7384, 7396, 7403, 7536, 7581, 7643.

768 Plummer, John F. 'The Woman's Song in Middle English and its European Backgrounds.' *Vox Feminae: Studies in Medieval Woman's Song.* Ed. John F. Plummer. Studies in Medieval Culture 15. Medieval Institute Publications. Kalamazoo, MI: Western Michigan U, 1981. 135–54.

Relates ME woman's song to European forms, to argue against the perception of a popular form distinct from the 'courtly' lyric, and to imply 'that woman's songs and the male-voiced love lyric arose from fundamentally different social and cultural milieux.' Woman's song is more narrative and realistic, dealing with love and sex, carnal in *ethos*, and 'within *stilus humilis*,' with 'the *fabliau*, the *pastourelle*, and the farce' (135). It is of the boundaries of courtly experience (unlike the central male-voiced lyric) and it may be related to dance songs and carols. Although it seems popular in origin, like the *chanson de toile*, woman's song may be revealed as 'archaizing, sophisticated artifice,' just as the 'open sensuousness' of Walter von der Vogelweide's 'Under der linden' is 'an artistic male creation' (139). The songs include the *chanson de mal mariée* and ironic lament of the abandoned maiden. The latter often involves a clerical seducer, and this aspect may be conveyed in macaronic verse, by juxtaposition of Latin and vernacular lines. The '[g]libness and trickery' often mentioned by the maiden are 'proverbial attributes of the clergy in medieval anticlerical satire and in the *fabliaux*' (143), as in the *Miller's Tale* [*4019*], *Dame Siriʒ* [*342*], and the *Interludium de Clerico et Puella* [*668*]. Such a character does not appear in male love songs. The maiden and her lover are stereotypes and treated unsympathetically. Some woman's songs express the woman's satisfaction in her sexual activities. Plummer sees a pattern in such songs. He questions the idea that 'O lorde so swett ser Iohn dothe kys' [*2494*], 'one of the best of the English wanton woman's songs' (148), is 'realistic and popular' (149), but finds the Scots *chanson d'aventure* 'Wa Worth Maryage' antifeminist. In ME songs the woman enunciates 'a non-courtly position,' frequently involving 'either a headstrong carnality or a hapless sexual carelessness' (150). Antifeminism and class feelings contribute, but neither of these is the only explanation. The ME song must be seen as 'one branch of a lyric tradition as old as European vernacular lyrics in themselves' (151). Plummer supplies a list of ME woman's songs (151–2).

225, 342, 377, 438, 445, 668, 1008, 1091, 1265, 1286.5, 1269.5, 1330, 1849, 2236, 2494, 2654, 3174, 3409, 3418, 3594, 3832.5, 3897.5, 3902.5, 4019, 7286.

769 Pope, Nancy P. 'An Unlisted Variant of *Index to Middle English Verse* No. 2787.' *Notes and Queries* 226 (1981): 197–9. [Edition.]

'*Quant homme deit parleir videat que verba loquatur*' [*2787*] is a collection of macaronic proverbs found in Trinity College, Dublin MS 517. Pope explains its relation to other texts of the work, with a table of variant lines. She prints it, with notes on variants and some words.

2787.

770 Stemmler, Theo. 'Die englische Literatur.' *Europäisches Hochmittelalter.* Ed. Henning Krauss et al. *Neues Handbuch der Literaturwissenschaft.* Ed. Klaus von See et al. Vol. 7. Wiesbaden: Akademische Verlagsgesellschaft, 1981. 513–34. 9 vols. 1972–83.

A general historical study illustrated with numerous examples, many of which are lyrics (524–33). Stemmler supplies a German translation for some of the texts. He first discusses changing patterns in the use of languages in England, particularly after the Norman Conquest. These patterns tended to make English a spoken language, scarcely represented in literature until the thirteenth century. He contrasts Provençal, French, and German literature which flowered earlier. In the explication of earlier works he compares 'The Grave' [*3497*] and 'The Soul's Address to the Body' [**2684.5*]; he examines 'The Owl and the Nightingale' [*1384*] and compares passages with various lyrics (518–21) . Stemmler suggests reasons for the scarcity of early lyrics, and remarks that many poems must have circulated orally. Common characteristics of those preserved include their brevity, religious themes, paired rhymes, and connections with the life of a saint. These features are exemplified in St Godric's hymn, 'Seinte marie clane uirgine' [*2988*], and a hymn to St Thomas Becket, 'Haly thomas of heouenriche' [*1233*]. Stemmler describes in detail the earliest secular lyric preserved, '[þ]eh þet hi can wittes fule-wis' [*3512*], which precedes courtly poetry such as the Harley lyrics. Most early lyrics are religious, and Marian, Passion, or *memento mori* poems. Their mood is serious until the replacement of this kind of piety by the joyous Franciscan style later in the thirteenth century. Stemmler offers close analysis of several lyrics. He notes similarities to 'The Owl and the Nightingale' in *3512* and in 'Leuedi sainte marie moder and meide' [*1839*], and considers implications of the seemingly fragmented text of 'Mirie it is while sumer ilast' [*2163*].

445, 631, 1233, 1272, 1384, 1395, 1839, 2070, 2163, 2164, 2305, 2320, 2988, 3497, 3512, 7258.

771 Stevens, John. '*Angelus ad virginem:* the History of a Medieval Song.' *Medieval Studies for J.A.W. Bennett* Aetatis Suae LXX. Ed. P.L. Heyworth. Oxford: Clarendon, 1981. 297–328. [Edition.]

A detailed account of the Latin lyric, its sources, and musical settings. Stevens finds evidence of its popularity in two ME translations, one accompanying it in BL Arundel MS 248 ['Gabriel fram evene king,' *888*], and another, by John Audelay, in Bodleian Library, Douce MS 302 ['The angel to þe virgyn said,' *3305*]. He prints both translations. The Arundel version seems to be 'little more than a loose paraphrase of the Latin,' whereas Audelay's translation represents 'the pith of the Latin text in almost every line.' Audelay preserves the scheme of metre and rhyme 'almost intact,' and is 'more consistently close to the metre of the Latin,' although variations in numbers of syllables suggest that 'he was writing a *contrafactum* to the melody.' The 'most curious feature' in Audelay's work is his omission of the stanza of 'the Virgin's humble acceptance of her divine mission' and the insertion of 'an extra stanza which turns out to be a close translation of the stanza unique to the Digby MS [147]' (310).

888, 3305.

772 Stouck, Mary-Ann. 'A Reading of the Middle English *Judas.*' *JEGP* 80 (1981): 188–98.

Surveys representations of Judas to trace the change from 'the archvillain of Christian history' to 'something of an archunderdog' (188). Stouck summarizes 'Judas' [*1649*], comparing readings of Schueler, **660**, and Baum, **142**, and relates the poem to the Gospels, to show that the most significant additions are in 'Judas' encounter with the woman and his subsequent agreement with Pilate' (191). She probes Judas' motivation and the significance of the sum of 30 pieces of silver in its contemporary value. The latter includes the sum's associations with 'the price of a slave,' its use 'to buy a burial field' (193), and a possible relation to the price of the ointment used to anoint Christ at Bethany. The last factor hints that materialism obscures the disciples' understanding of the divinity of Christ signified in the anointing. It reveals Judas as 'one whose concepts of discipleship and Christ are hopelessly inverted,' so that he sees Christ 'as a figure of vengeance rather than mercy'; this is 'consistent with his later despairing suicide' (195). This perception is opposed to Peter's resolution, through faith, of his denial of Christ. Association of the woman who anoints Christ with Mary Magdalene implies a comparison with the woman who influences Judas. The latter woman represents 'the unredeemed daughter of Eve, as Mary Magdalene represents the redeemed in medieval tradition' (196). The poem presents Judas in a way that is 'neither tragic nor particularly sympathetic,' to explain his motivation as that of 'one who consciously abuses his own free will to follow the typical pattern of Christian sin,' compounding duplicity with despair, 'for which forgiveness is impossible' (196).

1649.

773 Bazire, Joyce. 'Mercy and Justice.' *Neuphilologische Mitteilungen* 83 (1982): 178–91. [Edition.]

An edition of the poem that Bazire calls 'Mercy and Justice' ['Bi a forest as y can walke,' *560*] from Chichester MS Cowfold (C). Kurvinen, **580**, previously printed the Porkington MS version with the title 'Mercy and Righteousness,' and designated it P. Bazire, however, calls that version H/P, since the manuscript is now 'in the National Library of Wales and designated MS Harlech 10' (178). Bazire describes the Cowfold Parish Account and Memoranda Book, 1460–1485, and lists significant features of dialect that differ from versions H/P, A (BL Add. MS 31042), and L (Lambeth MS 853). These features point to the general area of Horsham, including Cowfold, and possibly mid-south Surrey. Bazire prints the text (181–4), and follows the numbering of stanzas and lines in Kurvinen's edition, although H/P has 26 stanzas to the 15 of C. She provides textual footnotes and comment, a table to relate the four versions (186), and explanatory material. C differs significantly in its introductory stanza (which could be explained by 'an oral transmitter's inability to remember the whole stanza') and in the abrupt conclusion in the fifteenth stanza. In H/P, A, and C, Mercy debates with *Ryȝth* (called '"Justice" rather than "Righteousness,"' by Bazire), but with a Sinner in L, 'undoubtedly the correct debater' (187). The figure of Mercy is masculine. The versions differ in rhyme words and pattern. A seems most specifically Northern in character, and varies most from the others, although each version has 'peculiarities which vary against the other three' (189). Comparison of the four versions demonstrates 'how a poem could "develop" in the course of transmission, both oral and scribal' (191).

560.

774 Bennett, J.A.W. *Poetry of the Passion: Studies in Twelve Centuries of English Verse.* Oxford: Clarendon, 1982.

Surveys works on the Passion, beginning with the OE *Dream of the Rood*, in 'A Vision of a Rood' (1–31). 'The Meditative Movement' (32–61) traces developments of the theme, in particular attention paid to the 'new figure, the Virgin,' and to 'the marred beauty of the body of Christ.' These have the effect of making the poet write as one 'emotionally involved in the scene' (35). Bennett compares Latin and English verses, and finds the latter 'eloquent in their stark economy' (37), and intended to induce pity and tears. Some details recur in the presentation of the image 'in wood or stone, paper or vellum' (39), including 'the whiteness of the flesh, the pallor of the face' (48). The adjective *unkind*, for man, is balanced by *sweet*, used of and by Christ. Prose meditations on the Passion tend to be ample, but the lyrics are characteristically bare and simple, although not artless, and they may recall the *imago pietatis*. The notion of life as warfare inspires the image of '*Christus Miles*' (62–84), which presents Christ as a lover-knight who rescues a besieged lady who represents 'the soul, that dwells in a tenement of clay' (64). The imagery further represents Christ's body through the knight's pierced shield, with allegories of his armour, arming, weapons, wounds, and combat. Canticles inspires imagery here, as it does in the meditations. In the martial imagery the Cross symbolizes triumph. Bennett discusses 'The Passion in *Piers Plowman [1459]*' (85–112) and 'The Scottish Testimony' (113–144), before proceeding to more recent poetry of the Passion.

143, 248, 324, 497, 498, 583, 776, 1119, 1125, 1235, 1274, 1308, 1406, 1459, 1460, 1463, 1752, 1761, 1781, 1921, 1922, 1930, 1943, 2250, 2273, 2320, 2574, 2824, 3112, 3144, 3242, 3310, 3691, 3825, 3906, 4019, 4088.

775 Benning, Helmut. '"þis wommon woneþ by west": epische Allusionen in englischen Gedichten des MS Harley 2253.' *Festschrift für Karl Scheider zum 70. Geburtstag am 18. April 1982.* Ed. Ernst S. Dick and Kurt R. Janofsky. Amsterdam: Benjamins, 1982. 433–7.

Presents evidence for Celtic influence on the ME lyric, with examples taken from the Harley lyrics, which were compiled in Leominster, in an area of English and Welsh interaction. Although Benning does not posit a direct relationship, he notes associations with Celtic epics in allusions in *Sir Tristem [1382]* and in Gottfried von Strassburg's story of Tristan. These links imply the involvement of Welsh bards whose repertoire included the Tristan material. He discerns references to the wife of the king of Ireland and mother of Isolde; to Tristan and Isolde, the wife of King Mark; and to Tristan's marriage to Isolde, the daughter of the Duke of Brittany.

105, 1382, 1504, 2359, 4194.

776 Benskin, Michael. 'Marian Verses from a Hedon Manuscript: Some New Materials for the Middle English Dialectology of the East Riding.' *Revista Canaria de Estudios Ingleses* 5 (1982): 27–58. [Edition.]

Four Marian lyrics not noted in *S/IMEV* are preserved 'on the dorse of a rental [Humberside County Record Office DDHE 19] that belonged formerly to the borough corporation of Hedon' (27). Benskin presents 'an account of the manuscript, a diplomatic transcript, and an examination of the linguistic provenance,' rather than literary comment. He finds that Text I [']e-/]⟨at⟩ be fe[/]lilio/[y]^e frut of y^e . . ./[w]as nalyd on a tre,' *7651*; an acephalous lyric] and Text IV ['None/And hyr/So fayr so/

Take hyr to,' *7379*; the text lacks many line-ends] are 'seemingly conventional.' Text II ['A semly song I wyƚƚ ȝow syng,' *7019*] is 'distinctive and accomplished.' Text III ['lystyng lordyngs I wyƚƚ ȝow tell,' *7309*] is 'at least unusual' (28) in its presentation of the Nativity. Compilation of the manuscript, in the time of the chamberlain William Molscroft and a king who may have been Henry IV, V, or VI, was piecemeal but not protracted. The document seems to have remained in Hedon until it was acquired by the antiquarian Gillyat Sumner. Thus the verses were written, but not necessarily composed, in Hedon, and the manuscript is 'at most a fair copy, for the texts are written without hesitation or correction' (30). Some errors of sense imply copying, rather than composition, from a dialect not substantially different from that of the scribe. Benskin compares the dialect with Northern ME forms, with particular attention to the substitution of *y* for *þ*, which he uses as a guide to authorship. The manuscript's association with the chantry of St Mary at Hedon, which was maintained for a time by rent charges, may mean that it represents 'the financial and devotional aspects of but a single enterprise' (32). Benskin prints the texts, with conjectural readings where there is damage to the manuscript, supplying a summary of each poem and brief notes. Text I compares the tree of Eden and the Cross, and requests intercession. Text II alone is intact: it is 'an imaginary encounter between the narrator, and a maiden accompanied by an old man.' Although the work tells of Mary and Joseph, the incongruities of age and the maiden's child recall 'cuckoldry and the *mal mariè(e)* of secular poetry' (34). Text III is of the Annunciation and Nativity: it presents the latter through reference to the Passion, and shows the Circumcision as a type of the Crucifixion. Text IV is a meditative love lyric to the Virgin. There are three appendices: 'The language of the Hedon verses compared with the language of the East Riding documents' (38–47); 'A note on the Hedon scribe's use of the letters *y* and *þ*' (47–9); and 'A note on the texts and authors of Durham Dean and Chapter Muniments Locellus XXV numbers 18 and 27' (49–52). In the first, Benskin notes several documents, with a map locating their sources, and compares phonological categories, grammatical suffixes, and lexical categories. He discerns many similarities in letters written by Richard Cliff and Robert Babthorpe, and considers that they may have colluded in recommending a candidate for the choral vicary of Hemingborough.

7019, 7309, 7379, 7651.

777 Burrow, J.A. *Medieval Writers and Their Work: Middle English Literature and its Background 1100–1500.* Oxford: Oxford UP, 1982.

In his discussion of ME lyrics in 'Major genres' (56–85), Burrow explains that, in the context 'ME lyric,' the last word 'usually means no more than a short poem.' He confines his attention to 'short poems which speak in the first person, usually to a second person,' to illustrate 'the most characteristic *axis* of lyric poetry: the "I" addressing the "you." ' The 'I' of many medieval first-person poems may be a type rather than an individual, for example 'a lover, a penitent sinner, or a devotee of the Virgin' (61). Burrow demonstrates similarities in secular and religious lyrics and the development in English poetry of the fixed forms of Provençal love lyrics (such as Chaucer's roundel 'Your yëen two wol slee me sodenly' [*4282*]). He compares *4282* and 'Nou goth þe sonne under wode' [*2320*], since both employ 'the generic I' and are 'general compleynyngs.' A more specific kind of dramatic lyric is the *chanson de femme*. 'As I went on Yole day in oure prosession' [*377*], for instance, demonstrates the important 'internal, generic relation between literary forms and social class,' which is more significant than 'the external, sociological relation' (65). The *chanson d'aventure* is clearly defined, and tells of the speaker's riding out and encounter with another, 'who herself (it is usually a woman) may sing a *chanson de femme*.' Religious lyrics include dramatic examples of the complaint of Christ, such as 'ȝe þᵗ passen be þe weyȝe' [*4263*], which modifies 'a verse in the Lamentations of Jeremiah (1:12)' (66). The speaker of Burrow's last example is a woman, but not a betrayed maiden; her lyric is not a complaint, but rather 'a mysterious invitation . . . to come and dance with her in Ireland.' Her song, 'Gode sire pray ich þe' [*1008*], is perhaps a carol. The poem offers 'a forceful reminder that not all these lyrics can be understood in terms of known genres and traditions' (68).

100, 360, 377, 1008, 2037.5, 2320, 4019, 4263, 4282.

778 Heffernan, Thomas J. 'Unpublished Middle English Verses on the *Three Sorrowful Things.*' *Neuphilologische Mitteilungen* 83 (1982): 31–3. [Edition.]

Prints five previously unpublished examples of 'Wanne i ðenke ðinges ðre' [*3969*], which occurs in 14 versions. The theme of the Three Sorrowful Things, usually stated in three couplets, is 'the transience of human life, the lamentable fact of death, and the uncertainty of human salvation' (31). It is rarely seen before the twelfth century, but late in the thirteenth seems to be 'a commonplace on the transience of human life.' Heffernan includes 'þre þinges it ben þat I holde pris' [*3711.5*], not as a variant, but because its resemblances 'almost suggest a scribal parody of the more orthodox sentiments of *TST*' (32).

695, 3199.5, 3711.5, 3712, 3713, 3969.

779 Jeffrey, David L. 'Early English Carols and the Macaronic Hymn.' *Florilegium* 4 (1982): 210–27.

Considers functions of the fifteenth-century carol revealed by those in MS Cambridge Library Ee.1.12, which were composed or collected by James Ryman and edited by Zupitza, **10**. Of the 166 poems, the first 110 form 'a *compilatio* of sorts, more than a mere *collectio* . . . largely organized by the theme and liturgical occasion or calendar, concentrating especially on the seasons Advent, Nativity, and Epiphany' (211), anticipating 'specialization of the carol as a Christmas song.' They may be grouped according to address or function. More than 50 are concerned with the Virgin, 35 with Christ, and more than 12 with the Trinity, whereas 35 are catechal and 10 liturgical. There are also translations of Latin hymns and other forms of religious lyric, but the collection is 'dominated by carols' (212). The macaronic hymns are closely connected to the liturgy. The form of the lyrics shows that they were not intended 'for meditative, reflective use' (215). Some may have been sung by the preachers, '*to* a popular audience, if not likely *by* them' (218). In the carols, 'form and meter immediately suggest group singing . . . highly accessible even to the laity' (219). Thus they help to make 'divine service itself more accessible to the laity' (221). Some carols may seem garish, maudlin, or boring, but the best of them, 'with respect to their lyrics, are a blend of simplicity and unstudied elegance; with respect to meter and measure they are often "catchy" and eminently tunable' (314). Ryman's works show 'a definite rootedness of divine mystery and beauty in the tangibility of Christ's and the Virgin's humanity' (315). The collection is 'a signal contribution to the development in England of an accessible vernacular hymnody' (317). [Does not differ substantially from **831**.]

67, 328, 398, 434, 641, 781, 815, 1043, 2087, 2332, 2431, 2448, 2454, 2484, 2535, 2545, 2603, 2807, 3304, 3328, 3379, 3583, 3728, 3779.

780 Laing, Margaret, and Angus McIntosh. 'Bodleian Library, Rawlinson MS D.375: An Historical Puzzle.' *Notes and Queries* 227 (1982): 484–7. [Edition.]

A Northern or Scottish poem, 'In syfhyng sar I sit vnsauth' [*7265*], is printed, with notes on the text and dialect, and investigation of cryptographic possibilities. The work is 'not without literary merit,' and presents 'problems, textual, dialectal, historical and even cryptographic' (485). The authors expand abbreviations, and print *y* for þ and *y* (treated identically in the text). The language is 'somewhat idiosyncratic': features suggest that 'the original can scarcely have been composed anywhere south of Lincolnshire,' but this copy 'might have been written almost anywhere in the north' (486). The poem is a species of acrostic, but significant letters are placed within the stanzas, and form part of their meaning; *O* and *I* in the 'O and I' refrain may or may not be among them. The letters of stanza 4 spell *Angus* backwards, but it is difficult to decipher other words.

7265.

781 Machan, Tim. 'Etymology of *Helde* in the Eighth Harley Lyric.' *Comments on Etymology* 11 (1982): 2–4.

Surveys commentary on *helde*, which rhymes with *kelde* in 'The Meeting in the Wood' [*1449*]. Brook, **42**, in proposing a Kentish derivation, would assume 'a Kentish-Anglian rhyme,' but other evidence for Kentish influence is lacking. There is support for a derivation from **hældi*, but 'an apparent *hapax legomenon* must be assumed.' Machan suggests that the word's etymon is 'not OE *hyldu* but PrOE **hældi*' (4).

1449.

782 Malvern, Marjorie M. 'An Earnest "Monyscyon" and "þinge Delectabyll" Realized Verbally and Visually in "A Disputacion betwyx þe Body and Wormes," a Middle English Poem Inspired by Tomb Art and Northern Spirituality.' *Viator* 13 (1982): 415–33. [Edition.]

Represents a close examination of the poem ['In þe ceson of huge mortalitie,' *1563*] and its illustrations. Malvern aims to verify the work's worth and to relate it to 'late medieval literary and iconographic works that center on the death motif,' which show 'variations on poetic and homiletic traditions prevalent in Middle English literature' (415), particularly the conventions of 'the *débat* and of the *memento mori* topos,' and the 'intentional mingling of jest with earnest' (416). The poet's wish 'to delight and to instruct the reader,' although he acknowledges disease, death, and decay, 'leads to his animation of the body and worms depicted on the transi tomb' (417), in order to alleviate the fear of death. Malvern sets the poem in a context of affective piety which emphasizes the wounded Christ as *imago pietatis*. She compares it to contemporary religious drama, and notes that it is framed by 'a brief adaptation of the popular *danse macabre* poem and a short prose note on the *contemptus mundi* topos' (418) in BL MS Add. 37049. She considers first the picture of the tomb, which shows the Body as a beautiful woman, finely dressed, above a decaying corpse, consumed by worms, lizards, and toads. The tomb bears a preface, 'Take hede vnto my fygure here abowne' [*3252.5*]. In the 'Disputacion' the poet describes a pilgrimage in a time of mortality and desolation, and his visit to a church where he sees the tomb; here he prays before an image of the crucified, suffering Christ. In a dream, he observes the 'Disputacion,' which transforms 'the traditional debate between the Body and the Soul' (425), so that the Body learns from the Worms to recognize her sins and repent. The proud Body's first complaints incongruously resemble those of the humbled Job. The illustrations lend the Worms 'a choreographic vitality,' so that 'they seem to squirm in rhythm' (428). The Worms lead the Body to penitence, to learn '"the "wisdom" which the viewers of the Body's transi tomb are urged to learn from the "disputacion,"' to see her experience 'as part of fallen humanity's lot but not the final destiny for the devout Christian' (429). The lessons are imparted most strongly in an explication of the Ash Wednesday liturgy and in an exchange (about former lovers) which exploits the *ubi sunt* device. The illustrations show the Body's progress: in the last picture, 'the artist reverses the positions of the combatants and draws them nearer to each other.' When the Body has learned charity, she offers 'apologies to the Worms,' and begs 'that they be friends, kiss each other and dwell together in love until God calls her to the Day of Judgement' (432), again recalling Job. The Worms bring her 'from a state of miserable ignorance to a joyous state of

Annotations of Critical Works

"wisdom"' (434), to see decay as 'a necessary prelude to . . . ascent to eternal bliss' (436), a message reminiscent of Paul's teachings to the Corinthians. The poem unites 'seemingly disparate elements drawn from the Aesopic fable, the homily, the liturgy, the chivalric romance, the flyting match or the debate,' and reflects 'the heterogeneity evident in the various plays designed to promote spiritual health in Christian folk' (437). Malvern provides appendices on 'Perspectives on B.L. MS Add. 37049' (439–42) and 'Conjectures concerning the lacuna in "A Disputacion betwyx þe Body and Wormes"' (442–3), and reproduces pages of the manuscript and an illustration from *La danse macabre des femmes*. [See also Janofsky, **616**.]

603, 715, 1370.5, 1563, 2255, 2590, 2591, 3252.5.

783 Mantovani, Maddalena. 'La lirica "Mon in þe mon stond & strit" e la leggenda dell'uomo sulla luna.' *Quaderni de Filologia Germanica della Facoltà di Lettere e Filosofia dell'Università di Bologna* 2 (1982): 25–43.

Not seen.

2066.

784 Nicholls, Jonathan. 'A Courtesy Poem from Magdalene College Cambridge Pepys MS 1236.' *Notes and Queries* 227 (1982): 3–10. [Edition.]

'In maner whyche enlumynyth euery astate' [*1501*] is described in *IMEV* as 'another version of the popular late Middle English poem, *Stans Puer ad Mensam Domini*. The latter is usually attributed to John Lydgate,' but resemblances to the work are 'in the general messages of some of the precepts, not in verbal correspondences' (4). The Latin lines that prefix the stanzas are often attributed to Robert Grosseteste. This poem is generally closer to the Latin model than Lydgate's, which cannot always be considered a translation. The Pepys poet is more prolix than his source, and occasionally used 'a generalized knowledge of etiquette to give his translation more authority and detail where it was thought necessary' (4). A Paschal calendar and musical compositions in the manuscript suggest a date in the range 1450 to 1460. The work has 'few, if any, adroit poetical touches,' but is 'not without lexical interest,' since words of French origin – *rabyous* and *reitte* – may reveal 'the author's nationality or bilingualism' (5). Nicholls prints the poem, with expanded contractions and some additions, and offers footnotes on words and lines of interest.

1501.

785 Pickering, O.S. 'A Third Text of "Say Me Viit in þe Brom."' *English Studies* 63 (1982): 20–2. [Edition.]

Notes the two recorded occurrences of 'Say me viit in þe brom' [*3078*], in MSS Trinity College, Cambridge B.14.39 (323) and BL Add. 22579, and summarizes the rather different stories implied. In each poem a woman asks the 'wight' for advice about her husband: in the first she wants him to love her, but in the second she complains about him. The reply, in each case, is 'Hold þine tunke stille/& hawe al þine wille.' A third text, in Lambeth Palace Library 78, resembles the second poem, and is also found in a Latin story in a theological miscellany. Lambeth 78 is 'the only known manuscript of the *Speculum parvulorum*, a large-scale compilation by one William Chartham who was a monk of Christ Church, Canterbury from 1403 to 1448' (20–1). Pickering prints the story and the verse, noting independent occurrences of the wight's reply, other English sermon verses, and some previously unrecorded 'scraps of English' (21) in Lambeth 78.

142, 174, 1935, 2078, 2167, 2238.5, 3078, 3081, 3322.3, 3239, 3408, 7196, 7289, 7448, 7491, 7553, 7567, 7570, 7614, 7635.

786 Powell, Susan. 'Connections between the *Fasciculus Morum* and Bodleian MS Barlow 24.' *Notes and Queries* 227 (1982): 10–15.

The name 'Selk' has been noted as that of the compiler of sermons in Bodleian Library MS Barlow 24. Fletcher, **685**, proposes that he is 'one of two William Selks active in Oxford in the fifteenth century,' whereas Wenzel, **701**, suggests 'a Franciscan, Robert Selk (Selke, Silke).' Powell considers that Robert Selk is 'the likely author of the popular Latin treatise on the vices and virtues, the *Fasciculus Morum*, and that MS Barlow 24 shows connections with that work' (10). These connections are seen in 'three English lyrics otherwise unrecorded outside the *Fasciculus* and [in] an extended discussion of an anagram of *mors*, death' (11). She notes the lyrics and the couplet ['Mayde, wyff and moder whas neuer but ye/Well may such a Lady Goddys moder be'] 'quoted by Fletcher from "I sing of a maiden" [*1367*] ... in the 35th sermon ... on the Assumption of the Virgin.' A sermon on the Nativity of the Virgin has a Marian lyric related to 'Mary moder of grace we cryen to þe' [*2114*]. Two other lyrics come from the *Fasciculus* chapter on *memento mortis*. One of these translates Job 14. 1–2, as 'Mon iboren of wommon ne lyueth but a stounde' [*2058*]; the other, in a sermon that is 'largely ... an interpretation of the four letters of *mors*' (13), is related to 'Haue mynde on þyn endynge' [*1127*].

1127, 1367, 2058, 2114, 4035, 7065, 7328, 7402.

787 Revard, Carter. '*Gilote et Johane*: an Interlude in B.L. MS. Harley 2253.' *Studies in Philology* 79 (1982): 122–46.

Proposes that the French *Gilote et Johane* is an interlude placed in MS Harley 2253, in a trilingual collection that is 'not a miscellany but a *miroir*, not merely assembled but structured, [that] demonstrates both a principled *selection* of items and a principled *arrangement* of them' (127). In the selection of religious and secular works it may seem that *Gilote et Johane* is there 'to give the Devil his due, while in the *Harrowing of Hell* God was given his' (129). As analogies, Revard cites *De Arte Honeste Amandi* and *Canterbury Tales* [*4019*], and discusses the structure of fols. 75–6 of the Harley manuscript. He notes French as well as English poems, to display the juxtaposition of themes, 'in a sequence that appears planned rather than haphazard' (135). The study suggests that the manuscript is 'selectively and dialectically compiled as an anthology, with not only a deliberately wide variety of forms, genres, viewpoints, and themes, but also with a deliberate placement of its pieces in mutually illuminating relationships' (138). The diction and themes of *Gilote et Johane* present internal evidence to suggest a composer and an audience 'knowledgeable in academic and legal matters' (139). External evidence hints that the Harley scribe was a legal cleric. Revard supplies extensive biographical details of possible candidates, and finds Richard de Ludlow and James Wottenhull, senior the most likely, although there are objections to each.

694.5, 1365, 1678, 1705, 1921, 1922, 2236, 2359, 3211, 3236, 3963, 4019, 4037, 4177.

788 Stevens, John. 'Medieval Lyrics and Music.' *Medieval Literature: Chaucer and the Alliterative Tradition.* Ed. Boris Ford. Harmondsworth: Penguin, 1982. 248–76. Vol. 1 of The New Pelican Guide to English Literature. 9 vols. 1982–3.

Relates the words and music of medieval lyrics to general descriptions of their composition and preservation, including detailed discussions of particular examples. Through his explication of 'Bryd on brere y telle yt' [*521.5*], Stevens considers circumstances of authorship, purpose, and preservation. He also introduces the issue of editorial decisions about punctuation and meaning, to show that 'every edition is an interpretation' (249). Examination of ambiguities in texts indicates that 'a considered personal response' is indispensable 'in the study of medieval literature as of all other' (251). Although the words and music of *521.5* seem artless, the words are fresh, moving, and subtle, the melody 'well-wrought and tautly constructed.' The relation of the words and music does not show 'any direct intellectual or emotional response on the composer's part to the words of the song' (252). Stevens discusses ME lyrics in terms of the popular, clerical, and courtly traditions, and writes in detail on examples of each style. Among popular lyrics are 'Maiden in the mor lay' [*2037.5*], 'Nou springes the sprai' [*360*], and 'Of this martir make we mende' [*2665*]. He considers literary and social contexts of these and other lyrics, as well as the nature of carols. The clerical tradition may be more helpfully defined in terms of audience rather than of authorship. Stevens notes the relation of such lyrics to the liturgy. He takes 'What ys he þys lordling þat cometh vrom þe vyht' [*3906*] and 'My volk what habbe y do þe' [*2241*] as examples, and compares the approaches of William Herebert and George Herbert. Many lyrics survive in clerical manuscripts, but ownership was 'the condition of their survival, not evidence of any monopoly,' although 'all men in some kind of ecclesiastical orders . . . were the most numerous class of writers, in both senses of the word' (266). Variations on the theme of *contemptus mundi* were the source of many clerical lyrics. Traces of the French trouvère tradition can be observed in ME courtly lyrics, including 'Alysoun' [*515*] and Chaucer's 'Balade to Rosamond' [*2031*]. Stevens investigates 'In a gloryus garden grene' [*1450*] and its use of an *aubade* to counterpoint a song perhaps 'in honour of the white rose, Queen Elizabeth of York, the wife of Henry VII' (274), and to incorporate courtly symbols in a political context. Lyrics such as the 'Corpus Christi Carol' [*1132*] are liable 'to go on teasing us for ever with their enigmatic power' (275).

194, 298, 352, 360, 497, 515, 521.5, 1132, 1450, 1731, 1866, 2031, 2037.5, 2070, 2241, 2551.8, 2665, 3236, 3906, 3939, 4166.

789 ———. 'The Old Sound and the New.' Inaugural Lecture. University of Cambridge. 19 Jan. 1981. Cambridge: Cambridge UP, 1982.

This consideration of the relationship of sound and sense is also of the relationship of words and music. Stevens distinguishes literal and metaphorical mimesis, as he examines 'the proposition that the metaphorical range is far less extended in medieval poetry than in later, and that the mimetic function of sound is confined to the literal – the imitation of sound in sound' (4). His examples include 'Swarte smekyd smethes smateryd wythe smoke' [*3227*] (for literal mimesis) and *Pearl* [*2744*] (for metaphorical) through its 'intellectual metaphors of pattern and number' (5). Both mimetic qualities are discerned only when the poem's context is known. Stevens finds the relationship of words and music 'highly formalized and in verbal terms non-conceptual' (6). In its connection with speech, ME poetry is 'not strictly mimetic,' but rather 'consistently, very speech itself.' He points out differences in the use of speech by such poets as Browning, Tennyson, Eliot, and Yeats, and notes the difficulty of making such comparisons in the Middle Ages. Most medieval poetry is 'designed for live performance' (7), with style distinctions 'based on speech-categories' (7–8), and 'the author casts himself in the role of narrator' (8). Stevens decides that medieval poetry uses 'the mimetic and emotive resources of *prose*' (8) and 'metaphorical sound in the way speech does – naturally and without conscious artifice' (9). He questions iambic readings of Chaucer's verse (made by restoration of final *-e* in some editions) and shows that Chaucer exploits 'the rhythm of speech' (10), with a use of metaphor that is generally inconspicuous compared to Shakespeare's. He concludes that medieval poetry is 'semantically relaxed, open, unambiguous on the surface, linear, "melodic" rather than "harmonic," ' and contrasts the compression induced in metaphor. He further notes the analogical, iconographical, referential, lucid nature of medieval poetry. Of the 'old' and 'new' sounds, Stevens infers that the former was 'put together from phrases, units of speech,' whereas the latter is 'to be fabricated from words.' In conclusion, he examines works in 'the new metre – syllabic, relentlessly iambic and accentual' (11).

1459, 1978, 2163, 2744, 3227, 3327, 4019.

790 Turville-Petre, Thorlac. 'The Lament for Sir John Berkeley.' *Speculum* 57 (1982): 332–9. [Edition.]

The lament 'Seyng*ur*s þ*a*t solem weer se*m*bled he*m* al same*n*' [*7443*] is preserved on the back of a sheet, in 'a commission of sewers for the wapentakes of Bingham and Newark in Nottinghamshire' (332), Mi 01 in the Middleton Collection of Nottingham University Library. Sir John Berkeley of Wymondham died of a sickness after fighting in a campaign in Brittany, from which English forces withdrew in July, 1375. Turville-Petre supplies biographical details of Berkeley and his family and offers commentary on the poem. The latter mourns the loss from a hunting party, and is expressed in the contrast between the sorrowful occasion and former days of happiness in the company of the generous lord. The dialect of the *Lament* is that of the Northeast Midlands, employing 'the alliterative long line with end rhyme, usually in couplets.' It presents a man 'of local but not national importance' (334), who resembles Chaucer's Franklin; his life seems 'wholly admirable, and his good living as a proper and seemly adjunct to his social position.' The author pleasingly adapts Aesop's fable of the grasshopper and ant, and emphasizes loss at personal as well as public level, to produce a poem which is 'attractive, even if the poet's technical ability is not outstanding' (335). He presumably belonged to Berkeley's retinue, and perhaps revealed his name, Turnour, in his account of the dying knight's instructions. Turville-Petre prints the poem (336–8), with notes and commentary (338–9).

7443.

791 Wenzel, Siegfried. 'Pestilence and Middle English Literature: Friar John Grimestone's Poems on Death.' *The Black Death: The Impact of the Fourteenth-Century Plague.* Ed. Daniel Williman. Papers of the Eleventh Annual Conference of CMERS. MRTS, 13. Binghamton, NY: CMERS, State U of New York at Binghamton, 1982. 131–59.

Relatively few references to death in ME literature specify the Black Death, which is generally seen as God's punishment and call to reform. Wenzel examines ME lyrics of death for signs of changes in 'their representation of death and reaction to it . . . after the Black Death' (134). He compares preachers' tags of John Grimestone's Commonplace Book (written in 1372) with those of the *Fasciculus morum* (prepared shortly after 1300), in which the section on pride recommends meditation on death to encourage humility. The *Fasciculus morum* has 13 such verses in 55, whereas Grimestone has 28 poems on death among 246. This implies a greater preoccupation with death in the earlier work, emphasized in the greater length of the *Fasciculus* verses. Most ME poems in the collections can be related to Latin models. Grimestone's poems are indebted to Latin *proverbia* and *sententia*, 'the learned tradition of preaching,' divisions of sermons, lists of Signs of Death, and native proverbial commonplaces. Thus their origins and attitudes are from 'times long before the Black Death' (142), and express the transience of life and the warning of *memento mori*. In general they seem to differ little from earlier works, although their concentration on 'the gruesome details of corpse and grave' may have been 'caused or at least intensified by the ravages of the plague' (143). Wenzel discerns fewer changes in Grimestone's lyrics on death, except in the 'Visit to the Grave' ['Her sal I duellen loken vnder stone,' *1210.5*], than in those on topics such as the Passion, but the time of composition may have been 'too early for the full impact of plague experience to show in English lyrics on death' (147). Effects are seen in aspects of the Dance of Death, which may represent earlier traditions, including 'the *Vado mori*, the Three Living and the Three Dead, or simply the Visit to the Grave or a similar *Memento mori*' (148). The apparently slight effect of plague may come from English 'cheerfulness in the face of death.' This provides 'not only an excellent psychological defense' but also a possible 'medicinal value' (149), endorsed by Lydgate ['Who wil be hool and keep him fro sekenesse,' *4112*]. Wenzel concludes that the 'relatively insignificant impact' of the Black

Death on literature is related to the continuing perception of disorder in the world, caused by 'moral disorders in the heart of man' (152).

230.5, 296.3, 352, 353, 517.5, 703, 825.8, 1002, 1127, 1210.5, 1220, 1459, 1563, 1847, 2012, 2023, 2036, 2058, 2066.8, 2083, 2167, 2255, 2260, 2283, 2590, 2817, 2924, 3078.5, 3079.3, 3100.5, 3350, 3428, 3567.6, 3691, 3825, 3903, 3908, 3939, 3969, 4019, 4035, 4044, 4049.6, 4049.7, 4112, 4239, 4268, 7083, 7114, 7182, 7192, 7242, 7249, 7279, 7280, 7412, 7462, 7449, 7588, 7629.

792   Baker, D.C. '"De Arte Lacrimandi": A Supplement and some Corrections.' *Medium Ævum* 52 (1983): 222–6.

Supplements and corrects the edition of 'Now late me thought I wolde begynn' [*2347*], prepared by Garrett, **121**, from MS Harley 2274. Baker consults Bodley 423, Corpus Christi College F.261, and Trinity College, Dublin 160, and prints 'five stanzas in Bodley 423 not found in Harley 2274, and some corrections of the Garrett Harley text' (223). Bodley 423 is not signed, but appears to be in the hand of Stephen Dodesham. Although the texts differ in length, the shared contents agree quite closely, and it seems that no leaves are missing from the Harley and Trinity College versions. Thus Baker concludes that the poem 'grew in transmission, as is frequently the case with meditative materials' (225). The refrain 'Who cannot wepe com lerne of me' is shared with other *planctus*.

2347, 4189.

793   Barratt, Alexandra. 'A Middle English Lyric in an Old French Manuscript.' *Medium Ævum* 52 (1983): 226–9. [Edition.]

The lyric's 'interesting and somewhat unusual setting' is Paris, Bibliothèque Nationale, MS fr. 1830, 'a late xiii- or early xiv-century collection of three OF devotional treatises in prose: "Li douze services de tribulacion"' (226). The poem is a version of the levation prayer 'Ihesu lord welcom þow be' [*1729*]. Such prayers are sometimes the only examples of ME in Latin devotional works, but it is unusual to find them in manuscripts in other vernaculars. An inscription that may have stated ownership has been erased, but 'this MS was in the hands of an owner whose most reverent devotions naturally formed themselves in English' (227) when the verse was added. In her investigation of the manuscript's connections with England, Barratt records that it had been owned by François I, and so possibly by his grandfather, Jean d'Angoulême, or by his great-uncle Charles d'Orléans. The latter continued to collect books during his captivity in England, including French and Latin texts of *Li douze services de tribulacion*. The manuscript may have been in English hands before Charles bought it back, which could explain the erasure of an English note of ownership, and 'the ME lyric, which is homely and unsophisticated would perhaps not represent his own taste in poetry' (228).

1729.

794   Bergner, Heinz. 'Die mittelenglische Lyrik.' *Lyrik des Mittelalters: Probleme und Interpretationen.* Ed. Heinz Bergner. Vol. 2. Stuttgart: Reclam, 1983. 233–377. 2 vols.

First examines the cultural and socio-political background of ME lyrics. Bergner contrasts the situation in English and other courts, and proposes a growing audience for ME lyrics as the language gained acceptance and literacy became more widespread. He describes the range of ME lyrics and the factors important in their survival. The alliterative revival revealed increased national pride. Other influences on the lyrics were Latin hymns and sequences, and OF and Provençal lyrics, which generally affected secular ME poetry. Music for the poems is rarely preserved, although many must have been sung or accompanied. Bergner describes poetic forms, to conclude that classification must be based on topic rather than form, in contrast to French *formes fixes*. A few to events of her legendary life, and notes similarities to ballads. A few lyrics tell of the Dance of Death and the Last Judgement.

2, 14, 29, 37, 66, 72, 94, 115, 117, 225, 241, 254, 281, 298, 352, 359, 420, 420, 503, 515, 519, 640, 643, 651, 678, 688.3, 731, 744, 769, 772.5, 781, 785, 864, 933, 964.5, 1077, 1129, 1132, 1179, 1254, 1274, 1299, 1302, 1308, 1327, 1328, 1353, 1365, 1367, 1370.5, 1379, 1387, 1395, 1405.5, 1423, 1459, 1460, 1488, 1504, 1532, 1617, 1627, 1649, 1684, 1704, 1734, 1742, 1747, 1781, 1833, 1849, 1861, 1921, 1922, 1971, 1974, 1978, 2036, 2037.5, 2042, 2057, 2076, 2136, 2192, 2236, 2241, 2284.5, 2286, 2291, 2293, 2320, 2366, 2369, 2377, 2401, 2411, 2416, 2417, 2418, 2419, 2429, 2430, 2431, 2432, 2448, 2462, 2482.5, 2485, 2519, 2528, 2546, 2562, 2576, 2603, 2623.3, 2681, 2684, 2727, 2924, 3071, 3135, 3211, 3212, 3221, 3225, 3245, 3328.5, 3333, 3343, 3379, 3391, 3408, 3410, 3468, 3469, 3471, 3517, 3527, 3567, 3583, 3695, 3719, 3727, 3728, 3751, 3821, 3825, 3857.5, 3859, 3920, 3959, 3968, 4001, 4044, 4159, 4163, 4181, 4189, 4194, 4197, 4200, 4220, 4229.5, 4263, 7240, 7605.

828   Fulton, Helen. 'The Theory of Celtic Influence on the Harley Lyrics.' *Modern Philology* 82 (1984–5): 239–54.

Challenges the notion, proposed by Matonis, **582**, of strong Celtic influence on the Harley lyrics. Fulton offers examples from Harley poems, *Pearl*, and Irish and Welsh poetry to counter arguments concerning stanza linking, rhyme, and alliteration. She shows that Irish and Welsh poetic devices, such as *dúnad*, *saigid*, *aicill*, and *trebraid* rhyme, *breccad*, and *cynghanedd* do not correspond with the structures identified by Matonis. Although form does not demonstrate direct Celtic influence on ME poetry, contextual evidence shows 'the nature of the multilingual society that produced the Harley Lyrics and the types of literary traditions held in common by Continental and British poets' (248). Fulton examines the findings in *BrownXIII*, **36**, on names in 'Annot and John' [*1394*]; Welsh borrowings in 'Lenten ys come wiþ loue to toune' [*1861*] and 'Blow, Northerne Wynd' [*1395*]; and on resemblances between 'Svmer is icumen in' [*3223*] and a Welsh folk song. The work of Dafydd ap Gwilym may resemble *1395* in use of the device of a love-messenger. Fulton proposes that the Harley lyrics represent 'an English response to a popularizing lyric movement emanating from the Continent' (250), in a tradition 'native in origin but strongly overlaid with Continental material from the time of the Conquest.' She suggests that the work of Dafydd ap Gwilym exemplifies 'a corresponding movement in Wales in the fourteenth century,' and that there is 'evidence of a popular lyric movement in Ireland at about the same time' (251). The Harley lyrics demonstrate the native popular tradition and continental themes. Welsh words and names indicate 'the likely provenance of certain lyrics and the overlapping of languages, Anglo-Norman, English, and Welsh, around the border region' (252), with AN the medium for transmission of continental material, and French and Latin material the source of themes and images in English and Celtic poetry. Thus any Celtic influence discerned in the Harley lyrics must be considered 'minimal and indirect.' The diction and versification of the lyrics emphasize 'the importance of French and Latin . . . while the use of alliteration as the predominant form of ornamentation anticipates the revival of the native alliterative meter' (254).

515, 968, 1216, 1320.5, 1394, 1395, 1449, 1861, 1921, 2166, 2236, 2491, 2634, 2744, 3223, 3874, 4037.

829   Garbáty, Thomas J. 'Rhyme, Romance, Ballad, Burlesque, and the Confluence of Form.' *Fifteenth-Century Studies: Recent Essays.* Ed. Robert F. Yeager. Hamden, CT: Archon-Shoe String, 1984.

In a study concerned mainly with the connection between romance and ballad, Garbáty writes of works considered the earliest English ballads: 'Judas' [*1649*] and 'St Stephen and Herod' ['Seynt Steuen was a clerk in kin herowdis halle,' *3058*]. There is no record that they were sung, and they may have survived only because of their connection with religious literature. Garbáty wonders if there should be a new category, 'something like *un*ballads, or unsung ballads' (290), and suggests the term *rymes* to include these and similar works, including songs of Robin Hood, since ballads of the thirteenth, fourteenth and fifteenth centuries are 'simply "short, traditional, narrative rhymes."' The ballad before 1500 does not merely resemble other genres; rather the ballad '*was* the lyric, carol, romance, and things of that sort' (291).

1649, 3058, 4170.

830 Gray, Douglas. 'Rough Music: Some Early Invectives and Flytings.' *Yearbook of English Studies* 14 (1984): 21–43.

Surveys satirical invective and flyting, particularly the latter, 'an art form' that is 'essentially rhetorical,' involving 'an element of play and of "acting"' (22). Gray compares other traditional forms of satire and public ridicule such as the 'skimmingon ride' of *The Mayor of Casterbridge*. Dunbar, Minot, and Skelton make contributions in songs against particular people, such as the Duke of Suffolk, or against the Scots or English. Satirical poems against women may be general or particular. Drama affords examples of popular satire in the characters of Herod and Pilate. After remarks on Henryson's 'Sum practysis of Medecyne' [*1021*], Gray supplies a detailed account of 'The Flyting of Dunbar and Kennedie' [*3117.8*]. He demonstrates Dunbar's 'superb range and control of language, his gift for creating a fantastic or nightmarish "scene", a kind of satirical "speaking picture"' (34), whereas Kennedy's sections seem 'rather flat and long-winded.' The 'rough music' of the flytings 'really is a kind of music' (38), demonstrated in Skelton's 'Sithe ye haue me chalynged M[aster] Garnesche' [*3154.5*], when, among many insults, the poet stresses 'the similarity of Garnesche with the ranting idolatrous tyrants of the mystery plays' (41). The 'flamboyant display of "rough music" is concluded by a splendidly precise verbal image' (42) of the subject's knavish body, enshrined at Tyburn. Gray's dramatic examples of flyting culminate in an exchange between Vladimir and Estragon in *Waiting for Godot*.

1021, 1207, 1470.5, 1555, 1934, 1941.8, 2039.3, 2338, 2437, 2580, 2640, 2832.5, 3080, 3117.8, 3154.5, 3999.

831 Jeffrey, David L. 'James Ryman and the Fifteenth-Century Carol.' *Fifteenth-Century Studies: Recent Essays.* Ed. Robert F. Yeager. Hamden, CT: Archon-Shoe String, 1984. 303–20.

See **779**.

832 Miller, William Ian. 'A Relic of Divine Dispensation.' *Explicator* 42.4 (1984): 2–4.

The lyric 'We bern abowtyn non cattes skynnes' [*3864*] demands a sexual interpretation. Although 'the pocket with the two precious stones . . . and the powder that makes maidens' wombs swell . . . have only one correct and obvious referent' (2), the word *jelyf* is ambiguous. Miller questions previous interpretations as 'jelly,' hence 'semen,' since *powder* would then be repetitive. 'Penis' is more likely, but raises the problem of 'why a virile narrator would want to represent his penis by a jelly.' The scribe may have confused *j* with long *r* and *f* with *k*, and so copied *jelyf* for *relyk* in the unique copy of the poem. He may even have avoided irreverence by a deliberate substitution. Taken with the phrase *of godis sonde*, this would allow the poet to claim that 'his phallus is a genuine relic, proven so by the miracles it can perform – it can stand without feet and smite without hands,' to ensure that it is 'worthy the veneration of any damsel' (3). [See also Grennen, **871**.]

1449.

833 Moffat, Douglas. 'The Grave in Early Middle English Verse: Metaphor and Archaeology.' *Florilegium* 6 (1984): 96–102.

Offers examples in ME works of the image of the grave as a house for the corpse, and notes references to the image by Woolf, **522**, and Short, **661**. The metaphor's humour and irony are complicated, because 'Anglo-Saxon graves were often conceived of and built as houses' (97). Moffat cites archeological findings, and emphasizes that the image has 'a resonance that it has lost in its transformation into conventionality, a transformation of which we must be constantly aware if we are to achieve a clearer understanding of tone and meaning in literary artifacts, and of the imagination that created them' (100).

2684.5, 3497, 3517, 4044.

834 Newman, Florence. '*Christ Maketh to Man*,' Stanza Four: A Case for Interpolation.' *Neuphilologische Mitteilungen* 85 (1984): 454–61.

'Crist made to man a fair present' *[611]* presents the image of Christ on the Cross, offering his body as a token of love, and concludes with 'variations on the familiar theme of love and the gentle heart' (454), but its ideological focus is the paradox of 'the incomprehensible self-defeat of divine love' (456). The paradox of atonement creates a tone 'not of exhortation and accusation aimed at the reader but of awe centered upon the unsearchable ways of God' (455). The fourth stanza differs in metre and tone, and also concludes the lyric 'Loueli ter of loueli eyȝe' ['þu sikest sore,' *3691*]. Both Woolf, **522**, and Davies, **61**, assume that it is 'the author's own,' but Newman suggests that it was 'not "borrowed" by the original author, but supplied by a later interpolator uncomfortable with paradox' (456). The lyric *611* is of the genre of *planctus* or lament, and so not harmonious with the triumphant tone of the fourth stanza, which evokes 'a living Savior harrowing hell, not . . . a dying Savior pouring out his heart's blood for man's sins' (457). The lyric was probably inspired by the ME *Meditations on the Life and Passion of Christ*, a paraphase of John of Hovenden's *Philomena*, from which Newman cites passages relating to love allegory and 'the paradox of Christ's subjection to love – *Deus est caritas*' (458). There is a closer resemblance in 'Jacapone da Todi's *Laude* LXXXIII, "De l'amore de Cristo in Croce," which likewise expresses the poet's urge to emulate Christ's incomparable sacrifice' (459). Newman finds *611* complete without the addition of the fourth stanza, since imagery is sustained throughout the poem, and concludes '[t]hat the author himself should violate the high mystery he has so skillfully administered is inconceivable; that someone else has, is unfortunate' (461).

611, 1034, 3271, 3691.

835 Osberg, Richard H. 'Alliterative Technique in the Lyrics of MS Harley 2253.' *Modern Philology* 82 (1984–5): 125–55.

Examines 'ambiguities of alliterative and metrical practice that lurk in the tumbling line of the Harley lyrics' (125), to discern rules and patterns of structure and scansion, and to find influences on the composition and techniques of the verse. In an exploration of two stanzas of 'Annot and John' *[1394]* Osberg probes patterns of rhythm, metre, and alliteration, and objects to analyses of Brook, **42**, and Moore, **297**. He investigates scansion of alliterative Harley lyrics, in particular the 'accentuation of romance loan words; stress in compound nouns, noun phrases, and polysyllables; and the accentuation of personal pronouns, particles and clitic and enclitic adverbs' (128). He finds that the English poet of 'Mayden moder milde/*oeiz cel oreysoun*' *[2039]* applied English stress patterns to French verse, and offers examples of the patterns in Harley lyrics. Examination suggests that the rhythms originate 'neither in the Anglo-Saxon half-line nor in the accentual syllabic tradition,' but rather in 'the high style of rhythmical alliterative prose' (133). Osberg provides a comprehensive analysis of the patterns in prose works. Investigation of 'grammetrical' units in the Harley lyrics yields stress patterns in the half-lines to demonstrate that 'poets transposed, mixed, and varied their tumbling rhythms' (146) with ease. Comparison of alliterative structures and nonalliterative lyrics shows that 'lines of the alliterative lyrics admit more unstressed syllables than do those of the nonalliterative lyrics, but their half-lines are more frequently syncopated and more highly idiosyncratic' (149). Clashing stresses mark 'a major distinction between the two methods of composition' (150). Key stylistic differences include 'a different understanding of rhythm,' seen by comparing the half-lines; 'the characteristic swing of the alliterative lyric line'; the 'clashing stresses and extended numbers of unaccented syllables' of the alliterative lyrics; and the 'newly minted' character of the 'irregular alliterative cadences' (154). The structural nature of alliteration in Harley lyrics unites half-lines across the caesura. The rhythms are those of 'a broad spectrum of alliterative composition in lyric verse and prose' (155).

105, 515, 968, 1216, 1365, 1394, 1395, 1449, 1504, 1861, 2039, 2066, 2153, 2166, 2207, 2604, 3144, 3874, 3939, 4044, 4194.

836 Samuels, M.L. 'The Dialect of the Scribe of the Harley Lyrics.' *Poetica* [Tokyo] 19 (1984): 39–47. Repr. in *Middle English Dialectology: Essays on Some Principles and Problems by Angus McIntosh, M.L. Samuels and Margaret Laing.* Ed. Margaret Laing. Aberdeen: Aberdeen UP, 1989. 256–63.

Considers dialectal forms used by the scribe of MS Harley 2253, to answer the question: 'Was he a native of Hereford, or Ludlow, or elsewhere?' (256). Samuels examines disparate works of the Harley scribe to show the scribe's preferences for particular forms, and compares these with writings reliably located in particular places near Hereford, Leominster, and Ludlow. His citations tend to be general, indicating occurrences of words in whole manuscripts, rather than in particular works within them; they serve to locate the scribe's dialect in the area around Leominster. Localization suggests that 'the scribe acquired his linguistic and orthographic habits' in North Herefordshire, but does not reveal where he prepared the manuscript, although the evidence of Revard, **723**, points towards Ludlow. Samuels accepts connections with both Hereford and Ludlow, and also considers the prose recipes, written by another scribe in the manuscript. These show 'more southerly features,' to suggest that 'this scribe was from nearer Hereford.' Although the findings cannot determine whether the scribes or the book migrated, 'evidence for the dialect of the main scribe points clearly to Leominster rather than Hereford or Ludlow' (262).

1216, 1365, 2236, 3211.

837 Sichert, Margit. 'Liebe in den Mittelenglischen Pastourellen.' *Liebe-Ehe-Ehebruch in der Literatur des Mittelalters.* Ed. Xenja von Ertzdorff and Marianne Wynn. Giessen: Schmitz, 1984. 125–39.

An introduction to the pastourelle, with its pattern of a rural encounter between a young man of superior social rank, usually a knight or clerk, and a young shepherdess. Sichert summarizes comments of Gaston Paris [*Melanges de littérature française du moyen âge*], Paul Zumthor [*Language et techniques poétiques à l'époque romane*], and Michel Zink [*La pastourelle: poésie et folklore au moyen âge*. The pastourelle theme may be related to themes of Andreas Capellanus and the tradition of Circe, who is thought by Zink to represent a feminine Eros. Love in the pastourelle may be opposed to courtly love. Both forms, because they are linked with the changeable present, may be contrasted with love for the Virgin Mary, which is associated with an eternally peaceful afterlife. The antithesis resembles that of Eve and Mary. Sichert interprets the ME pastourelle in lyrics 'Als i me rod this endre dai' [*360*], 'As I stod on a day me self under a tre' [*371*], 'In a fryht as y con fere fremede' [*1449*], and 'Nou skr[yn]nkeþ rose & lylie flour' [*2359*]; and in ballads 'The Crow and the Pie,' 'Into a Sweet May Morning,' and 'The Knight and the Shepherd's Daughter.' In *1449* the characters are presented antithetically, with opposing social status and desires; in this case the girl refuses the gallant. Both characters of *360* feel the grief of love, since each laments a loss; here the knight comforts the girl. The dream-like poem *371* differs from other pastourelles in telling of a woman of higher social status. She is more active than the poet, who falls into her playful snare; the work contrasts ideal and reality, and the woman resembles Fortuna. Familiarity with the genre is assumed for the audience of *2359*, and there is a Christian interpretation. Instead of courting a shepherdess, the poet seeks forgiveness of sins through Mary, and the return of paradise, peace, joy, and unity with God, all lost by Eve. The ME pastourelle differs from French forms in the emphasis on morality and consequences. The girls want rational love and marriage; they scorn the knights and warn against sinful love, sometimes rejecting all earthly forms, and seeking only the spiritual love of God, through Mary.

360, 371, 1449, 2359.

838 Simons, John. 'An Early Sixteenth Century Lyric in National Library of Wales MS. Peniarth 369b.' *English Language Notes* 22 (1984): 1–5. [Edition.]

This lyric has been added to the fifteenth-century medical manuscript, 'in a small, rapid, secretary hand,' at some time 'between 1485 and the 1550's' (2). Simons prints the work, 'Hegh nony nony/nony no hegh' [*7200*], and indicates its similarity to lyrics in *RobbinsS*, **55**, 'O mestres why/Owtecaste am I' [*2518*] and 'Alone walking/In thought pleyning/And sore sighing' [*267*]. There is a dialogue in a dream vision which may be paraphrased: 'the man is troubled and insecure due to the absence of his lover, she appears and reassures him, he continues in his despair' (3). It seems to be a reconstruction of a song 'corrupted due to misremembering' (4).

267, 2518, 7200.

839 Stemmler, Theo. 'My Fair Lady: Parody in Fifteenth-Century Lyrics.' *Medieval Studies Conference Aachen 1983: Language and Literature*. Ed. Wolf-Dietrich Bald and Horst Weinstock. Bamberger Beiträge zur Englischen Sprachwissenschaft 15. Ed. Wolfgang Viereck. Frankfurt am Main: Lang, 1984. 205–13.

Defines parody, stating that its recognition depends on the author's indication of the parodied genre, rather than merely on exaggeration, incongruity, or deviation from a norm. Thus 'Annot and John' [*1394*] and 'The Fair Maid of Ribblesdale' [*2207*] are not parodies. [Cf. Ransom, **697**; Burton, **752**]. Chaucer's 'Rosemounde' [*2031*] is a doubtful case, but his *Tale of Sir Thopas* [*4019*] includes parodies of courtly-love lyrics. The 'Complaynt to his Empty Purse' [*3787*] and 'Merciles Beaute' [*4282*] are parodies that use deflation and reversal of motifs. Fifteenth-century techniques include ridicule of the lover as well as his lady. Stemmler offers examples that employ the 'juxtaposition of phrases taken from the repertoire of the courtly-love lyric and phrases which contradict the canon' (207); negation when 'a canonical motif is ridiculed not by contradiction . . . but by directly negating it' (208); and inversion of motif. The lady's beauty may be parodied in a portrait in which 'the author realizes his parodistic purpose by means of contradiction, negation, and irony' (209), with incongruous and exaggerated terms presented in the conventional order of description, as in Hoccleve's 'Praise of his Lady' ['Of my lady wel me reioise I may,' *2640*]. In poems such as 'O Mossie Quince hangyng by youre stalke' [*2524*], the poet adds 'sexual and scatological allusions,' so that 'the lady is not merely debunked but reviled' (210). 'O fresche floure most plesant of pryse' [*2437*] also ridicules the lover's epistle. The genre's climax comes in 'My fayr lady so fresshe of hew' [*2237*], which has been attributed to Lydgate, which has a description of 'hitherto

Annotations of Critical Works 315

unknown grossness' (211), with animal imagery and sexual allusions, and concludes with 'an inverted spring-opening which usually *introduces* a love-lyric' (212). The genre continues in the work of Shakespeare and Donne.

1280, 1300, 1394, 1957, 2031, 2207, 2237, 2437, 2524, 2640, 3787, 3879, 4019, 4209, 4282.

840 Wenzel, Siegfried. 'Medieval Sermons and the Study of Literature.' *Medieval and Pseudo-Medieval Literature.* The J.A.W. Bennett Memorial Lectures. Perugia, 1982–3. Ed. Piero Boitani and Anna Torti. Tübinger Beiträge zur Anglistik. Ed. Joerg O. Fichte and Hans-Werner Ludwig. Cambridge: Brewer; Tübingen: Narr, 1984. 19–32.

An exploration of connections between sermons and medieval poetry and of the notion that 'behind the actual sermons lie numbers of books and treatises which furnished the ingredients as well as guidance' (21). Wenzel offers several examples of investigation of this kind; he includes references to his earlier work on 'Maiden in the mor lay' [*2037.5*], **627**, and 'Haue mercie on me frere' [*1123*], **817**, and to evidence found for 'the popularity and spread of the vernacular songs cited by Bishop Ledrede next to his own Latin hymns' (22). He considers allegory in sermons, and expresses doubt about an audience's capacity to discern all the meanings of details. As an example he cites the use of a song of a deceived lover in a sermon that refers to 'those lukewarm Christians who after undergoing the cleansing experience of Lent and Easter return to their former sinful life' (24). The preacher explicates 'Ich aue a loue vntrewe' [*1301*] as a way to allegorize images of lovesickness in lyrics of secular love, in terms of Christ's spiritual love for mankind. This method implies a need to set images of *caritas* against those of *cupiditas*, and an awareness of separate systems of discourse. The medieval sermon had 'the status of a work of art,' and demanded 'quite sophisticated verbal, logical, and rhetorical skills' (26). The artistry involved is demonstrated in the collections of precepts for construction of sermons and in comments on and parodies of preaching found in other literary genres. Wenzel concludes by considering possible influences of sermon structure on the structure of Chaucer's works and the influence of medieval sermon language in passages in *King Lear*.

1123, 1301, 2037.5.

841 Whiteford, Peter. 'Unnoticed Verses from a Fifteenth-Century Sermon Collection.' *Notes and Queries* 229 (1984): 456–7. [Edition.]

Notes four ME verses in Bodleian Library MS e Musaeo 180, in which sermons are arranged for the church year. The verses are in *exempla*, and three of them are accompanied by Latin verses. The first 'Thu blynde in flessche has fall in a case' [*7534*] accompanies a miracle of the Virgin, in which a confessor removes a blood-stained glove from a sinful woman's hand, and explains the sins that are written on it in Latin. The verse in the second tale, 'Withe myne hert blod I the bowȝte' [*7634*], supplies inscriptions on a crucifix before which a man prayed. Although he had been shriven, the man had not forgiven a neighbour. The image bled and writing appeared on its breast, before and after the man left to offer forgiveness to his neighbour. The third story is of a repentant harlot, who died after hearing a sermon of St Austin, and was denied Christian burial. The roses springing from her mouth bore verses on their leaves, 'Thowe I were synfull deme [not me]' [*7539*]. The last tale is an allegory of four shields that bear enigmatic messages. The messages are interpreted by a clerk, who adds the verse 'In these scuchyns þat schynythe so bryȝt' [*7271*]. Whiteford supplies only the verse for the first shield 'Thy lyfe it is a law of dethe' [*7546*]. [See Fletcher, **651**.]

7271, 7534, 7539, 7546, 7634.

842 Wimsatt, James I. 'St. Bernard, the Canticle of Canticles, and Mystical Poetry.' *An Introduction to the Medieval Mystics of Europe.* Ed. Paul E. Szarmach. Albany, NY: State U of New York P, 1984. 77–95.

Explains teachings of Bernard of Clairvaux (based on a spiritual interpretation of the Canticle of Canticles) on the mystical experience of the soul's union with God, before considering the influence of Bernard's writings on ME poems that express 'affection for Jesus in his Passion.' This is shown in the lyric 'In a valey of þis restles mynde' [*1463*] which demonstrates 'the progress which Bernard postulates,' since 'the Passion meditation with which it begins turns neatly into a representation of contemplative union' (82). The lyric resembles secular love poems and meditative lyrics in its opening, which recalls the *chanson d'aventure*, and in the device of Christ the lover-knight, but its main source is Canticles and 'its tradition, led by Bernard, of mystical exegesis,' emphasized in the refrain 'drawn from Canticles (2:5, 5:8), "For I languish with love."' As the lover assumes many roles and relationships to the beloved, he stresses his affection, 'enumerating the proofs of his love that he has given the soul, and contrasting these sharply with what the soul has done to him' (83). References to his wounds lead to the Passion meditation and to 'a key transition to Christ's active wooing and winning of the soul in the second half of the poem' (84), especially in the image of the wound in the side as marriage chamber or nest for the soul. The image of windows, the senses, through which the soul apprehends the bed and chamber comes from Canticles 2.9. The soul's contemplative sleep is that of the Bride of Canticles, and signifies 'the ecstasy of communion with God' (86). The poem is 'thoroughly Bernardine,' although it was written 'nearly three centuries after Bernard.' Wimsatt compares the Latin 'Dulcis Iesu memoria,' of Bernard's time, 'which even more profoundly reflects his mystical thought' (87). To exemplify many ME imitations of the latter, he cites 'Iesu suete is þe loue of þe' [*1747*]. The ME poems show little poetic merit, and are 'not essentially mystical' (91). Among the factors that contribute to the effectiveness of *1463* and 'Dulcis Iesu memoria' are their grounding in coherent and profound Bernardine mystical theology; their narrative of the soul's progress; their emotional language based on affective, mystical love; and their Christian interpretation of Canticles. Wimsatt compares the mystical works of Mechthild of Magdeburg and of Richard Rolle and his followers with Bernard's, particularly those on love and Canticles. He concludes that Bernard's were the most important, 'the necessary catalyst for the outpouring of mystical literature based on Canticles that came after him' (94).

1463, 1747.

843 Ziolkowski, Jan. 'Avatars of Ugliness in Medieval Literature.' *Modern Language Review* 79 (1984): 1–20.

Surveys traditions of the description of appearance, comparing the conventional fixity of descriptions of beautiful young women with the wide range of those of the ugly. Sidonius Apollinaris, Matthew of Vendôme, Froumund of Tergensee, Geoffrey of Vinsauf, and Chrétien de Troyes are among those who establish the association of ugliness and depravity. This is seen in contrasting descriptions of 'a luscious young woman and a collapsing crone' that serve as 'an emphatic *memento mori* (or, to be more accurate, *memento senescere*)' (5), as in 'Death & Liffe' [*603*] and *Sir Gawain and the Green Knight* [*3144*]. The notion is based on physiognomy. Ziolkowski offers French examples, noting animal imagery, before alluding to a giant in the alliterative *Morte Arthure* [*2322*], and passing to 'an entire sub-class of late medieval English lyric poem which contain vituperative descriptions that invert the accepted catalogue of charms' (10). These include Hoccleve's 'Complaint' to Lady Money [*124*] and Lydgate's 'My fayr lady so fresshe of hew' [*2237*]. The former is a triple roundel, the latter an exhaustive description in the standard form; both poems exploit incongruous animal imagery. In a pair of lyrics, a verse letter to a lover ['Vnto you most froward þis lettre I write,' *3832*] has 'the only ironic catalogue of a man's handsomeness found in Middle-English lyric poetry' (13). The lover's reply to his mistress ['O fresche floure most plesant of pryse,' *2437*] counters 'with a retaliatory ironic catalogue of charms.' The absence of repetition in such poems confirms that 'the Middle Ages had more varieties of absolute ugliness than of absolute beauty' (14), as Ziolkowski demonstrates from the Cambridge ME lyrics. Actual people might be described, as in Dunbar's 'On ane blakmoir' ['Lang heff I maed of ladyes quhytt,' *1934.5*], on a woman offered 'as first prize in a joust in 1507'; and in Skelton's 'The Tunnyng of Elynour Rummyng' [*3265.5*], on 'an infamous barmaid' (16). Ziolkowski concludes by describing *blason* and *contre-blason* and the shattering of traditions by Shakespeare and Donne.

124, 603, 1300, 1934.5, 2237, 2322, 2437, 2524, 3144, 3265.5, 3832, 4019.

844 Albright, Daniel. *Lyricality in English Literature.* Lincoln, NE: U of Nebraska P, 1985.

This exploration of the nature of the lyric deals mainly with poems written after the Middle Ages, and examines the lyric as if it were 'a species of ether, having no commerce with the low world of solid forms.' In considering the antithesis of this partial truth Albright cites ME examples that are 'notably physical, corporeal, showing the surges, the spurtings, the muscularities, the thrusts of the body' in the 'deep embodiedness' (22) of such lyrics, among which he includes the 'Corpus Christi Carol' [*1132*] and 'Svmer is icumen in' [*3223*]. He notes the lyric's aspiration to be 'a wordless melody,' although 'it is verbal, nothing but verbal, exclusively a matter of verbal color, clamor, birdcalls, farts, grunts, yodels' (23).

1132, 1944, 3223 .

845 Baird-Lange, Lorrayne Y. 'Symbolic Ambivalence in "I haue a gentil cok."' *Fifteenth-Century Studies* 11 (1985): 1–5.

Probes the symbolism of 'I have a gentil cok' [*1299*], in particular 'the ambivalent *otherness* suggested in the opening and closing stanzas: the Christian priestly cock as awakener of the upright spirit juxtaposed to the upright cock as awakener of the priest' (1). The cock is an ecclesiatical symbol as *gallus deus* or *gallus Christus*; it is related to the pagan sun bird, 'messenger of the coming light of day,' and to Priapus. A third-century story of a resurrected cock persisted in the Middle Ages in *cock*-oaths, but 'after Prudentius and Ambrose, the cock-Christ was dropped from official church symbolism; instead, the cock was made symbol of the priest, as the *gallus praedicator*' (2). In many of the priest's functions the symbolism was 'accepted, repeated and elaborated upon by most of the Church Fathers' (3). It is seen in the fourteenth century 'in the mocking ironic-literal Chaucerian allusions to both the Nun's Priest and the Monk as treadfowls.' Thus the cock of the lyric suggests ecclesiastical and sexual symbols, as he maintains 'his gallinaceous integrity' (4), as 'the priest-cock who performs his matins, and the phallic cock who stirs the priest and puts to flight all other cocks' (5).

1299, 3058, 4019.

846 Barratt, Alexandra. 'The Lyrics of St Godric: A New Manuscript.' *Notes and Queries* 230 (1985): 439–45. [Edition.]

The new manuscript is Paris, Bibliothèque Mazarine 1716, 'a late-thirteenth-century collection of saints' lives written in Old French' (441), which contains a translation of Godric's life from the Latin of Reginald of Durham. Barratt notes other manuscript sources of the three ME lyrics and their contexts before describing the French manuscript. The lyrics, composed in visions by St Godric, are 'Seinte marie clane uirgine' [*2988*], 'Crist and saint marie swa on scamel me iledde' [*598*], and 'Sainte Nicolaes godes druð' [*3031*]. There are several accounts of Godric's life. Not all of them supply all the lyrics, but in Reginald's 'the first two lyrics appear at appropriate places in the text,' with 'a reference to the circumstances of composition of the third' (440). Mazarine 1716 belonged to Isabella of France, but was probably never in England; it has no other ME works or other evidence of English ownership. The lyrics' presence probably shows that 'Reginald's Latin life originally contained all three poems in context' (441). Barratt explores possibilities for the circulation of the lyrics and their music, noting that lines left may mean an intention to insert musical notation. Variations in details of the stories of composition concern the lyrics' original language – Latin in the French text and English in the Latin. She presents 'a diplomatic transcript of the Mazarine texts, accompanied by an attempt to reconstruct the translator's, or scribe's, Middle English exemplar' (443). The discrepancies reveal a lack of familiarity with 'letter forms found in early Middle English orthography but not in Old French' (444). Examination suggests that there were 'at least two stages in transmission,' and that the process illuminates 'the medieval attitude of respect for a saint's *ipsissima verba*' (445).

598, 2988, 3031.

847 Bazire, Joyce. '"Mercy and Justice"': The Additional MS 31042 Version.' *Leeds Studies in English* NS 16 (1985): 259–71. [Edition.]

Builds on previous editions [Kurvinen, **580**; Bazire, **773**] of 'Bi a forest as y gan walke' [*560*], prepared from the texts of MSS National Library of Wales Harlech 10 [formerly Porkington] (H/P), Chichester Cowfold (C), and Lambeth Palace 853 (L), with an edition of the version in BL Add. 31042 (A). Bazire repeats the table of **773**, to show variations in the stanzas, and notes differing features of dialect. Although a Northerly dialect is indicated for A, there is some evidence for the South-East or West Midlands, leading to the conclusion that 'one could only tentatively suggest an area towards the west of NEM' (263). Bazire prints the text, with footnotes on manuscript features, and more detailed comments, particularly on 'rhyme-patterns which are peculiar to A' (267). She closely examines the lines that vary, and finds that A shows 'most individuality in its lines.' The variations do not show connections between versions, to reveal 'which is closer to the original' or 'whether successive transmitters – in copying or orally – have tried to improve upon what they knew' (268). Inspection shows that variations and alterations have not resulted, 'on comparing it with H/PL, in the creation of a better work of art,' but they offer 'an interesting illustration of the possible fate of a short Middle English poem' (270).

560.

848 Boffey, Julia. *Manuscripts of English Courtly Love Lyrics in the Later Middle Ages.* Manuscript Studies 1. Gen. ed. Jeremy Griffiths. Woodbridge: Brewer, 1985.

Surveys manuscript sources of ME courtly love lyrics 'between c.1400 and c.1530' (4). Here a 'lyric' is 'essentially a non-narrative poem, and usually a short one' (3); 'courtliness' relates to 'implicit values' rather than to 'any connection with real, historical courts'; and the 'love' element is 'in many ways merely a function of their courtliness' (4). Boffey illustrates her findings with numerous examples.

In 'A Survey of the Manuscripts' (6–33), she describes the range of manuscripts, and notes hazards of drawing conclusions from the surviving texts. Using particular examples, she explains that of 'the hundred or so relevant manuscripts, only two complete volumes, BL MSS Addit. 17492 and Harley 682, and one section of . . . Bodl. Fairfax 16, are made up entirely (or almost entirely) of such poems' (7). The lyrics are found in anthologies, such as collections of Chaucer's works prepared by John Shirley, in commonplace books, and in songbooks; they may also be jotted on flyleaves, in manuscripts and early printed editions. Their 'literary status' seems slighter than that of their French counterparts, but 'writers and readers were clearly familiar with courtly love lyrics, and recognized them as handy for "autograph" purposes'; they were numerous, 'even if they did not circulate in impressively compiled collected editions' (33).

'The Presentation of the Poems' (34–60) examines the appearance of manuscripts, and warns that many lyrics are '"flyleaf" jottings, copied down with little or no regard for layout or visual impact' (34). Bodleian Fairfax 16 presents the most sumptuously decorated lyric in the amalgamation of the *Complaints of Mars and Venus* [*913, 3542*]. A *de luxe* manuscript, BL Royal 16 F.ii has six miniatures, three of which are associated with poems of Charles d'Orléans. Two songbooks, BL Add. 5465 and 31922, have decorated lyrics. Some manuscripts have such 'lesser ornamentation' as 'coloured flourishing of initial letters' (41), and gaps in other manuscripts containing lyrics show that 'decoration of some kind was projected but never completed' (43). The styles of illumination display French and Flemish influence, and there were English ateliers including William Abell's. The preoccupation with illumination of liturgical texts may explain why fewer than a third of lyrics are ornamented. French was the dominant language of secular literature. In continental manuscripts secular lyrics had been 'illustrated from the start' (49), and produced in luxurious and literary forms. There were intercalated lyrics in both French and English works. Some 'lyric utterances' may be the occasion for an illustration, perhaps shown only by a gap in the manuscript. English readers and compilers of manuscripts seem indifferent to the illustration of lyrics, and 'any English demand for beautifully-produced copies of lyrics was no doubt amply satisfied by the [readily available] foreign manuscripts' (59).

In 'Authorship and Composition' (61–86), Boffey examines internal and external evidence about the manuscripts, together with that elicited from her reconstruction of 'the compilation, copying, and subsequent history of individual manuscripts.' She extends her findings 'by scrutiny of the evidence of particular groupings of works, by scribal attributions and comments, and by information added to manuscripts by readers' (61). She considers the relationship between author and scribe; the value placed on the rare records of authorship, as in the cycle associated with Charles d'Orléans, in Harley 682; and the range of known authors. Names may be revealed in autobigraphical details; acrostics (which may also name the recipients); and mottoes (which sometimes inform only the poem's intended audience). Most of the individuals identified are scribes. Some rubrics, such as Shirley's, provide ascriptions and other information, although an author such as William de la Pole, Duke of Suffolk may have been named only to lend prestige to the manuscript. A lyric's context may imply a particular author, but such deductions tend to be speculative, unless it is known that lyrics were extracted from other works. Generally *centos* preserve 'the spirit of the works from which they are taken' (70–1), but the 'Canticus Troilii' has been put to several uses. Although Chaucer is often named, his dominance is statistically 'far surpassed by the supposed achievements of Charles d'Orléans (with or without the collaboration of his friend the Duke of Suffolk)' (74). Shirley's attributions also connect some lyrics with Lydgate. Evidence for Humfrey Newton's authorship of 17 lyrics is convincing. Two lyrics are attributed to Skelton, but attributions to Wyatt are difficult and uncertain. Associations can be made for a few others, but only the ascriptions to Marjery Brews ['And yf ye commande me to kepe me true wherever I go,' *303*] and Patrik Larrons ['I patrik larrons of spittale feyld,' *1338.5*] can claim 'satisfyingly incontrovertible evidence' (85). Of 600 poems, Boffey finds associations for 200 to 300.

'Currency and Transmission' (87–112) discusses the extent of circulation and the importance of examplars and oral transmission. Circulation seems limited, and few lyrics survive in more than one copy. Connections with music and with names, such as those of Chaucer, Wyatt, Charles d'Orléans, and Lydgate, are aids to survival. Some lyrics show evidence of reworking. Burdens and refrains may ensure 'musically-influenced transmission' (90). *Centos* reveal 'familiarity with the source works in a written form,' although borrowings may suggest oral or written sources and degrees of intermingling. Boffey surveys evidence for the circulation of groups of manuscripts (including Shirley's anthologies and the 'Oxford' group of manuscripts) and for the significance of music and its relation with the courtly lyrics. The bias towards Latin liturgical works meant that few musical settings for English secular songs are available; the preference for continental material influenced the demand for English lyrics. Centres of formal musical education, generally religious, were also sources of courtly love lyrics. Early printers seem not have noticed a demand for 'cheap, commercially-produced books of English songs' (97). Headings suggest melodies for singing some lyrics; other references, such as George Cely's notes, record the titles of lyrics which do not survive. Music used by minstrels has not survived, since they had no need for it, and there is little evidence of amateur performances. The most popular form was the *chanson*, usually with a three-part setting for voices or instruments. Many pieces, 'sung or played by musically illiterate amateurs' (104), were probably transmitted orally. Rhyme royal and ballade stanzas are often used, and most English courtly songs are settings of these forms, allowing the formation of *contrafacta*. More French than English songs survive, and English composers worked on the continent, leaving 'only settings for songs with French words' (106). Words and music were used and adapted freely. In the *quodlibet* 'the text is formed from the incipits (or other selected lines) of a number of other works, and the musical setting by means of a similar sort of cannibalism' (108). The links between words and music seem informal, casual, and improvisatory.

'Readers and Owners of the Manuscripts' (113–41) surveys 'the wider social context of courtly love lyrics – the nature of their audience, and the form and manner in which they circulated within it.' Boffey considers the identity of the audience, the libraries in which manuscripts were found, and the value placed upon them. The manuscripts can reveal 'who composed, copied, and read the contents.' Other documents can indicate 'ownership of particular books, and suggest certain habits and preferences,' to supply 'some idea of the original readership of courtly love lyrics, and . . . the possible discrepancy between what was demonstrably "available for reading" and what was actually recorded as "having been read"' (113). She treats with caution evidence drawn from dedications of manuscripts and records from wills of numbers of books or specific bequests, and finds many such records vague and unhelpful, 'fascinating yet baffling' (115). Provenance is complicated by many instances of courtly love lyrics found as additions to completed manuscripts. Only 30 provenances can be traced among 100 manuscripts. Boffey provides details of several of these, tracing their composition and ownership, in particular BL Add. 5465 (the Fayrfax MS), 31922, and 17492 (the Devonshire MS); Longleat 258; Bodleian Fairfax 16; BL Sloane 1212; and Cambridge University Library Ff.1.6 (the Findern anthology). Library collections demonstrated social standing, and some courtly works were acquired for this purpose. The clerical provenance of some manuscripts suggests that 'clerks of one sort or another formed the biggest audience for courtly love lyrics . . . just as they were . . . for written material of any kind' (127). Vague poetic terminology adds to the difficulties in interpreting evidence, so that the nature of a work, whether it is religious or secular, verse or prose, may not be clear. Courtly lyrics are not plentiful; they seem not to be considered 'desirable reading volumes' (130), and there are few in library records. Their occasional nature and the possibility that they were copied to 'thin, unbound booklets (even single leaves) which quickly disintegrated' (134) may contribute to difficulties. The dictates of taste and dominance of French seem significant, since troubadour and trouvère poetry have survived; English readers were likely to acquire French manuscripts of lyrics, which are found in several libraries. English courtly lyrics were enjoyed by 'all classes of cultivated reader,' particularly by those who 'could put them to some practical purpose – functionaries responsible for organizing court entertainments . . . or clerks of some kind . . . who were recording the poems . . . for similarly convivial uses' (140).

Boffey provides appendices of 'English Courtly Love Lyrics, c. 1400–1530' (142–86) and 'Manuscripts Containing Copies of English Courtly Love Lyrics, c. 1400–1530' (187–201), a 'Bibliography' (202–20), and 'Indices' (221–32).

.2, 3, 4, 9, 13.3, 13.5, 14.5, 15, 16, 19, 62, 84, 98.5, 113.5, 120.5, 120.6, 120.7, 133, 134, 135.3, 135.5, 136, 137, 138, 139, 140, 143.5, 144, 146, 146.5, 148, 151, 152, 154, 155.5, 157, 158, 158.2, 158.6, 158.8, 159, 159.5, 159.8, 164, 165, 175, 190.5, 231, 238, 263.3, 263.5, 263.8, 264, 266.3, 266.5, 267, 270, 296, 300, 303, 309, *317.5, 329, 335, 336, 337, 338, 340.5, 366, 370, 380, 382, 383, 402, 403, 409.5, 431, 440, 451, 460, 472, 479, 481, 482, 506.5, 509, 510, 517, 552, 553, 555, 556, 557.5, 564, 570, 571, 572, 590, 647, 649, 649.5, 650, 656, 657, 666, 675.8, 676.5, 681.5, 682, 688.8, 724, 729, 733.1, 734, 735, 737, 746, 751, 752, 753.8, 754, 763, 763.5, 764, 765.3, 765.5, 766, 767, 768, 810, 811.5, 813.6, 816, 823, 827, 828, 833, 835.5, 844, 852, 853, 855, 857, 865.5, 867, 868, 869, 870, 871.5, 922, 923, 924, 925, 926, 928.5, 932, 932.5, 960, 1010, 1017, 1017.5, 1018, 1022, 1023, 1086, 1088, 1120, 1176.5, 1176.8, 1180, 1187, 1214.7, 1237, 1238, 1239, 1240, 1241, 1250, 1256, 1257, 1270.2, 1273.3, 1288, 1295.8, 1305, 1309, 1313, 1316, 1328.2, 1328.5, 1328.7, 1328.8, 1329, 1329.5, 1331, 1333, 1334, 1338.5, 1339, 1344, 1345, 1349.5, 1356.8, 1385, 1388, 1403, 1404, 1409.3, 1413, 1414.5, 1414.8, 1418.5, 1420, 1420.5, 1422.1, 1422.3, 1422.5, 1424, 1440.5, 1449.5, 1450.5, 1485.5, 1487, 1489.5, 1496, 1500, 1510, 1529, 1549, 1562, 1581, 1598.3, 1607, 1620.5, 1628, 1768, 1789, 1826, 1829.8, 1838, 1841.5, 1858, 1864.5, 1866.5, 1926.5, 1933, *1944.5, 1999.5, 2013, 2015, 2016, 2017, 2027, 2028, 2028.5, 2028.8, 2029, 2030, 2031, 2032, 2161, 2175, 2176, 2177, 2178, 2179, 2180, 2181, 2182, 2182.3, 2182.6, 2183, 2184, 2185, 2188, 2195, 2195.3, 2195.5, 2196, 2197, 2198, 2200.3, 2203, 2204, 2205, 2206, 2217, 2223, 2224.5, 2230, 2231, 2236.5, 2243, 2244.6, 2245, 2245.1, 2245.3, 2245.4, 2245.6, 2246, 2247, 2249, 2250.3, 2250.5, 2254, 2259, 2261, 2261.2, 2261.4, 2261.6, 2263, 2265, 2266, 2267.5, 2271.2, 2271.6, 2272.5, 2274, 2275, 2276, 2277, 2277.5, 2277.8, 2278, 2279, 2281, 2281.5, *2284.3, 2289, 2293.5, 2294, 2295, 2297, 2299, 2300, 2307.5, 2308, 2308.8, 2311, 2318, 2325.5, 2349, 2350, 2358, 2378, 2379, 2381, 2384.8, 2386, 2406, 2407, 2412.5, 2421, 2422, 2423, 2424, 2424.5, 2425, 2427, 2436, 2437.5, 2438, 2439, 2439.5, 2440, 2449, 2450, 2455, 2456, 2457, 2458, 2475, 2478, 2478.5, 2479, 2482, 2488, 2491, 2496, 2498, 2510, 2517, 2518, 2529, 2530.5, 2531.5, 2532, 2532.3, 2532.5, 2535.5, 2547, 2547.5, 2548, 2550, 2558, 2560.5, 2564, 2567, 2577.5, 2579.3, 2581, 2583, 2588.5, 2594, 2595, 2597, 2599, 2602.2, 2619.5, 2623, 2626, 2634, 2648, 2657.5, 2669, 2699, 2736.8, 2753.5, 2755.5, 2756, 2757.3, 2758, 2768, 2782, 2794.4, 2798, 2813, 2819, 2821, 2822, 2823, 2827, 2828, 3074.6, 3097.6, 3099, 3124, 3125, 3128, 3131.5, 3132, 3134, 3140, 3141, 3142, 3144.5, 3162, 3162.5, 3163, 3163.5, 3164, 3165, 3168.4, 3179, 3180, 3181, 3228.5, 3229, 3255, 3256, 3271, 3291, 3297.3, 3297.5, 3370, 3376.5, 3396, 3413.3, 3414, 3418, 3426, 3439, 3447, 3458, 3461.5, 3461.8, 3465, 3486.5, 3488, 3498, 3498.5, 3534, 3541, 3542, 3586, 3601, 3613, 3622, 3626, 3631, 3633, 3645, 3670, 3678, 3688, 3702, 3703.5, 3706.7, 3706.8, 3706.9, 3707.3, 3707.8, *3721.5, 3722, 3723, 3724.5, 3751.3, 3752, 3758.5, 3768, 3785, 3794, 3795, 3804, 3806, 3808.5, 3836.5, 3844.5, 3849, 3860, 3875, 3878, 3880.6, 3885, 3890, 3897, 3899.3, 3903.8, 3911.5, 3912, 3913, 3914.5, 3915, 3916, 3917, 3917.8, 3941.5, 3946.5, 3947.6, 3949, 3956, 3960, 3962, 3995, 4014, 4027, 4044.6, 4057, 4058.3, 4059, 4069, 4070.5, 4075, 4112.5, 4120, 4143.3, 4143.5, 4161, 4186, 4190, 4191, 4192, 4195, 4199, 4201.3, 4201.6, 4209, 4210, 4213, 4213.5, 4217.6, 4241.5, 4242, 4256, 4272.5, 4281.5, 4282, 4283, 4283.5, 4284, 7014, 7030, 7094, 7155, 7184, 7228, 7373, 7390, 7391, 7397, 7399, 7401, 7405, 7595, 7622.

——— Review by Michael J. Franklin, *Medium Ævum* 57 (1988): 114–15. Commends the 'significant and scholarly substantiation of many central issues.' Among these are 'authorship,' including 'notions of authorial and textual integrity; clerkly audiences (both monastic and lay); clerical traditions of performing love lyric; the social and pragmatic functions of lyric; and the relative importance of the provinces and the court in terms of patronage and readership'; Franklin recommends development of the last of these. Although he notes Boffey's caution in making deductions, he advises rather more in her interpretation of survival of texts. He would prefer more attention to the manuscript contexts, but finds that the book has 'clarifying insights into the social and cultural milieu, and it could well prove instrumental in destroying facile assumptions concerning fifteenth- and early sixteenth-century love lyric' (115).

——— Review by David Fallows, *Songs and Musicians in the Fifteenth Century*, Variorum Collected Studies Series C5519 (Aldershot: Ashgate, 1996): III, 132 – 8 (first published *Journal of the Royal Musical Association* 112: 132–8). Emphasizes musical aspects of the lyrics, and contributes material on a poem ascribed to William de la Pole. Fallows develops Boffey's identification of a poem (perhaps the work of Charles d'Orléans) found in MSS Harley 7333 and Trent 87, by supplying a musical setting and extensive comments. Although he acknowledges Boffey's focus on the poems as literature, he welcomes the preparation of the handlist of courtly lyrics, even though she does not identify those, 'over one-fifth,' that 'either survive in a musical setting or are known . . . to have existed with music.' The study is based on 'a wide and intelligent reading of the work done in related disciplines, particularly musicology and art history' (137), and 'the result is an extremely useful contribution to our understanding of the subject' (138).

——— Review by E.G. Stanley, *Notes and Queries* 232 (1987): 66–7. Despite some reservation about the use of the term 'courtly love lyrics,' Stanley judges the book 'practical and useful,' and welcomes the series it begins. He predicts heavier use of the informative apparatus than of the text of the 'accurate and well-printed contribution' (67).

849   Cox, D.C., and Carter Revard. 'A New ME O-and-I Lyric and its Provenance.' *Medium Ævum* 54 (1985): 33–46. [Edition.]

The poem, on the dorse of a rental-roll, was copied 'at Lilleshall Abbey, by an employee of the abbey (if not by a canon or lay brother there), and very likely about 1370–2' (34). The love song has an O-and-I phrase in the fifth line of each stanza of six lines. By analogy with known *contrafacta*, paired religious and secular songs sharing the same tune, and from Chaucer's account of the Friar and his *yeddings*, the authors conclude that 'The Rejected Lover' ['y am by-wylt of a wyʒt þat worches me wo,' *7209*] has a religious counterpart, and that 'this particular *yedding* was composed and first performed by a friar' (34). They discuss resemblances to other O-and-I lyrics, and note that 'all but one of these others are didactic or religious' (35). The poem tells of a faithless lady who favours a worthless rival, causing the lover to renounce all women, 'more like anti-feminist commonplaces than like love doctrine.' It is perhaps meant 'as counterpart to a song praising the never-failing love of Mary or of Jesus,' as in 'The Way of Woman's Love' [*1921*] and 'The Way of Christ's Love' [*1922*]. The latter poems, from Harley MS 2253, which were copied 'not long before our Lilleshall scribe wrote his poem down . . . by a scribe working not far from Lilleshall,' have 'a refrain-phrase resembling the O-and-I refrain, with "Euer ant oo" taking the place of "wyt an on and an y,"' and there are resemblances to other Harley lyrics. Thus the Lilleshall song may be 'the secular half of such a pair, whose religious counterpart is not now known' (36). Cox and Revard print the poem (38–9), with alternative forms of some lines, and lexical notes. They provide an appendix on 'The Question of Authorial Revision' (42–3), with reasons for the poem's appearance of 'an author's own semi-final draft or revision of his poem' (42). The scribe's changes may suggest his use of another dialect, but he may 'simply have been exercising editorial privilege as well as poetic licence in reworking another man's original' (43).

412, 482, 701, 1001, 1320, 1320.5, 1504, 1921, 1922, 2003.5, 2021, 2287, 2614.5, 2663, 3069, 3098.5, 3363, 3567, 3719.5, 3874, 3921, 4019, 4083, 7209.

850   Diehl, Patrick S. *The Medieval European Religious Lyric: An Ars Poetica.* Berkeley: U of California P, 1985.

Surveys the religious lyric written in 'the liturgical and learned languages, namely, Latin and Greek; and the major and some minor vernaculars, namely Catalan, Old and Middle High German, Italian, Old and Middle English, Old French, Old Norse,

Portuguese, Provençal, and Spanish' (1). Diehl's focus is on 'the form and presentation of content' (3). He examines present day resistance to medieval piety, considering medieval culture 'centripetal, theocentric, and ecclesiological' whereas modern culture is 'centrifugal, anthropocentric, and sociological' (7). The purposes of the religious lyrics were not aesthetic, but they were achieved by aesthetic means, and so the poems can be read for their aesthetic value. They sought to establish or restore 'a proper relationship with the divine' (20), in verse intended to move the emotions. Diehl draws an analogy between the congregation of a medieval church and the audience at a modern reading of poetry, as he explores the role of rhetorical tradition and surveys modern criticism. He deals with the religious lyric in chapters on the functions, genres, forms and structures, and rhetoric, comparing lyrics written in the various European languages. The concluding chapter, 'Orientations,' summarizes his conclusions for each language, with bibliographical information, [for ME, 242–7].

229, 352, 239, 378, 631, 968, 1082.5, 1422, 1775, 1833, 1914, 2320, 2645, 2570, 3221, 3695, 3826.

851 Embree, Dan. ' "The King's Ignorance": A Topos for Evil Times.' *Medium Ævum* 54 (1985): 121–6.

The paradox of the King's Ignorance is 'a commonplace or topos of xiv- and xv-century satiric and didactic verse' (121). Embree cites examples from verses of complaint to demonstrate the assumption that anything wrong cannot be 'the fault of the commons or the King,' but instead of 'those who stand between them: local officials, church officials, magnates, and especially . . . corrupt and frivolous courtiers.' Analogies from the twentieth century include Russian peasants' affectionate regard for Lenin and the 'claims of executive innocence based on executive ignorance . . . made by the executive' (123). Although such claims are now used to contain problems, poems that employ the King's Ignorance topos generally issue 'enthusiastic and expansive attacks upon the administration or even . . . upon the King himself.' They offer advice, warning, and threats that are 'just below the polite surface,' even in the work of a poet such as 'the politically pious Hoccleve' (124). The poets generally speak for the middle class, with 'a fear of unchecked or capricious royal power only a little less than its fear of the unchecked or capricious power of the mob' (125). The topos emphasizes the need for 'the very medium in which it is found . . . the judicious commentary of a centrally located observer' who observes 'both the sufferings of the poor and the corruptions of the court' (125). Poems such as *Mum and the Sothsegger* [296.3] may show 'the simultaneous necessity and unlikelihood of having a sothsegger (or truthteller) present at court' as they advocate 'a reformulation of the theoretical relationship between the commons and the King' (125), perhaps to be achieved in the young Richard II's placation of the 'true commons' (126).

296.3, 817, 2229, 3113, 3448, 4165, 4261.

852 Horrall, Sarah M. 'A Poem of Impossibilities from Westminster Abbey MS 34/3.' *Notes and Queries* 230 (1985): 453–5

'I sei a sicte þat was vnseire' [*1355.5*], is one of the 'lying' or 'impossibility' poems that tell of 'situations which are either bizarre reversals of normal events . . . or logically impossible conditions' (453). These works are intended to amuse or 'to satirize the evils of the age, and, most often, as in the Westminster Abbey poem [*1355.5*], to point up the untrustworthiness of all women, or the unlikelihood that the poet's lady willl love him truly' (453–4). Poems may tell that 'plants bear unlikely fruit, normally timid animals chase their natural enemies, animals, birds, and fish perform human tasks, and unlikely sexual congresses occur.' Scottish poems report 'geographical and meteorological impossibilities' (454). Transmission of the works in Latin may result in the sharing of similar images; for instance two lines of *1355.5* are found in 'The hare wente þe markyth scharlyt forto syll' [*3372.5*]. Some elements of the lying songs are reworked in later poems. A poem copied by George Bannatyne, 'I ȝeid the gair that was nevir gane' that has 'conflated several traditions,' resembles *1355.5*, with similarities 'so pronounced that the Bannatyne poem must surely be considered, at least in part, as a later redaction of a poem very much like that in Westminster Abbey MS 34/3' (455).

1354, 1355.5, 3248.5, 3372.5, 3928.3, 3999, 4005.3, 4056.5, 4128.4, 4236.

853   Innes, Susan M. 'The Flower of God: A Note on Line 2 of "Now Goth Sonne Under Wode."' *American Notes & Queries* 23 (1985): 130–1.

Typical readings of *rode* in 'Nou goth þe sonne under wode' [*2320*] 'as "face," "visage," or "complexion,"' reflect associations in St Edmund Rich's *Mirror of Holy Church* that are 'typologically related to the appearance of Mary at her Son's deposition from the cross.' They obscure 'another, complementary reading of *rode* as an alternate spelling for *rud*, an obsolete name for the flower now known as the calendula, or marigold.' The flower's connection with the sun, in particular 'the observation that it opens with the rising of the sun and closes at its setting,' have prompted the names '*solsequium* ("follower of the sun") and *sponsa solis* ("bride of the sun") or, in Christian terms, *Oculus Christi* ("eye [bud, darling, jewel] of Christ") and "Seynte Marie rode" or adaptations or "Mary" + "gold" . . . variously alluding to Mary's roles as beloved and lover of God' (130). The associations enhance the image of the setting sun, adding 'the image of Christ as the "flower," or "faire rode," of Mary, as well as that of Mary as the "flower" of Christ,' to support and complicate 'the "criss cross" of allusion on which the poem is constructed' (131).

2320.

854   Keiser, George R. 'The Middle English *Planctus Mariae* and the Rhetoric of Pathos.' *The Popular Literature of Medieval England.* Ed. Thomas J. Heffernan. Tennessee Studies in Literature 28. Knoxville, TN: U of Tennessee P, 1985. 167–93.

Pathos is essential in the expression of late medieval affective piety. A particular example is the *planctus Mariae*; this is 'most often a free-standing lyric poem, but it can also be found imbedded in a dramatization or a narrative of the Passion,' as a monologue, or 'part of a dialogue with Jesus, the Cross, or St. Bernard.' It may be delivered 'as the Virgin stands at the foot of the Cross, as she holds the corpse of her Son, or as she looks back upon the events of the Passion from a later time' (168). The author must express the Virgin's sorrows and inspire the meditator's grief, and generally creates pathos through antitheses. In contrasting 'present sorrows and past joys,' the poets describe the Compassion to evoke the meditator's pity through allusions to 'earlier joys of the Nativity and Childhood' (170). They employ such motifs as Mary's freedom from pain in childbirth, her feeding the child at her breast, and her addresses to Gabriel or to other mothers. There are also references to Simeon's prophecy, and to the suffering of innocents. A significant contrast is that between the mourner and the dead, emphasized in Mary's feelings of separation, induced by the height of the Cross and the actions of the Jews. Since the tragedy of medieval *planctus* is mitigated by knowledge of the Resurrection, it is 'more apparent than real,' and should not be considered in terms of 'Frye's larger view of pathos as "low mimetic or domestic tragedy,"' (174) [Northrop Frye, *Anatomy of Criticism.*] Mary's eloquence has no connotation of insincerity, and 'the idea of clothing the words of the Virgin in the best rhetorical finery must have seemed wholly appropriate and decorous to the authors of the *planctus*' (175). The Jew is most often placed in antithesis to Mary, Jesus, or both. There may be an implied identification of the meditators or audience of Passion plays with torturers or Jews, enforced, for example, by describing the Jews and Jesus in terms of hardness and softness. Keiser concludes with an examination of a fifteenth-century prose 'Lamentacioun of Oure Lady.'

14, 95, 248, 377.5, 404, 548, 715, 716, 771, 1219, 1273, 1869, 1899, 2036, 2111, 2165, 2321, 2347, 2428, 2530, 2619, 2718, 3208, 3211, 3245, 3575, 3692, 3976, 4023, 4099, 4019, 4159, 4189.

855 Lerer, Seth. 'An Unrecorded Proverb from British Library MS Additional 35286.' *Notes and Queries* 230 (1985): 305–6. [Edition.]

The proverb 'bewar I say of hadywyste/harde it is a man to trust' [*7088*], in the margin of a mid-fifteenth manuscript of *Canterbury Tales* [*4019*], 'early in the text of the *Tale of Melibee*,' is an example of statements on '*Had-I-wist*, a word *OED* defines as "a vain regret, or the heedlessness or loss of opportunity which leads to it."' The couplet has 'no apparent relationship to the text at this point' (305), but its appearance suggests 'something of the reader's response to *Melibee* as a whole' (305–6), to which 'he appends a native fragment of familiar wisdom' (306).

4019, 7088.

856 Osberg, Richard H. 'Collocation and Theme in the Middle English Lyric "Foweles in þe Frith."' *Modern Language Quarterly* 46 (1985): 115–27.

Seeks to establish whether 'Foweles in the frith' [*864*] is a secular or religious lyric, 'the *cri du cœur* of one spiritually dead, or the lament of sinful Mankind himself' (115). Osberg sees the poem as religious, and the phrases *foweles in the frith* and *fisses in þe flod* as 'two significant elements in the theme of *lex aeterna* . . . that originated in Genesis and Psalm 8.' He traces those and associated ideas in ME poetry and prose, and remarks that *frith* can mean 'not only "woods," or "parkland," but "divine law" as well' (116). The analogy of associations with *muð imelen*, in 'On god ureison of ure lefdi' ['Cristes milde moder seynte marie,' *631*], demonstrates that 'a phrase that in most contexts has neither literary significance nor special linguistic resonance' may, by association, be linked to 'a theme that details the inability of human senses to assimilate Paradise fully' (117). From phrases, associations, and contexts Osberg establishes that 'four Middle English collocations, "foweles in þe frith," "foweles in flyght," "fisses in þe flod," and "foweles and fisses" are to be found commonly but independently associated with other significant details in the tradition of *locus amoenus*.' He concludes that they belong to the larger landscape beyond the garden, 'connected with the theme of *lex aeterna* and mankind's estrangement from that order' (120). Poems, plays, and homilies allude to 'a *lex aeterna* from which only mankind has been excluded . . . signaled by the fish and fowl collocations' (122). Adam's folly disrupts 'the due order,' and Original Sin condemns people 'to sorrow and pain in a natural world where they alone are not at home.' Thus the opening of *864* implies the contrast of 'the order and justice of the created world with the moral and even physiological disorder that . . . seemed a direct consequence of the Fall' (124). Varied occurrences of *beste of bon and blod* imply variable connotations for a medieval listener. Themes linked with the collocations supply 'a field of meaning in which the connotations of individual phrases may resonate' (126). Connotations of *frith* show 'the multiplicity of meaning in the *liber naturalis* itself, part divine gift, in which may be read God's beneficence and bounty, and part human penance, in which may be read Adam's loss of Eden and exile to the world' (127).

60, 542, 583, 603, 631, 635, 716, 864, 1272, 1273, 1395, 1459, 1608.5, 2025, 2153, 2207, 2951, 3213, 3413.

857 Ransom, Daniel J. *Poets at Play: Irony and Parody in the Harley Lyrics.* Norman, OK: Pilgrim, 1985.

Intends to demonstrate 'the ironic tone of four Harley poems and to reveal the parodic intention that underlies that tone' (xiii), from readings of 'The Poet's Repentance'

[*3874*], 'Annot and John' [*1394*], 'The Fair Maid of Ribblesdale' [*2207*], and 'A Wayle Whyt ase Whalles Bon' [*105*], and in extrapolation to other works. Ransom appraises 'rhetorical irony,' the expression of an idea in its opposite, through 'puns, ambiguities, allusions, and chop logic in achieving anticlimaxes or bathos or a general subversion of proper tone' (xv). 'Parody' means 'a species of rhetorical irony,' but 'not simple animadversion, since it is essentially imitative' (xviii). The Harley poets were probably 'clerics, not courtiers' (xx), familiar with Latin and French works. They seek amusement and 'playful ridicule,' rather than 'condemnation or rejection of the subject matter of their poems' (xix), most of which deal with the conventions of courtly love.

In 'Antifeminism, Irony, and *The Poet's Repentance*' (1–29) Ransom shows the basis for an ironic reading of *3874* and its glorification of Richard Hyrd, who attacked the poet 'for writing misogynic verse' (2). Incongruities in the poem imply an ironic tone, even in phrases used seriously elsewhere, in an apparently penitential lyric, written by one who 'has written unseemly poetry about women' (5). Inspection reveals the poet's technique of playful deflation of statements seemingly presented in earnest. This is confirmed in the extravagant praise of Richard that concludes a poem apparently designed to offer praise of women. The conclusion is probably intended 'to ironize, not lionize his rival,' and to preserve 'the concomitant irony of giving the poem's climactic praise to a man' (25).

'*Annot and John* and the Ploys of Parody' (31–48) has been published previously, and is annotated at **697**.

'Ribaldry in Ribblesdale, or The Fair Maid Reexamined' (49–63) probes the poet's manipulation of genres, in placing the styles of pastourelle and description to cause 'an ironic perspective on the courtly tone that seems to govern the body of our poem' (50). Ransom displays effects of disturbance of tone, incongruous associations of ambiguities, and exaggerations in the description of 'a monster, a poetic grotesque.' The ironies do not ridicule 'a poetic form or style,' but rather 'courtly love, and in particular its tendency to idealize the mistress,' and so produce 'a travesty of the idea' (56). The maid is hypothetical. The poet's use of conditional and indicative moods, embodied in poetic clichés, contributes to the creation of his idea; his juxtaposition of seemingly concrete and plausible details strains belief in 'even the probable' among them; apparently independent perceptions have 'the uncertain ring of hearsay' (58). Irreverent religious references further subvert the conventions and tone of courtly poetry and the notion of 'courtly love as a religion in conscious parody of the Christian religion' (60).

In '*A Wayle Whyt ase Whalles Bon*: An Ironic Reconstruction' (65–79), Ransom reads the poem as parody. He prints the reconstruction proposed in dissertations of Gibson [1914] and Stemmler [1962] and examines Stemmler's arguments and those of Degginger, **330**, who suggests a different reconstruction. Ransom shows how the poet's use of facetious tone, incongruous antifeminism, and misogyny undermine the courtly language. The envoi, of the poet's wish to be a male bird, introduces 'indelicate double-entendres that have no place in a courtly lyric' (70), in the *prestelcok* and *lauercok* that might shelter between the lady's kirtle and her smock, in images similar to those used by other poets, including Catullus and Skelton. Skelton parodies the elegy in 'Phyllyp Sparowe' [*2756.5*], but the poet of *105* 'parodies the love lament of the courtly tradition' (79).

Ransom extends his findings in 'Irony and Parody in the Middle English Lyric: A Survey of Possibilities in and after Harley 2253' (81–100), where he notes moments of irony or potential irony in some other lyrics. These include 'Blow, Northerne Wind' [*1395*], where the poet merely hints at ambiguities and inconsistencies, so that 'we are not inclined to notice the inherent incongruities and suggestive implications of some of his phrases' (82). Irony in the pastourelle 'The Meeting in the Wood' [*1449*] is 'somber, not satirical in tone' (85). 'De Clerico et Puella' [*2236*] is of the genre *contrasto*, but 'the lover's courtly poetic and the lady's traditional *danger* are patent shams and constitute a farcical enactment of conventional love' (87). Chaucer's lyrics lack allusions to or verbal echoes of Harley poems, but have similarly subtle ironic methods and attitudes, whereas fifteenth-century writers of parodic lyrics are 'blunt and obvious in their reversals of conventions' (93). Ransom attributes the decline in wit to a decline in encouragement at Henry IV's court, where lack of talent and interest produced 'an environment more conducive to broad comedy than oblique humour,' implying that 'the provincial lyric tradition had its culmination and its end in MS Harley 2253' (100).

66, 100, 105, 194, 377, 438, 515, 521, 532, 631, 694.5, 708, 718, 752, 762, 776, 780, 991, 1044, 1216, 1280, 1299, 1300, 1302, 1394, 1395, 1449, 1452, 1459, 1472, 1485, 1504, 1593, 1596, 1768, 1775, 1861, 1921, 2009, 2031, 2135, 2166, 2178, 2207, 2236, 2237, 2247.5, 2262, 2421, 2437, 2580, 2640, 2756.5, 3222, 3327, 3412, 3414, 3722, 3747, 3782, 3787, 3832, 3845.5, 3864, 3874, 3879, 3939, 4019, 4037, 4083, 4194, 4223.

———Review by Michael J. Franklin, *Medium Ævum* 56 (1987): 128–30. Finds Ransom 'tireless in pursuit' of parody, but questions his presupposition that 'any manifestation of game must be evidence' of it. Franklin doubts that the subtle and sophisticated audience Ransom posits would appreciate the sexual puns that he discerns in the lyrics, and suspects that his approach stems 'from a barely disguised feeling that mediaeval love-lyric is rather tedious ... unless viewed as parody or burlesque' (129). Ransom misses the opportunity to relate the *querelle des femmes* tradition to the Harley lyrics, and the book lacks 'any real attempt to illustrate the eclectic and experimental manner in which the Harley poets assimilated contemporary literary, artistic, intellectual and religious idiom' (130).

———Review by E.G. Stanley, *Notes and Queries* 232 (1987): 522. Although Ransom has given to 'the poets of some of the best [of ME lyrics] the credit of believing in their sophistication,' Stanley deplores his methods of discerning it. He concludes that Ransom is 'an author with enough ideas for a good article on a poem or two,' who 'should have resisted the urge to turn it into a book.'

858 Schmolke-Hasselmann, Beate. 'Middle English Lyrics and the French Tradition – Some Missing Links.' *The Spirit of the Court: Selected Proceedings of the Fourth Congress of the International Courtly Literature Society (Toronto 1983).* Ed. Glyn S. Burgess and Robert A. Taylor et al. Dover, NH: Brewer, 1985. 298–318.

Examines conventions of description and 'praise of a woman's character and beauty' (299), to establish influences, particularly those of French and Provençal poems, on ME love lyrics. Schmolke-Hasselman takes most of her examples from the Harley lyrics, where '50% consist predominately of lengthy descriptions of a noble girl or lady' (299). These typically English beauties differ from those of Provençal poems, although some details originate in Provençal works, including '[t]he healing effect [of the lady's beauty], the long neck, the "fyngres fair to folde"' (302), the gold wire in her hair, and the small breasts. All these characteristics appear in the thirteenth-century Provençal *saluts d'amor*, which evolved into the *complainte*, counterpart of the English *complaint*. Factors that are common to *saluts* and the Harley lyrics include the burden, stanza-linking, appeals to Christ or the god of love, and the nature topos. Inspection reveals that 'a French lady's eyes [are] invariably *vair* and an English lady's eyes always grey,' the latter adjective apparently used for alliteration with 'grete, gode, glass etc.' (309). Schmolke-Hasselman suspects alliteration's influence in the linking of *swan* and *swyre* for the neck; similarly 'British brows are brown, or black, and they are always bent' (310). The Provençal *salut* did not die in France 'before the end of the thirteenth century,' but lived on 'for another two centuries in Britain where its central portion, the praise of the lady, has enjoyed particular favour ever since the twelfth century' (317). It displays an eroticism that is 'absent from its French sources, but already discernible in Anglo-Norman narrative, and a remarkably little social distinction between the lyrical speaker and his paramour' (319). The bitterness felt by those whose features did not correspond to the conventions is expressed in 'the outcry of a woman with dark skin and black hair' (319), in 'Sume men sayon þat y am blak' [*3174*]. Schmolke-Hasselmann supplies a diagram to show the relations of the various verse forms.

105, 150, 366, 515, 694.5, 752, 1010, 1394, 1395, 1504, 1768, 2207, 2232, 2421, 2437, 2524, 2640, 3145, 3146, 3174, 3203, 3832, 4194, 4209.

859 Tarvers, Josephine Koster. 'A Hitherto Unnoticed Middle English Poem in University of Pennsylvania MS English 6.' *Notes and Queries* 230 (1985): 447–9. [Edition.]

'Whanne þou art stered to don amys' [*7604*], uniquely preserved in a vellum manuscript of the Wycliffite NT and written by a versifier 'not without technical skills,' presents 'moral commonplaces' (447). Although the manuscript's provenance is uncertain, it may have belonged to a bishop of Bath and Wells, perhaps Gilbert Bourne or Gilbert Berkeley. Tarvers prints the text, with abbreviations expanded and with emendations, the latter generally needed because of cropping. She arranges 25 long lines to make 6 stanzas of 8 lines, with two additional lines in the last stanza. In her notes she discusses difficult readings, patterns in word order, and possible emendations.

7604.

860 Weiss, Alexander. *Chaucer's Native Heritage.* American University Studies. Series 4. English Language and Literature 11. New York: Lang, 1985.

Examines the 'Englishness' of Chaucer's poetry, relating it to qualities of OE poetry and ME lyrics. The ME lyrics represent native tradition in style and range of subject; many probably had roots in OE poetry and were preserved orally. Weiss explores the continuity of tradition and the interaction of OE and Romance forms in 'The Middle English Lyrics and the Native Poetic Tradition' (23–84). He compares poems that are classified as lyrics because 'intense expression of personal emotion remains for many the essential criterion of lyric poetry,' although many ME poems display a 'very lack of such expression of personal emotion' (25). Some continental influences may have come through early ME lyrics, such as the Harley lyrics, where poets, 'in adopting various aspects of the continental tradition . . . also modified it in many respects . . . by incorporating elements from their own native tradition' (26). Distinction between religious and secular works is neither easy nor necessary; some lyrics may support both interpretations. 'Nou goth þe sonne under wode' [*2320*] and 'Foweles in the frith' [*864*] illustrate this ambiguity, and are similar in their simplicity and effectiveness. Resemblances to OE works include the didactic nature, exemplified in 'Worldes blis ne last no þrowe' [*4223*], and the visual concreteness of imagery of the lyrics, religious and secular. Scrutiny of several ME poems reveals their forceful, didactic nature, and effects of vigour, sincerity, vitality, and beauty. The English lyrists' objective approach differs from the subjective, self-conscious style of William IX, Bernart de Ventadorn, Conon de Béthune, and Gace Brulé. The orientation of ME secular love poems is external, whereas that of the French poems is internal, 'the poet addressing himself' (60). The 'stark plainness and simplicity . . . of the English religious lyrics' (64) differ from the elaborate metaphor and technique of French poems, which are addressed to the intellect rather than the emotions. The ME works seem intended for oral delivery, as were OE poems. Weiss notes the resemblance of repetitive and parallel structures in ME lyrics to parallel variation in OE poetry. In 'Bridging the Gulf: From *Beowulf* to Chaucer' (85–117), he examines the didactic purpose of the lyrics and relates this to the teaching in some of Chaucer's works. Chaucer's audience differed from that of early ME lyrics, as the latter did from that of OE poems. For Chaucer's audience poetry was 'a form of recreation, a pleasurable pastime' (91); they expected amusement as well as instruction. 'Chaucer and the Middle English Lyrics' (119–76), makes detailed comparisons of Chaucer's works with those that influenced them, including *An ABC* [*239*] with De Guileville's *Pèlerinage de la Vie Humaine*' and 'Cristes milde moder seynte marie' [*631*]; Weiss stresses the use of alliteration for emphasis in the English poems. Unlike De Guileville, Chaucer and ME lyric poets achieve a conversational effect. This effect may be linked to the relationship between poet and audience, accomplished through manipulation of syntax and metre, and exploitation of enjambement, using the half-line as a structural unit, as in OE poetry. Weiss illustrates the effect in 'Glade us maiden moder milde' [*912*] and 'Stond wel moder ounder rode' [*3211*]. 'Chaucer, the English Poet' (177–227) concentrates on Chaucer's own lyric poetry, comparing it with his narrative works and their sources. In the 'Conclusion' (229–30), Weiss uses the metaphor of Chaucer as gardener to propose that he 'cultivated the natural beauties of the [native English] garden . . . introduced beautiful flowers from France and Italy' and 'planted new seeds' (229).

28, 66, 100, 239, 293, 515, 631, 708, 809, 864, 912, 991, 1395, 1459, 1705, 1708, 1839, 1861, 1921, 2066, 2070, 2092, 2262, 2287, 2320, 2366, 2614.5, 2756, 2992, 3144, 3211, 3212, 3223, 3327, 3236, 3542, 3967, 4019, 4044, 4141, 4223.

861 Wenzel, Siegfried. 'Poets, Preachers, and the Plight of Literary Critics.' *Speculum* 60 (1985): 343–63. [Edition.]

Argues for careful examination of the manuscript context of medieval poems, using the case of 'I sayh hym wiþ fless al bi-sprad' [*1353*]. Here the context is a Latin sermon, and 'the text in question *is not a lyrical "poem" at all*, but the formal division of a Latin sermon put into English rhyming lines' (345). Wenzel surveys criticism by Kane, **292**, Manning, **443**, Reiss, **583**, Evans, **605**, and Hill, **803**, and their interpretations and notions of the poem's structure, with questions of 'whether the poem deals with Christ's Second Coming or his continuing concern for man's salvation,' and 'whether the printed text yields two stanzas or three' (344). The manuscript is a collection of sermons, compiled by John Sheppey, and the poem is found in 'a Latin sermon on the Ascension, on the biblical theme "Where do you come from, and where are you going?"' (346). The sermon expresses the joy of the angels greeting Christ on his return and the sorrow of the apostles at their loss. Answers to the questions refer to aspects of Christ's life and work. The divisions are four-fold, and involve not only the stanzas noted by the critics mentioned above, but two others on the Four Horsemen of the Apocalypse. The sermon may have been delivered in Latin or in English, with the Latin text used only as a guide to the preacher. The division, 'which required rhyme and other poetic devices, was worked out in advance and written down in the vernacular as well because its careful verbal craftsmanship could not be left up to the inspiration of the moment' (350). Wenzel translates the sermon and prints the complete text, with Latin and English verses, including 'An ernemorwe de dayliȝt spryngeþ' [*2684*] (353–63).

1353, 2684.

862 Bishop, Ian. 'Lapidary Formulas as Topics of Invention – from Thomas of Hales to Henryson.' *Review of English Studies* NS 37 (1986): 469–77.

Summarizes the lapidary description of a gem, to list 'its colour and other aesthetic characteristics,' followed by 'supposed medicinal or magical "virtues"' and sometimes 'a religious significance,' often with a reference to 'the ideal setting for the gem (usually gold)' and declaration that 'it is worthy to belong to a king or prince' (469). Bishop shows the exploitation of such formulas in 'A Luue Ron' of Thomas de Hales [*66*], the Harley lyric 'A Wayle Whyt ase Whalles Bon' [*105*], and 'The Tale of the Cock and the Jasp,' the first of Henryson's *Moral Fables* [*3703*]; he also makes many comparisons with *Pearl* [*2744*]. In *66*, Thomas describes the maiden's chastity as the most precious of gems. The poet of *105* resembles the *Pearl* poet in using *concatenatio* and numerology – it consists of 'the round number of 50 lines plus a pendant of 5 lines' (473) – and in the implication of the parable of the Pearl of Great Price, by employing mercantile language for 'the patently unbusinesslike transaction' (474) of his declaration of longing for the lady.

66, 105, 1394, 2744, 3703.

863 Colaco, Jill. 'The Window Scenes in *Romeo and Juliet* and Folk Songs of the Night Visit.' *Studies in Philology* 83 (1986): 138–57.

Locates the 'paradigm of the Night Visit, as it is found in English and European *Fensterlieder*,' in songs where a man 'makes the woman aware of his presence outside and asks her to let him in.' She replies first 'with surprise or disapproval,' but the usual ending for the song is her relenting and 'inviting her lover to enter' (140). The song with the burden 'Go from my window go etc.' ['* . . . ȝoure seruand madame,' *4284.3*] and a sixteenth-century religious parody are typical, whereas Alison's rejection of Absolon in the *Miller's Tale* [*4019*] makes a comic reversal and also recalls the Song of Songs. Colaco cites references in ballads and traces development of such scenes to the Plighting Scene in *Romeo and Juliet*, noting comments of Baskerville, **148**.

4019, *4284.3.

864 Datta, Kitty. 'The Absence of the Beloved: A Medieval Theme.' *Journal of the Department of English (Calcutta University)* 22 (1986–7): 25–36.

The theme of seeking the absent beloved, expressed in the Song of Songs, is rendered in many medieval works of prose and poetry in Latin and ME. Datta notes several poems that convey Christ's welcoming of Mary to reign in heaven, and the longing of the bride, the devout soul, for the heavenly bridegroom who knocks at the door. The poems tell of paradoxical relationships of the soul with Christ as 'father and mother, brother, sister and husband' (30), and those of Christ with Mary who is 'wife (*sponsa*) and mother, and is crowned queen by her son' (30–1). There are further paradoxes in Mary's mourning of her son, father, brother, and spouse, who is alive, although thought to be dead. Two complementary complaints of Christ and Mary express the search for the soul, and present the 'theme of *maistrye*, or who should be the dominant partner in a love-relationship . . . here extended with a nice twist to loving one's enemy,' in the paradoxical linking 'of sister and spouse, of Christ as husband and mother, of search with stillness' (32).

143, 404, 1460, 1781, 2007, 3225, 3825.

865 Dove, Mary. *The Perfect Age of Man's Life.* Cambridge: Cambridge UP, 1986.

The age considered perfect in man's life is 'mature adulthood, the stage of life lasting from the completion of bodily growth until the beginning of *elde*' (17). Dove cites numerous supporting literary references, including some to sermon lyrics in Grimestone's collection, and considers the images of Fortune's wheel, particularly in 'Somer Soneday' [*3838*], and the Wheel of Life, as it represents the Ages of Man. She compares these ideas of ages with those of longer works.

230, 349, 3838, 4277, 7102, 7210.

866 Edden, Valerie. 'Richard Maidstone's *Penitential Psalms*.' *Leeds Studies in English* 17 (1986): 77–94.

Shows Maidstone's purpose, to construct 'a single, continuous penitential meditation to be used in private devotion and in preparation for the sacrament of penance' (77), and investigates his audience. The poem 'To goddis worschipe þat dere us bouȝte' [*3755*] links seven psalms, through the penitent's reflection on sins and the trust that Christ will grant grace to repent and avoid further sin. The psalms, VI, XXXI, XXXVII, L, CI, CXXIX, CXLII (using Vulgate numbering, in Maidstone's order), have traditionally been interpreted 'in the light of David's remorse for his treatment of Bathsheba,' and have gained coherence 'by linking them to the seven deadly sins.' Day, **29**, connects them thus: VI and Anger; XXXI and Pride; XXXVII and Gluttony; L and Lust; CI and

Covetousness; CXXIX and Envy; CXLII and Sloth. Edden finds that Maidstone links 'the remorse of the sinner with the merits of the redemption' (78), and proposes instead to connect VI with acknowledgment of sin; XXXI with the penitent's need for clear conscience; XXXVII with Confession; L with prayer for grace; CI with dialogue between Christ and the sinner; CXXIX with contemplation of Judgement; CXLII with prayer to Christ for grace. This scheme seems to be influenced by the practice of reciting these psalms as well as the daily office and by a renewed interest in penance, rather than exegetical tradition. The context in which they were recited always connected 'the penitence of the individual sinner with Christ's passion and redemption.' Maidstone's interpretations tend to be spiritual, 'in which the penitent reader may become the speaker of the poems,' rather than literal, historical readings concerning David. He wishes to lead the reader through penitential, Christocentric meditation, with God 'as king (and feudal lord) and the penitent as his subject' (81). Maidstone varies most from the literal in Psalm L, which presents the speaker as 'the penitent sinner, addressing a God who has already made his redemptive love known in Christ' (83). His spiritual and allegorical reading of Psalm CI shows the poor man and the three birds (the pelican, night-crow, and sparrow) of the psalm to be Christ. Harrowing the earth represents Christ's torture and may be linked with *harrow*, the parchment-maker's frame, used 'figuratively for Christ's body drawn on the cross' (86). Maidstone's treatment is orthodox; his readers are likely to resemble those of the vernacular primers. They are often placed with Richard Rolle's, but Maidstone's works are 'quite unmystical, and ... more polished literary productions.' Edden notes the context of devotional, liturgical, practical, and political works in manuscripts that preserve Maidstone's psalms. She concludes that they met 'a need for vernacular devotional material of a penitential nature amongst the literate laity in the late fourteenth century' (89), with works 'theologically orthodox, pro-clerical and designed to supplement rather than replace the official prayers and liturgy of the Church' (90).

1961, 2157, 3755.

867 Fletcher, Alan J. 'The Sermon Booklets of Friar Nicholas Philip.' *Medium Ævum* 55 (1986): 188–202.

In his account of Oxford, Bodleian Library, MS Lat.th.d.I, a collection of sermon booklets prepared, but not necessarily composed, by Nicholas Philip, 'an English Franciscan friar of the earlier fifteenth century' (188), Fletcher describes a sermon 'on the theme "Qui custos domini sui gloriabitur,"' which is bedecked 'in a bewildering array of divisions and distinctions' (195). These divisions are achieved by sermon verses; they explain hospitality to be offered to Christ, the Christian's guest, and conclude with verses 'to be sung to God "devoutly in the heart"' (196).

636.5, 1938.5, 3727.5, 7021, 7104, 7291.

868 Franklin, Michael J. '"Fyngres heo haþ feir to folde": Trothplight in some of the Love Lyrics of MS Harley 2253.' *Medium Ævum* 55 (1986): 176–87.

The motif of folding a lady's fingers, found in several lyrics of love, has both 'a definite sensual significance,' and 'connotations of the ceremony of "trothplight", also known as "handfasting"' (176), which was considered 'sufficiently binding for the betrothal often to be consummated before the church ceremony' (177). Thus allusions in the Harley lyrics imply wish for contact in clasping the hands and for marriage. Indeed, in 'The Fair Maid of Ribblesdale' [*2207*], the next lines echo the medieval marriage service in the poet's wish to have and hold the lady, in 'the *pure paradys* or *paradys terrestre* of the marital estate, the "heaven" to be had here' (179). Franklin notes other possible references to trothplight in a translation of an AN 'A.B.C. a femmes, ' '*Bot fals men make her finges feld' [**552.8*], 'Nou springes the sprai' [*360*], Robert Mannyng's

Handlyng Synne [*778*], and in the Harley lyrics 'Advice to Women' [*1504*], 'The Meeting in the Wood' [*1449*], 'De Clerico et Puella' [*2236*], and 'The Lover's Complaint' [*4194*]. The lyrics speak of truth in love and courtship, expressing the wish for 'a blissful love which is both settled and quiet' (184), in allusions to *seete, reste, ro,* and *pees.*

105, 360, 515, 552.8, 778, 1216, 1394, 1395, 1449, 1504, 1861, 1921, 2207, 2236, 3144, 4194.

869 Glasscoe, Marion. 'The Fair Maid of Ribblesdale: Content and Context.' *Neuphilologische Mitteilungen* 87 (1986): 555–7.

In spite of using conventional and formulaic descriptions, 'The Fair Maid of Ribblesdale [*2207*] seems to avoid stereotypes and 'to come alive with an ambivalent blend of imaginative idealism and sexual frankness wittily asserted with blasphemous bravado.' It is startling to find that the poet uses 'language of undeniable sexual innuendo' to number the 'paragon of bright loveliness' among 'wanton (*wilde*) women' (555). Linguistic evidence confirms the internal credentials of provenance from names in the poem. In the district around Ribblesdale, many Cistercians lived austerely, with rules that prohibited women even in 'the abbey precinct or outer walls of granges' (556); pressure on these isolated men might have come from 'the statutes themselves.' Glasscoe finds the 'physical deprivation and spiritual aspiration in the bleak Pennines . . . a convincing context for the tonal extremes of this lyric,' and considers the possibility of composition by a Cistercian 'for whom the all too real attractions of a ride out in local Ribblesdale held more allure than the distant equestrian splendour of the Pope' (557).

117, 1459, 2207, 4037.

870 Gray, Douglas. 'A Middle English Secular Illustrated Poem.' *Journal of the Department of English (Calcutta University)* 22 (1986–7): 1–4.

The lyric 'By thys fyr I warme my handys' [*579*] is 'a rare example in English of an illustrated poem that is secular, not religious, in subject' (1). Gray describes the illustrations in the two manuscripts in which the poem survives, Bodleian Library, Digby 88 and BL Add. 22720. In Digby 88, each line is briefly illustrated by 'a simple emblematic depiction of the relevant instrument or idea,' whereas the more expansive Add. 22720 shows the activities being performed, 'in the traditional manner of a calendar with pictures of the labours of the Months' (2), together with pictures of the signs of the Zodiac.

579

871 Grennen, Joseph E. 'We Ben Chapmen.' *Explicator* 44.3 (1986): 3–5.

Strives for accuracy in glossing 'We bern abowtyn non cattes skynnes' [*3864*], in particular *Ielif|jelyf|jelif.* Unlike other editors Grennen finds that the singer 'and his congeners . . . are *not* chapmen,' but rather 'sexual opportunists whose offerings have merely a smirking resemblance to peddlers' wares.' Explication of the allusions would cause him to blush, but 'logic insists that "jelif" can not mean "jelly," nor is Greene's supposition [**86**] that it is slang for penis at all convincing.' He proposes that the character Greene reads as *j* and Robbins as *I* [*RobbinsS*, **55**] could resemble either letter, 'presumably pronounced as the dental spirant [dʒ] in the former instance and as the palatal [j] in the latter.' The latter phonologically resembles *yelf|yelve,* a garden fork, and 'would fit the context . . . especially in the light of the sexual innuendo of a poem such as "I have a newe gardin" [*1302*] (child in womb = garden under cultivation).' A connection with *yelver,* a young eel, involves a sound change '(from voiced [v] to unvoiced [f]) [that] would be more difficult to account for' (4). [See also Miller, **832**; Hala, **904**.]

1302, 1459, 3864.

872 Harrington, David V. 'The Harley Lyric WYNTER WAKENETH AL MY CARE.' *Explicator* 44.2 (1986): 3–4.

Presents a reading of 'Al that gren me graueth grene,' the eleventh line of 'Wynter wakeneþ al my care' [*4177*]. Interpretations of *BrownXIV*, **48**, Brook, **42**, and Silverstein, **73**, offer '"grein" for "gren," presumably to suggest the image of a seed buried, still unripe,' to evoke the speaker's complaint of 'his unfulfilled youth, now threatened by sudden death,' or 'a hope buried never to ripen.' Harrington does not find either of these satisfactory. Each of the alliterating words *gren*, *graueth*, and *grene* allows numerous readings. *Gren*, as a variant of *grin*, for trap or snare, must recall 'the preceding complaint about unavoidable and unwanted death,' and in this case '"trap" fits better if we imagine a pit or hole one might fall into.' Rather than 'buried,' as is often proposed, *graueth* seems 'a variant of greveth, or grieves, with any of its related meanings' (3). Harrington cites Chaucer's use of *graueth* in *Troilus and Criseyde* [*3327*] as 'to affect or influence.' Among meanings of *grene* is loss of colour in complexion, 'losing one's healthy bloom.' Thus the line reflects 'the speaker's discomfort at the thought of unavoidable death,' and could be rendered idiomatically as 'The thought of falling into such a pit causes me to turn pale' (4).

3327, 4177.

873 Hill, Thomas D. 'Androgyny and Conversion in the Middle English Lyric, "In the vaile of restles mynd."' *ELH* 53 (1986): 459–70

Explores the juxtaposition of images of 'In a valey of þis restles mynde' [*1463*] to show Christ first as a lover-knight and later as a nursing mother, with 'original and startling effect – a moment in which Christ's sexual nature is abruptly redefined' (459). Hill's explication assumes first a cast of two masculine figures – Christ and the narrator – and the feminine 'mannys soule.' Christ assumes the masculine role of hunter and later a passive one in the courtship of the soul, which involves union with the soul 'in a tender, loving, erotic relationship' (462), yet transformation to a maternal figure. Eventually there is a cast of two – Christ and the soul – since, 'just as Christ is transformed from lover-knight to nursing mother, the narrator is transformed from the wandering knight who traditionally narrates the *chanson d'aventure* to the faithful and loving "spouse" of Christ' (463). The images may be traced to the Canticle of Canticles, which is glossed by Bernard in his sermons. The reading of the narrator's conversion has its origin in 'the implicit narrative pattern . . . and the immensely commonplace medieval Christian *topos* that Christ is the *sponsus* of each faithful Christian's soul' (464). Hill explores the notion of mingling sexual identity in marriage, as it is implied in the gift of a wedding ring, when the bride offers a phallic gesture and the bridegroom a vaginal symbol. In the loving union of Christ and the soul, 'constraints of gender are swept away.' Although the ascription of any sexual role to God must seem 'arbitrary and to a degree absurd,' sexual figures may supply 'an appropriate and powerful mode of expressing the intensity of Christ's love for man' (465). The perception of confusion and lack of logic may explain the range of critical responses, for example those of Wimsatt, **680**, and Woolf, **522**, since it concerns 'some of the most powerful and primal desires that human beings can experience' (466), to which critics may have responded intuitively. Hill prints the poem in an appendix (467–70).

1463.

874 ———. '"Mary, the Rose-Bush" and the Leaps of Christ.' *English Studies* 67 (1986): 478–82.

After printing the best text of the carol, 'Lyth and lysten both old and ȝong' [*1914*] (entitled 'Mary, the Rose-Bush,' by Greene, **56, 86**) Hill elucidates its iconography. He takes issue with Greene's explanation that the five branches of the rose bush represent the Five Joys of the Virgin, and with Spitzer's explication, **303**. Hill contends that the lyric is also influenced by the 'leaps of Christ' theme, based on 'the traditional medieval exegetical understanding of Cant. 2:8' (480), which includes 'each event celebrated in "Mary, the Rose-Bush" except the coming of the Magi.' The poet plays on the word *spring* to indicate both growing and leaping, to convey the ideas that 'Jesus as the son of Mary the "rose" is a branch which sprang up at the Annunciation, the Birth, the Epiphany, the Harrowing and finally at the Ascension,' and also 'those great leaps which Jesus made when He leapt from heaven to the Virgin's womb, from her womb to the crib, and so on' (481). The poet grafts the Marian and Christological themes to mirror 'the love of Mary for her son and Jesus for His mother' (482).

1030, 1046, 1833, 1914, 2098, 2118, 2992.

875 Jones, F. 'A Note on *Harley Lyrics* 7.' *Neuphololologische Mitteilungen* 87 (1986): 142–3.

Questions Brewer's reply, **351**, to Chambers, **18**, that language in 'The Fair Maid of Ribblesdale' [*2207*] is conventional, 'so that the poem may not come from personal experience: a warning against treating poems as autobiography' (142). Instead, Jones proposes that there are two speakers, only one of whom has seen the girl, and that the second speaker, 'loves *solus solam* whereas the first wants the best of a *selection* of *wilde wymmen.*' Since, as noted by Brook, **42**, convention forbids naming the girl, names may be pseudonyms. Proper names could suggest provenance, but 'in this case the humour of the situation of a man riding off on hearsay evidence to find an unnamed girl somewhere around Ribblesdale would be increased proportionally to how far we could legitimately take the provenance away from Ribblesdale' (143)

2207.

876 Kane, George. 'Some Fourteenth-Century "Political Poems."' *Medieval English Religious and Ethical Literature: Essays in Honour of G.H. Russell.* Ed. Gregory Kratzmann and James Simpson. Cambridge: Brewer, 1986. 82–91.

Challenges ideas of Robbins, **423**, **724**, Kinney, **485**, and Elliot, **592**, who read some works as 'poems of "protest" and "dissent."' Kane finds their ideas unhistorical and anachronistic. He prefers to see the poems as estates satire, to describe a society which would function 'if all men behaved virtuously' (83), and to express a desire for 'a benevolent paternalism, good rule by the king, or rule by a good king,' not for 'individual right and its concomitant responsibility to participate in government' (84). The 'Song of the Husbandman' [*1320.5*] concerns excessive and dishonest taxation, an issue felt by more people than ill-treated serfs, and also considered in 'The Simonie' [*4165*]. Kane's view of the 'Satire on the Consistory Courts' [*2287*], as 'more social comedy than "complaint,"' accords with Revard's, **499**. The 'Satire on the Retinues of the Great' [*2649*] is not against 'the vanity of huge households' (87), which could be generously maintained, but rather 'a brilliantly malicious, very scurrilous lampoon against grooms, stable lads, horseboys, a companion piece to *The Blacksmiths* [*3327*]' (87–8). These, with 'The Song of Lewes' [*3155*], 'The Follies of the Duke of Burgundy' [*1939*], and 'The Papelard Priest' [*2614.5*] are examples of satire, which probably developed in England 'soon after 1154 in imitation of the *sirventes*' (88). More serious works include *4165*, which shows that 'present sufferings of people are divine visitations for their sins' (89), 'Pierce the Ploughman's Crede' [*663*], and 'Mum and the Sothsegger' [**296.3*]. Only the writings of Wyclif and the Lollards could be called revolutionary, not that of John Ball. The serious works have in common only 'concern about the inadequacy of human conduct, the consequent malfunctioning of the social order, the loss of hope' (91).

296.3, 663, 1320.5, 1459, 1939, 2287, 2614.5, 2649, 3155, 3327, 4165.

Annotations of Critical Works

877 Maddicott, J.R. 'Poems of Social Protest in Early Fourteeth-Century England.' *England in the Fourteenth Century: Proceedings of the 1985 Harlaxton Symposium.* Ed. W.M. Ormrod. Woodbridge: Boydell, 1986. 130–44.

These songs were written in ME, French, and Latin. They survive haphazardly if they have no associations with a particular event or background, leaving only the suspicion that 'there were once many more of them' (131). If the chronicles record no allusions to the songs, it is impossible to know if they were '"popular" in any real sense' or represented 'the voice of the people' (131). Maddicott considers 'The Song of the Husbandman' [*1320.5*] and 'On the Evil Times of Edward II' or 'The Simonie' [*4165*], in ME; 'The Song against the King's Taxes,' in French and Latin; and 'The Outlaw's Song of Trailbaston,' in French. The literature crosses linguistic boundaries and shares characteristics. It attacks those in authority, for 'corruption, graft and venality,' and failure 'to correspond to the pretensions of their offices'; it expresses sympathy for the poor and dislike of those who oppress them; it sometimes appeals to God. The complex form and style imply that the poets were 'clever and technically skilled craftsmen,' probably members of the clergy, rather than the poor. Two possible authors are Master Ralph Acton and William of Pagula. Circulation of the poems was probably not wide, but some appear in more than one manuscript. The letters of John Ball and others with allegorical names, distributed in the Peasants' Revolt of 1381, recall the poems in 'theme, style, phrasing, [and] possible circles of authorship'; they change 'the language of mere grievance . . . into the language of sedition' (139). Considering the effect of language, Maddicott notes that the poems in French could circulate as easily as those in English, and that the Latin phrase *si dedero* recurs in *4165* and a letter of Jack Trueman. Works of social protest are related to the genres of estates and venality satire. As conditions became worse 'the poetry of passive complaint became for an instant the literature of active resistance' (144).

1320.5, 3155, 3352, 4144, 4165.

878 O'Mara, Veronica M. 'A Middle English Versified Penance Composed of Popular Prayer Tags.' *Notes and Queries* 231 (1986): 449–50. [Edition.]

The penance, 'Swete Ihesu/þat was of maydyn borne' [*7470*], in MS Cambridge University Library Add. 2829, has 11 lines and a prose introduction; it has been added to 'a sermon in English addressed to intending communicants on Easter Day.' The first lines are not listed in *IMEV* or *SIMEV*, but 'could be embedded in longer poems and so be listed under a different incipit.' O'Mara notes similarities in other lyrics, to demonstrate that the verse 'is drawing on ideas and expressions common in popular medieval prayers' (449). Lines 6–9, in particular, provide a version of the prayer 'Jesus for thy holy name/And for thy bitter passion/Save us from sin and shame/And endless dampnation,' and were 'so widely known . . . that they could be incorporated into other poems without any hint of quotation' (450).

1703, 1738, 1759, 7470.

879 Peck, Russell A. 'Social Conscience and the Poets.' *Social Unrest in the Late Middle Ages.* Papers of the Fifteenth Annual Conference of the CMERS. Ed. Francis X. Newman. MRTS, 39. Binghamton, NY: CMERS, State U of New York at Binghamton, 1986. 113–48.

Relates the poetry of social comment to religious and political issues, in particular to Lollard doctrines and to the Peasants' Revolt. Peck considers letters of John Ball ['John Ball Saint Mary priest,' *1791*; 'Johan the Muller hath ygrownde smal smal,' *1796*], which 'epitomize the spirit of much of the subsequent reform literature' (114). Ball's tone is evangelistic and urgent; he supports unity and appeals to truth; 'in Chaucer, Langland, Gower, *Richard the Redeles,* or *Mum and the Sothsegger* [**296.3*], the advice to seek truth and liberation guided by one's "gost" appears again and again' (116). Peck *ite* in the text. Grennen proposes that here 'O' and 'I' stand for *oculi* and *ictu*. This resembles Greene's suggestion, taken from Dante's *Inferno*, 24: 97–102, but Grennen stresses the difference between 'o' *or* 'i' and 'O and I,' although the treatment of judgement in both poems is significant. In cases of variations of the refrain, such as 'I and E,' 'O and V,' 'A and I,' and 'E and O,' Grennen suggests 'unless those poems are merely imitations of misunderstood exemplars [that] they must be based on different texts' (624), although other possibilities remain.

412, 701, 1001, 1320, 1353, 2003.5, 2021, 2614.5, 2663, 3069, 3098.5, 3363, 3567, 3719.5, 3921, 4083.

891   Kennedy, Ruth. '"A Bird in Bishopwood": Some Newly-Discovered Lines of Alliterative Verse from the Late Fourteenth Century.' *Medieval Literature and Antiquities: Studies in Honour of Basil Cottle.* Ed. Myra Stokes and T.L. Burton. Cambridge: Brewer, 1987. 71–87. [Edition.]

An edition of the lines that begin 'In a sesone of somere þat souerayne ys of alle' *[7255]*, found on 'a blank portion of a parchment roll: GL MS 25125/32 – a rental and account of 1395/6,' one of the 'surviving muniments of St Paul's Cathedral . . . consigned to the care of the Guildhall Library, London.' The verse is of 'a walking-out in May to the bishop's woods outside London and of an unfulfilling encounter with a bird there' (71). Kennedy describes the rolls and their history, with evidence to suggest that the poem was composed by John Tickhill, 'Collector of Rents of the Dean and Chapter of St Paul's' (72). She provides details of the 'fairly neat and fluent cursive anglicana' of the manuscript, 'a literate clerical hand which is rather similar to that ascribed to Chaucer in CUL MS Peterhouse 75' (74). The work is a draft, with many alterations and enigmatic punctuation, probably set down 'before mid-1398 when John Tickhill became rector of St Gregory's and resigned both his chantry and his office' (77). Its 'traces of non-London dialect' suggest the work of 'a South Yorkshireman who had been living and working in London for the greater part of the previous seventeen years' (78). The work is most likely 'a lyrical vignette of a familiar bipartite narrative structure, where the walking-out precedes a meeting in the wood' (79), and seems complete. Kennedy describes its structure, alliteration, and spelling. The dialect is South-East Midland, with Northern features. The bird resembles the turtle-dove of bestiary tradition; other features recall the works of Langland and Hoccleve. Kennedy provides details of her 'Editorial Procedure' (82), before printing photographs of the lines, as in the manuscript, and of the opening lines with a diplomatic transcription, the edited text (83), and 'Notes to the Text' (84–7).

7255.

892   Kooper, Erik. 'Slack Water Poetry: An Edition of the *Craft of Lovers*.' *English Studies* 68 (1987): 473–89. [Edition.]

The poem 'To moralise ⟨a similitude⟩ who list these ballet sewe' *[3761]*, from 'the slack water between the high tides of Chaucer and Spenser,' is preserved in MSS Harley 2251 (H), BL Add. 34360 (A), and Trinity College, Cambridge, R.3.19 (T). These manuscripts are miscellanies, A and H 'didactic, moralistic or religious,' and T 'definitely courtly.' All originated 'in the office of that avid fifteenth-century collector and diligent copyist, John Shirley' (473). Kooper briefly traces the texts' history, including their use by John Stow, whose edition was freely used by Alexander Chalmers in his own of 1810. Kooper supplies a new edition (475–84), based on H, which records variations from Stow's (S), based on T. He offers extensive notes, pointing out manuscript variations and stanzas which have appeared in other contexts (in poems with the titles 'Lady of Pite' ['Lady of pite for þy sorowes þ^t þ^u haddest,' *1838*] and 'The X Commaundements of love' ['Certes fer extendeth my Reason,' *590*]) edited by Robbins, *RobbinsS*, **55**, **336**. Kooper's

'Commentary' (484–89) notes points of interest in the text, relating it to other works, and extending comments of Moore, **296**. The poet exploits connotations including those of Marian lyrics, Job and his association with riches, and numerous classical references.

181, 590, 1838, 2208, 2594, 2791, 3761, 4004, 4043.

893 Moser, Thomas C., Jr. '"And I Mon Waxe Wod": the Middle English "Foweles in the Frith."' *PMLA* 102 (1987): 326–37.

The only context of 'Foweles in the frith' [*864*] is its place on a leaf of a manuscript 'otherwise devoted mostly to legal writings.' It is unusual in being preserved with music, and has remained mysterious. Moser focuses on 'ways that a late thirteenth-century auditor would be most likely to interpret this fine small love poem' (326). He prints the work and summarizes its structure of harmonious *Natureingang*, the poet's incongruous madness, apparent clarification of the source of distress, and the enigmatic conclusion that remains 'confusing, casting doubt retrospectively on our understanding of the rest of the lyric' (327). Moser concentrates on *beste of bon and blod*, the cause of *sorw*, and the references to birds and fishes. He surveys earlier criticism of the lyric, with concentration on puns and other ambiguities and scope for religious and secular interpretation, and notes instances of 'single pieces of music attached to both secular and sacred words' (328). His interpretation probes religious associations of the *Natureingang* and the ambiguity of the last line. He connects birds and fishes with Adam's domination of the earth's creatures at creation, and the 'uniquely unhappy state' (329) of sin in which Adam's descendants must live. The *Natureingang* evokes Christ's death in spring, with NT references to foxes' holes and birds' nests in contrast to his poverty. The latter topos draws on OT passages, and there are parallels in other lyrics and plays of the Towneley and York cycles. Although the images evoke Christ's suffering, not that of the poet-meditator, they imply that 'we all must participate in that sorrow.' Thus Moser paraphrases *864*: 'The birds (have their natural homes) in the woods and the fish in the sea and I am in anguish; I sorrow as I go walking because (I think) of (the son of God who is) the best man that ever lived (but who on the cross had no place to rest)' (331). He examines exegetical meditations of Bernard of Clairvaux and Bonaventure, to show the lyric's intellectual background; notes a similar passage in *Piers Plowman* [*1459*]; refers to examples recorded by Wenzel of contemporary comment on and interpretation of secular lyrics, **627**, **840**; and offers linguistic evidence for a *beast-best* pun in the last line. The lyric will allow many interpretations, leaving 'a marvelously ambiguous and moving song about the human heart, one whose brevity, isolation, and wealth of reference place it just beyond easy solution' (334).

715, 864, 1273, 1301, 1395, 1459, 1523, 2025, 2207, 2481, 3221.

894 Powell, Susan. 'Another Manuscript of *Index of Middle English Verse* No. 2627.' *Notes and Queries* 232 (1987): 154–6. [Edition.]

A medical herbal 'Of erbis xxiij' [*2627*], beginning with the herb betony, is recorded, with much variation, in 15 manuscripts, two of which have only the verses on betony. A third such version is found in York Minster Library XVI.E.32, a medical manuscript compiled by William of Killingsholme. Powell prints these verses, and notes variations from the two full versions of the herbal, 'one from Stockholm Royal Library MS X.90, pp. 49–78, and the other from British Library Add. MS 17866, fos 5r–21v' (155). [See Garrett, **128**.]

2627, 3754.

(9), and with the Soul. The loss of self when the narrator is identified with the Soul is significant in Bernard's teaching, since 'loss of self is a prerequisite for the highest degree of contemplation' (10); the poet considers an earlier stage. By emphasizing Christ's role, he affirms 'the need for grace, and Christ's willingness to provide it' (11).

1460, 1463.

900 Woodbridge, Linda. 'Black and White and Red All Over: The Sonnet Mistress Amongst the Ndembu.' *Renaissance Quarterly* 40 (1987): 247–97.

Investigates use of the colours red, white, and black, in the literature and folklore of several cultures, including that of the Ndembu. Woodbridge concentrates on the connection between fertility rites and conventions, and on the clichés of love poetry, particularly in the sonnet. Surveying the literary background to Renaissance works, she examines colour imagery and symbolism in secular and religious medieval works, including Chaucer's. 'Red-and-white imagery, sometimes adding black' (265) frequently appears in love poetry, chiefly in descriptions of the beloved, and often expressed in terms of lilies and roses. There is similar imagery in the religious lyrics that centre on 'the story and rites of one of Europe's foremost fertility myths, the springtime sacrificial death of Jesus.' Poems of the eucharist stress 'the inseparability of body and blood.' Lyrics of the Virgin may also involve red and white, as in carols in which 'the red rose is Mary, the white lily Christ.' It is easier to understand veneration of the Virgin and of the courtly lady in images involving 'the "sexual" colors red and white . . . if both are connected with fertility myths, including Christ's sacrificial atonement' (266). Woodbridge reviews the place of symbolic colours in Arthurian romance, classical sources, rituals, and games; she includes Morris dancing and May games, ecclesiatical vestments, imagery of Christmas, chess, playing cards, and riddles, and particularly considers the underlying ritual and its effects on Renaissance love poetry.

65, 100, 161, 550, 769, 991, 1001, 1306, 1627, 1893, 1914, 2178, 2421, 2437, 2576, 2640, 2654, 3144, 3171, 3174, 3327, 3583, 3638, 3779, 4019, 4088, 4170, 4197, 4221.

901 Bawcutt, Priscilla. 'A Miniature Anglo-Scottish Flyting.' *Notes and Queries* 223 (1988): 441–4. [Edition.]

Two stanzas beginning 'I was ane hund and syne ane hair' [*7235*], on a page originally left blank in the Aberdeen Sasine Register, preserve insults directed between Scots and English during the Wars of Independence. The 'quasi-dramatic . . . miniature flyting between two speakers, an Englishman and a Scot' (441) depicts them alternately as hare and hound, where 'the hound suggests bold pursuit, while the hare suggests speed only in flight, and therefore implies cowardice.' Scottish composition is confirmed by the presence of the Scottish rhymes and the awarding of the last word to the Scot. Bawcutt notes the resemblance to *The Flyting of Dunbar and Kennedie* [*3117.8*], and its membership of 'that tradition of popular abuse and invective that helped to shape *The Flyting.*' The insult '"Rocht-futtit Scot" is countered by "Talyt tyk" and "Inglis Rumpill."' The first term refers to the Scots' shoes 'of untanned leather, still rough and hairy, for which the common term was *riveling* or *rilling*' (442), used in an English verse in Peter of Langtoft's AN chronicle, 'Tprut Scot riueling' [*3799.3*], and by Minot and Skelton. The charge that the English had tails probably came from a legend of St Augustine of Canterbury, who was ill treated by the English. Because they pelted the saint with fish-tails, 'as a divine punishment [they] henceforth wore tails themselves.' The story had 'a wide distribution in medieval Europe, and a long history' (443). Englishmen were accused 'of bearing the tails of rats, swine, serpents, or scorpions,' but most commonly those of dogs. In its use of *tyk*, 'mongrel,' a term 'even more opprobrious than *canis*, the Aberdeen piece carries the insult one stage further' (444).

1822.5, 1931.3, 3117.8, 3799.3, 3801, 7235.

902 Breeze, Andrew. 'The Virgin's Tears of Blood.' *Celtica* 20 (1988): 110–22.

Examines the motif of the tears of blood wept by the Virgin at the crucifixion, and in particular its appearances in Celtic literature. The tradition was recorded first 'during the thirteenth century in Latin, German and English poetry,' and was 'clearly known in the fifteenth to Welsh and Irish bards.' The topos seems already familiar in German secular uses, but Celtic appearances are related to influences from England and the continent, rather than to 'the secular tears of blood frequently mentioned in early Irish literature' (110). Breeze traces the motif in ME lyrics and accounts of the Passion, and notes that it would also be disseminated in 'statues, carvings, images and book illustrations' (114). He cites various Welsh, Cornish, and Irish occurrences.

293, 328, 648, 771, 776, 1318, 1650, 1869, 1907, 1943, 2347, 3211, 3221, 3366, 3692, 4154.

903 Fein, Susanna Greer. '*Haue Mercy of Me* (Psalm 51): An Unedited Alliterative Poem from the London Thornton Manuscript.' *Modern Philology* 86 (1988–9): 223–41. [Edition.]

'God þou haue mercy of me' [*990*] paraphrases one of the Seven Penitential Psalms. In translated form, it was 'the one most often excerpted from the others,' and was included '(in Latin) in the liturgy, in books of hours, and (in English) in the Primer' (228). Fein presents the version from Robert Thornton's London Manuscript (BL Add. 31042), which is 'densely alliterative, with concatenation and a twelve-line stanza, known elsewhere in alliterative verse only in *Pearl* [*2744*]' (223). She records contents of Thornton's manuscripts which form the psalm's context; suggests reasons for its having remained unedited; and notes observations of earlier editors on the stanza form. Works similar in metre, rhyme scheme, and tone include the Northern *Metrical Old Testament* [*944*], *Pety Job* [*1854*], and *Pearl*. Fein compares verse 6 of the psalm in several versions, comparing the treatment of words and themes. The poems are in the Auchinleck MS (Advocates 19.2.1) ['Lorde god to þe we calle,' *1956*], in Richard Maidstone's Penitential Psalms ['Lord in thyne anger vptake me nouȝt,' *1961*; 'Mercy god of my mysdede,' *2157*; 'To goddis worschipe þat dere us bouȝte,' *3755*], in the Surtees Psalter ['This blessyd boke that here begynneth,' *3576*], and in Thomas Brampton's Seven Penitental Psalms ['In wynter whan the wedir was cold,' *1591*]. She prints Thornton's version, with the Latin verses, and includes footnotes on points of interest, a description of the manuscript (232–4), the dialect and date (235–6), and her editorial method (236).

560, 583, 990, 994, 1591, 1732, 1854, 1956, 1961, 2153, 2157, 2410, 2573, 2744, 3533, 3576, 3755, 3774.

904 Hala, James. 'We ben chapmen.' *Explicator* 46.3 (1988): 3–4.

An answer to the reading (proposed by Grennen, **871**) for *jelif*, in the carol with the burden 'We ben chapmen' ['We bern abowtyn non cattes skynnes,' *3864*]. Grennen's suggestion is 'a hypothetical form, "ielif," as a variation of "yelf" (fork),' consistent with other *doubles entendres* in the poem, whereas Hala's is 'a gelatin used in cooking, which is to say something soft that gets hard and is used in the creation of a new substance.' Such a word conforms to 'the extended metaphorical comparison between the sale of domestic goods and sexual seduction.' The singer and his comrades are chapmen, but not of 'the *usual* domestic merchandise.' Examination of the burden leads Hala to conclude that 'the "foul weyes" they must flee are enraged fathers and husbands, *foul*-tempered *men* who have been made *fools* by these chapmen.' He finds confirmation for his ideas in other ambiguities. They reside in the line '*Damsele, bey some ware of me*: "Damsel, buy some wares from me" and "Damsel, be somewhat wary of me" ' (3); in the word *assayed*, which could suggest experiencing the qualities of materials or of the other considering the use of verse in sermons, and suggesting that a poem of a complaint of the Virgin could have been combined with a legend of her descent from a tower, to create the *Miracle*, as 'the product of one conscious creation' (236).

239, 373, 404, 583, 880, 1031, 1041, 1083, 1310, 1402, 1455, 1459, 1460, 1596, 1769, 1841, 1854, 2080, 2092, 2192, 2522, 2574, 2678, 2744, 2800, 3225, 3420, 3451, 3484, 3533, 3612, 3925, 3996, 4121, 4135, 4145, 7400.

909 ———. 'An Early Middle English Verse Inscription from Shrewsbury.' *Anglia* 106 (1988): 411–14. [Edition.]

Although Lambeth Palace Library MS 499 had been thought to have only one ME item, 'Wanne i ðenke ðinges ðre' [*3969*], there are secular lyrics and 'a copy of even earlier verses' (410), 'Her lis arfaxat fader brandan' [*7198*], which Pickering prints here. He describes the manuscript and supplies a detailed account of the work, which was 'found on a certain leaden vessel outside under the foundation of the structure of the Chapel of the Blessed Virgin at Shrewsbury.' The inscription records the burial or resting place of 'two people, Arfaxat and Coroune, who are said to be the father and mother of three saints, Brandan, Kolmkilne, and Cowhel' (412). The last line, 'þat komen in to bretene sautes to seke,' may suggest that they had come to Britain as refugees, or 'it may be the *sautes* is a mistake for *saules* "souls", which would give good sense if the line were taken to refer to the three saints' (413). It is hard to reconcile the account of Arfaxat and Coroune with the Irish saints Brendan, Columcille (Columba), and Comhgall (Comgall), and the saints were not related. Pickering suggests that the verse is a work of fiction.

3939, 7198.

910 Scattergood, John. 'A Graveyard Formula in *Hamlet* V.i.115–131.' *Notes and Queries* 223 (1988): 470–1.

The question and answer formula of Hamlet's dialogue with the Gravedigger is found in some earlier epitaphs. In that of Edward Courtenay, third earl of Devonshire, and Maud, his wife, the body replies 'I the good Erle of Devonshire;/With Maud, my wife, to mee full dere,' in answer to the question: 'Hoe! Hoe! who lies here?' [*7204*]. There are similar epitaphs for Robin of Doncaster and Margaret ['How, howe, who is here?/I, Robin of Doncaster, and Margaret my feare,' *7203*], and for one of Henry VIII's fools ['Stay, traveller, guess who lies here,' *7467*]. The closest analogy is preserved in 'a vellum roll in the College of Arms Library, Box 21 No. 16 in the form of a "dialoge betwix a seculer askyng and a frere answeryng at the grave of Dame Johan [Joan] of Acres", who died in 1305, showing the succession of the lords of the honour of Clare from 1248 to 1456.' Scattergood cites a passage to demonstrate that the friar's 'rather unhelpful preciseness . . . here anticipates Shakespeare's Gravedigger, though this is probably not meant to be comic' (471). Since it is unlikely that Shakespeare read the document, Scattergood concludes that he probably encountered the formula in epitaphs.

7203, 7204, 7467.

911 Stemmler, Theo. 'Das Überleben alt- und mittelenglischer Lieder in Prosatexten.' *Mündlichkeit und Schriftlichkeit im englischen Mittelalter*. ScriptOralia 5. Ed. Paul Goetsch, Wolfgang Raible, and Hans-Robert Roemer. Tübingen: Narr, 1988. 65–74.

Some songs have been preserved in prose form, for example those inserted in sermons and in the prose of other authors. Stemmler investigates the process and purposes of such works. He suggests that the Canute song ['Merie singen þe munaches binnen Ely,' *2164*] was intended to note Canute's visit, and that its form demonstrates the change from oral to written record. Manuscripts preserve different forms of St Godric's hymns, showing additions by another author. In 'Haly thomas of heouenriche' [*1233*], William of Canterbury, an eyewitness, documents Thomas Becket's murder, perhaps to persuade the pope that he should be canonized. The survival of the poems is not coincidental; they had religious, political, and propaganda purposes, as well as aesthetic ones. The prose form may have aided their survival.

1233, 2164, 2988, 3031.

912 ———. 'The Problem of Parody: *Annot and John*, for Example.' *Genres, Themes, and Images in English Literature: From the Fourteenth to the Fifteenth Century.* Ed. Piero Boitani and Anna Torti. The J.A.W. Bennett Memorial Lectures. Perugia, 1986. Tübinger Beiträge zur Anglistik 11. Tübingen: Narr, 1988. 156–65.

After citing medieval and modern parodies which recall an Old Provençal lyric and the 'Cuckoo Song' ['Svmer is icumen in,' *3223*], Stemmler discusses the difficulty of recognizing parody and 'the character of the author's deviation from the traditional canon' (158). He warns of the unreliability of exaggeration and apparent incongruity, and its encouragement to the 'peculiar variety of philological hunter . . . the parody-hunter.' Among recently discovered examples of parody in 'the thickets of Middle English texts,' he finds victims of '*ironic fallacy*' (160). He uses 'Annot and John' [*1394*] for his analysis, and refers to Ransom, **697**. The poem is a conventional catalogue, in diversified alliterative verse, and Stemmler disagrees with Ransom about perceived incongruity and monotony. He finds no puns on *coynte* as a variant of *queinte*, or *cunde* of *cunte*, and no ambiguity in comparison with flowers and herbs. His reading of 'the totally innocent words *licoris* and *leche*, [mandrake and parrot]' (164) leads Stemmler to find that 'Annot is not "a bundle of contradictions" . . . but of perfection, and the poet is not ambiguous but straight' (165).

683, 1327, 1394, 3223.

913 Thompson, John J. 'Literary Associations of an Anonymous Middle English Paraphrase of Vulgate Psalm L.' *Medium Ævum* 57 (1988): 38–55. [Edition.]

Presents a previously unpublished 'fragmentary Middle English paraphrase of the fiftieth Vulgate Psalm' ['God þou haue mercy of me,' *990*] from BL MS Add. 31042, 'an important and well-known anthology of Middle English verse items compiled in the middle years of the fifteenth century by Robert Thornton of East Newton in North Yorkshire' (38). The psalm was well known and used more often than other penitential psalms; it was available in Primers and Books of Hours, and so familiar to many of the devout laity. It was used to encourage confession, for meditation, and to offer comfort. Thompson explains its context in Add. 31042, noting its proximity to a Latin text of *Veni Creator* and a prose *Reuelacyon schewed to ane holy woman now one late tyme*. He describes works of this kind available to the private reader, including treatments of the psalm by Richard Rolle, Richard Maidstone, and Thomas Brampton, and considers the influence of Peter Lombard's commentary on the Psalter and interpretation of David's composition. The text has been affected by Thornton's 'uncharacteristically cramped presentation of his copy,' and a lacuna in a 'particularly fragmentary and troublesome section of the manuscript, in an exceptionally large and composite gathering which shows signs of considerable disarrangement' (43); Thompson delineates these problems, and comments on the likely structure of this section. He compares the text of the psalm with other works of similar metrical composition, including *Pearl* [*2744*], *Pety Job* [*251, 1854*], and the didactic refrain poems in the Vernon and Simeon MSS. In an appendix, he prints the text, with notes.

251, 355, 560, 583, 990, 1031, 1041, 1051, 1083, 1369, 1379, 1406, 1591, 1854, 1961, 2157, 2744, 3533, 3755, 3861, 4135, 4246.

Harrowing of Hell, 'Ondo ʒoure ʒatys, p*r*incys, to me!' [*7569*]. The latter perhaps recalls a scene that had 'taken root in his [Philip's] imagination from any of many sources in literature, art and drama' (166).

672.5, 1938.5, 3490.6, 4225.5, 7024, 7245, 7283, 7518, 7569.

920 Green, Richard Firth. 'The Two "Litel wot hit any mon" Lyrics in Harley 2253.' *Mediaeval Studies* 51 (1989): 304–12.

Examines the relationship of the two lyrics called 'The Way of Christ's Love' [*1922*] and 'The Way of Woman's Love' [*1921*], and considers a similar address to the Virgin 'A Song of the Love of Our Lady' [*1923*], found as a fragment in MS BL Egerton 613. Green sees *1922* and *1923* as *contrafacta* 'of a very distinctive kind' (306) of the secular *1921*. He demonstrates the resemblance of these lyrics to those of a puy at which 'matched pairs of *amoureuses* and *serventois*' (308) were composed. Points of resemblance include the verbal echo of first lines, lexical and syntactical echoes, and the stanza structure. However the Harley lyrics differ from French *contrafacta* in presenting the poems together, suggesting that 'the English compiler was particularly eager to draw attention to the fashionable parallelism between the two pieces.' Green poses the question: 'might the "Way of Christ's Love" have been written for a puy – have been in fact the winner of a competition to produce a *serventois* on the "Way of Woman's Love"?' (311).

322, 888, 1921, 1922, 1923, 3223.

921 Jansen, J.P.M. 'Charles d'Orléans and the Fairfax Poems.' *English Studies* 70 (1989): 206–24.

Comments on criticism of poems ascribed to Charles d'Orléans and to William de la Pole, Duke of Suffolk. Jansen is particularly interested in the suggestions of MacCracken, **129**, that Suffolk wrote the 'nine English poems in Charles's personal manuscript (Paris, Bibliothèque National f.fr. 25458), a manuscript that appears to have served as an *album amicorum*'; that he was 'also the author and translator of the English poems of Charles in Harley 682'; and that he wrote a series of courtly love poems in Fairfax 16, one of which is also found in the personal manuscript. Jansen summarizes the arguments offered and investigates various poems in detail, concentrating on 'the subject matter and the use of imagery, formal aspects (prosody), and the language (including the rhymes)' (208); he illustrates each point with numerous examples. Explorations show many differences between the lyrics of Fairfax 16 and Harley 682. Although Charles could have written the Harley works when he had less familiarity with writing in English and the Fairfax poems later, it is more likely that the differences suggest two authors, and that the author of the Fairfax poems was an Englishman.

3, 129, 133, 136, 140, 144, 148, 151, 157, 164, 165, 264, 296, 300, 335, 382, 403, 440, 451, 460, 472, 509, 510, 552, 553, 555, 571, 656, 682, 816, 827, 833, 867, 1023, 1088, 1239, 1240, 1250, 1256, 1257, 1313, 1316, 1385, 1403, 1404, 1413, 1420, 1500, 1529, 1549, 1826, 1858, 2027, 2032, 2175, 2177, 2178, 2180, 2182, 2197, 2203, 2204, 2205, 2206, 2230, 2243, 2265, 2266, 2276, 2278, 2295, 2300, 2308, 2309, 2349, 2350, 2378, 2406, 2407, 2422, 2424.5, 2427, 2436, 2438, 2455, 2456, 2458, 2482, 2488, 2535.5, 2548, 2550, 2558, 2560.5, 2564, 2567, 2581, 2583, 2595, 2623, 2648, 2669, 2758, 2768, 2813, 2819, 2823, 2824, 2828, 2831, 3099, 3124, 3131.5, 3132, 3140, 3141, 3163, 3327, 3360, 3396, 3439, 3447, 3458, 3488, 3541, 3586, 3601, 3622, 3626, 3752, 3794, 3795, 3860, 3875, 3885, 3897, 3912, 3913, 3915, 3949, 3956, 3960, 3962, 3972, 4024, 4188, 4191, 4192, 4213, 4242, 4283.

922 Lawton, David A. 'The Diversity of Middle English Alliterative Poetry.' *Studies in Honour of H.L. Rogers*. Ed. Geraldine Barnes, et al. *Leeds Studies in English* NS 20 (1989): 143–72.

A study of alliterative poetry, to discover where it was written and for whom, 'who copied it, who read it, when, where and . . . how?' (164). After surveying the issues generally, Lawton offers a more detailed consideration of particular aspects and texts, including 'The Disputation between the Blessed Virgin and the Cross' [*2481, 2718*], for which he compares manuscript versions and the use of imagery and alliteration, and explains its development from the source, 'the poem *O Crux de te volo conqueri* by Phillip de Greve' (155). He examines the significance of 'þe disputisoun betwen þe bodi and þe soule' [*351*] in manuscripts that preserve *2481/2718*, and the influence of AN works. Lawton's examination of 'Four Stanzaic Poems from Yorkshire' (158–61) relates 'The Pistill of Susan' [*3553*] and *2481/2718*, and elicits similarities with 'The Quatrefoil of Love' [*1453*], '*De tribus regibus mortis*' [*2677*], and 'Somer Soneday' [*3838*]. He notes too, the relationship of these poems to plays of the York Cycle. The thirteen-line stanzas express themes that are linked numerologically, since 'thirteen is the number of epiphany' and thus 'suitable for expressing the joys and sorrows of the Virgin' (161). Among works in these stanzas are '"Memento Mori" Poems' (162–3). There are connections between *3838* and *351*, and to other alliterative works, and a relation between the stanza and the body and soul debate, implying 'a cultural continuity from Old English in the literary importance of the Body and Soul theme' (163).

351, 1453, 1566, 1718, 2481, 2677, 2678, 2718, 3227, 3415, 3481, 3553, 3838.

923 Matsuda, Takami. 'Death and Transience in the Vernon Refrain Series.' *English Studies* 70 (1989): 193–205.

Considers the 'reflective and non-homiletical quality' of the Vernon refrain lyrics that demand 'a didactic rather than ascetic response' and offer 'secular wisdom for winning salvation and avoiding discomforts in life.' Matsuda finds the source of the didacticism and style of expression in Ecclesiastes, which teaches contempt for the world but is 'sometimes ostensibly indifferent to the fate of the afterlife' (193). There are similar attitudes in 'I wolde witen of sum wys wiht' [*1402*], 'In a Pistel þat poul wrouȝt' [*1455*], and 'Whon Men beoþ muriest at heor Mete' [*3996*], all of which deal with death and transience and are 'indebted particularly to Ecclesiastes' (194). 'I wolde writen' suggests that striving to know of the afterlife is vain curiosity, and offers 'more pragmatic wisdom for life in this world' (195); in one stanza it presents 'the *carpe diem* attitude, a reminder of transience based on the *contemptus mundi* tradition, and a brief but orthodox admonition to clean life' (196). 'In a Pistel' stresses the need for self-knowledge, evading consideration of the afterlife, and concerning itself with the pragmatic. It urges man to seek knowledge of God through knowledge of self, but acknowledges the 'sinful and sorrowful conception of man' and the 'transience of joy, fame and life' (198), and teaches 'self-scrutiny through conscience' (199). 'Whon Men beoþ muriest' stresses death as 'the ultimate end,' and 'the antithesis of life and non-life, rather than this life and after-life' (200); it has 'more pragmatic and materialistic concern with death and salvation' (201) than others in the series. The poems deal with this life rather than any other, with 'intellectual resignation rather than ascetic contempt of the world.' Matsuda compares other Vernon poems on death 'which do not borrow consciously from Ecclesiastes' and have 'a more plainly homilic manner,' to trace the 'gradual secularization of the traditional Christian virtues and vices' (202), pragmatic attitudes to salvation and possibility for control of the afterlife by individual will, through varying concepts of Purgatory. Belief in the possibilities for salvation are reflected in another Vernon poem 'Nou Bernes Buirdus bolde and blyþe' [*2302*]. The poems show how 'the inevitable transience of life can be intellectually accepted and the anxiety of death sublimated, without necessarily dismissing the world as false and vain' (205).

563, 679, 769, 817, 1402, 1443, 1455, 2088, 2091, 2235, 2302, 2865, 3420, 3925, 3996, 4135, 4158, 4268.

924 Mooney, Linne R. 'Lydgate's "Kings of England" and Another Verse Chronicle of the Kings.' *Viator* 20 (1989): 255–89. [Edition.]

Examines an anonymous chronicle of kings of England [listed separately as 'At Westm. Wyllyam j-crovnyd was,' *444*; 'The myghty William Duk of Normandy,' *3431*]. The chronicle is thought to be the work of Lydgate and a redaction of his 'Kings of England sithen William Conqueror' ['This myghti William Duk of Normandie,' *3632*], by MacCracken [*Lydgate: Secular Poems*: 710–16, 717–22]. The poems stress the 'hereditary right to succession and . . . power of the Crown,' and seem to have been 'written – and received – as political propaganda' (256). In a detailed account of *3632* (256–63), Mooney relates it to Lydgate's translation of Laurence Calot's 'The Title and Pedigree of Henry VI' ['Trouble hertis to sette in quyete,' *3808*], and establishes the date of composition. The Lydgate work's wide circulation and preservation in 35 manuscripts demonstrate that it was 'not only a prototype but a paragon of English political propaganda.' Close study of the anonymous 'Kings of England' reveals differences from Lydgate's work 'in verse form, content, and tone, the latter two revealing the change in political climate . . . in the course of Henry VI's reign' (263). It survives, generally with a pedigree of kings, in 16 manuscripts, six of them rolls. The two chronicles circulated 'side-by-side in the fifteenth century'; they were 'sometimes combined or confused with one another,' and some scribes 'must have had both texts in front of them' (264). From variations in the use of some of Lydgate's lines and the length of stanzas, Mooney names two groups of manuscripts of the anonymous work the 'Lydgate family' and the 'longer family.' She compares stanzas on King Stephen to demonstrate their differences. Those of the longer family seem 'to represent the earlier as well as the standard version of the poem' (266). It was probably composed for the marriage of Henry VI and Margaret of Anjou in 1445, implied in the discreet emphasis on pedigree and succession, omitting 'such references . . . as would insult the sensibilities of the bride' (268). Additions were made to some manuscripts to record later events, and some rolls were hung for display. Some copies were altered to remove details of uprisings, so that they 'express a different view vis-à-vis Henry's right to the French throne' (273). Other verse chronicles survive, and have varying degrees of debt to the works that 'established the use of brief versified chronicles of the kings as political propaganda, to establish a monarch on the throne, to glorify his accession, or to bolster aristocratic or popular support for him during his reign' (276). Mooney supplies appendices: 'Manuscripts of Lydgate's "Kings of England"' (277–8) and 'Manuscripts and Editions of the Anonymous "Kings of England"' (278–89), the latter with full textual and explanatory notes.

444, 3431, 3632, 3808, 4174.3, 7270.

925 Moore, Bruce. 'The Reeve's "Rusty Blade."' *Medium Ævum* 58 (1989): 304–12.

A didactic poem, 'Envy' ['þe worm on þe treo,' *3506*], uses the image of rust on a knife in its description of 'the destructive and corrosive power of envy,' as it expresses 'qualities which are especially relevant to the Reeve' (307), in metaphors of disease, rust, corrosion, mould, rot, and burning, the last of which produces 'coals of vice' (308) rather than a purifying fire. The rustiness of his blade 'hints at . . . potential for envy, rancour, vice and discord' (309), used by Chaucer in his characterization.

3506, 4019.

926 Schwetman, John. 'Minor Middle English Poems: A Context for Medieval Studies.' *Teaching the Middle Ages* 3. Ed. Robert V. Graybill, et al. Studies in

Medieval and Renaissance Teaching. Warrensburg, MO: Central Missouri State University, 1989. 107–17.

Discusses topical and political poems that could introduce students 'to medieval England' (107). The poems could achieve this by indicating their context in details such as the Wheel of Fortune motif in 'The Lamentacioun of the Duchess of Glossester' ['Thorow owt a pales as I can passe,' *3720*]; interpretation of the earthquake of 1382 ['ȝhit is god a curteys lord,' *4268*]; and the mixed sympathies of 'On the Rebellion of Jack Straw' ['Tax has tenet us alle,' *3260*]. The poems of battles offer a more realistic picture of warfare than chivalric romances. Schwetman finds those of Minot, 'a front man for Edward III,' the best, and 'most typically chauvinistic' (113), with a jingoistic, nationalist style, unlike the ideals of knighthood, although some knightly deeds are to be found in Laȝamon's *Brut* [*295*]. Most important of the benefits of studying the minor poems is the possibility for developing criteria 'for evaluating the major works that we concentrate on' (117).

295, 987, 3080, 3155, 3260, 3720, 3796, 3801, 4268.

927 Smallwood, T.M. '"God was born in Bethlehem . . .": The Tradition of a Middle English Charm.' *Medium Ævum* 58 (1989): 206–23. [Edition.]

A detailed study of a fourteenth-century charm against thieves, 'God was iborin in bedlem' [*993*], its antecedents, derivatives, and related works. Smallwood summarizes investigation of the charm, preserved 'at f. 193rb of the manuscript Paris, Bibliothèque nationale, MS nouv. acq. lat. 693 . . . a manuscript from England,' before printing a 'near-diplomatic transcription' (206) and an 'edited version' (207), with comprehensive notes on modifications, motifs, and the unusual use of the letter p, which accounts for this version's name of 'P charm.' Motifs of the charm include Christ's Baptism in the Jordan (often invoked to stanch blood, since the river was believed to stop flowing at the time); a journey to Jerusalem (the Presentation in the Temple or the visit at the age of twelve); a prayer for protection against wolf and thief; and an invocation of saints, here probably John and Luke. The charm ends in a spell to immobilize thieves, in which p is frequently repeated. Smallwood prints a 'First Derivative' (209–10), 'recognizable as a reworking and simplification of the P charm' (210), with the addition of a prose passage and omission of the motifs of the visit to Jerusalem and the wolf. A Second Derivative, in prose, survives in eight manuscripts which agree closely, although the dates of copying range from the fourteenth to the sixteenth centuries. Modifications suggest use of both the First Derivative and the P charm, and some seventeenth-century copies mention the wolf and thief and the Baptism. Smallwood comments on the recording of charms, first to be used as treatments, and later as occult curiosities. A French derivative of the P charm invokes fifteen saints and 'various other sacred powers,' in 'the form more of a fulsome personal prayer than the arbitrary, formulaic and rigidly conventional English charm' (214). Antecedents of the P charm are in an AS charm against theft and a tenth-century Latin work 'set down in a High German-speaking area' (215). The Baptism in the Jordan occurs later in HG charms to stop bleeding. The use of the motifs of the visit to Jerusalem, the Baptism, and the wolf and thief within one charm seems confined to English and German examples. It implies 'a contact of educated minds, able to carry and translate relatively sophisticated charms, or to transport a written text' (219). An appendix supplies the history and possible date of the Paris manuscript (219–20). [Cf. Gray, **610**.]

993, 3771.

928 Allen, Mark. 'Middle English Drama and Middle English Lyrics.' *Approaches to Teaching Medieval English Drama.* Ed. Richard K. Emmerson. New York: Modern Language Association of America, 1990. 106–10.

Explains the advantages of linking ME lyrics and ME drama, 'using the lyrics to discover nuances in the plays and vice versa' (106). Thus lyrics of *contemptus mundi* and of the nativity can enhance the study of the Wakefield *Second Shepherds' Play*, and lyrics of death that of *Everyman*. Allen does not cite particular lyrics.

929   Astell, Ann W. *The Song of Songs in the Middle Ages.* Ithaca, NY: Cornell UP, 1990.

Two chapters of this study of 'medieval reader response – both interpretive and imitative – to the Song of Songs' (177), have particular significance: 'Religious Love Lyric and the Feminine "I"' (136–58) and 'Biblical Drama, Devotional Response and the Feminine "We"' (159–76). In the first Astell elucidates the voice and audience of lyrics of religious love, explaining the 'masculine/feminine polarity' in texts and traditions of poems that present the Virgin as a courtly heroine or Christ as the mystical Bridegroom. She compares the polarity of secular love songs in which 'the central consciousness and voice is almost invariably masculine,' with a lover's words 'about his beloved, not to her' (137), so that the songs define the feminine as 'nameless, absent, exterior, and unattained.' In contrast religious lyrics such as those of Rolle and his school 'enforce the constant rhetorical presence of the feminine as a role to be played,' to express 'love-longing for the Savior in the form of apostrophe or prayer.' Thus the audience identifies with the Bride, in 'a receptive surrender to the Divine' (138). There are similarities in the conventions of religious and secular love but differences in the love object, with Christ and Mary in place of an earthly lover or lady. The auditor's response to Mary in her function as Mediatrix, 'along the vertical line of human ascent (masculine) and divine descent (feminine),' is typically 'contrasexual (first masculine, then feminine)' (141). Astell illustrates responses to 'Mary the Lady' (141–3). She scrutinizes the convention of 'Christ the Lover' (143–540), through lyrics that show 'Prayer: The Feminine "I"' (144–5); 'Prosopopoeia: The Feminine "Thou"' (145–54), (in which she examines 'In a valey of þis restles mynde' [*1463*]); and 'Dialogue: "I" and "Thou"' (154–8). In each case, she traces imagery from the Song of Songs, to appraise effects that 'engage the auditor in an intensely personal religious experience of Christ as Bridegroom' (158).

Considering biblical drama, Astell probes the connection between lyric and the drama, and notes the influence of the lyric mode and the presence of lyrical passages (some of which are isolable), within many religious plays. Although the Song of Songs is both dramatic and lyrical, there is no 'Play of Solomon, and direct verbal allusion to Canticles is rare.' There are few borrowings, even in 'New Testament scenes most closely assimilated to the Song in the commentary tradition – the Annunciation, the Crucifixion, the Appearance to Mary Magdalene, and the Assumption of the Virgin' (160), although the York Assumption play has songs from the Marian liturgy that use texts from the Song of Songs. Astell summarizes commentary on the Song of Songs as a dramatic work for four voices: the Bride, her maidens, the Bridegroom, and his attendants. She examines the work of Mary as Medium and Mother through consideration of 'The Medial Woman and the Lyrics' (169–72), tracing 'the reciprocal pattern in the lyrics of salutation' (169). Mary's role in expressing the audience's love for Christ is seen in 'The Mother-Bride and Exemplification' (172–6). Here Astell considers illustration in words of the Virgin, Christ and Joseph; her examples are taken from the York cycle, 'in its entirety . . . a "song of songs"' (176), in which the church and the audience's responses are feminized.

110, 359, 1407, 1460, 1463, 1663, 1684, 1715, 1761, 1781, 1930, 1940, 1943, 2012, 2042, 2241, 2260, 3109, 3236, 3365, 3825, 3826, 3836, 3862, 4088, 4263, 7009, 7035, 7172, 7174, 7175, 7177, 7178, 7366, 7531.

——— Review by Marjory Rigby, *Review of English Studies* NS 43 (1992): 543–4. Finds some difficulty with parts of the argument that 'wherever love and longing are evoked [in the treatment of religious lyrics] the reader is being feminized.' Rigby is sceptical when she is 'directed in the epilogue to modern reception theory' (543), and in Astell's engagement with Woolf's findings. She does not agree that cocreation can extend to the mystery cycles or to biblical drama generally.

930   Axton, Richard. 'Interpretations of Judas in Middle English Literature.' *Religion in the Poetry and Drama of the Late Middle Ages in England.* Ed. Piero Boitani and Anna Torti. The J.A.W. Bennett Memorial Lectures. Perugia, 1988. Cambridge: Brewer, 1990. 179–97.

Examines the apocryphal stories of Judas which are intended to explain his betrayal of Christ. Axton first discusses the gospel narratives, with their 'three explanations: avarice, diabolic possession, and the fulfilment of prophecy or divine necessity' (180). He then examines the dialogue *Lucidus and Dubius* [*3352.5*]; stories that present Judas as Oepidus; the *Legenda Aurea*; English legendaries; and ME and French drama. He finds the ME 'Judas' [*1649*] 'the most intriguing' (190) of the interpretations. He describes and prints the text, with possible reasons for the mark '.ii.' near three of the lines, and for the poem's length of 33 lines, which in 'a poem which tells of the betrayal of Christ, might be thought significant' (191). Axton analyses episodes in the poem, and comments on its density, a characteristic of other works in the manuscript that argues against incompleteness. Judas seems the obsessed victim of a temptress; the tearing of his hair, in a 'haunting portrait of demonic possession, isolation, and suffering' (195), recalls Samson's betrayal. The ballad begins and ends with prophecy. Eventually it shows Judas without moral sense and reveals Peter's weakness, as 'the extravagance of his boast contrasts beautifully with the quietness of Christ's prophecy' (196). The accounts answer the need to understand and assign motivation to Judas, since 'the man who had to betray Christ and then hang himself must have a special destiny, finely balanced between misfortune and wickedness.' In popularizing the story, the friars showed the bargain as 'a double destiny that is both psychologically and theologically disturbing,' and evinced some equivocal sympathy, 'at the expense of St Peter, the rock of the established Church' (197).

1303, 1649, 3352.5, 3561.5.

931   Barratt, Alexandra. '"I am Rose" Restored.' *Notes and Queries* 235 (1990): 270. [Edition.]

The fragment 'I am Rose wo is me' [*1279*], apparently 'a woman's lament,' deserves clarification. Barratt describes its source, in Cambridge University Library MS Hh.6.11. This has suffered cropping at a point where it seems to translate a Latin couplet, which she reconstructs from Oxford, Trinity College 7. This allows an improved transcription, which Barratt prints: 'I am Rose: wo is me, sutere þat i snete þe!/þat i wacs, weylawey! Cherles hand me þristet ay.' She supplies notes on *sutere* and *snete*. The revision suggests that 'the poem may refer to a specific Mistress Rose Souter, who had both an undeserving husband, and a clerical admirer who wrote Latin verse.'

1279.

932   Brehe, S.K. 'Reassembling the *First Worcester Fragment*.' *Speculum* 65 (1990): 521–36. [Edition.]

The *First Worcester Fragment* ['Sanctus beda was iboren her on bretone mid us,' *3074.3*], which is written as prose, records a decline in learning, teaching, and language, from more pious AS days to Norman times. Brehe surveys previous criticism, and cites the titles assigned to the work, including *The Disuse of English*, *Sanctus Beda*, the *Beda Fragment*, and *Sicut oves absque pastore*, before printing it, using the lineation of Varnhagen [*Anglia* 3 (1880): 423–5]. There are two passages of prose: a list of AS bishops and words of God expressed in the Latin of the Vulgate. In this form it may seem not to belong to 'that metrical form represented by the *Soul's Address* ['* ... on earde/and alle þeo i-sceaftan þe to him to sculen,' *2684.5*], the *Proverbs of Alfred [433]*, and Laȝamon's *Brut [295]*' (523), where there is alliteration in most lines, but 'in a minority of lines in all these poems, verse rhyme, not alliteration, unites the two verses in each line' (524). Brehe compares the list of bishops to similar sections in *Brut* and the ME *Bestiary [3413]*, noting the use of end rhyme. The passage from the Vulgate can be arranged to assume a metrical form similar to Laȝamon's metre, and to yield both alliteration and rhyme within the first line. Further rearrangement of lines that apparently lack alliteration and rhyme can offer a longer line that binds long verses with alliterating syllables, as in the *Brut* and the *Soul's Address*. Brehe prints the new lineation, in verse without prose, and in a form generally consistent with Laȝamon's, with a MnE translation. Apparent confusion of the names Ælfric and Alcuin in the list of bishops may suggest an honorific, such as 'Ælfric Alcuin,' 'to distinguish Ælfric, translator of Alcuin, from the several other Ælfrics of the Anglo-Saxon era' (531). Citing the Pentateuch, by which 'the poet filled out his line and achieved verse rhyme,' also presents a reminder of Israel's 'struggle against faithlessness and foreign oppression' (531), a theme linked with Ælfric's works as well as the *First Fragment*. The list of bishops, formerly thought to be random, moves from north to south and records the resting places of relics of these bishop-saints, rather than their sees. Selection of these individuals may be linked to 'achievements related to the poem's theme' (533), and a wish to revive interest in their work. The *Fragment* expresses regret for the leadership 'that English bishops had provided before the conquest' (535). The rearrangement renders it 'more coherent in form and content, and more interesting than its editors have realized' (536).

*295, 433, *2684.5, 3074.3, 3413.*

933 Burrow, John. 'The Shape of the Vernon Refrain Lyrics.' *Studies in The Vernon Manuscript*. Ed. Derek Pearsall. Cambridge: Brewer, 1990. 187–99.

Investigates 23 lyrics, all with 'stanza forms derived from the French *balade*,' but variations in number of lines and rhyme scheme. They are found, in identical order, in the Vernon and Simeon MSS; sub-stanzaic textual variations suggest that they were copied 'from a common exemplar, VS' (187), rather than from each other. Burrow is concerned with their shape, generally with the order of stanzas, and particularly with variations in nine poems also found in other manuscripts. Only 'Mercy Passes All Things' ['Bi west vnder a wylde wode syde,' *583*] is not varied; the rest display at least one other shape. Three poems are also found in another pair of manuscripts, BL Cotton Caligula A.ii and Princeton Garrett 143, which in each case 'agree on a shape different from that in VS' (190). Burrow notes difficulties in determining the original shape, and the role of the refrain in fixing this. 'Ever More Thank God of All' ['Bi a wey wandryng as I went,' *562*], has 'six distinct shapes' in seven manuscripts, 'with only V and S agreeing' (191). Only the VS version has five stanzas that Burrow sees as an interpolation of an *exemplum* of Job's patience. He compares a similar passage found only in the VS version of 'Who Says the Sooth, He Shall be Shent' ['þe man þ^t luste to liuen in ese,' *3420*], to contrast a flatterer with a surgeon who speaks frankly and 'cures wounds by painfully probing them' (193). In other cases, he inspects links between stanzas, omissions, and differences in order. He questions the shape of some lyrics that are found only in VS. His proposal to reorder two stanzas of 'This World Fares as a Fantasy' ['I wolde witen of sum wys wiht,' *1402*] is based on the aptness of the penultimate stanza to end the poem, since the last, 'with its elaborate *exemplum* of the growing and rotting tree, has none of the marks of a conclusion' (198). Burrow suggests that 'the stanzas in question represent an addition to the original.' Their nature implies 'the work of the same hand that interpolated stanzas' in *562* and *3420*; the three unique passages 'exhibit a peculiarly learned and curious mind, with an interest in the concrete exemplifying instance' (199). [See also Sajavaara, **503**; Thompson, **943**.]

5, 253, 349, 373, 374, 378, 404, 562, 563, 583, 872, 1379, 1402, 1443, 1448, 1455, 1460, 1532, 1596, 2108, 2280, 2302, 2619, 2790, 3420, 3522, 3925, 3996, 4157, 4158, 4268.

934 Deyermond, Alan. 'Sexual Initiation in the Woman's-Voice Court Lyric.' *Courtly Literature: Culture and Context: Selected Papers from the 5th Triennial Congress of the International Courtly Literature Society, Dalfsen, The Netherlands, 9–16 August, 1986.* Ed. Keith Busby and Erik Kooper. Utrecht Publications in General and Comparative Literature 25. Amsterdam: Benjamins, 1990. 125–58.

This survey of poems that describe sexual initiation in the woman's voice discusses lyrics in several languages. Three ME works are in the category of 'seduction followed by pregnancy and the man's abandonment of the young woman' (143). Deyermond finds the woman's voice authentically presented in 'Y louede a child of this cuntrie' [*1330*], but he argues that it is 'a mere cover – and a fairly transparent one – for the male point of view' in the lyrics 'As I went on Yole day in oure procession' [*377*] and 'Ladd Y the daunce a Myssomur Day' [*1849*].

377, 1330, 1849.

935 Dronke, Peter. 'On the Continuity of Medieval English Love-Lyric.' *England and the Continental Renaissance: Essays in Honour of J.B. Trapp.* Ed. Edward Chaney and Peter Mack. Woodbridge: Boydell, 1990. 7–21.

Investigates the extent to which continuities with similar OE works may be traced in ME love lyrics. Dronke examines three early lyrics, '[þe]h þet hi can wittes fule-wis' [*3512*], 'He may cume to mi lef but by þe watere' [*1142*], and 'Atte wrastlynge mi lemman i ches' [*445*]. In each case, his emendations and critical commentary provide texts and interpretations that diverge from previous readings and remove some possibilities of certainty. He notes recurring motifs of separation (especially by water) and of enclosure (particularly within stone walls), and shows that the 'persistence of narrative enigma within lyric is one of the principle continuities between Old and Middle English examples' (9). The early lyric *445* is a woman's complaint of 'erotic invective' (11), but also used as an allegorical sermon verse. Dronke traces techniques and images in fourteenth-century works 'We schun maken a ioly castel' [*7577*] and 'Wer þer ouþer in þis toun' [*3898*], and offers a 'more reflective' reading for *3898*, which hints at 'muted anguish,' rather than the 'operetta world' (13) of the title, 'A Toast to His Lost Mistress' in *RobbinsS*, **51**. Uncertainties in text as well as poetic style contribute to the enigmatic nature of the works, in 'narrative and dramatic hints . . . only half-given, so that they will work upon the imagination of the audience,' as in similar OE short lyrical poems, where there is 'the sense of lyric reaching out towards narrative' (14). Dronke considers expressions of sorrow, separation, and captivity in OE in *Wulf and Eadwacer*, *The Husband's Message*, and *The Wife's Complaint*, and motifs in a Welsh lyric of Tristan and Wolfram von Eschenbach's *Titurel*. In a woman's lyric of the Findern anthology, 'Yit wulde I not the causer faryd amysse' [*4272.5*], the poet 'pays homage to her medieval predecessors in the art of uniting lyrical and narrative-dramatic impulses with compelling directness' (20). The techniques point towards Wyatt's in 'They fle from me that sometyme did me seke,' where the poet alone, without imagery of the outer world, employs 'narrative transitions' that are 'psychological,' although 'there is still a continuity with the lyrics of earlier centuries in a knowing use of enigma' (21).

445, 1142, 3512, 3898, 4272.5, 7577.

936 Fein, Susanna Greer. 'Why did Absolon put a "Trewelove" under his Tongue? Herb Paris as a Healing "Grace" in Middle English Literature.' *Chaucer Review* 25 (1990–1): 302–17.

Absolon's use of a truelove plant before he visits Alison in the *Miller's Tale* [*4019*] is based on extensive popular and poetic tradition. Fein explains the symbolic significance of the herb paris, its associations with good luck in love, and its use as an emblem of divine love, although it fades 'like fickle love.' Seeking it involves the *double entendre* of looking both for 'the desired plant and . . . an ideal faithful mate' (303). The leaves resemble a cross and a lover's knot, and it appears as a herbal remedy in continental herbals, although ME records suggest that 'the curative power of truelove . . . acted on spirit rather than body' (304). ME religious lyrics link it with meditation on the Passion and the visualization of Christ's wounds, indicating 'truest love . . . in Christ's suffering for man,' so that 'affective remembrance of the Crucifixion will help men to love God faithfully in return' (305). The image of Christ the Lover-Knight recurs in the search for the plant, as in the lyric 'In a valey of þis restles mynde' [*1463*]. Although this poem, found in early fifteenth-century texts, may not have influenced Chaucer, distorted traces of 'associated images: herb paris, divine love, the cross, the wounded Christ as Lover-Knight' (306), may be discerned in the tale. Elements are also found in 'That ilke man wole lerne wel' [*3279*], known as 'Loue þat god loueth,' and in 'The Foure Leues of the Trewlufe' ['In a mornynge of May when medose schulde sprynge,' *1453*; 'On a dere day by a dale so depe,' *2678*], which Fein describes in detail. The cluster of four leaves symbolizes the Trinity and Mary, who represents 'true love expressed within the human sphere' (309). A bird in *1453* explains biblical history, 'a drama of the four leaves joining in companionship, tragically suffering disunion during the Crucifixion, and at last joyfully reunited in the Resurrection and Mary's Coronation as Queen of Heaven.' The poem employs 'a delicate pun upon the four-leaved "gras" and "grace"' (308), a figure seen in other works. Although the milieu of the *Miller's Tale* differs from that of the religious lyrics, there are analogies in Absolon's wish to be gracious, 'to have the verbal grace of a courtly lover, to win the favour of his lady' (310); in 'the triangle of Nicholas, Alisoun, and John [that] parodies Gabriel, Mary and Joseph'; and in the 'incongruous likeness to Christ' of each male character 'through a specific association with a type for the Savior and cross' (311). The herb has immediate effect in curing Absolon's love-longing. In the late fifteenth century it symbolizes secular love.

196, 252, 420, 498, 1328.7, 1453, 1463, 1583, 1718, 2007, 2107, 2153, 2678, 3279, 3281.5, 3802, 3805, 4019, 4154, 7476.

937 Jones, F. 'The Unity of Harley Lyrics 4.' *Neuphilologische Mitteilungen* 91 (1990): 251.

Comments on the yearning expressed by the poet of the Harley lyric 'Alysoun' [*515*]. This culminates in lines 35–6, 'Betere is þolien whyle sore/þen mournen euermore,' apparently offering 'a choice between a brief torment and one which will last always,' and resembling 'the earth-heaven opposition' expressed in another Harley lyric, 'A Winter Song' [*4177*]. Thus, although the poet's suffering in love service expresses his love for Alysoun, 'not loving her is *itself* Hell.' The paradox unites the sorrow of the stanzas with the joy of the refrain.

515, 4177.

938 Kessel-Brown, Deidre. 'The Emotional Landscape of the Forest in the Mediaeval Love Lament.' *Medium Ævum* 59 (1990): 228–47.

The wild forest is the landscape most frequently associated with sorrow in love, and it is often a setting for lamentation. It may reflect the chaos of an unhappy lover's mind, when he flees 'from the exposure of the city to woodland privacy,' to isolation linked with 'the mediaeval myth of the wild man,' because he is 'at odds with environments in which social harmony exists' (229). Kessel-Brown illustrates the idea with literary references, including 'Lenten ys come wiþ loue to toune' [*1861*]. The forest may also be a place of spiritual refuge, leading to spiritual reflection. Emblematic presentation of the forest generally offers 'the common depiction of the spring wood as a *locus amoenus*' (232), to remind the lover of happier times and perhaps sharpen grief. A narrator may speak of contrasts, as in *chansons d'aventure* and pastourelles. The forest is then receptive to 'expressions of loss and lamentation,' a sympathetic listener to confidences, 'often invested with the qualities of a living being which possesses sense and intelligence.' Intimacy in the relationship 'between lamenter and landscape' (235) is heightened when a specific tree is addressed. A lover may be driven into the forest, perhaps hunted in the 'allegorical chase of love' (237); if he is wounded he will not recover. The wild wood is linked to visions of hell; apprehension of an enforced exile expresses a lover's sorrows. The figure of a man lamenting beneath a tree is used in *The Book of the Duchess* [*1306*] and *The Squire of Low Degree* [*1644*], and is associated with the theme 'Christ in Distress,' the powerful image of the opening of 'In a valey of þis restles mynde' [*1463*]. The lyric exemplifies the use of the forest 'as a vehicle for the expression of emotional disturbance wrought by failure in love' (245).

359, 864, 1306, 1333, 1463, 1644, 1861, 2236, 3187, 3868, 4019, 4037.

939 Kohl, Stephan. 'Genre Development and Perennial Truth: The Case of the Middle English Religious Lyric.' *REAL: Yearbook of Research in English and American Literature* 7 (1990): 1–18.

Examines the progress of the religious lyric, from its 'flowering' in the thirteenth and fourteenth centuries, to 'dull didactisicm' and 'forced poetic elaboration' in the fifteenth, and its absence from literary life until the seventeenth. Kohl relates this course to 'changing aesthetic qualities . . . to correspond with differing social functions' (1). The needs 'to evoke love of God, or fear of death, or compassion for Christ,' and to be 'a mass medium for religious education' (2) prompted different presentation. The conflict of 'pastoral demand for unchanging repetition, and the literary demand for defamiliarizing variations . . . led to the lyric's decline and near-disappearance in the fifteenth and sixteenth centuries' (3). Poems of the thirteenth and fourteenth centuries are original in using the vernacular for the 'lyrical presentation of the speaking suffering Christ' (4), without didacticism, a method for 'an audience whose allegiance is beyond doubt' (6). In contrast, the fifteenth-century complaints of Christ present authoritative and 'explicit theological teaching,' perhaps to counter 'effects of a growing habitualization' (7), or in reaction to Wyclif and his school. Later works discourage 'emotionally involved, concentrated meditation on the Passion': they offer instruction, and 'it is man who asks for love and mercy, no longer Christ' (9). Many lyrics address man 'as a rational being' (10), to appeal to intellect before emotion. Complaints became 'rational explications' (12) and lost lyrical qualities; reliance on prose meditations increased. Even didactic lyrics were not part of 'contemporaneous theological controversies.' Thus fifteenth-century lyrics did not follow 'changing ways of feeling and thinking,' and had no 'element of unfamiliarity' (13). The genre does not re-emerge until the seventeenth century, exemplified in works of Donne and Herbert, whose lyrics meet 'the demand of defamiliarizing their subjects' (15).

497, 550, 1308, 2081, 2240, 2241, 3826, 3845, 3862, 4263.

940 Marx, C.W. 'The Middle English Verse "Lamentation of Mary to Saint Bernard" and the "Quis dabit."' *Studies in The Vernon Manuscript*. Ed. Derek Pearsall. Cambridge: Brewer, 1990. 137–57.

Relates the fourteenth-century ME 'Lamentation of Mary to Saint Bernard' ['Lewed men be not lered in lore,' *1869*], in the Vernon MS, to the thirteenth-century Latin work

'*Quis dabit* or *Liber de passione Christi et doloribus et planctibus matris eius*, frequently attributed . . . to St. Bernard or St. Augustine,' and to 'an intermediary, a thirteenth-century AN verse text, the *Plainte de la Vierge*' (137). The examination considers the tension between 'emotional excesses' of lyrics on the Compassion of the Virgin (so characterized by Woolf, **522**) and the restraint of those on Christ's Passion, attributed to teaching on the Passion's contribution to redemption. Marx explores the 'tension between grief and faith' of the *Quis dabit* in the speaker's wish to know and utter the grief of Mary, who, 'because she has been glorified (*glorificata*) . . . cannot weep.' The text presents human and spiritual attitudes, to show that experience of 'the human emotion of grief in response to the passion of Mary and Christ . . . is a sign of grace' (141). The AN and ME texts demonstrate 'policies of revision,' implying 'different literary contexts' and responses to 'problems in the *Quis dabit* itself, and . . . to doctrinal and literary pressures.' Marx discerns attitudes and something of the reception of the *Quis dabit* in the vernacular texts. Whereas the Latin text has the 'divine authority of the Virgin' (147), the others have St Bernard, John's gospel, and medieval material 'responding to the broader traditions and legends which grew up around the scriptural account of the passion' (150). The ME text is a dialogue, but the AN has narrative shared by Bernard and Mary. The ME text shows Mary's grief ambiguously. It offers 'less emphasis on the sorrows,' but more prominence for Mary, who 'relates the events of the passion' (151). Marx compares examples of the expression of Mary's grief with corresponding passages in the *Quis dabit*, to display the *Lamentation*'s resolution of 'grief and doctrine or faith' (154). Changes suggest that 'one of the purposes of the ME text was to present a balance between faith and grief' (155), to show Mary 'as a symbol of faith,' and present her 'genuine human grief . . . within a doctrinal framework,' to show compassion as 'a sign of grace and a defence against the devil' (156).

170, 245, 323, 512, 771, 1034, 1718, 1869, 1907, 3428.

941 Reed, Thomas L., Jr. *Middle English Debate Poetry and the Aesthetics of Irresolution.* Columbia, MO: U of Missouri P, 1990.

Focuses on 'debate poetry's local manifestations in England between roughly 1200 and 1450' (2), including some shorter works in the examination. In 'The Middle English Tradition' (153–218) Reed examines 'the literary context in which poems like *The Owl and the Nightingale* [*1384*] and *The Parlement of Foules* [*3412*] came to be written' (153). He considers dialogues that involve supernatural figures; abstractions (such as death, youth, and age) and human beings; and debates on love and women conducted by birds, abstractions, deities, and humans. Among lyrics of the Nativity and Passion are dialogues of the Virgin and Christ; between Christ and Man; and some between Mary and Gabriel, saints, and the Cross. Others take the form of struggles for the souls of the dying, sometimes involving angels and devils. There are debates between the Body and the Soul. Debates of secular love include the pastourelles, 'The Meeting in the Wood' [*1449*] and 'De Clerico et Puella' [*2236*], and the 'happy affair . . . preserved in two macaronic lyrics from the fifteenth century, the *De Amico ad Amicam* [*16*] and its *Responcio* [*19*]' (163). Another pair of lyrics offers mocking descriptions of the lover ['Vnto you most froward þis lettre I write,' *3832*] and his lady ['O fresche flour most plesant of pryse,' *2437*]. The flyting style is seen in the contests of Holly and Ivy. Henryson and Charles d'Orléans are among poets who favour the genre, and contribute debates of abstractions and love exchanges. Reed considers Chaucer's exploitation of '"Implied Debate" and *The Canterbury Tales*' (179–204), and compares other dialogues. He concludes that debates, often unresolved, demonstrate that 'humans do not live in a world of perfect intellectual clarity and volitional control'; they must explore 'the difficulty of pursuing dimly perceived and occasionally conflicting ideals in a realm of distracting phenomena' (204). He looks in detail at 'The Thrush and the Nightingale'

[*3222*], *Death & Liffe* [*603*], and 'The Parlement of the thre Ages' [*1556*], as examples of the 'search for resolution' (218).

16, 19, 100, 150, 167, 285, 295.5, 296.3, 344, 351, 360, 370, 467, 603, 658, 995.4, 1086, 1195, 1384, 1406, 1449, 1452, 1459, 1461, 1475, 1503.5, 1556, 1563, 1751, 1921, 1922, 2018, 2213, 2236, 2437, 2481, 2520, 2551, 2590, 2591, 2662, 2718, 2735, 2784, 2831, 3028, 3137, 3144, 3222, 3247, 3327, 3361, 3396, 3412, 3458, 3461, 3642.5, 3761, 3825, 3832, 3845.5, 3942, 3992, 4019, 4026, 4169.

942 Stevens, John. 'Chaucerian Metre and Early Tudor Songs.' *Chaucer Traditions: Studies in Honour of Derek Brewer*. Ed. Ruth Morse and Barry Windeatt. Cambridge: Cambridge UP, 1990. 139–54.

Uses musical settings of songs in the Fayrfax MS for an investigation of 'verse-sound, and therefore possibly the *spoken* performance of verse,' accepting that 'the basis of courtly metres in the fifteenth-century high style was courtly speech itself' (140). The settings of final and medial syllables and their accentuation offer evidence of word-sound, but this may not be unambiguous. The problem of the mid-line break or pause is 'most important and baffling' (146). Intonation may be 'the most intractable' among 'problems of historical phonology,' and few settings can tell 'the truth about everyday speech-melody formalized in verse.' Enjambement is rare, and melismas 'much more prominent' (149). The musical treatment of the stanza is formal and conventional, involving the *formes fixes*, carol, and rhyme-royal. The effects are variable, and may not suggest the spoken performance. When syllable counts seem irregular or unusual, the setting may help establish the rhythm of the line and display '*armonia* of proportioned words and phrases,' in works that seem irregular 'if an anachronistic "iambic" regularity is looked for' (152). The 'unusually sensitive musical renderings of the text' show that iambic lines 'represent *only one way* of creating a "harmonical concent." ' The renderings offer contemporary readings that show 'the poetic line as a stable, separable unit,' significantly without 'a norm so insistent that any deviation from it will be heard as creating a tension between "voice" and metrical pattern' (153).

13, 155.5, 497, 557.5, 1273.3, 1328.5, 1636.5, 1731, 1866.8, 2277, 2394.5, 2547.5, 3131, 3206.5, 3297.3, 3437, 3724.5, 3845, 3903.8.

943 Thompson, John J. 'The Textual Background and Reputation of the Vernon Lyrics.' *Studies in The Vernon Manuscript*. Ed. Derek Pearsall. Cambridge: Brewer, 1990. 203–24.

Studies the relationship between Vernon and Simeon copies of the lyrics in the *Sowlehele* section of the manuscripts, commenting on differences observed and suggesting possible reasons for them. Thompson notes that, when readings do not agree, 'the superiority of the Vernon text is not automatically guaranteed.' He cites instances where the Simeon offers 'equally viable alternative readings or, much less often . . . makes better sense' (205). To investigate the idea that the Simeon was copied from the Vernon, he notes differences in punctuation, decoration, and the anonymous insertion of words in the Vernon copy of some lyrics in places where this is apparently not editorial correction against another copy. The decoration provides information about a possible sequence of preparation and about the work of scribes and limners. Thompson considers related works in other parts of the manuscripts. He notes points of transition between scribes and differences in methods of punctuation, spacing, and planning, and speculates on effects of availability of copy text. Many of the lyrics survive only in these manuscripts, but some are found or mentioned in other sources, which Thompson describes in detail, suggesting circumstances of gathering and preserving the texts. They are in collections that include those of Robert Thornton, Richard Hill, and John Northwood, and in various religious anthologies; Thompson shows the connections with other works. He concludes that, as the 'enormous sister volumes' were being prepared, 'a number of different types of small anthologies were probably also circulating as written exemplars.' These probably had thematic connections, but since they have not survived, there are limits to the possibilities for making decisions about editorial work in the Vernon and Simeon MSS. The tendency to call the lyrics 'songs' implies that they were to be 'memorised, sung or recited' (222). The large size of the Vernon and Simeon MSS suggests that they were to be consulted as 'substantial and permanent written records of what had been or was being written in English to assist "Sowlehele"' (224). [See also Sajavaara, **503**; Burrow, **933**.]

5, 83, 220, 244, 247, 251, 257, 355, 358, 374, 378, 406, 471, 506, 560, 561, 562, 563, 583, 606, 678, 707. 750, 820, 872, 880, 1028, 1030, 1032, 1041, 1055, 1081, 1108, 1111, 1259, 1286, 1342, 1379, 1402, 1433, 1446, 1448, 1454, 1455, 1460, 1491, 1503, 1532, 1591, 1596, 1653, 1718, 1781, 1815, 1854, 1962, 2108, 2119, 2157, 2167, 2233, 2250, 2270, 2280, 2302, 2385, 2410, 2573, 2607, 2714, 2718, 2770, 2790, 3184, 3371, 3420, 3501, 3533, 3685, 3687, 3715, 3774, 3793, 3861, 3925, 3996, 4056, 4150, 4154, 4155, 4157, 4158, 4160, 4200, 4268.

944 Waldron, Ronald. '"Maiden in the Mor Lay" and the Religious Imagination.' *Langland, the Mystics and the Medieval English Religious Tradition: Essays in Honour of S.S. Hussey.* Ed. Helen Philipps. Cambridge: Brewer, 1990. 215–22 [cited.] Repr. in *Unisa English Studies* 29 (1991): 8–12.

After a summary of commentary on 'Maiden in the mor lay' [*2037.5*], Waldron proposes a context in the 'singing-games of children,' based on 'the coherence and . . . persuasiveness of the resulting reading.' He cites nineteenth-century games of 'the enactment of a funeral, usually of a young person, often a young maiden or her bridegroom-to-be' (217), in particular that of 'Jinny Jo,' in 'a dialogue . . . of a group-courtship followed by a funeral' (218). The works proceed in questions and answers. In 'Jinny Jo' this has 'the poetic and dramatic function of delaying the recognition of the maiden's death and of mitigating its horror (though emphasizing its poignancy)' (219–20). The first line 'Maiden in the mor lay' can then be read literally, rather than as a statement that the maiden lives on the moor. After references to the *OED* and *MED* on *lay* and *moor*, Waldron proposes 'A/The maiden lay buried in the mire' (221). Thus the poem can be 'the effort of a child's mind to take in and comprehend the fact of death (specifically the death of another child)' (221). This culminates in the 'note of acceptance struck by the repeated *Welle was hire . . .* found in the later poem in the final *And that will just do*' (221–2). Questions in *Pearl* [*2744*] offer another analogy to the 'profound and universal human need for reassurance in the face of mortality' (222).

2037.5, 2744.

945 Wilson, Edward. 'Local Habitations and Names in MS Rawlinson C 813 in the Bodleian Library, Oxford.' *Review of English Studies* NS 41 (1990): 12–44.

A close study of works in the manuscript compiled by Humphrey Wellys, considering those that mention names and places associated with him, to identify them and their relevance in his life. The lyric verses are 'some thirty-nine courtly love lyrics; five poems concerned with death in the form of two epitaphs, two lamentations, and a testament (of a buck); four humorous or light poems; and three moral and admonitory ones' (12). Other works in verse and prose include five political prophecies; their references to contemporary events allow dating of the manuscript. An inscription in cipher identifies Wellys as the owner, and poems styled 'letters' provide further evidence. Wilson prints 'A letter send by R.W. to A.C.' ['Right wel beloved prentise,' *2827.5*] (15–16) and 'A letter sende by on yonge woman to anoder, which aforetyme were ffelowes togeder' ['My loving frende amorous Bune,' *2261.8*] (23–4). He supplies details of people and places mentioned in each poem, and the implications of metaphors and descriptions; he adds further notes in appendices on the two verse epistles (42–4). The references establish the Staffordshire provenance and many yield information about Wellys and his family. Wilson notes biographical material available in his account of Wellys's life and work. He emphasizes Wellys's career as an administrator; his recusancy, although his will acknowledges Elizabeth as Defender of the Faith; and his connections with the Chatwyn family through marriage to Mary Chatwyn. The manuscript is carefully compiled, and Wellys's selection of texts shows 'not the happenstance of the commonplace book . . . but rather a concentration on, and physical separation of, two principal genres, the lyric and the political prophecy' (30–1). It preserves 'The epytaphe of Lobe, the Kynges foole' ['O Lobbe Lobe on thy sowle God haue mercye,' *2482.5*], and 'The Lamentatyon of Edward, late Duke of Buckyngham' ['O dere God beholde þis worlde so transytorye,' *2409.5*], probably copied from texts belonging to William Chatwyn, Wellys's father-in-law, who had been involved in litigation with Buckingham. The latter text displays 'a public figure who is an exemplum of deservedly punished pride,' whereas another Buckingham lament, in the John Colyns's commonplace book, 'Alas to whom shuld I complayne' [*158.9*] shows 'a victim of fortune and treachery . . . with humane anxieties about his family' (34–5). There is other commentary on contemporary events in an extract from Skelton and in 'The Testament of the Bucke' ['As I stode in a parke streite vp bi a tree,' *368*]; the latter work seems particularly apt, because Wellys's arms included a buck's head. The political prophecies are 'pro-papal, and on occasion, anti-Henrican' (40), a dangerous position, although Wellys's belief in supremacy of the papacy did not blind him to its faults. Wilson sees the manuscript 'not as a passive repository, nor even as the "mere" ordering of a categorizing mind, but as a *compilatio* which is the result of the interanimation of family and personal ties with the literary, moral, religious, and political concerns of a Staffordshire gentleman' (42).

158.9, 194.5, 368, 813.3, 870.8, 1215, 1253.5, 1768, 2228, 2261.8, 2409.5, 2482.5, 2496, 2532, 2532.5, 2552.5, 2757.3, 2744, 2822, 2827.5, 3917.8, 3962.5.

946   Boffey, Julia. 'Early Printers and English Lyrics: Sources, Selection, and Presentation of Texts.' *Papers of the Bibliographical Society of America* 85 (1991): 11–26.

Investigates short English poems in early printed books and the factors that influenced their presence there. The surviving works are of many kinds: the lyrics, 'printed on single sheets, or individually in short pamphlets,' are the '[m]ost ephemeral of all' (12). The range of printed poems suggests that 'printers recognized and catered for an audience for this kind of material' (13). Boffey records details of numerous lyrics, including topical works, convivial songs, and carols. She suggests that some were 'used as padding' (15), in books printed by Caxton and de Worde, to accompany major works of Chaucer and Lydgate. Some poems circulated in quarto volumes, in contexts similar to those of their manuscript form. Chepman and Myllar's printing of lyrics seems concerned more 'with space to be filled than with overall theme' (17). Caxton at times practises 'economy-filling of this kind' (18), but may include works to add prominence to his name as a translator or printer. Many poems printed by other early printers, are 'dedications, prologues, and envoys' (19); their presence can indicate the printing history of major works. Lyrics composed in English or in translation were in the earliest books; they include some 'embedded in longer works, and merely reproduced in context' (20), and others in miscellanies. Boffey explores the survival, in printed form, of lyrics that were not preserved in manuscripts, finding that some 'were likely to circulate easily by word of mouth,' and that the 'logical conclusion to this . . . comes in those manuscript copies of printed lyrics which have been jotted into empty spaces in other printed books' (22). Some 'flimsy and ephemeral handwritten copies' (23) used by printers have not survived. The links between author and printer account for some losses of manuscript copy, exemplified in the asssociations of Woodville and Caxton and of Skelton and Rastell.

The English enthusiasm for French lyrics may explain the scarcity of collections of English lyrics. The reluctance of English printers to produce such collections is demonstrated in the circulation of Wyatt's lyrics in manuscript form during his life, although he was acquainted with printing.

33.5, 42.5, 272.5, 324, *338.5, 448.5, 467, 513, 524, 658, 679, 731.5, 761, 860.3, 913, 920, 1168, 1466.5, 1501, 1507, 1587.8, 1598, 1618, 1619, 1703, 1725, 1808.7, 1829.2, 2139, 2233, 2264, 2578.5, 2579.5, 2654.5, 2663.5, 2695.5, 3074, 3074.8, 3117.8, 3190, 3327, 3348, 3412, 3492.3, 3503, 3521.5, 3540, 3542, 3558, 3563.5, 3651, 3656.3, 3661, 3670, 3747, 3787, 3818, 3917.3, 3943, 4064, 4101, 4106, 4106.5, 4109.5, 4137, 4181, 4187.8.

947 ———. 'Middle English Lyrics: Texts and Interpretation.' *Medieval Literature: Texts and Interpretation.* Ed. Tim William Machan. MRTS 79. Binghamton, NY: CMERS, State U of New York at Binghamton, 1991. 121–38.

Probes effects of the problems of definition and 'the peculiar history of the currency of the language' in generating 'different editorial and critical imperatives' (121), with the result that 'lyric scholarship . . . has no unassailable common core of concern' (122). Boffey surveys critical methods, noting their benefits and problems, and commends the tendency to see lyrics 'as part of a larger cultural context' (123). She demonstrates the need for context study by comparing 'radically divergent interpretations of particular poems made by uninformed and informed critical understanding' (124). This need is demonstrated in 'the history of misapprehension concerning a poem conventionally known as "How Christ Shall Come" ['I sayh hym wiþ fless al bi-sprad,' *1353*],' which is a plan for a sermon rather than a lyric. [See Wenzel, **861**.] Two poems in Sloane MS 1212, 'Mercy me graunt off þat I me compleyne' [*2161*] and 'Myn worldly Ioy vpon me rewe' [*2188*], called 'courtly' in *RobbinsS*, **51**, reveal the ramifications of close study of manuscript copies and context. Boffey prints the poems, 'keeping the layout and punctuation of the manuscript' (125), including lines drawn by the scribe, producing an arrangement which is unlike Robbins's. The poems are indebted to Lydgate's *Temple of Glas* [*851*], to which Boffey compares them, to determine the purposes and extent of the borrowing. Different effect of the poems are revealed in this light, but not seen in 'the tidied, independent poems which might catch the eye of the casual browser through Robbins's anthology' (130). In context, with other extracts from poems of Lydgate, including some that echo works of Chaucer, 'open allusiveness, to texts both in the manuscript and outside it, seems entirely at home,' and perhaps implies a process 'by which one poem answers, anticipates, or spawns another' (131). Marginal annotations of family names and mottoes around *2188* seem to offer ways to identify readership and provenance, but such speculation is unreliable. It is difficult to determine the status and purpose of poems that are extracts. Some parts of longer works, such as sermon lyrics and isolable carols in plays, 'were expressly designed to be extracted' (135–6). Particular extracts from *Troilus and Criseyde* [*3327*] survive 'as discrete "lyrics"' (137) in other situations. Separation and context may modify meaning. The study of context and relations reveals opportunities, with 'disquieting and yet also exhilarating' possibilities 'to modify if not completely undermine prevailing interpretations' (138).

99, 147, 729.5, 848.5, 851, 1168, 1353, 1418.5, 1422.1, 1470.5, 1926.5, 2161, 2188, 2219, 2229, 2388.5, 2577.5, 2820, 3327, 3327, 3503, 3535, 3651, 3911.5, 4019.

948 ———, **and Carol M. Meale**. 'Selecting the Text: Rawlinson C. 86 and Some Other Books for London Readers.' *Regionalism in Late Medieval Manuscripts and Texts: Essays Celebrating the Publication of* A Linguistic Atlas of Late Medieval English. Ed. Felicity Riddy. York Manuscripts Conferences: Proceedings Series. University of York, Centre for Medieval Studies. Gen. ed. A.J. Minnis. Cambridge: Brewer, 1991. 143–69.

A detailed study of Rawlinson MS C.86 and some related manuscripts, their contents and owners. The authors list the contents of Rawlinson C.86 and describe its four sections, with comment on materials, scribal methods and hands, and relations of the works copied. They consider the gatherings and their ordering, suggesting that some were left for a long time before binding. The range of contents implies a commonplace book, where miscellaneous scraps of information 'take the form of random jottings,' but the formal, professional copying suggests a planned work, and short pieces that accompany the major works seem to be 'pragmatic filling of space during the process of copying' (149). They compare this manuscript and others with similar contents, and note the resemblance of Egerton 1995, apparently a professional production, to commonplace books such as those of Richard Hill and John Colyns. Associations of Rawlinson C.86 connect it with 'London at an early stage of its existence' (156); these links include signatures and inscriptions, and references to particular places. Associations of the Warner family and their service of Elizabeth Woodville and Elizabeth of York may explain a lyric to 'Quene Elyzabeth,' copied in the hand of the scribe who copied a Latin elegy on Edward IV. Comparison with similar works in Richard Hill's commonplace book can establish 'a sense of the intermingling civic and social circles in which court functionaries and members of merchant families moved together.' Other works in Rawlinson C.86 typify 'the tastes of middle-class, usually mercantile, readers' (160); the booklets are thematically linked, and generally appeal to a metropolitan audience. Booklet IV stresses civic pageantry and royal genealogy, to evoke 'past glories, and hopes for future national success' (163). 'The Expedition of Henry V' ['God that all this world gan make,' *969*], included there, appears in other sources that suggest its milieu, and the 'political and historical nature of the material . . . demonstrates its London affiliations particularly clearly' (164). Booklet II implies links with John Shirley and 'London scribes who had access to his exemplars' (165). Booklets II–IV were probably copied 'when printed versions of vernacular texts were readily-available,' and display 'the main subject areas on which early English printers concentrated' (167). After summarizing the history of compilation and connections between works in the booklets, the authors conclude that '[t]he pronounced conceptual and physical differences between the various sections of this manuscript reflect something of the range of predominantly vernacular sources available in this period to metropolitan readers and compilers' (169).

71, 100, 186, 401, 404, 444, 658, 675.5, 700, 824, 969, 977, 1447, 1460, 1511, 1636.8, 1841, 1907, 1916, 2179, 2233, 2464, 2584, 2625, 2719, 2737, 3113, 3203, 3431, 3503, 3531, 3612, 3651, 3798, 3799, 3847, 4019, 4020, 4082, 4090, 4137.

949 Camargo, Martin. *The Middle English Verse Love Epistle.* Studien zur englischen Philologie. Neue Folge 28. Ed. Lothar Fietz, et al. Tübingen: Niemeyer, 1991.

The ordered, consistent style of collections of model letters demonstrates a lack of consciousness of genre and the influence of the *ars dictaminis*. In contrast to more private works, the collections may have been 'no more than elegant compliments or pleasant opportunities to practice classical versifying' (2). Camargo examines the letters' structure, to show that all are 'documents that *address* the recipient directly, *speaking for* the writer who cannot be physically present' (13). He explains the form and function of love letters and the genre's defining tensions. It is closely related to the complaint, and it may be hard to distinguish secular letters of love from works of praise for the Virgin Mary. The ME verse epistle shares the difficulties of classification of the ME lyric, which is resistant, 'especially by comparison with the Provençal or even the Old French lyric' (15). Among precursors of the ME verse love epistle, Camargo considers the Provençal *salutz* and AN *saluts d'amour*; he also refers to other works, including *Ancrene Wisse*, and the Harley lyrics 'The Way of Woman's Love' [*1921*] and 'The Way of Christ's Love' [*1922*]. The pair *'De amico ad amicam'* [*16*] and

'Responcio' [19] is rare in being a macaronic letter and response 'preserved in more than one manuscript' (45). Camargo traces Ovid's effect on Chaucer and the latter's on other poets, noting that Chaucer's shorter love poems recall the complaint rather than the epistle. He compares the 'Litera Troili' and 'Litera Criseydis' in *Troilus and Criseyde [3327]* with passages of Boccaccio's *Filostrato*, to display Chaucer's modifications of character and form. The historical study of love epistles has the problems of the study of ME lyrics. The epistles are generally anonymous, and rarely found in large numbers, although some survive in commonplace books, such as the Findern Anthology, 'compiled by many hands over periods as long as a century.' Sixteenth-century collections, such as the Devonshire, and Bannatyne MSS, preserve poems of 'a century or more prior to the compilation' (87), and some works in Harley 682 and Fairfax 16 'can be dated with certainty to the period before 1450' (87). The latter manuscripts are connected with Charles d'Orléans and perhaps with his English friend, William de la Pole, Duke of Suffolk; they show the influence of contemporary French literature. Camargo distinguishes fixed forms including *salut d'amour,* ballade, and complaint, and finds the love letter and legalistic love document most popular among English secular epistles. His examination of epistles in Harley 682 and Fairfax 16 reveals that 'the formal conventions of the genre are the main subject matter' (121); the earliest Fairfax letters closely resemble the 'Litera Troili.' Gower, Lydgate, Hoccleve, and Humfrey Newton are among few known poets, and a sequence in the Devonshire MS is perhaps 'verse correspondence of Lord Thomas Howard and Lady Margaret Douglas, composed during their imprisonment for their "impolitic" marriage' (182). The genre was most popular in England in the early sixteenth century, but less so by *c.*1540. Camargo places the verse epistle as lover's gift in the social context of the game of love. He explores the intertextuality in the use of stanzas from such works as *Troilus and Criseyde* and Hawes's *The Pastime of Pleasure [4004]*. Parody, to ridicule or adapt to religious use, shows consciousness of the genre and conventions of style and theme, although in '"external form" – stanza, meter, and total number of lines – the verse love epistle was always "open"' (146).

16, 19, 231, 303, 366, 481, 556, 724, 729, 735, 737, 751, 752, 754, 763.5, 765.3, 768, 811.5, 833.1, 868, 927, 929, 1017.5, 1121, 1180, 1238, 1241, 1309, 1329, 1344, 1349.5, 1360, 1510, 1768, 1789, 1838, 1921, 1922, 1926.5, 2182, 2184, 2217, 2223, 2230, 2245, 2247, 2263, 2267.5, 2271.6, 2281, 2308.8, 2311, 2318, 2383, 2384.8, 2412.5, 2421, 2437, 2478, 2478.5, 2496, 2497.5, 2510, 2517, 2529, 2532, 2532.5, 2547, 2560.5, 2597, 2821, 2822, 2823, 2824, 3291, 3321, 3327, 3498, 3785, 3785.5, 3804, 3832, 3878, 3917.8, 4004, 4190, 4192, 4199, 4201.6, 4210, 7026, 7051, 7111, 7157, 7183, 7229, 7256, 7299, 7367, 7368, 7373, 7278, 7385, 7392, 7416, 7555, 7556, 7589, 7611.

—— Review by Carol M. Meale, *Archiv* 230 (1990): 164–6. Summarizes the formidable problems of studying medieval lyrics, to show the value of Camargo's 'important contribution to a modern-day understanding of the genre' (164). Meale demonstrates 'the slipperiness of generic definition' experienced in the study and Camargo's sensitivity in perception. The scope of the book's arguments is wide, although its 'rather schematic lay-out . . . can seem a little restrictive . . . and it tends to inhibit the flow of discussion' (165); nevertheless, the system is helpful for reference. Meale finds the book one 'to be highly recommended: it is scholarly, informative, and stimulating' (166).

—— Review by H.L. Spencer, *Review of English Studies* NS 45 (1994): 87–8. Summarizes the argument of the book, relating it to other instances of love epistles. Spencer has some regret that Camargo has emphasized *qualis*? 'at the expense of other questions' to be asked of the texts, but judges the work 'a competent and informative introduction to his chosen subject' (88).

950 Davenport, W.A. 'Bird Poems from *The Parliament of Fowls* to *Philip Sparrow*.' *Chaucer and Fifteenth-Century Poetry*. Ed. Julia Boffey and Janet Cowen. King's

College London Medieval Studies 5. Gen. ed. Janet Bately. London: King's College London Centre for Late Antique and Medieval Studies, 1991. 66–83.

An account of bird imagery, chiefly as it is found in the work of known poets. Davenport considers first Chaucer's exploitation of bird lore in the lists and classifications of *The Parliament of Fowles* [*3412*] that display the poem's social themes. Chaucer's influence persists in the employment of birds as characters in other poems, including Clanvowe's 'The Book of Cupid/The Cuckoo and the Nightingale' [*3361*] and James I's *The Kingis Quair* [*1215*]. The nightingale has various roles as love's messenger; an attacker or defender of women; and, through the story of Philomena, 'as sacrificial victim and hence as a figure of the bleeding Christ' (70). Birds are teachers in 'The Bird with Four Feathers' ['By a forest syde walkyng as I went,' *561*], 'Revertere' ['In a noon tijd of a somers day,' *1454*], Lydgate's 'The Churl and the Bird' [*2784*], *The House of Fame* [*991*], Henryson's 'The Preaching of the Swallow' [*3703*], and Holland's 'The Buke of the Howlat' [*1554*], among others. Dunbar and Skelton display 'the rich resource' (78) of bird-lore and bird poems, particularly in 'The Thrissil and the Rois' [*3990.5*], 'Speke Parott' [*2263.5*], and 'Phyllyp Sparowe' [*2756.5*]. The birds can be 'mirrors of human activity'; 'their natural qualities of colour, grace and sweet sound' appeal to the poets' imagination, making their poems 'sensitive and truthful about feelings and ideas,' and sometimes 'sophisticated and funny' (82).

417.5, 561, 913, 931, 991, 1215, 1384, 1388, 1452, 1454, 1498, 1503.5, 1554, 1556, 2263.5, 2375, 2756.5, 2784, 2820.5, 3137, 3327, 3361, 3412, 3448, 3703, 3990.5, 4019.

951 Easting, Robert. 'Double-Meaning in *Atte ston castinges*.' *Notes and Queries* 236 (1991): 160.

Explains innuendoes of the poem 'Atte wrastlynge mi lemman i ches' [*445*] in 'the phallic ambiguities of *fel* . . . and *stonde*'; in the 'happy equation of sexual intercourse and a wrestling bout'; and particularly in the notion that '*ston* can mean "testicle."' Thus it conveys the disappointed reaction of a girl who gave 'her big-shot hero at least two tries.'

445.

952 Green, Richard Firth. 'Jack Philipot, John of Gaunt, and a Poem of 1380.' *Speculum* 66 (1991): 330–41.

Questions the date of 1388 suggested by Wright, **2**, for the poem 'On the Times' ['Syng I wold butt alas *decedunt prospera grata*,' *3113*]. Green proposes 1380, and finds 'the historical importance of its satire on contemporary abuses . . . considerably increased once we accept that it was composed on the eve of the Peasants' Revolt' (330–1). Wright took extravagant court fashion to indicate the reign of Richard II, which Green accepts, although some details and the king's youth suggest the earlier date. He does not agree with Wright that 'the retreat of "Jacke" accompanied with "Jacke Noble," to "regna romata," in all probability refers to the flight of the king's favorite Robert de Vere duke of Dublin, with Michael de la Pole earl of Suffolk, to the continent' (331). Green prints lines that refer to *iak* and *Iak*, and rejects identification of Robert de Vere as 'Iak' and Michael de la Pole as 'Ion,' in line 109 ['Goode Iak, wher is [thi] Ion']. The *iak* of lines 105–8 may play on senses of a quilted tunic and a coin; thus allusions to 'those forced to wear on their backs the *jakkes* they would rather have in their purses' hint at 'the burden of wartime taxation' (334). In his investigation of references to war that include activities on land and sea, Green examines campaigns of John of Gaunt and Thomas of Woodstock. As the 'Goode Iak' he proposes 'a prominent London citizen and former mayor called John Philipot who made a conspicuous contribution to the war effort,' by hiring ships and paying for armour which soldiers pawned to buy their food. Thus Philipot provided 'jacks that paid for the jacks on the backs of Woodstock's ill-fed soldiers' (336). John of Gaunt could plausibly be 'Ion,' but the implication that he was on good terms with Philipot is 'at odds with standard accounts of the period' which tend to show Philipot 'as leader of an anti-Lancastrian faction.' (337). Green demonstrates that, although 'Walshingham portrays Gaunt as a war profiteer and Philipot as a disinterested philanthropist, the account books do not entirely bear him out' (338); Philipot could have expected Gaunt to reward him. Relying on details of Gaunt's northern campaigns, Green places the poem in autumn 1380. He compares a similar macaronic work, 'Tax has tenet us alle' [*3260*], and finds it 'tempting to see these two pieces as the work of a single author . . . writing on the eve and on the morrow of the Peasants' Revolt' (341).

892, 3113, 3260.

953 Hinton, Rebecca. 'Dialogue between Our Lady and Jesus on the Cross.' *Explicator* 50.1 (1991): 5–7.

A note on implications of the word *reu*, which is found in line 13 of 'Stond wel moder ounder rode' [*3211*] only in the version of Royal MS 12 E.i. Other sources, Digby 86, Harley 2253, and Cambridge 111, have *rew* or *rewe*. In each, line 13 can be interpreted as 'Mother have pity on your child!' In the Royal 12 E.i version, *reu* in line 43 could bear 'a twofold interpretation,' considered 'in the light of its spelling, the conjugative pattern of Middle English verbs, and a passage from Saint Jerome that may have influenced the particular author.' Here it could be 'the imperative of *reuen*, meaning "to take or deprive." ' (5). Mary's grief prevents her from comprehending Christ's command to be 'blithe,' and she asks what she should do. He tells her 'to have compassion (reu) on her universal children, particularly other woman,' linking 'her present emotional pain with the pain that other women experience in childbirth.' He calls her 'clene mayden *man*,' where the last word is 'an impersonal pronoun denoting either a man or a woman.' This may suggest 'that Mary has now forgone (in a psychological sense) her womanhood,' a reading supported by Jerome's contention that a woman who serves Christ will be called a man. *Claene* may refer to lack of encumbrance as well as purity. Thus Mary, having severed her maternal bond, is 'free, or unencumbered, to undertake her new spiritual role: the motherhood of all people on earth' (7).

3211.

954 Lambdin, R.T. 'The Thrush and the Nightingale.' *Explicator* 50.1 (1991): 2–5.

Considers the surprising end to the debate of 'The Thrush and the Nightingale' ['Somer is comen wiþ loue to toune,' *3222*], in the 'hypothetical resolution to the problem of compromise between adherents of the Pauline Doctrine and those of the cult of the Virgin.' The thrush offers specific examples for the case 'that women are false, lustful, and reponsible for the fall of man.' In contrast the nightingale offers 'emotional, rather unsubstantiated "proofs," ' until the last speech, which cites 'the virtue of the Virgin Mary' and 'turns the debate in her favor.' The thrush's arguments express 'traditional thinking of medieval England' (2), following 'the teachings of the Church.' The thrush seems to shift position by admitting that even 'five of every hundred women are pure' (3), perhaps 'foreshadowing that startling reversal that immediately follows,' in the nightingale's only 'tangible proof . . . that women are good.' The shift could indicate failure to resolve confusion from 'the Pauline doctrine that woman are evil and its contradiction, that Mary, Mother of Jesus, is holy' (4). Thus the poem accomplishes 'a difficult task by providing a clear illustration of an abstraction firmly dependent on faith; the paradox of the degradation of women and the glorification of Mary is resolved without further ado' (4–5).

3222.

955 Louis, Cameron. 'A Yorkist Genealogical Chronicle in Middle English Verse.' *Anglia* 109 (1991): 1–20. [Edition.]

An edition of a Yorkist genealogical chronicle 'found in the papers of the Earl of Aylesford at Packington Hall, West Midlands' (2). Louis describes the manuscript, a roll, which preserves two chronicles, a prose paragraph of kings of England, and a list of mayors of Coventry. He edits the first chronicle, 'Thys londe was furste Be goddys ordynaunce/Inhabyt withe Brytons full longe Agone' [*7528*]. The other, 'At Westm. Wyllyam j-crovnyd was' [*444*], is 'interspersed among the branches of a genealogical tree' that 'serves as a kind of "gloss" to make it prove the legitimacy of Edward IV's ascent to the throne,' although it is 'not written with a Yorkist slant,' and is 'quite complimentary to the Lancastian kings' (3). [See Mooney, **924**.] Annotations (which express 'a Yorkist point of view') made on the list of mayors commemorate events in the Wars of the Roses, when allegiances in Coventry changed. Except in the prose paragraph, the manuscript's contents suggest that 'the compiler's scholarly interests . . . seem to have been secondary to his political preoccupations' (4). The first chronicle is intended to justify Edward IV's succession, which, with the slant of other entries, hints that it was compiled in his reign, probably in Coventry, as propaganda and to show loyalty, perhaps with some 'official or public function' (5). Louis prints the poem, describes its content and purpose in the selection of events, and supplies notes (6–20).

444, 882, 3431, 3632, 7528.

956 ———. 'Two Middle English Doomsday Poems.' *Neuphilologische Mitteilungen* 92 (1991): 43–6. [Edition.]

Presents two poems, not previously printed, 'that deal with the subject of Doomsday alone' (43), without mentioning signs of the Last Judgement. The first, 'When slepe had slipt out of my heade' [*4015*], 'written on a fly-leaf of St. John's College Cambridge ms. 31 (B9), which otherwise contains saints' lives in French, along with *Somme le roi*,' is a 'dream vision,' with visions 'derived from various parts of Apocalypsis' (43). The second, 'When þe day of dome sall be/It is in gods pryuyte' [*4030*], written 'in the main body of British Library Additional ms. 37049, a collection of religious poems and prose pieces from the first half of the fifteenth century,' complements 'a preceding prose description of the Last Judgement,' in 'a vividly drawn picture of the purging of the universe by fire' (44).

3967, 4015, 4030.

957 Lynch, Andrew. '"Now, fye on youre wepynge!": Tears in Medieval Romance.' *Parergon* NS 9 (1991): 43–62.

Questions the application of current perceptions of weeping as 'a sign of weakness, and as a feminised action,' by demonstrating that in some medieval contexts it was encouraged, 'as a purposive form of behaviour' (43). Lynch cites examples from *Ancrene Wisse*, and notes references in ME religious lyrics, where weeping is recommended to express sorrow and repentance, 'as part of the soul's cure' (48). Tears may be related to the sacramental liquids, water and wine, and to the blood shed by Christ and martyrs; indeed 'tears for Christ crucified are clearly a kind of surrogate martyrdom' (50). Weeping was recommended to add force to prayer. The 'highest endorsement' came from the effect of Christ's tears, shed 'before the raising of Lazarus' (51).

1132, 2007, 2250, 3211, 3691, 3874, 3961, 3964.

958 McNamer, Sarah. 'Female Authors, Provincial Setting: The Re-Versing of Courtly Love in the Findern Manuscript.' *Viator* 22 (1991): 279–309. [Edition.]

Anonymous love lyrics of Cambridge University Library MS Ff.1.6, the Findern MS, or Findern Anthology, have been seen as the work of male authors, writing in the playful genres of courtly love; many have been awarded titles such as 'To His Mistress.' McNamer examines their context, considering the 'amateur character' of the manuscript, its 'provincial provenance, and the appearance of several women's names in it' (280). These are features that caused Robbins, **54**, to see the poems as works enjoyed by women and copied by them during visits to Findern. McNamer describes the manuscript and people connected with it, and reads the lyrics as works composed by women, with an autobiographical element. [Cf. Hanson-Smith, **712**.] The presence of items such as household accounts implies that the lyrics were not valued. It suggests that the manuscript ceased to be 'a collection of secular works to be treasured and added to as a kind of public entertainment' to become rather 'a place for insignificant personal jottings which were not necessarily meant to be shared.' Emendations, apparently 'motivated by poetic concerns' (283), confirm that the manuscript is a holograph, used when it was sufficiently less valuable and private enough 'to encourage experimentation' (284). The pronouns used and possibilities for correspondence with the lives of women who might have written in the manuscript suggest a woman's point of view. The lyrics of the pain of separation need not have been written by men as part of the game of courtly love, since they could express the feelings of provincial women parted from their husbands. Thus the use of 'playful terms' of courtly tradition might be 'in the service of sincere self-expression' (289). In support, McNamer cites poems of the *trobaritz* and Margery Brews's letter ['And yf ye commande me to kepe me true wherever I go,' *303*] to 'her future husband John Paston III' (288). When disease is mentioned it seems more likely to be physical illness than 'lovesickness.' In lyrics of separation the speaker is likely to blame Fortune rather than the absent lover, and not to use the courtly style of blaming a cruel mistress. McNamer compares poems of Charles d'Orléans and William de la Pole, Duke of Suffolk. She relates the theme of imprisonment in those male-voiced poems to that of the confinement of the Findern women, and notes in some Findern lyrics 'psychological depth and movement – rare qualities of the courtly lyric before Wyatt' (295). Pledges of loyalty seem to be part of the courtly tradition, but they echo the bride's marriage vows of service and obedience, hinting that they are not 'playful metaphors,' but 'statements of literal truth' (298). Thus context and manuscript evidence suggest that the lyrics were indeed 'composed by the women living at or near the Findern estate.' McNamer comments on implications for ideas of female authorship, previously discounted, and on ideas of the lyric. She notes that the term was 'not used in the Middle Ages,' that it has associations from other periods, and is percieved as not necessarily 'an autobiographical genre' (299). She discerns in the Findern lyrics 'the authentic woman's lament,' distinguished from 'popular' examples that seem 'laden with clerkly and courtly irony.' The Findern works offer 'a curious reversal of the standard definition of parody' in their appropriation of 'an essentially playful idiom' to invest it with 'seriousness and meaning' (300). In an appendix (302–9), McNamer prints 14 lyrics she believes to be the work of women. She supplies a title for each, and notes the titles provided in other sources.

139, 303, 383, 657, 734, 2269, 2279, 2640, 3125, 3193.5, 3613, 3849, 3878, 3917, 4059, 4241.5, 4272.5.

959 Morgan, Gwendolyn. 'Erthe Toc of Erthe.' *Explicator* 49.4 (1991): 199–200.

Erthe in 'Erthe upon Erthe' [*3939*] has been interpreted as man, Eve, and Mary. Morgan proposes that certain instances refer to 'Christ, the human (earthly) form of God,' so eliminating a grammatical problem and indicating a consistency otherwise unnoticed. If one reads the first *erthe* in the poem as Christ, *toc* (in 'Erthe toc of erthe erthe wyth woh') is a suitable simple preterite. Thus 'God, the Creator of both *erthes*, takes up human form as Christ,' with the woe of 'the sins of man . . . or a foreshadowing of the

Crucifixion.' Then the second line ('Erth other erthe to the erthe droh') means 'earth (man) brings to death an "other" earth, the *erthe* that is different and set apart from himself.' The third line ('Erthe leyde erthe in erthene throh') then means that 'man laid this "other earth" in the grave.' The fourth line ('Tho hevede erthe of erthe erthe ynoh'), in either of two interpretations, suggests that 'Christ's passion is sufficient for the salvation of man' (199). Thus the poet alludes to Adam's creation and humanity's flesh and soul. The poem's movement shows God's descent to, burial in, and rising from the earth; it draws on typology and allegory, and emphasizes salvation.

3939.

960 Rubin, Miri. *Corpus Christi: The Eucharist in Late Medieval Culture.* Cambridge: Cambridge UP, 1991.

Studies the central place of the eucharist in the culture of the late Middle Ages in Europe. Rubin traces the growth of its importance; the significance of symbolism and doctrine; teaching and reception of the sacrament; establishment of the feast of Corpus Christi and associated sermons, ceremonies, fraternities, and drama; and variations in interpretation. She draws on Latin and vernacular works, including 'The Lay Folk's Mass Book' [*3507*], that are intended to explain and interpret the eucharist, and to allow the congregation's participation. 'Beyond design: teaching and reception of the eucharist' (83–163) includes references to works intended to instruct the clergy (83–98) and the laity (98–108); these explain doctrine, preparation, and procedures. Various works illuminate understanding of eucharistic symbols. Prayers for the congregation mark moments such as the elevation and communion, to evoke the most fitting frame of mind.

10, 298, 406, 448, 457, 498, 778, 779, 961, 1034, 1071, 1132, 1249, 1323, 1372, 1389, 1459, 1627, 1640, 1703, 1718, 1729, 1935, 1941, 1986, 2076, 2413, 2663, 2832, 3217, 3434, 3443, 3507, 3583, 3606, 3834, 3882, 3883, 3884, 3920, 4019, 4052, 4154, 4245, 4246, 4249, 4250.

961 Sichert, Margit. *Die mittelenglische Pastourelle.* Studien zur englische Philologie. Neue Folge 27. Ed. Lothar Fietz, et al. Tübingen: Niemeyer, 1991.

Investigates the existence of 'a Middle English equivalent to the French popular genre of the *pastourelle*' (205) through exploration of the French genre, preceding an analysis of relevant ME poems. Sichert considers the pastourelle in the socio-psychological and cultural settings of southern and northern France, as 'a "genre of relief," for the French aristocracy, and later for the clergy and the burgesses, from social, moral and religious rules which were too strict to be persistently followed.' It is thus 'an anti-genre opposed to the courtly love lyric.' The ME poems differ from the French works in their 'didactic and moralistic stance.' She presents a detailed examination, with tables to summarize information, and relates her findings to ME poems often considered pastourelles, 'De Clerico et Puella' [*2236*], 'In a fryht as y con fere fremede' [*1449*], 'As I stod on a day me self under a tre' [*371*], and 'Nou springes the sprai' [*360*], and to related ballads, 'The Knight and the Shepherd's Daughter,' 'Into a Sweet May Morning,' 'The Crow and the Pie,' and 'The Over Courteous Knight.' Sichert deems the ME poems 'examples of an anti-genre opposed to the French genre,' and concludes that the pastourelle 'never existed in England' (206).

360, 371, 1449, 2236.

962 Stanbury, Sarah. 'The Virgin's Gaze: Spectacle and Transgression in Middle English Lyrics of the Passion.' *PMLA* 106 (1991): 1083–93.

Explores aspects of the female gaze, especially that of the Virgin in Passion lyrics. Stanbury's first examples of gazing women include Beatrice and Lucrece, who support ideas of the gaze as 'cupidinous, seductive, aggressive, thoroughly transgressive,' and 'most invitingly marked by its absence,' characteristics demonstrated in Bernard of Clairvaux's use of Eve and Dinah to illustrate 'ocular sins.' It is conventional in horror films to punish 'women who are visually assertive' (1084). In ME literature, Marian laments and Passion lyrics offer 'the most systematic portrayal of a woman's gaze' (1085), in the Virgin's gazing on Christ's dead or dying body. Stanbury discloses implications of this gaze, conventionally forbidden, yet permitted because 'maternal and compassionate, entitled by a mother's right,' and because 'a nearly dead body is hardly an erotic spectacle.' The lyrics offer a drama of 'sanctified transgression' (1086), in the paradoxical relationships of the Holy Family and Christian readers, some of whom plead to receive the Virgin's gaze. Effects of the 'assertive command of Christ's body' and the 'deferral in which her own looking turns her into a spectacle' are dramatized in 'Stond wel moder ounder rode' [*3211*]. In her analysis of this poem Stanbury reveals Christ's recognition of the power of the 'gaze of maternal pity,' which compels him to explain 'the complicitous cycle of suffering.' Mary's gaze 'entitles her to a subtle control' (1088) despite grief, and 'reestablishes the primal order of mother and infant,' although it shows 'Christ's ambivalence toward maternal power.' The gaze enables 'a transfer of pain from the body on the cross to the woman below, and even to all women' (1089). In lyrics, Christ or the Virgin may speak to a traveller who observes the Crucifixion. The command to the poet to look at the Virgin's countenance stresses 'her own role as spectacle rather than as spectator' so that the lines of sight in the poem are those of 'the passerby, the sinful man of reason' (1090). The Virgin's gaze transgresses tradition; it 'touches Christ's body, coercing us to confront the spectacle of her act of looking' (1091).

100, 207, 404, 420, 776, 1048, 1073, 1119, 1318, 1365, 1459, 1761, 1836, 2036, 2619, 3211, 3245, 3412, 3691, 3692, 3700, 3904, 4189.

963 Stemmler, Theo. 'Miscellany or Anthology? The Structure of Medieval Manuscripts: MS. Harley 2253, for Example.' *Zeitschrift für Anglistik und Americanistik* 39 (1991): 231–7.

Considers Harley MS 2253, its compilation, and comments of Pearsall, **672**, and Revard, **787**. Stemmler finds the manuscript 'neither a miscellany – a somewhat arbitrary, casual collection of texts – nor a well-wrought book carefully made up of mutually corresponding parts,' but rather 'an anthology, a careful collection of texts selected as representative specimens of various genres' (232). Using a table (232), Stemmler demonstrates possible parameters for ordering the texts, according to authors, language, form, genre, content, and association. He shows that the Harley scribe used all of these except authors. The scribe's approach is that of a compiler rather than an editor, and his 'over-riding principle . . . is the distinction between verse and prose' (233). Stemmler describes groups of texts according to their relations; he notes that some texts seem to be together by coincidence, from resemblances in the appearance of words rather than sense. The poems may be linked by content, tone, or rhyme. Examinations reveal correspondences in subject; complementary pairs of poems; poems so closely related in metre and style that they appear to be the work of one poet; and groups united in genre and content. Stemmler attributes the increasing disparateness towards the end of the first part of the manuscript (the first 79 items), to 'the haphazard order in which they became disposable to the compiler.' Although he finds 'no traces of a sustained organizing principle,' Stemmler considers the manuscript 'an anthology rather than a miscellany' (236), in which many poems are arranged according to associative grouping. He supplies a table to illustrate the methods used by the compiler (237).

105, 166, 185, 205, 359, 694.5, 968, 1104, 1115, 1196, 1216, 1320.5, 1365, 1395, 1407, 1449, 1461, 1504, 1678, 1705, 1747, 1861, 1889, 1894, 1921, 1922, 1974, 2039, 2078, 2207, 2236, 2287, 2359, 2604, 2649, 3155, 3211, 3236, 3310, 3939, 3963, 3989, 4037, 4177, 4194.

964 Taylor, Andrew. 'The Myth of the Minstrel Manuscript.' *Speculum* 66 (1991): 43–73.

Questions 'the codicological category "minstrel text"' (43), and scrutinizes manuscripts 'that have been explicitly linked to English minstrels and to a few obvious French analogues' (43–4). Taylor examines 'Manuscripts Containing *Chansons de Geste*' (44–53); 'Manuscripts Containing Middle English Romances' (53–60); 'Anthologies of Lyrics' (60–5); 'Manuscripts Signed by Minstrels' (65–7); 'Rolls' (67–70); and 'Scraps and Fragments' (70–2). Three anthologies, small 'plain paper volumes without any extensive decoration' (60), with religious and secular lyrics, have been called minstrel texts by Wright [*Songs and Carols*] and in *RobbinsS*, **55**. The manuscripts are BL Sloane 2593; Bodleian Library, Eng. Poet.e.1; and St John's College, Cambridge S.54. Taylor examines three Sloane lyrics, called by Robbins 'An Unwilling Minstrel' ['If I synge ʒe wyl me lakke,' *1417*], 'The Minstrel and his Wares' ['We bern abowtyn non cattes skynnes,' *3864*], and 'A Minstrel's Begging Song' ['*Omnes gentes plaudite*/I saw myny bryddis setyn on a tre,' *2675*]. He argues against an association with minstrels, citing Greene on *1417* [**460**], and *2675* [**86**]. The other anthologies seem not to have belonged to minstrels. Arguments from appearance of the documents ignore 'a substantial nonminstrel readership of moderate means' (65) who may have travelled with their books; Taylor favours clerical connections. Bodleian Library Douce 302, and Cambridge University Library, Add. 5943 have been signed by minstrels, but their appearance does not suggest minstrel ownership. Although rolls seem better suited than other forms to being carried by minstrels, Taylor thinks only BL Add. 23986 'could have begun life as the property of a minstrel herald' (69). The most likely minstrel text is 'a single sheet . . . now bound as the first folio of Oxford, Bodleian Library, MS Rawlinson D 913' (71), with English lyrics and an AN lyric and call to dinner. The scribe's hand hints that although he 'might have been a minstrel . . . he might well have been a bureaucrat at some point as well' (72). Difficulties in making 'the distinction, always tenuous and hypothetical, between minstrel manuscript or commercial text' mean that 'direct access to medieval oral narrative must be postponed' (73).

668, 1008, 1417, 1953, 2037.5, 2675, 2716, 3864.

965 Thompson, John. 'Textual Instability and the Late Medieval Reputation of Some Middle English Religious Literature.' *Text* 5 (1991): 175–94.

Probes the effects of transcription and transmission on texts, and the interpretive difficulties of editors who must 'construct critical texts of items that survive in unstable forms in extant copies' (175) because copyists were editors as well as scribes. Chaucer's 'An ABC' [*239*] differs from others in its acceptance as a stable text of a passage of De Guileville's *Le Pèlerinage de la vie humaine*; it was inserted in two translations of the French work – an anonymous prose version, and a verse work in the style of Lydgate. Extant versions of the latter have spaces for 'An ABC,' but lack the poem; it is anticipated in an encomium in the text and a note in John Stow's manuscript, which has another Marian lyric, 'O blyssed mayde fflour off alle goodnesse' [*2395*]. Thompson demonstrates that copyists of such collections as the Vernon and Simeon MSS were able to consult several copies of the works. He pays particular attention to the *Cursor Mundi* [*2153*], noting the appearance of the 'Discourse between Christ and Man' ['Ihesu was of Mary borne,' *1786*], which is seen elsewhere as an independent work. This is inserted in three northern manuscripts of *2153* and is written in a deictic style, standing 'in dramatic contrast to the formal and restrained Passion narrative that precedes it' (185). Some scribes had access to a wide range of material, and the composition of miscellanies was influenced by availability of texts and by the tastes of readers. For such reasons, 'questions of textual integrity, or of "authorial responsibility" and "scribal role" (as the medieval scholastic writer or the modern reader might want to understand them) often tended to get confused with other, parallel, production issues' (187).

239, 1786, 2153, 2395.

966 Whaley, Diana. '*Nowelis Flood* and Other Nowels.' *Language Usage and Description: Studies Presented to N.E. Osselton on the Occasion of His Retirement.* Ed. Ingrid Tieken-Boon von Ostade and John Frankis. Amsterdam: Rodopi, 1991. 5–16.

Explores implications of *Nowelis flood*, the term used by John the carpenter in the *Miller's Tale* [*4019*], and distinguished from *Noes flood*, generally used by Nicholas. In this context *Nowel* is 'Chaucer's joke, deliberate and rather unusual,' to evoke associations of a personal name and the cries repeated in carols of the Nativity and at other joyful occasions. Whaley traces the word's etymology, and finds 'two principal uses in late ME, both of which correspond with French uses . . . as a cry of celebration . . . and . . . a word for the feast of Christmas or the Nativity' (7). She cites numerous occurrences in carols, where it is 'very frequently . . . all or part of the burden' (8). The French word fits easily in carols in English or Latin, to add 'a resounding chime to festive songs' or to be fragmented 'in playful jubilation.' It is even used in the burden of a Passion lyric, 'Mary moder cum & see/þi sone is nayled on a tre' [*2111*], 'to transform a sacred poem into a carol' (9). It offers metrical and rhyming possibilities and can be used in word-play. Through a connection with *nouvelles*, it also carries the meaning of 'news,' and it may also be 'a call for attention.' In 'þis world is falce I dare wyll say ' [*3654*], a poem of 'the vanity of earthly life,' the effect is 'inept or strikingly ironic' (10), since the word more often suggests a joyful occasion. Secular examples include poems for the birth of a prince or celebration of a victory. It was apparently used only rarely as a personal name, and such use is assumed to be connected with Christmas. Particular associations with the *Miller's Tale* include the possibility that the tale was to be told in the Christmas season, and the implication of John's resemblance to Joseph 'not only in his occupation but also in his advanced age and his fear of being cuckolded by his young wife,' the theme of several carols on the 'trouble of Joseph' (13). The word recalls the joyful cry and the season, 'while at the same time, by delicate implication, putting its immorality in a proper religious perspective' (14).

20, 527, 651, 667, 681, 753, 889, 1004, 1043, 1322, 1471, 1473, 1744, 1802, 1984.5, 2111, 2113, 2312, 2343, 2384, 2733, 2735, 3144, 3315, 3652, 3654, 3736, 3736, 3742, 3877, 4019.

967 Wimsatt, James I. 'Chaucer and Deschamps' "Natural Music." ' *The Union of Words and Music in Medieval Poetry.* Ed. Rebecca A. Baltzer, Thomas Cable, and James I. Wimsatt. Austin, TX: U of Texas P, 1991.

In his discussion of the 'natural music' of verse, so classified by Eustache Deschamps, in his *Art de Dictier*, Wimsatt compares Guillame de Machaut's ballade 'Tout ensement com le monde enlumine' with 'The Fair Maid of Ribblesdale' [*2207*] and Chaucer's 'To Rosemounde' [*2031*]. 'Tout ensement' and *2207* deal mainly with 'description and praise of the speaker's ladylove' (141), but 'in versification and content they contrast sharply' (142). Wimsatt cites differences in versification, diction, and imagery. For instance, although both resemble the sun, 'on the one hand there is the refined lady of the French court whose excellence illuminates the world, and on the other a jolly English girl whose complexion shines like the sun' (143). 'The associations of "To Rosemounde" clearly are with the French' (144), and the 'only argument with any force for connecting "To Rosemounde" with poems like the "Maid of Ribblesdale" is the matter of stress' (145).

2031, 2207.

968 Breeze, Andrew. 'New Texts of Middle English Verse 3513.' *Medium Ævum* 61 (1992): 284–7. [Edition.]

Adds seven new sources of 'They thou the vulf hore hod to preste' [*3513*]. This poem warns against a wolf which, 'though hooded as a priest and set to learn psalms, remained a wolf in his habits.' Breeze prints the three versions noted in *IMEV* and the others, all found as 'an English "inset" in fable 22 of *Liber Parabolarum* written *c.* 1219 by Odo of

Cheriton' (284). There is a parallel in lines found in *Ancrene Wisse* '"euer is þe eie to þe wude leie,/þerinne is þet ich luuie" [*734.5*] – perhaps the refrain of a lost love lyric.' (286). It seems that 'this would help date *Ancrene Wisse*,' but another occurrence suggests that 'the first line at least was as perennial as a proverb' (286). The text is found in Berlin, Staatsbibliothek zu Berlin – Preussischer Kulturbesitz (Haus Unter der Linden) MS Phill. 1904; it has belonged to Battle Abbey, probably in the library of Brecon Priory, and has Welsh material. In the Welsh version of Odo's fable, 'the wolves are monks of the present day' (287); the fable is presented in Welsh and concludes with the ME verse.

734.5, 3513.

969 ———. 'The Instantaneous Harvest and the Harley Lyric *Mayden Moder Milde.*' *Notes and Queries* 237 (1992): 150–2.

Examines the lines 'Of the sprong the ble/*Ly souerein creatour*' in the Harley lyric 'Mayden moder milde/*oeiz cel oreysoun*' [*2039*], particularly considering *ble*. Although the word refers elsewhere to '"colour, face, complexion, appearance"', these meanings do not suit here'; Breeze proposes an allusion to 'the miracle of the Instantaneous Harvest on the Flight into Egypt,' in the reading '"Through you [and] the Sovereign Creator sprang up the Harvest"': a miracle occurring through God's power at the Virgin's intercession.' He recounts the legend, and notes a link to 'an English version of the lyric's first stanza (*IMEV* 2034) used by Michael of Northgate to close *Ayenbite of Inwyt,* itself a translation of *Somme des Vices et des Vertues* by Lorens of Orleans.' A reference in *2039* offers 'precious evidence for the legend in England about 1300' (151). It links the Virgin and Christ, then carried in her arms, to make 'an especially fitting allusion for a poem which, honouring Christ through devotion to the Virgin, seeks her protection for the sake of his love' (151–2). It would be more significant if the poet were imprisoned, pondering 'a miracle by which fugitives escaped capture at the hands of unjust agents of law,' and would render the poem 'a more suble and sombre work than has previously been realized' (152).

2034, 2039.

970 Donaldson, Kara Virginia. 'Alisoun's Language: Body, Text and Glossing in Chaucer's "The Miller's Tale."' *Philological Quarterly* 71 (1992): 139–53.

To explain that 'Alisoun is both the product and object of a male discourse that has maintained power over women by separating women from both their bodies and language' (141), Donaldson considers lyrics of clerical seduction. She notes use of the name *Alisoun* for the Wife of Bath and for the seduced girl of 'As I went on Yole day in oure prosession' [*377*]. Nicholas's physical approach resembles 'that described by the "woman" narrator of the male poet's lyric,' 'Lad Y the daunce a Myssomur Day' [*1849*]. The narrator's 'expression of sexual enjoyment' with the clerk who controls her implies no 'wrongdoing in using force' (143). The gulf between Absolon and the clerks of courtly lyrics adds to the humour of the *Miller's Tale* [*4019*]. Absolon sees himself as that kind of lover, and defines himself 'through his use of courtly language gaining the voice of authority' (144). Alisoun's realistic language and her rebellious body answer him: she 'destroys his ability to control discourse by asserting her own gloss of her body's language' (150).

105, 225, 377, 708, 1849, 2161, 2359, 4019, 4037.

971 Duncan, Thomas G. 'Textual Notes on Two Early Middle English Lyrics.' *Neuphilologische Mitteilungen* 93 (1992): 109–20. [Edition.]

Explains some difficulties of using corrupted texts of lyrics, which may be 'hardly readable as poems.' Following Dobson, **87**, Duncan advocates textual reconstruction to emend 'defects in metre, rhyme and sense,' and cites an example in 'Leuedi sainte marie moder and meide' [*1839*], in which 'a striking anomaly in the order of its final stanzas may have passed unnoticed on account of undue deference to manuscript authority' (109). The penitential work seems complete after the tenth of its eleven stanzas. Duncan proposes that Stanza 11 was originally 8, and an error from use of *drede* as rhyme-word of the last line in the two stanzas caused misplacement. Thinking he had copied stanza 8 instead of 7, the scribe moved on to the next, which was originally stanza 9; realizing his mistake, he added the missing stanza at the end. This may have happened in the copy text or in the unique surviving copy in MS BL Add. 27909. After reordering, the lyric, 'as is usual with poems of contrition and supplication, ends appropriately with an appeal to the Virgin and through her to Christ.' Duncan relates his reconstruction of 'A Wayle Whyt ase Whalles Bon' [*105*] to comments of Gibson [MA diss. 1914], Brook, **42**, Davies, **61**, Stemmler, **444**, and Degginger, **330**. He stresses that *105*, 'typically a song lyric albeit without music . . . is a kind of poem in which metrical regularity is to be expected' (111), and compares other Harley lyrics. Following Gibson, he transfers lines that seem superfluous to Stanza 6 to the end of a defective first stanza, and places Stanza 7 as the second. To emend 'three apparently defective first lines,' Duncan proposes to add words from the last lines of preceding stanzas, to satisfy metre, sense and stanza-linking. He considers that 'omission of the same words in the second of two consecutive lines is just the kind of mistake a medieval copyist was liable to make' (113). Other emendations address apparent metrical irregularities, some of them 'attributable to linguistic variants introduced in the course of scribal transmission.' Any change is 'inevitably conjectural,' but Duncan asserts that 'a plausible emendation, albeit uncertain, which has the merit of rectifying the metre, must be counted a significant improvement in itself' (116). He prints the emended poem, with stanzas in the order proposed by Gibson.

105, 359, 708, 1115, 1216, 1272, 1394, 1407, 1839, 2166, 2207, 4194.

972 Fein, Susanna Greer. 'Form and Continuity in the Alliterative Tradition: Cruciform Design and Double Birth in Two Stanzaic Poems.' *Modern Language Quarterly* 53 (1992): 100–25.

Studies 'a previously unrecognized combined motif in two poems in the thirteen-line alliterative stanza' (100) ('The Dispute between the Blessed Virgin and the Cross' ['Oure ladi freo on Rode treo make hire mone,' *2718*] and 'The Four Leues of the Trewlufe' ['In a mornynge of May when medose schulde sprynge,' *1453*]), to indicate 'focused attention upon Mary and the Cross, symbols of incarnation and resurrection.' This focus causes 'an original development of *planctus Mariae* conventions'; reenactment of 'a metaphoric "birth" at the center, with an actual opening of gates'; and 'chiasmic symmetry of paired antitheses and parallels, as if imitating in poetry the shape of the cross' (101). Fein comments on the slight attention paid to the works, and compares others that are similar in theme and style. The poems' didactic nature fits them for 'the classification "popular piety,"' with 'strange but undeniably arresting conceits of the Cross debating and correcting the Virgin and of a turtledove sermonizing a maiden upon the spiritual meaning of a cross-shaped herb' (104). The poems, 'shaped to become themselves cruciate emblems against demonic powers' (105), emphasize Mary's compassion and the Cross as signs of grace to defend against the devil. Fein scrutinizes their symbolism and patterned structure. She deals first with *2718*, to reveal intertwined themes of incarnation and resurrection, symmetrically arranged in stanzas assigned to the two speakers. Her interpretation of stones, barriers, and gates, in images of birth, relates them to Christ's painless, immaculate birth and the Virgin's pain at the Passion, and also to humanity's cleansing second birth, which makes the Cross '*actually* become a second mother of mankind through Christ's suffering humanity' (111). In a crossing over of symbolism, 'just as the Cross is a mother, so too Mary is a tree' (112). The spirit of *1453* is more gentle, but there are resemblances in its 'related stanza forms, identical overall length of apparent numerological value, a meditative focus upon Mary at the Cross, and a climactic central event with gates opening' (113–14). Fein elucidates the poem's stanzaic and symbolic structure, to show the significance of the lovelorn maiden, mourning under a tree and searching for the truelove plant, who first evokes a 'human soul in fallen separation from God.' Her secular love-longing is considered spiritual and 'the basis for a sermon, delivered by the turtledove, upon the Trinity and Mary, who are rhetorically likened to the four leaves of the herb' (115). Here the imagery of gates depicts the Harrowing of Hell, and offers, 'a parallel, if different, rendition of the theme of second birth' (117), in 'the exit of his [Christ's] "bon chylder"' by means of the Cross' (118). Mary's reversal of the Fall is symbolized in the rejoining of the truelove's leaves. The stanzas of the maid and sermon show 'mirror imaging . . . between the two halves, suggesting a chiasmic reversed symmetry' (121). The poems 'subordinate the lament impulse to a framework of doctrinal instruction' (122); Fein compares them with other shaped and alliterative poems.

583, 1232, 1328.7, 1453, 2320, 2481, 2718, 3211, 3357.

973   Frankis, John. 'St Zita, St Sythe and St Osyth.' *Nottingham Medieval Studies* 36 (1992): 148–50.

In 'Kytt hathe lost hur key' [*1824.8*] a reference to 'Seynt Sythe,' invoked 'in cases of lost property,' whose 'emblem was a key' uses the pronoun 'him.' If there is no error in the poem, this implies 'devotion at a popular level at which there was ignorance of the saint's sex' (148). It may be that '*Sythe* is to be identified with St Osyth' (148). Frankis explores possibilities of variation in the name, suggesting such identification in a poem attributed to Lydgate, 'Heyl hooly Sitha maide of gret vertu' [*1050*], to celebrate St Zita. He finds 'no evidence that St Sithe's Church in London . . . was originally dedicated to St Osyth,' but it 'was a centre of devotion to Zita by the mid-fourteenth century, though it may not have been officially dedicated to her' (150).

1050, 1824.6.

974   Frese, Dolores W. 'Marie de France and the "Surplus of Sense": A Modest Proposal Concerning the *Lais*.' *De Gustibus: Essays for Alain Renoir.* Ed. John Miles Foley. Center for Studies in Oral Tradition, U of Missouri. New York: Garland, 1992. 216–33.

Explores Marie de France's use of the 'deliberate obscurity assiduously cultivated by ancient writers to guarantee that future generations of readers might supply continuing significance to the written text – *la lettre* – by glossing it with insights from their own wisdom – *lur sen*' (216). Each of Marie's *Lais* involves 'imaginative readjustment whereby the *aventure* of an ancient *lai* is recontextualized by her effort both to recollect a past performance, and to reinvent it poetically by her present investment in the activity of writing' (217). The *lai* can be seen 'as a lyric and as a narrative form.' Frese considers in particular the *lai* 'Yonec,' and a lyric she identifies as 'clearly coordinate' (220). 'Yonec' is written in OF, but 'The Corpus Christi Carol' [*1132*] survives in ME and preserves the poetic essence of the *lai* which is its story version. Frese prints both the lyric and a résumé of 'Yonec,' elucidating correspondences in motifs of the two works. She relates the term *lai* to OIr *laid/loîd* and Latin *laus/laudis*, and considers implications of the falcon's arrival at the hour of Lauds, to conclude that '"Yonec" stresses the poetically inevitable connection of love and suffering whose essential anguish in the face of embodied displacement, demise and survival had been profoundly rehearsed and propagandized in connection with the Christian Doctrine of the Incarnation' (230). Frese's discussion indicates that '[t]he "fortunate fall" in "Yonec" is more than a theopoetic parody' (232), and that 'in the Middle English lyric which so clearly conserves a digest of Marie's essential poetic meaning, we may begin to retrieve a chapter in the literary history of generic passage from one form of poetry to another' (233).

1132.

975 Green, Richard Firth. 'John Ball's Letters: Literary History and Historical Literature.' *Chaucer's England: Literature in Historical Context.* Ed. Barbara A. Hanawalt. Medieval Studies at Minnesota 4. Minneapolis: U of Minnesota P, 1992. 176–200.

Examination of *Pierce the Ploughman's Crede* [*663*] and critical comment on it reveal the differing approaches of the literary critic and the historian. Green considers John Ball's letters ['Jack Miller asketh helpe to turn his Mill aright,' *1654*; 'Jacke Trewman dothe you to vnderstand,' *1655*; 'John Ball greteth you wele all,' *1790.8*; 'John Ball Saint Mary priest,' *1791*; 'Johan the Muller hath ygrownde smal smal,' *1796*], to show that phrases and themes, such as 'nowe is tyme' and 'trewthe,' can be related to occurrences and echoes in other texts. There are variations in the interpretation of similar proverbial material, for instance 'now is time' and 'speak, spend, and speed.' The letters fit the social context of popular preaching. Green draws on analogues to assess 'Ball's individual contribution to the actual texts'; to see 'how closely we should identify the themes of these letters with the events of 1381'; and to ascertain 'how closely these letters might affect our interpretation of the Peasants' Revolt itself.' He finds the first of these aims 'a largely literary matter'; the second 'a matter of literary history'; and the third 'a historical question' (188). Ball's letters differ from traditional complaints against Abuses of the Age. They have been thought conservative and reactionary, opposing the Peasants' Revolt, although some passages, on truth and judicial corruption, may link them to it. Their effect on interpretation of the Revolt turns on 'the role played by men like Ball in directing, or at least inspiring, the rebellion' (190), a role estimated by assessing Ball's use of traditional and contemporary issues. Green concludes that 'the tradition of popular preaching and the complaint literature associated with it may be said to have helped inflame deeply banked resentments in 1381' (190–1). Ball, who criticized the friars, nevertheless drew on material used by them, and was 'anything but a typical Lollard' (191). Perhaps to avoid implication in the rebellion, the friars in turn attempted to show that the Lollards were trying to blame them, so that John Ball's 'alleged confession,' which apparently incriminates Wyclif, seems to be 'a Carmelite forgery.' The Lollards' hostility to the friars reflects 'the mutual antipathy of radical and reactionary' (192). In *Pierce the Ploughman's Crede*, Green finds 'signs of a discontent with the source of cultural authority more profound than anything in John Ball's letters' (193). He prints Ball's letters in an appendix (193–5).

190, 312, 663, 836, 906, 1020, 1139, 1459, 1654, 1655, 1790.8, 1791, 1796, 1798, 2008, 2167, 2319, 2340, 2356, 2500, 3274, 3282, 3802, 3922, 4098.3, 4165, 7246, 7596, 7615.

976 Hargreaves, Henry. '*Stirps Anne Beate*: An Unpublished English Poem.' *English Language Notes* 31 (1992–3): 9–18. [Edition.]

A poem 'Menksful and myȝty in mynde modyr of maries iij' [*2153.5*] in Aberdeen University Library MS 123 tells of St Anne, mother of the Blessed Virgin, and her extended family. Hargreaves describes the manuscript and the poem's context of works of computation, numerology, and astragalomancy; historical events on significant dates; and works on St Ursula. Preceding the poem is a diagram; this sets out 'the relationships presented later in it, showing at the head Anne, below her her three successive husbands, Joachym, Cleopas and Salome, and lower again the three Marys who were the children of these marriages, each with her husband's name alongside in his own cartouche, and on the bottom line the grandchildren of Anne by these daughters' marriages' (10). A line links Anne to her sister, here named 'Emery,' the grandmother of John the Baptist. A similar diagram in the manuscript specifically sets out Henry VI's descent from St Louis of France. Hargreaves describes and prints the poem, the language of which is 'a mixture which might well be expected in the Northwest of England' (13), but does not conform closely with linguistic profiles recorded for places near Warrington. There are no exact parallels to the work's unusual metrical structure, with alliteration and a bob, but Hargreaves notes several similar poems. The matter of the poem resembles the *Legenda Aurea* of Jacobus de Voragine and Caxton's translation, but differs in 'the name of Anne's sister, who has no place in the Latin poem.' The Latin verses follow *Stirps Anne Beate* in the manuscript, 'with an additional two lines on the death of some of the apostles' (15). Hargreaves concludes with comments on other poems on the life of St Anne.

208, 888, 1889, 2153.5, 2392, 2421, 3694.3, 3838.

977 McClellan, William. 'Radical Theology or Parody in a Marian Lyric of Ms Harley 2253.' *Voices in Translation: The Authority of 'Olde Bookes' in Medieval Literature. Essays in Honor of Helaine Newstead.* Ed. Deborah M. Sinnreich-Levi and Gale Sigal. New York: AMS, 1992. 157–68.

An examination of 'Ase y me rod þis ender day/by grene wode to seche play' [*359*], to show the conflation of the secular genre of pastourelle with that of religious lyric detailing the joys of Mary. The descriptive language, although it was used 'in erotic "secular" poetry to describe courtly ladies, was also used in Marian lyrics to describe the attributes of the Virgin' (158). Many words suggest 'an ambiguity regarding the poet's declaration of love' (159). McClellan argues for parody as 'the operative mode governing the poem's discourse,' but states that 'the parodic appropriation moves in *two* directions, not just one.' There is 'sacred parody' in 'the movement towards a religious transvaluation of the secular erotic elements,' qualified and limited by 'secular parody,' in 'a movement towards a travesty of the sacred image of Mary' (160). He supports his contentions by reference to Revard, **787**, Howell, **736**, and Bakhtin's theories of dialogic discourse and parody. From the 'erotic/spiritual opposition' of the dialectical movement, the poet produces 'a radical interpretation of the Christian theological concept concerning the physical resurrection of the body, and in the process claims a special and intimate relationship with Mary' (162). McClellan derives the last notion from reading the last lines of the ninth stanza, 'Crist, leue vs alle wiþ þat wymman/þat ioie al forte sene,' as an extension of the concept of the glorified, resurrected body, with erotic and spiritual significance and many possibililties for interpretation. Thus the 'parodoxical movement of parody' shows the site where 'the material body is transfigured and the spiritual body is eroticized,' so that '*eros* and spiritual bliss dialectically intersect' (167).

359, 1861.

978 Means, Laurel. '"Ffor as moche as yche man may not haue þe astrolabe": Popular Middle English Variations on the Computus.' *Speculum* 67 (1992): 595–623. [Edition.]

Some adaptations of the computus, intended 'for the literate or semiliterate layman,' depended 'less upon written form than upon fingers and memory' (595). Means surveys forms of the computus first developed by Bede, and proceeds to adaptations for specific tasks. These are related to 'the position of the moon and its relation to the tides, days of fasting, names of the days of the week, the number of days and weeks in the year, and the length of days, nights, seasons, and shadows' (597). She describes the presentation of information, 'from the highly technical to the popular and simplistic' (598), in such forms as calendars, tables, notes, canons, diagrams, and volvelles, considering how widely the knowledge was spread among laymen, many of whom had 'neither written resources . . . nor mechanical computational instruments (602). ME mnemonic techniques included rhyming verses and use of the hands and fingers. Means prints several verses, and explains calculation of Leap Years, Sunday Letters, Easter, Ember Days, seasons, months, saints' days, and numbers of days in the months and year.

426, 579, 633.5, 1396, 1502, 1721, 2750, 3571, 7558.

979 Orme, Nicholas. 'Medieval Hunting: Fact and Fancy.' *Chaucer's England: Literature in Historical Context.* Ed. Barbara A. Hanawalt. Medieval Studies at Minnesota 4. Minneapolis: U of Minnesota P, 1992. 133–53.

Surveys aspects of hunting, including hunters, their methods, and game. Its importance ensured that it was often mentioned in literature, in formalized language, one function of which was to make social links and distinctions. Orme considers allusions to hunting, for example in tales of Sir Gawain and the legend of 'The Three Dead and the Three Living.' Poems that purport 'to give the animals' point of view' (147) include 'The Mourning of the Hunted Hare' ['Bi a forrest as I gane fare,' *559*] and 'Wyl Bucke his Testament' ['As I stode in a parke streite vp bi a tree,' *368*]. In fact they endorse established rituals of hunting rather than expressing sympathy for the hunted creatures.

368, 559, 710, 1306, 1317, 1399, 1459, 1556, 1566, 3144, 4019.

980 Parker, David R. 'The Act of Supremacy and the Corpus Christi Carol.' *English Language Notes* 30.2 (1992–3): 5–10.

The context of the 'Corpus Christi Carol' [*1132*], in Richard Hill's commonplace book (Balliol College MS 354), helps explicate the allegory. Hill copied many puzzles, and his 'taste for enigmas sheds a powerful light on the enigmas of Corpus Christi.' Parker sees the carol as a riddle in which 'the listener hears of the contents of each container within each larger container' (5). He connects it with 'particular physical circumstances of the Mass as it was performed in England in the early 1500s,' to suggest that the first verses 'figuratively portray the church and altar during the Mass' (7) in a Lenten celebration. Thus the 'orchard brown' can be 'the dark interior of a columned church or cathedral' and 'the hall "hangid with purpill & pall" . . . the altar structure.' Red cloth was frequently ordered for Lenten services, since it symbolized 'the red earth of the grave, and therefore the entombment of Christ, as well as the blood of the Passion.' Parker reads the 'bede' as a paten, and the bleeding knight as 'the body of Christ as communion wafer, perhaps bleeding because it has just been dipped in the communion wine.' The stone with the words 'Corpus Christi' may be 'the super-altar, where the consecration of the Host took place' (8). He agrees with Greene, **418**, that the white falcon represents Anne Boleyn, but does not see Catherine of Aragon as the narrator. Parker finds the carol a riddle, to which 'the answer is "the Holy Communion," but more specifically "the Holy Communion in the Roman church."' Henry VIII's Act of Supremacy separated the churches of England and of Rome; the falcon bore away not Henry but the Roman church. The riddle of maid and bleeding knight shows a 'female communicant . . . weeping over this tragedy,' in an image that may recall a *pietà.* The Act seemed to reopen Christ's wounds, 'and surely Mary was weeping over the freshly opened injuries,' adding further meaning to the allegory and 'a moving lament' for the Roman church 'which evoked the beauty and mystery of the Roman ritual' (9).

1132.

981 Pickering, O.S. 'Newly Discovered Secular Lyrics from Later Thirteenth-Century Cheshire.' *Review of English Studies* NS 43 (1992): 157–80. [Edition.]

Discusses and prints eight lyrics from 'the margins of a Latin manuscript, now Lambeth Palace Library MS 499, written at Stanlow (or Stanlaw) Abbey, Cheshire, almost certainly in the 1270s.' The brief, sophisticated, heavily alliterative poems deal with the following topics: '(**A**) a knightly assembly ['I holde hendeburne her . worthli water ant wys . i world as i wene,' *7227*], (**B**) hunting ['busken bernes . boues bryten . blithe burdes botes beden,' *7093*], (**C**) the natural world in winter ['faste fresen fennes fule. frostes fre is foules foo,' *7137*], (**D**) a fugitive in the hills ['faste ifunde fer on folde . frode fryth is feire fre,' *7138*], (**E**) keeping a lady's love ['I haue to a semly that i bi sete . send mine sonde selliche sete,' *7225*], (**F**) bad weather ['welkes werren . waies weten . windes walken w[e?]de wo,' *7584*], (**G**) unsuccessful wooing ['Bi bele arn briddes breme on bowes,' *7097*], and (**H**) characteristics of four named places ['Littel is lithe bi lythum . wen stormes arn stronge upon strike warth,' *7312*]' (157). Pickering describes the manuscript and its history, and finds that the lyrics were written 'while the scribe was officially occupied with . . . a treatise of Augustine on the Trinity' (161). He prints the texts (161–8), with 'a rendering into modern English . . . and textual notes' (162). Although date and provenance can be determined, linguistic information is less certain. The text suggests the North-West Midlands, but some more Southern features almost certainly show the lyrics' early date; they may reveal that the scribe was not the author, and that 'the poems were composed somewhat further south than Stanlow Abbey' (169); the place-names suggest 'a general north-western scatter' (170). In discussing the lyrics' verse-form and metre (170–6), Pickering considers rhyme-schemes, alliteration and assonance, word play, and metre. There is also a possibility that the poems were not composed in very long lines, but that 'a scribe pressed for space in the bottom margin of a page might have reduced the poems' vertical length by running two or more lines together.' He divides the works into two groups: '**AEH** and **BCDF**, with which the "short line" lyric **G** is closely linked in terms of metre and alliteration' (170); these may be the work of different poets. In detailed comment on the first group, he arranges the poems in shorter lines. **BCDFG** alliterate 'wholly or virtually wholly on a single letter, and . . . each is decidely homomorphic,' (173). Pickering examines rhyme and metre in the poems, and relates them to contemporary ME verse (176–80). Comparisons reveal that '[i]n their confident and playful use of the courtly-love tradition, as in their cleverness with words, their exploitation of verse-form, their mixture of metres, and their sometimes ironical stance, the Lambeth poems have most in common with the somewhat later lyrics of MS Harley 2253' (177). There are parallels in Welsh, Irish, AN, and Latin techniques, and the author (or authors) may have been 'deliberately experimenting with verse-form, and even setting himself exercises in composition' (180).

515, 585, 872, 1394, 1395, 1402, 1504, 1861, 1921, 2003, 2162, 2163, 2649, 3080, 3117, 3874, 3899, 4177, 7093, 7097, 7137, 7138, 7225, 7227, 7312, 7584.

982   Saint Paul, Thérèse. 'A Forgotten Heroine in Medieval English Literature.' *A Wyf Ther Was: Essays in Honour of Paule Mertens-Fonck*. Ed. Juliette Dor. Liège: L³-Liège Language and Literature, 1992. 247–55.

Investigates 'Tegeu,' who appears in ME literature only in the 'rather cryptic' (247) 'Annot and John' [*1394*]. There are Welsh influences in the style and content of the poem, which resembles the eulogistic genre of Welsh court poetry, with some techniques of the Welsh *awdl* or ode. The name Tegeu or Tegau is Celtic. It is linked with legends of testing the chastity of Caradoc's faithful wife and of 'a courageous, virtuous woman who sacrifices one of her breasts to free her loved one from a serpent coiled around his arm' (251–2); in some versions, she acquires a golden breast. These tales are in the French *Livre de Caradoc*. Saint Paul traces the occurrence of the names '*Tergau Euvron* "Tegau Gold Breast,"' as *Caradawc Vrechvras's* ("Strong Arm") faithful wife in the Welsh Triads' (253), but without a 'serpent tale.' She explores possible explanations for the changes, suggesting that the name could represent 'a *souvenir* of a tale which had been attached on the Continent to the hero Carodoc Brech/f-bras and his lady whose fidelity was well-known' (254), perhaps through the 'serpent tale.' Contact with the OF Carodoc story could have revived Old Welsh traditions.

1394.

983   Smithers, G.V. 'Notes on the Middle English Poem *The Four Foes of Mankind.*' *Neuphilologische Mitteilungen* 93 (1992): 199–205.

In his elucidation of problems in 'The Four Foes of Mankind' ['þe siker soþe who so seys,' *3462*], Smithers refers to *BrownXIV*, **48**, and to emendations proposed by McIntosh, **694**. By analogy with lines before and after it, line 82 ['Long lyopon and lened' in *BrownXIV*] should contain two past participles. Emendation of *lyopon* to *ly opon* yields a participle, and an instance of zeugma, a 'not altogether common' (199) ME construction. Lines 81–2 can then be 'an idiomatically acceptable way of saying "when you have accumulated and harvested [your possessions], and over a long period have leant over and hung over [them] and have been reluctant to be parted [from them] . . ."' (200). Smithers rejects McIntosh's emendation '*Longly opon land lened* . . . interpreted as "for a long time have relied upon the land for sustenance"' (201). He offers several reasons for reading lines 43–4 as 'þe warld tirneþ ous touȝ/Fram wawe to wawe,' and declines McIntosh's suggestion to read *tirneþ* as *tirueþ*. Instead he proposes that the word evokes Fortune's wheel, mentioned elsewhere in *BrownXIV* and *BrownXV*, **39**, and notes 'a little network of similarities that link certain passages and phrases in a handful of these lyrics to one or another among them, when one in isolation would be cryptic and unintelligible' (202). There is a similar reference in the *Ormulum* [*2305*], 'in an orthodoxly allegorical disquisition on the early verses of *Luke* II (*Ormulum* 3494 ff.),' although this wheel is not Fortune's, but is 'symbolised by Galilee, and itself symbolises life in this world and its affairs' (203). The idea of uncontrollable change and turning persists. Thus *wawe* is more satisfactorily read as 'misery' than as 'wave,' and line 44 is then 'the last, and the climactic, point in a presentation of the usual motif of the vicissitudes of fortune in life in the world' (204), confirmed by philological comparisons with analogous forms. [See McIntosh, **992**.]

12, 351, 433, 1114, 1448, 1459, 2025, 2153, 2280, 2305, 2576, 2744, 3400, 3408, 3462.

984   Wentersdorf, Karl P. 'Pandarus's *Haselwode*: A Comparative Approach to a Chaucerian Puzzle.' *Studies in Philology* 89 (1992): 293–313.

Investigates Pandarus's references to *haselwode*, in *Troilus and Criseyde* [*3327*]. Wentersdorf looks at each of these in context, and compares similar passages in ME and other languages, relating them to Chaucer's innovations in retelling the story of Troilo and Criseida. He supplies examples of erotic allusions to hazeltrees and gathering their nuts as occasions for rustic lovemaking. Pandarus's last reference includes *joly Robyn*, which is often the name of a rural lover in pastourelles. Wentersdorf notes varying implications of hazeltrees in a range of poems. These include 'The Thrush and the Nightingale' ['Somer is comen wiþ loue to toune,' *3222*], where it underlines the coming of love; 'The Reply of Friar Daw Topias' [*4098.3*], where it seems to suggest that the Wycliffites might as well write poems of love as hope to enter heaven; and 'Lovely lordynges ladys lyke' [*2018*], where the bird observed 'should not have left the cage of virtue for the wildness of singing, however blissfully, in a hazeltree' (307). Such instances and the link with Pandarus, 'a man knowledgable in the *jeux d'amour*,' imply dangerous and erotic possibilities, confirmed in the knowledge that Pandarus 'as a man of the world . . . believes that those who enter the hazelwood cannot count on lasting happiness in love or even on mutual fidelity' (313).

683, 1091, 1459, 2018, 2092, 2831, 3222, 3327, 4098.3.

985 Boffey, Julia. 'The Treatise of a Galaunt in Manuscript and Print.' The Library 6th Series 15 (1993): 175–86.

Traces the origins and history of 'The Treatise of a Galaunt' ['Lyke as grete wateres encresyn into floods fele,' *1874*], and other appearances of the motif of excesses in fashion to indicate sin and evils of the times. Boffey compares textual and contextual features of surviving manuscript copies: Rome, English College A.347 (R); the former Astor A.2 (A); and Trinity College, Cambridge, R.3.21 (T). She observes differences in order, transpositions of lines, omissions of stanzas, and variant forms, such as acrostic stanzas on the seven deadly sins. In addition, she notes the difficulties of determining local meanings and understanding variations and processes of transmission. Boffey considers movement of the text to print, the process and the changes it may entail. She compares four editions associated with Wynkyn de Worde, relating them to manuscripts. The comparisons reveal that the version most closely resembles R. The poem's success and long life were probably helped by contemporary feelings against the French and against excesses in dress, also expressed in the sumptuary laws. Attribution to Lydgate, implied by the context of 'more reliably Lydgatian pieces' and a reference by Bishop John Alcock of Ely, may have seemed to de Worde 'reason enough for keeping it alive.' Its interest is in 'its all-purpose topicality and in the changes which can be observed between its initially flexible manuscript appearances and more fixed printed form' (185).

143.8, 299.8, 892, 1497, 1585.8, 1874, 2832, 3682, 4165, 4254.5, 4255.

986 Boklund-Lagopoulou, Karin. '*Judas*: The First English Ballad?' Medium Ævum 62 (1993): 20–34.

Considers whether 'Judas' [*1649*] is indeed the first English ballad. Since it is 'a narrative poem . . . composed almost exclusively of event and speech with . . . the narrator reduced to a bare minimum and very little overt indication of personal bias,' the issue becomes 'whether the poem can be considered "a folksong."' Boklund-Lagopoulou weighs the oral and written transmission of ballads and their development from ME metrical romances and folksongs. Recognition of 'Judas' as a ballad would 'reshape the discussion over the origins of the popular ballad' (21) by acknowledging its existence 150–200 years before other accepted texts. Classification of the poem as a religious folksong by David C. Fowler [*A Literary History of the Popular Ballad*] would not vitiate 'the possibility that it is an ancestor of the popular ballad' (22). Most works in the manuscript (Cambridge, Trinity College B.14.39) are religious; some secular pieces, perhaps collected by the friars for didactic purposes, are closely related 'to an oral poetic tradition' (23). This does not prove 'Judas' a ballad, but offers 'a legitimate interpretative context for the poem in vernacular folksong' (24). It can also be compared with the vernacular saints' lives and Gospel tales in the manuscript. Other comparisons can be made with such works as 'The Corpus Christi Carol' [*1132*] and 'St Stephen and Herod' [*3058*], which resemble both folksongs and ballads. Narrative analysis establishes the poem's actantial structure. Its religious, spatial, temporal, economic, sexual, familial, and erotic codes show their relation to the poem's social world, to conflicts of loyalty, and to plot structure. Boklund-Lagopoulou demonstrates the resemblance to 'the most common form of the later popular ballad, the romantic and tragic ballads' (29). Her stylistic analysis includes the effects of 'sudden shifts of scene, the lack of transitions, and the consistent use of direct dialogue [that] place the entire action, as in the mediaeval drama, squarely in the everyday world of ordinary men and women to give the familiar narrative and doctrine fresh impact.' Presenting Christ as feudal lord enhances the ambiguity of the betrayal, 'a typically feudal conflict of loyalties' with 'elements of both family and erotic relationships' (30). Techniques of incremental repetition, action, and direct speech are ballad conventions, as is the sense of movement towards the tragedy of Judas. She does not claim to have proved the work a ballad, but Boklund-Lagopoulou suggests that the features that make 'Judas' memorable, suggestive, and unique are those 'it has in common with the popular ballad' (31), and that a Franciscan would be an excellent candidate for its collector or composer.

1132, 1389.5, 1649, 1935, 3058, 3078.

987   Braekman, Martine. 'A New Source for *The Pains of Love* in Rawlinson MS. C.813.' *Neophilologus* 77 (1993): 127–34.

Investigates the 'common practice for medieval poems to be considered and treated as communal property by contemporary writers,' so that poems were composed when compilers 'interlaced Chaucer, Gower or Lydgate's verse with other anonymous lyrics' (127). Braekman notes several anthologies that have such poems, and compares commonplace books, before considering Rawlinson MS C.813, owned by Humphrey Wellys, which was arranged deliberately. She shows that 'Loo he that ys all holly your3 soo free' [*1926.5*] was composed from stanzas of *Troilus and Criseyde* [*3327*], when the poet 'adapted, rearranged and altered the lines to form a new, independent lyric' (128). She offers similar examples of borrowings from Hawes's *The Comfort of Lovers* [*3357.5*] in 'The Pains of Love' ['O loue most dere o loue most nere my harte,' *2496*]. The Hawes work is not the only source. The last six stanzas, previously thought to be the poet's own, are in a ' "courtly love aunter" composed by William Walter and printed by Wynkyn de Worde probably in 1533,' where they are 'interspersed with other lyric material' (130). Braekman prints the relevant passages in parallel columns (130–1), and notes differences in the texts. They suggest that the Rawlinson scribe's dialect is 'predominately western and perhaps to be situated in a region adjoining northern Wales' (131), consistent with the notion of Wellys as compiler and scribe. These stanzas and others in 'O my lady dere bothe regarde & se' [*2532*], adapted from Hawes's *Pastime of Pleasure*, [*4004*] correspond more closely to their sources than do those of *1926.5*, although *2532* alters the sense of the lines. Examination of Walter's poem discloses that lines 64–70 are printed in two colums to reveal the acrostic 'William Walter,' not preserved in Rawlinson C.813. The discovery prompts doubt about accepted dates of composition for both poems, 'as Walter flourished around 1520 and the *Spectacle* is dated [1533?],' although the acrostic hints that 'Walter's works were written at a date earlier than their printed publication' (133).

851, 1926.5, 2532, 3327, 3357.5, 4004.

988   Breeze, Andrew. '*Bounting* "Corn Bunting" in the Harley Lyric *A Wayle Whyt ase Whalles Bon*.' *Archiv* 230 (1993): 123–4

A stanza of the lyric 'A Wayle Whyt ase Whalles Bon' [*105*] expresses the poet's desire to be 'A bounting other a laverok . . . Bitwene hir curtel and hir smok.' *Bounting* refers to a bird, 'of which the commonest species in Britain is the Corn Bunting,' but the word seems to be 'a Welsh loan in Middle English' (123). Skeat aligned it with 'Welsh *bontin* "the rump" and *bontinog* "large-buttocked." ' Breeze cites instances of these words, noting that they occur 'only in poetry of a popular kind.' He suggests that the Corn Bunting may have had a 'less polite' name, before '*bras yr ŷd* "fat one of the corn", first recorded in a Welsh-English-Latin dictionary of slightly before 1592.' This would accord with the description of the bird as ' "large and plump" . . . showing a broad spread tail in flight,' with the English descriptive name '*wheatear* . . . "white rump" ' (124), and with the occurrence of other Welsh loanwords in the Harley lyrics.

105.

989   ———. 'Celtic Etymologies for Old English *Cursung* "Curse", *Gafeluc* "Javelin", *Stær* "History", *Syrce* "Coat of Mail", and Middle English *Clog(ge)* "Block, Wooden Shoe", *Cokkunge* "Striving", *Tirven* "To Flay", *Warroke* "Hunchback." ' *Notes and Queries* 238 (1993): 287–97.

The note on '*Warroke* "hunchback"' in *Jolly Wat the Shepherd* (296–7) explains a crux in 'Dog, kepe well my shepe fro the corn,/And warn wel Warrok when I blow my horn,' which contains 'Wat's farewell to his sheep and dog as he sets off for Bethlehem,' in 'The shepard upon a hill he satt' [*3460*], the 'famous much-edited Christmas carol' (296). Breeze summarizes comments on *warroke*, and suggests that it may refer to Wat's assistant and be a Scottish or Yorkshire word for a 'stunted child.' There are also connections with words for 'stoop' and 'hunchback.' He proposes a Celtic loanward, from Cumbric, 'a sister-language of Welsh spoken in Cumbria and Strathclyde up to the twelfth century (when shepherds were no doubt among its last speakers).' He notes further that 'anyone with a spinal deformity would be unfit for the bending and lifting of much farm work, but might be able to help another tend sheep.' The poet shows 'a sharp ear for the language of shepherds, and the unflattering name a deputy shepherd might have' (297).

3460.

990 ———. 'Middle English *Tromchery* and Irish *Tromchroí* "Liver."' *Notes and Queries* 238 (1993): 16.

A note on *tromchery*, a *hapax legomenon* used in 'A Satire on the People of Kildare' [*1078*], and explained by Sisam and Sisam, **69**, as 'rubbish' in the *hory* dwelling of the market women, the *hokesters* who sell 'tripe, cows' feet, and sheep's heads.' Breeze perceives the word as 'a loan from Irish *tromchroí*, "liver" (literally "heavy heart"),' likely to make the dwelling *hory* since the liver is filled with blood. The poem may also suggest a location for the dwellings, since '*hokesters down by the lake* may refer to Dublin, with its *dublind* "black pool."' The lake might be the Liffey, near the 'flesh shambles' in Fishamble St, 'at high tide, when its flow is held back.' His use of the language reveals the poet's 'ear for common speech,' and offers comment on medieval attitudes to the use of Irish: whereas '[b]eyond the Pale, it enjoyed high status . . . [w]ithin the Pale . . . [i]t was the language of slaughtermen and offal-sellers.'

1078.

991 ———. 'Welsh *Mil* "Animal" and the Harley Lyric *Lenten Ys Come*.' *Notes and Queries* 238 (1993): 14–15.

Surveys critical comment on the word *mil* in the lyric 'Lenten ys come wiþ loue to toune' [*1861*], to show fairly general agreement on a Welsh origin. This notion 'makes sense in the context; it avoids emendation; it accords with the lyric's West Midland provenance.' However, there are several ideas of the nature of the animal to which it refers. Breeze investigates the range for which *mil* is used in Welsh, and notes related forms in Old and Modern Irish, Old Cornish, and Middle Breton. The Welsh word is used for monsters and other creatures. Originally, like ME *deer*, it included any quadruped, with 'the diminutive *milyn* for the salmon.' It was a familiar word for a hunted or a domestic animal. Breeze concludes that the poet wished to mention in the lyric 'the shy, elusive creatures of the forest whose love might well be as quiet as *strem that striketh stille*' (15).

1861.

992 McIntosh, Angus. 'A Supplementary Note to the Middle English Poem *The Four Foes of Mankind*.' *Neuphilologische Mitteilungen* 94 (1993): 79–81.

In answer to Smithers, **983**, McIntosh offers more evidence for the change from '*lyopon* to the two-word phrase *ly opon*' in line 82 of the lyric 'þe siker soþe who so seys' [*3462*]. Although he agrees with the proposal, he questions rendering '"ly opon and lened" as "leant over and hung over."' He wishes also to investigate the use of *ly* 'as a past participle form of the verb *lien* which is valid for *this* poem' (79). He finds similar forms in the hand of Scribe 1, who copied the text in the Auchinleck MS and *Lai le Freine* [*3869*], and notes that, in *3462,* '*ly* nestles discretely there, midway between *long* and *opon*' (80). As an example of findings that offer a similarly salutary message to the investigator, McIntosh offers the modification of *sone* to *loue* (line 56) in *BrownXIV*, **31**; the subsequent proposal of *sone* by Menner, **229**; and the silent restoration of *sone* in Smithers's edition of *BrownXIV*, **48**.

1382, 2153, 3462, 3869.

993 Moffat, Douglas. 'Rage, Play, and Foreplay in Middle English Literature.' *Neuphilologische Mitteilungen* 94 (1993): 167–84.

Investigates 'sexual connotations for the Middle English . . . verb *ragen* "rage"' (167), with examples, including some from ME lyrics. Moffat examines the verb's semantic background, and compares OF *ragier*. He traces links with children's wild romping and with exuberant flirtation or 'innocent, though probably high-spirited, frolicking between young people of the opposite sex.' He observes that '"raging" might lead to *outrage*, a noun whose connection with *ragen* is often established by rhyme' (170). *Ragen* may imply 'capacity for sexual intercourse' (174), but it emphasizes 'the pleasure of anticipation and preparation' (175). Moffat demonstrates the collocation of *ragen* and *pleien*, to suggest that occurrences of *ragen* offer 'linguistic evidence' for 'a general tendency toward a rehabilitation of sexual pleasure in the later Middle Ages' (180).

129, 1845, 3764, 3784.6, 4157.

994 Waldron, Ronald. 'The Vernon Refrain Poems: Didacticism into Art.' *Unisa English Studies* 31.2 (1993): 1–10.

Considers poetic rather than didactic merits of the Vernon and Simeon lyrics. The works do not seem to be the work of one author, although 'striking overall similarities of form and subject-matter' point to 'some degree of common authorship' (1). Metrical patterns and structure reveal 'a particular combination of homely reasonableness of address with a fair degree of artificiality of form,' and several points of resemblance to *Sir Gawain and the Green Knight* [*3144*] and *Pearl* [*2744*]. The style and scribal dialect are 'compatible with the South West Midlands provenance' (2), although the rhymes are 'consistently those of an East Midlands origin.' Most of the poems are moral or didactic. Their theme of the universality of death leads to 'the transitoriness of earthly things, and contempt for the world, . . . regret for one's own follies,' to 'warnings to others to reform in time,' and to 'specific social complaint and satire' (4). There are allusions to the horrors of death rather than descriptions. The *ubi sunt* motif and 'homely illustrations' show links to sermons, and anticipate metaphysical images such as Herbert's. Alliteration and rhythmic devices enforce the themes. Waldron explores the poems' sermon-like qualities. They are not 'sermons in verse,' in spite of their themes, and the 'sermon-elements are used . . . in a shifted literary context' (7). Some poems use conventions of fictional frameworks such as pastourelle and *congé*. The varied Vernon manuscript is 'a repository of vernacular texts suitable for reading aloud at mealtimes to a fortuitous assembly of lay guests'; the lyrics seem 'near the literary end of this spectrum, and . . . in them a didactic purpose is in process of being itself absorbed into an aesthetic mould' (9).

5, 66, 372, 445, 562, 563, 583, 1379, 1402, 1448, 1455, 1459, 1532, 2302, 2607, 2744, 3144, 3310, 3420, 3996, 4135, 4157, 4158, 4268.

995 Whiteford, Peter. 'Too Dull for Words? A Neglected Middle English Lyric.' *Of Pavlova, Poetry and Paradigms: Essays in Honour of Harry Orsman*. Ed. Laurie Bauer and Christine Franzen. Wellington, NZ: Victoria UP, 1993. 139–48.

Counters the dismissal (by Woolf, **522**) of 'A son take hede to me whas son þou was' [*14*] as a 'dull' work. Whiteford scrutinizes the lyric, beginning with the Latin lines that introduce its brief speeches. Here he finds an attribution to John Chrysostom, and an indication of 'another speaking voice,' perhaps 'the translator and versifier' (141). The voice and context, in two manuscripts containing sermons, suggest a sermon lyric to emphasize two opposed moments to which affective literature gave conspicuous devotion. The contrast of joy at Christ's birth and grief at his death are declared in the preceding sermon verse, 'At his burth thou hurdist angell syng' [*427.5*]. The traditional expression, in *14*, of the Virgin's sorrow and Christ's doctrinal reply and entrusting of his mother to John's care, links 'concerns or focuses of interest.' The author articulates and contrasts 'a human complaint and a divine response.' The relationship of mother and son intensifies the tension of human and divine, which is also seen as that of the 'emotions and the reason, between despairing grief and the certainty of faith and knowledge' (143). This is revealed spatially and temporally, in the lyric's emphasis on separation and manipulation of the tenses, through the simultaneous presentation of events of past, present, and future. The style is restrained and seems plain, but the poet is 'consciously exploiting the resources of the language.' He stresses 'the fundamental tension between human and divine perspectives' and 'a universal human relationship,' to relate them to his sermon and 'a particular devotional response in his listeners' (146), creating 'a simple but moving lyric which operates in a rather more subtle way than may first be suspected' (147).

14, 427.5, 3211.

996   Amati, Antonietta. *Ichot a burde in a bour: il sapere scientifico nella lirica inglese del Trecento.* Fasano: Schena, 1994.

Not seen. Bibliographical information indicates that it deals with the relation between science and literature expressed in fourteenth-century ME poetry.

997   Breeze, Andrew. 'Middle English *Cammede* "Bow-Legged" in *Swart Smekyd Smethes.*' *Notes and Queries* 239 (1994): 148–50.

Explains the *cammede kongons* of 'Swarte smekyd smethes smateryd wythe smoke' [*3227*]. They have been seen as misshapen individuals with misshapen noses, by analogy with *camus*, the adjective used to describe the noses of the miller and his daughter in *The Reeve's Tale* [*4019*]. Breeze summarizes critical comment, and argues for *cammede* as a derivative of the Welsh *cam* (bent), not a description of the smiths' noses, since 'noses are not mentioned,' and because '*cammed* < Welsh *cam* . . . is easy to accept, but *cammed* < *camus* is not.' *Cam* can describe a range of deformities, including 'hunch-backed' and 'bow-legged,' and is related to other words concerned with the leg. 'Bow-legged' is more likely than 'snub-nosed,' because 'a lame man with strong arms would naturally become a smith,' rather than a farmer, soldier, or hunter. 'Hunch-backed' is not likely, since this 'makes strenuous work impossible' (149). *Cammede*, 'bow-legged,' a deformity, is more fitting than 'snub-nosed' to describe *kongons*, which is 'better translated "changelings, misshapen creatures" than "rascals, brutes, bastards"', once we grasp the medieval belief that a changeling was "an ill-favoured, often deformed or imbecile child believed to be the offspring of fairies and to have been substituted by them for a normal child"' (149–50). The variant *kammede* in *The Reeve's Tale* and *Promptorium parvulorum* may mean a twisted rather than a snub nose. A last argument comes from allusions to lame devils and the hellish setting, in references that 'echo the gospel ones to Hell as an outer darkness, a furnace of fire, a place of wailing and gnashing of teeth' (150).

3227, 4019.

998 ———. 'Two Bardic Themes: The Virgin and Child, and *Ave*-Eva.' *Medium Ævum* 63 (1994): 17–33.

Compares early (before *c.* 1300) and unusual treatment of themes of the Virgin and Child, and the play of *Ave* and Eva in early Welsh poems and ME lyrics. Breeze first considers a poem of Friar Madog ap Gwallter, whose emphasis on the poverty of the Nativity suggests that he was a Franciscan. He compares the poem with Latin works and with ME verses from a friars' preaching-book (Trinity College, Cambridge MS 323) that stress 'the pathos of the Incarnation,' with 'delicate emphasis on the Virgin Mary' (19). He contrasts it with an earlier Welsh poem that stresses the Christ Child's power, yet anticipates Madog's work by evoking 'the intimate bond of mother and child' (21). Madog's conclusion mentions the Virgin's 'active and explicit role as our intercessor now and at the Last Judgement' (22), as in earlier Irish works. The contrast of Eve and Mary and word play on Eva and *Ave* in the angelic salutation was 'variously developed throughout Europe' (23). Breeze cites examples in Latin, English, French, Provençal, Galician, and Catalan works, before examining Welsh treatments of the theme. He shows the range of the wordplay in medieval poetry; the misunderstandings in works that state it is a patristic topos; and the imaginative nature of the Welsh treatments by Gruffud ap Maredudd and Rhys Goch Eryri.

889, 1024, 1054, 1601, 2644, 2645.

999 Duncan, Thomas G. 'Two Middle English Penitential Lyrics: Sound and Scansion.' *Late-Medieval Religious Texts and Their Transmission: Essays in Honour of A.I. Doyle.* Ed. A.J. Minnis. York Manuscripts Conferences: Proceedings Series 3. Cambridge: Brewer, 1994. 55–65.

An investigation of the metre of ME lyrics, illustrated in two penitential works, 'Mirie it is while sumer ilast' [*2163*] and 'Louerd þu clepedest me' [*1978*]. Duncan surveys criticism, noting that Brook, **42**, sees resemblances to MnE and OE metre, whereas Stevens, **789**, recognizes the relation to the rhythms of speech. Dobson, **87**, distinguishes between 'literary' lyrics and songs, and emends lines freely. Duncan disagrees with some aspects of Dobson's work, in particular concerns about headless lines and 'the matching of rhythm and word stress' (57), although he acknowledges the stricter constraints of the song and its music. To demonstrate sound and scansion, Duncan offers the musical setting of *2163* supplied by Stevens, with some revisions to produce 'arguably a more faithful presentation of the original music and text' (61). Since many lyrics are not songs, Duncan also considers the stress pattern of the work as a spoken poem. He presents a similar analysis for *1978*, referring to Stevick, **62**, and proposes fewer stressed syllables after elision and syncope. He finds the reading of Oliver, **549**, of 'What is this worlde but oonly vanyte' [*3909*] anachronistic, since it fails to recognize 'the speech-like quality of Middle English verse.' Duncan concludes that 'all metrical syllables, and not just accented syllables, must be taken into account in the appraisal of the Middle English lyric verse,' and that the rhythm of this verse was 'that of speech rather than any insistent pattern of metrical stress' (65).

352, 1978, 2070, 2163, 2678, 3909.

1000 Margherita, Gayle. *The Romance of Origins: Language and Sexual Difference in Middle English Literature.* Philadelphia: U of Pennsylvania P, 1994.

In 'Women and Riot in the Harley Lyrics' (60–81) the study explores 'courtly discourse, and the extent to which it succeeds in repressing the primal violence of tropological substitution, a violence whereby the feminine body is ob*lite*rated ("written out") in a poetic struggle for dialectical resolution or transcendence' that Margherita calls 'lyrical' (60). Within courtly lyrics women are generally depicted as absent love-objects to be 'celebrated, entreated, mourned and blamed.' Margherita uses some Harley love lyrics to focus on 'the points of resistance in the semiotic system' (61). She surveys criticism and depicts the lyrics as 'fundamentally transgressive' (62), through examination of 'the relationship between sexual difference and figural language' in 'Annot and John' [*1394*], 'The Fair Maid of Ribblesdale' [*2207*], 'The Meeting in the Wood' [*1449*], 'De Clerico et Puella' [*2236*], and 'The Poet's Repentance' [*3874*]. (She provides texts and translations of the poems in an appendix [163–77].) In *1394* and *2207* 'the instability of language is inscribed across the body of woman' (65). In *1394*, the love-object is described in visual terms, in many comparisons, and she is eventually reduced to 'a "note of the nightegale," that is, to a pun' that seems to reveal her name. However the poem also promises 'the satisfaction of a desire to see both the feminine body and the "derne deeds"' mentioned in the poem. Thus the 'rhetorical extravagance' produces a veil over Annot that 'serves as a lure for the reader/hearer' (68). Margherita finds a similar strategy in *2207*, in the focus on the belt buckle 'as a fetishistic substitute for the female genitalia' (69). The lyrics have a prurient appeal directed 'not toward the absent woman, but rather toward the implicitly present voyeur' (71). Margherita's analysis of *3874* shows it as 'the setting for a confrontation between two men, the poet and "Richard, riht of reson rote," who emerges as the addressee' (72). The poem presents vices and virtues of women through the antithesis of Eve and Mary, in which women and language are shown to correspond in their unruliness. The pastourelle, *2236*, demonstrates this genre's potential for violence. Through rape, 'the female voice is submerged in the female body' (77), even though the genre is ambivalent and unstable, and many pastourelles show the woman's triumph. There is more emphasis on the feminine character of *1449*, which compels the reader 'to identify with the feminine position, rather than that of the would-be lover/ assailant' (78). The poem ends ambiguously, with a wish for 'a man who means what he says' (80). The place of the feminine speaker of the pastourelle, aware of the duplicity and negativity of language, is 'at the borderline, the place of the mother, the abject, and the poet' (81).

1394, 1449, 2207, 2236, 3874.

1001 Ogden, James. 'From Lyric to Limerick.' *Notes and Queries* 239 (1994): 529–31.

Finds ancestors of the first English limericks in ballads and lyrics, and asserts that the limerick's genealogy is 'more respectable than is generally thought.' 'Svmer is icumen in' [*3223*] illustrates 'aspects of both form and content' (529) in its metre and spirit. A fourteenth-century description of the lion, 'The lion is wonderliche strong,' in 'þe formest of þese bestes þre' [*3353*], on the Lion, Bear and Dragon, 'brings the limerick closer' in its metrical form, and in the 'emphatic conclusion . . . about a character named at the beginning' (530). Ogden observes that 'the name limerick seems to be a trisyllabic version of lyric' (531). [See Bibby, **682**.]

3223, 3353.

1002 Scase, Wendy. '"Proud Gallants and Popeholy Priests": The Context and Function of a Fifteenth-Century Satirical Poem.' *Medium Ævum* 63 (1994): 275–86.

Traces the motif of the 'gallant' in satirical and didactic literature (chiefly of the fourteenth and fifteenth centuries) particularly in 'Ye prowd galanttes hertlesse' [*4255*], with its account of extravagant, lewd attire and comparisons with priests' apparel. Scase calls it '"Proud Gallants and Popeholy Priests" to highlight its yoking of dandies with clerics' (275), and prints the text (275–6). There are striking similarities in the rhyme words of the first stanza and those of 'a popular quatrain directed against the attire of Englishmen,' 'Longe berde hertelles' [*1934*]. The second stanza deals with priests' clothing, and is related to a popular song, 'a biting denunciation of over-dressed priests which begins with the line "Ye popeholy prestis fulle of presumcyoun" [*4254.5*]' (276). Scase compares versions of *4255* in MSS BL Harley 372; University College,

Oxford 154; and Trinity College, Cambridge O.2.53. The second, without 'the opening "Proud gallants" verses . . . has a kind of preface to the "Popeholy priests" attack,' in a stanza, 'Sing lorel syng' [*3114*] that ridicules the gallant's exaggerated shoe. Variations suggest 'not simply a version of a popular song, but literary experiments which adapt popular material' (278). The quatrain's presence in *The Brut* [*295*] and John Benet's commonplace book shows its use in preaching. Palaeography, costume, and contemporary references suggest that *4255* was composed late in the fifteenth century, coinciding with 'renewal of interest among the authorities in standards and modes of dress' (279) for laity and clergy. Comments on clerical dress compare it unfavourably with that of gallants, and stress that there should be marked differences between the two, to allow priestly attire to stress authority. Scase compares *4255* and documents in the register of Thomas Bourgchier, archbishop of Canterbury. She finds 'the same "official" language and stereotype,' but a different use of language. The perspective of documents 'on offending priests and lower clergy is from above' (281), whereas the poem's is 'from below, that of the priests' proud subjects.' *The Vision of Edmund Leversedge*, written shortly afterwards by a minor cleric and subject of Bourgchier, has 'the viewpoint of the gallant' (282), in a prose account of Leversedge's vision of an angel who instructs him about his clothing. Its part in official discourse on the authority of the clergy is the independent one of 'satirical exploitation of popular song' (284).

295, 892, 1934, 3113, 3114, 4254.5, 4255.

1003 Schwetman, John W. 'Feudal Chivalry in Popular Medieval Battle Poems.' *The Rusted Hauberk: Feudal Ideals of Order and Their Decline.* Ed. Liam O. Purdom and Cindy Vitty. Gainesville, FL: U of Florida P., 1994. 229–44.

Not seen.

1004 Willmott, Adrian. 'Another Middle English Verse Rendering of Job 14: 1–2.' *Notes and Queries* 239 (1994): 148. [Edition.]

Discerns another expression of Job 14.1–2, 'Man þat is of womman born' [*7340*], in 'the sermon for the fourth Sunday after Epiphany' in MS Longleat 4, 'a sumptuous volume that contains a complete set of Sunday sermons in English, *Pore Caitif*, and *The Charter of the Abbey*.' The sermons are the work of a Franciscan, the author of *Dives and Pauper*. Wenzel, **701**, and Fletcher, **685**, have noted a variant, 'Mon iboren of wommon ne lyueth but a stounde' [*2058*]. Willmott concludes that 'there are other versions . . . waiting to be discovered.' [See Powell, **786**.]

2058, 7340.

1005 Wilson, Edward. '*The Testament of the Buck* and the Sociology of the Text.' *Review of English Studies* NS 45 (1994): 157–84.

A study of 'The Testament of the Buck' ['As I stode in a parke streite vp bi a tree,' *368*] and its sources, relating it to other testament poems. The sources are 'two manuscripts and one printed edition, all of the sixteenth century: Bodleian Library, Oxford MS Rawlinson C 813, fos. 30–31ᵛ; British Library MS Cotton Julius A V, fo. 131ᵛ; and *wyl bucke his Testament*, printed in London by Wyllam Copland (no date)' (157); Wilson describes all of these. He also describes the life of Humphrey Wellys, who first owned and perhaps copied Rawlinson C.813, and notes that recipes follow the testament in the print. He supplies a descriptive list of 23 testaments in verse and prose, and observes a general preference for verse and for human testators, apart from 'the allegorical human heart . . . and the abstract Heresy' (163), the buck of *368*, a parrot, a fox, and a crab-tree. The genre's purposes can be 'moral and religious . . . amatory . . . instructional . . . satiric . . . and memorial' (164). The wills are generally satiric, and only *368* is without humour;

its content is related to 'straightforward and pedagogic hunting treatises' (166). References to the death of hunted deer are found in *As You Like It* and *The Merry Wives of Windsor*, and there are Latin and French animal testaments. The genre has no restrictions of 'time, country, or language,' but 'the circumstances, manuscript and print, of its preservation' (167) are determined and can reveal intentions, as Wilson illustrates. He considers the bibliographical contexts of *368* and effects of its appearance: on a leaf pasted into Cotton Julius A V; within woodcut borders in the Copland print (with another stanza and recipes, perhaps composed by John Lacy); and in Rawlinson C.813, paying greatest attention to the last. He relates the poem to 'Wellys's interest in the ceremony and ritual of hunting' (174) and to its surroundings. To illustrate the significance of these rituals, he cites the hunting and preparation of the St Mary Day Buck of Needwood (174–6), and Erasmus's mocking account of the breaking of a deer (176), and notes that Wellys's coat of arms included a deer's head. The manuscript is carefully arranged, and 'The Testament' is 'the last of a sequence of four poems which treat of death.' The framing of the second and third poems ['The Epytaphye of Sir Gryffyth ap Ryse,' *3962.5*; 'The Lamentatyon of the Ladye Gryffythe,' *2552.5*], concerning 'the death of a member of the Welsh gentry with court connections,' with 'The Epytaphye of Lobe, the Kynges Foole' [*2482.5*], and 'The Testament of the Bucke,' discloses, in the quartet, the 'mortality we share with the foolish and the animal.' The fool's epitaph emphasizes 'both our common folly and our common mortality' (178). Wilson finds a similar deflationary effect in Dr Johnson's reaction to the making of a will, and reflects on 'the supervenient grace of a meaning conferred by a new context created by Humphrey Wellys' (181). In conclusion he describes some treatments of 'The Testament,' including those of Copland and Wellys, as acts of executors.

194.5, 285, 368, 813.3, 1018, 1018.5, 1330.5, 1382, 1459, 1488, 1556, 1820.5, 1826, 1863.5, 2092, 2261.8, 2409.5, 2464, 2482.5, 2496, 2532, 2532.5, 2541, 2552.5, 2757.3, 2822, 2827.5, 3144, 3227, 3428, 3917.8, 3962.5, 4019, 4020, 4099, 7310.

1006 Griffiths, Jeremy. 'Unrecorded Middle English Verse in the Library at Holkham Hall, Norfolk.' *Medium Ævum* 64 (1995): 278–84. [Edition.]

Describes previously unrecorded ME verses found in the manuscript library of Holkham Hall. A macaronic poem 'O gracyous Ihesu bothe trysty and kynde' [*7393*] is written on the vellum wrapper of Holkam Hall, MS 755, a legal miscellany which Griffiths describes extensively and associates with the Scarning family. Although the poem seems discrete, the recurring phrase 'Spes mea in deo est' appears 'as the refrain of an alliterative song . . . "When lordschyp ys loste & lusti lekyng with all" [*3988*].' The phrase suggests a family motto and proverb; together with the line, 'To trust on this world hit is but treson,' it contributes to 'some flavour of the tone and origins of the piece' (280). Another legal manuscript, Holkam Hall 229, has variants of a grace 'Crist þat breed brak' [*620*] and a carol to the Virgin 'Ther is no rose of swych vertu' [*3536*], the latter based on 'the image of the Virgin Mary as a rose' and 'the familiar paradoxes of the Nativity' (281). Griffiths describes the manuscript, and records other occurrences of the works and differences in the versions. He prints the texts (281–2) with the titles: 'Spes mea in deo est' [*7393*], 'Gode þat hys brede brake' [*620*], and 'þer ys no rose of suche vertu' [*3536*].

620, 3536, 3988, 7393.

1007 Lindström, Bengt. 'Middle English *Withoute(n) More.*' *Notes and Queries* 240 (1995): 21–2.

In the phrase *withoute(n) more*, 'a line-filler and rhyme-tag,' *more* has been thought 'the comparative of *muchel*.' Thus the *OED* and *MED* offer the meanings 'without anything further or additional,' 'without delay,' and 'unhesitatingly.' Lindström suggests that 'an aphetic form of the Old French and Middle English noun *demore* "delay"' (21) should be considered. Among the examples he cites is 'The Song of the Battle of Lewes' [*3155*], in which *dude more* in the line 'Ant so he dude more' may be a periphrastic past tense form of the verb *demore(n)*, with the meaning 'did hesitate,' or 'did prevaricate' (22).

1993, 2153, 2574, 2662, 3155, *3281.5.

1008 Millet, Bella. 'The Song of Entertainers and the Song of the Angels: Vernacular Lyric Fragments in Odo of Cheriton's *Sermones de Festis.*' *Medium Ævum* 64 (1995): 17–36.

Examines the use of secular lyrics in preaching, in particular one 'which occurs as part of a moralized exemplum on confession in a notebook compiled by the cleric John Dygoun in the early fifteenth century' (31). Dygoun tells of a knight who finds a maiden at a bubbling fountain under a hawthorn, described in 'At a sprynge wel vnder a þorn' [*420*], and revealed as representing the Virgin standing near the fountain of Christ's wounds which supply the healing and cleansing water of regeneration. Millet finds a precedent in *Sermones de Festis*, a collection compiled by Odo of Cheriton in the thirteenth century, and probably preached in Toulouse. They use Provençal lyrics, broadly classified as *chansons de femme*, and apparently written for secular purposes. Odo's disapproving comments on secular song, in a sermon on John the Baptist, imply a wish to use 'profane material for religious ends' (21), by denouncing and exploiting aspects of secular culture. The allegorical linking of 'hawthorn and spring with the crown of thorns and the wound in Christ's side' (30) by Odo and Dygoun suggests that the latter drew on established custom, although it is hard to distinguish between use of an independent ME secular song and composition of an English song inspired by the French sermon tradition. Odo's conversion of lyrics 'from profane entertainment to mnemonic links between this world and the next' makes a bridge 'between the songs of entertainers and the songs of angels' (31).

360, 420, 7333.

1009 Newhauser, Richard. '"Strong it is to flitte" – A Middle English Poem on Death and Its Pastoral Context.' *Literature and Religion in the Later Middle Ages: Philological Studies in Honor of Siegfried Wenzel.* Ed. Richard G. Newhauser and John A. Alford. MRTS 118. Binghamton, NY: CMERS, State U of New York at Binghamton, 1995. 319–36. [Edition.]

Comments on the value of the manuscript contexts of ME lyrics, and the need to investigate the manuscript's source. Newhauser considers a lyric on death 'Strong it hus to flitte/Fro worldes blisse to pitte' [*3219*] in Bodleian MS Bodley 29, 'a familiar type of friar "miscellany"' (321). He demonstrates its Franciscan connections, particularly in 'the allegorical presentation of the physical characteristics and dress of what appears to be the Franciscan friar as *pugil domini contra diabolum*' (324), in the treatise containing the verse. The poem has three couplets, which are arranged according to the message to be imparted. In Bodley 29, where 'the friar's victory in spiritual warfare is to be emphasized, the poem ends with a reminder of heaven's bliss,' in the lines 'But werst it is to misse/of heuene-riche blisse.' However, in BL Harley 7322, the last lines are 'Strengest is to wende/To pine witouten ende,' since 'where sin must be cured, the poem's audience is left with the warning of the pains of hell' (328). The motif of the corpse's journey has developed from a lyric of the thirteenth century, 'If man him biðocte' [*1422*], which stresses the descent that begins when the body is moved 'from the bed to the floor immediately after death,' continues 'when the corpse is placed in the grave,' and is extended, 'in the poetic imagination, by the descent into hell' (329). Later lyrics on this theme preserve the rhyme words. Although the theme would have appeal in Franciscan preaching, 'there is no necessary connection between the lyric in its many forms and the

Annotations of Critical Works

Franciscans in most of its manuscript appearances' (331). In an 'Appendix' (331–6), Newhauser prints the Latin treatise containing the ME lyric, from Bodley 29, with notes on biblical references (334), and a translation (334–6).

1422, 3201, 3219, 4033, 4047, 4129.

1010 Nichols, Stephen G., and Siegfried Wenzel, eds. *The Whole Book: Cultural Perspectives on the Medieval Miscellany.* Ann Arbor, MI: U of Michigan P, 1995.

Not seen.

1011 O'Mara, V. M. 'Another Copy of "Who-so him beþouete/Inwardlich & ofte."' *Notes and Queries* 240 (1995): 30–1.

Notes the occurrence of the mortality lyric 'Who-so him biþouete' [*4129*] 'at the end of the Huntington Library copy of the early printed text, *The Seven Sheddings of the Blood of Jesus Christ.*' The poem has been entered 'after the colophon in an early-sixteenth-century hand . . . that annotates the text elsewhere' (31). This may have been thought to be a site where accidental discovery could enhance its effect, as on tombstone and mural inscriptions.

4129.

1012 Platzer, Hans. 'On the Disputed Reading of *Uerteþ* in the "Cuckoo Song."' *Neuphilologische Mitteilungen* 96 (1995): 123–43.

Offers cultural, lexicographical, linguistic, and semantic evidence on *uerteþ* in 'Svmer is icumen in' [*3223*]. Platzer summarizes comment on the date and localization of the manuscript [Harley 978], before examining proposed readings derived from AN *vert*, 'seek the green' and 'harbour in the green'; from Latin *vertere*, verbs of motion such as 'caper,' 'gambol,' and 'leap'; and from OE *feortan*, 'break wind.' The first seems 'least probable,' since a 'de-adjectival verb' would imply 'become green' (124); the second and third are more likely; the third most often proposed. Platzer's investigation does not support 'prejudices towards medieval culture . . . responsible for both the erotic interpretations of the "Cuckoo Song" and the adoption of the translation of "break wind"' (126), which seems not to have been socially acceptable. Lexicographic examination does not show an established loan form from *vertere*, although there is 'a record of a complex verb with the base -*vert* at about the time of the composition of the lyric (ante 1300)' (136). The Latinate setting of the poem's composition and demands of its rhyme scheme make a 'nonce borrowing of Lat. *vertere* seem plausible' (128). Study of voicing of ⟨f⟩ and ⟨v⟩ leads to the conclusion that 'mere probability favours the loan over the voiced variant' (136). Semantic and stylistic considerations favour a verb of fast motion for *uerteþ*, with a parallel relation to *sterteþ*; such a word would be a loan from *vertere*. Platzer prints the text in an appendix (137).

3223.

1013 Reichl, Karl. '"No more ne willi wiked be": Religious Poetry in a Franciscan Manuscript (Digby 2).' *Literature and Religion in the Later Middle Ages: Philological Studies in Honor of Siegfried Wenzel.* Ed. Richard G. Newhauser and John A. Alford. MRTS 118. Binghamton, NY: CMERS, State U of New York at Binghamton, 1995. 297–317.

Examines Bodleian MS Digby 2 and the possibility that it is a Franciscan manuscript, in the light of 'the all-pervasive influence of Franciscan spirituality on the early Middle English religious lyric' proposed particularly by Robbins, **230,** and Jeffrey, **639.** Reichl summarizes the manuscript's contents, mainly 'computational writings, philosophical treatises, and poetry' (300) in Latin, ME, and French. The lyric of the intention to become a friar 'No more will i wiked be' [*2293*] and a note of the feast day of St Francis hint at Franciscan origin, in spite of possible connections with the Dominicans, and Reichl places the manuscript 'in the Franciscan house of Oxford' (299). The contents imply that the manuscript's compilers and readers were 'clerics, whose life revolved both around their studies and around their religious calling' (314), disclosed in their interests in computation, astronomy, and medicine. Music with several works suggests 'professional musical skills in at least some of the scribes' (315), who were were 'well-versed in the lyrical production of their time' (316). The tone of 'fervent and subjective religiosity . . . is particularly associated with Franciscan poetry' (317), but neither religiosity nor such poetry was exclusively Franciscan. Reichl finds the moral stance of *2293* more convincing evidence of Franciscan origin.

888, 1066, 1365, 1697, 2293, 3432, 3963, 4223.

1014 Bitterling, Klaus. 'Additional Bibliographical Information for the *Index of Middle English Verse*.' *Notes and Queries* 241 (1996): 18–19.

Notes sources not listed in the entries for two works in *IMEV* and *SIMEV*. A poem on Fortune's wheel, '*ʒutte y se but fewe canne sece' [**4267.5*], has been printed from Bodleian Library MS Douce 78 'as Appendix G . . . of the *Chronicque de la Traïson et Mort de Richart Deux Roy Dengleterre mis en lumière* . . . par Benjamin Williams à Londres: Aux dépens de la Société, 1846' (18). Bitterling prints six stanzas of the poem as it appears in this source, which omits two previous stanzas printed by Bowers, **412**. 'Maydenes of Engelande sare may ye morne' [*2039.3*], a Scottish song to express scorn of the English after the Battle of Bannockburn, is preserved in several chronicle manuscripts. Bitterling notes its appearance 'in *Tytler's History of Scotland . . . New & Greatly Enlarged Edition*, 4 vols. (London and Glasgow, n.d.), I, 299, [which] has escaped notice so far' (19) and prints the text.

2039.3, *4267.5.

1015 Duncan, Thomas G. 'The Maid in the Moor and the Rawlinson Text.' *Review of English Studies* NS 47 (1996): 151–62. [Edition.]

An examination and reconstruction of 'Maiden in the mor lay' [*2037.5*], in which Duncan assesses previous editions and comments. He prints the poem as it is found in MS Rawlinson D.913, 'copied out as prose, in a seemingly casual manner' (151), and considers various edited versions, including those of Sisam, **30**, and Robbins, *RobbinsS*, **51**. The relation of *2037.5* to Richard de Ledrede's *Peperit virgo*, noted by Greene, **314**, influenced later editions, such as those of Sisam and Sisam, **69**, and Dobson, **87**. Greene argues for following the Latin in restructuring the English text, whereas Dobson prefers the English form. Duncan sees significance in repetition in both poems. [See **886**]. He urges caution in comparisons of the Rawlinson text and the Latin lyric, 'for however likely it is that the Rawlinson scribe and the Irish bishop knew the same tune and therefore the English poem in exactly the same form, this cannot be assumed' (155). Duncan proposes that the Rawlinson scribe was 'reluctant to waste space and effort,' and so reduced 'copying of repeated material to a minimum.' To avoid obscuring the poem's form, he showed the pattern of full and partial repetition in the first stanza, and abbreviated as he continued to write. Duncan offers a reading (158–9) which expands abbreviated lines and adds final -*e* as necessary; he reconciles this with the stanzaic and metrical structure of *Peperit virgo*. Considered thus, 'the text as found in the Rawlinson MS is on the whole fairly accurate' (160), with few cases of suspect metrical structure. Duncan suggests that the scribe was also a performer, 'or at least . . . someone who could readily make sense of the system of abbreviation in the light of and guided by the music' (161). To think of the work as a dance song could 'further undermine the credibility of

Annotations of Critical Works

interpretations of this lyric as sophisticated Christian allegory,' [see Robertson, **298**], but it 'loses nothing of its curious combination of simplicity and enigmatic allure' (162).

2037.5.

1016 Edwards, A.S.G. 'An Unrecorded Copy of *Index of Middle English Verse* 3724.5.' *Notes and Queries* 241 (1996): 403. [Edition.]

Notes the occurrence, not previously recorded, of the lyric of a variable mistress 'Thus musyng in my mynd gretly mervelyng' [*3724.5*] in University of Chicago MS 253, 'a copy of the Middle English prose *Brut*.' Edwards prints the lyric, indicating variants from BL Add. 5465.

3724.5.

1017 Hunt, Tony. 'The Poetic Vein: Phlebotomy in Middle English and Anglo-Norman Verse.' *English Studies* 77 (1996): 311–22. [Edition.]

Bloodletting in medieval medicine was used for diagnosis, prognosis, and as a treatment for many disorders. As well as prose treatises on the subject, there were verses of instruction. Hunt summarizes some uses of the procedure and presents an extract from John of Mirfield's *Breviarium Bartholomei*, before his edition of 'Veynes þer be XXX^{ti} and two' [*3848*], from MS BL Sloane 2457, which here begins 'The maystres that usen blood-lettyng.' The work explains the veins and methods to be employed. Hunt includes an AN poem for comparison, and notes variations in other manuscript sources for the ME composition. He prints two other ME poems on bloodletting, 'To knawe the vaynes to let blode one' [*7551*] and 'A man may be laten blod in two and twenti stedis' [*7015*], in an appendix (321–2). [See also Mayer, **214**.]

3848, 7015, 7551.

1018 Jager, Eric. 'The Book of the Heart: Reading and Writing the Medieval Subject.' *Speculum* 71 (1996): 1–26.

Investigates the book of the heart, 'a trope that dates from the birth of the codex in late antiquity and that ever since has haunted our ideas about writing and the subject' (1). Among Jager's numerous examples are the metaphor of the Charter of Christ, which 'likens the suffering Savior's body to a written document' (13), and a poem of the Passion, 'Ihesus þat hast me der abouȝte' [*1761*], which 'urges Christ to write a record of each event on the believer's heart' (14).

239, 1761, 3700.

1019 Keiser, George R. 'A New Text of, and New Light on, the *Supplement to the Index of Middle English Verse*, 4106.5.' *Notes and Queries* 241 (1996): 15–18.

Interprets texts of 'Who that mannyth hym with his kynne' [*4106.5*], from 'a small collection of witty and wise proverbs and precepts . . . in the *Boke of St Albans*' (15). It is found in manuscript form on blank leaves in a print of Alliaco Petrus's *Meditationes*, and is printed in *Here be Certayne Questyons of Kynge Bocthus*. Keiser has found another manuscript copy in BL MS Add. 30338, 'a medical miscellany,' which he prints (16). The manuscript was probably copied in a monastic institution, a surprising setting for these verses 'with their emphasis on practical, worldly matters.' Comparison with the copy in the *Boke of St Albans* reveals 'the skilful and amusing display of wit,' from 'an educated clerical mind, trained in language and rhetoric.' The printed text seems debased, 'probably resulting from a period of oral transmission and presenting a literal-minded reworking of the original.' The manuscript sheds more light on some wayward acts. It is unwise to expect support from one's kin and to surround a garden with cherry trees (so 'drawing those whom they are meant to keep out'). Making a fire of spoons is 'an act of foolish extravagance.' The warning against unwise love depends on the sense of *gromes*: as someone 'below one's station,' if the word is *grom*, or 'of coming to love through anger,' if it is *gram*. The error in 'fetching ale in tankards . . . at first defies easy explanation' (17), since *tankard* was a vessel for storage or for drinking when the poem was written. The reader must choose between 'the folly . . . of fetching ale in a drinking vessel, which might leave a thirst unslaked, or . . . in a barrel . . . which will lead to drunkenness,' which Keiser favours. Omission of this line in the printed version may mean that the meaning changed while the verse was transmitted orally, to result in 'the reconstructed and far less interesting version printed by the Schoolmaster Printer of St Albans' (18). [See Bühler, **448**.]

36, 761, 3848, 4106.5.

1020 Cartlidge, Neil. 'Orthographical Variation in the Middle English Lyrics of BL Cotton Caligula A.ix.' *Neuphilologische Mitteilungen* 98 (1997): 253–9.

Two spelling systems of 'The Owl and the Nightingale' [*1384*] in BL MS Cotton Caligula A.ix. (copied in one hand) suggest that the scribe's exemplar [X] was 'the work of two scribes whose spelling practices were markedly different from each other [X1, X2]' (253). The other copy of *1384*, in Jesus College, Oxford 29, has fewer traces of the differences, but was apparently copied from X. Among other works probably derived from X are six ME lyrics, which Cartlidge examines for orthographic variation; for signs that other ME texts were copied by X1 and X2; and for traces of any other hands in X. The lyrics are 'Doomsday' ['Hwenne ich þench of domes dai ful sore i me adrede,' *3967*], 'The Last Day' ['þene latemeste dai wenne we sulen farren,' *3517*], 'An Orison to Our Lady' ['On hire is al me lif ilong,' *2687*], 'Death's Wither-clench' ['Mon may longe lyues wene,' *2070*], 'A Lutel Soth Sermun ['Herkneþ alle gode men and stylle sitteþ adun,' *1091*], and 'The Ten Abuses' ['Hwan þu sixst on leode,' *4051*]. 'Will and Wit' ['Hwenne so wil wit ofer-stieð,' *4016*], in Caligula A.ix, was probably lost from Jesus 29. When they are found together in these manuscripts, they retain the same order. Some of the lyrics are also found (generally singly) in other manuscripts. Cartlidge's scrutiny of the frequency of characters and forms reveals three possible kinds of variation. These are caused by 'dialectical properties of the lyrics before they were copied into X' (254); by the possibility of several X scribes with different orthographical practices; and by inconsistencies of the Caligula A.ix scribe. Most variations are of the second type. He finds two groups within the five longer texts: *3967* and *3517*; and *2070, 2687,* and *1091*. Analysis suggests that there were four scribes, with the possibility of six. This number suggests that X must also have contained 'a substantial number of English texts that were not copied into [Caligula A.ix]' (256); some are perhaps found in Jesus 29.

295, 1091, 1384, 2070, 2687, 3517, 3967, 4016, 4051.

1021 Lerer, Seth. 'The Genre of the Grave and the Origins of the Middle English Lyric.' *Modern Language Quarterly* 58 (1997): 127–61.

Explores the earliest ME lyrics and relates them to OE poems. Lerer examines first 'Ic añ witles' ['[þe]h þet hi can wittes fule-wis,' *3512*], apparently 'the earliest piece of Middle English lyric poetry' (128), to reveal implications of standards of form and language and 'the idea of the lyric voice itself and . . . the birth of subjectivity in the vernacular' (129). Since most first-person OE texts involve 'a speaking object or narrativized versions of Christian doctrine' (130), the lyric is foreign. Lerer considers the literary culture of the period and the expression of emerging nationhood in the use of ME. The tropes of 'architectural form and topographical manipulation' are significant in articulating 'new Norman projects of castle building, cathedral reorganization, and forest management,' and AS concerns with 'the transitoriness of human works and with death and burial'

(132). 'The Rhyme of King William' ['Castelas he let wyrcean'], in the *Peterborough Chronicle*, renders his life in 'verse forms of the Conqueror's own court' (134). Among the loanwords, *castelas* 'emblamatizes the Conquest to the English chronicler' (135), and emphasizes the imposition of foreign buildings and Norman barons. Wulfstan of Worcester employs 'principles of Continental verse against a Continental subject' (137), by using an architectural metaphor to lament the church's interest in creating Norman buildings rather than caring for souls; his is the first English work in rhymed couplets. 'Durham' ['Is ðeos burch bretome geond Breotenrice,' *1608.5*] and *The First Worcester Fragment* ['Sanctus beda was iboren þer on bretone mid us,' *3074.3*] recall life before the Conquest in the style of OE verse, and thus 'inhume Anglo-Saxon England' (138). Poems such as 'The Soul's Address to the Body' ['* . . . on earde/and alle þeo i-sceaftan þe to him to sculen,' **2684.5*], 'The Grave' ['ðe wes bold ȝebyld er þu i-boren were,' *3497*], and 'The Latemest Day' ['þene latemeste dai wenne we sulen farren,' *3517*] retain 'preoccupations with the structure of burial, with the architecture of death' (141), in '[t]he trope of the grave, and of the body, as a house' (143). The soul's house is beautiful in Godric's hymn, 'Sainte Nicolaes godes druð' [*3031*]. Images of OE verse preserved in *3512* (perhaps written by the Tremulous Hand responsible for *3074.3* and **2684.5*), lead Lerer to see it 'not as Carleton Brown's first Middle English poem [*BrownXIII*, **36**] but, perhaps, as the last Old English one' (146). He discerns the OE heritage in poems that reveal 'features of the grave verse of late Anglo-Saxon and post-Conquest England' (147), such as 'Foweles in the frith' [*864*], 'Mirie it is while sumer ilast' [*2163*], 'Wen þe turuf is þi tuur' [*4044*] and 'Bryd one brere' [*521*]. He proposes 'a new, historically minded understanding of the fragments *as fragments*' (151) and of 'expressions of the alienation that provokes the lyric statement and, in historical terms, locates the speaking subject in a landscape of displacement' (152). This is voiced in 'The Owl and the Nightingale' [*1384*], which Lerer examines at length. The poem is followed, in Cotton Caligula A.ix, by 'Death's Wither-Clench' ['Mon may longe lyues wene,' *2070*], a sharp, sombre comment on the debate of two lively birds. In early ME lyrics, Lerer finds voices 'from castles and from graves [to] remind the readers of conquest's "wither-clench" and of the afterlife of Old English idioms and genres in later lyrics' (161).

521, 694.5, 864, 1384, 1608.5, 1861, 2070, 2163, *2684.5, 3031, 3074.3, 3497, 3512, 3517, 4037, 4044.

1022 Stanbury, Sarah. 'Regimes of the Visual in Premodern England: Gaze, Body, and Chaucer's *Clerk's Tale.*' *New Literary History* 28 (1997): 261–89.

The body of Christ crucified is the spectacular body in medieval representation; it is the object of a gaze of devotional desire, of the 'eye of piety' (267), and thus 'independent of gendered prohibitions or distinctions.' In some Passion lyrics, the Virgin's empathetic, suffering gaze can engage 'his returned look as well as the gaze of the reader/spectator' (268). The effect is 'to fracture visual distance through meditation.' It is seen in 'Man and wyman loket to me' [*2042*], a command from 'the speaking body on the Cross . . . to stop and study his wounds, setting in motion a move to a tactile close-up' (269), to efface boundaries to the reader/viewer's intimate engagement, without loss of the voice's authority. Stanbury explains various representations of the Crucifixion scene and implications of gazes of those gathered around the Cross, before relating the politics of the visibility of the body to Chaucer's references to Griselda's body in the *Clerk's Tale.*

110, 497, 1073, 2042, 3109, 3211, 3862, 4019, 4263.

Works Cited but not Annotated

The works listed here have been mentioned briefly in the introductions and annotations, sometimes through references in the works which have been annotated.

Auden, W.H. *The Dyer's Hand.* London: Faber, 1963.
Batho, Edith C. *The Ettrick Shepherd.* Cambridge: Cambridge UP, 1927.
Block, K.S. *Ludus Coventriae or The Plaie Called Corpus Christi, Cotton MS Vespasian D.viii* . EETS ES 120. London: Oxford UP, 1922 *for* 1917; rpt 1961.
Böddeker, K., ed. *Altenglische Dichtungen des MS. Harl. 2253.* Berlin, 1878.
Brown, James Walter. 'An Elizabethan Song-Cycle' and 'Some Elizabethan Lyrics.' *Cornhill Magazine* 48 (1920): 572–9; (1921): 285–96.
Burke, Kenneth. 'Three Definitions.' *Kenyon Review* 13 (1951): 173–92.
Chaucer, Geoffrey. *The Riverside Chaucer.* 3rd edn. Gen. ed. Larry D. Benson Oxford: Oxford UP, 1987.
Fowler, David C. *A Literary History of the Popular Ballad.* Durham, NC: Duke UP, 1968.
Frye, Northrop. *Anatomy of Criticism.* Princeton: Princeton UP, 1957.
Furnivall, F.J., ed. *The Digby Mysteries.* London: Trübner for the New Shakspere Society, 1882.
Gilbert, J.T. 'Archives of the See of Ossory.' *Historical MSS Report* 10. Appendix, Part V (London, 1859).
Graves, J. 'English and Norman Songs of the 14th Century.' *Notes and Queries* 2 (1850): 385–6.
Guest, Edwin. *A History of English Rhythms.* London: Pickering, 1838.
Hirsch, E.D. *Validity in Interpretation.* New Haven, CT: Yale UP, 1964.
Langer, Susanne. *Feeling and Form.* New York: Scribner, 1953.
MacCracken, Henry Noble, ed. *The Minor Poems of John Lydgate. Edited from all available MSS., with an attempt to establish The Lydgate Canon.* Vol. 1. Religious Poems. EETS ES 107. London: Kegan Paul; Frowde, Oxford UP, 1911 *(for* 1910).
———. Vol. 2. Secular Poems. EETS 192. London: Milford, Oxford UP, 1934 *(for* 1933).
Newman, Ernest. *A Musical Motley.* New York: Knopf, 1925.
Olson, Elder. 'The Lyric.' *Papers of the Midwest Modern Language Association* 1 (1968): 59–66.
Paris, Gaston. *Mélanges de littérature française du moyen âge.* Paris: Champion, 1912.
Peck, Russell. *Chaucer's Lyrics and* Anelida and Arcite: *An Annotated Bibliography 1900 to 1980.* The Chaucer Bibliographies 1. Toronto: U of Toronto P, 1983.
Ridley, Florence H. 'Middle Scots Writers.' *A Manual of the Writings in Middle English 1050–1500.* Gen. ed. Albert E. Hartung. New Haven, CT: Connecticut Academy of Arts and Sciences, 1973.
Robbins, Rossell Hope. 'The Lyrics.' *Companion to Chaucer Studies.* Ed. Beryl Rowland. Toronto: Oxford UP. 313–31.

Rosenstein, Roy. '*Mouvance* and the Editor as Scribe: *Trascittore Traditore?*' *Romanic Review* 80 (1989): 159–71.

Scheps, Walter, and J. Anna Looney. *Middle Scots Poets: A Reference Guide to James I of Scotland, Robert Henryson, William Dunbar, and Gavin Douglas.* Boston, MA: Hall, 1986.

Schlüter, A. 'Über die Sprache und Metrik der mittelenglischen weltlichen und geistlichen lyrischen Lieder des MS. Harl. 2253.' *Archiv* 71 (1884): 153–84, 357–88.

Spargo, John Webster. 'Chaucer's Love-Days.' *Speculum* 15 (1940): 36–56.

Steele, R. ed. *The English Poems of Charles d'Orléans.* Vol. 1. EETS 215, 220. London: Oxford UP, 1941. Vol. 2. Ed. R. Steele and Mabel Day. 1946 *for* 1944. Repr. as one vol., 1970.

Toulmin Smith, Lucy, ed. *York Plays: The Plays Performed by the Crafts or Mysteries of York on the Day of Corpus Christi in the 14th, 15th, and 16th Centuries.* Oxford: Clarendon, 1885.

Varnhagen, Hermann. 'Ein fragment des 12. jahrh.' *Anglia* 3 (1880): 423–5.

Wanley, Humfrey. *A Catalogue of the Harleian Collection of Manuscripts . . . in the British Museum.* London, 1759.

Warton, Thomas. *The History of English Poetry, from the Close of the Eleventh to the Commencement of the Eighteenth Century.* London: Dodsley, 1714.

White, Beatrice. 'Frederick James Furnivall.' *Essays and Studies 1952* NS 5. Ed. Arundel Esdaile. London: Murray, 1952. 64–76.

Whiting, E.K., ed. *The Poems of John Audelay.* EETS 184. London: Oxford UP, 1931. New York: Kraus, 1988.

Willeumier-Schalij, J.M. 'On Indexing Mediaeval Songs and Poems.' *Neelandica Manuscripta: Essays Presented to G.J. Lieftinck, III.* Litteras textuales. Amsterdam: van Gendt, 1972. 15–17.

Wimsatt, James I. *Chaucer and His French Contemporaries: Natural Music in the Fourteenth Century.* Toronto: U of Toronto P, 1991.

Wimsatt, W.K., Jr., and Monroe C. Beardsley. *The Verbal Icon.* Lexington, KY: U of Kentucky P, 1954.

Wright, Thomas. *Songs and Carols Printed from a Manuscript in the Sloane Collection in the British Museum.* London, 1836.

Zink, Michel. *La pastourelle: poésie et folklore au moyen âge.* Paris: Bordas, 1972.

Zumthor, Paul. *Langage et techniques poétiques à l'époque romane.* Paris: Klincksieck, 1963.

Index of Scholars and Critics

References in this index are to the numbers of annotations. Numbers in bold face indicate the author or editor of the work annotated; those in regular typeface indicate a reference to the scholar in that annotation. A lower-case *r* following the annotation number denotes the reviewer of the work annotated at that number.

Abel, Patricia **469**
Ackerman, Robert W. **483**
Adams, Robert **260**
Adamson, Margot **35**
Albright, Daniel **844**
Allen, Mark **928**
Allen, Judson Boyce **821**
Allison, Alexander W., et al. **67**
Alspach, Russell K. **238**
Amati, Antonietta **996**
Anglo, Sydney **438**r
Anonymous reviewer of *BrownXIII* **36**r
Anderson, J.J. **728**
Anderson, George K. **275**
Arens, Werner **914**
Arngart, O. **255**
Astell, Ann W. **929**
Audiau, Jean **146**
Axton, Richard **930**

B., R. **244**r
Baird-Lange, Lorrayne Y. **845**
Bakhtin, Mikhail 977
Baker, D.C. **523**, **792**
Baldwin, Charles Sears **165**
Barratt, Alexandra **100**, **630**, **793**, **822**, **846**, **931**
Baskerville, Charles Read **147-8**, 863
Bateson, F.W. **276**
Batho, Edith C. **345**
Baugh, Nita Scudder **56**
Baugh, Albert C. **277**
Baum, Pauli Franklin **142**, 772
Bawcutt, Priscilla **901**
Bazire, Joyce **322**, **773**, **847**
Beadle, Richard, and A.E.B. Owen **84**
Bell, H. Idris **131**, 133
Benedikz, B.S. **748**
Bennett, J.A.W. **440**, **774**
———, and G.V. Smithers **65**, **562**, **732**
Bennett, Josephine Waters **386**, 636
Benning, Helmut **775**
Benskin, Michael **776**
Bergner, Heinz **681**, **794**, **823**
Berry, Francis **345**, **387**
Bessai, Frank **560**
Besserman, Lawrence C. **729**

Besserman, Lawrence L., Gail Gilman, and Victor Weinblatt **541**
Best, Larry G. **705**
Bibby, Cyril **682**
Birney, Earle **198**
Bishop, Ian **862**
Bitterling, Klaus **706**, **1014**
Blake, Norman F. **542**, **665**
Blanchfield, Lynne Sandra **884**
Bloomfield, Morton W. 749
Böddeker, Karl 166, 171, 239, 255, 273
Boenig, Robert **707**
Boffey, Julia **750**, **795**, **848**, **946-7**, **985**
———, and Carol M. Meale **948**
Boklund-Lagopoulou, Karin **986**
Bolle, Wilhelm **127**, 134
Booth, Mark W. **708**
Bornstein, Diane **631**
Borroff, Marie **648**
Bowers, R.H. **60**, **199**, **267**, **285-7**, **306-11**, **322**, **326-7**, **346-50**, **364**, 370, **374**, **386**, 403, **412**, **447**, **493**, 683, 1014
Bowie, Linda Julian **824**
Bowra, Maurice **426**
Boyer, Raymond **683**
Braddy, Haldeen **297**r
Bradford, Melvin E. **543**
Bradley, S.A.J. **632**
Braekman, W.L. **730**
Braekman, Martine **987**
Braekman, Willy L. **587**, **684**
———, and Peter S. Macaulay **524**, **561**
Breeze, Andrew **885**, **902**, **915**, **968-9**, **988-91**, **997-8**
Brehe, S.K. **932**
Brett, Cyril **157**
Brewer, Derek S. **47**r, **351**, **470**, **796**, 875
Brian, Beverley **573**
Brice, Douglas **397**
Brink, Bernhard ten 107
Briscoe, Marianne G. **882**r
Brockman, Bennett A. **588**
Brook, G.L. **36**r, **39**r, **42**, 166, 171, 273, 330, 530, 586, 732, 781, 835, 872, 875, 971, 999
Brown, Beatrice Daw **153**, 167
Brown, Calvin S. **261**
Brown, Carleton, *BrownXIV* **31**, *BrownXIII* **36**, **37**r, *BrownXV* **39**, 87, 132, 143, 153, 158,

Index of Scholars and Critics

160, 170, 186, 211, **213**, **224**, 227, 229, 239, 250, 255, 270, 273, 332, 336, 381, 404, 497, 500, 536, 574, 578, 599, 603, 626, 646, 732, 819, 828, 872, 890, 983, 992, 1021
——, rev. G.V. Smithers, *BrownXIV* **48**, 481, 621, 645, 992
Brown, Huntington **243**, 246, 249, 248
Brunner, Karl **180–3**, **200**
——, and Karl Hammerle **162**
Buckley, Vincent **508**
Bühler, Curt F. **201**, **205**, **288**, **328**, **352**, **375**, **388**, **398**, 410, **413**, **427–8**, **448**, **457–8**, **471**, **525**
Bukofzer, Manfred F. **206**, **234**, **244**, 252, 263, 265, 268
Burrow, John A. **85**, **709**, **777**, **933**
——, and Thorlac Turville-Petre **101**
Burton, T.L. **751–2**
Bynum, Caroline W. **639r**

Calwell, John **880r**
Camargo, Martin **731**, **949**
Cartlidge, Neil **1020**
Casieri, Sabino **441**
Casling, Dennis, and V. J. Scattergood **602**
Cawley, A.C. **55r**, **289**
Chambers, E.K. **247**, 329, 351
——, and F. Sidgwick **18**, 407, 708, 875
Chewning, Harris **312**
Chickering, Howell D., Jr. **562**
Child, Francis 514
Chu-chin Sun, Cecile **797**
Colaco, Jill **863**
Coleman, Janet **753**
Colledge, Edmund **603**, 803
Collins, Fletcher **172**
Comper, Francis M.M. **38**
Conlee, John W. **97**
Cook, Albert Stanburrough **26**
Cooling, June **399**
Cooper, Helen **87r**
Copeland, Rita **825**
Copley, J. **329**, **389–90**, **400**, **429**
Cottle, Basil **59r**, **526**
Cox, D.C., and Carter Revard **849**
Crampton, Georgia Ronan **732**
Croft, P.J. **754**
Cross, J.E. **391**, **574**
Crowther, J.D.W. **563**, **633**
Curry, Jane L. **430**, **459**, 484
Cutler, John L. **248**, **313**, **353**, 368, 404
Cutts, John P. **376**, **826**, 377

D'Angelo, Benito **798**
Datta, Kitty **864**
Davenport, Tony **799**
Davenport, W.A. **950**
Davidson, Clifford **634**
Davies, J. Glyn 131, **133**
Davies, R.T. **61**, **79r**, **81r**, **86r**, 87, 461, 492, 497, **539r**, 574, 595, 663, 732, 834, 971

Davis, Norman **65**, **321r**
Day, Mabel **29**, 468, 866, 884
Dearmer, Percy, R. Vaughan Williams, and Martin Shaw **34**, 396
Degginger, Stuart, H.L. **330**, 602, 857, 971
Dent, E.J. **190**
Deyermond, Alan **934**
Dickins, Bruce, and R.M. Wilson **47**, **202**, 536, 732
Diehl, Patrick **850**
Dobson, E.J., and F.Ll. Harrison **87**, 886, 971, 999, 1015
Dodds, Madeleine Hope **154**
Donaldson, E. Talbot **79**, **290**, **414**, 567
Donaldson, Kara Virginia **970**
Dove, Mary **865**
Downing, Janay **527**
Dronke, Peter 79, **431**, **472**, **509**, **604**, **649**, **710**, **935**
Dubois, Marguerite-Marie **442**
Dudley, Louise **137**
Duncan, Thomas G. **87r**, **104**, **880r**, **886**, **971**, **999**, **1015**
Dunn, Charles W., and Edward T. Byrnes **76**
Dunning, T.P. **509r**, **575r**, **583r**
Dutka, J.A. **87r**
Dyboski, Roman **19**

Easting, Robert **951**
Eberly, Susan S. **916**
Edden, Valerie **866**
Edwards, A.S.G. **528–9**, **589–90**, **1016**
——, and A.W. Jenkins **591**
Einarsson, Stefán **432**
Elliot, Thomas J. **592**, 876
Embree, Dan **851**
——, and Elizabeth Urquhart **887**
Erb, Peter C. **564**, 647
Ericson, Eston Everett **207**, 248, 291
Erlebach, Peter **917**
Evans, W.O. **495**, 861
Everett, Dorothy **321r**

Fain, John Tyree **256**, **291**
Fallows, David **650**, **848r**
Farnham, Willard **150**
Fehr, Bernhard **11–12**, **14**
Fein, Susanna Greer **888**, **903**, **936**, **972**
Fenton, Iain **88b**
Fifield, Merle **449**
Finlayson, John **918**
Fletcher, Alan J. **651**, **666**, **685**, **786**, **800**, **867**, **919**, 1004
Fletcher, Bradford Y. **91a**, **686**
Flügel, Ewald **7–8**, **15**
Förster, Max **4**, **27**, **144**
Fowler, Alistair **889**
Fowler, David C. **827**, 986
Frankis, John **973**
Frankis, P.J. **354**, **365**, **401**, **415**, **450**
Franklin, Michael J. **848r**, **868**

Frese, Dolores W. **974**
Frey, Charles **652**, **711**
Friedlander, Carolynn VanDyke **687**
Friedman, Albert B. **392**, **402**, **606**–**7**
Friend, Albert C. **331**
Fries, Maureen **733**, **755**
Frost, William 45
Frye, Northrop 854
Fulton, Helen **828**
Funke, Otto **40**
Furnivall, Frederick J. **4**–**5**, **9**, **13**

Garbáty, Thomas J. **90**, **829**
Gardner, Helen **75**
Gardner, John **565**
Garrett, Robert Max **120**–**1**, **128**, 792
Gellrich, Jesse M. **608**
Gerould, G.H. 37r
Giaccherini, Enrico **688**
Gibińska, Marta **609**, **653**
Gibson, J.A. 445, 971
Gierasch, Walter 355
Gilbert, J.T. **676**
Gilchrist, Annie G. **125**
Gillespie, Vincent **882**r
Glasscoe, Marion **869**
Gneuss, Helmut **416**
Gradon, Pamela **566**
Graves, J. 676
Gray, Douglas **81**, **91**, **102**, **417**, **433**, **444**r, **451**, **496**, **510**, **544**, **575**, **610**, **756**, **801**, **830**, **870**
Green, Richard Firth **654**, **920**, **952**, **975**
Greenberg, Cheryl **757**
Greene, Richard Leighton **37**, **39**r, **59**, **78**, **86**, **87**, **173**, **225**, 236, **314**, 329, **332**, **377**, 396, 407, **418**, **434**, **460**–**2**, **484**, 567, 581, 606, **611**–**12**, 663, 676, 693, 732, 871, 874, 890, 964, 980, 1015
Greg, W.W. **122**, **36**r
Grennen, Joseph E. **871**, **890**, **904**
Gretsch, Mechthild **92**
Griffith, Richard R. **452**
Griffiths, Jeremy **1006**

Hala, James **904**
Hall, Joseph **28**, 94a
Halliburton, David G. 79, **511**, 595
Hallwas, John E. **613**–**14**, **655**, **667**
Hammerle, Karl **184**
Hammond, Eleanor Prescott **112**–**13**, **123**, **152**
Hands, Rachel **576**
Handschin, Jacques **268**
Hanham, Alison **378**
Hanna, Ralph, III **530**, **734**
Hanson-Smith, Elizabeth **712**
Harbert, Bruce **516**r
Hardman, Philippa **689**
Hardy, Adelaide **473**
Hargreaves, Henry **531**, **668**, **976**
Harley, Marta Powell **905**

Harrington, David V. **872**
Harris, Joseph **567**
Harvey, Carol J. **690**
Haskell, Ann S. **66**, **577**
Hatto, Arthur T. **333**, **474**
Heffernan, Thomas J. **636**, **758**–**60**, **778**, **802**
Heidtmann, Peter **568**
Helterman, Jeffrey A. **593**
Hench, Atcheson L. **203**
Heningham, Eleanor K. **226**
Henry, Nat 379
Heuser, W. **16**, **108**–**9**, **114**–**15**, 168, 185, 194, 238
Hieatt, A. Kent, and Constance Hieatt **545**
Hill, Betty **463**, **578**, **691**
Hill, Thomas D. **637**, **692**, **803**, 861, **873**–**4**
Hinton, Rebecca **953**
Hirsch, E.D. 658
Hirsh, John C. **512**, **546**, **615**, **669**, **713**–**14**
Hodder, Karen **513**
Hodgart, M.J.C. **334**
Hodgson, Phyllis 51r, 297r
Hoepfner, Theodore C. 243, **245**–**6**, 249, 248
Hogg, James **735**
Holland, Norman 380
Holthausen, Ferdinand **145**, 168, 185, 194
Horrall, Sarah M. **804**, **852**
Horstmann, Carl **9**
Howell, Andrew J. **736**, 977
Hunt, Tony **1017**
Hussey, Maurice **393**
Hussey, S.S. 48r

Immaculate, Sister Mary [Creek] **227**
Innes, Susan M. **853**

Jacobs, Nicolas **101**r
Jager, Eric **1018**
Janofsky, Klaus **616**
James, Thomas Beaumont **94a**
Jansen, Sharon L., and Kathleen H. Jordan **98**
Jansen, Johannes Petrus Maria **95**, **921**
Jauss, David **805**
Jeffrey, David L. **569**, **638**–**9**, **715**, **779**, **831**, 1013
Jemielity, Thomas 79, **532**
Jeremy, Sister Mary [Finnegan] **269**, **497**, 562
Johnston, G.K.W. **381**, **403**
Johnston, Jeanette **693**
Jones, F. **875**, **937**
Jones, William Powell **164**
Jungman, Robert E. **716**

κ, ε.τ. **105**, 125
Kail, J. **17**
Kaiser, Rolf **49**
Kane, George **292**–**3**, **404**, **491**, **574**, **579**, **585**, 658, 861, **876**
Kar, G. **174**
Keiser, George R. **854**, **1019**
Keller, Joseph R. **533**

Kendrick, Laura **717**
Kennedy, Ruth **891**
Kenyon, John S. **248**
Ker, N.R. **64**, **475**
Kerrigan, John **99**
Kessel-Brown, Deidre **938**
Kiernan, Kevin S. **640**
King, Pamela M. **761**
Kinney, Thomas L. **485**, 876
Kittredge, G.L. **156**
Klinefelter, Ralph A. **315**
Knowlton, Sister Mary Arthur **594**
Kohl, Stephan **939**
Kooper, Erik **892**
Kreuzer, James **44**, **208–9**, 219, **294**
Kurvinen, Auvo **323**, **580**, 773, 847

Laing, Margaret, and Angus McIntosh **780**
Lambdin, R.T. **954**
Langenfelt, Gösta **419**
Lasater, Alice E. **617**
Lass, Roger **476**
Lawton, David A. **922**
Le May, Sister Marie de Lourdes **169**
Lees, Clare A. **93**r
Lepow, Lauren **718**
Lerer, Seth **855**, **1021**
Levy, Bernard **737**
Lewis, Arthur O., Jr., 379, **366**
Lindström, Bengt **1007**
Linn, Irving **210**
Lockwood, W.B. **435**
Löfvenberg, M.T. **251**
Long, Mary McDonald **356**
Loomis, Roger Sherman, and Rudolph Willard **43**
Louis, Cameron **955–6**
Lucas, Peter J. **719**, **762**
Luisi, David **498**
Luria, Maxwell S., and Richard L. Hoffman **79**, 732
Lynch, Andrew **957**

Mabbott, T.O. **278**
McBryde, J.M., Jr. **116**
McClellan, William **977**
MacCracken, Henry Noble 88, **117**, **129**, 213, 224, 315, 360, 468, 591, 921, 924
MacDonald, Alasdair **906**
McFarlane, K.B. **57**r
McGarry, Sister Loretta **195**
Machan, Tim **781**, 815
McIntosh, Angus **670**, **694**, 983, **992**
McNamer, Sarah **958**
Maddicott, J.R. **877**
Malone, Kemp **186**, **211**, **367**, 381, 481, 530
Malvern, Marjorie M. **782**
Manning, Stephen **394**, **404**, **420**, **443**, **461**, **486**, 491, 511, 562, 585, 595, 605, 645, 658, 708, 803, 861, 886
Mantovani, Maddelena **738**, **783**

Manzalaoui, Mahmoud **477**
Margherita, Gayle **1000**
Marx, C.W. **940**
Mason, H.A. **405**, **581**
Matheson, Lister M. **806**
Matonis, A.T.E. **582**, **763**, 828, **907**
Matsuda, Takami **807**, **923**
Maxwell, J.C. **436**
Mayer, Claudius F. **214**
Maynard, Theodore **178**
Mead, Elizabeth V. **421**
Meale, Carol M. **949**r
Means, Laurel **978**
Medcalf, Stephen **764**
Meech, Sandford B. **228**
Meier-Ewart, C. **641**
Menner, Robert J. **229**, **252**, **270**, 530, 992
Meroney, Howard **239**, **257**, 270, 530
Miller, Catharine K. **279**
Miller, Lewis H., Jr. **487**
Miller, William Ian **832**
Millett, Bella **1008**
Miskimin, Alice S. **575**r
Mitsui, Tōru **514**
Moe, Phyllis **534**
Moffat, Douglas **93**, **833**, **993**
Monda, Joseph B. **547**
Mooney, Linne R. **765**, **808**, **924**
Moore, Arthur K. **79**, **258**, **271–2**, **280**, **295–7**, **464**, 491, 540, 708, 835, 892
Moore, Bruce **925**
Moran, Virginia A. **595**
Moran, Jo Ann Hoeppner **395**
Morgan, Gwendolyn **959**
Morris, Richard **6**
Moser, Thomas C., Jr. **893**
Mossé, Fernand **50**
Muir, Kenneth **41**
Müller, Alexander **130**
Müller, Wolfgang G. **809**
Muraoka, Yu **535**
Murray, Hilda M.R. **23**
Mustanoja, Tauno F. **357**, **548**

Newhauser, Richard **1009**
Newman, Florence **834**
Nicholls, Jonathan **784**
Nichols, Stephen G., and Siegfried Wenzel **1010**
Nicholson, John 25
Nicholson, R.H. **720**
Nitecki, Alicia K. **766**
Norton-Smith, John **88**
Nwuneli, M.L. **721**

Oakden, J.P. **163**
———, and Elizabeth R. Innes **187**
Obst, Wolfgang **810**
O'Donoghue, Bernard, and Christopher Woolgar **739**
Ogden, James **1001**

Ogilvie-Thomson, S. **618**
Oliver, Raymond 79, **549**, 658, 999
O'Mara, Veronica M. **878, 1011**
Onions, C. Talbut **119**, **170**, **262**, 393
Orme, Nicholas **979**
Osberg, Richard H. **671, 722, 767, 835, 856**
Owen, Lewis J. **536**
———, and Nancy H. Owen **72**
Owst, G.R. **175**

Padelford, Frederick Morgan **25, 134**
———, and Allen R. Benham 127, **20**
Paden, William D. **94**
Palmer, Barbara D. **695**
Panofsky, Richard J. **740**
Paris, Gaston 837
Parker, David R. **103r, 980**
Parr, Johnstone 316
Patterson, Frank Allen **24, 33**
Pattinson, Bruce **37r**
Payne, Robert O. **297r**
Pearsall, Derek **672**, 963
Pearson, Lu Emily **196**
Peck, Russell A. **642, 879**
Perényi, Erzsébet **643**
Perkins, George **437**
Person, Henry A. **39r, 53**
Peterson, Clifford **741**
Phillips, William J. **149**
Pickering, O.S. **596, 696, 785, 908–9, 981**
Pirotta, Nino **263**
Platzer, Hans **1012**
Plummer, John F., III **644, 768**
Pope, Nancy P. **769**
Porter, Peter, and Anthony Thwaite **619**
Powell, Susan **786**, 800, **894**
Pratt, John H. **656**
Prins, A.A. **51r**
Pullein, Catharine 884

Raby, F.J.E. **188**
Rankin, J.W. **151**
Ransom, Daniel J. **697, 857**, 912
Raw, Barbara C. **422**, 511
Raymo, Robert R. **368, 488**
Reed, Edward Bliss, **21, 135, 159**, 621, 645
Reed, Thomas L., Jr. **941**
Rees, Elinor **233**
Reichl, Karl **80, 895, 1013**
Reimer, Stephen R. **94a**
Reiss, Edmund 79, **453, 478, 515**, 517, **550–3**, 562, **583**, 708, 803, 861, 886
Renwick, W.L., and Harold Orton **215**
Revard, Carter **499, 698, 723, 787**, 963, 977
Rhys, Ernest **138**
Rickert, Edith **22, 176**
Riddenhough, Geoffrey B. **259**
Riddy, Felicity **500**, 574
Rigg, A.G. **489, 501, 516**
Ringler, William **358**
Rios, Charlotte R. **742**

Rissanen, Matti **743**
Ritson, Joseph **94a**
Robbins, Harry Wolcott **155**
Robbins, Rossell Hope **46**, *RobbinsS* **51**, **54**, *RobbinsS* **55**, *RobbinsH* **57**, **58**, 59, **59r**, **86r**, 212, **216–21**, **230–1**, **235–7**, **240–1**, **281**, 313, 322, 324, 327, **335–41**, **359–62**, **369–71**, **382**, **406–8**, **423**, 430, **444r**, **454–6**, 460, **465**, **479**, **490**, 515, **517–19**, **537–8**, **554–5**, 556, 573, **584**, 599, 606, 618, 626, **657**, 712, **724–5**, **744**, 838, 871, 876, 892, 935, 947, 958, 964, 1013, 1015
Roberts, P.D. **597**
Robertson, D.W., Jr. 79, **298**, 414, 567, 1015
Robinson, F.N. 316
Robinson, Pamela **88a**
Rogers, William Elford **585**, 658
Root, Robert K. **126**
Ross, Thomas W. **383–4**, 918
Ross A.S.C. **189**
Rossetti, W.M. 4
Routley, Erik **396**
Rowland, Beryl **502**, **699**
Rubin, Miri **960**

Sabol, Andrew J. **264**
Sahlin, Margit Rigmor 59, **232**, 279, 407
Saint Paul, Thérèse **982**
Saíz, Próspero **659**
Sajavaara, Kari **503**
Salter, Elizabeth **504, 598, 726, 811**, 918
Saltmarsh, John **190**
Samuels, M.L. **836**
Sampson, George **32**
Sandison, Helen Estabrook **139**, 574
Scase, Wendy **1002**
Scattergood, V. John **505, 520, 556–8, 570**, **620, 645, 812, 896, 910**
Schelling, Felix E. **140**
Schibanoff, Susan **673**
Schlauch, Margaret **372**
Schlüter, A. 171
S[chmidt], A.V.C. **91r**
Schmolke-Hasselmann, Beate **858**
Schoeck, R.J. **42r, 299–301, 317**, 567
Schofield, B. 263, **265**, 268
Schreiber, W.L. 278
Schueler, Donald G. **660**, 772
Schulz, H.C. **222**
Schwetman, John W. **926, 1003**
Seaton, Ethel **57r**, **373**
Seymour, St John D. **161**
Shannon, Ann 621
Short, Douglas D. **661**, 833
———, and Porter Williams, Jr. **674**
Sichert, Margit **837, 961**
Sidgwick, F. **31r**, **110**, 125
Sikora, Ruta **466**
Silverstein, Theodore **73**, 872
Simons, John **94a, 838**
Sisam, Celia **61r, 480**, 751

Index of Scholars and Critics

———, and Kenneth Sisam **69**, 645, 732, 990, 1015
Sisam, Kenneth **30**, 514, 1015
Sitwell, Gerard **282**
Skeat, Walter W. 119, **136**, 514
Smallwood, T.M. **599**, **927**
Smith, A.H. **302**
Smith, Sarah Stanbury **675**
Smithers, G.V. **273**, **481**, **897**, **983**, 992
———, ed. (of *BrownXIV*) **48**, 229, 992
South, Helen Pennock **191**
Spalding, Mary Caroline **141**
Spearing, A.C., and J.E. Spearing **82**
Spears, James E. **622**
Speirs, John 79, **385**, 511, 567, 595, 621, 709
Spencer, H.L. **949**r
Spitzer, Leo 79, **303**, **318**, 732, 874
Stanbury, Sarah **962**, **1022**
Stanley, E.G. **409**, **646**, 723
Steele, R. 468
Stemmler, Theo **70**, **444**–**5**, **467**–**8**, **623**–**4**, **647**, **676**, **700**, **770**, **839**, 857, **911**–**12**, **963**, 971
Stevens, John **52**, **83**, **86**r, **283**, 329, **438**, **522**r, 650, **771**, **788**–**9**, **880**, **942**, 999
Stevick, Robert D. **62**, **103**, **424**, **491**, 732, 999
Sticca, Sandro **898**
Stobo, Marguerite **813**
Stone, Brian **63**
Stouck, Mary-Ann **772**, **899**
Stugrin, Michael **745**
Sweeney, Patric M. 355, **363**, 366
Szittya, Penn R. **881**

Tarvers, Josephine Koster **859**
Taylor, Andrew **964**
Taylor, George C. **111**, **118**
Taylor, F. Sherwood **266**
Telfer, J.M. **319**
Ten Brink, Bernhard, *see* Brink
Thayer, C.G. **320**, 404
Thompson, John J. **913**, **943**, **965**
Thompson, E.M. **106**
Thomson, S. Harrison **179**, **192**, 393
Thornley, Eva **506**
Tierney, Frank **571**
Tillyard, E.M.W. 301, **304**, 567
Townsend, Brenda **600**
Trapp, J.B. **77**
Travis, James **625**
Tristram, Philippa **662**
Tucker, Susie I. **69**r
Turner, F.McD.C. **190**
Turville-Petre, Thorlac F.S. **89**, **96**, **626**, **677**, **790**, **814**
Tydeman, William **71**

Utley, Francis Lee **253**–**4**

Vann, J. Daniel, III **410**
Varnhagen, Hermann 932
Vincent, Sister Mary **325**
Virginia, Sister Marie **492**

Wagner, Bernard M. **193**
Waldron, Ronald **944**
Wanley, Humfrey 646
Warren, Robert Penn **242**
Watts, V.E. **815**
Wawn, Andrew **816**
Weber, Sarah Appleton **539**, 585
Wehrle, William O. **177**
Weiss, Alexander **860**
Wells, Celia Townsend **586**
Wells, John Edwin 239
Wentersdorf, Karl **984**
Wenzel, Siegfried **572**, **627**–**9**, **663**–**4**, **701**, 786, **791**, 800, 802, **817**, 840, **861**, **882**, 893, 1004
Whaley, Diana **966**
Whitbread, L.G. **818**
White, Natalie 407
Whiteford, Peter **841**, **995**
Whitfield, D.W. **702**
Wilhelm, James J. **74**
Wilkins, Nigel **883**
Williams, O.J. **124**, 131
Williams, Margaret **274**
Willmott, Adrian **1004**
Wilson, Edward **88**b, **98**r, **482**, **601**, **639**r, **678**–**9**, **727**, **746**–**7**, **819**, **1005**
Wilson, Kenneth G. **342**–**4**, 415
Wilson, R.M. **57**r, **61**r, **197**, **204**, **223**, **321**
Wilson, Sarah **411**
Wimsatt, James I. **680**, **842**, 873, **967**
Wimsatt, W.K., Jr., and Monroe C. Beardsley 658
Wolley, R.M. 199
Wolpers, Theodor **284**, **521**, **703**–**4**
Woodbridge, Linda **900**
Woolf, Rosemary 79, **446**, **522**, **540**, **559**, 574, 585, 701, 833, 834, 873, 940, 995
Woolgar, C.M., and B. O'Donoghue **820**
Wright, C.E. **305**
Wright, Thomas **1**–**3**, 315, 952, 964

Young, Karl **31**r
Yunck, John A. **425**

Zesmer, David M. **439**
Zettersten, Arne **507**
Zink, Michel **837**
Ziolkowski, Jan **843**
Zumthor, Paul 837
Zupitza, J. **10**, 779

Subject Index

References in this index are to the numbers of annotations, shown in bold face. There are some references to *S/IMEV* numbers of poems, in italics. The manuscripts listed under 'manuscripts' are listed as the subjects of some discussion and as the sources of poems. Those manuscripts which have attracted more comprehensive study are noted separately, under the names used most frequently, such as 'Harley MS 2253,' 'Vernon MS,' etc. The lyrics associated with such manuscripts are also listed separately from the term 'lyric.'

Aaron **422**
abandonment **934**
Abell, William **848**
abject **1000**
Absolon, *Miller's Tale* **290**: and Jankyn **563**; and truelove **936**; and Night Visit **863**
Abuses of the Age/Evils of the Times **57**, **132**, **341**, **362**, **570**, **720**, **799**, **905**; and fashion **985**; in sermons **882**
abuse, personal **359**
acrostics **46**, **114**: ANGUS **780**; in courtly poems **247**; IESV **613**; KATYRYN **342**; in love lyric **456**; MARIA **185**; MORS SOLVIT OMNIA **353**, **368**; PIPWEL **185**; on Seven Deadly Sins **985**; WILLIAM WALTER **987**
Act of Supremacy **980**
Acton, Master Ralph **877**
Adam: creation **959**; descent from **607**; *felix culpa* **675**; and sin **856**, **893**; stock figure **259**
Adam de Madderley **463**
Adam of St Victor **59**
Adonis **543**
advice: to lover **308**; verses **471**
adynata **673**
Ælfric, scribe **818**
Ælfric, sermons **226**
Ælfric Alcuin **932**
Aëliz **623**
Æneid **726**
afterlife **923**
age: old **651**, **766**, **897**; perfect **865**
Age/Elde, personified **662**
Ages of Man **865**
aʒeyn star **700**
Agincourt, *see* battles
aicill **582**, **828**
Agnes, name **723**
Alabaster, William **825**
alba **659**, **755**
Albertus Magnus **803**
alchemy **266**, **742**
Alcock, Bishop John of Ely **44**, **985**

ale-wives **455**, **538**
Aled, Tudur **915**
Alis, name **548**
Alison/eleyson **548**
Alison: in *Miller's Tale* **290**, **640**, **970**; name **548**; and Night Visit **863**
All Saints **518**
allegory **443**, **549**: in *2037.5* **414**, **1015**; allegorical figures **139**; *arbor caritatis* **916**; Christ as lover-knight **169**, **446**, **522**; Christ as king **169**; dissociative allegory **705**; interpretation **298**; Man in the Moon **585**; poet's capture **303**; religious life **301**; in sermons **840**; soul as besieged lady **774**. *See also* Charter of Christ; Christ, knight.
alliteration **763**, **767**: binding or concatenating **582**; Celtic patterns **907**; in descriptions **858**; in Harley lyrics **300**, **736**, **828**, **835**; Northern, revised by a Southerner **542**; phrases **449**; OE patterns **163**, **907**; poetical use **46**, **96**, **130**, **187**, **240**, **343**, **677**; and rhyme **349**; Scottish **677**; sound effects **526**; structural **671**; in Vernon lyrics **994**. *See also* cynghanedd.
———— alliterative assonance **300**
———— alliterative prose **671**, **835**
———— alliterative revival **240**, **445**, **677**, **794**
———— alliterative verse **726**, **811**, **888**, **922**, **972**, **981**; twelve-line stanza **903**; thirteen-line stanza **626**, **670**, **922**
Alliaco Petrus, *Meditationes* **1019**
alod **170**
aloddin **170**
allusions: classical **892**; heraldic **753**; historical **717**; musical **608**; scatological **839**; sexual **839**
almanacks **216**
Alphabet of Tales **760**
Alysoun, name **623**
amarscled **270**, **743**
Ambrose **340**, **845**
Amfortas **345**
amphibole **341**

Subject Index 411

amoureuse **920**
anagram **456**: *mors* **786**
Ancrene Wisse **968**: allegory of Christ as knight **169**; and lyrics **522**, **603**
Andreas Capellanus **837**
androgyny **873**
angel: fallen **805**; guardian **81**; struggle with devils **561**
Angelus ad virginem, translations **771**. See also Nicholas, *Miller's Tale*.
anger **209**
angr (ON) **209**
animals **991**: noises **305**. See also imagery, animal.
Ann, name **723**
Anne, St **976**
Annot, name **1000**: diminutive of *Agnes* **723**; and *Johon* **211**, **646**
Annunciation **737**. See also lyrics.
Anoelius **494**, **683**
Anselm, St **24**, **38**, **642**
Anthelmus, St **683**
anthology, and commonplace book **987**
Antichrist, and friars **881**
antiphon: and carols **37**, **86**; processional **58**
antithesis **443**
apology, scribe's **471**
Apostles, careers **349**. See also under individual names.
apophthegms **448**
appeals, in religious lyrics **939**
April, dew **422**
arbor caritatis **916**
arbor cupiditatis **916**
architecture **1021**
Arfaxat **909**
Aristotle **668**; *ABC of Aristotle* **714**
Arma Christi/Arms of Christ/Arms of the Passion **218**, **220**, **512**, **575**, **756**
arming **446**
armonia **942**
armour **446**, **774**
ars dictaminis **949**
Ars Nova **707**
Arthur **345**
Ascension **60**: sermon **861**
asceticism **304**
Ash Wednesday, epistle, Joel 2.12–19 **584**
Ashby, George **570**, **654**; and peace **260**
assayed **904**
assignation, place of **430**
assonance, alliterative **300**
astrology **150**
aubade **788**
aube **135**, **277**, **401**, **474**, **559**, **659**, **673**; motifs **148**
Auchinleck MS [Edinburgh, National Library of Scotland, Advocates 19.2.1] **145**, **384**, **520**, **536**, **887**, **903**, **918**: copy of *3462* **694**; and Langland **504**; Scribe 1 **992**
Audelay, John: and *2677* **626**, **670**, **763**; and Bede **630**; *Angelus ad virginem* **771**; carols **37**, **38**, **59**, **86**, **247**, **389**, **400**; historical poems **570**, **704**; and mortality **417**; religious lyrics **18**; and St Thomas Becket **693**; treatise on Deadly Sins **816**
Augustine of Hippo **38**, **522**: and Abuses of the Age **362**; *Candet Nudatum Pectus* **653**, **825**; cosmology **642**; *Quis dabit* **940**. See also translation.
Augustine of Canterbury, and English **901**
Austin, St **841**
authority: clerical **1002**; criticism of **485**
awdl **982**

background, to ME literature **483**
badges, armorial **570**
Babthorpe, Robert **776**
backbiters **326**
Ball, John **419**, **423**, **704**, **753**, **876**, **877**; confession **975**; letters **592**, **879**; lost works **321**; proverb **607**; and Three Estates **724**
balada **392**
balade **165**, **392**
ballad **392**, **796**, **829**; of Agincourt **809**; broadside **392**; characteristics **986**; chronicle **809**; English **90**, **142**; and folksong **986**; French **567**; historical **809**; of Mary Magdalene **567**; and ME lyrics **61**, **334**, **509**; and pastourelle **164**, **961**; Scandinavian **567**; Wendish **142**
ballade **61**, **135**, **392**, **571**, **650** **794**, **821**: of Charles d'Orléans **468**; and ME **883**; and ME love epistles **949**
ballata **392**: and carol **37**, **86**
ballette **277**, **392**
Bannatyne, George **852**;
Bannatyne MS [Edinburgh, National Library of Scotland, Advocates 1.1.6] **127**, **335**, **340**, **675**; love epistles **949**; version of *1270.2* **581**
Barbara, St **440**
Barclay, Alexander **672**; and fashion **896**
barfote **817**
Barkley, Nicholas **632**
Barlaam **182**
Basilius **494**
battles: Agincourt **25**, **57**, **809**; Bannockburn **445**, **794**, **801**, **1014**; Northampton **57**; Otterburn **57**; poems of **1003**; Whitby Haven **555**
beatitudes **558**
Beauchamp, Richard **744**
Beatrice **962**
beauty: catalogue **92**, **843**; notions of **351**. See also description.
Bede **630**, **978**: and Song of Songs **680**
Bedynham, John **650**
beetle **719**
Bele Aeliz **401**
Benet, John **555**, **584**, **1002**
Bequory **754**

bereavement **543**
Berengaudus **803**: Commentary on the Apocalypse **603**
Berkeley, Bishop Gilbert **859**
Berkely, Sir John **790**
Bernard of Clairvaux, St **522**, **794**: and *1699* **153**; allegory of *arbor caritatis* **916**; and *Candet nudatum pectus* **825**; *De diligendo Deo* **899**; influence **24**, **38**, **59**; *Meditationes piisimae de conditione humana* **391**, **893**; mystical lyrics **653**; *Quis dabit* **940**; *Sayings of St Bernard* **391**; *Sermones de diversis* **603**, **899**; sermons on Song of Songs **680**, **842**, **873**
Bernardino of Siena **639**
Bernart de Ventadorn **486**, **860**
beste of blod and bon/*beste of bon and blod* **856**, **893**
betony **128**, **894**
Bible:
——— brief references: Apocalypse **603**, **956**; Col. 2: 13–14 **421**; Eccles. **282**, **923**; 2 Esdras 9 **477**; Job 17, **782**, **892**, 14: 1–2 **786**, **1004**; Joel 2: 12–19 **584**; John 12: 24–5 **621**; Lam. 1: 12 **777**; Luke 2 **983**, 24: 13 ff. **492**; Matt. 6: 19–20 **586**, 23 **881**; Paul **782**; Song of Songs 2: 5, 2: 9, 5: 8 **842**, 2: 8 **874**; Wisdom **510**
——— Job: influence **17**; patience **933**; and riches **892**
——— Psalms: 6 **44**; 32 **44**; 38 **44**; 50 **913**; 51 **44**; 51 and Maidstone **585**; 102 **44**; 130 **44**, **541**; 143 **44**; penitential **294**, **866**, **903**; *see also* Brampton; Maidstone
——— Song of Songs **522**, **680**, **864**: and *3221* **604**; bridal images **737**; commentary **821**; imagery **774**, **873**, **899**; influence **169**, **680**, **710**; and NT **929**; and Night Visit **863**; and Office of the Assumption **591**; reader/audience response **929**; sermons of Bernard **680**, **842**
Bicornis **368**
Binchois, Gilles **707**
birds **139**, **893**: names **305**; noises **305**; as soul **699**
birth, and death **661**
bishop-saints, AS **932**
Black Death **791**
blacksmiths **550**, **726**, **997**
blason **843**
blasphemy **752**, **869**
Blickling Homilies **226**
ble **969**
blood: of Christ **94a**; drops in Christ's heart **383**; drops shed by Christ **512**; in family relationships **432**; of Hayles **253**
bloodletting **214**, **1017**
blues **425**
body:
——— of Alison, *Miller's Tale* **970**
——— of Christ, *see* Christ

——— journey of corpse **1009**
——— and soul, **380**, **922**: dialogue **23**; *exemplum* **226**; soul's house **1021**
——— woman's **1000**
——— and worms **616**. *See also* debate poetry.
bocche of deth cruell **822**
Boccaccio, *De Casibus* **113**
Boethius: *Consolation of Philosophy* **332**, **457**; prisoner **654**
Boke of St Albans **448**, **1019**
Bokenham, Osbert **518**, **570**
Boleyn, Anne: and *1132* **418**, **461**; and *2281.5* **611**, **716**; motto **716**; as white falcon **980**; and Wyatt **716**
Bonaventure, St **38**, **639**; cosmology **642**; *Lignum Vitae* **573**; *Meditations* **111**, **714**, **893**
bone, family relationships **432**
bontin **988**
bontinog **988**
The Book of Privy Counselling **899**
books:
——— commonplace **948**: and anthologies **987**; John Colyns **324**, **541**, **945**; Glastonbury miscellany **516**; John Grimestone **212**; William Herebert **94a**; Richard Hill **19**; Humfrey Newton **46**, **795**; *see also* individual compilers.
——— courtesy **438**, **631**
——— elementary **395**
——— of the heart **1018**
——— of Hours **218**, **525**, **756**; Beauchamp **756**; Talbot **756**
——— miscellany, medieval **1010**
——— printed **358**, **448**, **471**, **522**, **946**, **948**
——— song **438**
Bordsley Abbey **56**
Bothe, family of Barton **822**
Bourgchier, Thomas **1002**
bounting **988**
Bourne, Bishop Gilbert **859**
Bovo **494**
bow leg **997**
boy, kitchie **469**
Bozon, Nicholas: and carols **59**, **247**, **382**, **445**; *Contes moralisés* **204**, **473**; paradoxes **641**; translated by William Herebert **94a**, **798**
Bradshaw, Henry: and carol manuscript **490**, **754**
Bradwardine, Thomas **282**
Brampton, Thomas **44**; Psalm 50 **913**; Seven Penitential Psalms **903**
Brandan **909**
Braque, Georges **811**
bras yr ŷd **988**
bread **235**
break, mid-line **942**
breast: of BV Mary **802**; of Fair Maid of Ribblesdale **805**; golden **982**
breccad **582**, **828**
Brendan, St **909**

Brews, Margery **100**, **731**, **848**, **958**
'The Bridal of Polmood' **461**
bribery **473**
Bridius **494**
Brinstan **88b**
Brinton, Bishop **607**
Britius of Auxerre **683**
broȝir **817**
Bromyard, John **607**, **663**: *Summa Predicantium* **666**
BrownXIII **36**; emendations **186**, **229**, **239**, **257**
BrownXIV, **31**, **48**; emendations **229**, **367**, **481**, **983**, **992**
BrownXV **39**, **983**
Browning, Robert **789**
Brulé, Gace **860**
Brunetta **368**
Bruno, St **494**, **683**
Brynkele, Robert **739**
buck, St Mary Day **1005**
Buckingham, Edward Stafford, Duke of **744**, **945**
buckle, of belt **1000**
Bull, Papal **190**
burden **139**, **396**, **537**: and carol **37**, **86**; French influence **858**. *See also* carol; lyric.
Buryton, John **88b**
burlesque **198**: courtly **544**
Burgundy, court of **88b**, **234**
bunting **401**, **699**, **988**
Bunting, Bessy **401**

c, dominical letter **501**
cacce **263**
Cadiou, Androw **883**
Cain **453**
Calais **378**
calendar **978**: Church **827**; with tables **427**; verses of **525**
calendula **853**
Calot, Laurence **924**
cam **997**
cammede/kammede **997**
camp **450**
camus **997**
can **425**, **711**
Candet nudatum pectus **825**. *See also* Augustine, Bernard.
canon, Summer **244**
canso **609**
Canticle of Canticles, *see* Bible, Song of Songs
Canticus Troilii **848**; *see also* Chaucer, extraction, *Troilus and Criseyde*
cantilenae **37**, **86**
Canute, song of monks of Ely **178**, **321**, **911**
Capet/Valois descent **94b**
Capgrave, John **726**
capitalism **704**
captivity **935**
caritas, and *cupiditas* **653**, **840**
Carmina Burana **566**

Carodoc/*Caradawc Vrechvras* **982**
carol, AN **22**
carol, French **22**
carol, Latin **22**, **37**, **52**, **86**; tradition **407**
carol, macaronic **37**, **59**, **86**
carol, ME **37**, **52**, **59**, **86**, **385**, **522**:
—— of Christ **10**, **408**, *see also* Christ; lyrics
—— of Christmas **8**, **22**, **58**, **86**, **149**, **259**, **329**, **408**, **454**; of boar's head **622**; noel **396**; *see also* lyrics
—— 'Corpus Christi' [*1132*]: ballad **105**, **110**; Derbyshire **387**; Hill version **345**, **387**, **418**; Hogg version **345**, **387**, **461**; interpretation **110**, **125**, **418**, **543**, **980**; Staffordshire **387**; and 'Yonec' **974**; *see also 1132*.
—— and dance **889**; of Ireland **380**, **709**
—— editions **18**, **19**, **22**, **25**, **34**, **37**, **52**, **58**, **59**, **83**, **86**; of James Ryman **10**
—— of events and times: of Agincourt **809**; fifteenth-century **329**; Tudor **283**;
—— folk **397**; origin **606**; transmission **606**
—— and Franciscans **212**; *see also* friars
—— literary qualities: ballad **105**, **110**, **396**; burden **236**; nowel **966** and cantilena **390**, **407**; evolution **22**; fragments **513**; humorous **37**, **86**, **247**; lullaby **247**, **522**, **588**, *see also* Mary; mysogynistic **747**; narrative **149**; of nature **149**; numeral **149**; origins **22**, **407**; political **37**, **86**, **809**; ribald **490**, **754**; satirical **37**, **86**; survival **225**; traditional **125**; in woman's voice **768**
—— of Mary **10**, **149**; and Joseph **408**, **966**, *see also* Mary; lyrics
—— and music **52**, **241**, **389**, **400**, **406**, **942**
—— and plays **764**, **947**: Coventry [*2251.8*] **376**, **377**, *see also 2551.8*; in *Gammer Gurton's Needle* **612**; shepherds' **826**, **988**
—— religious **37**, **52**, **86**, **247**, **389**, **396**, **779**: of the Annunciation **10**; as *conducti* **279**; of Epiphany **149**, **408**; liturgical **86**, **779**; of the Nativity **10**, **169**; of the Passion **345**; processional **279**, **382**; of saints **408**, *see also* individual saints; of the Trinity **10**, **408**
—— secular **37**, **52**, **86**, **247**, **396**: amorous **37**, **86**; of betrayed maidens **755**, *see also* laments.
See also individual authors.
carole **58**, **59**, **247**, **880**: and *2037.5* **627**
carpe diem **522**
Carthusian order **575**, **735**: founding **281**, **494**, **683**
Cassius, St **202**
castle **1021**
Cat and the Candle **524**, **557**
Catherine of Aragon: and *1132* **418**, **461**, **980**; and *2281.5* **611**, **716**
Catullus **857**
cauda **644**

Cavalcanti, Guido **634**
Caxton, William **448**, **946**; text of *Monk's Tale* **91a**; translation of *Legenda Aurea* **976**
Cayphas **638**
Cely, George **378**, **848**
cento **848**; *see also* extraction
century, fourteenth **801**
cēte (OE) **251**
chace **263**
Chalmers, Alexander **892**
chamber, bridal **680**
changeling **997**
chanson **848**:
——— *d'amour* **24**, **135**
——— *d'aventure* **139**, **289**, **559**, **721**, **768**, **777**, **794**, **895**, **938**: and *1460* **574**; as complaint **99**; knight **873**; and penitential lyric **506**; religious **139**, **169**; Scottish features **139**; symbolism **139**; women in **139**
——— *de carole* **135**
——— of Charles d'Orléans **468**
——— *courtois* **18**, **135**; and ME lyric **277**
——— *à danser* **37**
——— *dramatique* **139**, **289**
——— English **206**
——— *de femme* **777**; used in sermon **1008**
——— *de mal marié* **695**; *see also* lament
——— *de mal mariée* **540**, **559**, **695**, **709**, **768**; *see also* lament
——— *à personnage* **24**
——— *populaire* **18**
——— *à refrain* **330**
——— *de toile* **135**, **768**
——— *des transformations* **540**
chapmen **871**, **904**
charity: Christian **758**; and cupidity **298**, **805**; *see also* caritas.
Charles d'Orléans: abstract style **566**; captivity **958**; courtly poet **85**, **544**, **848**; and Fairfax 16 **921**, **949**; and François I **793**; French manuscripts **795**; and game of love **438**; and Harley 682 **949**; influence on ME poetry **672**; and Jean d'Angoulême **793**; love poems **796**, **889**; refrain poems **537**; and religious works **61**; and William de la Pole, Duke of Suffolk **88**, **129**, **468**, **883**
charms **575**: against thieves **116**, **388**, **410**, **610**, **927**; against enemies **116**; P **927**; against smallpox **202**; to stanch blood **116**, **610**, **927**; against wolf **927**
Charter of Christ **141**, **144**, **421**: and book of the heart **1018** and Bozon **641**; Irish forms **885**; and mystery plays **118**; Welsh forms **885**
Chartham, William, *Speculum parvulorum* **785**
Chartier, Alain **883**
chastity **530**, **737**: gem **862**; maid's treasure **749**
Chatwyn, Mary **945**
Chatwyn, William **945**
Chaucer, Geoffrey **385**:

——— *ABC* **885**;
——— *Canterbury Tales* **787**: *Clerk's Tale* **1022**; *Knight's Tale* **316**; *Manciple's Tale* **557**; *Miller's Tale* **172**, **290**, **440**, **726**, **936**, **996**; *Nun's Priest's Tale* **282**; *Pardoner's Tale* **726**, **766**; *Reeve's Tale* **925**; *Tale of Melibee* **855**
——— criticism: and aube **148**; and ballade **392**; and complaint **949**; and conventions **405**; and courtly love **634**; courtly poet **85**, **99**, **544**, **744**, **848**; descriptions **152**, **351**; Englishness **860**; implied debate **942**; interpolation of lyrics **295**; irony **857**; musical allusions **608**, **880**, **332**; parody **839**; pastoral style **709**; perception and perspective **642**; refrain poems **537**; and rondeau **571**; speech **789**; use of vernacular **798**; and woman's song **755**;
——— comments: on Friar **453**, **849**; on loveday **636**; religious views **526**; on his times **704**, **753**, **764**; on truth **816**, **879**
——— extraction of passages **373**, **947**, **987**
——— imagery: birds **950**; cock **845**; colour **900**
——— influence: of Chaucer **82**, **91a**, **98**, **127**; of Chaucer circle **213**, **672**
——— influences on Chaucer: Eleanor of Aquitaine **657**; French works **405**, **777**, **788**, **883**; friars **881**; Guillaume de Guileville **585**; Machaut **967**; ME lyrics **860**; OE **860**; patronage **821**; sermons **840**
——— lyrics **50**, **61**, **70**, **71**, **88**, **104**, **577**: French works **657**; Marian lyrics **284**, **703**
——— texts: black-letter editions **312**; concern for text **665**; iambic readings **789**; printed works **946**; Stow's edition **686**
——— *Troilus and Criseyde* **438**, **801**, **807**, **872**, **984**
cheerfulness, in face of death **791**
chees **523**
þe chelde water of þe welle-spring **567**
Chepman, Andro **946**
chete, and words for 'hut' **251**
chevaldour **78**
ching [sense] **797**
ch'ing [feeling] **797**
chivalry **631**, **1003**
Chrétien de Troyes **843**
Christ **60**:
——— attributes: age **547**; appearance **285**, **805**; body **421**, **962**, **1018**; conqueror of death **363**; Crown of Thorns **916**; divinity **667**, **772**; Fifteen O's **201**, **615**; heart **521**, **703**; humanity **745**; name **546**, **822**, *see also* cult, of Holy Name; nature **633**; power **667**; Son of Man **605**; suffering **14**, **745**, **972**; tears **957**; wounds **451**, **496**, **521**, **547**, **604**, **630**, **774**, **842**, **885**, **1008**
——— figures **345**: bird **866**; bread **696**; bridegroom **522**, **603**, **653**, **680**, **737**, **864**, **873**, **929**; brother **680**, **864**; Christian's

guest **867**, **919**; deer **604**; doctor **696**; *erthe* **959**; father **864**; fertility spirit **276**; feudal lord **986**; flower **303**; food **696**; hunter **680**, **873**; husband **605**, **680**, **864**, **899**; judge **94a**, **605**, **890**; king **94a**, **492**, **605**, **615**; knight **169**, **446**, **522**, **523**, **603**, **604**, **613**, **703**, **774**, **842**, **873**, **899**, **980**; lily **900**; lover **749**, **825**; merchant **603**, **605**; mother **680**, **864**, **873**, **899**; nightingale **319**, **950**; parchment-maker's frame **866**; Passover lamb **696**; pilgrim **603**, **605**; suitor **680**; warrior **605**; wheat **696**
—— life events: Ascension **861**; baptism **927**; betrayal **772**; birth **995**; childhood **149**; Crucifixion **116**, **521**, **825**, **834**; death **995**; deposition **853**; earthly life **605**, **615**; Flight into Egypt **969**; infancy **94a**; Nativity **521**; Passion **94a**, **774**, **940**; Presentation **927**; sold **633**, **660**; second coming **605**; visit to Jerusalem **927**
—— in literature: address to Christ **703**; address to mankind **817**; appeal for sinner **802**; appeals to man **939**; Complaint **777**, *see also* Charter of Christ; in Distress **938**; exclamation **652**; lament **139**, **628**; Leaps **874**; reproach **269**; words from Cross **630**, **919**
—— and others: executioners **604**; Judas **930**; Mary **854**; *Miller's Tale* characters **936**; object of gaze **1022**;
See also lyrics, prayers, specific events, and entities.
Christ Child **718**
Christus miles **774**
Christina of Markyate **575**
chronicles: Geoffrey of Monmouth **741**; Gregory's **362**; historical **359**; John Harding **741**; Peter Langtoft's **1**; Yorkist **955**
Chronicque de la Traïson et Mort de Richart Deux Roy Dengleterre mis en lumière . . . **1014**
Churches: of England and Rome **980**
Circe **837**
Cistercians, rule **869**
Clanvowe, Sir John **88**, **744**; bird imagery **950**
Clement V **717**
cleo **749**
Cleopas **976**
Clerk, William **724**
clerks, writers of lyrics **107**
clichés/stock phrases **335**, **644**; of description **486**; used in religious and secular lyrics **338**
Cliff, Richard **776**
Clifford, Lewis **213**
clothing, in pastourelle **895**
The Cloud of Unknowing **899**
cock: crowing at dawn **148**, **474**; symbol **699**, **845**
coins, clipping **425**
collocations **856**
Colucille/Columba, St **909**

Colyngbourne, Wyllyam **724**
Colyns, John, *see* books, commonplace.
comedy, ribald **398**
Comhgall/Comgall, St **909**
commentary: historical **526**; political **526**; social **720**
commerce, foreign policy **3**, **369**, **914**
commonplace books, *see* books
Compassion, and *planctus Mariae* **854**
compilatio, distinguished from *collectio* **779**
complaint **61**, **485**, **753**, **777**, **821**; of betrayed maiden **777**, *see also* lament; of Christ **777**; and epistle **949**; female **99**; of lover **858**; morality **328**; of the times **533**, **592**, **720**, **851**, **887**, *see also* Abuses of the Age
complainte **858**; *complaint d'amour* **725**, **744**
computus **978**
Conan, substituted for Owan **741**
concatenatio **728**, **862**
conductus, secular **562**
confession **561**: prayers of **56**
congé **994**
connotations **856**
Conon de Béthune **860**
contemplation **680**
contemptus mundi **463**, **473**, **528**, **592**, **662**, **749**, **758**, **788**, **928**; and *ubi sunt* **807**
context, of poems **85**, **811**: changing **892**; effect **947**, **1005**; and genre **709**; importance **1009**
Constitutions of Clarendon **693**
continuity, of OE to ME lyric **935**
contrafacta **87**, **848**, **849**, **920**; of *Angelus ad virginem* **771**
contrasto **895**
contre-blason **843**
convention, violations of **752**; *see also* descriptions
coop, poultry **600**
Cooper, Dr **7**
Copland, William **1005**
corn, winter **645**
Cornish, William **7**, **8**
Coroune **909**
Corpus Christi, feast **195**, **960**
'Corpus Christi Carol,' *see 1132* and carols
cortasye **495**
counsel, Christian **758**
counterpoint, rhythmic **707**
court: archdeacon's **499**; ceremonies **283**; consistory **499**; entertainments **283**; of Love/Venus **308**; Tudor **438**
Courtenay, Edward **910**
Courtenay, Maud **910**
courtesy, poem **784**; courtesy book, *see* books
courtliness **848**
Coventry, allegiances **955**
covetousness **473**
Cowhel **909**
cows, and song **460**
Cranmer, Thomas, Book of Common Prayer **764**

Creed, Apostles' **349**
Criseyde, vows **673**
criticism, literary and historical **975**
crook **484**
Crophill, John **538, 556, 570**
Cross: and Herebert **94a**; as knight's horse **446**; as mother **972**; sign of grace **972**; symbol of triumph **774**; words from **630**
cross row **398**
crow **474**
Crown of Thorns **916**
crucifixion: of thieves **116**; of Christ, *see* Christ, life events; representation of **1022**
cryptogram **750, 780**
cuccu **708**
cuckoldry **776**
cuckoo **244, 394, 474, 824**; and cuckoldry **593**
cults: Five Wounds of Our Lord **451, 575**; Holy Name **575, 594**; Precious Blood **451, 575**; Sacred Heart **451**; the Virgin **954**
culture, medieval **850**
Cuthbert, St, translation of **154**
Cupid **470**
cupidity, opposed to charity **298, 805**; *see also caritas*
cupping **364**
Cwicwine **726**
cymeriad **907**
cynghanedd **133, 582, 763, 828, 907**
Cyprian, and Abuses of the Age **362**
Cyrcetur, Thomas **106**
cȳte (OE) **251**

Dafydd ap Gwilym **189, 828**
Dame Siriȝ **768**
dance: of Ireland **709**; lessons **378**; signifying marriage **380**
Dance of Death/Makabre **118, 182, 782**; **791**
Dante Alighieri: and courtly love **634**; *Inferno* **434**; self-description **692**
The Dancers of Colbek **729**
daughter, merchant's **469**;
David, composition of Psalms **913**
dawn, poetry of **474**
Days, Last **533**
De Arte Honeste Amandi **787**
De Duodecim Utilitatibus Tribulationis **209**
death **61, 324, 553, 778, 872**: architecture **1021**; and birth **661**; of a child **944**; common fate **599**; diagnosis **554**; and Ecclesiastes **923**; and grave **137**; imagery **661, 906**; poverty of **666**; power of **182**; signs of **522, 554, 706**; warnings **522**, *see also memento mori*.
Death, personified **522, 626, 662, 799**: plea to **342, 353**; and young **353**; *see also* Dance of Death
débat **135, 443, 736, 782**
debate poetry **97, 941**: alliterative **97**; birds **97**; body and soul **93, 97, 616, 782, 941**; body and worms **616, 782**; didactic **97**; Latin **97**; Mary and the Cross **972**; Mercy and Justice **773**; Mercy and Righteousness **580**; nightingale **319**; Nurtur and Kynd (Cat and Candle) **524, 557**; Thrush and Nightingale **536, 954**; about women **280, 319**. *See also* dialogue.
deer **991**
deer: figure for Christ **604**; hunting **1005**
delicacy **752**
demore(n) **1007**
Denarius, personified as Dan Denarius **425**
dereworpliche **732**
derne **578**; *derne love* **290**
Deschamps, Eustache **2**: adapted by Chaucer **883**; *Art de Dictier* **967**; and rondeau **571**
descort **107**
description: conventions **92, 290, 609, 623, 640, 752, 843, 858**; formal **152, 351, 472**
descriptio pulchritudinis **92**
devil **550**: lame **997**
dew, April **422**
Devonshire MS [London, BL Add. 17492] **41, 373, 405, 438, 581, 848**; love epistles **949**;
dialect **47, 90, 92**: comparisons **847**; Derbyshire **54, 712**; East Midland **384, 820**; Harley scribe **836**; Herefordshire **416**; Irish-English **16**; Kentish **781**; Kentish-Anglian **781**; Middlesex **694**; normalization **62, 103, 424**; Northern **399, 694, 776**, copied by Midland scribe **209**; Northern and Middle Scots **335**; North Midland **500, 689**; NE Midland **458, 790**; NW **981**; SE **603**; SE London **54, 712**; SE Midland **547, 596, 891**; SW Norfolk **602**; SW Midlands **94a**; **416**; Southerly **773**; Western **987**
dialogue: body and worms **182**; Christ and Mary **139, 443, 854, 953**; Cupido and Diana **296, 336**; friar and devil **488**; lovers **139**; Mary and Cross **854**; Mary and St Bernard **854, 940**; Morien and Merlin **266**; soul of dying person and others **182**. *See also* debate poetry.
dice **730**
Dictes and Sayings of the Philosophers **375**
diction: aureate **247, 343, 566, 703**; conventional **644**; courtly **970**; of men **733**; Scottish **415**; of women **733**
didacticism **994**
dignitas non moritur **616**
Dinah **962**
disillusionment, of waking **365**
displacement **1021**
dissent **724**
dit amoureux **725, 744**
divination, methods **730**
document, love epistle **949**
Dodesham, Stephen **792**
dogged **473**
Doomsday **956**
Donne, John **351, 385**: and *769* **811**; descriptions **839, 843**; religious lyrics **939**

Subject Index

Douglas, Gavin **672**, **792**
Douglas, Lady Margaret **41**, **405**; correspondence **949**
Li douze services de tribulacion **793**
Drake, Raff **7**
drama, religious **638**. *See also* plays.
dream: erotic **365**; interpretation **732**; private **642**; public **642**; religious **365**
dress: of clergy and laity **1002**. *See also* fashion.
drinkers, fraternity of **281**
Dublin **990**
Dublin, Robert de Vere, Duke of **952**
dublind **990**
dude more **1007**
Duenna, *Le Roman de la Rose* **557**
Dufay, Guillaume **707**
dúnad **828**
Dunbar, William **385**, **672**, **764**: aureate diction **566**; bird imagery **950**; and *chevalour* **78**; courtly poet **61**, **85**; descriptions **843**; flyting **830**, **901**; and French tradition **883**; and friars **881**; and limerick **682**; and London **704**; macaronic hymns **177**; and mortality **417**; Passion meditation **906**; patronage **821**; refrain poems **537**; religious poet **794**; and woman's song **755**
Durham: Hymnal **340**; Prior of **154**, **197**
Dunstan, St **726**
dyfalu **907**
Dygoun, John **1008**

e: final **121**; final, inflected **656**; unstressed **87**
eagle **824**
earth **959**
East, as symbol: of birth and Incarnation **605**
Easter, date of **216**, **501**, **808**, **978**
echoes, verbal in *1367* **429**
Eden **856**
Edmund Rich, St, Archbishop of Canterbury **24**, **155**, **856**; subject of 'Kinges Note' **172**
education, medieval **395**; religious **720**
Edward I: and *1857* **717**; and degeneracy **520**; reign **1**
Edward II: and *1857* **717**; and *3838* **160**, **361**, **599**, **626**, **704**; evil times **384**; reign **1**; and Piers Gaveston **520**, **614**
Edward III **94b**; and *5* **704**; campaigns **753**; and Hundred Years War **445**; parliament **800**; reign **2**, **361**, **764**
Edward IV: carol **809**; lament **807**; reign **3**, **11**, **361**, **570**; succession **955**
Edward V: reign **570**
Edward de Courtenay, Earl of Devon, epitaph **352**
ego, lyric **821**
Egwin of Evesham **726**
Eleanor of Aquitaine: and Chaucer **657**; influence on poetry **50**, **146**
Elias **637**
Eligius, St **726**

Eliot, T.S. and speech **789**
elision **999**
Elizabeth I, Defender of the Faith **945**
Elizabeth of Hungary, St **445**
Elizabeth of York, wife of Henry VII **788**, **948**
Ember Day **978**
embryology, human **668**
emerald **697**
Emery **976**
Emmaus, castle of **492**
englyn **907**
enigma, narrative **935**
enjambement **942**
Enoch **637**
envoi: conventions **644**; and Charles d'Orléans **468**
envy **925**
Epiphany **922**
epistles, verse: of love **46**, **271**, **336**, **731**, **750**, **949**; satiric **237**
epitaphs: questions **910**; verse **433**, **575**
Eros **355**, **837**
erthe **959**
Erthe upon Erthe, edition of poems **23**
esquyer **191**
estrif **107**, **736**
Eucharist/Holy Communion/Mass: in *1132* **980**; lyrics of **38**, **195**, *see also* lyrics, eucharistic; in culture **960**; Elevation **195**, **718**, **793**; enclosure of Sacrament **345** imagery **696**
Eve **567**, **962**: archetype **733**; children of **607**; as *erthe* **959**; and BV Mary **675**, **837**, **998**, **1000**
Evils of the Time, *see* Abuses of the Age.
exaggeration **752**
exempla **561**, **564**: bleeding crucifix **841**; blood-stained glove **841**; Gayus **663**; leper **684**; miracle of BV Mary **802**; repentant harlot **841**; St Martin **684**; shields with enigmatic messages **841**; Theobaldus and the Leper **760**
explosives **440**
extraction, of stanzas, **725**, **947**, **987**; *see also* individual poets
eyes: colour **623**

f **832**: voicing, **1012**
fable, of lion, fox, wolf, and ass **473**
fabliau, and women **768**
Fairfax/Fayrfax MS [BL Add. 5456] **12**, **83**, **88b**, **283**, **438**, **848**, **942**; polyphonic songs **650**; songs **746**
Fairfax poems [Oxford, Bodleian MS Fairfax 16] **921**
faith, and reason **632**
falcon **418**, **461**, **543**
Fall, Fortunate **974**
fallacy, ironic **912**
Fardyng, Thomas **7**
Farne, monk of **575**

Farnelay, Robert **349**
Fasciculus Morum **572, 701, 786**: authorship **800**; date **800**; and death **791**; exemplum of Gayus **663**; Franciscan **798**; ME verses **628**; preacher's aid **664**; signs of death **554**
fashion **896**: excesses **985**
fel **951**
felix culpa **224, 675**
Fensterlieder **863**
feortan **1012**
fetishism **1000**
Fifteen O's of Christ **201, 615**
Findern MS [Cambridge UL Ff.1.6] **53, 54, 84, 848**: anthology **54**; autograph album **795**; feminist interpretation **712, 958**; love epistles **949**; and Welsh version of *2742* **915**; woman's lyric, *4272.5* **935**
Findern, family **54**
fingers **670**
First Worcester Fragment **932**
Fisher King **543**
fishes **893**
fisses in þe flod **498, 856**
Fitzrobert, Robert, of Lascawe **157**
flatterer, motif **933**
Flemings **402, 450**
flicke **136, 897**
flowers **912**
ffluyd **7**
flyting **830, 901, 941**: Holly and Ivy **941**; *see also* Dunbar; Kennedy
foetus, position of **668**
fool, Henry VIII's [Lobbe] **910**
forest, and lover **938**
fork **904**
formes fixes **794, 942**
forma tractatus **821**
formulae: gravedigger **910**; lapidary **862**; religious **820**
Fortune: personified **342, 575, 626, 628, 662, 837, 958**; Wheel **412, 599, 712, 865, 888, 926, 983**
fortune-telling **730**
foule weyes **904**
fountain **1008**
Four Daughters of God **60**
fourthe **656**
foweles in the frith **498, 856**
fox, and goose **311, 322, 437**
France, English claim to **3, 94b**
Francis, St **37, 284, 569, 639**; carol **10**
François I **793**
Franklin, *Franklin's Tale* **790**
Freemasonry **386**
French, poems against **359**
frere **817**
Froumund of Tergensee **843**
friars:
―― in *Canterbury Tales* **453**; *see also* Chaucer
―― Carmelite **975**
―― Dominican **575, 1013**: sermons of **158, 701**
―― Franciscan **569, 575, 1013**: carols **37, 59, 86, 212, 247, 397**; in fire **890**; of Lynn **702**; lyrics **230, 443, 575, 638, 639, 703**; mentality **798**; and Nativity **998**; at Oxford **94a**; preaching **158, 463, 638, 639, 701**, of Judas **930**; poems about **57**; and polyphony **562**; *pugil domini contra diabolum* **1009**; satire **488, 573**; and secular poetry **569, 715, 796**; sermons **158, 638**; spirituality **569, 715, 798**; and vernacular material **986**; and Waldensians **569**; wall-paintings **573**
―― friar and nun theme **754**
―― at grave **910**
―― miscellanies **672**
―― rivalry with secular clergy **499**
―― verses against **447, 488, 526, 879, 881**; and Cain **453, 881**; and Judas **453**
frith **856**
Froissart, Jean **94b, 295**
Frost, Robert **487**
Frye, Walter **234, 883**
fully **273**

Gabriel **737**: and Mary **854**
galaunt **799**, *see also* gallant
Galen **556**
Galfridus de Anglia **650**
Galilee **983**
gallant, satire **799, 896, 1002**
gallus Christus **845**
gallus deus **845**
gallus praedicator **845**
game, hunting rituals **979**
games, funeral **944**
Gaveston, Piers **520, 614**
Gawain-poet and society **764**
gay **663**
Gayus **663**
gaze **962, 1022**
gelatin **904**
genre: and context **709**; criteria **731**
Geoffrey de Mandeville **402**
Geoffrey of Monmouth, *Historia Regum Britanniae* **741**
Geoffrey of Vinsauf **351, 843**: conventions of description **640**; *Poetria Nova* **726**
George, St: carol **390, 408**; Hours of **184**; patron saint of England **172**
Gerveys, *Miller's Tale* **550**
Gesta Romanorum **572**; Story of the Three Cocks **564**
ghost, of dead lover **649**
Giles of Rome **668**
Gilote et Johane **787**
girdle **805**
'Go little book' **271, 317**
God: creator **959**; healer **758**
Godefroy of St Victor **87**
godendgaghes **450**

Godric of Finchdale, St **575**, **703**, **770**, **911**: hymns **61**, **87**, **151**, **163**, **284**, **321**, **509**, **906**; influence on Chaucer **178**; manuscript sources **846**; and soul's house **1021**
gonne **440**
Goodall, Alice, name **750**
goose: and fox **311**, **322**, **437**; symbol **699**
Gospels of the Twelve Apostles (Coptic) **142**
gossips **455**
Gottfried von Strassburg **775**
Gower, John: courtly poet **85**, **146**, **544**; epistles **949**; extraction of stanzas **987**; French *ballades* **883**; and friars **881**; influence on other poets **672**; and money **720**; musical allusions **880**; patronage **821**; political poems **3**, **570**, **753**; and truth **879**
grace **899**, **940**, **972**, **1006**
grammar **387**
grand chant courtois **821**
grave, as house **661**, **833**, **1021**; *see also* imagery
graven **621**
gravedigger **910**
Graves, Robert **355**
graueþ **645**, **872**
Great Whore **805**
Green, Richard, chorister at King's College **754**
Gregory, Pope **573**
gren **159**, **645**: and *grein* **621**, **872**
grief, and faith **940**
Grimestone, John **882**: carols **37**, **59**, **61**, **86**, **247**, **382**, **407**, **522**; Commonplace/Preaching Book [Edinburgh, National Library of Scotland, Advocates' Library 18.7.21] **212**, **601**, **753**; and death **791**; Franciscan **798**; prose **825**; religious verse **672**; secular works **37**, **59**, **61**; sermon lyrics **101**, **521**, **522**, **639**, **865**
grin **872**
Griselda, *Clerk's Tale* **1022**
gromes/grom/gram **1019**
Grosseteste, Robert **138**, **784**: *De Virtutibus et Viciis* **179**
grotesque **888**
Gruffud ap Maredudd **998**
Sir Gryffyth ap Ryse **1005**
Gryffyth, Lady **1005**
grysly **729**
Guenevere, meeting with mother **626**; *see also* Wyrwein
Guillaume de Guilleville: *Pèlerinage de l'âme* **522**, **597**; *Pèlerinage de la vie humaine* **597**, **860**, **965**
Guillame de Machaut **967**
guilt, human **660**
Gurney MS [London, BL, MS Egerton 3245] **221**, **284**
Gybbe, William **762**
gymel **562**

Hadewijch **604**
had-I-wist **855**
haldan **815**
*hældi (PrOE) **781**
half-line **835**
half wakyng half slepyng **692**
Halgrinus, John **404**
hall **461**
Halsham, John **191**, **672**
Halsham, Philippa **191**
Hamlet, and Gravedigger **910**
handfasting **868**
hapax legomenon **681**: *helde* **781**; *tromchery* **990**
Harcourt (family) **302**
Harding, John, *Chronicle* **741**
hare **189**;
Harley lyrics **61**, **96**, **101**, **138**, **297**, **441**, **444**, **472**, **643**, **811**, **835**:
——— alliteration **163**, **677**, **736**, **828**, **835**, **907**: alliterative assonance **300**; alliterative phrases **449**
——— criticism: collation of texts **166**; conventions **736**; cruces **700**; date **445**; dittography **436**; reconstruction **330**, **971**
——— edition (Brook) **42**
——— influences: AN **828**; Celtic **775**, **828**; French **828**, **858**, **907**; Latin **828**; Provençal **233**; Welsh **907**; troubadours **146**
——— language: dialects **171**; macaronic **598**; Welsh loanwords **998**
——— literary qualities: allusion **736**; descriptions **290**, **351**, **486**, **858**; imagery, of gems **862**; irony **736**, **857**; stanza-linking **602**, **828**, **858**; stress patterns **835**; style **445**, **566**
——— moralizing poems **704**
——— names **723**; *see also* names
——— parody **857**: in *1394* **697**; in *2207* **92**, **752**
——— topics: handfasting **868**; love **688**, ways of **578**, **849**, **920** **949**; political **753**, **763**; of women **1000**
Harley MS 2253 **672**: anthology **963**; clerical compiler **906**; compilation **963**; copying **330**; dialect **836**; facsimile **64**; *miroir* **787**; scribe **723**, **787**, **836**; structure **787**, **963**; themes **787**
Harpsfield, Nicholas **418**
harrow **866**
Harrowing of Hell **787**, **919**, **972**
Haselwood, Joseph **309**
Hawes, Stephen **98**, **127**, **672**: epistles **949**; extraction of stanzas **987**
Hawghton, John **689**
hawk **255**
hawthorn/may **916**, **1008**
Haymo **475**
hazeltree **984**
he cam **523**
head, of boar **622**

heart, health of **732**; of Christ, *see* Christ
heald **815**
healdan **815**
health, god of **506**
Heaven **403**
hedging **270**
Hedon **776**
Heege, Recardu*m* **689**
helde **781**, **815**
Hemingborough **776**
hende: ase ha[u]k in chete **251**, **255**; *as hawk in halle* **255**
hendest in helde **815**
Henry II: and St Thomas Becket **693**
Henry III: and *1857* **717**; reign **1**
Henry IV: court **857**; reign **3**, **570**, **776**, **914**
Henry V: and *822* **704**; and Agincourt **809**; and St George **390**; reign **570**, **776**, **914**
Henry VI: and *822* **704**; carol **809**; complaint **361**; reign **570**, **776**; and succession **924**; support **371**
Henry VII **337**; reign **570**
Henry VIII **283**: and *1132* **418**, **461**; and *2281.5* **611**; and *2737.5* **716**; and Act of Supremacy **980**; and game of love **438**; and Lobbe **299**; and papacy **945**; songs of the court **193**
Henry VIII's MS [London, BL MS Add. 31922] **283**, **438**, **848**
Henryson, Robert **672**: bird imagery **950**; courtly poet **85**; debate **941**; and friars **881**; gem imagery **862**; refrain poems **537**; satire **830**; and woman's song **755**
hent **732**
Herbert, George **598**: and *769* **811**; and Charter of Christ **885**; and William Herebert **788**; religious lyrics **939**; and Vernon lyrics **994**
Here be Certayne Questyons of Kynge Bocthus **1019**
Herebert, William **94a**, **522**, **575**, **641**, **672**: adaptor **37**, **61**; carols **37**, **59**, **86**, **247**, **382**, **407**; consonants **416**; and George Herbert **788**; religious lyrics **38**, **94a**; translator **94a**, **382**, **416**, **703**, of Nicholas Bozon **798**; vocabulary **416**
herbs **128**, **912**; herbal, medical **427**, **894**
Hereford **836**
Herod, stock figure **259**
hi **162**
Hickling, manor of **739**
Hichecoke, W. **309**
Hill, Richard: collection of texts **943**; commonplace book [Oxford, Balliol College 354] **19**, **200**, **405**, **908**; and items in Trinity College, Cambridge O.9.38 **489**; proverbs **812**; version of *1132* **345**, **387**, **418**; taste for enigma **980**
Hilton, Walter, *The Scale of Perfection* **899**
Hippocrates **556**
hire loue **732**

his ponkes **700**
history, OT **183**
ho **162**
Hoccleve, Thomas: advice to king **851**; and ballade **392**; courtly poet **85**, **88**, **704**, **744**; descriptions **839**, **843**; epistles **949**; and fashion **896**; fragments from poems **373**; and French forms **61**; and Guillaume de Guileville **597**; historical **570**, **704**; *La Male Regle* **506**; and money **425**, **720**; patronage **672**, **821**; political comment **570**; and peace **260**; *Regement of Princes* **726**; and rondeau **571**
hocket **707**
Hogg, James, version of *1132* **345**, **387**, **461**
hokesters **990**
Holcot, Robert **510**
Holland, Richard, bird imagery **950**
Holly, personified as man **256**, **258**, **662**, **733**, **941**
Holton, John **724**
Holy Ghost, gifts of **347**
Holy Grail **19**, **543**: Damsel of **125**
Holy Name **522**
Holy Rood Day **154**, **517**
Holy Thorn of Glastonbury **916**
homo viator **713**
Hopkins, Gerard Manley **292**
Horace **726**
hore **728**
horse, analogy of Cross **446**; appearance **576**
Horsemen, of the Apocalypse **603**, **861**
hory **990**
hospitality **510**: work of mercy **684**
Host (eucharistic) **235**
hound **418**
hounsculles **450**
Howard, Lord Thomas **41**, **405**; correspondence **949**
Hubert **453**; hedger **560**; name **743**
huff **799**
Hugh of Avalon, St **494**, **683**
Hugh of St Cher **803**
humanism, Italian **88b**
humanities, study of **158**
Humphrey, Duke of Gloucester **360**
hunchback **997**
hunting **979**
Hurd, Agnes **723**
The Husband's Message **935**
Hwmffre ap Hywek **915**
hyldu (OE) **781**
hymns:
——— Latin **33**, **165**, **200**, **340**, **598**, **882**: liturgical **521**; processional **407**; sanctus, of Eastern Church **388**, **410**
——— macaronic **177**, **779**
——— ME **882**: eucharistic **195**; of Jesus **109**; Marian **200**; to St Thomas Becket **200**; translated from Latin **33**.
See also lyrics, prayers.

Hyrd/Hird/Herd/Hurd, Richard **646**, **723**, **857**, **1000**
hyrd, identification **646**

I, of lyric **559**, **777**, **821**
ich **644**
identity, sexual **873**
Idley, Peter **724**: and fashion **896**
.ii. **514**
illumination, of manuscripts **848**
imagery **443**: associations **811**; Celtic **543**; technique **585**
——— of human life: birth **972**; blood **604**; bridal **737**; clothing **799**; grave **616**, **661**; heraldic **461**; heroic figures **697**; gates **972**; martial **774**
——— of nature: animal **461**, **570**, **839**, in *1132* **418**; birds **697**, **824**, **857**, **950**; corruption **925**; decay **661**, **925**; dew **420**, **422**; disease **925**; fire **94a**; flower **303**, **420**, **422**, **567**; gem **805**, **862**; herbs **697**; light **94a**; lily **805**; quaternions **603**; rose **337**, **570**, **805**; rust **925**; spices **805**; spray **420**, **422**; spring **422**; water **604**
——— religious **521**: of Christ **94a**, **680**; Christ's body **774**; Christ's wound **680**; Christian **543**; eucharistic **543**, **585**, **696**; Magdelenian **567**; Marian **94a**, **567**, **585**; Passion **585**, **615**, **774**; soul **680**
——— and symbolism **705**; *see also* symbolism
imagination **585**
imago pietatis **522**, **630**, **774**, **782**
impossibilia **673**
Improperia, for Good Friday **382**
in oculi ictu **890**
Incarnation **38**, **595**
IMEV: additions **531**, **719**, **734**, **765**, **1014**; emendations **294**, **529**, **596**, **676**, **765**, **819**
inflexion **47**
Inglis rumpill **901**
Innocent III **766**
initiation, sexual **934**
inscriptions, as devotional verses **496**
instability, textual **965**
insults: Scottish and English **901**
Interludium de Clerico et Puella **768**
interpolation, of lyrics **295**; *see also* extraction
intonation **942**
invective **830**; *see also* flyting
Iris **355**
irony **805**: in Harley lyrics **736**, **857**; medieval **198**, **341**
Isabella of France **846**
Isabella, wife of Richard Beauchamp, Earl of Warwick **117**
Isolde, daughter of Duke of Brittany **775**
Isolde, wife of King Mark **775**
ite **890**
Ivy, personified as woman **256**, **258**, **662**, **733**, **941**

j **528**, **832**
Jack, name **548**
Jacob's Well **760**
Jacobus de Voragine **976**
Jacopone da Todi **569**, **834**
Jacques de Vitry **561**, **760**
jakkeliak/Iak **952**
James I: bird imagery **950**; and French tradition **883**
James IV **461**
Janet, name **548**
Jealousy **470**
Jean d'Angoulême **793**
Jean de Meun **881**
jelly **871**
ielif/jelyf/jelif **832**, **871**, **904**
Jerome, St **953**
Jesse **303**: rod **422**
jeux d'amour, *see* love, games
Jevan ap Rydderch ap Jevan Lloyd **124**, **907**
Jews **14**, **854**: stock figures **259**
'Jinny Jo' **944**
Joachym **976**
Joan of Acres **910**
Job, *see* Bible
Johane, name **548**
John, name **548**
John, reign **1**
John the Baptist **976**, **1008**
John de Brompton **723**
John Chrysostom **995**
John, St, the Evangelist **38**, **114**, **522**: care of BV Mary **995**
John of Fécamp **825**
John of Gaunt **952**
John of Hovenden **834**: *Philomena* **188**
John, *Miller's Tale* **966**
John of Mirfield, *Breviarium Bartholmei* **1017**
John de Multon **820**
John Peter **882**
John of Salisbury **720**
John de Wotton **723**
Johnson, Samuel **1005**
Johon, name **211**, **646**, **723**
joly Robyn **984**
Josaphat **182**
Joseph, St: husband of BV Mary **511**; trouble of **966**; in York cycle **929**
Joseph of Arimathea **125**
jottings, in printed books **205**
Judas Iscariot: apocryphal lives **930**; and betrayal **986**; and friars **453**; bargain with Pilate **633**; despair **772**; guilt **660**; motivation **142**, **772**; preaching about **930**
Judgement: Day **552**, **684**, **782**, **890**; God's **720**; Last **60**, **93**, **956**
Julian of Norwich **575**: and ME lyrics **594**; *Revelations of Divine Love* **522**, **899**
Jung, C.G. **634**
Justice, personifued **773**, **847**
Juvenal **726**

k **832**
Katherine, name **548**
Katherine of Alexandria/Sinai, St **114**, **168**, **194**; Capgrave's life of **726**
Katherine Group **671**
Kempe, Margery **575**
Kennedy, Walter: flyting **830**; refrain poems **537**
Kentish insurrection **321**, **419**
kettill-hattes **450**
Kildare, Friar Michael **16**, **18**, **161**, **238**, **575**: Franciscan **798**
Kildare Poems **16**, **238**: Franciscan **798**
King Lear, influence of sermons **840**
King's Ignorance **851**
kings, commemoration of **599**
knight, wandering **873**
Knights Templar **384**
Kolmkilne **909**
kombir-flet **651**
kongon **997**
-kyn suffix **402**

labours, of the months **870**
labourers **419**
Lacy, John **1005**
Laȝamon **670**, **672**, **926**, **932**
lai, as lyric **974**
Lai le Freine **992**
laid/loîd **974**
lament: betrayed maiden **139**, **559**, **768**, **777**; Christ **196**; chorister **254**; Henry VI **361**; husband, *mal marié* **139**, **695**, **776**; lover **139**; BV Mary **139**, **196**, **521**, **854**; Mary Magdalene **196**; old man/Maximian **766**; Procne **319**; wife, *mal mariée* **139**, **695**, **776**, **931**; woman **958**
Lament of the Redeemer, *see* Charter of Christ
Lamentatio Mariae **898**
Lancaster, warfare with York **3**
Lancelot, and Grail **692**
Langland, William: and *4165* **504**, **918**; and blacksmiths **726**; and friars **881**; and loveday **636**; social comment **423**, **720**, **753**, **764**; and speech **789**; and Three Estates **724**; and truth **816**, **879**
languages:
———— Celtic **991**: Cumbric **988**; Irish **990**, **991**; Welsh **991**, and Harley lyrics **828**, loanwords **988**
———— French **318**, **848**: and ME **657**
———— Latin **318**
———— ME **318**, **665**; use of ME **672**, **724**
———— patterns of use: AN, Latin, and ME **690**, **753**, **770**; AN, ME, Welsh, and Harley lyrics **828**, **907**
lapides **754**
lark **474**
Last Judgement **60**, **93**, **956**
Last Supper **660**

Last Things **81**
Lauds **974**
Launceston Priory **465**
lauercok **857**
laus/laudis **974**
laws, sumptuary **896**, **985**. *See also* fashion.
lawyers **425**
lay **227**, **944**
Lay Folks Mass Book **24**, **960**
Lazarus **957**
leaf, and love **333**
Leap Year, calculation **978**
leche **912**
lechery: accusation **499**; warnings against **370**
Legenda Aurea **976**
Leicester, Earl of **402**
Lent **272**, **333**, **759**
lenten **272**
Leominster, cell of Reading Abbey **265**, **775**, **836**
leper: OT treatment **696**; and St Theobaldus **760**; sheltered by a woman **684**
lessons: dancing **378**; music **378**
letters, verse, *see* epistles
la lettre **974**
Leversedge, Edmund **1002**
lex aeterna **856**
leyd **897**
liber naturalis **856**
Liber Parabolarum, Welsh translation **968**
libraries **848**
licoris **912**
lien **992**
life: Christian **81**; earthly **81**, **923**; as pilgrimage **316**
Liffey **990**
lime tree **333**
limerick **682**, **1001**
limners, work of **943**
linde, and love **333**
line: iambic **942**; long alliterative **163**
linguistics **16**, **62**, **103**
Litera Criseydis **949**
Litera Troilii **949**
literacy **570**, **720**
literature: affective **745**; Gothic **796**; lost **197**, **204**, **321**
litigation **915**
liturgy **539**: for Ash Wednesday **782**
liver **990**
Lobbe, jester **299**, **910**, **1005**
Locket, Lucy **502**
locus amoenus **856**
logic **549**
Lollards **3**, **57**, **753**, **876**: hostility to friars **975**; Lollardry **713**, **724**, **748**; and love poems **984**; and truth **816**
Lombard, Peter **890**; commentary on psalms **913**
Londe, Robert **727**
London **948**

Lord's Prayer, *see* Paternoster
Lorens of Orléans **969**
Lostkey, Kitt **502**
loue, and *sone* **992**
love:
———— courtly **61**, **66**, **297**, **303**, **438**, **472**, **609**, **634**, **669**, **712**, **751**: initiation to life **634**; parody **857**; woman's view **958**
———— religious **61**, **634**: Christian **81**; divine **463**, **628**, **749**; mystical **842**; spiritual **38**, **749**, **837**
———— secular **61**, **463**, **837**, **984**: games **984**; and hazeltrees **984**; joy of **644**; love-longing **568**; service, **644**, **937**
Love, personified **732**
Love, Nicholas, translation of *Meditationes vitae Christi* **288**
loveday **307**, **386**, **636**
lovesickness and Christ's love **840**
lover, as poet **438**, **486**; suffering **937**
Lucrece **962**
Ludlow **836**
lullaby: in *1132* **543**; in mystery plays **196**; prophetic **61**, **316**; *see also* carols
ly oponl/yopon **983**, **992**
Lydgate, John **575**:
———— ascriptions **315**, **489**; doubtful ascriptions **113**, **213**, **360**, **566**, **654**
———— comment: antifeminist advice **210**; on fashion **896**; on money **720**; on peace **260**; political comment **570**; on sins and virtues **882**; on society **724**, **764**; on succession **924**
———— literary qualities: aureate diction **566**; and ballade **392**; bird imagery **950**; and carols **59**; courtly poet **544**, **672**, **744**, **848**; descriptions **839**, **843**; poet **27**, **85**, **88**, **99**, **127**, **522**, **630**; and rondeau **571**; style **91a**
———— own works: and *1050* **973**; and *4112* **791**; courtesy poem **784**; epistles **949**; *Fall of Princes* **741**; macaronic hymns **177**; Marian lyrics **284**; monitory verses **247**; on nightingale **319**; printed works **946**; refrain poems **537**; religious lyrics **703**, **794**
———— and others: extraction of stanzas **947**, **987**; and John Halsham **191**; imitated **965**; influence **19**, **98**, **127**; and Song of Songs **566**; translator of *Criste qui lux es et dies* **340**; translator of Deschamps **883**; translator of *Stella celi exstirpauit* **822**
lying-song **120**; *see also* satire, songs
lyric, AN **858**
lyric, Celtic **625**, **998**: Old Irish **625**; Medieval Welsh **625**
lyric, European **426**, **478**, **509**, **598**, **998**; of courtly love **623**; religious **850**
lyric, French **24**, **107**, **472**, **509**, **549**, **823**, **848**, **858**, **998**: trouvère **788**
lyric, German **472**, **509**, **549**, **823**
lyric, Latin **107**, **472**, **478**, **549**, **564**, **575**, **598**, **823**, **998**: devotional **78**; 'Furibundi' **604**
lyric, macaronic **61**, **318**, **598**, **768**, **779**

lyric, ME **61**, **107**, **135**, **138**, **439**, **443**, **478**, **549**, **770**, **777**, **794**, **823**, **848**, **860**, **906**:
———— of Christ **130**, **277**, **509**, **575**, **779**; *see also* Christ
———— criticism: and art **545**; and ballads **334**, **509**, **649**; circulation **946**; classification of religious and secular **338**; and Chinese **797**; context **788**, **795**, **947**; critical methods **491**, **577**, **579**, **583**, **947**; definition **68**, **73**, **848**; editing **788**; evaluation **292**; fragments **321**; and limerick **1001**; and music **297**, **788**; provenance **848**; purposes **549**, **788**; reconstruction **330**, **971**, **1015**; simplicity **466**; and song **140**, **443**, **650**, **708**; structure **466**, **467**, **549**, **751**, **850**; style **619**, **651**; survival **223**, **788**; technique **292**; themes **223**; unity **24**, **330**; voice **755**, **768**, **934**
———— courtly **84**, **98**, **438**, **544**, **559**, **725**, **744**, **768**, **788**, **795**, **820**, **848**, **858**: parody **330**
———— of death **292**, **506**, **509**, **522**, **526**, **559**, **575**, **594**, **651**, **666**, **685**, **791**, **928**, **1009**, **1011**
———— fifteenth-century **39**, **795**; parody **839**
———— Findern, *see* Findern lyrics; Findern MS
———— fourteenth-century **31**, **48**, **801**, **811**
———— Harley, *see* Harley lyrics; Harley MS 2253
———— influences **794**: Augustine **174**; ballads **442**; Celtic **582**, **775**; *chanson d'aventure* **61**, **104**; earlier forms **275**; European **65**; Franciscan **569**; French **24**, **61**, **104**, **223**, **277**, **522**, **579**, **617**, **848**, **1021**; German lyrics **472**; Irish **582**; *kharja* **472**; Julian of Norwich **594**; Latin **24**, **61**, **223**, **443**, **522**, **579**, **582**, **609**; liturgy **24**, **539**; mysticism **594**; OE **104**, **226**, **1021**; Provençal **277**, **486**, **579**, **609**, **617**, **777**; Richard Rolle **594**; theology **539**; troubadours **140**, **146**, **165**, **334**, **442**, **486**, **644**; trouvères **644**; Venantius Fortunatus **174**; Welsh **582**
———— isolable **195**, **196**, **767**, **947**; 'Hail' **718**
———— of love **18**, **70**, **98**, **104**, **135**, **277**, **297**, **342**, **426**, **509**, **858**, **882**, **917**: divine **594**, **653**, **929**; love epistles, *see* epistles; *see also* love
———— Marian **11**, **14**, **130**, **135**, **277**, **443**, **509**, **522**, **539**, **575**, **776**, **779**, **794**, **892**, **962**, **977**; *see also* Mary, BV
———— meditative **292**, **526**, **714**; of the Passion **231**, **714**, **774**
———— MnE translation **35**, **43**, **63**
———— other subgenres: allegorical **19**; alliterative **163**, **187**, **449**, **671**, **767**; bookplate **112**; cautionary **476**; clerical **788**; comic **223**; complaint **91**, **882**; devotional **104**, **130**, **292**, **512**; didactic **811**; emblem **383**, **521**; female voice **934**; flyleaf **590**; folk **147**; Holy Name **594**; of instruction **91**, **395**, **765**; intercalated **848**; invocatory **757**; literary **999**; male-voiced **755**, **768**; mnemonic **747**, **757**; moral **19**, **104**, **292**; of

lyric, ME (*cont.*)
    nature **487**; popular **559**; satirical **704**, *see also* satire
    —— penitential **24, 44, 104, 180, 467, 506, 594, 999**
    —— political **1, 2, 3, 4, 11, 17, 57, 91, 223, 526, 753, 794, 926**; prophecy **882, 945**
    —— Rawlinson, *see* Rawlinson lyrics
    —— religious **31, 38, 39, 48, 60, 81, 102, 223, 277, 284, 292, 443, 508, 521, 522, 539, 559, 575, 598, 703, 779, 794, 796, 811, 823, 827, 850, 882, 939**; classification **508**; Elevation **195, 718**; eucharistic **195**
    —— of religious events: Annnunciation **108, 539, 575**; Christmas **14**; Crucifixion **539**; Nativity **11, 522, 539, 559, 575, 928, 998**; Passion **14, 509, 522, 559, 575, 590, 594, 653, 679, 774, 825, 902, 962, 1022**; Resurrection **596**; *see also* carols
    —— of saints, *see* individual saints
    —— secular **11, 14, 19, 51, 55, 84, 98, 130, 297, 559, 598, 704, 794, 796, 811, 827**
    —— sermon **144, 175, 204, 564, 572, 628, 629, 638, 639, 647, 651, 685, 703, 706, 753, 785, 786, 823, 840, 841, 861, 867, 882, 919, 947, 995, 1004**; in *Fasciculus Morum* **664, 701**; Franciscan **638, 639, 1013**; John Grimestone **601**; William Herebert **94a**; secular **1008**; *see also* friars
    —— sixteenth-century **21, 838**
    —— thirteenth-century **36, 449**
    —— of Trinity **779**
lyric, Provençal **486, 509, 823, 858, 998**; and love epistles **949**
lyricality **844**

Mac an Leaghas **885**
Machaut, Guillaume de **295**
macke . . . berde **322**
Madog ap Gwallter **998**
Magnificat **196**
magpie **270**
maiden in the mor lay **567**
maiden, betrayed **99, 459, 559**; *see also* lament of
Maidstone/Maydestone, Richard **585, 672**: Oxford fragment of Psalms **884**; Psalms **294, 866, 903**; Psalm 50 **913**; *see also* Bible, Psalms
maistrye **864**
makeles **511, 595**; *see also* Mary; word-play
makers, courtly **85**
mal marié(e), *see* lament of
males **681**
Malkin, name **548**
Malory, Sir Thomas **692**
man: as *erthe* **959**; and God **282**; wild **938**; and worms **528**
man, impersonal pronoun **953**
Man in the Moon **783**: allegory **585**; and Cain **453, 585**; comic character **743**; confessional

satire **499**; dramatic monologue **499**; hedging **270**; and Judas **453**; political poem **560**; punished by God **203**
mandrake **912**
Manning, Robert **138**
Manning, Stephen **79**
manuscript, ME, **848**: as a library **689**; minstrel **964**, study of **519**
manuscripts, detailed discussions:
    —— Cambridge, Trinity College R.3.19 **91a**
    —— London, BL, Add. 22283, *see* Simeon MS; 31042, *see* Thornton MS; 39574 [Wheatley MS], edition **29**; 60577 [Winchester Anthology] **88b, 819**; Egerton 613, **691**; Harley 2253, *see* Harley 2253: lyrics, *see* Harley lyrics; Sloane 2593, edition **14**
    —— Oxford, Bodleian Library, English Poetry a.1, 3938, *see* Vernon MS; Rawlinson C.813 [12653], *see* Welles Anthology; Rawlinson D.913, *see* Rawlinson lyrics
manuscripts mentioned briefly, as sources of poems:
    —— Aberdeen, Blairs College **756**; University Library 123 **976**
    —— Arras, Bibliothèque de la Ville 184 (254) **331**
    —— Army Medical Museum and Library 4 **214**
    —— [former]Astor A.2 **985**
    —— Berlin, Staatsbibliothek zu Berlin, Preussischer Kulturbesitz (Haus Unter der Linden) Phill. 1904 **968**
    —— Bicester Priory Bursar's Accounts Roll **505**
    —— Cambridge, Cambridge University Library: 111 **953**; Add. 2829 **878**, 4407 (19) **897**, 5943 **87**, **406**, **964**; Dd.1.1 **307**, **493**, **596**, **636**, Dd.5.16 **53**, Dd.5.64 **411**, Dd.6.1 **53**, Dd.8.2 **53**, Dd.11.89 **60**; Ee.1.12 **10**, **779**, Ee.4.35 **53**; Ff.2.38 **53**, **209**, Ff.5.48 **53**, Ff.6.31 **488**; Gg.4.12 **53**, Gg.4.27 **795**, Gg.4.31 **180**, Gg.4.32 **53**; Hh.4.12 **53**, Hh.6.11 **931**; Ii.3.8 **564**, **647**, Ii.4.9 **347**, **587**, **684**, Ii.6.40 **155**, Ii.6.43 **53**; Mm.4.41 **53**; Pepys 1584 **209**; Fitzwilliam Museum, McLean 182, **529**
    —— Cambridge colleges: Caius 383 **200**, 512 **578**; Corpus Christi 294 **53**, 405 **53**; Emmanuel 27 **53**; Gonville and Caius 174/95 **53**, 176/97 **53**; King's College 21B **754**; King's College Muniments 2 W.32 **190**; Magdalene College 13 **905**, Pepys 1236 **784**; Pembroke 307 **53**, **342**; Peterhouse 104 **384**, **504**, **887**, **918**; St John's G.28 **53**, 15 **825**, 112 **520**; Trinity 3.19 **440**; B.2.18 **53**, B.14.39 (323) **53**, **80**, **122**, **183**, **785**; O.1.29 **53**, O.2.40 **53**, O.2.53 **53**, O.9.38 **53**, **489**, **516**, **808**; R.3.19. **53**, **635**, **686**, **795**, **892**, R.3.20 **129**, R.3.21 **762**, **985**; 263 **342**, 323 **825**, **998**, 599 **343**, 652 **342**, 1230 **400**, **407**

Subject Index

―――― Cambridge, MA, Harvard University, Houghton Library 1032 **760**
―――― Chicago, University of Chicago 253 **1016**
―――― Chichester, Cowfold [Parish Account and Memoranda Book] 773, **847**
―――― Cleveland, Public Library, W q091.92-C468 **534**
―――― Copenhagen, Royal Library, Thott 4° 110 **632**
―――― Dublin, Trinity College 157 [D.4.11] **335**, 160 **792**, 212 [D.4.1] **812**, 516 [E.5.10] **371**, **555**, 517 **769**; Blage [D.2.7] **470**, **523**, **581**
―――― Durham, Dean and Chapter Archid. Dunelm.: 60 **399**; A.III.12 **825**; Muniments Locellus XXV, numbers 18 and 27 **776**
―――― Edinburgh, National Library of Scotland, Advocates 18.7.21 **101**, **905**; 19.3.1 **689**; 23.7.11 **668**
―――― Eton College 34 **572**, **719**
―――― Glasgow, University Library Hunterian 83 **241**; 230 **354**
―――― Harlech, Porkington 10 [National Library of Wales 10] **173**, **323**, **354**, **773**, **847**; Peniarth [National Library of Wales] 395 **537**, 369b **838**
―――― Hawkesbury, court roll **409**
―――― Holkam Hall, 229, 755 **1006**
―――― Humberside, County Record Office DDHE 19 **776**
―――― Leeds, University of Leeds, Brotherton 501 **908**
―――― Lichfield, Lichfield 10 **748**
―――― Lilleshall Abbey rental roll **849**
―――― Lincoln, Lincoln Cathedral 91 **288**, 129 **590**; Lincoln Archives Office, MS 2 Tennyson D'Eyncourt K/1 **814**
―――― London, BL Add. B.66 **615**, 5465 **1016**, 17492 **462**, 17866 **894**, 18752 **21**, 22283 **282**, 22579 **785**, 22720 **870**, 23986 **964**, 27909 **971**, 30338 **1019**, 31042 **513**, **542**, **773**, **847**, **903**, 31922 **7**, 32578 **349**, 34360 **123**, **360**, **589**, **635**, **892**, 37049 **60**, **285**, **500**, **735**, **782**, **956**, 38666 **750**, 39996 **349**, 45896 **302**, 46919 **94a**, **416**, **641**, 47214 **702**, 60577 [Winchester] **746**, **819**; Arundel 248 **771**, 285 **181**, 292 **254**, **726**; 'Bassus' **8**; Cotton Caligula A.ii **933**, A.ix **1020**, **1021**, Domitianus.xviii **337**, Galba E.ix **94b**, **315**, Julius A.v **1005**, Tiberius B.iii **756**, Titus A.xxvi **455**, Vespasian A.iii **596**, E.v **265**, Vitellius D.xii **455**; Egerton 613 **578**, **920**, 1624 **364**, 1995 **948**, 2810 **346**, 3245 [Gurney] **221**, **618**, 3307 **407**; Harley 45 **346**, 55 **818**, 172 **88b**, 293 **741**, 665 **340**, 682 **468**, **848**, **921**, **949**, 913 **16**, **161**, **238**, **473**, **798**, 978 **244**, **265**, 1002 **305**, 1260 **340**, 1706 **558**, **714**, **905**, 2202 **287**, 2247 **706**, 2251 **123**, **360**, **589**, **591**, **635**, **892**, 2252 **447**, 2253 **796**, **897**, **953**, 2274 **121**, **523**, **792**, 2383 **267**, 2942 **454**, 3362 **795**, 3954 **587**, **684**, 4011 **750**, 4012 **678**, **679**, 4826 **590**, 7322 **4**, **1009**, 7333 **123**, 7578 **348**; Lansdowne 418 **238**, 762 **350**; Printed Book IB 55242 **253**; Royal 2 B.x **286**, 12 C.xii **64**, **897**, 12 E.i **953**, 16 F.ii **129**, **848**, 17. C.xvii **60**, 18. A.vi **342**, 18. A.x **326**, 18. B.xxiii **561**; Royal App. 58 **7**; Sloane 747 **808**, 1212 **848**, **947**, 2457 **1017**, 2593 **14**, **122**, **796**, **886**, 4031 **310**
―――― London, Guildhall Library 25125/32 **891**
―――― London, Lambeth Palace 78 **785**, 265 **375**, 306 **4**, 352 **817**, 499 **909**, **981**, 541 **339**, 559 **618**, 853 **5**, **411**, **773**, **847**
―――― London, Public Records Office, E. 163/22/1 **190**
―――― London, Wellcome Historical Library 406 [Loscombe] **214**, **507**, 1493 **293**
―――― London, Westminster Abbey 34/3 **852**
―――― Longleat, Longleat 4 **1004**, 29 **173**, **411**, **618**, 30 **222**, 258 **848**
―――― Madrid, Escorial B **206**; Madrid University Library, Faculty of Law, 116²⁰.3 **628**
―――― Melbourne, State Library of Victoria **597**
―――― New York, Bühler 21 **427**; Glazier 39 **458** Pierpont Morgan Library, Morgan 298 **628**, 486 **201**, 775 **205**;
―――― Nottingham, University Library MS Mi 01 **790**
―――― Oporto, Oporto 714 **650**
―――― Oxford, Bodleian Library: A.106 **542**; Arch. Selden B.24 [3354] **344**, **354**, B.26 **400**, **407**; Ashmole 59 **591**, **762**, 176 **193**, 750 **132**; Barlow 24 **685**, **786**, **800**; Bodleian 26 **798**, 29 **1009**, 48 **887**, **918**, 315 [2712] **465**, 423 **792**, 789 **714**, 2322 **523**, 3554 **476**, 29734 **241**, **253**; Digby 2 **13**, **655**, **798**, 55 **825**, 86 **13**, **145**, **391**, **536**, **798**, **953**, 88 **870**, 102 **17**, 147 **771**; Don. c. 13 **167**; Douce 1 **512**, 54 [21628] **546**, 78 [21652] **412**, **1014**, 302 **771**, **964**, 322 **17**, **500**, 381. 87: Douce Fragments 94, 94v **8**; Eng. Poet a.1 **9**, b.4 **341**, e.17 [32690] **884**; Fairfax 16 [3896] **113**, **129**, **152**, **312**, **848**, **921**, **949**; Gough Eccl. Top. 4 [17680] **356**; Hatton 20 **818**, 30 **244**, 96 **651**; Lat. Misc. c 66 [olim Capesthorne MS] **46**, **240**; Lat. th. d. I **867**; e Museo 180 **651**, **841**; Rawlinson A.389 **884**, C.86 **948**, C.813 **354**, **1005**, D.328 **228**, D.375 **780**, D.913 [13679] **238**, **354**, **709**, **964**, poet. 36 [14530] **237**, poet. 118 **762**; see also Rawlinson lyrics, Welles anthology; Rolls 22 [30445] **114**; Tanner 201 **905**, 346 [10173] **88a**, **312**; Wood empt. 18 [8606] **576**
―――― Oxford colleges: All Souls 33 **741**; Balliol 354 **15**, **241**, **253**, **808**, **812**; Corpus Christi 61 **308**, 155 **349**, F.261 **523**, **792**; Jesus 29 **1020**; Lincoln Lat 129 (E) **727**,

manuscripts mentioned briefly (*cont.*)
Lat. 141 **747**; Magdalen, Deeds: Multon Hall 39a **820**; Trinity 7 **931**
——— Paris, Bibliothèque Nationale fr. 25248 **129**, **921**, fr. 1830 **793**, nouv. acq. lat. 693 **927**
——— Paris, Bibliothèque Mazarine 469 **822**, 514 **822**, 1716 **846**
——— Pavia, Bibliotheca Universitaria MS 69 **179**
——— Philadelphia, University of Pennsylvania: English 6 **859**; Latin 35 **462**, **581**
——— Princeton, Garrett MS **126**; Garrett 143 **933**
——— Rome, English College, 1306 **315**; A.347 **985**
——— Salisbury, Cathedral Library 82 **119**, 126 **106**
——— San Marino, Huntington Library HM 142 [Bement] **222**; Huntington 183 [*olim* Phillips 8923] **309**; HM 501 **180**; HM 503 **434**; various **734**
——— Sidney Sussex 80 **618**
——— Stockholm, Royal Library X.90 **894**
——— Stonyhurst College XLIII **618**
——— Throckmorton, Coughton Court, court roll **176**, **678**
——— Windsor Castle, St George's Chapel E. I. I. **804**
——— Worcester, Worcester Cathedral F.154 **132**, F.174 **93**
Mapes, Walter **720**
Marcabru **895**
Marcolphus **524**
mare reȝ mysse/mareregȝ mysse **325**
Margaret of Anjou **361**, **924**
Margaret of Doncaster **910**
marginalia **428**
Marie de France **974**
Maries, daughters of St Anne **976**
marriage **695**, **873**, **958**: ceremony **868**
Martial **726**
Martin, St **684**
Marvell, Andrew **616**
Mary, name **548**
Mary, Blessed Virgin **38**, **81**:
——— attributes: archetype **733**; compassion **953**, **972**; description **805**; focus of emotional response **94a**; gaze **962**, **1022**; grief **854**, **940**, **953**, **995**; Joys **114**, **168**, **181**, **185**, **194**, **227**, **827**, **874**, **922**, **977**, **995**; *makeles* **420**; mateless **511**; mediatrix **60**, **758**, **929**, **969**, **998**; miracles **572**, **802**, **908**; mother **284**, **511**, **864**; pain **972**; peerless **511**; praise **949**; protector against plague **822**; queen **574**, **864**, **936**; relationships **703**; reversal of Fall **972**; Sorrows **181**, **922**; sufferings **745**; tears of blood **902**
——— images **585**, **703**: beloved lady **929**; castle of Emmaus **492**; and colour symbolism **900**; *erthe* **959**; flowering rod **422**; Maid of the Moor **298**, **567**; maiden **511**, at fountain **1008**; mother-bride **929**; noble lady **284**; rose **303**, **900**, **1006**; second Eve **675**; tree **972**; weeping maid **980**; wife **864**
——— life events **181**: Annunciation **737**; Assumption **356**; childbirth **854**, **953**, **972**; at deposition **853**; Immaculate Conception **522**, **595**
——— texts **56**: prayers **81**, **118**, **757**
Mary of Egypt **304**
Mary Magdalene **518**: appearance of Christ **929**; archetype **733**; Flemish clerk's vision **692**; Maid of Moor **304**, **567**; redeemed daughter of Eve **772**
mass **38**, **195**; lover's/Venus **113**; *see also* lyrics, eucharistic
Matthew of Vendôme **351**, **842**
Maud, wife of Edward de Courtenay, Earl of Devon, **352**
Mawley, Maud/Matilda **191**
Maximianus **766**
May Day **405**
The Mayde's Metamorphosis **376**, **377**
The Mayor of Casterbridge **830**
meaning: double **951**; historical **515**; implied **502**; poetic **276**; medieval and modern **487**
Mechthild of Magdeburg **842**
medicine, medieval **668**
meditation **443**, **866**: on *Arma Christi*/Arms of Christ **218**; on the crucifixion **218**, **220**; for indulgence **220**; mystical **231**; lyric **939**; prose **939**; *see also* lyrics, meditative
Medwall, Henry, and fashion **896**
meles **681**
melisma **942**
Mellon Chansonnier **234**, **252**; literary relationships **354**
memento mori **144**, **165**, **353**, **575**, **628**, **782**, **922**; verses on tombs **761**
Memorare Novissima **666**
menske **728**
Meredith, George, *The Ordeal of Richard Feverel* **207**, **291**
merchants **423**
mercury **266**
mercy: works of **684**
Mercy, personified **773**, **847**
messes & meskins **450**
metaphor, in ME lyric **549**
metre **62**, **85**, **92**, **103**, **130**, **549**: discrepancy in *117* **886**; early ME **687**; iambic **789**; limerick **1001**; structure **913**
mice **202**
Michael of Kildare, *see* Kildare
Michael of Northgate, *Ayenbite of Inwyt* **969**
Michael de la Pole, Earl of Suffolk, *see* Suffolk
mil **991**
mil(es) **681**

milyn **991**
Minot, Laurence **94b, 811**: battle poems **794, 801, 26**; Edward III's campaigns **753**; invective **830**; ironist **198**; political poet **50, 359, 526**; and Scots' shoes **901**; songs **914**; stanza-linking **602**
minstrels, manuscripts **964**
miracle: Instantaneous Harvest **969**; of BV Mary **908**; *see also* exempla
Mirk, John: exemplum of truth-telling **816**; *Festial* **356**
mnemonics, of calendar **216**; *see also* lyrics
mode: courtly **90**; lyric **372**; popular **90**; religious **90**
Molscroft, William **776**
mon **497**
monarchs **57**
Monasteries, Dissolution of **465**
money: plea for **506**; power of **425, 704**
Money, personified as Lady Money **425**
monologue, dramatic **499**
moon **150**
moor **567, 944**
Moore, Henry **811**
Mopso **376, 377**
morality, and fashion **896**
more **1007**
More, Sir Thomas **264**
morphology **103**
Morris, William **607**
mortality **662, 888, 944, 1005**: commonplaces of **417**
Morton, Robert **650, 883**
motet **263**
movements, religious: Bernadine-Franciscan **188**; mystical **188**
muchel **1007**
music **36, 438**: analysis **514**; and literature **707**; liturgical **848**; for lyrics **68, 261, 625**; melismatic **707**; natural **967**; neumatic **707**; secular **848**; settings **942**; and song **880**; syllabic **707**; and theology **707**; transcription **880**; and words **789, 880**
musicians, amateur and professional **283, 438**
mutability **553**; personification **626**
muð imelen **856**
Mydwynter, Johannes **267, 403**
Myllar, William **946**
mysticism **842, 899**: influence of **218**
mystics **522**
myths **642**: of courtly love **634**; fertility **900**

nails, for Crucifixion **726**
names: concealed **211, 646, 697, 750, 723**; conventions **875**; of hare **189**; of plants **727**; significance **548, 743, 984**. *See also* individual names.
narrative: codes **986**; in ME lyrics **935**; scriptural **549**
narrator of *1463* **873, 899**

Nativity: paradoxes **1006**; themes **998**; *see also* carols, lyrics
nature **568**: in lyrics **487**; order in **498**
Nature, personified **662**
Natureingang **644, 893**; *see also* reverdie
Navigatio Brendani Sancti **726**
Ndembu **900**
nere **415**
Nettleton, John **513**
Newton, Humphrey: alliterative poem **240**; commonplace book **46, 795**; courtly lyrics **848**; epistles **949**; versification **313**
Nicasius St, of Rheims **202**
Nicholas, *Miller's Tale*, **172, 290, 966**: and *Angelus ad virginem* **608**
Nicholas, St: hymn to **509**
Nigel de Longehamps, *Speculum Stultorum* **368**
Nigellus **720**
Night Visit **148, 559, 863**
nightingale **824, 950**: debates **319**; defender of women **319**; song **148**; symbolism **319, 474**
Nine Worthies **814**
Noah, children of **607**
Noël **135**
Noes flood **966**
normalization, of language **62, 79, 103, 424**
Norman Conquest **1021**
North, as symbol: of Synagoga and the world **605**
Northampton, council of **693**
Northern Homily Cycle **760**
Northwood, John **56, 943**
nose, snub **997**
nostalgia **807**
notation: mensural **244, 263**; musical **249, 268, 810**; musical, black-and-red **283**
nou, conjunctional **262**
nouvelles **966**
nowel **966**
Nowels flood **966**
numerology **545, 862, 922**
numbers: five **551**; eight **551, 552**; 12 **742**; 29 **551**; *see also* symbolism

Oculus Christi **853**
Odo of Cheriton **968**: fables **204**; *Sermones de Festis* **1008**
Oedipus **930**
of godis sonde **832**
Offices: of Assumption **591**; of the Dead **173**; Hours of the Compassion **630**; Hours of the Passion **630**; Hours of the Virgin **630**
Oldcastle, Sir John **260**
olod **170**
orchard brown **461**
Origen: and Abuses of the Age **362**; and Song of Songs **680**
Original Sin **856**
Ormulum **983**

orthography: Middlesex **694**; ME and French **846**; variation **1020**
Osyth, St **973**
Other **821**
Oton de Granson, adapted by Chaucer **883**
outrage **993**
Owen, Wilfred **300**
owl **824**
'The Owl and the Nightingale' **770**: displacement **1021**; spelling systems **1020**. *See also 1384*.
oye **722**

pacifism **260**
painting, and lyrics **545**
Palden **286**
Pale **990**
pallor **872**
Pandarus, *Troilus and Criseyde*, **984**
paradox **439**, **443**, **552**: defeated love **834**; *dignitas non moritur* **616**; faith **632**; freedom **675**; of Nativity **1006**; prisoner of Christ's love **675**; relationships of Mary **574**; religious **598**; religious life **713**; queen in poor array **574**; soul's relationships with Christ **864**
parerga **305**
paris [herb] **936**
Paris, Matthew, *Historia Anglorum* **402**
Parker, monk of Stratford **7**
The Parlement of the Thre Ages, and old age **766**
parody: in *344* **143**; in *359* **977**; in *762* **198**; in *1394* **697**; in *2207* **92**, **752**; of aureate diction **296**; of Christianity **506**; courtly **544**; of courtly love **296**, **697**; in Harley lyrics **857**; recognition **752**, **839**, **912**; of religious life **637**; religious parodies of secular songs **212**, **247**; of religious songs **212**, **977**; sixteenth-century **522**
parrot **600**, **912**
Parzival **588**
Passion **38**, **60**: English poetry **521**, **774**, *see also* lyrics; instruments of **421**, **512**, **512**, **575**, *see also Arma Christi*; Latin poetry **521**; and *planctus Mariae* **854**; and redemption **940**
pastiche **725**
Paston, Sir John **378**
pastourelle **61**, **135**, **164**, **277**, **297**, **559**, **609**, **755**, **821**, **837**, **895**, **941**; and *chanson d'aventure* **104**, **139**; characters **837**; clothing **895**; convention **728**, **994**; as debate **97**, **941**; edition **94**: English **540**, **961**; French **961**; Harley **659**; milieu **854**; rape **1000**; and religious lyric **977**; themes **566**
Paternoster **119**, **179**, **393**; seven petitions **476**
patience **413**
pathos **854**: cult of **61**
patronage, courtly **672**
Patta **818**

peace **57**
Pearl, and *2037.5* **944**; *see also 2744*
Pearl of Great Price **862**
peasants, rebellious **423**
Peasants' Rebellion/Revolt **560**, **656**, **877**, **952**, **975**; *see also* insurrections
Peccantem me cotidie **173**
Pecock, Bishop Reginald **632**, **724**
peddlers **871**
pees **868**
Pellam **345**
penance **584**, **759**
penis **832**, **871**
penitence **81**, **575**, **720**, **758**, **888**; *see also* lyrics, penitential
penny, silver **425**
Penny, personified as Sir Penny **425**
Pentateuch **932**
Peperit virgo **1015**; *see also 2037.5*
perception: human and divine **995**; medieval and modern **642**
performance, oral **743**, **942**, **999**
Percival (scribe) **458**
Percy, Henry **321**
Percy, Sir Ralph **191**
personae, female **100**, **712**
personifications **662**; *see also* Death, Fortune, Mercy, Justice, Righteousness, etc.
perspective: female and male **712**; medieval and modern **642**
Perspice christicola **708**, **810**
pes **644**
Peter, St **660**, **772**: and Judas **930**
Peter/Piers de Bermingham **161**
Peter of Blois **209**
Peter of Langtoft, AN chronicle **901**
Peterborough Chronicle **1021**
Petrarch, Francesco **88b**, **801**
Petruchio, *The Taming of the Shrew* **754**
pheasant **699**
Philip, Duke of Burgundy **359**
Philip, Friar Nicholas **867**, **922**
Philip of Valois **94b**
Philipot, John **952**
Philippe of Harvengt **404**
Phillip de Greve **922**
Philomena **950**
Philosopher's Stone **266**
phlebotomy, *see* bloodletting
phonology **62**, **103**
physiognomy **843**
Picasso, Pablo **811**
Piers Plowman: and *864* **893**; and *4165* **504**, **918**; first line imitated **470**; and old age **766**; *see also* Langland
Pietà **521**, **522**, **980**
piety **522**: affective **451**, **575**, **782**, **796**; Christocentric **60**, **81**, **451**; fourteenth-century **60**; Franciscan **284**, **569**; Marian **522**; medieval **850**
Pilate, Pontius **307**

Subject Index

pilgrimage **81**; life as **316**
Pipewell **114**, **185**; *see also* acrostics
plague, bubonic **364**, **791**
Plainte de la Vierge **940**
planctus **755**, **792**, **821**: dramatic **111**; non-dramatic **111**; *planctus Beatae Virginis Mariae* **99**, **111**, **854**, **898**, **972**
planets **66**
planh **107**
Plato **457**
plays:
—— attributes: comment on society **175**, **764**, **767**; isolable lyrics **196**, **767**
—— religious **175**: mystery **135**, **397**, **718**; Chester **111**, **196**, **898**; Corpus Christi **118**, **718**; Coventry **196**, **898**; Digby **111**; *Everyman* **928**; Hegge **111**; Shrewsbury Fragments **826**; Towneley **898**; York **196**, **898**
—— of shepherds: Coventry, *Pageant of the Shearmen and Taylors* **376**, **377**, **826**; Rouen, *Officium Pastorum* **826**; Towneley **718**; Wakefield, *Shepherds' Plays* **826**
pleien **993**
Pliny, and nightingale **319**
pneuma **266**
poems: alphabetical **398**; context **811**; courtesy **784**; historical **57**, **359**, **877**, **955**; illustrated **756**, **870**; Lancastrian **371**; mnemonic **346**; political **2**, **17**, **337**, **359**, **914**, **924**, **955**; public **914**; Yorkist **371**
poésie populaire **135**
poet: as lover **438**, **486**; as entertainer **438**
poetry, pure **242**; OE **860**
point of view: female **958**; male **934**
polarity, masculine/feminine **929**
policy, commercial **3**, **369**, **914**
Pollard, Walter **228**
polyphony **263**: song repertory **650**; vernacular **562**. See also Chaucer.
posy **648**
powder **832**, **904**
Powers, family **161**
prayers **81**: to the Cross **589**; Elevation **235**, **793**; eucharistic **960**; to Jesus **118**; to BV Mary **81**, **118**; private **180**, **218**, **339**; penitential **757**; petition **757**; popular **217**; of repentant sinner **118**; to saints **81**, **518**; tags **878**; technique **292**; to the Trinity **56**, **288**; vernacular **218**, **221**, **235**; and weeping **957**. *See also* Christ; BV Mary; individual saints; lyrics.
preaching: and Lollardry **753**. *See also* friars; lyrics; sermons.
predictions **57**: of cuckoo **350**; from New Year's Day **541**; political **98**, **945**; from the Prime **541**; from thunder **527**; and weather **216**, **527**, **541**
pregnancy **934**
premerain **822**
Priapus **845**

Pride of Life **132**: personification **662**
priests, clothing **799**
prime **808**
primereyn **822**
processionals: Sarum **407**; York **407**
Procne **319**
prologue, of play **399**
Promptorium parvulorum **997**
pronouns, significance **756**
Proprietates Mori, Signs of Death **575**, **666**; *see also* death
prose: alliterative **671**; devotional **671**; and lyrics **522**; of the mass **37**, **86**; rhymed **356**; verse written as **908**, **911**
protest, political **423**
proverbs **19**, **27**, **228**, **557**, **804**: macaronic **769**
Proverbs of Hendyng **136**, **628**
Prudentius **845**
Prymer **630**, **672**, **757**
Psalms, *see* Bible
Psalter, paraphrased in prayer **339**
pseudo-ballade **392**
punctuation, effect on meaning **208**, **219**
pungere **754**
Purgatory **403**, **923**
purpill and pall **461**
purposy **648**
Putta **818**
puy **24**, **920**
Pygott **7**
pykes **450**
pyn **600**

quadrenramp **450**
quaternions **603**
querelle des femmes **736**
La Queste de Saint Graal **692**
quest, spiritual **713**
questions, and answers **27**, **910**
quid profuit **807**
Quis dabit/Liber de passione Christi et doloribus et planctibus matris eius **940**
Quis est hic qui pulsat **603**
Quixley, John **883**
quodlibet **848**
quoniam **754**

r long **832**
R. de Burgate **265**
Raby: Lord Neville of **154**, **197**, **321**; stag **154**
rabyous **784**
Radcliff, family of Barton-upon-Irdwell **822**
Rageman **730**
ragen **993**
ragier **993**
Raimbaut d'Aurenga **486**
rain, small **355**, **363**, **379**, **652**, **674**
Rastell, John **946**
rats **202**
Rawlinson lyrics [Oxford, Bodleian Library, MS Rawlinson D. 913] **101**, **431**, **709**

Sidney, Sir Philip **634**
Sidonius Apollinaris **843**
Sigurd, and nightingale **319**
Simeon MS [London, BL, Add. 22283], and Vernon MS **503**: Midlands connections **748**. *See also* Vernon MS.
simplicity **405**
sincerity **486**
Sins, Seven Deadly **985**; *see also* vices
Sintram, Friar Johannes, of Würzburg **628**
'Sir David Graeme' **461**
Sir Gawain and the Green Knight **46**, **240**, **979**; poet **670**; *see also 3144*
Sir Isumbras **726**
Sir John, name for priest **459**
Sir Tristem **775**
sirvente **359**, **876**
Skelton, John **672**, **764**, **946**: and ballade **392**; bird imagery **857**, **950**; descriptions **843**; and gallant **799**; heraldic imagery **461**; invective **830**; refrain poems **537**; and rondeau **650**; and Scots' shoes **901**; and his times **619**; and truth-telling **816**
sky, as parchment **210**
sleep **692**
smallpox **202**
snete **931**
Socrates **556**
soht (OE) **897**
soliloquy, poet's **139**
Solomon **524**: stock figure **747**; temple **749**
solsequium **853**
somer **272**
sone, and *loue* **992**
songs **25**, **297**, **385**, **880**:
——— edition **87**
——— folk **821**: archetype **437**; French **164**; Italian, of Mary Magdalene **567**
——— historical: in chronicles **197**; political **1**, **2**, **3**, **175**, **297**; soldiers' **197**; of wars against Scots **321**
——— of love **190**, **408**: courtly love **83**; maiden's joy **139**; Night Visit **148**, **559**, **863**; wooing **709**
——— lying **120**, **156**, **253**, **673**, **852**
——— and other genres: and lyric **652**; in mystery plays **196**; and poem **708**
——— religious **19**: to saints, *see* saints and individual names; to Trinity **38**
——— secular **19**: court **283**; dance **382**, **709**; at dinner **460**; drinking **61**, **408**, **709**; forester **438**; minstrels' **115**; occasional **283**; polyphonic **650**; early Tudor **746**
——— woman's **758**, **895**; in ME and Middle Scots **755**
Song of Solomon *see* Bible, Song of Songs
Song of Songs, *see* Bible
sonnebem **805**
sonnets: English **21**; imagery **900**; Petrarchan **571**
sophistication **405**

soul: bride **680**, **873**, **899**; Christ's executioner **604**; fate of **553**; salvation of **802**; struggle for **572**; wooed by Christ **842**
sound **549**; changes **700**; and sense **789**; of words **942**
Souter, Mistress Rose **931**
South, as symbol of Ecclesia **605**
South English Legendary, *Quadregesima* **759**
souvenir, of tale **982**
sowlehele **943**
Spalding, Richard **114**, **168**, **194**
Speculum Ecclesie, of St Edmund Rich **155**, **853**
Speculum Parvulorum **785**
Speculum Peccatoris **714**
Speculum Sacerdotale **692**
speech: common **990**; and ME verse **999**; rhythms **789**, **999**
Speght, Thomas **635**
spells **575**
spelling, French forms **756**
Spenser, Edmund **672**, **744**
sponsa Christi **463**, **749**
sponsa solis **853**
sprent **415**
spring **272**: celebration **394**, **568**; lovemaking **366**; return **644**; and sorrow **593**; symbolism **422**. *See also Natureingang, reverdie.*
sprite, of wood or water, as Maid of the Moor **627**
squiere **191**
Staffordshire **748**, **945**
stage **173**
Stanbrook Abbey **475**
Stanfeld, Friar Thomas **538**
Stanlow/Stanlaw Abbey **981**
stanza **942**: ballade **848**; bob and wheel **313**, **542**; French influence **858**; *Golden Targe* **344**; in Harley lyrics **828**; interpolation **834**; linking **582**, **602**, **858**; rhyme royal **343**, **848**, **942**; thirteen-line **626**, **670**, **922**
Stella celi exstirpauit **822**
Stephen, King **924**
Stephen, St, carol **408**
stertep **1012**
stille **523**
Stokys, Richard **213**, **672**
ston **951**
stonde **951**
Story of Asneth **224**
Stow John **213**, **528**, **635**, **892**: edition of Chaucer **91a**, **686**; texts **965**
strem that striketh stille **991**
stress patterns, English, French **835**
structure, poetic **549**, **583**, **603**; triple **394**. *See also* lyric.
style: courtly **958**; ME **566**
succession, of kings of England **924**
Suffolk, Michael de la Pole, Earl of **952**
Suffolk, William de la Pole, Duke of **88**, **95**, **129**, **731**: captivity **654**, **958**; and Charles

d'Orléans **468**, **883**; courtly poet **544**, **744**, **848**; and Fairfax 16 **921**, **949**; and Harley 682 **949**; love poems **796**; poems against **830**
sulch **698**
sully **273**
summer **272**
Sumner, Gillyat **776**
sun, setting of **250**, **435**
Sunday Letter **978**
SIMEV: additions **479**, **719**, **734**, **765**, **1014**; emendations **294**, **765**
surgeon, motif **933**
Surrey, Howard, Henry, Earl of **71**, **438**: lyrics **744**
Surtees Psalter **903**
sutere **931**
swallow **474**
swannes swyre **805**
sweet **774**
swype **436**
syllables **942**: accented **999**
symbolism: alienation **916**; birds **474**, **697**, **699**, **824**, **866**; black **900**; cock **845**; colour **546**, **900**; compass points **605**, **803**; courtly **788**; dew **422**, **523**; fertility **916**; flowers **298**, **303**, **523**; flowering rod **422**; four **742**; gates **972**; holly **256**; ivy **256**; letters M, I, X, C **167**; lily **900**; lust **916**; martial **774**; mother **972**; nightingale **319**, **950**; numbers **66**, **298**, **545**, **546**, **551**, **552**, **803**; pain **916**; red **125**, **404**, **900**; rose **788**; seven **467**; spray **523**; thorn **125**; three **742**; tree **474**, **972**; truelove **936**; twelve **742**; virginity **916**; white **900**
syncopation **707**, **886**
syncope **999**
syng **389**
syntax **549**
Sythe, St **973**

TER **375**
Tadh Óg **885**
tageliet **659**
tags: prayer **878**; preaching **629**; vernacular **664**; *see also* lyrics, sermon
tail, of English **901**
Talbot, Johanna **723**
Talbot, Richard **723**
talyt tyk **901**
tankard **1019**
Tawddgyrch Cadwynog **133**
tears: of blood **902**; and other liquids **957**
technique, verse **583**
Tegeu/Tegau/*Tergau Euvron* **907**, **982**
temple, Solomon's **749**
tenso **609**
testaments/wills **1005**
Testament of Christ, *see* Charter of Christ
texts: abbreviation **886**; copying **665**; corruption **751**; editing **635**, **711**; parallel-text edition **887**; problems **624**; punctuation **711**; reliability **676**; revision, authorial **620**, **849**; revision, scribal **756**, **887**; transcription **712**
texture, of verse **604**
tey vp ȝour ky **460**
þat **728**
theology, Bernardine **842**
þewes **586**
thieves **586**
Thomas Aquinas: influence **24**
Thomas Becket, St: carol **408**; hymn **200**, **770**, **911**; reasons for martyrdom **693**
Thomas of Erceldoune **445**
Thomas de Hales: and Annunciation **737**; imagery **805**, **862**; 'Luue Ron' [**66**] **169**, **463**, **703**, **749**, **796**, **798**; *see also 66*; religious poet **18**, **37**, **86**, **138**, **247**, **575**
Thomas of Woodstock **952**
Thoms/Toms/Thomas, Samuel **754**
Thornton, Robert **513**, **913**; assembly of texts **943**
Thornton MS; Robert Thornton's London MS [London, BL, Add. 31042] **903**, **913**
þoro **227**
Three Estates **310**, **724**, **877**
Three Living and Three Dead **522**, **626**, **791**, **888**, **979**
Three Sorrowful Things **758**, **778**
þrestlecok **857**
Throckmorton, Dame Margaret **678**
thrush **699**
thunder, prophecy **527**
Tickhill, John **891**
timor mortis **173**, **522**
tirneþ/tirueþ **983**
tituli **575**
to lede bi lagmon **670**
toc **959**
tollum **754**
tools, shoemakers **747**
tomb, cadaver/double/transi **616**, **761**, **782**
trade, woollen **3**, **369**, **914**
transience, of earthly life **528**, **778**, **923**, **994**
translation: *Candet nudatum pectus*, **192**; *Criste qui lux es et dies* **340**; to MnE **274**, **565**, **740**; More epigram **264**; *Vox Christi* and *Responsio peccatoris* **192**; work of Charles d'Orléans **468**, **921**, work of William Herebert **94a**
transmission, oral **345**
tre **250**
trebad/trebraid **582**, **828**
treatises, medical **427**
tree: family **432**; figure for BV Mary **972**; in love poetry **333**; and lover **938**; motif **933**
Tremulous Hand **1021**
Trinity, see lyrics, prayers, songs
Tristan **775**: and nightingale **319**; Welsh lyric **935**
trobaritz **958**
tromchery **990**
tromchroí **990**

trothplight **868**
troubadours **468**; *see also* lyrics, influences
Troy **529**
truelove **936**, **972**
Trueman, Jack **877**
truth: and falsehood **720**; telling **816**
tuet **381**
Turnour **790**
turtle-dove **891**

ubi sunt: in lyrics **334**, **522**, **547**, **575**, **662**, **749**, **782**; and *contemptus mundi* **807**; motif **118**, **165**, **182**, **391**, **439**; and place in manuscript **93**; in Vernon lyrics **994**
ugliness, description **843**
Ugolino, *Monk's Tale* **588**
unkind **774**
Uriel **477**
Usk, Thomas **654**
usury **346**

v, voicing **1012**
Vache, Philip **213**
vade mecum **714**
vado mori **182**, **791**
Valley of the Shadow **543**
variation, orthographical **1020**
venesection **364**
Veni Creator **913**
venite **890**
Venus, court of **308**
vernacular **579**, **939**; expression of subjectivity **1021**
Vernon lyrics: and *3144* **994**; and *2744* **994**; context **943**; editions **9**, **13**; poetic merits **994**; refrain poems **537**, **913**, **923**; shape **933**; structure **994**; style **994**; truth-telling **816**; *ubi sunt* **994**
Vernon MS [Oxford, Bodleian Library English Poetry a.1, 3938] **9**, **13**, **126**, **138**, **672**; and Simeon MS [London, BL, Add. 22283] **282**, **503**, **933**; ballade form **392**; Gothic poetry **796**; purpose **994**
vers de société, satirized **296**
verses: of advice **471**; against the Scots **741**; complaint **485**; calendar **525**; courtly **544**; for display **465**; early ME accentual **687**; emblem **383**; macaronic **690**; mnemonic **525**, **808**; nonsense **544**; OE **687**; political **485**, **570**, **620**, **717**; practical **765**, *see also* lyrics of instruction, mnemonic; social comment **485**; written as prose **908**, **911**
versification **67**, **114**, **549**
versus tripartitus caudatus **107**
vert **1012**
vertere **1012**
uerteþ/verteþ **207**, **243**, **245**, **246**, **248**, **249**, **291**, **1012**
Vexilla regis prodeunt **919**
vices: seven, in Ostienic order **587**; in sermons **882**; triumph **533**; and virtues, *see* virtues

Vices of the Times, *see* Abuses of the Age
villeins **419**
vinculum amoris **675**
virelai **117**, **206**, **571**, **744**, **794**, **821**
Virginia **907**
Virgins: 11,000, invoked for chastity **339**; wise **574**
virtues: cardinal **558**, **803**; remedies for sins **493**, **587**, **720**; in sermons **882**; seven **278**, **587**; theological **558**
vise, Scandinavian **164**
Visit, Night *see* Night Visit
voice, woman's **1000**
'The Vows of the Heron' **94b**

w **528**
W. de Wicumbe **265**
W. de Winton **265**
Waiting for Godot **830**
wake **484**
wakefulness **692**
Waldo Peter **569**, **639**
Waldensians **639**
Walsingham, Thomas **952**
Walter of Châtillon **895**
Walter von Vogelweide **768**
Walter, William **987**
Walton, John **332**, **457**
war **57**: poems of **570**
Warner, family **948**
warroke **988**
Warwick, Richard Beauchamp, Earl of **117**
Wassail **149**
Wat, shepherd **988**
water, of regeneration **1008**
wawe **983**
Way, William **88b**
weather, and poet's mood **425**; predictions **527**
weder is went **667**
weeping **957**
wela hay **289**
well: holy **459**; wake beside **459**, **484**
welle was hire . . . **567**, **944**
Welles/Wellys Anthology [Oxford, Bodleian Library, Rawlinson MS C.813, 12653] **20**, **127**, **134**, **335**, **365**, **945**; arrangement of works **987**; literary relationships **354**
Welles/Wellys, Humphrey **98**, **1005**: compiler and scribe **987**; recusancy **945**
Werkens, T. **222**
West, as symbol: of death **605**; of Crucifixion **605**
weth **450**
whale **805**: whalebone **805**
wheatear **988**
Wheatley MS [London, BL Add. 39574] **29**
Wheel: of Fortune **865**, **926**, **983**; of Life **865**
wheelwright **626**
wher he were **743**
Whethamstede, Abbot **361**
whetstone, sign of a liar **156**

The Wife's Complaint **935**
wilde **805**: *wilde wymmen* **875**
will, free **282**
will **322**
William IX **821**, **860**
William of Canterbury **911**
William the Conquerer **1021**
William of Killingsholme **894**
William of Leicester **179**
William of Nassington **18**
William of Pagula **877**
William de la Pole, Duke of Suffolk, *see* Suffolk
William of Shoreham **18**, **138**, **492**, **566**, **672**
Williams, William Carlos **642**
Willimot **818**
wills/testaments **1005**
Winchester **265**: Winchester Anthology [London, BL, Add. 60577] **88b**, **819**; [lost] Winchester Codex **244**
winter **553**: and Death **593**
wind, western **355**, **363**, **366**, **379**, **425**, **652**, **674**
Wingfield, Dame Anne **678**, **679**
wisdom, proverbial **812**, **855**
wit **443**
withoute(n) more **1007**
þe *Wohunge of ure Lauerd* **603**
Wolfram von Eschenbach **935**
Wolsey, Cardinal **461**
Woman of the Apocalypse **574**
women: authors, **99**, **100**, **958**; characteristics **733**; depiction in *Miller's Tale* **768**; frigid **530**; images **733**; lecherous **530**; Pauline Doctrine **954**; in punctuation poem **219**; satire **61**, **120**, **253**, **695**, **830**
Woodville, Elizabeth **948**
Worcester, copying centre **818**;
Worcester Fragments: edition **93**; tone **137**; OE precursors **226**
word play **443**, **583**: *Alison-eleyson* **563**; *Annot-a note* **1000**; *beast-best* **893**; *bey some ware* **904**; *coynte-cunde-cunte* **697**, **912**; *Eva-Ave* **998**; *gome* **697**; *gras-grace* **936**; *Maria-lady* **420**; *matchless-mateless* **420**; *sun-son* **404**; *weder* **667**
words: Flemish **450**; and music **789**
world: rejection of **552**; riddle **642**; upside down **533**
worms: and body **616**; and man **528**
Wottenhull, James, *senior* **787**
Wounds, Five, of Christ **451**; Blazon of the Five Wounds **451**. *See also* Christ, wounds
Wulf and Eadwacer **935**
Wyatt, Sir Thomas **41**, **61**, **71**, **365**, **385**, **438**: and *1270.2* **581**; and *2281.5* **611**; and Anne Boleyn **716**; carol **462**; and Charles d'Orléans **405**; and Chaucer **405**; circulation of lyrics **946**; lyrics **744**, **848**; and ME poetry **405**, **634**, **672**, **795**, **935**; refrain poems **537**; and rondeau **571**
Wyclif, John **3**, **704**, **876**: incrimination **975**; and lyrics **939**; social comment **423**; NT **748**; and Three Estates **724**
Wycliffites, *see* Lollards
wyll/wylt **711**
Wynkyn de Worde **542**, **946**, **987**; and *1874* **985**
Wyrwein/Gyrwein **907**

y: for unstressed *e* **121**; for þ **776**; Welsh vowel **124**
Yeats, W.B. **238**; 'Leda' **523**; and speech **789**; 'The Mother of God' **523**
yeddyng **499**, **849**
yelf/yelve **832**, **871**, **904**
yelver **871**
'Yonec,' in *1132* **974**
York, warfare with Lancaster **3**
youth **897**
Youth, personified **662**

Zephyrus **674**
zeugma **983**
Zita, St **973**
Zodiac **870**

Index of First Lines

This index lists the poems mentioned in the works annotated, including those noted only in the lists that accompany the annotations, many of which are not lyrics; the index includes poems cited to establish contexts, and in comparisons and similar brief references. The numbers in bold face indicate annotations with a reference to a poem in the text of the annotation, rather than only in the list following it. A poem not followed by an annotation number may have been noted as part of the context of another poem which is described in greater detail and so mentioned in the work, or have been noted in a work such as an edition or a book of criticism, for which the annotation has taken the form of an overview. The forms of the first lines, and most ascriptions and titles are those of *IMEV* and *SIMEV*. The titles of Harley lyrics are those of Brook's edition, **42**. The titles of other poems, e.g. 'The Maid of the Moor,' 'The Thrush and the Nightingale,' are used in criticism, as are some ascriptions from the works annotated. 'BR+' indicates a poem not listed in *IMEV* or *SIMEV*, with a number assigned by an author using the methods of *IMEV* and *SIMEV*.

.1	A for Alyn Mallson þat was armyde in a matt	
	398	
.2	A a my hert I knowe yow well	
1	A blessid Ihū hough fortunyd this	
2	Ha cruell deeth contrarious to creatures in kynde	
	224	
3	A Daunger here y cast to thee my gloue	
	Translated from the French of Charles d'Orléans	
4	A dere god haue I deseruyd this/This dere destyny to drede	
	55	
5	A dere God what may this be/That alle thing weres etc.	
	361, **704**	
6	A ihesu criste crovne of maydenes alle	
	Life of St Katherine	
	John Capgrave	
	726	
7	A iesu so fair an fre/Suettest of all þinge	
8	A Ihū þow sched þi blode/ffor dred of pyn þ^u wyst sold be	
	231	
9	A lo myn hert what tolde y the	
	Associated with Charles d'Orléans	
10	A lord crist of heuene blisse þou art kynge	
12	A Mercy fortune haue pitee on me	
13	A myn hart remembir þe well	
	Richard Davy	
13.3	A most fayre and true/ye cause me rue	
13.5	Ah my hart/ah this ys my songe	
	193	
13.8	A Robyn gentyl robyn/Tel me how thy lemman doth	
	Attributed to Thomas Wyatt	
14	A son take hede to me whas son þou was	
	995	
14.5	A the syghes þat cum from my hart	

Index of First Lines

15	A wel myn hert but wol ye not ben wise
	Associated with Charles d'Orléans
16	*A celuy que pluys eyme en mounde*/Of alle tho that I have found/*Carissima De amico ad amicam*
	318, 795, 941, 949
18	*A patre unigenitus*/þorw a maiden is com to vs
19	*A soun treschere et special*/ffer and ner and oueral/In mundo
	Responcio to 16
	318, 795, 941, 949
20	A babe is born al of a may/In þe sauasyoun of vs
21	A babe is born of hey nature/the prince of pees etc.
	400
22	A babe is born our blysse to brynge/A maide ther was etc.
	225
23	A barge to beren fro depe grounds
28	A blisful lyfe a peseable and a swete
	Etas Ptima/Former Age
	Geoffrey Chaucer
29	A child is boren amonges man
	798
30	A chyld ys borne e-wys/þ^t all þis word xall blys
	59, 225
31	A childe ys born of a mayde/in redempcion of vs all
33	A cros was maad al of rede/In þe bigynnyng of my book
	John Trevisa
33.5	A faythfull frende wold I fayne fynde
33.6	A fals begininge
33.8	A fals by-hetyng/A lyeres auansyng/A bitynde fonding
34	A ferly thing it is to mene/That a mayd a chyld etc.
34.5	A floure is sprongen þat shall never faile
	597
35.5	A fryer an heyward a fox and a fulmer sittyng on a rewe
36	A ffroward knave pleynly to descryve
	'A Satyrical Ballad against Jack Hare.'
	John Lydgate
37	A God and yet a man/A mayde and yet a mother
37.3	A gulden begh in a soghes wrot/A faire wyman and a sot
37.5	A gode begynnyng/makyth a gode endyng
39.5	A good scoler yf þou wilt be/Arise erly & worship þe trinite
42.5	A grehounde shulde be heded like a snake
44	A hole confessoure þ^u were hone/& leuydist in contemplacion
	John Audelay
	389
52	A kinge out of the North shall come
54.5	A kynges sone and an emperoure
60	A levedy and my love leyt the bole bigan to belle
61	A lady þat was so feyre and briȝt/*velut maris stella*
62	A ladies hert forto want pite
	Associated with Charles d'Orléans
63	A litil childe þer is i-bore/I-spronge owt of Iesses more
63.5	A lyoun raumpaund wit his powe
64	A letyll tale Y wyll yow tell/Y troye hit wyll lyke yow well
65	A lytyll tale I will you tell/The very trowth how it befell
66	A Mayde Cristes me bit yorne/þ^t ich hir wurch a luue ron
	'A Luue Ron'
	Thomas de Hales
	169, 463, 566, 585, 653, 662, 703, 737, 749, 796, 798, 805, 827, 862
66.5	A mayde perles/hathe borne godys Son
67	A Meyden myelde hath borne a chielde
	James Ryman
68	A man may a while/nature begile

71	A man that lovith ffisshyng and fowlyng bothe
	Piers of Fulham
72	A man þ^t xuld of treuþe telle/W^t grete lordys he may not dwelle
73	A man þ^t will of wisdam lere/Herkyn to þe boke etc.
76	A man was þe fyrst gylt/and therefor he was spilt
77	A man w^t out mercy mercy shall mysse
78	A mervelus þyng I hafe musyd in my mynde
79.5	A new songe anewe/vnto yow louers blynde
80	A newe song i wil begynne/Of kyng Edmund þat was so fre
81	A nywe werk is come on honde/þorw my3t & grace etc.
81.5	A nyce wyfe A backe dore/Makyth oftyn tymes a ryche man pore
83	A nobull story wryte y fynde/A pope h^t wrote etc.
	The Trentale of St Gregory
84	A pak a pak madame my lode alight
	Associated with Charles d'Orléans
86.3	A pyte withowten trewthe
87.5	A prety wenche may be plesur
88	A pryncypal poynth of charyte/it is so mery for to be
91	A schelde of red a crosse of grene
92	A solytarye soore compleynyng/Sat weping by a water syde
	A complaint for my Lady of Gloucester and Holland
	John Lydgate
93	A songe to syng y haue god ry3t/& myrþ to make in þis presens
94	A sory beuerech it is & sore it is a-bouth
95	A soule that list to singe of loue/Of Crist that com till vs etc.
98.5	A thorne hath percyd my hart ryght sore
99	A thowsand storijs kowde I me reherse
	'Balade in Commendation of Our Lady'
	John Lydgate
	566
100	A thousand tymes have I herd men telle
	The Legend of Good Women
	Geoffrey Chaucer
	50, 70, 75, 295
101	A tokne of godes louiinge/A sheld of mithful wynninge
102	A tresour of gret Richesse/A virtue of douthtynesse
102.3	A . . . vpon a strawe/Cudlyng of my cowe
103	A virgyn pure/this is full sure/Gabriell dide her grete
103.5	A war wys lokere/A war wys kepere
105	A wayle whyt ase whalles bon
	'A Wayle whyt ase Whalles Bon'
	171, 330, 401, 602, 857, 862, 971, 988
106	A vidue pouere was & freo
106.5	A wyld beest a man may tame/A womanes tunge will never be lame
107	A woman a mayd in thought & dede
108.5	A woman oftymes will do/þat she is not bede to do
109	Abel wes looset in treunesse/Habraham in bousumnesse
110	Abyde gud men & hald yhour pays/And here what god etc.
111	Abyde I hope it be the beste
112	Abowt the fyld thei pyped ful right
	376, 377, 397
112.5	Aboffe all thynge/Now lete us synge
113	Aboue all th[i]ng thow art a kyng
113.5	Absens of 3ou causeth me to sygh and complayne
113.8	*Accipe* that longeth to the
114	Adam alas and waylaway/A luþer dede dedest þou þ^t day
114.5	Alas for lake of her presens
115	Adam and Eve did geve concent/Vnto the feende etc.
	James Ryman
116	Adam and Eve thatte were unwyse/Were putte etc.
	James Ryman

Index of First Lines

117	Adam lay I-bowndyn bowndyn in a bond
	224, 259, 583, 675, 886
118	Adam our fader was in blis/And for an appil of lytil pris
120	Adam scryveyne if euer it þee byfalle
	'Chaucer's wordes unto Adam.'
	Geoffrey Chaucer
	642, 665
120.2	Adam that ys ower father be kynde
120.4	Adew adew le company/I trust we shall mete oftener
120.5	Adewe adewe my hartes lust
	William Cornish
120.6	Adew corage adew/Hope & trust
120.7	Adew der hart/be man depart
124	After that hervest Inned had his sheves
	'Complaint'
	Thomas Hoccleve
	843
129	Aftir the day that made is for travayle
	Translated from the French of Charles d'Orléans
133	Afftir wyntir the veer with foylis grene
	Associated with Charles d'Orléans
134	Ayens the comyng of may/That is full of lustynes
	Charles d'Orléans
134.5	Ageynst þe frenchemen in the feld to fyght
135.3	Agwillare habeth stan diff yn lantern chis tale me [t]old
135.5	Alac alac what shall I do
136	Alak y kan yow nethir loue nor my
	Translated from the French of Charles d'Orléans
137	Alas a thousand sith alas
	Humfrey Newton
138	Alas alas Alas is my chief song
	234, 252
139	Alas alas and alas why/hath fortune done so crewelly
140	Allas allas how is hit heth gen entresse
	Translated from the French of Charles d'Orléans
141	Allas alas *si haut si bas*/so lenger so werchs yc was
142	Alas alas þat I was born
143	Allas allas vey yuel y sped/for synne Jesu fro me ys fled
	238
143.5	Alas dere hart what ayleth the
143.8	Alasse Dethe alasse a blessful thyng ye were
	799
144	Allas deth who made thee so hardy
	Translated from the French of Charles d'Orléans
145	Allas diceyte þat in truste ys nowe
	John Lydgate's *Fall of Princes*?
146	Alas departynge is grounde of woo
	234
146.5	Alas for lak of her presens
147	Allas for thought and inward peyne
	'Supplicacio Amantis'
	John Lydgate
	725
148	Alas fortune alas myn hevynes
	Translated from the French of Charles d'Orléans
149	Allas ful warly for wo may I synge
	'The Harper'
	383
150	Alas good man most yow be kyst
151	Allas how evyr kouthe the god of kynde
	Associated with Charles d'Orléans

152	Alas howe schale my hert be lyght	
154	Allas I wooful creature/Lyving betweene hope and dread	
	John Lydgate	
	99, 497	
155	Allas in gret sinne alle beʒete we were	
155.5	Alas it is I that wote nott what to say	
156	Allas Iesu þi loue is lorn	
	John Grimestone	
157	Alas madame what maner stryf	
	Associated with Charles d'Orléans	
158	Alas mercy wher shall myn hert yow fynd	
	Charles d'Orléans	
158.2	Alas myn eye whye doest þou bringe	
158.3	Ellas mornyngh y syngh mornyng y cal/our lord ys deyd that bogthe ovs al	
158.4	Alas my childe how haue ye dighte	
158.6	Alas poor man what chans hav y	
158.8	Alas to whom should I complayne	
158.9	Alas to whom shuld I complayne	
	Edward Stafford, Third Duke of Buckingham	
	945	
159	Alas what planet was y born vndur	
	54	
159.5	Alas what shall I do for love	
	Ascribed to Henry VIII	
159.8	Alas what thing can be more grevous payne	
161	Allas what schul we freris do	
	359, 881	
162	Allas wo sal myn herte slaken	
163	Ale mak many a mane to styk at a brere	
164	All be hit so y selde haue of yow sight	
	Translated from the French of Charles d'Orléans	
165	All be that of my fare or sely case	
	Translated from the French of Charles d'Orléans	
166	Alle beon he bliþe/þat to my songe lyþe	
	The Gest of King Horn	
167	Alle bliþe mote þei be/þat folyes bleþeliche wole fle	
168	All besy swymmyng in the stormy flood	
	The Court of Sapience	
169	All chylder þᵗ wyll clergy kone/Take hed how Catoun etc.	
	Cato's *Distiches*	
170	All cristen men both more and les/þat in þis werld etc.	
171	All cristyn men y bid ʒou cum	
	John Audelay	
172	All crysten men þat wawkys me bye/Behold & see etc.	
173	Alle cristen peple listeneth ye & here/Of an holi bisshop etc.	
174	Al day we preche: al day we vse to teche	
175	All desolat from ioy or hertis hele	
	Associated with Charles d'Orléans	
177	Al fram ehvuele þinge/me schulde Iesus þat may	
179	Al gold Ionet is þin her	
	431, 709	
180	Alle hayle and wel y-met/Alle ʒee schulleþ beo þe bet	
	Cayphas	
181	All haile lady mother & virgyn immaculate	
182	All heyle Mary and well you be	
	'Salue sancta parens'	
	236, 241	
183	All hayle Mary ful of grace/Oure lord of heven is with þe	
185	Alle herkeneþ to me nou/a strif wolle y tellen ou	
	The Harrowing of Hell	

186	All hast ys odyus whereas dyscrecyoun
	John Lydgate
187	Alle his frendes he shal beo loþ/And helud shal ben etc.
187.5	Al holy chyrch was bot a thrall
190	All hyt is fantom þ^t we wiþ fare/and for oþer mennes goode etc.
190.3	Alle it is for woo/þat þe hen synges in þe snowe
BR+190.5	All lust and lyking I begyn to leue
	'Let Pyte Comfort Your Daungernesse'
	343
191	Alle monkyn tornithe in welle & þat on wonder gyse
193.8	All mi blod for þe is sched/Reu on me þat am for bled
194	Al nist by [þe] rose rose/al nist bi the rose I lay
	431, 583, 709
194.5	All noble men of this take hede
	John Skelton
196	Al oþer loue is lych þe mone/þat wext and wanet etc.
*196.5	*All owr mischeuis haue in þy syht
197	Al oure wele & al oure lif/sum time þoru pride was for-lore
197.5	Al oure wonder & al oure wo/is torned to wele & blisse al so
197.8	Alle perisches and passes þat we with eghe see
	Richard Rolle
199	Al rightwisnes doth now proceed
	'Rammeshorne'
	John Lydgate
BR+199.3	All schall be drawn at the syde/And honestly rosted withouten pride
200	All synnes sal þ^u hate thorow castyng of skylle
	Richard Rolle
205	Alle þat beoþ of huert trewe/a stounde herkeneþ to my songe
	'An Elegy on the Death of Edward I'
	136, 171, 700
206	Alle þat euer gon and riden/þat willeȝ godes merci abiden
207	Alle þat gos and rydis loket op on me
208	Alle þ^t haues lykyng for to here/Off prophetes sawes etc.
210	All that I may swink or swete
212	Alle þ^t loue to here þis lessoun/Crist graunt hem his benisoun
	493
214	Alle þ^t thenke to beo shriuen/And out of dedly sinne to liuen
215	Alle þ^t well a stownde dwelle/lysten I xal ȝou telle
	347
220	Alle þat welyn of wysdam ler/lestyn to me and ȝe schal her
221	Al þe ioȝe of oure herte nou is went a-wey
222.5	Alle þe wordis þat drawen to senne/þenk þat wenym is þerinne
223.5	Al thyngys contryued by mannys reason
	John Skelton
225	All this day ic han sought/Spyndul ne werne ne wond Y etc.
	827
226	All this worlde was ful of grace
228.5	Alle to late all to late/When þe weyne is at þe ȝate
229	All vanitese forsake if þ^u his lufe will fele
	Richard Rolle
230	Alle wandreths welthis in lykingis/by chaunce or happe etc.
230.5	Alle we liuien hapfulliche
231	Al hoolly youres withouten others part
231.5	All wyth a throwe and a lowe and lully/I haue Ioly a pryn for þe mastry
232	All women have vertues noble & excelent
	Richard Hattfeld
233	Al worshippe wisdam welthe & worthinesse
	'The Aungelles Songe within heuene,' De Guileville's *Pèlerinage de l'Ame*
234	All werthy men that luffes to here/Off cheuallry etc.
	The Sege of Melayne

235	Alle ȝe mowyn be blythe & glade
	696
236	Alle ȝe mouwen of ioye synge/fro heuene ys come etc.
237	Alle ye that passe bi thys holy place
238	Almes yowre mercy me my swete
	Associated with Charles d'Orléans
239	Almighty & al mercyable quene/To whom all the world etc.
	'ABC hymn to the Blessed Virgin Mary'
	Geoffrey Chaucer
	585, 860, 885, 908, 965
240	Almyȝty godde conserue vs fram care
241	Almyghty god fadir of heuene/ffor cristis loue þat dyde etc.
	618, 714
242.5	Almyghty god in trenite/fadir and sone and holy gost/as wis as y believe in the
	410
244	Alle-mighty god in trinite/fader and son and holy gost/þat is one god etc.
245	Almighty god in trinite/In wham anely es persouns thre
	Speculum Vite
	William of Nassyngton
246	Almighty god in trinite/Inwardly I thanke þe
	288
247	Almihti god in Trinite/leeue vs wel to spede
	'Luytel Caton'
248	Alle-myȝty god yn trynyte/Now & euer wyþ vs be
	Robert of Brunne
251	Almyȝty god lord me spare/ffor soþe my dayes werkys etc.
	The Lessons of the Dirige
	17, 913
252	Allemyghty god maker of alle/Saue you my souereyns etc.
253	Almiȝti God maker of Heuene/Erthe and Eyre Watur etc.
254	Almychty god our fader of hewyne abuf
255	Almyȝti god so merciable/In fedinge þou make us resonable
257	Almyghty god þ^t made all thyng/aftir his owne ordynaunce
	209
263	Allmyghti lord oure blisful kyng Ihesu
	'The Aungelles Songe,' De Guileville's *Pèlerinage de l'Ame*
263.3	Alone alone alone alone alone alone/alone in wyldernes
263.5	Alone alone/here y am myself alone
263.8	Alone alone/murning alone
264	Alone am y and wille to be alone
	Associated with Charles d'Orléans
265	Allone as I went vp and doun/In ane abbay etc.
	'The Abbay Walk'
	Robert Henryson
265.5	Allon he drawys from company
266	Alone I lyve alone and sore I syghe for one
	190
	[*SIMEV*: Burden to 2293.5.]
266.3	Alone y lyue alone
266.5	Alone I leffe alone/And sore I sygh for one
267	Alone walkyng/In thought pleynyng/And sore sighing
	838
268	Also crist steȝ vp hastely . In on stonde so fer to go
269	Also take hede to þis insawmpyl here/þat is lykend etc.
	'The Falcon'
	60, 383
269.5	Also þe lanterne in þe wynd þat sone is aqueynt
	William Herebert?
270	All þof I kan no farer make in her presen[ce]
271	Al-weldand god of myhttis most/ffadir & sone & holy gost
	221

Index of First Lines

*272.5	* . . . am I lent by diuyne prouidence/ . . . we mankynde
274	Amonge al merthes manny/We chol seng of o lady
276.5	Amang thir freiris within ane cloister
	William Dunbar
	906
277	Ane aigit man twyss fourty yeiris
	Walter Kennedy
278	An angelle bright/came down w^t light/A message for to do
	James Ryman
279	An angelle came vnto thatte mayde/And knelyd downe etc.
	James Ryman
280	An angelle came with fulle grete light/And seyde Haylle etc.
	James Ryman
281	An aungell fro hevin gan lyth/A greth a maydyn etc.
282	An angelle seide to thatte meyde so fre/Hayle etc.
	James Ryman
283	An angelle that was fayre and bryght/Came to Mary etc.
	James Ryman
285	Ane doolie sessoun to ane cairfull dyte
	The Testament of Cresseid
	Robert Henryson
	755
286.5	An evyll favouryd and a fowle blacke wyf
292	An holy prayer here begynnes/In remedy of seue dedly synnes
	John Audelay
BR+292.5	An hoote wynter, a tempestly somer/Plenty of corne, of frute goode caster
293	On leome is in þis world ilist/þer of is muchel pris
	662
294	An old said sawe: on-knowen on-kyste
	812
295	An preost wes on leoden/Laȝamon wes ihoten
	Brut
	Laȝamon
	670, 926, 932, 1002
*295.5	*And a woman of hauntynge moode
	'*Disputacio inter Clericum et Philomenam*'
296	And as for yow that most ar in my mynde
	Duke of Suffolk
*296.3	* And as I passid in my preire þer prestis were at messe
	Mum and the Sothsegger
	816, 851, 876, 879
*296.6	*And as þy worde came on þys wyse/To þe thefe
298	And by a chapell as y Came/Mett y whyte Iesu etc.
	236
299	And endyd my complaynt in this manere/one knocked etc.
	'*Dialogus cum amico*'
	Thomas Hoccleve
	425
299.8	And for swet smell at thi nose stink sall thou find
300	And god before the greef and gret ennoy
	Translated from the French of Charles d'Orléans
302	And I yt los and yow yt fynd
302.5	And I war a maydyn/As many one ys
303	And yf ye commande me to kepe me true wherever I go
	Margery Brews
	100, 731, 848, 958
304	And loue þi god ouer al þyng/þi neȝbore as þi self I say
	John Audelay
*306.5	*And sayde I dreede no threte/I haue founde youe here
	The Jeaste of Syr Gawayne

306.8	And save thys flowre wyche ys oure kyng
	337
309	And so be now that y my purpos lesse
	Translated from the French of Charles d'Orléans
310	And swa mai men kenne
	359
*310.5	*And suffred for ȝow wondes smert
311	And þen þe apostles togeder went/And mayde þe crede etc.
312	And þerfor ȝe lordingis þᵗ louedays wile holde
	307, 386, 636
313	And tus may you here
314	And we fynd writen of ane hermite/þat liued lange etc.
	230
*316.3	*And whan they had resceyved her charge
316.6	And wyth the noyse of them two
317	And ye will please god gretly/Use preuey penaunce discretly
*317.5	*And ȝouthe that ȝeldes newe ioyes
320	Anoder yere hit may betyde
322	Ar ne kuthe ich sorghe non nu ich mot manen min mon
	87
323	Ar þe fulþe of tim was comen/Satenas al folke aued nome
324	Aryse erly/Serve god deuoutly
327	Als a se flouwende
328	As Aaron yerde wᵗoute moisture/Hath flourisshed etc.
	James Ryman
329	As by the purchas of myn eyen twayne
	Translated from the French of Charles d'Orléans
333	As dyuers doctours hath wryt of the vertu/In herynge of etc.
334.5	As flowers in feeld thus passeth lif
335	As for farewel farewel farewel farewel
	Associated with Charles d'Orléans
336	As for the gyft ye haue vnto me geve
	Translated from the French of Charles d'Orléans
337	As for yowre prayers yn fame that is vpbore
	Translated from the French of Charles d'Orléans
338	As he that no thing may profite
	Translated from the French of Charles d'Orléans
*338.5	*[As] her am I sent by diuyne prouidence
	278
340	As holy kyrke makys mynde/*Intrauit ventris thalamum*
340.5	As I came by a bowre soo fayre
341	As I cam by a forrest syde/This endyrs day in one mornynge
342	As I com bi an waie/Of on ich herde saie
	Dame Siriȝ
	768
343	As I cam [walkyng] by þe way/I sawe a sight semly to see
344	As I cowthe walke because of recreacioun
	143
345	As I fared in a frith/in somer to hure fowlis syng
346	As I fared thorow a forest free/There byrdis song etc.
349	As Y gan wandre in my walkinge/Bisidis an holt etc.
350	As I gan wandre in on evenyng/Betwen the cornys etc.
351	Als I lay in a winteris nyt/in a droukening bifore the day
	'þe disputisoun betwen þe bodi and þe soule'
	93, 922
352	Als i lay vp-on a nith/alone in my longging
	539, 588
353	Als i lay vpon a nith/I lokede vpon a stronde
354	As I lay upon a nyȝt/My þowt was on a mayde bryȝt
355	As I me lay aloone in bed/And sikenes revid me etc.
	Thomas Brampton

Index of First Lines 445

356	As I me lend to a lond/I herd a schepperde etc.
	341
357	As I me lenyd vnto a Ioyful place/lusty phebus etc.
358	As I me rode in a mey mornyng/I loked abowte etc.
359	Ase y me rod þis ender day/by grene wode to seche play
	'The Five Joys of the Virgin'
	40, 48, 171, 227, 977
360	Als i me rod this endre dai/O mi [pleyinge]
	A Love Adventure, with refraid 'Nou springes the sprai' etc.
	94, 99, 262, 289, 583, 609, 710, 751, 788, 837, 868, 895, 961
361	As I me ros in on morwenyng/My þowte was on a mayde ȝynge
362	Als I me sat my self allon/In my hart makand my mon
363	As I me walked ouer feldis wide/When men began to Ere etc.
364	As I me walked this endurs day/To þe grene wode for to play
366	As I myselfe lay thys enderȝ nyght/All alone etc.
	365
368	As I stode in a parke streite vp bi a tree/Mi Arowe in mi honde
	'The Testament of the Bucke'/'Wyl Bucke his Testament'
	John Lacy
	945, 979, 1005
369	As I stod in a ryalle haulle/Where lordys and ladys etc.
370	As I stod in stydyenge allone
371	As I stod on a day me self under a tre
	94, 837, 895, 961
372	As I walkyd my self alone
	'God Amende Wykkyd Cownscell'
	361
373	As I walkyd vppon a day/To take the eyre of fylde & flower
	882
374	As I wandrede her bi weste/ffaste vnder a forest syde
	'Ay Merci God and Graunt Merci'
374.5	As I was so be ye
	352
375	As I went in a mery mornyng/I hard a byrd boþe wepe etc.
	417
376	As I went me fore to solase/I hard a mane syghe etc.
377	As I went on Yole day in oure prosession
	55, 563, 777, 934, 970
377.5	As I went this enders day/alone walkyng
378	As I went þrow a gardyn grene/I fond an erber etc.
378.5	As I went to þo kyrk wepand
379	As y yod on ay mounday bytwene Wyltinden and Walle
380	As in my remembrauns non but ye alone
382	As in writyng y put haue my wisshis
	Translated from the French of Charles d'Orléans
383	As in yow resstyth my Ioy and comfort
398	As longe before prophesy seyde/W^t vs to dwelle now etc.
	James Ryman
399.5	As moche as gnawes/Bestes long inneþ dawes
	John Trevisa
400	As myche a was wyrchepe
401	As of hony men gadren oft swetnesse
	John Lydgate
402	As ofte as syghes ben in herte trewe
403	As oon swete look of your eyen twayn
	Charles d'Orléans
404	As Reson Rywlyde my Rechyles mynde
405	As storys wryght and specyfy/Sent Thomas etc.
406	Als that a gret clerk shewes in his bokes/Of all the creatures
	The Lay Folk's Catechism.
	John de Gaytryge (or Gaysteke, Caterige, etc.)

407	As þᵗ I walkid in the monethe of May/Besyde a groue etc.
	Translated from the French by William Hoccleve.
407.6	As the Child Merlin sat on hys fathers knee
	266
409.5	As the holy growth grene
	Ascribed to Henry VIII
411	As þe see doþ ebbe & flowe/So fareþ þe world etc.
412	As þou for holy church riȝt/bare þe blody face
	109
412.5	As þou Lord dyddest stope and staye
	610
413	Als þᵘ ware marter & mayd clene
	John Audelay
	389
417.5	As ȝung Awrora with cristall haile
	William Dunbar
418	At a place where he me sett/He bad me etc.
419	At a sarmoun þer I seet/A comely clerk Ich herde crauen
420	At a sprynge wel vnder a þorn/þer was bote of bale etc.
	385, 1008
424	At domes day we solen vp-rise/& wenden fort foles & wyse
425	Att domys day when we shall ryse/And cum before etc.
426	Ate feste of seint benedist
427.5	At his burth thou hurdist angell syng
	995
428	At london in Englond noȝt full longe sythene
429	At matyne hours in middis of þe nicht
	Walter Kennedy
430	At my begynning Criste me spede/in grace and vertue etc.
430.5	At my begynnyng Crist me spede/In vertv and lernyng for to spede
430.8	At my howse I have a Jaye
	305
431	At nede thi frendis preven what thei be
	Translated from the French of Charles d'Orléans
432	At owur begynnyng god be owur spede/In grace etc.
433	At Sifforde seten þeines manie/fele Biscopes etc.
	The Proverbs of Alfred
	932
434	Atte sumtyme mery at sume tyme sadde
	James Ryman
435	At þe begynnyng of þe chartirhows god did schewe
	281, 494, 683, 735
436	At the begynnyng of the mete
437	At the end of Somer when wynter began
	George Ashby
438	At the northe end of seluer whyte
	430
440	At the short game of fablis forto play
	Translated from the French of Charles d'Orléans
441	At þe time of matines lord þu were itake
442	At þis ȝate þe laghe is sette/Poure men here ne slepes etc.
	510
444	At Westm. Wyllyam j-crovnyd was
	924, 955
445	Atte wrastlynge mi lemman i ches
	144, 935, 951
447	Atween mydnyght and the fresssh morwe gray
	John Lydgate
448	Atwixte dreed and tremblyng reuerence
	John Lydgate
BR+448.5	Auctor of gramarye, was whilom Precyan

Index of First Lines 447

449	Auctor of helthe Crist haue in myende/That thou etc.
	James Ryman
451	Avaunce thee hope as myn affyaunce
	Translated from the French of Charles d'Orléans
452	*Ave gracia plena* devooide of all trespace
453	*Ave maria* I say to þat blessyd mayde/þat modur ys etc.
454	*Aue maris stella* þe sterre on þe see
454.5	*Ave* quene of heven/ladi of erthe welle of all bownte
455	Awake lordes awake and take goode hede
455.5	Awake synner out of thi slepe
456	Away ffeynt lufe full of varyaunce
456.5	Ay besherewe yow be my fay
	Perhaps by John Skelton
457	Ay bitwene þou loken on me
460	Baladis songis and complayntis
	Translated from the French of Charles d'Orléans
461	Bare was þ^t quite brest/& red þe blodi side
	825
462	Be gladde and blythe quene of blysse
	John Mirk
463	Be glad lordynges beþe more & lesse/I bring you tidinges etc.
465	Be glad of al maydens flourre/þat hast in heuene swich etc.
465.5	Be hit beter be hit werse/folo hym þat berit þe pursse
466	Be it knowen and vnderstand/This Cite shuld be free honoure
467	Be it right or wronge/Thes men amonge/On wymen etc.
	The Notbrowne Mayde
	280
468	Be lou & louende/Be meke & murnende
469	Be meke and mylde of herte and tunge
470	Be mery & suffer as I the vise/wher euer thow sytte or rise
471	Be neuer to Aunterous to Amerous ne Angre þe nat to moche
472	Be nyse myn hert as purse is of an ay
	Associated with Charles d'Orléans
474.5	Be pes ye make me spille my ale
475	Be ryȝtwys man what euer be-tyde/To god and man etc.
	558, 714
478	Be thou pacient in thyn aduersite/ffor when god wyll etc.
	413
479	Be trewe and hold that ye haue hyȝte/ȝe haue my louys etc.
480	Ber þe wel an quemfuliche/Spek seldom & skilfuliche
481	Beaute of you burne in my body abydis
	Humfrey Newton
482	Befor my deth this lay of sorow I sing
	'The Lay of Sorrow'
	344, 415
486	Beholde a clere voice soundith in/That alle derkenes etc.
	James Ryman
487	Beholde a voyce of plesant armony
488	Beholde & se how that nature/Chaungith here lawe etc.
	James Ryman
488.5	Beholde & see how byrds dothe fly
489	Behold and see o lady free/*Quem meruisti portare*
	James Ryman
490	Beholde and se this gloriows fygure/which sent luke etc.
	John Lydgate
490.5	Beholde he saide my creature
491	Beholde here as þou may se/A man standyngg in a tree
	182
492	Behold how good & iocunde it is/Brothers to dwell etc.
	James Ryman

493	Behald man and þi þoght vp lede/To heuen with al þi spede
	735
494	Behold man wat is my wo/þer hange vp-on þe tre
495	Byholde mon what peyne I drye
496	Behalde merueylis a mayde ys moder
497	Beholde me I pray þe with all þi hole reson
498	Beholde myne woundes how sore I am dyȝthe
499	Beholde þe þornes myn heued han þrongen hou sarpe þ^t it ben
500	Beholde þis grete prynce Edward þe Secounde
	John Lydgate
501	Behold þu man her myth þu se/þe armes þ^t i bar for þe
502	Biholt þou man wiþ Routhful herte/þe sharpe scourge etc.
502.5	Behold we wrecches in this world present
503	Behold what lyfe that we ryne ine/Frayl to fayl etc.
504	Be-hold womman a dolful sith/þis is þi sone etc.
505	Byleue in god þat alle haþ wrouȝte
	558, 714
506	*Benedicta sit sancta trinitas*/þ^t all this world hath etc.
506.5	*Benedicite* whate dremyd I this nyȝt
	264
507	Benyng lady blessed mote thow be
509	Besechyth mekly in ryght lowly wyse/Now in hys nede etc.
	Duke of Suffolk
510	Bisichith this vnto yowre regally
	Translated from the French of Charles d'Orléans
512	Bitid þe time Tiberius/rewled Rome with realte
513	Better is to suffre and fortune abyde
514	Bytwene a þousend men on y kouþe etc.
515	Bytuene mersh and aueril/When spray biginneþ to springe
	'Alysoun'
	171, 297, 351, 385, 426, 442, 568, 623, 640, 644, 733, 788, 801, 813, 937
517	Bewar y rede yow loke here not vpon
	Translated from the French of Charles d'Orléans
517.5	Bewar man I come as thef
519	[B]idde huue with milde steuene/til ure fader þe king etc.
520	Bydynge al alone with sorowe sore encombred
521	Byrd one brere
	190, 1021
521.5	Bryd on brere y telle yt/to non oþer y ne dare
	788
522	Bisete þine poueþis sire eode
524	Blak be thy bandis and thy wede also
	741
526	Blissed ben men pore w^t wil
527	Blyssis be þat mayde mary/born he was of here body
527.5	Blessid by the swettest name of our lord/Jhesu crist
	William Caxton
528.5	Blisside be þou holy trinite
	597
529	Blissyd Denys of Athenys cheef sonne
	John Lydgate
532	Blessid god souereyn goodness/mercy to me etc.
	180
533	Blessed lady O pryncesse of mercy/Moder ecallyd etc.
	John Lydgate
534	Blessed mary moder virginall
535	Blessid mot be oure heuen quene/ffore vergyn & maydyn etc.
	John Audelay
536	Blessid mot þ^u be þ^u berd so bryȝt/Moder & maidon etc.
	John Audelay

Index of First Lines

537	Blessid Sebastian goddis martir and knyght
	518
539	Blessing ȝeue hem Ihū crist/þat listeneþ Iohan etc.
540	Blisful lord on heigh what schall I do/or in what place etc.
	The Piteous Complaint of the Soul, De Guileville's *Pèlerinage de l'Ame*
541.5	Blyth Aberdeane thow berial of all tounis
	William Dunbar
541.8	Blood swetyng/Herd byndyng
542	Blodles & bonles blod has non bon
543	Blowyng was mad for gret game
544	Boothe be ware bisshoppe thoghe thou be
546	Bothe yonge and olde take hede of this/The cours etc.
	James Ryman
547	Bothe ȝonge & oolde wheþir ȝe be/in cristis name etc.
548	Bowght & sold full traytorsly/& to a pylar bownde
548.3	Breke owte & not blynne
549	Bring us in no browne bred for that is made of brane
550	Brother abyde I the desire and pray/Abyde abyde etc.
550.5	Bird us neure bliþe be/Wen we þenke on þinges þre
	758
551	Burgeys thou hast so blowen atte the Cole
	348, **359**, **370**
552	Brennyng desire to see my fayre maystres
	Translated from the French of Charles d'Orléans
552.5	Busy in stody be þou child
*552.8	*Bot fals men make her finges feld/& doþ hem wepe wel
	868
553	But for bi cause that deynte lo is leef
	Associated with Charles d'Orléans
553.5	But god that good may geue
554	But i me be-thouthte/Inderliche & ofte/Wat crist dreu etc.
*554.3	*But y the goste of guydo him
554.5	But yf that I maye have trwly
	612
555	But late agoo went y my hert to see
	Translated from the French of Charles d'Orléans
556	Bot on thynge mastres greues me ful sore
	Humfrey Newton
556.5	But Suthfolke Salesbury and Say
557.5	But why am I so abusyd
558.3	By a banke as I ley/musyng In my mynd
558.5	By a bancke as I lay/musyng my sylfe alone
559	Bi a forrest as I gane fare/Walkyng al myselvene alone
	'The Mourning of the Hunted Hare'
	979
560	Bi a forest as y gan walke/W^t out a paleys in a leye
	'Merci Passith Riȝtwisnes'
	580, **773**, **847**
561	By a forest syde walkyng as I went/desport to take etc.
	'The Bird with Four Feathers'
	495, **545**, **950**
562	Bi a wey wandryng as I went/Sore I syked etc.
	'Thank God of all'
	126, **820**, **933**
563	Bi a wode as I gone ride/Walkyne al mi self alone
	'For þi Sunnes Amendes make'
	126
564	Be cause that teres waymenting and playnte
	'The Lufaris Complaint'
	344, **415**
565	Be dedes of dayne I swere to the

567	Be doughty Artous dawes/þat held Engelond yn good lawes
	Thomas Chestre
570	Bi god but oon my verry plesaunt Ioy
	Translated from the French of Charles d'Orléans
571	Bi god of loue comaundid lo am y
	Translated from the French of Charles d'Orléans
572	By god of loue set I nothyng
	Humfrey Newton
573	By granting charters of peace/To false English without lease
576	Bi sapience tempre þy courage/Of hasty yre etc.
	293
579	By thys fyr I warme my handys/And w^t my spade etc.
	662, 870
580	Bi þis tokninge of þare rode for fram me mote floe
581	Bi thi burthe þ^u blessed lord/ys made of variance now etc.
	236
583	Bi west vnder a wylde wode syde/In a launde etc.
	'Mercy Passes all Things'
	370, 495, 933
585	Calays men now mai ȝe care/And murning mun ȝe haue etc.
	'The Siege of Calais'
	Laurence Minot
	704
*586.5	*Cassamus roos aftre this talkynge
	54
588	Kavser of my goy helthe and comford
	'Katyryn'
	342
590	Certes fer extendeth my Reason
	'The X Commaundementes of Love'
	634, 892
591	Chaunge þis name þov man of pride
591.5	Change þi lawe if þou wolt wel spede
592	Charite chaste pite arn waxin al colde
593	Charite is brithe of word/Charite is milde of mod
593.5	Charite is chasyd al abowte
597	Childryn of Eve both grete and small
	James Ryman
597.5	Chyldern profyt & lycor faylyng
598	Crist and saint marie swa on scamel me iledde
	St Godric
	130, 151, 846
600	Cryst buggere of al y-coren/þe uadres olpy sone
	William Herebert
601	Crist crid in cradil moder ba ba/þe childer of israel etc.
602	Christ criȝede wan he preyede forȝefnesse of oure senne
	John Grimestone
603	Christ christen king y^t on the crosse tholed
	Death & Liffe
	843, 941
604	Cryst crosse me spede & seynt nicolas/A. b. c. A doth etc.
605	Crist crowned kyng þat on cros didest
606	Crist ȝiue vs grace to loue wel holi chirch
607.5	Crist is offred for mannes sake/Of senne fre man to make
607.8	Crist ys woundid for oure wikkednesse
608	Cryst kepe vs all as he well can/*a solis ortus cardine*
609	Crist lay on londe gredde
610	Cryste made mane yn þis maner of wyse
611	Crist made to man a fair present/His blody body etc.
	794, 834

Index of First Lines 451

612	*Criste qui lux es et dies*/O Iesu crist þe verray lycht
	340
613	Crist that ayene has made free/*Ex patre* etc.
	James Ryman
614	Crist that art both day and light/And sothfast sonne etc.
	John Lydgate
615	Cryst þat art [boþe d]ay & lyht/thow vnhilist þe mirkness etc.
	618
616	Cryst þ^t art boþe ly3t & day/Derkenesse of ny3t etc.
	340
617	Crist thatt arte light and day also/Derkenes of nyght etc.
	James Ryman
618	Criste that art light and day so bright
	James Ryman
619	Crist that light clerenes and day/Derknes of nyght etc.
	James Ryman
620	Crist þat breed brak/at þe soper þer he sat
	'Gode þat hys brede brake'
	1006
620.5	Cryst that day ert and lyght
	340
621	Cryste þ^t dyed on þe rode
623	Crist þ^t was crucifyd on cros for our synnus sake
	John Audelay
624	Crist that was in Bedelem born/& bapteisyde was in flum iordan
	610
625	Criste that wold all men reydeme and bye
628	Cristes blod þe heye of lif þre þingges it hat vndon
629	Cristes bodi malt3
631	Cristes milde moder seynte marie/Mines liues leorne etc.
	794, 860
631.5	Christene man þu lerne of loue
	421
633.5	Cir-cum-staunt-ly thre Kings came by nyght
	525
634	*Claritas Sapiencie.* Clernesse of vnderstondingge
635	Clannesse who so kyndly cowþe comende
	'Cleanness'
635.5	Clym clam the cat lepe over the damme
636	Closter of Christ riche recent flour-de-lyss
	Walter Kennedy
636.5	Close þi herte from enwye
637	Cum folow me my frendes vnto helle/Ay to dwelle etc.
	'The Invitation'
	383
639	Cum lord vr makere Holigost/þe þouhtes of þyne forte sene
640	Cum maker of gaste þou ert/þouhtes of þine etc.
641	Come my dere spowse and lady free/Come to thy sonne etc.
	James Ryman
642	Come now gud lord now come owr savyour
642.5	Come ouer the woodes fair & grene
643	Come shuppere holy gost of-seth oure þouhtes
	William Herebert
644	Cometh nere ye folkes temtyd in dreynes
647	Comaunde me what ye will in everi wise
	Translated from the French of Charles d'Orléans
648	Compatience persis reuth & marcy stoundis
649	Compleyne I may wher soo euer I goo
649.5	Complayne I may whereuyr I go
650	Compleyne ne coude ne might myn hert neuer
651	Conceyued man how may that be by reason broght abowte

653	Consider wel with euery circumstaunce/Of what estate etc.
	John Lydgate
655	Consideryng effectually the gret diuersite/Of sectys etc.
656	Constraynt of payne thou3t and hevynes
	Associated with Charles d'Orléans
657	Continvaunce/Of remembraunce/withowte endyng
	54
658	Controuersies plees and al discord
	John Lydgate
	4
660	Conseil þe redeles & þe wille/Chasty þe wanton etc.
662	*Credo in deum*/þat ys w^towt begynnyng and ende
663	Crose and curteys Christ thys begynnyng spede
	Pierce the Ploughman's Crede
	753, 876, 879, 881, 975
664	[Cross] of ihesu criste be euer oure spede/And kepe vs etc.
*664.3	* . . . crowne of thorne so scharpe & kene/throw my heyde
666	Cupido vnto whos commandement/The gentil kynrede etc.
	Thomas Hoccleve
667	Dayly in Englond meruels be fownd
668	Damishel reste wel/Sir welcum by Saynt Michel
	Interludium de clerico et puella
	768
670	Danger me haþ vnskylfuly
	87
671	Doutter 3if þou wilt ben a wif and wisliche to wirche
	'How the Good Wiif tau3te Hir Dou3tir'
672	Dauyd þat prophet was ay/In þe sawter boke þus etc.
672.3	Dere is þe hony bou3t/þat on thornes is sou3t
672.4	Dethe began by cause of syn
672.5	Deth bringith down lowe þat ben bolde
673	Ded is strong and maystret alle thing
674	Deceyt deceyuyth and shal be disceyued
	John Lydgate
675.5	Deme þe best of euery dowt/Tyll the trowth be tryed owt
675.8	Demyd wrongfully/In absent
676.5	Departure is my chef payne/I trust ryght wel of retorn agane
	Ascribed to Henry VIII
678	*Deus caritas est*/A deore god omnipotent
679	Deuise prowes and eke humylitee
680	*Dic erodes impie*/what awayleth thy cruellis
681	Dievs wous garde byewsser tydynges Y yow bryng
681.5	Dysdayne me not wythout desert
682	Displesere thought wrath woo ne heuynes
	Translated from the French of Charles d'Orléans
683	Diuers is þis myddell erede/To lewed men and to lerede
	Kyng Alisaunder
	295
684	Do do nightyngale synges ful myrie
687.3	Dou way Robin the child wile wepe
687.5	Do well whill þou art here/& þou shalt haue well els wher
688	Doctoures woordes mowe not vari/seyen þat aries leo etc.
688.3	Done is a battell on the dragon blak
	William Dunbar
688.8	Downbery doun/Now am I exild my lady fro
693	Dred of deþ sorow of syn/Trobils my hert ful greuysly
	John Audelay
	693
694	Drightin dere wit blisful beildes/þat all þe werld etc.
694.5	*Dum ludis floribus velud lacinia*
	'Dum Ludis Floribus'

Index of First Lines

695	Yche day me cumeþ tydinges þreo
696	Ich heredemen vpo mold make muche mon
	The Song of the Husbandmen
697	Eche man be ware that bereth a state/Of counseil etc.
698	Eche man folwith his owne fantasye
	John Lydgate
700	Erly in a somerstide/y sawe in London as y wente
701	Erliche in þe morwenyng Ihu the Iewes gunne take
702	Erly on morwe and toward nyght also
702.5	Erth goyth vpon erth as mold vpon
703	Herde maket halle/& herde maket boure
	A variant of 'Erthe upon Erthe' (A version)
	23
704	Erth owte of erth is wondyrly wroght/for erth hath geten etc.
	'Erthe upon Erthe' (B version)
	23, 662
705	Erthe vpon erthe is waxin and wrought/Erthe takys on etc.
	'Erthe upon Erthe' (C version)
	23
707	*Ecce ancilla domini*/Seyde tho virgyn withowtyn vice
708	Edi beo þu heuene quene/folkes froure & engles blis
	562, 585
709	Edward oure cumly king/In Braband has his woning
	Laurence Minot
	50
710	Edward the third that was king of this lond
	John Hardyng
*711.5	* . . . eke to þe sowlys þy mercy
	Dominus Iohannes arcuarius Canonicus Bodmine
715	*Ego sum alpha et o*/I am the first the last also
	The Towneley Series of Mystery Plays
	170
716	*Ego sum Alpha et O*/*primus et nobilissimus*/It is my etc.
	The Chester Plays
717	VIIJ ys my love ʒif IX go before
	551
718	Elde makiþ me geld/and growen al grai
	161
722	Emperoures & kynges be kende/Erlys & barunnys bolde
724	*En Ihesu roy soueraign*/You lady fare and fre
725	Enmy herowde þ^u wokkyd kyng/qwy dredis þ^u etc.
726	Enforce thy wyttes for to lere
729	Entierly belouyd & most yn my mynde
	271
729.5	Arectyng my syght towarde the zodyake
	'The Garland of Laurell'
	John Skelton
730	*Esperaunce en dyeu*/Truste in hym he is moste trew
731	Eternall god fader of light/Thatt madist al thyng etc.
	James Ryman
731.5	Eternall lawde to god grettest of myght/Be hertely
	John Trevisa
732	Eterne maker of all oo god one live
733.1	Evyn as mery as I make myght
734	Euer yn one with my dew attendaunce
734.5	Euer is the eie to the wude leie/þerinne is þet iche luuie
	968
735	Euerlastyng lof to me I haue tane
	Humfrey Newton
735.3	Euer lenger þe wors/Lokys þe blynde hors
737	Euer souereyn swete swettist in siʒt
	Humfrey Newton

738	Euery day before ye go to youre bede/Serche wel etc.	
	George Ashby	
738.5	Eueri day me comeʒ tiþinge þre	
739	Euery day þ^u myʒt lere/To helpe þ^i self qwil þ^u art here	
	663	
740	Eueriche freman hath to ben hende/for to be large etc.	
741	Every man and woman hath grete nede	
	558	
742	Euery man delytyth hyly in hijs degre	
743	Euery mane in hys degre/Cane say yf he avysed be	
744	Euery man schulde teche þis lore/To hise children etc.	
746	Euery maner creature/Disposed vnto gentylnesse	
	John Lydgate	
746.5	Euerich nyʒt þere a cok/Wakeþ som man or it dawe	
	John Trevisa	
750	Ensample may we rede and se/Of Ierusalem etc.	
751	Exemple sendyng to yow rowte of gentylnes	
752	Excellent soueraine semely to see	
	Perhaps by a Duke of York	
752.5	*Exilium* is contrari to his Ioyeng	
753	*Exortum est* in loue & lysse/Now cryst hys grace etc	
753.8	Fayre and discrete fresche wommanly figure	
754	Fair fresshest erthly creature/That ever the sonne overshone	
754.5	Faire laydis I pray yow tell me/Whos this ij fayre children be	
	482	
755	ffayre maydyn who is this barne/that þ^u beriste in thyn arme	
	482	
759	Falseness and couetys er feris/Wil neþer oþer be-sweke	
761	Far from the kyn cast the	
762	Fur in see bi west Spaygne/Is a lond ihote Cockaygne	
	'The Land of Cockaygne'	
	161, **198**, **238**, **637**, **665**	
763	Fareth wele wirchepe and goodnesse	
763.5	Fare well fare well/All fresh all chere	
	176	
764	Fare-wel fare-wel my lady and maystres	
	Associated with Charles d'Orléans	
765	Farewell my frends the tide abideth no man	
765.3	Fairweill my Hairt fairweill boyth freind and fa	
765.5	Farewell my joy and my swete hart	
766	Fayre-wele my Ioye my comfort and solace	
767	Farewell now my lady gaye	
768	Farewell þat was my lef so dere	
	Humfrey Newton	
769	Farewell this world I take my leue for-euer	
	'Farewell, this World is but a Cherry Fair'	
	433, **811**	
771	Fader and sun and hali gaste/almighti god in trinite	
772.5	ffader & son and holy gost/Gret god in trinite	
773	Fadyr and sone & holy gost/Grete god in trinite	
774	Fadyr & sone & holy gost/Gret god in trinite	
775	Fadur and sone and Holigost/Lord to þe I crie and call	
776	Fadur & sone & holi gost o god in trinite/To þe y make etc.	
777	Fader and sun and haligast/þat anfald God es ay stedfast	
778	Fadyr and sone & holy goste/þat art o god of myʒtes moste	
	'Handlyng Synne'	
	Robert Mannyng of Brunne	
	729, **868**	
779	ffadur and sone & holy gost/þat i clepe & calle most	
780	Fader and sun and hali gast/To þe I cri and call most	
	618	

Index of First Lines 455

781	Fader and sonne & holi goost/We knowledge the in euery coost
	James Ryman
782	ffadyr I am þin owyn chylde/and born of mary meke etc.
783	Fadir in god benigne and reuerent/My lord etc.
	Thomas Hoccleve
785	Fadere of blisse omnipotent/For thou has made and create us
	James Ryman
789	ffader sum tyme what was þou
790	ffadyr sone and holy gost/Almyhtty god sittend in trone
790.5	Fader sone and holy goost/Lord to the I make my moone
792	ffede þe hungere þe þirste ȝif drenke
	John Audelay
795	*Fetys bel chere*/drynk to þe fere
796	Fiftene toknen ich tellen may/Of XV dayes er domesday
797	Fire cold and tereshatyng/dred worme and weping
798	ffyre water wynde & lond
803	First myn vnkunnynge and my rudenesse/Vnto yow all etc.
	312, 730
804	Fyrst þou sal make knawledge to god of heuen
	735
806	Fyrst whan a man or a woman drynk more/Any tyme etc.
808	Flen flyys and freris *populum domini male caedunt*
809	Flee fro the prees and dwelle with sothfastnesse
	'Truth' or '*Balade de bon conseyl*'
	Geoffrey Chaucer
810	Fleth the shott of swete regard
	Translated from the French of Charles d'Orléans
811	Fleshly lustys and festys/And furres of divers manner of bestys
811.5	Folke discomforted bere heuy countenaunce
	The Boke of Fame, Pynson
813	For a man þat is almost blynd
813.3	For age is a page/for the courte full vnmete
	John Skelton
	98
813.6	For as ye lyst my wyll ys bent
	Ascribed to Thomas Wyatt
	462
814	For boule bred in his boke
	359
815	For cause alle men shall vnderstonde/My lordes etc.
	James Ryman
816	For ded y lyf my lyv & deth y wite
	Associated with Charles d'Orléans
817	For drede ofte my lippes y steke/ffor false reportours etc.
818	ffor feer or for favour of ony fals mane
819	For foules lustes I wistod
820	For god is lord of alle þing/As prophetes tellen i-mene
822	Fore he is ful ȝong tender of age
	John Audelay
	389, 704, 809
823	for he is true/and will pursue
824	For helth of body couer for colde thyn hede
	John Lydgate
	27
825	ffor his love þ^t bowght vs all dere/Lysten lordyngis etc.
825.5	ffor I am dughti of dede wo so will me knowe/be þe kyte he may se þe pocok and þe crowe
825.8	For I ham pore withouten frendes
826	For I wend when any foly me felte/In þought or speche etc.
827	For Ipocras nor yet Galien
	Associated with Charles d'Orléans

827.5	for it is mery to ben a wyfe/deye I wylle and lese my lyfe
828	For lac of sight grete cause I haue to pleyne
829	ffor lore of godes i wepe soore/But more for lore of day
830	For loue i morne & sorwe make/for mornige y perische etc.
831	ffor loue is loue & euer schal be/& loue has bene etc.
	John Audelay
833	For loue of god as kepith remembrance
	Translated from the French of Charles d'Orléans
834	For loue of Iesu my swete herte/y morne and seke etc.
835	for me loue he ys nou asslawe
*835.5	*ffor my pastyme vpon a day
836	For no myrþe be þ^u to gladde/Ne for no sorow etc.
837.5	For nowe vpon þis first day I will my choys renuwe
	John Lydgate
838	ffor on a tewsday thomas was borne/& on a tuysday etc.
	John Audelay
	693
840	ffore pride in herte he hatis alle one/worchip ne reuerens etc.
	John Audelay
841	For Scottes/Telle I for sottes
844	For the reward of half a yere
	Charles d'Orléans
846	ffor þe I wax al rody opon þe rode
847	For þe man Y suffre schame/Wo and peyne and gret blame
848	For thar wer thai bal bred
	359
848.5	for thylke grounde þat beareth the wedes wycke
849	ffor þu art comen of good blood
850	For þou were Meke an laftuste pruyde/Wite blisse etc.
851	For thou3t constreint and greuous heuines
	'The Temple of Glas'
	John Lydgate
	295, 725, 947
*851.3	* . . . for þi sake man to whom yf þou call at a
852	Forto biholde the bewte and manere
	Translated from the French of Charles d'Orléans
853	ffor to p[reue]nte/And after repente/hyt wer ffoly
	54
853.2	for to saye havyng non atorryte
	Jhon Mereley
853.8	For whan the roof of thy hous lyth upon thy nese
854	For why that God is inwardli the witte/Of man etc.
	Benedict Burgh
854.5	For Winefrede virgine pure/That ouercomminge
855	For you my lady I am ne3 slayn
	Humfrey Newton
856.5	fformynge in me the maner of my lyffe
	457
857	For-seek in woo and fer from ioyous hele
	Translated from the French of Charles d'Orléans
860	Fortune alas alas what haue I gylt
	123, 654
860.3	Fortune ys varyant ay tornyng her whele/He ys wyse þat is ware or he harm fele
BR+861.7	Four thyngis dullith a mannys reson
861.8	Vour þynges 3e ofte ysoeth
864	Foweles in the frith/þe fisses in þe flod
	79, 466, 478, 497, 498, 562, 568, 583, 698, 856, 860, 893, 1021
865.5	ffree lusti fresch most goodly
867	Fresshe bewtie riche of youthe and lustynes
	Translated from the French of Charles d'Orléans
868	Frishe flour of womanly nature/ye be full gentill

Index of First Lines

869	ffresshe lusty beaute ioyned with gentylnesse
	John Lydgate
870	Fresshest of colour and most amyable
870.5	ffrere gastkyn wo ye be
870.8	ffrere tamas stanfeld/god almegtheie hem it ȝelde
	John Crophill
	538
871	Freers freers wo ȝe be *ministri malorum*
	359
871.5	Frende of that ere I knew/& I lowe and schal
872	Frenschipe faileþ & fullich fadeþ/ffeiþful frendes fewe etc.
	48
873	frenchipe is felounie/Manchipe is vileynie
873.5	ffrendschupe þat chawnachit nowth/Enles lordschupe þat deyth nouth
874	Ffrom all mysrewle in ȝowthe exercisyd by me
	339
876	Fra god was sent ane angel bright/Gabriel for soth etc.
877	From heouene in to eorþe god gretynge he sende
878	From hevyn was sent an angell of light
880	From þe tyme þat we were bore/Oure ȝouþe passeþ etc.
	662
881	ffrome thens þ^t phebus w^t hys bemys bryght
882	Froom tyme of Brute auctours do specefye
	John Lydgate
884	Fulfylled ys þe profe[s]y for ay/þ^t merly sayd & many on mo
	341, 884
885	Ful feir flour is þe lilie
	551
887	Gabriell bryȝther then the sone/graciusly grette etc.
888	Gabriel fram evene king/Sent to the maide swete
	539, 608, 771
889	Gabryell of hyȝe degre/Cam down from the Trenyte
	236, 241
890	Gabriell that angell bryȝt/Bryȝter than the sonne is lyȝt
891	Gayneth me no garlond of greene/Bot hit ben of etc.
	78
892	Galawnt pride thy father is dede
	236, 359, 892
892.5	Galauntis purse penyles *per vicos ecce vagrantur*
893	Game and ernest euer among/And among al othyr degre
894	*Gaude felix anna* þe moder of mari
	John Audelay
895	*Gaude maria* cristis moder/mary mylde of the I mene
	John Audelay
896	*Gaude* of uirgins þe freshest floure/In maydenhede etc.
897	*Gaude* the flowre of virginyte/In hevyn thow hast etc.
898	*Gaude* to whom gabryell was sent/from nazareth to galalie
899	*Gaudete iusti in domino*
900	Gay gay þou art yhent
	663
903	Jentill butler bell amy/Fill the boll by the eye
	665
905.5	Get the hence what doest thou here
906	Gifte hys made domesman/gyle is mad chapman
	132
909	Glad & blithe mote ȝe be/All that euer y here now se/Alleluya
910	Glade in god call hom ȝoure herte/In ioye & blisse etc.
	820
911	Glade in god þis solempne fest/Now Alleluya is vnloken
912	Glade us maiden moder milde/þurru þin herre etc.
	539, 860

912.5	Gladlythe thoue queyne of Scottis regioun William Dunbar
913	Gladeth ye foules of the morwe gray 'Compleynt of Mars' Geoffrey Chaucer **659, 848**
914	Glorieux crosse that with the holy blood/of Christ Ihū etc. **756**
916	Glorious god had gret pite/how long mans sowle etc.
918	Glorius god in trinite/well of man & pyte
919	Glory vnto God laude and benysoun/To Iohn to Petir etc.
920	Goo forth kyng reule the by sapyence John Lydgate
921	Goo forth lybell and mekly schew thy face/Afore my etc. 'On the English Commercial Policy' **3, 914**
922	Go forth myn hert wyth my lady/Loke what ye spar etc. Charles d'Orléans
923	Go forth mine owne true heart innocent
924	Go forthe thi way my feithfull deservaunce Translated from the French of Charles d'Orléans
925	Go hert hurt with adversite/and let my lady thi woundes see
926	Go litull bill and command me hertely Humfrey Newton **317**
927	Goe lytyll byll & doe me recommende/Vnto my lady etc.
927.5	Goo lityl book and submytte the/Vnto al them William Caxton
928.5	Go lytyl boke for dredefull ys thy message
929	Goo litle book of commendacioun/I pray to god etc. **317**
931	Go lityll quayere And swyft thy prynses dresse John Lydgate **46, 319**
932	Goo lytell ryng to that ylke suete **317**
932.5	Go piteous hart rasyd with dedly wo John Skelton
933	God against nature thre wonders haith wrought
935	God almighty saue and conferme our kyng John Lydgate and Benedict Burgh
936	God allmyghty saue and conserue owre kynge
937	God Almihti þat all þing weldes/Windes watres etc. Robert of Brunne
939	God & sient Trinite/as I bylyue on þe
940	God be in my hedde & in my understonding St Richard of Chichester
941	God be oure gyde/and then schulle we spede **321**
944	God fader in heuyn of myghtes most/That mad etc. *Metrical Old Testament* **903**
945.5	God grant me gras to gehte agayn/þe luffe þat I haue loste
947	God haþ graunted grace vnto our lernyng John Audelay
951	God in thy name make me safe and sounde John Lydgate
952	God is a substance foreuer dureable
955	God lord þᵗ sittes in trone/Nu & euere þu here my mone
956	God made Adam the fyrst day of þe moone
956.5	God maker of alle thyng/Be at oure begynnynge

Index of First Lines

957	God of hewine that shoepe Erthe and helle/ȝyf me grace etc.
960	God of thi grace the good sowle now pardon
	Associated with Charles d'Orléans
960.1	God prosper long our noble king
961	God seyth hym self as wryten we fynde/That whenne etc.
	John Mirk
962	God sende vs pese & unite/In engelande w^t prosperite
964.5	God spede þe plouȝ/and send us korne I-now
965	God þat al hast mad of nouht/ffor loue of mon etc.
968	God þat al þis myhtes may/in heuen & erþe þi wille is oo
	171, 325, 467, 758
969	God that all this world gan make/And dyed for us on a tre
	'The Expedition of Henry V'
	Perhaps by John Lydgate
	948
970	God þat all þis world hath wrouȝt/And all mankinde etc.
972	God þ^t all þis word has wroȝth/and w^t precius blod etc
973	God that art of myghtes most/Fader and sone and holy gost
974	God þat art of mihtes most/ffader and Sone and holigost
975	God þat art of mihtes most/þe seuen ȝiftus of the holigost
977	God that deyde ffor vs all/And drancke aysell and gall
979	God that dyde apon a Tre/And boughte vs etc.
980	God þat is in mageste/One God and persons thre
981	God þat ys myghtfull/Spede all ryghtfull
981.5	God þat is so foul of meght/Saue hare solys bothe day & neght
	John Crophill
985	God þat madist al þing of nouȝt
987	God þat schope both se and sand/Saue Edward king etc.
	Laurence Minot
990	God þou haue mercy of me/After thi mercy mekill of mayne
	903, 913
991	God turne us every dreem to gode
	The House of Fame.
	Geoffrey Chaucer
	950
993	God was iborin in bedlem
	927
994	God wiht hise aungeles i haue forloren/Allas ȝe while etc.
*995.2	*Godes boure as tu gane bilde/us fra sinne and syame sylde
	758
995.3	Goddys chosyn who so wil be
995.4	Goddis grace is redy bothe erly & late
	'The Debate between Nurture and Kynd'
	524, 557
996	Goddis son and lord omnipotent
997	Godes sonne for þe loue of mane/Flesshe and blode etc.
998	Goddys sonne is borne/his moder is a maid
999	Goddys son oo shynyng bryght splendowre
1000	Goddys sone passyng frome place supernall
1001	Godys sone þat was so fre/into þis world he cam
	109, 357
1002	Gold & al þis werdis wyn/Is nouth but cristis rode
	552, 583
1003	Goode bydder goode werner
1004	Go day Syre crystemas our Kyng/for euery man etc.
1005	Good god make me for þi love & þi desyre
1007	Goodman fool ass lovte/That tearest a Book etc.
1008	Gode sire pray ich þe/For of saynte charite
	238, 380, 385, 709, 777
1009	Gode werkemen foul of werynes
1010	Gracius and gay on hyr lyytt all my thoȝth

1011	Gracyous lord for thy bytter passyon/Accept my prayers etc.
	451
1011.5	Grant gracious God grant me this time
1011.8	Grant me þe will of wepynge/With teris
1014.5	Gret huntyng by ryuers and wode/Makythe a manys here to growe thorowe hys hoode
1017	Grettere mater of dol an[d] heuynesse
	John Lydgate
1017.5	Grene flowryng age of your manly countenance
1018	Grevus ys my sorowe/Both evyne and moro
	55
1018.5	Grevouse ys my sorowe/both Even & morow
1020	Gyle & gold togedere arn met/couetyse by hym is set
1021	Guk guk gud day schir gaip quhill ȝe get it
	'Sum practysis of Medecyne'
	Robert Henryson
	830
1022	Had y as moche of worldly goodis
	Translated from the French of Charles d'Orléans
1023	Hadde y hertis a thousand thousand score
	Associated with Charles d'Orléans
1024	Heil & holi ay be þi name/Fulsum leuedi hende and swete
	108
1026	Haile be þou hende heuen qwene/þ^t thugh chastite etc.
1027	Heyle be þ^u ladye so bryȝt/Gabriel þ^t seyde so ryȝt
1028	Heile be þou marie cristis moder dere
1029	Haile be þu mari maiden bright/þu teche me þe wais right
1030	Heil beo þou Marie Mylde qwen of heuene
1031	Heil be þow Marie Moodur and May/Mylde and Meke etc.
1030.5	Hayle be thou Mary most of honowr
1032	Heil be þou marie þe modir of crist/Heil þe blessidest etc.
1033	Hayll be þu qwen of gret honour/our lord þi hert has fild etc.
1034	Heyl be þ^u sone of þe fader aboue/þ^t man bycome etc.
	188
1034.5	Ayl be þow ster of se/godis moder blessed þow be
1036	Hayl blessid flour of virginite/þat bare this time etc.
1037	Hayle blessyd lady the moder of cryst ihū
	John Lydgate
1038	Hayle bot of bale blissed qwene
1038.5	Hayle cheftane Cristes aghen confessour
1039	Hayl comely creature curteys of kynde
1040	Haill Cristin knycht haill etern confortour
	Walter Kennedy
1041	Heyle fairest þ^t euyr god fonde/Heyle modyr & mayden free
1041.3	Haile festivale day with al honoure
	597
1041.5	Hayle flower of virgynyte
1042	Haile ful of grace criste is w^t the/Of alle women blessed etc.
	James Ryman
1043	Hayle full of grace criste is w^t the/To Mary seide aungel etc.
	James Ryman
1044	Haill Glaid and glorius/Haill virgin hevinnis queyne
1045	Hayle glorious lady & heuenly quene/Crownyd etc.
	John Lydgate
1046	Heyl gloryous virgyne ground of all our grace
1047	Heyl god ye schilde modyr holy kyng bere milde
1048	Heyle goddes moder dolorous/By þe crosse stonding etc.
	200
1049	Hayle holy fader of the high cuntrey/Of frere mynours etc.
	James Ryman

Index of First Lines 461

1050	Heyl hooly Sitha maide of gret vertu
	Perhaps by John Lydgate
	973
1051	Haile holy spyritt & Ioy be vnto the
1052	Hayle Iesu Godys Sone in forme of bred
	235
1053	Heyle Ihū my creatowre of sorowyng medicyne
	Richard Rolle
1054	Heyle leuedy se-steorre bryht/Godes moder edy wyht
	William Herebert
1055	Hayle louely lady laymand so lyght/hayle myghtyfull etc.
1056	Hayle luminary & benigne lanterne/Of Ierusalem etc.
	John Lydgate
1057	Heil Mayde cheef of alle/þorw whom þe blessed Mon
1059	Hayle mayden of maydyns thorȝt worde consaywyng
	108
1060	Heyl Mayden ouer Maydenes vchon/Modur wiþ-outen pere
1061	Heil marie an wel þu be/Of loue gunne þu lere
1062	Heil marie ful of grace/God is wiþ þe in euerich place
	108
1064	Heil marie ful of wynne/þe holy gost is þe wiþinne
1066	Hayl mari hic am sori/haf pite of me and merci
1070	Hayle Marie wele the be/Full of grace God is with the
1070.5	Hayl most myghty in þi werkyng
1071	Heyle my lord in wom ich leue/sothfastliche god & man
	235
1072	Hayle oure lod sterre both bright & clere
	James Ryman
1073	Hayle oure patron & lady of erthe/Qwhene of heven etc.
	200
1074	Haile perfect trone of Salamon/Haile flore and flease etc.
	James Ryman
1075	Hayle prynce roiall most amyable in sight
1076	Hayle quene of blisse of grete honour/Moder of crist etc.
	James Ryman
1077	Haill quene of hevin and steren of blis/Sen þat þi sone etc.
1078	Heil seint Michel wiþ þe lange sper
	'A Satire on the People of Kildare'
	161, **238**, **990**
1079	Hayle se-sterne gods modyr holy/Pray þou þi swete son etc.
	200
1080	Haile spowse of criste oure savioure/Hail lilly floure etc.
	James Ryman
1081	Heil sterre of þe See so briht/þow graunt vs to ben vr gyde
1082	Heile sterne on þe se so bright/To godes heli modir dight
1082.5	Hale sterne superne hale in eterne
	'Ane Ballat of Our Lady'
	William Dunbar
	566, **794**
1083	Haile þe fayrst þer euer god fond
	John Audelay
1085	Heil wrth þou King of Englis erde/kynges knyth etc.
	172
1086	Half in a dreme not fully awakid
	Perhaps by Sir Richard Ros, translated from Alain Chartier
1088	Half in dispeyre not half but clene dispeyrid
	Associated with Charles d'Orléans
1088.5	happe is harde grace hath no pere/Rych is nygarde worshippe is dere
1089	Harde gates I haue go

1091	Herkneþ alle gode men and stylle sitteþ adun
	'A Lutel Soth Sermun'
	1020
1104	Herkeþ hideward & beoþ stille/y preie ou ȝof hit be or wille
1105	Herkeneþ hiderward ȝe lordlynges/ȝe þat wollen ihure etc.
BR+*1105.5*	He that in youthe no care will take
	428
1107	Herkyns now bothe more and lasse/I wille yow telle etc.
1108	Herkneþ now boþe olde & ȝyng/ffor Marie loue þᵗ swete þyng
1111	Herkyns serys þᵗ standys abowte/I wyll ȝow tell etc.
1113	Herkeneþ þat loueþ honour/Of Kyng Arthour and hys labour
1114	Herknet to me gode men/Wiues maydnes and alle men
1115	Herkneþ to mi ron/As hic ou tellen con
	766
1116	Herkyn to my tale I schall to yow schew
	341
1119	Herkyne wordis wonder gud/How iesu crist wes done on rud
1120	Have all my hert and be in peys/And þink I lowfe you etc.
	55, 338
1120.5	Haue god day my leman
1121	Haue gooday nou mergerete/wiþ grete loue y þe grete
1122	Haue Ioye Marie Modur and Maide/As þe Angel Gabriel etc.
1123	Haue mercie on me frere/Barfote that Y go
	817, 849
1123.8	Haue mercy vppon me oo god
1124	Haue myende for the how I was borne
	James Ryman
1125	Haue myende how I mankynde haue take/Of a pure etc.
	James Ryman
1126	Haue mynde on the blys þᵗ neuer schall blyne
1127	Haue mynde on þyn endynge
1129	Hawe on god in wrchipe
1131	He abit þolemodliche/He scurget litliche
1132	He bare hym vp he bare hym down
	'Corpus Christi Carol'
	19, 59, 105, 110, 125, 169, 345, 385, 387, 418, 442, 461, 543, 642, 788, 796, 827, 844, 974, 980, 986
1133	He ȝaf him self as good felawe/Whan he was boren etc.
1134	He haȝt a swete song loude icried
1136.5	He is no good swayn/þat lettith his Iorney for þe rayn
1137	He is wel siker þat hat clennesse
1137.5	He ys wyse and wel y-taȝth/þat beryth a horne & blow hym noȝth
1139	He is wys ȝat kan be war or him be wo
1140	He Iesus is myth and waxit wan
1140.5	He makt himself in gret richesse/þat nith & day flet wrechednesse
1142	He may cume to mi lef but by þe watere
	935
1143	He rod vpon a whit hors in þet
BR+*1143.5*	He may lightli swim/that is hold vp by þe chin
1145.5	He sthey open þe rode þat barst helle clos
	William Herebert
1147.8	He þat hadd inou to help him self withal/Sithen he ne wold I ne wile ne I ne schal
1147.9	He that had London for-sake/Wolde no more to hem take
1148	He that harborythe a ffrere harborythe fesyke
	447
1149.5	He that heweth heweth to hye/þe chippis will fall in his ye
1150	He þat hem reuen hoe reuen ful sore
1150.5	He that in youthe no care will take
1151	He that in ȝouthe no vertu usit/In age all honure hym refusit
1151.5	He that in youthe to sensualite/Applythe his mynde

Index of First Lines 463

1152	He that intendith in his hert to seke/To loue etc.
	John Lydgate
1156	He that lovyth welle to fare
1157	He that made bothe Heuene and Helle/Man and woman etc.
1162	Hee that made with his hand/both winde water and lande
	Arthour and Merlin
1162.8	He is no good can nor non will lern
1163	He þ^t owith mych & hath nowght/& spendith mych etc.
1163.5	He þat smythth with a stafe off oke
1165	He þat stelys this booke/shul be hanged on a crooke
1167	He þ^t was al heuene w^t him þ^t al hat wrouth
1168	He þat whilom did his diligence
	Fall of Princes
	John Lydgate
	113, 295, 360, 741
1170	He that wilbe a lover in euery wise
	'Advice to Lovers'
	342
1171	He þat wol herkyn of wit/þ^t ys witnest in holy writ
	The Dayes of the Mone
	150
1172	He þat wyll hys sowle leche/Lysteneth to me and y woll etc.
	4, 505
1174	He þt wylle rede ouer þis boke/& w^t hys gostly high etc.
	885
1174.5	He that wyll with the devyll ete/A long spone must he gete
BR+*1176.5*	Harte be tru and don not amys/& thynk one them that gaue you this/& euer among remember me
1176.8	hartte be trwe and true loue kepe
1179	[H]Euen it es a richʒ ture/Wele bies im þat itte may winne
1180	Hevy thoughtes & longe depe sykyng
	271
1182	Helpe crosse of tymbris thre
1184	Hende in halle and ʒe wole here/Off eldres þat
	Sir Isumbras
	726
1185	Henry haitspours haith a halt
	321
1186	Henrie seth my Sone as thi Sufferayne haith the sembly assyned
1187	Her hert I wold I had I-wis
	Humfrey Newton
1189	Here begynnes a new lessoun/Off crystys ressurrectioun
	60
1190	Her begynys A tretis fyne/Made in ynglis owt of latyne
	364
1192	Here begynneth of Saynt Margarete/The blessed lyfe etc.
1193	Here bigynneþ þe soþ to say/A noble book wiþout nay
	The Pricke of Conscience
	Robert Manning?
1194.5	Here beside dwellithe a riche barons dowghter
1195	Her commys Holly þat is so gent
1196	Her commensez a bok of sweuenyng/þat men meteþ etc.
1198	Here haue I dwellyd with more and lasse
1199	Here I ame and fourthe I mouste/and in Ihesus Criste etc.
1201	Her I was and her I drank
1202	Heer is a good Confession/þat techeþ mon to sauacion
1204	Here is comen þat nomon wot
1206	Heir lyis Erle George þe Brytan
1206.6	Here lyth John Brigge under this marbil ston
	761
1206.7	Here lythe Rychard þe sone and þe Eyer

1206.9	Here lith the fresshe flour of Plantagenet
1207	Here lyeth under this marbyll ston
1210.5	Her sal I duellen loken vnder stone
	791
1211	Here schul ȝe here a trew lessoun/Hou fayþ & charyte etc.
	John Audelay
1212	Herode þ^t was bothe wylde & wode/ful muche he shadde etc.
1213	Herodes þou wykked fo/Whar of ys þy dredinge
	William Herebert
1214.4	Hay how the cheualdoures/woke al nyght
	238
1214.5	Hay how the mavys on a brere
1214.6	Hey now now
1214.7	Hey troly loly loly/my loue is lusty plesant and demure
1215	Heigh in the hevynnis figure circulere
	The Kingis Quhair
	James I of Scotland
	741, 950
1216	Heȝe louerd þou here my bone/þat madest middelert & mone
	'An Old Man's Prayer'
	48, 171, 443, 602
1217	Hey priuetȝ gritliche/hey Robbetȝ holliche
1218	Hiegh towers by strong wyndes full lowe be cast
1219	His body is wappyd all in wo/Hand and fot he may not go
1220	His colour blaket/his mirthe slaket
1220.5	Hys sighe ys a ster bryth
1221	Hoccleue I wole it to thee knowen be/I lady moneie etc.
	Thomas Hoccleve
1222	Hogyn cam to bowers dore
1223	hol & helyng soth & sorwyng
1224	Holde up oure yong kyng *Ave benigna*
1225	Holver and Heivy made a grete party
1226	Holy berith beris rede ynowgh
	256, 662
1229	Holi gost þi miȝtte/Ous wisse and rede and diȝte
1230	Holy maydyn blyssid þou be/Godis sone is born of þe
1231	Holy maker of sterres bright/Of feithefull men etc.
	James Ryman
1232	Holy moder þat bere cryst buggere of monkunde
	William Herebert
1233	Haly thomas of heouenriche/Alle apostles eueliche
	770, 911
1234	Holy Writ seyȝt whech no thyng ys sother
1235	Holy wrouhte of sterres brryht/Of ryht byleue etc.
	William Herebert
1237	Honour and beaute vertue and gentilnesse
1238	Honour and Ioy helthe and prosperyte
1239	Honure and prays as mot to hym habound
	Translated from the French of Charles d'Orléans
1240	Honure ioy helth and plesance
	Associated with Charles d'Orléans
	566
1241	Honowre wit all manere of heyll/Be vnto yow ffayre etc.
1242	Honured be þis holy feste day/In honour of þe etc.
	Thomas Hoccleve
	597
1243	Honured be þu blisful heuene queene/And worschepid etc.
	Thomas Hoccleve
	597
1244	Honured be þou blisful lord aboue/þat vouched saaf etc.
	Thomas Hoccleve

Index of First Lines 465

1245	Honoured be þu blisseful lord benigne/That now vnto etc.
	Thomas Hoccleve
1246	Honured be þu blisful lord Ihesu/and preysed mote etc.
	Thomas Hoccleve
1247	Honowred be þu blisful lord on hye/That of the blisful etc.
	Thomas Hoccleve
1248	Honured be þou holy gost on hie/þat vnto poeple etc.
	Thomas Hoccleve
	597
1249	Honured be þou Ihesu oure saueour/þat for mankende etc.
	Thomas Hoccleve
1249.5	Honoured be þou lorde of myghte
	597
1250	Hope hath me now fresshe gladsum tidyng brouȝt
	Translated from the French of Charles d'Orléans
1251	Hope is hard ȝer pap is foo
1252	Hoppe hoppe Wilekin hoppe Wilekin/Engelond is min etc.
	402
1253	Hote and moyste ys Aquarius as ys the Eþe[n] men tellyth etc.
1253.5	How a lyon shal be banished and to Berwyke gone
1254	Howe cometh al ye That ben y-brought/In bondes etc.
	332
1255	How darest thou swere or be so bold also
1256	How how myn hert opyn þe gate of thought
	Translated from the French of Charles d'Orléans
1257	How is hit how haue ye forgoten me
	Translated from the French of Charles d'Orléans
1259	How mankinde dooþ bigynne/Is wondir for to scryue so
1260	How mankende furst bygan/In what manschepe now ys man
1261	How schal a mann in pes abide
	W. Hichecoke
	309
1262	Hou sort a feste it is þe ioyȝe of al þis werd
1263	How schowld I bot I thoght on myn endyng day
1264	How suld I now þ^u fayre may fall apone a slepe
1265	Hou shold y with that olde man
	238, 314
1265.5	How slely þe deth schal robben ham
1266	How that Abell sumtyme had a double corne
1267	Hou þi fairnisse is bi-spit/Hou þi swetnisse etc.
1268	I am a chyld & born ful bare/And bare out of þis word etc.
1269	I am a fol i can no god/ho þ^t me houit hi halde him wod
	614
1269.5	I am a woman I may be bold
1270	Ich am afert Lo whet ich se
1270.2	I ham as I ham and so will I be
	Attributed to Sir Thomas Wyatt
	462, 560
1272	Ic eom eldre þanne ic wes a wintre and a lare
	'Poema Morale'
	691
1273	I am gracyus and grete god withoutyn begynnyng
	The York Plays
1273.3	I am he that hath you dayly servyd
1273.5	I am he that wyl not fle/Gyfe me a stafe for charity
1274	I am iesu þ^t cum to fith/w^{t}outen seld & spere
	613
1276.8	I am not unkynd to love as I ffynd
1278	I am olde whan age doth apele
1279	I am Rose wo is me
	931

1280	I am sory for her sake
1286	I boste and brage ay with the best
1286.5	I can be wanton and yf I wyll
1288	I can not half þe woo compleyne
	Richard Beauchamp, Earl of Warwick
	117
1289	I come vram þe wedlock ad a suete spouse etc.
1290	I comawnde alle þe ratons þat are here abowte
	202
1292	I conyoure the laythely beste with that ilke spere
1293	I coniure þe woundes blyue/by þe vertu of þe woundes fyue
1293.5	I coniure hem in the name of the ffader
1294	I counsell what-so-euer thow be/Off polycye forsight etc.
	John Lydgate
1295	Iche Edward Kynge/Have yeoven of my forest the keping
1295.8	I fly/constraynyd am I/with wepynge eyes/to morne & pleyne
1296	I Grace dieu quen and heuenly princesse
	Thomas Hoccleve
1297	I had my syluer And my frend/I lent my syluer etc.
	739
1298	I hadde richesse I had my helth/I had honoure etc.
	James Ryman
1299	I have a gentil cok/Croweth me day
	699, 845
1300	I haue a lady where so she be
	53
1301	Ich aue a loue vntrewe
	840
1301.5	Ich aue a mantel i-maket of cloth
	709
1302	I have a newe gardyn and nowe is begunne
	665, 871
1303	I have a ȝong suster fer beȝondyn þe se
1303.3	Y haue ben a foster long and meney day
1303.5	I haue bene a foster/long & many a day
1304	Y haue for-ȝeue take hede þer-to/y charge þᵗ þᵘ no more do so
1305	I have grete marvell off a byrd/That wᵗ my luff is went away
1306	I have gret wonder by this lighte
	The Book of the Duchess
	Geoffrey Chaucer
	70, 631, 938
1308	I haue laborede sore and suffered deyȝth
1309	I have non English convenient and digne/Myn hertes etc.
1310	I haue nowe sett myne herte so hye/my luff alone is one etc.
1311	I hafe set my herte so hye/Me liket no lufe that lowere is
1312	Ie have so longe kepe schepe on the grene
1313	I haue the obit of my lady dere
	Translated from the French of Charles d'Orléans
1314	I have xii oxen þat be fayre and brown
1315	I haue y-soȝte in many a syde/to fynde water to washe etc.
1316	I here many peple playne
	Translated from the French of Charles d'Orléans
1317	I herde a carpyng of a clerk/Al at ȝone wodes end
	Robyn and Gandelyn
1318	I hard a maydyn wepe/ffor here sonnys passyon
1319	I herd a playnt of grete pyte
1320	I herd an harping on a hille as I lay vnder lynde
1320.5	Ich herde men vpo mold make muche mon
	'The Song of the Husbandman'
	171, 582, 704, 794, 876, 877, 914
1321	I honge on cros for loue of the

Index of First Lines 467

1322	I iosep wonder how this may be/That Mary wex gret etc.
1322.5	I Julius cesar your high emperour
	507
1323	I knowe to the god ful of myght/And to his moder etc.
	The Lay Folk's Mass Book
1324	I knowlech to god with veray contricion
1326	I leue in godd almicten fader/ðat heuene and erðe etc.
1327	I loue a flour of swete odour
	337
1328	I loue a louer that loueth me well
	James Ryman
1328.2	I loue and ffynde cause
1328.3	I loue and y dare nouȝt
1328.5	I loue loued & loued wolde I be
1328.7	I loue so sore I wolde fayne descerne
1328.8	I love trewly without feynyng
1329	I loue on louyd I wotte nott what loue may be
1329.5	I loue vnloued suche is myn aventure
1330	Y louede a child of this cuntrie
	99, 405, 934
1330.5	I maister Andro Kennedy/*Curro quando sum vocatus*
	William Dunbar
1331	I may woll sygh for greuous ys my payne
1332	Y morne for loue þou may see/þat makide me deye for þe
1333	I muste go walke þe woed so wyld
	236
1334	I ne haue Ioy plesauns nor comfortt
1335	I ne mai a liue/For Benoit ne for Ive
	402
1336	I ne may leuen on no manere/ne leten for no þing
1337	I ne wot quat is loue/Ne i ne loue ne louede nouth
1338.5	I patrik larrons of spittale feyl
	Patrik Larrons
	497, 848
1339	I prayse no thing these cossis dowche
	Translated from the French of Charles d'Orléans
**1339.5*	*I pray daily ther paynys to asswage
1340	I pray þe lady þe moder of crist/Praieth ȝoure sone etc.
1341	[I] praye þe spirit þat angell arte/To whom y ame betake
1342	I pray ȝowe all my frendes dere/Sumwhat of bokes etc.
1344	I pray you M to me be tru
	Humfrey Newton
1344.5	I pray yow maydens eueryrchone/Tell me
	490, 754
1345	I put my silf unto yowre mercy lo
	Translated from the French of Charles d'Orléans
1347	I rede þat þou be ioly and glad
1349.5	I recommende me to yow with harte and mynde
1350	I sawe a doge sethyng sowse/And an ape thechyng an howse
	156
1351	I saw a fayr maydyn syttyn & synge
1352	I saw a swete semly syght/A blisful birde a blossum etc.
1353	I sayh hym wiþ ffless al bi-sprad/I sayh him wiþ blod etc.
	583, 603, 605, 803, 861, 947
1354	I saw iij hedles players at a ball
1354.5	I say withowte boste/that the smoke stereth the roste
1355	I see a Rybane Ryche and newe/Wyth stones and perles etc.
1355.5	I sei a sicte þat was vnseire
	852
1356.3	I seche a þouthe þat eldyth noȝt
	713

1356.5	I seik about this warld unstabille
	William Dunbar
1356.8	I serue wher I no truyst can ffynde
1358	I schalle pray for hys sowle that God gyff him rest
1359	Y shall say what ynordynat loue ys
	632
1360	I shall telle you a tale
	John Pympe
1362	I shall you tell a full good sport/How gossippis gader etc.
	455
1363	I shall you tell a gret mervayll/how an Angell for owr avayll
1363.5	I schal you tell þis ilk nyght
1364	I schal yowe tel wyth hert mode/Of the kynggys etc.
1364.5	I shall you tell without leyssinge
	Attributed to George Ripley
1365	I syke when y singe/for sorewe þat y se
	171, 521, 655
1367	I syng of a myden þ^t is makeles/kyng of alle kynges etc.
	79, 122, 303, 405, 420, 422, 424, 429, 439, 511, 521, 532, 539, 551, 566, 583, 595, 685, 703, 707, 764, 786, 796, 906
1367.5	I slepe and my hert wakes/Wha sall tyll my lemman say
	Richard Rolle
1368	I þank þe ihū of al þy goodnesse/I cry þe mercy etc.
1369	I þonke þe lord god ful of miht/wiþ al þat euer I con & may
	503, 748
1370.5	I that in heill wes and gladnes
	'Lament for the Makaris'
	William Dunbar
	417, 442, 827
1372	I þe honoure wiþ al my miht/In forme of brede as y þe see
	235
1373	I þinge al day I þinge of nowth
1373.5	I thocht lang quhill sum lord come hame
	William Dunbar
1374	I trow in god fader of myghte þ^t all has wroghte
	349
1376	I trow in god þe fader Almythy/makare of hewyne etc.
1377	I wowe to god scho [mais grete stere]/The Scottis wenche etc.
1378	I wayle I wepe I sobbe I sigh ful sore
	John Skelton
1378.5	Y wandryng ful wery and walkynge þe ways
	727
1379	I warne vche leod þat liueþ on londe/And do hem dredles etc.
1380	I warne you euerychone for ye shuld vnderstonde
1382	I was a[t erþeldoun]/wiþ tomas spak y þare
	Sir Tristem
	775
1383	I was born In a stall/Betwen beistis two
1384	Ich wes in one sumere dale
	'The Owl and the Nightingale'
	319, 372, 565, 770, 796, 824, 941, 1020, 1021
1385	I was long tyme oon of the company
	Translated from the French of Charles d'Orléans
1386	I was w^t pope & Cardynall/and w^t byshoppes & prestis etc.
1387	I Wende to dede a kyng y-wys
	182, 583
1388	I which that am the sorwefulleste man
	An Amorous Compleint *(Compleint Damours)*
	Geoffrey Chaucer
1389	I wole be mendid ȝif y say mys/Holy chirche nes noþer etc.
1389.5	Ic chule bere to wasscen doun in þe toun/þat was blac ant þat was broun

Index of First Lines 469

1392	I winked I winked whan I a woman toke
1393.5	[I] wote a boure so bricht/es kidde with kaiser and knicht
	758
1394	Ichot a burde in a boure ase beryl so bryht
	'Annot and John'
	36r, 171, 472, 566, 600, 646, 697, 699, 700, 723, 806, 828, 839, 857, 907, 912, 982, 1000
1395	Ichot a burde in boure bryht/þat fully semly is on syht
	'Blowe, Northerne Wynde'
	42, 171, 273, 303, 351, 432, 472, 566, 640, 732, 794, 828, 857
1396	I wot a tre xii bowys betake
1399	I wold ffayn be a clarke/but yet hit is a strange werke
1401	I wald noght spare for to speke wist I to spede
	Laurence Minot
1402	I wolde witen of sum wys wiht/Witterly what þis world were
	'This World Fares as a Fantasy'
	48, 282, 526, 923, 933
1403	I wrecche fulfillid of thouȝd and hevines
	Associated with Charles d'Orléans
1404	I yelde my-silf to yow save me my lyf
	Associated with Charles d'Orléans.
1405	Ic ou rede ye sitten stille/& herknet wel wid god wille
	183
1405.5	I-blessyd be Cristes sonde
1406	Y-blessed be god ofer alle þynge
1407	I-blessed beo þu lauedi ful of houene Blise
	'Blessed Be þou, Leuedy'
	171, 691
1408	Iff a man or womman more or less/In his hede haue grett etc.
	128, 427
1409.3	Yf all the erthe were parchment scrybable
1409.5	Yff anye man aske a question of the/In thine answer
	471
1410	If ony persone stele this boke
BR+*1410.5*	ȝyf ony thevis com ny my good
1411	Yf Crystmas day on the monday be/A trobolus wynter etc.
1412	Yf god send þe plentuowsly riches/than thank hartely etc.
1413	Iff y koude make my wanton wisshis flee
	Translated from the French of Charles d'Orléans
1414.5	Yf I had space now for to write/my mortal paynes
1414.8	Iff I had wytt for to endyght/of my lady
1415	If y halde the lowe Asyse/and take aray of lytel pryse
1416	Iff y lye bacbyte or stele/Iff y curse scorne or swere
1417	If I synge ȝe wyl me lakke
	460, 964
1417.5	If it be loste & you it finde
1418.5	Yf it be so that ye so creuel be
1419	If it befalle that god the lyste visyte/w^t ony tourment etc.
1420	If hit plese yow yowre cossis forto selle
	Translated from the French of Charles d'Orléans
1420.5	If Loue now reyned as it hath bene
	Ascribed to Henry VIII
1421	Yf luste or anger do Thy mynde assayle
	In the hand of Thomas Lower
1422	If man him biðocte/Inderlike and ofte etc.
	144, 1009
1422.1	Gif no luve is o God quaht feill I so
	'Song of Troyelus'
	725
1422.3	Yf on the rockes of Scilla and caribdis I doe chaunce
1422.5	Yf onely sight suffyse/my hart to lose or bynde

1423	Giff sanct Paullis day be fair and cleir **827**	
1424	Iff so were that ye knowe my woo trewly Translated from the French of Charles d'Orléans	
1426.1	If the day of Saint Paule be cleere	
1426.4	Yf the lord byddyth fle/The stewward byddyth sle	
*1426.8	*If þai do so he wil þaim safe/as walnot barke his hare 'The Portrait' **285, 383**	
1428	ȝyf þou comest to me/wordlich blisse ic by-hote þe	
1430	Yf thow fle idelnes/Cupide hath no myght	
1431	ȝef þu ȝeuest him eten inou þanne must him slepen	
1432	ȝef þu sekest loue & wilt him finde/In holinesse etc.	
1433	If þou serue a lorde of prys/Be not to boystous etc.	
1434	Yf thou thy lyfe in synne haue ledde/Amende the now etc. James Ryman	
1436	ȝef þu wilt ben strong in fith	
1436.3	[If þou wylt goo in] to the partes of the este	
1436.5	If þou wyse be wil/six kep þou whilke I þe kenne	
1439.5	If þi horse have iiij white feet give him to þi foo **576**	
1440.5	Gif ȝe wald lufe and luvit be Attributed to William Dunbar.	
1441	I-hereþ my one lutele tale þat ich eu wille telle	
1443	Ilke a wys wiht scholde wake/And waite with werk etc. **48**	
1444	*Illa iuventus* that is no nyse/*Me deduxit* in to vayn devise	
1445.5	In a busshell of wynnynge/ys not a hondfull of cunnyng	
1445.6	In a day go we to the tyre wyth hay hay	
1446	In a chambre as I stode/There lordys were and Barenis bold	
1447	In a chyrch as I gan knelle/Thys endres dey for to here messe	
1448	In a Chirch þer I con knel/þis ender day in on Morwenynge **537**	
1448.5	In a drem late as I lay/me þought I hard/a maydyn say	
1449	In a fryht as y con fere fremede 'The Meeting in the Wood' **42, 79, 94, 171, 540, 582, 659, 728, 781, 815, 837, 857, 868, 895, 941, 961, 1000**	
1449.5	In a garden vnderneth a tree	
1450	In a gloryus garden grene/Sawe I sytting a comly quene **337, 401, 788**	
1450.5	In a goodly nyght as yn my bede I laye **365**	
1451	In a merie morewynyngge of May/whan the svnne etc.	
1452	In a mornyng of May as I lay on slepyng/To here a song etc. **319**	
1453	In a mornynge of May when medose schulde sprynge 'The Quatrefoil of Love'/'The Foure Leues of the Trewlufe' **542, 599, 657, 677, 922, 936, 972**	
1454	In a noon tijd of a somers day/þe sunne schoon ful myrie etc. 'Revertere' **699, 950**	
1455	In a Pistel þat poul wrouȝt/I fond hit writen etc. **923**	
1455.5	In a plesante arboure very queynte & quadrante	
1456	In a semely someres tyde/Als I gan walke in a wolde woude 'Mesure is best of all thynge'	
1459	In a somere sesoun when softe was þe sonne *Vision of Piers Plowman* William Langland **75, 160, 293, 303, 470, 504, 636, 720, 726, 753, 766, 774, 789, 816, 893, 908, 918**	

Index of First Lines 471

1460	In a tabernacle of a toure/As I strode musyng on the mone
	48, 99, 143, 500, 574, 908
1461	In a þestri stude y stod/a lutel strif to here
	93
1463	In a valey of þis restles mynde/I souȝte in mounteyne etc.
	143, 566, 680, 842, 873, 899, 929, 936, 938
1466	In alle maner þrifte y passe alle þingge
1466.5	In all oure gardyn growis thare no flouris
	Attributed to William Dunbar
1467	In all this worlde ys none so true/As she that bare our Lorde Jhesu
1468	In all this warld [n]is a meryar life/Than is a yong man etc.
1470	In Aprell and in May/when hartys be all mery
	401, 1470
1470.5	In autumpne whanne the sonne in Virgine/By radyante hete
	'The Bowge of Courte'
	John Skelton
	799, 816
1470.8	In baill be blyth for þat is best
1471	In Bedleem in that fair cete/A child was born of a maden fre
	513
1472	In bedlem is a child i-born/sal comen a-mongus vs
1473	In bedlem this berde of lyf/Is born of marye maydyn & wyf
1475	In blossemed buske I bode boote/In riche array etc.
1478	In Cloþyngge ys lyue y-hyd
1480	In erth there ys a lityll thyng
	55, 704
1483	In eueri place men mai se/Whanne children to scole etc.
1484	In euery plas qwere þat I wende/My purse is my owene frende
1485	In euery place ye may well see/That women be trewe etc.
	341
1485.5	In fayth ye be to blame/for my good wyll me to dyffame
1487	In Feuerier whan the frosty moone
	John Lydgate
1488	In iiij Poyntys my Wyll ys or I hens departe
1489	In ffull grette heveness myn hert ys pwyght
1489.5	In hond and [herte] true loue kepe
1490	In hert clene & buxum
1490.5	In hevene and erth aungell and man
	597
1491	In Heuene shal dwelle all cristen men/That knowe etc.
1492	In euyn yer sitte a lady [?schene]/Of all women etc.
*1492.5	*In hel ne purgatore non oþer plase
	John Audelay
	816
1493.5	In hys beyng he [is] god in persons tre
1494.5	In holy Churche of cristys fovndacion
1495	In holy sauter me may rede/Hou god etc.
	William of Shoreham
1496	In honour of þis heghe fest of customs yere by yere
	John Lydgate
1497	In Iuyli whan the sonne shone shene
	'The Siege of Calais'
	315, 359
1498	In Iune whan Titan was in Crabbes hede
	John Lydgate
	319
1500	In louers paradise as them among
	Translated from the French of Charles d'Orléans
1501	In maner whyche enlumynyth euery astate
	784

1502	In March after þe fyrst C/Loke the prime &c.	
	501, 808	
1503	In Mattheus gospell as we fynde	
1503.5	In May as that Aurora did upspring	
	William Dunbar	
	319	
1504	In may it murgeþ when hit dawes	
	'Advice to Women'	
	171, 736, 868	
1504.5	In may that lusty sesoun	
1505	[In Ma]y when euery herte is lyghte/[And f]ayre flour flourys etc.	
1506	In May whan euery herte is lyȝt/And floures frooschely etc.	
1507	In May when Flora the fresshe lusty quene	
	'The Complaint of the Black Knight'	
	John Lydgate	
1508	In my conscience I fynde/And in my soule I here & se	
1509	In my defens god me defend	
1510	In my hertt is ther nothynge off remembraunce	
1511	In my ȝowþe full wylde y was	
1512	In nome of him Alweldyng/þat is vr heiȝe heuene-kyng	
1513.5	*In nomine patris* at my Crowne	
1514	*In nomine patris* god kep me *& filii* for cherite	
	'Boke of Kervyng & Nortur'	
	John Russell	
	631	
1522	In patras þer born he was/þe holy buschop seynt Nycholas	
1523	In place as man may se/Quan a chyld to scole xat set be	
1524	In prophesy thus it is saide/The whiche no wyse may etc.	
	James Ryman	
1527	In secreit place this hyndir nycht	
	William Dunbar	
1528	In Septembre at the fallyng of the leef	
	'The Boke called Assemble de Damys'	
	Ascribed to Chaucer	
	725	
1529	In slepe beb leyd all song daunce or disport	
	Associated with Charles d'Orléans	
1531.5	In sory tyme my lyf is y-spent	
	409	
1532	In Somer bifore þe Asceniun/At Euensong on a Sonundai	
1533	In schomer when the leves spryng/The bloschems etc.	
1534	In somer when þe shawes be sheyn/And leves be large etc.	
1539	In the begynnyng of this dede/Pray we god that he us spede	
1540	In the begynning of this litell werke/I pray to god etc.	
	Peter Idle	
1540.5	In þe begynnyng off thys yere	
1541	In the cheiftyme of Charlis that chosin chiftane	
	The Taill of Rauf Coilȝear.	
1542	In the cite callyd Assyse/*Vir trahens tunc originem*	
1543	In the contre herd was we	
	419	
1544	In the day of faste and spirituelle afflixione	
1545	In the daye of Seynte Svythone/Rane ginneth rinigge	
1549	In the forest of noyous hevynes	
	Translated from the French of Charles d'Orléans	
1551	In þe londe of liue Y hope to se/Ioy and blisse etc.	
1552	In the londe of more bretayne	
1554	In the myddis of May at morne as I ment/Throw myrth etc.	
	'The Buke of the Howlat'	
	824, 950	
1555	In the monethe of May when gresse groweth grene	

1556	In the monethes of Maye when mirthes bene fele	
	'The Parlement of the thre Ages'	
	766, 941	
1561.5	In the sacrament I am contenyd bothe god and man	
1562	In the season of Feuierere when it wase full colde	
1563	In þe ceson of huge mortalitie/Of sondre disseses etc.	
	'A disputacion betwyx þe body and wormes'	
	182, 616, 782	
1565	In þe space of halu a day made þis schorte geste	
1566	In the tyme of Arthur an aunter by tydde	
	'The Awntyrs off Arthure at the Terne Wathelyne'	
	160, 189, 599, 626	
1567	In the tyme of Arthur as trew men me told	
	Golagrus and Gawain	
	160	
1568	In þe vale of abraham/Cryst hymself he made Adam	
1570	In þee god fadir I bileeue/þe firste persoone etc.	
1571	In þine honden louerd mine/Ich biteche soule mine	
1570.8	In thyn adversyte thanke thi gode	
1574	In þis time a chyld was born/to saue þᵒ sowle þᵗ wern forlorn	
1575	In þis tyme cryst haȝt vs sent/his owyn sone in present	
1575.5	In this tyme of Chrystmas	
1577	In thys tre es alle hys myth	
1578	In this vale of wrecchednesse	
1580.5	In thought dispered not knowyng remedy	
1581	In thought in wisshis and in dremes soft	
	Translated from the French of Charles d'Orléans	
1583	In tyberies tyme the trewe Emperour	
1585	Yn time of wele þenke on þi wo/for þe wele of þis world etc.	
*1585.8	* . . . in torne clothis	
1586	In troble & in thrall/vnto the Lord I caull	
1587	In xxᵗⁱ yere of age remembre we euerychon	
1587.8	In welth be ware of woo what so þe happes/& bere þe evyn for drede of after clappes	
1588	In wat order or what degre/Hole cherch haþ bownd þe to	
	John Audelay	
1589	In whom is trauthe pettee fredome and hardynesse	
1589.5	In wyldirnes/ther founde I Besse	
1591	In wynter whan the wedir was cold/I ros at mydnyȝt etc.	
	Thomas Brampton	
	903	
1592	In womanhede as auctors al write	
1593	In women is rest peas and pacience/No season etc.	
	219	
1595	In word in ded in wil in þoȝt/ȝour maydyn hede etc.	
	John Audelay	
1596	In worschupe of þat Mayden swete/Mylde Marie etc.	
1596.5	Infynite laude wyth thankynges many folde	
	Walter Hilton	
1596.8	Instruckt well thy familie/Sucor the pore	
1597	Insuffischaunce of cunnyng and of wyt/Defaut of langage etc.	
	John Walton	
1598	In-tyl ane garth wnder ane reid roseir/ane ald man etc.	
	Robert Henryson	
1598.3	Into my Hairtt emprentit is so sore	
1599	Intoe þine honden Louerd bitech Yh gost minne	
1599.5	Into thir dirk and drublie dayis	
	William Dunbar	
1600	In-to þi handes lorde I take my soule	
1601	In-to this worlde this day dide come/Ihū Criste bothe god etc.	
1602	Inwardliche lord bi-seche i þe/Al my trespas for-ȝiue etc.	

1605	Ipocras this boke made ȝare/And sente it to the emperor etc. **531**	
1605.5	*Ipse mocat me*/An aple is no pere tree	
1606	Is a priue pouyson	
1607	Is she not full of all goodly manere Translated from the French of Charles d'Orléans	
1608	Is tell yw my mynd anes tayling dame **907**	
1608.5	Is ðeos burch breome geond Breotenrice 'Durham' **1021**	
1609	Is þer any good man here/That will make me any chere	
1609.5	Ys thys a fayre avaunte ys thys honor	
1610	Is wan of beting	
1611	*Iste puer* is a prynce þ^t is perles	
1615	Hit beoþ þreo tymes on þo day/þat soþe to witen me mai	
1617	Hit bilimpeð forte speke to reden & to singe	
1618	Hit cometh by kynde of gentil blode	
1619	Hit falleth for every gentilman	
1620	Yt fell abowght the Lamasse tyde/Whan husbondes etc. 'The Battle of Otterburn' **704**	
1620.5	Is it not sure a deadly pain **190**	
1622	It fell ageyns the next nyght/The fox yede etc. 'The Fox and the Goose' **236, 311, 322, 437**	
1625	Hiȝt is a marchaund and spendeȝt nouth **564**	
1627	It is bred fro heuene cam/ffleych & blod of mary it nam	
1628	Hit is doon ther is no more to say Translated from the French of Charles d'Orléans	
1628.5	It is first þe floritif of fairnes	
1629	Hit is ful harde to knowe ony estate/Double visage etc.	
1630	Hit is ful heue chastite/w^t mene maydyns now o-day John Audelay	
1631.3	Het is i-cume to þis tune/Godith and Godrun	
1632	Hyt is y-founde in holy wryt/That þe dede seyde to þe quik	
1632.5	Hit ys in heruyst cartes to clater **305**	
1633	Ittes knowyn in euery schyre/Wekyd tongges have no pere	
1634	Hit is lawe þat failleþ noth/Hit it ouer al þat mai beo etc.	
1634.5	Hyt is mery in hall/when berdys waggyth all	
1636	Is it nouth worth to a child his frendis gode	
1636.5	hit is so praty In euery degre	
1636.8	It is þe properte of a gentelman/To say the beste þat he can	
1637.2	It is to me a ryght gret joy	
1637.6	hit is vnknowe/what man bulde þis cete nowe John Trevisa	
1637.8	It is well fownde a passyng grete damage	
1638	Hit nis bot trew I-wend an afte/forte sette *Nego* etc.	
1639	Hit resteþ and hit quemeþ/hit richeþ and hit demeþ	
1640	Hyt semes quite and is red/hyt is quike and semes dede	
1641	It was a kniȝt beȝonde þe se/þat riche man was wont to be	
1641.5	It was a mayde of brenten ars	
1644	It was a squyer of lowe degre/That loved the kings etc. *The Squire of Low Degree* **189, 938**	
1645	Hit was an Erl of muche miht/Bi-ȝonde þe see etc. **760**	

Index of First Lines

1649	Hit wes upon a screreþorsday þat vre louerd aros
	'Judas'
	61, 90, 142, 334, 509, 514, 633, 660, 705, 772, 796, 829, 930, 986
1650	It wern fowre letterys of purposy/M and A, R and I
	648
1651.5	Iuy is both fair & gren
BR+*1651.8*	Y-wandrynge ful wery & walkynge þe wayes
1652	I-wyss I-wyss I remember me
1653	I-writen I fynde a goode stori/þe Pope hit wrot seint Gregori
	The Trental of St Gregory
1653.5	Jack dawe þou habest blasfemed & reson hast
	Jack Upland's Rejoinder
	677
1654	Jack Miller asketh helpe to turn his Mill aright
	Jack Miller's Song
	975
1655	Jacke Trewman dothe you to vnderstand
	Jack Trueman's Epistle on the Abuses of the Age
	975
1657.5	Jerusalem reioss for joy
	Attributed to William Dunbar
1659	Ihesu almyghty and mary maydyn fre
1662	Ihesu as þ^u art our sauyour/þat þ^u saue vs fro dolour
1663	Ihesu als þow me made & broght/þu be my lufe & all my thoght
1664.5	Jhesu be þou my ioy al melody and swetnes
	Richard Rolle
1666	Jhesu by the my sowle
	339
1669	Ihesu crist al þis worldes red/þat for oure sunnes etc.
	The Proverbs of Hendyng
	136
1672	Ihesu crist godis sone of heuene/Boþe god & man i-borne etc.
	615
1674	Ihesu Criste haue mercy one me/Als þ^u erte kynge of mageste
1677	Ihesu cryst heuyn kynge/Be at my begyninge
1678	Iesu crist heouene kyng/ʒef vs alle god endyng
	'Iesu Crist, Heouene Kyng'
	171
1679	Jhesu cryste i beseche the for the clennes of thyn incarnaciun
1680	Ihesu crist I the be-seche/Thow here my prayere etc.
1682	Iesu Crist kepe oure lippes from pollucion
	589
1684	Ihesu crist my lemmon swete þat diʒedest on þe Rode-tre
1687	Ihesu crist of Nazareþ/That for vs all suffridist deþ
1691	Ihesu cryst ryhtful Iustyce/King and lord ouir alle kyngis
1692	Ihesu cryste saynte Marye sonne/Thurgh whaym þis werlde etc.
1693	Ihū cryste þat dyed on tre/And sofurred pyne for Adam syn
1695	Ihesu Crist þat is so fre/to Monnes soule spekeþ he
1697	Iesu cristes milde moder/stud biheld hire sone o rode
	404, 539, 562
1698	Ihesus descended for to cum/To a cete þat hight capharaum
1699	Ihesus doþ him by mene/and spekeþ to synful man
	153, 269, 896
1700	Ihesu for þe mourne I may/As turtel þat longeþ etc.
1700.5	Jhesu for thi blysful blod/bryng thoo soulis in to thi blis
1701	Ihesu for thi blode þou bleddest/And in þe firste tyme
1703	Ihū for thy holy name/And for thy bytter Passioun
	496, 546
1704	Ihesus for þi holy name/& for thi beter passyon

1705	Iesu for þi muchele miht/þou ȝef vs of þi grace	
	'Iesu, for þi Muchele Miht'	
	171	
1706	Iesu for Thy precius blod/And Thy bitter Pascion	
1707	Ihesu for þi precius blood/þat þ^u schaddist for oure good	
	714	
1708	Ihū for þyn precius blode/þat Thow shedest for owre good	
	370	
1709.5	Jesu for þi woundes fiue/þou kepe he weil in al þaire lyue	
1710	Jhesu for thy wondes fyff/Saue fro shedyng Cristayn blode	
1711	Ihesu for þi wondis wide/wiþ þi meeknesse fordo mi pride	
1714	Ihesu god is be-comen man/Ihū mi loue & my lemman	
1715	Ihesu god sone lord of mageste/Send wil to my hert etc.	
	411, 585	
1717	Ihesu grete loue meued þe/To suffur þe peyne etc.	
1718	Ihesu kyng of heuen & hell/Man & woman I will þe tell	
	885	
1719	Ihesu kyng of hie heuen aboue/Vnto Michael my chief etc.	
1719.5	Jesu lythe my sowle with þi grace	
	339	
1720	Ihū lord blyssed þ^u be	
1721	Ihesu lorde for thy holy cyrcumsicioun	
	John Lydgate	
1723	Ihesus Lord of miȝt/Keppe vs boþe day and niȝt	
1724	Ihesu lorde of myȝtes most/Fader and sone and holy gost	
1725	Iesu lorde oure heuyn kynge/Graunte vs all etc.	
1726	Jhesu lord owr heavenly kyng	
	281	
1727	Ihesu lord þat madist me/And wiþ þi blessid blood hast bouȝt	
	Richard de Caistre	
	46, 218, 618	
1728	Ihesu lorde þi blesside life/help and counforte etc.	
1729	Ihesu lord welcom þow be/In forme of bred as I þe se	
	235, 793	
1730	Ihesu mercy and graunt mercy	
1731	Ihesu mercy how may this be/That god hymselfe for sole etc.	
1732	Ihesu mercy mercy I cry/myn vgly synnes þou me forgyfe	
1732.5	Jesu most swettest of any þynge/To love ȝow I haue grete longyng	
1733	Ihesu my lefe Ihesu my loue: Ihesu my couetyne	
	Possibly Richard Rolle	
	167	
1734	Ihesu my lord welcom þ^u be/In flesch & blode I þe see	
1735	Ihū my luf my ioy my reste/þi perfite luf close in my breste	
1736	Ihesu my louer and my delite/In þi loue make me perfite	
	339, 822	
1737	Iesu my suete with/þ^t alle þingge hast wrouth	
1738	Ihesu of a mayde þou woldist be borne/to saue mankynde etc.	
1739	Ihesu of his moder was born/For vs he werde garlond etc.	
1739.5	Iesu of Nazareth/þat þoledest for mannes soule deth	
1741	Ihesu of whayme all twewe luffe sprynges	
1742	Iesu oure raunsoun/Loue and longynge/Louerde god etc.	
	William Herebert	
1744	Ihesu restyd in a may/xl wekys and a day	
1746	Ihesus seynge peplys comynge hym tylle/He styed etc.	
	558, 714	
1747	Iesu suete is þe loue of þe/noþing so suete may be	
	171, 231, 842	
1748	Ihū that alle this worlde has wroghte/And of a clene virgyn etc.	
1749	Ihesu þat al þis world haþ wroȝt/haue merci on me	
	48	

1750	Iesu that all thys worlde hathe wroght/Heven & erthe etc.
	Palden
	286
1751	Jhesu that arte a jentyll ffor joye off thy dame
1752	Iesu þat art heuene kyng/Sothfast God and mon also
1755	Ihesu þat borne was of a may/In amendement of mankynde
1757	Ihesu that diede one the rude for þe lufe of me
1758.5	Jhesu that deyed vp on a tre/owr sowlys for to wynne
1759	Ihesus þat diȝedest vppon þe tre/And þoledest deþ etc.
1760	Iesu þat for vs wolde die/And was boren of maiden Marie
1761	Ihesu þat hast me der abouȝte/Write þ^u gostly in my þouȝte
	1018
1762	Ihesu þat heuyn & erthe begane/And aftyr hys forme etc.
1768	Iesue that ys most of myght/& made aboffe all thyng
1769	Ihesus þat sprong of iesse roote/As us haþ prechid þi prophete
1772	Ihesu þ^t was borne of Mare fre/As he hase power etc.
1775	Ihesus þat walde after midniȝt/þi sqete face þat was so briȝt
1776	Iesu þat wolde for vs dye/& was boren of mayde marie
1777	Ihesu þat woldist for manys sake
1779	Ihesu the sonne of mare mylde/The seconde parsone in trinyte
	679
**1779.5*	*Iesu thow do me loue the so
1780	Ihesu þi name honourde miȝt be/with al þat any lyfe is in
1781	Ihesu þi swetnes whoso myȝte it se/And þerof haue etc.
	806
1785	Ihesu was born in bedlem Iude/Of mayde mary þus fynde we
1786	Ihesu was of Mary borne/ffor synfull man þat was forlorne
	'Discourse between Christ and Man'
	965
1786.5	Iesu whom ye serue dayly/Vppon ȝour enemys
1787	Ihesus woundes so wide/ben welles of lif to þe goode
1789	Iuellis pricious cane y non fynde to selle
1790.8	John Ball greteth you wele all
	John Ball
	975
1791	John Ball Saint Mary priest/Greeteth well all etc.
	John Ball
	321, **592**, **753**, **879**, **975**
1793	Ion blessis hom alle þat þis boke redem/Wit gode entent etc.
1793.5	John Barton lyeth under here/Sometimes of London
1793.6	Ion Clerke of toryton I dar avow
	475
1793.9	Ion Ion pyke a bone/tomorrow þu schall pyke none
1796	Johan the Muller hath ygrownde smal smal
	John Ball
	419, **753**, **879**, **975**
1798	Joly chep [er]te of Aschall downe/can more on loue etc.
1799	Jolyfte Jolyfte/Maket we to the wode the
1802	Iosephe wold haue fled fro that mayde
	James Ryman
1803	Ioye and blisse wyȝt outen endyng
1804	Ioy blissid lady with pure virgynal floure
1808.5	Joy winefred virgine that ouercommynge youthful lures
BR+*1808.7*	Iuball was fader and fynde[r] fyrst of songe
1810	Iuce of lekes with gotes galle/For evyl herynge help it shalle
1811	Justyce loke thu stedfast be
1813	Katereyn þe curteys of all þat I knowe/cumlyest keping etc.
	Richard Spalding
	114, **168**, **194**
1814	Kateryne with glorious Margarete/that be virgines etc.
1815	Kepe thy syght fro vanyte/that þ^u coveite not þ^t evil may be

1817	Kepe well x & flee from sevyn/sspende well v & cum to hevyn **551**
1817.5	Kepe well thy cowncele as tresor in cheste
1818	Kyndeli is now mi coming/into ʒis werd wiht teres and cry
1820	King conseilles/Bissop loreles **161, 799**
1820.5	King hart in to his cumlie castell strang *King Hart* Attributed to Gavin Douglas
1821	Kyng hext of alle kynges þat hauest non endyng William Herebert
1822	Kynge I syt & loke about
1822.5	Kynge Jamy Jomy your Ioye is all go Attributed to John Skelton
1823	Kynge of grace & ful of pyte/Lord of heuyn I-blyssed þou be
1824.8	Kytt hathe lost hur key **502, 973**
1825	Knele down man let for no shame/To wurshupe ihc̄ etc.
1826	Knelyng allon ryght thus I may make myn wylle Duke of Suffolk **744**
1828	Knowyn alle men that are & schuln ben/That I Ihc̄ etc. **885**
1829	Know er thow knytte Prove er thow preyse yt
1829.2	Know or þou knyte & then þou mayst slake
1829.8	Knolege acquayntance resort favour with grace John Skelton
1830	*Kyryleyson Cristeleyson/Pater de celys deus* to the we crye
1831	*Kyrieleyson* have mercy good lorde/*Xpeleyson* we crye etc. **222**
1832	Lefdy blisful of muchel miʒt/heyere þanne þe sterres liʒt
1833	Leuedy for þare blisse/þat þu heddest at þe frume **539**
1834	Lady for þi sonne sake/Saffe me fro þes fendes blake **182**
1836	Leuedi ic þenke þe wid herte suiþe milde **466, 794**
1837	Ladye marye maydyn swete/that art so good fayre and free
1838	Lady of pite for þy sorowes þᵗ þᵘ haddest/ffor Ihū þu son etc. 'A Lover's Appeal' Signed 'Chaucer' **343, 892**
1838.5	Ladi quene y pray the to govern me in gode lore
1839	Leuedi sainte marie moder and meide/þᵘ wisie me nuþe etc. **770, 971**
1840	Leuedi swete and milde/For loue of þine childe
1841	Late as I wente one myne pleynge/I set my herte all in solase
1841.5	Late on a nyght as I lay slepyng **365**
1842	Late whane Aurora of Tytane toke leue John Lydgate
1842.5	Laude honor prasingis thankis infynite *The XIII Bukes of Eneados* Translated by Gawin Douglas
1844.5	*Le roy cuuayte nos deneres*
1845	Lerne bodyly to lyue/þy seruaunt non hyre þᵘ pay
1846	Leerne þou vnkynde man to be kynde
1847	Leorne to loue as ich loue þe/On alle my lymes þou mith seo
1848	Leche oþ þe lasours lawfulliche y-lenyd
1849	Ladd Y the daunce a Myssomur Day **405, 794, 827, 934, 970**

1850	Leve in yi rokke ne is no thef/Take oyer manez wulle etc.
1851	Leve is the wrenne/Abouten the schowe renne
1852	Leve lystynes to me/Two wordes or three
1854	Lyef lord my soule thow spare/the sothe I sey now sykerly
	Pety Job
	17, 903, 913
1856.5	Leue men þis beoþ þe ten heste
1857	*Len puet fere et defere/Ceo fait il trop souet*/It nis nouther wel ne faire
	520, 620, 717
1858	Lende me yowre praty mouth madame/Se how y knele etc.
	Charles d'Orléans
1859	Leynte comeþ þer afterward þ^t six wike i-lasteþ
	759
1860	Lenten is an holy tyme/In which folke wile hem schryue
	759
1861	Lenten ys come wiþ loue to toune/wiþ blosmen etc.
	36r, 40, 272, 385, 426, 566, 568, 583, 681, 736, 759, 794, 828, 938, 991
1863.5	Let fal downe thyn e & lift up thy hart
1864	Late lef him þ^t michil spekt/ffor gret spekere treuthe brekt
1864.5	Lett lowe to lowe go kyndly and sowfte
	354
1865	Lat no man bost of cunnyng ne vertu
	'Midsomer Rose'
	John Lydgate
	566
1866	Lett no man cum into this hall
	55, 454
1866.5	Let not vs that yong men be
	Perhaps by Henry VIII
1866.8	Lett serch your myndis ye of hie consideracion
1868	Lat vs avvise thys dey primordiall
1869	Lewed men be not lered in lore/As clerkes ben in holi writ
	'A Dialogue between St Bernard and the Virgin Mary concerning the Passion'
	596, 940
1871	*Lex* is layde and lethyrly lukys/*Iusticia* is exyled etc.
1871.5	Ly þow me ner lemmon in þy narms
1872	Lyft vp the Ieen of youre aduertence/ye that beth blynde etc.
	John Lydgate
1873	Lyft vp your hartis & be glad/In crystis byrth the angell bad
1874	Lyke as grete wateres encresyn into floods fele
	'A Treatise of a Galaunt'
	799, 985
1877	Lysteneth all and ye shall her/How the gode man taght etc.
1887	Lustneþ Lordes leoue in londe/Soþeli sawes I wol ȝou telle
1888	Lystennyth lordynges A lyttyll stonde/Of on þat was etc.
	Syre Gawene and the Carle of Carelyle
1889	Lystneþ lordynges a new song Ich ulle bigynne
	'The Execution of Sir Simon Fraser'
	171, 700, 704
1891	Listhiþ lordingis and ȝe schulen here/How þe wise man etc.
1892	Lestenytȝ lordyngis boþe grete and smale/I xal ȝu telyn etc.
	693
1893	Lestenyt lordynges boþe elde and ȝynge/How þis rose etc.
	303
1894	Lystneþ lordinges boþe ȝonge ant old/Of þe Freynshe etc.
	'The Song of the Flemish Insurrection'
	171, 198
1896	Lestenit lordynges I you beseke/There is no man worght etc.
1897	Lystenyþ lordynges y yow pray/How a merchand etc.
1898	Lustneþ lordynges leof and dere/ȝe þat wolen etc.
1899	Listyns lordingus to my tale/And ȝe shall here of on story

1900	Lystyn lordyngys qwatte I xall sey/A grete maruell tell I may
1902	Lystne man lystne to me/Byholde what I thole for the
1903	Lustne mylde wrouhte oure bones with woepinge
	William Herebert
1905	Listenythe nowe & ye shall hyre/Talkynge of a goode matere
1907	Lystenys now I wyll ʒowe tell/Of mykell pyte I may ʒow spell
	The *Northern Passion*
	596
1914	Lyth and lysten both old and ʒong/How the rose begane etc.
	874
1915	Lithe and listen gentlemen/That be of free born blood
1916	Lythe and listenyth the lif of a lorde riche
	The Weddynge of Sir Gawen and Dame Ragnell
1917	Liþer lok and tuinkling/Tihing and tikeling
1918	Lytyll and mykyll olde and yonge/Lystenyth now etc.
1919	Lytle childe sythen youre tendre infancie
1920	Lytyll cheldryn here ʒe may lere/Moche cortesye etc.
1921	Lutel wot hit anymon/Hou derne loue may stonde
	'The Way of Woman's Love'
	171, 297, 578, 827, 849, 920, 949
1922	Lytel wotyt onyman hu derne loue was funde
	'The Way of Christ's Love'
	171, 578, 827, 849, 920, 949
1923	Litel uotit eniman ou trewe loue bi-stondet
	'A Song of the Love of Our Lady'
	691, 920
1924	Liuis firist and licames hele
1925	Lo fol how the day goth
1926	Lo he that can be Cristes clerc
1926.5	Loo he that ys all holly yourʒ soo free
	987
1929	Loo here two kynges righte perfit and right good
	John Lydgate
1929.5	Lo kyng Artour ful manly and ful wyse
1930	Lo lemman swete now may þou se/þat I have lost my lyf etc.
1931	Lo moises bush shynynge vn-brent/þe floures faire etc.
1931.3	Lo these fonde sottes/And tratlynge Scottes
	John Skelton
1932	Lo wordly folkes thouʒ þis processe of dethe/Be not swete etc.
1933	Logge me dere hert in yowre armys twayne
	Translated from the French of Charles d'Orléans
1933.5	London thou art of townes a per se
	'The City of London'
	William Dunbar
	19, 303, 704
1934	Longe berde herteles/peyntede hoode wytles
	359, 1002
1934.5	Lang heff I maed of ladyes quhytt
	'On ane blakmoir'
	William Dunbar
	843
1935	Longe slepers and ouerlepers
1936	Long wilbe water in a welle to keche
1937	Looke before the how thi lyfe wasteth/Looke behynde etc.
	905
1938	Loke er þin herte be set/Lok þou wowe er þou be knet
1938.5	Loke his wonnyng be clere a dytʒte
	919
1939	Loke how Flaundres doþ fare wiþ his folyhede
	'The Follies of the Duke of Burgundy'
	876

1940	Loke man to iesu crist hi neiled an þe rode
	48
1940.5	Loke nu frere/Hu strong ordre is here
	321
1941	Loke on þis wrytyng man for þi devocion
1941.8	Loke out here Maier with thy pilled pate
1942	Loke þat þu for no frend be
1943	Loke to þi louerd man þar hanget he a-rode/and wepe etc.
	48, **161**, **825**
1944	Looke well about ye that louers be
	'Beware the blind eat many a fly'
	210, **489**
*1944.5	* . . . [lo]kyng for her trew love/long or that yt was day
1946	Louerd ass þu ard on god ever buten hende
	183
1947	Lorde be þ^u my kepere
	339
1949	Louerd crist þou hauest vs boust/þou madest al etc.
1948	Louerd crist ich þe grete/þu art so mylde and swete
1950.5	Lorde god alweldande/I beteche todaye into þi hande
1951	Lord god as þou art al good/And of myght þat al may
1952	Louerd godd in hondes tine/I bequeðe soule mine
1952.5	Lord God in Trinite/Fader and Sone and Holy Gost
	388, **410**
1953	Lord God in trynite/Yeff heme hevene for to see
	Sir Degrevant
1956	Lorde god to þe we calle/þat þou haue merci on ous alle
	903
1957	Lord how shall I me complayne
1958	Lord I bidde boþe day and nyth/cum to my feste etc.
1959	Lord I ȝelde me gulti/þat I neuere fedde þe hungri
1960	Lord in hondes thine/I be take sowle mine
1961	Lord in thyne anger vptake me nouȝt/and in þi wrap etc.
	Richard Maydestone
	903
1961.5	Lord Iesu Cryst goddes sone on lyve/haue mercy on vs
1962	Lord Ihū crist in Trinite/þreo persones In vnite
1963	Lorde iesu cryste leuand god sone/þu set þi deyde þi cros etc.
1965	Lord iesu þin ore/I sorwe & sike sore
1967	Lord my God al Merciable/I þe be-seche wiþ herte stable
1968	Louerd shyld me vrom helle deth at þylke gryslich stounde
	William Herebert
1969	Lord sunged haue I ofter/In my fyue wittes etc.
1970	Lord swete Ihū crist Haue merci of me
1971	Lord þat art of myȝtis moost/ffadir & sone & holy goost
1974	Lord þat lenest vs lyf ant lokest vch-an lede
	'On the Follies of Fashion'
	171
1975	Lorde þat suffrydist harde turment/And on the rode etc.
1977	Loverd þi passion/wo þe þenchet arist þaron
1978	Louerd þu clepest me/An ich naȝt ne ansuared þe
	491, **658**, **999**
1979	Lord thu kyng off glorye/Whyche grace and uyctorye
	Richard Coer de Lion
	295
1982	Lord what is thys world wele/Rychesse reule and ryche Aray
1984	Lordus ȝif ȝe wol lusten to me/Of Croteye þe noble Cite
1984.5	Lordes & ladyes all bydene/For your goodnes & honour
1986	Lordyngis & ȝe wyl lythe/Of o thyng I xal ȝ^u kythe
1989	Lordynges I warne yow al beforne/yef þ^t day that Cryste etc.

1992	Lordyngis leue & dere listneþ to me a stounde	
	384	
1993	Lordynges lystniþ to my tale/þat is meryer þan þe ny3tyngale	
	Sir Beues of Hamtoun	
1995	Lordynges that be now here/If ye wille listene and lere	
	Robert of Brunne	
1996	Lordynges þat bene hende and Free/Herkyns alle etc	
1999.5	Loue fayne wold I/yff I coude spye	
2001	Loue god ouer all thyng	
2002	Loue god þat loued the	
2003	Loue hauith me bro3t in liþir þo3t/þo3t ic ab to blinne	
	'A Rhyme-Beginning Fragment'	
	161, 238	
2003.5	Loue hym wrouste/and loue hym brouste	
	302	
2005	Loue is a selkud wodenesse	
2006	Loue is blisse in mannis mynde/& loue is fre etc.	
2007	Luf es lyf þ^t lastes ay þar it in Criste es feste	
	'Love is Life'	
	Richard Rolle	
	411	
2007.5	Loue is naturall to euery wyght	
2008	Loue is out of lond i-went/Defaute of loue þis lond etc.	
2009	Loue is sofft loue is swet loue is goed sware	
2010	Luffe luffe where es þi reste/Of Englond I am oute-keste	
2011	Loue made crist in oure lady to lith	
2012	Loue me brouthe/& loue me wrouthe	
*2012.3	* . . . love shuld com/On euery syde þe way she pryde	
2013	Love þat is powre it is w^t pyne/Love that is riche etc.	
	205	
2014	Loue þou art of mikel mit/Mi day þou tornis into nit	
2015	Love wyll I and leue so yt may befall	
2016	Luf wil I with variance	
2017	Loue wolle I withoute eny variaunce	
2017.5	Loued be þou king & thanked be þou kyng	
	Richard Rolle	
2018	Lovely lordynges ladys lyke/Wyves and maydynus ryallyke	
	984	
2021	Luke in his lesson leres to me/How gabryel etc.	
	109, 302	
2022	Luke in his lesson leres vs þus/Vnto his desciples etc.	
2023	Lullay lullay litel child reste þe a þrowe	
2024	Lullay lullay litel child/þ^u þ^t were so sterne & wild	
2025	Lollai lollai litel child whi wepistou so sore	
	161, 198, 316, 588, 745	
2025.5	Lusti yough should vs ensue	
	Ascribed to Henry VIII	
2026	Lyarde es ane olde horse and may noght wele drawe	
2027	Madame a trouthe not wot y what to say	
	Translated from the French of Charles d'Orléans	
2028	Madame as longe as hit doth plese yow ay	
	Translated from the French of Charles d'Orléans	
2028.5	Madame d'amours/All tymes ar ours	
2028.8	Madame defrayne/Ye me retayne	
2029	Madame for your newe fangelnesse	
	'Against Women Inconstant' or 'Newfangelnesse'	
	Perhaps by Geoffrey Chaucer	
2030	Madame y wold bi god alone	
	Associated with Charles d'Orléans	

Index of First Lines 483

2031	Madame ye ben of al beaute shryne
	'A Balade to Rosamond'
	Geoffrey Chaucer
	788, 839, 967
2032	Madame ye ought well know to my semyng
	Translated from the French of Charles d'Orléans
2033.5	Mayde and moder eke thou be
2034	Mayde and moder mylde/uor loue of þine childe
	48, 969
2034.5	Mayde whether go you/I go to the medewe etc.
	895
2035	Mayde wiþoute make/Behold þow qwat I craue
2036	Maiden & moder cum & se/þi child is nailed to a tre
	513
2037	Maidin and moder þat bar þe heuene king
2037.5	Maiden in the mor lay
	'The Maid of the Moor'
	78, 79, 298, 301, 304, 314, 385, 405, 414, 459, 477, 484, 509, 567, 583, 627, 709, 788, 817, 827, 880, 944, 1015
2038	Mayden Modur and comely Qween/þat art in heuene etc.
2039	Mayden moder milde/*oeiz cel oreysoun*
	'A Prayer for Deliverance'
	171, 703, 835, 969
2039.3	Maydenes of Engelande sare may ye morne
	1014
2039.5	Make we mery in hall and boure
2040	Man a-mong þi myrþis haue in mynde/From whens etc.
2041	Man and woman in every place/God hath ȝow sent etc.
2042	Man and wyman loket to me/u muchel pine ich þolede for þe
	1022
2044	Man be mery I the rede/but be whar what merthis þ^u make
2046	Man by-hold hou nou wytȝ my hand
2047	Man bihold what ich for þe/þolid up þe rode tre
2048	Man be war of wikkid counsaile/He wol the lede etc.
2050	Man be war þe way ys sleder
2050.5	Man com & se yow schal alle dede be
2051	Man folwe Seint Bernard's trace/And loke in ihū cristes face
2052	Man from myschefe thou þou amende/And to my talkynge etc.
2053	Man haue in mynde how here byfore/for thy mysdede etc.
2054	Man haue hit in þy þouȝt/Of what matere þ^u maked is
2056	Man have this in thi mynd
2057	Man hef in mynd & mend þi mys/Quhill þow art heir etc.
2058	Mon iboren of wommon ne lyueth but a stounde
	786, 1004
2059	Man ȝyf þat þou wylt fle synne/Neuer more to come þer-inne
	587
2060	Man yff thou a wyse man erte/Of thy goodes take thy parte
2061	Man if þ^u hast synnyd owth/chaunge redely þi þowth
2062	Man ȝyf þ^u wylt here/Ryth good thyng þ^u myth lere
	684
2063	Man in Heuyn hyt ys mery to dwll
	Johannes Mydwynter
	267, 403
2066	Mon in þe mone stonde and strit
	'The Man in the Moon'
	171, 223, 270, 385, 453, 499, 560, 585, 743, 783
2066.5	Man in what state that ever thou be
2066.8	Man is but a frele þing
2070	Mon may longe lyues wene/Ac ofte him lyeþ þe wrench
	'Death's Wither-clench'
	1020, 1021

2072.6	Man Remembre whens þou com & wheþer þou shalt
2073	Man sigh & sorw for þi synnes/þan semeþ þi synnes as slayn
2074	Man siker helpe hast þ⁽ᵘ⁾ & prest/þe moder þe sone sewet etc.
2076	Man þᵗ in erth abydys here/Thov mvst be-leve wᵗowten dure
2077	Man þᵗ lyf up-holdest/thenk whan þᵘ art oldest
2077.5	Man þat was in wurchipe tok no hede/And þerfore last his worchup for is mysde[de]
2078	Mon þat wol of wysdom heren/At wyse Hendyng he may leren
	The Proverbs of Hendyng
2079	Man þenke here on ofte tyme/What helpuþe sowles etc.
	Iohannes Mydwynter
	267, 403
2079.5	Man þu haue þine þout one me
2080	Man þus on rode I hyng for þe/fforsake þi syn for luf of me
2081	Man to reforme þyne exile and þi losse/ffrom paradys etc.
	'Complaint þat Crist maketh of his Passioun'
	John Lydgate
2082	Man vpon molde whatsoever þou be/I warn utterly etc.
	704
2083	Man wenit euere to liuen/He þinket nouth þᵗ he sal deyȝe
2085	manhed & mercy þis lond haueth ichached hout
2086	Mankend I cale/wich lyith in frale/For loue I mad the fre
2087	Mankyende was shent and ay forlore/For synne etc.
	James Ryman
2088	Mannys soule is sotyl & queynt/shal neuere ende etc.
2090	Many a man blamys his wyffe perde/Yet he ys more to etc.
2091	Many man is loþ to here/Repref of vices & werkis ylle
2092	Many men seyn that in sweveninges/Ther nis but fables etc.
	The Romaunt of the Rose
	Geoffrey Chaucer
	880, 908
2093	Many men wened/þat he ne wene ne þarf
2095	Manie ȝeres ben i-went/siþen treuthe outȝ of londe is lent
2097	Mary flowr of flowers all/hath born a chyld in an oxstall
2098	Mary for the loue of the/Glad and mery schal we be
2099	Mary for thine yoys fyve/teche me þe vey to ryth lyve
2100	Marie ful of grace weel ðe be/Godd of heuene be wið ðe
2101	Marye goddis moder dere/Socoure & helpe us etc.
2103	Mary is a lady bryȝt/Sche hyȝt a sone of meche myȝt
2107	Marye mayde mylde and fre/Chambre of þe trynyte
	William of Shoreham
	492, 566
2108	Marie Mayden Moder mylde/þat blisful Bern in bosum bere
2109	Mari milde haþ boren a chylde/crist lyþ in cradul bonde
2110	Marie Modur and Mayden: Euere wel þe be
2111	Mary moder cum & se/þi sone is nayled on a tre
	513, 966
2113	Mary moder meke & mylde/from schame & synne etc.
2114	Mary moder of grace we cryen to þe
	786
2115	[M]ary moder of mercy & pyte/And seynt Kateryn pray for me
2116	Marie Modur Qwen of heuene/þenk on me etc.
2118	Marie Modur wel þe bee/Modur and Mayden þenk on me
	222
2119	Mary moder well thou be/Mary mayden þenk on me etc.
	618, 757
2121	Mary of help both day and nyght/I pray þe etc.
	618
2122	Mary so myelde and good of fame/By vertu of the holy goost
	James Ryman
2124.5	Mary thou were greet with lovely cheere

Index of First Lines 485

2125	Marie ȝow quen ȝow moder mayden briht
2128	Master Geffray Chauser that now lyth in grave
2128.5	Mayster Johan eu greteþ of Guldeuorde þo
2129	Maistur in mageste maker of Alle/Endles and on euer to last
2130	Maisters Gower Chauucer and Lydgate/Primier poetes etc.
	'Active Policy of a Prince'
	George Ashby
	260
2131	Maysters that was of craftes seere
2133	Matheu hat mad a grete gestenyng/te Iesu at home etc.
2135	May no man slepe in ȝoure halle/for dogges madame etc.
2136	Maist thou now be glade with all thi fresshe aray
	'A Mirror for Young Ladies at their Toilet'
	353, 368
2138	Me lykyþ euer þe lengere þe bet
2139	Me merveillis of this grit confusioun
	'The Want of Wise Men'
	Robert Henryson
2141	Me þingkit þou art so loueli/so fair and so swete
	669
2142	Mekely Lordyngis gentylle and fre
2145	Men hem bimenin of litel trewth/It is ded and ȝat is rewthe
2146	Men hem compleynes of vntrewyth/lawe es dede etc.
2148	Men may leue all gamys/That saylen to Seynt Jamys
2149	Men may rede in romance right/Of a grete clerk
	'The Battle of Crecy'
	Laurence Minot
2150	Men rent me on rode/Wiht wudes woliche wode
2153	Men ȝernen iestes for to here/& romance rede etc.
	Cursor Mundi
	965
2153.5	Menkskful and myȝty in mynde modyr of maries iij
	'Stirps beate Anne'
	976
2154	Mercyful quene as ye best kan and may/After your sone etc.
2155	Merci abid on loke alday/War man fro senne wil wende awey
2156	Mercy and Trowthe met on a high monteyne
	'A Praise of Peace'
	John Lydgate
	260
2157	Mercy god of my mysdede/For þi mercy þat mychel ys
	Paraphrase of the Fifty-first Psalm
	Richard Maydestone
	294, 585, 903
2158	Mercy is hendest whore sinne is mest/Mercy is lattere ȝere etc.
2159	Mercy es maste in my mynde/for mercy es þ^t I mast prayse
	Richard Rolle
2160	Mercy Marie maydene clene/þu let me neuer on sinne duele
	157
2161	Mercy me graunt off þat I me compleyne
	55, 947
2162	Murie a tyme I telle in May/Wan bricte blosme brekez on tre
2163	Mirie it is while sumer ilast
	424, 553, 583, 770, 999, 1021
2164	Merie singen þe munaches binnen Ely
	The Canute song, quoted by Thomas of Ely
	178, 321, 642, 911
2165	Merie tale telle ihc þis day/Of seinte Mary þ^t swete may
2166	Middelerd for mon wes mad/vnmihti aren is meste mede
	'The Three Foes of Man'
	42, 171, 239, 273, 300, 530, 582, 586

2167	Might is right . . . Light is night
2168	Myght wisdom goodnesse of the Trinite/Mi naked sowle etc.
2171	Myldeste of moode & mekyst of maydyns alle
	114, **168**, **185**, **194**
2172	*Miles Rogerus* by ten mile wons he to neer us
	374
2173	Mynd resun vertu & grace/humelete chast & charete
	John Audelay
2174	Myn angel that art to me y-send
2175	Myn hert hath sent abowt ye fer and nere
	Translated from the French of Charles d'Orléans
2176	Myn hert hath send glad hope in hys message
	Charles d'Orléans
	468
2177	Myn hert if so that y good tidyng here
	Translated from the French of Charles d'Orléans
2178	Myn hert ys set and all myn hole entent/To serue etc.
	Perhaps by the Duke of Suffolk in reproof of Lydgate
2179	Myne hert is set uppon a lusty pynne
	Poem ascribed to Elyzabeth, Queen to Henry VII
2180	Myne hert the schepe off fresche fedyng
	Translated from the French of Charles d'Orléans
2181	Myn hert thou fondis bi this light
	Associated with Charles d'Orléans
2182	Myn hertes Ioy and all myn hole plesaunce
	Duke of Suffolk
	731
2182.3	Myne hartys luste
2182.6	Min hartys lust & alle my plesure
2183	Myn hertis lust sterre of my confort
	234, **252**
2183.5	Myne high estate power & auctoryte
	Thomas More
2184	Myn only ioy my lady and maystres
	Translated from the French of Charles d'Orléans
2185	Myn owne ladi dere ladi fair and fre/Y pray yow in herte etc.
2186	Myne awen dere sone & þᵘ will lere/Of sundry wittis etc.
2187	Myn oȝen deþ and cristes and mi wikedhede
2188	Myn worldly Ioy vpon me rewe
	55, **947**
2189	Minot with mowth had menid to make/Suth sawes etc.
	'The Sea fight at Sluys'
	Laurence Minot
2190	M. Merowre/ys deth/of gostly schewyng
2192	*Miseremini mei* ye that ben my ffryndys/This world hath etc.
	The lamentation of the soul of Edward IV
	Attributed to John Skelton
2193	*Misit deus angelorum*/A-downe fro heuen blysse
	James Ryman
2195	Masteres Anne/I ame your man/As you may well espie
	280
2195.3	Mastres your maners are hard to know
	Nycholas Wikes
2195.5	Moaning my hart doth sore oppresse
2196	More speche madame is of your goodlynes
	Associated with Charles d'Orléans
2197	More then body hert good and servise
	Associated with Charles d'Orléans
2198	More than the deth nys thinge vnto me leef
	Translated from the French of Charles d'Orléans

Index of First Lines 487

2200	Moost cristen Princesse by influence of grace
	Probably by John Lydgate
2200.3	Most clere of colour and rote of stedfastness
2202	Most glorius quene Reynyng yn hevene/Stere of the se etc.
2203	Most goodly fayre aboue alle þo lyvyng
	Translated from the French of Charles d'Orléans
2204	Most goodly fayre as lust hit yow to here
	Translated from the French of Charles d'Orléans
2205	Most goodly fayre if it were yowre plesere
	Translated from the French of Charles d'Orléans
2206	Most goodly yong O plesaunt debonayre
	Translated from the French of Charles d'Orléans
2207	Most i ryden by Rybbesdale
	'The Fair Maid of Ribblesdale'
	42, 92, 171, 297, 351, 436, 472, 752, 805, 839, 857, 868, 869, 875, 967, 1000
2208	Most mercifull lorde by thyne habundant goodnesse
2211	Most noble prince of Cristen princes alle/Flouring in youþe
	John Lydgate
2213	Mooste noble Prynce with support of Your Grace
	John Lydgate
2214	Most prepotent prince of power imperiall
2215	Most prudent prince of pruved prevision
2216	Most reverend rightwose regent of this rigalitie
2217	Most soueren lady comfort of care
	Humfrey Newton
2217.5	Moost soueryn Lorde Chryste [Jesu]/Born of a mayde
2218	Most souerayn lord O blysfull cryste Ihū/ffrom owre enemyes
	John Lydgate
2219	Most worthi prince of whome the noble fame/In vertue etc.
	John Lydgate
2220	Moder milde flur of alle/þu ert leuedi swuþe treowe
2221	Modir of god and virgyne vndeffouled/O blisful queene etc.
	Attributed to Thomas Hoccleve
2223	Moder of norture best beloved of al
2224	Mourning mourning/Thus may I sing
2224.5	Morning my hart doth sore oppresse
2226.5	Musing allone this hinder nicht
	Possibly William Dunbar
2227	Musyng alone voide of consolacion
	Henry Baradoun
2228	Musyng vppon the mutabilite/Off worldlye changes etc.
2229	Musyng vpon the restles bisyness/Which that this etc.
	De Regimine Principium
	Thomas Hoccleve
	260, 726
2230	My best belouyd lady and maistresse/To whom I must etc.
	Duke of Suffolk
2231	My cares comen euer anew
2231.5	My darlyng dere my daysy flour
	John Skelton
2231.8	My doȝter my derlyngge/Herkne my lore y-se my thechyng
2232	My dere an dese þat so fayre ys
2233	My dere child first thi seue enable/With al thyne herte etc.
	Stans Puer ad Mensam
	John Lydgate
2233.5	My dere frendes I you pray/four thingis in your hertis bere away
2234	Mi dere lemman behold þu me
2235	My dere sone wnderstande this buk/þow study & reid etc.
	'Ratis Raving'

2236		My deþ y loue my lyf ich hate for a leuedy shene
		'De Clerico et Puella'
		280, 297, 469, 566, 857, 868, 895, 941, 961, 1000
2236.5		My dely wo
2237		My fayr lady so fresshe of hew
		839, 843
2238		My fader above beholdyng thy mekeness/As dewe etc.
		882
2238.5		My felowe for his sothe sawe/hath loste his lyf and lythe ful lawe
2240		My folk now ansuere me/qwat haue I to the gylt
2241		My volk what habbe y do þe/Other in thyng toened þe
		William Herebert
		788
2243		My gostly fader I me confesse/First to God etc.
		Associated with Charles d'Orléans
2244		My guddame wes ane gay wyfe bot scho wes rycht gend
		William Dunbar
2244.3		My heid did ȝak yester nicht
		William Dunbar
2244.6		My herte ys yn grete mournyng
2245		My hert ys so plungit yn greffe
2245.1		My harte ys sore but yett noo forse
2245.3		My hart ys yowrs now kyp het fast
2245.4		My harte ys yours ye may be sure/And so shall be
		Signed 'Bourscher Richard Daniel'
2245.6		My hart my mynde & my hole poure
2246		My hertly love is in your governauns
		Translated from the French of Charles d'Orléans
2247		My hertes Ioie all myn hole plesaunce
2247.5		My hartis treasure and swete assured fo
		William Dunbar
2248		My hope mayden I ask & crafe/In þˢ trans þᵗ þᵘ me safe
2249		My joye it is from her to here
2250		My kyng þe watur grett/and þe blod he swett
		Richard Rolle
2250.3		My Ladye hath forsaken me/that longe hathe ben her man
2250.5		My lady hath me in that grace
2250.8		My lady went to Caunterbury
2251		My ladyes and my maistresses echone/Lyke hit unto etc.
		Ragmanys Rolle
2254		My lefe ys faren in londe
		665
2255		Mi leeue lyf þat lyuest in welþe/in mete and drinke etc.
		714
2255.3		My lytell fole/Ys gon to play
2255.6		My lytell prety one my prety bony one
2256		My lyue y hynde in sorwe & wo/Man to hyme fro ys fo
2257		My lord whan ye thys boke ouyr redde
2258		Mi lord with herte I preyȝe þe withouten vois wol stille
2258.5		My lordis of Chalker pleis ȝow to heir
		William Dunbar
2259		My love and lady whom y most desere
		Translated from the French of Charles d'Orléans
2260		Mi loue is falle vpon a may/ffor loue of hire i defend etc.
2261		My love only my ioy and my maystress
		Translated from the French of Charles d'Orléans
2261.2		My loue she morns ffor me
2261.4		My love sche morneth/For me for me
		William Cornish
2261.6		My loue so swyte/Iesu kype

Index of First Lines

2261.8	My loving frende amorous Bune	
	'A letter sende by on yonge woman to anoder . . .'	
	945	
2262	My maister Bukton whan of Criste our kyng	
	L'Envoy de Chaucer à Bukton	
	Geoffrey Chaucer	
2262.3	My mayster ys cruell and can no curtesye	
	'The Five Dogs of London'	
	371	
2262.5	Mi mind is mukel on on þat wil me noȝt amende	
2263	Mi Mornynge M greues me sore	
	Humfrey Newton	
2263.5	My name is Parott a byrde of paradyse	
	'Speke Parott'	
	John Skelton	
	950	
2264	My noble sones and eke my lordis dere/I your fader etc.	
	Scogan	
2265	My paynid gost enforsith me complayne	
	Associated with Charles d'Orléans	
2266	My poore hert bicomen is hermyte	
	Translated from the French of Charles d'Orléans	
2267	My prince in God gif the guid grace	
	William Dunbar	
2267.5	My ryght good lord most knyghtly gentyll knyght	
2268	My self Alon I mak grete m[one]/And sigh full sore etc.	
2269	My-self walkyng all allone/ffull of thoght of ioy desperat	
2270	My sange es in syhtyng/my lyfe es in langynge	
	'Cantus amoris'	
	Richard Rolle	
2271.2	My soverayn lorde for my poure sake	
2271.4	My soverayne saveoure to þe I calle	
	597	
2271.6	My swetharte & my lyllye floure	
2272	My thoght ys full hevy/and greuith me Ryght sore	
2272.5	My thought oppressed my mynd in trouble	
2273	My trewest tresowre sa trayturly was taken/Sa bytterly etc.	
2274	My verry ioy and most parfite plesere	
	Translated from the French of Charles d'Orléans	
2275	My wele my ioy my love and my lady	
	Translated from the French of Charles d'Orléans	
2276	My wille my loue my verry sorse of blis	
	Translated from the French of Charles d'Orléans	
2277	My wofull hart in paynfull weryness	
	Signed 'Sheryngham'	
2277.5	My wofull hert of all gladnesse baryeyne	
2277.8	My whofull herte plonged yn heuynesse	
	54	
2278	Mi woful hert þat slepis lo in care	
	Translated from the French of Charles d'Orléans	
2279	My woofull hert thus clad in payn	
	54, 99	
2280	Mi word is *Deo gracias*/In world wher me be wel or no	
2281	My worshipfull and reuerent lady dere	
	Humfrey Newton	
2281.5	My yeris be yong even as ye see	
	Thomas Wyatt	
	462, 611, 716	
2282	Nakyd into þis warlde born am I	
	306	
2283	Nas ter neuer carayn so loþ/As man wan he to putte goþ	

*2284.3	* . . . nature y-sette in ȝowr ymage
*2284.5	*Naueþ my saule bute fur and ys
	583
2286	Ne haue þou no god botin on/Idel oth ne suere þou non
2287	Ne mai no lewed lued libben in londe
	'A Satire on the Consistory Courts'
	171, 499, 704, 763, 876
2288	Ne saltou neuer leuedi Tuynklen wyt þin eyen
	Signed 'Robertus seynte Mary, Clericus'
	321, 480, 751
2288.5	Ne sey neruer such a man a Iordan was/and went he to gogeshale panyles
	709
2289	Ne were my trewe innocent hert
	Charles d'Orléans
2289.3	Nede not y loue wher men loue me
2289.5	Neuer to ȝelden & euere to crauen/Maket man fewe frendis to hauen
2290	Next þe derke nyght þe gray morewe/So is Ioye next etc.
	Impingham
2291	No god no haue þov boten on/Hijs name þov naȝt etc.
2293	No more will i wiked be/Forsake ich wille þis worldis fe
	230, 798, 1013
2293.5	No wondre thow I murnyng make
2293.8	Non sigheth so sore/as þe glotoun that mai no more
2294	Nar that y drede displesen yow only
	Translated from the French of Charles d'Orléans
2295	Not far fro marche in the end of feueryere/Allon I went etc.
	Duke of Suffolk
2297	Not long agoo purposyd I and thought
2298	Nout mannes steuene but good wille/Nout mirthe etc.
2299	Not oft y prayse but blame as in substaunce
	Translated from the French of Charles d'Orléans
2300	Not wot y now what wise to bere my chere
	Translated from the French of Charles d'Orléans
2300.3	Noghte yo lyke þow me to lake/For this schrowyll byhynd my bake
	458
2300.6	Now all men mowe sen be me/That wordys Joye is vanyte
2302	Nou Bernes Buirdus bolde and blyþe/To blessen ow her etc.
	923
2303	Now blissid lorde as I haue trust in þᶜ/þᵗ euerlastyng etc.
2305	Nu broþerr Wallterr broþerr min afterr þe flaeshess kind
	Ormulum
	Orm
	983
2306	Now Criste Iesu soþfast preest and kynge
	222
2306.5	Now culit is Dame Venus brand
	William Dunbar
2307	Now deþ is at myn hede/Iᶜ may wel sege alas
2307.5	Now do I know you chaungyd thought
2308	Now drede y daungere nor yet noon of his
	Translated from the French of Charles d'Orléans
2308.5	Now fayre fayrest off euery fayre
	William Dunbar
2308.8	Now fayreste of stature formyd by nature
2309	Now felle me when þis Jubile þus was made
	Associated with Charles d'Orléans
2310	Now forto syng I holde it best/And lete all care etc.
	James Ryman
	454
2311	Now fresshe floure to me that ys so bryght

Index of First Lines 491

2312	Now gyneth the devel to wrathen him sore
	Merlin
	Henry Lovelich
2313	Now gladly shall the clergy singe/To seint Fraunceys etc.
	James Ryman
2315	Now god almythy doun hath sent/The holy gost etc.
2316	Now god almyghty haue mercy on me/For maryes prayers etc.
2317	Now god þat syttyst an hygh in trone
2318	Now good swet hart and my nane good mestrys
2319	Now goot falshed in eueri flok/And trewth is sperd etc.
2320	Nou goth þe sonne under wode/Me riweth marie þi etc.
	An English quatrain in *Speculum Ecclesie*
	St Edmund Riche
	79, 155, 215, 250, 262, 303, 320, 372, 404, 435, 478, 509, 566, 583, 642, 777, 821, 853, 860, 906
2321	Now gracyous god groundyd of all goodnesse
	Ludus Coventriae
2322	Now grett glorious Godd thurgh grace of hym selvene
	Morte Arthure
	160, 189, 599, 843
2323	Now herken euery man bothe more and lesse/What mede etc.
	St Augustine
	762
2323.3	Now has Mary born a floure/all þis world to gret honour
BR+*2323.4*	Now hathe ye harde bothe olde & yonge
2323.5	Now haw y vryt alle/ȝyf me drynk of gode ale
2323.8	Now helpe fortune of thy godenesse
2325.5	Now holde him silf from loue let se þat may
	Translated from the French of Charles d'Orléans
2327	Now holy gost owr verry Counfortowre
2329	Now ich haue þat I wyle
2331	Nou ich wille þat ye ywryte hou hit is y-went
2332	Now in Betheleme that holy place/To bringe man oute etc.
	James Ryman
	454
2333	Now ys Crystemas y-cum/ffadyr and Son to gedyr in oon
2334	Now ys cum owre saueowre/And now hathe mare borne etc.
2335	Nowe is Englond perisshed in fight/With moche people etc.
2336	Now is mon holi & seint/& huuel him muit in mund
2338	Now is the Fox drevin to hole hoo to hym hoo hoo
2339	Now is þe twelþe day icome/þᵉ fader & sone togeder etc.
2340	Now ys tyme to sle & tyme to hele
2342	Now ys wele & all thing a-ryȝt/And crist is come as a trew kniȝt
2343	Now ys ȝole comyn wᵗ gentyll chere/Of merthe & gomyn etc.
	55, 184
2344	Now ihc̄ for derworþ blode/þat þou schaddist for mankyn
	161
2345	Now Ihū lord welle of all goodnes
2346	Now Ioy be to the trynyte/ffader son & holy goste
2347	Now late me thought I wolde begynn/My synfyll etc.
	121, 523, 792
2348	Now let vs be mery bothe all and some
	454
2349	Now lyst fortune thus for me to purueye/That I ne may etc.
	Duke of Suffolk
2349.5	Now lufferis cummis with larges lowd
	'The Petition of the Gray Horse, Auld Dunbar'
	William Dunbar
2350	Now must I nede part out of your presence
	Duke of Suffolk
2352	Now now Ihū for thy circumcisioun/Whan thou was kut etc.

2356		Now pride ys yn pris/Nou couetyse ys wyse
2357		Now rightwis Iuge crist lord Ihū/of kyngis kyng etc.
2358		Now say me lo myn hert what is thi reed
		Translated from the French of Charles d'Orléans
2358.5		Now shall youe her a tale fore youre dysport
		455
2359		Nou skr[y]nkeþ rose & lylie flour
		'An Autumn Song'
		171, 662, 703, 837
2361		Now sly3tes of cure wylle I preche/How somme mete etc.
		Liber Cure Cocorum
		189
2361.5		Now þe bok takeþ on honde/Wales to fore Engelonde
		John Trevisa
2362		Now the deys sterre in hys hevenly spere
2364		Nowe the lawe ys layde be clere conscience
		208
2366		Nu þis fules singet hand maket hure blisse
		122, 303, 420, 429, 511, 539, 796, 906
2367		Nowe this tyme *rex pacificus*/Is man become for loue of vs
		James Ryman
2369		Nu þu unseli body upon bere list
2370		Now to do well how shalt þᵘ do/herke to me & shall the telle
2371		Now to speke will I noght spare/Sen speche has made etc.
		476
2373		Nowe vnderstonde boþe more and lesse/What mede etc.
		St Augustine on the Virtues of the Mass
		762
2375		Now welcome somer with thy sonne softe
		A roundel inserted in two MSS of *Parlement of Foules* [*3412*]
		Geoffrey Chaucer
		571, 801
2376		Nowe well and nowe woo/now frend and nowe ffoo
2377		Now wel may we merthis make/ffor vs ihc manhode etc.
2378		Now what tidyng my lady and mastres
		Translated from the French of Charles d'Orléans
2379		Now will ye lordis wesshe or shall y wesshe
		Associated with Charles d'Orléans
2381		Now wold I fayne sum myrthis make
		650
2382		Nou 3e alle beo glad and bliþe/For i come to leden ou etc.
2383		Now 3ee that will of loue here/I counsell yow þᵗ 3e cum nere
		'The Parlement of Love'
		725
2384		Nowel el boþe eld & 3yng/Nowel el now mow we syng
2384.5		O altitude of alle science
		597
2384.8		O beauteous braunche floure of formosyte
		'To the Floure of Formosyte'
		343
2385		O Angel dere wher euer I goo/Me that am comytted etc.
2386		O bewtie pereles and right so womanhod
2387		O best maker of lyght and of creatowre
2388		O blesse god in trinite/grete cause we haue to blesse thy name
		279
2388.5		O blessid Albone O martre moste benygne
2390		[O] Blissed god þᵗ art almi3ti/þu arte ful of goodnesse
2391		O blessed ihū hyghe heuens kynge/I most synfull etc.
2392		O blessed Ihū that arte fulle of myght/The wonder of etc.
2392.5		O blessyd Johan the Euangelyst
2393		O blyssed king so full of vertus

Index of First Lines 493

2393.5	O blessed lord how may this be
2394	O blyssid lord my lord O crist ihū/Welle and hedspryng etc.
	John Lydgate
2394.5	O blessed lord of heuyn celestiall
2395	O blyssed mayde fflour off alle goodnesse/On alle synfull etc.
	John Lydgate
	965
2396	O blessid mayde moder and wyffe/Graunter of pease etc.
	James Ryman
2397	O blessed mary the flowre of virgynitie/O quen of hevyn etc.
2398	O blessid quene about the sterrid heuene
	Perhaps by John Lydgate
2400	O blyssedfull berd full of grace/To all mankynd etc.
2401	O cryste Ihū mekely I pray to the/To lete thy name etc.
2402	*O Criste rex gencium*/Whoyse kyngdom hath non ende
	James Ryman
2403	O crist þᵗ art þe parfyt partnere/Of fadyrs lyght etc.
2404	O closed gate of Ezechiel/O plentevous mounte of Daniel
	James Ryman
2405	O closed gate of Ezechiell/O plentevous mounte of Daniel
	James Ryman
2406	O come to me sum gladsum tidyng newe
	Translated from the French of Charles d'Orléans
2407	O cruell daunger all myn aduersarye/Of whom alle etc.
	Duke of Suffolk
2408	O cruell deth paynfull & smert/On the to thenke etc.
	James Ryman
2409	O Dauid thow nobell key/cepter of the howse of israell
2409.5	O dere God beholde þis worlde so transytorye
	'The Lamentatyon of Edward, late Duke of Buckyngham'
	945
2410	O dere god pereles prince of pece/With all my power I etc.
2411	O deth how byttere ys þe mynde of the
2412	O dethe whylum dysplesant to nature/Where duellyst etc.
	'Come Death'
	342
2412.5	O desirerabull dyamvnt distinit with diversificacion
2413	O deuout people which kepe an obseruance/louly etc.
	John Lydgate
2414	O dredefull deth come make an ende/Come vnto me etc.
	James Ryman
2415	O emperesse the emperoure/*Quem meruisti portare*
	James Ryman
2416	O endles god bothe .iij. and one/Fader and sonne and etc.
	James Ryman
2417	O endles god of maieste/*Alpha et oo quem vocamus*
	James Ryman
2418	O endles god of maieste/On in godhede in persons thre
	James Ryman
2419	O endles god of mageste/*Te patrem rite vocamus*
	James Ryman
2420.5	O eternall and persones three
2421	O excellent suffereigne most semely to see
2422	O fayre y wot ye haue in remembraunce
	Translated from the French of Charles d'Orléans
2423	O fayre madame all though that there be noon
	Associated with Charles d'Orléans
2424	O fayre madame crist wold ye knew my payne
	Associated with Charles d'Orléans
2424.5	O fayre madame if so ye dare not loo
	Associated with Charles d'Orléans

2425	O fayre madame no more vnto me write
	Associated with Charles d'Orléans
2426	O fayre Rachel semely in syght/Ther is no spotte of syn etc.
	James Ryman
2427	O fayrist flowre o floure of flowris alle
	Associated with Charles d'Orléans
2428	O fader god how fers and how cruel/In whom the list etc.
	Thomas Hoccleve
2429	O fader of eternall blys/*Qui semper es ingenitus*
	James Ryman
2430	O fader of high maieste/O sonne and holigost all thre
	James Ryman
2431	O fader of high maieste/The sonne and holigost w^t the
	James Ryman
2432	O fader w^{t}oute begynnynge/O sonne and holigoost also
	James Ryman
2433	O first fownder and hevenly creature
2434	*O flos campi* of swete odoure/Moost fayre of hue etc.
	James Ryman
2435	O floure of all uirginite/O moder of oure sauyeoure etc.
	James Ryman
2436	O Fortune dost thou my deth conspyre
	Translated from the French of Charles d'Orléans
2437	O fresche floure most plesant of pryse
	237, 359, 665, 839, 843, 941
2437.5	O ffresches flour
2438	O fy fortune fy thi dissayt and skorne
2439	O fy love fy amende yowre gouernaunce
	Associated with Charles d'Orléans
2439.5	O gentyll & most gentyll Ihesu yow save
2440	O gentyll fortune I thonke yowe I wys
	'Thanks, Gentle Fortune'
	342
2440.5	O glorious feste among al other
	597
2441	O gloryus God oure governor gladin alle this gesttyng
2442	O glorius god redemer of mankynde/Whiche on the crosse etc.
	512
2443	O glorius Iohan evangelyste/Best belovyd with Ihū Cryst
2444	O glorius lady and virgyn imaculatt/Succur hus etc.
2445	O gloryous Martyr wiche of deuout humbles/ffor crystes etc.
	John Lydgate
2446	O glorius mother and mayd off pety/The Swerd off sorow etc.
2448	O god & man sempiternall/That hast made vs free etc.
	James Ryman
2449	O God how that she lokith verry fayre
	Translated from the French of Charles d'Orléans
2450	O god so as hit enioyeth me
	Associated with Charles d'Orléans
2451	O god swete lord ihū crist that madest me
	618
2451.5	O god þat in tyme all thingis did begin
	John Skelton
2453	O god we pray to the in specyall/ffor all the saulis etc.
2454	O good Herry the sixte by name/Both of Inglond etc.
	James Ryman
2455	O good swet hert my ioy and soul plesaunce
	Associated with Charles d'Orléans
2456	O goodly fayre sith y have doon and shall
	Associated with Charles d'Orléans

2457	O goodli faire which y most loue and drede
	Charles d'Orléans
2458	O hert more hard then roche of any ston
	Associated with Charles d'Orléans
2459	O Hevenly sterre most Comfortable of lyght
2460	O heuenly sterre so clere and bright/In whome did light etc.
	James Ryman
2461	O Hie Emperice and quene celestiall
2462	O highe ffader of heuen blys/Sith crist thy sone oure broder is
	James Ryman
2463	O hope in nede þ^u helpe me/Gods moder I pray to þe
	182
2464	O howe holsom and glad is the memorie/Of Cryst Ihu etc.
	John Lydgate
2466	O Iesse yerde florigerat/The fruyt of lyff is sprung of the
2467	O Iesse yerde florigerat/The fruyte of liffe is sprung of þe
	James Ryman
2468	O Ihū crist hongyng on cros/vij. wordis þ^u sayest w^t myld voys
	John Audelay
	630
2469	O Ihū cryste of euerlastynge swettnes/Thou god in þi etc.
	222
2470	O Jhesu grant me þi will of wepynge
	201
2471	O Ihū lett me neuer forgett thy byttur passion
2472	O Ihū mercy what world is thys
2473	O Ihū þat madest þe heuenes clere/Enlumined etc.
	222
2474	O Ihū to all thy true louers/Graunt peace of hert etc.
2475	O kendly creature of beute perleȝ
2476	O king of grace and indulgence/By whome alle thynge etc.
	James Ryman
2477	O lady dere o condite clere/O well of vertue & of grace
	James Ryman
2478	O Lady I shall me dres with besy cure
2478.5	O Lady myne to whom thys boke I sende
	'The Lover's Book'
	343, 725
2478.8	O lady sterre of iacob glorie of israel/Of all blessid
2479	O lewde book with thy foole rudeness
	312
2480	O lilly flowre of swete odowre/In whois chast bowre etc.
	James Ryman
2481	O litel whyle lesteneþ to me/ententyfly so haue ȝe blys
	'A Disputation between the Blessed Virgin and the Cross'
	696, 922
2482	O lo myn hert syn ye wol gone your way
	Associated with Charles d'Orléans
2482.5	O Lobbe Lobe on thy sowle God haue mercye
	'The Epytaphye of Lobe, the Kynges Foole'
	299, 945, 1005
2483	O Lord allmyghty blissid thou be/That hast me formyd etc.
2484	O lorde by whome alle thing is wrought
	James Ryman
2485	O lorde by whome al thing is wrought
	James Ryman
2486	O lord God O Ihū Crist/O sueit saluiour I þe salewe
	630
2488	O lord god what yt is gret plesaunce
	Duke of Suffolk
2491	O lord of loue here my complaynt

2494	O lorde so swett ser Iohn dothe kys **236, 768**
2495	O lord þ^t art maker and creature/Of thynges all o lord etc.
2496	O loue most dere o loue most nere my harte 'The Pains of Love' **271, 987**
2497.5	O lusty flour of ȝowth benyng and bricht William Dunbar
2498	O lustye lyllye þe lantorne of all gentylnes
2499	O maker of hevyn immensurable
2500	O man beholde before the how thy lif wastith **905**
2500.5	O man more than madde what ys þi mynde
2501	O man of molde/mekely beholde/How god mankynd etc. James Ryman
2503	O man thow marrest in thy mynd/To muse how god etc.
2504	O man vnkynde/hafe in mynde/my paynes smert **383, 703**
2505	O man vnkyende pryente in þi myende/The perfecte loue etc. James Ryman
2506	O man whiche art the erthe take froo/Ayene into erthe etc. James Ryman
2507	O man-kynde/hafe in þi minde/my passion smert
2508	O meke Hester so mylde of mynde/Thatte hast fownde etc. James Ryman
2510	O merciful and o mercyable/king of kinges and father of pitee
2511	O marcyfull god maker of all mankynd/What meneth etc.
2512	O merciful ihū for merci to the i crie **235**
2514	O meichti ladi owr leding tw haf Jevan ap Rydderch ap Jevan Lloyd **124, 131, 133, 907**
2516	O myghty Mars that wyth thy sterne lyght *Troy Book* John Lydgate
2517	O maistres myn til ȝou I me commend **365**
2518	O mestres whye/Owtecaste am I **838**
2519	*O mors mordens aspere* yn gyle þou haste noo pere
2520	O mortall man behold tak tent to me 'The Ressoning betuix Deth and Man' Robert Henryson
2521	O Mortall Man By grete exaltacion/In ryches awtoryte etc. **324, 370**
2522	O Mortall man call to Remembraunce/The day shalle etc. **541**
2523	O mortall man masyd w^t pompe and pride/of vayne glorye etc. **528**
2524	O Mossie Quince hangyng by youre stalke **53, 359, 440, 839**
2525	O most blessid Fader omnipotent/O light most glorius etc.
2526	O moste famous noble king thy fame doth spring and spreade John Skelton
2527	O moder mylde mayde vndefylde/Thatte we so wylde be etc. James Ryman
2528	O Mother of God Inuolat virgin mary/Exult in Ioy etc.
2529	O my dere harte the lanterne of lyght
2530	O my dere sonne why doest thou soo/why doest thou etc. James Ryman
2530.5	O my desyre what eylyth the

Index of First Lines

2531	O my good brother/You ar ne nother	
	488	
2531.5	O my hart and O my hart	
	Attributed to Henry VIII	
2532	O my lady dere bothe regarde & se/my harte vppon yow etc.	
	987	
2532.3	O my lady dure/I am your prisoner	
2532.5	O my swete lady & exelente goddes	
2533	O of iesse thow holy rote/that to thi pepill arte syker merke	
2533.5	O orient lyghte & kinge eterne	
	597	
2534	O orient light shynyng moost bright/O sonne of right etc.	
	James Ryman	
2535	O oure fader that art in blisse/Sanctified the name mote be	
	James Ryman	
2535.5	O painefull hart in peiyns syȝht	
	354	
2536	O penful harte that lyes in travvail	
	341	
2536.5	O pereles Prynce of Peace/And Lord of Lordes all	
	328	
2538	O precious tresor inconparable/O ground and rote etc.	
	La Male Régle de T. Hoccleve	
	Thomas Hoccleve	
	506	
2539	O prince of peas & king of grace/O endeles lorde etc.	
	James Ryman	
2540	O prynces of eternall peas/O lady of all angellis bright	
	James Ryman	
2541	O prudent folkes takeþe heed/And remembreþe in youre lyves	
	John Lydgate	
2541.5	*O quem mirabilia* good Lord thy werkys been	
2542	O quene of blisse thy son Ihesus/*Quem meruisti portare*	
	James Ryman	
2543	O quene of grace and of conforte/Whose vertu we cannot etc.	
	James Ryman	
2544	O quene of mercy and of grace/O oure comforte in euery case	
	James Ryman	
2545	O quene of pitee and of grace/O swete lady to thy dere chielde	
	James Ryman	
2546	O Radiant luminar of light eterminable/Celestiall father etc.	
2547	O resplendent floure prynte þis in your mynde	
2547.3	*O Rex regum* in thy realme celestialle	
	The House of Stanley: *Flodden Field.*	
2547.5	O rote of trouth o princess to my pay	
	746	
2548	O Royalle hope to long y se the slepe	
	Translated from the French of Charles d'Orléans	
2549	O sapiencia of þe ffader surmountyng all thyng	
2549.5	O Schotland thow was flowering/in prosperus welthe	
2550	O sely Ankir that in thi selle	
	Associated with Charles d'Orléans	
2551	O sinfull man in to this mortall se/quhilk is the vaill etc.	
	'The Thre Deid Pollis.'	
	Robert Henryson	
2551.8	O sisters too/how may we do	
	376	
2552	O sonne supernall proceding/Fro the fader sumtyme goyng	
	James Ryman	

2552.5	O soorowe of all sorowes my harte doeth dere
	'The Lamentatyon of the Ladye Gryffythe'
	1005
2554	O spowsesse most dere most bry3t most clere
	James Ryman
2555	O spowsess of Crist and paramour/Most of vertu etc.
	James Ryman
2556	O sterre of Iacob glorye of Israell/Of all blissed etc.
	John Lydgate
	794
2557	O sterne so brycht þat gyfys lycht/til hewyne and haly kirk
2558	O Stedfast trouth displaye thi baner
	Translated from the French of Charles d'Orléans
2559	O stronge Iudith so full of myght/By thy vertu we be made fre
	James Ryman
2560	O Swete angell to me soo deere/that nyght and day etc.
2560.5	O swete harte dere & most best belouyd
2561	O sweete Ihesu so meke and mylde/*Fili Marie virginis*
	James Ryman
2562	O swete Ihesu we knowlege this/Thatte thow art kyng etc.
	James Ryman
2563	O sweete lady o uirgyn pure/*O mater summi iudicis*
	James Ryman
2564	O Swete thought y neuyr in no wise
	Translated from the French of Charles d'Orléans
2565	O swettest bawm of grettest excellence/Lady of this etc.
2567	O thou Fortune which hast the gouvernaunce
	Charles d'Orléans
2568	O þou fortune why art þou so inconstaunt/To make þis etc.
	54
2570	O thow ioyfull lyght eternall ye shyne/In glory etc.
	John Lydgate
2573	O thou pereles prynce of pees/With all myne herte y þe pray
2574	O thou3tful herte plunged in distresse/With slombir etc.
	John Lydgate
2575	O tryclyn of the trinite/Replete with all diuinite
	James Ryman
2576	O Vanite off vanytes & all is vanite
2577	O vernacule I honoure him and the/þat þe made etc.
	The *Arma Christi* or 'Arms of Christ'
	218, 220, 512, 756
2577.3	O uery lyfe of swetnes and hope
2577.5	O very lord o loue o god alas
2578	O uirgyn chast both furst and last/That in tyme past etc.
	James Ryman
2578.5	[O wauering W]orlde all wrapped in wretchidnes
	Perhaps Stephen Hawes
2579	O welle of swetnesse replete in euery veyne
	John Lydgate
2579.3	O what a treasure ys love certeyne
2579.5	O when be dyvyne deliberatioun/Of persons thre
2580	O wicket wemen wilfull and variable
	359
2581	O wooful hert forcast with heuynes
	Associated with Charles d'Orléans
2582	O woofull hert make thy complaynt/Why art thou etc.
	James Ryman
2583	O wofull hert profound in gret duresse
	Duke of Suffolk
2584	O wofull worlde deceyver of mankynde
2586	O worthy lord & most of myght/*Eterne rex altyssime*

Index of First Lines

2587	O worthi noble kyng Henry the ferthe/In whom the etc. John Gower **3**
2588.5	O ye all that ben or haue byn in dyssease 'Help Me to Weep' **343**
2589	O ȝe al whilk þ^t by me cummes and gothe/Attende etc. **182**
2590	O ye creatures that be resonable/the lyffe desyring etc. 'Dance of Macabre' John Lydgate
2591	O ye folkes that bene hard harted as a stone 'Dance of Macabre' John Lydgate
2593	O ȝe holy Angeles in ȝoure Ordres nyne/Patriarkes etc. **518**
2594	O ye lovers that pletyn for youre ryght **308**
2595	O ye louers which in gret heuynes/Haue led your lyfe etc. Duke of Suffolk
2596	O ȝe men þ^t by me wende/abyde a whyle & loke on me
2597	O ye my emperice I your seruant þis to you say Humfrey Newton
2599	O ye prynces þat prechyd hase my hert **338**
2602.2	*Oblesse oblesse que porar obler*/All hevy thought Associated with Charles d'Orléans
2602.6	Of a day of wel & of a day of wo
2603	Of a mayde Criste did not forsake/Mankyende to take etc. James Ryman
2604	Of a mon matheu þohte/þo he þe wynȝord wrohte 'The Labourers in the Vineyard' **171**
2605	Off a trewe loue clene & derne/Ichaue I-write þe a Ron **585**
2607	Off alle floures feirest fall on/And þat is Marie Moder fre **284, 331**
2608	Of all mankynde þat he made þat maste es of myghte **114**
2609	Of alle mennys disposicion naturalle/Philosophyrs wryten etc.
2610	Of alle þe bryddus þat euer ȝeyt were
2612	Offe al the enmys y^t I can fynd
2613	Of alle þe ioyus þat in þis worlde may be **60**
2613.5	Of al þe merueile of merlyn how he makys his mone
2614.5	Of Alle þe witti men and wise I warne Alle i þe wache 'The Papelard Priest' **302, 499, 876**
2615	Of alle þese kene conqueroures to carpe is oure kynde
2618	Of all þi frendes sche is þe flowre/Sche wyll the bryng etc.
2619	Off alle wemen þat euer were borne/That berys childer etc.
2619.2	Of all werkys in this worlde that ever were wrought
2619.5	Of bewtie yet she passith all
2622	Of euerykune tre/Of euerykune tre/þe haweþorne etc. **385, 431, 709**
2623	Off fayre most fayre as verry sorse and welle Associated with Charles d'Orléans
2623.3	Off Februar the fiftene nycht William Dunbar
2624	Of yiftis large in love hathe gret delite

2625	Off God and kynde procedith al bewte	
	John Lydgate	
2626	Of gretter cause may no wight him compleyne	
	'Complaint to my Lodesterre'	
	Perhaps by Geoffrey Chaucer	
2627	Of erbis xxiij/I wyl þe telle by and by	
	128, **388**, **427**, **894**	
2632.5	Off Lentren in the first mornyng	
	William Dunbar	
2634	Off lufe and trewt w^t lang continwans	
2635.5	Of mary a mayd withowt lesyng/this day was borne	
	490, **754**	
2636	Off mary crist was bore/w^{t}oute wem of aney hore	
2640	Of my lady wel me reioise I may	
	Thomas Hoccleve	
	839	
2644	Of one stable was is halle	
2645	Of on þat is so fayr and briȝt/*velud maris stella*	
	691	
2646	Of vr vife wittes a wel witiynge	
2647	Off oure lordes disciples þilke day tweye	
2648	Off passid tyme the plaster of no care	
	Translated from the French of Charles d'Orléans	
2649	Of Rybaudȝ y ryme and rede o my rolle	
	'Satire on the Retinues of the Great'	
	171, **704**, **763**, **799**, **876**	
2652.5	Of saynt Steuen goddes knyght/That preched the fayth	
2654	Off seruyng men I wyll begyne/Troley loley	
BR+2654.5	Of seuen scyences called lyberall	
2656	Of spayn take the clere light/þe rede gumme þat is so bright	
	Ascribed to Richard Carpenter in one MS	
2657	Off stryvys new and fraudulent falsenesse	
	Perhaps John Lydgate	
	359	
2657.5	Off seche cvmplayn	
2659.6	Of the blessed martire saynt Sebastyane/Whos greuous paynes non tell can	
2661	Of theyre nature they gretly theym Delyte	
2662	Of hem that writen ous tofore/The bokes duelle etc.	
	Confessio Amantis	
	John Gower	
	880	
2663	Of thes frer mynours me thenkes moch wonder	
	573, **890**	
2663.5	Of these sayynges Cristyne was aucteuresse	
	Earl Rivers	
2664	Off thynges all O myghty mayntoure	
2664.5	Of this chapell se here the fundacyon	
2665	Of this martir make we mende/*qui triumphauit hodie*	
	788	
2667	Of Troye throw hard fechynge/In half thirde yeris slew etc.	
2668	Of wyne awey the moles may ye wash	
2669	Oft in my thought full besily haue y sought	
	Translated from the French of Charles d'Orléans	
2671	Okure þrowe crafte of okerrers/Schewis hit on mony maners	
	346	
2674.5	*Omnes gentes plaudite*/Car nostre saueyour est ne	
2675	*Omnes gentes plaudite*/I saw myny bryddis setyn on a tre	
	964	

Index of First Lines

2677	An a byrchyn bonke þer bous arne bryʒt
	'De tribus regibus mortis'/'The Three Dead Kings'
	John Audelay
	96, 313, 626, 670, 677, 763, 888, 922
2678	On a dere day by a dale so depe/As I went thorow etc.
	'Fortis vt mors dileccio'
	936
2681	On Cristis day I vnderstond/An ere of whet of a mayd sprong
2682	On clife þat castell so knetered
	Perhaps by Humfrey Newton
	46, 240, 313
2683	On days when I am callit to þe scole/de matre et matertera
	184
2684	An ernemorwe de dayliʒt spryngeþ
	861
*2684.5	* . . . on earde/and alle þeo i-sceaftan þe to him to sculen
	'The Soul's Address to the Body'
	93, 226, 677, 770, 932, 1021
2685	On esterne day in þe dawing Ihū ros fro deth to lyue
	'The Story of the Resurrection'
	596
*2685.5	*On folie was myn silwyr leyd
	[Replaces *1580*.]
	136
2686	On grene/That kynered kene
	359
2687	On hire is al me lif ilong/Of hwam ich wule singe
	'An Orison to Our Lady'
	1020
2688	On hooly hilles whecche beoþe of gret Renoun
	John Lydgate
2689	On the rode I was put for þ^e/þ^u þ^t synneste sease for me
2690	On xij^{the} day came kingis thre/W^t golde encense etc.
	James Ryman
2691	On xij^{the} day this sterre so clere/Brought kings iij oute etc.
	James Ryman
2691.5	O beggur is wo/þat anoþer in þe town goo
2695	On hit is and ne haueþ noþer/sone ne suster ne nouþer broþer
2695.5	One only god thou shalt loue and worship perfytely
	525
2696	Oon sleyth the deer wythe an hookid arwe
	287
2699	Oppressid with thought langoure and hevynes
	Associated with Charles d'Orléans
2700	Or Crist into clouds gan flyeʒ vp so swiftly/þe pater etc.
	Robert Farnelay
	349
2702	Oure fader in heuen halowed be þi name/As Ihesus þi etc.
2703	Ure fader in heuene riche/þi name be haliid euer i-liche
2704	Vre fader in heuene y halʒed be þy name/þy kinedom etc.
	179, 393
2708	Oure fader þ^t art in heuen onon/I-blissed be þi name
2709	Vre feder þ^t in heouene is þ^t is al soðful iwis
	178
2710	Hure wader þat is in euene/þyn oli name beyn olid
	106, 119, 393
2711.5	Our gracyous god moost in magnyfycence
2714	Oure gracious god prynce of pite/That all this worlde etc.
	William Lychefelde

2716	Owre kynge went forth to Normandy
	The Agincourt Carol
	809
2717	Oure lady dude hyre churche gonge as felle in þe lay
2718	Oure ladi freo on Rode treo made hire mone
	'The Disputation between the Blessed Virgin and the Cross'
	696, 796, 922, 972
2719	Oure lady hade a childe bothe fryssh and gaye
2721	Our lord Ihc̄ crist, did appere/To saynt Edmunde etc.
2723.5	Ur lauerd þat alle michtes may/In even and erthe þi wille þou mai
2727	Our shyp is launched from the grounde/Blessed be God etc.
	236
2729	Oure wysdam þis world has be-raft/Pees of lond is lost etc.
2730	Out of þe blosme sprang a þorn/quan god hym-self etc
2731	Oute of the chaffe was pured this corne/& else the cherche etc.
2732	Owt of þe est a sterre shon bright/ffor to shew thre kynges lyght
2733	Owt of ȝour slepe aryse & wake/For God mankynd nowe etc.
	423
2734	Oute of youre slepe arryse and wake/For god oure etc.
	James Ryman
2735	Ouer all gatis that I haff gon/Among yᵉ grovys so fayer etc.
2736.2	Pallas Euander his song lieþ here
	John Trevisa
2736.4	Palmers all our faders were
2736.6	*Parce mihi* o lord most excellent
2736.8	Pardon alas why saye I so
2737	Passe forþe þou pilgryme and bridel wele þy beeste
2737.5	Passetyme with good cumpanye/I loue and shall unto I dye
	Attributed to Henry VIII
	716
2738	*Pater noster* most of myȝt/þᵗ al þys world hast wrot
2739	Pacience is a poynt þaȝ hit displese ofte
2740	Pacyens is peyntid with pride
2741	Pees and horkynt hal ifer/Ric and por yong and hold
	The Pride of Life
	132
2741.5	Pes lordyngs I prai ȝow pes/And of ȝour noys
	399
2742	Pees maketh plente/Plente maketh pride
	583, 915
2743.5	*Pecunia* maket wrong rith
2744	Perle plesaunte to prynces paye/To clanly clos in golde etc.
	Pearl
	255, 325, 789, 862, 903, 913, 944, 994
2745	Perles pryncos of euery place/Of heuen of erthe of see etc.
	James Ryman
2747	Peny is an hardy knyght/Peny is mekyl of myght
	55, 704
2749	Petir Petir prynce of aposteles alle
	Benet Howe
2750	Petyrs cheyre begynnethe Ver
2751	Phebus fonde first the craft of medicine
2753.5	Persyd wyth payne wounded full nygh the hart
2754	Piket hym and diket hym/On scorne saiden he
	321
2755.5	Petyously/Constrayned am I
	Sometimes ascribed to John Skelton
2756	Pitee that I haue sogthe so yere ago
	'The Compleynt unto Pite'
	Geoffrey Chaucer

Index of First Lines 503

2756.5	Pla-ce-bo/Who is there who
	'Phyllyp Sparowe'
	John Skelton
	857, 950
2757	Playn word entereth the hert/I-flarysched the eeres feedyt
2757.3	Please ytt your grace dere harte to gyff audyence
2757.5	Pleasure yt ys/to here Iwys
	Probably by William Cornish
	8
2758	Plesaunt bewte had woundid sore my hert
	Translated from the French of Charles d'Orléans
2762	Pore and hungri þat han nede
2763	Pore of spirit blessed be/þouȝ he be lord of richesse fele
2766.8	Pray we to God that all may gyde
2767	Prefulgent in pretyousness O synope the quene
2768	Presence of yow causith my comfort
	Associated with Charles d'Orléans
2769	Prute Couertise Slevþe Wreþe and Onde
2770	Pryde ys hede of alle kynne synne/þat makeþ mannes etc.
2771	Pryde is out & pride is ine/And pride is rot of euery synne
2773	Pride pierlies/envie endeles
2774	Pryd pryd wo thow be *mater uisyorum*
2775	Pryde þ^t is ouergart/algate has unquart
2776	Pryde wraþ and enuye/Scleuþe glotony and lechery
	106
2777	Preste ne monke ne ȝiy chanoun/Ne no man of religioun
	'The Orders of Cain'/'Against the Friars'
	453, 704
2778	*Primum nomen istius prisone vocatur*/A place to bury etc.
2779	Prince duke & erle lord knyght & squier
	James Ryman
2781	Princes most excellent born of blode riall/Chosen quene etc.
2782	Princesse af youth and floree of god-li-hede/[t]he per-fight etc.
	206, 650
2784	Problemes of olde lykenes and figures
	'The Churl and the Bird'
	John Lydgate
	950
2786	Put out his hed lyst nat for to dare
	John Lydgate
2787	*Quant homme deit parleir videat que verba loquatur*
	769
2789	Quene of hevyn make thou myrth/And prayse god etc.
2790	Qween of heuene Moder and may/Saue hem alle now etc.
2791	Quene of heuyn of helle eke Emperesse/lady of thys world etc.
	John Lydgate
2792	Quene of parage paradyse repayred I-wysse
2794	Rabe moyses þe good clerke/Spekes and preueþ a wunder etc.
2794.4	Rasyd is my mynde
2794.6	Reche me mi rocke quet alfled
*2797.5	* . . . red rosse fayre and sote
2798	Refresshe the castell of my poore hert
	Translated from the French of Charles d'Orléans
2799	*Regem regum* A mayde hath borne/To Save mankynde etc.
2800	*Regina celi* and Lady *letare*/Lemyng lely & in place of lyght
	292
2801	*Regina celi letare*/ffor crist thy sonne so dere
	James Ryman
2802	*Regina celi letare*/In whome fyrste þis worlde began
2803	*Regina celi* qwene of thy sowth

2803.5	Reioyse England/And vnderstande
	John Skelton
2804	Rejoice ye reames of Englond and of Fraunce
2805	Religious pepille leuyn in holynesse
	'The World Upside Down'
	341
2806	Remember man the paines and smarte/the Christ etc.
	590
2806.5	Remember man the payne and smart/Wich Christ
	590
2807	Remembre wele thou man mortall/And pryente wele etc.
	James Ryman
2808	Remembyr with reuerens the Maker of mankynde
	3
2809	Remembryng on the grete vnstabilness/The pleasaunt etc.
	John Lydgate
2811.5	Renowit ryall right reuerend and serene
	William Dunbar
2813	Retorne for shame retorne retorne ageyne
	Associated with Charles d'Orléans
2816	*Rex salamon summus* of sapience/The which the sterrid etc.
	591
2817	Riche and pouere ȝong and eld/þer whiles þou hauest etc.
	Hendyng
2819	Right as y herde this othir day tofore
	Translated from the French of Charles d'Orléans
2820	Ryght as pouerte causeth sobreness/and febleness etc.
	'On the Evils of Prosperity'
	457, 476
2820.3	Right as the rose excelleth all floures *inter ligna floriga*
2820.5	Ryght as the sterne of day begouth to schyne
	'The Golden Targe'
	William Dunbar
	344, 566
2821	Right best beloved & most in assurance
2821.3	Rycht airlie on Ask Weddinsday
	William Dunbar
2821.5	Rycht fane wald I my quentance mak/withe Sir penny
2822	Ryght gentyll harte of greane flouryng age
2823	Ryht goodly flour to whom I owe seruyse
	Duke of Suffolk
2824	Ryht godely fressh flour of womanhode
	H. Bowesper
2825	Riht myhty prynce and let it be your wille/Condescende etc.
	John Lydgate
2827	Right ny myn hert with my bosom lo
	Translated from the French of Charles d'Orléans
2827.5	Right wel beloved prentise/I commande me to your gentilnesse
	'A letter send by R.W. to A.C.'
	945
2828	Right yongly fayre replet with goodlihed
	Associated with Charles d'Orléans
2829	Riȝtful dom is ouer cast/& troupe is fer agon
	Bishop Bartholomew of Exeter
2830.5	Robyn Hod in scherewod stod
2831	Robene sat on gud grene hill/Kepand a flok of fe
	'Robene and Makyne'
	Robert Henryson
	164, 297, 755
2831.4	Rome no þing is þere to þe
	John Trevisa

Index of First Lines 505

2831.6	*Rorate celi desuper*/Hevins distill your balmy schouris
	William Dunbar
2832	Ronde in schapynge
2832.2	Rutterkyn is com vnto oure towne
	Perhaps by John Skelton.
2832.5	Rowe the bote Norman/rowe to thy lemman
2833	Royal Banerys vnrolled of the kyng/Towarde his Batayle etc.
	Ascribed to John Lydgate
2835	Sayde þys vntrewe man himself for to schende
2864	Seynt Bernard seiþ and soo seye I/In her counseill etc.
	326
2865	Seint Bernard seiþ in his Bok/þat Man is worm etc.
2880	Seint Cudbert was i-bore here in Engelonde/God dude etc.
2886	Seint edmund þe confessour þ^t lyþ at pounteneye
2892	Seint elene I þe pray/To helpe me at my last day
2902	Saynt George of kyngryk of Capidous so clere
	184
2903	Seynt Iorge our Lady kny3th/He walked day he walked noy3th
2924	Seynt Iohn for grace þou craue/þat of his mercy etc.
2942	Saynte Ione þe gospellere vs telles
2951	Seinte Iuliane com of hey3e men as we findeþ i-writ
2963	Seynt luke in his godspel bryngeth ous to munde
	William Herebert
2988	Seinte marie clane uirgine/moder ihū cristes nazarene
	St Godric's hymn to the Virgin
	St Godric
	61, 130, 151, 178, 284, 703, 770, 846
2992	Seinte marie leuedi brist/Moder thou art of muchel mist
	381
2993	Seint marie magdalene lady ffair and brithy
	518
2995	Seinte Mari moder milde/*mater salutaris*
3012	Sayn Matheu sais in our godspelle/þat crist com dunward etc.
3027	Seynt Mi3el & sint gabriel/And alle goddes angelis also wel
3028	Saint Michael goddes angell clere/and saint Austin etc.
	'The Gast of Gy' (*Spiritus Guidonis*)
3031	Sainte Nicolaes godes druð/tymbre us faire scone hus
	Prayer to St Nicholas
	St Godric
	130, 151, 509, 846, 906, 1021
3033	Seynt Nicholas þe holie Man þat guod confessour was
3034	Seynt Nicholas was of gret poste/for he worchepid etc.
3038	Sent Patrik thorow god all myght/Kam for to preche etc.
3040	Saynt paule þe apostyl þus sais he/Dos al your workys etc.
3057	Saynt steuen þe first martere/He ched his blod in herþ here
	John Audelay
3058	Seynt Steuen was a clerk in king herowdis halle
	90, 829, 986
3065	Sainte valentyne of custome yeere by yeere
	'Valentine to Our Lady'
	John Lydgate
3069	Salamon sat & sayde many soth sawes/Wordis þ^t walkys etc.
	162
3070	*Saluator mundi domine*/ffader of heuene y-blessed þu be
3071	*Saluator mundi domine*/To the Ihesu make I my moon
3072	*Salue decus pauperum*/In whom be vertuys ryve
	James Ryman
3074	*Salue* wyth all obaysans to God in humblesse
3074.3	Sanctus beda was iboren her on bretone mid us
	The First Worcester Fragment
	226, 932, 1021

BR+*3074.4*	Sanguine is þe fyrst, þe ii fleumatyk
3074.6	Sauns remedye endure must I
BR+*3074.8*	Saturne disposyth a man to melancolye
3075	Saviour of the world saue ous
3076	Savyoure of this worlde we pray/Lord that has saved etc.
	James Ryman
3077	Saver of world lord and mantenowr
3078	Say me viit in þe brom/teche me wou i sule don
	785
3078.5	Sey nou man quat þinket þu
3079.3	Sey þu vessel of wrechednesse
3079.7	Saye well ys a worthy thyng
3079.8	Say well or be styll/Suffyr and haue all thy wyll
3080	Skottes out of Berwik and of Abirdene
	'The Battle of Bannockburn'
	Laurence Minot
	76, 359, 704, 794, 801
3081	See & here & held þe stylle/If þou wylt leue & haue þi wylle
3083	Se meche sey lytyll and lerne to suffre in tyme
	Ascribed to R. Stokys
	213
3085	Semenaunt is a wonder þing/It begylyt boþe kny3t and kyng
3087	Serve þi God trwly/And þe world bysely
3088	Sette and saue yf thow wyll haue/Waste and wante etc.
3092	Shalle I by whome all thing began/Dere moder shalle I soo
	James Ryman
3093	Shall I dere moder as I wille/Dere moder shall I soo
	James Ryman
3094	Shalle I moder mayden & wyfe/My dere spowse shall I soo
	James Ryman
3095	Shalle I that am so high in trone/Moder shalle I doo soo
	James Ryman
3096	Shalle I that heuen & erth did make/Dere moder shall I soo
	James Ryman
3097	Shalle I that wrought althing of nought/Dere moder etc.
	James Ryman
3097.6	She is gentyll & also wysse
3098	Sche saw y^{eis} women all bedene/both for sorow and for tene
3098.3	She þat hathe a wantan eye/& can convey ytt wysselye
3098.5	Sche þat I loue alle þermost & loþist to begile
	434
3099	Shulde y me make a lady newe fy fy
	Associated with Charles d'Orléans
3100	Schrude and fede and drench and hereborior þe pouere
3101	Siknes of hire synne sorfulliche was i-schowid
3100.5	Siker to dele to alle maner men/To tellen of is time nouere no man kan
3102	Si3e and sorwe depeli/moorne and wepe inwardli
	100
3104	Silly sicht i seich vnsembly forte se/A fwil ar hit was etc.
3104.5	Simenel hornes/ber non þornes/alleluya
3106	Sinne & fulþe onli for sake/to clennesse of lif for mi loue tac
3109	Senful man be-þing & se/Quat peine i þole for loue of þe
3110	Synful man loke vp & see/how reufulli I hyng on rode
3111	Synful man ne dred þe nouth/þou þe þenke a wikke þouth
3112	Synful man thou art vnkynde
3113	Syng I wold butt alas *decedunt prospera grata*
	'On the Times'
	952
3114	Sing lorel syng/Euell Ioye the wyng
	1002

Index of First Lines

3115	Synguler shepperde gardeyn of cristis folde
	Attributed to John Lydgate
3117	Sir Dauid þe Bruse was at distance
	'The Battle of Neville's Cross'
	Laurence Minot
	198, 359, 704
*3117.4	* . . . sire he seis and sonenday is nouwe
3117.5	Schir I complane off injuris
	William Dunbar
3117.7	Schir Jhon Sinclair begowth to dance
	William Dunbar
3117.8	Schir Johine the Rose ane thing thair is compiled
	'The Flyting of Dunbar and Kennedie'
	William Dunbar
	830, 901
3118.5	Sur songe in tyme past hath ben doune a doune
3118.6	Schir ȝe have mony seruitours
	William Dunbar
*3119.5	* . . . sit amonges the knyghtes all/ . . . at te counsell
3121	Syn alle men naturally desyre/To konne o eterne etc.
	Thomas Hoccleve
3122	Syth alle that in thys world hath been *in rerum natura*
	417, 819
3123	Sith Criste hath take both flesshe & blode/For thy clennes etc.
	James Ryman
3124	Syn cursid deth hath taken my maystre
	Translated from the French of Charles d'Orléans
3125	Sith fortune hathe me set thus nethis wyse
	54
3126	Sith Gabriell gan grete/Vre ledi Mari swete
	Sir Pers of Birmingham
3127	Sithe god hathe chose þe to be his knyȝt
	809
3128	Syn y may not askape me fer nor nere
	Translated from the French of Charles d'Orléans
3129	Syth in thys world þer can no þyng be sewre
3131	Sith it concluded was In the trinite/that the son of god etc.
3131.5	Sin it is lo/that I muste goo/& pass yow ffroo/my lady dere
3132	Syn hit is so we nedis must depart
	Associated with Charles d'Orléans
3133	Sithyn law for wylle begynnyt to slakyn
3134	Syn loue hath cast me banysshe etc.
	Translated from the French of Charles d'Orléans
3135	Soethþe mon shal hoenne wende/And nede deȝen at þen ende
	William Herebert's translation of Bozon
3136	Sith of right thou mayst not forsake/Mankyende etc.
	James Ryman
3137	Sythene that Bretayne was biggede and Bruyttus it aughte
	Wynnere and Wastoure
3140	Syn that y absent am thus from yow fare
	Translated from the French of Charles d'Orléans
	365
3141	Syn that y am yowre haue been and shall
	Translated from the French of Charles d'Orléans
3142	Syn that y haue a nonnparall maistres
	Charles d'Orléans
3143	Syth that ye lyste to be my costes/And in your boke etc.
	John Lucas
3143.5	Sythen the furste þat were here or may be
	555

3144		Siþe þe sege and þe assaut watȝ sesed at Troye
		Sir Gawain and the Green Knight
		45, 189, 240, 313, 622, 843, 895, 970, 994
3144.5		Syne the tyme I knew yow fyrst
3145		Syth the tyme þat cryst ihesu/Thorough hys grace and vertu
		Guy of Warwick (First version)
3146		Sythe þe tyme þat god was borne/And Crystendome etc.
		Guy of Warwick (Second version)
3147		Sithen þis world was ful of honde
3148		Sith thou hast born the kyng of grace/That sittith etc.
		James Ryman
3149		Sith thou hast born the kyng of grace/The lorde etc.
		James Ryman
3151		Sen trew vertew encressis dignytee
3152		Sith thy sonne is both god and man/And by thy meane etc.
		James Ryman
3154.5		Sithe ye haue me chalyngyd M[aster] Garnesche
		John Skelton
		799, 830
3155		Sitteþ alle stille and herkeneþ to me/þe Kyng of Alemaigne etc.
		'The Song of the Battle of Lewes'
		171, 223, 297, 704, 876, 914, 1007
3157		Sluggy & slowe in spetynge muche/Cold & moyst etc.
3160		So as I lay this other nyght/In my bed tournyng vp so doun
3161		So blessid a sight it was to see/how mary rokked etc.
3162		So fayre so fresche so goodely an to se
		Charles d'Orléans
3162.5		So fer I trow from remedy
3163		So fresshe bewte so moche goodlynes
		Associated with Charles d'Orléans
3163.5		So gret vnkyndnes wythoute diseruyng
3164		So hath myn hert caught in remembraunce
		'Womanly Noblesse – Balade that Chauncier made.'
		Geoffrey Chaucer?
3165		So ys emprented in my remembrance
		Signed 'Walterus ffr'
		234, 252
3167.3		So longe ic haue lauedi/yhoued at þi gate
3168		So noble medesyne ne so sovereyne
		Perhaps by Lydgate
3168.4		So put yn fere I dare not speke
		746
3170		Solomon seyth ther is none accord
3171		Sum be mery and sum be sade
3172		Som do entende/there yowthe for to spende
3173		Svm man goth stille of wysdam and resoun
		Perhaps by John Lydgate
3173.5		Summe maner mater worlde I fayne meve
		'De Veritate & Consciencia'
		293
3174		Sume men sayon þat y am blak
		858
3179		Some tyme Y loued as ye may see
3180		Somtyme Y louid so do Y yut
3181		Sum tyme y was a poore serviture
		Associated with Charles d'Orléans
3182		Som tyme in Fraunce dwelled a plowman
3184		Some tyme in Rome a pope þer was/þat hade a moder etc.
3187		Some tyme þer was a noble man/Whos name was clepyd etc.

Index of First Lines

3190	Some tyme this world was so stedfast and stable
	'Lak of Stedfastnesse'
	Geoffrey Chaucer
3193.5	Somewhat musing/and more mourning
	Earl Rivers
	744
3194	Sum while ich was wiþ sunne i-bounde/And sunne me etc.
3197	Son of Priamus Gentyll paris of Troy
3199	Sonderliche his man astoned/In his owene mende
	William of Shoreham
3199.3	Son crokith the tre/that crokid will be
3199.5	Sore I sye & sore I may
3199.8	Sore this dere strykyn ys
3200.5	Sorwe of his kare/ioye of his weilfare
3201	Sori is þe fore/from bedde to þe flore
3203	Sothly by Arthwrys day/Was Bretayne yn grete nobyle
3206	Souerayne Immortal euerlastyng god
	Epitaphium eiusdam Ducis Glowcestre, AD 1447
	Perhaps John Lydgate
	360
3206.5	Souerayn lorde in erth most excellent
3206.8	Soveraygne lorde welcome to your citie
	John Lydgate
3207	Souereyns and serys ȝyf it be ȝour wylle
3208	Spel yet I wals spek if I cuþe/War ani mirþis etc.
3209	Spend and God schal send/Spare and armor care
3209.5	Stanche blood stanche blood/So dyd Noes flood
	610
3211	Stond wel moder ounder rode/Bihold þi child etc.
	'Dialogue between the Virgin and Christ on the Cross'
	171, 230, 539, 860, 953, 962
3212	Steddefast crosse inmong alle oþer
3213	Stedes ther stumbelyd in that stownde/That stod stere etc.
	'The Battle of Agincourt'
	704
3214	Stel is gud I sey no odyr/So mowyn wemen be kaymys brodyr
**3216.5*	* . . . stod ho þere neh/þat leueli leor wid spald ischent
3217	Storyis to rede are delitabill/Suppose that thai be nocht etc.
	Bruce
	John Barbour
3218.3	Straunge men þat needeþ/þat lond
3218.5	Stroke oul and schape oule and evere is oule oule
3219	Strong it hus to flitte/Fro worldes blisse to pitte
	1009
3220	Such a lady seke I neuer non/*Sicut tu maria*
	454
3220.7	Such as ye be sone time ware wee/Suche as we are suche schall ye be
3221	Somer is comen & winter gon/þis day biginniz to longe
	604, 691
3222	Somer is comen wiþ loue to toune
	'The Thrush and the Nightingale'
	72, 145, 272, 319, 536, 565, 609, 736, 824, 941, 954, 984
3223	Svmer is icumen in
	'The Cuckoo Song'/Summer Canon/Reading Rota
	40, 79, 207, 243, 244, 245, 246, 248, 249, 263, 265, 268, 272, 291, 297, 394, 426, 466, 483, 583, 593, 625, 682, 704, 708, 810, 821, 828, 844, 912, 1001, 1012
3224	Somer þat rypest mannes sustenance/With holsum hete etc.
	Thomas Hoccleve
3225	*Surge mea sponsa* so swete in sight/Com se thy sone etc.
3225.5	*Surrexit Dominus de sepulchro*/The Lord is rissin
	Attributed to William Dunbar

3226	*Sustine abstine* kepe well in yowr mynde
3227	Swarte smekyd smethes smateryd wythe smoke
	385, 526, 550, 726, 789, 801, 811, 997
3228	Swete and benynge moder & may/Turtill trew etc.
	William Huchen
3228.3	Swete harte be trwe/chavnge for [no] newe/Come home to me agene
3228.5	Swet harte I loue yow more feruent than my fader
3229	Swet hert/mercy/For smert/Avert
	Associated with Charles d'Orléans
3231	Swete Ihesu crist to þe/A gulti wrecche Ich ȝelde me
3232	Swete ihesu crist to þe/a synful wreche I ȝelde me
3233	Swete ihesu crist to þe/Culpable wrecche y ȝeld me
3234	Swet ihc̄ hend and fre/þat was i-strauȝt on rode tre
	Friar Michael Kildare
	161, 238
3235	Swet Ihesus is cum to vs/This good tym of Crystmas
3236	Suete ihū king of blysse/my huerte loue myn herte lisse
	171
3238	Swete Ihesu now wol I synge/To þe a song of loue longinge
	822
3238.3	Swet Ihesu that on the Rode/Boutast us
3239	Swete Ihesu hwar was thy gylt
3240	Swete lady now ȝe-wys/As ȝe bene quene of heuen blys
	200
3241	Swete leuedy synte marie/fful of grace and curteysie
3242	Suete leman Y deye for þi loue
3242.5	Swete lamman dhin are
3243.3	Sweit rois of vertew and of gentilness
	William Dunbar
	682
3244	Swete saynt anne we þe beseche/þᵘ pray fore vs etc.
	John Audelay
3245	Suete sone reu on me & brest out of þi bondis
	539
3246.5	Swynes halle/fendes falle
3247	Swiþe muche neode hit is/þat vche mon be war and wys
3248.5	Take a wobster þat is leill
3251	Take hede man how þe Iewes dyd cry
3252.5	Take hede vnto my fygure here abowne
	616, 782
3254	Take no god but oon in heuen
3255	Take take this cosse atonys my hert
	Translated from the French of Charles d'Orléans
3256	Take þe sevenþ in ordre sette/Lyneal of þe ABC
	'Devenayle par Pycard'
	456
3258	Tancret that was prynce of Salern
3256.1	Take thou this treatise thi time therin to vse
3259	Tappster fyll another ale
	55
3260	Tax has tenet us alle/*probat hoc mors tot validorum*
	On the Rebellion of Jack Straw (1381)
	926, 952
3261	*Te deum Laudamus* to the lord sovereyne
	Attributed to John Lydgate
3262	Teche ich man with charyte/To kepe godys bydyngs etc.
3264	Tel nouth þi frend al [þᵗ þu wost]
3265	Tell we nowe of þᵗ ȝere/that begynnyth wᵗ Ienyver
	216
3265.5	Tell you I chyll/If that ye wyll

Index of First Lines 511

	'The Tunnyng of Elynour Rummyng'
	John Skelton
	843
3267	That archaungell shynyng full bright/Came vnto Marie etc.
	James Ryman
3270	þat good þenkeþ good may do/And god wol helpe him þer-to
3270.5	That goodly las/When she me bas
3271	That hart my hart hath in suche grace
3272	That holy clerke seint Augustyne/Seith now is tyme etc.
	James Ryman
	569
3273	That y ȝaf þat ys myn
3274	þat I hete & þat I drinke may I haue
3275	þat y spende þat I had
3277	þat I wrecche þᵗ senful was/Mouwe fynde merci etc.
3278	þat ylke day be out of Muinde
3279	That ilke man wole lerne wel/To loue god wiþ al etc.
	'Loue þat god loueth'
	143, 936
3281	þat ys mery to be a wyf
*3281.5	þat it apertly was apayed for profit þat he feld
	William of Palerne
3282	That lawe hathe noo ryȝte
3283	That lord þᵗ lay in asse stalle/cam to dye for vs Alle
3284	That meyden mylde here childe did kepe/As moders etc.
	James Ryman
3287	þat mantell þe kinge to Vlfride lente
3289	þat may ȝe be saynte martyne se/ffor in his lif þus writen etc.
3291	That pasaunte Goddnes the Rote of all vertve
	271, 365
3292	þat schort was turned into longe
3293	þat þu crye to hy[m]/wiþ sorwe of herte etc.
3297	That was Ihū oure saueour/The oonly sone of gode myghty
3297.3	That was my ioy is now my woo and payne
3297.5	That was my woo is nowe my most gladness
	746
3302	þat ȝe forbere ȝow fro alle vylene
3302.5	The aunciente acquaintance madam between vs twayn
	John Skelton
3303	The aungell seide of high degree/Haile ful of grace etc.
	James Ryman
3304	The aungell seyde of high degree/Haill full of grace god etc.
	James Ryman
3305	The angel to þe virgyn said
	John Audelay
	771
3305.8	The armes of crist both god and man/Seynt Pieter þe pope discryued
3306	The ax was sharpe the stokke was hard
	656
3306.3	The bakarse boy is vere cranke
3307	The best tre ys ye take entent/*Inter ligna fructifera*
3308	The bysshope Scrope that was so wyse/Nowe is he dede etc.
	809
3310	þe blessinge of heuene king/And of his moder þat swete þing
	'The Sayings of St Bernard'
	171, 391, 547
3311	þe blisse of oure herte al it is ago/Al vre wele etc.
3312	þe borys hed haue we in broght
3313	The boris hed in hondes I brynge
	622
3314	The boris hede in hond I bryng/With garlond gay in etc.

3315	The borys hede that we bryng here/Betokeneth a prince etc. **59**
3318	The boke of marchalsie here shall begyn
3318.2	The bred is flesche in our credance
3318.4	The burne ys this worlde blynde
3318.7	The catte the ratte and Louell our dogge/Rulyth all England vnder a hogge Wyllyam Colyngbourne
3321	The chief gynnyng of grace and of vertue/To exclude etc. John Lydgate
3322	The cyte is bond that shuld be fre
3322.3	The cok seithe in his songe/that thow dost thin husbonde wrong
3324	The krycket & þe greshope wentyn here to fy3gh[t] **327**
3325	þo dedtur (?) so is fals and falende/Stille and eke stalkinge
3327	The double sorwe of Troilus to tellen *Troilus and Criseyde* Geoffrey Chaucer **70, 75, 148, 271, 295, 317, 577, 741, 755, 807, 872, 876, 947, 949, 984, 987**
3328	The false fox came vnto oure croft 'The False Fox' **55, 357**
3328.5	The ffather of heuyn from aboue/Hathe sent his son **490, 754**
3329	The Fader of Heuene his owyn Sone he sent
3330	The Fadyr of pytte and most of myserycorde/That alle etc.
3331	The faders sonne of heven blis/By a virgine to vs come is James Ryman
3332	The faders sonne of heven blis/Of a pure mayde man etc. James Ryman
3333	The ffaders sonne of heuen blis/Of a pure mayde man etc. James Ryman
3334	The faders sone of heuen blys/Thatte is the lord etc. James Ryman
3339	þe fende oure foe ne may vs dere
3343	þe ferste day of 3ol han we in mynde/how man was born etc.
3344	The fyrst day wan crist was borne/There sprong a rose etc.
3346	þe furst h^t is þi heryng/loke þu turne away þyne ere John Audelay
3347	þe ferste Ioye as I 3^u telle/w^t mary met seynt Gabrielle
3347.5	The first vj yeres of mannes byrth and aege **525**
3348	The first stok-fader of gentilesse/What man etc. 'Gentilesse' Geoffrey Chaucer
3350	þe flesches lust may þ^u nou3t olyue bettur quench
3352	The fote folke/Puthe the Scotes in the polke
3352.5	The formyst fadere þat formed 3ou alle *Lucidus and Dubius* **930**
3353	þe formest of þese bestes þre/is worst of alle astou mait se **682, 1001**
3354.5	The frutefull sentence and the noble werkes
3356	þe garlond þ^t of þorn is wroth/an stikid on my crune
3357	þe 3ates of parais þoruth eue weren i-loken
3357.5	The gentyll poets under cloudy figures *The Comfort of Lovers* Stephen Hawes **987**
3359	The gladsom Byrd þe deys mesanger
3360	The god Cupide and Venus the goddes Translated from the French of Charles d'Orléans.

Index of First Lines

3361	The God of loue A benedicte
	'The Book of Cupid'/'The Cuckoo and the Nightingale'
	Sir John Clanvowe
	312, 319, 824, 950
3361.3	þe gode mon on is weie
	709
3363	The good wyf wold a pylgremage/vnto þe holly londe
3365	þe grace of godde and holi chirche/þroȝ uertu of þe trinite
	161
3366	þe grace of god ful of miȝt/þat is king and euer was
	161
3367	þe grace of ihū fulle of miȝte/þroȝ prier of ure swete leuedi
	161
3370	The gret disese of seekfull anoyaunce
	Translated from the French of Charles d'Orléans
3371	The grete god full of grace/Of whome all goodness grew & gan
	126
3372.1	The gret vertus of oure elders notable/Ofte to remembre
	The moral proverbs of Cristyne
	Translated by Anthony Woodville, Earl of Rivers
3372.5	The hare wente þe markyth scharlyt forto syll
	852
3374	The heuenly sterre so bright & clere/That fedde etc.
	James Ryman
3375	The hedgehoge will the cookcok fed
	350
3376	The high Astrapotent auctor of all/Vnder whos clayme etc.
3376.5	The hye desire that Y have for to se
3378	The high fader of blisse aboue/Hathe sent his sonne etc.
	James Ryman
3379	The high fader of blisse aboue/Sent his owne sonne etc.
3381	The herrere degre þe more wys/þe gretter worschip etc.
3382	The hyere men clymmeth the sorere ys the falle
3385	The holy gost is to the sent/ffro the fadyr omnypotent
3390	The incorrupt wombe virginall/Hath borne the king etc.
	James Ryman
3391	The infinite power essenciall/Me thoght I sawe verrement
3396	The ioly tyme the first fresshe day of may
	Translated from the French of Charles d'Orléans
3397	þe ioye of oure herte is ago/oure song is turnyd into woo
3398	The ioye or ur hert is withere to wo/The floures of ur etc.
3400	þe king of heuen mid us be/þe fend of helle fram vs te
	161
3402	The Kyng of Kynges regnyng ouer al/Which stablisshid etc.
	Thomas Hoccleve
3403	þe kinges baner bigan to sprede/On þe crouch etc.
3405	þe kynges baneres beth forth y-lad/þe rode tokne etc.
	William Herebert
3405.5	The knyght knokett at the castell gate
3406	The laborous and the most mervelous werkes
3407	The laddre of heuene I meene charitee/Comandith vs etc.
	'Address to Sir John Oldcastle'
	Thomas Hoccleve
	260
3408	The lade dame fortune is bothe frende & foo
3409	The last tyme I the wel woke
	459, 484
3410	The law of god be to þe thy rest/The flesh þy sacrifice etc.
3411	þe lif of þis world/Ys Reuled wiþ wynd

3412	The lyfe so shorte the crafte so longe to lerne
	The Parlement of Foules
	Geoffrey Chaucer
	571, 801, 824, 941, 950
3413	ðe leun stant on hille/and he man hunten here
	The Bestiary
	932
3413.3	The lytyll prety nyȝhtygale among the leuys grene
3413.6	The lyver maketh a man to love
3414	The longe nyghtes whan euery creature/Shuld have etc.
	'The Balade of Pite' or 'A Complaint to his Lady'
	Geoffrey Chaucer
3415	The lord þat is a howsholder/wᵗ fayer festis folk
	696
3416	þe luf of god who so will lere/In his hert þe name of Ihū etc.
3416.5	The lover trwe/In colour blew
3418	The man that I loued altherbest/In al thys contre etc.
3419	þe mon þat is of wommon I-bore/His lyf his heere but a þrowe
3420	þe man þᵗ luste to liuen in ese/Or eny worschupe etc.
	'Who Says the Sooth, He Shall be Shent'
	537, 816, 933
3421	þe mon that þe hare i-met/Ne shal him nevere be the bet
	189, 907
3422	þe man þᵗ wylle of lechecraft lere/Rede over þis boke etc.
	531
3423	The man that wol to the to hond swerd lere bothe close etc.
3424	The masse is of so high Dignytee/þᵗ no thing to it etc.
3426	The mede is flowe the grace is goon
	Associated with Charles d'Orléans
3428	þe might of þe ffader Almihti/þe wit of þe sone Alwitti
	The Pricke of Conscience
	118
3431	The myghty William Duk of Normandy/By iust tale etc.
	John Lydgate
	924
3432	The milde Lomb i-sprad o rode/Heng bi-hornen al o blode
	539, 794
3433	þe mynde of þy swet passion Iesu teres it telles
3434	The merthe of alle þis londe/maketh þe gode husbonde
3435	The mone in the mornyng merely rose
	341
3436	The more I go the further I am behynde
	191
3437	The more I goo the ferther I am behinde
	191
3438	þe most worthye she is in towne
3438.3	The moder full manerly & mekly as a mayd
3438.6	The mowse goth a brode/When þe cat is not lorde
3438.8	The name of Iohan wel prays I may
3439	The next tyme my lady and mastres
	Translated from the French of Charles d'Orléans
3439.5	þe nyȝtyngale synges/þat all þe wod rynges
3443	The nowmer of Ihū cristes wowndes/Ar fyve þowsande etc.
	512
3443.5	The nunne walked on her prayer
	490
3444	The ordre of foolis ful yore agoon begonne
	John Lydgate
3445	The *pater noster* to expone may no man hit prise
	John Audelay
3444.5	The owle to þe stone and the stone to the owle

Index of First Lines

3445.5	The Perse owt off Northombarlande and a vowe to God mayd he
	The Hunting of the Cheviot
3446	The parfyte life to put in remembraunce
	Probably by John Lydgate
3447	The plesaunt lemys of yowre eyen clere
	Associated with Charles d'Orléans
3448	The plowman plucked up his plow/Whan midsomer etc.
	The Plowman's Tale
	879
3449	The propyrte of every shyre/I shal you telle and ye will here
3450	The prophesy fulfilled is/Of the prophetes now alle & sume
	James Ryman
3451	The prophete in his prophecye/lernith vs yn an holy lore
	584
3452.8	þe rede stremes renning
3454	The ryȝth wey to heuen Ihesu þ^u me shewe
	339
3455	The Rote is ded the Swanne is goone
3457	The Ros it es the fairest flour
3458	The secund day of fayre fresshe lusty may
	Translated from the French of Charles d'Orléans
3460	The shepard upon a hill he satt
	989
3461	The shype ax seyd unto the wryght
3461.5	The sigh . . . ysse
3461.8	The sight which ferst my hart dyd strayne
3462	þe siker soþe who so seys/Wiþ diol dreye we our days
	'The Four Foes of Mankind'
	48, 694, 983, 992
3463	The synne of pryde nys noȝt in schroude
3464	þe slauwe man is but a driȝe tre þ^t no froit wil beren
3464.5	The smaller pesun the more to pott
3465	The smyling mouth and laughyng eyen gray
	Associated with Charles d'Orléans
	566
3467	The sonne of god and king of blis/Whoos ioye and blis etc.
	James Ryman
3468	The sonne of god hath take nature/Of mylde Mary etc.
	James Ryman
3469	The sonne of god oure lorde Ihesus/Ys man becum etc.
	James Ryman
3470	The sone of god so full of myght/Came downe fro heuen trone
	James Ryman
3471	The sonne of god thatte all hath wrought/To take nature etc.
	James Ryman
3472	þe sunne of grace hym schynit in/in on day quan it was morwe
3473	The son of the fader of hevyn blis/Was born als thys day etc.
3474	þeo soþe luue a-mong vs beo/Wyþ-vten euch endynge
3475	þe saule haskis ryȝt as wrytin is in storie
3476	þe saules þat to purgatory wendes
3477	The Sofferent thatt seithe evere seycrette/He saue you all etc.
	The Pageant of the Shearmen and Taylors, a Coventry Corpus Christi Play
	295
3477.6	The stern of heven modre Marye
3479	Ye sonne ys here in his syne/þ^t is seson forto reyne
3481	þe sononday is godis oun chosyn day
	John Audelay
3482	The sermoungynge pleasure who can expresse
3483	The ten commawndementis that I haue broke
*3483.5	*þe tent ioy had our lady at þe feste of Architriclyne
3484	The tixt of holy writ men sayn/Hit sleep but glose be among

3485	þe þing þᵗ þu mauth lesen clepet nouth þin owen
3486.5	The thowghts within my brest
	Ascribed to Henry VIII
3487.5	The tyme of youthe is to be spent
	Henry VIII
3488	The tyme so long the payn ay more and more/That in etc.
	Duke of Suffolk
3490.6	þe Tree of þe cros is wol bryȝte
	Friar Nicolas Philip
	919
3491	The trewe processe of Englysch polycye
	'The Libel of English Policy'
	260, 369, 914
3492.3	The xij degres of pacyence thou mayst beholde her
3493	The vnware woo that commeth on gladnesse
3496	þe way of sleythe & of sothnes
3496.6	The wednesdayes/astynence and holy fast
3497	ðe wes bold ȝebyld er þu i-boren were
	'The Grave'
	93, 137, 226, 661, 677, 687, 770, 1021
3498	The well of vertwe and flour of womanheid
3498.5	The whele of fortune who can hold/or stablysh yt
3499	The wisdome of þe fadir/þe treuþe of þe hiȝ king
3500	þe wise herte & understondingge/Sal kepen him selue etc.
3501	þe wyse mon in his bok haþ þis seying/þat þe biginnyng etc.
3502	The wysman seyde to hys sones/thenk on þise prouerbis etc.
3503	The worlde so wyde the ayre so remuable/The sely man etc.
	191
3504	The worlde so wide th'aire so remuable/The cely man
	191
3505	þe werd wᵗ is faired/þᵗ be-nemet man is sith
3506	þe worm on þe treo/and þe hul on þe see
	925
3507	þo worthyest þing most of godnesse/In al þis world is þo messe
	The Lay Folk's Mass Book
	960
3510.5	þe þanne we beseken þi seruans do good
3512	[þe]h þet hi can wittes fule-wis/of worldes blisse habbe etc.
	770, 935, 1021
3513	They thou the vulf hore hod to preste
	968
3515	Then all your doyngs schold here in earthe/Present the etc.
3515.5	þan creu cacces An þan was it dey rybaude
3516.5	þanne is abstinence of worþinesse/Wan man fastet fro wikednesse
3517	þene latemeste dai wenne we sulen farren
	'The Latemest Day'/'The Last Day'
	93, 1020, 1021
3518	Then shall stynte þat now is kud
3520	þer as al þe herte of man
3521	þer ben foure thinges causing gret folye
	632
3521.5	Ther be iiij thynges full harde for to knaw
3522	Ther ben iij poyntis of mischeff
3522.5	There ben women there ben wordis/There ben gese there ben tordys
	699
3523	þer beoþe foure thinges þat makeþ man a fool
	632
3525	There blows a colde wynd todaye todaye
	236
3526	þer is a babe born of a may/In saluacion of vs
3527	Ther ys a blossum sprong of a thorn/to saue mankynd etc.

Index of First Lines 517

3529	þer is a busch þat is forgrowe/Crop hit welle etc.
3530	There is a floure spronge of a welle/To alle mankyende etc.
	James Ryman
3530.5	Ther ys a saying bothe olde & trwe
3531	Ther is full lytel sicurnesse/Here in this worlde etc.
	Possibly John Lydgate.
3533	There is no creatour but oon/Maker of all creaturs
*3533.5	*þer ys no merth yn noþir/A man þat haþ yteyd hym vp
3534	Thayr ys no myrth under the sky
3535	Ther is no more dredfull pestilens
	'The Tongue'
3536	Ther is no rose of swych vertu/As is þe rose etc.
	707, 1006
3537	þer is non gres þ^t growit in ground/Satenas ne peny round
3538	þere is none so wyse man but he may wisdame leere
3538.5	There may to slouthe no nother qw . . .
3540	Ther ne is dangyer but of a vylayn/ne pride but of a etc.
	Perhaps by Alain Chartier
3541	Ther nys in me comfort or gladnes
	Associated with Charles d'Orléans
3542	There nys so high comfort to my plesaunce
	Complaint of Venus, from the French of Sir Oton de Graunson
	Geoffrey Chaucer
	848
3543	There stod besyde the crosse of Ihū/Hys modyr etc.
3546	There was a man that hadde nought
3550	There was suim teme byfalle a cas
3552	þer wer iij wylly 3te wyly þer wer/a fox a fryyr and a woman
3553	þer woned in Babiloine a bern in þat borw riche
	'The Pistill of Susan'
	96, 160, 599, 922
*3553.5	*Therefore be thyn own frend
*3553.8	*These be the diue techynges expresse/The which giveth
3556.5	Thir ladyis fair that makis repair
	William Dunbar
	280
3557	These lettris þre wiþ þe titil/Arn mochil of myht etc.
3558	Thise make perfyte charite after poulis epistyll
3558.5	These scaterand scottes/hold I for sottes
3559.5	These xij aposteles under figure/I shall declare in short manere
3560.5	þies woundes smert bere in þi hert
3561.5	þeues frend and louerdes porse/Comune chest & crystes corse
3562	þin herte w^t spere stiked/þin heued w^t þornes priked
3563	þyn heritage ȝef þou wolt wynne
3563.5	Thinke and thanke prelate of grete prise
3564	Thenke hertely in þy þouȝt/Of what matere þou etc.
3565	þenc man of mi harde stundes
3565.5	Thenke man thi life mai not ever endure
3566	Thynk man qwerof þ^u art wrout/Powre and nakyd etc.
	702
3567	Thyke man qware off thou art wrought/þ^t art so wlonk etc.
	162, 167
3568.5	Thynke on hym and haue god mynde/That to the was soo kynde
3571	XXX^{ti} days hath novembre/June Aprill and Septembre
3572	XXXII teth that beþe full kene
3574	This babe to vs that now is bore/Wundyrful werkys etc.
3575	Thys blessyd babe þ^t thou hast born/Hys blessyd body ys etc.
3576	This blessyd boke that here begynneth/full of louyng etc
	Richard Rolle
	903
3580	Thys boke is one and God's kors ys anoder

3581	This booke late translate here in syght/By Antony Erle etc.	
	Earl Rivers	
	375	
3583	This brede geveth eternall lyfe/Both vnto man to chielde etc.	
	James Ryman	
3584	This breuit Buke of sober quantite/Off Synnaris etc.	
	Friar William of Touris	
3585	This chielde is was and ay shall be/One in godhede etc.	
	James Ryman	
3586	This dyane day the first in moneth of may	
	Translated from the French of Charles d'Orléans	
3587	This day ys borne a chylde of grace	
3593	Thys indrys day befel a stryfe/Totwex an old man and etc.	
3594	þis endyr day I mete a clerke/And he was wylly in his werke	
	99	
3595	This ender day wen me was wo/Naghtgale to meue me to	
3595.6	Thys yonders nyght/I herd a wyght	
3596	This endrys ny3t/I saw a sy3th/A mayde a cradyll kepe	
3597	This endurs nyght/I sawe a syght/all in my slepe	
3598.5	Thys enders nyte/When sterres shone bryte	
3599	This hindir yeir I hard be tald/Thair was a worthy king	
	The Bludy Serk	
	Robert Henryson	
3600	þis fals mannes thogt was all in synne/for drede of god etc.	
3601	This fer from yow am y lady maystres	
	Translated from the French of Charles d'Orléans	
3603	þis flour is faire & fresche of heue/Hit fades neuer etc.	
	John Audelay	
	389	
3604	þis hardy foole þis bridde victoryous	
	John Lydgate	
3606	This high feste for to magnifye/Now fest of festis etc	
	John Lydgate	
3607	þeos holy gostes myhte/Vs helpe and rede and dihte	
3608	This holy tyme make 3ow clene/Burnysche bry3t etc.	
	362	
3609	This holy tyme oure lord was borne/To saue mankynd etc.	
3610	þis is a wondir merie pley & longe ssal laste	
3612	This is goddis owne complaynt/ffro man to man þ^t he etc.	
3613	This ys no lyf alas þat y do lede	
	54	
3619	This is the songe þat 3e shul here/god is come from his Empere	
3620	This is the stone kut of the hille/Thus seith the prophete etc.	
	James Ryman	
3622	This ioyous tyme this fresshe cesoun of may	
	Translated from the French of Charles d'Orléans	
3625	This litill prose declarith in figure	
	John Lydgate	
3626	This long dilay this hope without comfort	
	Associated with Charles d'Orléans	
3627	This louely lady sat and song/And to her child con say	
3628	Thys mayden hy3th mary she was full mylde	
3631	This may that loue not lusten forte slepe	
	Associated with Charles d'Orléans	
3632	This myghti William Duk of Normandie	
	John Lydgate	
	924	
3632.3	This mynon ys in London	
3632.6	þys nome ys also on honikomb þat 3yfþ ous sauour and swetnesse	
	William Herebert	
	94a	

Index of First Lines 519

3633	This monthe of may withouten pere princesse
	Associated with Charles d'Orléans
3634.3	This nycht befoir the dawing cleir
	William Dunbar
	682
3634.6	This nycht in my sleip I wes agast
	William Dunbar
3635	This nyght there is a child born/that sprange owt of etc.
3635.5	This other day/I hard a may/Ryght peteusly complayne
	289
3637	This present book legeble in scripture/Here in this place etc.
3638	This rose is railed on a rys/he hath brouȝt þe prince of prys
3638.6	þis rewle ys gode/for lettynge of blod
3640	þis ȝynful man yn dede and thouȝt/His lord god he etc.
3641	þis synnere in him-self he sayde/þ^t he schulde synne etc.
3642	This solemne ffest to be had in remembraunce/Of blissed etc.
	The Digby Play of the Slaughter of the Innocents
3642.5	Thys the parlament of byrdys/Of hygh and low
3643	þis tyme is born a chyld ful good/he þat vs bowt vpon þe rod
3644	þis time man haþ ouercome þe fende and Robbed helle
3645	This tyme when lovers alþermost defie
	Associated with Charles d'Orléans
3645.5	This vnryghtwys man said in is sawe
	561
3645.8	This voyce both sharp & also [shryll]
3647.5	þis wondir wel vndir þis trone
3649	þis worlde fyle ys & clansyt lyte
3650	þis world hym pleyneȝ of mikel ontrewe
3651	Thys world ys born vp by astates seuyn
3652	This worlde ys but a vanite/subtile & false etc.
3654	þis world is falce I dare wyll say/and man xall fade etc.
	966
3656	This worlde is ful of variaunce/In euery thinge etc.
BR+*3656.3*	This worlde is mutable thus sayth sage/Therfore gader in tyme or thou shall falle in age
3658	þis word lordlinggis I vnderstode/may be lyknyd etc.
3659	This worle wondreþ of al thynge/howe a maide etc.
3660	This wardly Ioy is onely fantasy/Of quhich none erdly etc.
3661	This wrecched worldis transmutacioun/As wele and wo etc.
	'Balade of Fortune'
	Geoffrey Chaucer
3662	Thys ȝol thys ȝol/þe beste red þat yc kan
	406
3662.5	Thomas Albone is my name/With hande and pene I write
	Thomas Albone
	471
3667	Thou art solace in alle oure woo/And thou art etc.
	James Ryman
3668	Thow cruell herode thow mortall enemye
3669	Thow Dereste Disciple of Ihū Criste/Most best belovid etc.
3670	Thou ferse god of armes Mars the rede
	Anelida and Arcite
	Geoffrey Chaucer
	99
3671	Thowe first moever þat causest al thinge/To haue his etc.
	John Lydgate
3672	Thow gracious lord graunt me memory
3673	Thow heuenly quene of grace oure loode-sterre
	John Lydgate
3674	Thow holy douȝter of Syon/Princesse of hierusalem

3676	þou kyng of woele and blisse/louerd iesu crist
	William Herebert
3677.5	Thow man envired with temptacion
3678	þu man þ^t wilt knowen þiself loke quat þu hast þouth
3680	þou most fort wit wele or wo
3681	þou opene myne lyppen Lord/Let felþe of senne etc.
	William of Shoreham
3682	Thow Phellippe foundour of new falshede
	359
3684	þu salt hauen na god buten an/Idel adh ne swere etc.
3685	Thou schalte haue on god and no moo/And ouer all etc.
3687	Thou shalte loue god with hert entier
3688	Thou shalt no more rewle me my hert
	Associated with Charles d'Orléans
3689.5	Thou shalt worshyp one god onely
	525
3690	þu scendest me sore w^t þi loking
3691	þu sikest sore/þi sorwe is more
	'Loueli ter of loueli eyȝe'
	667, 834
3692	Thou synfull man of resoun þ^t walkest her vp & downe
3694.3	Thow þat has cast iij sixes her/Shalt haue þy desyr
	730
3695	Thow that in prayeris hes bene lent/In prayaris etc.
3696	þu þad madest alle þinc
3697	þou þ^t sellest þe worde of god/Be þou berfot etc.
	359, 881
3698	þou þat werred þe crowne of thornes/Fell dovne þe pryde etc.
3699	þou vs ast shend þoru þi fol loking
3700	þou wommon boute vere/þyn oun vader bere
	William Herebert
	94a, 566, 640, 703, 798, 885
*3700.5	*þou wost wol lytil ho is þi foo
3701	þw wreche gost wid mud y-det
3701.5	Thocht all þe wod vnder the hevin þat growis
	210
3702	Though daunger have the speche biraft me here
	Translated from the French of Charles d'Orléans
3703	Thocht feinȝeit fabilles of ald poetrie/Be not all etc.
	Moral Fables
	Robert Henryson
	755, 862, 950
3703.5	Thofe I doo syng my hert dothe wepe
3704	þo ihū crist an eoþe was . Mylde weren his dede
3706.2	Thowgh peper be blake/hit hath a good smakke
3706.4	Though poetts fayn that fortune by her chaunce
3706.5	Though sum saith that yough rulyth me
	Ascribed to Henry VIII
3706.7	Thow that men do call it dotage
	Attributed to Henry VIII
3706.8	Though that she can not redresse
3706.9	Tho that ye cannot Redresse/Nor helpe me of my smart
3707	þow þ^u be kyng of tour & town/þow þ^u be kyng etc.
3707.3	Though ye my love were nere a ladye fayre
3707.8	Thoythis fre þat lykis me
	335, 365
3709	Thre gude brether are ȝe/Gud gatis gange ȝe
3710	Thre kingis on the xijth daye/*Stella micante preuia*
	James Ryman
3711	Thre thinges ben in fay/That makith me to sorowe etc.

Index of First Lines 521

3711.5	þre þinges it ben þat I holde þris **778**
3712	Tre thinges þat eren þ^t done me sigh sore
3713	Thre woys mosthe wyt thowth/nyth and day etc.
3713.5	Through a forest as I can ryde/to take my sporte
3715	Throwe a towne as y com ryde/Y saw wretyn etc.
3716	þourghe ferly dethe to gedur arn falde
3718	Thorugh gladde aspectis of þe god Cupyde/And ful etc. John Lydgate
3719	Thurgh grace growand in god almyght
*3719.5	*Throw hys hond wyth hammur knak þai mad a gresely wound **184**
3720	Thorow owt a pales as I can passe/I hard a lady make etc. 'The Lamentacioun of the Duchess of Glossester' (1447) **620, 926**
*3721.5	* . . . thus hath mayd my payne
3721.8	Thus he sought in euery side
3722	Thus y compleyne my grevous hevynesse
3723	Thus in a pece of tyre y most delite Associated with Charles d'Orléans
3724	Thus it is seide in prophecye/I take witnesse of Ysay James Ryman
3724.5	Thus musyng in my mynd gretly mervelyng **1016**
3725	Thus seide Mary of grete honoure/My soule my lord etc. James Ryman
3726	Thus to her seide an aungell thoo/Haile full of grace etc. James Ryman
3727	Thy begyning is barane brutelness/w^t wretchitnes wofull
3727.5	þi broþer in heuen is maister & kyng
3728	Thy creatures terrestriall/*Te patrem nostrum inuocamus* James Ryman
BR+3729.7	Thy grehounde moste be heddyd lyke a snake
3730	þi ioy be ilke a dele to serue thi godd to paye Richard Rolle
3731	þy lord of heuene loue wel/Take not ys name yn ydul **106**
3732	Thy myghty mercy kyng of blis/My syn and me be þou etc.
3733	þi tunge is mad of fleych & blod/Evele to spekyn etc.
3735	Tydynges I bryng ȝow for to telle/What me in wyld forest befell
3736	Tydynges trew þer be cum new/Sent from the trynyte
3737	Tydings trew tolde ther ys trewe/iesu to be born of a mayde
3740	Til his decipeles said Iesus/Als sain matheu her tellis us
3742	Tyll home sull wylekyn this joly gentyl schepe
3743	*Timor mortis conturbat me*/This is my song in my olde age **173**
3743.6	To a fowle syngyng
3744	To Adam and Eve Crist gave the soueraignte Probably John Lydgate
3746	To alle folkys vertuouse/That gentil bene and amerouse *Reson and Sensuallyte* John Lydgate
3747	To-broken been the statuts hye in hevene 'Lenvoy de Chaucer à Scogan.' Geoffrey Chaucer
3750	To Caluery he bare his cross with doulfull payne Gilbert Banaster
3751	To Crist Ihesu thatte lorde and kyng/Of whois kyngdome etc. James Ryman
3751.3	To complayne me alas why shulde I so

3752	To fle the sect of alle mysgouernaunce/I am truly etc.
	Duke of Suffolk
3753	To geff pees to men of good wyll
3754	To God that is owre best leche/Owre hele holy we be-teche
	238
3755	To goddis worschipe þat dere us bouȝte/To whom etc.
	Version of the Seven Penitential Psalms
	Richard Maydestone
	866, 884, 903
3756	To have in mynde callyng to remembraunce
3758.5	To leve alone comfort ys none
3759	To London once my steppes I bent
	'London Lickpenny'
	425, 704
3760	To loue Ichulle beginne/Ihū boþe day and nihte
3761	To moralise ⟨a similitude⟩ who list these ballets sewe
	'The Craft of Lovers'
	296, 336, 343, 635, 657, 892
3764	To pleyȝen & ragen is for þi pru/Wanne suldest þu etc.
3768	To shewe y haue not forgoten yow
	Translated from the French of Charles d'Orléans
3768.2	To sorow in the morning
	George Cely
	378
3769.8	To þe blisful Trinite be don all reuerens
3771	To the holy goste my goodes I bequeth/that in this place be set
3774	To the maist peirlas prince of pece/With all my power etc.
3775	To the shepeherdes keping theire folde/That Crist was etc.
	James Ryman
3776	To the now cristis dere derlyng/that were a maydyn etc.
3779	To this roose aungell Gabriell/Seide Thou shalt bere etc.
	James Ryman
3782	To onpreyse wemen yt were a shame
3782.5	To veri god & to alle trewe in Crist
	'Jack Upland'
	677, 816, 879
3783	To waxen riche w^t gret blame/I ne make no force etc.
*3783.5	*to weri with my heued
3784.6	To you beholders cowde I say more þan þis
3785	To ȝou hie worschip and magnificence
3785.5	To yow mastres whyche haue be longe/a feynd louer
3787	To yow my purs and to non other wyght
	'Complaynt to his Empty Purse'
	Geoffrey Chaucer
	839
3788.5	Today in the dawnyng I hyrde þe fowles syng
	305
3790	To-day sain Louk telles us/In our godspell that Iesus
3792.5	Tonge breketh bon/wher bon he hathe non
3793	To Amerous to Aunterous ne Angre the nat to muche
3794	To longe for shame and all to longe trewly
	Translated from the French of Charles d'Orléans
3795	Toforne loue haue y pleyd at the chesse
	Translated from the French of Charles d'Orléans
3796	Towrenay ȝow has tight/to timber trey and tene
	The Siege of Tournay
	Laurence Minot
3797	Toward Aurora in the monyth of decembre/Walkyng etc.
3798	Toward the Eende of ffroosty Ianuarye/Whan watry etc.
	John Lydgate

Index of First Lines

3799	Towarde the ende off wyndy Februarie
	John Lydgate
3799.3	Tprut Scot riueling/wiþ mikel mistiming/crop þu ut of kage
	321, 901
3799.6	Trendel an appull never so ferre/hyt will be know fro wheyre he comyth
3800.5	Trolly lolly loly lo/Syng Troly loly lo
3801	Trew king þat sittes in trone/Vnto þe I tell my tale
	'Battle of Halidon Hill'
	Laurence Minot
3802	Trewe loue among mene þat moste is of lette
3803	Trewe loue is a lawe þat semeþ he had not riȝt
3804	Trew loue to me yn harte soo dere
3805	Trewloue trewe on you I truste/Euermore to fynde etc.
	338
3806	Trew on wam ys al my tryst
3807	*Tronos celorum continens*/Whos byrthe thys day etc.
3808	Trouble hertis to sette in quyete/And make folkys theire etc.
	John Lydgate
3808.5	Trust in my luf hy schall be trw
3809	Trusty seldom to their ffrendys uniust/Gladd for to helpp etc.
	208
3812	Tutiuillus þe deuyl of hell/He wryteþ har names etc.
3815.3	Twenty wynter glad and blyth
3815.5	Two frereus and a fox maken þre shrewes
3818	Two wyman in one howse
3819	Vncomly in cloystre i coure ful of care
	254
3820	Vnder a forest þ^t was so long/As I me rod etc.
3820.5	Vnder a law as I me lay/I herd a may
	289
3821	Vndir a park ful prudently pyght/A perillous path etc.
3822	Vnder a tre/In sportyng me/Alone by a wod syd
3825	Vndo þi dore my spuse dere/Allas wy stond i etc.
	583
3826	Vnkynde man ȝif kepe to me/And loke what payne etc.
3827	Vnkinde man take heed of me/Loke what peyne y etc.
3828	Hounseli gost wat dest þou here/þou were in helle etc.
3830.5	Vnto the holy and vndeuyded trynyte/Thre persones
	William Caxton
3831	Vnto the rial egles excellence/I humble Clerc etc.
	Thomas Hoccleve
	497
3832	Vnto you most froward þis lettre I write
	237, 843, 941
3832.5	Vp I arose *in verno tempore*
3834	Apon a day saynt gregore/Song his mas at rome truly
	John Audelay
3835	Vpon a lady fayre & bright/so hartely I have set etc.
3836	Vpon a lady my loue ys lente/Withowtene change of etc.
3836.5	Apon a mornyng of may
3837	Vpon a nyght an aungell bright/*Pastoribus apparuit*
	James Ryman
3838	[O]pon a somer soneday se I þe sonne
	'Somer Soneday'
	96, 160, 361, 565, 599, 626, 677, 704, 865, 888, 922
3844	Vpon my Ryght syde y me leye/blesid lady to the y pray
3844.5	Upon temse fro london myles iij/In my chambir
3845	Vp-on the cros naylled I was ffor the/Suffred deth etc.
	John Lydgate

3845.5	Apon the Midsummer evin mirriest of nichtis 'The tretis of the tua mariit wemen and the wedo.' William Dunbar **755**
3846	Vpon þe rode I am for þe/þ^t þu sennest let for me
3847	Vtter thy langage wyth gud avisement/Reule the by etc.
3848	Veynes þer be XXX^{ti} and two **214, 1017**
3849	Veryly/And truly/I schall nat fayne **54**
3851	Vertues & good lyuinge is cleped ypocrisie **341**
3852	Vycyce be wyld and vertues lame/And now be vicyce etc.
3854	Victorious Kyng our lord ful gracious/We humble lige etc. Thomas Hoccleve
3857.5	Wel and wa sal ys hornes blaw **154, 197, 223, 321, 478, 515, 517, 583, 642**
3858	Waich & wreschede þou art in sith
3859	Wake man slepe not rise vp and thynk þat erth thou art
3859.5	Wake wel annot/þi mayden boure
3860	Walkyng allon of wyt full desolat/In my spyrytes etc. Duke of Suffolk
3860.6	Was hit neverre mi kind/Chese in welle to finde
3861	Wast bryngeth a kyngdome in nede/Mede maketh etc.
3862	Water & blod for þe i suete/& as a þef i am i-take
3863	We ben executors of þis dede
3863.5	We be maydyns fayr & gent
3864	We bern abowtyn non cattes skynnes/Pursis perlis syluer etc. **832, 871, 904, 964**
3866	We fynde wryttyn .x. thyng sere/That venial synnes etc.
3868	We redyn ofte and fynde ywryte/As clerkes don us wryte Sir Orfeo
3869	We redeth oft and findeth y-write/And this clerkes wele etc. Lai de Freine **992**
*3870.5	*We Tib/Telle on
3872	Wele heriȝyng and worshype boe to crist þat doere ous bouhte William Herebert
3873	Weole þu art a waried þing vn-euene constu dele
3874	Weping haueþ myn wonges wet 'The Poet's Repentance' **171, 251, 255, 297, 300, 582, 723, 857, 1000**
3875	Welcome and yit more welcome bi þis light Translated from the French of Charles d'Orléans
3876	Welcome be thys blissed feest/Off Iesu Christ in trinite
3877	Wolcum be þu heuene kyng/Wolcum born in on morwenyng **196**
3878	Welcome be ȝe my souereine/The cause of my ioyfull peine **54**
3879	Welcome be ȝe whan ye go
3880	Wellecome Edwarde oure son of high degre
3880.6	Welcum ffortune wellcum agayne
3881	Welcom full high and nobull prince to us right speciall
3882	Welcome lord in forme of bred/ffor me þ^u polidest etc. **235**
3883	Welcome Lord in fourme of Bred/In þe is boþe lyf and Ded
3884	Wolcome louerd in likinge of bred/ffor me on rode þat etc.
3885	Welcome my ioy welcome myn hertis ese Associated with Charles d'Orléans
3889	Wel may I pleyne on yow Lady moneye Thomas Hoccleve

Index of First Lines 525

3889.5	Well on my way as I forth went/ouer a londe
3890	Wel wanton ey but must ye nedis pley
	Associated with Charles d'Orléans
3892	Wel were hym þ^t wyst/to wam he myȝt tryste
3893	Wele were him þat wiste/to whom he might trust
3895	Wenest þu husch w^t þi coyntyse
	199
3896	Wenne Wenne Wenchichenne
3897	Were y a clerk then wold y say yow grace
	Associated with Charles d'Orléans
3897.5	Were þat þat is ido iet for to donne
3898	Wer þer ouþer in þis toun/ale or wyn
	431, 709, 935
3899	War þis winter oway wele wald I wene
	The Taking of 'þe castell of Gynes'
	Laurence Minot
	359
3899.3	Westron wynde when wylle thou blow
	242, 261, 276, 355, 363, 366, 379, 452, 478, 583, 649, 652, 674, 711, 797
3899.6	Waylowy so dere boht þat it sal þus ben
3900.5	Weilawei þat ich ne span/þo ich into wude ran
3901	Weylawey þ^t i was boren/for sinne vnschriuen i am for-loren
3902	Wei-la-wey what me is wo/now rote ik in molde
3902.5	Vaylaway whi ded y so/now ich am in alle wa
3903	Wat heylet man qui is he prud/Wat ned hat he of riche scrud
3903.3	What art þou & art so ȝynge
3903.5	What can it auayle/To dryue forth a snayle
	'Colyn Cloute'
	John Skelton
3903.8	What causyth me wofull thoughtis to thynk
3904	Quhat dollour persit our ladyis hert/Quhan scho hard etc.
	'The Houris of oure Ladyis dollouris'
	181
3905	What helpithe it man to be vnstable
3906	What ys he þys lordling þat cometh vrom þe vyht
	William Herebert
	583, 703, 788
3907	Wat is he þis þ^t comet so brith/wit blodi cloþes al be-dith
3908	Wat is more dred/& wat is more fled/þan pouerte etc.
3909	What is this worlde but oonly vanyte/Who trustith etc.
	999
3909.4	What lyf is þer here/þe lyf her is deye
	William Herebert
3910.5	What man that wille of huntyng leere
3911	What manere of ivell thou be in Goddes name I coungere the
3911.5	Quhat meneth this Quhat is this windir vre
	John Lydgate
3912	What menyst thou hope dost thu me skoffe and skorne
	Translated from the French of Charles d'Orléans
3913	What shall I say to whom shall I complayn/I wot not etc.
	Duke of Suffolk
3914	What shul þees cloþes þus many folde
	Sometimes attributed to Chaucer
3914.5	What shuld I say sithe faith is ded
	Thomas Wyatt
	405
3915	What shulde me cause or ony wyse to thynk/To haue etc.
	Duke of Suffolk
3916	What so be that y say parde
	Translated from the French of Charles d'Orléans

3917	What so men seyn/Love is no peyn
	54
3917.3	What thynge maye sown to gretter excellence
	Wynkyn de Worde
3917.8	Whatt tyme as Paris son of kyng Priame/lay sleping in a garden
3918.5	What wenes kynge Edwarde with his longe shankes
3919	What why dedist þou wynk whan þou a wyf toke
3920	Qwete is bothe semely and sote
3921	When adam delf & eue span spir if þᵘ wil spede
	48, 170
3922	Whan adam delffid & eve span/who was than a gentilman
	704
3923.5	Quhen Alexander our kyynge wes dede
3924	Whanne alle a kyngdom gadrid ysse/In goddis lawe etc.
3925	Whon alle soþes ben souht and seene/Euerichone at etc.
	537
3926	When all this ffresche feleship were com to Cauntirbury
	The Tale of Beryn
3927	When Alleluya is alofte/I go gay and syt softe
3927.6	Whanne bloweþ þe brom/þanne wogeþ þe grom
3928	When briȝte phebus passed was þe ram/Myd of Aprille etc.
	The Siege of Thebes
	John Lydgate
3928.3	Qwan brown beryth apelys and homulok hony browin
3929	When charite is chosen with states to stonde
3930	Whenne Criste was borne an aungell bright
	James Ryman
3931	Qwan crist was borne in bedlem/þer rose a stere etc.
3932	When cryst was born of mary fre/In bedlem in þᵗ fayre cyte
	59
3939	When erþ haþ erþ i-wonne wiþ wow/þan erþ mai of erþ etc.
	'Erthe upon Erthe' (A version, MS Harley 2253)
	23, 161, 583, 642, 665, 742, 959
3940	Whanne eorthe hath eorthe wiþ wrong i-gete/And eorthe etc.
	'Erthe upon Erthe'
3941.5	Whan euery woo hathe easse/And euery wyshe his wylle
3942	Quhen fair flora þe goddes of al flowris
	'A Reasoning between Age and Youth'
	Robert Henryson
3943	When feithe fayles in prestys sawes/And lordys willes etc.
	Attributed sometimes to Chaucer and sometimes to Merlin
	46, 341
3944	When fals Iudas her son had solde/To the Iewes wikked etc.
	James Ryman
3946	When fishes in the water leve their swimming
3946.5	When Flora had oerfret the firth/In May
3947	Whan Flora the quene of plesaunce
	The Isle of Ladies, or 'Chaucer's Dream'
*3947.3	*When folk are festid and fed fayn wald þai here
	The Wars of Alexander the Great
3947.6	When Fortyne had me avaunsyd
3948	When Fortune list yewe here assent
	236
3949	When fresshe phebus day of seynte valentyne
	Translated from the French of Charles d'Orléans
3950	When god was borne of mary ffre/Herod the kyng etc.
3952	Whon grein of whete is caste to grounde/But ȝif hit die etc.
	503, 696
3955	When I aduertyse in my remembraunce/And se how fell etc.
	'Parvus Cato'
	Benedict Burgh

Index of First Lines   527

3956	When y am leyd to slepe as for a stound
	Translated from the French of Charles d'Orléans
3957	When I bethenke me hertli/How fele men erren greuousli
3958	When I compleyne ther is no Resone
3959	Quan I haue in my purs inow/I may haue both hors etc.
3960	When y last partid fro myn hertis swete
	Translated from the French of Charles d'Orléans
3961	Wen i o þe rode se/ffaste nailed to þe tre
3962	When y revolue in my remembraunce
	Translated from the French of Charles d'Orléans
3962.5	When I reuolue yn my remembrance/Thys lyfe fugytyue
	'The Epytaphye of Sir Gryffyth ap Ryse'
	1005
3963	When y se blosmes springe/ant here foules song
	'A Spring Song on the Passion'
	169, 171, 521
3964	Quanne hic se on rode/ihū mi lemman
	583
3965	Wenne his soe on rode i-don/ihc̄ mi leman
3967	Hwenne ich þenche of domes dai ful sore i me adrede
	'Doomsday'
	1020
3968	Qvanne I zenke onne þe rode/quorupe-one þu stode
3969	Wanne i ðenke ðinges ðre/ne mai hi neuere bliðe ben
	144, 424, 778, 909
3971	Wan ic wente byyond the see/Riche man for te bee
3972	When in myn hond was tan me þis patent
	Associated with Charles d'Orléans
3975	When ihūs criste baptyȝed was/The holy gost descended etc.
3976	Whan ihesu crist was don on rod/And þolede deþ etc.
3976.5	When Jesus Christ was twelve yeare olde
3985	Whan lyf is most louyd & deþ ys most hatid
	'Erthe upon Erthe' (B version)
	23, 293
3986	Whan lordes wol leese þeire olde lawes
	Attributed sometimes to Merlin and sometimes to Chaucer
3987	Whan lordschype fayleth/gode felawschipe avayleth
3988	When lordechyppe ys loste & lusti lekyng with all
	1006
3989	When man as mad a kyng of a capped man
3990.5	Quhen Merche wes with variand windis past
	'The Thrissil and the Rois'
	William Dunbar
	950
3992	Whanne marye was greet w^t gabriel/And had conceyued etc.
3995	When me bithought is of my ladi dere
	Associated with Charles d'Orléans
3996	Whon Men beoþ muriest at heor Mete/Wiþ mete & drink etc.
	923
3998	Wanne mine eyhnen misten/and mine heren sissen
	44, 583, 662
3999	When nettuls in wynter bryng forth rosys red
	120, 253, 341, 673
4001	Whane noþing whas but God alone/The fadyre the holly etc.
4002	When oure lord ihū so fre/Was born in bedleem of Iude
4004	Whan Phebus entred was in Gemyny/Shynynge aboue etc.
	The Passetyme of Pleasure
	Stephen Hawes
	317, 949, 987

4005	Whan Phebus in the Crabbe had nere hys cours ronne	
	The Assembly of Gods	
	Perhaps by John Lydgate.	
4005.3	Quhen phebus fair wt bemis bricht	
4006	When pride is most in prise/And couetus most wise	
4007	When Rome is removith into England	
4008	Qwhen Rome is removyde into Inglande	
4012	Whan seynt Stevyn was at Ieruȝalem/Godis lawes etc.	
4014	When shal thow come glad hope from your vyage	
	Charles d'Orléans	
	468	
4014.5	When shall yor cruell stormes be past	
4015	When slepe had slipt out of my heade	
	956	
4016	Hwenne so wil wit ofer-stieð/þenne is wil and wit for-lore	
	'Will and Wit'	
	36r, 1020	
4018	When Sonday gothe by D and C	
	730	
4019	Whan that aprill with his shoures sote	
	The Canterbury Tales	
	Geoffrey Chaucer	
	75, 295, 472, 577, 588, 608, 636, 640, 642, 665, 704, 722, 726, 755, 766, 768, 787, 839, 855, 863, 882, 936, 941, 966, 970, 997	
4020	Whan that Bachus the myghti lorde/And Juno eke etc.	
	Colyn Blowbols Testament	
4020.3	When that byrdes be brought to rest/Wythe joy & myrth	
4020.6	When þat I wowe/goold is in my glove inowe	
4021	Whan that in old tyme by awnsyent antyquety/trubilis etc.	
	529	
4023	Whan þᵗ my swete sone was xxxᵗⁱ wynter old	
4024	When that next approchen gan the fest	
	Translated from the French of Charles d'Orléans	
4025	Whane that phebus beemes schynyng as golde	
4026	Whan that Phebus his chaire of gold so hy/Had whirled etc.	
	The Flower and the Leaf	
4027	When that ye goo/Then am y woo	
	Associated with Charles d'Orléans	
4028.3	Qwan the belle ys solemply rownge	
4028.6	When the clot klyngueth and the cucko syngith	
	305	
4029	When þe cock in þe northe hath byld his neste	
4030	When þe day of dome sall be/It is in gods pryuyte	
	956	
4031	When þe hee beginnis til turne	
4033	Whanne þe ffet coldetȝ/And þe tunge ffoldetȝ	
	666	
4034.6	When þe game ys best/yt ys tyme to rest	
4035	When þe hede quakythe *memento*	
4036.5	Wen þe nese blakes and þe lyppe quakes	
4037	When þe nyhtegale singes þe wodes waxen grene	
	'When þe Nyhtegale Singes'	
	171	
4040	When the prime fallythe vppon Sonday	
	541	
4040.6	When þe rofe of þyn hous lithe on þe nese/Alle þe worldis blisse ys noth worthe a pese	
4042.5	When þe snail renneþ and þe see brenneþ	
	730	

Index of First Lines

4043	When the son the laumpe of heuen ful lyght
	'How a Lover Praiseth his Lady'
	152, 725
4044	Wen þe turuf is þi tuur
	583, 906, 1021
4044.3	Whan the whelpe gameth/the old dogge grenneth
4044.6	When the wyntar wynddys ar vanished away
4045	Wonne þin eren dinet and þi nese scharpet
4046	Wenne þin eyen beit i-hut/& þin heren beoit i-dut
4047	Whanne þyn hewe blokeþ/And þi strengþe wokeþ
4049.2	When tho herd hat Rome
4049.6	Wen tho lest wenis *veniet mors te superare*
	819
4049.7	When þou lyes vnder þe ston
4051	Hwan þu sixst on leode
	'The Ten Abuses'
	1020
4052	When þ^u seyst þ^e sacrement
	John Audelay
4053	When thonder comeþ in Januere/þou shalt haue þat etc.
	527
4056	Qwen wil þu come & comforth me/& bryng me out of kare
	Richard Rolle
4056.3	Wanne hol man is turned into half man
4056.5	When wreneys weare wodknyves Cranes for to kyll
4056.8	When ye fflemyng wer fressh florisshed in youre flouris
	359, 450
4057	When Zepheres eeke withe his fresshe tarage
	Humfrey Newton
4058.3	Wher be ye/My love my love
4058.8	Where ffrom euer thys boke be com
4059	Where y haue chosyn stedefast woll y be
	54
4060	Where I loue rigth wele/And where I kysse I loue etc.
	'Where I Love'
	342
4062	Where is this Prynce that conquered his right
	361, 807
4064	Where so euer ye fare by fryth or by fell/My dere chylde etc.
	Book of Hunting
	Dame Juliana Berners
4065	Qwhereas Adam cawsed þe sinne/Owre nature thus etc
4066	Whereas þat this land wont was for to be/Of sad byleeue etc.
	Thomas Hoccleve
	704
4068.6	Wherfore shuld I hang up my bow
4069	Wherfore wherfore make ye pre nayes whi
	Associated with Charles d'Orléans
4070	Where-of is mad al mankynde/Of seuene þynges etc.
4070.5	Wherto shuld I expresse/My inwarde heuynesse
4073.5	Quyles I am ȝong whom schold I dred
4074.5	While I haue in mynde/The blode of hyme that was so kynde
4075	Whylome I present was with my soffreyne
4076	Whils I satte in a chapel in my prayere/A heuenly sounde etc.
4077	While y was ȝonge & hadde corage/I wolde play w^t grome etc.
4078	Qwyll mene haue her bornys full/þerof Y thynk my pert etc.
4079	Whil ȝat i was sobre sinne ne dede i nowht
4079.3	While the fote warmith/the shoe harmith
4079.6	While the gresse growith/the hors stervith

4082	Whylome þer was an hygh and myghty prynce
	'The Tale of Guiscardo and Ghismonda'
	Gilbert Banester
4083	While þᵘ hast gode & getest gode for gode þᵗ miȝt beholde
	890
4084	Wil time is of forȝeuen
4085	Hwile wes seynte peter i-cleped symon/þo queþ vre louerd etc.
4087	Wyt is þi nachede brest and blodi is þi side
	'Candet nudatum pectus'
	192, 825
4088	Wyth was hys nakede brest and red of blod hys syde
	Augustine's 'Candet nudatum pectus'
	48, 192, 509, 825
4089	Who can the sorrow conceyue allas/That thou hadde etc.
4090	Who carpys of bryddys of grete gentrys
4091.6	Wo hath non herynde feethe synde
4092	Wo hath þᵗ conyng by wysdam or prudence/To know etc.
4094.3	Who is my loue/but god aboue
4094.5	Who is so wounded or ille bate
4094.8	Ho may þe lynne fle þat by þe wode went
4096	Who redes þis boke of ymagerie/hit wil hom comfort etc.
4098	Hwa se þis writ haueþ ired
4098.3	Who shal graunten to myn eye a strong streme of teres
	The 'Reply of Friar Daw Topias' to 'Jack Upland' [*3782.5*]
	677, 816, 984
4098.6	Who shall haue my fayre lady
*4098.8	*Whoe shall haue the egge saye ye
4099	Who shal yeve vn-to myn hed a welle/Of bitter terys etc.
	John Lydgate
4101	Who that byldeth his howse all of salos
4102	Hoo that comyȝt to an howse
4104	Ho that lust for to loke/or for to rede on this boke
4106	Who that maketh in Cristemas a dogge to his larder
4106.5	Who that mannyth hym with his kynne/And closith his croofte
	448, 1019
4107	Ho þat siþ him on þe Rode/iesus his lemmon
4109	Who þat wole knowe condicion/Of parfyt lyf in alle degre
4109.5	Who that wol lodge hymself herynne
	William Caxton
4111	Who was ded ande never borne/Adam þᵗ was oure first etc.
4110.3	Wo þe þer be seþ Iesus my suete lif
4112	Who wil be hool and keep him fro sekenesse
	John Lydgate
	791
4112.5	Quha will behald of luve the chance
	William Dunbar
4116	Quho wald do weill he mon beginn at weill
4120	Whoso biholdith wel as with my eyȝe
	Associated with Charles d'Orléans
4121	Whoso kon suffre and hald hym still/I trow he schall etc.
4126	Who so euer thys booke fynde
4126.5	Who so euer thou hearest be it good or badde
4129	Who-so him biþouete/inwardlich & ofte
	1011
4132	Hoo so luste olde stories to rede/He shalle fynde etc.
	Parthenope of Blois (Version A)
	722
4134	Whoso levyth in flescly wylle
	370

Index of First Lines

4135	Who-so loueth endeles rest/þis false world þen mot he fle
	'But he say soth he schal be schent'
	503, **816**
4135.5	Who loueth wel to fare
4137	Who-so off welth takyth non hede/he shall fynd defawt etc.
4138	Ho so on me doth loke/I am . . . . .. boke
4141	Wose seþe on rode ihs̄ is lef mon
4143	Whoso spekyth of þyng þ^t is vnwreste
4143.3	Whoso that wyll all feattes optayne
	Ascribed to Henry VIII
4143.5	Whoso that wyll for grace to sew
	Ascribed to Henry VIII
4143.8	Whoso that wyll hymselfe applye
4144	Whose þenchiþ vp þis carful lif/Niȝte and dai þat we beþ inne
	'A Song on the Times'
	161, **238**, **473**
4145	Who-so wele thinkes wele may say/ffor of gode thoghtes etc.
	The Myrour of Lewed Men, a translation of Grosseteste's *Château d'Amour*
	908
4146	Ho so wyl a gardener be/Here he may both hyre and se
4148	Who so wylle be ware of purchassyng
	46
4149	Whose wol boþe wel rede and loke/he may fynde wryte etc.
	386
4150	Who-so wyll haue helle/he must do as we hym telle
4150.3	Wo-so wile in soule hanne blisse
4151	Whoso wolle noȝt when he may
BR+*4151.8*	Wo-so wol this oureson saie/Be nyȝth other be daie
	388
4154	Who-so wyll ouer rede thys boke/And w^t his gostlye ye etc.
	The 'Long Charter of Christ' (B text)
	885
4154.8	Wo-so wol this oureson saie/Be nyȝth other be daie
4155	Who-so wilneþ to be wijs & worschip deiriþ
	'The ABC of Aristotle'
4156	Wo-so woneþ hym noȝt to goude furst all in hys youth
4157	Hose wolde be-þenke him weel/Ou þis world is went I-wis
4158	Hose wolde him wel a-vyse/Of þis wrecched world etc.
4159	Wy haue ȝe no reuthe on my child/Haue reuth on me etc.
	539
4160	Whi is þis world biloued þat fals is & veyn
	Cur mundus militat
	534
4161	Whi loue y yow so moche how may þis be
	Translated from the French of Charles d'Orléans
4162	Hwi ne seue we crist and secheþ his sauht
4162.5	Whye shulde man dowtefully questyons make
4163	Why sittist thou so syngyng þenkyst þou nothyng
4165	Why werre and wrake in londe/And manslaught is y-come
	'The Simonie'/'On the Evil Times of the Reign of Edward II'
	384, **504**, **876**, **877**, **887**, **918**
4165.5	Quhy will ȝe merchantis of renoun
	William Dunbar
4166	Wikked Herode thou mortall foo/That Criste shulde etc.
	James Ryman
4169	Wol ȝe here/a wonder thynge/Betwyxt a mayd etc.
4170	Wolle ye i-heren of twelte day/Won þe present was i-broust
4174	Wille Gris Wille Gris/Thinche twat you was/and qwat etc.
4174.3	Wyllyam conqueror Duke of Normandie/Conquered ynglond
4175	Wyne of natur propurtees hath nyne

532   Index of First Lines

BR+*4175.1*	Wyn of nature hath propreties ix
4176.5	Wynter etyth/what somer getithe
4177	Wynter wakeneþ al my care/nou þis leues waxeþ bare
	'A Winter Song'
	40, **159**, **171**, **487**, **553**, **569**, **583**, **621**, **645**, **662**, **703**, **715**, **872**, **937**
4180	Wisman wranglere/Richeman robbere/nedi man gadere
4180.6	Wyst euery man how brettel were his shen bon
4181	Witt hath wunder that reson ne tell can/hogh maiden etc.
	Often ascribed to Reginald Pecock
	632
4182	Wite thou wel that this bok ys leche/To all thyng that etc.
	531
4184	Wyteth now all þat ben here/And aftyr shall ben leef & dere
	The 'Short Charter of Christ'
	144, **885**
4185	With a garland of thornes kene/My hed was crowned etc.
	705
4185.5	Wyt a . . . so wondyrleche grete/þe comb yt ys of red coral
4186	Wyth all myn Hool Herte entere/To fore the famous etc.
	'Lover's Mass'/'Venus Mass'
	Perhaps John Lydgate
	113, **634**
4187	Wyth bodylye ffode Encreasyng in quantitee
	370
4187.8	Wyth empty honde men may no hawkes lure
4188	With axcess shake forsekid and forfaynt
	Associated with Charles d'Orléans
4189	With fauoure in hir face ferr passyng my Reason
	292, **583**, **692**
4189.5	Wiþ four hors all snowe white/þou schalt sire Emperore wende
4190	With greate humylyte I submytt me to your gentylnes
4191	With hert body and hool puysshaunce
	Translated from the French of Charles d'Orléans
4192	With hert repentaunt of my gret offence
	Associated with Charles d'Orléans
4193	Wytȝ lawe and wytȝ ryte
4194	Wiþ longyng y am lad/on molde y waxe mad
	'The Lover's Complaint'
	171, **472**, **566**, **868**
4195	With my trewe herte content of ioy and wele
	Translated from the French of Charles d'Orléans
4196	With notis cleer & vois entuned clene/lyk the ravisshyng etc.
4197	With paciens thou has vs fedde
4198	With pety movyd I am constreyned/To syng a song etc.
4199	W^t ryth al my herte now y yow grete
4200	Wyth scharp þornes þat beth kene/Myn hede was etc.
4201.3	With sorowfull syghs and grevos payne/Thus ever to endure
4201.6	Wyth sorowful syghes and wondes smert/my hert ys persed
	Margaret Howard?
4202	With þis betull be he smytte/þat all þe world well it witt
	719
4204	With this rynge I wedde the and with this golde etc.
4205	With tymoros hert and tremblyng hand of drede
4206	With wiel my herte is wa/And closyd ys w^t care
4207	Wyþ what mastrie he hat man y-wrouȝht
4208	Wiþ wo & drede I am born/Al for adam y am lorn
4209	With wooful hert & gret mornyng
	640
4210	With woofull harte plungede yn dystresse
4211	Vid word & wrid ic warne þe sire ode

Index of First Lines 533

4213	Within the tresoure haue y of my thought
	Translated from the French of Charles d'Orléans
4213.5	Withowt dyscord/And bothe accorde
	Attributed to Henry VIII
4217.6	Womans herte vnto no creweltye
	Thomas Hoccleve
4218	Wymmen ben fayre for to . . .
4219	Wymmen beþ boþ goud and schene/On handes fet etc.
4220	Worldys blys haue good day/No lengur habbe ych þe ne may
4221	Worldes blys haue god day/Nou fram min herte etc.
	583
4222	Werdis blisse maket me blind/þᵗ of my det I make etc.
4223	Worldes blis ne last no þrowe/Hit wit ant wend etc.
	880
4224	Worldis blisse strif hat wrout/for it is wit serwe etc.
4225	Werdis ioyȝe is menkt wᵗ wo/He is more þan wod etc.
4225.5	Werdys lowe lestyth but a qwyȝle
4227.5	Worldly love is in herte bysy þouȝt
4229	Worshyp be þe birth of þe/*quem portasti Maria*
4229.5	Worschip of vertu ys þe mede
	390
4230	Worship wymmen wyne and vnweldy age/Make men etc.
	632
4235	Wos maket of a clerc hurle/And prelat of a cheurle
4236	Wold god þᵗ men myȝt sene/Hertys whan thei bene
	341
4237	Wald my gud lady lufe me best/and wirk eftir my will
	'The Garmont of Gude Ladeis'
	Robert Henryson
4239	Wreche mon why art þᵘ prowde
	798
4240	Wrey þy self als a þef doȝ
4241	X for crystes him selfe was dyth/As clerkys redyn etc.
4241.5	Ye ar to blame to sette yowre hert so sore
	54
4242	Ye are to moche as in my dette madame
	Translated from the French of Charles d'Orléans
4242.5	Ȝe ben my fader my creacion
	475
4245	Ȝee deuout people which haue obseruance/Mekely etc.
	John Lydgate
4246	Yhe folkes alle whiche han deuocioune/To here masse etc.
	John Lydgate
4249	Ye holy prestes remembreth in your herte/Toward masse etc.
	John Lydgate
4250	Ȝe lewede Man takeþ hede/ffor þeos clerkes haþ no nede
4251	Yee lordes eek shynynge in noble fame
	Thomas Hoccleve
4253	Ye mene that wysdome will lerne
	541
4254	Yee maistresses myne and clenly chamberys
	Sometimes attributed to John Lydgate
4254.5	Ye pop holy pristes full of presumcion
	1002
4255	Ye prowd galanttes hertlesse
	359, 1002
4256	Ye schal be payd after your whylfulnes
	Charles d'Orléans
*4256.3	* . . . ye xall etc.
4256.5	Ȝe suln/rediliche/withouten abiding

4256.8	Ye Sir [þat is] idronken/dronken ydronken
	321, **431**, **709**
4257	Ye that ar comons obey yovr kynge and lorde
	310, **370**
4258	Ye þat be bi comen wikked and eny werke wol byghyne
4259	ȝe þat be þis wey pace/abidid & behaldit my face
4260	Yee that deyre in herte and have pleasaunce
	John Shirley
	112
4261	Ye that have the kyng to demene/And ffrauncheses gif etc.
4262	Yee þat lengen in londe Lordes and ooþer/Beurnes or etc.
4263	ȝe þ^t passen be þe weyȝe/Abidet a litel stounde
	777
4263.3	Ye þat put your trust & confydence
	Ascribed to Thomas More
BR+4264.2	Ye that wyll lette gude men blode/And wyn þerwyth all youre liues fode
4265	Ye worldly folk avyse yow betymes/Wych in thys lyff etc.
	Translation of De Guileville's *Pèlerinage de la vie humaine*
	John Lydgate
4265.5	Ye wryng my hand so sore/I pray yow do no more
*4267.5	*ȝutte y se but fewe canne sece
	412
4268	ȝhit is god a curteys lord/& curteysly can schaw etc.
	'The Insurrection and the Earthquake'
	423, **926**
4272.5	Yit wulde I not the causer faryd amysse
	54, **935**
4273	ȝissinge and glosing and felsship beon riue
4273.8	Yone that haue redd the contentes of thys booke
	375
4276	ȝong & olde More and lass/fful god hit is to here a Masse
4277	Yong and tender child I am & souke my moder tete
4278	ȝyng men I red that ye bewar/That ȝe cum not in the snar
4279	Ying men I warne you everichone/Elde wives take ye none
	424
4280	Yung men of Waterford lernith now to plei
	238
4281	ȝyng me þ^t bern hem so gay/þey þink not on domys day
4281.5	Yowre counturfetyng/with doubyll delyng
4282	Your yëen two wol slee me sodenly
	'Merciles Beaute'
	Geoffrey Chaucer
	571, **777**, **839**
4283	Yowre goodlihed myn hertis lady dere
	Associated with Charles d'Orléans
4283.5	Your light grevans shall not me constrayne
4284	Yowre mouth hit saith me bas me bas swet
	Translated from the French of Charles d'Orléans
*4284.3	* . . . ȝoure seruand madame
	215, **354**, **863**
4284.5	Youre vgly token/My mynd hath broken
	John Skelton
4285	Yougth luste reches or manhod/Trustyth in any of thes etc.
4286	ȝungþe ne can nouth but leden me wil/Ne elde etc.

Temporary Index of First Lines not noted in *IMEV* or *SIMEV*

These lines are in the forms cited by the authors of the works annotated, and any comment is drawn from those works. The numbers allotted are temporary ones, chosen to avoid confusion with those of *IMEV* and *SIMEV*. The references are to page numbers, in the annotated works or in others cited by the authors, unless otherwise noted. Doubtless some poems should not be included, because they were composed in a time or place beyond the limits of *IMEV* and *SIMEV,* or because the form represents a variant of a poem already listed. The list includes some poems in which the first line is incomplete [*7648–51*], and some for which no first line was specified [*7652–8*].

7001   A! A! A! how myn hert is colde!/A! hert hard as ston, how mayst thou lest?
        Dramatic planctus, Hegge Plays, Coventry XXVIII, *The Betraying of Christ*: 286–7.
        Taylor, **111**: 613.

7002   A, A, my dere sone I*esus*! A, A, my dere sone I*esus*! . . ./Stonde still, frend*es*! hast ye not soo!
        Dramatic planctus, *The Digby Mysteries*, *The Burial of Christ*, lines 450, 456–8, 470, 478–507, 515–46, 556–62, 565, 567–99, 603–5, 612–791, 793–6, 802–9, 813–18, 820–21, 823–8.
        Taylor, **111**: 613.

7003   A! blessid body, þat bale wolde beete,/Dere haste þou bought man-kynne
        Mary Magdalene mourns Christ's sacrifice, York XXXIX, *Jesus appears to Mary Magdalene*, lines 110–25.
        Osberg, **767**: 326.

7004   A, blyssedful mayden and modyr, þis is a wonderful change
        On giving the Blessed Virgin to the care of John.
        Wenzel, **882**: 159–60.

7005   A, Iesu Crist that ous is boue/For his swete moder loue
        Silverstein, **73**, no. 11.

7006   A lord what ys thys worldes wele
        Winchester Anthology, item 131.
        Wilson, **88b**: 26, 37.

7007   A! mercyfull maker, full mekill es þi mighte,/þat all this warke at a worde worthely has wroghte
        Praise of God by seraphim, York I, *Creation, and the Fall of Lucifer*, lines 41–8.
        Pearson, **196**: 233.

7008   A, mercy! mercy! myn owyn sone so dere,/Thi blody face now I must kysse!
        Dramatic planctus, Hegge Plays, Coventry XXXIV, *The Burial of Christ*: 336.
        Taylor, **111**: 613.

7009   A! mygtfull god, ay moste of myght . . ./I thanke þe, John, with wordis fune
        Dramatic planctus, York XLIII, *The Ascension*, lines 179–92, 202–4.
        Taylor, **111**, 612; Astell, **929**:175.

7010   A! my good Lord, my sone so swete!/Why hast thou don? why hangyst now thus here?
        Dramatic planctus, Hegge Plays, Coventry XXXII, *The Crucifixion of Christ*: 321–3, 326–8.
        Taylor, **111**: 613.

7011   A praye we now alle to the Holy Trynyte
        Mirk's *Festial*, Sermon 40, *De Festo Trinitas*.
        Long, **356**:14.

7012   A body tendur of complexion/And nobelyst in kynde
        Christ's Passion from four aspects--*causae*.
        Stemmler, **647**, no. 29.

7013 A gurdul of gile—-/Ich wolde go a mile/To see þe mordaunt
Bennett and Smithers, **65**: 128; Wenzel, **882**: 224.
7014 A lady bry3t, fayre *and* gay,/Made hir mone and seyd in fay
Early Tudor song. Winchester Anthology, item 172.
Wilson, **88b**: 30, 37; **746**: 294; Boffey, **848**: 142.
7015 A man may be laten blod in two and twenti stedis/Of þe whilke in þe hevyd are two faste behinde þe eris
On bloodletting.
Hunt, **1017**: 322.
7016 A moder and mayde a childe hath borne/As Gabriell hath tolde beforne
James Ryman
Zupitza, **10**: 193–4, XXVI.
7017 A pri*n*ce is clad i*n* cloþ3 of dul/for þe deiing of hijs mak*e*
Quatrain in a sermon on Good Friday.
Wenzel, **629**, no. 2.
7018 A scholer must in youth bee taught
Translates 'Discipulus teneris est instituend*us* ab annis' etc.
Bühler, **471**: 651.
7019 A semly song I wy̅ll 3ow syng/Is of a maydyn mylde
A Marian lyric, an imaginary encounter between the narrator and a maiden (Mary) accompanied by an old man (Joseph).
Benskin, **776**: 34–5.
7020 A selcouth sight yonder now is . . ./All myghty god, how may this be? etc.
Dramatic planctus, Towneley XXIX, *The Lord's Ascension*, lines 298–307, 348–63, 372–9.
Taylor, **111**: 613.
7021 A tapy3te of trewthe,/A dosser*e* of cle*n*nesse
Allegory of household furniture to be prepared for Christ, the Christian's guest, in sermon book of Friar Nicholas Philip.
Fletcher, **867**: 195.
7022 A white hors vp þe hille. A blacke horse down'/þe hille. A gray hors in a gr*a*vell' way. And' a brown bay is best at all 'assay
Hands, **576**.
7023 A wonder mete þat god hat hetth,/Hit3 ha3t newe name, wyde kyd
Sermon, *Panem nostrum cotidianum da nobis hodie* . . .
Stemmler, **647**, no. 16.
7024   (plenyng of his woo,
A word off (ffor3iuing to his ffoo
On Christ's seven utterances from the Cross.
Fletcher, **919**: 165.
7025 Above this horse blacke and hydeous
Woolf, **522**: 353–4.
7026 Absent I am rycht soir aganis my will/My lang absens causss me mekle wo
From Bannatyne MS: ff. 237[r], ed. Ritchie, Vol. 3: 319.
Camargo, **949**: 183.
7027 Adonay, thou god veray,/Thou here vs when we to the call
Abraham's prologue, Towneley IV, *Abraham*, lines 1–48.
Pearson, **196**: 236.
7028 After þat þe appel was eten withouten det3 passed non of alle
De Peccato.
Wilson, **601**, no. 144; Wenzel, **882**: 109.
7029 A3en my felawes þat I haue spoken/And with my tungge wroth hem wo
De Detraccione.
Wilson, **601**, no. 59; Wenzel, **882**: 120.
7030 Allac þat euer scho bewte bar
A courtly love lyric.
Boffey, **848**: 144.
7031 Alas alas *and* wele away/þat evyr towchyd I þ*e* tre
Eve's lament, *Ludus Coventriae, Fall of Man*, lines 378–90.
Pearson, **196**: 234.

Temporary Index of First Lines 537

7032 Allas, allas, þis werdis blisse lestet but a stounde
De Leticia Huius Mundi.
Wilson, **601**, no. 103.

7033 Allas! for my maistir þat moste is of myght,/That 3ister-even late, with lanternes light
John's lament, York XXXIV, *Christ led up to Calvary*, lines 107–142.
Pearson, **196**: 247.

7034 Alas, for my son dere,/that me to moder chese!/Alas, dere son for care/I se thi body blede
Mary offers to carry the Cross, Towneley XXII, *The Scourging*, lines 315–19.
Taylor, **111**: 613.

7035 Allas! For my swete sonne I saie . . . Allas! þat þou likes noght to lende etc.
Dramatic planctus, York XXXVI, *Mortificacio Christi*, lines 131–43, 148–52, 157–60, 170–73, 181–2, 261–6.
Taylor, **111**: 612; Astell, **929**:173.

7036 Allas! For syte and sorowe sadde,/Mournynge makis me mased and madde
Adam's lament, York VI, *Adam and Eve driven from Eden*, lines 81–122.
Pearson, **196**: 234; Osberg, **767**: 325.

7037 Allas! for syte, so may I saie,/My synne it passis al mercie
Cain's punishment is too great to bear, York VII, *Sacrificium Cayme and Abell*, lines 117–27.
Osberg, **767**: 325.

7038 Allas! for syte, what schall I saie,/My worldly welthe is wente for ay
John laments the judgement passed on his master, York XXXIV, *Christ led up to Calvary*, lines 117–42.
Osberg, **767**: 326.

7039 A Allas for sennes þat I haue wrouth;/M Merci, Iesu, þat hast me bouth;
De Peccato. Preceded by 'Quilibet peccator potest dicere "Amen."'
Wilson, **601**, no. 148.

7040 Alas her is ifalle a reuful cas/a poynt was byloken in a compas
Verse from a sermon.
Erb, **564**: 78.

7041 Allas i am icast adoun,/Alas i am in hard presoun
Verse from a sermon.
Erb, **564**: 79.

7042 Alas! In languor now I am lent!/alas, now shamfullie I am shente!
Adam's lament, Chester II, *The Creation*, lines 345–60.
Pearson, **196**: 234.

7043 Allas, in þis worlde was neuere no wight/Walkand with so mekill woo
Lament of Mary Magdalene, York XXXIX, *Jesus appears to Mary Magdalene after the Resurrection*, lines 1–21.
Pearson, **196**: 249; Osberg, **767**: 326.

7044 Alas, it is a reuful mange/Of myth strong and wyl wrong
Sermon, *Sermo de ascensione domini* . . .
Stemmler, **64**, no. 40.

7045 Alas, moche wes þat senninge,/þat to al mankende was damninge
Sermon, *De passione Christi* . . .
Stemmler, **647**, no. 12.

7046 Alas! my love! my lyfe! my lee!/Alas! mowrning now madds me
Mary's lament, Chester XVI, *The Passion*, lines 625–44/8.
Pearson, **196**: 245.

7047 Alas! my love, my life, my lere,/Alas! nowe mournynge, woes me!
Dramatic planctus, Chester XVII, *The Crucifixion*, lines 239 ff., 331 ff.
Taylor, **111**: 613.

7048 'Alas my sone' seide heo/'Hu may ihc liue? hu may þis beo?'
Assumption of Our Lady, lines 36–42.
Taylor, **111**: 607.

7049 Alas! now lorne is my lykinge/for woe I wander and handes wringe.
Mourning of Mary Magdalene [and Maria Iacobi?], Chester XVIII, *Christ's Resurrection* (40–41), lines 309–24.
Osberg, **767**: 324

7050 Alas! now weale is went away,/myne owne my maister ever I may.

Mourning of Luke, Chester XIX, *Christ appears to two Disciples*, lines 1–8.
Osberg, **767**: 324.

7051   Alas that men be so vngent/To order me so creuelly!
From a sequence in the Devonshire MS, thought to be correspondence composed during their imprisonment by Lord Thomas Howard and Lady Margaret Douglas.
Muir, **41**: 263, no. 10; Camargo, **949**: 182.

7052   Alas! the doyll I dre/I drowpe, I dare in drede!/Whi hyng*y*s thou, son, so hee?/my bayll begynnes to brede
Mary's lament, Towneley XXIII, *The Crucifixion*, lines 309–38, 361–4, 382–99, 406–15, 424–46.
Taylor, **111**: 613; Pearson, **196**: 245.

7053   Alas! to dy with doyll am I dyght!/In warld was neuer a wofuller wight
Mary Magdalene laments the death of Jesus and Mary Jacobi faints to think of his wounds, Towneley XXVI, *The Resurrection of the Lord* 334–45, 346–51.
Osberg, **767**: 325.

7054   Allas! what schall nowe worþe on me,/Mi kaytiffe herte will breke in three
Lament of Mary Magdalene, York XXXVIII, *The Resurrection; Fright of the Jews*, lines 270–86.
Pearson, **196**: 248.

7055   Alle for joie me likes to synge,/Myne herte is gladder þanne þe glee
Mary Magdalene rejoices, York XXIX, *Jesus appears to Mary Magdalene*, lines 134–41.
Pearson, **196**: 248–9.

7056   Alle godes bote on þu salt forsaken./Ne saltou nout his nome on idel taken
The Decalogue in English verse.
Wenzel, **629**, no. 3.

7057   All my lufe, leif me not/Leif me not, leif me not
Wilson, **321**: 183.

7058   Al oure wonder and al oure wo/Is torned to wele and blisse al-so
Sermon, *Se[r]mo in navitate domini* . . .
Stemmler, **647**, no. 34.

7059   Al þat ys shal com to was/and eue*ry*lke was [?] shal blynne
Quatrain warning against death.
Wenzel, **629**, no. 4.

7060   Al þe wey þat God goth by/[I]s sothfastnesse and mercy
De Via Christi.
Wilson, **601**, no. 243.

7061   Alle þe warld wyde and brade/Oure Lord specyally for man made
Poem comparing the world to a sea, a wilderness, and a forest. Item 50 in a Carthusian miscellany.
Hogg, **735**: 271–2.

7062   All þe worschipe þou hast of cunde/as someres flour it will a-swynde
Translates a Latin poem on three kinds of honour.
Wenzel, **629**, no. 6.

7063   All under the leaves, and the leaves of life,/I met with virgins seven
Rickert, **22**: 145; Sandison, **139**: 135, R1; Phillips, **149**: 40; Routley, **396**; Gray, **575**: 222.

7064   Also Adam wyt lust and likynge/Broght al his ken into wo and wepynge
Joy after redemption.
Gray, **575**: 75.

7065   And hys yen wexyth dym,/And his nose wexyth þyn
Cum senescit. Signs of death, in a sermon collection assembled by 'Selk.'
Fletcher, **685**: 108; Powell, **786**: 12.

7066   And yff thou wyst what thyng yt were
Winchester Anthology, item 125, in the hand of Thomas Dakcomb.
Wilson, **88b**: 25, 37.

7067   Als a clerk withnesset of wisdom þat can/herte of tunge meister is, as man of womman
De Lingua. The tongue's subordination to the heart. Grimestone Lyric 102.
Wilson, **601**, no. 102; Wenzel, **882**: 110

7068   Ase a gost schewyng,/Ase a wynd wyrlyng
Sermon, *De corpore Christi* . . .
Stemmler, **647**, no. 23.

Temporary Index of First Lines

7069   As A ravaschyd man whos witt is all gon/grett mornynge I make ffor my dredfful dowte
Lament of Thomas, *Ludus Coventriae, The Appearance to Thomas* 353–92.
Pearson, **196**: 249.

7070   As holy wrytt wytnesse and telle,/Three thingis shull neu*er* ben fulfelle.
On vicious women.
Hanna, **734**: 239, no. 2.

7071   As I did walk onys be ane medo side
Laing, *Select Remains*: 361; *Early Popular Poetry* I: 112.
Sandison, **139**: 130.

7072   As I me walkid in A may morning
Winchester Anthology, item 217 [music].
Wilson, **88b**: 35, 37.

7073   As mekyll as þer schal be hewynes/qwan Crist schal sey, 'Go ȝe me froo!'
Quatrain translating the Latin couplet 'Quantus est luctus . . .'
Wenzel, **629**, no. 7.

7074   At moost mischief/I suffre grief/For of relief/Sins I have none
'My lute and I.'
Thomas Wyatt
Davies, **61**, no. 185.

7075   Ave maria gratia plena Dominus tecum./Heyl fful of grace god is w*ith* the
Gabriel hails Mary, *Ludus Coventriae, The Parliament of Heaven/The Salutation and Conception,* lines 216–20.
Pearson, **196**: 237.

7076   Backe bent smocke rent
Person, **53**, no. 65.

7077   Barred girdel, wo þe be,/mi maidenhed he les fo þe
Lament of a fallen woman.
Wenzel, **629**, no. 8.

7078   Be þe wel, be þe wo, be þeself mynde/þat þu dost quiles þu liues þat saltu fynde
De Ingratitudine.
Wilson, **601**, no. 91.

7079   Bewty is subiect vnto age/Sicknes the same will stayne
Wilson, **321**; Bühler, **428**.

7080   Byfore the gate of Galile,/Saynte Petur ther sate hee
'A goode charme for sore teþ^e.' Written as prose in a series of recipes, preceded by 'In nom*ine* † p*at*ris † & filii † & sp*iritus* s*an*cti † amen.'
Hanna, **734**: 239–40, no. 5.

7081   Behold man what þou arte
Winchester Anthology, item 170.
Wilson, **88b**: 30, 37.

7082   Beholde myn woundes and have hem in þine þouȝte
Woolf, **522**: 48.

7083   Behold nou, man, quat þu salt be/þat al þis werd nou drawith to þe
De Superbia.
Wilson, **601**, no. 228; Wenzel, **791**: 154.

7084   Behold, þu wreche, withouten strif,/Quat det I suffre for þi lif.
De Passione Christi.
Wilson, **601**, no. 216.

7085   Betre is þe pore in his si[m]plesse/þan þe riche þat liuet with vnrithfulnesse
De Diuiciis.
Wilson, **601**, no. 70.

7086   bytwene a þousend men mo*n*y on y koupe r*e*yme/to wo*m* my c*o*nsel y durste schowe
Verse from a sermon.
Erb, **564**: 72.

7087   Biware howe thou the body keytte,/For the blode may not to faste out fleitte
On the influence of the signs of the Zodiac on venesection.
Hanna, **734**: 240–1, no. 6.

7088   bewar I say of hadywyste/harde it is a man to trust
Proverb on *Had-I-wist* (vain regret etc.) in a fifteenth-century manuscript of *CT*, in margin of the *Tale of Melibee*.
Lerer, **855**: 305.

7089 Blak be thy bankes/and thy ripes also/Thow sorowful Se/ful of Stremes blak
An invitation to the seas to grieve that they must touch the Scottish shore, based on the envoy to Lydgate's *Fall of Princes* and (the first stanza) after the copy of *Troilus and Criseyde* in the *Kingis Quhair* manuscript.
John Harding.
Peterson, **741**: 202–3.

7090 Blissed moten þo pappes be/þat Godes sone sak of þe
De Benediccione.
Wilson, **601** no. 36.

7091 Blysse *and* Ioye *and* heryng/Be to þe, lord kyng
ME poem translating a Latin hymn, found in Worcester Cathedral MS F.124, fol. 30ᵛ.
Wenzel, **701**: 71.

7092 Bisiliche ȝef þe to lore/Als þu suldest liuen eueremore
De Ocupacione (no 140), De Tempore (no 236).
Wilson, **601**: nos. 140, 236.

7093 busken bernes . boues bryten . blithe burdes botes beden .
Alliterative lyric on the hunt.
Pickering, **981**: 163, **B**.

7094 But now I se even then/My mystrys dos me love
Courtly love lyric.
Hanna, **734**: 241, no. 7; Boffey, **848**: 149.

7095 By a blody weye/Crist wente in-to his contreye
Sermon, *De passione Christi* . . .
Stemmler, **647**, no. 11.

7096 Be a wildernes/As I did passe
See Padelford, *XVI Cent. Lyrics*: xliii, note.
Sandison, **139**: 146, M 11

7097 Bi bele arn briddes breme on bowes ./Boles blosmes breden brode .
A lyric of love, where *bele* may be either a place-name or a pet form of Isabel.
Pickering, **981**: 166–7, **G**.

7098 Be chance bot evin this vthir day.
Bannatyne MS: 358.
Sandison, **139**: 131, A 6.

7099 By west off late as I dyd walke
Ritson, *The Caledonian Muse*, (London 1785, 1821): 172. Laing, *Select Remains*: 367, *Early Popular Poetry* II: 74.
Sandison, **139**: 131, A 9.

7100 Cadwalladyre sall Owan call./And Walys sall busk þaim forto ryse
Based on 'Prophecies of Merlin' passage in Geoffrey of Monmouth's *Historia Regum Britanniae, Book VII*. Substitutes Owan for Conan and Wales for Scotland.
Peterson, **741**: 203.

7101 Child i was *and* child i am/*and* euer wil be for sinful man
Verse from a sermon.
Erb, **564**: 75.

7102 Children ben litel, brith and schene, and eþe for to fillen/Suetliche pleyende, fre of ȝift and eþe for to stillen
De Condicione Puerorum. Characteristics of children. Grimestone Lyric 50.
Wilson, **601**, no. 50; Dove, **865**: 26; Wenzel, **882**: 121.

7103 Crist had rest at hys nede/--cum dicitur, quod sedit--
Sermon, *Sermo de ascensione domini* . . .
Stemmler, **647**, no. 37.

7104
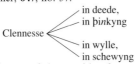

The 'dossere of clennesse' has four corners. Allegory of household furniture to be prepared for Christ, the Christian's guest. A verse from the sermon book of Friar Nicholas Philip.
Fletcher, **867**: 196.

Temporary Index of First Lines 541

7105 Cok craw thou quhill day
        In *Cockelbie Sow*.
        Baskerville, **148**.
7106 Com hider, love, to me!
        Stevick, **103**: 175.
7107 Com, my swete, com my flour
        Sisam and Sisam **69**, no. 143; Long, **356**: 324; Woolf, **522**: 299.
7108 Cum, þe man, ne dred þe nast./Mi sune þat þe haueþ so dure ibo3t
        The Virgin appeals by baring her breast.
        Wenzel, **629**, no. 9.
7109 Comet, 3e children, me for to heren;/þe dred of God I sal 3ou leren
        De Doctrina Sine Gracia.
        Wilson, **601**, no. 72.
7110 Complayne we maye miche ys amise
        Winchester Anthology, item 124.
        Wilson, **88b**: 25, 37.
7111 Considdir hairt my trew intent/Suppois I am no^t eloquent/To wryt 3ow anser reponsyve
        From Bannatyne MS, ed. Ritchie: ff. 235^v–236^r, Vol. 3: 315–16.
        Camargo, **949**: 183.
7112 Corrupciun of synne/þat we han fallun inne
        Recommends penance.
        Wenzel, **629**, no. 10.
7113 Ded is a wol comwn thing/for it ne sparet erl ne king
        On death.
        Wenzel, **629**, no. 11.
7114 Deth is a Dredful Dettour;/Deth is an Elenge hErbergour
        De Morte. Preceded by: 'Mors habet quatuour litteras, videlicet DETH, et possunt designari quatuor condiciones mortis. Nam per D:' etc.
        Wilson, **601**, no. 112; Wenzel, **791**: 154.
7115 Deth is lif; id est, mors Christi est vita nostra, etc.
        De Nouis.
        Wilson, **601**, no. 132.
7116 Desine, fle, narra, corrige, perfer, habe;/Let and wep, tell and bet, hold and haue
        Nota: Legitur in gestis Romanorum . . .
        Stemmler, **647**, no. 10.
7117 Diabolus, þoru pride of herte and heynesse,/Caro, with lust, likingge, and vnclennesse
        De Hostibus. Preceded by 'Contra istos quatuour sunt hostes, videlicet.'
        Wilson, **601**, no. 88.
7118 Diverte a malo: for drede,/Fac bonum: ffor mede
        Sermon, *Declina a malo et fac bonum*.
        Stemmler, **647**, no. 31.
7119 Diues and lazarus þe scripture saythe plaine
        Winchester Anthology, item 211.
        Wilson, **88b**: 35, 37.
7120 Downe by 3one riuer I ran
        Religious ballad, in *Gude and Godlie Ballatis*: 168.
        Sandison, **139**: 137, R 16.
7121 Drau þe neuere to man/þer is lif is wan
        De Murmuracione.
        Wilson, **601**, no. 108.
7122 Dred and loue, hate an good/Turnen mannis with and maken him wod
        De Fatuitate. Fear, hatred, love and property often turn the right minds of men.
        Grimestone Lyric 79.
        Wilson, **601**, no. 79; Wenzel, **882**: 127.
7123 Drunkenchipe brekt/Al þat wisdom spekt
        De Ebrietate. Grimestone Lyric 77.
        Wilson, **601**, no. 77; Wenzel, **882**: 127
7124 Erle at the day doue
        W. Dauney, ed., *Ancient Scottish Melodies* (Edinburgh: Bannatyne Club, 1838): 49.
        Sandison, **139**: 131, A 10.
7125 Earthly man, that I haue wrought,/awake out of thy sleepe!

Christ's exhortation, Chester XVIII, *Christ's Resurrection*, lines 154–73.
Pearson, **196**: 248.

7126   Erthly man, that I haue wroght,/wightly wake, and slepe thou noght!
Lament of Jesus, Towneley XXVI, *The Resurrection of the Lord*, lines 226–333.
Pearson, **196**: 247.

7127   Egge ou*re* hertes, lord of myth,/þi so*n*ys weyis do to dyth
Couplets in a Latin sermon, translating the collect of the Second Sunday in Advent.
Wenzel, **629**, no. 12; **701**: 85.

7128   Emperasse of helle, heven quene,/My socour thou be in sorow and tene
Poem isolated from Lambeth Palace MS 559: f. 47^v.
Ogilvie-Thomson, **618**: 393.

7129   evyn as you lyst my wyll ys bent
Reed, **21**, no. XIX.

7130   Eu*e*rech kokewold*es* dore stondeþ anyne, etc.
A song mentioned in a sermon.
Wenzel, **629**, no. 14; **701**: 84.

7131   Eueri prechour/Is godes owe harpour
Sermon, *Tene, quod habes . . .*
Stemmler, **647**, no. 18.

7132   Eyne to seing;/Eres to hering
De Obediencia. Preceded by: 'Totum interius se colligit vt imperantis in se colligat voluntatem. Anglice.'
Wilson, **601**, no. 137.

7133   Fare well all clene Melawdy/Fare well all ladys and . . .
Verse on a pillar of Landwade St Nicholas.
Wilson, **321**: 179.

7134   Farwell Crystmas fayer and fre
In *Early English Ballads*, 'Songs and Carols': 57.
Taylor, **118**.

7135   ffarwell! the frelyst that eu*er* was fed!/ffarwell! floure more fresh the*n* floure de lyce!
John apostrophizes Jesus, Towneley XIX, *Iohn the Baptist*, lines 257–72.
Osberg, **767**: 325.

7136   Farewele, þou schynyng schappe þat schyniste so schire,/Farewele, þe belle of all bewtes to bide here
Thomas bids farewell to the *belle* of all beauties, York XLVI, *The Appearance of Our Lady to Thomas*, lines 202–8.
Osberg, **767**: 326.

7137   faste fresen fennes fule . frostes fre is foules foo .
On winter.
Pickering, **981**: 163–4, **C**.

7138   faste ifunde fer on folde . frode fryth is feire fre .
On 'Frode Fryth,' probably a place, 'frog wood' or, more likely, 'Frod's wood.'
Pickering, **981**: 164–5, **C**.

7139   Fewe hereres,/Feynte wereres/Manie bacbiteres
De Veritate. Preceded by 'Veritas habet.'
Wilson, **601**, no. 242.

7140   Fill the cup, Philip,/And let us drink a dram
Chambers and Sidgwick, **18**: 228.

7141   First at prude ich wol begin
Heuser, **16**: 121.

7142   First, lerges, the King my cheife/Quilk come als quiet as a theif
Burden: 'Lerges, lerges, lerges ay:/Lerges of this New Yeirday.'
William Stewart, 1527.
Nat. Lib. of Scotland, MS Advocates 1.1.6: f. 95^v.
Greene, **86**, no. 121.2.

7143   Fyrst qwen I wrought þis worlde so wyde,/Wode and wynde and watters wane
God's speech, York VIII, *The Building of the Ark*, lines 1–24.
Pearson, **196**: 235.

7144   fle, forsake *and* wytstond/*and* ihc þe take þis croune in hond
Verse from a sermon.
Erb, **564**: 80.

Temporary Index of First Lines 543

7145   Fle þe dich of senne/þat þu fal nouth þerinne
       De Peccato. Beware of the pits, that you may not perish through them!
       Grimestone Lyric 143.
       Wilson, **601**, no. 143; Wenzel, **882**: 130.

7146   Flowres in myn herbere thay growe grene
       Florete flores crescunt viride.
       Winchester Anthology, item 132 (m).
       Wilson, **88b**: 27, 37.

7147   For pes to mak I com in lond,/man fre to mak þat was bond
       Couplets spoken by Christ.
       Wenzel, **629**, no. 17.

7148   For summer is a come unto day
       Refrain of processional for May Day--Padstow Hobby Horse.
       Baskerville, **147**.

7149   For þat appel þat Eue tok/Al mankindde Crist forsok.
       De Peccato. Preceded by 'Pro vetito pomo corruit omnis homo.'
       Wilson, **601**, no. 146.

7150   For þing þat is askyn/With stedefast herte and lesten [. . .]
       Manuscript damaged.
       Wilson, **601**, no. 2.

7151   Forto ȝyue pes to men of good wyll.
       Mirk's *Festial*, sermon on the Nativity.
       Long, **356**: 14.

7152   Furth ouer the mold at morrow as I ment
       Bannatyne MS: 774.
       Sandison, **139**: 131, A 12.

7153   Furth throw ane forrest as I fure
       Bannatyne MS: 118.
       Sandison, **139**: 141, D 17.

7154   Furth throcht yone finest [sic]
       Line 13 of poem begins 'Wa is the man that wantis.'
       The Miscellany of the Spalding Club (Aberdeen, 1841–53, 1842): xxvii, n. 1.
       Sandison, **139**: 142, D 18.

7155   Fortune, vnfrendly þou art vnto me./My dyligent seruise to my soverayne--
       Early Tudor song. Winchester Anthology, item 175.
       Wilson, **88b**: 30, 37; **746**: 294; Boffey, **848**: 153.

7156   Fresch and new I haue in mynde/þe blod of hym þat was kynd
       Couplet in an exemplum of a princess who is to keep her knight's heart as a remembrance.
       Wenzel, **629**, no. 18.

7157   ffresche fragrent flour of bewty souerane/my hummill seruice tak no^t in disdane
       From Bannatyne MS: ff. 219^v–220^r, ed. Ritchie, Vol. 3: 266–9.
       Camargo, **949**: 182.

7158   ffro this worlde be gynyng,/vnto þat cyte of rome makyng
       A rudimentary historical and topographical description of Rome, found with *The Stacions of Rome*.
       Scattergood, **505**: 279–82.

7159   Gawde, Vergine and mother beinge/To Criste Jhesu, bothe God and Kinge/By the blissed eyare him consevinge/*Gabrielis nuncio*
       Prayer of Eleanor Percy, written by her sister, Anne Arundel, in a Book of Hours, introduced by 'Oratio Elionore Percie/Ducissa Buckhammie.' A translation of the Latin hymn 'Gaude virgo, mater Christi.'
       Barratt, **100**: 279–81.

7160   Ȝef þi godis wil it ben þine,/þat after þi detȝ þu haue no pine
       De Diuiciis.
       Wilson, **601**, no. 68.

7161   God of his goodnesse and of grace grounde/By whoys gloryous power all thyng is wrought
       Noah's prologue, *Ludus Coventriae*, *Noah*, lines 1–26.
       Pearson, **196**: 235.

7162 God ouer alle þingge,/Himself withouten wemme of senningge
De Hostibus. Preceded by 'Hoc debet diligere, videlicet.'
Wilson, **601**, no. 87.

7163 Good awdience, harken to me in this cace
Wright, ed., *Songs and Ballads*: 129.
Sandison, **139**: 131, A 13.

7164 Grete god! þat all þis worlde has wrought,/And grathely gouernes goode and ill.
Abraham prays that he may not rebel. York X, *Abraham's Sacrifice of Isaac*, lines 173–80.
Osberg, **767**: 325.

7165 Grett god, þat all þis world has wrought,/And wisely wote both gud and ille
Abraham's prologue, York X, *Abraham's Sacrifice of Isaac*, lines 1–52.
Pearson, **196**: 236.

7166 Gret heynesse of blod/Richesse and wele of good
De Superbia.
Wilson, **601**, no. 227.

7167 Gula is samel[es];/Luxuria is laweles
De Peccatis Mortalibus. Modo. Cf. *1791.*
Wilson, **601**, no. 219; Wenzel, **882**: 174.

7168 Hale and howe Rumbylowe/Stire well the gode ship and lete the wynde blowe
Sea song entered in Tolsey Court Book, 1487–97.
Wilson, **321**: 178.

7169 Haile be thou, Mary, maiden free,/full of grace! god is with thee
Gabriel hails Mary, Chester VI, *The Nativity*, lines 1–4.
Pearson, **196**: 237.

7170 Haill! blyssed babb, that Mary bare,/And blyssed be thy mother, Mary mylde
Simeon hails the babe and the mother, York XLI, *The Purification of Mary: Simeon and Anna prophesy*, lines 354–73.
Osberg, **767**: 326.

7171 Hail, comly and clene,/Hail, yong child!
Song of the Shepherd in the *Secunda Pastorum* of Towneley Plays [*715*].
Chambers & Sidgwick, **18**; Phillips, **149**; Cutts, **826**: 268.

7172 Haill floscampy and flower vyrgynall,/The odour of thy goödnes reflars to vs all
Simeon's salutation, *The Purification*, (*York Plays*, ed. Beadle:158).
Astell, **929**: 170.

7173 Heyle floure of flourys fayrest i-fownde/Heyle perle peerles prime rose of prise.
Song of the Shepherds, *Ludus Coventriae*, *The Adoration of the Shepherds*, lines 90–118.
Osberg, **767**: 325.

7174 Hayle! jentilest of Jesse in Jewes generacion,/Haile! welthe of þis worlde all welthis is weldand
Thomas praises Mary, the gentle, courteous, and beloved, York XLVI, *The Appearance of Our Lady to Thomas*, lines 132–43.
Osberg, **767**: 326; Astell, **929**: 171.

7175 Hayle! Marie! full of grace and blysse,/Oure lord is with þe
Salutation of Mary, York XII, *The Annunciation, and Visit of Elizabeth to Mary*, lines 145–52.
Pearson, **196**: 237; Astell, **929**: 169.

7176 hayll, mary, gracyouse!/hayll, madyn and god*is* spouse!
Gabriel hails Mary, Towneley X, *The Annunciation*, lines 77–88.
Pearson, **196**: 238.

7177 Hayle, myghtfull Marie, Godis modir so mylde,/Hayle be þou, roote of all reste, hayle be þou, ryall
Gabriel summons Mary to heaven. *The Death of the Virgin* (*York Plays*, ed. Beadle: 386).
Astell, **929**: 171.

7178 Hayle my lord God! hayle prince of pees!/Hayle my fadir, and hayle my sone!
Mary worships the child, York XIV, *The Journey to Bethlehem; the birth of Jesus*, lines 57–70.
Pearson, **196**: 238; Osberg, **767**: 325; Astell, **929**: 170.

7179 Hayll! prophette, preued withouten pere,/Hayll! prince of pees schall euere endure

Temporary Index of First Lines 545

        Hail lyric spoken by eight burgesses, York XXV, *The Entry into Jerusalem upon the Ass*, lines 490–545.
        Pearson, **196**: 240; Osberg, **767**: 325.

7180 Hand, heued, foot, herte/Criȝet Crist for wondis smerte
        De Passione Christi.
        Wilson, **601**, no. 159.

7181 Harkried alle gode men, and stille sitteth adun
        Religious Songs (Percy Society XI: 81).
        Taylor, **118**: 31.

7182 Haue detȝ in mende:/Neuere sal senne þi soule schende
        De Morte.
        Wilson, **601**, no. 119; Wenzel, **791**: 154.

7183 Haif hairt in hairt ȝe hairt of hairtis haill/Trewly sweit hairt ȝour hairt my hairt sal haif
        From Bannatyne MS: f. 228^r, ed. Ritchie, Vol. 3: 293–4.
        Camargo, **949**: 183.

7184 Have I not cause to morne alas
        Courtly love lyric.
        Boffey, **848**: 155.

7185 He cryth *and* wepyth streyt ibownde/in clowtys and cloþys wrappyd *and* wownde
        Verse from a sermon.
        Erb, **564**:73.

7186 He taket oþer coloures arith/And oþere coloures sewith to mannis sith
        De Colore. Preceded by 'Nota quod color albedo quatuor habet in se condiciones propter quas consciencie munde comparari potest.'
        Wilson, **601**, no. 48.

7187 He þat alle þing doth wel/His preyȝere is herd eueridel
        De Benediccione.
        Wilson, **601**, no. 35.

7188 He þat hathe an euyll bylle
        Winchester Anthology, item 132 (f).
        Wilson, **88b**: 26, 37.

7189 He þat is all weldy*n*g haþ takyn a lytul In./þo ky*n*g of *p*aradys is komen of sempul kyn
        Three *mirabilia* of the Incarnation.
        Wenzel, **629**, no. 21.

7190 He þat is king of alle londis/At soper sith among hem tuelue
        De Corpore Christi.
        Wilson, **601**, no. 55.

7191 He þat louet his frend and fo,/His loue ne werchet him no wo
        De Amore Proximi (no. 28), De Dileccione (no. 64).
        Wilson, **601**: nos. 28, 64.

7192 He þat time borwith fro morwe to morwen/And ȝelth with þe mouth
        De Morte.
        Wilson, **601**, no. 114; Wenzel, **791**: 154.

7193 He that will not whan he may/Whan he would, he Shall have nay
        Baskerville refers to the date 1562.
        Baskerville, **147**.

7194 Here and see and say noght./Be wyse and war*e and* telle noght
        ME Verse 6 of *Fasciculus Morum*.
        Wenzel, **701**: 140.

7195 Help God, and haue all
        Det Deus auxilium, et fiat omne suum.
        Rigg, **516**: 83.

7196 Here I sytte be thy wyff that am qwene of heuene
        English scrap in Latin theological miscellany, MS Lambeth Palace Library 78: f. 264^v.
        Pickering, **785**: 21.

7197 Here lieth Marmaduke Cunstable of Flaynborght knyght
        Verses on cadaver tomb of Marmaduke Constable, Flamborough, N. Yorkshire (1520).
        King, **761**: 495.

7198 Her lis arfaxat fader brandan/ant kolmkilne ant cowhel þer halewe/ant dame courne moder þeyre halewe/þat komen in to bretene sautes to seke

	Records the burial or resting place of Arfaxat and Coroune, father and mother of three saints, Brandan, Kolmkilne, and Cowhel.

Pickering, **909**: 412.

7199 Here maist thou learne thyselfe how to be-haue/Within this curteous booke of curtesie
To the reader.
Bühler, **471**: 652.

7200 Hegh nony nony/nony no hegh/hegh nony nony/nony nony nony no hegh/y lay alle nyght/a sorowfull wight
A sixteenth-century love lyric.
Simons, **838**: 1–2.

7201 Hay now the day dallis
Baskerville, **148**; Hatto, **474**: 510.

7202 Hyghe and almyghty creator of alle
Winchester Anthology, item 130.
Wilson, **88b**: 26, 37.

7203 Howe, howe, who is here?/I, Robin of Doncaster, and Margaret my feare
Epitaph for Robin of Doncaster and Margaret (dated 1579).
Scattergood, **910**: 470.

7204 Hoe! Hoe! who lies here?/I, the goode Erle of Devonshire;/With Maud, my wife, to mee full dere,/We lyved togeather fyfty-fyve yere
Epitaph for Edward Courtenay, third earl of Devonshire (d. 1419) and his wife Maud.
Scattergood, **910**: 470.

7205 Hold yowre tung and sey the best/And let yowre neghboure sitte in rest
Verse on a mazer.
Gray, **575**: 48.

7206 Holy water wel y-mad,/Schyl song to mak men glad
Four things used in blessing a church.
Wenzel, **629**, no. 22.

7207 Hou hard it was, and wat distresse/My deʒ þe sewith þis liknesse
De Passione Christi.
Wilson, **601**, no. 156.

7208 I am blisse of michil lith/To hem þat leden here lif orith.
De Gloria Eterna.
Wilson, **601**, no. 85.

7209 y am by-wylt of a wyʒt þat worches me wo,/ʒerfore wemmen y warye in world ʒwer y go
'The Rejected Lover,' with an *O-and-I* refrain phrase in the fifth line of each stanza.
Cox and Revard, **849**: 38–9.

7210 I am despysid as man for-sake,/Curys with erth to wurmys make
Couplets translating hexameters on an *imago humilitatis*.
Wenzel, **629**, no. 23; Dove, **865**: 17.

7211 I am fel and mercy haue none,/for euery man to deth shall gone
Couplets spoken by Death.
Wenzel, **629**, no. 24.

7212 I am soore astoned whan I remembre me
Verse translation of the Proem and Book I of Petrarch's *Secretum*.
Winchester Anthology, item 72.
Wilson, **88b**: 21–2, 37.

7213 I am weddere/Ego sum ille cui aliqua nubet
The English may be verse of a sort.
Winchester Anthology, item 132 (c).
Wilson, **88b**: 26, 37.

7214 I aske thys sowle for to wynne,/qwech I know ful of synne
ME dialogue inserted in a Latin sermon, of the struggle for a sinner's soul, spoken by a devil, Mary, Christ, the Father and an angel.
Wenzel, **572**: 84–5.

7215 I bitake þe, holy gost, þis place here ysette,/And þe fadir and þe sone, þeues for to lette.
'*Coniuracio bona pro latronibus venientibus ad domum,*' a charm against thieves.
Gray, **610**: 66.

7216 I brene and euermore must/For synne þat neuer man wist!
Exclamation of the damned soul.
Wenzel, **882**: 81.

Temporary Index of First Lines

7217   I come hider to wowe. . . .
      Stevick, **103**: 176.

7218   I comende me on to ȝow • þou trone of þe trinyte/O mekest mayde now þe modyr of jhesu
      Speech of Gabriel, *Ludus Coventriae, The Salutation and Conception*, lines 333–8.
      Osberg, **767**: 325.

7219   I dye for sorowe, I peyne for þowht,/I brenne in fyyr þat queyncheth nowht
      Lines spoken by a dying sinner.
      Wenzel, **629**, no. 26; **701**: 72.

7220   I god that all the world have wrought,/heaven and earth, and all of nought
      God's speech, Chester III, *The Deluge*, lines 1–16.
      Pearson, **196**: 235.

7221   I haue a hole aboue my knee
      Person, **53**, no. 63; Gray, **91**: 368.

7222   I have a thing and roughe yt is.
      Person, **53**, no. 64.

7223   I haue for-yef the all thyng,/take no more to euell lyuyng
      Inscriptions on tunic and ring of emperor's daughter . . . in a moralized story from *Gesta Romanorum*.
      Wenzel, **629**, no. 27.

7224   I haue hard many men make their mone/That lawyers frendly weare to none;/But whether y^t be true or no,/It is not lawfull to saye so
      Poem in Huntington MS 906, f. 59^v.
      Hanna, **734**: 243, no. 18.

7225   I haue to a semly that i bi sete . send mine sonde selliche sete .
      A gift to a beautiful lady.
      Pickering, **981**: 165, **E**.

7226   I hard lately to a ladye
      Wright, ed., *Songs and Ballads*: 28.
      Sandison, **139**: 132, A 15.

7227   I holde hendeburne her . worthli water ant wys . i world as i wene .
      Lyric on a river, perhaps Hendeburne.
      Pickering, **981**: 162–3, **A**.

7228   I love good alle þat ys no fayle/by þis ye may fynde hyr
      Cryptogram of lady's name, perhaps 'Alice,' perhaps 'Goodall.'
      Boffey, **750**: 21; **848**: 157.

7229   I may well say with joyfull harte/As neuer woman myght sat beforn
      From a sequence in the Devonshire MS, thought to be correspondence composed during their imprisonment by Lord Thomas Howard and Lady Margaret Douglas.
      Muir, **41**: 264, no. 12; Camargo, **949**: 182.

7230   I pray to god he spede ȝour way/and in sowle helth he mote ȝow kepe
      Mary speaks to Joseph, *Ludus Coventriae, The Betrothal of Mary*, lines 474–86.
      Osberg, **767**: 324.

7231   I syr Ector most honorable, þat prynce was of Troye,/xix kyngys att þat sege I slowe with myn handys
      Poem on the Nine Worthies.
      Turville-Petre, **814**: 81–3.

7232   I spende, I gife, I welde, I werned myne,/I had, I haue, I lost, I pyne
      Variant of ME Verse 50 of *Fasciculus Morum*?
      Wenzel, **701**: 192.

7233   I thanke þe as reuerent rote of oure reste,/I thanke þe as stedfast stokke for to stande
      Thomas overflows with thanks, York XLVI, *The Appearance of Our Lady to Thomas*, lines 170–82.
      Osberg, **767**: 326.

7234   I thanke the lord God of thy greet grace,/That thus haith sparyd me a space
      Simeon's prayer, York XLI, *The Purification of Mary: Simeon and Anna Prophesy*, lines 386–426.
      Pearson, **196**: 243.

7235   I was an ane hund and syne ane hair/Anys I fled, I fle no mair./Rocht-futtit Scot, quhat says thow?

Anglo-Scottish flyting in the Aberdeen Sasine Register.
Bawcutt, **901**: 441.

7236 I wil [. . .]/And þus I haue [. . .]
Manuscript damaged.
Wilson, **601**, no. 1.

7237 I wolde be absent daye and nyght
Winchester Anthology, item 228.
Wilson, **88b**: 36, 37.

7238 I you assure/Full well I know
'To Mistress Margaret Tilney.'
John Skelton
Davies, **61**, no. 161.

7239 Ibore and euer bifore of ancestrie/And noun þoȝt myȝcte and maystrie
Sermon, *Dominus hiis opus habet*.
Stemmler, **647**, no. 13.

7240 If Candlemas day be dry and fair,/The half o' winter's to come and mair
Rhyme for predicting the length of winter.
Fowler, **827**: 65.

7241 Iff hit so betyde
Si tibi contingat
Winchester Anthology, item 132 (g).
Wilson, **88b**: 26, 37.

7242 Ȝef preyȝer or mede/Mith of Detȝ maken meistre
De Morte. If death could be overcome by prayer or bribe, man would be free of it.
Grimestone Lyric 118.
Wilson, **601**, no. 118; Wenzel, **791**: 154; **882**: 132.

7243 If that a yong man wold atain/Unto worship, must him refrain etc.
BL MS Royal 19 B.iv: f. 98a (*c.* 1500).
Sisam and Sisam, **69**, no. 325.

7244 Yif þe blynde wile haue is bone/crist is þe sunne and marie þe mone
Verse from a sermon.
Erb, **564**: 71.

7245 ȝif þou art por*e*, þa*n* art þou fr*e*./ȝif þou be riche, þa*n* woo is þe
Fletcher, **919**: 164.

7246 ȝif þou be icast adoun/aris vp *and* tak þe beth
Verse from a sermon.
Erb, **564**: 79; Green, **975**: 187.

7247 If þu be rych *and* wyse also/*And* of bewte fressh þerto
ME Verse 8 of *Fasciculus Morum*.
Wenzel, **701**: 142; **882**: 192–3.

7248 [Ȝ]ef þu be riche and wys in lore,/In tunge gracious
De Superbia.
Wilson, **601**, no. 223.

7249 Ȝef þu 'wilt' ben riche or cleped holi,/Ler to flateren, for þei ben laten wel bi
De Adulacione. A commonplace on flattery. Grimestone Lyric 16.
Wilson, **601**, no. 16; Wenzel: **791**: 154; **882**: 104.

7250 Ȝif þu wilt flen lecherie,/Fle time and stede and cumpanie.
De Luxuria. If you want to avoid Venus, flee the respective places and times.
Grimestone Lyric 99.
Wilson, **601**, no. 99; Wenzel, **882**: 109.

7251 Ȝif þu wilt nouth here, but spekt wordis manie and veyne/Betre þu were to han on ere and mouþes to haan tweye
De Multiloquendo. Translation of a Latin hexameter. Grimestone Lyric 104.
Wilson, **601**, no. 104; Coleman, **753**: 182; Wenzel, **882**: 127.

7252 Ȝyf þou wlt well schriue boen,/Sixth kep þat I þe kene
The (six or seven) circumstances of sin.
Wenzel, **882**: 81.

7253 Ȝef ȝe liuen after þe flesses red,/He sal ȝou bringgen to det withouten dred
De Carnalitate.
Wilson, **601**, no. 53.

Temporary Index of First Lines 549

7254 In a sartayn place apoynted for pleasur
Wright, ed., *Songs and Ballads*: 133.
Sandison, **139**: 132, A 18.

7255 In a sesone of somere þat souerayne ys of alle
'A Bird in Bishopswood.'
John Tickhill
Kennedy, **891**.

7256 In all this warld no man may wit/Thair no power nor knawlege may
From Bannatyne MS: ff. 257ʳ–258ᵛ, ed. Ritchie, Vol. 4: 19–22.
Camargo, **949**: 183.

7257 In an arber of honor set full quadrant
Wright, ed., *Songs and Ballads*: 136.
Sandison, **139**: 132, A 19.

7258 In on efnigge, stille þer I stod
A Passion lyric.
Stemmler, **770**: 533–4.

7259 In Bowdoun on blak monunday
Pinkerton, ed., *Ancient Scotish Poems* I: 135.
Sandison, **139**: 132, A 20.

7260 In December, when the dayes draw to be short
Percy, ed., *Reliques* II, Bk 2, No. 3: 112 (129).
Sandison, **139**: 146, M 19.

7261 In euer same maden and wythe my eye
Winchester Anthology, item 123.
Wilson, **88b**: 25, 37.

7262 In gret blode,/In myche gode,/In gret bewte,/And in frut of body
Sermon, *Se[r]mo in navitate domini* . . .
Stemmler, **647**, no. 32.

7263 In May in a morning, I movit me one
Bannatyne MS: 647.
Sandison, **139**: 132, A 21.

7264 In May qhen that hert ys lyȝt,/Euer make thy praer to God almyȝt,/And then heuen for the shall be byȝt
Poem in a column originally left blank, in the middle of *The Pricke of Conscience*.
Hanna, **734**: 247, no. 24.

7265 In syfhyng sar I sit vnsauth/& oft mon murnyng myye
Cryptogram in Bodleian Library Rawlinson MS D.375: 216.
Laing and McIntosh, **780**.

7266 In soumer seson, as soune as the sonne/had breydid his bemes on beris and bouddes Ielosy.
Brewer, **470**: 85.

7267 In sommer tyme I dyd prepaire
Ed. Böddeker, *Jb. f. rom. u. engl. Spr. u. Lit*, N.F. III: 103.
Sandison, **139**: 138, R 22.

7268 In somer quhen flouris will smell
Conlee, **97**: 308–12; Sandison, **139**; Jones, **164**; Reichl, **895**: 54.

7269 In þe ys all my blysse, in þe ys all my þouht,/Fayr *and* fals, suche ys þys world
Inscriptions on a chest made by a usurer and a priest.
Wenzel, **629**, no. 30.

7270 In this litill tretis men may se and be in[tro]dusyde/To the reyngne of the kingis of Inglande & ther namys with-all
Prefatory stanza to a verse chronicle which seems a redaction of Lydgate's 'Kings of England' [*3632*], extending to Henry VIII.
Mooney, **924**: 274.

7271 In these scuchyns þat schynythe | so bryȝt/there is doctrine to the pepyll of gostly well
Sermon lyric in allegory of shields with enigmatic messages.
Whiteford, **841**: 457.

7272 In tyme to come the wodde shall wante and waters shall increase,/And vice shall steke from yonge and olde here (?) vertue to release
In a hand of the first half of the sixteenth century.
Hanna, **734**: 257, no. A2.

7273	In waylyng and weping, in woo am I wapped,/ In site and in sorowe, in sighing full sadde Lament of Thomas, York XLVI, *The Appearance of Our Lady to Thomas*, lines 1–104. Pearson, **196**: 250; Osberg, **767**: 326.
7274	In ȝour name Maria • ffyve letterys we han/M. Mayde most mercyfull *and* mekest i*n* mende Angel's song to Mary, *Ludus Coventriae*, *Mary in the Temple*, lines 244–51. Pearson, **196**: 244; Osberg, **767**: 325.
7275	Into a mirthfull May morning Iohn Forbes, *Cantus, Songs and Fancies* etc. Sandison, **139**: 133, A 28.
7276	Is a robour of rentis and londis;/It is a prisoun of stronge bondis De Luxuria. Luxuria. Wilson, **601**, no. 100; Coleman, **753**: 182.
7277	Iste liber me pertinet, and bear it wel in mynde,/Per me Gulielmum Downes, so gentelle and so kynde;/A vinculis doloris Iesue do hym brynge/Ad vitam etername, to lyfe everlastynge. A bookplate. Hanna, **734**: 247, no. 25 (second).
7278	Iste liber pertinet, beare it well in mynde,/Ad me Georgiu*m* Savagium, boothe curteyes and kynde:/A penis inferni Iesyesu him bringe,/Ad gaudia celestia, to ioye euerlastinge. Amen. A bookplate. Hanna, **734**: 247, no. 25 (first).
7279	It doth harm, and hat don harm,/To putten forth þe time De Morte. On delay. He who is not ready today will be less so tomorrow. Grimestone Lyric 113. Wilson, **601**, no. 113; Wenzel,**791**: 154; **882**: 129.
7280	It is bitter to mannis mende;/It is siker to mannis kende De Morte. Mors. Wilson, **601**: no 111; Wenzel, **791**: 141, 154;
7281	It is doute in mannis richesse/Wer mo louen his godis or is worþinesse De Diuiciis. Wilson, **601**, no. 67.
7282	It is wol lithliche iborn/þer good wil wilcomet beforn De Obediencia. Wilson, **601**, no. 136.
7283	It pesys þo*m* þat be wroth,/It cle*n*sith he*m* þat be lothly Translates the preceding Latin lines on the five virtues of Christ's Blood. Fletcher, **919**: 165.
7284	It strengþit man in is fiting/Agenis felle fon. De Corpore Christi. Preceded by 'Effectus corpus Christi digne sumentibus.' Wilson, **601**, no. 57.
7285	Yt will stant sincke into mans brayne Subscribed 'Dictis w wey.' Winchester Anthology, item 224. Wilson, **88b**: 36, 37.
7286	Ianekyn of Londone/Is loue is al myn Bennett and Smithers, **65**: 128; Barratt, **100**: 19; Mustanoja, **548**: 65; Plummer, **768**: 152; Wenzel, **882**: 225.
7287	Ihesu Crist and al mankende/Dampnen þe man þat is vnkende De Ingratitudine. Condemnation of the ungrateful person. Grimestone Lyric 90. Wilson, **601**, no. 90; Wenzel, **882**: 128.
7288	Jhesu, my loue and my delyt,/In þi loue make me perfyt. Lyric from MS Mazarine 514: f.7^v. The first line is very similar to that of *1736*, and it has been entered there in *SIMEV*. Barratt, **822**: 26.
7289	Jhesu, my spowse good and trewe,/ne take me to noon other newe

Prayer of a virgin to the crucifix; lament of the devil; drops of blood as tokens of Christ's love.
Wenzel, **629**, no. 31; Pickering, **785**: 21.

7290 Jhesu, hy þat by þe stode/of lof teres wepede and flod
'Unde de isto dolore [matris] dicit quidam Donatus . . .'
Wenzel, **629**, no. 32.

7291 Ihesu, þat woldist for manys sake/Comen ffrom heuen to oure wendyng
Verses in sermon book of Friar Nicholas Philip, to be sung to conclude the sermon on preparation for Christ, the Christian's guest.
Fletcher, **867**: 196.

7292 Iob † in a donghill laye †./Thre wormis † did hem fray †.
'For wormis in children,' a charm.
Hanna, **734**: 247–8, no. 27.

7293 John bury, off care Be war, y rede the off Clare./Lest þu mysfare, now hede þu tak to my lare
The scribe's demand for promised payment.
Wenzel, **629**, no. 33.

7294 Joly lemman dawis it not day.
In *Cockelbie Sow*.
Baskerville, **148**.

7295 kar bon ostel auerez/e veraiment auerez/riche e bon ostel/kar a la curt ihesu crist vendrez/ ky est rey del cel/od ky vus saunz fin serrez/[A]nd salt fare swyþe wel
AN piece with English line in MS Egerton 613.
Hill, **691**: 495.

7296 Kyng, be þu redy, wach *and* wake./Or þu be ware I woll þe take
In a Middle English sermon, letters of a tyrant (i.e. Death) besieging the castle of the soul.
Wenzel, **629**, no. 34; Bitterling, **706**: 102.

7297 Kunne to speke worchipe is; worchipe is cunne be stille/[þ]is to ȝif þu cunne mith, no word ne saltu neuere spille
De Sapientia.
Wilson, **601**, no. 231.

7298 Lladi myn, whyche clleped Clleo,/Help me nev in thys meserable case
Fragment which, with additions, could produce an acceptable Chaucerian distich.
Hanna, **734**: 248, no. 28.

7299 Lanterne of lufe and lady fair of hew/O perle of pryce most precius and preclair
From Bannatyne MS: ff. 235ʳ, ed. Ritchie, Vol. 3: 312–13.
Camargo, **949**: 183.

7300 Lait lait on sleip as I wes laid
Bannatyne MS: f. 233ʳ, STS 26: 308.
Frankis, **365**.

7301 Lawe an los and rich, worchipe and of lore drede/And defaute of rith, maket man to sueren in nede
De Iuramento.
Wilson, **601**, no. 94.

7302 Lawe is leyd vnder graue,/For þe demeres hand hat idrawe
De Lege.
Wilson, **601**, no. 96; Coleman, **753**: 182.

7303 Leef hen. Whanne hue Leyth/Loth whanne hue clok seyth
Proverb on the hen, added to MS Egerton 613.
Hill, **691**: 406.

7304 Lete þe cukewald syte at hom/And chese þe anoþer lefmon
A wife should not abstain from taking a friend in place of her ill-favoured husband.
Wenzel, **882**: 216–17.

7305 Let us rejoice and sing/And praise that michty King
Burden: 'La-lay-la.'
Before 1567.
Rickert, **22**: 38.

7306 Lettres of gold written I fand
Bannatyne MS:138.
Sandison, **139**: 143, D 29.

7307	Lyke as the daye his course doth consume/And the new morowe springyth agayne as faste
Epitaph of Robert Fabian (d. 1511), at St Michael Cornhill.
Gray, **575**: 290.
7308	Lyke as women haue facis
Winchester Anthology, item 106.
Wilson, **88b**: 24, 38.
7309	lystyng lordyngs I wyll ȝow tell/how ⟨h⟩et owr lady gabryell
A Marian lyric on the Annunciation and Nativity.
Benskin, **776**: 35–6.
7310	Lystyne lordys veramont/How the sowter hath made hys testament
Burden: 'Pyrdow, pyrdow, pyrdow, wows se bone/Trenket sowterly.'
A Shoemaker's Testament.
Wilson, **747**: 22; **1005**: 160.
7311	Lystenythe a while and thenke ye nott longe
Quis Ascendit in montem domini. Verse sermon on Psalm xxiii. 3–4.
Winchester Anthology, item 121.
Wilson, **88b**: 25, 38.
7312	Littel is lithe bi lythum . wen stormes arn stronge upon strikewarth
On various places.
Pickering, **981**: 168, **H**.
7313	Longe Y was a gygelot,/Yyl þou was on lyue
Prayer of a young girl for her rich husband's soul.
Wenzel, **882**: 217.
7314	Longingge, likingge, lestingge on reuthe/Schewede þat in loue was miche treuth/Ihesus
De Fidelitate.
Wilson, **601**, no. 78.
7315	Loke, such as we ar, such schall ye be
Verse on a cadaver tomb, unnamed, Grantham, Wooburn, Bucks (c. 1520).
King, **761**: 496.
7316	Lord, for þi holy blyssed name/schelde vs alle from syn *and* schame
Prayer.
Wenzel, **629**, no. 35.
7317	Lovert þe mincginge of þe it is so swete
Woolf, **522**: 373, n. 2.
7318	Lorde wherto ys this worlde soo gaye
A translation of the *Cur mundus militat*.
Winchester Anthology, item 120.
Wilson, **88b**: 25, 38.
7319	Lord! wyth a lastande luf we loue þe allone,/Þou mightefulle maker þat markid vs and made vs
A cherub praises God, York I, *The Creation, and Fall of Lucifer*, lines 57–64.
Osberg, **767**: 325.
7320	lord wyth þine eres/þou heire mine teres
Verse from a sermon.
Erb, **564**: 70.
7321	Lordings, listen to our lay—/We have come from far away
Anglo-Norman carol.
Tr. F. Douce.
Rickert, **22**: 134; Phillips, **149**: 96.
7322	Lou, lou, lou! wer [h]e goþ!/A lou, lou, lou! wer [h]e goþ!/For hir i les myn [h]alywater, -ter, -ter, lou!
Song in Dublin, Trinity College, MS D. 4. 9 (270), f. 37^v.
Dobson and Harrison, **87**: 198–9, no. 19.
7323	Luue bendes me bindet
An image of love bonds used for Christ's fetters.
Wenzel, **882**: 222.
7324	Love did him fra heuen comen,/Love did him man be-comen
Divisions of a sermon for Good Friday.
Wenzel, **882**: 151.
7325	Loue him bothe morow and eue,/for loue is fresche and euer newe

Couplets inscribed on the two halves of the open heart displayed by an image of the God of Love in Athens.
Wenzel, **629**, no. 36.

7326 Loue is knotte of mannes hertes,/Loue is mette of mannes werkes
As love is the measure of all human acts, so it is the knot of minds.
Wenzel, **882**: 223.

7327 Loue me and Yche þe,/And þenne schal we wrendes boe
Proverbial wisdom on temperance.
Wenzel, **882**: 88.

7328 Love noȝtte þe world, ne ffalsenysse,/Ne no þynge þat in hym euyll ys
Lyric in sermon collection, assembled by 'Selk.'
Fletcher, **685**: 108; Powell, **786**: 12.

7329 Lownes and humylyte,/Clennes and chastyte,/Love and charyte,/Mercy and pyte
Virtues.
Hanna, **734**: 248, no. 29.

7330 Magister redyngge,/Riche emperour
Sermon, *De corpore Christi* . . .
Stemmler, **647**, no. 21.

7331 Magnificat a*ni*ma mea d*omi*num;/My saull luf*ys* my lord abuf
Mary's song of praise, Towneley XI, *The Salutation of Elizabeth*, lines 49–78.
Pearson, **196**: 241.

7332 'magnificat,' while I have tome,/'anima mea dominu*m*'
Mary's song of praise, Chester VI, *The Nativity*, lines 69–112.
Pearson, **196**: 241.

7333 Maiden stod at welle and wep: 'Weilawei,/Late comet þe lith of dai'
The BV's suffering.
Wenzel, **882**: 226; Millet, **1008**: 22.

7334 Make the poure to pray well/Be stylle or ellis saye well
Proverbial remarks of birds, in a window in Yarnton, Oxfordshire.
Gray, **575**: 50.

7335 Maker of mankynd, O God in trynyte,/Of thyn high mercy grant me this bon
Memento mori verse on cadaver tomb of Joan Walrond, Childrey, Bucks (1477).
King, **761**: 495.

7336 *Version A*: Makyn here mone/þat now no ys in þe world no god but gold alone
Version B: þer nas no god but gold alone . . . [Latin] . . ./þat God schal be god, wan gold nys none
Sermon, *Dominica 23 post festum Sancte trinitas* . . .
Stemmler, **647**, no. 42.

7337 Man is mold/þi þryȝte is ysolde
Verse from a sermon.
Erb, **564**: 77.

7338 Man, loke and se
Woolf, **522**, 355.

7339 Man ne hat nouth grace for God ȝef hit nouth/But for it is nouth rediliche of man isouth
De Gracia.
Wilson, **601**, no. 81; Coleman, **753**: 181.

7340 Man þat is of womman born/He lyuyth but a lytyl stounde
Rendering of Job 14. 1–2.
Willmott, **1004**: 148.

7341 Mon, þu bihode þat hic thole for þe
Woolf, **522**: 373.

7342 Mon, wi seestu loue ant herte
Early Bodleian Music, II: 7.
Reed, **135**: 51.

7343 Man withoute mercye mercy schal mysse
Winchester Anthology, item 152.
Wilson, **88b**: 28, 38.

7344 Meni ma*n* syngat/Wan he ho*m* in bringat/A fayr yunge wyf . . .
Rhymed proverb found in *The Proverbs of Hendyng* and *The Proverbs of Alfred*.
Wenzel, **701**: 95.

7345 Mirke my wordes well/& ber thym in my[nde]:/Appli thy loves in syth--/In age thou shal be [blynde]
Some letters were lost when the folio was cropped; thus 'syth' may read '3owth.'
Hanna, **734**: 248, no. 30.

7346 Mary Moder, mayden clere,/Pray for me, William Goldwyre
Epitaph of William Goldwyre, d. 1514, Coggeshall, Essex
Gray, **575**: 277.

7347 Marie wyth wepy[n]g greth/Wach Cristes feth
Sermon, *Lacrimis cepit rigare pedes eius.*
Stemmler, **647**, no. 24.

7348 Mater of murnyng ys þus cloþ/Y-coloured wyþ rede for our sake
Christ's Passion from four aspects--*causae.*
Stemmler, **647**, no. 30.

7349 Me think*es þat* I haue gode right/To s*er*ue *þat* semely to my sight
Poem in Magdalen College, Oxford, deeds: Multon Hall 39*a*, dorse.
Woolgar and O'Donoghue, **820**: 218–19.

7350 M*emo* God and houre lady that best may,/Sawe al m*a*rchaunt*es* be hyght and be day,/And be ther sped. Amen q*uo*d Willme
Added after the explicit of *The Pricke of Conscience.*
Hanna, **734**: 242, no. 13.

7351 M*er*cy *and* treuthe to-gydd*ur* han mette,/redempciouo*n* ys mad for mannys syne
Paraphrases Psalm 84.11.
Wenzel, **629**, no. 39.

7352 Mercy, ih*es*u, rew on me/my hande is blody of thi blode!/Mercy, ih*es*u, for I se/thi myght that I not vnderstode!
Lament of Thomas, Towneley XXVIII, *Thomas of India*, lines 316–39.
Pearson, **196**: 249.

7353 Mightfull god, thou vs glad!/That heuen and erthe and all has mayde
Simeon's prayer, Towneley XVII, *The Purification of Mary*, lines 1–72.
Pearson, **196**: 242.

7354 Myth mylde and strong,/Syth schort and long
Sermon, *Sermo de ascensione domini* . . .
Stemmler, **647**, no. 39.

7355 Myghtfull god veray/Maker of all that is,/Thre p*er*sons withoutten nay/oone god in endles blis
Noah's prologue, Towneley III, *Noah and the Ark*, lines 1–72.
Pearson, **196**: 236.

7356 Myn hert is sore, I may not synge
One line, apparently an allusion to a song: Man in tribulation.
Wenzel, **629**, no. 40; **882**: 221.

7357 Myn hertes ioye is went a-way,/to wo *and* sorwe ys t*ur*ne my play
Translates Lamentations 5.15–16.
Wenzel, **629**, no. 41.

7358 Myrth I make till all men,/with my harp and fyngers ten
David's song, Towneley VII, *The Prophets*, lines 109–62.
Pearson, **196**: 237.

7359 Mystrys Barnarde gave her thys boke;/God sende her well heuyn to loke
A bookplate.
Hanna, **734**: 249, no. 32.

7360 Mystrys Dorethe god bovth save and se,/And gravnte enow that she may know the verete
A bookplate.
Hanna, **734**: 249, no. 33.

7361 Mystrys Dorethe, this is yovr boke;/Who wovll you deny,/Cavle me to recorde/I wyll saye ly
Bookplate.
Hanna, **734**: 249, no. 34.

7362 More loue may no man schewe/Maiorem caritatem nemo habet, etc.
De Passione Christi. Robbins includes this, with no. 192, as *2258.*
Wilson, **601**, no. 193.

7363 Most myghty maker*e* of Sunne and of mone/Kyng *of* kyng*ys and* lord ou*er* all

Temporary Index of First Lines 555

       Abraham's prologue, *Ludus Coventriae 5*, *Abraham and Isaac*, lines 1–8.
       Pearson, **196**: 236–7.

7364   Mod*er* and maiden þat neuer did mysse,/*intrauit castellum* of ioy and blisse
       Couplet at the beginning of a sermon on 'Intravit castellum' (Luke 10.38).
       Wenzel, **629**, no. 42.

7365   Mysyng gretly yn my mynde
       Reed, **21**, no. XVII.

7366   Mi chosen childir, comes vnto me,/With me to wonne nowe schall ȝe wende
       God's invitation to the upright. *The Last Judgement* (*York Plays*, ed. Beadle): 415.
       Astell, **929**: 176.

7367   Ma co*m*mendationes w^t humilitie/I send vnto hir fay^{t}full womanheid
       From Bannatyne MS: ff. 223^{r-v}, ed. Ritchie, Vol. 3: 278–80.
       Camargo, **949**: 182.

7368   My dullit corss dois hairtly reco*m*mend/My faythfull se*r*uice vnto my lady bricht
       From Bannatyne MS: ff. 238^{r-v}, ed. Ritchie, Vol. 3: 322–3.
       Camargo, **949**: 183.

7369   My folk, what haue I done to the,/That thou all thus shall tormente me?
       Lament of Jesus, Towneley XXIII, *The Crucifixion*, lines 244–71, 274–94.
       Pearson, **196**: 245; Osberg, **767**: 325.

7370   My jornay lat as I dyd take
       Wright, ed. *Songs and Ballads*: 97.
       Sandison, **139**: 133, A 31.

7371   My joye it is ffrom here to hyre
       Reed, **21**, no. XXV.

7372   Mi lordes lemman is liche þe mone/for hire loue chaungeȝ alto sone
       Verse from a sermon.
       Erb, **564**: 72.

7373   my owne dere hart I grete you well/yevyn as hit is my mynde
       A love epistle.
       Boffey, **750**: 20; **848**: 165; Camargo, **949**: 187.

7374   Ne bring þu nouoth þeself to lowe/With lust þat lestet but litel þrowe
       De Peccato.
       Wilson, **601**, no. 147.

7375   Ne sal it wite no man, wite no man,/Hu Ich go ibunde for me lemmon
       A sermon lyric on love's bonds.
       Wenzel, **882**: 225.

7376   Nesciat dextera, quid faciat sinistra./Let noȝt þi lyft hand: our lord techeþ
       MS Douce 104; cf. EETS 54: 46.
       Heuser, **16**: 223.

7377   Nis no[þunc?] on liue þat maketh wimman/swo sore to wipen as here lefmon
       A marginal note.
       Wenzel, **629**, no. 44.

7378   No woundir is altho^t my hairt be thrall/To ȝow I wiss þe flour of courtesy
       From Bannatyne MS: ff. 234^{r-v}, ed. Ritchie, Vol. 3: 309–11.
       Camargo, **949**: 183.

7379   None/And hyr/So fayr so/Take hyr to
       A love lyric to the Blessed Virgin. It lacks many line endings.
       Benskin, **776**: 37.

7380   Not long agoo/it chaunsed soo
       Wyatt, *Poetical Works*, Aldine edn.: 130; Padelford, *C16 Lyrics*: 12.
       Sandison, **139**: 133, A 33.

7381   Now begy*n*nys to go þe banner of o*u*r lord þe kyng,/now kun [*or* gun?] spryng wide þe crose tokenyng
       Translates the first stanza of the hymn 'Vexilla regis prodeunt.'
       Wenzel, **629**, no. 45.

7382   Nu hur is goo wroth [*corrected from* worth]/and hyre frendes loth
       The miseries of a fallen girl.
       Wenzel, **629**, no. 46.

7383   Now I p*er*ceue yo*u* chaungyd thought.
       Reed, **21**, no. XXVI. (Version of IX.)

7384   Nowe maiden meke and modir myne,/Itt was full mekill myrþe to þe

	The five joys of Mary, words of Jesus, but spoken by six angels, according to the rubricator, York XVLII, *The Assumption and Coronation of the Virgin*, lines 113–44. Pearson, **196**: 244; Osberg, **767**: 326.
7385	Now may I morne as one off late/Dryuen by force from my delyte From a sequence in the Devonshire MS, thought to be correspondence composed during their imprisonment by Lord Thomas Howard and Lady Margaret Douglas. Muir, **41**: 261–2, no. 7; Camargo, **949**:182.
7386	Now she that I/Louyd trewly/Beryth a full fayr face Burden: '[Care awey, a]wey, awey,/Mornyng awey.' John Rastell. Greene, **86**, no. 470.1.
7387	Now that I have cape and hood, Longer will I do no good! Spoken by a devil who received a cape and hood from this landlord for work done at a handmill. Wenzel, **701**: 97. Son [?] so he hauet coperu*n* and te hod,/ne wil he nomre don non god On growing slack after entering a religious order. Wenzel, **629**, no. 55.
7388	Now the lady lechery, you must don your attendans Isolable lyric in *Mary Magdalene, The Digby Plays*, ed. F.J. Furnivall, EETS ES 70 (1896; repr. 1967): 70, lines 422–5. Robbins, **744**: footnote 37.
7389	Nu te wude, Marie, al sa ro./Ne sal hit wite noman wuder hith go Mary Magdalene's flight to the desert. Wenzel, **882**: 227.
7390	O cruell ffortune to me most contrarye Courtly love lyric. Boffey, **848**: 168.
7391	O Cupid I graunt thy might is much/for sure thov loveth the dart 'to' shout at soch . . . Lyric in hand of George Conyers. Hanna, **734**: 249, no. 36; Boffey, **848**: 169.
7392	O cupid king quhome to sall I complene/or call for confort in þis cairfull cace From Bannatyne MS: ff. 224^v–5^r , ed. Ritchie, Vol. 3: 282–3. Camargo, **949**: 183.
7393	O gra*c*yous Ihe*s*u bothe trysty and kynde/Spem meam to put in the me thynketh best 'Spes mea in deo est,' in the vellum wrapper for a legal manuscript in Holkham Hall. Griffiths, **1006**: 281–2.
7394	O Lady Ven*us* what aylyth the Reed, **21**, no. XXII.
7395	O Lorde, have marssye one my soull,/Whyne that to marssye he dose it call./Amen. Finis. George Conyers Lyric in hand of George Conyers. Hanna, **734**: 249, no. 37.
7396	O! maker vnmade, full of myght,/O! Jesu so jentile and jente Longeus receives his sight from Jesus' blood, York XXXVI, *Mortificacio Christi [and Burial of Jesus]*, lines 300–12. Osberg, **767**: 326.
7397	O splendent spectakyll most comlyeste of hewe Courtly love lyric. Winchester Anthology, item 164. Wilson, **88b**: 29, 38; Boffey, **848**: 172.
7398	O that fface t*h*at ffragraunt fface Reed, **21**, no. XIV.
7399	O that my tovng covld but expres Courtly love lyric. Hanna, **734**: 249, no. 38; Boffey, **848**: 172.
7400	O þou my brothyr haue in thy mende/ . . ./How thy flesh and thy blood ys ordeynd Verses hidden in a ME prose Miracle of the Virgin. Pickering, **908**: 231–4.
7401	O verre rote Courtly love lyric. Boffey, **848**: 173.

Temporary Index of First Lines

7402   Of all þat he was wont to haue/is left hym oonly but his graue
In a Middle English funeral sermon.
Wenzel, **629**, no. 47.
Of all þat I was wont to haue/To me alone y^s lefte my graue
In a collection of sermons assembled by 'Selk.'
Fletcher, **685**: 108; Bitterling, **706**: 102; Powell, **786**: 12.

7403   Of grete mornyng may I me mene,/And walk full werily be þis way
Joseph, old and weak, is ashamed that he has wedded a young wife, York, *Joseph's trouble about Mary*, York XIII, lines 1–20.
Osberg, **767**: 325.

7404   Of my husband giu I noht,/Another hauet my luue ybohit
I do not care for my husband.
Wenzel, **882**: 216.

7405   Of one accorde owre harttes be knytt
Courtly love lyric.
Stevens **438**: 449; Boffey, **848**: 173.

7406   Of þe graces þat God hat þe sent/Of þe godis þat God hat þe lent
De Reddenda Racione. Preceded by 'Oportet te reddere racionem.'
Wilson, **601**, no. 222.

7407   Of the VII dedly synnys now will I telle
MS Laud 416.
Heuser, **16**: 207

7408   Of wysdom I haue most plente./þat godeness sterys bot lytyl me
Translates a dialogue between a king and four philosophers.
Wenzel, **629**, no. 48.

7409   Omnis sanctus in tempore oportuno/þan consciens comford vs: boþ clerge and scriptour
Cf. EETS 54: 264.
Heuser, **16**: 264.

7410   On bowes of tre of gret myght/Hengen thre bodys be day light
A charm against thieves.
Gray, **610**: 67.

7411   On folie was myn silwyr leyd/And folileke it betaght
Carefree youth and wretched old age.
Smithers, **897**: 455-6.

7412   On mo[r]ewe morwen comet al oure care/Wan borwed ware wil nom fare
De Morte.
Wilson, **601**, no. 117; Wenzel, **791**: 154.

7413   On þe tre he hatȝ iborn/Oure sennes for whiche we weren forlorn
De Amore Dei. 'He himself has borne our sins in his body on the cross.'
Grimestone Lyric 24.
Wilson, **601**, no. 24; Wenzel, **882**: 107.

7414   On 3 crosses of a tree/3 dead bodyes did hang
A charm against thieves.
McBryde, **116**: 169.

7415   Ons in your grace I knowe I was,/Even as well as now is he
'What once I was.'
Thomas Wyatt
Davies, **61**, no. 187.

7416   Only to ȝow in erd þat I lufe best/I me commend ane hundreth thowsand syiss
From Bannatyne MS: ff. 237^v–238^r, ed. Ritchie, Vol. 3: 321–2.
Camargo, **949**: 183.

7417   Oure gladnesse of herte ys awent,/To sorwe *and* wo oure murþe is went
Translates Lamentations 5.15–16.
Wenzel, **629**, no. 49; **701**: 84.

7418   Ower kynges baneres byth foorþe y-bore,/now schynes þe crouches þat raþer was pryuee
Translates the first stanza of the hymn 'Vexilla redis prodeunt.'
Wenzel, **629**, no. 50.

7419   Our lord god in trynyte,/Myrth and lovyng be to the
Praise of God by Cherubin, Towneley I, *Creation*, lines 61–76.
Pearson, **196**: 232.

7420 Oure lorde Ihesu Criste/Ouer a den roode.
'For armes or legges that ar/myswreyght say thes wordes,' a charm.
Hanna, **734**: 249–50, no. 42.

7421 Oure peynes ben grille and felle/Be war of þe pit of helle
De Inferno.
Wilson, **601**, no. 93.

7422 Over yonder's a park, which is newly begun/All bells in Paradise I heard them a-ring
Down in yon forest there stands a hall/The bells of Paradise I heard them ring
The heron flew east, the heron flew west/The heron flew to the fair forest
Down in yon forest be a hall,/Sing May, Queen May, sing Mary
Traditional versions of *1132*, from North Staffordshire, Derbyshire, Scotland, and USA.
Rickert, **22**: 194; Greene, **37**, **86**, **461**, no. 322 A, B, C, D, E; κ, ε.τ., **105**; Sidgwick, **110**; Gilchrist, **125**: 52; Berry, **345**, **387**.

7423 Parauenture hit may hapen/yet yt is but hazarde
Reed, **21**, no. XXIII.

7424 Pes be/In vertu of þe/Fiat pax in virtute tua
De Pace.
Wilson, **601**, no. 150.

7425 Peccator assimilatur/To a fals tresorer
De Peccato
Wilson, **601**, no. 142.

7426 Peccatum est vitandum propter quatuor: For it is/A filthe þat God almithten hateʒ
De Peccato.
Wilson, **601**, no. 145.

7427 Plana sine paliacione . . . Opyn wyʒt-oute leyseyngge
Sermon, *Dominus hiis opus habet.*
Stemmler, **647**, no. 14.

7428 Pouerte ys tornd in-to couetynge,/Trevth in-to trecherie
Evil changes taking place.
Wenzel, **882**: 183.

7429 Prai for hym þat made þis scryte/þat God make hym and vs of synnys quyte
Follows the explicit of the final dominical sermon of 'The Northern Homilies' [*2940*].
Hanna, **734**: 250, no. 44.

7430 Pride of herte and hey beringge;/Of þi time euel spendingge
De Temptacione. Prededed by: 'Periculosissima temptacione est nulla temptacione pulsari, quia qui non temptatur quatuor mala incurrit que sunt.'
Wilson, **601**, no. 240.

7431 Queramus ergo istum puerum/þat rotyth nowth
Sermon, *Sermo in natali domini* . . .
Stemmler, **647**, no. 47.

7432 Quod Perkyn þe ploughman: be seint Peter of Rome
Cf. EETS 54: 139.
Heuser, **16**: 227.

7433 Rax ande wax
Exalta adole.
Winchester Anthology, item 132 (k).
Wilson, **88b**: 26, 38.

7434 Remember that there be in hell
Subscribed 'w.w.'
Winchester Anthology, item 117.
Wilson, **88b**: 24, 38.

7435 Riche apparell, costly and precius/Makithe a man lusty, cumly and gloryus
Poem in wall paintings at Leconfield.
Wilson, **321**: 177.

7436 Ryght and no wrong, it is amonge
Woolf, **522**: 193–4, 398, 409.

7437 Ryght noble and blessede fader to whom of excellence
Addressed to William Waynflete as Bishop of Winchester.
Winchester Anthology, item 74.
Wilson, **88b**: 22, 38.

Temporary Index of First Lines 559

7438 Robbers me beyte and made me bonde
Ex vespilionibus egomet vapulabam et ab eis colbertus fiebam
Winchester Anthology, item 132 (n).
Wilson, **88b**: 27, 38.

7439 Robyn Hode in Barnysdale stode/And lent hym tyl a mapyll thystyll.' Burden: 'Downe downe downe &c.'
John Rastell, c. 1517, *A new interlude and amery of the Nature of the iiij. elementes.*
Greene, **86**, no. 473.1.

7440 Reuthe made God on mayden to lithe
Woolf, **522**: 169; Gray, **575**: 39.

7441 Sainte wynwall and saint braston and saint tobas/and sonne that shineth so bright
'To binde a house/a gaynste theffes,' a charm against thieves, written as prose.
McBryde, **116**: 170.

7442 Salue sancta parens: my moder dere/All heyl modyr with glad chere
Christ's greeting to Mary, after the Resurrection.
Jeffreys, **638**: 22.

7443 Seyngurs þat solem weer sembled hem al samen,/þat were gra[c]ious & glad of þer gamen
'The Lament for Sir John Berkeley,' possibly by 'Turnour.'
Turville-Petre, **790**: 336–8.

7444 Seldome seene ys swetyst, and pretye thingis be strange
Rigg, **516**:143.

7445 Seth faste þi fot on rode-tre;/In Cristis bodi mak þi se
De Passione Christi.
Wilson, **601**, no. 157.

7446 Shall she neuer out of mynde
Reed, **21**, no. XV.

7447 [S]alt dreden God for he wrouthte þe;/Salt louen God for he bouthte þe;
De Via Christi. Manuscript damaged.
Wilson, **601**, no. 245.

7448 Schame and drede long lyfe and nede . . . the book the bord the bowh the staf
English scrap in Latin theological miscellany, MS Lambeth Palace Library 78: f. 306 ʳ.
Pickering, **785**: 21.

7449 Sort arn mennis dayȝes; his monis ben told also;
De Morte.
Wilson, **601**, no. 109; Wenzel, **791**: 154.

7450 Schort was turned in-to longe/--quando homo erat deus--
Sermon, *Se[r]mo in navitate domini . . .*
Stemmler, **647**, no. 33.

7451 Sic uite peniteas ȝif heuene thow thynk to wynne/Cor simul inspiceas and clense the clene from synne
Macaronic penitential lyric. Cf. *1297.*
O'Donoghue and Woolgar, **739**: 498.

7452 Synne is so on my breste/þat non so bitter loue is of prest
A nun in love with a priest.
Wenzel, **629**, no. 52; Stemmler, **647**, no. 2.

7453 Sen he fro vs will twynne etc.
John, help me nowe and neuere more/That I myght come hym tille
Dramatic planctus, York XXXIV, *Christ Led up to Calvary* lines 143–60, 202–3.
Taylor, **111**: 612.

7454 Since I for love, man, bought thee dear,--/Thyself the sight thou mayst see here
Makculloch MS.
Adamson, **35**: 126–7.

7455 Since mercie nowe in men doth rest,/Assaie what lyes in womans breste
Distich in a sixteenth-century hand.
Hanna, **734**: 251, no. 49.

7456 Sa sal i luue the, sal i luue the,/sal i neuer for thi luue wanner be
Perhaps from a popular song.
Wenzel, **629**, no. 54.

7457 Softeliche senne gennet in wende,/But it bitet as a neddere at þe end.
De Luxuria.
Wilson, **601**, no. 101.

7458 Salomon þe wyse he tawt in his lyf/To all maner men þat cast hem for to wyffe
Burden: 'All ffresche, all fresch, fresch is my song etc.' An anti-marital carol.
Wilson, **747**: 25.

7459 some men offrenden hym boistes of riche spicerie/some men maden hem bysi aboute here marchandie
Verse from a sermon.
Erb, **564**: 71.

7460 Sum tyme I haue you seyn/yn hygh estate full strange
Reed, **21**, no. XIII.

7461 Some tyme I was a persone here,/Of thys churche of Wadson
Verse on cadaver tomb of Hugh Brystowe, Waddeson, Bucks (1548).
King, **761**: 496.

7462 Sorfulhed of detȝ þat stant an waitet þe;/Reufulhed of Cristes blod þat schad was on þe tre
De Ocupacione.
Wilson, **601**, no. 138; Wenzel, **791**: 154.

7463 Sors maris, ira fere,/dolor anguis, agunt miserere./ dred of þis gryslich lyon/and gyle of þys felle dragoun
Verse from a sermon.
Erb, **564**: 80.

7464 Sothliche with trewe sennes forsakingge;/Erliche with hastif penance takingge
De Resurexione. Preceded by: 'Nota quod resurexio Christi fuit multipliciter, in signum qualis debet esse resurrexio peccatoris a culpa. Nam Christus resurexit, ita homo vere. Vere per detestacionem peccatorum'
Wilson, **601**, no. 221.

7465 Sowters haue a nyse pryde
Sutores vtuntur quadam pompa frenola
Winchester Anthology, item 132 (h).
Wilson, **88b**: 26, 38.

7466 Spere and cros, nail, detȝ and þorn/Schewen hou I bouthte man þat was forlorn.
De Passione Christi.
Wilson, **601**, no. 158.

7467 Stay, traveller, guess who lies here
Epitaph for one of Henry VIII's fools.
Scattergood, **910**: 470.

7468 Still vndir þe levis greene
Maitland MS. Pinkerton, *Ancient Scotish Poems* II: 205. Sibbald *Chron. Scot. Poetry* I: 201. Laing, *Early Popular Poetry* II: 34. Furnivall, *Captain Cox*, cl. G.G. Smith, *Specimens of Middle Scots*: 64.
Sandison, **139**: 134, A 36.

7469 Sunt infelices, qui[a] matres sunt meritrices/þere sch is weld wiþ ony kyng: wo is þe reme
Cf. EETS 54: 52.
Heuser, **16**: 225.

7470 Swete Ihesu/þat was of maydyn borne/my body nor my sowle/lett þem neuer be lorne
Versified penance composed of popular prayer tags, 11 lines with a prose introduction.
O'Mara, **878**: 449.

7471 Suich semblant Crist sal maken to þe aboue/Suich as þu makest her nou for his loue
De Eleemosyna.
Wilson, **601**, no. 76.

7472 tak þis in mynde of me/and wanne ich am ago/þou þenc on me
Verse from a sermon.
Erb, **564**: 76.

7473 þat fastingge withouten elmesse is of mith/As is þe lampe with 'oten' olie and lith
De Ieiunio. Fasting without almsgiving is like a lamp without oil.
Grimestone Lyric 95.
Wilson, **601**, no. 95; Wenzel, **882**: 108.

7474 þat ich haue ben longe about,/al haf i lorn a-pon þis niȝt
Apparently the speech of a devil frustrated by a knight's timely repentance.
Wenzel, **629**, no. 56.

7475 þat is on Ynglysche þus to say/He says, Thynk on þine endyng daye

Temporary Index of First Lines

A poem on death, item 47 in a Carthusian miscellany.
Hogg, **735**: 266–7.

7476 þat knotte þat is knytte scholde not be brokone./Trw loue in hertus to-gydur scholde be lokone
'In wedlocke.'
Wenzel, **629**, no. 57; Fein, **936**: 314.

7477 That mi lef askes wit sare weping,/Ne mai Ic it werne for nane kinnes thing
God will not refuse to listen to insistent prayer.
Wenzel, **882**: 222.

7478 Det peruynkkle hed ykowmbyrght owre town,/Tyl vs het ybent hys boghe
Burden: 'Man of mightt, that al hed ydyght/An knowys heuery wronge.'
County Archives Office, Maidstone, Kent. K.A.O.U. 182ZI.
Greene, **86**, no. 424.1; Müller, **809**: 165.

7479 The ape the lyon the foxe the ase/Descrybes manes nature as in a glase
Bühler, **428**: 22.

7480 þe bred þat fedoȝ vs eueri day,/þou graunte vs, lord, þis esterday!
Sermon, *Panem nostrum cotidianum da nobis hodie* . . .
Stemmler, **647**, no. 15.

7481 þe day taket his lith, Misericordia/þeues taken here flith Demones
De Gracia. Sermon divisions, preceded by 'Wanne þe sunne rist.'
Grimestone Lyric 82.
Wilson, **601**, no. 82; Wenzel, **882**: 122.

7482 þe dew of Aueril/Hauetȝ y-maked the grene lef to sprynge
Spring song of a Cistercian abbot who escaped eternal damnation by a hair's breadth.
Wenzel, **882**: 223.

7483 The fyrst commandment off all þe lawe
MS Arundel 20.
Heuser, **16**: 206.

7484 Thee flourys in a nyȝt can spryng;/Frome euery flowur a streme rennyng;/A clerk, among the flourys lyyng,/Hem fond, but noȝt durst say or syng
'For drede of the Maie.' Apparently concerns clerical indiscretion.
Hanna, **734**: 252, no. 55.

7485 þe foot of þi wil be bounde in þe bond of chastete/þe hond of þi werk be bounde in þe bond of charite
De Religione. Preceded by: 'Nota quod si religiosus esse volueris quod stringaris vinculis. Oportet.'
Wilson, **601**, no. 220.

7486 þe ȝate is opun,/þe kyng commun,/þe couenand is brokun,/And þe sesi[n]g is nomun
Sermon, *Sermo de ascensione domini* . . .
Stemmler, **647**, no. 35.

7487 þe ȝefte faliȝet nouth with skil [no. 74]
þe ȝifte of hand faliȝet nout with skil [no. 75]
De Eleemosyna.
Wilson, **601**: nos. 74 and 75.

7488 The God of Love, that sits above,/Doth know us: Doth know us
Translation, from Douce Fragments.
Comper, **38**: no 70.

7489 The heyer that the ploumes be,/The heyer that the tres
In a hand of the late sixteenth century, and followed by two indecipherable lines.
Hanna, **734**: 253, no. 56.

7490 þe ioie of oure herte is a-wei y-went,/Oure song is to sorwe isent
Erroneously registered as a variation of *3397*.
Stemmler, **647**, no. 3.

7491 The kyng is wode and fowle doth fare./The qwene wepyth and makyth gret care
Sums up an exemplum from the *Life of Kentigern*.
Wenzel, **629**, no. 60; **701**: 71; Pickering, **785**: 21.

7492 þe leuys sothyn in wit wyn/Schal make her f⟨or⟩ to grow will & fyn
On 'þe vertu of rose mary.'
Scattergood, **556**: 338.

7493 The maidens came/When I was in my mother's bower etc.
'The Bridal Morn' (Gardner).

Extract from a longer poem in Harley 7578, printed *Archiv* 106: 61 (ed. Fehr).
Chambers and Sidgwick, **18**: 82; Gardner, **75**: 19.

7494 The mil gothe and let hir go so merely
[Music.]
Winchester Anthology, item 217.
Wilson, **88b**: 35, 38.

7495 þe mone chaungeȝ his shap/þe mone chaunges his heu
Verse from a sermon.
Erb, **564**: 71.

7496 The old dog þe old dog as he lay in his den a buffa
[Music.]
Winchester Anthology, item 217.
Wilson, **88b**: 35, 38.

7497 The [p..as] & singgest of pype . . ./can not dow away your gestinge of I woll & canne/
That I can I can/& dow I wyll
Reed, **21**, no. X.

7498 þe pore man oueral litȝ stille/Quil is pours is nouth at is wille
De Paupertate.
Wilson, **601**, no. 153.

7499 The proverbes of Salmon do playnly declare
Potentially a product of the early court of Henry VIII.
Hanna, **734**: 253, no. 58.

7500 *[Form A]* The ryche ne rychesse god ne hatyth,/But who-so for rychesse god forsakyth
[Form B] Neiþer þe rychesse/Ne þe ryche man God ne hatyþ
ME Verse 42 of *Fasciculus Morum*, perhaps considered part of Verse 41.
Wenzel, **701**: 180–1.

7501 The sede of man *and* woman clere as cristal it is/Owre lorde hym selfe it made for man jwis
De spermate hominis, on human embryology.
Hargreaves, **668**.

7502 þe schip in þe seyling,/Treuthe in michil speking
De Periculo. Preceded by 'Tria versantur cotidie in periculo, vidilicet.'
Wilson, **601**, no. 151.

7503 The ship saileth over the salte fom/Wyl brynge etc.
Stevick, **103**: 176

7504 þe soule of þis synful withe/þoru contritioun þat on hir lith
Angel's message in an exemplum about a contrite incestuous woman.
Wenzel, **629**, no. 63.

7505 þe vnseli man seyde of God þat hyme no rouhts
Speeches of four devils seen carrying off the body of a rich man.
Wenzel, **629**, no. 64.

7506 þe wyte skyn haȝ a sori lak/for nouu hit is wyte and *nou* hit is blak
Verse from a sermon.
Erb, **564**: 69.

7507 The wyse man his sone for bede/Masons crafte and all clymbynge
Lass, **476**: 175.

7508 the blynd I thynk my lady dere
Reed, **21**, no. XX.

7509 Hem þat ben naked ȝif cloþing;/Hem þat ben hungri ȝef feding
De Misericordia.
Wilson, **601**, no. 105.

7510 þer I luuie, þer leik i noth./þer his min hie, þer is all my þouth
Couplet adapting the Latin proverb 'Ubi amor, ibi oculus.'
Wenzel, **629**, no. 65.

7511 Ther ys a thyng as I suppose
Person, **53**, no. 66.

7512 *Version A*: þer is on,/And swsch a nothur was neuere non
Version B: He is swsch on,/þat swsch a noþur nas neuere non
Version C: He is on,/And swch anoþer was neuer non
Sermon, *In natali domini*. Entered in *IMEV* as last lines of *1611*.
Stemmler, **647**, no. 43.

7513	þer ys on in þys hous/þat doþ wornge to oure spouse Verse from a sermon. Erb, **564**: 83.
7514	þer nys no God but gold alone A *communis cantus* mentioned in a sermon that condemns various social vices. Wenzel, **882**: 220.
7515	Ther was a ladie leaned her back to a wall Person, **53**: no 61.
7516	þei ben noth wel for to leuen/þat with manie wordis wil quemen De Adulacione (no. 14), De Decepcione (no. 61). Grimestone Lyric 14. Wilson, **601**: nos. 14 and 61; Wenzel, **882**: 104.
7517	þei þat ben trewe is louingge,/Alone in god is here restingge De Dileccione. Wilson, **601**, no. 66.
7518	þin ffadere was a bond mand,/þin moder curtesye non can An opinion of high birth in sermon remarks on contrition. Fletcher, **919**: 164.
7519	þenk, man, þi loue was dere ibouth:/For loue of werdli þing þu les et nouth Lamentacio dolorosa. Wilson, **601**, no. 207.
7520	þeynk on þe doom þat now us myn/for ful sone such schal be þyn Couplets warning of death. Wenzel, **629**, no. 67.
7521	þis boke heyght yppocras/þe best surgyon þat heuer in þis world was Scattergood, **556**: 337.
7522	þis boke wrot [a large erasure]:/God kepe hym fro syn and schame Follows the explicit of *4164*. Hanna, **734**: 253, no. 59.
7523	This daye is Fridaye/Faste while we maye 'Friday spell.' W. Sparrow-Simpson, *J. Arch. Ass.* xlviii: 46. Gray, **575**: 164.
7524	þis is my bodi, als ȝe mov se,/þat for ȝou sal peined be De Corpore Christi. Preceded by 'Hoc est corpus meum.' Grimestone Lyric 56. Wilson, **601**, no. 56; Wenzel, **882**: 117.
7525	Thys ys my mystrys boke,/Who ovtyth hym forto have;/Whoso whovlde agenstey loke,/He ys a vere knave Probably 'agenstey' should be emended to 'agensey.' Hanna, **734**: 253, no. 60.
7526	This is the time Man hath o'ercome/The fiend, robbed hell Harl. MS, *c.* 1370 Adamson, **35**: 60; Le May, **169**.
7527	þis is þe wylle *þat* god is inne/þat ȝe be clene of dedlyche synne Verse from a sermon. Erb, **564**: 70.
7528	Thys londe was furste Be goddys ordynaunce/Inhabyt withe Brytons full longe Agone *Titulus Regis Edwardi Quarti ad Coronam Anglie Sanguine Bruti et Cawaldi Quondam Regis Britonum*, a Yorkist chronicle to support the succession of Edward IV. Louis, **955**: 10–20.
7529	This picture presentythe to yore remembrance/The last semblytude of alle yore bewty and and fame *Memento mori* verse on cadaver tomb of Elizabeth Thame, Shipton-under-Wychwood, Oxfordshire, (1548). King, **761**: 496.
7530	þis saule I chalange for to wyne,/þat I knaw is ful of syne Dialogue between the Devil, Death, the Soul, an Angel, the BV, Christ and the Father. Heffernan, **802**: 235.
7531	þis teene for thi trespace I take/Who couthe þe more kyndynes have kydde/Than I?

Jesus addresses the larger audience, speaking of his wounds. *The Death of Christ* (*York Plays*, ed. Beadle: 326).
Astell, **929**: 173.

7532 þis woman þ*at* deyde in doloor/is qwytt*er* þen þe lili flour
Inscription on tomb of a sinful woman converted by a vision of Christ.
Wenzel, **629**, no. 69.

7533 Thomas Beech is my name/And with my pen I write the same
Cf. *3662.5*.
Bühler, **471**: 649.

7534 Thu blynde in flessche hast fall in a case/þu hast geven to þe fende þing*is* þ*at* riche was
Sermon lyric from a tale of a miracle of the Virgin, in which a Latin verses spell out a woman's sins on her blood-stained hand.
Whiteford, **841**: 456.

7535 þu faire fles þat art me dere,/Nou art þu fo, nou artu fere
De Tempore. Grimestone Lyric 234.
Wilson, **601**, no. 234; Wenzel, **882**: 132.

7536 Thow maker þat is most of myght,/To thy mercy I make my mone
Joseph praises the Lord for his grace and regrets his weakness, York XVIII, *The Flight into Egypt*, lines 1–24.
Osberg, **767**: 325.

7537 þu þat hangest þer so heye,/þu art mi sone—-I ne haue no mo
De Passione Christ.
Wilson, **601**, no. 183.

7538 þu wysdom þat c*re*pedest out of Godes mouþe,/þat rechest frame est too west, fra*m* norþ to souþ
Couplets translating the Advent antiphon 'O Sapientia.'
Wenzel, **629**, no. 70; **701**: 86.

7539 thowe I were synfull deme [not me]/MS me not
Sermon lyric of a repentant harlot.
Whiteford, **841**: 457.

7540 Thoughe my pycture be not to your pleasaunce
Woolf, **522**: 354.

7541 þoȝ þou habbe a fayr [face],/ne treyst þou noȝt to meche þeron
Translates Latin lines 'O formose puer' etc., Virgil, *Eclogues*, II: 17–18.
Wenzel, **629**, no. 71.

7542 þeȝ þou habbe caseles *and* toures,/halles, chau*m*bres, semeliche boures
Triplets translating the Latin: 'Si tibi magna domus, si splendida mensa, quid inde?'
Wenzel, **629**, no. 72.

7543 þoru suetnesse of lore in preching,/þoru fair conuersacioun in leuing
De Doctrina Sine Gracia. Preceded by: 'Tu qui habes curam animarum tripliciter debes eas pascere et custodire, videlicet.'
Wilson, **601**, no. 71; Coleman, **753**: 181.

7544 Thus he preuet our fay
Mirk's *Festial*, sermon *De Festo Sancti Thome Apostoli*.
Long, **356**:13–14.

7545 þus þay þat ben dampnet to hell
Mirk's *Festial*, homily for Advent Sunday.
Long, **356**:13.

7546 Thy lyfe it is a law of dethe,/A strengthe of dome the to begyle
Fletcher, **651**: 342; Whiteford, **841**: 457.

7547 þi lust þat lasteþ but a wile, þou it be breme and like,/it deþ þe for to sike sore *and* lite loue *and* sore for to sike
Two long lines, on *voluptas carnis*.
Wenzel, **629**, no. 73.

7548 Tintful, tantful,/Al is þis lond ful./Yehc I go al dai,/Ne habbe Ich min hond ful
A riddle of fog.
Wenzel, **882**: 219.

7549 To eueri preysing is knit a knot./þe preysing wer good, ne wer þe 'but'
De Detraccione.

Temporary Index of First Lines 565

If it were not for the 'but,' everyone would be perfect. But none has been found who lacked 'but.'
Grimestone Lyric 58.
Wilson, **601**, no. 58; Coleman, **753**: 181; Wenzel, **882**: 131.

7550 [T]o his grace I will me ta,/With chastite to dele
Mary's words before she sings the *Magnificat* (stage direction: 'Magnificat, *tunc cantat*), York XII, *The Annunciation, and Visit of Elizabeth to Mary*, lines 233–40.
Pearson, **196**: 242.

7551 To knawe the vaynes to let blode one/3e that wyll lette gude men blode
On bloodletting.
Hunt, **1017**: 321–2.

7552 to loughe to smyll to sporte to play
Reed, **21**, no. VI.

7553 To the fend of helle I am betawth,/hwan Cryst me clepyd ne herd I hym nawth
Exclamation of a damned soul.
Wenzel, **629**, no. 74; Pickering, **785**: 21.

7554 To þe whech mercy God bryng you and me
Mirk's *Festial*, Sermon 9, *De Innocentibus*.
Long, 356:14.

7555 To 3ou þat is þe harbre of my Hairt/And creatour in quhome my confort lyis
From Bannatyne MS: ff. 218^v–219^r, ed. Ritchie, Vol. 3: 264–5.
Camargo, **949**: 182.

7556 To yowr gentyll letters an answere to resyte,/Both I and my penne there to wyll aply
From a sequence in the Devonshire MS, thought to be correspondence composed during their imprisonment by Lord Thomas Howard and Lady Margaret Douglas.
Muir, **41**: 265, no. 13; Camargo, **949**: 182.

7557 Toldiri toldiro
An ancient lyrical burden or refrain, surviving in English popular music.
Wenzel, **882**: 218.

7558 Tred eke the kennyth/Sonday whate letter on rennyth
Written around a calendar wheel in Daniel's *Liber uricrisiarum*, to explain Book II, chapter 6.
Hanna, **734**: 254, no. 62; Means, **978**: 606.

7559 Trol þe bol and drinke to me
[Music.]
Winchester Anthology, item 217.
Wilson, **88b**: 35, 38.

7560 Trewe withouten quey[n]tise and feiningge;/Lestingge withouten deceyte and chaunggynge
De Dileccione. Prededed by 'Nota quod vera dileccio debet esse.'
Wilson, **601**, no. 65.

7561 Treuloue is large, fre *and* hende,/*and* loue 3if alle þins[?] bleþeli to his frende
Couplet translating the Latin: 'Diliget ardenter sic dat amico cuncta libenter.'
Wenzel, **629**, no. 75.

7562 Trewþe ys turnyd in-to trecherye,/chast loue in-to lecherye
Couplets translating a distich: 'Ingenium dolus est, amor omnis ceca voluntas . . .'
Wenzel, **629**, no. 76.

7563 Turn þe to vre louerd./Foro widerward so þu wlt fle
Based on Eccli. 17.21.
Wenzel, **629**, no. 77.

7564 Two stones hathe yt or els yt is wrong
Person, **53**, no. 62.

7565 Under ane brokin bank ane by
Pinkerton, ed., *Ancient Scotish Poems* II: 200; Sibbald, *Chron. Scot. Poetry* III: 197.
Sandison, **139**: 135, A 42.

7566 Vndyrnethe a lovere
Sub lodio
Winchester Anthology, item 132 (l).
Wilson, **88b**: 27, 38.

7567 Undyrstande what thow were and art,/ffor sum tyme thow dreue thy fadyr cart
Exemplum of an English bishop of low birth who reminds himself of his origins.
Wenzel, **629**, no. 78; **701**: 73; Coleman, **753**: 287.

7568   Undo your dore
       Baskerville, **148**.

7569   Ondo ȝoure ȝatys, p*r*incys, to me!/Helle ȝatis, oppen ȝe!
       On the Harrowing of Hell.
       Fletcher, **919**: 165.

7570   Vnkende men I haue fownde therfore I smyte wyth dethy wownd
       English scrap in Latin theological miscellany, MS Lambeth Palace Library 78: f. 266ᵛ.
       Pickering, **785**: 21.

7571   Walkyng allone amang thir levis grene
       Bannatyne MS.
       Sandison, **139**: 144, D 36.

7572   Waloway! my lefe deres/there I stand in this sted,/sich sorow my hart sheres/for rewth I can no red
       Peter's lament for Jesus, Towneley XXVIII, *Thomas of India*, lines 65–79.
       Pearson, **196**: 249.

7573   Walterius Pollard *non est* but a dullard;/I say that Pollard is none mery gollard
       Bodl. MS Rawlinson D. 328: f. 162a (*c*.1450), given to Walter Pollard of Plymouth, 1444–5.
       Sisam and Sisam, **69**, no. 316.

7574   Was thou noght, Franceis, with thi wapin
       Baldwin, **165**.

7575   We ben heled þat eer wer seke./Iblissed be þat wonder leche
       De Passione Christi.
       Wilson, **601**, no. 160.

7576   Wee happie hirdes men heere/maye singe and eke reioice
       Carol, perhaps from a medieval pageant.
       Friedman, **606**: 300–1; Cutts, **826**.

7577   We schun maken a ioly castel/on a bank brysden a bry*m*me
       Apparently an allusion to a Latin popular song.
       Wenzel, **629**, no. 79; **882**: 228; Dronke, **935**: 11.

7578   Whe schold neuer lust, hop, ne dawnce,/Noþer syng no song of þis new ordenance
       Wilson, **321**: 183.

7579   Wedde me Robyn and brynge me home
       Tibi nubam Roberte et me ducas domum
       Winchester Anthology, item 132 (i).
       Wilson, **88b**: 26, 38.

7580   Weddyng withoutyn luffe,/Deth withoutyn sorow,/Synn withoutynn schame
       Tres abusiones seculi.
       Wenzel, **882**: 179–80.

7581   Welcome! blyssed Mary and maydyn ay,/Welcome! mooste meke in thyne array
       Anna welcomes the bright star, York XLI, *The Purification of Mary: Simeon and Anna Prophesy*, lines 324–39.
       Pearson, **196**: 243; Osberg, **767**: 326.

7582   Welcum illustrat layde and oure quene!
       In *Bannatyne MS*, Vol. 2: 235.
       Taylor, **118**.

7583   Welcom, my Lord! welcom, my grace!/Welcome, my sone, and my solace!
       Dramatic planctus, Hegge Plays, Coventry XXXV, *The Resurrection*,: 347–8.
       Taylor, **111**: 613.

7584   welkes werren . waies weten . windes walken w[e?]de wo .
       On wild weather.
       Pickering, **981**: 166, **F**.

7585   What menethe this? When I lye alone/I tosse, I turne, I sighe, I grone
       'What does this mean?'
       Thomas Wyatt
       Davies, **61**, no. 186.

7586   What no, perdy, ye may be sure!/Think not to make me to your lure
       'No! indeed.'
       Thomas Wyatt
       Davies, **61**, no. 184; Tierney, **571**:38.

Temporary Index of First Lines

7587   What schulde physyke but yf sekenes were
Winchester Anthology, item 79.
Wilson, **88b**: 23, 38.

7588   Wat so þu art gost her be me
Woolf, **522**: 88–9; Wilson, **601**, no. 115; Wenzel, **791**: 154; **882**: 129.

7589   What thyng shold cawse me to be sad?/As longe (as) ye rejoyce wyth hart
From a sequence in the Devonshire MS, thought to be correspondence composed during their imprisonment by Lord Thomas Howard and Lady Margaret Douglas.
Muir, **41**: 262–3, no. 9; Camargo, **949**: 182.

7590   Whan Crist for vs wold be ded,/he made his body of þis bred
On the Eucharist.
Wenzel, **629**, no. 83; **882**: 94.

7591   Whan Dame Flora/In die aurora
The Armonye of Byrdes, ed. John Wright. Collier, Percy Soc. VII. W.C. Hazlitt, *Remains of Early Popular Poetry of England* III: 184.
Sandison, **139**: 139, R 27.

7592   Wanne frend schal fram frende go/into Unkuhelonde
On the separation at death.
Wenzel, **629**, no. 84.

7593   Wan is heyn turniþ,/And is breþ stynkyþ
Fletcher, **651**: 342.

7594   Whan I þinke on cristes blod
Extract from *Dives and Pauper*.
Comper, **38**: 135; Gray, **81**, no. 34; Woolf, **522**: 39 n. 2.

7595   Whan I wold fayne begynne to pleyne/And tell my wofull hevynesse
Early Tudor song. Winchester Anthology, item 171.
Wilson, **88b**: 30, 38; **746**: 294; Boffey, **848**: 183.

7596   When myght and will *and* ryght wer ane,/þen was welthe in ilk a wane
On the evils of the times.
Wenzel, **629**, no. 86; Green, **975**: 186.

7597   Quhen Phebus in the ranie cloude
Pinkerton, ed., *Ancient Scotish Poems*: 192.
Sandison, **139**: 143, D 32.

7598   When sturdye stormes of stryfe are paste/Shall qui[e]te calmes app[.]ere?
In a hand of the first half of the sixteenth century.
Hanna, **734**: 257, no. A6.

7599   Quhen Tayis bank wes blumyt brycht
Bannatyne MS: 660. Laing, *Select Remains*: 220; *Early Popular Poetry* I: 169.
Sandison, **139**: 134, A 35.

7600   When that Aurora illumynath lyȝght/I rose vp to haue a syȝght
Reed, **21**, no. I; Sandison, **139**: 147, M23; Greene, **418**.

7601   Wan þat is wyte waxit falou/And þat is cripse waxit calau
Fletcher, **651**: 342.

7602   Whanne þo hillus smoken, þanne Babilon schal haue an eende./But whan þey brenne as þo fyyr, þanne eerthe schal henus weende
Fourfold prophecy, attributed to Daniel.
Wenzel, **629**, no. 88.

7603   When þe hounde knawithe þe bone,/þan of felishippe kepeþ he none
Worldly friendship likened to the friendship between dog and master.
Wenzel, **882**: 80.

7604   Whanne þou art stered to don amys,/bihold þisilf *and* þenk on þis
Written in a Wycliffite New Testament, U of Pennsylvania MS English 6, f. 4ʳ.
Tarvers, **859**: 448.

7605   When thou from hence away are past/To Whinny-muir thou comest at last
'Lyke-Wake dirge,' burden: 'This ae night, this ae night,/Every night and all' etc. Also cited thus: 'This ean night, this ean night,/every night and awle.'
Allison et al. **67**: 61; Gray, **575**: 222–4; Porter and Thwaite, **619**: 22–3; Fowler, **827**: 79.

7606   Wanne þo lokest in þis stone . . .,/þonk on hur from wham it com
Christ speaks of love in a token.
Wenzel, **882**: 221.

7607   Wan þu makst ingong,/Beþenk þe so to ben þolmod
De Periculo.
Wilson, **601**, no. 152.

7608   When thy frende by enemyte
A translation of 'Si sit amicus factus iniquus scismate dante,' item 36.
Winchester Anthology, item 37.
Wilson, **88b**: 20, 38.

7609   Quil men and wemmen woniȝen togidere/þe fendes brand sone comet þidere
De Luxuria. Translates Jerome, 'If women live together with men, the devil's fire will not be absent.' Grimestone Lyric 97.
Wilson, **601**, no. 97; Wenzel, **882**: 128.

7610   Wil þu art in welthe and wele/þu salt hauen frendis fele
De Ingratitudine.
Wilson, **601**, no. 89.

7611   Who hath more cawse for to complayne/Or to lament hys sorow and payne?
From a sequence in the Devonshire MS, thought to be correspondence composed during their imprisonment by Lord Thomas Howard and Lady Margaret Douglas.
Muir, **41**: 264, no. 11; Camargo, **949**: 182.

7612   ho her hys fot set opene þe seewaȝ[e]/bote hys schou wete [not], ared me þys saȝe
Verse from a sermon.
Erb, **564**: 69.

7613   Qwo set euere hys fote abouyn þe seys wawe/bot yf he it wete? tw red me þis saw
Riddle of the Sphinx, solved by Oedipus.
Wenzel, **629**, no. 91.

7614   Hwo so etyth of thys bred he schal leue and nawth be deed
English scrap in a Latin theological miscellany, MS Lambeth Palace Library 78: f. 307^r.
Pickering, **785**: 21.

7615   Quo sabet [i.e. whoso habet] longe ligge in sinne,/nu is tyme þat e blinne
Warning against delay in conversion. Exhortation to penance.
Wenzel, **629**, no. 92; **701**: 95; Green, **975**: 187.

7616   Woso louet nouth to don orith,/Treuliche he hatit lith
De Peccato.
Wilson, **601**, no. 149.

7617   Woso þouthte of his birthe/And wider he sal wende
De Occupacione.
Wilson, **601**, no. 139.

7618   Whoso will a white entrete make,/Wirgyn waxe & honny he muste take
'Forto make a white entret,' a recipe for a plaster.
Hanna, **734**: 255–6, no. 70.

7619   Woso wile ben riche and hauing,/He fallet in þe fendes fonding
De Diuiciis.
Wilson, **601**, no. 69.

7620   [W]ho þat wol nyde clippe and kisse aboute mydnyth,/he scheld duelle in þe pyne of helle mid þat ys rith
Couplet against lechers.
Wenzel, **629**, no. 90.

7621   Ho that wil sadly beholde me with his ie/May se hys owyn merowr and learne for to die
Verse on cadaver tomb of John Baret, Bury St Edmunds, Suffolk (1467).
King, **761**: 495.

7622   Why dare I not compleyn to my lady?/Whie woll I not aske grace in humble wyse
Early Tudor song. Winchester Anthology, item 173.
Wilson **88b**: 30, 38; **746**: 293; Boffey, **848**: 184.

7623   Wy hastou me forsake þat mad þe of noght?/Why hastou me forsake þat þe so dere bought?
Christ's lament on the Cross.
Wenzel, **629**, no. 93.

7624   Why should earthes gentry make herself so good
Woolf, **522**: 210.

7625   Wyd is swete armes/vus acolera/and myd milde steuene/ducement dirra
Macaronic quatrain in MS Egerton 613.
Hill, **691**: 495.

Temporary Index of First Lines 569

7626 Wylt thow and I by one assent—/Thow thieselfe shall chuse or no—
      Rigg, **516**: 143.
7627 Wyse men of gret sley3e,/Riche men of gret eyte
      Sermon, *De corpore Christi* . . . Cf. *4180.*
      Stemmler, **647**, no. 20.
7628 Wyth a fairness of lyt and knoulechyngg/þou hast i-mad, lord, þi clo3yngg
      Sermon, *De corpore Christi* . . .
      Stemmler, **647**, no. 22.
7629 With a sorwe and a clut/Al þis werd comet in and out
      De Morte.
      Wilson, **601**, no. 116; Wenzel, **791**: 154.
7630 With bittirfull bale haue I bought,/þus, man, all þi misse for to mende
      Lament of Jesus, York XXXVI, *Mortificacio Cristi [and Burial of Jesus]*, lines 183–95.
      Pearson, **196**: 246.
7631 W^t fyd & fy, w^t fy./Off my lady m*argery* at h*ur* god I *wylle* gyn,/To nu*m*bre (?) hyr beute bothe cheke & chyn
      Probably in the hand that has added accounts for the parsonage of Witchford, Cambs. for 1530.
      Hanna, **734**: 257, no. A4.
7632 With fles al bespred,/With blod al bebled
      De Via Christi. Preceded by 'Venit.'
      Wilson, **601**, no. 246.
7633 With humble prayer I beseech thee/That this scripture shall here or see
      Moran, **395**: 53.
7634 Withe myne hert blod I the bow3te/to wassche þe owte of synne
      Sermon lyric of a man who had not forgiven his neighbour and prayed before a crucifix which bled. Verses appeared on the image's breast, changing after the man had forgiven his neighbour. Cf. *7635.*
      Whiteford, **841**: 456–7.
7635 Wyth myn owyn herte blod/I wysch the owt of synne
      Inscriptions appear on a crucifix, in an exemplum. Cf. *7634.*
      Wenzel, **629**, no. 94; Pickering, **785**: 21.
7636 Wo is me, wo is me, for loue y go ibunden
      Allusion to an English song in a sermon.
      Wenzel, **629**, no. 95; **882**: 222.
7637 Wordes ben so knit with sinne/Tis strong to knowen a þouth withinne
      De Decepcione.
      Wilson, **601**, no. 63.
7638 Worliche blysse and joye al so/Endite3 in sorwe and wo
      Mourning takes hold of the end of joy.
      Wenzel, **882**: 117.
7639 Wordely rychesse me haþ a-blend,/*and* lecherye me haþ yschend
      Speech of a sinful woman who would not forgo her sin.
      Wenzel, **629**, no. 97.
7640 worst is best/strengthe is akaste
      Verse from a sermon.
      Erb, **564**: 76; Wenzel, **882**: 117.
7641 Writ þus oððe bet oððe þine hyde forlet
      Doggerel scribal jotting warning against poor penmanship. 'Write well thus or pay the cost,/Your own hide must else be lost.'
      Whitbread, **818**: 198.
7642 Writ þus oððe bet ride aweg
      Doggerel scribal jotting warning against poor penmanship. 'Write thus or pay/(And) ride away.'
      Whitbread, **818**: 199.
7643 3a 3a all Olde men to me take tent/*and* weddyth no wyff in no kynnys wyse
      Joseph's speech to Mary, *Ludus Coventriae, Joseph's Return*, lines 49–61.
      Osberg, **767**: 325.
7644 Ye blessed sterre of sterris emperice/That nurryssed Oure Lord wit*h* youre tetes tweyn

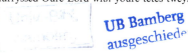

Translation of *Stella celi exstirpauit*, a Latin hymn to the Virgin for protection from the plague, MS Mazarine 469: f. 104^v.
Barratt, **822**: 24.

7645   ye men of galylee,/wherfor meruell ye?
Song of two angels at Christ's ascension, Towneley XXIX, *The Lord's Ascension*, lines 254–93.
Pearson, **196**: 241.

7646   Ye þat stonde in welthe and grete plesaunce
Winchester Anthology, item 150.
Wilson, **88b**: 28, 38.

7647   ʒe þat wilen heuene winne,/Withdrau ʒou fro flesli senne
De Luxuria.
Wilson, **601**, no. 98.

The following poems lack a complete first line.

7648   [. . .] wil is good wel for to do/[. . .]t quan my liking comet, good wil is go
De Voluntate.
Wilson, **601**, no. 241.

7649   [. . .]ness an buxumnesse;/[. . .]uerte and sarpnesse
De Via Christi. Preceded by: 'Nota quod via Christi vel vita fuit.'
Wilson, **601**, no. 244.

7650   (-) l(o)se þat (m)an wil hard be stad, þat d(-) noght thi(n-) angry thoght
Poem in Magdalen College, Oxford, deeds: Multon Hall 39*a*, dorse.
Woolgar and O'Donoghue, **820**: 218.

7651   ]e-/]⟨at⟩ be fe[/]lilio/[y]^e . . ./[w]as nayled on a tre
First complete line (13): [Mar]y modyr aftyr þ^i son
A Marian lyric, Text I of a Hedon MS.
Benskin, **776**: 33–4.

No first line has been specified for the following poems.

7652   In the *Wheatley MS*, ed. Day, EETS 15: 6–15.
Knowlton, **594**: 100.

7653   In *The Lay Folks' Mass Book*. Ed. T.F. Simmons. EETS 71: 28.
Knowlton, **594**: 130.

7654   Prayer to Jesus in *The Processional of the Nuns of Chester*. Ed. J.W. Legg. *Henry Bradshaw Society*, Vol. 18. 26–7.
Knowlton, **594**: 134.

7655   In the *Wheatley MS*, ed. Day, EETS 15: 6–15.
Knowlton, **594**: 166.

7656   In Huntington MS 1087, f. 145^v, in a hand of the early sixteenth century. See Schulz *et al.*, *Ten Centuries*, p. 6.
Hanna, **734**: 248, no. 31.

7657   Cf. 'Justyce loke thu stedfast be' [*1811*], which lacks a first line. Seems to be part of Trevisa's translation of Higden, *Polychronicon*, Book III, Chapter 8.
Hanna, **734**: 251–2, no. 50.

7658   A poem in a fifteenth-century hand. See Greene, **86**: 452, notes to carol no. 401.
Hanna, **734**: 256, no. 72.